D0848658

AMERICAN NATURE WRITERS

AMERICAN NATURE WRITERS

JOHN ELDER
Editor

VOLUME II

Peter Matthiessen
to
Western Geologists and Explorers

CHARLES SCRIBNER'S SONS
Macmillan Library Reference USA
Simon & Schuster Macmillan
NEW YORK

SIMON & SCHUSTER AND PRENTICE HALL INTERNATIONAL
LONDON   MEXICO CITY   NEW DELHI   SINGAPORE   SYDNEY   TORONTO

Library of Congress Cataloging-in-Publication Data

American nature writers / John Elder, editor.
   2 vols.   cm.
   Includes bibliographical references and index.
   Contents: v. 1 Edward Abbey to John McPhee—v. 2 Peter
Matthiessen to Western Geologists and Explorers.
   ISBN 0-684-19692-1 (2-vol. set :alk. paper)
   1. American literature—Dictionaries. 2. Nature in literature—
Dictionaries. 3. Authors, American—Biography—Dictionaries.
4. American literature—Bio-bibliography—Dictionaries. 5. Nature
in literature—Bio-bibliography—Dictionaries. 6. Natural history—
United States—Historiography—Dictionaries. 7. Natural history—
United States—Bio-bibliography—Dictionaries.   I. Elder, John,
1947–   .
PS163.A6   1996
810.9'36—dc20   96-31237
                                      CIP

10 9 8 7 6 5 4 3 2 1

PRINTED IN THE UNITED STATES OF AMERICA

The paper used in this publication meets the minimum requirements of the
American National Standard for Information Sciences—Permanence of Paper
for Printed Library Materials, ANSI Z39.48-1984.

CONTENTS

Volume I

v

CONTENTS

Volume II

CONTENTS

PETER MATTHIESSEN
(b. 1927)

DANIEL G. PAYNE

PETER MATTHIESSEN'S remarkable literary oeuvre is primarily composed of two related but discrete bodies of work. It was as a writer of natural history and travel books and essays that Matthiessen first came to prominence, and his work in this area alone is enough to rank him with the best writers of nonfiction in this century. One of his books in this genre, *The Tree Where Man Was Born* (1972), was nominated for a National Book Award and another, *The Snow Leopard* (1978), won this honor. With powerful—and often remarkably innovative—novels such as *At Play in the Fields of the Lord* (1965), *Far Tortuga* (1975), and *Killing Mister Watson* (1990) to his credit as well, Matthiessen must be considered one of the premier American writers of the twentieth century. His adventurous life is thoroughly intertwined with his literature, and the intensely spiritual quality of his work has led one commentator to refer to him as "one of the shamans of literature" (Cobbs, p. 223).

Early Life and Work

Two of the most powerful recurring motifs in Matthiessen's work, his love of nature and his distrust of a life of unearned privilege, have their roots in his own sheltered childhood. Born on 22 May 1927 to Erard and Elizabeth Carey Matthiessen, his father was a successful New York architect; even the Great Depression, Matthiessen recalled, "had no serious effect on our well-insulated family, which maintained a summer house on Fishers Island, a country house with a fine view of the Hudson, and a comfortable apartment . . . [on] Fifth Avenue" ("New York: Old Hometown," p. 56). He attended private schools: St. Bernard's in Manhattan (where he met lifelong friend George Plimpton) and the prestigious Hotchkiss boarding school in Connecticut. Although he admitted to "a lot of rich-boy fun" (p. 66), Matthiessen later traced his sense of social justice to the "uneasiness about unearned privilege" that he felt regarding his family's wealth (p. 60). During his teenage years this uneasiness principally took the form of unfocused rebellion at home and at school. As he would later remark, "My formative years left me unformed; despite kind family, superior schooling, and all the orderly advantages, I remained disorderly" (Wakeman, p. 956).

Despite the recurring discipline problems of his youth, Matthiessen's early years also served to instill in him the love of nature that pervades his writings. He and his younger brother, George Carey (who would later become a marine biologist; they also have an older sister, Mary Seymour), shared a "passion for snakes" (Smith, p. 241) as boys. Other fond childhood memories for Matthiessen included the Central Park Zoo and the American Museum of Natural History in New York City. Most importantly, summers at Fishers Island exposed Matthiessen to the sea, an experience that later brought him to Long Island, where he worked as a fisherman for a time in the 1950s. Recalling these idyllic summers in *Men's Lives: The Surfmen and Baymen of the South Fork* (1986) he wrote, "For many years as a boy in the late thirties, I had gone deep-sea fishing off Montauk with my father, and to this day I cannot see that high promontory of land with its historic lighthouse without a stirring of excitement and affection" (1988 ed., p. 102).

Immediately following his graduation from Hotchkiss in 1945, Matthiessen joined the navy and was assigned to duty at Pearl Harbor. World War II was nearly over by the time Matthiessen enlisted, making his stint in the armed forces a relatively uneventful one. He served as a ship's laundryman at Pearl Harbor, where he also managed the boxing team and wrote sports articles for the Honolulu *Advertiser*. There was, however, one vitally important incident that took place while at sea that he would later describe in *The Snow Leopard*:

> One night in 1945, on a Navy vessel in Pacific storm, my relief on bow watch, seasick, failed to appear, and I was alone for eight hours in a maelstrom of wind and water, noise and iron; again and again, waves crashed across the deck, until water, air, and iron became one. Overwhelmed, exhausted, all thought and emotion beaten out of me, I lost my sense of self, the heartbeat I heard was the heart of the world, I breathed with the mighty risings and declines of earth, and this evanescence seemed less frightening than exalting. Afterward, there was pain of loss—loss of *what*, I wondered, understanding nothing." (pp. 42–43)

As Matthiessen later characterized it, this disquieting sense of exhilaration during the storm became one of the defining moments of his spiritual development. Both ego and time were momentarily obliterated as he "breathed with

. . . the earth," and felt for the first time an identification with the larger forces of nature that were then imperiling his life. As William Dowie has suggested, the constant voyaging, in both a physical and spiritual sense, that characterize Matthiessen's life and literature might be read as an attempt to recapture this first transcendent moment.

Several months after his discharge from the navy in 1946, Matthiessen enrolled at Yale University, where he majored in English and enjoyed some phenomenally early literary success. He also continued to work on the reportorial skills that are so evident in his later work, cowriting a series of hunting and fishing articles for the *Yale Daily News* called "Two in the Bush." His junior year was spent in France, where he studied at the Sorbonne and where he met Patsy Southgate, whom he would marry two years later. Following his graduation from Yale in 1950, Matthiessen took a position as creative writing instructor at the school. Matthiessen's first big literary break came when "Sadie," a story he wrote for a creative writing class at Yale, won the *Atlantic* "First" award for 1951. Just a few months later, the *Atlantic Monthly* published another story by Matthiessen, "The Fifth Day." Both of these stories are notable chiefly because of their presaging of themes such as the conflict between the primitive and the civilized, often linked to the conflict between rich and poor, that Matthiessen explored further in his early novels.

Largely on the strength of this early literary success, Matthiessen and his new wife decided to return to Paris in late 1951, where a group of young American writers formed an artistic community that some would compare to that of the 1920s. William Styron, Harold Humes, George Plimpton, James Baldwin, and Ben Bradlee were all part of a literary circle who met regularly for cocktails and conversation, often at the Matthiessens' apartment on the Rue Perceval. It was at these gatherings that tentative plans for a new magazine were bandied about; as William Styron, one of the principals, recalled in *This Quiet Dust* (1982), "Later that spring [1952], as the idea of a new magazine grew less far-fetched

... we convened in an apartment ... that belonged to Peter Matthiessen, to whom credit is due for having originated the idea for the magazine." The first edition of the *Paris Review*, with longtime Matthiessen friend George Plimpton as editor in chief, came out in 1953. Matthiessen served as the magazine's first fiction editor, and has remained on the editorial board (in an emeritus capacity) ever since. Matthiessen's two years in Paris were enormously productive, despite what William Styron referred to as "a nearly inexhaustible supply of scotch" (Nicholas, p. xiv), and a growing aversion to urban life. In addition to his work on the *Paris Review*, he drafted his first novel, *Race Rock*, wrote a number of short stories, and fathered his first son, Lucas Carey.

Much of Matthiessen's early fiction—in particular his first three novels: *Race Rock* (1954), *Partisans* (1955), and *Raditzer* (1961)—drew on his own privileged youth for their main themes. His own feelings toward the subject may best be summed up by a character in "The Fifth Day," a "Rich Kid" who fails to respond to the mean-spirited ribbing of a poor associate because "there was nothing to offer in defense of a wealthy family" (p. 61). All three novels are conventional bildungsromans featuring an intelligent young man from a fairly wealthy family as the protagonist. In *Race Rock*, George McConville, the scion of a wealthy old New England family, is forced to deal with a number of personal crises, including his girlfriend's unforeseen pregnancy and his sense of guilt over his family's wealth; the most dramatic confrontation, however, is with Cady Shipman, a brutal but fascinating figure from McConville's childhood. In its examination of the theme of vital but savage primitivism (represented by Cady Shipman) versus corrupted civilization (represented by George McConville), *Race Rock* sketches out some of the same territory that Matthiessen would later explore to greater effect in more mature works such as *At Play in the Fields of the Lord* and *Killing Mister Watson*.

Partisans is centered on a young American journalist's search for a Marxist guerrilla leader, Jacobi, a near mythical figure from his childhood. The personal and allegorical implications of this novel—Jacobi serves as something of a father figure to Sand, who is emotionally estranged from his own father, an American diplomat—have been justifiably criticized as heavy-handed. Although *Raditzer* was published several years after the first two novels (and just four years before Matthiessen's breakthrough novel, *At Play in the Fields of the Lord*), it is both thematically and structurally closer to Matthiessen's earlier novels. In this work, Charlie Stark, a wealthy young idealist who has enlisted in the navy, is befriended by Raditzer, a poor and despicable character whose humanity is only vaguely apparent. As in *Race Rock*, *Raditzer* prefigures the tension between the savage and the primitive that Matthiessen would develop more fully in later novels.

Leaving Paris in August 1953, Matthiessen and his small family moved to eastern Long Island, where he worked as a commercial fisherman. The brutally hard work appears to have allowed Matthiessen to exorcise at least some of his lingering guilt about his privileged background: "Doing hard labor with my hands, I felt more free, less malcontent, than at any time in all my life" ("New York: Old Hometown," p. 70). He also found the seasonal, out-of-doors life of commercial fishing to be an excellent complement to writing. In the spring and fall he dug for shellfish and worked on a haul-seining crew; during the summer he captained a charter fishing boat, the *Merlin*. As for the rest of the year: "From November to April, I wrote steadily, and on days of bad weather as well; this was the best year-round working schedule that I ever devised" (Wakeman, p. 957). *Men's Lives*, in which Matthiessen recalls his own experiences on the water and examines the history and economically precarious present of the Long Island fishing industry, is both a social history of and a tribute to the fishing families of eastern Long Island. By 1956, however, Matthiessen's life as a fisherman came to an abrupt halt despite the feeling of well-being it gave him; as he later wrote, "This well-being, alas, was not reflected in my marriage, which dissolved, and for the next five years I did some of the world wandering

I had always longed for" ("New York: Old Hometown," p. 70).

Wildlife in America

Matthiessen's first stretch of "world wandering" involved a tour of the wildlife refuges of the United States that resulted in *Wildlife in America* (1959), his first book of natural history. Where Matthiessen's early novels had shown numerous rough edges for all their promise, *Wildlife in America* was immediately recognized as a work of unusual accomplishment. Although this was Matthiessen's first foray into environmental literature, the depth and scope of his scholarship was impressive and the prose clear and assertive. Matthiessen begins this history of humankind's often disastrous impact on the wild creatures of the North American continent with the killing of the last great auk in 1844, a passing that was as symbolic as it was tragic, because the auk represented "the first species native to North America to become extinct by the hand of man" (rev. ed., p. 21). Since then several other species have also passed into extinction, and many others, despite recent attempts to spare them, were "hovering at the abyss of extinction."

Perhaps the most impressive aspect of *Wildlife in America* is that—unlike other great ecological historians of the twentieth century such as Aldo Leopold and Rachel Carson—Matthiessen's training in the environmental sciences was largely restricted to a few science classes in college; as he has stated in an interview, "I'm not really trained in any of the disciplines; I'm what the 19th century would call a generalist—I have a lot of slack information, and for my work it's been extremely helpful" (Smith, p. 241). Nevertheless, Matthiessen's history is authoritative and, where he discusses the root causes of the great decline in North American wildlife, persuasive. Matthiessen surveys the history and present status of America's endangered wildlife region by region, combining his own observations with meticulously documented research. In addition to covering such familiar ground as the

extinction of the passenger pigeon and the near extinction of the bison, Matthiessen also considers less well known cases, such as those of the endangered gila monster and desert pupfish, and the Eskimo curlew (a species presumed extinct since 1945), of which Matthiessen writes movingly: "One prefers to think that the last curlew fell naturally to a fox or coursing gyrfalcon in *Keewatin*, the land of the north wind, rather than that some farm boy, in Nebraska or Saskatchewan, blew it forever from the face of the earth with a single, senseless blast of a cheap gun" (p. 164).

For all the damage done by hunting, however, Matthiessen persuasively argues that the human role in habitat degradation has generally been even more harmful to animal populations. Man's adaptability makes it possible for him to survive in nearly all of earth's many climates, Matthiessen writes, "and less resourceful creatures have no choice but to make room for him during his stay on earth. He cannot be condemned for adjusting to his world as best he can, for all animals do that; he *can* be condemned for fouling his own nest" (pp. 211–212). Having said that, Matthiessen addresses the question of "less resourceful" species that are currently hovering on the brink of extinction, such as the California condor and the whooping crane, and argues that although there is a "certain logic in the view which advocates the relinquishment of doomed creatures to eternity" (p. 257), man bears a measure of responsibility for such "senile" species since, "had mankind not altered the shape and nature of the land, their withdrawal from the earth would have been a slow one, lived out gracefully over centuries to come. And so we must assume responsibility, even for these" (p. 264).

Over the next thirty years, Matthiessen would get a firsthand look throughout the world at the effects of environmental degradation caused by human activity. Even in the most remote regions of the earth he would observe areas of deforestation, erosion, and desertification that were attributable directly to humans and their domestic animals. Matthiessen early recognized that untouched wilderness areas all around the globe were becoming increasingly scarce, and this is one of the main factors behind his unrelenting travel to distant places. Like Francis Parkman (whose classic *The Oregon Trail*, 1849, is cited by Matthiessen in *Wildlife in America*), Matthiessen is driven to see the last wild places on earth before they are forever altered by the hand of man. In a 1986 interview he addressed this compulsion, stating, "I've always been interested in wildlife and wild places and wild people. I wanted to see the places that are disappearing" (Smith, p. 241). In works such as *The Cloud Forest, Under the Mountain Wall*, and his books on Africa, Matthiessen serves not just as a chronicler of the wilderness but as a witness and an advocate of sorts for the "wild people," the preindustrial civilizations fast disappearing as the world becomes smaller and more culturally homogeneous.

The Cloud Forest

Following the success of *Wildlife in America*, Matthiessen was looking next to extend his studies of natural history to the South American continent when the *New Yorker's* legendary editor William Shawn took an interest in his work and sponsored the trip. As Matthiessen later recalled, that fortuitous decision "launched the whole theme of my life" (Smith, p. 241). The series of descriptive, informative, somewhat rambling articles that he wrote about his travels for the *New Yorker* are typical of the nature/travel articles that he would continue to write for that magazine and others for the next thirty years. *The Cloud Forest: A Chronicle of the South American Wilderness* (1961)—which like the *New Yorker* articles was based on the journal he kept during the trip—is composed of two parts. The first is a straightforward account of his voyage to Peru, and his travels in the Amazon region, the Andes, and Tierra del Fuego. Although his travels through these regions are relatively uneventful, his descriptions, particularly of the Amazon jungle, are remarkably vivid, as when he describes the first time he entered the jungle:

One steps through the wall of the tropic forest, as Alice stepped through the looking glass; a few steps, and the wall closes behind. . . . The trees themselves are so tumultuous and strange that one sees them as a totality, a cumulative effect, scarcely noticing details; there is a strange, evilly spined palm trunk, though, and a crouching plant with gigantic fronds, and a fantastic parasite, like a bundle of long red pipe-cleaners studded with olive nuts, fastened here and there to the high branches, and the looming trunk of a silk-cotton, seen only when one is right on top of it; it soars off through the leathery green canopy overhead. (p. 38)

Although the first half of *The Cloud Forest* is a wonderfully descriptive pastiche of information, there is little display of the narrative talent that distinguishes Matthiessen's best travel writing. As one critic has noted, however, in the second half of the book, "something radically different happens. . . . Matthiessen's aimless trip becomes a journey. . . . His story thereby assumes direction and accrues a mythic dimension" (Dowie, p. 49). While in a remote Amazon village, Matthiessen hears a barroom rumor of a giant fossilized mandible hidden deep in the jungles of Peru. This story, improbable though it might be, gives him the urge to "scrape up an expedition and go plunging off into those imperturbable green walls" (p. 56). His fascinating account of the resulting expedition is in the tradition of earlier travelers to this remote region, but it also prefigures—and probably helped to inspire—the new generation of "gonzo" nature/travel writers like Tim Cahill.

At Play in the Fields of the Lord

Written several years after *The Cloud Forest*, Matthiessen's powerful novel *At Play in the Fields of the Lord* might be seen as a fictional continuation of his experiences in the South American jungle. His firsthand knowledge of the region gives the book the rich density of detail that helps make it so vivid, but the novel form made it possible for him to imaginatively explore some of the issues he had merely touched on in *The Cloud Forest*. The most important of these concerns the role of missionaries—even well-meaning ones—in destroying native culture in the process of "saving" the souls of the Indians. In *The Cloud Forest*, Matthiessen had briefly noted the effect of the missionaries, writing that their contact with a primitive tribe "is followed more often than not by its extinction, through the subsequent exploitation, mixed breeding, alcohol, and disease that arrive not with the advent of the Word but with civilization" (p. 133). In *At Play in the Fields of the Lord* he developed this theme to marvelous effect, creating a fictional account of the first contact of the Niaruna, a primitive and warlike tribe, with American missionaries.

The conflicts that drive the narrative of *At Play in the Fields of the Lord* are multifaceted, primarily involving the Niaruna; the missionaries; Guzmán, commandant of the garrison of Madre de Dios, the sole outpost of civilization in the province; and Lewis Moon, an American adventurer. Moon, under the influence of *ayahuasca*, a powerful local hallucinogen, takes the plane (bearing the inscription "Wolfie & Moon, Inc.—Small Wars & Demolition") in which he and his partner had arrived in Madre de Dios. He flies deep over the jungle where the Niaruna are located and he bails out, leading the Niaruna to hail him—albeit somewhat suspiciously—as a god. Matthiessen's comments in *The Cloud Forest* on how a preindustrial people become "infected" once they come in contact with Western civilization are played out in a literal sense in *At Play in the Fields of the Lord*. The missionaries bring influenza with them (transmitted by the unwitting conduit, Moon), a disease for which the Niaruna have no resistance—but in addition to this dramatic but preventable infection, Matthiessen suggests that the missionaries also carry the spores of a material and spiritual illness with them. They infect the Indians with material desires in order to trap them into converting, and seek to supplant not just the Indians' way of life, but their religion and their whole way of seeing the world as well. The final irony is that in the attempt to equate Christian dogma

with the Niaruna gods, an error in translation (giving Jesus the equivalent name of an evil god) is largely to blame for the Niaruna's intractable resistance to the missionaries' proselytizing.

Although Matthiessen does not present the Niaruna as sentimentalized "noble savages"—for instance, when Lewis Moon attempts to form the Indians into a confederation to resist the depredations of Guzmán, the Niaruna fall into drunkenness and bickering—he suggests that in many ways the primitive has a clearer view of the world (similar in some ways to the Zen philosophy that he would later study) than does the civilized person. After Moon (who is half American Indian himself) has lived among the Niaruna and adopted their ways, he finds himself adapting to a new way of seeing the world around him: "He laughed at the extraordinary experience which had befallen him—the *perceiving*, through the Indians of a wilderness which heretofore had seemed to him a malevolent nether world, poisonous and stagnated, miasmal" (p. 191). By the end of the story, Moon has lost the sense of self so central in Western thought, and has attained a state that is painfully pure in its transcendence of the self and integration with nature:

> He felt bereft, though of what he did not know. He was neither white nor Indian, man nor animal, but some mute, naked strand of protoplasm. He groaned with the ache of his own transience under this sky, as if, breathing too deeply, he might rise on the wind as lightly as a seed, without control or intimation of his fate. He was the nameless beetle probing the pores of his own toe; he twitched in the wind like the dull scale that loosened on the flank of the rotten fish. His was the bald eye of the vulture forming its halo over the mute landscape; far beneath, he saw the solitary man on the humble mud. (p. 372)

While this is a moment of transcendence for Moon, it is also a moment of unutterable pain, a letting go that seems less triumphant than humbly submissive. The scene is reminiscent of Matthiessen's account of his own experience during the 1945 storm in the Pacific described in

The Snow Leopard, and seems to intuitively anticipate his later studies of Zen.

At Play in the Fields of the Lord was critically well received, and was compared to such works as Herman Melville's *Typee* (1846). Matthiessen won praise for the lush realism of the novel, with one reviewer calling him "the psalmist of the umblemished wilderness" *(Newsweek* 66:114, 8 November 1965). *At Play in the Fields of the Lord* was also nominated for the National Book Award, and recent critics have for the most part agreed with the early assessment of the book, although one critic, Bruce Bawer, has argued that at the heart of the novel is a cultural double standard whereby Matthiessen judges the ethnocentrism of the white American missionaries as a flaw and that of the Indians as a virtue.

Under the Mountain Wall

In the years following his journeys through South America, Matthiessen engaged in a peripatetic lifestyle that took him to the far reaches of the globe. In 1961 he accompanied the Harvard-Peabody Expedition (which received substantial media attention due to the death of one of its members, Michael Rockefeller) that traveled to Netherlands New Guinea to study the Kurelu, a tribal people who had up to that time had no contact with modern cultures. The purpose of the expedition was, as Matthiessen stated in *Under the Mountain Wall: A Chronicle of Two Seasons in the Stone Age* (1962), "to live among the people as unobtrusively as possible and to film and record their wars, rituals, and daily life with a minimum of interference, in order that a true picture of a Stone Age culture—one of the few in which both war and agriculture are important—might be preserved" (p. xiii). In its respectful portrait of a primitive culture, *Under the Mountain Wall* might be said to resemble the anthropological studies of writers such as Margaret Mead and Claude Lévi-Strauss. Although Matthiessen is not an anthropologist, the tone of the work is rather scholarly, incorporating maps, diagrams, and glossaries of native terms, although he skillfully develops a narrative struc-

ture that keeps the book from sounding too much like an academic tome. He gives a sense of the daily lives of the Kurelu by following the actions of several tribespeople, some of whom, like the chieftain U-mue, are developed into full-fledged characters.

As is generally the case with Matthiessen's explorations of indigenous cultures, he is clearly enthralled by the opportunity to study a people who live so close to nature and who have (at least up to this point) escaped the homogenizing influence of Western civilization. Although the life of these people is marked by a constant and highly ritualized warfare with their ancestral enemy, the Wittaia, Matthiessen presents this as just another aspect of tribal culture and refuses to make any indictment (which would probably ring rather hollow in any case) of this as a proof of savagery. Instead, as in his description of the death of Weake, a young boy mortally wounded in a raid by the Wittaia tribe, Matthiessen emphasizes the sympathetic response of the Kurelu to the boy's death:

> In the pilai crouched Asikanalek, twisted by grief. Against the wall, where sunlight filtered through the chinks, sat Weake's small silhouette, already arranged in the position he would be given in the chair. Asikanalek went to him and carried him outside into the day. Still holding the boy, he kneeled in the bright sun before the pilai and, staring upward at the sky, lamented. The men about him looked disheveled and distraught, and Asikanalek's shoulders were smeared with yellow clay. Weake's appearance in the yard had caused a stir among the women; the long day of fierce wailing had begun. (p. 157)

In his narrative, Matthiessen strives for the same dispassionate recording of fact that the camera's eye would record (and did—Robert Gardner's film *Dead Birds* was shot on this same expedition). He dutifully records some of the less pleasant aspects of Kurelu culture and tradition, but his description of such customs is uniformly nonjudgmental. At times, Matthiessen's objectivity is perhaps too pronounced, as in his chilling description of the ritual severing of young girls' fingers as a sign of mourning for a deceased male relative.

Matthiessen concludes his account of the Kurelu with an ominous development—the descent of a man with "white skin . . . accompanied by black men dressed like himself" down to the valley (p. 256). This encroachment of the modern world into the lives of the Kurelu is meant to signal that the old way of existence for these people is about to undergo an enormous transformation. The anticipated invasion of missionaries and soldiers began soon after the expedition left, and Matthiessen bitterly surmises that "by the time this account of them is published, the proud and warlike Kurelu will be no more than another backward people, crouched in the long shadow of the white man" (p. xiv). As several commentators have pointed out, however, the presence of the Harvard-Peabody Expedition itself signaled the end of the Kurelu's traditional way of life, and raises some significant questions about the role of these researchers themselves in "corrupting" the Kurelu. Throughout *Under the Mountain Wall* Matthiessen employs the fiction of omitting any reference to himself or to the other members of the expedition, "not only because the first reactions of a wild people to the white man . . . have been well documented, but because the Kurelu offered a unique chance, perhaps the last, to describe a lost culture in the terrible beauty of its pure estate" (p. xiv). Still, Matthiessen's disclaimer notwithstanding, lingering doubts about the ethical propriety of such an intrusion remain.

During the 1960s and 1970s Matthiessen continued to travel widely, and he wrote a number of articles for the *New Yorker* and other magazines. These articles, and books such as *Oomingmak: The Expedition to the Musk Ox Island in the Bering Sea* (1967), *The Shorebirds of North America* (1967), and *The Wind Birds* (1973), solidified Matthiessen's reputation as one of America's premier natural history writers. Other works, such as *Blue Meridian: The Search for the Great White Shark* (1971), which chronicled the oceanic research expedition that shot the first undersea film of the great white shark (commercially screened as *Blue Water, White Death*), continued to demonstrate that Matthiessen's narrative powers and his taste for adventure—literally diving into the proverbial shark-infested waters—were also undiminished. He was accorded a steady stream of honors for his work as a nature writer; in 1965 he was named a trustee of the New York Zoological Society (he resigned in 1978), in 1974 he was elected to the National Institute of Arts and Letters, and in 1985 he received a Gold Medal for Distinction in Natural History from the Academy of Natural Sciences in Philadelphia.

Far Tortuga

In 1967 Matthiessen embarked on a voyage that ultimately resulted in the novel *Far Tortuga* (1975), a stylistic tour de force that drew comparisons to the work of Robert Louis Stevenson and Joseph Conrad, with one critic ranking it as "second only to *Moby-Dick* among America's great sea novels" (Bender, p. 229). The genesis of *Far Tortuga* was a trip to the Grand Cayman Islands sponsored by the *New Yorker* that Matthiessen described in "To the Miskito Bank." In this article, Matthiessen described his frustrating but ultimately successful attempt to get the captain of the *Lydia E. Wilson*, one of the last full-masted turtle schooners in the West Indies, to allow him to "go along on a turtle voyage the following spring" (p. 128). When he showed up at the Grand Caymans the next year, Matthiessen was shocked to find that the *Lydia E. Wilson* had been clumsily converted to a motor vessel with its name, now the *Wilson*, truncated like its once majestic masts. In a spirit once again reminiscent of literary adventurers such as Parkman and Melville, Matthiessen bitterly notes:

I had vaguely dreaded the discomforts of the voyage . . . but now these matters seemed of small importance. A chance to witness something old and marvellous had been lost; it seemed inconceivable that a full-rigged schooner could operate even one more year, and the market for green turtles, like the green turtles themselves, could disappear. (p. 134)

Realizing this, Matthiessen went through with his original plans and accompanied the *Wilson* (paying a "fot fee" for the privilege of doing so) on its turtling voyage. The article describing this voyage in the *New Yorker* is a straightforward bit of reporting enlivened chiefly by Matthiessen's portrait of the ship's captain, Cadian Ebanks, and by his skilled rendition of the crew's idiomatic conversation during the course of the journey. The relative flatness of the piece is attributable to Matthiessen's decision (made with the blessing of the *New Yorker's* William Shawn) to hold back some of the best material for *Far Tortuga*.

The novel's plot is stripped down to a simple framework centered around the ill-fated voyage of Captain Raib Avers and the crew of the turtle schooner *Lillias Eden* (a converted motor vessel like the *Wilson*) to the mysterious Far Tortuga Cay. The book is allegorically rich, however, weaving together such themes as the effect of "modern times" on the crew and their industry, the dispassionately Darwinian forces of nature, and Raib's doomed attempt to stave off ruin despite forces beyond his control. The aspect of *Far Tortuga* that has drawn the most attention, however, is Matthiessen's style. The layout of the book, with all its "white space," is as spare as the plot. Matthiessen also dispensed with many of the conventions of the novel, including such seemingly indispensable details as identifying which character is speaking.

In an interview with the *Paris Review* Matthiessen explained that he used this style "to achieve resonance, to make the reader receive things intuitively, hear the silence in the wind, for instance, that is a constant presence in the book" ("The Craft of Fiction in *Far Tortuga*," p. 80). While the effect of this can be confusing until the reader gets acclimated to Matthiessen's innovations, there is considerable merit to his claim that "once the reader gets the feel of the new form, the book is quite straightforward," and that by the time it really matters, the reader is able to identify the characters by their idiosyncratic speech. Matthiessen's experimentation in *Far Tortuga* has elicited a wide range of critical responses, with several reviewers referring to it

as an excellent but flawed work. Others were less equivocal in their praise; in his review for the *Atlantic Monthly* (June 1975), Edward Weeks wrote: "Peter Matthiessen has lived with the potential that at some time he would write an exceptional novel. This is it" (p. 92).

Africa

During the period between his turtling voyage in 1966 and the publication of *Far Tortuga* in 1975, Matthiessen continued to travel widely. Of all the places he visited in his travels, perhaps none has elicited the kind of long-standing fascination that he has had with Africa. On his way to New Guinea in 1961 to join the Harvard-Peabody Expedition, he traveled south from Egypt through Sudan to Kenya, "wishing to see the Egyptian temple of Abu Simbel, up the Nile, the warrior-herdsmen of the south Sudan, and the great animal herds of the Serengeti Plains, all of which, in 1961, seemed on the point of disappearance" (*The Tree Where Man Was Born*, Author's Note). Over the next thirty years Matthiessen returned to Africa several times, drawn both by its wildlife and by his interest in its peoples, particularly the remnants of the hunter-gatherer cultures of the vast forests of that continent. Matthiessen wrote three books (excluding *Shadows of Africa*, which draws from all three) about his African experiences: *The Tree Where Man Was Born* (1972), *Sand Rivers* (1981), and *African Silences* (1991).

The Tree Where Man Was Born (which was nominated for the National Book Award) alternates between Matthiessen's trip to Africa in 1961, one to Kenya in 1969, and a journey with photographer Eliot Porter to the Northern Frontier District of Kenya in 1970. His travels in Africa, like most of his journeys to far-off places, were inspired by a fear that much of the wildlife of Africa might soon disappear: "With the collapse of colonial governments, the destruction of wildlife by rampaging Africans had been widely predicted, and a glimpse of the last great companies of wild animals on earth was the main object of my trip to Africa in 1961" (p. 38).

Matthiessen notes that although the worst has not come to pass—in fact, the size and number of East African parks and game reserves have actually increased since independence—widespread poaching still presents an imminent danger to Africa's wildlife.

Where the object of Matthiessen's journey through East Africa in 1961 had been to see the wildlife, in his travels there in 1969 and 1970 his main desire was to see the "Small People," the hunters of the African bush whose numbers, never large in the first place, were dwindling rapidly. Matthiessen's interest in these people is partly anthropological in nature, but, as was the case with the Kurelu of New Guinea and the primitive Indian tribes of South America, it is their relation to nature that most intrigues him. These gentle, quiet people, he writes, live "in harmony with the land and the changing seasons, with none of the aggressiveness and greed that the domestication of plants and animals, with its illusion of security and permanence, brought to mankind" (p. 51). When Matthiessen finally meets some of these hunters (a tribe called the Hadza) in 1969, he is struck by how easily they blend into their environment, marveling, "they have no idea of wilderness, for they are part of it" (p. 232). In a passage that strongly correlates to his Zen studies, he writes, "For people who must live from day to day, past and future have small relevance, and their grasp of it is fleeting; they live in the moment, a very precious gift that we have lost" (p. 232).

Sand Rivers, Matthiessen's second book on Africa, describes a 1979 safari into the Selous Game Reserve in Tanzania, the largest wildlife sanctuary in Africa, "said to be the greatest stronghold of large wild animals left on earth" (p. 3). As in *The Tree Where Man Was Born*, Matthiessen's primary motivation for this journey is to observe the unique wildlife of Africa before it disappears. As Matthiessen and Brian Nicholson, the former warden of the Selous, travel through the preserve, Nicholson frequently observes that in the short period since his retirement as warden in 1973 the number of elephants and other large animals has drastically decreased, primarily due to the depredations of poachers. However, as Matthiessen notes, it is not simply a matter of cracking down on the local hunters who kill the animals, since it is the "demand for rhino horn and ivory [that] has put the animals in danger" (p. 153).

In many ways, *African Silences*, which describes Matthiessen's first visit to West Africa, is the bleakest of his Africa books. As he and primatologist Dr. Gilbert Boese travel throughout the region "on an informal survey of what was left of West Africa wildlife" (p. 3) he remarks on how the "new African" with his adopted Western ways and contempt for "old Africa's" people and wildlife was in the process of making the same environmental mistakes that are endemic in the West. In Senegal, the first country Matthiessen visited, he points out the role that humans (and their domestic animals) have played in impoverishng the land, spreading the deserts of North Africa by overgrazing and deforestation. In a strikingly symbolic passage, he describes a train ride in the Ivory Coast where, "staring outward at the forest, deep black against that other black of the night sky, I saw under the stars and moon an enormous burning tree of the doomed African forest" (p. 30).

The Snow Leopard

For all the sheer joy of exploring the unknown that is reflected in Matthiessen's marvelous descriptions of his "world wanderings," there is also a driven quality to his constant traveling that hints at an underlying motive for this restlessness. In *The Snow Leopard*, Matthiessen touches on this aspect, writing: "I already had what Kierkegaard called 'the sickness of infinitude,' wandering from one path to another with no real recognition that I was embarked upon a search, and scarcely a clue as to what I might be after. I only knew that at the bottom of each breath there was a hollow place that needed to be filled" (p. 43). This sense of spiritual emptiness led him to experiment with hallucinogenic drugs during his 1959 trip to Peru, where he used *ayahuasca*, a powerful hallucinogen used by the Amazon tribes to induce a visionary state.

Upon his return to the United States he continued to use various hallucinogens, including LSD, for several years, a period about which he wrote: "Now those psychedelic years seem far away; I neither miss them nor regret them. . . . The drug vision remains a sort of dream that cannot be brought over into daily life. Old mists may be banished, that is true, but the alien chemical agent forms another mist, maintaining the separation of the 'I' from true experience of the One" (*The Snow Leopard*, p. 47).

One of the reasons Matthiessen has been so strongly drawn to primitive peoples like the Kurelu of New Guinea, the Indians of the Amazon jungle, and the bushmen of Africa is that they have not yet developed the dualism between the self and nature that is characteristic of adults in the West. As children, he writes, we are not yet conscious of any wall between ourselves and the outer world; a child is "at rest in the very center of the universe, a part of things, unaware of endings and beginnings, still in unison with the primordial nature of creation, letting all light and phenomena pour through" (*The Snow Leopard*, 1987 ed., p. 41). Likewise, children and primitive cultures retain the ability—greatly admired by Matthiessen—to live in the present to a degree not generally possible for civilized people, who always seem to be planning for the future or regretting the past. The few moments in his journeys where Matthiessen is able to recapture this ability to live in the "now" are described in transcendent terms, such as a moment when he is on the bow of the turtle schooner *Wilson* as it courses through the sea on the way to the Far Tortugas: "On a bright, fresh day at sea, the ocean wind against your cheek and the tropical sun on your bare feet can restore childhood's sense of being at the center of time, with no time passing" ("To the Miskito Bank," pp. 148–149).

In August 1969 Matthiessen returned to his home in Sagaponack, Long Island, following a series of journeys in Africa that had lasted several months, to find three Zen monks standing in his driveway. The men were the teachers of his second wife, Deborah Love (they were married in 1963), but due partly to marital tensions exacerbated by his long absences, he later characterized this first contact with Zen masters as inauspicious. Eventually, however, Matthiessen found himself drawn to the study of Zen, an interest that he shared with Love until her death from cancer in 1972.

In 1973 Matthiessen accompanied the noted wildlife researcher George Schaller to the remote mountains of the Inner Dolpo in Nepal, a trip described in *The Snow Leopard*. Schaller's principal purpose in organizing the expedition was to study the bharal, the Himalayan blue sheep. Matthiessen went partially in the hope of spotting the rare Himalayan snow leopard, but also out of a desire to visit the Crystal Monastery of Shey Gompa; as he wrote in *The Snow Leopard*, this "was a true pilgrimage, a journey of the heart" (p. 3). Although Matthiessen had already begun his Zen studies at the time he left on the expedition, he was still a novice. Before he departed the United States his Zen teacher, Eido Roshi, warned him to "expect nothing" in the way of enlightenment, to go "into the light and silence of the Himalaya, without ambition of attainment" (p. 298). Despite this warning, he still hoped to see the revered Lama of Shey and "entertained visions of myself in monkish garb attending the Lama in his ancient mysteries . . . I suppose I had hoped he would be my teacher" (p. 191).

As in earlier travel books such as *The Cloud Forest*, the narrative structure of *The Snow Leopard* follows the journal entries that Matthiessen made during the journey. To some extent the book is similar in pattern and approach to his earlier travel books: he journeys through a remote region of the globe studying the wildlife and ecology of the area and observing and learning from indigenous cultures. In *The Snow Leopard*, however, Matthiessen's newfound interest in Zen provides a philosophical focus and context for his actions and observations that help to make this one of his finest books. As always, Matthiessen's descriptions of the land, the wildlife, and the people of this remote region of the world are precise and insightful, conveying a sense of the harsh beauty of this mountainous region as well as the ecological dangers that beset it. As Matthiessen and the other members of the expedition—George Schaller, four Sherpa guides, and a variable cast of porters—travel deeper into the mountains, leaving the twentieth century behind, Matthiessen experiences the same sense of euphoria that he exhibits in many of his other books describing journeys to far-off places. The ecological destruction that seems inevitably to accompany the presence of people is found here as well, however, and Matthiessen documents the deforestation, overgrazing, erosion, and flooding that are characteristic of the region, "the whole dismal cycle of events that accompanies overcrowding by human beings" (p. 14).

When the expedition sets up camp near the Crystal Monastery at Shey Gompa, Matthiessen finds that the monastery he hoped to visit (and perhaps study at) has been locked up and abandoned for the winter. This disappointment, he wrote, "might be read as a karmic reprimand to spiritual ambition, a silent teaching to this ego that still insists upon itself, like the poor bleat of a goat on the north wind" (p. 192). The other main goal of Matthiessen's journey, the desire to catch a glimpse of the rare snow leopard, also eludes him; although he finds leopard signs, he never actually sees a leopard. Despite this disappointment, however, he is already beginning to understand that the true nature of his quest has little to do with reaching goals or achieving either temporal or spiritual ambitions. He realizes that it is not absolutely necessary to see a leopard for the trip to be a successful one: "I think I must be disappointed, having come so far, and yet I do not feel that way. I am disappointed, and also, I am not disappointed. That the snow leopard *is*, that it is here, that its frosty eyes watch us from the mountain—that is enough" (p. 242).

When Matthiessen does finally meet the Lama of Shey—who, as it turns out, is living in a hut not far from the camp—the two main purposes of Matthiessen's journey converge in an unexpected way. Through an interpreter, Matthiessen asks the monk, whose legs are badly crippled, how he feels about the fact that he will in all likelihood never be able to leave the mountains

again due to his physical condition. The monk cheerfully responds, "Of course I am happy here! It's wonderful! *Especially* when I have no choice" (p. 246). The lama's enthusiastic acceptance of what is, of conditions that are beyond his power to change, makes Matthiessen feel "as if he had struck me in the chest." The lesson as applied to the other part of his quest becomes apparent to him, as he asks the rhetorical question, "Have you seen the snow leopard?" and answers it with the only answer that now seems appropriate: "No! Isn't that wonderful?" (p. 246).

The Snow Leopard, which won the National Book Award in 1979, is generally considered to be Matthiessen's finest nonfiction book. Reviewers used words such as "masterly" and "brilliant" in discussing the work, although some found the Zen to be a bit "watery" (Robert M. Adams, *New York Review of Books* 25:8, 28 September 1978). Matthiessen's second book concerning Zen practice, *Nine-Headed Dragon River: Zen Journals 1969–1985* (1986) is a far more didactic account of his personal experience with "the religion before religion." He has admitted that he was hesitant about writing the book, and only did so reluctantly, out of a desire to raise funds for a Zen center in Riverdale, California. Still, as either an introduction to Zen or as a means of approaching Matthiessen's writing from a spiritual perspective, this work can be quite useful.

The ways in which Matthiessen's nature writing and his studies of Zen tie together are intriguing. As he wrote in *The Snow Leopard*, "debasement of our vision, the retreat from wonder, the backing away like lobsters from free-swimming life into safe crannies, the desperate instinct that our life passes unlived, is reflected in proliferation without joy, corrosive money rot, the gross befouling of the earth and air and water from which we came" (p. 42). While it was by no means inevitable that his love of nature would lead him to Zen—in fact, he wrote that "If I had found an American Indian teacher . . . willing to work with me, I might well have chosen a North American tradition over an Asian one" (*Nine-Headed Dragon River*,

Matthiessen on a research expedition at the black-necked crane sanctuary in Phobjika, Bhutan, 1992

p. 180)—Zen espouses some of the same things, such as sublimation of the self and living in the present, that Matthiessen admired in the primitive cultures he studied. He frequently contrasts these attitudes with those of civilized cultures, in which a debasement of the spirit has accompanied pervasive pollution and environmental degradation.

Social Criticism

In *Nine-Headed Dragon River*, Matthiessen says: "Since from a Zen point of view, the absolute and the relative are not different, I cannot dwell in the absolute calm of my black [meditation] cushion and ignore the chaos of the relative world pounding past the zendo doors" (p. 188). Matthiessen's social activism has manifested itself in several books, beginning with *Sal Si Puedes: Cesar Chavez and the New American Revolution* (1969), a hagiographic account of Cesar Chavez's attempt to unionize the farm workers of California. Matthiessen's longstanding fascination with the American Indian has led him to write two books about ongoing political conflicts between the Indians and the United States government: *In the Spirit of Crazy Horse* (1983) and *Indian Country* (1984). Both of these books are bitter diatribes on the perfidy of U.S. government agencies and their corrupt allies in the Indian community. *In the Spirit of Crazy Horse*—an exhaustive defense of the American Indian Movement (AIM) and Leonard Peltier, who was convicted of the murder of two FBI agents at the Pine Ridge Reservation in 1975—gained a great deal of notoriety from a well-publicized libel suit brought against Matthiessen and his publisher by two principals in the case. After a six-year legal battle that effectively halted distribution of the book, Matthiessen was exonerated in a decision that had significant First Amendment repercussions.

For the most part, Matthiessen's social criticism does not measure up to the best of his nature and travel writing. The openness and objectivity that serve him well in examining primitive cultures often makes his social criticisms seem overly, perhaps even naively, credulous. A significant exception is *Men's Lives*, Matthiessen's social history of the fishermen of Long Island's South Fork. Matthiessen's personal experience here gives his writing an intimacy and an authority that, despite his characteristically meticulous research, is absent in his other books of social criticism. Ironically, his personal interest in Long Island's fishermen and the political and economic hardships they face gives this book a less strident, yet more passionate, tone than his other books in this genre.

Conclusion

For all his success as a writer of nonfiction, Matthiessen has expressed a preference for writing fiction, stating, "I've always thought of nonfiction as a livelihood, my way of making a living so I could write fiction" (Smith, p. 241). In 1989 he published a collection of short stories, *On the River Styx and Other Stories*, and in 1990 he published *Killing Mister Watson*, a critically acclaimed work that employs the device of multiple narrators to examine the death of E. J. Watson, who was murdered in 1910 by his neighbors in a rural community in Florida. Despite this increased attention to fiction and the critical acclaim that he has received for his novels, many still regard his nature writing as his most significant work. Regardless of whether he is thought of first and foremost as a novelist or as a nature writer, however, there is little doubt that Matthiessen's work ranks him as one of the most significant American writers of the last half of the twentieth century.

Selected Bibliography

WORKS OF PETER MATTHIESSEN

NONFICTION

Wildlife in America (New York: Viking, 1959; rev. ed., New York: Viking, 1987); *The Cloud Forest: A Chronicle of the South American Wilderness* (New York: Viking, 1961; repr., New York: Penguin, 1987); *Under the Mountain Wall: A Chronicle of Two Seasons in the Stone Age* (New York: Viking, 1962; repr., New York: Ballantine, 1969; New York: Penguin, 1987); *Oomingmak: The Expedition to the Musk Ox Island in the Bering Sea* (New York: Hastings House, 1967); *The Shorebirds of North America*, ed. by Gardner D. Stout, text by Peter Matthiessen (New York: Viking, 1967); *Sal Si Puedes: Cesar Chavez and the New American Revolution* (New York: Random House, 1969; rev. ed., 1973); *Blue Meridian: The Search for the Great White Shark* (New York: Random House, 1971); *The Tree Where Man Was Born* (New York: Dutton, 1972; repr., New York: Dutton Obelisk, 1983); *The Wind Birds* (New York: Viking, 1973), an expanded edition of *The Shorebirds of North America*; *The Snow Leopard* (New York: Viking, 1978; repr., New York: Penguin, 1987); *Sand Rivers* (New York: Viking, 1981); *In the Spirit of Crazy Horse* (New York: Viking, 1983); *Indian Country* (New York: Viking, 1984); *Men's Lives: The Surfmen and Baymen of the South Fork* (New York: Random House, 1986; repr., Vintage, 1988); *Nine-Headed Dragon River: Zen Journals 1969–1985* (Boston: Shambhala, 1986); *African Silences* (New York: Random House, 1991).

FICTION

Race Rock (New York: Harper & Brothers, 1954; repr. as *The Year of the Tempest*, New York: Bantam, 1957; New York: Vintage, 1988); *Partisans* (New York: Viking, 1955; repr. as *The Passionate Seekers*, New York: Avon, 1955; New York: Vintage, 1987); *Raditzer* (New York: Viking, 1961; repr., New York: Vintage, 1987); *At Play in the Fields of the Lord* (New York: Random House, 1965; repr., New York: Vintage, 1987); *Far Tortuga* (New York: Random House, 1975; repr. New York: Vintage, 1988); *Midnight Turning Gray* (Bristol, R.I.: Ampersand, 1984), short stories; *On the River Styx and Other Stories* (New York: Random House, 1989; repr., New York: Vintage, 1990); *Killing Mister Watson* (New York: Random House, 1990).

CHILDREN'S BOOK

Seal Pool (Garden City, N.Y.: Doubleday, 1972).

SELECTED ARTICLES

"Sadie," in *Atlantic Monthly* 187 (January 1951); "The Fifth Day," in *Atlantic Monthly* 188 (September 1951); "The Wolves of Aguila," in *Harper's Bazaar* (August 1958); "Annals of Crime," in *New Yorker* 34 (1 November 1958); "Slaughter and Salvation," an excerpt from *Wildlife in America*, in *Sports Illustrated* 11 (16 November 1959); "The Last Wilderness: Amazonas Journal," in *New Yorker* 37 (8 July 1961); "The Last Wilderness: Brazilian Chronicle," in *New Yorker* 37 (12 August 1961); "The Last Wilderness: Peruvian Journal," in *New Yorker* 37 (9 September 1961); "The Tree Where Man Was Born: Notes from Travels in Equatoria," in *Reporter* 26 (21 June 1962); "Death of Weake," an excerpt from *Under the Mountain Wall*, in *Harper's Magazine* 225 (October 1962); "Sand and Wind and Waves," in *New Yorker* 41 (3 April 1965);

"Ovibos Moschatus," an excerpt from *Oomingmak*, in *New Yorker* 41 (5 February 1966); "The Wind Birds I," in *New Yorker* 43 (27 May 1967); "The Wind Birds II," in *New Yorker* 43 (3 June 1967); "To the Miskito Bank," in *New Yorker* 43 (28 October 1967); "Lignumvitae: The Last Key," in *Audubon* 74 (January 1972); "The Tree Where Man Was Born I," in *New Yorker* 48 (16 September 1972); "The Tree Where Man Was Born II," in *New Yorker* 48 (23 September 1972); "The Tree Where Man Was Born III," in *New Yorker* 48 (30 September 1972); "The Craft of Fiction in *Far Tortuga*," an excerpt from *Far Tortuga* and interview, in *Paris Review* 15 (winter 1974); "Happy Days," in *Audubon* 77 (November 1975); "A Track on the Beach," in *Audubon* 79 (March 1977); "The Snow Leopard I," in *New Yorker* 54 (27 March 1978); "The Snow Leopard II," in *New Yorker* 54 (3 April 1978); "Travels Through Indian America," in *Nation* 236 (12 February 1983); "Our National Parks: The Case for Burning," in *New York Times Magazine* (11 December 1988); "New York: Old Hometown," in *Architectural Digest* 46 (November 1989); "Congo Basin: The Search for the Forest Elephant," in *Antaeus* 63 (autumn 1989); "The Blue Pearl of Siberia," in *New York Review of Books* 38 (14 February 1991); "Who Really Killed the FBI Men," in *Nation* 252 (13 May 1991); "The Trials of Leonard Peltier," in *Esquire* 117 (January 1992); "The Last Cranes of Siberia," in *New Yorker* 69 (3 May 1993); "Alighting upon the Daurian Steppes," in *Harper's* 286 (June 1993).

BIBLIOGRAPHIES

D. Nicholas, *Peter Matthiessen: A Bibliography: 1951–1979* (Canoga Park, Calif.: Orirana Press, 1979); James Dean Young, "A Peter Matthiessen Checklist," in *Critique* 21, no. 2 (1979).

AUTOBIOGRAPHY

World Authors: 1950–1970, ed. by John Wakeman (New York: H. W. Wilson, 1975).

BIOGRAPHICAL AND CRITICAL STUDIES

Bruce Bawer, "Nature Boy: The Novels of Peter Matthiessen," in *New Criterion* 6 (June 1988); Bert Bender, "*Far Tortuga* and American Sea Fiction Since *Moby Dick*," in *American Literature* 56 (May 1984); Kay Bonetti, "An Interview with Peter Matthiessen," in *Missouri Review* 12, no. 2 (1989); John L. Cobbs, "Peter Matthiessen," in *American Novelists Since World War II: Second Series*, vol. 6 of *Dictionary of Literary Biography*, James E. Kibler, Jr., ed. (Detroit: Gale Research, 1980); William Dowie, *Peter Matthiessen* (Boston: Twayne, 1991); Trip Gabriel, "The Nature of Peter Matthiessen," in *New York Times Magazine* (10 June 1990); James P. Grove, "Pastoralism and Anti-Pastoralism in Peter Matthiessen's *Far Tortuga*," in *Critique* 21, no. 2 (1979); Michael Heim, "The Mystic and the Myth: Thoughts on *The Snow Leopard*," in *Studia Mystica* 4 (summer 1981); Pico Iyer, "Laureate of the Wild," in *Time* 141 (11 January 1993); Deborah Love, *Annaghkeen* (New York: Random House, 1970); Richard F. Patteson, "*At Play in the Fields of the Lord*: The Imperialist Idea and the Discovery of the Self," in *Critique* 21, no. 2 (1979), and "Holistic Vision and Fictional Form in Peter Matthiessen's *The Snow Leopard*," in *Bulletin of the Rocky Mountain Modern Language Association* 37 (1983); Paul Rea, "Causes and Creativity: An Interview with Peter Matthiessen," in *Re Arts and Letters: A Liberal Arts Forum* 15 (fall 1989); Wendy Smith, "PW Interviews Peter Matthiessen," in *Publisher's Weekly* (9 May 1986); Gay Talese, "Looking for Hemingway," in *Esquire* 60 (July 1964); W. Ross Winterowd, "Peter Matthiessen's Lyric Trek," in his *The Rhetoric of the "Other" Literature* (Carbondale, Ill.: Southern Illinois Univ. Press, 1990), and "Reading (and Rehabilitating) the Literature of Fact," in *Rhetoric-Review* 8 (fall 1989).

ENOS MILLS
(1870–1922)

JOHN DOTSON

ENOS ABIJAH MILLS discovered his place in the American West as a young man; he dedicated his life to learning about that place and to telling its story to the world. With a grand vision of the future, he fought to exhaustion to preserve his place and places like it for future generations.

An understanding of Mills's legacy is important to an understanding of the Rocky Mountain region. Among the great figures in the history of the state of Colorado, Enos Mills incontestably earned his place as Father of Rocky Mountain National Park. A self-made man who discovered himself at Longs Peak at age fourteen, Mills never lost his connection with the mountain. No matter how widely he traveled or how deep the demands that drew him away, Mills knew that this place was the origin of his life's work and his destiny.

Finding His Place

A penchant for westward migration winds through Mills's Quaker ancestry. His parents, Enos Abijah Mills, Sr., and Ann Lamb Mills, had trekked from Indiana to Iowa and on to southeast Kansas where Enos, Jr., was born in a plains farmhouse near Fort Scott on 22 April 1870, third-youngest of eleven children.

Ann Lamb Mills had traveled in the Rocky Mountains with her husband at the time of the Breckenridge gold rush in 1859, and it was his mother's tales of her Colorado adventures that early kindled her son's curiosity and imagination.

In the summer of 1884 Mills traveled by rail to Denver and then went northward into the rugged mountain resort area by Estes Park. Mills had a family connecton there in the Reverend Elkanah Lamb, who had cut the first road into Longs Peak Valley (now Tahosa Valley). It was in calling on Lamb that Mills first caught sight of Longs Peak.

At 14,255 feet, Longs exceeds the elevation of all peaks to the north of it in the Rocky Mountain chain. Kit Carson likely trapped in its vicinity in the 1840s. The first recorded climb was led by explorer John Wesley Powell in 1868. Enos Mills would eventually reach the summit three hundred times, forty times solo, attaining the top at every hour of day and night, in all months and seasons, the first to do so in winter, and the first to do so by way of the precipitous North Face.

After working the summer at Elkhorn Lodge in Estes Park, Mills supported himself as a ranch hand for his first winter in Colorado. Employed by Lamb in the summer of 1885, Mills was guided to the summit of Longs for the first time. He then staked his claim—tentative until his twenty-first birthday—and began raising his own homestead cabin facing Longs Peak on the eastern slope of Tahosa Valley.

Mills helped construct the Longs Peak hiking trail in the summer of 1886 while finishing his cabin. The sensibilities of this somewhat physically frail youth during this period are recounted in the story "Love Song of Little Blue," collected in *Bird Memories of the Rockies* (1931):

> I frequently talked to the birds in a natural, conversational way, apparently to their great enjoyment. I always talked about something definite, told stories or endeavored to speak sympathetically as though talking to a child. I avoided detached words and meaningless chatter. Often I have won the attention and sometimes the affection of an animal or bird simply by talking calmly, kindly to it. (pp. 27–28)

Mills befriended a family of bluebirds nesting in the rafters of his unfinished cabin. His account of a subsequent "tragedy" indicates his developing sensibility and outlook to have been in sharp contrast to typical expectations of young male behavior. While Mills was on the trail,

> a boy from a tourist camp near by . . . enthusiastic over barbaric sport, to which he had been reared . . . amused himself by shooting at the bluebirds [and] carried the mangled birds to camp to recount his feat to proud parents. I can never know how much or how deeply this tragedy influenced and colored my life. I had planned simply to enjoy seeing the parents feed and train these children for their brief and busy existence. Thence came the sad event that changed the even tenor of passing days and asked me to be far more than I had ever been and different than I had ever dreamed of being. (p. 11)

In the summer season of 1887, Mills climbed Longs Peak solo for the first time, and then he journeyed to Butte Hill in the Montana Territory, "the Richest Hill on Earth," and apprenticed as a tool boy at the Anaconda Copper Mine. Mining was his livelihood for the next sixteen winters as he advanced through the

ranks to become a licensed stationary engineer. Doing so allowed him to earn the financial base that supported his dreams and adventures.

Learning His Place in the World

With no formal education, Mills made his way to the Butte Public Library, reputedly "the best library in the West," where he directed his own reading toward Darwin, T. S. Huxley, Spencer, and other prevailing scientific and social theorists. He also became familiar with the literature of Shakespeare, Burns, Byron, Walter Scott, Dickens, and Robert Louis Stevenson, and he later cited Washington Irving, Ralph Waldo Emerson, Henry David Thoreau, Walt Whitman, John Muir, and John Burroughs as significant American literary influences.

Mills was deeply attracted to the heroic pattern of Thomas Paine's life. Like Mills, Paine was a self-educated man and an unaffiliated believer in a universal deity. Both men were occasionally tactless activists for noble causes who often roused strong feelings toward themselves, both positive and negative. Mills was a long-term subscriber to *The Free Thought Press*.

Two pivotal events took place in Mills's nineteenth year. In the summer of 1889, he guided his first party to the summit of Longs Peak, and that autumn he set out for the West Coast. There, a chance encounter with John Muir profoundly influenced the future course of Mills's life.

Mills observed a small Muir expedition examining a specimen of yerba buena on a beach in San Francisco. His curiosity piqued, he joined the party and engaged in conversation with Muir during their four-mile hike through the area where Golden Gate Park was taking shape. The encounter brought an invitation to visit Muir at home in Martinez.

Muir lent structure to the young man's ambitions by suggesting that Mills organize his knowledge of the Rockies and develop the necessary speaking and writing skills to bring his knowledge to the world and make his place his cause. Mills's feeling for Muir as his mentor was immediate, deep, and abiding. Muir would later become an ally in the battle to establish Rocky Mountain National Park, and in the advocacy of other national parks. The suggestions of both Muir and Mills were important in establishing the National Park Service.

In 1890, Mills acquired his only formal education at Heald's Business College in San Francisco. He delivered his first lecture on forestry in the city the following year. In 1891, he served a stint with a U.S. Geological Survey team in Yellowstone National Park. In 1892, he made his first journey to Alaska. He traveled to Chicago for the World's Columbian Exposition in 1893. An 1894 Alaskan journey ended in Juneau after an unplanned two-hundred-mile solo trek.

Later journeys included tracing the Missouri River from its source in Montana to its confluence with the Mississippi and onward to the Gulf of Mexico. Mills often mentioned that he had "sat by a camp-fire all alone" in every state in the Union, Alaska, Canada, and Mexico. All these adventures originated from and led back to the homestead cabin with its window facing Longs Peak.

In 1896 Mills began his writing career by filing reports of resort life in Estes Park for the *Denver Times and Republican*. Marking his thirtieth birthday at the turn of the century, Mills gained a global perspective by traveling widely in Europe with Elkanah Lamb. Their five-week tour included Shakespeare's Stratford-on-Avon, the birthplace of Robert Burns, the Paris Exposition, the Swiss Alps, and a climb up Mount Vesuvius.

In 1901 Mills terminated his career as a miner and liquidated his savings to purchase the Lamb property of 160 acres in the Tahosa Valley of Colorado. The next year saw him purchasing Longs Peak House from Lamb and publishing an article in *Outdoor Life*. Fortuitously, this appearance in print coincided with a widespread public awakening to the need to protect America's scenic wonders and to conserve natural resources.

In 1903 Mills achieved the first winter ascent of Longs Peak. Also that winter, he entered an extraordinary two-year contract to become

Mills in the Rocky Mountain forest

"snowman" for the state of Colorado. Officially, his position was that of Snow Observer for the State of Colorado Irrigation Department. To accomplish this experimental work, Mills hiked the upper slopes of the Rockies through the frozen months sending data to Denver so that projections could be made of the summer water supply for the lowlands. Mills demonstrated his winter mountaineering skills, and he accomplished such feats as hiking the Great Divide the full length of the state—from Wyoming to New Mexico—and once trekked 120 miles in six days.

The ever-restless Mills established in 1904 a singular means of bringing his knowledge to the people and bringing people to the place of his knowing. He transformed the Longs Peak House into the Longs Peak Inn. Years later, in the preface to *Bird Memories of the Rockies*, writer John J. Jacobs aptly characterized the inn:

Long's Peak Inn [was] one of the quaintest, one of the most original inns in the world. It was built for expression of himself, just as he wrote his books. . . . It was Enos Mills—the grounds, the buildings, the great lobby, the fireplaces, the dining-room, the quaint rules . . . the collections of books and flowers, and the uncanny totem-poles from timber-line— all are Enos Mills. . . . Into this place he threw all his intense energy, all his money, all his fierce craving for self-expression, all his genius and all his sense of the fitting and the proper. (p. xvii)

Enos Mills's simple but staunch ideals were reflected in such instructions to guests as the following: "Spare the flowers. Thoughtless people are destroying the flowers by pulling them by the roots or by picking too many. Neither the roots nor the leafy stalk should be taken, and flowers, if taken, should be cut, not pulled. WHAT DO YOU WANT WITH AN ARMFUL OF WILD FLOWERS?" (Hawthorne and Mills, p. 106).

Longs Peak Inn became a highly successful enterprise. The rituals of the inn were intended to bond guests with one another, with the community of forest and mountain creatures, and with the whole environment. Mornings began with Mills's legendary query, "Glad you're living?" Throughout the day, if not guiding a peak expedition, Mills might ask, "What's up?" or "Why don't you start something?"

He kept no piano, allowed no dancing, discouraged card games or "talk of movies," and tolerated no religious services. Posted throughout the inn were other injunctions, such as "*Go light! Take camera, binoculars, hatchet, matches, raisins, notebook, raincoat.*" (Believing them to be an ideal energy food for hikers, Mills persuaded a national producer to market raisins in individual-serving-size boxes.) He would deliver after-dinner nature talks and then usher guests outdoors—on occasions of particular excitement for Mills, into the rain.

Famous guests at Longs Peak Inn included novelist and playwright Edna Ferber; labor leader Eugene V. Debs, a close friend of Mills's; novelist Gene Stratton Porter; lawyer Clarence Darrow; jurist Charles Evans Hughes; activist and writer Jane Addams, recipient of the Nobel Peace Prize in 1931; educator David Starr Jordan; and actor Douglas Fairbanks, Sr.

To keep up his extensive connections and expanding responsibilities, Mills financed his own private telephone line into Tahosa Valley and established and played the role of postmaster at the Longs Peak Post Office.

Mills was indefatigable in carrying his stories, his learning, and his truths to the world. Gathering reminiscences of early settlers to Estes Park, Mills self-published his first book, *Story of Estes Park and a Guide Book* (1905). In the summer of 1906, his last to serve officially as a mountain guide, Mills led at least seventy-five parties to Longs Peak, thirty-two ascents in the month of August alone. He went on an autumn lecture tour of eighty eastern cities, during which he formed an acquaintance with John Burroughs, and then completed his last winter as Snow Observer in Colorado.

Early in 1907, Mills's reputation caught the attention of President Theodore Roosevelt, who invited Mills to become Government Lecturer on Forestry. In the autumn of 1908, Mills traveled to fourteen states and delivered fifty-four addresses to high schools and colleges, teachers' organizations, women's clubs, and civic and business meetings.

Mills's first nationally distributed book, *Wild Life on the Rockies*, was published in 1909 by Houghton Mifflin of Boston, publishers of Muir and Burroughs, both of whom Mills would routinely outsell. Mills resigned his presidential appointment and began what he termed his life's "most stimulating and growth-compelling" activity, the campaign for the establishment of Rocky Mountain National Park (*Enos Mills of the Rockies*, 1935, p. 150).

Mills not only campaigned for the park, but also continued crusading and frequently lobbying

Congress in Washington on behalf of diverse environmental issues.

Telling His Story to the World

By his fortieth birthday, Mills was writing prolifically and had contributed sundry articles to magazines such as *Sunset, Harper's Weekly, Atlantic, Collier's, World's Work, Craftsman, American Boy, Youth's Companion,* and *Country Life in America.* Over the course of his career, he published more than fifty pieces with the *Saturday Evening Post* alone. Mills often consolidated, reworked, and published articles in variant versions before collecting them as chapters in his popular books. This practice—rooted in his rather frenetic drive to communicate and to express himself—contributed to the disorganization that sometimes plagues his work.

The context of the radically changing American society in which Mills establishes his persona as a Western nature writer is evidenced in the September 1910 issue of *Country Life in America,* which marked his first appearance in that magazine. Adjacent advertisements are headlined "Make the Farm Pay, Complete Home Study Courses," "A Word of Advice to the Home Maker from an Expert House Decorator, Department of Decoration, Murphy Varnish Company, Fifth Avenue New York," and "All Star Performance Right in your own home whenever you want to hear it on the Victor-Victrola, $15, Music by Sousa's Band and Victor Herbert's Orchestra." A brief news item reports: "AERIAL TRAVEL. No trip to Europe this year will be complete without a voyage on one of the ships of the Zeppelin Aerial Line . . . run under the auspices of the City of Munich."

At the foot of the column appears "ENOS A. MILLS, MOUNTAINEER," with the following description: Men of the type of Henry D. Thoreau, John Burroughs, and John Muir are becoming more and more rare. . . . But their mantle has fallen upon one who, though still a young man, has already proved himself worthy—Enos A. Mills. . . . He is a man who has

something to say, and what he says is worth reading.

The article so introduced, "At the Stream's Source," exemplifies Mills's contribution to the science of his time. Mills was among the first popular writers to address such natural interconnections as that of beaver dams in the heights and flood prevention in the lowlands. Also advancing solid information drawn from direct personal observation, Mills anticipated dendrochronology by nearly a decade. Mills's most popular and most frequently told story consisted of his interpretive reading of the rings of a veteran pine.

Mills's public spiritedness was deep and genuine. He often wrote for the youth who encountered his articles in classrooms across the country and for whom he stood as an exemplar. In his writing, as in his speaking, Mills entertained while educating, informing and promoting his "noble causes" with enthusiasm. An important aspect of his endeavor to communicate was his use of a Kodak reflex camera to create over twenty thousand negatives, producing slides for his lectures, prints for his books, and postcards for Longs Peak Inn.

Stylistically, first-person narration is central in Mills's stories. His relentlessly earnest tone blends a meticulous perfectionism with an outspoken zeal that can at times be preachy and moralistic to the point of self-righteousness. Beyond his rhetoric, however, Mills's aim was to present facts and solid information that would change readers' attitudes and lead them outdoors, and the tenor of his narratives remains extrovertive and self-effacing.

Mills's work has received scant critical attention or analysis in the later twentieth century. His powers of expression were limited by his narrow, self-directed reading and by the naive tastes of the Gilded Age reading public for whom he wrote. Also, his work tends to perpetuate the highly individualistic and public persona he sought to create. Mills may not have been the intellectual equal of Thoreau or Muir—for one, he did not enjoy the same advantages of higher education—and as a self-taught writer was never required to discipline himself or study or accept the influence of another writer. He was seldom required to submit his ideas or his style to formal criticism.

At times Mills's prose is sentimentalized and ornamented with mixed metaphors, abstract and convoluted diction, inverted sentence order, and passive verb forms. He often oversimplifies, which reflects his conviction that the benign and cooperative side of nature predominates over the violent and brutal. References to animals as "folks" and other anthropomorphic associations evoke the "nature faker" controversy of the early 1900s, though he wrote after this issue had largely subsided. Mills's contemporary readers, many of whom had daily contact with farm or work animals, were nevertheless comfortable with his prose style and language.

Major Themes

Mills's major themes are reverence for nature, the integrity of animals, the rightful place of human beings in nature, and the ennobling effects of both knowing and protecting nature for the common good.

Mills strongly asserts that contact with nature brings health to body, soul, and society. The cycle of human life, as of all living creatures, includes insuring the young the opportunity to survive, helping the mature to thrive, and allowing the old to die with integrity. He urges receptivity to new perceptions of what is real and what is possible beyond the scale of a single human lifetime. Mills assumes that the majority of his readers acknowledge some form of transcendent deity and are at least somewhat familiar with the philosophies of Emerson and Thoreau. Mills speaks in his own manner of divine immanence and pastoral myth.

Mills employs upper case letters frequently; for example, in one sentence he referred to wilderness as "No Man's Land, the Undiscovered Country, the Mysterious Old West, the Land of Romance and Adventure." He often alludes to having left the ordinary polarities and oppositions of the human condition behind at lower altitudes.

In *Your National Parks* (1917), he evokes feelings for nature as Great Mother:

If you are dulled and dazed with the fever and the fret, or weary and worn,—tottering under burdens too heavy to bear,—go back to the old outdoor home. Here Nature will care for you as a mother for a child. In the mellow-lighted forest aisles, beneath the beautiful airy arches of limbs and leaves, with the lichen-tinted columns of gray and brown, with the tongueless eloquence of the bearded, veteran trees, amid the silence of centuries, you will come into your own. (p. 338)

Mills wrote extremely detailed descriptions of his own encounters with the primary elements of wind and fire. One of his most expressive chapters is "Wind Rapids on the Heights," published in *The Adventures of a Nature Guide* (1920). Having reached an altitude of twelve thousand feet and achieved his objective of retrieving a wind meter (recording wind speeds of up to 170 miles an hour), he chose to continue onward to the summit of Longs Peak. The personification may seem awkward, but it may also have been necessary for the expression of what was for Mills a deeply interactive experience:

I eased myself upward in the rushing wind, crawling close, holding with hands, and anchoring and holding rear down by hooking feet behind and beneath rocks. . . .

Just before reaching the top of the narrow ridge and the precipice, I felt the wind getting the better of me and feared that a slightly more violent rush or surge would tear my holds loose. . . . Putting a shoulder against a rock point, I allowed the wind to push my legs around, then forward. I was then going up feet foremost instead of head foremost. The gully was so extremely steep that I was almost standing or walking on my head. . . . There was no climbing; the wind sucked, dragged, pushed, and floated over me ever upward. . . .

Why did I . . . venture precipices and go up into the sky on a peak nearly three miles above the seven restless seas?

Irresistible is nature's call to play. This call comes in a thousand alluring forms. It comes at unexpected times and sends us to unheard-of places. We simply cannot tell what nature will have of us, or where next. But from near and far, ever calls her eloquent voice. . . . She pictures alluring scenes in which to rest and play; in mysterious ways she sends us eagerly forth for unscaled heights and fairylands. . . . She fascinatingly commands and charms us to other scenes. We rush to respond and fix our eyes on a happy horizon. . . . It was seriously splendid to play with these wild winds. There is no greater joy than wrestling naked handed with the elements. (1990 ed., pp. 82–88)

Mills continually asserts that the spell of the high country can transform human nature through an immediate and profound consciousness of freedom. He preached this belief in *Your National Parks:*

Stirring and wild, wonderful scenes are encountered during storms on mountaintops, by the lakeshore, and in cañons. The dangers in such times and places are fewer than in cities. Discomforts? Scarcely. To some persons life must be hardly worth living. If any normal person under fifty cannot enjoy being in a storm in the wilds, he ought to reform at once. (p. 322)

For Mills, when the continuity of sensation and environment is intact, life is lived more abundantly. Vulnerability to elemental powers heightens the senses, awakens mental faculties, and liberates powers of imagination. Nature is benign and instructive and yields inexhaustible adventure. Peril and injury are simply part of the wilderness experience.

Mills profoundly respected the integrity of animals (although he occasionally lapsed into a bias against a particular species, as in his dislike of the ways of the mountain lion). Mills did not accept the notion of wilderness as a bloody battleground of unceasing hostilities, but rather he observed "the greater wilderness of coöperation" and found animals to be companions, helpers, and guides contributing distinctive intelligence to the organic whole. Mills possibly gathered more firsthand knowledge of the culture of grizzlies than has any other human being and lived to mourn the loss of the last grizzly in Rocky Mountain National Park. He recorded observations of one beaver colony for thirty-six years, and he drew from that experience salient lessons not only in animals' tenacity but also in their playfulness and enjoyment of life despite ruination and upheaval.

This passage from *Rocky Mountain Wonderland* (1915) exemplifies his acute powers of observing animal behavior:

I spent hours reading the news, observing the illustrations, and studying the hieroglyphics on the snow. Whether footprints in the mud or snow may have suggested printing cannot be told, but it is certain that the tracks, stains, and impressions in snow print the news and record the local animal doings. Here the rabbits played; there the grouse searched for dinner; while over yonder the long, lacy trail of a mouse ends significantly between the impressions of two wing feathers. One sees a trail made by a long-legged animal and another by a fellow with a long body and short legs— perhaps a weasel. At one place near the foot of an old tree a squirrel had abandoned a cone and run home. Near by was the trail of a porcupine who was well-fed, well-protected, and though dull-witted, not at all afraid. Apparently he hadn't any idea where he was going and did not care whom he should meet; for at one place he came face to face with a fox and the fox turned aside. (in *Radiant Days*, 1994, p. 181)

In addition to the grizzly and beaver, Mills developed considerable expertise in understanding the bighorn, or wild mountain sheep. The following passages are from *Rocky Mountain Wonderland:*

Wild mountain sheep are perhaps the most accomplished and dare-devil acrobats in the animal world . . . [I]n descending dizzy precipices and sheer walls the bighorn sheep are unrivaled. When sheep hurriedly descend a precipice, the laws of falling bodies are given a most spectacular display, and the possibilities of friction and adhesion are tested to the utmost. . . .

There was one long pitch that offered nothing on which to stand and no place on which to stop. Down this the old ram plunged with a series of bouncing drops and jumps,—falling under control, with his fall broken, checked, and directed, without stopping, by striking with the feet as frequently as was necessary. First came three or four straightforward bouncing dives, followed by a number of swift zigzag jumps, striking alternately right and left, then three or four darts to the right before again flying off to the left. At last he struck on a wide ledge, where he pulled up and stopped with masterly resistance and stiff-legged jumps! Mind controlled matter! This specialty of the sheep requires keen eyesight, instant decision, excellent judgement, a marvelous nicety in measuring distances, and a complete forgetfulness of peril. Each ewe in turn gave a similar and equally striking exhibition; while the lambs, instead of breaking their necks in the play of drop and bounce, did not appear to be even cautious. They showed off by dropping farther and going faster than the old ones! This was sheer frolic for these children of the crags. (pp. 24–26)

Mills continually and unwaveringly urged individuals, "Go out into nature alone." A man who spent great portions of his lifetime traveling alone above timberline through long winters, Mills was convinced that direct contact with nature ennobled human character, as did striving to protect nature for the common good. The Quaker sensibility in Mills's ancestry seems as least to be latent in this appeal in *Your National Parks:*

To bring the capitalist and the laborer—all classes—together in the Park's august scenes, is bound to encourage acquaintance and to prevent misunderstandings. All this means unity, friendship, and will keep war drums in the background. He who feels the spell of the wild, the rhythmic melody of falling water, the echoes among the crags, the bird-songs, the wind in the pines, and the endless beat of wave upon the shore, is in tune with the universe. And he will know what human brotherhood means . . . Nature is universal . . . The supreme triumph of parks is humanity. (p. 386)

Although he did not and could not fully appreciate the magnitude of the effects of rapidly expanding industrialism, Mills was aware that he lived in a time of great transition. On his travels he noted the dehumanizing effects of industrialized society and observed, "Blue Monday did not originate outdoors" (*Your National Parks*, p. 382).

He understood that the last spreads of wilderness in the American West were threatened by private interests. Longs Peak Inn was frequently the target of vandalism perpetrated by petty enemies who resented his zeal in setting western lands aside for preservation and recreation rather than leaving them open for private investment. To his dying day, he remained a populist agitator in the pattern of Thomas Paine.

Preserving His Place

Mills's battles were not limited to ideology. What he termed his "missionary work" moved individuals and legislators to action. As an interpreter of nature to the nation, Mills was a preeminent shaper of values and contributed to the higher appreciation of the aesthetic qualities of nature in his time.

As he began the extended campaign to create a national park, he dreamed at first that Colorado's entire Front Range, from Wyoming to New Mexico, might be set apart as a "playground for the nation." His popular volume *The Spell of the Rockies* (1911), appearing near the apex of his influence, makes appeal for the preservation of his place: "It is close to the geographical centre of the country, is easily accessible, has an excellent climate, and as a National Park it would become a scenic resource of enormous and exhaustless richness" (1989 ed., p. 348).

Mills realized what he considered to be his great life achievement on 26 January 1915, when President Woodrow Wilson signed the bill establishing Rocky Mountain National Park. Enos Mills stood as master of ceremonies at the park dedication on 4 September. He could also take credit when Congress created the National Park Service in the Organic Act of 1916, legislation about which both Muir and Mills had been consulted.

The climate in which Mills could enjoy his public triumph changed abruptly in 1917. The nation was assuming a new role on the world stage and entering combat in the First World War. Public attention to conservationist causes vanished overnight, and Mills's rhetoric broadened and grew more strident, as evidenced in *Your National Parks*, published that year:

> It is but little less than folly to spend millions on forts and warships, on prisons and hospitals, instead of giving people the opportunity to develop and rest in the sane outdoors. The population of the United States now numbers a hundred millions and is growing with amazing rapidity. The harassing, exacting life of to-day makes outdoor life more important than ever before. (p. 382)

In *The Adventures of a Nature Guide* (1920), both Mills's breadth of vision and loss of pragmatism in the face of changing public priorities are reflected in his call for a national department of parks and recreation—"for all time and for all people"—with a director "separate from and independent of all Cabinet positions" (p. 16).

In the summer of 1918, forty-eight-year-old Enos Mills married his protégé, Esther A. Burnell, twenty years his younger, in a ceremony at his original homestead cabin. He then took fresh initiative in establishing the Trail School—the first of its kind—for training nature guides (of both genders, as Mills always insisted) and for conducting summer programs. He watched over the thriving inn operations himself while continuing to prepare numerous manuscripts.

Recognizing the need for nature interpreters in the parks, the first director of the National Park Service, Stephen Mather, consulted Mills as the pioneer of the art and science of nature interpretation. Mills's ideas figured significantly in the development of the role of the ranger naturalist. However, a deep and irreconcilable conflict grew between Mills and Mather. Park Service policies that were developed to protect the parks restricted use of long-established roads to monopolistic concessioners. As a result, Mills and his employees were prevented from conducting excursions in the park he had fought so hard to establish. Mills felt personally persecuted.

In 1919, the year his daughter Enda was born, Mills sued Mather. The struggle sent Mills back to the lecture circuit to argue the issue publicly. World War I had brought complex economic and social changes, and in the postwar environment, Mills sensed that many people had become "pleasure bent" and "money mad." About twenty-two million persons, five hundred thousand in the United States, died in a worldwide outbreak of influenza, the worst pandemic since the Black Death. In the face of such upheaval, Mills did not succeed in kindling wide interest in his arcane dispute with the Park Service.

His celebrity, however, was undiminished, as reflected in a feature article in *Country Life in America* for May 1920: "Mr. Mills is still a young man . . . still active and hardy, and may be said to be only fairly launched upon his career" (Chapman, p. 61). That same year, in *The Adventures of a Nature Guide*, Mills revealed some of his most lyrical prose:

> I wish every one could have a night by a campfire—by Mother Nature's old hearthstone. When one sits in the forest within the campfire's magic tent of light, amid the silent, sculpted trees, there go thrilling through one's blood all the trials and triumphs of our race. The blazing wood, the ragged and changing flame, the storms and calms, the mingling smoke and blaze, the shadow figures that dance against the trees, the scene and figures in the fire—with these, though all are new and strange, yet you feel at home once more in the woods. A campfire in the forest is the most enchanting place on life's highway by which to have a lodging for the night. (1990, p. 249)

The end of his life journey was, ironically, induced by a jarring subway accident in New York City in January 1922. Within months, an emotionally exhausted Mills succumbed to an infection caused by an abscessed wisdom tooth and died on 21 September, the autumnal equinox. At his funeral in the lobby of Longs Peak Inn, a close friend, Judge Ben B. Lindsey of Denver, eulogized, "some of these men like Zebulon Pike discovered the bodies of our mountains. Mills discovered their souls" (Hawthorne and Mills, p. 255). British novelist Thomas Hardy sent his condolences: "It is as if a mountain peak had sunk below the horizon" (p. 257). Mills's ashes were later scattered from an airplane over Longs Peak.

Subsequent to Mills's death, other volumes of collected essays were published. An estimate of Mills's influence in his time is drawn in the preface to the final publication of his writings in that era. In *Bird Memories of the Rockies* (1931), John J. Jacobs states his prediction regarding the homestead cabin built by young Enos Mills: "In years to come this cabin will be as much a shrine as the spot where Thoreau's cabin stood on the shores of Walden Pond" (p. xvi). Increasing numbers of visitors to Mills's cabin, and increasing attention to and republication of his work, lend support to these sentiments.

Selected Bibliography

WORKS OF ENOS MILLS

BOOKS

Story of Estes Park and a Guide Book (Self-published, 1905); *Wild Life on the Rockies* (Boston: Houghton Mifflin, 1909); *The Spell of the Rockies* (Boston: Houghton Mifflin, 1911; repr., Lincoln: Univ. of Nebraska Press, 1989); *In Beaver World* (Boston: Houghton Mifflin, 1913); *The Story of a Thousand-Year Pine* (Boston: Houghton Mifflin, 1914); *The Rocky Mountain Wonderland* (Boston: Houghton Mifflin, 1915); *The Story of Scotch* (Boston: Houghton Mifflin, 1916); *Your National Parks* (Boston: Houghton Mifflin, 1917); *Being Good to Bears and Other True Animal Stories* (Boston: Houghton Mifflin, 1919); *The Grizzly, Our Greatest Wild Animal* (Boston: Houghton Mifflin, 1919); *The Adventures of a Nature Guide* (Garden City, N.Y.: Doubleday, Page, 1920; repr., Friendship, Wis.: New Past, 1990); *Waiting in the Wilderness* (Garden City, N.Y.: Doubleday, Page, 1921); *Watched by Wild Animal* (Garden City, N.Y.: Doubleday, Page, 1922); *Wild Animal Home-steads* (Garden City, N.Y.: Doubleday, Page, 1923); *The Rocky Mountain National Park* (Garden City, N.Y.: Doubleday, Page, 1924); *Romance of Geology* (Garden City, N.Y.: Doubleday, Page, 1926); *Bird Memories of the Rockies* (Boston: Houghton Mifflin, 1931); *Radiant Days*, ed. by John Dotson (Salt Lake City: Univ. of Utah Press, 1994).

ARTICLES

"Dangers of Snowslides," in *Harper's Weekly* 48 (24 December 1904); "At the Stream's Source," in *Country Life in America* 18 (September 1910); "Racing an Avalanche," in *Country Life in America* 19 (November 1910); "A Park for the Nation," in *Colliers* 49 (8 June 1912); "The Story of Scotch," in *Country Life in America* 22 (May 1912); "Beautiful America; IX. The Rocky Mountain Region," in *Country Life in America* 22 (August 1912); "Touring in Our National Parks," in *Country Life in America* 23 (January 1913); "The Forest Fire," in *Country Life in America* 27 (January 1915); "The Battle Along the Timberline," in *Country Life in America* 31 (December 1916); "Twisted Trees," in *Country Life in America* 37 (January 1920); "A New National Park," in *The Saturday Evening Post* (5 March 1910); "The Proposed Estes National Park," in *Sierra Club Bulletin* (June 1910); "Who's Who—and Why: Enos A. Mills Himself, By Himself," in *Saturday Evening Post* (1 September 1917); "Children of My Trail School," in *Saturday Evening Post* (1 March 1919); "A Home of Forest Fire Logs," in *Sunset Magazine* 46 (May 1921).

BIOGRAPHICAL AND CRITICAL STUDIES

Arthur Chapman, "Enos A. Mills, Nature Guide," in *Country Life in America* 38 (May 1920); Hildegarde Hawthorne and Esther Burnell Mills, *Enos Mills of the Rockies* (Boston: Houghton Mifflin, 1935); Lloyd K. Musselman, *Rocky Mountain National Park: Administrative History, 1915–1965* (Washington, D.C.: U.S. Department of the Interior, National Park Service, 1971); Peter Wild, *Enos Mills* (Boise, Idaho: Boise State Univ., 1979), and *Pioneer Conservationists of Western America* (Missoula, Mont.: Mountain Publishing Company, 1979); Kent Dannen, "Rocky Mountain Men," in *Westways* (August 1976); LeRoy Jeffers, "A Lover of Nature and the Mountains," review of *The Adventures of a Nature Guide*, in *The Bookman* (March 1920); Ben B. Lindsey, "The Passing of Enos Mills," in *Sunset Magazine* 50 (January 1923); Grace D. Phillips, "Guardian of the Rockies," *National Parks Magazine* (January/March 1955); "Rocky Mountain Life and Scenes," review of *Wild Life on the Rockies*, in *New York Times Book Review* (24 April 1909); "The Rocky Mountain Wonderland," review of *The Rocky Mountain Wonderland*, in *New York Times Book Review* (8 August 1915).

JOHN HANSON MITCHELL
(b. 1940)

TERRELL F. DIXON

JOHN HANSON MITCHELL is among the most traditional and the most original of contemporary American nature writers. He is, by virtue of where he lives and what he chooses to write about, one of the twentieth century's most Thoreauvian of nature writers. Mitchell lives in Littleton, Massachusetts, not far from Thoreau's Walden, where, as he describes in *Living at the End of Time* (1990), he built and made his home in a small cabin. As he pointed out, no one who does this in the United States "does so without at least a nod to Henry Thoreau" (p. 5). His own work features more than a nodding acquaintance with Thoreau, however. *Living at the End of Time* includes an extensive study of Thoreau's journals and life, and it provides what is very much a Thoreauvian commentary on contemporary life. This book also parallels Thoreau's work in its insistence on the importance both of nearby nature and of those characters—eccentrics and outcasts—whose ways of being in the natural world take them outside the village norms.

Mitchell is also an innovator, a highly individualistic writer whose prose is decidedly his own mix of personal experience, nature observation, and environmental concern. *Ceremonial Time: Fifteen Thousand Years on One Square Mile* (1984) embodies a distinctive approach to nature writing. In it, Mitchell compresses the landscape studied to one square mile while expanding the temporal scope to include fifteen thousand years of history. He carries out this narrative exploration through an innovative method that he calls ceremonial time, a technique for knowing the world that he learned from his Native American friends.

Mitchell wrote these two major works only after a significant apprenticeship, and some of the key ideas expressed in them first found expression in earlier and different types of texts. His first books are two collaboratively produced nature guides—*Hiking Cape Cod* (1978) and *The Curious Naturalist* (1980)—and *The Energy Book* (1979), a coedited collection of essays about the energy crisis. A third nature guide, *A Field Guide to Your Own Back Yard*, was a solo project first published in 1985. Unlike those hiking guides that are resolutely factual in their approach, focusing on trail markers and distances, or those that include some pre-packaged aesthetic perspective, telling the reader where to point a camera, Mitchell's prose in *Hiking Cape Cod* demonstrates the depth and vision that found fuller expression in *Ceremonial Time* and *Living at the End of Time*.

Early Works

Hiking Cape Cod was begun by John Bennett and William Kutik, who turned the project over to

Whit Griswold—a writer, fishing guide, teacher, carpenter, and political organizer—and to John Hanson Mitchell. Mitchell had recently resigned as director of the Roaring Brook Nature Center in Canton, Connecticut, to work as assistant editor of publications for the Massachusetts Audubon Society; he hoped the move would allow him to have more writing time. *Hiking Cape Cod* provides an early example of his ability.

The book's opening chapter, titled with a version of an old Irish blessing, "May the Wind Be at Your Back," sounds what will be central themes in Mitchell's work—the joys, the importance, and the wildness of nearby nature. The authors describe themselves as walking the beach near Race Point in Provincetown, heading out toward the lighthouse on "one of those heartlessly cold days" (p. 13). A near gale forces them to walk backward to make any progress at all. Although they are able to cover only about a hundred yards before seeking shelter, Mitchell's reflection on that experience will resonate throughout his writing career:

> Needless to say, perhaps, we were alone that day. There were no jeeps on the beach, no joggers or fishermen. Here, not three miles from the nearest coffee shop, we had achieved the so-called wilderness experience, for which more ambitious and better financed hikers spend an inordinate amount of time and money to match. We had found a place where the elemental forces of the planet displayed themselves in such fury that we would have perished there in a matter of hours, had we stayed. (p. 14)

Like Thoreau, Henry Beston, Annie Dillard, and others central to the tradition of American nature writing, Mitchell wants his readers to realize that nature and wildness exist everywhere, not only in far-off and exotic locales. For Mitchell, this hiking guidebook is a way to teach his readers about more than trail signs in unfamiliar territories; it also, somewhat paradoxically, given that a substantial part of the readership for such a book is likely to be tourists—visitors from afar seeking guidance in an area new to them—begins Mitchell's advocacy for nearby nature.

Other significant topics also emerge here. In the chapter called "Glacier!" Mitchell provides this description of a glacier: "There is something sublime, if not terrifying, in the image of a layer of ice as much as a mile thick moving slowly southward, purposefully, undeniably, and preceded by dizzying fogs, blizzards, and iron-fisted frosts" (p. 19). The terror comes because he holds the view, set forth by the geologist Barbara Blau Chamberlain in her book *These Fragile Outposts: A Geological Look at Cape Cod, Martha's Vineyard, and Nantucket* (1964), that we are living in an "inter-glacial age" (p. 24), that the glaciers will return. Another chapter provides a brief history of humankind's years on the Cape, anticipating a similar exploration of place that occurs in *Ceremonial Time*.

Whereas *Hiking Cape Cod* illustrates Mitchell's interest in outdoor activity and nature observation, *The Energy Book*, coedited with Wayne Henley as part of a series by the Massachusetts Audubon Society, features his environmental concern. The essays collected in it discuss the energy crisis from a variety of perspectives and range from the history of fuel use in the United States to a photographic description of the alternative energy landscape of aquaculture and biological farming at the New Alchemy Institute at Woods Hole, Massachusetts.

Mitchell's individual contribution to *The Energy Book* is a personal essay called "Scyther's Complaint," which is placed at the end of the book. Unlike the other essays collected here, this is a literary meditation, one that offers Mitchell a way to introduce what will be another major underlying concern of his work: American food production. Here he emphasizes the connection between how Americans produce food and the energy crisis. At the heart of his essay is a contrast between past farming practices—represented by the scythe that Mitchell uses to cut his meadow—and modern food production systems—represented by a fast-food wrapper found in this meadow, a full twelve miles from the nearest McDonald's.

In this, his initial essay about the part of Massachusetts that will be featured in *Ceremonial Time* and *Living at the End of Time*, Mitchell describes growing rye, and how he cuts, winnows, and grinds it into flour for bread. This "thorough little ritual, half-sacred, half-profane," is to make the point, one too easy to overlook in our time, "that flesh is grass" (p. 168). His three loaves, prepared on a one-time basis, contrast sharply with the output of the industrialized American bread-production system.

Had our rye crop failed that year we could have gotten into one of the two vehicles, fired up the engine, and steered the machine along a special roadway, blacktopped with petroleum products, to a market. Inside the climate controlled building we could have bought a loaf of rye bread. The bread itself would have a complicated history. It would be created by wheat flour grown in the Midwest and rye flour grown in Canada. The two flours would have been mixed with sodium proprionate, manufactured, I would guess, in a place like Newark, New Jersey. The various ingredients would be mixed together in a climate-controlled bakery in Greenwich, Connecticut, by stainless steel machinery run by electrical current generated in Bridgeport from fossil fuels brought over from Saudi Arabia. Once the machines had completed the process of mixing, kneading, and baking the ingredients, the finished loaves would have been loaded onto trucks and brought to the supermarket through a series of highways and superhighways, one of which would undoubtedly have been Route 495 which runs through the former grain fields and apple orchards in this once agricultural community. (pp. 169–170)

This devastating perspective on food preparation in American and global culture fits Mitchell's view of a culture that destroys the Amazon to get meat for McDonald's. The one hope he offers is that civilization may well run out of fossil fuels before all the rain forests are destroyed. In a collection that is, as the preface notes, "an essentially optimistic book" (p. v), Mitchell's last word offers a fairly grim prospect.

The Curious Naturalist and *A Field Guide to Your Own Back Yard* develop variations on another type of text: the nature teaching guide. *The Curious Naturalist* is a handbook for those who teach children about the natural world; it originally appeared in magazine form, put out by Mitchell and others for the Massachusetts Audubon Society. It was then published in an eight-by-eleven-inch handbook format as a part of the excellent PHalarope series for amateur naturalists, a series that also included books by such figures as the astronomer Chet Raymo and the nature photographer Stan Osolinski.

The Curious Naturalist, unlike *A Field Guide to Your Own Back Yard*, has various audiences in mind. The primary readers will be teachers, but the goal of the handbook—to pique children's interest in the natural world—determines the kinds of crafts, games, and other activities presented here. Thus the handbook contains many large illustrations and careful, simple explanations about how to make an aquarium, a twig belt, maple sugar, and a log-sided owl house.

Mitchell's introduction, however, is aimed at a broad readership. Like his other early writings, these sections begin the consideration of issues and topics that Mitchell develops more fully in later works. Several such themes are set in motion, for example, by the word "curious" in the title. Mitchell clearly has in mind the naturalist who is inquisitive about the ways of the natural world, but the term also points to the unusual, the odd, the eccentric. His introduction begins with the story of Gilly Robinson, an old man who "more or less served as the unofficial naturalist for the children of the community" during Mitchell's childhood:

In retrospect, I realize that Gilly was the mildly eccentric sort of social misfit who nowadays might be living off state aid or institutionalized in some old people's home. But to us, in those days, he was pure hero, a man who fell somewhere between wild Indian, Pan, and a benevolent woods-dwelling Santa Claus. The thing I remember best about Gilly is not his ability to identify plants and animals, but the long Saturday morning rambles we would take with him. . . . He seemed energized by the presence of trees and birds and would virtually leap from point to point as he described, in animated detail, the characteristics or uses of some obscure plant. He had an odd habit of holding any interesting object he had found as close to his face as he could, as if he needed to smell the thing, or inspect it in minute detail in order to identify it. This is the image of him I remember best, a skinny goatlike man hopping from tree trunk to tree trunk, pointing out a variety of local natural wonders to his accompanying tribe of children. (pp. 1–2)

Gilly, Mitchell laments, is dead, not only literally but figuratively as well; there is no one in the present generation to continue teaching as he taught. The child with a question about some aspect of nature therefore faces a void. To get an answer, this child will most likely go to a school science department or library or nature center; the information will come not from a person in the woods but from a book. While such books providing specific factual answers can often be found, Mitchell argues that something very important is missing.

What the children, and their parents, lack today are those "little tidbits of interesting fact and folklore about common plants and animals" (p. 2) once passed on by Gilly and other unofficial teachers like him. Mitchell laments that there is now "a small empty nook in the body of the subject that was once the place of the less scientific but in some ways more humane side of the natural world" (p. 3). Stories, such as the one in which the butternut tree was designated by Gilly as the witches' tree because "once a year the witches would come out and wander through the night woods ironing flat all the rough bark of the butternut trees" (p. 2), no longer enrich our relationship to the natural world. With their absence, "the spirit of the woods and fields," that "sense of the complexities and richness of the outdoors" (p. 3), has become much harder to acquire. Missing, too, is the excitement that such tales engendered. They served to inculcate

what Mitchell feels is an absolutely crucial feature of any education about the natural world: a sense of mystery.

In his introduction to *The Curious Naturalist*, Mitchell disavows any aim to offer the kind of information formerly provided by Gilly, suggesting that the printed page cannot supply what Gilly taught his listeners. Nonetheless, even as Mitchell explains to his multiple audiences just what it is that a naturalist does, his prose engages the reader in its presentation of intriguing aspects of nature. We are introduced to the woodcock, who, Mitchell tells us, spends eleven months of the year "facing downward toward the dank soil where it feeds," only to go skyward during its mating dance.

It will climb higher and be lost to view. Then, in splendor, it will drop. The descending flight is punctuated with barrel rolls, loop-the-loops, side flight, twists, and similar acrobatics, and all the while, the wind wails through specialized primary feathers so that the flight is accompanied by a series of soft warbles and whistles. It is only after this elaborate display that the woodcock lands, usually only a few feet from its original takeoff point, to begin the whole process over again. (p. 12)

The Curious Naturalist moves through the calendar year with a series of similarly engaging descriptions of such diverse creatures as dragonflies, frogs, and migratory birds.

A Field Guide to Your Own Back Yard, the last of Mitchell's books to be designated as a guidebook, carries over some material from *The Curious Naturalist*. Gilly Robinson, the woodcocks, and Mitchell's idea to divide the year into eight seasons, rather than four, are among the subjects that reappear. They are in the context of much new material, however, and Mitchell's envisioned audience for this text transforms even these familiar subjects.

Despite its name, this book barely fits into the confines of the field guide category. As Mitchell himself mentions, the field guide reference in the title is employed loosely here; the book comprises essays intended to bring adult suburbanites into closer contact with nature. Its scope,

Mitchell at his home in Littleton, Massachusetts

as no less an authority on field guides than Roger Tory Peterson states in a blurb on the book's back cover, clearly exceeds that of the usual guidebook. "This well-written book by John Mitchell goes beyond identification. Its purpose is to open our eyes to the galaxy of living and growing things nearby."

A Field Guide to Your Own Back Yard contains a substantial amount of natural history writing. Whereas in *The Curious Naturalist* the nature writer occasionally broke through the bounds of the educator's sourcebook, *A Field Guide to Your Own Back Yard* reverses that balance, making only a few concessions to the handbook form in its collection of short natural history essays on particular subjects. Instead of a few essays with a preponderance of craft and calendar illustrations, this book provides occasional illustrations keyed to a substantial text of nearly seventy short essays.

These essays range in subject matter from purple grackles to Jefferson's salamanders to orange hawkweed to such wintering insects as the oak apple gall. They combine natural history observation, scientific information, personal experience and anecdotes, literary quotations, and tidbits of legend and folklore in an intriguing mix that makes them very much akin to a written adult version of Gilly Robinson's nature stories for children. Like *Ceremonial Time*, which was published during the same period, this book marks Mitchell's emergence as a full-fledged nature writer.

Ceremonial Time: Fifteen Thousand Years on One Square Mile (1984) is John Hanson Mitchell's first in-depth investigation of those aspects of American nature and culture that most interest him. The site chosen for this ambitious exploration is a small piece of land located thirty-five miles west of Boston. Before moving to this area, Mitchell explored a variety of other landscapes, some of them more and some less isolated from other humans. He was born in what he calls "the cutting edge of New York City," in Englewood, New Jersey, where he lived with his father, an Episcopal minister, and his schoolteacher mother. After graduating from Columbia University with a degree in education he lived "in the middle of some sixty thousand acres of state forestland in northwestern Connecticut," and then "[took] care of a sixty-acre property on Martha's Vineyard" (p. 72). His relocation to Scratch Flat, the square-mile landscape featured in *Ceremonial Time*, is described in somewhat casual terms: "There happened to be an old house for sale there and my wife and I were looking for a place to live in the general area" (p. 8). But, once there, he came to know and love the old farm where they live on four semi-wild acres of "forgotten overgrown landscape" (p. 9) near a stand of pines and the square mile of land that encloses it.

The folkname of Scratch Flat, Mitchell speculates, was probably assigned back in the nineteenth century because the land was cultivated so thoroughly. As he lays out its boundaries, we learn that "it is bordered on the south by a highway, known locally as the Great Road" (p. 3), that runs from Concord, Massachusetts, to southern New Hampshire, and on the east and north by a stream known as Beaver Brook that empties into a shallow lake called Forge Pond. The western edge is "a deep pine forest and a brooding larch swamp" (p. 4). Mitchell carefully characterizes this landscape in terms that are only seemingly paradoxical; it is crucial to his view of the world that Scratch Flat is both a "demi-paradise" (p. 9) and an "insignificant little patch of the planet" (p. 13).

This landscape is a perfect place for Mitchell's rambles into "that undiscovered country of the nearby, the secret world that lurks beyond the night windows and at the fringes of cultivated backyards" (p. 7). One such excursion he lauds as "a genuine nature walk, filled with the kind of small epiphanies that make exploration of the natural world such a continuing adventure" (p. 178). He comes across an unfamiliar cerulean warbler, a western tanager, a parula warbler, and the spectacularly striped Blackburnian warbler. In Beaver Brook, he encounters "an immense otter," a least bittern, a snapping turtle—one of those "great lumbering relics of the Cretaceous period that have survived into our era" (pp. 181–182)—a painted turtle, and a fox. The

symbolic, historic, and endangered status of this walk emerges more clearly as we learn the history of Scratch Flat.

Mitchell's exploration into the full fifteen-thousand-year relationship of the humans to the land takes shape, as the subtitle suggests, by focusing on the relatively small geographical space of Scratch Flat as the site for an excavation into time. He provides something akin to what William Least Heat-Moon, writing seven years later in *PrairyErth*—a somewhat similar book about a very different part of the country—designated as "a deep map" or "verticality." To make his history deep in history as well as dense in real-life detail, Mitchell learns from his own dreams, memory, and experience and from the cultural memory, the stories, tales, and rituals of those humans whose presence has been on the land the longest: the Indians. He learns this history in himself and others through the method that gives the book its title.

> Every morning between April and November, weather permitting, I take a pot of coffee up to that grove to watch the sun come up over the lower fields and to think about things. More and more now I find myself thinking there about time, how it drifts in from the future, how it brushes past us briefly in the present, and then drifts off again to become the past, and how none of these stages, neither past, nor present, nor future, are really knowable. Presented with this dilemma, I have come in recent years to accept the primitive concept of ceremonial time, in which past, present, and future can all be perceived in a single moment, generally during some dance or sacred ritual. Ceremonial time was perceived easily by the people who lived on the land around the plum grove for most of human history. The Pawtucket Indians would summon it up regularly during certain periods of the year, and I have found that it is a convenient method of understanding the changes that have taken place on this particular patch of earth over the last fifteen thousand years. (pp. 1–2)

Mitchell first experiences this sense of ceremonial time in a ritual enacted by his Native

American friends Nompenekit (Fred Williams) and Tonupasqua (Linda Waters) and their friend White Bird. The ceremony takes place, with Mitchell in attendance, on a point of private land that extends into Forge Pond—Indian artifacts found at the site suggest that it was once used for religious ceremonies. During a long dance that continues until after dawn, Mitchell comes to feel that they are momentarily apart from the temporal world, "a mere island of four individuals afloat in time" (p. 42). There is, also, as he senses and later hears about from Nompenekit, the shadowy presence of another figure in this ceremony: something halfway between a bear and a man—"a spirit man." Between bouts of worry that the late-night ceremony will be interrupted by the police, Mitchell absorbs what he feels was the spirit of the first humans to inhabit the land.

As Mitchell develops his narrative, he explains the notion of ceremonial time with care, de-emphasizing the supernatural: "I don't claim to have experienced these things in some previous experience. It was simply a heightened experience or perception of the ways things must have been." Yet it is, he explains, more than a simple mental picture; it is also a chance actually to see, hear, smell, and "for just a flash, a microsecond if you care to measure things, I would actually be there, or so it seemed" (p. 12).

In the early chapters, Mitchell works to build a comprehensive history by blending the knowledge gained from ceremonial time with what he learns in other ways. The chapter called "The Kingdom of Ice," for example, talks about the impact of the glaciers from both the scientific and the personal points of view. As Mitchell's friend the Red Cowboy (whose name is Vernon Stafford and who speaks with the authority of a glaciologist) explains it, this area was obliterated by ice a mile thick for fifty thousand years. The ice sheet wore down, rounded and shaped the land, creating the lakes, hills, and ridges on which human history has been played out, and it also laid down a thick layer of good soil that has shaped much of humanity's agricultural endeavors on Scratch Flat.

Mitchell parallels this scientific explanation with his personal experience of how the kingdom of ice still influences us. He describes a powerful childhood dream in which he felt himself astride a huge wall of endless ice. As an adult out for a walk on a cold January night, Mitchell feels himself go "into a wilderness that might as well have been ten thousand miles from the nearest human settlement" (p. 24). When a snowshoe breaks, he finds himself "one-footed and alone in the emptiness of winter" (pp. 24–25). He faces the fact that he might not make it home and then sees "Scratch Flat as it must have been fifteen thousand years ago." "The place that I saw, the Scratch Flat that had endured for some fifty thousand years, was neither cruel nor kind; it was simply inhuman, totally devoid of meaning.... The essence of the experience, brief though it was, was that I had seen into the heart of the glacier" (p. 25).

Mitchell uses a similar mix of materials from science, personal experience, and cultural memory as he traces the long period of post–Ice Age and pre-European settlement on this land. As he proceeds chronologically through, in archaeological terms, the Paleo-Indian time, the Archaic Indian period, and the time of the Eastern Woodland Indians, he blends various kinds of knowledge to re-create the period of the large mammals and the humans who hunted them. Changes in weaponry depicted by museum artifacts, for example, evoke the movement away from the time of the great woolly mammoths to a period of smaller animals suited to different hunting methods.

Mitchell adds to this the views both of the paleontologist who traces change back to the further retreat of the glaciers and the consequent advance of the conifer forests and of Tonupasqua, who tells stories about how T'Chi Manitou, the Maker, or creation deity, in her tales, helped her people by bringing about a change to smaller creatures. His purpose in putting the theories of the anthropologists and the archaeologists alongside the stories that come from Tonupasqua's Wampanoag and Algonquian tradition and with those that come from his own experience of ceremonial time seems not so much simply to reconcile science and story; he does show us where they differ as well as how they fit together. He wants rather to present all the versions of the history, to provide us with multifaceted and comprehensive perspectives on the land, to make his history of Scratch Flat have cultural width as well as temporal depth.

His inclusiveness does not mean an absence of judgment, however; all cultural attitudes toward the land are not equal in Mitchell's opinion. As he works out the differences between Native American views of man's relationship to the earth and those held by the European settlers, Mitchell lets us know his preference. Although he is careful here, as elsewhere in his writing, not to turn his narrative into a sermon, Mitchell honors the beliefs of those Native Americans, the Pawtucket, Micmac, Wampanoag, and Algonquian, who have inhabited this part of the world. Nompenekit, as he tells Mitchell about another important figure—the bear-man or spirit figure who was present for awhile at the Forge Pond ceremony—explains these views.

> We're made of this, the marshes here, the trees. No different, see what I mean? You don't understand this because you look on this world as something that is not you. But Indian people believe that we are no different than a squirrel or a bear, just a different form. We're all the same, squirrel, bear, me. Okay? (p. 48)

Although Mitchell values such Native American beliefs, his balanced views prevent *Ceremonial Time* from becoming a jeremiad. This is especially evident as Mitchell returns to questions of food supply in a humorous chapter called "Eating Scratch Flat," a story of what happens when he and the Red Cowboy try to sustain themselves as the early Woodland people must have done. Their hunter-gatherer experiment involves fortifying themselves with "noncaloric drugs—i.e., black coffee" (p. 74) before setting out each morning in search of wild foods, and, fortunately for them, it takes place in the summer.

Blueberries, black bass, bluegills, and catfish keep them going at first, but by the end of the second day they are getting desperate. A hilarious attempt to dive for painted turtles yields only a stew with a "dull pondlike taste to it" (p. 75) and very little meat. Their staples—cattails and arrowhead tubers—get boring; they fail to catch an old woodchuck who lives in the area, and they finally call off the experiment early rather than eat insects. Mitchell describes a similarly disastrous experiment undertaken by his friend Toby Beckwith, who attempted to create a modern version of a Woodlands Indian garden, and here Mitchell's humor makes a complex point. His environmental values are tempered by an ironic and honest awareness of our limitations. He recognizes his, and humanity's, difficulty in moving away from the comforts of late-twentieth-century culture.

The second half of *Ceremonial Time* traces the changes wrought by the European settlers, those quiet yeomen who brought with them a sense of land ownership that replaced the natural boundaries. This history of the last three to four hundred years is determinedly unofficial as Mitchell focuses on the local stories, the word-of-mouth histories, the land-ownership records, and the poor farm records (to see who actually did the work). In doing so, he describes such local characters as Henry Hodgson, who fathered twelve children in a one-room structure. As Hodgson's family grew, he ended up living in the woodshed behind the house and wandering the roads at night. Mitchell reports that this old curmudgeon did, however, honor the most important biological dictates: he stayed alive and he reproduced himself.

A sadder, symbolic piece of history involves a black man named Johnny Putnam who lived on Scratch Flat in the early 1800s. Putnam and a white hunter killed a black bear in the same hemlock grove where Mitchell goes to contemplate time and the changes wrought by humans on the landscape. As the animals' habitat has declined over time and as the story of this killing has been handed down from one generation's local historian to the next, the individual death has taken on wider importance: it becomes "as if this bear were dying for all bears" (p. 136). Its death thus raises Mitchell's fears about the passing of wilderness.

Intertwined with his sense of loss is Mitchell's belief that the long flow of history has reached a very significant point of fulcrum. It is true that there have been many other changes before those manifested in the present time. Mitchell, in fact, sees that serious alteration of the landscape has been part of the human interaction with the land for much of human history. It started when the Woodland Indians burned parts of the forest to increase deer habitat, and it increased when they started to farm. The European farming culture, however, distanced itself from the land in ever increasing ways. In present times, the opening of an interstate highway, Route 495, in 1964 was for Scratch Flat both the symbol and the culmination of this accelerating process. Such major highways and the commuter populations who use them now separate those who live on the land from the land. There are no longer real needs that tie people to a particular place. "Now, in Scratch Flat, the people tend to alter their environment to suit their needs; and in fact they could live pretty much in the same way anywhere in the United States" (p. 56). This consequence of a commuter population may well signal the end of interaction with the natural world. Soon, the land may no longer support the kind of nature walk that Mitchell has experienced on Scratch Flat.

Mitchell's tracing of the fifteen thousand years of the human past on this one square mile ends at this critical juncture, enabling him to discuss important recent area environmental battles won and lost and then to conclude *Ceremonial Time* by looking at possible futures for the land. In a battle won, Toby Beckwith and a man named Bradford Thurston, the health inspector for the town, battle with developers about water quality. It is a nasty fight, complete with bomb threats and an appearance by the FBI, but it leads to clean-water protection. The women of the town also organize a campaign that halts construction of a shopping mall. Nonetheless, the overall struggle to preserve the land appears to be a losing cause. Mitchell's memorable walk where he saw the warblers, the otter, and the fox already feels to him like a historic event. As development takes away the habitat that has supported them, the songbirds and animals begin to disappear. Nompenekit and Tonupasqua move away from the area, and Mitchell himself is about ready to give up. "I felt that I was more cut off from the past than ever, and my frustration was made all the worse by the fact that my nonwestern guides had deserted me and that without them, all my exploration through the experience of ceremonial time was at an end" (p. 198).

In the last chapter of the book, fittingly entitled "Nompenekit's New World," Mitchell turns to a consideration of three possible scenarios for the future of Scratch Flat. One possibility—annihilation by nuclear war—is both the least pleasant and, Mitchell feels, the least probable. Even with nuclear war and the fallout of nuclear winter, he holds the hope that the world could be repopulated by a remnant population of postholocaust individuals. Uncontrolled growth would also bring about a dark future for Scratch Flat, leaving room only for "those few species such as starlings, rats, and pigeons which can survive well in the highly developed human community" (p. 213). A third, more positive scenario emerges in a conversation with Toby Beckwith, who draws on the ideas of Nompenekit for suggestions about remaking the world. Such reshaping would have its base in a lessening of American materialism: the realization that less is more. Beckwith ties this to "the creation of a postindustrial tribe," a community "bound together by a common belief, existing in a common territory with enough natural resources to supply themselves with food and fuel and shelter" (p. 220). The Indians, he says, will "come back as an idea" (p. 221).

None of these possibilities, however, provides the last word in *Ceremonial Time*. As Mitchell walks home in the cold after his dinner at Toby's, his thoughts turn away from communes, resources, and the formation of postindustrial tribes and back to the glacier. He suggests that all now is merely interlude, that the present interglacial period will give way to winter as the great ice pack moves south to cover Scratch Flat again. Mitchell's ultimate comfort, cold though it may be, is that the great forces of nature are ultimately in control. In the stretch of geologic time that embraces and blends the past, present, and future, the changes wrought by humans do not amount to much.

Living at the End of Time

Living at the End of Time examines Mitchell's Massachusetts landscape from a different perspective. Its emphasis is on individual experience, both Mitchell's own and that of his neighbors who, like himself, choose small, out-of-the-way lives lived close to the natural world. Consciously placing himself in the tradition of such "champions of the small life" (p. 4) as Gilbert White of Selbourne, England, and Henry David Thoreau of nearby Concord and Walden Pond, Mitchell relates his encounters with such locals as Megan Lewis, a gardener of mythic abilities, and Prince Rudolph, the surly town drunk who sleeps outdoors because it is too warm inside.

He also reads and responds to the journals written by Thoreau and the men of his own family. As he talks and reads, Mitchell works out the personal dimensions of the views expressed in *Ceremonial Time*. With its different emphasis on the same landscape, *Living at the End of Time* can be read either as an independent piece of nature writing or as a companion piece to the earlier work, a more personal and a more traditional natural history narrative that complements the earlier book's innovative historical emphasis.

By this time, Mitchell's personal situation has changed and his immediate neighborhood is also undergoing significant alterations. He is separated from his wife, and he has moved to a different part of his property. As he, helped by a friend, builds a cottage on the edge of a meadow behind the main house, he watches Digital Equipment Corporation erect a new complex directly across the highway. As the buildings go up, it is clear that the highway divides this landscape into two very different worlds. Mitchell's small cottage follows the plans of the mid-nineteenth-century architect Andrew Jackson Downing; it is without electricity and running water and Mitchell works to make it as open to the natural world as he possibly can.

The huge Digital building and parking lot across the highway proceed in a very different fashion. Built where a beautiful orchard used to be, the plans for it elicit some modest protest from the community. "But, as there was no law prohibiting the construction of office buildings in pear orchards" (p. 14), construction goes forward. Crews slice off the top of the hill and dig a foundation for two buildings and parking lots large enough to accommodate four thousand commuting workers. Mitchell notes Digital's encroaching presence even as he delights in the life in and around his cottage, his "excellent refuge from the world at large" (p. 16).

Mitchell terms this now-bifurcated place "an ironic landscape." His wild ridge, with "its mysterious, forgotten forest" (p. 12), is located only thirty-five miles west of Boston and not far from Route 128, America's Technology Highway, and only a little more than a mile from Route 495, another beltway circling Boston. Mitchell, however, can still find abundant wildlife on his ridge and meadow. He hears whippoorwills and raccoons on his first night in the new cottage, and there is also an unknown creature who looses a mysterious scream before fleeing deep into the woods. Mitchell finds four different kinds of snakes, four varieties of frogs and toads, foxes and skunks, robins and flickers, juncos, flycatchers, swallows, and bats in the area. There are also twenty different herbaceous plants in the meadow, and on one morning he sees "twelve dew-bejeweled webs of the orb web weaver spider glistening in the morning sun" (p. 23).

For Mitchell, the humans in this landscape, and especially those who live close to the natural world, are also compelling. He consciously chooses to live near the meadow—a locale that is both accessible to the village and on the edge of the forest, a middle ground between the encroaching chaos of the industrial community and "the mysterious wooded slopes" (p. 4). Like Thoreau in *Walden*, Mitchell delights not only in wilderness but in those unconventional small lives lived close to the natural world.

Two of the women pictured here illustrate the healing powers of nature. Megan Lewis is one of these. "She was in some ways a human version of her gardens—half-tended, her hands dirty with good soil, strands of grey hair falling from under a straw hat, and bits of grass and seeds clinging to her" (p. 44). Megan has a horror of the neatly tended suburban yards now creeping up in the town, and she advocates, instead, controlled disorder "as the most harmonious landscape" (p. 47). Mourning the death of her husband, she voices an important concern for this book, one that brings the philosophical observations of *Ceremonial Time* into play at the personal level: nature goes on despite individual human loss and death, and its power to restore us comes directly from the fact that it does not need us. Alice Dart, a researcher at Harvard on early Woodland Indians' basket making, offers a similar view on nature's healing powers. After the breakup of her marriage, the woods became her home, and it was her rediscovery of life and self in nature that brought her out of depression.

Emil and Minna, brother and sister émigrés from Austria, and a character called Bill, who was featured in "The Green Man" chapter of *Living at the End of Time*, illustrate another facet of the small life lived in harmony with nature: self-sufficiency. The brother and sister live an almost entirely independent life on the other side of the ridge, growing their own food and collecting wood from the forest for their fuel. Bill's appearance is unusual; he has a full beard, a long tangle of hair, and he wears a motley combination of denim and khaki and furs, complete with an animal skin pouch and a deerskin cap. Equally striking is his unusual knowledge of nature, especially of how to live and gather food in the mysterious woods, those "forested wild edges just beyond the grazed meadow" (p. 114).

As the modern-day counterpart of the woods-dwelling peoples discussed in *Ceremonial Time*, Bill is the successful hunter-gatherer who does what Mitchell and the Red Cowboy tried to do in their humorous attempts to live off the land in Scratch Flat. Bill, the Green Man, harkens back to *Ceremonial Time* and to Mitchell's cultiva-

tion of the ability to know life from another time. As an adult counterpart to the tales that Gilly Robinson once told his young listeners, Bill is, as Mitchell tells his readers, "not so much an entity as a possibility" (p. 115), evoking that part of nature's mystery represented by the deep woods.

As *Living at the End of Time* moves from May through summer and fall and then on into winter, it becomes less descriptive of day-to-day life and more contemplative. As the weather cuts Mitchell off from the outside world, he turns to the journals that he has brought with him to the cottage. Winter here, as in *Ceremonial Time*, brings with it thoughts of death, but this time Mitchell explores such thoughts on the personal, rather than the societal, level. His exploration comes partially through his journal reading; Mitchell has with him in the cottage not only Thoreau's journals but journals kept by several men of his family: his grandfather, father, brother, and cousin.

These journals, the theme of death developed in them, and Mitchell's own contemplations on life and death give his title personal as well as public ramifications. His reference to "the bitter end of the twentieth century" suggests that "we all could be living at the end of time" (p. 213), and he writes from a midlife vantage point that envisions the end of his own time. Since the journals he has brought with him all reinforce these considerations, much of the last part of this book becomes a personal meditation on death. He reads the record of the death of Thoreau's brother, Thoreau's own death, his father's death, and the death of the member of his family most like himself in his dedication to nature, his cousin, Dr. John.

Mitchell meditates as well on the new DEC building, asking what its construction means both for him and for the direction of life in the late twentieth century. The focal point of his contrast shifts as the book progresses, however. Instead of juxtaposing the corporate building and his own cottage, Mitchell contrasts the man DEC employees call Uncle Kenny—Kenneth Olsen, the founder and executive officer of DEC—with Henry David Thoreau. Throughout this discussion, Mitchell scrupulously emphasizes the good qualities of Olsen and his company. Olsen is fair, he cares about his employees, and he demonstrates this concern in tangible ways. He is an unassuming man who mows his own lawn, goes to the market dressed in a flannel shirt and khakis, and for vacations he takes canoe trips in Maine.

Despite Olsen's attractive personal features, Olsen's company brings its four thousand commuter employees into the farmland and forest country that Mitchell loves. Thus, Olsen embodies the power of twentieth-century civilization to separate the people from the land, evoking in Mitchell what he describes as "a Digital Dream." He imagines himself boarding a trolley where DEC employees sit obediently in neat rows, being transported across the valley from Mitchell's farm to their work building. The driver is Kenny Owens, and, as Mitchell boards the train, he notices at the back, in the dim light, an odd-looking individual staring at the driver. The man is immediately recognized by Mitchell as Thoreau, and he has "a sort of cynical, resigned smirk on his face as if to say, 'You see, I knew it would come to this'" (p. 170).

This technological pull of American society away from Thoreau's values shapes the climax of *Living at the End of Time*. In the final, title chapter, two crucial scenes, one set on each side of the highway, emphasize Mitchell's delight in the natural world and his fears for the place of nature in American society. The first scene is a nature walk that Mitchell takes one morning toward the end of May, after he has been living in his cottage almost a year. It begins when Mitchell is led out of the hemlock grove (and also away from his despair over the future of Scratch Flat) by a mysterious yellow bird that he follows through a small terrace of pines and then over a stone wall. He realizes that he is lost, and as he rests on the ground he hears an unfamiliar birdsong. Mitchell opens his eyes to a Canadian warbler—a species he has not seen for twenty years. Stillness descends, and a red fox comes to look at him. He follows it and encounters five white-tailed deer. The deer and the man watch each other. As the deer run away, one of them

stops, stamps its right leg elegantly, and faces him for a full two minutes.

This series of small surprises from nature leads him to a kind of revelation. Mitchell hears, or thinks he hears, or perhaps only thinks, a name. Whatever its immediate source, however, the name is much more powerfully present for him than a thought: it seems to Mitchell that the words ring out among the trees. This name so powerfully evoked is that of T'Chi Manitou—the name given to the spirit of nature by the Native Americans who once lived in the area. This persistence of their vision of humans and nature is a powerful event, restoring some of the hope lost with the disappearance of bears and their habitat in *Ceremonial Time*.

The second scene relates Mitchell's visit to the Digital Equipment plant, now grown to its full size of two large buildings, and it stands in sad contrast to the scene of natural richness previously described. Once inside, on a visit arranged by the special efforts of a longhaired guide named Virgil, Mitchell notes conference rooms named after Thoreau, Ralph Waldo Emerson, and Margaret Fuller, and a solitary maple tree lost between the two buildings. He looks out of the climate-controlled environment to see the wind moving the trees and grass, but from this vantage point it is only "a silent film of nature" (p. 216).

Despite this bleakness, Mitchell's final words in *Living at the End of Time* emphasize community, his sense of connectedness with nature and with other like-minded humans. On the summer solstice, the date chosen for the original move into his cottage, he hears a flicker let out a long, mysterious whinny from the woods. He feels "a strange sense of communion with the bird—a fellow traveler in the experiment of life," and a similar human communion as he sees the light in the house below the meadow: "I felt that I and my family, my friends and allies and acquaintances, were all shrinking down into the small, wild spaces of the world" (p. 220).

It is not that the threat of development represented by the Digital building has suddenly gone away or that the promise/threat of the glacier's return has vanished, but simply that Mitchell acknowledges that there can be, even in the midst of the great flow of geologic time and the sad limits of personal time, moments of peace grounded in community. The community as it is presented here is not so grand as the postindustrial tribe envisioned by Toby Beckwith at the end of *Ceremonial Time*, but the recognition remains that the joys of the small life have a place and that these joys can be shared. This hopeful recognition leads Mitchell to stay on in his cabin.

A brief epilogue reveals that Mitchell did, two years later, leave the cottage, but that he has kept his ties to the landscape by building another replica of a Downing cottage, this one complete with insulation, electricity, and running water. The lessons of the first year, however, stay with him; the time "has sharpened those things I already knew about myself: that I find great solace in living close to the cycles of the natural year, and that living in this way, I feel more in touch with deeper, less evident cycles in the universe, closer to the moving spirit of the land." His experience also taught him firsthand a lesson hard to learn otherwise in Western culture; he learned "as Henry Thoreau so often taught, that the essence of civilization is not the multiplication of wants but the elimination of need" (p. 223).

By the conclusion of *Living at the End of Time*, Mitchell has become not exactly a contemporary version of Gilly Robinson, but certainly a writer who has incorporated the values that he admired in his teacher into the broader vision of his own writing. The engaging descriptions of the natural world that characterize Mitchell's writing from *Hiking Cape Cod* through *Living at the End of Time* do teach his readers appreciation of the natural world. They also foster the kind of appreciation that celebrates, rather than reduces, the mysteries of nature. In *Ceremonial Time*, Mitchell adds to this his own fascination with the great sweeps of geologic time and human history, and he traces an intelligent, absorbing, even humorous, pathway through fifteen thousand years of human interaction with the one-square-mile landscape of Scratch Flat.

Living at the End of Time celebrates the small lives of those whose existence is intertwined with nearby nature, and it demonstrates also Mitchell's commitment to the preservation and transmittal of this unofficial local history. Mitchell's fascination with the life and journals of Thoreau and the lives lived and written about by the men in his own family contributes yet another dimension to the text. By looking at the personal dimensions of time and examining individual lives, including his own, bounded by the knowledge of death, Mitchell expands the range and the depth of his writing. There are, of course, real dangers for any contemporary writer choosing to live, walk, and write in such physical and philosophical proximity to Walden and Thoreau, but Mitchell's work is equal to the task. His nature writing has the grace and the complexity necessary to blend literary history and personal experience into important literature that illuminates our human place in nature and history at the end of the twentieth century.

Selected Bibliography

WORKS OF JOHN HANSON MITCHELL

LITERARY NONFICTION

Ceremonial Time: Fifteen Thousand Years on One Square Mile (Garden City, N.Y.: Anchor Press, 1984); *A Field Guide to Your Own Back Yard* (New York: Norton, 1985); *Living at the End of Time* (Boston: Houghton Mifflin, 1990).

COLLABORATIVE AND EDITED WORKS

Hiking Cape Cod, with Whit Griswold (Charlotte, N.C.: East Woods, 1978); *The Curious Naturalist*, with the Massachusetts Audubon Society (Englewood Cliffs, N.J.: Prentice Hall, 1980); *The Energy Book: A Look at the Death Throes of One Energy Era and the Birth Pangs of Another*, with Wayne Hanley (Brattleboro, Vt.: Stephen Greene, 1980).

BIOGRAPHICAL AND CRITICAL STUDIES

John N. Cole, "Looking Back at Time," review of *Ceremonial Time: Fifteen Thousand Years on One Square Mile*, in *Washington Post Book World* (16 July 1984), sec. B; James Corpora, "The New Totemism:

The Use of Animal Images in Recent American Nature Writing," in *Midwest Quarterly* 32 (autumn 1990); George Johnson, "Paperbacks: New and Noteworthy," review of *Living at the End of Time*, in *New York Times Book Review* (26 May 1991); Don Lessem, "*Living at the End of Time* by John Hanson Mitchell," in *Smithsonian* (January 1991); Sam Pickering, "Driving Life into a Corner," review of *Living at the End of Time*, in *Sewanee Review* (summer 1992); Donald Scheese, "Review of *Ceremonial Time*," in *Winterthur Portfolio: A Journal of American Material Culture* 21 (summer/autumn 1986); John R. Stilgoe, "Thoreau with Bottled Gas," review of *Living at the End of Time*, in *New York Times Book Review* (13 May 1990); John Anthony West, "Scratch Flat Is and Was the World," review of *Ceremonial Time: Fifteen Thousand Years on One Square Mile*, in *New York Times Book Review* (12 August 1984).

N. SCOTT MOMADAY
(b. 1934)

MATTHIAS SCHUBNELL

THE KIOWA WRITER and painter N. Scott Momaday is widely regarded as one of the most eminent Native American artists of the later twentieth century. His first novel, *House Made of Dawn*, received the 1969 Pulitzer Prize for fiction; *The Way to Rainy Mountain* has become a classic among American memoirs; and the retrospective exhibition of his paintings at the Wheelwright Museum in Santa Fe in 1992 has affirmed his reputation as a painter of stature. However, as a nature writer, Momaday has received little recognition, even though his work, from the very beginning, has sought to define an appropriate relationship between human beings and the natural world from the vantage point of his Native American heritage.

One of his first published poems, entitled "Eve My Mother, No," reveals that Momaday approaches questions related to nature and ecology from a non-Western, non-Christian perspective. His poem instills the commonplace of "Mother Earth" with fresh meaning in its emphasis on the vitality, endurance, and sacredness of creation. The persona's looking, listening, and moving within a sacred landscape suggests a daily communion with the earth. Nature here manifests not a material resource to be appropriated but a spiritual presence that willingly nurtures those who care for her. This bond finds ceremonial expression in a dance to honor the earth's generosity, patience, and endurance. The physical and spiritual immersion in the natural order celebrated in this poem is a far cry from the increasingly distant and impersonal relations to nature prevalent in modern civilization.

Momaday's recent pronouncement that "The land, the earth, is the foundation of all belief, all wonder, all meaning in the story of human existence" (foreword to *Earth Is My Mother*, p. xvi) confirms that nature remains a focal point for him as a writer and conservationist. When he writes about the landscapes of Arizona, New Mexico, Oklahoma, and Colorado, he seeks to convey the mystery and beauty of the world and to teach the ethical and moral imperatives regarding the earth that have come down to him from his Kiowa ancestors. These concerns are central to all his writings, his nonfiction prose as well as his fiction and poetry.

Mythic Landscapes and the Remembered Earth

To behold nature through Momaday's eyes is to share in "a vision beyond time and place." In an essay of this title, Momaday explains how he shares his characteristically native perception of the world with an old Kiowa man, Cheney, whom he never knew but whose existence persists in Momaday's imagination. In his daily prayer to the rising sun, Cheney paid tribute to the mystery of renewal inherent in nature's rhythms. By worshiping each dawn as a reenactment of creation, he connected himself to its originative powers and affirmed his own place in the universe.

Cheney's vision of nature is a paradigm for Momaday's own. The native view of nature integrates sense perception and memory, fusing the visible with collective and personal wisdom about the universe. Central to this process is the oral tradition that shapes and perpetuates the understanding of the earth. To look at a landscape and take possession of it in the mind involves an understanding of the past, both historical and mythic. One of Momaday's recurrent assertions is that "events take place" and persist within that locality. The stories surrounding a particular tribal geography or migration route convey the human involvement inherent in them across time. In the tribal mind, nature is both material and experiential, physical and imagined. This fusion of visible nature with myth and memory is the defining feature of a concept of nature that Momaday refers to as "the remembered earth."

Momaday's personal induction into the mythic landscape of his ancestors occurred when he was two years old. An old Kiowa man, Pohd-lohk, had given him the name Tsoai-talee, Rock Tree Boy, which connects him to one of the most sacred places along his tribe's migration route from the Yellowstone area to the Staked Plains, the imposing rock formation today called Devils Tower. When the Kiowas beheld this awesome sight, they needed to account for it by creating a myth, and in order to affirm the significance of this myth in the life of their son, Al and Natachee Momaday traveled with him to Wyoming.

In this creation myth of Devils Tower, seven sisters and their brother are transformed into the stars of the Big Dipper and a bear, respectively. The children are at play when the boy mysteriously turns into a bear and chases his terrified sisters to the stump of a tree. The tree speaks to the girls and carries them into the sky, where they become the seven stars. The boy-bear, forced to abandon his chase high up in the tree,

grudgingly slides down the trunk, scraping the bark with his claws. The tree then metamorphoses into Rock Tree, Devils Tower. The Kiowa oral tradition is replete with such stories of humans turning into animals or natural objects, affirming the close kinship between all forms of life, but none is so important to Momaday as this one. It appears in many of his essays and addresses; in his major prose works *House Made of Dawn*, *The Way to Rainy Mountain*, *The Names: A Memoir*; and as the central unifying myth in *The Ancient Child*.

The story of Tsoai is an account of loss and gain, of separation and reconnection, and of the sacred bond between human and nonhuman forms of life. The tribe's loss of eight of their young ones could be borne only by the belief in their eternal presence in the night sky. There, they persist as a visible reminder of the Kiowas' connectedness to the universe. For Momaday, as a modern incarnation of Tsoai-talee, the power of the bear resides in his name, Rock Tree Boy, linking him to the mythic worldview of his ancestors.

In *The Way to Rainy Mountain* (1969), Momaday offers numerous other examples of how his perception of the land is colored by the Kiowa myths that occupy his imagination. As he enters the northern Great Plains on his journey along the Kiowas' migration route, he is startled by the light and expanse before him, and he takes stock of every detail in the vision plane. This moment affords him a personal reexperience of the Kiowa emergence from the hollow log into the world, as well as an imaginative participation in his tribe's transition from the mountains to the plains, which marks the beginning of their golden age.

In another passage, Momaday recalls crossing a mountain meadow and seeing a male pine grosbeak high up in a lodgepole pine whose branches appeared to float in the sky. This lyrical sketch dramatically evokes the northern landscape, and its association with another Kiowa myth reveals how Momaday's understanding of geography is infused with a sense of the sacred. The mythic underpinning of Momaday's vignette relates the story of a little Kiowa girl resting in her cradle in the branches of a tree, being watched over by a redbird. Inexplicably, the tree begins to grow, carrying the two into the sky, where the girl turns into a woman and the bird into the sun god. This story captures another crucial moment in the mythic evolution of the Kiowas, for from this time on, they were related by marriage to their most powerful deity, the sun. The intersection of place and myth in Momaday's sketch is an example of how he brings himself and his readers to experience the landscape as a sacred geography, the common ground of ancestral and personal encounters.

Momaday's American Land Ethic

The concept of nature is fundamentally different in Native American cultures from what it is in modern, Western civilization. For this reason, Momaday formulated his philosophy of an American land ethic. Concerned with the increasing detachment of modern society from the natural world and its prevailing view of nature as an object, useful only as a commodity that can be exploited without any emotional involvement or fear of retribution, Momaday has offered his land ethic as an alternative. It rests on the conviction that the natural world is the physical manifestation of the sacred and has found expression in his numerous calls on modern America to come to a moral understanding of nature. "We must live according to the principle of a land ethic," Momaday contends in "The Man Made of Words": "The alternative is that we shall not live at all" (in Costo, ed., *Indian Voices*).

This ethical regard for the land requires an act of the imagination, as Momaday explains in "Native American Attitudes to the Environment." In this essay, he calls for an imaginative involvement in the natural world by way of a "reciprocal appropriation" that ties us into our natural context and creates personal landscapes of the mind. This process relies, in native cultures, on the racial experience that is perpetuated through the oral tradition.

Another key feature of this land ethic is appropriateness. It is a moral concept that guides all aspects of the Indian's interaction with nature. Momaday cites as an example a hunter's refusal to kill a deer despite the fact that he and his pregnant wife have gone hungry for some time. Because the couple are expecting the gift of a child, it would be inappropriate to take another creature's life. Material need is surrendered to an ethical imperative, expressed through a gesture of respect and thanksgiving for the gift of life.

In *House Made of Dawn* (1968), the contrast between Abel's and Francisco's adherence to the tribal hunting code is another illustration of this idea of appropriateness. When Abel captures an eagle, he is overcome with pity for the bird and kills it rather than taking it to the village where it would have remained in captivity to ensure the tribe's good relations to the gods. Unfamiliar with the hunting tradition, Abel acts inappropriately, in contrast to Francisco, who adheres to traditional ceremonial practices in his killing of the bear. He patiently waits until the bear is ready to give itself up for the benefit of the tribe, and after the kill he appeases the animal's spirit by praying and consecrating it with corn pollen. Francisco demonstrates that respect for life and the taking of life can be reconciled if the hunt is conducted as a spiritual activity, governed by moral imperatives and ritual practices.

Momaday believes that this attitude of reciprocity is the outcome of a long evolutionary process. In "A First American Views His Land," he contrasts the environmental impacts of prehistoric and modern Indian hunters. The Paleo-Indian of perhaps ten thousand years ago had developed a formidable technology to survive, but his ability to control nature had not yet been tempered by a moral code. This disparity between technological and ethical sophistication held the potential for degrading the very ecosystems on which his existence relied. In contrast, the hunter of the modern period— Momaday chooses a Woodlands Indian of the fifteenth century as his example—has acquired an ecological awareness and diversified his economy to the point where he can ensure a sustainable subsistence. In the course of time, the idea of nature as a sacred presence has taken hold in the tribal mind and formed the basis for a conservationist ethic.

Despite the fact that Momaday traces the evolution of an appropriate land ethic in Native American cultures, he avers that it remains latent in all of us, waiting to be reintegrated into modern life He finds it in the old inhabitants of Colorado mining towns who acquired "a sense of place that is nearly lost upon us whose minds are fixed upon the immediate world" (*Colorado*, p. 30), and in his own ancestors who transformed the wilderness of the South into agricultural land without forgetting that the value of their tobacco crop consisted "not only in the cash for which it is given in trade, but also in the remembered wilderness that was given up for it" (*The Names*, p. 19). Momaday believes that while it is impossible for humans to live in nature without altering it, they must strive to maintain a moral and empathic relation with it to ensure a viable balance. This requires an intimate knowledge of place that each individual is obliged to acquire. Momaday poses this challenge in one of his most frequently quoted passages from *The Way to Rainy Mountain*:

> Once in his life man ought to concentrate his mind upon the remembered earth, I believe. He ought to give himself up to a particular landscape in his experience, to look at it from as many angles as he can, to wonder about it, to dwell upon it. He ought to imagine that he touches it with his hands at every season and listens to the sounds that are made upon it. He ought to imagine the creatures there and all the faintest motions of the wind. He ought to recollect the glare of the noon and all the colors of the dawn and dusk. (p. 83)

By internalizing the earth through an imaginative process and by adopting a native land ethic as a corrective to our modern preoccupation with the control and exploitation of nature, we can restore our balance with the earth and ensure the continuing survival of all life on it. This simultaneously new and ancient attitude also holds the promise of reinvigorating modern society by reconnecting it to the sources of vitality inherent in the natural world. This idea is at the center of Momaday's essay "I Am Alive" and his poem "The Delight Song of Tsoai-talee," and it recurs throughout his *Colorado: Summer, Fall, Winter, Spring* (1973).

The Living Earth

In "I Am Alive," Momaday defines the Indian sense of vitality and well-being in terms of a comprehensive set of relationships that encompasses the geographical, spiritual, aesthetic, and moral. A good relation to the earth rests on the premise that nature is a living organism, to be cherished and protected as the source of all life and well-being. Because of this emphasis on ecological and communal considerations—communal in the broadest sense, including human and animal interests—traditional Native American views of the earth have always seen as alien the Western concept of land as private property, with the owner's implicit right to use nature at his or her discretion for personal gain. Momaday suggests here that the Indian's physical and spiritual integration into the living community offers an alternative model to the modern anthropocentric attitude toward nature.

The spiritual aspect of this relationship is reflected in the ceremonial practices of Native American peoples. The Pueblo dawn runners exert themselves physically to offer some of their strength to the rising sun, thus contributing ritually to its ongoing cycle. Their observance of a solar calendar, which governs the ceremonial life of the village, reflects their immediate relation to place and time, for it is through the reading of the sun's position relative to the tribal landscape that the community organizes its spiritual and economic activities. Their harvest and hunting ceremonies dramatize their empathy and closeness to other life forms; they acknowledge that without a good relation to animals and plants, their very existence as a community is at stake.

The appreciation of the earth as beautiful represents another facet of the Indian's complex relation to the natural world. Momaday argues that this aesthetic sense is highly developed, and that this ability to discern order, balance, proportion, and symmetry in the natural world finds lasting expression in Native American art, ranging from pottery and weaving to drama, from music and dance in Indian ceremonies to the oral tradition.

Lastly, Momaday's assertion that in order to be fully alive, the Indian must stand in good relation to other human as well as nonhuman members of the earth community, describes the profound morality of his vision. It is a moral responsibility to exercise restraint, charity, and neighborliness in the daily conduct of life, because this is the first prerequisite for realizing one's humanity.

In the canon of Momaday's writing there is perhaps no better expression of these ideals than in his poem "The Delight Song of Tsoai-talee" (in *In the Presence of the Sun*). It is a love poem in a personal and cosmic sense. The persona delights in his "good relation to the daughter of Tsen-tainte," but significantly this relationship is mentioned last, following the more important relations to the earth, the gods, and the beautiful. Momaday makes numerous equations between the persona and the natural world. These identifications—with horse, fish, eagle, and deer; shadow and light; rain, snow, and cold—blur the line between the various forms of creation. The poem celebrates an ecological awareness that breaks down the divisions within nature and conjures up the unifying power of the life force. Through his chant, the persona becomes part and parcel of the natural world.

The work that perhaps best fits into the category of nature writing and reflects Momaday's sense of the living earth is his collaboration with the photographer David Muench on a portrait of Colorado. This book stands in the tradition of Ansel Adams and Mary Austin's *Taos Pueblo* and Ansel Adams and Nancy Newhall's *This Is the American Earth*. Momaday's brief prose pieces in *Colorado: Summer, Fall, Winter, Spring* indeed capture the spirit of the place and its people. What is more remarkable about this book, however, is Momaday's ability to reach beyond the surface of the landscape, which he depicts in masterful detail, to convey its evolutionary past as well as its spiritual dynamics. The latter, on rare occasions, afford him the mystical experience of flowing into the motion of nature's processes. These moments, when he knows he is inextricably connected to the web of creation, assure Momaday that he is most fully alive.

Momaday's rendering of surfaces, colors, textures, and shades and shadows in the Colorado landscape testifies to his extraordinary ability to paint with words. Whether he captures the blueness of Blue River, of columbine and sky, or celebrates the profusion of colors bordering the mountain lakes, as in the following passage, it is always apparent that such vision results in the beholder's integration into something larger than himself or herself.

> On closer view there are white and blue and sand-colored stones among the bells and buttercups. There is at once an elaboration and a disintegration of color, confusion in the best sense. It is not easy to see clearly into the physical world, but it is eminently worthwhile to try. I am told by an old Indian that it is good for the eye to behold a sky-blue stone. (p. 110)

Momaday's pun on eye/I here expresses his conviction that this process of beholding the natural world, far from maintaining a distance between the perceiver and the thing perceived, in fact is capable of instilling a sense of well-being and connection in the beholder.

When Momaday describes the patterns in a winter landscape, he conveys the starkness and fragmentation of nature in the grip of a deep freeze. The "frozen filigree" of cottonwood trees in January is the focal point within the vision plane, seemingly arresting the onlooker as the tree itself is held in the grasp of the cold. Yet there are also passages that emphasize nature's exclusion of human life, as in this passage where Momaday creates an image of winter in its hard magnificence, defying any human presence: "The cold is a splintering of planes. Splinters of light inform the winter dawn and dusk, glance at water and glacial lees. The sky is splintered at the brittle limbs of a tree, and here and there in the snowfields are thin radial shadows at the drifts, splinters of long grass and grain" (p. 84).

The notion that nature persists separate from human existence becomes most apparent when Momaday shifts his attention from nature's surfaces to the processes that have given rise to the landscape of Colorado.

His geological perspective on the formative processes at work in the natural world reminds us of the relatively recent arrival of humans in the larger scheme of evolutionary time and evokes an appropriate sense of humility in the face of eternity. The idea of cosmic time that measures the evolution of stars and planets is captured in this passage: "A black spine of rock lies like a great snake on the hills, as if to verify an ancient conflagration, a remote and planetary fire" (p. 39). When Momaday reflects on the topography of the Front Range canyons, he sees "the remote possibilities of Creation. Here and there are monoliths against the sky. They seem to stand in peculiar relation to time, or in no relation whatsoever, as if eternity were their element" (p. 59). His meditation on the relation between mountains and the sea reveals the geologic processes that inexorably transform a seemingly changeless landscape. Water is not only the quintessential element of life, it is also the agent of continual if unobtrusive metamorphosis:

> Only water, in its pure, persistent life, is equal to the mountain. The river is the ribbon of light at the bottom of a dark gorge—and a line drawing of geologic time. At noon, in a frame of dark growth, I have come upon a waterfall in the mountains and seen in it the flare of the first dawn. (p. 43)

In these passages, Momaday magnifies the natural world's evolution through the ages in order to put the human presence into perspective. His contrast between the fleeting human presence in Colorado mining towns, many of which are now abandoned, and the ancient landscape underscores the relative significance of the human place in nature.

This idea also echoes in Momaday's claim that the landscape of Colorado offers "an organic resistance, a wildness" against human efforts to control it. Yet those who open themselves up to the mountains are rewarded by experiencing "a keen sense of the original earth, of its deep, definitive life" (p. 7). Such experiences often reach the level of mystical communion, affording the individual the feeling of being carried along by planetary currents: "Nothing is so exhilarating as this, to stand just here on the rim of the plain, at midmorning, and feel the world's turning—the slow, persistent spinning of the planet in its universe" (p. 7). In other instances, the moment of intuitive connection with nature generates the feeling of being infused with the life force. This impulse of life, for Momaday, is located particularly in bristlecones, "the thorns of the ancient earth." In the presence of these oldest of trees, Momaday affirms his participation "in the irresistible continuum of life itself," and catches a glimpse of immortality (p. 51). And when his sight follows the immense vistas of the Colorado landscape, "a stirring of the mind and of the blood" affects him, and he comes to understand his place in the world: "the wilderness fulfills my sphere of instinct, and I am as intensely alive as I ever was or will be" (p. 86). Climbing down from the mountains into deep valleys, too, can bring "a strange and perfect exhilaration" (p. 76), testimony to the possibility of a vital, mystical connection to the living earth.

Nature and Technology

Momaday does not condemn technology indiscriminately. Yet in many of his works the intrusion of the machine into the garden recurs as the central metaphor for modern society's degradation of the natural world. In "The Man Made of Words," Momaday points to the rise of technology as the cause of our modern detachment from the earth. He claims,

> We have suffered a kind of psychic dislocation of ourselves in time and space. We may be perfectly sure of where we are in relation to the supermarket and the next coffee break, but I doubt that any of us know where he is in relation to the stars and to the solstices.

Our sense of the natural order has become dull and unreliable. (in Costo, ed., *Indian Voices*)

If one applies this statement to both *House Made of Dawn* and *The Ancient Child*, it becomes readily apparent that the respective protagonists must first come to terms with their stake in a tribal homeland before they can overcome their crises of identity. Significantly, this reattunement to place must be accomplished against the uprooting force of a modern, technological, and primarily urban civilization.

Although it is important to recognize that the protagonist's disorientation in *House Made of Dawn* first manifests itself before he leaves his tribal community, it quickly becomes evident that his personal and cultural alienation correlates with his emotional and geographical distance from his ancestral land. Abel's experiences in the remote theater of World War II and subsequently in the anonymity of Los Angeles deepen his inner conflicts of identity. Momaday brings Abel's confrontation with a modern world at war with itself into sharp focus in a scene that dramatically illustrates the terrifying potential of misused technology. Here, Abel faces "the machine" in the form of an enemy battle tank bearing down upon him in a wooded landscape littered with dead leaves and bodies. Momaday's depiction of the tank as "looming . . . in front of the sun" (p. 26), seemingly suspended "apart from the land" as it races toward Abel (p. 26), makes the machine a memorable symbol for technological man's deadly efficiency.[1] How totally dominant over nature this force has become is revealed through Momaday's strategy of conveying the tank in organic terms, as if it had insinuated itself into the defenseless body of the earth. The machine seems to grow and take shape, "as if it were some upheaval of the earth, the eruption of stone and eclipse, and all about it the glare, the cold perimeter of light, throbbing with leaves" (p. 26–27). Even as it comes crashing down an incline, it moves "slow as a waterfall, thunderous, surpassing impact, *nestling*

almost into the splash and boil of debris" (p. 27). Abel faces here the ruthless assault of a death force threatening all life, and much of his subsequent healing process requires a new definition of his own relation to the earth.

Upon his return to his native community, Abel attempts to sing a creation song that would have affirmed his homecoming and reintegration into the tribal universe, but he fails. Only years later, Ben Benally's celebration of the Night Chant restores Abel's place in the "house made of dawn," the Navajo metaphor for the universe. Abel consummates his restoration by participating in his community's dawn run, a ceremonial race specifically aimed at affirming the vital connection between communal life and the cycles of creation.

The quest for an indigenous identity in *The Ancient Child* (1989) also proceeds in the tension between nature and modernity. When Locke Setman, a Kiowa painter who has found success in modern America at the expense of his tribal identity, returns to his native Oklahoma to begin, unbeknownst to him, the rediscovery of his roots, he views the land from an airplane window. What he sees is an expanse of geographic patterns, the signature of modern land use, in competition with "the opposing aesthetic of the wilderness." This vision represents an accurate reflection of Setman's psychological landscape, because just like "the green belts slashing through the boxes like limbs of lightning, like sawteeth and scythes" (p. 57), the remnants of his tribal self need to reassert themselves against the patterns of modern life that overlay and repress it.

After confronting the mysterious image of a boy, the ancient child and mythic tie to Setman's bear identity, near his relatives' home, Momaday's protagonist takes a close look at his native soil. It is essential that he move from the aerial view facilitated by modern technology to the close perspective of a down-to-earth, rooted inhabitant in order to recognize his native soil as the place where geography, myth, and personal bloodlines converge: "He could not remember having seen earth of that color; it was red . . . or catlinite, the color of his father's name" (p. 63).

---

1. All page citations for *House Made of Dawn* refer to the 1989 reprint edition.

Although Setman is not yet able to comprehend fully the intricate connections between himself and this place, he does know that he is in the presence of "some ancestral intelligence," of "something profoundly original" (p. 64). As in *House Made of Dawn*, Momaday measures the restoration of his protagonist's sense of self in terms of his reintegration into a spiritually significant landscape.

Just as the battle tank in *House Made of Dawn* symbolizes the destructive potential of modern civilization, so the nuclear laboratories at Los Alamos become the focus of Momaday's protest against man's quest for ultimate control over nature in his early poem "Los Alamos." Published in 1959, in *New Mexico Quarterly Review* (vol. 29, no. 3), it contrasts the magnificent Jemez Mountains—the geographical backdrop to Momaday's childhood home—with the nightmarish world of destructive technology that gave birth to the nuclear age. Because this poem is not readily accessible, it is quoted here in full:

Steel spans and spurns our filtered vision
To the crossed hairs of promise, the
    magnified self-image.
In the near distance, audible in time,
Exiled voices hover and collide.
Beneath gray girders skaters groove the
    water
and crumble bread for snowbirds.

Children, though uprooted and wedged
    from the earth,
Humanize this statuary.

Machinery is scattered over the earth like
    hurled coins.
I have heard the angry monotone
Retching into troughs the pins of war
When I walked in the wood to hear rain.

The stark, impersonal lamps on the bridge
Destroy the symmetry of her straining
    shadows.
The desert smiles and waits
and there the night settles, transfixed by
    the moon.

Confidently,
Uniformed men pace the corridors of
    Purgatory
And every wrist and wall is shackled to a
    timepiece
That, through the disinfected chambers,
Rap against the unknown like a blind
    man's cane.

I have dreamed a city peopled
By one sufficient man
and faithful reproductions.

The bridge Momaday describes spans Los Alamos Canyon, connecting the town with the atomic laboratories. As "the magnified self-image" of a technological civilization, the structure offers subtle violence, "the crossed hairs of promise." This imagistic rendering of the bridge's structural elements not only evokes the cross-hairs of a gunsight, designed to make the delivery of deadly technology even more efficient, but also implies, through the pun on "crossed," that the development and application of technology for destructive purposes undermines and betrays the promise of the scientific age. This

N. Scott Momaday

idea is reinforced by Momaday's reference to the bridge's spurning "of our filtered vision" of technology as an unqualified triumph.

In the tension between the natural world (water, snowbirds, children, the forest, rain, desert, night, and moon) and a man-made, surrogate world (the bridge, machinery, bombs, underground corridors, disinfected chambers), Momaday develops his theme that unchecked progress based exclusively on advances in technology ultimately blinds and enslaves humans in a sterile, artificially controlled environment. The persona's nightmare of a cloned population inhabiting a totally homogeneous city foreshadows what might become of modern civilization if its seemingly irrepressible urge to remake nature cannot be curbed.

The Creatures of the Wild

Momaday's fascination with animal life finds expression in such poems as "The Bear," "Buteo Regalis," and "Pit Viper." All three poems are meditations on the mystery and grace inherent in these creatures. What sets Momaday's "The Bear" apart is that it reveals both the resilience of nature and its gradual decline under the assault of a utilitarian modern society. The poem is Momaday's self-conscious poetic reexpression of the central scene in William Faulkner's "The Bear," in which Ike McCaslin encounters Old Ben. For both writers, the bear is the embodiment of the wilderness, a ghost inhabiting a doomed natural order. In Faulkner's story, Ike, who is being initiated into the mysteries of nature by Sam Fathers, an old man of Black and Chickasaw descent, finally confronts the bear after leaving his gun, compass, and watch behind. Having disavowed the trappings of civilization, Ike undergoes a formative experience with the bear that ultimately leads him to reject his inheritance of the land. The two bears are described in almost identical terms. Momaday's bear is "forever there, / dimensionless, dumb, / in the windless noon's hot glare" (*In the Presence*, p. 3); in Faulkner's story "[the bear] was just there, immobile, fixed, in the green and windless noon's hot dappling" (*Go Down,*

Moses, p. 209); they both appear and disappear at will; and both carry the scars of their battles with the encroaching civilization. In Faulkner's work, the bear's death signifies the impending doom of the wilderness at large; Momaday suggests as much by emphasizing the bear's age, disfigurement, and the "pain [that] slants his withers, / drawing up the crooked limb" (*In the Presence*, p. 3), even though at the end of the poem the bear blends back into the woods.

Whereas "The Bear" reflects the tension between civilization and wilderness, "Buteo Regalis" focuses on the hawk's magnificent adaptation to its natural habitat. In this poem, Momaday marvels at the grace and cold efficiency with which the bird of prey descends upon a rodent. Despite the prey's intuitive knowledge of impending danger, the "unheard, / Unseen" (*In the Presence*, p. 4) approach of the predator, depicted in an impressionistic image of color and motion, symmetry and speed, inevitably leads to the kill.

"Pit Viper" centers on a fascinating moment of renewal in nature, the snake's sloughing of its skin. As such, the poem mediates on the persisting life force in all of creation. As the seemingly new snake emerges from its old skin, Momaday shifts the perspective from the observing persona to that of the pit viper. The effect is startling: "Blurred eyes that ever see have seen him waste, / Acquire, and undiminished: have seen death — / or simile — come nigh and overcome" (*The Gourd Dancer*, p. 12). By placing the reader into the snake's consciousness, Momaday allows for an unmediated experience of this process of rejuvenation. Implicit in the poem is the endless cycle of life, as the snake's wasting, acquiring, and remaining undiminished indicates. Like the bear, the pit viper is "alone among its kind, old, almost wise" (p. 12). But whereas the bear symbolizes the death of nature, the pit viper seemingly defies death, if not as an individual specimen, then as a species.

The same theme is at the center of one of Momaday's greatest poems, "Angle of Geese." Here Momaday contrasts the death of a child with that of a wild goose and explores the implications of these deaths in their respective human and natural contexts. Confounded by the child's death, the mourners grapple with the ultimate incomprehensibility of death, recognize the ineffectuality of language and ceremony to find repose or reason for the loss, and finally accept that despair and grief must be experienced in isolation.

The dead child's impact on the human consciousness is contrasted with that of a "huge, ancestral goose," the progenitor of the flock, which falls out of the V shape and meets death without "hope and hurt," while the other geese fly on in their archetypal formation. The "margin of repose" that eludes the mourners in the first half of the poem is "longer in the watch,/As if forever,/Of the huge ancestral goose" (*In the Presence*, p. 21). As in "Pit Viper," the readers assume the animal's perspective at a critical moment, allowing them to share the goose's final sight of the flock disappearing in the distance: "So much symmetry!—/Like the pale angle of time/And eternity./The great shape labored and fell." The difference between the human response to death and death in nature is evident, for the goose, "quit of hope and hurt," fixes its gaze "On the dark distant flurry" (p. 21) of its surviving offspring and finds repose in it. Whereas death appears inexplicable and arbitrary to those who grieve for the child, the ongoing flight of the flock stands as an uplifting symbol of immortality, for Momaday is concerned here with the ongoing evolutionary process in nature. The ancestral goose has done its part in the chain of life. Even though humans are subject to the same evolutionary laws, death as an integral part of life remains a difficult reality to accept.

Momaday's nature writings convey the wonder and delight, the awe and humility, with which he confronts the mysteries of creation. They allow us to accompany him on his travels beyond time and space into the mythical past of his Kiowa ancestors, and remind us that we are defined as people by the places we call home. Momaday also cautions us that the loss of this "remembered earth" inevitably brings with it a loss of identity that represents as dangerous a threat to our spiritual wholeness as the degradation of nature poses to our physical well-being.

In a brief essay titled "Sacred Places," Momaday challenges us to connect with the numinous in nature and protect the sacred grounds on this continent. For him, Devils Tower, Rainy Mountain, Canyon de Chelly, the Cahokia Mounds, Barrier Canyon, Utah, among others, are spiritual sites that link ancestral dreams with those of future generations. It is our duty to take responsibility for the equivalent places in our lives, to make them a part of our imagination, and to ensure their physical survival. As Momaday puts it in "Sacred Places," "It is good for us to touch the earth. We, and our children, need the chance to walk our sacred earth, this final abiding place of all that lives. We must preserve our sacred places in order to know our place in time, our reach to eternity."

Selected Bibliography

WORKS OF N. SCOTT MOMADAY

NOVELS

House Made of Dawn (New York: Harper & Row, 1968; repr., Harper Perennial, 1989); *The Ancient Child* (New York: Doubleday, 1989).

AUTOBIOGRAPHIES

The Way to Rainy Mountain (Albuquerque: Univ. of New Mexico Press, 1969); *The Names: A Memoir* (New York: Harper & Row, 1976).

COLLABORATIVE WORK

Colorado: Summer, Fall, Winter, Spring, with photographs by David Muench (New York: Rand McNally, 1973).

SELECTED ARTICLES

"An American Land Ethic," in *Sierra Club Bulletin* 55, no. 8 (1970); "The Man Made of Words," in *Indian Voices: The First Convocation of American Indian Scholars*, ed. by Rupert Costo (San Francisco: Indian Historian Press, 1970); "A Vision Beyond Time and Place," in *Life* (July 1971); "I Am Alive," in *The World of the American Indian*, ed. by Jules B. Billard (Washington, D.C.: National Geographic Society, 1975); "A First American Views His Land," *National Geographic Magazine* (July 1976); "Native American Attitudes Toward the Environment," in *Seeing with a Native Eye*, ed. by Walter Holden Capps (New York: Harper & Row, 1976); Foreword to *Earth Is My Mother, Sky Is My Father: Space, Time, and Astronomy in Navajo Sandpainting*, by Trudy Griffin-Pierce (Albuquerque: Univ. of New Mexico Press, 1992); "Sacred Places," in *Sacred Places: Native*

American Sites (San Francisco: Sierra Club Special Edition Calendar, 1993).

POETRY

"Eve My Mother, No," in *Sequoia* 5, no. 1 (1959); "Los Alamos," in *New Mexico Quarterly Review* 29, no. 3 (1959); *Angle of Geese and Other Poems* (Boston: David Godine, 1974); *The Gourd Dancer* (New York: Harper & Row, 1976); *In the Presence of the Sun: Stories and Poems, 1961–1991* (New York: St. Martin's Press, 1992).

EDITION

The Complete Poems of Frederick Goddard Tuckerman (New York: Oxford Univ. Press, 1965).

INTERVIEW

Charles L. Woodard, *Ancestral Voice: Conversations with N. Scott Momaday* (Lincoln: Univ. of Nebraska Press, 1989).

BIOGRAPHICAL AND CRITICAL STUDIES

Peter G. Beidler, "Animals and Human Development in the Contemporary American Indian Novel," in *Western American Literature* 14 (1979); Lawrence J. Evers, "Words and Place: A Reading of *House Made of Dawn*," in *Critical Essays on American Indian Literature*, ed. by Andrew Wiget (Boston: G. K. Hall, 1985); Mick McAllister, "The Topology of Remembrance in *The Way to Rainy Mountain*," in *Denver Quarterly* 12, no. 4 (1978); Carole Oleson, "The Remembered Earth: Momaday's *House Made of Dawn*," in *South Dakota Review* 11, no. 1 (1973); Kenneth M. Roemer, "Bear and Elk: The Nature(s) of Contemporary Indian Poetry," in *Journal of Ethnic Studies* 5, no. 2 (1977), *Landmarks of Healing: A Study of* House Made of Dawn (Albuquerque: Univ. of New Mexico Press, 1990), and as ed., *Approaches to Teaching Momaday's* The Way to Rainy Mountain (New York: Modern Language Association, 1988); Matthias Schubnell, *N. Scott Momaday: The Cultural and Literary Background* (Norman: Univ. of Oklahoma Press, 1985), reprints Momaday's poem "Los Alamos."

John Muir
(1838–1914)

THOMAS J. LYON

JOHN MUIR is one of the most reliably affirmative American writers. In the typical Muir essay, the participant-narrator (Muir himself) progresses through study, adventure, difficulty, or danger toward a perception of the immortal unity of all things. The beauty of the natural world is the signature of its sacredness, and the human ability to perceive wild beauty indicates human participation in the greater whole. This "yea-saying" philosophical position is consistent throughout Muir's work.

Muir translated the precepts of his philosophy into action in the public arena with extraordinary effectiveness. As a founder of the American environmental movement, he helped create a lobby for nature, and in particular for wilderness, at a time (the Progressive Era) when the United States, having achieved its main territorial ambitions, was beginning to take a more critical look at itself. In the last decade of the nineteenth century and the first of the twentieth, America was beginning to emerge from a more or less thoughtless expansionary mentality. Muir's great contribution was to give forthright literary expression to the human passion for wild nature, and to the significance of wilderness, which had long been on the margins of American intellectual debate. Regarding the environment, no literary figure has had greater impact on the actualities of American politics and history. A founder of the Sierra Club in 1892, Muir was instrumental in the establishment of a national parks system and had a direct influence on other important preservation legislation.

The simplicity and consistency of John Muir's thought, along with his prominence as a public and historical figure, may have worked against his critical reception as a writer. For a long time after his death in 1914, most critics, if they thought about Muir at all, did not dig below the surface of either his ideas or his place in American life. In 1923, in *Nature in American Literature*, the literary historian Norman Foerster declared that "one does not go to John Muir for a criticism of life" (pp. 254–255), and apparently the literary establishment agreed with him. For another half century, there was very little interpretation or analytic study of Muir. After the environmental awakening symbolized by the first Earth Day in 1970, however, interest in Muir was revived. Perhaps he did have a criticism of life that ought to be investigated, after all. Albert Saijo, a California writer, opened the modern era of Muir criticism with a thoughtful essay in *Backpacker* magazine's "Elders of the Tribe" series, in which he described Muir as philosophically profound, a person with a modern, ecological vision. Saijo portrayed Muir as ahead of his time—someone to whom the present age, in its time of crisis, should pay serious attention. Next, William and Maymie Kimes's thorough bibliography, published in 1978 and revised in 1986, filled a need as a modern trail guide to Muir's life as a writer. Stephen R. Fox's *John Muir and His Legacy: The American Conservation Movement*, published in 1981, centered its analysis on an insightful biography of Muir. Other important events in Muir scholarship included a biography by Michael P. Cohen, *The Pathless Way: John Muir and American Wilderness* (1984), a major study of Muir as a thinker and political activist by Frederick Turner III, *Rediscovering America: John Muir in His Time and Ours* (1985), a complete cataloging of Muir's papers by Ronald H. Limbaugh and Kirsten E. Lewis (1986), and the reprinting of a number of long-unavailable texts by Muir himself. In addition, Linnie Marsh Wolfe's 1945 biography, *Son of the Wilderness*, was reprinted in paperback (1978), as was Edwin Way Teale's 1954 reader, *The Wilderness World of John Muir* (1976). This critical activity and mass-market republication, amounting to a veritable flood of books, indicated a whole new life for John Muir's thought.

Life

John Muir's father was an exacting and repressive force during the writer's childhood, and the embodiment of civilized, anthropocentric thinking against which the mature Muir pitted his own nature-oriented philosophy. Daniel Muir was a Christian fundamentalist who believed the Bible to be the sole and sufficient source of truth, and a Calvinistic thinker with a strong sense of mankind's inherent sinfulness. Orphaned in youth, he had had a conversion experience at the age of fifteen, an apparently life-shaping incident. Ever after, a true believer's intensity marked his way.

In *The Story of My Boyhood and Youth* (1913), Muir portrayed his father as a man of stern proscriptions and an adherent to the puritan work ethic. His mother, Ann Gilrye Muir, was much gentler. In the seacoast town of Dunbar, Scotland, where Muir was born on 21 April 1838 and where he spent his first eleven years, Daniel Muir attempted to curb his children's natural urges to run free in the nearby fields. Young John was "solemnly warned that I must play at home in the garden and back yard, lest I should learn to think bad thoughts and say bad words" (p. 2). It is well to remember that by 1908, when he dictated *The Story of My Boyhood and Youth* to a secretary, John Muir's sense of the opposition between the tame and the wild, and his own allegiance to the wild, were completely developed, and perhaps cast a distinctive, shaping light over his recollections. Invariably, Daniel Muir is pictured as the stern and oppressive enforcer of restrictive, indoor, abstract values. John is the wild child of nature, irrepressibly drawn to the freedom of the open landscape. "In spite of the sure sore punishments that followed like shadows, the natural inherited wildness in our blood ran true on its glorious course as invincible and unstoppable as stars" (p. 2), Muir wrote of himself and his childhood playmates. This retrospective view from the vantage point of 1908 may be somewhat simplified and "pat"; nevertheless, it is clear that John Muir's upbringing was marked by conflict. Daniel Muir's universe was a battleground—most fundamentally between God and Satan, good and evil, but also, and relatedly, between progress and sloth, civilization and wilderness. He wanted to be quite sure that his children were on the right side in this universal warfare. Linnie Marsh Wolfe, in *Son of the Wilderness*, termed the Muir farmstead in Wisconsin, to which Daniel Muir had brought his family in 1849, a "concentration camp" (p. 7). The father by necessity enlisted the energies of all family members in the struggle to convert the wilderness into productive farmland. Thus the Muirs' early years on their two south-central Wisconsin farms enacted in microcosm the early, puritan era of American life. Under the rule of the patriarch, and with fundamentalist principles kept daily before them, they waged a ten-year struggle against nature.

Even so, the woods and lakes and rolling hills of south-central Wisconsin made a positive impression upon young John Muir. "Oh, that glorious Wisconsin wilderness!" he later wrote in *The Story of My Boyhood and Youth* (p. 63). He was particularly attached to Fountain Lake, a pond on the first of the family farms. In 1867 (well before achieving any sort of financial stability), he made an unsuccessful attempt to buy the lake in order to preserve it as a wildlife sanctuary.

If Muir's early life, with its heavy-handed religion and daily toil of wilderness-breaking, recalls aspects of seventeenth-century New England life, it is also true that he had traits of Yankee ingenuity, mechanical skill, and thrift, characteristic of what might be termed the Benjamin Franklin era of American history. He early showed himself to be an amazingly apt inventor and fabricator. As a teenager, he fashioned pendulum-driven clocks (one of them several feet in diameter, mounted on the barn) and sensitive, bimetallic thermometers that were marveled at by neighbors. One of his alarm clocks was connected by levers to his bed, rigged to dump him on the floor at one in the morning so that he could pursue his studies. (Daniel Muir had forbidden him to stay up late reading, but had no argument with his son's getting up early.) The evidence is of a highly motivated, technically skillful, rather ascetic young man.

Muir's first move toward independence came in 1860, when he exhibited some of his devices at the Wisconsin State Fair in Madison, and was persuaded to enroll at the recently founded University of Wisconsin there. At first a special student making up for the absence of a high school education, Muir soon began scientific studies, particularly in botany and geology. In his five semesters at Wisconsin, he owed much to Dr. Ezra Carr, who taught chemistry and geology and stressed fieldwork; to Carr's wife, Jeanne, an apparent philosophical mentor with whom Muir maintained an important correspondence for many years; and to Dr. James D. Butler, a classics professor who helped Muir gain confidence as a writer. All three of these people, as it happens, had been strongly influenced by the person and teachings of Ralph Waldo Emerson (1803–1882). Here at Madison, Muir began to come out from under the dark creed of human sinfulness taught by his father into the positive light of Emerson's recommended self-reliance. If his upbringing was puritan, Muir can now be

seen as entering the transcendental era of American intellectual life. The basic principle of transcendentalism is the unity of the world: the essential oneness of divinity, humankind, and nature. "I am part or particle of God," Emerson had declared early in his first book, *Nature* (1836), challenging the Calvinists' concept of a distant and angry deity who is unreachable by fallen, sinful mankind. Emerson had also written, in "The American Scholar," that "the ancient precept, 'Know thyself,' and the modern precept, 'Study nature,' become at last one maxim," again positing a nonhierarchical unity. It is important to note that Emerson always couched these ringing, influential statements in terms of personal experience and study. Human beings are capable of learning the basic truths of existence for themselves. This is very different from following the authority of a historical text or church.

Also in college, under the tutelage of "the Doctor, who first laid before me the great book of Nature," as he described Professor Carr (*Letters to a Friend*, p. 13), Muir was gaining a conception of the immense age of the earth and learning about the effects of glaciers. In his botany courses, which emphasized taxonomy, he began to see pattern and relationship in nature. Years later in an encyclopedia entry, Muir would pay high honor to the pioneer taxonomist Carolus Linnaeus as an enlarger of humanity's worldview, and it is clear that his own understanding of botany, even early on, went well beyond rote learning. He was developing a picture of the world as an interdependent system of great age and complex development, in which plant life, geologic history, and his own developing consciousness played a part. This newly emerging feel for the natural world as a logical, observable, and unified home place was founded in important measure on Emersonian confidence. A religious response to existence was an ingrained part of Muir's makeup; in his early twenties, under the influence of both science and transcendental philosophy, he began to see divinity as interwoven with nature. Thus he carried out and reported on his studies, then and ever after, in a state very like exaltation. The simultaneity of his immersion in science and in Emersonian thought allowed his easy accommodation of religion and modern, post-Darwinian natural philosophy. Unlike many in the latter nineteenth century, Muir happily united the sense of the sacred with the methods and findings of empirical investigation. Every new fact he learned about natural history, every new discovery he made about the glacial past, he saw as simply a part of the living, divine totality. The foundations of this holistic and dynamic worldview were laid at Madison, and the tremendous energy with which Muir invested his lifework was liberated there.

Muir neither volunteered nor was drafted for service in the Civil War, and he spent much of 1864, all of 1865, and the first few months of 1866 in Canada. He botanized there and worked in a broom factory in Ontario. Returning to the United States, he found employment in an Indianapolis wheel factory. There he drew up an immensely detailed plan of the factory's operation, from the incoming raw materials to the finished product, complete with notes on how procedures might be made more efficient. He was offered a partnership. But an accident at the factory, in which Muir stabbed himself in the right eye with the sharpened end of a file, enforced a four-week period of reflection while the eye healed. When Muir emerged from the darkened convalescent room, his life and thought had formed around a new purpose. He would travel the world, absorbing the beautiful light, studying the natural, divine patterns of creation. After a brief farewell trip home to Wisconsin, he began the new regimen in the fall of 1867 with a solo walk from southern Indiana to Florida. The journal he kept on this trek, later published as *A Thousand-Mile Walk to the Gulf* (1916), documents a milestone in the development of his thinking. In an entry made at the Cedar Keys in Florida, where he recuperated from chills and fever, he bade a formal farewell to the God of his father, "as purely a manufactured article as any puppet of a half-penny theater" (p. 137). Thus declaring himself his own man, he codified the philosophical freedom symbolized in the long, solo walk.

In the spring of 1868, Muir arrived by ship in San Francisco, attracted by an illustrated brochure he saw describing Yosemite Valley. With a chance companion, he walked through the Coast Ranges, across the San Joaquin Valley, and on into Yosemite. Curiously, in view of what the valley later came to mean to him, he stayed only a week or so, returning to the foothill country to find employment at a ferry crossing and on ranches near Coulterville. During the next several months he kept his journal, wrote letters to Mrs. Carr, and perhaps in part because of her longtime urging began to try his hand at essays. One of his efforts from this time, "Twenty Hill Hollow"—appended later to *A Thousand-Mile Walk to the Gulf* by its editor, William Frederic Badè—demonstrates a high degree of literary finish. Careerless at age thirty-one, working as a ranch hand, living alone, Muir seems to have begun to consider writing as some part of his vocation. In the late spring of 1869, he was favored with what turned out to be one of the great opportunities of his life when a rancher named Patrick Delaney, apparently seeing something out of the ordinary in Muir, hired him to accompany a band of some two thousand sheep on their summer trail to the High Sierra. Since Delaney already had a sheepherder, Muir was something of a supernumerary on this journey. He had considerable freedom to roam the mountains by himself, and a great deal of time in which to write extended journal entries. The months from June through September of 1869, memorialized in one of the major texts of American nature writing, *My First Summer in the Sierra* (1911), were absolutely crucial to Muir's development as a thinker and writer.

The herders' first base camp, according to *My First Summer in the Sierra*, was established on the north fork of the Merced River on 7 June, at an elevation of three thousand feet. Situated at a bend in the river in a "picturesque hopper-shaped hollow formed by converging hill-slopes" (pp. 41–42), this camp was shaded by Douglas fir and incense cedar. Vistas of the alpine sort were lacking, but the surroundings were brightened by Washington lilies, saxifrage, and a ground-cover plant Muir particularly liked,

Chamoebatia foliolosa. The sheep were corralled at night on Brown's Flat, a meadow located an uphill half mile from camp. Water was obtained from the river. The herders made racks for dishes and provisions, and set up "beds of fern fronds, cedar plumes, and various flowers, each to the taste of its owner" (p. 42). For the next month, Muir explored the surrounding area, making entries in his journal that for passionate response to nature have no superior in his work. Upstream from camp, a large flat-topped boulder lay in the stream. Muir found that resting on this rock was conducive to a meditative state of mind. "When I climbed on top of it to-day and lay down to rest, it seemed the most romantic spot I had yet found. . . . The place seemed holy, where one might hope to see God" (pp. 64–65).

As the summer days passed and Muir immersed himself more and more thoroughly in his richly vegetated surroundings, walking miles each day over varied terrain, his transcendental concept of unity took on ecologically specific content. He learned new plants and birds—the water ouzel became a favorite at this time—and his spirits rose to a kind of ecstasy as he contemplated the living, relational quality of nature. Ponderosa pines called forth a typically strong response: "Were they mere mechanical sculptures, what noble objects they would still be! How much more throbbing, thrilling, overflowing, full of life in every fibre and cell, grand glowing silver-rods—the very gods of the plant kingdom, living their sublime century lives in sight of Heaven, watched and loved and admired from generation to generation!" (p. 70). When on 7 July the time came to move the sheep higher to new feedgrounds, Muir summed up the effect of his month on the North Fork: "Never while anything is left of me shall this first camp be forgotten. It has fairly grown into me, not merely as memory pictures, but as part and parcel of mind and body alike" (p. 111). In a catalog of personally meaningful images, he included the rather startling formulation, "the landscape beaming with consciousness like the face of a god" (p. 113).

Two weeks later, on 20 July, having moved to a new camp above the cliffs of Yosemite, Muir gave a fuller indication that a significant development in his consciousness had occurred. While sketching on North Dome, looking down on the great, still chasm of Yosemite Valley below him, he jotted notes on the question of whether or not his sketching and writing would have any life beyond his journals and letters. Quite suddenly, in the midst of these somewhat mundane, personal worries, the journal records what seems to have been a decisive insight: "No pain here, no dull empty hours, no fear of the past, no fear of the future. These blessed mountains are so compactly filled with God's beauty, no petty personal hope or experience has room to be" (p. 174). After six weeks of sleeping, eating, and walking daily in the midst of wild nature, Muir was tuned and paced to her. Clearly, he now felt himself an aspect of the greater stream: *no petty personal hope or experience has room to be.*

This conception of Muir's represented a major departure from the historical norm of Western consciousness. The civilization that shaped John Muir is founded on the rock of personal, separate identity, given cogent statement in René Descartes' "I think, therefore I am." In this approach to existence, there are inherently two realms of being: "subject" (mind) and "object" (matter); "me" and "not-me"; "man" and "nature"; "civilization" and "wilderness." Generally speaking, the acceptance of this frame of reference is pervasive and unthinking in the Western world. It has the unfortunate effect, however, of keeping the individual from a clear perception of relationship, interdependence, inter-impingement: the cornerstone of ecological awareness. So long as one's primary conception of oneself is as an island of consciousness, looking out upon a world of likewise discrete objects, one can have at best only a theoretical understanding of ecology. A biocentric orientation begins with the capacity to see relationships.

The inward transformation, Muir's writing argues, requires more than a simple taking up of new ideas. Intuition, emotional awareness, and a certain physiological sensitivity come into play. It is instructive to note how Muir finishes the 20 July entry: "Drinking this champagne water is pure pleasure, so is breathing the living air, and every movement of limbs is pleasure, while the whole body seems to feel beauty when exposed to it as it feels the camp-fire or sunshine, entering not by the eyes alone, but equally through all one's flesh like radiant heat, making a passionate ecstatic pleasure-glow not explainable" (p. 174–175).

At this point we confront John Muir's essential significance within Western culture. Muir made the transition from an egoistic, dualistic standpoint to a relation-perceiving, ecological view, demonstrating a complete trust in nature. This is the root of his passion for wildness, the source of his effectiveness as a writer and a public spokesman for the wild. To ask after the source of his charisma is to conclude that to a great degree Muir actually lived out his deepest thought. Nature was more than a benign concept to him. He was energized—by others' accounts, made volubly passionate—by the release from a limited sense of self. The central importance of Muir's 20 July 1869 journal entry is that it records the transformative move beyond the alienated tradition of his upbringing into a holistic awareness.

The summer of 1869 was John Muir's confirmation in his new theology, and his profound opening was the root of his later success, but it took a geological argument to provide him with a vocation. The controversy was over the formation of the dramatic canyons of the Sierra Nevada, in particular Yosemite Valley. The state geologist of California and author of *The Yosemite Guide-Book*, Dr. Josiah D. Whitney, had laid out the accepted theory before Muir ever arrived in California. A catastrophist in his geological theorizing, Whitney believed that the great monoliths and cliffs of Yosemite had been brought into being in sudden shocks. Half Dome, Whitney wrote, was "split asunder in the middle, the lost half having gone down in what may truly be said to have been 'the wreck of matter and the crush of the worlds'" (quoted in *John Muir's Studies in the Sierra*, 1960, pp. xvi–xvii). Glaciation had played no significant role in the area. Muir, on the other hand, was unable to accept catastrophe as an explanation.

His vision, founded in his own experience, was of a seamless unity in which change was a matter of minute adjustments rather than great revolutions. In Ezra Carr's classes at Wisconsin, Muir had learned about glaciation, which at that time was a new theory propounded by the Swiss geologist Louis Agassiz, author of *Études sur les glaciers* (1840). Glaciation fitted Muir's general perception of earth history: glaciers grew naturally and slowly as part of the hydrologic cycle, and when they began to slide downhill from their birthplaces in the mountains, they moved with majestic slowness, heavily grinding and shaping the earth beneath. On a July day in the summer of 1869, Muir had come upon some "erratics," pieces of rock not native to the area in which he found them. Such rocks were important in Agassiz' theory; along with moraines and striations (the actual marks of glacial passage, carved in bedrock), they were primary evidence for glaciation. They could only have been transported to their new homes by glaciers. "A fine discovery this," Muir had written in his journal on 11 July 1869 (*My First Summer in the Sierra*, p. 134). It was the first piece of evidence for his later hypothesis that glaciers had carved the features of the Sierra and Yosemite Valley.

In 1870 and 1871, while living in Yosemite Valley and working as a sawyer for the hotel owner James Hutchings, Muir began telling visitors that Yosemite had not resulted from "the wreck of matter and the crush of the worlds" at all, but had been shaped much more slowly, by an ancient glacier. Encouraged by several scientifically distinguished visitors to whom he had related his theories, Muir determined to make a serious study of the Sierra Nevada, in particular the watersheds of the Merced and Tuolumne Rivers, to find indisputable evidence of glaciation. By 5 December 1871 his quest had propelled him into print in the *New York Daily Tribune*, one of the most prominent newspapers in the country, with an article entitled "Yosemite Glaciers: The Ice Streams of the Great Valley; Their Progress and Present Condition; Scenes Among the Glacier Beds." He spent a great part of the years 1870, 1871, and 1872 in this pursuit, becoming in the course of this time a glaciologist of some standing and a writer with a distinctive flair for uniting enthusiasm and natural history. In terms of his overall development, the glacier study was important as the period of his life most consistently devoted to science. The discipline helped give factuality and intellectual rigor to his writing, and it made him a published authority on matters pertaining to mountains.

Muir's style of scientific expedition was amazingly simple. After drying several loaves of bread, he broke them into crumbs and put the crumbs, along with some cheese and a bit of tea, into a cloth sack. Picking up his notebook, some matches, and a couple of tins to boil water in, he strode off, many times leading what must have been a lightly loaded packhorse, leaving Yosemite Valley for the higher elevations. No tent, no sleeping bag, no sleeping pad—the list of what Muir did without would be long indeed. He knew what he was looking for and in short order began finding it: erratics, moraines, striation, glacial "polish." He capped the search by discovering sixty-odd remnant glaciers, all alive and still active. Following the scientific method, he thrust stakes into suspect surface layers and using these as markers ascertained that in fact he was observing moving glaciers. (Snowfields stay put.) He eventually took an earned place as one of the gifted amateurs of nineteenth-century natural history. A reading of the seven articles on Sierran glaciation that he published in the *Overland Monthly* beginning in May 1874 (reprinted as *John Muir's Studies in the Sierra*), however, makes it clear that as much as empirical data-gathering, Muir relied upon a more general, intuitive sense of the landscape's history. The drawings accompanying his analysis reveal a strongly sensuous perception; it seems evident that Muir's haptic sensibility was aroused, and perhaps as well a physical feeling of identification with the mountain and valley forms. A profound synthesis appears to have been going on within Muir—after all, the same Sierra Nevada terrain had been studied by the trained scientists of the California Survey, beginning in 1861, and they had not seen the glacial history that to Muir's eyes was obvious. After the publi-

cation of his series of articles in 1874–1875, Muir's argument against catastrophism in the Sierra Nevada essentially carried the day. Modern geologists agree with Muir's thesis, except that it is now believed not one but several glaciers, in turn, buried and carved the range.

In this period, Muir was a riveting figure to many Yosemite visitors, embodying the spirit of wildness that permeated the then-remote, dramatic valley. Therese Yelverton, for example, a British author who came to Yosemite in 1870, memorialized Muir as the character "Kenmuir" in her 1872 novel, *Zanita: A Tale of the Yosemite*. Kenmuir was described as an amazingly agile, Pan-like free spirit, with "bright intelligent eyes" and a remarkable spiritual unity with nature. Then, in the summer of 1871, Emerson himself came to Yosemite, traveling with an entourage. Muir made it his business to meet and talk with the Concord sage. Emerson in turn was genuinely impressed by Muir. When he returned to Concord, he entered Muir's name on his list of "My Men," eighteen individuals whom he had met and considered superior in insight and accomplishment. The first name on that list was Thomas Carlyle's; Muir's was the last.

The early 1870s, then, marked the consolidation of science and spirituality in Muir's philosophy and the beginning of his influence as a guide, at first on foot and then increasingly in writing. His journals from this period are replete with instances of ecological insight. As the natural world unfolded its secrets to him and he became more sure of his vision, he ventured interpretive statements on the nature of reality and the process of seeing itself. An entry from October 1871, made at a camp high in the mountains, is instructive:

In streams of ice, of water, of minerals, of plants, of animals, the tendency is to unification. We at once find ourselves among eternities, infinitudes, and scarce know whether to be happy in the sublime simplicity of radical causes and origins or whether to be sorry on losing the beautiful fragments which we thought perfect and primary absolute units;

but as we study and mingle with nature more, the pain caused by the melting of all beauties into one First Beauty disappears, because, after their first baptismal submergence in fountain God, they go again washed and clean into their individualisms, more clearly defined than ever, unified yet separate. (*John of the Mountains*, pp. 79–80)

This passage demonstrates that Muir was analytic as well as rhapsodic. He saw an essential paradox—that the various components of the world have both individual being and flowing participation in a greater whole. Stated another way, reality is both "particle" and "wave." Years later, in *The Mountains of California*, Muir would write of the sights and sounds of the mountains as "leading one far out of himself, yet feeding and building up his individuality" (p. 56), showing again that he had had primary experience of this paradox. Although, as Linnie Marsh Wolfe pointed out, Muir "studied . . . to keep himself and his mystical interpretations of nature in the background" (p. 166), it is apparent that his experience and reflection were complex, including both the mystical and rational dimensions. This depth underlies his work.

In another revealing statement of a general or normative nature, this one made in an 1875 journal entry, Muir recorded his broadened and diffused conception of deity. "No synonym for God is so perfect as Beauty. Whether as seen carving the lines of the mountains with glaciers, or gathering matter into stars, or planning the movements of water, or gardening—still all is Beauty!" (*John of the Mountains*, p. 208). In its conception of deity and its positive tone, this statement is as distant from his father's world as could be imagined.

By 1875, Muir had published over fifty articles in newspapers and magazines and had become known to the readership of the *Overland Monthly* and the *San Francisco Daily Evening Bulletin*, especially, as a natural-history expert and an interpreter of experience in the wild. In February 1876, he published a strongly conservation-oriented article on forests in the *Sacramento Daily Union*, and thus by mid-decade can be

said to have fairly started on his life's calling as a voice for wild nature. In the latter half of the decade, he was able to take excursions to Nevada and Utah, sending articles back to the *Daily Evening Bulletin* and widening his field of activity beyond California. He was also by this time publishing essays in *Scribner's Monthly* and *Harper's New Monthly Magazine*, important national periodicals. By the time he became engaged to Louie Wanda Strentzel, the daughter of a Martinez, California, physician and fruit-grower, in 1879, he had made a distinctive mark in the world.

Three months after the couple's marriage in 1880, Muir was off on a trip to southeastern Alaska, where he traveled the Inside Passage and explored the gigantic, ocean-reaching glaciers of the future Glacier Bay National Park. On his Alaska trips, Muir's journal reflects heightened appreciation for Native Americans, a group he had scarcely noticed previously. Aside from this, however, the main lines of his ideas were in place by the 1880s. As a man in his thirties, he had experienced the wild world of the Sierra Nevada at an extraordinarily intense level, had developed out of that encounter an original philosophy of life, had studied the actual workings of nature, thus supplying a realistic dimension to his thought, and had begun to communicate his ruling passion to others.

His marriage marked a turn toward the practical side of life, first in fruit ranching and then in public policy. Activity in the self-described "real world" would occupy his remaining thirty-four years. To begin with, Dr. Strentzel had given the couple an impressive wedding present, a working fruit ranch. No stranger to hard agricultural work, Muir managed the Martinez acreage with skill. Within ten years, he had cleared over one hundred thousand dollars, a significant sum in the pre-income-tax days of 1890. During these years, with the exception of editing a volume entitled *Picturesque California and the Regions West of the Rocky Mountains from Alaska to Mexico* (1888), Muir was considerably less active as a writer. He also went several years without an extended wilderness trip. In this period, he devoted himself to his family (daughter Annie

Wanda was born in 1881, and Helen in 1886) and to his work with pears and Tokay grapes. He also grew thin and increasingly nervous. He described himself as only "doggedly contented, as wild animals in cages" (quoted in Wolfe, p. 233). In 1889 his wife pointed out to him that the success of the fruit enterprise now made leisure possible, and urged him to get back to the basic source of his happiness, the mountains. Muir did go back to the Sierra Nevada, his home range, several times in the next few years. But the twenty-odd intervening years had made a new and different life for Muir, now in his fifties and a family man, and the mere fact of his responsibilities militated against a simple repetition of the past. The journals from this period are less incandescent than his earlier logs.

For its own part, the Sierra was not as it had been. Unremitting pressure from mining, grazing, and logging had stripped the range of its wild virginity. Even Yosemite Valley, which had been given a special, reserved status by President Abraham Lincoln in 1864, had deteriorated as a result of heavy, unregulated visitation and various inappropriate uses. Nationally, there was a movement for legislation that would protect Yosemite Valley and some of the surrounding mountain land as a national park. In June 1889, John Muir received a visitor at Martinez who aimed to enlist his person and talents in the struggle. Robert Underwood Johnson, associate editor of *Century* magazine and a man with influence in Washington, persuaded Muir to write articles giving reasons for Yosemite's preservation. "The Treasures of the Yosemite" (*Century* 40, August 1890) and "Features of the Proposed Yosemite National Park" (*Century* 40, September 1890) are detailed in their natural history, inspiring in their dramatization of rejuvenative experience in the mountains, and cogent in their sociopolitical reasoning. The two essays, appearing in one of the best-edited, most widely read magazines of the day, had a considerable impact. Meanwhile, working with Johnson, Muir had drawn up a boundary along watershed lines for the proposed Yosemite National Park, and had suggested terms for the legislation that specifically protected the area's status as largely undeveloped wilderness. (Yellowstone, founded in 1872 and the world's first national park, had no such provision, having been proposed as mainly a recreation ground.) Muir's suggestions were enacted in the Yosemite Act, passed and signed into law in September 1890. He was now, rather suddenly, embarked on the choppy seas of public policy as an important spokesman—perhaps *the* important spokesman—for wild nature.

It is well to pause for a moment now and consider the times, in order to gauge Muir's contribution. In 1890, twenty-five years following the conclusion of the Civil War—a quarter century of unprecedented growth, almost unimaginable creation of wealth, and practically unrestricted violence to the environment—America had just fulfilled its manifest destiny. The Census Bureau, in an appendix to the official 1890 census, announced what had already become apparent to some: there was no more frontier. The Gilded Age, marking the ascent to full power of industrial capitalism, was over. As if awaking from a dream of gluttony, American society now found itself contemplating a land denuded of some of its finest forests, all but empty of bison—which just a few decades earlier had made up probably the largest assemblage of herbivores the world had ever seen—and crisscrossed with close to two hundred thousand miles of railroad track, the source of enormous fortunes but also the chief facilitator of long-range, large-scale disruption of nature. The American sky was now all but empty of passenger pigeon flocks, counterpart of the bison as symbols of the former, unequaled New World abundance. Along with environmental destruction, the growth-inflamed post–Civil War period had also seen the creation of an urban underclass, widespread carelessness and pollution in the food-packaging industries, and the growth of political corruption. An atmosphere of disillusion began to color American literature, where economic determinism and other "naturalistic" themes became prevalent.

A counterweight to all this was the increasing activity of public-spirited and in some cases environmentally conscious citizens making up

Muir (right) with fellow naturalist John Burroughs

the Progressive movement. For more than two decades, until World War I, redressing excess became a part of the American agenda. On the environmental front, the legislation creating Yosemite National Park, protecting wilderness as it did, was symbolic of the new national self-consciousness dawning in the post-frontier era. In the next year, 1891, President Benjamin Harrison created some thirteen million acres of "forest reserves," the forerunners of the national forests. In 1892, a number of prominent San Francisco Bay Area citizens joined with John Muir to found the Sierra Club, and immediately made Muir the club's president, a post he held until his death in 1914. The Sierra Club, though nowhere near as militant as it became in the environmental wars of the 1960s, was nevertheless an organized constituency for wild nature, one of the first in history. In 1893, historian Frederick Jackson Turner promulgated his immensely influential "frontier thesis," which held that the wild land to the west of expanding American civilization had shaped the country's economy, politics, and general temper. The cor-

ollary to the Turner thesis seemed obvious: if the wilderness had indeed played such an important role in building American character and institutions, we would do well to preserve it for the benefit of future generations. In 1894, urged by friends and responding to the new audience for wildness, the fifty-six-year-old Muir gathered several essays and molded them into his first book, *The Mountains of California*. It became an important text in the growing environmental movement.

By 1896, when Muir became an adjunct member of the presidentially appointed Forestry Commission (also known as the Sargent Commission) and traveled with that body to survey the status of the nation's forests and make recommendations about policy, it had become apparent to many that he championed a decidedly philosophical, nonmaterialistic perception of wild land. Mainstream conservation thought at that time (and today, for that matter) held to the concept of active management, very much oriented toward the production of goods. Forests were to be managed as tree farms, so that society could continue to harvest logs securely into the future. This was a step forward from the "cut and run" philosophy of the recent past, to be sure, but to Muir it was woefully lacking. To him, a forest was first of all a portion of the sacred scheme of things, and as such should be treated (like any other aspect of nature) with spiritual respect. Its highest use was essentially revelatory. "Happy the man to whom every tree is a friend," he wrote in his journal on 4 September 1908, "who loves them, sympathizes with them in their lives" (*John of the Mountains*, p. 437). He also specifically recognized material values in preserving forests whole. Wild forests are sources of water, for example, and natural preventers of downstream flooding and erosion, as he wrote as early as 1876. But in the deliberations of the Sargent Commission, and increasingly in the public eye, Muir became identified with the contemplative *preservation* of wild nature, as opposed to the utilitarian *conservation* of what became known simply as "natural resources." His opposite number was Gifford Pinchot (1865–1946), the first chief of the Forest Service when that agency was created in 1905, and a vigorous champion of the management-oriented, "commodity" concept of forest conservation. In the terms developed later by the Norwegian philosopher Arne Naess, Pinchot represented "shallow ecology," and Muir, "deep ecology." There can be little doubt, historically, that Pinchot's side has been dominant, but the values represented by John Muir were given significant standing in the formation of the National Park Service in 1916, and made inroads even in the U.S. Forest Service as early as 1924, when the first national forest primitive area was established. In later years, the more profound valuation of nature expressed by John Muir surfaced again in the struggle for the Wilderness Act, passed into law in 1964, and in the deep ecology and "green" movements of the 1970s and later.

But in 1896, Muir was distinctly a minority voice. Despite his gift for persuasion, he found the other members of the Sargent Commission, with a couple of exceptions, essentially immovable. The national forests would be treated as material resources to be grown, cut, and sold with the greatest efficiency possible. Gifford Pinchot, politically astute and confidently embodying the majority's viewpoint, carried the day. He approved of sheep grazing within national forests and later played a key role in the placing of a dam at Hetch Hetchy, within Yosemite National Park. An incident occurring in the summer of 1897, in Seattle, illustrates the differences between Muir and Pinchot, and also offers a good insight into Muir's style. For many years, going back to the summer of 1869, Muir had seen direct evidence of the damage domestic sheep could do to mountain and forest vegetation. Calling them "hoofed locusts," he wrote that "the harm they do goes to the heart." Herded in vast numbers over the Sierra Nevada, as in other western mountain ranges, sheep had significantly altered the native ecology in many places, and by destroying the plant cover had contributed to erosion and flooding. Muir's outrage at the devastation had a distinctly moral and religious quality. When he found, for example, that a herd of sheep had destroyed a beautiful mountain meadow, he noted, "The money-changers were in the temple" (*The Mountains of California*, p. 116).

Overgrazing was not simply a technical matter to him, something that might be mitigated by adjustments in management, but a sign of humanity's self-centered arrogance and spiritual unconsciousness. To Muir, it should be national forest policy to strictly limit or eliminate sheep grazing, and he carried moral fervor into the Sargent Commission's discussions. Pinchot, for his part, also knew of the damage sheep did. A graduate of the famed Sheffield Scientific School of Yale University and a longtime student of forest practices in Europe, he was certainly able to interpret on-the-ground evidence. But he lacked Muir's ecological and moral perception of nature, and was able to make political compromises with wool growers, in order more easily to secure government control over traditional grazing lands. To get a mountain range safely into the national forest domain, he would allow sheep grazing to continue. But then in a speech in Seattle he went one crucial step further by declaring, against his own knowledge, that sheep did little harm to forests. When Muir, traveling with the Sargent Commission, read an account of the speech in a Seattle newspaper, he was furious. Confronting Pinchot in a hotel lobby, he asked the forester if the newspaper account were true. When Pinchot owned up to his remarks, Muir said, "Then if that is the case, I don't want anything more to do with you" (quoted in Wolfe, pp. 275–276).

In better circumstances, though, enjoying the right interpersonal chemistry, Muir could be charming and effective. In 1903, for example, he had the chance to take President Theodore Roosevelt on a three-day camping trip in Yosemite. Making the most of the opportunity, Muir spoke feelingly about the need for greater forest protection. The president became convinced of the wisdom of federal protection for Yosemite Valley (it had been under the very loose control of California), and a day after parting from Muir, lengthened the Sierra forest reserve northward to Mount Shasta. He later followed Muir's advice and preserved a portion of the Grand Canyon as a national monument. Roosevelt's authority for this executive action was the Lacey Antiquities Act of 1906, legislation inspired by Muir, as it happens, and much used throughout the twentieth century. Using this piece of legislation, presidents have saved much of Jackson Hole for Grand Teton National Monument, and Capital Reef and Arches National Monuments in Utah, all of which became national parks, among many other sites. Perhaps the most spectacular use of the 1906 Antiquities Act occurred in 1980, when outgoing President Jimmy Carter spared some fifty-six million acres of Alaskan wilderness until it could be permanently protected under National Park, National Wilderness Preservation System, and National Wildlife Refuge auspices.

Muir's inherent tendency to see environmental battles as religious in nature, and to fight them with prophetlike thunder, is nowhere better illustrated than in the last struggle of his life, the fight over the Hetch Hetchy Valley. Beginning in 1882, the city of San Francisco had developed and promoted plans to dam the Tuolumne River in Hetch Hetchy, a valley to the north of

Yosemite Valley and somewhat similar to it, in order to have a reliable supply of drinking water and to generate electric power. Even after the Yosemite Act of 1890, which of course protected Hetch Hetchy in its wild state, San Francisco politicos and their allies continued to press for special legislation that would allow the desired dam. Their bills were introduced almost yearly, but always, up to 1913, were beaten back. John Muir led the forces dedicated to saving Hetch Hetchy and keeping Yosemite National Park intact. In the absence of a national park service with an enabling act spelling out a general policy for national parks, Muir relied chiefly on trying to convey his philosophy of wild integrity and the cultural importance of wilderness. His arguments, written out in several magazine articles and in *The Yosemite* (1912), made much of the inspirational and health-giving powers of wild places, and damned the shortsighted and greedy who would drown one of the most beautiful valleys in the Sierra and put much of one of its great rivers into a pipe. Allied with San Francisco were Gifford Pinchot and Congressman William Kent of California, who in 1908 had given the land for Muir Woods National Monument and suggested that it be named for Muir. As the struggle grew in intensity, Muir threw in more of his time and resources. Articles such as "The Tuolumne Yosemite in Danger" (*Outlook* 87, 2 November 1907), and "The Hetch-Hetchy Valley: A National Question" (*American Forestry* 16, May 1910) forthrightly laid out the moral and cultural dimension of the question. The 1911 publication of *My First Summer in the Sierra*, the journal Muir kept back in 1869, may have been inspired by the heat of the Hetch Hetchy campaign. Certainly it contains the most personally revealing of Muir's writing published during his lifetime. But Muir's passion rose to a peak in 1912 with the publication of *The Yosemite*. "Dam Hetch Hetchy!" he exclaimed on the book's last page. "As well dam for water-tanks the people's cathedrals and churches, for no holier temple has ever been consecrated by the heart of man" (p. 262).

In the end, San Francisco had its way with Hetch Hetchy. The special legislation was passed in 1913, O'Shaughnessy Dam was con-

The Hetch Hetchy Valley as it appeared before the O'Shaughnessy Dam was built

structed, and Hetch Hetchy has remained under water to the present. John Muir, exhausted by the long and losing battle, traveled to the Mojave Desert to visit his daughter Helen, who lived there for health reasons. He worked on a manuscript that would become *Travels in Alaska*. In the fall of the following year he contracted pneumonia and was taken from the desert to a hospital in Los Angeles. There, with his book-in-progress laid out on the bed around him, he died on Christmas Eve, 24 December 1914.

It has been pointed out that though the immediate battle for Yosemite's integrity was lost, the fighting of it had greatly enlarged the constituency for wild places, and likely contributed to the founding of the National Park Service just three years later in 1916. Significantly, the enabling act spelled out that an important part of the service's mandate, coequal with providing recreation, would be preservation of the wild resource itself.

Muir as a Writer

The key to John Muir's effectiveness as a writer was his liberation from conventional Western perception. Transcending his culture's philosophical dualism and perceptual predilection for static, hard-bordered entities, he became better able to see the dynamic and ever-changing relationships in nature. His task as a writer was to find ways to convey this.

Of the two primary modes of human consciousness, one of which works in terms of wholes and configurations and the other in entities and linear sequence, it is clear that Western civilization is oriented toward the latter. The entire structure of Western economics, politics, behavioral norms, and ideology is built upon entity-bound perception. Most Westerners live their daily lives on what could be called the "Gifford Pinchot" model. Indeed, historically, at least since the time of Aristotle, some of the most important thinkers in the Western tradition have honored the entity-focused mode of consciousness, and have declared the configurative mode secondary. Aristotle held that what he called "Reason" was the "highest and best part of man." René Descartes (1596–1650) argued that linear-sequential consciousness, which he referred to simply as "thought," defined human existence itself: "I think, therefore I am." John Locke (1632–1704) similarly celebrated dualistic awareness in his influential *Essay Concerning Human Understanding* in 1690. (It

663

bears mentioning here that the church of John Muir's father, the Disciples of Christ, explicitly endorsed Locke's theories of human consciousness.) The problem with entity-bound consciousness is that it can result in mechanistic interpretations of existence and in a lack of creative, feeling engagement with the world.

The other fundamental mode of awareness, the ability to perceive in wholes and configurations, is essential to all creativity and the arts, and in any situation where perceiving and understanding relationships are paramount. But in a culture venerating what it sees as practical and rational, the "heart" or the "right brain" or "intuition" (three common shorthand terms for holistic consciousness) receive strictly limited praise. The preponderant weight of cultural valuation falls on the egoistic, anthropocentric, and materialistic side of life.

Despite the coercive power of the general cultural ideology, and the specific authoritarian pressure of his father, Muir believed that he was never quite defeated, never quite tamed. Apparently the spark of wildness remained alive and resistant. It was still viable when, in his thirties, not yet "settled down," he came to the Sierra Nevada. Away from the built environment, surrounded by essentially nonegoistic nature, Muir's native intelligence blossomed. The ahistorical, holistic, intuitive, and ethical side of his consciousness rose toward its rightful place. Interestingly, the first tangible result of this opening of awareness in Muir was the writing of a journal. Traditionally, writing and language are associated with the "left-brain," linear-sequential mode of consciousness. Certainly, Muir often complained that mere words, lined up in a book, could not reproduce the full glory of the mountains. "I find this literary business very irksome," he declared in 1873 (quoted in Wolfe, p. 166), and there is evidence that the difficulty remained with him all his life. "I have a low opinion of books; they are but piles of stones set up to show coming travelers where other minds have been. . . . Cadmus and all the other inventors of letters receive a thousand-fold more credit than they deserve. No amount of word-making will ever make a single soul to *know* these

mountains," he had written in 1872 (*John of the Mountains*, pp. 94–95). But despite his skepticism, Muir's writing at its best expresses the synthesis of the two major modes of consciousness. Though necessarily couched in the linear forms of the English language, his sentences nevertheless manage to convey the nonlinear richness of nature.

Some of Muir's most successful images appear to spring from simple perception and are presented as mere reportage. They emphasize natural things in movement, and do not offer a substantial secondary layer of adjectival or adverbial modification. These images dramatize the moment of perception before categorization, and have the effect of evoking experience itself rather than description and judgment. The narrative situation in which they occur thus has the feel of continuing discovery and unfolding action. The reader is there with Muir, sharing in unembroidered perception. (In his later years, as a successful writer and public man living at a certain distance, perhaps, from his experience of wild nature, Muir worked hard to eliminate adjectives from his written recollections. This chastening process may be seen as his attempt to recapture the feeling of being at the source.) The journals, not surprisingly, often record relatively unembellished moments. A plain and straightforward account may seem to resonate with ethical content, perhaps because the precision implies respect for what is before the writer's eyes. In mid-July 1869 Muir described an attempted stream crossing, later published in *My First Summer in the Sierra*:

> The drivers and dogs had a lively, laborious time getting the sheep across the creek, the second large stream thus far that they have been compelled to cross without a bridge; the first being the North Fork of the Merced near Bower cave. Men and dogs, shouting and barking, drove the timid, water-fearing creatures in a close crowd against the bank, but not one of the flock would launch away. While thus jammed, the Don and the shepherd rushed through the frightened crowd to stampede those in front, but this would only cause a break backward, and away they would scam-

per through the stream-bank trees and scatter over the rocky pavement. (pp. 147–148)

Images with movement in them are typically much more compelling than static scenes. Muir's consciousness of this truth seems to have been native, to inhere in his own sensitivity to the living quality of nature. He simply did not see the natural world as a collection of static objects. The record of one of his best-known adventures exemplifies this. In December 1874, on the forested divide between the Feather and Yuba Rivers on the west slope of the Sierra Nevada, he found a new way to enjoy a windstorm. Selecting a tall Douglas fir, Muir climbed to the top and "clung with muscles firm braced, like a bobolink on a reed."

In its widest sweeps my tree-top described an arc of from twenty to thirty degrees, but I felt sure of its elastic temper, having seen others of the same species still more severely tried— bent almost to the ground indeed, in heavy snows—without breaking a fiber. I was therefore safe, and free to take the wind into my pulses and enjoy the excited forest from my superb outlook. The view from here must be extremely beautiful in any weather. Now my eye roved over the piny hills and dales as over fields of waving grain, and felt the light running in ripples and broad swelling undulations across the valleys from ridge to ridge, as the shining foliage was stirred by corresponding waves of air. Oftentimes these waves of reflected light would break up suddenly into a kind of beaten foam, and again, after chasing one another in regular order, they would seem to bend forward in concentric curves, and disappear on some hillside, like sea-waves on a shelving shore. (*The Mountains of California*, p. 252)

Indeed, it is difficult to find a standing-still image of nature in Muir's writing. His mind, clearly, was unconstrained, and at its best partook of the moving and living quality of wild nature. As readers, we respond to the dynamic connection between Muir and his surroundings as much as to his particular subjects, and feel vivified, our

capacities renewed. (This recapturing of perception and experience may in fact be the core attractiveness of modern nature-writing.)

Muir's literary attention to the relational aspect of nature also proceeds from his holistic awareness. Where the conventional mind sees "natural resources" stacked up like so many inert blocks, presumably waiting to come alive and meaningful in some sort of human use, Muir sees a vital, sanctifying connectedness among all things. Relationship embodies the life principle, makes unity possible. Thus his images are almost always couched in terms of interaction, layers of relationship and response. In *The Mountains of California* Muir wrote of the Douglas squirrel, ubiquitous in the Sierra Nevada, "Every wind is fretted by his voice, almost every bole and branch feels the sting of his sharp feet" (p. 226). In the same text he described the water ouzel: "I have often observed him singing in the midst of beaten spray, his music completely buried beneath the water's roar; yet I knew he was surely singing by his gestures and the movements of his bill" (p. 283).

Muir's ebullience is obvious, and like his feeling for movement, it tends to be contagious. He wrote quite literally as a man in love, in a state of extreme sensitivity to impression, and again, readers respond to the lively quality of his mind and heart as much as to the subjects of his attention. During that heady summer of 1869, recorded in *My First Summer in the Sierra*, he wrote, "God himself seems to be always doing his best here, working like a man in a glow of enthusiasm" (p. 80)—as Muir himself worked. His prose is often exclamatory: "Who wouldn't be a mountaineer! Up here all the world's prizes seem nothing" (p. 153). A state of ecstasy could not be maintained permanently, of course, yet even in his most sober scientific work, the seven glaciology articles published under the title *John Muir's Studies in the Sierra*, Muir's enthusiasm for the whole mountain experience—not simply or separately the geological history—runs along just under the surface, and frequently bursts forth. In an early description of Yosemite Valley, he begins with the valley's monolithic walls, clearly relevant to the geological thesis, but after a few sentences his feeling for the valley as a whole compels a more inclusive view:

> The average height of the walls is about 3,000 feet, made up of a series of sublime rock forms, varying greatly in size and structure, partially separated from one another by small side cañons. These immense wall-rocks, ranged picturesquely together, do not stand in line. Some advance their sublime fronts far out into the open valley, others recede. A few are nearly vertical, but far the greater number are inclined at angles ranging from twenty to seventy degrees. The meadows and sandy flats outspread between support a luxuriant growth of sedges and ferns, interrupted with thickets of azalea, willow and brier-rose. The warmer sloping ground along the base of the walls is planted with noble pines and oaks, while countless alpine flowers fringe the deep and dark side cañons, through which glad streams descend in falls and cascades, on their way from the high fountains to join the river. The life-giving Merced flows down the valley with a slow, stately current, curving hither and thither through garden and grove, bright and pure as the snow of its fountains. (p. 18)

The student of John Muir must sooner or later confront his use of the "pathetic fallacy." As with his emphasis upon image, movement, and relationship, and his tone of enthusiasm, Muir's personification of the elements of nature derives from his basic perceptual stance. The pathetic fallacy is a result of his way of thinking and responding to the world. The term was used by the British critic John Ruskin in Volume 3 of his *Modern Painters* (1856) to describe the attribution of human emotions or states of mind to nonhuman things such as leaves, primroses, waves, wind, and so forth. For Ruskin, such an assignment of feeling ("pathetic" in this case from the Greek *pathos*, passion) was illogical, and thus a fallacy, though it might have a certain poetic power. He thought the very first rank of writers—Homer, Shakespeare, and Dante, for example—did not indulge in the pathetic fallacy. For John Muir, however, the world did not sort out neatly into human and nonhuman categories. Like the Romantics Keats and Wordsworth,

and the American writers Emerson and Whitman, he saw a streaming unity above all, and simply did not believe that humanity was some sort of special or separate creation. Muir's concept of human evolution was that Homo sapiens had "flowed down through other forms of being and absorbed and assimilated portions of them" (*John of the Mountains*, p. 138). Thus connection is the ground truth; in the great relational play of life, metaphor is basic, constant, and obvious. Muir therefore uses the pathetic fallacy forthrightly and virtually continuously. For just one example, he writes that when we travel high in the mountains where the tarns and the glaciated landscape, only recently emerged from the ice, seem raw and grim, our affirmation may be tested.

> However perfect the season and the day, the cold incompleteness of these young lakes is always keenly felt. We approach them with a kind of mean caution, and steal unconfidingly around their crystal shores, dashed and ill at ease, as if expecting to hear some forbidding voice. But the love-songs of the ouzels and the love-looks of the daisies gradually reassure us, and manifest the warm fountain humanity that pervades the coldest and most solitary of them all. (*The Mountains of California*, p. 124)

Given Muir's systematically relational outlook, symbolism and parable are pervasive in his work. Absolutely everything can be seen as a sign of the divine intention, the flowering unity of nature. What his writing amounts to, in effect, is an explanation of the ways of God (that is, beauty, the totality), a sort of rewriting of the Bible in ecological and nonanthropocentric terms. Instead of genealogical and historical concentration on humanity, Muir offers a spiritually democratic universe in which the human species is one among many. His "neighbor" who should be loved as oneself is the "handsome grasses," the "sunny air . . . tingling with infinite wing-beats of newborn insect people," the "massive, snowless gray walls of the valley," the "symmetrical spire" of the Ponderosa pine. In Muir's thought, anything can open the eyes and inspire the heart. A detailed description of *Pinus aristata* (bristlecone pine) takes a typical turn: "Again in the same woods you find trees that are made up of several boles united near the ground, spreading at the sides in a plane parallel to the axis of the mountain, with the elegant tassels hung in charming order between them, making a harp held against the main wind lines where they are most effective in playing the grand storm harmonies" (*The Mountains of California*, pp. 218–219). Always, the upshot of a description, the ultimate theme, is the role that any particular thing plays in the "grand harmonies."

Some elements and inhabitants of the natural world seemed especially well suited to Muir's symbolic imagination. Sierran and Alaskan glaciers were quintessential: they were created by a slow accretion, season upon season, of uncounted millions of snowflakes, which in turn had been produced by the rising and cooling of moisture-laden air coming off the Pacific, which in turn was the product of the sun's evaporation of ocean water and the global swirls of air currents and weather systems. When the glaciers began to flow, bearing down on the land, they created rock dust, moraines, and beds for lakes and streams, setting up the conditions for soil accumulation, forests, meadows, squirrels, and flowers. The streams fed by melting glaciers eventually made their way back to the ocean, completing a circle, a harmony. This cycle never failed to arouse Muir's sense of wonder and reverence for nature. One of the denizens of the mountain streams, the water ouzel, also caught Muir's symbolic attention readily. The ouzel seemed perfectly wedded to its environment: as Muir explained, this bird stays intimately close to the water, building its nest on midstream boulders or even behind waterfalls, hunting its food (water insects) by wading or diving in the stream, in all seasons, and even following the meanders of a meadow stream exactly, if scared into flight. The ouzel's wrenlike song is also seemingly waterborne: "nearly all of his music is sweet and tender, lapsing from his round breast like water over the smooth lip of a pool, then breaking farther on into a sparkling foam of melodious notes" (*The Mountains of California*,

p. 282). Muir's essay on the water ouzel is, in the end, an allegory on the proper way to live, emphasizing that the bird leads a nature-embedded life in harmony with its surroundings. Undaunted by winter, storm, white water, or even the din of a sawmill, it sings cheerily.

But Muir's most important carrier of the theme was, of course, himself. Necessarily, he was the protagonist of the encounter with hallowed wildness. His adventures were almost always overlaid with an implication of sacred journeying; sometimes the figuration seems overt. His description of the climb of Mount Ritter, for example, which took place in October 1872, would be hard to see as anything other than a "grail" story. Early in the month, Muir had been high in the mountains, measuring the movement of some stakes he had planted in a glacier. He had climbed "more than twenty-four thousand feet in these ten days," as he wrote to Jeanne Carr upon his return to Yosemite Valley, and was terribly weary. But two days later he was on his way back into the high country, guiding three artists who wanted to paint some classic alpine views. After taking them to an appropriate standpoint, Muir went on his way alone, toward unclimbed Mount Ritter. As described in *The Mountains of California*, on the mountain proper, he "made [his] way into a wilderness of crumbling spires and battlements, built together in bewildering combinations, and glazed in many places with a thin coating of ice" (p. 63). The climbing became increasingly dangerous, until finally Muir found himself unable to move either up or down. "My doom appeared fixed. I *must* fall," he wrote.

When this final danger flashed upon me, I became nerve-shaken for the first time since setting foot on the mountains, and my mind seemed to fill with a stifling smoke. But this terrible eclipse lasted only a moment, when life blazed forth again with preternatural clearness. I seemed suddenly to become possessed of a new sense. The other self, bygone experiences, Instinct, or Guardian Angel,—call it what you will,—came forward and assumed control. Then my trembling muscles became firm again, every rift and flaw in the rock was seen as through a microscope, and my limbs moved with a positiveness and precision with which I seemed to have nothing at all to do. Had I been borne aloft upon wings, my deliverance could not have been more complete. (pp. 64–65)

From the summit, Muir enjoyed an unlimited 360-degree view of wild mountains, canyons, lakes and streams, and the unbounded sky. As Herbert F. Smith has pointed out, the contrast with the framed scenes sought by the artists has inevitable satiric content. The painters were working well within romantic convention, but Muir was seeking direct experience of the sublime. On his quest, he took almost no care for comfort ("I had not even burdened myself with a coat"), and at early stages, when retreat might still have been possible, refused to listen to his "better judgment," or safety-consciousness. In effect, he threw himself upon the mercy of the wilderness in one of its coldest and most merciless-seeming forms, the shady side of an unscaled, rocky summit, miles from any sort of help. Something—"call it what you will"—brought him through the "terrible shadow" into the sunlight flooding the peak, and granted a new perspective. Using the term "deliverance" only makes the religious parallel obvious.

The climb of Mount Ritter may have been more fraught with physical danger than the events described in other of Muir's narratives, but it is typical in its general plot and symbolic movement. His central urge as a writer was to convey the beauty, the sustaining quality, the astonishing diversity, and the sacredness of nature as he had experienced them himself. Muir's writings argue for a higher range of mind as well as for a learner's attitude of humility. As human beings witness more and more of the unsought side effects of utilitarianism and resource-management "conservation," Muir's nonmaterialism and his unwavering reverence for the whole of nature may come to seem increasingly instructive. His writings demonstrate that spiritual delight in the world is surely one of the most endearing human capacities.

Selected Bibliography

WORKS OF JOHN MUIR

COLLECTED WORKS

The Writings of John Muir: Manuscript Edition, ed. by William Frederic Badè 10 vols. (Boston: Houghton Mifflin, 1916–1924); *John of the Mountains: The Unpublished Journals of John Muir*, ed. by Linnie Marsh Wolfe (Boston: Houghton Mifflin, 1938; Madison: Univ. of Wisconsin Press, 1979); *John Muir's Studies in the Sierra*, ed. by William E. Colby (San Francisco: Sierra Club, 1960); *South of Yosemite: Selected Writings of John Muir*, ed. by Frederic R. Gunsky (Garden City, N.Y.: American Museum of Natural History, 1968); *The Wilderness World of John Muir*, ed. by Edwin Way Teale (Boston: Houghton Mifflin, 1954; repr., 1976); *To Yosemite and Beyond: Writings from the Years 1863 to 1875*, ed. by Robert Engberg and Donald Wesling (Madison: Univ. of Wisconsin Press, 1980); *John Muir Summering in the Sierra*, ed. by Robert Engberg (Madison: Univ. of Wisconsin Press, 1984); *Muir Among the Animals: The Wildlife Writings of John Muir*, ed. by Lisa Mighetto (San Francisco: Sierra Club, 1986); *Northwest Passages: From the Pen of John Muir in California, Oregon, Washington, and Alaska* (Palo Alto, Calif.: Tioga, 1988); *The Eight Wilderness Discovery Books* (Seattle, Wash.: Mountaineers, 1992).

NONFICTION

The Mountains of California (New York: Century, 1894; Garden City, N.Y.: Doubleday, 1961; Dunwoody, Ga.: Norman S. Berg, 1975; Berkeley, Calif.: Ten Speed Press, 1977; New York: Penguin, 1985; San Francisco: Sierra Club, 1989); *Our National Parks* (Boston and New York: Houghton Mifflin, 1901; New York: AMS, 1970; Madison: Univ. of Wisconsin Press, 1981; San Francisco: Sierra Club, 1991); *Stickeen: The Story of a Dog* (Boston and New York: Houghton Mifflin, 1909; Dunwoody, Ga.: Norman S. Berg, 1971; Garden City, N.Y.: Doubleday, 1974; Berkeley, Calif.: Heyday Books, 1981); *My First Summer in the Sierra* (Boston and New York: Houghton Mifflin, 1911; Dunwoody, Ga.: Norman S. Berg, 1972; Boston: Houghton Mifflin, 1979; New York: Penguin, 1987; San Francisco: Sierra Club, 1989); *The Yosemite* (New York: Century, 1912; Garden City, N.Y.: Doubleday, 1962; Madison: Univ. of Wisconsin Press, 1987; San Francisco: Sierra Club, 1989); *Edward Henry Harriman* (New York: Doubleday, Page, 1912); *The Story of My Boyhood and Youth* (Boston and New York: Houghton Mifflin, 1913; Madison: Univ. of Wisconsin Press, 1965; Dunwoody, Ga.: Norman S. Berg, 1975; San Francisco: Sierra Club, 1989); *Travels in Alaska* (Boston and New York:

Houghton Mifflin, 1915; New York: AMS, 1971; Boston: Houghton Mifflin, 1979; San Francisco: Sierra Club, 1988); *A Thousand-Mile Walk to the Gulf*, ed. by William Frederic Badè (Boston and New York: Houghton Mifflin, 1916; Dunwoody, Ga.: Norman S. Berg, 1969; Boston: Houghton Mifflin, 1979; San Francisco: Sierra Club, 1992); *The Cruise of the Corwin*, ed. by William Frederic Badè (Boston and New York: Houghton Mifflin, 1917; Dunwoody, Ga.: Norman S. Berg, 1974); *Steep Trails*, ed. by William Frederic Badè (Boston and New York: Houghton Mifflin, 1918; Dunwoody, Ga.: Norman S. Berg, 1970).

CORRESPONDENCE

Letters to a Friend: Written to Mrs. Ezra S. Carr, 1866–1879, by John Muir (Boston and New York: Houghton Mifflin, 1915; Dunwoody, Ga.: Norman S. Berg, 1973); *The Life and Letters of John Muir*, ed. by William Frederic Badè (New York: AMS, 1973); *Dear Papa: Letters Between John Muir and His Daughter Wanda*, ed. by Jean Hanna Clark and Shirley Sargent (Fresno, Calif.: Panorama West Books, 1985); *Letters from Alaska*, ed. by Robert Engberg and Bruce Merrell (Madison: Univ. of Wisconsin Press, 1993).

MANUSCRIPTS AND PAPERS

The largest collection of John Muir's papers is held at the University of the Pacific, Stockton, California. Consult *The Guide and Index to the Microform Edition of the John Muir Papers, 1858–1957*, ed. by Ronald H. Lumbaugh and Kirsten E. Lewis (Alexandria, Va.: Chadwyck-Healey, in collaboration with the University of the Pacific, 1986).

BIBLIOGRAPHIES

William F. Kimes and Maymie B. Kimes, *John Muir: A Reading Bibliography* (Palo Alto, Calif.: William P. Wrenden, 1978), 2d ed., rev. and enl. (Fresno, Calif.: Panorama West Books, 1986); Ann T. Lynch, "Bibliography of Works by and About John Muir, 1869–1978," in *Bulletin of Bibliography* 36 (1979).

BIOGRAPHICAL AND CRITICAL STUDIES

William Frederic Badè, *The Life and Letters of John Muir*, 2 vols. (Boston: Houghton Mifflin, 1924); James Mitchell Clarke, *The Life and Adventures of John Muir* (San Francisco: Sierra Club, 1979); Michael P. Cohen, *The Pathless Way: John Muir and American Wilderness* (Madison: Univ. of Wisconsin Press, 1984); Richard F. Fleck, *Henry Thoreau and John Muir Among the Indians* (Hamden, Conn.: Archon, 1985); Norman Foerster, *Nature in American Literature: Studies in the Modern View of Nature* (New York: Macmillan, 1923); Stephen R. Fox, *John Muir and His Legacy: The American Conservation Movement* (Boston: Little, Brown, 1981); Edith Jane Hadley, "John Muir's Views of Nature and Their Consequences" (Ph.D. diss., University of Wisconsin, 1956); Holway R. Jones, *John Muir and the Sierra Club: The Battle for Yosemite* (San Francisco: Sierra Club, 1965); John P. O'Grady, *Pilgrims to the Wild: Everett Ruess, Henry David Thoreau, John Muir, Clarence King, Mary Austin* (Salt Lake City: Univ. of Utah Press, 1992); Albert Saijo, "Elders of the Tribe 2: John Muir (1838–1914)," in *Backpacker* 1 (summer 1973); Herbert F. Smith, *John Muir* (New York: Twayne, 1965); Frederick Turner, *Rediscovering America: John Muir in His Time and Ours* (New York: Viking, 1985); Linnie Marsh Wolfe, *Son of the Wilderness: The Life of John Muir* (New York: Knopf, 1945; repr., Madison: Univ. of Wisconsin Press, 1978); Samuel Hall Young, *Alaska Days with John Muir* (New York: Fleming Revell, 1915).

GARY PAUL NABHAN
(b. 1952)

SARA L. ST. ANTOINE

IN THE AMERICAN Southwest, where Gary Paul Nabhan makes his home, a prehistoric flutist named Kokopelli is said to have roamed from village to village, trading crop seeds and swapping stories. Ignoring the flutist's less respectable reputation as an unpredictable prankster, one could say that Gary Nabhan has become his modern-day successor. Nabhan is an ethnobotanist—one who studies the relationship between plants and peoples—who has worked to sustain the heirloom seeds of indigenous groups in the desert Southwest. Like Kokopelli, he is a traveler, gracefully circulating among the Anglo, Native American, and Mexican communities around his desert home and comfortably navigating the varied disciplines of field botany, conservation biology, anthropology, education, and nature literature. Culturally and intellectually, Nabhan is a master of cross-pollination. He applies holistic thinking to scientific fields dominated by specialists, and insists on concomitant attention to culture and nature in all of his work. Not surprisingly, his essays and books span a broad spectrum of topics and styles. That range is both a reflection of his versatility and a tribute to the many intricate associations he sees among plants, animals, and cultures.

One might doubt that Gary, Indiana—the industrial city where Nabhan was born (on 17 March 1952) and grew up—would be a fertile environment for an aspiring naturalist, but Nabhan has often cited its advantages. Local schools had benefited from educational reforms and innovations led by John Dewey in nearby Chicago. Lake Michigan afforded a dune-swept playground—"a hodgepodge of buried forests, quaking bogs, and mountains of sand"—where Nabhan could explore wilder terrain (*Geography of Childhood*, p. 38). The neighborhood boasted immigrants from around the world, including Nabhan's relatives—second-generation Lebanese who passed on to him a love of working among diverse communities that was a product of their centuries-old heritage as cross-cultural traders.

As an adolescent, Nabhan grew restless with public schooling, especially the confinement it imposed. In his entire primary and secondary school education, he recalls taking only a handful of field trips out-of-doors. Convinced that he had more to learn outside the four walls of a high school classroom, Nabhan took to going truant, spending hours alone along Lake Michigan, and ultimately dropping out of high school.

For several months he worked as a manual laborer around Gary. Whenever possible, he chose jobs that allowed him to stay outdoors. One afternoon, on the railroad tracks near his home, he caught sight of six herons searching for a place to land in a region that had long ago been converted from marshes and swales to factories and junkyards. Watching as the herons finally gave up and flew on, Nabhan had something of an epiphany about his own future path:

> I stood there for another moment, imagining their trail toward other primordial pitstops, following the path of their predecessors for millennia. . . . It was then that I had my own magnetic encounter with an encoded legacy — a continuity with former generations of my own kind — that had buried deep within my own consciousness. I realized that no matter where I was, I had the capacity to see the world as freshly as any naturalist could.
>
> (*Geography of Childhood*, p. 36)

Turning this vision into an academic orientation, Nabhan attended Cornell College in Iowa before transferring to Prescott College in Arizona, where he acquired a B.A. degree in 1974 with an emphasis in environmental biology and Western American literature. It was a change not only of schools but also of homes. Despite strong nomadic tendencies, Nabhan has made Arizona his home base ever since.

After college, Nabhan wrestled with the seeming duality of his passions. Friends and family insisted that he choose between biology and poetry, but he was reluctant to abandon either interest. In order to sort out his dilemma, he holed away for several months in a converted chicken coop — writing, studying biology texts, and reading the journals of Henry David Thoreau. In his preface to Thoreau's posthumously published *Faith in a Seed* (1993), Nabhan recounts the effect Thoreau had on him during this period of his life: "In Thoreau, I first encountered someone who saw no polarity between poetry and nature's economy, but instead envisioned a vast ecology that spanned both and enriches our senses, our hearts, and our minds" (p. xii).

Determined to combine disciplines himself, Nabhan received a master's degree in plant science from the University of Arizona in 1978, and completed his Ph.D. in the university's Arid Lands Resources Program in 1983. He attributes his decision to work in deserts more to chance than to choice, noting that he was first fascinated by plains and prairies. "I really feel a lot more baffled and intrinsically mystified by the grasslands," he told Stephen Trimble in an interview for *Words from the Land* (p. 264). But when he found an Arizona botanist whose interests matched his own, he made a corresponding shift from grassland to Sonoran desert ecology.

Nabhan's dissertation concerned arid lands ethnobotany and agricultural ecology among the Papago (O'odham) people of southern Arizona. His conversations and shared time with Papago families provided material for his first book, *The Desert Smells Like Rain: A Naturalist in Papago Indian Country* (1982).

The Desert Smells Like Rain

The Desert Smells Like Rain explores the relationship between the Papago people and the arid home they have inhabited for centuries. While outsiders always focus on the fact that there is so little water to be found in the desert, the Papago simply concentrate on living in a way that accommodates its ebb and flow. As Nabhan himself notes, "The desert is unpredictable, enigmatic. One minute you will be smelling dust. The next, the desert can smell just like rain" (p. 9). Thus, the Papago's farming practices, their ceremonies, and even their language are shaped by the uncertainty of the rains in their lives. Nabhan's spare portraits illuminate the manifestations of this extraordinary connection in a world increasingly marked by alienation between humans and their local terrain.

In the acknowledgments for the book, Nabhan writes that he has constructed composite personalities out of different Papago people he has known. He wants to respect their privacy, he explains, and he knows that no individual feels comfortable being singled out as the expert on the community. Nabhan goes on to explain, "Likewise, I can neither 'possess' the desert, nor the knowledge they have shared. And despite the help of many Papago, nothing here is meant to convey an 'official' Papago viewpoint" (pp. ix–x).

Humility and deference, as well as respect, underlie Nabhan's ethnographic account. He follows in the tradition of colleagues Richard Nelson and Barry Lopez, both of whom deny their own authority on the cultures or ecosystems they describe. Nabhan apprenticed himself to the region and its native inhabitants, and his depictions guide his readers to become as respectful of the desert community as he is.

In an early chapter, Nabhan joins several Papago as they climb Baboquivari Peak in search of the cave of I'itoi, the Papago creator. He weaves in stories regarding the sacred peak, giving them full credence as cultural history instead of passing them off as quaint legends. When the group loses its way and begins to give up the search, they hear the voice of an elder companion "singing a path" from the base of the peak: "Suddenly, behind a jojoba bush, the last rays of the day's sun flashed on an opening in the rock. Then the sun was gone. A vertical slit beginning waist high allowed passage through a vein of brecciated porphyry" (p. 21). Such mysteries are common in Nabhan's writing; they express his belief in forces beyond his understanding and control.

The Desert Smells Like Rain is not a collection of mystical or romantic portraits, however. Nabhan is intent on complicating every stereotypical notion of the Papago; in one chapter he does so with a dose of harsh reality. Travel magazines, he explains, have provided glossy images of the Papago organ-pipe wine ceremony over the years: women in long dresses gathering fruit, old men singing down the rains. Nabhan presents the real picture: a drunken matriarch heckling her visitors, and the endless cycle of drinking and vomiting that accompanies the four-day ceremony. But although descriptions of regurgitation quickly shatter the travel writer's romantic veneer, Nabhan also uncovers the powerful symbolism behind this behavior: "This purging and subsequent physical relief tie in so well with the ceremonial start of the Papago's annual cycle. As they are being cleansed, they are bringing in the rains to renew the land and to break the heat" (pp. 36–37). No travel magazine with a glossed-over version of the Papago ceremony could ever reveal such insights.

In other essays, Nabhan presents the modern-day challenges facing these desert people—the effects of water diversion projects, a Westernized diet, imposed political borders. Nabhan never suggests that the Papago should be forced to maintain their traditional ways. Instead, he continually points out the scope of their local knowledge and the value of incorporating that into modern approaches. Papago knowledge of hydrology and crop productivity has never been bettered by modern irrigation projects. Their traditional diet includes vitamin-rich native plants that seem to provide calories without altering sugar levels or fat production. Even modern notions of wilderness protection are complicated by the discovery that a desert oasis recently farmed by the Papago supports a greater diversity of birds than a protected oasis located in nearby Organ Pipe Cactus National Monument.

The Desert Smells Like Rain offers understated glimpses into the Papago way of life. The scenes are ephemeral—like a desert stream—and short. But many of the themes Nabhan lightly touches on in this first book become the central topics of his later writing.

Gathering the Desert

Following completion of his doctorate, Nabhan worked as a research associate for the Office of Arid Lands Studies at the University of Arizona, and later as an adjunct assistant professor of botany at Arizona State University. In 1983, he joined with three colleagues to found the non-profit organization Native Seeds/SEARCH.

Native Seeds/SEARCH works to conserve the traditional crops, seeds, and farming practices that have sustained native people throughout the U.S. Southwest and northern Mexico. Still active with approximately four thousand members, the organization is based in Tucson with affiliates throughout the Southwest. Native Seeds/SEARCH is not a static seed bank. From the beginning, the group has emphasized the history and culture that surround heirloom seeds. Educational programs highlight the suitability of indigenous seed varieties to the desert climate and soils, their health benefits, and the stories and ceremonies that have accompanied their planting, harvest, and consumption.

Nabhan records his own fascination with these and other desert plants in *Gathering the Desert* (1985), which won the 1986 John Burroughs Medal for outstanding nature writing. Each chapter describes three plants from the Southwest which, whether wild or domesticated, have been used by desert peoples for centuries. Included in the volume are creosote bush, desert palms, agave, sandfood, mesquite, organ-pipe cactus, amaranth greens, tepary beans, chiltepines, devil's claw, panicgrass, and desert gourds. Nabhan looks at how each of these plants has been used as a food, a medicine, a symbol, and more by human cultures of the past and present. He does not claim that there is, or should be, one fixed set of uses for desert plants; rather, he is interested in the changing dynamics of utilization and how they affect all desert dwellers.

As always, Nabhan incorporates art, stories, historical anecdotes, and technical explanations into one seamless essay. Published at a time when sociologists began defining the different ways people value natural resources, Nabhan's well-rounded portraits offer something for everyone. He delineates cultural, utilitarian, ecological, aesthetic, and other values of these plants that, taken together or apart, support the need for their protection.

Still, it is Nabhan's well-rounded appreciation, not mere conservation savvy, that governs the book's structure. In a chapter on wild agaves (also known as century plants), Nabhan chats with a Mexican mescal maker about the process of converting the plants to potent alcohol, and draws comical portraits of young workers passing out from too many taste tests. Paragraphs later, he provides a detailed botanical background on agaves—quickly switching his subject but maintaining a colorful and bemused tone: "It has been said that century plants kill themselves reproducing—not a bad way to go,

when you think about it" (p. 41). Nabhan then describes the pollination of agaves by bats, and seeks a solution to the chicken-and-egg dilemma regarding the recent depletion of both species. Is the extirpation of local bat populations severely reducing agave reproduction? Or is overharvesting by bootleggers reducing one of the most important food sources for migratory bats? Either way, the culprit ends up being human. After sharing archaeological records on the eight-thousand-year-old relationship between humans and agave, Nabhan writes, "At our levels of increasing population, it may be that the harvest of wild agaves for spirits or for any other intensive use is approaching parasitism" (p. 47). He drives the conservation message home but stops short of a political lecture. Instead, he finishes with a gentle poetic nudge:

> Choose a moonlit night in the summer, and hike through the scattering of agaves in bloom. . . . Listen for the flutter of wings, watch for the bats, their shoulders clouded in a coat of pollen, shining in the night like a poncho made of Precolumbian golden thread. Follow them back down to the scent of agave blossoms, where plants and animals again dance to an ancient American rhythm. (p. 48)

Through his varying of tone and topic, Nabhan shows that agaves have value for a diverse community that includes bootleggers, biologists, poets, and bats.

If a celebrity could be featured in her biography as having the wide-ranging importance and appeal of Nabhan's agave, she would undoubtedly be thrilled. For Nabhan, it reflects a rare gift that he can do so much not just for this one plant but also for the eleven others he described in the volume. His depictions of these rich mutual relationships show just how much is lost when cultures, creatures, or plants disappear.

Enduring Seeds

Soon after publishing *Gathering the Desert*, Nabhan produced another compelling volume on the importance of protecting wild plant species.

Gary Nabhan examines the local flora on Camelback Mountain, Phoenix, Arizona.

Enduring Seeds: Native American Agriculture and Wild Plant Conservation (1989) examines the evolving relationship in North America between agriculture and wild plants, and argues that modern farming practices that reduce wild plant diversity diminish the health and quality of domesticated crops.

Nabhan first traces the evolution of plant life in North America and the development of an interdependence between plants and animals. As insect, bird, and mammal populations grew across the continent, plants evolved to take advantage of the pollination and dispersal services these creatures could provide. Diversity flowered, Nabhan explains, as plants and their seeds adapted to a variety of different climates, soils, and animal communities. Then humans entered the picture.

Many paleoecologists emphasize the destructive role humans played when their population grew and pushed big game into extinction. Nabhan, whose philosophy is often one of grounded optimism, focuses on the important relationship that subsequently developed as humans and plants came to depend upon each other without

other large animals in the picture: "cultures were left without large herds of grazers and browsers, but they did have the gourds, calabashes, yucca fruit, and other plants that evolved under these animals' influence. Did these Neotropical dwellers take up the gourd, and its seeds, to become their agents of dissemination and increase?" (pp. 14–15). Nabhan believes that humans did come to aid in seed dissemination, and he describes a second flowering of plant diversity as "the cornucopia of domesticated plants that the America's have offered the world" (p. 15).

In subsequent essays, Nabhan travels from Guatemala to Florida to Wisconsin, investigating past and present relationships between humans and wild plant diversity. The spectrum is expansive. Nabhan visits Tepehuan Indian fields in Chihuahua, Mexico, where small-scale chile farmers are intimately familiar with the wild chile species lurking on the edges of their fields, delighting in the extra-fiery taste the wild varieties provide when cross-pollinated with their domestic chiles. He travels to southern Florida, where commercial sugar farmers seem to pay no heed to the wild gourds destroyed by their irrigation systems or to the wild sugar varieties being lost worldwide. As Nabhan points out, this indifference is ironic, given that domestic sugar crops once almost succumbed to a pest infestation until they were crossbred with a resistant wild variety tracked down in Indonesia.

This reduction in resilience becomes Nabhan's most critical concern. Although we can look back in time and to other cultures to find examples of successful coexistence between humans and wild species, modern United States society ignores or destroys almost everything except a handful of commercial crop plants. Nabhan argues that domestication for a narrow purpose, such as convenience in shipping or efficient harvesting, results in a dangerous reduction in genetic diversity. Losing biodiversity diminishes the viability of the species that remain.

One colorful example of this point appears in Nabhan's discussion not of plants but of turkeys. Bred to have hefty amounts of meat over their breastbones in order to satisfy modern consumers, commercially raised turkeys have become too fat to mate. They must be fertilized through artificial insemination. They have become so stupid, it is said, that they will drown looking up—beaks agape—at the falling rain.

As for plants, Nabhan describes the way commercial white corn languishes under dry conditions in which the native Hopi corn can still flourish. He records the superior taste of true wild rice harvested from canoes around the Great Lakes, as compared with varieties grown domestically in California, where modern equipment is used and chemicals control competing species.

Nabhan also asserts that when we lose these wild species, we are losing the long cultural heritage to which they are tied; similarly, when the integrity of cultures is diminished, we tend to lose the species they sustained. In looking at cultures that have survived through times of change, he notes that they have developed an "ecology of the heart"—an emotional binding to the domestic and wild species of their region: "A cultural community that persists in its farming tradition does not simply conserve indigenous seedstocks because of economic justifications; the seeds themselves become symbols, reflections of the people's own spiritual and aesthetic identity, and of the land that has shaped them" (p. 85).

Nabhan does offer visions of hope in this era of destruction of wild plants. He describes modern approaches to seed protection—seed exchange groups like his own Native Seeds/SEARCH, botanic gardens, biosphere reserves, and seed banks. But he emphasizes the danger of *ex situ* (out-of-site) conservation. Imagine a seed sealed away in cold storage, he writes. When it is reintroduced years later, how equipped will it be to survive in the present-day conditions? Not very, Nabhan argues, for the seed will not be adapted to modern climatic conditions, pollution, and other changing variables.

Thus integration is essential. Nabhan emphasizes the need for a dynamic balance of domestication and wildness in the plants we grow around us. The isolation of a seed, a genetic strain, or even a community leads to its weakening and demise. Having evolved through interdependence, we can only survive through interdependence.

Songbirds, Truffles, and Wolves

Nabhan has often been regarded as a spiritual thinker, but in no book is his personal spirituality so exposed as in *Songbirds, Truffles, and Wolves: An American Naturalist in Italy* (1993). In a trip that can only be called a personal pilgrimage, Nabhan journeyed to Italy after his divorce from his first wife, and traveled by foot along the paths of Tuscany and Umbria that St. Francis of Assisi once followed.

Nabhan cites a number of missions in his trek. He wanted to return to the Mediterranean region of his ancestors—the Old World from which he is descended. He hoped to gauge the health of the Italian landscape—the depth and abundance of the wounds of civilization. And, finally, he hoped to discover some of the spirit of his favorite saint.

Nabhan's identification with St. Francis is more than superficial: for several years he studied to be a member of the Franciscan order, but found little acceptance of his proposal to work among his own notion of the poorest of the poor—endangered plants. In *Songbirds, Truffles, and Wolves*, he explains that he first became curious about St. Francis when he read one of his quotes: "All which you used to avoid will bring you great sweetness and exceeding joy." The line makes a fitting epigraph for the book, for as he escapes both career and relationships for a trek on unfamiliar terrain, Nabhan cannot help but make constant intellectual and emotional connections to home.

His first connection occurs in a marketplace in Genoa, where Nabhan spies prickly pear cactus fruit from the United States–Mexico border. He instinctively traces the origins of other familiar fruits and vegetables in the market: avocados from Central America, pears from Asia Minor, cucumbers from Peru. He has no professional purpose in engaging in this geographical sorting but suggests that "once trained, perhaps [my eyes] could see the world no other way" (p. 11).

On the long trek, Nabhan regards the landscape with his discerning ethnobotanical eye. His discoveries about food plants give the book its educational substance—and colorful humor—as he ferrets out the local lore about truffles, polenta, chestnuts, and other specialties. Though far from the people and cultures he knows best, Nabhan seems to have no trouble engaging local people in animated and informative conversations.

As to the vitality of Italy's wild plants and agriculture, the situation seems grim: Nabhan is amazed and often disturbed by the domestication of the countryside. Forested lands turn out to be plantations that yield a product for human consumption. Areas set aside as refuges seem devoid of bird life, not to mention the wolves and other large mammals that once roamed there.

Meanwhile, Nabhan covers ground on his personal quest. In discussions with his travel companion, he expresses the pain and bewilderment of divorce and the nascent hope for recovery. Even when these topics are not being discussed

directly, it is clear that they affect Nabhan's experiences and observations of the places he visits. Thus the distinctions between personal and natural histories break down. In one chapter, Nabhan finds himself feeling the impatience of a chestnut tree, which takes forty years to heal its wounds. In another, he regards with perhaps more than just ecological concern the dangerous stagnancy of a prized woodland that has not been allowed to burn down or otherwise biodegrade to make room for new life. It is through these reflections, as much as through discussions with his companion, that Nabhan begins to heal his own emotional wounds.

As Nabhan concludes his trek in Assisi, he struggles to find the essence of St. Francis amid a festival of Hare Krishnas, songbird hunters, and animal rights activists. He wanders, claustrophobic, out of a cloister and stumbles into a moss-covered courtyard—St. Francis' own spiritual space. Here, under the trees in the full open air, Nabhan concludes that his idea of religion—and life—is one that does not separate the inside and the outside, humans and the natural world they inhabit.

Songbirds, Truffles, and Wolves is a complex book because of its variety of questions and purposes. But Nabhan is able to link them, mostly by integrating issues one might ordinarily separate: natural and personal history, spirituality and ecology, order and wildness. Likewise, in journeying far afield, he has in fact journeyed deep within.

Counting Sheep

In 1992, Nabhan organized a number of leading naturalists, wildlife biologists, and writers for a conference titled "Writing the Lives of Plants and Animals." Intrigued by how anthropologists have grappled with the dilemma of accurately depicting cultures they can never truly know, Nabhan had come to believe that writing about other species presented many of the same challenges. Creatures, like people, have complex lives that cannot be evoked completely in an essay or a data table. Nabhan called for a break from traditional essays in which wildlife is merely the object of the writer's musings or, worse yet, theories, and for a new dedication to original forms of nature writing.

Concern about this issue also led Nabhan to compile a series of essays on the desert bighorn sheep. He writes in the introduction to *Counting Sheep: Twenty Ways of Seeing Desert Bighorn* (1993), that the book is "an attempt to broaden what the natural history essay can be. . . . It is also a challenge to our imaginations to consider what other lives are like" (p. xi).

Nabhan brought together well-known nature writers (including Ann Zwinger, Charles Bowden, and Peter Steinhart) and people from other fields concerned with the desert bighorn sheep—among them, an American anthropologist, a Mexican policymaker, and an O'odham educator and folklorist. The variety of tone and topic makes it clear that the human conception of other species is subjective and personal. Terry Tempest Williams decries the military maneuvers conducted over sheep territory, and describes her dreams of the now elusive bighorns. Kermit Roosevelt recounts the adventures of a bighorn sheep hunting expedition (first published in 1912). Wildlife biologist Harley Shaw reports controversies over mountain lions, predators of the desert bighorn.

Nabhan's own essay chronicles four days spent conducting a sheep count in Cabeza Prieta Wildlife Refuge. In the introduction to his essay, Nabhan warns the reader that the essay may fail to "take itself too seriously." But he makes no apology: "Most nature writing has become burdened by gravity; except for [Edward] Abbey, David Quammen, and perhaps John Graves, it is as though humor is taboo in the genre" (p. 156).

The tone of the essay is wry and crusty. Nabhan admits to his failure to spot any sheep on a count several years earlier, and marvels that he has returned to do another: "Somehow, I had been sentenced to four days of sweating until I had salt around my rim, drinking warm beer, listening to lonesome doves droning, watching the full moon shining and turkey vultures soaring, occupied with endless wondering: will the sheep ever show?" (p. 158). Humor does not preclude thoughtful commentary, though. Aware that this sheep count, too, may be futile, Nabhan suggests that daring to see nothing is a necessary part of an ecologist's work. Scraping data out of an unsuccessful venture is an unfortunate job requirement; in fact, fruitless pursuits should be acknowledged as part of the discovery process.

The essays Nabhan assembled reveal much about the lives of the desert bighorn, but they cannot completely articulate its life or its essence. Rather, through their own personal filters, the writers provide a snapshot of the sheep they encounter, and the result is a collage of interpretations, not a unified or definitive portrait.

The Geography of Childhood

In 1994, when Nabhan published *The Geography of Childhood: Why Children Need Wild Places*, he was the father of two children of elementary school age, and increasingly interested in the way children learn about the natural world. The book, written with Nabhan's friend and colleague Steve Trimble, examines the formative experiences of nature that they and their children have had, and ponders the significance of these encounters in their lives. Like *Songbirds, Truffles, and Wolves*, this is an exceptionally personal book, but Nabhan works earnestly to draw out generalizations that any parent or educator can take home.

In his opening essay, Nabhan frames one of his primary concerns. Having just taken his children camping in northern Arizona, he drives home through densely urbanized sections of Phoenix, pondering the lives of children who live there: "Their lives may be rich socially, but are they given the range of environments in which to express themselves, to express the variety of human talents and emotions that are part of our genetic inheritance from having evolved in wild environments?" (p. 10). Nabhan does not answer the question outright, except to admit, "I don't know." Although the book does not attempt to answer every question it raises, Nabhan's ruminations on his topics are rich.

Nabhan advocates the benefits of "going truant"—finding unstructured, spontaneous time out in the wild. Not only did such experiences fill a personal need for him in his early adolescence, but they seem to connect to the initiation rites that were once nearly ubiquitous among indigenous cultures. Nabhan suggests that without such experiences, children "remain in an arrested state of immaturity." He describes the success of programs across the country—such as Vision Quest, Walkabout, and Human Beginnings—that have renewed outdoor rites of passage for teenage girls and boys.

Nabhan further explores the important knowledge children traditionally gained through firsthand experience of nature and through family stories, experience that has been undervalued if not lost in modern educational programs. In the summer of 1992, Nabhan interviewed Anglo, Mexican, and Native American children living in and around the Sonoran Desert to ascertain the source and extent of their nature knowledge. The results, first published as a chapter in Stephen Kellert and Edward O. Wilson's collection, *The Biophilia Hypothesis* (1993), indicate that children are becoming less intimately familiar with the plants and animals around them as the mediated experience provided by television, science lessons, and textbooks replaces firsthand experience. Some of the results are startling. Most children interviewed knew general science facts about wildlife but could not name the time of day when birds sang loudest. Few could identify which desert tree smells strongest in the rain. Without reinforcement, knowledge that was once essential for survival is now lying dormant.

In his final essay, Nabhan describes his own history with reptiles and amphibians—first as a snake-scared boy, then as an assistant researcher on horned lizard projects, then as a father of two lizard-loving children. As in the preceding essay, he suggests that firsthand experience of these and other creatures is essential:

The lizardness within us is our wild side. . . . Because we put ourselves on pedestals above the rest of the animal world, we find it hard to acknowledge our affinity to lizards and snakes. . . . People who flee for comfort zones in the presence of snakes and lizards are often the same ones who respond to their own vestigial behaviors with fear, distrust, or shame. (p. 154)

It should not be surprising that the writer who has sung the virtues of wildness in seeds, crops, conservation, and religion should now suggest that the human spirit, too, must embrace wildness.

Desert Legends: Re-storying the Sonoran Borderlands

Looking over the scope of Nabhan's books, one sees that although certain common themes appear in each volume, the style and structure have varied greatly. This is not an accident. Nabhan is an exceptionally innovative writer, always seeking to push the boundaries of nature writing beyond its traditional forms. He varies his own voice according to the project at hand.

When Nabhan started writing the essays collected in *Desert Legends: Re-storying the Sonoran Borderlands* (1994) he quipped that the book would be the first marriage of natural history writing and magical realism. The suggestion is not that far-out. Nabhan's sketches of life along the United States–Mexico border include a visit to a Mexican *curandera* for relief of his chronic joint pain, and to a desert camp-out unwittingly set up amid the discarded lingerie of a nearby brothel.

The Sonoran Desert, as Nabhan sees it, is no barren wasteland. It is a loud, life-filled land with "raucous white-necked ravens making fun of me, big-eared antelope jackrabbits who don't miss a snitch of gossip, bean-eating bruchid beetles who spoil all my food, skinny-assed coyotes who steal me blind, as well as tree lizards and pincushion cacti and other lives too numerous to mention" (p. 2).

Slapped down across this lively land nearly 150 years ago is a line—Nabhan calls it a window or a mirror—more than two hundred miles long called the United States–Mexico border. An arbitrary political stroke on a map, the border makes little sense for the plants and peoples that once moved freely on both sides of it. The first set of Nabhan's essays depicts the border as an impediment to Sonoran communities; the second set shows how the boundary can and should be blurred.

The surrealistic touches in the essays are Nabhan's tribute to the absurd distortions of the borderland regions, to the tendency images and ideas have to warp and waver like a desert mirage: "[The border] has sliced through the desert's heart to remind us that the cultures on either side of the line affect this land in distinctive ways. It seldom makes us look pretty, and often makes us look absurd. We have become the fools in the desert's funhouse mirror. The stories that follow play on those marvelous distortions, the peculiar ways we come to see some subtle truths about ourselves" (p. 6).

A broader purpose of these essays is to resuscitate the stories bound up in the culture and ecology of the borderland region. In an essay titled "Re-storying the Sonorous Land," Nabhan visits Sonoran farmers who can point to cottonwoods and tell the history of floods that have inundated them. He records the powerful family histories one Seri man has committed to memory. Both of these examples portray the deep connection people feel to a region when its stories are their own. Nabhan suggests that restoration ecology—a field devoted to reintroducing plants and animals into their former habitats—must simultaneously restore the oral tradition that has occupied that region: "To restore any place, we must also begin to re-story it, to make it the lesson of our legends, festivals, and seasonal rites. Story is the way we encode deep-seeded values into our culture" (p. 193). Ultimately, the greatest contribution of Nabhan's book is not in recounting ancient legends but in proving how lively and enriching one person's regional storytelling can be.

Other Works

Nabhan's books offer only a partial glimpse of his expansive scholarship. He has worked on conservation programs in Arizona and Mexico as an ecologist for Conservation International, studying the ecology of the desert ironwood tree and guiding programs to aid Seri Indian and Mexican artisans who carve ironwood in Sonora. He has joined with ecologists and health practitioners in the United States and Australia to probe the relationship between diabetes and the loss of a native foods diet among indigenous desert dwellers. In addition to being a confessed chile addict, he has directed chile conservation programs as part of his work for Native Seeds/SEARCH, including an annual chile festival of storytelling, chile-eating contests, and unusual chile foods. He teaches at writing conferences, lectures at ethnobotanical meetings, and serves as a mentor for undergraduate and graduate students starting their own ethnobotanical careers. And he and his new wife, Caroline Wilson, have collaborated on a book about the canyons of Utah.

Nabhan's achievements have not gone unrecognized. In 1990 he was named a MacArthur Fellow and a Pew Scholar on Conservation and Environment. In 1991 he received Sicily's Premio Gaia award for working toward a "culture of nature."

But the real strength of Nabhan's lifework is that it grows out of a genuine love for the peoples and issues that have defined his career. For example, his trips through the desert still include frequent stops at Papago households—not as objects of study, but as lifelong friends.

It is undoubtedly this integrity that accounts for Nabhan's great popularity as a nature writer. He was "multicultural" and "interdisciplinary" long before these terms became fashionable. His writing provides relevance and significance to these critical approaches, helping to save them from becoming superficial trends.

Moreover, Nabhan has never been a predictor of gloom. He is aware of the ecological wounds on the landscape and is attuned to the problems that create them, but he is not cynical. With a realist's mind and an optimist's heart, he confronts head-on the issues of the day while seeking reasons for hope, moments of grace, and flashes of beauty.

As Nabhan's work makes clear, he is an unflagging proponent of integration—of the dynamic possibilities that exist when ideas, disciplines, and cultures are cross-pollinated. Remarkably, Nabhan integrates without sacrificing difference. It is not a monochrome world he seeks but a dynamic and diverse community that celebrates the uniqueness of every species, genus, person, and profession while embracing the human and wild natures that unite us all.

Selected Bibliography

WORKS OF GARY PAUL NABHAN

BOOKS

The Desert Smells Like Rain: A Naturalist in Papago Indian Country (San Francisco: North Point Press, 1982); *Gathering the Desert* (Tucson: Univ. of Arizona Press, 1985); *Saguaro* (Tucson: Southwest Parks and Monuments Assn., 1986); *Arizona Highways Presents Desert Wildflowers* (Phoenix: Arizona Highways, 1988), edited with Jane Cole; *Enduring Seeds: Native American Agriculture and Wild Plant Conservation* (San Francisco: North Point Press, 1989); *Counting Sheep: Twenty Ways of Seeing Desert Bighorn* (Tucson: Univ. of Arizona Press, 1993); *Songbirds, Truffles, and Wolves: An American Naturalist in Italy* (New York: Pantheon, 1993); *Desert Legends: Re-storying the Sonoran Borderlands* (New York: Henry Holt, 1994); *The Geography of Childhood: Why Children Need Wild Places* (Boston: Beacon Press, 1994), with Steve Trimble; *Canyons of Color: Utah's Slickrock Wildlands* (San Francisco: HarperCollinsWest, 1995), with Caroline Wilson and Jeff Garton (photographer).

CHAPTERS IN BOOKS AND ANTHOLOGIES

"Replenishing Desert Agriculture with Native Plants and Their Symbionts," in *Meeting the Expectations of the Land: Essays in Sustainable Agriculture and Stewardship*, ed. by Wes Jackson, Wendell Berry, and Bruce Colman (San Francisco: North Point Press, 1984); "Wild Desert Relatives of Crops: Their Direct Uses as Food," in *Plants for Arid Lands*, ed. by G. E. Wickens, J. R. Goodin, and D. V. Field (London: George Allen and Unwin, 1985), written with Richard S. Felger; "The Sonoran Desert," in *Arizona: The Land and the People*, ed. by Tom Miller (Tucson: Univ. of Arizona Press, 1986); "New Crops for Small Farmers in Marginal Lands? Wild Chiles as a Case Study," in *Agroecology and Small Farm Development*, ed. by Miguel A. Altieri and Susanna B. Hecht (Sarasota, Fla.: CRC Press, 1990), written with M. Slater and L. Yarger; "Conservation and Use of Rare Wild Plants by Traditional Cultures of the U.S./Mexico Border States," in *Biodiversity: Traditional Management and Development of Biological Resources*, ed. by M. Oldfield and J. Alcorn (Boulder, Colo.: Westview Press, 1991), written with D. House, L. Hernandez S., W. Hodgson, and H. Suzan A.; "Native Plant Products from the Arid Neotropical Species: Assessing Benefits to Cultural, Environmental, and Genetic Diversity," in *Sustainable Harvest and Marketing of Rain Forest Products*, ed. by Mark Plotkin and Lisa Famolare (Washington, D.C.: Conservation International/Island Press, 1992); "Learning the Language of Fields and Forests," in Henry David Thoreau, *Faith in a Seed: The Dispersion of Seeds and Other Late Natural History Writings*, ed. by Bradley P. Dean (Washington, D.C.: Island Press/Shearwater, 1993); "The Loss of Floral and Faunal Story: The Extinction of Experience," in *The Biophilia Hypothesis*, ed. by Stephen R. Kellert and Edward O. Wilson (Washington, D.C.: Island Press/Shearwater, 1993), written with Sara L. St. Antoine.

RICHARD K. NELSON
(b. 1941)

JOHN TALLMADGE

RICHARD NELSON occupies a distinctive place in American nature writing. Whereas most authors bring to the genre a background in natural science or belles lettres, Nelson began as an anthropologist. He received his education from American university professors and Native American subsistence hunters, and all his works, from the early ethnographies to the autobiographical *The Island Within* (1989), use hunting as a lens through which to view the natural world. His professed goal has been to build bridges between cultures, to show how the wisdom of native teachers can help human beings develop a wiser, richer, and more sustainable relationship to the earth. His work is noteworthy for its intercultural vision, its richness of information, the vividness and grace of its style, and the profundity of its deep-ecological thinking.

Nelson was born on 1 December 1941 in Madison, Wisconsin, to Robert King, who was employed by the state, and Florence Olson. From an early age Nelson loved animals and the outdoors. "Emphatically opposed" to hunting in his youth, he intended, upon entering the University of Wisconsin in 1960, to major in zoology, but he found natural science dry and mechanical: he wanted to know what animals *were*, not just how they worked inside. "Ultimately," he told Michael Armstrong, "the reason I chose anthropology as a career was because of my feeling that the way to learn about nature was through the traditions of native people, that their

knowledge of nature was much greater and more profound than the knowledge I was getting from my zoology professors."

Nelson soon came under the influence of William Laughlin, a legendary professor of arctic anthropology who introduced him to Alaska via archaeological digs on Kodiak Island and in the Aleutians. In 1964, Nelson entered the master's program at Wisconsin, and Laughlin, who had heard of a United States Air Force project to develop an arctic survival manual, asked him if he would like to spend a year with the Alaskan Eskimos. Nelson's introduction to the Inupiat was abrupt. The pilot landed on the beach at Wainwright, dumped out his bewildered passenger, and flew away. Fortunately, says Nelson, "the people took care of me and kept me alive." The local schoolteacher helped him get a dog team and suggested that the best way for Nelson to learn about hunting was to go out with the hunters. That winter marked the beginning of what critic Sherman Paul calls Nelson's "conversion." Impressed by the passion that Eskimos brought to the hunt, Nelson grew to admire their skill and resourcefulness, the depth of their natural history knowledge, and their eagerness to learn about animals. He also discovered the difference between a view of nature based on detached observation and one based on ecological engagement. "What struck me most about hunting," he told interviewer Jonathan White, "was that for the first time in my life I was engaged in the entire process of keeping myself alive; it was a tremendous breakthrough in my understanding of where my life comes from."

From the Eskimos, Nelson received not only initiatory hunting experiences but also the first lessons in the spiritual and epistemological perspectives that would inform his nature writing. These perspectives included a sense that animals and other beings in nature have spirits that can be angered if they are not treated with respect, that the animal gives itself to the hunter in a transaction that is both spiritual and physical, and that the success of the hunter therefore depends upon luck (or grace) as much as on skill. Nelson also began to realize that hunting cultures evolved as sustainable societies based upon pragmatic ecological principles and that the views of nature held by these societies were more inclusive, and thus perhaps wiser, than those of Western science.

In Nelson's early works, these themes are treated implicitly, often submerged in a wealth of detail that speaks to the expectations of a professional audience. The Wainwright studies yielded two reports for the air force and a master's thesis that became *Hunters of the Northern Ice* (1969). Although Nelson's first book is refreshingly readable for a work of social science, it still follows ethnographic conventions. The voice is that of an expert lecturer; the tone relaxed, businesslike, and reportorial; the presentation categorical and sequential; and the emphasis throughout on facts rather than on character, narration, or ideas. The narrator himself keeps an extremely low profile; his aim is to minutely observe Eskimo hunting. As a result, the book's primary interest derives from its "lore." Only in the two brief final chapters does Nelson venture to generalize about the character of the hunters and the challenges posed to their way of life by seductive American culture. But these comments are closely circumscribed by the mode of objective reportage. The narrator, for all his acquired expertise, remains "outside" Eskimo culture. He never reveals how, or even if, he has been transformed by his experiences.

After his sojourn with the Inupiat, Nelson entered the doctoral program at the University of California in Santa Barbara. In 1969 he undertook another year of fieldwork, this time among the Kutchin Athapaskan Indians of interior Alaska, where he studied subsistence methods and knowledge of the environment. He reported the results in a dissertation that became *Hunters of the Northern Forest: Designs for Survival Among the Alaskan Kutchin* (1973). This work also presents itself as an ethnography devoted to hunting, trapping, fishing, and other subsistence activities, and the presentation is organized according to key resource species. The narrator is an expert academician, well versed in the technical literature of anthropology and accomplished in field observation.

Although the primary interest of these ethnographies lies in their technical detail, they contain elements of nature writing that prefigure Nelson's later work. Both incorporate substantial amounts of natural history in their descriptions of climate, landscapes, and resident species. As Nelson reminds us again and again, subsistence hunters' lives depend on their knowledge and skill; they must thoroughly acquaint themselves with the habitat, behavior, and personality of their quarry. Under their tutelage Nelson begins to see the world with the eyes of a native naturalist, even though his professional mode of discourse does not permit us to witness this transformation. By letting the facts speak, he defers to his teachers and his material. Nevertheless, the luminous descriptions, the fascinating lore, and the intense, intimate contact with nature evoked on every page compel us, as literary readers, to wonder what it would be like to live in such a way, to learn from such a people, and to make a life of comparable richness, energy, and spiritual depth in our own culture. In short, we want to get from the outside to the inside of such experiences, to move from science to story.

Shadow of the Hunter

While at Santa Barbara, Nelson began to work on a fictionalized account of Eskimo life that would take the reader inside the hunter's mind.

Having little confidence in his literary abilities, he set the work aside after completing only one chapter. After graduation in 1971, he took a series of one-year teaching jobs, the first at the University of Hawaii, where he learned to surf and returned to writing with renewed confidence and eventual passion. "I'd surf until I was tired," he told Michael Armstrong, "then go home and write. It's a wonderful way to write." In 1974 he moved back to Alaska, where he supported himself with freelance ethnography, research, and consulting while he finished *Shadow of the Hunter* (1980), his first literary work.

Shadow of the Hunter consists of ten stories named for lunar months of the Eskimo year. Each focuses upon a particular type of hunting or fishing and reveals not only the techniques but also the emotional and moral dimensions of the enterprise. In this work, Nelson is very conscious of stretching ethnographic models. In his preface he explains that he chose fictionalized narrative over the usual exposition and analysis because he wanted to evoke the experience of living in a culture from the point of view of the people themselves. The quickest way in appeared to be through hunting, which is not only the principal economic activity but also the organizing passion of Eskimo life. Nelson's choice of fictional narrative allows him to create stories that are both realistic and representative, respecting the facts while dealing with values, meaning, and emotions. In this way, he realizes what he has called the "idea of anthropology as an art form." He is also able to write for audiences in both cultures, and the book therefore serves more than one purpose. For Eskimos, the book can be seen as a celebration of their way of life. Nelson reports that he sent copies to Wainwright "with some trepidation" and was overjoyed when an Eskimo friend finally mentioned to him that he found the book accurate. For a Western reader, the book not only evokes an exotic and admirable way of life but also provokes critical reflection upon Western culture, especially regarding attitudes toward hunting, conceptions of native peoples, and our relationship to the natural world. *Shadow of the Hunter* is Nelson's first truly intercultural work.

In these stories men go out on the sea, the ice, or the tundra to stalk and kill large, wary, powerful animals—the seal, the walrus, the whale, the caribou, and the polar bear. The action is dramatic, full of risk and suspense with the outcome always in doubt right up to the end. Except for one chapter in which a teenage girl struggles to choose between her own culture and that of the outside world she encounters at school, the stories deal with men and take place away from the village. Nelson explains in his preface that Eskimo men do most of the hunting and that he chose to write about hunting because that was the aspect of the culture that he knew best.

These stories engage the American literary tradition in several ways. As Sherman Paul observed, the Eskimo hunter cuts a heroic figure amid the epic vastness of Arctic sea and ice. The hunt poses great dangers; requires extraordinary courage; demands skill, knowledge, and fortitude; inflicts suffering; and affirms or challenges personal identity, thus carrying an aspect of adventure. The central and archetypal character is Sakiak, the oldest, wisest, and most successful hunter in the village. He invites comparison with other notable hunters in American literature, such as Natty Bumppo, Sam Fathers, and Captain Ahab, but he is a more complex and well-rounded figure. Sakiak has too much humor and compassion for a Deerslayer, too much gentleness, fatherly sensitivity, and emotional balance for an Ahab. "Indeed," Nelson comments, "there were few predators as cunning and deadly as this man, who was at once also gentle and full of laughter" (p. 245). The book opens with Sakiak stalking and killing a seal on the ice and ends with a midwinter festival during which, having just vanquished a polar bear, he dances ecstatically to the beat of drums.

In Western culture, hunting is commonly seen as a form of recreation pursued only by certain types of people (mostly men) and viewed with marked ambivalence by the rest. The hunt is either glorified as a heroic, initiatory adventure that pits human skill and intelligence against the power and instincts of wild nature, or it is condemned as a blood sport in which persons of dubious character slaughter innocent creatures

685

with high-tech weapons, seeking regeneration through violence. Either way, hunting takes place in the wilderness, remote from society and its institutions. But for the Eskimos, hunting is work, not sport; it is the sustaining activity of their lives, and to it the men devote their best intellectual, physical, and spiritual efforts. Nelson's detailed accounts of how Sakiak and his companions stalk, kill, and dismember their prey may make us squirm but they fill us with admiration. We learn that butchering a walrus can be as honorable an activity as open-heart surgery.

These stories also lack the elements of demonism sometimes found in American hunting stories. Although the animals are certainly "other," they never become objects of irrational fear or hatred. The polar bear may be the most dangerous animal in the north, but when Sakiak kills one of these creatures there is no hint that this act somehow redeems or saves the village. Although these stories demonstrate a comparable love of natural history and technologic detail, it is hard to imagine an Eskimo *Moby-Dick*. Part of the reason may be that in Eskimo culture there is no clear distinction between wilderness and civilization. The hunter and his quarry occupy the same world, in which both are predators.

Like Nelson's ethnographies, these stories contain a great deal of natural history, but they also challenge conventional modes of nature writing, in which a spirit of romantic amateurism often prevails. Modern natural history began as a pursuit of clergymen, travelers, and other self-taught philosophers, and Romanticism reinforced this amateur spirit by permitting the self to assume its own authority. But Nelson's hunting stories depict authority as conferred by the animals (who give themselves to the hunter) or by the community (which honors his success). The hunter is a consummate professional who, in the enactment of his craft, fulfills his culture's highest expectations and so becomes a hero. Like the naturalist, the hunter must be a meticulous observer, but his knowledge of the land must be deeper and more comprehensive, because his very life depends upon it. Indeed, "observer" is

hardly an adequate term, for no detachment or objectivity is permitted the hunter. Hunting requires not only knowledge but also intimacy and a willingness to take life, to go beyond the contemplative relationship. One must engage the other, not merely watch and report. Accounts of such truly ecological relations are rare in American nature writing, and these stories offer an implicit critique of the genre and its epistemological bases in science and Romanticism. Every time Sakiak or his companions take an animal, a transaction occurs: the hunters give honor and respect in return for food. Spirit, in other words, is exchanged for matter, and so life is passed from one species to another.

In his preface, Nelson says that these stories are not only *about* the Inupiat but *for* them. They are an apprentice hunter's gifts to his teachers, and Nelson's respect is conveyed by the manner in which he effaces himself from the narrative. Sherman Paul sees him appearing indirectly in the figures of the novice hunters Pamiuk and Patik, whose errors provoke much teasing from the elders. But Nelson's persona also reveals acute powers of observation, empathy, and a concern for moral values. The choice of an omniscient narrator and a point of view that shifts from one sentient character to another allows Nelson to write about arctic hunting in a way that honors the Eskimo outlook while providing the abundance of information that a non-Eskimo reader would need. Whereas Nelson's early ethnographies dealt exhaustively with technique, this book deals equally with values and individual behavior, setting the stage for larger questions of epistemology and character. Having demonstrated his respect, the apprentice hunter is now ready to come forward on his own.

Make Prayers to the Raven

During the 1970s, Nelson lived nomadically in Alaska, supporting himself on grants, lectureships, consultancies, and government research projects. He spent several summers "hanging out" in the country along the Koyukuk River, a major tributary of the Yukon that flows along the south side of the Brooks Range. It was there that he made the acquaintance of the Koyukon Athapaskan Indians, whose ecological wisdom and spiritual view of nature impressed him deeply. Subsequently, he lived for a year in the Koyukon villages of Hughes and Huslia, under contract to study native subsistence patterns in and around the Gates of the Arctic National Park. But his personal goal was to find out how the Koyukon integrated their land-use practices into their intellectual culture. He was fortunate to have excellent teachers, and the experience marked a second "conversion," the results of which he described in *Make Prayers to the Raven: A Koyukon View of the Northern Forest* (1983).

Whereas Nelson's first two books focused on hunting techniques and his third moved beyond skills to questions of character, *Make Prayers to the Raven* broadens the outlook to communal values and worldview, with a corresponding increase in literary sophistication. Nelson uses the ethnographic model in novel ways to engage not one, but two cultures simultaneously and thereby achieves a stereoscopic view of the natural world. "Through the Koyukon," he writes in his introduction, "I became aware of a rich and eloquent natural history that extends into realms unknown or ignored in my own culture" (p. xiv). His stated purposes are to present an ethnography of Koyukon life, to write a "native natural history," to evoke the "power and substantiality of a view of nature that differs vastly from our own," and, finally, to "serve the Koyukon people" by honoring and preserving part of their cultural heritage (pp. xiv–xv).

For the Koyukon, as for the Inupiat, hunting is not recreation but work. Because they depend upon it for their livelihood, they are forced into a much deeper and more intimate engagement with the land than that required by the inhabitants of industrialized societies. The Koyukon approach combines an extraordinary capacity for observation and pragmatic ecological thinking with a highly developed spiritual regard. This attitude is far from mere superstition, for, as

Claude Lévi-Strauss demonstrates in *The Savage Mind* (1962), "attentive, meticulous attention turned entirely on the concrete finds both its principle and its result in symbolism" (1966 English trans., pp. 222–223). The Koyukon world is alive and watchful. Everything has a spirit and must be treated with respect; otherwise, bad luck in the form of hunting failures, accidents, or disease will surely follow. Koyukon natural history, like that of other aboriginal peoples, rests upon an extensive classification scheme, which as Lévi-Strauss notes, is also a system of meaning. Plants, animals, places, and other natural phenomena are construed according to the kind and power of spirit they possess. An elaborate system of taboos and protocols helps people maintain appropriate relations with these beings on whom their lives depend. Like other hunting peoples, the Koyukon both love and honor the animals they kill for food, inhabiting a world that is full of beauty, energy, uncertainty, and danger. Nature does not operate like a machine, according to immutable laws, but like a novel, where powerful personalities interact in an unfolding story. In such a world, survival will likely depend more on diplomacy than on engineering. For the Koyukon, therefore, humility and respect form the bedrock ethical principles that sustain every aspect of their subsistence practice.

How to embody this attitude of respect is a key problem for Nelson the writer, who must satisfy not only his professional audience of Western anthropologists but also the internalized audience of his Koyukon teachers. He solves it ingeniously, honoring both traditions in the structure and rhetoric of his book. Western natural history and ethnographic conventions are engaged in the book's framing and exposition. Nelson begins with demographic and geographic overviews of the region, then discusses its natural history in detail, proceeding chapter by chapter from plants and invertebrates up through fish, birds, and small mammals to large mammals and major predators. The book concludes with speculative chapters comparing Koyukon and Western culture in terms of conservation practices, worldviews, and conceptions of nature.

Prefatory labeling statements and abundant scholarly apparatus reinforce the impression of Western-style expertise, and Nelson's authorial voice is often learned and academic. He maintains a cool, professional manner, employs scientific concepts in his analysis (drawing freely from biology, ecology, and anthropology), and engages the pertinent scholarship. Like a good field observer, he also quotes occasionally from his journal to emphasize a point, but he generally understates emotions and downplays his own adventures.

But the text also honors Koyukon tradition in multiple ways. The book's overall theme, of course, is respect for the Koyukon worldview, and this respect is gently argued on every page while, simultaneously, it is implied in the choice of material and the design of individual chapters. Nelson constructs his text using multiple voices, some Western (as above) and some Koyukon. The latter include direct quotations and stories from his teachers, who appear as superior but complex human beings resistant to stereotypes of noble savage or childlike primitive. They are rich and vital characters, fallible, quirky, wise, resourceful, and dynamic. They adhere to traditional ways while pragmatically embracing selected aspects of Western culture. For instance, they will pray to the Christian God or to Raven as the occasion requires, and they find no contradiction in doing so; indeed, they see the two deities as complementary—as Nelson points out, Christianity may provide moral wisdom but offers little guidance for living with the ecology of a particular place. Similarly, the Koyukon have adopted snowmobiles, steel traps, rifles, the English language, and other useful Western devices. Nelson admires their bicultural fluency while realizing that he will always remain a novice in comparison. He reports how one old man teased him: "I understand what you're interested in, because for my whole life I been studying the white people!" (p. 252).

Another sort of Koyukon voice emerges in "Distant Time" stories—origin myths pertaining to animals, places, or traditions. These tales represent the culture's collective voice, speaking the distilled wisdom of centuries of experience.

In the Distant Time, the bear and lynx were talking. The bear said that when humans began hunting him they would have to treat him right. If he was mistreated by someone, that person would get no bears until he had gray hairs on his head. But the lynx said that people who mistreated him would never get a lynx again in their lives. (p. 156, italics in original)

In addition, Nelson quotes Koyukon riddles, native teaching aids that both require and promote intimate engagement with the land. They work rather like Zen koans, expanding the mind while containing an element of humor:

Wait, I see something: Tiny bits of charcoal scattered in the snow.
Answer: The bills of ptarmigan. (p. 98)

Finally, Nelson makes abundant use of Koyukon words, often in instances where they correlate with animal behavior. Thus, Koyukon culture is allowed to speak directly. An example is the word *ggaagga*, which means "animal" but is also an onomatopoeic transcription of the raven's cry. When a raven utters this call while tucking its wing and rolling over in midflight, hunters take it as a signal that game is near. They recognize that the raven will remain nearby in hopes of gleaning scraps from their kill. Such terms collapse the distinction between "human" and "natural" language, making it impossible to separate nature and culture or to ascribe any transcendent referent to natural phenomena.

The effect of these multiple voices is to embody the principle of respect at the deepest level of textual construction, creating a kind of expressive form. Sherman Paul called this Nelson's "collagist mode," a term that conveys an appropriate sense of richness, variety, and artistry. But the voices are also linked in a pattern of successive mediations between beings in nature and the reader. Animals most often speak a behavioral language that must be interpreted, and Koyukon culture has evolved the means to do so, through language, riddles, Distant-Time stories, classification, taboos, and protocols. The culture speaks to the elders, who have been born into it, followed its wisdom, and observed the results in their particular lives. They, in turn, speak to Nelson the apprentice, and he speaks to the reader through his text. This chain of successive mediations embodies respect insofar as each participant or level confesses its own limitations. Koyukon culture does so by remaining open to acculturation and new learning. The elders do so by confessing their ignorance about animals and behaving with respect toward all beings. Nelson does so by assuming the role of apprentice and keeping his own self in the background. And the text confesses its own limits by incorporating multiple voices rather than granting hegemony to the synthesizing, academic, authorial voice of the ethnographer. Such use of multiple voices is rare in both ethnography and nature writing, but it is entirely in keeping with Nelson's professed intent to write a "native natural history" for both native and nonnative readers.

The Koyukon emerge from this text as a fundamentally centered people with a durable scale of values and an abundant store of wisdom. They have maintained themselves for hundreds, perhaps thousands, of years in a challenging environment. Moreover, they have achieved sophisticated ecological relations that are economically sustainable, spiritually rich, and open to pragmatic modifications. This portrait offers an implicit critique of agro-industrial human ecology. Whereas that system is ecologically self-defeating, the Koyukon way provides sustenance without depleting the game or scarring the landscape. (Westerners, Nelson points out, have difficulty imagining how a landscape can be intensively used while remaining "natural" and "pristine.") Moreover, the Koyukon system deserves respect because of its antiquity and proven survival value. Finally, Koyukon spirituality and ethics are fully integrated into the people's daily lives, while Western spiritual and ethical practices remain dubious, confused, and abstracted from the earth. The Koyukon have no need of prophetic nature writers to change their angle of vision. And Nelson, for his part, eschews the opportunity to engage in Thoreauvian jeremiad. His criticism of Western culture remains gentle and indirect, consonant with his overall humil-

ity. But it is a powerful critique nonetheless, pointing out the hubris that lurks in an ethnocentric ignorance.

Although *Make Prayers to the Raven* does not advertise itself as a work of nature writing, it calls into question the ways of understanding, engaging, and writing about the natural world to which Western readers are accustomed. Whereas Ralph Waldo Emerson, who set the terms for so much American nature writing, maintained that the "use of natural history is to give us aid in supernatural history," the Koyukon occupy a world where every being is both natural and supernatural. Their world is both vividly concrete and relentlessly symbolic, an apocalyptic reality in which Raven can be both a black scavenging bird and the demiurge. Needless to say, it makes no sense for the Koyukon to distinguish between "wilderness" and "civilization" or "humanity" and "nature." In moving toward and within their way of life, Nelson finds himself struggling with such inherited constructs. By the book's end, we see him as a man caught between two cultures. Now, when a raven appears, he wonders what it is. "Bird-watchers and biologists know," he writes. "Koyukon elders and their children who listen know. But those like me, who have heard and accepted them both, are left to watch and wonder" (p. 248).

Although Nelson is always present as narrator in the text, all his personal reactions and moments of insight are placed at the service of the argument. Yet his journal extracts, brief and sparse as they are, reveal a person of great sensitivity, passion, and intellect, a romantic narrator who, oddly, shuns romanticism. The sense of restraint is palpable, and Nelson's humility is admirable. But we also want to hear more from that "learning self," the person who undergoes transformation in contact with nature. Certainly *Make Prayers to the Raven* stands as testimony to all that Nelson has learned, but the process of transformation has only been hinted at, not told. It would undoubtedly make for an exciting story: the journal passages are some of the most engaging in the book. But the learning self will emerge only in Nelson's next work, when the apprentice, having learned his lessons, seeks to apply them toward making a home for himself in a new place.

The Island Within

In 1983, Nelson and his wife Nita settled on the southeast coast of Alaska because he felt strongly attracted to a nearby island in the Pacific. He had discovered the island by accident, "like bumping into the person you fall in love with," yet it soon became the focus of a long-term experiment in blending the knowledge gained from his native teachers with his own inherited culture. For the first three years in this new environment he engaged in miscellaneous writing and editing projects—including a television series for the Public Broadcasting System based on *Make Prayers to the Raven*—while developing a subsistence lifestyle centered upon the island. The extensive journals he kept during that period became the basis of his next book, *The Island Within*, which won the Burroughs Medal. With this work, Nelson entered fully into the tradition of nature writing, evoking the character of a special place, reporting its lessons, wrestling with its challenges, and sharing the possibilities it suggests for a richer and fuller life.

In his preface, Nelson characterizes the book as a progress report on his process of learning from the island. At first, he says, he was just interested in exploring the terrain, learning the natural history, and getting food, but the island soon wove itself into his personal and professional life. He began to realize that the "particular place I'd chosen was less important than the fact that I'd chosen a place and focused my life around it." The book, therefore, is "not . . . a travel guide but . . . a guide to nontravel (p. xii). Whereas *Make Prayers to the Raven* was a native natural history, *The Island Within* is a personal ecology, a Thoreauvian experiment in living deliberately according to the combined wisdom of two cultures. It is not a prescription, but an exemplum. With appropriate modifications, it might be imitated anywhere.

Richard K. Nelson

The book's structure follows the cycle of a hunter's year, beginning and ending with the taking of the deer that feed Nelson's family. In between, ten chapters record various excursions to and around the island for hunting, fishing, exploration, or adventure. Nelson stalks, observes, snorkels, surfs, hikes, camps, and climbs, often alone but sometimes with family or friends. He recounts his experiences in a style that combines dramatic, first-person, present-tense narrative with descriptions of stunning lyric intensity. From time to time he pauses, like a dolphin surfacing, to reflect on how an experience might be viewed by Koyukon or Western minds. These epiphanic moments provide thematic continuity and needed relief from the intense absorption in detail. But Nelson means for the reader to experience the island as vividly as he does and to ground every insight in direct, concrete encounter.

The first chapter, "The Face in a Raindrop," sets the tone and pace of the book. In mid-December Nelson hunts deer on the island. He is a predator dependent on the land for his food, and his relation to it, as one might expect, proves more complex, emotionally charged, and morally ambiguous than that of most nature writers to their chosen ground. Nelson experiences the hard and anxious work of subsistence hunting. But the hunt also fosters the virtues of patience, self-control, attentiveness, humility, intimacy, reverence, and faith. Nelson shows respect for the deer by learning its ways and refraining from taking a doe with her fawn. When he finally manages to shoot a buck, the reader shares the electrifying moment and feels the tremendous release of tension that brings the hunter to tears. The deer, it seems, has given itself to Nelson because of Nelson's devotion; the episode conveys the vivid sense that all life is a gift passed from one organism to another, something Western culture has forgotten. Predator and prey participate in a sacred communication that it would be salutary to acknowledge. Hunting appears as an ethical transaction rooted in mystery, the energizing core of Nelson's practice and his text.

But taking the deer is only the climax of this particular excursion. The long, fruitless hours of searching and stalking also provide what Aldo Leopold, another hunter-naturalist, would have called an abundance of distractions. Nelson experiences the island in all its moods, and his account reveals a romantic temperament suggestive of William Wordsworth or Henry David Thoreau. But despite the high level of physical and mental adventure, Nelson makes clear that all this is part of his normal life. His relation to the island is less like a romance than a marriage:

powerful, stormy, dangerous, charged with energy and beauty, changing like the weather, but above all committed and ongoing. He's in it for life, and his island adventures are part of the larger enterprise of making a home. But in this enterprise he suffers disadvantages compared with the Koyukon. First, he was not born into the landscape, and his subsistence relations are partial at best. Second, he has no community to sustain him in his practice; he's a sort of cultural pioneer, living on the edge of industrial society. The Koyukon are far away; he must learn directly from nature with only their remembered lessons to guide him. He's on his own, and this situation accounts, in part, for the microscopic intensity of his style. He writes as if he were seeing everything for the first time, because to write is a way to pin things down, to penetrate mystery, to be sure about Raven and his world.

The problem of two cultures emerges clearly in the second chapter, the title of which, "The Forest of Eyes," alludes to the "watchful world" of the Koyukon. This time Nelson comes to the island to surf, an activity that provides another kind of intimate contact with nature. But the beach where he lands is littered with plastic bottles, chunks of Styrofoam, and other flotsam of the industrial age. The old logging road he follows to the surfing beaches takes him across an ugly clear-cut that contrasts painfully with the lush old-growth forest along the shore. But despite the agony he feels over such desecration and loss—the wood has been sold to Japan for pulp—Nelson refuses to repudiate his own culture. He recognizes that he and the loggers are members of the same society, and that all must share the guilt. He cannot reject his culture without repudiating himself. All he can do is to "strive toward a different kind of conscience, listen to an older and more tested wisdom, participate minimally in a system that debases its own sustaining environment, [and] work toward a different future," presumably by setting an example in his life and work (p. 57). A raven appears to punctuate this insight—something that will happen repeatedly in the book—and we realize that Nelson, unlike the loggers, also belongs to another world.

The next chapter, "A Frenzy of Fish," evokes the superabundance of nature, as brown bears, commercial fishermen, and Nelson's own family gather along the strait to exploit the herring run. The fishing vessels fascinate Nelson, representing "the primal endeavor of people at work in nature, set incongruously within the context of big business" (p. 71). To succeed, the expensive ships must make a huge catch, whereas Nelson and his family can afford to fish modestly for their own needs. The spectacle of jostling vessels and a captain shouting frenziedly at his crew hint at the spiritual impoverishment of a culture in which fish are a product and people are cut off from the lives that feed them.

In "Awakening to a World of Dreams," Nelson goes exploring with a surfer friend named Topaz. Their conversations turn on Nelson's quest for the wild, for sensual intimacy with the island, and for a spirituality grounded in nature. Nelson confesses his "secret dream" that he might someday touch a deer on the island (p. 247). It would be an act of extraordinary intimacy, a direct contact with mystery. Pondering his other experiences in nature, Nelson concludes that they have as much value as any university education. Indeed, the Koyukon would say that experience is the best way to learn. But Nelson realizes that reflection and assimilation are also necessary. Everything he has learned is being gradually woven together to form what he calls the "island in my mind," a process his text both celebrates and enacts.

By the fifth chapter, "The Hidden Island," it is June, and Nelson's family are fishing for halibut, who seem to avoid the boat because of his overconfident predictions. But here again nature provides an abundance of distractions. The title refers to the marine world beyond the island's shore, which casts up extravagant images of death, abundance, and playfulness: a sperm whale carcass gnawed by bears, sea lions cavorting with the boat, screaming flocks of gulls and oystercatchers. Nelson loves being out on the sea with his family, who are sustained by wild foods like all the other creatures surrounding them. But he finds himself oppressed by thoughts of his mother-in-law's illness. "The mysteries of the island fascinate and excite me," he says, "but the mysteries of the people I love nurture my deepest fears" (p. 129). He concludes that the "completeness and certainty of nature makes possible an unreserved love, makes tomorrow's awakening bearable, makes the deep stains of human anguish fade away, makes the fear of judgment tolerable, makes the frailty of human existence endurable. There is everything to trust in an island's sustaining, inhuman love" (p. 129). This is a strong and radical credo, challenging to the reader and to Nelson himself. By the end, Ethan, his stepson, has caught a halibut.

In the sixth chapter, "The Island's Child," Nelson visits a smaller adjacent island that night-flying petrels have colonized with innumerable nesting burrows. Comparing his experience to that of ornithologist Joseph Grinnell, who was once stranded there overnight, Nelson imagines the lush, guano-enriched forest as a complex organism that he enters with the stealth and intimacy of a microbe. He ponders the limitations of biology as a means to know nature, explaining his preference for anthropology as "descriptive science." Passing a sea cave, he decides to risk exposing himself to the percussive blast released by a wave breaking inside. "I've never been kissed so vehemently," he exults. "It's moments like this that fire the deepest passion for being alive" (p. 168). Such intense, eroticized responses to nature remind us of John Muir, who also visited Alaska. Yet despite Nelson's manifest love for this place, he insists that all places are special, made so "by the relationships people sustain with them" (p. 171). He realizes that places wait only to be known and that his purpose is "to understand myself in relationship to a natural community of which I am, in some undefinable way, a part" (p. 172). Seeking to define that way is always the task of a nature writer, to which enterprise Nelson reveals that he has finally turned. In a climactic epiphany, he realizes that the "exploration has turned inward, and I have slowly recognized that I am not an outsider here. . . . The island is not just a place to pleasure my senses—it is my home, my ecological niche, my life broadly defined" (p. 172). He concludes by wondering, as Thoreau might have done, how Western culture would be transformed "if each person, at some point in life, set aside a time to become thoroughly engaged with a part of the home community" (p. 172). Koyukon wisdom, he believes, offers a clue.

In "The Bird in the Backyard," Nelson's focus shifts momentarily to his own house, his family life, and his writing practice. His wife has gone back to the States to visit her mother, who is dying of cancer, and Nelson is left alone to write and think about the "island of home." This chapter is full of comic elements. At one point, Nelson goes out to weed the garden, where anemic vegetables and domestic flowers struggle against the wild exuberance of local species that press in from all sides. Later, Nelson opens his study windows to let in the hummingbirds that come to his feeder. His house is more like a den, with ragged, porous edges through which the wild can enter. When threatening weather keeps him housebound, he ponders how his writing practice both depends upon and isolates him from nature. When the storm arrives, he opens the windows, reveling in the wind that bursts into the house. "While the storm is something outside me, it also expresses itself through me," he exults. "I *become* the storm. Even these words, like swells rolling against the island's shore after the wind has passed, are the storm's echoes, given life through it and becoming part of its life. I am a tunnel the wind blows through" (p. 202). So nature writing becomes a part of Nelson's devotional practice, a complex act of discovery, recognition, worship, and transformation.

Clearly, Nelson brings as much discipline and effort to writing as he does to hunting and adventure. But, one may well ask, why write at all? As Sherman Paul observed, it is unlikely that the Koyukon dream secretly about touching deer, nor, one might add, do they engage in nature writing. But for someone in Nelson's position, it makes sense to interpret the act of writing in ecological terms. Writing is a way of making return for gifts of food and wisdom; it's a devotional ritual, like saying grace. Thus, it connects

him to his sources of inspiration, the island and the Koyukon. But it also connects him to his own culture, through a community of readers who are interested in learning from the land and deepening their own relationship to the earth. Writing is a way to make a place for oneself in cultural space; it's like building a house. It allows Nelson to settle and cultivate the frontier between worlds.

In his searching and astute commentary on Nelson's work, Sherman Paul faults *The Island Within* for employing a "correspondential method that appropriates the world and turns everything into self, that displaces things with mind, a proprietary way of seeing at odds with Koyukon propriety" (p. 158). Paul located this turn of mind in the simile, which is frequently used in *The Island Within*. No doubt Nelson's romantic temperament makes him susceptible, both as protagonist and as narrator, to such an Emersonian turn of mind. But the simile can also be seen as an appropriate figure to give the reader, who comes from a faraway place, the sort of intense vicarious experience that would make Nelson's insights credible. It is also important to note that the self in this work undergoes a change with each experience, rather than assimilating the world in the romantic manner; it is plastic, evolving, continually enlarged by the island. But perhaps it would be most accurate to say that self and world merge to form a new relationship with each encounter. Ultimately, of course, Nelson finds the duality of self and world to be an illusion, in the manner of Buddhist and Koyukon thinking. The simile can be seen as a vehicle for this notion of "interbeing."

In "A Mountain in My Hand," Nelson returns to the island with his friend Topaz to climb the dormant volcano at its center. As they ascend, he ponders the risks inherent in loving any wild place and the grief he feels at his mother-in-law's approaching death. The summit view gives him an encompassing perspective, and he returns momentarily to the "unshakable sanity of the senses" (p. 227). But death and grief still concern him in the penultimate chapter, which takes him back to the island for another hunt. In late autumn, after the spawning runs, he finds the streams clogged with dead and dying salmon. American readers are familiar with the heroic side of the run, the salmon battling upstream, resplendent in their breeding colors, but Nelson shows the other side: the spent fish turning to garbage, their torn bodies gray with fungus, a feast for scavengers. There is little in this spectacle to console him. He remembers how, after his mother-in-law's funeral, he hiked through her suburban neighborhood and noticed fragments of the landscape's original flora and fauna, including birds also known to the Koyukon. He realizes that his culture has somehow forgotten that it too, depends for sustenance on the natural world. He writes, "The anthropologist inside me judged this abandoned sense of physical and spiritual connectedness to be among the greatest transfigurations of the human mind, as important as the origin of tools, the development of agriculture, and the rise of urban life. And the citizen of North America inside me wondered if it might be possible to resurrect this hidden world, drawing from the insights of Western science and the time-proven wisdom of Native American people, who listened to the continent's own voices for thousands of years" (p. 244).

Moving deeper into the forest, Nelson once more experiences the island as an organism. When he comes upon a young deer that lets him approach to within ten feet, he confesses once more his dream of touching a full-grown deer on the island. He realizes that all living things are merely instances of the earth expressing itself. Life is neither created nor destroyed, but only passed from one organism to another. His profound connection to the island becomes clear. "There is nothing in me that is not of earth, no split instant of separateness, no particle that disunites me from the surroundings. I am no less than the earth itself. . . . The life of the earth is my own life" (p. 249). A raven's cry underscores this ecologic epiphany. "I am the deer and the deer is me," Nelson writes. "These hands that write of the island are also made from it; and the heart that loves the island has something of the island's heart inside" (pp. 249–250). Now he can mourn for the dying salmon and his

mother-in-law without despair, since their life, too, will flow on into other forms. This earth-bound view is enough for him: "I ask no heaven but this Raven's world" (p. 256).

That such a world can be charged with grace is beautifully evoked in the last chapter, "The Gifts of Deer," in which Nelson finally realizes his secret dream. It is winter again, near the end of hunting season, and Nelson still needs meat for his family. Once more the reader experiences the discipline and suffering of the hunter, but now the enterprise seems richer and more significant in light of all that has been learned. When Nelson kills and butchers a deer, the reader shudders and rejoices with him, knowing what he feels when he eats fresh venison, that sense of a "special intimacy in living directly from nature, nourishing my body from the same wildness that so elevates my spirit" (p. 268). The reader can now appreciate the profundity of this communion and is prepared for the dazzling moment when Nelson comes upon a doe at the precise moment a buck is approaching her, and she, unaccountably, chooses Nelson. As the deer draws near, Nelson is spellbound, a "watcher craving inhuman love" (p. 274). She comes right up to him, and he touches her on the top of her head, feeling the "flaming strength and tension that flow in her wild body as in no other animal I have touched" (p. 275). The moment lasts until Nelson, "by the flawed conditioning of a lifetime among fearless domesticated things," drops his hand to her nose. She takes in the "affliction" of his human scent and leaps away, followed by the buck. Nelson comes off this encounter, surely the most vividly realized of its kind in American literature, thinking of his Koyukon teachers, whose behavior is governed by a "few simple principles: Move slowly, stay quiet, watch carefully, be ever humble, show no hint of arrogance or disrespect" (p. 277). They would have understood, and perhaps the reader can, too. "Two deer came and gave the choices to me. One deer I took and we will now share a single body. The other deer I touched and we will now share that moment. These events could be seen as opposites, but perhaps they are identical.

694

Both are founded on the same principles, the same relationship, the same reciprocity. Both are the same kind of gift" (p. 277).

The Island Within is Nelson's most personal and ambitious work, engaging the nature-writing tradition while opening exciting new vistas for the genre. The correspondential view of nature, espoused by Emerson and his followers, reinforces the dualities of mind/matter, culture/wilderness, and human/natural that Nelson's experiences taught him to question. The nature he knows, while charged with spirit, never points toward any higher reality. Raven is both a scavenger and a god, and for Nelson he symbolizes the mystery inherent in the world. That sense of mystery and attendant possibility Nelson believes are redemptive.

At many points Nelson's adventures recall those of other nature writers. For instance, his epiphany of a living earth in the title chapter invites comparison with Thoreau's disturbing existential vision on his descent from Mount Katahdin, when he saw all nature, including his own body, as made of raw matter indifferent to human concerns. But Nelson's conception of the flow and exchange of life offers a way to see matter and spirit together. Likewise, his erotic encounters with the island recall the adventures of John Muir, who crept over the lip of Yosemite Falls and climbed into swaying treetops during storms. But all Nelson's adventures take place in the context of a long-term commitment, like a marriage. His is a true "practice of the wild," in which he cultivates a relationship to the island as assiduously as Wendell Berry might tend to his farm.

Nelson's economic dependence on the island sets him apart from most other nature writers in the Western tradition, for whom observation is the primary form of engagement. Even Thoreau did not live off the land, for all his boasting about the desire to eat woodchucks raw, and Muir had to have bread and tea wherever he went. The natural historian, the traveler, and the philosopher can all contemplate a world that does not feed them directly. The sanitary distance thus created can allow the projection onto nature of

any paradisal or demonic fantasy. Correspondential seeing, devout preservationism, and messianic development all spring from this basic dualism, which Nelson's work both exposes and seeks to overcome. In Raven's world there is no separation between matter and spirit, living and nonliving, nature and human beings. We do not see this world because our culture has enabled us to forget the ecological transactions that sustain us. Because they have forgotten where this food comes from, they have, in a deep-ecological sense, forgotten who they are. They must begin the life's work of making a home, and Nelson's books constitute a manual for that undertaking.

Selected Bibliography

WORKS OF RICHARD K. NELSON

NONFICTION

Hunters of the Northern Ice (Chicago: Univ. of Chicago Press, 1969); *Hunters of the Northern Forest: Designs for Survival Among the Alaskan Kutchin* (Chicago: Univ. of Chicago Press, 1973); *The Athabaskans: People of the Boreal Forest* (Fairbanks: Univ. of Alaska Museum, 1983); *Make Prayers to the Raven: A Koyukon View of the Northern Forest* (Chicago: Univ. of Chicago Press, 1983); *The Island Within* (San Francisco: North Point Press, 1989; repr., New York: Vintage, 1991; taped version by Audio Press, 1991).

FICTION

Shadow of the Hunter: Stories of Eskimo Life (Chicago: Univ. of Chicago Press, 1980).

ARTICLES

"Cultural Values and the Land," in *A Study of Land Use Values Through Time* (Fairbanks: Cooperative Park Studies Unit, Univ. of Alaska, 1978); "A Mirror on Their Lives: Capturing the Human Experience," in *Sharing Alaska's Oral History*, ed. by William Schneider (Fairbanks: Univ. of Alaska Press, 1983); "The Gifts," in *On Nature: Nature, Landscape, and Natural History*, ed. by Daniel Halpern (San Francisco: North Point Press, 1987); "Shooting a Buck," in *Harper's* 276 (January 1987); "Hunters and Animals in a Native Land: Ancient Ways for the New Century," in *Orion* 89 (spring 1989); "Alaska: A Glint in the Raven's Eye," in *Wilderness* 54 (winter 1990);

"An Elder of the Tribe," in *Gary Snyder: Dimensions of a Life*, ed. by Jon Halper (San Francisco: Sierra Club Books, 1991); "The Embrace of Names," in *Northern Lights* (1992); "Exploring Eskimo Science," in *Audubon* 95 (September/October 1993); "Searching for the Lost Arrow: Physical and Spiritual Ecology in the Hunter's World," in *The Biophilia Hypothesis*, ed. by Stephen R. Kellert and E. O. Wilson (Washington, D.C.: Island Press, 1993).

INTERVIEWS

Rob Baker and Ellen Draper, "Exploring the Near at Hand: An Interview with Richard Nelson," in *Parabola* 16 (summer 1991); Bruce Hampton, "An Interview with Anthropologist Richard Nelson," in *The Leader* 6 (November 1990); George Russell, "Ways of Knowing: An Interview with Richard Nelson," in *Orion* 9 (autumn 1990); Jonathan White, "Life-Ways of the Hunter," in his *Talking on the Water: Conversations About Nature and Creativity* (San Francisco: Sierra Club Books, 1994).

BIOGRAPHICAL AND CRITICAL STUDIES

Michael Armstrong, "Richard Nelson: Man of Words and Waves," in *We Alaskans* (10 July 1983); Richard Leviton, "The Island Within," in *Yoga Journal* (January/February 1992); Sherman Paul, "The Education of a Hunter: Reading Richard Nelson" and "A Letter from Richard Nelson," in *For Love of the World: Essays on Nature Writers* (Iowa City: Univ. of Iowa Press, 1992); Pete Sinclair, "Unbounded: Notes on the Life and Work of Richard K. Nelson," in *North Dakota Quarterly* 59, no. 2 (spring 1991).

SIGURD F. OLSON
(1899–1982)

JOHN COOLEY

SIGURD OLSON'S writings reveal him as a storyteller, a runic bard of the north country. Although some of Olson's wilderness tales were passed on to him from Indian and French-Canadian traditions, most are about his own experiences in the boundary waters region of Lake Superior National Forest in northern Minnesota and the adjoining Quetico Provincial Park in southwestern Ontario. Olson spent all of his adult life in this region, exploring the countless lakes and rivers of the Quetico-Superior. The most comprehensive and authoritative writer about this area, Olson merits being considered among North America's foremost nature writers.

In *Runes of the North* (1963), Olson commented on his writing career:

I have listened to the rapids of rivers, to the winds of summer and winter, and to the waves of many lakes. I have known mountains and glaciers, forests and tundras, and have gathered runes wherever I have gone. Only a few are part of the legendry of the past; most have to do with what I have known and done, thoughts and impressions which have come to me in my home country of the Quetico-Superior. . . .

My runes have come from the wilderness, for in its solitude, silence, and freedom, I see more clearly those values and influences that over the long centuries have molded us as a race. (p. 3)

Olson was a teller and a writer of tales, or runes, of nature's magic and mystery. Educated in both earth science and ecology, his initial and primary apprehension of nature was aesthetic, with special emphasis upon the auditory and the visual. He listened with heightened sensitivity to the sounds and silences of the natural world, to the singing of the wilderness, the focusing concept for most of his writing. To follow Olson's narratives is not only to hear and see the identifiable flora and fauna of his heartland, but also to hear what he called the "pipes of Pan"—the natural music of the wilderness.

Olson first published much of his writing as articles and essays in journals including *National Audubon, North Country,* and *National Parks Magazine.* This work was subsequently reshaped into individual chapters in his eight books of nature writing. With the exception of his autobiography, *Open Horizons,* individual chapters in his books are not anchored in place by strong chronological, seasonal, or narrative elements. Although his chapters function as parts contributing to a whole, many are also independent, self-standing essays, worthy of consideration as part of the important tradition of the American nature essay.

Since Olson's works are interrelated and rooted in a cluster of core concepts about the relationship of humans to wild country, they can be read in any order, as one might listen randomly, rather than sequentially, to the lifework of a poet or composer. Although Henry David Thoreau is the strongest literary influence upon Olson's writing, Walt Whitman's "Song of Myself" presents a useful conceptual analogy. Olson's songs are indeed his own experiences as a traveler, explorer, and professional guide in the Quetico-Superior wilderness, but they are much more. He also sings the landscape of North America, describing the glaciers and their shaping influence on the geography of the area, and the plant, animal, and human communities of the bioregion. Like Whitman's, his song of songs is inclusive of all natural processes and is filled with radiance. It is sensuous and visceral, yet develops depths and heights of spiritual and visionary wisdom as it unfolds.

With these lyric and mystical elements of a powerful and largely romantic imagination, Olson combined his formal training in geology and ecology, his experience as a high school and college teacher, and his practical skills as a professional guide to the Quetico-Superior wilderness. Each of these strengths finds its way into his essays. Olson's compelling adventure narratives are informed by the inclination of the teacher to edify and of the wilderness guide to showcase the woods and waters he loves. During Olson's mature years, and with the publication of his first two books of essays, *The Singing Wilderness* (1956) and *Listening Point* (1958), he was much sought after as a consultant on conservation and wilderness issues. A tireless worker for wilderness status protection of the Quetico-Superior, he was appointed to a presidential committee on the Quetico-Superior, and became a wilderness conservation consultant to the Department of the Interior in 1962. He was president of the National Parks Association from 1954 to 1960. A member of nearly every national environmental organization of his day, Olson served as council member and then as president of the Wilderness Society, and was a consultant to the Izaak Walton League of America. He was honored by the Sierra Club with its prestigious John Muir Award in 1967.

Upbringing in Nature

Sigurd Ferdinand Olson (or "Sig" as he was known to his friends) was born in Chicago on 4 April 1899. He spent his boyhood in rural Wisconsin, and that is where the story of his love of the natural world begins. His earliest childhood recollections were not of toys or pets but of his first encounters with nature. One such recollection was of holding his mother's hand and walking through a blazing grove of maples at the height of their fall color. Vividly etched into his memory was the intensity of the colors around him and, as the wind started to blow, the sensation of being drenched with color. Soon young Olson and his mother were running through the grove, and they ran until they sank, exhausted, to the leaves. As Olson expressed it in his self-described "autobiography in nature" *Open Horizons* (1969), "Color and beauty became part of my life. So vivid is the memory, I can still hear the rustling of the leaves in my dreams and see the wild, free bursts of exploding color" (p. 4). Blest with a vivid memory as well as powerful sensory perception, Olson, at the age of seventy, recalled this and other childhood steps that led to his lifetime love for and commitment to wilderness. He described these peak early experiences as nudges in the direction his life would take.

As a boy Olson was entranced by an alder thicket that separated the family garden from a swamp. He burrowed his way into the very center of this maze and made a hideout there. In this cozy, warm nest he lay, listening to and watching nature's sounds and sights. If he stayed still long enough in this hidden refuge, he could watch the mice come down their tiny runways and the rabbits follow their own hidden trails. This image of being hidden away, listening to and watching nature reveal its secrets, is also central to the adult Olson's approach to nature. Looking back on such places and times of hidden refuge in nature's protective arms,

Olson recalled, "I became part of all the beauty, the tiny sounds, and everything around me" (p. 5).

Olson's father, Lawrence J. Olson, a Baptist minister, and his mother, Ida May Cedarholm, gave young Sigurd and his brothers a steady, nurturing environment of modest material means. Although there were no luxuries, there were no worries about the future either, with a prevailing family belief that God and the church would provide. In addition to its Christian religious centering, the Olson household overflowed with books, music, and ideas. Although his parents knew about their young son's compelling attraction to nature, this powerful early response seems to have come from the core of young Sigurd's being rather than from reinforced family values. In *Open Horizons*, Olson introduced a succession of older peers and adult men who guided and encouraged his budding interest in the natural world.

The formative events of his childhood had less to do with town, church, school, and friendships than with that monumental challenge to a young boy living in the country: becoming a successful hunter and angler. Olson recalled that he had never even seen a brook trout until the first time an older neighbor boy took him fishing. His fishing tackle consisted of a thin branch of tamarack, some black sewing thread, a one-penny fishhook, and some grasshoppers. To his amazement, he caught a trout after just a few casts. He flung it on the bank and threw himself upon it. With its icy coldness and radiant colors, the trout had in fact caught Olson, pulling him into a lifetime of fishing. The fish and, later, the game that Olson brought home were always a welcome addition to, and sometimes the mainstay of, the family larder. This obsession with fishing the cold waters of the northern Midwest is one of many points of similarity between Olson's autobiographical essays and Norman Maclean's short stories in *A River Runs Through It* (1976). Both Olson and Maclean believed that fishing, and particularly trout fishing, was a spiritual act, a religious experience that brought one closer to the creative and holy spirit than could any church service.

Music was an important element of Olson's family and religious life, and he described an early initiation into the music of nature's songs. Olson attributes such songs to the "pipes of Pan." (Olson refers to Pan and his pipe music not with an interest in worshiping the Greek god of wilderness, but as a classical representation of the diverse music of the "singing wilderness.") His rather generalized mythological references enlarge the scope of his calling from Christian to classical, with hints that he was exposed at a young age to the same natural music that has compelled humans for millennia to live in intimacy with and knowledge of wild country. The backdrop to each new discovery, each new plateau of experience in and knowledge of the outdoors, was the singing of nature, Pan's pipes beckoning Olson further afield. Such music is continuous, Olson asserted, but especially audible at moments of peak excitation and revelation. He maintained that nature's songs must be heard when one is young and receptive to its calls; then, the singing of the wilderness becomes integral to every nature experience. As Olson expressed it in *Open Horizons* in regard to the act of fishing, the "sense of surprise, the eternal wonder of a fish coming out of the water, the deep inherent sense of primitive accomplishment in getting food by simple means, and the Pipes always playing softly in the background—no wonder all boys love fishing" (p. 7).

Olson became a dedicated, intense watcher of nature in all its guises. He also developed a strong sense of the nonrational and extraordinary, relying on urgings from his dreams and intuition as well as on knowledge gained from reason and science. Unlike Huckleberry Finn, whose prayers for pies went unanswered, causing him to give up the practice, young Sigurd once successfully relied on a dream that told him how and where to catch two fish. He continued to heed promptings from within and from mysterious sources even as an adult. Especially during times of uncertainty or crisis he would make himself accessible to extraordinary sources of knowledge.

Olson recalled that his young imagination was filled with the romantic frontier adventures of

Kit Carson, Natty Bumppo, Daniel Boone, and Henry Ware of the Altscheler books. Long before he was allowed access to guns, Olson built a hunting shelter along a tiny spring-fed creek overshadowed by a great stand of hemlocks. With a slingshot, snares, and fishhooks, he experimented with catching and cooking squirrels, rabbits, birds, and fish. In his simple wilderness camp not far from home, Olson dreamed of being the Deerslayer and other romanticized wilderness heroes. A neighbor, Old John, sensed the boy's readiness to become a hunter, and in a series of scenes reminiscent of the nature education of William Faulkner's young Ike McCaslin in "The Bear," taught young Olson the skill and patience required to become a hunter. During what Olson called his "Daniel Boone days," he bought his own .22-caliber rifle and brought home enough small game to feel he was an important contributor to the family economy.

As a teenager, Olson spent several summers with Soren and Kristine Uhrenholdt, Danish immigrants who were struggling to clear land and establish a productive homestead farm in northern Wisconsin. Young Olson joined this family, with their four boys and four girls and learned the strenuous labor involved in doing farm chores and in clearing scrubland to make new pastures. He experienced the satisfying exhaustion that comes from long hours of physical work and shot his first buck.

Olson completed high school in Ashland, Wisconsin, on the south shore of Lake Superior, where his family had moved. He took two years of basic studies at Northland College before giving serious thought to a career direction. His father believed there were only three worthy professions: the ministry, farming, and teaching. Although he never discussed the topic with Sigurd, there was an unspoken family assumption that he would choose one of the three. Thus, when Olson arrived at the University of Wisconsin, he entered the School of Agriculture. Although he liked his studies, especially in botany and geology, Olson recalled feeling displaced in the city and big urban university, and numb with longing for the woods. He soon shifted his studies to science and education and after his

graduation in 1920 decided to seek a post teaching geology and biology.

His first teaching job was at a frontier high school in Nashwauk, Minnesota, located on the Mesabi Iron Range. Even though the land had been decimated by lumbering and open-pit iron mining, the lakes of the region were glorious. At the suggestion of Al Kennedy, one of the best woodsmen of the region and a new friend, Olson went to Ely, Minnesota, as soon as his first teaching year was over, to explore the Quetico-Superior region. Olson fell in love with the area and vowed to join the faculty of a two-year college that was being established in Ely. In August 1921, Olson married Elizabeth Uhrenholdt, whom he had met on the Uhrenholdt farm as a teenager. Olson was appointed head of the biology department at the newly opened Ely Junior College in 1922, and in 1931 he received his M.S. in ecology from the University of Illinois.

The Singing Wilderness

After years of writing newspaper feature articles and hunting and fishing stories at the behest of editors, Olson began following his own inclinations in his work. The result was a collection of essays titled *The Singing Wilderness*, published by Alfred A. Knopf, who published nearly all his books.

The title metaphor of Olson's first book evokes the distinctive sounds of the wild, which Olson contended hold the power to capture and transform the listener. As this book demonstrates repeatedly, Olson's ears were sensitively tuned to the full range of nature's sounds, from the inaudible to the "rushing thunder" of great rapids, as he traveled by pack and canoe over the time-etched trails of Indians and French-Canadian voyageurs. Like many nature writers in the Thoreauvian, pastoral tradition, Olson questioned modernity, seeking closer ties with wilderness and with human cultures that live simpler, more natural lives. He stated his case mildly. There is, he wrote, a "restlessness within us, an impatience with things as they are, which modern life with its comforts and distractions does not seem to satisfy" (p. 6). Olson spoke for his readers, assuming that his search for greater proximity to nature mirrored their needs as well. He reassured readers that even if they don't know what to listen for, the search for the "singing wilderness," and for the solace it can bring, is instinctive.

Olson's politely restrained critique of civilization contrasts with Thoreau's strident attack upon his neighbors in *Walden* (1854) for living in a "fool's paradise" and for rapidly becoming "tools of their tools." Similarly caustic attacks on American society have been unleashed by many American nature writers, such as John Muir, Edward Abbey, and Wendell Berry, but such was not Olson's style. He was more at home in his essays with a mild chiding of his readers for misguided habits and values. Even though he worked hard and long for national protection, including wilderness status, for the Quetico-Superior, and saw the threats to this region from resource exploitation, hydroelectric development, and recreation, his restrained arguments thus stand in contrast to such early clarion calls to avert impending environmental catastrophe as Rachel Carson's *Silent Spring* (1962).

Olson recalled that the first time he heard the singing wilderness was at the age of seven. It was during a summer vacation with his family on Lake Michigan. He described hiking alone through deep woods until, "frightened and breathless," he came to the boulder-strewn shore of the big lake. Olson expressed being overwhelmed by a sense of wonder and awe at this solitary, uninhabited spot, experiencing what we might call an ecological "peak experience." Throughout his life a similar feeling came over him in such moments of discovery and participation in the essence of wildness. "That day I entered into a life of indescribable beauty and delight," Olson wrote. "There I believe I heard the singing wilderness for the first time" (p. 8).

In his descriptions of nature's wild songs, Olson emphasized the importance of removal from the sounds of human civilization in order to hear and experience nature on its own terms.

If one is to "know the glory" of the full range of nature's sounds, one must keep the sounds of human civilization out of wild country and out of mind. Of course, many other nature writers emphasized sounds. Thoreau included a chapter on auditory experience in *Walden* and complained of the frequency with which his pastoral retreat was invaded by the sounds of the railroad. Muir captured the music of falling water on rock and of windstorms in pine forests in his beloved Yosemite Valley, but Olson is probably America's most sound-sensitive nature writer. He was, for example, so upset by the intrusion of noisy, low-flying amphibious planes over the Quetico-Superior, bringing in weekend fishing parties and violating the very essence of wilderness, that he lobbied President Harry S. Truman to sign an executive order establishing the nation's first airspace reservation, which banned flights below four thousand feet.

The Singing Wilderness includes a number of vividly remembered incidents from Olson's childhood. One of these boyhood memories is of a hike Olson took in backcountry, presumably alone. He found a "spring hole" at the headwater of a little river and from a shelf of rock watched a school of speckled trout below. Olson's bolder boyhood adventures are closely connected with, and perhaps influenced by, the rich vein in American literature devoted to boys' adventures in nature. For example, Olson's tales of early love for the big hemlock forests, for trout fishing and hunting, are in a certain way similar to Ernest Hemingway's Nick Adams stories. Nick knew some of the same north country—the woods and trout streams of the Petoskey-Charlevoix region of Lake Michigan and of Michigan's Upper Peninsula—and like his creator, he was about the same age as Olson. Trout fishing was at the center of their young lives, and aside from the practical satisfaction of providing food for the table, fishing and hunting became symbolic experiences for both Nick Adams and Olson, rather than trophies and badges of achievement in themselves. A parallel reading of these two trout-fishing contemporaries would reveal many further philosophical similarities. Toward the end of nearly all his recollections of boyhood adventures, whether in watching or catching fish, finding a deserted lakeshore, or shooting his first deer, Olson concludes, "There, too, I heard the singing wilderness" (p. 9).

Most of Olson's essays describe solo experiences or trips with fellow guides and voyageurs, though occasionally he makes reference to his wife, Elizabeth, and his two sons, Sigurd Thorn and Robert Keith. In "Pools of the Isabella," Olson fishes the little river north of Lake Superior that over the years has "become a part of me," but he is also fishing his memory, for each pool brings to mind a story. The uppermost pool below the headwaters "belongs," he writes, to one of his sons, who landed his first real trout while fly-fishing there. "His face was beaming, and in his eyes was a glory that comes only once in the lifetime of a boy, when he knows he has measured up at last" (p. 94). Despite the intensity of the achievement, Olson adds that for father and son the real catch had been the entirety of the experience—the rock pools, the white-throated sparrow's song—the "trout was only a symbol" of the whole. He also admits that the "boy standing there at the upper end was me" (p. 93). This allusion to William Wordsworth's "My Heart Leaps Up" adds an important dimension to Olson's conception of time, continuity, and perpetuation. The operative line in Wordsworth's poem is "the Child is Father of the Man." Although Wordsworth is speaking of the power of memory to revivify childhood experiences in adulthood, Olson has the added advantage of experiencing vicariously through his son's first real trout an event and a feeling that happens but once in a lifetime. Olson draws from Wordsworth's romantic ecology as well as from Thoreau's transcendental pastoralism.

The Singing Wilderness contains an introduction and thirty-three essays arranged seasonally, from earliest spring to late winter. In addition to many fishing adventures and boyhood recollections, Olson writes about canoeing, portaging, and camping in the Quetico-Superior, about wild geese, northern lights, and timber wolves. He writes about events and topics that have excited him and changed his life direction, given it meaning and focus. Early spring was for Olson a

time "ripe for signs," and in this book he describes himself as like a hound, sniffing through winter-starved nostrils for the earliest talismans of the coming season. His first trip of the year was usually a solo voyage, so that he could take his time and "have it all to myself." On one such early spring foray he describes himself as driving the porcupine from an otherwise empty trapper's cabin, restocking the firewood, catching a trout for supper, and spending several hours reading Thoreau in the cozy environment. In "The Loons of Lac La Croix," he describes loon behavior and the wild, excited calling of these wilderness-loving birds. On one early spring evening their calls grew in number until the "entire expanse of the lake was full of their music" (p. 46). Spring loon music epitomized for Olson the "wild harmony" that could be found in nature and that he continually craved.

Singular among these essays is "Forest Pool," the most overtly environmental piece in the collection. "Forest Pool" is a tragic story of the decline and death of a pool of water in deep pine forest. The pool was a reliable source of water for moose and caribou and a web of smaller woodland creatures. For several winters a trapper lived in a cabin he had built near the water source. After he had exhausted the game in the region, he moved on. Soon the "timber-cruisers" arrived. Roads were built and a logging operation settled in. The loggers stayed for two winters and stripped the forest in all directions, leaving barren slashing for as far as the eye could see. A forest fire further ravaged the land, fueled by the tinder-dry slashings left by the loggers. The next season a settler arrived to clear the land for farming and to establish a homestead there. As the farm progressed, the forest pool, separated from its sustaining environment, became a liability to the farmer, an "unsightly swamp hole" that defied draining and bred mosquitoes. After losing a horse in the swamp hole, as Olson tells his story, the settler waited until the swamp had dried out, then "tamped in a charge of explosive, and lit the fuse." The following summer, after the homesteader had cleared and planted corn where the forest pool had been, he could finally feel that the "whole field belonged to him and there was no longer the smell of the swamp, no longer anything to remind him of the old wilderness" (p. 121).

Given the wilderness orientation of Olson's life and writing, the irony contained in this time-line march of human progress is discernible. But Olson also worked on farms as a teenager, clearing fields of stumps and similar remnants of the old wilderness. The conflicting forces of clearing land and preserving wilderness may have forced him to employ the ambiguity inherent in this story. One could hope for fuller debate in subsequent essays of these two powerful forces in American westward expansion: to clear and use (exploit) the land for human "progress" or to conserve the land for human appreciation of wilderness and for its own evolutionary process.

In "Timber Wolves" in the winter section of the book, Olson, wearing snowshoes, sets out on an excursion on a bitterly cold night. After setting up temporary quarters in a remote cabin, he decides to explore a nearby lake. That morning, he had seen wolf tracks and the carcass of a large, elderly buck that the predators had clearly killed and eaten from. Now, at the narrowest point in the lake, he sees two wolves running toward him. As Olson describes it:

> Nearer and nearer they came, running with that easy, loose-jointed grace that only the big timber wolves seem to have. . . . About fifty feet away they stopped and looked me over. In the moonlight their gray hides glistened and I could see the greenish glint of their eyes. Not a movement or a sound. We stood watching each other as though such meetings were expected and commonplace. (p. 243)

This was the closest encounter Olson had ever had with wolves, close enough to see the glint in their eyes. Of course, Olson knew a great deal about wolf behavior: he observes in this essay that over the past twenty-five years there has never been an instance of an "unprovoked attack on man" (p. 240). Olson also cites the all-too-numerous instances of needless bounties and senseless killings of this magnificent top predator of the Quetico-Superior, and he argues the wolf's importance to a balanced ecology. His defense of the wolf and of its place in the north country is his most passionate argument for environmental protection in this first collection.

Readers of Aldo Leopold's *A Sand County Almanac* (1949) will find many similarities between these two writers of the upper Great Lakes region. Although Leopold's famous narrative of his farm retreat is far more domestic and rural in subject than any of Olson's writings, Leopold also had much to say as a champion of wilderness. After Thoreau, Olson leaned more toward Leopold for ideas and reinforcement than to any other writer. He made specific reference to the holistic vision in Leopold's famous essay "Thinking Like a Mountain" of a forest ecology with its top predators in place. In this essay Leopold admitted to habitually shooting predators in order to maximize game populations. He made this his practice until one day he saw the "green fire die" in the eyes of a female wolf he had just killed. Olson came unarmed to his wolf encounter and rejoiced in the living "greenish glint of their eyes." Both writers reached similar conclusions about the need for a wilderness preservation, even though Leopold's "land ethic" was far more searching and embracing than Olson's pragmatic wilderness philosophy. Leopold's evolved conservation ethic, promulgated in "The Upshot" section of *A Sand County Almanac*, has had a major influence on contemporary environmental ethics — a topic about which Olson had relatively little to say.

Later the same evening Olson sits before his cheery cabin fire and hears the sounds of the singing wilderness he has awaited, the "long-drawn quavering howl" of the wolves (p. 244). He draws from his pack a "brush-worn" copy of Thoreau and reads from his mentor: "We need to witness our own limits transgressed and some life pasturing freely where we never wander" (p. 245). Even though Thoreau found the Maine wilderness uncongenial, if not frightening, his words capture for Olson the chief rationale for preserving wilderness and its top predators. *The Singing Wilderness* was widely reviewed and received quick recognition as an important contribution to the nature-writing field. It was chosen by the American Library Association as one of forty-two significant books published in 1956, and it was honored during the Minnesota Centennial of 1957 as one of the ten best books of the century by a Minnesota writer. With this recognition Olson had also created a readership and assured the publication of his next books.

Listening Point

Olson's second book, *Listening Point*, continues his emphasis on the sounds of a singing wilderness. In contrast to the point of view of his first book, that of a wilderness guide on the move, exploring widely throughout the Quetico-Superior, this collection is centered on a fixed point from which he listens to and watches nature's dramas. Olson exploits the opportunities that come from knowing and describing one place well, rather than many places fleetingly. "Listening Point" is the name Olson gave to a rocky promontory of Burntside Lake. One of his favorite wilderness locations, the lake was close enough to Ely to allow him to visit it frequently. In a chapter titled "The Cabin," he describes the process of planning and constructing his listening outpost. The proper siting of the cabin on the promontory was crucial: it had to access the panoramic view the site afforded, yet provide protection from wind during stormy and winter weather. The site deliberation yielded a back-country compromise: a south-facing location with plenty of sun and a decent view, but also adequate wind protection. Also imperative was that the cabin blend with its surroundings. After a lengthy search of the Ely environs, Olson and his wife found an abandoned log cabin that fit the bill: local jack pine, hand-hewn logs weathered to a silvery-gray, with tightly mortised corners.

Listening Point, of all Olson's books, comes closest to the form and focus of Thoreau's Walden Pond experience. Like Thoreau, Olson "recycled" an existing dwelling on a location with a "lake view" of his own choosing. Thoreau's dictum "simplify! simplify!" guided Olson's re-construction of the cabin, restraining him from building a porch, a dock, and outbuildings. As Olson expressed it, his cabin "would be a symbol of a way of life, an extension of an ideal that was all involved with Listening Point" (p. 24). It would emulate the simplicity and stark beauty of the forests and lakes of the Quetico-Superior.

Philosophically, Olson embraced and reinforced many Thoreauvian ideas. His is, as previously noted, a gentler, less combative relationship with his readers than Thoreau's. It is not his task to wake his neighbors up, in the manner of Thoreau's rooster at dawn, but rather to bring them quietly, persuasively, to experience nature with reverential "awe" and to be transformed by "wonder" over nature's complex beauty. Thoreau mused that everyone should build their own Walden (a suggestion taken literally by some of his readers); Olson put it this way: "Everyone has a listening-point somewhere. It does not have to be in the north or close to the wilderness, but some place of quiet where the universe can be contemplated with awe" (p. 8). No doubt Olson wished his readers well in finding their own Walden or Listening Point, but not on the shores of his Burntside Lake or, for that matter, within the Quetico-Superior, which should remain wild and nearly inaccessible. In this and nearly all development and environmental issues Olson was a classic advocate of "not in my backyard."

The essays in *Listening Point* cover an unusually wide range of topics, even for a nature writer. Earth science is well represented by essays dealing with glacial activity and the shaping of the landscape, an essay on rose quartz, and an essay on the origin of the diverse rocks and sands that make up Olson's wilderness beach. There are essays on bobcats, pileated woodpeckers, beavers, and loons. Interspersed with these essays are others on the history of humans on Burntside Lake and the surrounding wilderness, on Indian Pictographs, on French-Canadian voyageurs, fir harvesters, and lumberjacks. Olson's most colorful portrait is of his friend Canada Jack, from whom he learned much about backcountry. Olson tends to lionize and heroize the past, especially those hardy men

Olson at his "Listening Point" cabin on Burntside Lake

who, like Canada Jack, trapped, lumbered, and established the portages that link the myriad lakes of the region. One could get the impression from Olson's essays that women never set foot in the wilderness (and probably few white women did) or were not sufficiently interesting subjects for his essays.

Olson describes a "bygone reckless era" (p. 115) in which Canada Jack, Austrian George, Gunder Graves, and other "river pigs" organized the big lumber drives down the rivers and through the rapids of the Quetico-Superior. As Olson wrote, "to be a river pig in those days was something to be proud of" (p. 114). To Olson, men like Canada Jack "were of the old tradition, as much a part of the country as the forests themselves" (p. 115). The wilderness men of Canada Jack's vintage, in Olson's thinking, "owned it, and the country owned him"

(p. 118). This sense of reciprocity and a resulting stewardship are central features of Olson's optimistic conception of human nature. Throughout his writing he voices the feeling that human beings carry with them their wilderness heritage, their attachment to and love for nature. Thus, Olson's task is to reconnect his readers (and those he physically guides) to the wildness that runs in their blood. Once humans find a listening point from which to hear the singing wilderness and become reacquainted with nature's ways and deeds, they will be less inclined to harm the biosphere. Olson's inclination toward romantic primitivism is reminiscent of Whitman's poems about the heroic exploits of pioneers and frontiersmen in *Leaves of Grass* (1855).

In "The Breaking" Olson describes the day the bulldozer arrived to grade a narrow driveway back to his cabin. As soon as the dozer began pushing aside pines and boulders he began to regret his decision away from Thoreauvian simplicity and toward convenience. Olson likens his engineering project to the impulse of settlers of the North American continent to "[change] the earth itself to suit their needs" (p. 33). By historicizing his personal project, Olson sees in it "our unlimited ingenuity and enthusiasm for changing the face of the land" (p. 34). As if a cautious but permissive answer to his concerns, the clear flutelike notes of a hermit thrush sounded from the tangled landscape of his new driveway. So long as man's scratchings on the earth's surface are modest, restrained by common sense and a love of nature, even the shy hermit thrush will continue to sing, this essay implies.

As in the foregoing incident, Olson frequently brings the wisdom of his years of experience as a teacher, guide, and conservationist to bear on his writing. His essays usually begin with a contemporary human event, but soon digress to consider a pertinent slice of human history and then perhaps to a lesson in the biological and geological history of the region. The bedrock upon which Olson's historicity founds itself is the last glacial retreat, some ten thousand years ago, and the gradual emergence of the landforms and biota of the present age. His restless, inquiring mind asks such questions as: How did this boulder get here? Where did it come from? How was my beach at "listening point" formed? Such questions may take a full essay to answer. Through this process of rhetorical questions and artful answers Olson tells the story of his north country.

After hiking to a high, rocky ridge, Olson looks down on Listening Point and the lake beyond. He registers a note of concern for the future of this undeveloped landscape, but optimistically concludes, "Nothing would ever destroy this lookout point of mine to the undeveloped north" (p. 236). While this projection may be technically accurate, the last decades of the twentieth century witnessed waves of change as Americans moved in unprecedented numbers from cities to suburbs and into rural and wild country. Surrounded by vast, untouched wilderness, Olson often gives readers the impression that it is impregnable and will always remain intact to revivify the senses and to expand the soul. It is not until the publication of *Open Horizons* that we read of his deep involvement in the struggle by conservationists and the general public to secure the integrity of the Quetico-Superior as a part of the national wilderness system.

Runes of the North and *Open Horizons*

In *Runes of the North* Olson takes his readers on extended travels beyond the Quetico-Superior to the rivers and lakes of Manitoba, Saskatchewan, the Yukon, and Alaska. Olson introduces this adventure by saying, "There is magic in venturing into the unknown for the first time, especially when one is young" (p. 19). And magic along with "wonder" and "awe" make up the aesthetic equipment of the romantic naturalist, to accompany the requisite packs, canoes, and other tangible equipment of wilderness exploration. Here again Olson stresses auditory apprehension, instructing his readers to clear their ears, eyes, and minds of civilization in order to hear the "pipes of Pan." Even though his pastoral metaphor may seem out of place in these forests of fir and balsa, Olson is the goatherd piper enticing the reader with the "inner music" of this remote singing wilderness.

Olson's title emphasizes his evolving narrative role as a teller of Indian myths, such as "The Dream Net," and colorful legends of the French-Canadian voyageurs: he is intent on keeping alive the oral tradition of the north country. He makes clear early in *Runes of the North* that his aim is not only to entertain but also to engage the reader in a metaphysical historical voyage. His goal, through his wilderness narratives, is to restore a vision of wholeness to and of balance between human culture and wilderness. "Should the reader catch even a glimmering of the almost forgotten joys of simplicity, contentment, and fullness that are found in wilderness," he writes, "that is enough" (p. 4).

In the second part of *Runes of the North*, Olson takes his readers from Hudson Bay across the tundra and Barren Grounds to the Yukon and Alaska. As he travels north of Lake Superior, over routes familiar to him from an earlier trip, he is disturbed by the signs of change. Hudson Bay trading posts have been replaced by shopping markets, canoe routes by roads, guided parties by tourists with cameras and fishing rods. He is appalled by the "cars and bridges, the hurrying, well-dressed tourists who knew nothing of the past" (p. 147). To his dismay, he meets Indians who have lost touch with their own culture and traditions. He comes upon Teal Lake, once a round jewel of a wilderness lake, now marred by an eighty-foot gap that has been blasted through the mountains to bring a highway into the valley. Thus is his "pastoral whirled away," as Thoreau expressed it, and the "hidden haunt of moose and ducks" rendered into a settling for "Kodachromes." In Olson's ideal world, the wilderness would remain unchanged and of limited access; the Indians would remain in their established territories and maintain their traditional culture, because "they have so much to give that civilization needs" (p. 156). Although Olson's idea about insulating native cultures against change is both unrealistic and controversial, it is characteristic of that nostalgia for an unchanging past which pervades cultural primitivism. Olson's dilemma is that he understands evolution and the dynamics of biological systems, including human cultures, yet he maintains a desperate need for stasis. Why? To preserve a natural and cultural heritage, he argues, that could balance, even renew, a stressed and tortured urban, industrial civilization.

Open Horizons is Olson's "autobiography in nature" and provides our clearest pictures of his personal life. Even here he is never a confessional writer; if there were crises or difficult times in his personal and domestic life, Olson does not reveal them. His wife and two sons remain names rather than personalities. Still, the book provides a sense of Olson's growth from a young biology teacher and wilderness guide into a conservationist and writer with a coherent wilderness philosophy. Reviewer David McCord commented aptly about the autobiography: "Suddenly you are not looking at another man . . . you are thinking his thoughts." We experience Olson's evolving perspective in *Open Horizons* from a nature-loving youngster to a competitive fisherman and daring wilderness adventurer to a mature naturalist holding a vision of unity with wilderness and the biosphere. Olson's title implies a life journey toward "ever widening horizons" of thought as well as action.

In *Open Horizons* Olson presented a portrait of himself as a natural science teacher who spent, Thoreau-style, as little time in the classroom as possible. As the head of the biology department at Ely Junior College, Olson spent his summer vacations apprenticed to experienced wilderness guides; before long he knew all the rivers and portages within several days of his home, and he was ready to hold his own as a regular guide for Wilderness Outfitters of Ely. Along with developing competency as a guide, he felt obliged to learn the mythic tales of the Cree and Ojibwa, as well as the oft-repeated stories of the French-Canadian voyageurs.

In "The Maker of Dreams," Olson describes a visionary moment that transformed his life. While paddling toward his home one early autumn day, he saw a shaft of light suddenly illuminate a little raft of ducks. Something about the clarity and singularity of this image spoke to his uncertainty about the direction of his life. The challenge before him came into focus: to describe the Quetico-Superior region to those who had not traveled there and to share his experiences and wilderness philosophy. "Suddenly the whole purpose of my roaming was clear to me, the miles of paddling and portaging, the years of listening, watching, and studying. I would capture it all" (p. 178). Finding his voice as a writer was as challenging to Olson as learning to be a wilderness guide. During his early years as a nature writer, he responded to the call for newspaper features describing hunting and fishing exploits. But he longed for an outlet for the longer essays he was also writing, essays that captured the scale and complexity of the land and water that surrounded him. The success of his first book, *The Singing Wilderness*, validated his efforts.

His essay "Battle for a Wilderness" tells the story of those, including Olson, who worked for two decades to establish wilderness status for the Quetico-Superior. The first step toward significant protection was a U.S. Forest Service decision to stop all road building within Superior National Forest. The steady efforts of the conservation community came to fruition in 1934 when, after nine years of study and debate, the International Joint Commission established the Quetico-Superior Wilderness. The last essay in *Open Horizons*, "Landscape of the Universe," conveys Olson's strongest, most direct argument for environmental education and for restraint in population growth and resource utilization. With optimism he concludes, "If we can develop love and stewardship, we can look forward to the future with hope and confidence" (p. 225).

Later Works

Olson's last two books, *Reflections from the North Country* (1976) and *Of Time and Place* (1982) are written from the retrospective, reflective viewpoint established in *Open Horizons*. The essays in both volumes recall and recount the great voyages and adventures of Olson's young adult and middle years. His associative memory mirrors the interconnecting waters of the Quetico-Superior; each remembered name brings dozens of others to mind. These two books complete the portrait begun in his earlier works of Olson and his country. They have neither the intensity nor the artistic complexity of the earlier volumes, but they gain from the richness of Olson's lifetime of experience in the outdoors.

Reflections from the North Country illustrates the clarity of thought and enlarged, unifying vision Olson came to toward the end of *Open Horizons.* This collection of skillfully crafted essays represents, as Olson put it, a "partial summing up of personal beliefs." The thirty-seven essays in *Of Time and Place* were published shortly after Olson's death on 13 January 1982. As he wrote this final collection, Olson had outlived most of his backwoods friends; he pays tribute to many of them here. In "Friends of the Trail" he sketches fellow guides, fishing partners, and Forest Service rangers—men he never took the time to describe in earlier books.

The essay "Mavericks" in *Of Time and Place* is an apt illustration of his late work. Here Olson describes individuals he knew or admired who chose their own unconventional way rather than the "expected mold" of the commonplace. His collection of mavericks would make a good anthology of nature writers and conservation activists: Jack London, the naturalist John Burroughs, wilderness explorer Bob Marshall, the novelist Zane Grey, Supreme Court Justice William O. Douglas, and Thoreau. Olson praises Justice Douglas, an independent thinker and a lover of wilderness, as epitomizing the maverick spirit. He recalls the occasion when Douglas joined him for a hundred-mile canoe trip in the Quetico-Superior. After that "he fought for wilderness wherever it was threatened" (p. 34). Douglas gives a vivid portrait of Olson and of this same trip in his book *My Wilderness: East to Katahdin* (1961). He considered Olson "one of the stalwarts" in efforts to protect the Quetico-Superior wilderness from road building and hydroelectric projects. Olson's wild-country maver-

icks are, of course, reflections of the maverick nature of his own experience.

Olson's final sketch in this essay is of Thoreau. Here Olson candidly admits he "took [Thoreau's] life-style as my own. For years I carried one of his books with me wherever I went" (p. 35). It was more than Thoreau's life-style that Olson emulated; America's arch-maverick had a shaping influence upon Olson's writing life. In this late essay Olson speaks directly of the scope of this influence: "I have adopted his philosophy and made it mine" (p. 36). He quotes one last time the line from Thoreau he had used several times before: "In wildness is the preservation of the world." This line from Thoreau's essay "Walking" is the central concept around which Olson weaves his thought about the relationship of human life to the earth and its biosphere.

The last chapter in *Of Time and Place*, "An Ethic for the Land," similarly brings to the fore the influence of fellow north country wilderness writer Leopold. By comparison with Leopold's "Land Ethic," which shaped a generation of thought on environmental values, Olson's contribution to environmental philosophy was not as an original thinker about wilderness but as an articulate adapter of Leopold's and especially Thoreau's ideas to the region he knew and loved. As a pastoral guide to the wilderness, Olson sought to awaken ears and eyes to nature's wonders. He believed that guided wilderness experiences and education were capable of transforming lives and values in an industrial society that was making wrong choices and wandering in dangerous directions.

As a follower of Thoreau, Olson could proudly state that he "chose not to live in quiet desperation" but to "live wisely." In *Open Horizons,* Olson's meditation on Thoreau's celebrated line about the wilderness can be taken as a summary of his own writing career:

When I first read the sage of Walden Pond, it took a long time before I knew what he meant. Only after years of watching what is happening to America did the full impact of his words strike home—that in wildness, and all it entails in the broadest connotation of the term, is the preservation of the world and the human spirit. His magic formula has never varied for me, and the memories I bring back from the out-of-doors are the same as they have always been. These are the eternal values he talked about, spiritual dividends, abiding satisfaction and simple joys often forgotten in the excitements and diversions of a machine age. These are the moments of revelation, these the great imponderables for which we live. (pp. 226–227)

Selected Bibliography

WORKS OF SIGURD F. OLSON

BOOKS

The Singing Wilderness (New York: Knopf, 1956); *Listening Point* (New York: Knopf, 1958); *The Lonely Land* (New York: Knopf, 1961); *Runes of the North* (New York: Knopf, 1963); *The Hidden Forest* (New York: Viking, 1969); *Open Horizons* (New York: Knopf, 1969); *Sigurd F. Olson's Wilderness Days* (New York: Knopf, 1972); *Reflections from the North Country* (New York: Knopf, 1976); *Of Time and Place* (New York: Knopf, 1982).

BIOGRAPHICAL AND CRITICAL STUDIES

Silence B. Bellows, "An Autobiography in Nature," in *Christian Science Monitor* (26 June 1969), review of *Open Horizons*; William O. Douglas, *My Wilderness: East to Katahdin* (Garden City, N.Y.: Doubleday, 1961), pp. 99–125; David McCord, "Open Horizons," in *New York Times Book Review* (28 September 1969), review; Stanford E. Marovitz, "Romantic Echoes of Sigurd Olson: Conservationist with a Fly Rod," in *The Old Northwest* 16, no. 2 (1990); Jim Dale Vickery, *Wilderness Visionaries* (Merriville, Ind.: ICS Books, 1986), pp. 188–236, 246–247, 257–259.

NOEL PERRIN
(b. 1927)

CYNTHIA HUNTINGTON

NOEL PERRIN'S move to Vermont in 1959 set in motion the transformation of a self-confessed city slicker into a part-time farmer, countryman, and committed environmentalist. While his early work is literary and scholarly, including essays about Henry James and early American book titles as well as forays into Japanese history, he has become best known as a chronicler of country life. Discovering the New England countryside at the age of thirty-two, he has kept his amateur standing intact while publishing essays in such magazines as *Vermont Life* and the *Country Journal* as well as *New York* magazine and the *New Yorker*. The first collection of these country essays appeared in 1978 as *First Person Rural: Essays of a Sometimes Farmer*. Well received by readers and critics alike, *First Person Rural* was followed over the next fourteen years by *Second Person Rural: More Essays of a Sometime Farmer* (1980), *Third Person Rural: Further Essays of a Sometime Farmer* (1983), and *Last Person Rural: Essays by Noel Perrin* (1991). Throughout, Perrin, who says he dislikes sequels, has continued to insist that each collection will constitute the final entry. ("A series of three is the absolute maximum" permitted by the laws of English grammar, he states in the foreword to *Second Person Rural*.) In 1992, having at last, as he says, "run out of grammar," he published *Solo*, a very different book that offers a firsthand account of

his adventures and trials in purchasing an electric car and attempting to drive it across the country.

Life and Early Works

Perrin's earlier books include *A Passport Secretly Green* (1961), *Dr. Bowdler's Legacy: A History of Expurgated Books in England and America* (1969), and *Giving Up the Gun: Japan's Reversion to the Sword, 1543–1879* (1979). *A Passport Secretly Green* is a collection of essays, many written during Perrin's time in England while he was studying at Cambridge. His passport is "secretly" green because he has a young man's desire, as the "most inconspicuous American in residence," to pass as an Englishman. The book contains discussions about the cries of nightingales, English social customs, and Noah Webster's revision of the Bible (Webster found much of the King James Version obscene and was supported in this by the president of Yale and by most of the Congregational Church). Many of these essays first appeared in the *New Yorker*, *Punch*, *New Statesman*, and *Vogue*, and some were later reprinted in *A Noel Perrin Sampler* in 1991, along with new work. *Giving Up the Gun*, a portion of which was originally published in the *New Yorker* (20 November 1965), is a lively monograph that sets out to show how military values mirror the culture of a society. Although Japan used guns for more than one hundred years, beginning in 1543 with the initial contact with the Portuguese, for over two hundred and fifty years the use of firearms was voluntarily abandoned in favor of the sword, mainly for reasons of samurai honor and aesthetics. In clear contrast to the subject matter of these early works are some typical essays from *First Person Rural*, with such titles as "Buying a Pickup Truck," "In Search of the Perfect Fence Post," and "Raising Sheep."

Soon after arriving in 1959 at Dartmouth College in Hanover, New Hampshire, to assume a post as assistant professor of English, Perrin bought a one hundred-acre hill farm outside nearby Thetford Center, Vermont (population 200), and quickly took up part-time farming and began to write about his experiences. Praised for their wit and relaxed, unaffected style, Perrin's essays convey his enthusiasm for the life he has chosen without attempting to idealize country life. He maintains a voice of unromantic realism throughout, whether he is discussing making a pond, buying farm equipment, or building stone walls or arguing against overdevelopment and pollution in the name of progress.

Noel Perrin was born in New York City on 18 September 1927, the son of Edwin Oscar Perrin, advertising executive, and Blanche Browning Chenery. After serving in the army from 1945 to 1946, Perrin studied at Williams College, receiving his B.A. in 1949. He earned his M.A. from Duke University in 1950 and an M.Litt. from Trinity Hall, Cambridge, in 1958. Called up to the army again during the Korean War, he became a first lieutenant and received the Bronze Star. Before beginning his teaching career, Perrin worked as a copyboy for the *New York Daily News* and was associate editor of *Medical Economics* in Oradell, New Jersey. He began teaching at the Woman's College of the University of North Carolina as an instructor in 1956. In 1959, after he had finished his thesis and received his M.Litt. from Cambridge, he accepted a position at Dartmouth College, where he has taught ever since. He has been a professor of English at Dartmouth and served as chairman of the English department from 1972 to 1975. Later, he took on a joint appointment as Adjunct Professor of Environmental Studies. Partly retired, he continues to teach literature and writing in the Environmental Studies program at Dartmouth, finding himself, as he says, "out of sympathy" with much of the contemporary literary theory that prevails in English studies today.

Perrin married his first wife, Nancy Hunnicutt, in 1960. They were divorced in 1971, having had two daughters, Elisabeth and Amy. In June of 1975 he married Annemarie Price, from whom he was divorced in 1980. He writes, in a somewhat bemused tone, that his wife (he does not say which one) left "not even for someone else, but just to be rid of me" ("A Part-Time Marriage," from *A Noel Perrin Sampler*). Both marriages find their way into the subject matter of Perrin's essays, along with the pleasures he finds in his growing children and stepchildren, neighbors, chores, crops, and animals. Perrin's enthusiasm for family life, despite its uncertainties, is evident. It seems a farm is just not as much fun alone. He requires, as he writes in the foreword to *Last Person Rural*, "people to raise beans for and discuss bean culture with, and maybe even to help with the hoeing. Properly done, farming is a social activity . . . and a farm family remains one of the very few truly functional units in modern America."

In 1988 Perrin married the novelist Anne Spencer Lindbergh. Lindbergh, who died in 1993 at the age of forty-six, proved a kindred spirit, whose love for literature and the country life nearly surpassed his own. He describes her as, like himself, an eager convert, "harder to pry loose from our two farms than I am. A one-day trip to Boston, and you'd think she was never going to see the horses or pigs or chickens again." She appears briefly in the essay "Barn Hospitality," in *A Noel Perrin Sampler*, as a "wonderful woman" with her own barn, which for Perrin is surely the highest recommendation. In the foreword to *Last Person Rural*, Perrin explains their "part-time marriage," set up to accommodate the fact that each of them had their own farm when they met. The couple spent their years together commuting back and forth between the two places, forty-eight miles apart, hers in Barnet, Vermont, and his in Thetford, taking turns mowing fields and cutting wood, an arrangement devised as a temporary, though not an unsatisfactory, measure.

Various other aspects of Perrin's life as teacher, writer, and transplanted urbanite enter the essays at several points over the years. He particularly enjoys his double identity as farmer and English professor, taking great pleasure at being mistaken in either role. His greatest delight, he writes in *Second Person Rural*, is "to have a close-up encounter . . . and to emerge from it with disguise intact" ("A Passable Farmer"). One particularly funny incident shows him delivering wood to the home of a junior colleague whose father-in-law mistakes him for a handyman and reproaches his son-in-law for helping "this fellow"—speaking of Perrin in the third person—unload wood from his truck. The gentleman's consternation when he is introduced to "Professor Perrin, my superior in the English department" is enough to make Perrin characterize this incident as the "supreme encounter of my life so far." Another essay finds him positively gleeful when, while helping a friend cut some trees, he is condescendingly offered more work by the friend's next-door neighbor. Perrin relishes the irony along with what he considers a rare opportunity to witness class conflict from the other side. Part joker and part provocateur, he cannot resist testing assumptions based on appearance or prejudice.

First Person Rural

In general, the essays in the four *Rural* books fall into a few distinct categories, consisting of advice or how-to pieces, appreciations of country life, and arguments and speculation. While many of the essays actually mix these categories somewhat engagingly, this list provides a broad overview of their range. In addition, the mixture changes from book to book, beginning in a more pragmatic vein and gradually growing more concerned with political and ecological realities

that threaten the future and character of New England.

First Person Rural is a sort of primer for the novice, containing twenty essays "all concerned with country-ish things." Perrin fills most of the book with (ostensibly) practical advice, including essays on the hows and whys of barter, buying a pickup, buying a chain saw, and raising sheep. He tries to clarify the meaning of grades of maple syrup and to cope with burst water pipes on a bitter Vermont morning. One essay discusses the merits of various types of fence posts (alders are lousy), another offers an appreciation of the pleasures of unpasteurized milk. Most are written in a sort of light adventure mode, as Perrin recounts the pitfalls and surprises of the new life he is learning.

First Person Rural pretends to educate the reader while really recounting the story of Perrin's own education. He says himself that he doesn't expect his information to be of any help to a real farmer, who presumably knows it already. Much of the interest in these essays comes from Perrin's brisk and entertaining style. Sometimes compared with E. B. White, he makes what many of us would regard only as dreary labor sound like fun.

Some of the essays don't pretend to be practical at all. He has extended, though imaginary, conversations with roadside billboards, challenging their claims of "friendly" service at a nearby motel or of "garden fresh" frozen vegetables. He contemplates the differences in how animals are believed to talk in other languages (Russian pigs say "khru"). And in "Grooming Bill Hill," he explains the value of a hillside pasture, declaring that Vermont is prettier than New Hampshire precisely because Vermont still has farmers, whose cows continue to keep pastures groomed right up to the edge of stone walls and wooded hills. His contribution to the "ranks of those who maintain Vermont," eighteen acres of recovered hillside pasture, is aesthetic as much as useful. "There will be cows against the skyline, and there will be four new stone walls visible. It will be no bad legacy to leave."

In Perrin's country essays there is little talk of fall foliage, spring flowers, or views of hills and sky (unless the view is newly earned by mowing a hill). What he likes about farm life is the work. In "Selling Firewood in New York," he characterizes himself gleefully as "once a New Yorker, now a peasant." More interested in sheep than in wildlife, he'd rather figure out the best way to soak fence posts that contemplate a sunset. Perrin likes to putter around and to experiment, and he is as ready to document his failures as his successes. They include his inability to adequately sharpen a chain saw, his burning a batch of maple syrup, and the time he ran out of heating oil at twenty-six degrees below zero; in each case the mistake or ineptitude becomes an excuse for some new improvisation. In "Selling Firewood in New York" he trucks a load of maple and birch logs into New York to sell, not seeming to care so much how much money he makes, but simply to see whether it can be done.

A signature essay in this collection testifies to the downside of country life. In "The Other Side," Perrin rebuts the city dweller's idealization of rural ease and quiet with some less romantic facts. True, in the country there are no sanitation strikes (you simply haul your own garbage to the smelly dump on Saturday afternoon, a twelve-mile round-trip), and there is no urban racket (unless you count chain saws, rifle shots, and snowmobiles. "If mosquitoes were six feet long and powered by gasoline engines, they would sound like snowmobiles," he advises the reader). There are no traffic jams or crowded subways (and no taxis or bus service most places either), and the country offers pure clear water, unless your well runs dry, which happens regularly. In short, life in the country is no simpler than anywhere else: in fact, Perrin claims it is probably easier to live in Manhattan.

Still, he clearly feels lucky to live where he does and does not want to see it change. In warning others away, his motives may be suspect. Insisting on the rigors of farm life, he tries to counter a prominent attitude toward rural America, which might be termed the "Currier and Ives view," a sentimental idealization that oversimplifies and thus endangers authentic country life. Perrin insists on the importance of keeping the urban and the rural separate, fearing the city's tendency to overwhelm whatever it touches and its propensity to turn the rest of the country into its backyard or vacationland. This need to defend the countryside from those who love it too well is a note he will sound more frequently and more urgently in succeeding books.

Second Person Rural

Perrin's foreword warns that *Second Person Rural* will be even less practical than the first collection, less concerned with the how of part-time farming than the why. (As for why, there is one short answer—he likes it.) After twenty years in Vermont, he is beginning to pick up more than just pragmatic knowledge and to become more interested in differences of psychology. This book has fewer particulars on how to do farm chores and more about the differences between city and country people, but Perrin continues to bring the reader along with him as he learns, now concentrating on behavior and on how the two groups perceive each other. In these essays, predictably, the city dweller usually comes up short, offending the neighbors without knowing why, largely through a lack of understanding of what Perrin calls "country codes." They include the Power Code (never give orders and avoid making demands), the Non-Reciprocity Code (never call in your debts), and the Stoic's Code (do not complain). To violate any of these codes is to show yourself as an outsider. Once, while working on a hot day with two neighbors, helping put hay bales in a barn loft, Perrin repeatedly complains about the heat and at last flops down for a rest (while thinking privately that they should really go for a dip in the river). One neighbor "has never really respected me again, to this day," though the other "made allowances for my background and forgave me."

In "Vermont Silences," the New England work ethic is seen as accounting for some of the lapses in rural conversations. Conversation, Perrin says, "should never be sought for itself, but should just sort of happen. Deliberately to plan some occasion when you do nothing but talk (e.g., a cocktail party) is certainly foolish and probably immoral." Instead, if you really want to talk, plan to share a job with someone, "and if there happens to be a steady stream of conversation while you stitch or pound, well, you're just as surprised as everybody else. You came to work." He illustrates the lack of privacy in a small community in "Life in the Fishbowl" and tries to determine what makes a native (a condition all outsiders in New England aspire to) in "The Natives Are Restless."

This expanding catalog of differences in outlook and expectations culminates in the famous immigration test outlined in "The Rural Immigration Law." Perrin's theory is that the "immigrant," seduced by visions of country life, tries to bring too much with him (starting with a "series of unconscious assumptions") and so ends up destroying the world he tried to join. He imagines a typical couple from Boston who leave to take up residence in Vermont. At first they are delighted with their new life, raising vegetables and taking up cross-country skiing, but gradually they become aware of certain problems. The school's programs do not meet their expectations, and a new building is needed (at a cost of 2.8 million dollars). The area really needs a better airport, quicker access to Boston. Pretty soon it's golf courses and French restaurants and, of course (and most seriously), higher taxes to pay for services and in response to increased land values. Next, small farmers are being taxed out of existence, and the rural town has become a suburb of the nearest city.

There ought to be a law, Perrin says. He fantasizes about communities adopting an immigration law, which would not actually keep people out, but rather require them to learn rural values in order to be allowed to stay. Under his dispensation, newcomers would be issued one-year visas. At the end of their trial year they would have to appear before a board "composed entirely of native farmers, loggers, and road-crew men" to show evidence that they had adapted. Tests would include "proof of having taken complete care of the two farm animals of at least

pig size, or of one cow, for at least nine months." In the case of elderly people or hardship cases, Perrin would allow them to substitute undelegated volunteer work, particularly at church suppers. ("A cash donation would get them nowhere.") Failing the test, the immigrant would be given another chance, but in the meantime his taxes would be doubled. ("What about all the second-home owners who aren't residents anyway? That's easy. Double all their taxes right now.")

However amusingly he frames his proposal, Perrin's point is serious, as he takes it upon himself to defend the country as a separate entity, not simply a place for weekenders to relax. Continuing in this vein, he goes on to demonstrate the extent of his own adaptation. Other essays praise the joys of raising animals and crops, making one's own butter (his wife makes the butter and he watches, but . . .), tapping trees for real maple syrup and what to do with it when you get it, besides pour it on pancakes. (Even real Vermonters don't eat pancakes every day.) Unable to resist the excitement of passing along newly won knowledge, particularly when it comes to appropriate technology, he tells the reader how to use a peavey, an all-purpose logging tool that Perrin characterizes as the "best little woods tool going."

Perrin's interest in behavior isn't limited to the human sphere. Some of his sharpest observations are reserved for the lives of farm animals, from a spirited defense of pigs to a humorous account of failed romance among the chickens. Just as he attempts a summary in *First Person Rural* of the "advantages" of country life apart from the city dweller's wistful projections, here he attempts an accounting of the practical side of his venture. In "One Year's Yield," he figures out what he makes farming, counting his sales of firewood and other wood products, maple syrup, and cider and the raising and butchering of four lambs. The total comes to over six hundred hours for about sixteen hundred dollars in cash or products. While this may not seem impressive (it works out to just over $2.50 an hour), Perrin juggles the figures at the last moment, adding on a whopping, and arbitrary

"$10,000 worth of amusement." That, of course, is a great part of the point.

Third Person Rural and *Last Person Rural*

After twenty-four years, Perrin is finally so secure in his new life that he can declare in "Class Struggle in the Woods": "I am so deeply into rurality that my own (suburban) childhood conditioning has almost been overcome" (*Third Person Rural*). How far this is true is obvious in the detailed descriptions contained in "A Country Calendar," a portrait of Vermont in *Third Person Rural* that lovingly records the twelve-month cycle of the Vermont year (which he says contains six seasons: the usual four, plus "locking" before deep winter and "unlocking" before real spring). There are pages on snow, on the beauty of pastures, historical glimpses, a meditation on the farm as a work of art, on the wealth of late summer harvests, and on snow again. All these show a familiarity with the rounds of the year and his affection for the varying moods and circumstances of his land.

At the same time, his hard-won resident status has afforded him the right to speak even more forcefully on behalf of the landscape he inhabits. As usual he writes of practical farm matters, comparing varieties of potatoes, explaining how to remove porcupine quills.

He also is concerned with the fact that land speculation has driven the value of farmland past the means of small farmers. The latter half of *Third Person Rural* contains the most overtly political writings of any of his books so far (though one of the strongest pieces, an essay titled "Nuclear Disobedience," is reprinted from *A Passport Secretly Green*). His convictions favor the small-time farmers, those who are self-sufficient against the pressures of developers and corporate land raiders. He defends the idea of farming "badly," by which he means avoiding high technology, being content with moderate yields and old equipment, and accepting limits.

"The Beef Cow's Plea to the Vegetarians" attempts, in the voice of a two-year-old Hereford steer, to correct some popular misconceptions about the place of beef cattle in agriculture. While defending the treatment and use of farm cattle, he points his finger at the feedlot system. Farm cattle live on grass and hay, consuming perhaps one sack of grain per year for three cows. They graze in steep pasture on poor soil that would otherwise not be farmed. The true abuse of animals as well as of resources, according to Perrin (speaking as a steer), occurs in industrial feedlots where cattle are fattened quickly on grain, soybeans, and molasses and kept under conditions "that can best be described as institutionalized cruelty." The intertwined destinies of cattle and men over thousands of years deserve better. By doing away with the feedlot system and raising beef on farms, "normally," we could save millions of tons of grain a year, help keep American farms going, provide "honorable jobs for human beings," and also do away with needless animal suffering.

In "Nuclear Disobedience" Perrin announces that he is about to play the part of the sweating Jehovah's Witness at the Episcopal picnic, to be the one "waving his arms and making the same point over and over." The point is that we possess weapons which are too powerful for us and which may at any time destroy us and the world "without anyone's ever quite having meant to." What can we do when we realize that we're all implicated and that all usual means of educating and persuading seem ineffective? He quotes Henry David Thoreau, who said in "Civil Disobedience": "They hesitate and they regret, and sometimes they petition; but they do nothing in earnest and with effect." On matters of total conscience, more is needed than a signature on a petition, Perrin says, yet his response is uncharacteristically tentative, consisting mostly of wistful speculation about tax resistance and other forms of "loyal disobedience."

In a postscript, written in 1983, he does say that he has joined an organization, Conscience and Military Tax Campaign, whose members have signed a pledge to begin weapons-tax refusal as soon as they number one hundred thousand. Perhaps, to his credit, he is realistic enough not to promote more than he can deliver.

His real purpose in this essay is one of witness, attempting to overcome the very human desire to repress or reject bad news by discounting the messenger as hysterical. He imagines a council of Blackfoot Indians in 1800 discussing a rumor that white men are moving in with terrible weapons. Alarmists predict disaster, while the council pooh-poohs them: "Don't be so excitable. You'll be predicting the end of buffalo next," says the voice of reason.

Last Person Rural continues several of the arguments begun in the third book, advocating a return to organic farming and expressing an antipathy toward corporate technology and agribusiness. Here also are the expected pleasures of these country essays, the straightforward, self-deprecating voice rehearsing the pleasures of state fairs and old farm equipment, devising a scheme to use child labor to pick milkweed from a field (a penny for five stems, a dollar for five hundred), and the satisfaction of owning a power winch. While the interest of the individual essays remains fresh, by this time the alert reader can predict their subjects. But Perrin is now fully immersed in farm life and no longer writes with the newcomer's wide-eyed astonishment at every turn. Instead he has grown uncomfortably aware of outside influences that threaten his farm and others like it. A major theme in this book is displacement: the loss of family farms, and the skills they nourished, to agribusiness; the loss of the environment to acid rain and other pollution; and the loss of open space to development.

"My Farm Is Safe Forever" appropriately ends the series with a look to the future, beyond the author's own lifetime. By signing over the development rights to his farm, Perrin has ensured that his land will remain farmland in perpetuity. Protecting the farm will have the effect, in the short run, of lowering his taxes and, in the long run, of devaluing his estate, since the land will not be available for speculation. But he is concerned with a longer time frame. As development pressure continues to turn fields and pasture into house lots, closing in the land and putting greater demand on town services, his eighty-eight protected acres remain open. "Eco-

logically, aesthetically, and morally," he says, this was the right thing to do.

On a first view, these farm essays may seem not to belong in the mainstream of American nature writing, which has often been preoccupied with solitude and wilderness experiences. Although they are rooted in a deep awareness of nature, the emphasis of these essays is on stewardship, focusing on the human impact on the landscape. An appreciation of nature in these terms carries immediate responsibility for all the ethical implications of our actions, seen "ecologically, aesthetically, and morally."

These essays also carry an emphasis on work and on acquiring practical skills, rather than on contemplation. One of the values of Perrin's work lies in his effort to recover lost skills, attempting to restore a natural competence once taken for granted among civilized beings. After ten thousand years of humans' working the land, we have forgotten how we fit into the natural patterns and how to function efficiently with them. Perrin's growing commitment to his piece of land and to farming as an art worthy of the highest attention and delight aims to renew this bond, not just with the land but also with our deeper selves.

Perrin's preferred engagement with the world is through work. Seeming at times to be a kind of droll puritan, not much interested in wilderness but rather in improving things through a dedication of wit and labor, he is fired with an entrepreneurial spirit — and seems willing to try anything once. Perrin demonstrates in these essays his belief in the role of the true amateur, learning to do many things as well as possible rather than one thing perfectly. In this sense, his identity as a farmer, part-time, low-tech, and provisional, can be seen not as a retreat from the world but rather as a limited engagement, on redefined terms. For all our national ideals about the importance of the small family farm, less than three percent of the population of this country now farms for a living, and their economic base has been severely eroded by the demands of industrial capitalism. Perrin's return to the farm "part-time" can be seen as a pragmatic compromise — if the farm can't support a

Perrin at his farm in Thetford, Vermont, 1986

family entirely, then maybe a family can support a farm. While the rest of our civilization moves away from primary work and from an intimate connection with its food and livelihood, Perrin aims to restore lost connections and to renew a firsthand contact and partnership with nature.

Amateur Sugar Maker

Perrin's celebration of work can be read clearly even before the publication of *First Person Rural*. *Amateur Sugar Maker*, first published in 1972, gives a blow-by-blow account of Perrin's first foray into maple sugaring, from building his sugarhouse, buying the boards, and pouring the concrete to purchasing equipment, including the ignominious pink and yellow plastic buckets with which he begins his first season. (One neighbor asks him if he expected Snow White and the Seven Dwarfs to help him.) He keeps strict accounts of his expenses throughout this business venture, setting himself up in half-humorous competition with Thoreau, who

painstakingly documented his economies in building the cabin at Walden Pond. (Even allowing for inflation, he finds it impossible to beat the master.) Along the way he talks about how sugaring was done by early settlers, about the current threat to maple trees from pear thrips, and about the welcome discovery that firing up the evaporator in the sugarhouse is an invitation for neighbors to drop by, one or two at a time.

In this account, the influence of Thoreau on Perrin's career comes suddenly into focus — not the Thoreau who lay on his stomach for hours staring through the ice of Walden Pond to watch the fish swim below, but the Thoreau who kept strict accounts and would always stop work to talk to a neighbor. Like Thoreau, Perrin is particularly interested to discover how little money he can spend and still do what he wants. (To do what he wants is a crucial point, without which his economies are to no purpose.) A similarity, or line of descent, also exists between Perrin and Thoreau in the competitive, experimental agitator, the one who says "why not?" to every "you can't," particularly when a principle is at stake.

718

Solo

The spirit of Perrin's *Solo* is experimental, a comic moral tale of the difficulties and surprising rewards of stubbornly acting out of conviction and against one's own convenience. Here he tells the story of his search for and purchase of an electric car (named "Solo") and his attempts to drive it from California to Vermont. The whole adventure begins with a challenge from a student in Environmental Studies I, who wants to know how Professor Perrin, who lives thirteen miles from campus, gets to work. Blushing, he confesses to driving, in a "gas-guzzling, air-polluting farm truck" (p. 9). Perrin says he doesn't mind looking foolish in class, but he does mind polluting the air on his way to teach a course in environmental studies, and he makes himself a promise: by the end of term he will have a pollution-free way to get to class.

In the end it takes him a year to settle on and locate an electric car for his commute. Meanwhile, on every corner he sees car dealers, gas stations, and parking lots, all ready to serve the gasoline engine. Gradually, he comes to the obvious conclusion: the whole world wants you to get in your own car and drive and burn gas. Predictably, this awareness of bucking the system fires his determination even more. From the first, Perrin meets with skepticism, even from his dealer, on the second part of his plan: to drive the car from Santa Rosa, California, to Vermont. Counting on a sixty-five-mile range (with solar panels), he expects to get home within a month or six weeks and imagines the trip as a romantic odyssey, a historic journey across America. The first day out he makes it twenty-seven miles, to a Travelodge in Novato, California.

Perrin's real troubles begin, though, trying to cross Donner Pass. The owner's manual of his new car says "Avoid steep hills," and Donner Pass is over seven thousand feet, the equivalent of driving up the side of the Empire State Building six times. Defeated, he finally turns back and spends four days looking for a pickup and a tow bar to tow Solo home to Vermont. Part of the book's appeal lies in Perrin's descriptions of people he meets along the way. The electric car, whether driven or towed, attracts attention, and people seem eager to talk to him about it. He risks a few generalizations: Californians are enthusiastic, Utahans scornful, and Wyomans pretend not to see the car. As for the Midwest— they even have an electric car museum!

Once home, commuting presents problems that Perrin attacks with gusto. The first is how to recharge the batteries in town if he is doing errands and not going straight home. Ever resourceful, he tries to park on the grass and plug in through his office window before he finally persuades the college to install an outlet in a parking lot. Winter is a challenge, and after several attempts he concludes that commuting to Anne's farm, almost sixty miles from campus, is too uncertain. He retreats to using the truck for these trips. This is the word, for now, on electric cars, he concludes. They are impractical and expensive, their range is short, and they present all sorts of difficulties. They also produce zero emissions. Perrin is not discouraged. He has the attitude of a pioneer: he is concerned only with proving that something *can* be done, and he relies on further trial and experiment to make it more efficient. He believes that his role as a trailblazer includes taking on initial difficulties and learning to improvise around them, in an attempt to define the territory for future efforts. The word, for now, on Perrin is that he can be seen driving his second electric car (Solo was demolished in an accident having nothing to do with its power source), which he plugs in behind Town Hall in Hanover, New Hampshire, whenever he goes in to teach.

Selected Bibliography

WORKS OF NOEL PERRIN

BOOKS

A Passport Secretly Green (New York: St. Martin's, 1961); *Dr. Bowdler's Legacy: A History of Expurgated Books in England and America* (New York: Atheneum, 1969; repr., New York: Macmillan, 1970); *Amateur Sugar Maker* (Hanover, N.H.: Univ. Press of New England, 1972; reissued, 20th Anniversary Edition, 1992); *Vermont in All Weathers* (New York: Viking, 1973); *The Adventures of Jonathan Corncob, Legal American Refugee* (Boston: David Godine, 1976), Perrin as ed.; *First Person Rural: Essays of a Sometime Farmer* (Boston: David Godine, 1978), illus. by Stephen Harvard; *Giving Up the Gun: Japan's Reversion to the Sword, 1543–1879* (Boston: David Godine, 1979); *Second Person Rural: More Essays of a Sometime Farmer* (Boston: David Godine, 1980; New York: Penguin, 1981), illus. by F. Allyn Massey; *Third Person Rural: Further Essays of a Sometime Farmer* (Boston: David Godine, 1983), woodcuts by Robin Brickman; *Mills and Factories of New England: Essays* (New York: Abrams, 1988), with Kenneth Breisch, photographs by Serge Hambourg; *A Reader's Delight* (Hanover, N.H.: Univ. Press of New England, 1988); *A Noel Perrin Sampler* (Hanover, N.H.: Univ. Press of New England, 1991); *Last Person Rural: Essays by Noel Perrin* (Boston: David Godine, 1991), illus. by Michael McCurdy; *Solo* (New York: Norton, 1992).

CRITICAL STUDIES

BOOK REVIEWS

Christopher Andreae, review of *First Person Rural*, in *Christian Science Monitor* (23 August 1978); James N. Baker, review of *First Person Rural*, in *Newsweek* (7 August 1978); Helen Bevington, review of *First Person Rural*, in *New York Times* (23 July 1978); Roy Blount, Jr., "One Pig Jumped," in *New York Times Book Review* (26 October 1980), review of *Second Person Rural*; Miriam Davidson, review of *Last Person Rural*, in *New York Times Book Review* (17 April 1988); Doris Grumbach, "Fine Print," in *Saturday Review* (14 October 1979), review of *First Person Rural*; Margaret E. Guthrie, review of *Solo*, in *New York Times Book Review* (15 November 1992); Patti Hagan, review of *Third Person Rural*, in *New York Times Book Review* (8 January 1984); Maria Lenhart, review of *Second Person Rural*, in *Christian Science Monitor* (10 November 1980); Richard Skidmore, review of *A Reader's Delight*, in *New York Times Book Review* (17 April 1988).

BRENDA PETERSON
(b. 1950)

LISA KNOPP

"A NEW BREED of essayist is aborning in America, especially in the American West," writes Pat Monaghan in the 15 September 1990 *Booklist*. "Writing about nature, they write of spirit; writing about humanity, they give voice to the animals in us all. Their work attempts to breach the Cartesian mind-body split by joining us more fully with the world around us. Brenda Peterson exemplifies this new essayist." The occasion for Monaghan's lyrical prophecy was the 1990 publication of Peterson's slim volume of nature essays *Living by Water: Essays on Life, Land, and Spirit*. In this collection, Peterson leads her readers on a journey into, rather than over, the Northwest landscape—into the earth, into the being of other creatures. While it would be easy to dismiss Peterson as "New Age" because of her interest in dolphins, yoga, tarot cards, goddess religions, jin shin jytsu, Taoism, and Native American spirituality, Monaghan is correct in noting that she brings something fresh and necessary to American nature writing and environmentalism: the ability to not only observe but to actually become the other. In her essays, Peterson offers that experience to her readers.

In "Shadow People," the opening essay of *Living by Water*, Peterson says she chose to become rooted in Seattle after having lived in so many other places because she suspects Washington is a shamanistic state. Peterson defines a shaman as a healer who undertakes journeys to the spirit world to witness, experience, and willfully bring back visions that will heal others and the self. There is much about shamanism that Peterson finds necessary to proper living: the shaman recognizes the "aliveness" of all things; the shaman turns inward to connect "the visible world with the invisible one that parallels our daily lives"; the shaman heals the self and the world "not by an external, established authority . . . but by changing on the inside, telling the story" (p. 5). These are the themes to which Peterson repeatedly returns. This is the journey she undertakes for her readers.

Life and Early Works

Peterson had the ideal childhood for a nature writer. Born in Glidden, California, on 8 August 1950, she spent her first seven years in an isolated Forest Service cabin in the Plumas National Forest in northern California's High Sierras. Her father, Max Peterson, was a Forest Service employee whose office was the forest; her mother, Janice Peterson, was "a would-be writer who, in her own words, 'had babies instead of books'" (*Nature and Other Mothers*, p. xiii).

721

Peterson's first rattle was made from a diamondback rattlesnake. So far from supermarkets, she grew up eating "venison and squirrel, rattlesnake and duck," as she writes in "Growing Up Game" (*Living by Water*, p. 8). Her family used every part of an animal: if her father killed an elk, they made steaks, stews, salamis, and sausages, and the elk's head and horns were placed on the wall. Every Christmas Eve Peterson's family made moccasins for the new year out of whatever her father had tanned. Because of her early wilderness experience, Peterson grew up believing herself one with nature. In *Nature and Other Mothers: Reflections on the Feminine in Everyday Life* (1992), she writes that she "memorized the forest floor as I would my mother's body. This forest skin smelled like pine sap and sweet rot that stained my diapers green and perfumed my hair. . . . It never occurred to me those early years on the forest that I was human. The small tribe of foresters and their families were not separate or, to a child's eyes, distinct from the forest" (p. xiii).

Even though Peterson left the forest when her father accepted a fellowship at Harvard University and moved his family to a Boston suburb in 1957, the wilderness remained in her. "Because of that original body-bond, I long ago made a newborn's assumption that stays with me still: I am loved by nature, as I first loved her" (p. xiv).

Peterson's family moved every five years because of her father's career. Several moves took the family cross-country, "zigzagging from California to New England, from Boston to Montana to Virginia, back to California, and then on to Georgia" (*Nature and Other Mothers*, p. xiv). Despite the urban address of many of his jobs, Peterson's father always located his family "next to a forest, a river, or an ocean—all of which were expansive and natural enough to absorb our wildest play" (*Living by Water*, p. 14). What saved Peterson from being rootless were her parents' southern ties—her mother is from a "wild, Wabash railroading" past in Tennessee; her father, who is Cherokee, Seminole, and French Canadian, but passed as white, is from a dirt farm in the Ozarks.

Twice, Peterson nearly drowned. Incredibly, she was two before she left the forest for the first time, according to Peterson, to visit the ocean, where "I threw wide my short arms and ran shouting, straight into the Pacific, where an undertow reached out to embrace me. I still remember the spinning upside-down whirlpool of warmth like the womb I'd so recently swum my amphibious way out of" (*Living by Water*, p. 111). She did not struggle, but "remembered" to breathe water. Once the wave released her onto the sand, her father pumped air back into her chest. "This drowning felt to me then like a second, distinct birth, with nature now as a vast body of water, as well as woods" (*Nature and Other Mothers*, p. xiv).

Her second near-drowning occurred when she was fourteen and her family was moving yet again. They stopped to spend the night in a Nebraska motel. Even though it was dark, they swam in the motel pool. Peterson's father played a dunking game with his children. He pushed them down; when they surfaced, they gasped and he pushed them down again. Because it was dark, he did not see that when his daughter surfaced, she "forgot to breathe or else got confused and breathed water" (*Living by Water*, p. 119). The latter is not hard to imagine, since in Peterson's dreams she often envisioned herself as finned and gilled, sleeping or drifting on the ocean floor and breathing water. Her father gave her a mighty shove to the bottom of the pool and held her there. Because it was dark, he could not see her last air bubbles; because it was noisy, he could not hear her screams. Her father saved her, but not before she felt her legs turn into an amphibious tail. According to Peterson, as she was beginning to drown in that Nebraska pool she had a moment of lucidity: "*Oh*, I thought, and was suddenly grateful, *this again*. Then the calm as my body returned to its watery rhythms."

Following her graduation from the University of California at Davis in 1972, with a double major in English and comparative literature, Peterson worked as an editorial assistant at the *New Yorker* for the next four and one-half years.

During this time she wrote her first novel, *River of Light* (1978), in which she paid her "southern dues." Set during the Great Depression in the Yellow River country of north Georgia where Peterson once lived, it is the story of dirt farmers, migrant workers, mysticism, and fundamentalism. During her last year at the *New Yorker*, Peterson asked Rachel MacKenzie, the editor of Isaac Bashevis Singer, Saul Bellow, and Anne Tyler, to read her novel. MacKenzie, who was dying of congestive heart failure, read and edited the manuscript. *River of Light* was accepted by Alfred A. Knopf, the first publisher Peterson sent it to, within three weeks of its arrival at the company. Within two days of publication, the novel sold out and went into a second printing.

From 1977 to 1982, Peterson lived on a farm near Denver that her family had inherited. There she farmed, was a fiction editor for *Rocky Mountain Magazine*, and served as writer-in-residence at Arizona State University in Tempe, commuting twice a week by plane. While in Arizona, Peterson gathered material about the Hopis for *Migrations*, a historical novel set during the Depression in which she pays her "Native American-Anglo half-breed dues" (personal interview). The manuscript that had taken her four years to write was rejected; her editor told her to let no one see it for three years. Peterson says this rejection cut deeply: "I was ashamed because I was writing about my mix-bloodedness. I re-experienced my father's shame of needing to pass to get along in the world" (personal interview).

After reading *Migrations* in 1981, Rosalind Drexel, a fellow writer at Arizona State, challenged Peterson to send off three excerpts from the novel. All three were published—"Abner Molton" (1980), "Flute Ceremony" (1980), and "Lullaby of Dust" (1982)—and two won awards. Peterson realized her novel wasn't "a monster and a stillborn," but had been "delivered into a vacuum"—before Native American fiction became popular; before the magical realism of Louise Erdrich, Isabel Allende, and others was accepted by the general reading public (personal interview).

When Peterson found herself "staring at an Arizona sun boiling up over the horizon, heat glazing the low, red rocks like a mirage, [she] realized [she] had to do more than a rain dance for relief" (*Living by Water*, pp. 127–128). So, she traded two water shares from her great-uncle's farm irrigation ditch company—her only inheritance—accepted a teaching position in Seattle, and moved there in 1982. Because of budget cuts, the teaching job was eliminated, so she took a position at Recreation Equipment Incorporated (REI), a cooperative that channeled a percentage of its profits into environmental and wilderness programs. From 1983 to 1989, Peterson was a wilderness and environmental writer at REI, picking her way between "the pitched camps and philosophies of the environmental movement" (*Living by Water*, p. 97), a battle that would decide, in the words of her friend Joseph Meeker, "whether nature belongs to us or we to it." One of her main adversaries was her father, then chief of the U.S. Forest Service.

During this time she wrote and published *Becoming the Enemy* (1988), a novel based on her experiences at the *New Yorker*. In the background is the takeover of the Cowley and Pelzner publishing house by a corporation more interested in profits than in books and excellence; in the foreground are the lives and loves of five different editors.

In 1989, Peterson left her position at REI so she could write full-time. During this period, she made a conscious decision to commit herself to nature writing. Unlike Gretel Ehrlich and Annie Dillard, Peterson does not approach nature writing as a largely intellectual activity; nor does she see herself as an urban person "reconnecting" with nature. Because of her early preverbal and physical bonding with the forest, Peterson's approach is more instinctive, primal, and romantic.

Peterson teaches writing and is a contributing editor to *New Age Journal*. The novel *Duck and Cover* appeared in 1991; *Nature and Other Mothers*, a second collection of essays, was published in 1992. *Sister Stories: Taking the Journey Together*, about women modeling themselves upon feminine instead of masculine models, is scheduled for publication by Viking Penguin in 1996. In 1995 Peterson was at work on *Wolf Medicine*, a "nature memoir" set in the Alaska Wolf Summit and at Yellowstone. *Wolf Medicine* will be about the double message she received from her father about nature as something to be part of and as something to control. This book is expected to explore the different ways in which males and females look at nature and will include the history of wolf management. Peterson says *Living by Water* was a "love letter" to her father; *Wolf Medicine* will explore his dark side. In 1995, Peterson was also compiling, with Deena Metzger and Linda Hogan, an anthology titled *Between Species: Woman and Animals*, scheduled for publication in 1996.

Connecting with Nature

In his 1836 essay *Nature*, Ralph Waldo Emerson divides the universe into Nature and the Soul. In the strictest sense, "all that is separate from us, all which Philosophy distinguishes as the NOT ME, that is, both nature and art, all other men and my own body, must be ranked under this name, NATURE." Even though Emerson believed that through nature one came to know the self ("so much of nature as he is ignorant of, so much of his own mind does he not yet possess") and that through nature one could experience the divine ("behind nature, throughout nature, spirit is present"), he saw nature as something separate and other than the self, something one walked over or through or around, but did not enter into: "NOT ME."

Henry David Thoreau accepted the main tenet of his teacher's idealism—that the divine may be known through nature—but surpassed Emerson's understanding by suggesting that nature is not merely a symbol of the divine, but actually is the divine. In *A Week on the Concord and Merrimack Rivers* (1849), Thoreau wrote: "May we not *see* God? Are we to be put off and amused in this life, as it were with mere allegory? Is not

Nature, rightly read, that of which she is commonly taken to be the symbol merely?" Words such as these led the Reverend George Ripley to accuse Thoreau of pantheism—the doctrine that all the laws, forces, and manifestations of the self-existing universe are God, that God is everything and everything is God.

For Walt Whitman, there is nothing that is "not me." He not only erased the boundaries between nature and the divine as Thoreau did, but went a step further, erasing the boundaries between himself and the rest of creation. In "A Song for Occupations" he observes that "objects gross and the unseen soul are one." In the 1856 version of "Crossing Brooklyn Ferry" he writes, "We realize the soul only by you, you faithful solids and fluids." After the speaker's body and soul merge in the fifth canto of "Song of Myself," Whitman writes that he had the "peace and knowledge that pass all the argument of the earth . . . that the hand of God is the promise of my own . . . that the spirit of God is the brother of my own . . . that all the men ever born are also my brothers, and the women my sisters and lovers." Also included in his limitless self are leaves, ants, stones, elder, mullein, and pokeweed. Whitman, with his nonhierarchical, subjective view of nature, had an intimate relationship with creation that was distinctly feminine.

It was typical for white male nature writers of the nineteenth and early twentieth centuries to travel widely in their experience of nature (via tours; immigration; scientific, military, or hunting expeditions) rather than encountering nature at home, as home. In *The Land Before Her: Fantasy and Experience of the American Frontiers, 1630–1860* (1984), Annette Kolodny examines the conflicting metaphors by which white men and women viewed the American landscape. White men, for instance, conceived of America as a virgin who would bear fruit after being conquered and penetrated. This metaphor was not operative for females, who instead conceived of America as a garden, a "potential sanctuary for . . . domesticity" (p. xiii), a safe space carved out against the howling wilderness.

Thus, females were more likely than males to see nature not as separate and removed, but as an extension of home. Though these metaphors have been revised or changed with time, what Annette Kolodny identifies as the images of the virgin and the garden still influence how we perceive the natural world. Thus, it is no wonder that many men (and those women who absorbed male metaphors, language, and perspective) saw and continue to see nature as something to enter and to exit and, above all, to remain superior to and separate from. Indeed, Brenda Peterson is "a new breed of essayist," in that she gives voice to an ignored or suppressed but absolutely essential point of view.

Still, vestiges of these old metaphors remain. Peterson says that most male nature writers—John McPhee and Edward Hoagland are the two she names—still see nature as a distant object which they approach intellectually, as scientists and professionals. McPhee, for instance, apprentices himself to a specialist; then he observes that observer, so he is two times removed from the animal or the landscape. Such an approach to nature reveals a "horror of anthropomorphizing" (personal interview).

The nature writers Peterson feels most affinity with are those with a "feminine" perspective: Barry Lopez, who is willing to blur the distinctions between human and nonhuman; Victor Perera, who writes mystical, magical books about Guatemalan Indians and whales; Terry Tempest Williams, who sees the death of a salt marsh and her mother's death from breast cancer as equals; and such Native American writers as Joy Harjo, Leslie Marmon Silko, and Linda Hogan. Peterson also admires the abilities of such scientists as Dian Fossey (gorillas), Cynthia Moss (elephants), Jane Goodall (primates), and Elizabeth Marshall Thomas (dogs), who do not separate themselves from what they are studying, nor see themselves as superior to it. "It is condescension that is killing us," says Peterson. "We have broken our treaty with the animals by believing we are better and different than they are. If we are going to survive, we have to reach out and connect. We have to apprentice ourselves to other kinds of minds" (personal interview).

This theme of reaching out and connecting with other animals, other minds, is evident in both of Peterson's collections of nature essays. In *Living by Water*, she examines the connection in the most elemental sense: the act of becoming what we eat. Peterson was raised with the belief that animals were her kin who sacrificed their lives so she might live. But the animals we eat are more than just kin: we become their spirit and body.

These thoughts, from "Growing Up Game," lead naturally into the next essay, "Animals as Brothers and Sisters," in which Peterson writes about swimming with dolphins—her animal allies—in a Florida Keys research project "that reversed our society's usual prejudice against animals": humans were there for the dolphins to play with instead of the other way around, so researchers could study dolphin-human interactions in the cetacean's own environment (p. 15). Peterson insists that humans have much to learn from dolphins, since a cetacean's brain is not only larger than a human's, but has had thirty million more years of evolutionary development. Even more significant to Peterson is the theory that dolphins may exist in an alpha state (humans experience this in meditation) and never really sleep. Instead, they just switch sides of the brain being used, suggesting an extraordinary intelligence.

Peterson apprentices herself to cetaceans and they teach her how to live by water—that element she identifies with most and which surrounds her Seattle home. The dolphins teach her how to be more fully human, as well. "Animals do not change the world; they adapt. In my own life, the flexibility and adaptability of a dolphin mind, their sense of tribe and play, guides me. I can call upon the dolphin inside me for counsel as well as companionship" (p. 25).

In "Other Teachers Than Terror—from Dinosaurs to Dolphins," the opening essay in *Nature and Other Mothers*, the reader again finds Peterson swimming with her animal totem in the Florida Keys, marveling in the "simple

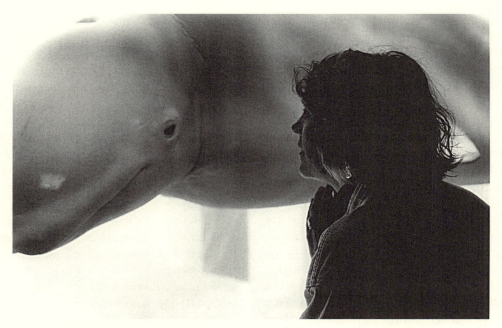

Brenda Peterson with Inuk, a beluga whale, at Point Defiant Zoo

but provocative" fact that cetaceans have a type of brain that is in some respects superior to humans. Sense receptors are scattered over various regions of the human brain, allowing us to respond quickly to danger. If we hear a loud noise, for instance, we don't have to wait for that stimulus to be integrated with other senses before the brain can respond: we fight or flee. The disadvantage of this system, according to Peterson, is that our neural functions can become isolated from one another: since we act without a grasp of the complete picture, we are prepared to fight or flee whether that loud sound signals delight or danger. In contrast, the paralimbic lobe in the dolphin brain synthesizes and integrates all senses so that the dolphin experiences the whole picture at once. Hologrammatic intelligence, Peterson calls it. As she sees it, if we are to survive we must acquire this integration of senses and mind and heart, since such an integration "trusts the world as if it were at one with us, our greater body" (*Living by Water*, p. 66). Further, if we would apprentice ourselves to cetaceans we could move beyond "the eye-hand manipulative skills of technological conquest" to the "synthetic, holistic mind" that whales possess (*Nature and Other Mothers*, p. 13). Peterson suggests that the presence of a paralimbic lobe explains why there are no dolphin wars or any recorded incident of a dolphin harming a human.

As a nature writer, Peterson consistently presents a view of nature that is partial, selective, and romantic. While there are "other teachers than terror," certainly we cannot ignore what terror has to teach. Unfortunately, Peterson's focusing only on nature's "friendly" forces gives a lopsided view of the natural world. In addition to being gentle, playful, and nurturing, nature can also be dangerous, violent, and to human eyes, cruel. If a full understanding of nature is what we are seeking, sharks have as much to teach us about the interactions between and within species as do the more lovable dolphins with which they share the waters.

Nonetheless, Peterson has learned well from her apprenticeship with dolphins. As David Miller notes in a review of *Living by Water*, Peterson "can establish connections with nature through other senses than sight . . . with a sense beyond the ordinary five" (p. 490). Frequently, she reveals this extraordinary sensitivity. When she is "sounded" by dolphins,—referring to the dolphins' sonar echolocation, their device for determining their surroundings—she feels her cells are being penetrated, seen, and accepted. In "Believing the Bond," in *Living by Water*, she describes feeling the sand tremble during a late-night walk near her Seattle home. Even though there was no storm, she believed "the sudden splash of phosphorous gleaming against me" was lightning, and there was electricity surging through her body. To ground herself, she plunged her hands into the sand and let the pulses pass through her. "I've never felt anything like this before. And yet it is familiar. I am afraid it will overwhelm me and my body will be blown out like an insignificant throwaway fuse by this electricity." Yet, it was not lightning, but the earth itself shaking her body. Finally, she cries that she has had enough. The result of this sensual epiphany is that the earth will never again feel the same to her. "I remember now that I live on a vibrant, breathing being that is a greater body encompassing mine" (pp. 48–49).

Mothering

In Peterson's novel *Duck and Cover*, one of the narrators, ten-year-old Daniella, observes, "The way nuclear families are put together . . . it just makes sense they would explode" (p. 129). In her nature essays, Peterson calls for a definition of family that includes all living creatures— trees, Earth, amoebas, whales. Since mothers are those who teach and heal, we should look for them beyond the confines of the nuclear family, beyond our own species. By learning to mother one another, we can defuse our families and the planet. Peterson explores and reveres a variety of mothers who continue to teach and heal her— "siblings, friends, mates, and lovers, dolphins, whales, grandparents, parents, and aunts who show me how to midwife my own life" (*Nature and Other Mothers*, p. xv). Neither are mammals her only mothers. *Living by Water*, is dedicated "To Puget Sound, who mothers me."

Nature and Other Mothers is filled with stories of Peterson's human family. In "In Praise of Skin" she tells of Vergie, her stepgrandmother, who mothered the living and the dead by massaging, by laying on hands and washing feet. In "Sisters of the Road" she tells of her father's three sisters, Nettie Mae, Mary Leola, and Donna Ruth, from the Ozarks' "piny woods," who mothered her when she was a child (" 'We never had no time or money for no doll babies,' Aunt Mary Leola explained in her deep, tobacco-rough voice. 'You young'uns were our toys' "), and who mother her still on wild, cross-country road trips. Peterson tells of the ways she mothers others—with lullabies, for instance—and of the ways she mothers herself—by taking luxurious baths, by doing daily chores, by swimming with dolphins.

"Power in the Blood" is Peterson's most complex and moving examination of mothering. She deftly alternates stories of her experience in a moon lodge—a teepee or hut in Native American and other indigenous communities that is used by women during menstruation—where she and other menstruating women mother each other with stories about how abortion has haunted her nuclear family: Peterson's mother unsuccessfully tried to abort her; a sister who aborted is now a vehement pro-lifer; Peterson miscarried before she had to abort. Peterson believes that the heart of the "war of the women" (the abortion controversy) is lack of acknowledgment for mothering: women join the pro-life movement to elevate "motherhood to a sacrament and the choice against it to a sacrilege" because the world so little honors them as mothers (p. 67). She suggests that the best way to disarm the combatants is for women to mother each other: "What if women's clinics were not based only on the masculine medical model of disease and surgical procedure but also on feminine healing? Why not a moon lodge near every abortion clinic, where a tribe of women meditate and comfort their own in the darkest phase of a woman's moon?" (p. 80).

Peterson speculates that her pro-life sister turned to the first group of women she could find who were focused on abortion. Years later, she is still comfortless. Peterson speaks compassionately of women who choose abortion and of their need for mothering. However, she does not extend sympathy to women (such as her sister) who, when faced with an unplanned and unwanted pregnancy, choose not to abort.

Peterson believes the lack of esteem in which our culture holds motherhood is founded in the Judeo-Christian creation story in which "God, without female mate, created man, who then gave birth to woman from his own body. This is biologically backward from all we know or experience" (p. 74). Just as the female counterpart of Jehovah is missing, the feminine in Jehovah's son is unrecognized. (Curiously, Peterson does not mention the Catholic adoration of Mary, the virgin mother, the impossible ideal, but a mother nonetheless.) Peterson finds solace in the woman-centered goddess religions. "There is so much to remember, to put back together of this feminine that has been so fragmented and forgotten" (p. 90).

In addition to human, supernatural, and natural teachers, Peterson is also mothered by ideas and experiences—personal disarmament, bodily illnesses, mourning, playfulness, humor, and daily chores, all of which can move us into more authentic ways of being and restore a sense of sacredness. In the final essay, "Killing Our Elders," she mourns the fact that in the past decade we have clear-cut 90 percent of our old-growth forests, in much the same way that we deny "our human elders a place in our tribe" (p. 211). Peterson calls us to think beyond family to tribe: "Aren't we all in a way native Americans now? Can we at last recognize that we are one tribe, one forest, that the last standing old trees in our country are crucial to our well-being, our own long-term growth?" (p. 215).

Politics and the Environment

The environment is Peterson's primary political focus in *Living by Water*. In "Oil Spill Eulogy," she mourns the devastation caused by the 1989 Exxon *Valdez* oil spill and speculates upon the "terrible symmetry [of] a man polluted by alcohol commanding a tanker that pollutes so beautiful a body of water" (p. 31). In addition to dealing with this as an environmental issue, Peterson says we must consider the underside of big businesses that have such farsighted insurance policies that they can weather even a financial loss of this magnitude. She believes that each of us must make this a personal issue as well: we must assign blame if no one is willing to step forward and accept it, and "along with mourning these lost animals, we must also be grateful for their sacrifice in showing us this sad truth: we human animals are out of balance and out of control." To commemorate their sacrifice, Peterson asks each of us to give up "one act of personal pollution" (p. 32).

In "Where the Green River Meets the Amazon," Peterson writes about her daily commute through the Green River Valley, "where the perpetrator of this country's longest series of unsolved murders takes his name and buries his bodies" (p. 77). At the same time, she thinks of the Amazon River, where colonials invaded, enslaved, and murdered Indians. Presently, the descendants of those conquered Indians are losing their rain-forest home at the rate of fifty-four acres per minute. Yet, says Peterson, it is hypocritical for those of us in "developed" nations to call for an end to the deforestation of the Amazon rain forests. After all, a century earlier we, too, deforested our own country in the name of development.

In Peterson's mind, the two rivers run together in a way that is not comfortable. "Do we lose our souls when we desecrate our land? And in those places like the Amazon or Green River basins where murderers, mass burials, wars over development are all inexorably linked, does this brutal confluence also summon the supernatural by drawing down the darkness?" (p. 81) Again, Peterson offers a solution. "Daily, slowly, in small, seemingly insignificant rituals we might someday summon back our own and the Earth's lost souls—by holding one funeral for one unknown victim of the Green River murderer;

paying one visit to Chief Sealth's grave to give thanks for the land the Indian tribes gave us; making one acknowledgment of the history, the people who died and are buried here in this land beneath us" (p. 82).

In *Nature and Other Mothers*, Peterson's political concern is still environmental, but even more, it is the post–cold war period "when ambiguity and reconciliation of seeming opposites will require all of our intelligence" (p. 180). It is a time when we must look for other teachers than "terror, intimidation, and physical force" (p. 20). It is a time when we can no longer give a foreign face to our enemies.

In the opening essay, "Other Teachers Than Terror—From Dinosaurs to Dolphins," Peterson writes that as a child, she lived with the knowledge that "Russia had all its missiles aimed right at our hearts" (p. 3). She grew up with emergency evacuations, fallout shelters, duck-and-cover drills, and "Red" alerts. She pondered why humans wanted to blow up their only home and go extinct. "There is a part of all of us that doesn't want to be here," she concludes. The official end of the cold war calls for a new way of living and imagining: "How can I parlay all my childhood civil defense survival skills into another way of facing the world—not hunched over with the dread and terror of nuclear death, but a posture of openness and flexibility?" Now, as she begins to imagine "a future without the simplistic morality play of Us and Them, [she] glimpse[s] a spacious new storyline that does not presume extinction for [her] own or others' species" (p. 7).

"War Diaries," the third group of essays in the collection, presents "a spacious new storyline" for the post–cold war era, so we may "evolve from murderers to visionaries" (p. 21). In "The War That Fell to Earth," Peterson explains how the roof of her house blew off in a rainstorm during the United States' Christmas 1989 invasion of Panama, a particularly frightening war since she feared her brother, a navy aviator, had been sent into the battle. Peterson's brother was not sent to Panama and her roof was repaired— more easily repaired than the damage caused by

a "missing in action" president. "Is it contempt or fear or unfamiliarity with the domestic that makes our country's masculine embodiment so busy in far-off places? Is President Bush simply a mirror of the man who long ago abandoned his family or any attempt at putting his own country's house in order?" (p. 173).

Two Christmases later, the United States is again attacking another country and again Peterson's roof blows off. Prepared for battle, she calls the man who fixed it before. His work is warranted; he will come immediately. Peterson almost weeps. In this workman, she finds the heroism and vision our country's leaders need. "He didn't tell me to ignore what was broken in my house; he didn't show contempt for my small domestic problems by proclaiming that he was out fighting Evil with a foreign face that only he seemed to recognize. He didn't tell me that he'd attend to it later, after worse damage had been done. He didn't promise a peace dividend that never came" (p. 174).

In "Saving Face," written during the final days of Desert Storm, Peterson remembers a college research paper she wrote on Japanese Americans who had been interned for the duration of World War II. These two war memories, the U.S. invasion of Panama in 1989 and the internment of the Japanese during World War II, lead her to consider the "divided face of war"—victory and defeat. While Americans were celebrating their victory, the Iraqis were in the midst of a scenario worse than the actual war—food shortages, epidemics, and a quarter million of their people dead. The United States has no memory of humiliating military defeat (she doesn't mention the defeat in Vietnam) as do the Japanese and the Iraqis; consequently, it is time for us to imagine "the face and feelings of defeat" so we can "present another face to the world [than that of victor]—one that is flexible, reflective, open to others who might not share our secure sense of strength" (p. 179).

The final essay in this section, "Arms and the Man," is about the 1976 death of Peterson's grandfather from pancreatic cancer. He bequeathed to her his World War I diaries, but more importantly, he told her the real story of war. As he lay dying, he saw his room filled with German soldiers he had killed. But at his death, they were there "to carry me on over" (p. 183). The last time Peterson saw him, two of the Germans had forgiven him, but he said there were many more he had to meet face to face. When Peterson asks if her uncle shouldn't hear the stories, her grandfather answers that his war stories aren't the type one passes on to a son. Perhaps, says Peterson, things might change if more men "broke the war-hero taboo and told the real story" (p. 183).

Stories of Nature and Spirit. Peterson prefers calling her prose pieces "ecological stories" rather than essays, since the purpose of a story is to "define and shape" life (p. 68). Thus the purpose behind each of her true stories is to effect a change in the way we see the environment and ourselves, so the reader practices ecology on "its more profound and healing level" (p. 69). Peterson tells stories of her family and her tribe; she retells Native American stories; she tells stories of our planet. Thus, she is a shaman who heals the world "not by an external, established authority . . . but by changing on the inside, [by] telling the story."

Conclusion

In "Wild at Heart," an essay published in the *New Age Journal*, Peterson tells about teaching a storytelling class for inner-city adolescents in Seattle. After a student shares the story of her friend's death in a drive-by shooting, Peterson asks the other students to imagine themselves as animals in the Amazon jungle, searching for the murderer they would bring to justice. Even though these city kids were afraid of nature and had only seen animals on television or in zoos, "they return instinctively to their animal selves. . . . Not because nature is 'out there' to be saved or sanctioned, but because nature is *in* them. The ancient, green world has never left us, though we have long ago left the forest" (p. 69). Memories of and alliances with the animals still live within her students.

Such imagining is no mere child's play. Peterson believes that imagination is a primal force, every bit as strong as lobbyists, boycotts, and endangered-species acts. To "claim another species not only as an imaginary friend, but also as the animal within—their ally"—is to change the external world, and that means practicing ecology "at its more profound and healing level" (p. 69).

When the second edition of *Living by Water* appeared in June 1994, it bore a new subtitle: *Essays on Life, Land, and Spirit* had became *True*

Selected Bibliography

WORKS OF BRENDA PETERSON

NOVELS

River of Light (New York: Knopf, 1978); *Becoming the Enemy* (St. Paul: Graywolf, 1988); *Duck and Cover* (New York: HarperCollins, 1991).

COLLECTIONS OF NATURE ESSAYS

Living by Water: Essays on Life, Land, and Spirit (Seattle: Alaska Northwest Books, 1990), repr. as *Living by Water: True Stories of Nature and Spirit* (New York: Fawcett, 1994); *Nature and Other Mothers: Reflections on the Feminine in Everyday Life* (New York: HarperCollins, 1992).

SHORT FICTION

"Abner Molton," in *Scottsdale Daily Progress*, Saturday magazine (12 April 1980); "Flute Ceremony," in *Rocky Mountain Magazine* (November/December 1980); "Lullaby of Dust," in *New America* 4, no. 3 (1982).

ARTICLES

"Baby Beluga," in *New Age Journal* (March/April 1993), pp. 84–87, 124–126, 128; "The New Eroticism," in *New Age Journal* (May/June 1993), pp. 62–68, 91–93; "Sister Against Sister," in *New Age Journal* (September/October 1993), pp. 64, 65–68, 142–145; "Wild at Heart," in *New Age Journal* (January/February 1994), pp. 667–669.

INTERVIEW

Personal interview with the author, 5 February 1994.

BIOGRAPHICAL AND CRITICAL STUDIES

Annette Kolodny, *The Land Before Her: Fantasy and Experience of the American Frontiers, 1630–1860* (Chapel Hill: Univ. of North Carolina Press, 1984); David Miller, review of *Living by Water*, in *Sewanee Review* 100 (summer 1992); Pat Monaghan, review of *Living by Water*, in *Booklist* 87 (15 September 1990).

ROBERT MICHAEL PYLE
(b. 1947)

MICHAEL PEARSON

FOR ROBERT MICHAEL PYLE the world is a text, an ever-changing story to be read by the thoughtful, careful observer. In his *Handbook for Butterfly Watchers* (1984) he says, "Most people are simply not aware of anything smaller than a robin; their senses are not adjusted to take in the small wonders" (p. 1). In his own life and work, Pyle has been fascinated by nature's diminutives—snails and butterflies and anonymous, forgotten landscapes.

Pyle received a B.S. in nature perception (1969) and an M.S. in nature interpretation and forestry (1973) from the University of Washington and a Ph.D. in ecology and environmental studies (1976) from Yale; his subsequent success as a writer enabled him to teach creative writing at colleges in the United States and at one university in England. He was also an assistant at the Peabody Museum of Natural History at Yale, a conservation consultant in New Guinea, a Rocky Mountain tour guide, a land steward for the Nature Conservancy, and a teacher of biology. He was a Fulbright scholar at Monks Wood Experimental Station in England, a fellow of the National Wildlife Federation, a Guggenheim fellow, and the founder of the Xerces Society, a group dedicated to the study and conservation of butterflies and other insects. The purpose of the society, which is named after the Xerces Blue (extinct since the 1940s and the first American butterfly to be extirpated by human develop-

ment), sounds the main theme that resonates through Pyle's books and essays: that humans can find peace in a reverence for nature.

In 1987 Pyle won the John Burroughs Medal for distinguished nature writing. Twice he was given the Governor's Writers Award, and in 1989 he received a Guggenheim to write essays on nature legends of the Northwest. Once a self-described "urban naturalist," Pyle wrote about city biology for *Horticulture* in the late 1970s, but he felt a growing need to live in the country. In the spring of 1979, he left his main employment with the Nature Conservancy in Portland, Oregon, and settled near Gray's River, in the state of Washington. He went there, he says in *Wintergreen* (1986), with the "romantic but semipractical notion of harvesting words grown out of the soil of the hills and the valleys" (p. 265). For a man trained in natural history, science, and conservation much more than in literature, the transformation from scientist into full-time writer was a daring step into *terra incognita*, a metamorphosis reminiscent of the butterflies he studies. Edwin Way Teale, one of his mentors, told him not to become a full-time writer until his work justified it, but Pyle's gamble paid off in his evolution as a writer and literary explorer. In the mid-1990s he was working on a collection of writings on Vladimir Nabokov's lepidopteran writings, and a novel (*Magdalena Mountain*) about three people who become intrigued with and even obsessed by the Magdalena Alpine butterfly, whose blackness may be as suggestive as the whiteness of Melville's whale. *Where Bigfoot Walks*, a book of essays on the Bigfoot myths, was published in 1995.

Early Life

Pyle first visted the rural Wahkiakum County, in southwestern Washington, at the end of the 1970s, and he moved there permanently in 1982. Gray's River, a stream and a little town, provided him with the necessary tranquillity he needed to write full-time. The old homestead where he settled, called Swede Park, a white Victorian farmhouse with a small arboretum in an area of rolling hills and gentle if ubiquitous rain, represented for him a "release from the stress and distraction of the city" (*Wintergreen*, p. 1). The small community provided fertile soil for his imaginative observations. Like Henry David Thoreau, Pyle retreated to the woods, not so much to escape as to confront the essential facts of life, to live deliberately, and to write about it.

Pyle's first awakening to nature took place in Colorado, "on the wrong side of Denver to reach the mountains easily or often" (*The Thunder Tree*, p. xv). He was born in Denver to Robert Harold Pyle and Helen Lee Miller on 19 July 1947. In *The Thunder Tree: Lessons from an Urban Wildland* (1993), Pyle explains that everyone who feels deeply connected to the natural world makes that connection *somewhere*, that there is always a particular place that is the catalyst for the love of land. It could be a vacant lot, a trickling stream, or an unadmired patch of woods. For Pyle it was the High Line Canal, an irrigation channel that runs along the tattered edges of the Great Plains and through the local suburbs on the backside of Denver. The length and breadth of this canal became his playground and schoolroom, offering him an "imaginary wilderness, escape hatch, and birthplace as a naturalist." It later became his "holy ground of solace" (p. xvi). This canal was his place of

initiation, the spot that taught him to explore the world, to examine it closely, and to take care of it. A sense of place permeates his work: "Place is what takes me out of myself, out of the limited scope of human activity, but this is not misanthropic. A sense of place is a way of embracing humanity among all of its neighbors. It is an *entry* into the larger world" (personal interview, 1994).

The first thing that Pyle loved upon entering the world of nature was the butterfly. Butterfly watching may have made him a social outcast at times among his teenage peers, but he never abandoned the activity because of social pressure, and finally he was rewarded for his loyalty. As he writes in *Handbook for Butterfly Watchers*,

> Personal peace is hard to find in the frenetic world we have made. Yet for me, no moments are more peaceful than those I spend among the butterflies, whether in Edenic landscapes or vacant lots. From my own experience, I commend spending time with the gentle, beguiling butterflies to anyone with tension to dissipate or stress to dispel. . . . I have found nature study, and in particular the contemplation of butterflies, to be the best tonic in my own search for serenity. (p. 7)

Butterflies became his eidolon in the contemporary landscape. Butterfly watching and collecting also gave him that sense of otherness, of being an outsider, that has distinguished many twentieth-century writers. His combination of idealism, independence, and literary persistence brought Pyle acclaim as an authority on butterflies. *Watching Washington Butterflies* was published in 1974, *The Audubon Society Field Guide to North American Butterflies* in 1981, and *The Audubon Society Handbook for Butterfly Watchers* in 1984 (reissued in 1992 as *Handbook for Butterfly Watchers*).

His youthful experiences along the High Line Canal also led him toward his conservationist's principles by making him aware of humble pieces of the earth, such as the damaged landscapes outside of Denver or in the Willapa Hills of Washington State. His best books are memoirs of place, love songs to wasted and scarred landscapes—clear-cut forests, stripped hillsides, neglected rivers. His conservationist ideals are memorably expressed in *Wintergreen: Rambles in a Ravaged Land* (1986) and in *The Thunder Tree*.

Wintergreen

Wintergreen is the story of Pyle's adult home-ground, the Willapa Hills of western Washington. It is a collection of sixteen essays that focuses equally on the "rain world," the creatures that inhabit it, mankind's effect on the ecology of the area, and finally the natives and naturalists who cherish it and make their lives on it. The Willapa Hills—bounded by the Olympic Mountains to the north, the Cascades to the east, and the Oregon coast and the Columbia River to the west and south—are a metaphor for wasted lands everywhere: "The woods of Willapa have been ravaged, along with its soils, rivers, and communities. It's a simple tale in many ways—great trees gone, boomtowns busted, fragments of forests struggling toward a kind of recovery, only to be logged again, too much, too fast" (*Wintergreen*, p. 146).

Willapa is the sort of anonymous and exploited environment that Pyle seems to have a particular affection for, a place without national forests or parks to protect it from the onslaughts of corporate greed. The Willapas have been stripped, the hills scarred, the rivers polluted. Pyle raises the moral argument that humanity has a responsibility to the earth, a responsibility to live *with*, not merely *on*, the planet:

> These are understated hills, not very high, made of lavas and mud, and nothing more. The fact that they once supported one of the greatest forests on earth is beside the point since that forest isn't there anymore—it's gone to sunken ships, secondhand furniture, derelict buildings, and yellowed newsprint. These are devastated hills, doing their best to recover, to grow green things in time for the next devastation. A ravaged land, awaiting the next ravages. It is no wilderness; and yet it is wild and elusive. (p. 29)

Pyle sees much beauty in the rivers and streams of this landscape. Growing up in dry Colorado, Pyle was mesmerized by his mother's stories of the moist Northwest. His grandparents, pioneer teachers in Washington, reinforced his "visions of a viscid, verdant place, dripping with mosses and ferns" (*Wintergreen*, p. 16). It is therefore only logical that he loves this wintergreen world, where streams and the ocean collaborate with the clouds to create a soggy landscape, where winter drips into a stretched-out spring "on a carpet of deeping green." Even the narrowest rivulet has something in common with the wide Columbia River: both drain the green sponge of the land. The streams allow the land to bear the burden of four meters of rainfall per year. It is a water-based ecological cycle—rain falling onto already damp soil and into rivers, river flowing into the sea, the sun drawing moisture into clouds, and then the cycle beginning all over again. The problem is that human hands have affected that pattern by cutting the trees that hold back erosion, dumping wastes, and damming rivers.

The activities of the logging companies affect the populations of species, such as bears, by eliminating the types of trees that bears feed on. Rather than attempting to supply the bears with alternative food sources, the companies engage in pogroms, hiring professional hunters or paying bounties. What these companies fail to acknowledge is an obligation to maintain the region's ecological balance:

> Bears should be viewed as a contribution to the vitality of the forest. If they entail costs to those privileged to harvest the forest resource, then the cost must be borne. Black bears should be a part of every working forest in Washington. Those glorious forests that built the industry should have all their working parts intact—that's how they were made in the first place. (p. 203)

But *Wintergreen* is not so much about the destruction of the Willapas as it is about the value of such a place, even in its diminished state. Pyle tries to appreciate the landscape for what it is now, he says, without focusing mournfully on what it once was. The heart of the book emphasizes the continuing worth and beauty of the Willapas and the surrounding area. The rivers still have "wild miles of green gorge walls and blue water-scooped holes" (p. 50). The flora of the area is varied, "all panels and pleats in the curtain of the forest fabric" (p. 72). Pyle discovers everything from bluebells and hound's-tongues to irises and water lentils, and although the tree species are fewer than in Costa Rica or even Connecticut, there are two or three thousand fungi and hundreds of mosses, lichens, and liverworts to make up a diverse green tapestry. There are also spiders, which are insects that disturb Pyle, and slugs, which fascinate him. In discussing spiders and slugs, Pyle joins the personal and the biological to make sense of both his fear and his attraction to certain species. In his careful examination of what he sees as the beautiful and the fearful in nature, he comes to a balanced perspective: "Both visions give me exactly the same reward—a solid sense of pleasure from beauty, fascination with form, and wonder at the elegance of evolution—as infatuation and phobia blend into equanimity toward all nature" (p. 99).

His first love, though, is butterflies, and he finds enough of them in the Gray's River area to satisfy his passion. He describes them with a loving specificity that is reminiscent of Annie Dillard in *Pilgrim at Tinker Creek* (1974), as in this description of white wings observed among plants:

> I recall one female I spied in the act, her body dusted with pollen, so heavy with eggs that she pulled the flowers nearly to the ground as she clambered among them. I feared that she might impale herself on a bramble thorn like a thick, stubby insect pin under her own weight. But she didn't and eventually she took wing in search of bleeding-heart foliage for her eggs, as if treading water on the hot summer air, so fat in her fecundity she could barely fly. (p. 108)

Pyle finds much to love in the wounded area of the Willapas. There are newts, coyotes, raccoons, opossums, moles, beavers, ducks, flickers, juncoes, and towhees. As a man who feels he owes his life to a hollow tree that saved him from a hailstorm, Pyle has a special affection for such pieces of the forest, "those mossy, rotting, wonderful stumps" (p. 232). A stump is also home to sword ferns and lichens, moss and foxglove, herbs and yellow violets. A sharp eye might see shamrocks or tiny mints. Pyle sees it as a microcosmic environment: "If a collecting party from another planet sought to bring back a single sample most reflective of our ecosystem, they could do worse than to select a fine stump" (p. 226). He even suggests that stumps are one more good reason to set aside the last of the old pristine forest, so that there will be a continuing supply of snags, hollow trees, and nurse logs for weevils, woodpeckers, and stump lovers.

For Pyle nothing in nature is useless or without beauty. Everything has its purpose. Even the big, old wolf trees, those left behind by the logging companies as "witness trees," stand for something, although they might not stand for much longer because of man's destructiveness. Pyle argues that the remaining old-growth forests provide more than just a habitat for certain endangered creatures. Such forests add to the human spirit: "The old-growth forests are important because they remind us of what the world can be in the absence of our hubris; and what it could be again if restoration were to outpace destruction" (personal interview, 1995). As Pyle says in *Wintergreen*, "What's left is not enough but it's all we've got, and nothing less than all of it will do" (p. 197). When Pyle writes about the stripped forests, damaged rivers, and the endangered wildlife, his anger sometimes rises to a polemical pitch, but usually his voice is filled with delight, as if, like Wordsworth, he finds "strength in what remains behind." There is still for Pyle a splendor in the grass and a glory in the flower. *Wintergreen* concludes with a description of the seasons as they come to the Pacific Northwest, where "the gentle influence of the sea wins out" (p. 283). The book ends with the winter rain pelting the bruised hills, bringing a promise of recovery to the land, a renewed greenness. Pyle is ready for the new year: "ready for the brand-new calendar without a mark upon it; like a fresh white page, ready to be written, the year itself stretches out before me" (p. 252).

The Thunder Tree

The Thunder Tree: Lessons from an Urban Wildland is different from *Wintergreen* in that it is about the nature of self as well as about nature. In this memoir of place Pyle focuses on the High Line Canal in Denver to dramatize his belief that human identity is directly linked to habitation and geography. A collection of twelve essays divided into four sections, *The Thunder Tree* interrelates the nature and history of his boyhood canal with his own upbringing and discovery of his vocation as a naturalist. Pyle believes that everyone who learns to respond to the earth discovers this lesson as he did—in a particular spot, often an ordinary piece of ground, a ditch, or a scruffy cluster of trees.

Robert Michael Pyle

The Thunder Tree begins with Pyle's epiphanic anecdote about an excursion he took with his older brother, Tom, in July of 1954. Looking for adventure they hiked from their suburban home in Hoffman Heights, on the outskirts of Denver, and headed for the High Line Canal. Soon after they reached the canal, lightning scratched the sky and thunder boomed in the distance. Next came hail the size of marbles, pounding down on them, ricocheting off their arms and faces, breaking eyeglasses, causing welts. In an old hollow cottonwood tree, once struck by lightning, they found sanctuary. Pyle and his bother came to call this poplar that had, as Pyle says, "surely saved our lives," the "thunder tree."

Appropriately enough, Pyle's book becomes an attempt to repay that debt, to save some small piece of the wildland. It is a plea to "keep the canals, the weedy fields between the mile roads . . . for these are the holdfast of the land in the hurricane of change" (p. 109). Pyle's voice is like the voice of the canary, the bird that the miners used to take down into the shafts to announce by its melancholy chirp that the air was no longer safe. Pyle is announcing that if we are to live, we must find a way of living with nature. He suggests we must not merely consider our rights as humans but also consider the rights of the voiceless but necessary elements of our world— be they watercourses, butterflies, or aged cottonwoods. He subscribes to Wendell Berry's opinion that "ignorance of when to stop is a modern epidemic" (personal interview, 1994). In Pyle's view, we ignore the natural and practical limits of human growth at our own serious risk. If we continue in the same purblind fashion, Pyle implies, we are headed toward a loss of experience, an exhaustion, entropy.

One of the most dramatic points he makes in *The Thunder Tree* concerns the extinction of experience. When we lose a species of animal or plant, even on the local level, we lose experience. Pyle notes that while many people are concerned about the global, or absolute, extinction of a species, few seem aware that local extinction is a serious problem with significant consequences. First, local extinctions affect "edge" populations, marginal species unable to adapt to environmental changes. Second, small losses soon add up to much larger ones. It often is only a short step from local extinction to the endangering of a species. Third, and perhaps most important, local loss means an extinction of experience for the people of the locality:

> Simply stated, the loss of neighborhood species endangers our experience of nature. If a species becomes extinct without our own radius of reach (smaller for the very old, very young, disabled, and poor), it might as well be gone altogether, in one important sense. To those whose access suffers by it, local extinction has much the same result as global eradication. (p. 145)

Local extinction is one more form of alienation. Already, as Pyle says, we lack a widespread intimacy with the natural world. Local extinction makes the gulf between humans and plants and animals even wider. And if it is the experience of place, particularly in the natural world, as Pyle contends, that makes us who we are, then this loss is truly a loss of self. Pyle underscores this idea by reflecting on his upbringing:

> Had it not been for the High Canal, the vacant lots I knew, the scruffy park, I'm not at all certain I would have been a biologist. I might have become a lawyer, or even a Lutheran. The total immersion in nature that I found in my special spots baptized me in a faith that never wavered, but it was a matter of happenstance too. It was the place that made me. (p. 152)

Pyle's point is that not only the wilderness but also our more localized and circumscribed natural areas must be preserved. Although he can be dramatic and beautifully descriptive in his writing, Pyle is essentially an unembarrassed editorialist for the voiceless in nature. He slips out of his narrative as readily as Henry Fielding does in *Tom Jones*, to speak directly and eloquently to his readers:

> If we are to forge new links to the land, we must resist the extinction of experience. We must save not only the wilderness but the vacant lots, the ditches as well as the canyonlands, and the woodlots along with the old growth. We must become believers in the world. (p. 152)

Pyle follows his own advice: he believes in the worth of the meanest flower that grows. Though he seems to feel, as the apostle Paul did, that we know only in part, he also believes that we are a part of what we know. Pyle's knowledge of the natural world, and it is extensive, is inextricably linked to his knowledge of himself. The botanical story he tells in *The Thunder Tree* of the cottonwoods *Populus sargentii*—which has heart-shaped leaves, an erect trunk, and the profile of an English oak—merges indiscernibly with the tale of his hiding from a storm in the belly of a hollow cottonwood. Even his scientific discussion of butterflies blends naturally into his recounting of his experiences with his mother and father, with his parents' divorce, with their deaths, and with his own social humiliations as a young man. In every case it is nature that points the way:

> We may imagine that we lead, but almost always we follow. . . . We still follow rivers and canals. We mark the ways of water and mimic its progress. We find our ways where we can: a gully, a narrow gorge, a green-brown stripe of winter wheat furrow; a sequence of steps from some foregone conclusion, a deer trail, a rabbit path; an imaginary line to the horizon or a crease in an old map, more alluring than any highway, blue or red: something, anyway, that draws the eye and points the foot. (p. 96)

Pyle's life has been one of looking for places where nature would lead him, always searching even amid the ruins for signs, however humble, of his connection to the world around him.

Conclusion

Robert Michael Pyle is a scientist, naturalist, essayist, and writer, but most profoundly he is an advocate for nature. From a very early age he was fascinated with what Charles Darwin called "the tangled bank." He has been influenced by a variety of voices, Darwin's in particular for its grace and knowledge. Edwin Way Teale, Gavin Maxwell, Kim R. Stafford, and Ann Zwinger he admires, but he also respects the nature observations of non-naturalists such as John Updike and the Supreme Court justice William O. Douglas. For Pyle, "Nature writing is everything. It is all-encompassing. True nature writers address themselves to the world. Eudora Welty and Thomas Hardy are nature writers too" (personal interview, 1994).

As a nature advocate, Pyle is a campaigner and a reformer: "I grew up as a conservationist in the 1960s. That comes out in my writing. However, my larger purpose is to persuade the reader to look more closely at the land. Ultimately, I want to find my themes in the narratives" (personal interview, 1994). Always, his story is about the land and how we find our humanity in a tender relationship with it. Pyle clearly and eloquently summarizes his philosophy in his essay "Receding from Grief" (1994):

> I believe that all the sadness in the world belongs to us. The land does not grieve. But as long as we live on the land, and among others, we shall know a state of permanent grief, for loss is continual, and always with us. After all, we are mortal. And as Aldo Leopold reminded us, the penalty of knowing nature is to live in a "world of wounds."
>
> Yet there is a balm, and it comes from the same source. F. Scott Fitzgerald, in *Tender Is the Night*, wrote that "Receding from a grief, it seems necessary to retrace the same steps that brought us there." That way is out, to the land, and love. (p. 3)

For Robert Michael Pyle, a love of the land and of all the creatures that inhabit it is the way to our own best and most human nature.

Selected Bibliography

WORKS OF ROBERT MICHAEL PYLE

BOOKS

Watching Washington Butterflies (Seattle: Seattle Audubon Society, 1974); *The Audubon Society Field Guide to North American Butterflies* (New York: Knopf, 1981); *Handbook for Butterfly Watchers* (Boston: Houghton Mifflin, 1992), repr. of *The Audubon Society Handbook for Butterfly Watchers* (New York: Scribners, 1984); *Wintergreen: Rambles in a Ravaged Land* (New York: Scribners 1986), repr. as *Wintergreen: Listening to the Land's Heart* (Boston: Houghton Mifflin, 1988); *The Thunder Tree: Lessons from an Urban Wildland* (Boston: Houghton Mifflin, 1993); *Where Bigfoot Walks* (Boston: Houghton Mifflin, 1995).

CO-AUTHORED BOOKS

Butterflies: A Peterson Field Guide Coloring Book, with R. T. Peterson and S. A. Hughes (Boston: Houghton Mifflin, 1983); *The IUCN Invertebrate Red Data Book*, with Susan M. Wells and N. Mark Collins (Gland, Switzerland: World Wildlife Fund, 1983); *Insects: A Peterson Field Guide Coloring Book*, with Kristin Kest (Boston: Houghton Mifflin, 1993).

SELECTED ESSAYS

"Death Row," in *Audubon* (November 1970); "Is There Wilderness in Western Europe," in *Living Wilderness* (winter 1970); "Can We Save Our Wild Places from Our Civilized Public," in *American West* (March 1972); "Butterflies and the National Parks," in *National Parks and Conservation Magazine* (spring 1975); "Silk Moth of the Railroad Yards: With Biographical Sketch," in *Natural History* (May 1975); "Bramble Patch Trap," in *Horticulture* (August 1976); "City Wildlife," in *Horticulture* (January 1977); "Butterflies: Now You See Them . . ." in *International Wildlife* (January/February 1981); "The Joy of Butterflying," in *Audubon* (July 1984); "Spineless Wonders," in *International Wildlife* (September/October 1989); "A Ditch in Time," in *Audubon* (March 1993); "Receding from Grief," in *Orion* 13 (winter 1994).

INTERVIEWS

Personal interviews with the author (1994, 1995).

BIOGRAPHICAL AND CRITICAL STUDIES

Andre Stepankowsky, "Metamorphosis of a Naturalist," in *Washington* magazine (July/August 1987); Jane Elder Wulff, "Dr. Robert Michael Pyle: A Meticulous Observer of Life," in *Peninsula* (fall 1992).

DAVID QUAMMEN
(b. 1948)

MARILYN CHANDLER McENTYRE

THE CRITIC Harold Bloom once addressed a large and distinguished university audience on the important of what he called "lunatic juxtapositions" in providing insight and generating creative thought. Such constructs allow apparently unrelated ideas and experiences to encounter one another and cross-pollinate, thus freeing the mind from the deeply cut channels of method and system and bringing into question what has seemed comfortably "known." In David Quammen's startling essays on what he calls "science and nature," his self-described "sidelong views" of the behavior, adaptiveness, and importance of the animals to whose lives and needs he draws our attention are triangulated frequently through the worlds of literature (as in "Sanctuary: William Faulkner and the California Condor"), art, and philosophy (as in "Jeremy Bentham, the *Pietà*, and a Precious Few Grayling"). An essay on "semelparity" (reproduction that takes place only once in certain species and results in death) takes a flying leap from popular culture to seventeenth-century poetry before it reaches the topic of biology.

David Quammen, born on 24 February 1948 in Cincinnati, Ohio, to W. A. and Mary (Egan) Quammen, was a Rhodes Scholar and a Guggenheim fellow. Quammen has been practicing leaps of imagination and landing on new islands of insight since 1981, as a freelance writer and as a contributing editor and writer of the "Natu-

ral Acts" column in *Outside* magazine, writing from Montana, his home since 1973. "I'm not a scientist," he reminds us in the introduction to his first collection of essays, *Natural Acts: A Sidelong View of Nature and Science* (1985): "I merely *follow* science" (p. xiv). The "merely" hardly does justice to the luminous originality, integrity, and usefulness of Quammen's scientific journalism. It does place him, along with Annie Dillard, John McPhee, and a host of other humanists, as an "outsider who is broadly curious," whose gift to the general reader is to make science accessible, compelling, and, not least important, entertaining. The range of publications in which Quammen's work has appeared testifies to its wide appeal. These include *Audubon, Esquire,. Harper's, New York Times Book Review*, and *Rolling Stone*, as well as *Outside*. Most easily classified as a "nature writer," Quammen, who majored in English at Yale and did graduate work on Faulkner at Oxford, has also published three novels and a collection of short fiction. His love of story informs his essays especially by means of anecdotes. His fans wait for his next piece in much the same spirit of proprietary expectancy as the London public is said to have awaited the weekly installments of Dickens's serialized novels. They look forward to a venture into some corner of the natural world or of scientific history with a guide whose habit of "constructive disorientation" interrelates an omnivorous curiosity with irreverence and rigorous journalistic and scientific accuracy.

Intent and Method

"I want to find ways to raise questions that get people to examine their presumptions," Quammen explained in a personal interview. One way he does that is to disestablish the genre of "nature writing." The primary focus of most of his essays is either a particular species of animal (occasionally a plant, as in the essay that begins by describing a particular tree in midtown Manhattan), a scientist (sometimes a mad scientist or pseudo-scientist) and his work and methods, or an environment (such as a section of tropical forest, an island, or a river valley). Once he has fastened himself to some branch of the scientific tree of knowledge, he weaves a web of historical, literary, mythical, folkloric, and personal connections that is rich with detail, humor, and surprise. The surprise often comes in the form of a question: What sort of life is it, to be an urban tree? How can durian both taste good and smell bad? Why don't owls have penises? Sometimes it comes as a bold or paradoxical proposition that serves as a trailhead, promising to lead us, if we will trust our guide, from apparent nonsense to sense and sometimes into wide reflection. Thus one essay in *Natural Acts* begins, "What this world needs is a good vicious sixty-foot-long Amazon snake" ("Rumors of a Snake"). And another, "A jellyfish is something much more than the sum of its parts, but that hasn't always been so" ("A Republic of Cockroaches"). Even as a biographer he can't always resist the impulse to begin with a slight jolt: " 'I don't give a shit *what* killed the dinosaurs,' says John R. Horner" ("The Excavation of Jack Horner").

Quammen has a love for the extended metaphor that links his habit of mind with that of the metaphysical poets (such as John Donne) whom he occasionally invokes, and an eye for the homely simile (a tarantula he sees has legs "the size of Bic pens"; a spider's eggsac is "the size of a Milk Dud"). Occasionally he indulges his fond-

ness for campy melodrama: "a decidedly ugly and disheartening prospect: our entire dear planet—after the final close of all human business—ravaged and overrun by great multitudes of cockroaches, whole plagues of them, whole scuttering herds shoulder to shoulder like the old herds of bison, vast cockroach legions sweeping as inexorably as driver ants over the empty prairies" (*Natural Acts*, p. 53).

Sometimes his observations of a particular animal assume philosophical or ethical dimensions. For example, he came to believe that experiments with talking chimpanzees question "some of the fundamental assumptions of Western culture, demanding new and careful thoughts on . . . the proper conduct of relations between mankind and other species" (p. 21). In a column on Washoe (*Outside*, July 1986), the chimpanzee who learned to use sign language not only imitatively but intentionally, Quammen details the close, emotionally varied, and cognitively sophisticated relationship Washoe had with his trainer and brings us, a little uncomfortably, to the question, What is a person?:

> "Person" . . . is an eloquent word, a richly connotative word, and one well suited for use in exactly that foggy no-man's land between humanity and the rest of the biological community. I think it's a word that is wasted if judged to be merely a synonym for *Homo sapiens*. To me it seems that a person is any creature with whom you—or I, or Roger Fouts [Washoe's trainer]—can have a heartfelt and mutual relationship." (pp. 25, 28)

Fouts and Washoe, he reflects in closing, "seem to have discovered something far more precious, and far more communicative, than language" (p. 28). Although his implied elevation of the chimp's status might easily be critiqued on a number of grounds, the question Quammen raises here about personhood is no sentimental anthropomorphism; it concerns the very basis of our ethical reasoning, our relationship to other species, and thus our place in nature.

The question of identity takes on a certain comical twist in essays like "The Selfhood of a

Spoon Worm" and "The Face of a Spider" (in *The Flight of the Iguana*, 1988), in which Quammen asks repeatedly, "How should a human behave toward the members of other living species?" He points out that most people who ask that question are focusing their attention on the " 'upper' end of the 'ladder' of life" (p. 6). Shifting the focus to the lower end, "down there among the mosquitoes and worms and black widow spiders" (p. 6), makes it trickier because it stretches us to the limits—and sometimes beyond—of our capacities for empathy and imagination. His prescription in the case of spiders, whom he confesses to regard with fear and loathing, is to settle the moral dilemma "To squash or not to squash" (p. 6) by making prolonged eye contact with "the beast, the Other" (p. 7), before taking action:

> No kidding, now, I mean get down on your hands and knees right there in the vegetable garden, and look that snail in the face. Lock eyes with that bull snake. Trade stares with the carp. Gaze for a moment into the many-faceted eyes—the windows to its soul—of the house fly, as it licks its way innocently across your kitchen counter. Look for signs of embarrassment or rancor or guilt. Repeat the following formula silently, like a mantra: "This is some mother's darling, this is some mother's child." *Then* kill if you will, or if it seems you must. (p. 7)

Behind the humor lies a humane ethics that is entirely unsentimental. In the same essay he insists, "I hold no brief for *ahimsa*" (p. 6), the extreme position represented most purely among India's Jains that one may not kill any living being. Quammen believes that moral responsibility involves honoring ambiguity, recognizing the complex weave of natural determination and human consciousness, and confronting as squarely as possible precisely those convenient categories that ensure one's sense of safety.

That ethical questions he raises are often philosophical curve balls, coming frequently from unexpected directions. Certainly Quammen is concerned with those central and urgent ethical dilemmas that define and unite what may

David Quammen

loosely be known as the "environmental movement," but he also pauses to consider the ethics of domestic dog ownership (isn't the life of many if not most urban and suburban dogs a study in unnatural restraint and neglect and in long-term loss of dignity for creatures bred to short-sighted human ends?), daring to throw darts at one of the most sacred of American icons, "man's best friend."

When Quammen raises a biological question, he rarely confines himself to a biological answer. One of his gifts as a writer is his profoundly interdisciplinary thinking. The appreciation of all modes of knowledge manifested in the essays might also be seen as large-hearted. Certainly there are moments of insight in many of his pieces that seem occasioned by emotional involvement and commitment—Quammen is, as Richard Wilbur once put it in his poem "The Eye," a "giver of due regard." The poem that contains this line is a petition for the grace to recognize beauty even in what we conventionally dismiss as ugly, deformed, or grotesque; in it the poet prays, "Charge me to see in all bodies the beat of spirit." Quammen sees and asks us to see that "beat of spirit" in the curious forms of animal behavior, in the ingenuities of creaturely adaptation, in the poetic and scientific imagination that allows us always to look again and see differently and deepen our understanding and enliven our curiosity.

In is this kind of seeing that makes Quammen's work so much more than scientific reporting. One principle he learned from a practiced animal tracker is "Learn to *see* before you think" (*Outside*, December 1986, p. 29). To do this is to resist the impulse to classify, categorize, hypothesize, or superimpose conventions on the thing observed—to allow for ontological indeterminacy and uniqueness before bringing the being or event into the comfort zone of comprehensibility. Once Quammen does begin to think, he works from observation to inference with both lucidity and ambiguity, involving his readers in complex moral reasoning without sermonizing and using life stories and biographical portraits as a means of promoting alternative perspectives and fighting the tide of homogeneous thinking. He teaches and models a contemplative habit of mind, passionate reverence for life, and commitment to intelligent and discerning conservation that resists the dangerous oversimplifications afflicting popular environmentalism.

Influences and Confluences

All these qualities contribute to and derive from habits of good writing. It is not insignificant that Quammen started his career on a literary path and spent his undergraduate and graduate years at Yale and Oxford in the grip of an enduring fascination with Faulkner, that wry, romantic, irreverent, and sometimes unscrupulous weaver of tales who eludes easy judgments or conclusions. "I was obsessed with Faulkner for years," he recalls. "You'll recognize his influence in my first novel, *Blood Line* [1988]" (personal interview). Faulknerian themes inform Quammen's interest in metaphor, parable, and metaphysics. For example, Quammen's essay on the chambered nautilus, a sea creature and the subject of a meditative poem ("The Chambered

Nautilus") by Oliver Wendell Holmes, invokes Faulknerian images of memory and mortality. "The Siphuncle: Chambers of Memory in the Ocean of Time" (in *The Flight of the Iguana*) brings together the story of Faulkner's death and Faulkner's notion of the presence of the past in its portrayal of the chambered nautilus as an embodiment of its own history. Quammen sees a penetration backward in space and time in the nautilus's series of sealed chambers, which are accumulated over time, and in their connection through the nautiloid siphuncle, "a conduit of blood and memory" (p. 261). Unusually confessional, the piece includes reflections on Quammen's own history and losses as sealed chambers of memory. The anatomy and physiology of the nautilus, precisely and scientifically described as an ingeniously designed buoyancy system wherein each sealed chamber contributes versatility, lends itself to parable, suggesting how we are borne up, sheltered, and accompanied by the past—how, as Quammen puts it, we accumulate our own "compartmented phases" and live with our pasts in ways that may either enlarge our worlds or contract them. There is no sure way to assess the present effects of the past or to take the measure of what we call "maturity," but, he concludes, "memory believes before knowing remembers. And the past lives coiled within the present, beyond sight, beyond revocation, lifting us up or weighting us down, sealed away—almost completely—behind walls of pearl" (p. 269).

Quammen's didactic impulses come out clearly in essays taking on the biological and ecological issues that have become the ante in high stakes political games. Here his characteristic love of the large and long view is fueled by an urgency that he shares with most environmental activists. Some of his most complex and artful writing may be found in the essays that combine his usual appeals to scientific curiosity and the story-making, story-loving imagination with a direct invocation of social conscience. For instance, "It's a Long River with a Long History" (1990), an ambitious essay on the Rio Grande, entwines three distinct narratives offering a multidimensional portrait of the river in terms of particular individuals and of agricultural, geological, political, and cultural issues. He starts with a wide-angle view of his subject:

It's a long river with a long history and a vast, confused inventory of contemporary problems, a river that winds out across centuries and cultures, draining one ecosystem through another into a third. Choked by dams and lakes, dividing neighbors in hatred, and forming a national boundary, the river is drawn in a wavering thin line from the depths of America's past into the present, and from the aspens of highland Colorado to the sabal palms of coastal Texas. (p. 68)

From here Quammen cuts to a scene from an abortive canoe trip down the river, in which a bent and broken canoe and gear is described as tossing around in the water. The writer is in his own kayak, safe. His guides stand, frustrated and dripping, on a small spit of sand. Written in the second person, the piece invites the reader to "imagine if you will . . ." The journalist sitting in his kayak on this ill-fated voyage, looking at the river as an obstacle, considers his responsibilities: "Lot of help you are. Then again, you're a journalist and not, anymore, a river guide" (p. 68). Interspersed between the close-up of the canoe trip and the epic tale of the river's history and fate are biographical sketches of individuals whose work to save the ecosystems and the human communities along that river from slow and certain destruction gives some perspective on what is being, and what must be, done to avert disaster.

Thus Clair Reiniger, a landscape architect from Harvard, is introduced, a citizen advocate for the Pueblo and Hispanic poor and mediator between those communities and the corporate entities who want their water rights. She is a champion of bioregional thinking, arguing that the American West should have been organized according to water drainages instead of state boundaries, since out there "water drives everything" (p. 74). Later Nita Fuller, biologist and associate manager of national wildlife refuges for Arizona and New Mexico, is featured. Quammen's interview with her furnishes an explana-

tion of the corridor theory, a plan initiated by the U.S. Fish and Wildlife Service, the Texas Department of Parks and Wildlife, and a loose coalition of private conservation groups: "If all these fragments of habitat, with their various ecological communities and their various ownerships, can just be linked together into a continuous corridor along the Lower Rio Grande, Fuller explains, the doom that otherwise awaits certain insularized species can perhaps be evaded" (p. 79).

Her message of hope counterbalances a sobering account of the problems of the beleaguered river valley, fallen prey, like so many other areas rich in resources, to short-sighted commodification. The river's recent history is of dams, water wars, and water shortages. As water was redistributed to growing urban centers in the Southwest, it became increasingly expensive: "Around the Santa Fe area these days, an acre-foot worth of water rights can be sold for as much as $10,000, or leased away even more lucratively" (p. 70). Economic pressure on local communities to sell water rights grew intense: "If a person or a community happened to have more water than money, they ought to be willing (even eager) to sell. Correct? . . . That came to be the commanding syllogism in modern, and ever-more-urban, New Mexico" (p. 73). "Out here in the Southwest," he goes on to say, "people like quoting a certain cynical adage: 'Water flows uphill to money'" (p. 73).

In the essay, the story of the canoe trip begins to assume parabolic significance in relation to the biological, geological, and cultural survival of the river valley and its inhabitants. The writer reflects upon his own responsibilities, recognizing his role in bringing about the canoe accident: he wanted to speed down the river. Yet, he comes to think, because the river takes its own time to form and flow, one is in some quite literal way wrong to foreshorten an experience, to "push the river." In the moment of this realization he sees a tarantula just before he might have stepped on it. He takes this incident, somewhat whimsically, as an omen.

The battle to preserve a wildlife refuge along the lower Rio Grande and to save a continuous corridor of ecosystem there "is crucial not just for the sake of the ocelot, or the Texas indigo snake, but because it's the same battle that will soon be fought everywhere" (p. 77). Quammen modulates this sobering reflection into a personal note that ties together the parts of this rich river story with a final shot of the canoeing party:

> Your head and your notebooks and your clothes have become filled with the multiplicity of this river. Many of the images you have gathered, many of the facts, are sad and ugly. Along much of its length the Rio Grande is defeated. Along much, it is abused. In some places it is just gone. But by good fortune you have experienced also a place called The Tight Squeeze in a canyon called Mariscal, beneath thousand-foot walls of Cretaceous limestone, where in defiance of all other reality the Rio Grande is still a proud untamed river, muscled and dangerous, capable of flattening human hubris. (p. 79)

The last word, "hubris," links this story to the Greek view of tragedy, which has deeply informed Western thought with its relation of individual ambition and communal, social, and metaphysical responsibilities. This kind of appeal to cultural legacies, to the imagination, and to compassion sounds the final note in Quammen's most powerful essays.

Subject Matter

Quammen is a writer with a remarkable sensitivity to the qualities and traits that distinguish individual people and places. It would be hard to find a portrait more full of tenderness and appreciation of another's gifts than Quammen's piece on Bedo, a local naturalist in Madagascar who was only twenty years old when he was murdered under mysterious circumstances. Quammen's feature piece in *Audubon* on Bedo, "A Murder in Madagascar," weaves together his reflections on the fate of endangered species in the fragmented tropical forests of Madagascar with stories of human and environmental inter-

dependence, a relationship that has been dangerously underestimated and disrupted.

The essay starts like a mystery novel: "At first there was uncertainty about whether this murder had actually happened. Some of the young man's friends, who got third-hand news of the killing across 12,000 miles of bad telephone connection, harbored a feeble hope that perhaps Bedo wasn't dead. His body hadn't been found. Maybe he had merely gone missing" (p. 50). The victim in question was "one of the most talented young naturalists on this troubled, otherworldly island off the east coast of Africa, with its hungry and fast-growing human population, its shrinking areas of tropical forest, its astonishing abundance of plant and animal species found nowhere else on Earth" (p. 50).

The essay has three keynotes: uniqueness, attunement, and mystery. Madagascar is almost unique in being "one of the last great reservoirs . . . of genetic and ecological diversity" (p. 50). One of its unique indigenous animals is a kind of lemur, the indri. Indri are monogamous, live in nuclear family groups; the young stay with their parents for as long as eight years. The haunting song of the indri carries about a mile: "It sounds like a cross between the call of a humpback whale and a saxophone solo by Charlie Parker. It may be one of the most beautiful and bizarre noises in all nature" (p. 51). No one knows for sure what it communicates; possibly a warning cry, it could also be used for territorial spacing between adjacent groups or for conveying information about the availability of young adults. The indri's song has been studied with "a real-time sound-spectrum analyzer, whatever that is," but Quammen prefers to document it in more humanistic fashion: "Listen with merely your ears, your heart, and you are more likely to hear the saxophone and the whale" (p. 51).

Attunement is the second keynote in the essay: Bedo's "attunement to the ecosystem was preternatural" (p. 53). The song of the indri blends with the particular sounds of its habitat to create a harmonic texture rich with meaning. Hearing the call of the indri, Bedo's "face lit in a special way. His face lit, I think, with love" (p. 53). Bedo's "identification with his environment influenced Quammen's own pursuit of scientific understanding. Quammen learned that knowledge without love is an empty thing and that love is enacted in the curiosity and attention that look for information and allow for mystery.

Mystery is the third keynote. Hoping to find out why Bedo was murdered, Quammen traveled to Madagascar and interviewed everyone he could find who had any connection to the boy or the event. The search yielded little:

> There didn't seem to be any facts, aside from the stark one that Bedo was dead. In place of facts, there was testimony. There were human voices. Angry ones, grief-weary ones, defensive ones. They spoke in French and in English and in Malagasy. I didn't discover truth; I collected versions. . . . I listened to the story ten or eleven times, in three languages, with and without help from a translator. Each time it was different. In Madagascar, as Alison Jolly [an indri biologist] warned me, 'things immediately move into the realm of myth. Usually within about a day." (pp. 57–58)

Speculation and unanswered questions surround and sometimes overtake events filtered through the meaning-making medium of village gossip.

Quammen's speculations on the causes of Bedo's death conflate finally with his speculations on the various causes of the gradual extinction of the indri. Some of the blame may lie with the foreign biologists and tourists who "paid handsomely for his skills, disturbing the equilibrium of his world" (p. 58). Bedo's nickname is "*babakoto*," also the nickname of the indri, which means "cousin to man." Our kinship with this "cousin" is not, he reminds us, so distant as we might like to think.

Quammen's interest in claiming that kinship as a way of revising common attitudes toward the nonhuman animal world informs many of his essays. He frequently highlights a species that possesses some quality or habit—some capacity for language or song or creative thought—that we like to think of as human. In this way, too, he attacks hubris and what he calls "xenophobia"—a term that he acknowledges refers most often to fear of foreignness among humans, but which Quammen extends to include fear of "nonhuman characters with the wrong number of legs or eyes, the wrong shape of face or jaws, the wrong sexual or alimentary deportment" (*The Flight of the Iguana*, p. x).

One form such hubris takes is the creationists' revered "proof-by-design"—the argument that the design of nature verifies a beneficent view of the Creator and His intentions. Quammen's response to this essentially anthropocentric argument is the African bedbug, a creature whose habits offer, he believes, a striking and embarrassing counterexample. At his comic best in "Nasty Habits: An African Bedbug Rebuts the Proof-by-Design" (*Outside*, February 1987), Quammen details the sexual practices of these creatures in appallingly human terms: sado-masochistic stabbing, hetero- and homosexual raping, and possessive sealing of female genitals as typical expressions of male bedbug sexual competition for maximum gene transmission. His sublimely ridiculous exposure of anthropocentric and anthropomorphic thinking concludes generously with an open-minded theological speculation that separates the Creator from the creationists: "My own instinct is to agree with Yogi Berra. If God does exist, He or She is probably patient enough to take the long view" (p. 19).

Just as we tend to fear what we regard as alien, we may conversely (and perhaps perversely) also feel a similar sense of alienation in recognizing some "human" quality in "lower" species. Quammen enjoys playing at the borders of anthropomorphism in essays like "The Miracle of the Geese: A Bizarre Sexual Strategy Among Steadfast Birds" (*Outside*, September 1986). The wild geese, he tells us with undisguised admiration, "live by the same principles that we, too often, only espouse. They embody liberty, grace, and devotion, combining those three contradictory virtues with a seamless elegance that leaves us shamed and inspired. When they pass overhead, honking so musically, we are treated to (and accused by) a glimpse of the same sort of sublime creaturehood that we want badly to see in ourselves" (p. 19). The ensuing explanation of the geese's economy of energy—the conservation of what might otherwise go into periodic mating rituals for long flights and intense periods of feeding—not only explains their monogamy in strictly biological terms, but by implication raises a curious set of questions about what we proudly call our own "moral" behavior. Fond of inversions like this as a means of "constructive disorientation," Quammen suggests that matters of the heart have a basis in biochemistry and that the practice and theory of biology have some bearing upon the habits of the human heart.

Stance

Quammen's appreciation of the role of the emotions in human consciousness extends also to a fascination with the way we frame questions to suit our romantic—or prurient—fancies. Rather than dismissing the apparently childish or undisciplined wanderings of the human mind, he takes intellectual digressions seriously as evidence of our own complexity as thinking creatures who don't quite know what to think. "There's a part of the human heart," he begins one essay ("Gardening on Mars"), "that desperately yearns for Martians." He goes on to consider why this might be so: "It's a matter of cosmic loneliness, I suspect, roughly the same character trait that makes itself so eagerly susceptible to religion, ghost stories, UFO sightings, cryptozoology, Shirley MacLaine, and news of higher communication among porpoises" (*Outside*, February 1989, p. 21).

In this same spirit of sympathetic curiosity about the odd proclivities of the inquiring mind, he devotes a whole essay to "Cryptozoology and the Romantic Imagination," in which he reflects on why the "romantic" imagination is drawn to the mysterious, the indeterminate, and the unverifiable—lore and legend and myth that train our vision on what seems to be just out of sight, possibly lurking in the shadows around the edges of what we know. Cryptozoology, he explains, is "loosely defined by its practitioners as 'the science of hidden animals.' . . . Cryptozoologists concern themselves with creatures that have

been rumored to exist in shapes, in places, in sizes, or in time periods whereby they somehow violate what is expected" (*Outside*, August 1986, p. 21).

Not a member but a relatively sympathetic fellow-traveler of the oddball association of marvel-hunters who designate themselves the International Society of Cryptozoologists and who produce their own newsletter for the exchange of theories, stories, and sightings, Quammen acknowledges, large-mindedly, "Truth and certainty are fine, as far as they go, but truth and certainty don't supply all the nourishment that the soul of our species seems to require. We also have a need for marvels, for facts that are stranger than truth" (p. 21). Quammen understands cryptozoology as "an epistemological enterprise as much as a zoological one," which puts the cryptozoologist in a position of "adjudicating the conflict between two belief systems: When scientific orthodoxy and local lore contradict each other regarding the existence of a creature, how often might local lore be proven correct?" (p. 21). To pose the question in itself places Quammen at what some scientific purists would consider an outer edge of respectability. It's also a place, however, of considerable vitality and convivial curiosity. Though he finally affirms that real science is sufficiently interesting to satisfy even the need for marvel and miracle, he sympathizes with the romantic longings such pursuits seem to represent. The romantic imagination, he concludes, "is itself a hidden animal, a wondrous and inextinguishable beast" (p. 23).

Perhaps it is their unorthodoxy as much as anything else that endears the cryptozoologists to Quammen, who occasionally undertakes to question even the most dearly held axioms of environmental science. For instance, the generally accepted proposition that the stability of an ecosystem is directly related to its complexity—stability is the ideal and that we must attempt to preserve complexity or diversity—is brought up for examination in his reflections on the "plague of starfish" that is threatening to consume the Great Barrier Reef, a tropical coral reef Quammen calls "the oceanic equivalent of mature rainforest" (*The Flight of the Iguana*,

p. 132). If, he argues reasonably, the unusual proliferation of the huge, toxic, coral-eating species *A. planci* is a result of some form of human tampering, then it would seem we have a responsibility, as with the rain forests, to mitigate the consequences of our own destructive intrusions. But if this "plague" is a natural catastrophe, like a lightning fire in a national park, perhaps we should let "unsentimental nature" have its way (p. 134). In other words, there may be times when systems naturally destabilize themselves and when the argument for preservation of species may not automatically prevail.

This is not merely an academic or even a practical question for a writer whose humanitarianism makes him an impassioned as well as a curious and skilled investigator of natural phenomena. The essay in which he considers the fate of the Great Barrier Reef is entitled "Agony in the Garden." Though it offers no final judgment about the ethics and ecological consequences of preservationist intervention, it does end on a note of poignant appeal for conscious consideration of what is at stake in words that refer to one of Western culture's most powerful myths: "Certainly the Great Barrier Reef is one of our planet's most mature ecosystems. And if it dies, under a crown of thorns, there may be no propect of resurrection" (*The Flight of the Iguana*, p. 139).

The large, ongoing contemporary controversies in the environmental sciences underlie most of Quammen's topical essays. Asked if there were any issues about which he felt particularly impassioned, he replied, "Well, I'm against anthropocentrism, of course—the presumption that mankind stands at the apex of creation. But beyond that I'm always looking for persuasive alternatives to the utilitarian argument for preservation of species and biological diversity. I think the utilitarian argument is dangerous" (personal interview). One of his most compelling anti-utilitarian statements is his provocatively titled essay "Jeremy Bentham, the *Pietà*, and a Precious Few Grayling" (in *Natural Acts*). Bentham, an eighteenth-century English legal scholar, founded the doctrine of utilitarianism whereby value is judged by utility to the community (the greatest good for the greatest number). The *Pietà* provides an example of an object of immense value that is not useful. And the grayling, a bony, scaly, endangered fish whose Rocky Mountain habitats are being disrupted, offers an example of a species whose claim to our attention may need to be made on something other than a utilitarian basis. "The whole argument by utility," Quammen writes here and elsewhere, "may be one of the most dangerous, even ominous, strategic errors that the environmental movement has made" (p. 112). He goes on to urge the development of a persuasive and clear argument for the protection of species who have "arrived . . . the hard way, the Darwinian way, across millions of years of randomness"; they represent "something far more precious than a net asset in potential utility" (p. 113). What, exactly, he admits, "isn't easy to say, without gibbering in transcendental tones. But something more than a floppy disc storing coded genetic lingo for a rainy day" (p. 113). Coming, in fact, close to Ralph Waldo Emerson's insistence that "beauty is its own excuse for being," Quammen makes his own final appeal for protection of the grayling on the basis of aesthetic experience as an avenue of moral enlargement:

You don't fish at them for the satisfaction of fooling a crafty animal on its own terms, or fighting a wild little teakettle battle handicapped across a fine leader, as you do with trout. The whole context of expectations and rewards is different. You catch grayling to visit them: to hold one carefully in the water, hook freed, dorsal flaring, and gape at the colors, and then watch as it dashes away. This is good for a person, though it could never be the greatest good for the greatest number. (p. 116)

The grayling, he concludes poignantly, are still around, "at least for now" (p. 118). Few writers have Quammen's clear-eyed combination of intelligence, imagination, humor, and pathos, and few train our focus more effectively on the losses we incur with the extinction of species.

Patterns of evolution and extinction are the focus of Quammen's work in progress (at this writing), *The Song of the Dodo: Island Biogeography in an Age of Extinctions*. Like most of his work, the study is designed to invite general readers to consider questions that may not have occurred to them, but which deeply involve us all. He focuses on "islands" as discrete systems that may offer significant case studies of evolution and extinction as well as teach us about the consequences of fragmentation. He uses the term "islands" to include natural areas that have been cut off or fragmented from a larger ecosystem such as an area in Madagascar where roads and rice fields have partitioned the tropical forest in ways that drastically constrain the movement and interactions of some species living there, and so threaten them. His hope as he finishes this work is twofold: first, and most importantly, to provide a wide general audience with an understanding of the way changes in the earth's population occur, and of how the patterns of change are themselves changing, so that we might recognize in a more informed way the role of human beings in these processes. Secondly, he says, he has wanted to pursue this eight-year research project to complete a stage in his own evolution as a writer. "I don't want to be known as just a writer of short essays." But those of us who know him as "only" an essayist with a few novels, a stack of reviews, and a wide network of public conversations with other nature writers and concerned environmentalists, already recognize that the size of Quammen's contribution to general understanding of the natural world is immense.

Selected Bibliography

WORKS OF DAVID QUAMMEN

NONFICTION

Natural Acts: A Sidelong View of Nature and Science (New York: Schocken, 1985); *The Flight of the Iguana: A Sidelong View of Nature and Science* (New York: Delacorte, 1988); *The Song of the Dodo: Island Biogeography in an Age of Extinctions* (New York: Scribner, 1996).

FICTION

To Walk the Line (New York: Knopf, 1970); *The Zolta Configuration* (New York: Doubleday, 1983); *The Soul of Viktor Tronko* (New York: Doubleday, 1987); *Blood Line: Stories of Fathers and Sons* (St. Paul: Greywolf, 1988).

ARTICLES AND ESSAYS

"Natural Acts," a regular column in *Outside*; "Yin and Yang in the Tularosa Basin," in *Audubon* 87 (January 1985); "The Miracle of the Geese: A Bizarre Sexual Strategy Among Steadfast Birds," in *Outside* (September 1986); "Seeking Refuge in a Desert: The Sanctuary Movement: Exodus redux," in *Harper's* 273 (December 1986); "The Keys to Kingdom Come," in *Rolling Stone* (18 June 1987); "Brazil's Jungle Blackboard: A Test for Conservation Deep in Amazonas," in *Harper's* 276 (March 1988); "Gardening on Mars: Cosmic Loneliness Confronts a Universe of Possibilities," in *Outside* (February 1989); "It's a Long River with a Long History," in *Audubon* 92 (March 1990); "A Murder in Madagascar," in *Audubon* 93 (January 1991).

INTERVIEW

Personal interview with the author, April 1995.

MARJORIE KINNAN RAWLINGS
(1896–1953)

BETSY S. HILBERT

We were bred of the earth before we were born of our mothers. Once born, we can live without mother or father, or any other kin, or any friend, or any human love. We cannot live without the earth or apart from it.
— *Cross Creek*

MARJORIE KINNAN RAWLINGS was destined by time and opportunity to describe the last frontier of the American South, a generation after it came into being and just a little while before it disappeared. In describing her own place in the world, portraying her neighbors and the extraordinary landscape that she and they inhabited, she classically defined the relationships among people who live close to the earth and their connections to the environment that shapes and sustains them. People depend on the earth that feeds them, she said, and they are subject to the laws of an ungovernable world, a world that they can experience but never completely possess.

Rawlings' lifetime spanned the flowering and decline of the Florida frontier. In 1928, when she arrived at the little community of Cross Creek in the north-central region of the Florida peninsula, the other inhabitants of the area were only one or two generations arrived. Spanish conquistadors and the original native inhabitants had earlier moved across the landscape and created small, scattered settlements—most visibly the

Spanish fort town of Saint Augustine—but not until the end of the Civil War did central Florida see the spread of the small village communities that are typical of frontier life. By the time of Rawlings's death in 1953, successive waves of land booms and development speculation had irrevocably changed the population and the way of life in the region. In a land and climate where growth is rapid and change comes quickly, she recorded the brief flowering of a frontier culture within the habitat that fostered it.

Early Life

Her childhood experiences fostered an early connection to the natural world. Born into a middle-class family on 8 August 1896 in Washington, D.C., she would later have strong memories of family vacations in Maine and of a dairy farm outside of Washington that her father, Arthur Frank Kinnan—an official in the U.S. Patent Bureau—had acquired as a combination hobby and investment. There were also long visits to her grandparents' Michigan farm. Despite the brief interludes in the outdoors, Marjorie's childhood was urban: raised by a mother who insisted on maintaining the status and proprieties incumbent on the family of a public official, Marjorie and her younger brother, Arthur Houston Kinnan (who in later years became a tour and fishing guide in Alaska), grew up in a politically and culturally astute social environment. The death of her father in 1913, while she was still in high school, was a devastating blow. A year later, Ida Kinnan moved with her two children to Madison, Wisconsin, so that Marjorie could attend the University of Wisconsin.

A bright, talented, outgoing, and apparently happy young woman, Marjorie Rawlings had already had some early success writing short stories and poetry and was inclined toward amateur theatricals. She entered the university in 1914 and graduated four years later with a bachelor's degree in English and a Phi Beta Kappa key. While at the university she became engaged to Charles Rawlings, who also wrote for the school's literary magazine, though they were separated soon after graduation when he joined the army. World War I was winding down, and Chuck was stationed on Long Island, just north of New York City. New York, the center of American publishing, was a beacon for Marjorie: she moved to the city to aim for the brilliant career her college successes seemed to guarantee, suffered through several low-level and ill-paying writing and editing jobs, and wrote her fiancé daily about her troubles and dreams for their future. Her letters from that period are passionate (for 1918) and tempestuous; already, the relationship was showing the distance between Marjorie's fierce temper and brilliance and Chuck's easy, unambitious approach to life. They were married in 1919 in New York City.

The young Mrs. Rawlings wanted to soar, but at the same time her dreams and expectations were wrapped in her generation's vision of happy domesticity. Given her high expectations, unfortunately, she had married the wrong person. Chuck Rawlings went through a number of jobs and found success at none of them; the couple moved to Rochester, New York, to be near the financial support of his family. They moved again, and again, both of them taking unchallenging newspaper and advertising jobs. Marjorie wrote feature and human-interest stories for several papers, and for two years turned out a daily syndicated half-humorous, half-sentimental series of poems titled "Songs of the Housewife."

At the close of *South Moon Under* (1933), Rawlings' first novel, there is a passage in which the central character considers the turns his life has taken: "A man ordered his life, and then an obscurity of circumstance sent him down a road that was not of his own desire or choosing. Something beyond a man's immediate choice and will reached through the earth and stirred him. He did not see how any man might escape it" (p. 327). In 1928, the thirty-two-year-old Marjorie Rawlings was seized by just such an obscurity of circumstance, in the way of an apparently simple decision to take a few weeks of vacation in Florida. Her life, her spirit, and her writing career were suddenly to take a decisive turn.

"Here Is Home"

Charles Rawlings had two brothers working in Island Grove, Florida, in the central part of the state. The couple sailed by steamer in March of 1928 to Jacksonville, met his brothers there, and continued into the interior. They toured the area, fished, hunted, and explored the countryside. By the time they went home to Rochester again, their decision to move south was made; the brothers were asked to find a place where all four could live and support themselves growing citrus, while Marjorie and Charles continued to write. Four months later, using money Marjorie had inherited and taking advantage of the collapse of prices following the 1920s land boom, the couple purchased seventy-four acres of Florida land, including orange and pecan groves, a run-down farmhouse, and various barns and outbuildings, in the tiny community of Cross Creek. Her first sight of home was in November 1928.

She now owned property; it would come in time to belong to her, as she would belong to it. Rawlings' emotional connection to that place, as she later described it, was immediate. She felt that she had at last found home. The overriding theme of her writing from then on would be the relationship of people to the land, the personal necessity of locating a place where one's spirit can find peace in connection to nature. "After long years of spiritual homelessness, of nostalgia," she would write of the grove in *Cross Creek* (1942), "here is that mystic loveliness of childhood again. Here is home. An old thread, long tangled, comes straight again" (p. 8).

The land to which she had come was half-wild and sparsely settled, a semitropical landscape raised eons ago from an ocean bottom. The landscape of the region is generally flat, with soft hills, crisscrossed by numerous rivers and creeks fed from rainfall and cold, crystalline springs. Hammock areas, slightly higher than the surrounding wetlands, provide ground for dense stands of hardwoods, with their wealth of accompanying plant and animal communities. The other ecosystem of the region is the local pine scrub, wide areas that are almost constantly dry because the rainfall drains immediately through the sandy remnant of the ancient ocean floor. The hammock and scrub are two distinctly different environments, and through them run the small, spring-fed rivers, dark and shallow, which then pass through stands of cypress and open into clear lakes bordered by cypress and water grasses.

Scattered among this landscape of scrup, swamp, and hammock were the clearings where settlers, chiefly from Georgia and neighboring southern states, had come to live, to raise whatever stock could withstand the climate and parasites, and to plant groves and crops. The landscape does not look much different today around Cross Creek and its neighboring towns—Orange Lake, Micanopy, Hawthorne—except that what little crop farming there once was has generally been abandoned, and house trailers with television-satellite dishes now stand in the clearings. Inhabitants who once made their living fishing and trapping (mostly illegally, though no one but the game wardens bothered to complain) now survive economically in other ways. The local springs of the area still run clear, and country roads still curve past pastures shaded by old oak trees bearing long scarves of Spanish moss. The Rawlings farmhouse is now a Florida state historic site, open regularly to visitors.

It was not an easy country to make a living in, the Rawlingses soon discovered, as earlier settlers had discovered before them. The warm winters of the area often give way to sudden freezes, which can destroy not only crops but entire groves; there is now no serious commercial citrus growing in the region. Dangerous animals were rare even by the time Marjorie Rawlings came to the Creek (the Florida panther is now one of the most seriously endangered animals of the world), but voracious mosquitoes and her neighbors' hogs were routine predators. From the numerous snakes she kept a respectful but intrigued distance, attempting to conquer her fear of them by going on at least one snake-hunting expedition with herpetologist Ross Allen. Staying on there at "the Creek" in the face of disasters from weather and various "varmints" required stamina. There was no electricity, telephone, or indoor toilet; the physical labor was punishing and competent workers difficult to find. Life was hard, but it contained at last the possibilities of peace and purpose. "When I came to the Creek, and knew the old grove and farmhouse at once as home," she writes in *Cross Creek*, "there was some terror, such as one feels in the first recognition of a human love, for the joining of person to place, as of person to person, is a commitment to shared sorrow, even as to shared joy" (p. 9).

Charles Rawlings' two brothers left when they realized that the homestead would never support them all. A few years later Charles left after he and Marjorie agreed to a divorce. Marjorie turned her attention to the work of field and typewriter, and she single-handedly took on the responsibility of making the grove financially productive. She worked on her property with the same focus and commitment with which she worked on the stories she had begun writing, stories about the people she was just coming to know and the countryside she had fallen in love with.

Cracker Stories

Rawlings' first two short stories about the region, "Cracker Chidlings" and "Jacob's Ladder," were sold to *Scribner's Magazine* in 1930, and established the pattern for the work she was to do over the next twelve years, the years of her greatest public and artistic successes. "Cracker Chidlings" is an extended description of the Florida Cracker, whose designation comes, Rawlings explains, from the crack of a whip over a team of oxen. "Chidlings" is a local version of "chitterlings," or hog intestines; its closest current synonym is "guts," and it is used in the same way: "He ain't got the chidlings to do it." "Cracker Chidlings" is subtitled "Real Tales from the Florida Interior," and the piece is a series of short vignettes, mostly humorous, told in the author's rendition of the local dialect. They portray local anecdotes and legends such as Fatty Blake's "big doin's"; the illegal whiskey still operated by 'Shiner Tim and his wife; a practical joke played on a stranger; a clever twist whereby a canny local outsmarts a rich man over the ownership of a beautiful piece of river property. "Jacob's Ladder" tells the story of a young couple suffering the hardships of the region in search of a place to settle; again, it explores the overriding Rawlings themes of love that survives adversity, the difficulties and beauty of the region, and the longing for connection to a place of one's own.

Rawlings' working methods were well established by the time "Cracker Chidlings" went to the publisher. Her work, for all its outward simplicity, was the product of intense labor: starting from extensive notes, every piece went through revision after revision. She wrote, for example, four complete drafts of *Cross Creek*. As a writer, particularly as a nature writer, she struggled constantly with the ways factual material may be transformed in fiction. "Facts themselves are not an open sesame to good writing," she once told a creative-writing class. "It is a common error to believe that travel, adventure, contact with many people and many kinds of people will automatically provide the writer with material. Whether they provide material or not depends on the writer's ability to absorb them into himself" (quoted in Bigelow, 1966, p. 131).

Her fascination with the countryside was apparent from the beginning of her Florida writing. She wanted to accurately describe and emotionally evoke the qualities of a landscape so different from anything she and most of her readers had ever known. In that attempt, she succeeded so well that place, in her work, becomes essentially a character. Florida was both farmland and Eden, territory and dreamscape. Rawlings did her research thoroughly, and she wrote from her own experience, turning fact into lyric. She was sensitive to differentiations and gradations of color and shape, to the feel of the landscape, and her lush, richly defined descriptions of the countryside suggest the emotional content of her stories. In "Jacob's Ladder," for example, the Florida landscape becomes a mystical universe, where sensory images float and flow into the characters'—and the readers'—consciousness: "On a night of full moon in April, Mart and Florry sat on the cabin steps. The palms were silver in the moonlight. The new growth of the oaks was white as candles. An odor grew in the stillness, sweeter than breath could endure. It seeped across the marsh like a fog of perfume. It filled the hammock. Yellow jasmine was in bloom" (*Short Stories*, p. 58).

Over the next seventeen years, she produced a steady stream of short stories and articles, nearly all of them with Florida settings and country people. While most of her short stories continued to be published in *Scribner's*, which had provided her start, stories sold consistently to other major national magazines, including *Saturday Evening Post*, *Women's Home Companion*, and *New Yorker*. Her collection of short stories *When the Whippoorwill*, published in 1940, shows the characteristic pattern of her short fiction, a pattern established at the very beginning with "Cracker Chidlings" and "Jacob's Ladder": local poor white folks "making do" within the constraints of a difficult way of life, relating in various ways to one another and the natural environment. They are portrayed as noble though not innocent, and humorous, though she never patronized them. Love and caring keep them together in difficult times;

disaster in the form of natural catastrophe or illness is a constant threat. They do the best they can, and it is—mostly—just enough.

Local Color and Regional Writing

The redirection of Rawlings' life and work at the time she found Florida was not only a change in subject, but of literary type and genre. Previously, she had been writing human-interest newspaper feature stories and trying to publish the kind of popular sentimental fiction that was then being written expressly for the large women's magazines. Now she had moved into the type of writing that is generally termed "local color" or "regional" writing. Though it was certainly not deliberate or probably even conscious on her part—no serious writer ever sets out to become part of a "type" or "group," though many find themselves cast within one or another—Rawlings is often regarded as one of the long tradition of American local colorists: writers who portray the inhabitants of a small, distinct region as "characters," usually as stereotypes, in generally humorous and sympathetic fashion. Writers of local color almost invariably try to re-create the regional dialect, with varying fidelity. The general themes of local color writing are the goodness and earthiness of plain country folk, uneducated but wise in life, and the disappearance of rural culture in an urban, industrialized nation; the writing is often tinged with sentimentality. The full flowering of American local-color fiction occurred in the late nineteenth century, with such southern writers as Joel Chandler Harris and George Washington Cable. Much of Mark Twain's writing is in the local-color tradition, as is that of Sarah Orne Jewett and Mary Eleanor Wilkins Freeman, though in all those cases the author's portrayals of character and theme go far beyond the stereotyping of local color and into the universal themes of the American regionalists.

"Regionalism" as a literary term is much broader than "local color," and it applies to the work of such writers as Kate Chopin and William Faulkner. The regional writer uses the setting of a particular time and place, usually a rural or isolated community, but the characters develop and grow, and their motivations are shown from the inside. The regional writer moves from intimate local knowledge to universal human experience. Perhaps the clearest distinction between local color and regional writers (and even this distinction tends to blur in practice) is that the local-color writer tends to make objects of the people he or she portrays, to point at, rather than to empathize with. The regionalist, on the other hand, provides a more interior view and portrays a greater depth of character. Local-color writing tends to focus on quaintness and sentimentality; regional writing, on significance and overriding themes.

Genres, types, and traditions in literature are defined by literary historians and critics, not by authors. Serious writers, even those who deliberately choose to work within a specific tradition, generally do not like to see their works pigeonholed into type. Rawlings would have hated being called "a writer of local color." About the designation "regional writer," she was more ambivalent. In an address to the National Council of Teachers of English, published in the February 1940 issue of *College English*, she wrestled with the defining term of her title: "Regional Literature of the South." (Rawlings had written the paper to be delivered as an address to the conference; but in characteristic fashion, she simply handed the written paper to the council secretary and spoke informally to the group, answering questions and charming the audience of English teachers.) The published paper reveals her distrust of the term "regional literature," and attacks the exploitation inherent in regional writing solely to satisfy public curiosity: "Regional writing done because the author thinks it will be salable is a betrayal of the people of that region. Their speech and customs are turned inside out for the gaze of the curious. They are held up naked, not as human beings, but as literary specimens." There are, however, Rawlings continued, regional books that are truly literature: "many of the greatest books of all time are regional books, in which the author has used, for his own artistic purpose, a background that he loved and deeply understood. Thomas Hardy is a compelling instance." Of the "regional" literary artists of her own time whom she most admired, Rawlings named Ellen Glasgow, Margaret Mitchell (though she expressed some reservations about *Gone With the Wind*), Julia Peterkin, Elizabeth Madox Roberts, and "the negress, Zora Neale Hurston."

Ellen Glasgow was a regional southern novelist with whom Rawlings exchanged letters for years, until Glasgow's death in 1945. Twenty-three years older than Rawlings, Glasgow had focused her work on attacking the shams and deceptions of the social conventions of her era; for the most part, her novels are set in cities such as her native Richmond, Virginia, though in her work the southern countryside serves often as a metaphoric foil for human struggle. Rawlings' last work, unfinished at the time of her death, was a posthumous biography of Glasgow. When *Cross Creek* was published, Glasgow wrote to Rawlings that the writing was like a "luminous web which captures and holds some vital essence of a particular place and moment of time" (quoted in Silverthorne, p. 208). The description is a classic definition of regional literature.

In 1930, however, all the literary terms and definitions that would later be applied by critics and scholars were completely immaterial to Marjorie Kinnan Rawlings, typing away in the wood-frame house at Cross Creek. She did not anticipate the next major opportunity of her life. Maxwell Perkins, the editor at Charles Scribner's Sons who was rapidly becoming a legend in the world of American publishing, took notice of "Cracker Chidlings." It was Perkins who had nurtured the reputation-making work of F. Scott Fitzgerald, Ernest Hemingway, and Thomas Wolfe, among many other great writers of the period. The kind of close, involved editing that Perkins provided his authors—cajoling, consoling, suggesting, supporting—was exactly the kind of mentoring Rawlings needed. Over the next seventeen years, they would struggle together. Rawlings always believed that Perkins

was responsible for much of her success as a writer. "Max had become a part of my thinking," she wrote, years after his death (*Selected Letters*, p. 370).

South Moon Under

Thus, in 1930, the great editor of new American writing sent a letter to an unknown woman writer in a tiny Florida hamlet, suggesting that she might wish to expand her Cracker material into a novel. Rawlings responded ecstatically: "I am vibrating with material like a hive of bees in swarm.... At present I see four books very definitely. Two of them need several more years of note-taking. Of the two I am about ready to begin on, one would be a novel of the scrub country. I managed to get lost in the scrub, the first day of the hunting season—and I encountered for the first time the palpability of silence. ... 'Jacob's Ladder' was, of course, over-written. If you will be patient with me, I can do better work" (*Selected Letters*, p. 43). Excited by possibility, she went to live in the Big Scrub for two and a half months with a local family in order to experience a way of life even more native than her own at Cross Creek, and to gather material for her first novel, *South Moon Under*.

South Moon Under was published in 1933 by Scribners. Despite the depth of the country's economic depression, the book sold reasonably well; it also received good critical reviews and was a Book-of-the-Month Club selection. It is the story of a man who has come to the Big Scrub to escape a clouded past. By nature and experience a loner, Lantry marries and clears a homestead on the edge of the Ocklawaha River, where the book is largely set. Here his favorite daughter Piety and her son Lant continue on, struggling for survival in the social order of interconnected families and the natural order of a beautiful but ungiving environment.

Piety Lantry is a figure of great stoicism, surviving the deaths of her husband and father and her increasing isolation from her family to go it alone in the Big Scrub. There are undoubtedly elements from Marjorie Rawlings' own life in the figure of Piety, and probably the theme of abandonment grew partly from her own growing feelings of estrangement from her husband. Through fourteen years of an increasingly strained marriage, Charles and Marjorie Rawlings had sought to balance their differences of temperament with their traditional view of marriage. Child of a warm, loving father and a cold, controlling mother, Marjorie looked to her husband for constant emotional support and approval, but neither was forthcoming. Charles simply could not produce what was expected of him, and the interactions between them grew ever more difficult. After their divorce in 1933, she wrote, "I am not riotously happy, not being interested in freedom for its own sake—I could have been a *slave* to a man who could be at least a benevolent despot—but I feel a terrific relief—I can wake up in the morning conscious of the sunshine, and thinking, 'How wonderful! Nobody is going to give me Hell today!'" (*Selected Letters*, p. 80).

She was not interested in freedom for its own sake, but independence came and she proved herself equal to it. Throughout her life, Rawlings was capable of deep, lasting friendships with women as well as men, but she had been conditioned early to look for support and encouragement from men; this pattern certainly marked her relationship to Max Perkins. The next few years, however, not only brought Rawlings financial independence through her earnings as an author, but also brought emotional growth as she managed her life and property on her own.

Independence and Creativity

The central characters of Rawlings' Florida fiction, both men and women, are strong, independent people. There is a repeated pattern in her fiction of warm, loving men married to distancing women, possibly a reflection of her early childhood, but another archetypal woman character is also consistently repeated: the woman who breaks the mold, who lives differently from her neighbors, and succeeds alone, either by choice or necessity. Camilla Van Dyne, the orange grower in Rawlings' second novel, *Golden Apples* (1935), is a woman very much like Marjorie Rawlings herself (or, perhaps, like Rawlings as she wanted to be): independent, tough-minded but generous, knowledgeable, and committed to her work. Later on in Rawlings' career, the Quincy Dover stories would also reflect a woman of this character (if of larger size) who is sharp-tongued but also warm-hearted and clever. The women in Rawlings' fiction do not choose solitude for its own sake, but when it is forced on them—by the death or desertion of a mate or father, as happens to Piety Lantry—they manage.

Later in life, Marjorie Rawlings married again: in 1941, to hotel keeper Norton Baskin, whom she had known for several years. Soon after their marriage, he opened the elegant Castle Warden Hotel in Saint Augustine and ran it as owner-manager. Though they owned a cottage at Crescent Beach, near Saint Augustine, and the penthouse suite of the hotel, Marjorie kept her house and land in Cross Creek as a constant retreat, just as she kept her independence of spirit and her pen name, Rawlings. By then, she had seen success, both artistic and financial. They did not worry about the local gossip that condemned Marjorie's necessary retreats to write in solitude. In that second marriage, there was apparently lasting affection spiked with the occasional storms that were part of her nature, made difficult by her emotional problems, eased by his quiet tolerance and their mutual sense of humor. "Long independence, and above all, the peculiar mental independence of the creative worker, is not the best of bases for a successful marriage," she wrote to Ellen Glasgow a few months after the marriage. "Yet the circumstances are such that I feel the odds are in its favor. . . . I believe that great happiness is probable" (*Selected Letters*, pp. 215–216).

Before she could achieve the independence that would allow her to envision a mutually nonrestrictive mature marriage between two people committed to their own professions, however, Marjorie Rawlings had years of struggle and growth before her. After the publication of *South Moon Under*, she left for England in 1933,

Marjorie Kinnan Rawlings at her home in Florida, 1939

spending some of the royalties from the first novel to begin research on her second, *Golden Apples*, completed late in 1934. Not much of the English countryside found its way into the final version of *Golden Apples*, for Rawlings, at Maxwell Perkins' urging, wisely decided to set the story entirely in her home region. The novel tells of a young member of the British landed gentry, unfairly banished from his home, who comes on remittance to central Florida in order to take over an abandoned orange grove. His "uppity" attitude toward the community and his relationship to the young brother and sister whom he finds as squatters on his property lead first to tragedy and then to his reconciliation to his life there.

The most interesting aspect of *Golden Apples*, for admirers of Rawlings' nature writing, comes from her balanced handling of different points of view of the countryside. Tordell, the English-man, sees the countryside as alien and malevolent, dark and jungle-like, a perspective that reflects his own bitterness and depression. By contrast, Luke, a native, is completely connected to place. For Luke,

Nothing was more important than growth. A man favored with the possession of land might choose what things he would grow; might make room for them to suit his will. He could not see how a man could ask more of living than to choose his crops and to command them; to merge himself with the earth; to follow the seasons and let the sun and rain unite the sweat of his body with the soil he tended; to dream in the long nights of shining groves and golden oranges. (p. 74)

Time, tragedy, a kindhearted doctor, and the love of Luke's sister, Florry, finally allow Tordell to achieve a semblance of peace with the region and himself, but the true understanding of growth and the natural world is only given to Luke, who has given himself to the land.

The Yearling

By 1936, with two published novels to her credit, Rawlings began intensive work on her best-known novel, *The Yearling*. Very early in their correspondence, Max Perkins had suggested a boys' book to her, and they agreed that it would be a book about a boy, though not specifically a work for children. Rawlings had been taking notes for the book for years, even joining a bear hunt so she could describe one. To work in solitude on the manuscript, she moved for several months to a cabin in North Carolina. Published in the spring of 1938, the novel almost instantly became a best-seller. At last, Rawlings had her major book, her resounding success.

The Yearling is the story of a lonely, solitary boy growing up in a cabin in the scrub. Child of a loving and—for the time and place—somewhat indulgent father, and an emotionally cold mother, Jody finds what amusement he can in the surrounding wilderness. Only after he rescues and raises a young fawn does he feel, finally, an end to his sense of alienation. But nature's laws are immutable: deer grow, and they eat crops. A family just barely surviving cannot afford the destruction and havoc a tame deer can wreak, and so Jody is ordered to shoot his pet. In agony, he does what he has to do, and then leaves home, only to discover that the world outside the scrub is harsh, unwelcoming, and unforgiving—and that his place is at home. *The Yearling* is a classic rite-of-passage story, as boy grows into man, and the fully rounded characters of the novel are shown as being both challenged and sustained by the countryside, living, by necessity, at one with nature.

The overwhelming popularity of *The Yearling* (which was reprinted in several editions and translated into at least fifteen languages) fueled a public taste to know more about both the author and the region she wrote about. Rawlings im-

mediately began work on a semiautobiographical book of nonfiction that would describe her own relation to the place and its people. She began to rework one or two short pieces that had appeared earlier in magazines, adding the bulk of the material from her memories and impressions of life in the little community and the surrounding countryside. *Cross Creek*, published in 1942, is both her most mature work and her finest achievement in nature writing.

Cross Creek

Cross Creek is a series of brief sketches about life in the land she had come to know intimately. None of the chapters is more than a few pages long, and each could stand alone as a complete, detailed miniature. The book opens with an overview titled "Cross Creek," which classically locates the human community in physical space. The first sentence, with its parallel pattern, establishes Rawlings' essential theme of humans in the balance of nature: "Cross Creek is a bend in a country road, by land, and the flowing of Lochloosa Lake into Orange Lake, by water" (p. 1).

Each prose piece in *Cross Creek* describes some aspect of the community with the same sinuous flow and the occasional perceptual flip that mark the opening sentence. Ensuing anecdotes tell the stories of her coming to the community, her struggles with grove and garden, her quizzical bemusement at the way that some of the community "characters" make their living. The book is told entirely from Rawlings' central point of view: a stranger who comes to the village, falls in love with the countryside, is intrigued by the community, and struggles to stay on. There are anecdotes about how she shoots the neighbor's pig that roots up her garden, how she deals with "toady-frogs, lizards, antses, and varmints," how she variously manages and doesn't manage the hired help. Her relations with a series of impossible though interesting maids are described in great detail; the poverty and struggles of the poor people are sympathetically recorded; the cow is elegized; and the "characters" of the community are described with humor and bemusement.

The places where *Cross Creek* rises above local color are in the descriptions of the country surrounding the village, in which the narrator's heightened perceptions of nature become almost pure lyricism. Rawlings manages the most difficult task for a nature writer—to present accurate, factual information within an emotional and thematic context. Her descriptions are sensuous, clear, exact, but also fired by metaphor: "The bees have slowed from their orgy in the orange blossoms and the pale gold honey is ready for gathering. They work leisurely, dipping into the long heavy sprays of the palmetto bloom, stabbing carelessly the pink tarflowers, the gallberries, the andromeda, and what may be left over of flowers in the garden. They know there will be long months of sweetness and there is no longer any hurry" (p. 268). *Cross Creek* has survived as a classic of nature writing largely because of the loving perspective from which it was written. Her description of the unpaved road outside her door embodies this perspective:

> Every pine tree, every gallberry bush, every passion vine, every joree rustling in the underbrush, is vibrant. I have walked it in trouble, and the wind in the trees beside me is easing. I have walked it in despair, and the red of the sunset is my own blood dissolving into the night's darkness. For all such things were on earth before us, and will survive after us, and it is given to us to join ourselves with them and to be comforted. (p. 6)

Unfortunately, one aspect of local culture that Rawlings recorded and to a degree shared was the ingrained racism of the times. There was only one extended black family at Cross Creek, but the demarcations of the social order were always very clear. Rawlings was an accurate recorder of the local speech and dialect, so the references to "niggers" throughout her works may be understood as a portrayal of attitudes of that time and in that place. The rampant racial stereotyping in many of her works, however, is far less forgivable. In *Golden Apples*, for example, the black girl Rhea is savage and unbalanced, mentally unstable, dirty, and consistently referred to as animal-like. Black people in *Cross Creek* are presented in almost entirely negative ways, with the exception of the wise, ancient Martha Mickens (also a stereotype). One episode in *Cross Creek*, told in Rawlings' own voice, is horrifying in retrospect but probably not unusual for the time: on the advice of friends who have told her to get a young and therefore trainable maid, Rawlings "buys" a young black girl, "somewhere between ten and twelve," from the child's widowed father. Predictably, the child proves "unteachable."

Rawlings' early prejudices, however, were balanced by her truly generous and empathic spirit. She understood racial issues historically, as she explains in *Cross Creek*: "[The Negro] could adapt himself to the injustice of his position and to the master white race only by being childish, carefree, religious, untruthful and unreliable" (p. 181). Unfortunately, she then goes on to a series of anecdotes about her black workers being childish, carefree, religious, untruthful, and unreliable. She tended to treat people cavalierly, according to Idella Parker, the "perfect maid" in Rawlings' terms. Parker, who was a constant over many years, later reported in her reminiscences that Rawlings was always "the boss," but she was also very generous and supportive in difficulties.

Possibly Rawlings' acquaintance with Zora Neale Hurston was a turning point for her; her consciousness of the socially required manner in which she treated Hurston may have given even more impetus to Rawlings' developing social conscience. Hurston, who much appreciated their friendship and enjoyed Marjorie's company, had to use the servants' entrance and back stairs when she came to visit at the Saint Augustine hotel. Idella Parker recalls how, on one visit to Cross Creek, Hurston was made to sleep in the maid's room in the tenant house, even though there were bedrooms available in the main house. A white woman of Rawlings' time and class simply could not associate on an equal social basis with a black woman.

Angered and ashamed by the injustice, Rawlings in her later years became an outspoken advocate of racial justice, taking every opportunity to condemn the evils of segregation. One piece she wrote advocating equality in the armed forces during World War II was turned down by the publisher because it was "controversial." She got into a major argument with the local school board because the school bus refused to pick up a "colored" child at Cross Creek. Her posthumously published children's book, *The Secret River* (1955), has a black child as heroine; while working on it Rawlings told Perkins that she had deliberately avoided Negro dialect: "No Uncle Remus or Little Black Sambo sort of stuff with its humorous, often deprecatory effect." (quoted in Silverthorne, p. 276). Once her eyes were opened, she threw herself into the fight for justice with her customary passion and zeal. She became a crusader for grants and scholarships for black artists and performers, and her will left part of her estate for scholarships for black students at the University of Florida. Rawlings' work offers an accurate and unsentimental portrayal of a place and a time in American history; although her early portraits of black people show her to have been a product of her times, she was also eventually ahead of her times.

If the local inhabitants of Cross Creek became "characters" for Rawlings, she was certainly one to them. The other residents of Cross Creek seem to have looked on her with curious uncertainty, valuing her honesty, giving and accepting occasional neighborly help, and tolerating her idiosyncrasies. As J. T. Glisson, who grew up at Cross Creek during the years Rawlings was in residence there, recalled in *The Creek*,

She exuded an aura of energy and controversy. She was charismatic and antisocial and unyielding, a force that could not be ignored. She smoked in public at a time when most women smoked in secret and publicized her taste for good liquor when most of the country buried their empty bottles. Her fast driving, reckless accusations, and occasional profanity all created an image not always admired but never ignored.... During the twenty-five years she was our neighbor, she came to our house to introduce her friends, fight with my dad, bring something she had cooked, apologize to my dad, invite me on a junket, fight with my dad, deliver her latest book, apologize to my dad, bring her holiday gifts, and fight with my dad. (pp. 86–87)

Cross Creek became, in the book that is named for it, a microcosm, a mythic space. It is as richly detailed a picture of a small Florida town as will probably ever be written. Glisson recalls his first reading of *Cross Creek* in the spring of his ninth-grade year, when Rawlings left a copy of the newly published book on his parents' front porch: "Mrs. Rawlings's version of the Creek was in some ways more vibrant, yet more simplified, than the real-life Creek. Even the truth laid bare was as savory as it was offensive. The book was a gift of a place and a time that was passing, though I was too young to know it" (p. 106). Other neighbors, according to Glisson, were less understanding: "She ought not to of wrote some of the things she did about some, even if it was true" (p. 106).

One of the people whom Rawlings describes in *Cross Creek* acted vigorously on the idea that the author had overstepped her bounds. Zelma Cason was one of Marjorie's oldest friends in Florida; she had met Marjorie and Charles Rawlings at the boat on their first trip to Florida, though over the years the tempers of the two women made for an off-again, on-again friendship. Rawlings describes Cason in the book as an "ageless spinster resembling an angry and efficient canary" (p. 48), mentioning Cason's warm heart, her concern for others, and her endless loud cursing. Cason decided to sue for invasion of privacy.

Rawlings saw the suit as an attack on a writer's freedom to express the truth and refused all settlement or compromise, even though the issue would drag on for years, sapping her emotional energy and her finances. She was also particularly bitter because, at Max Perkins' directive, she had gone to considerable trouble talking to some of her neighbors (though not Cason) about the book, trying to ensure that no one would be offended. She could not imagine Cason's objecting to so mild and humorous a description. In fact, as J. T. Glisson pointed out later, "Everyone who knew Zelma agreed that the description was probably the most accurate in the book" (p. 240).

The suit, which set an author's right to publish against a subject's right not to be held up to public ridicule, went to trial on 20 May 1946, following a long series of legal maneuvers, before the Florida Supreme Court, which finally held that Cason had a right to sue. Under questioning, Rawlings proved a match for the opposing lawyer, in a round of crossfire that delighted the packed audience. Her testimony explains her purposes in writing the book:

> To me, *Cross Creek* is a love story. It is a story of my love for the land, and for that particular portion of the land where I have felt that I belonged, which is Cross Creek. And when you love a person or a place, then their faults and peculiarities—that does not interfere with your love for them at all. (Acton, p. 111)

In the end, the Gainesville jury found the defendants, Marjorie and her husband, Norton Baskin (who under Florida law at the time had to be sued jointly with his wife), not guilty. It was a popular verdict among the local folk, and the jurors asked Marjorie to autograph their copies of the book. But Cason was not finished yet; she appealed and lost, appealed a second time to the Florida Supreme Court, and this time won, though the court ruled that while invasion of privacy had occurred, Cason was only entitled to recover "nominal damage and costs." Zelma Cason finally settled for $1.00 in damages, plus $1,050.10 in costs. It was a sad, drawn-out ending to a case which had pitted two feisty, strong-minded women, once close friends, against one another. Their graves are now a short distance apart, in the tiny Antioch Cemetery at Island Grove.

If *Cross Creek* is the story of Rawlings' love for the region, it is also a love song for the foods she had found there. Some of the most lyrical, sensuous descriptions in the book are given over to the delights of the kitchen, particularly in the chapter "Our Daily Bread." There are, for example, an elegy on mango ice cream and a delicious description of hush puppies fried fresh at the end of a fishing expedition. Rawlings was an accomplished cook who loved to entertain, and she followed *Cross Creek* almost immediately with a book of recipes, *Cross Creek Cookery* (1942), including her recipes for specialties such as Rum Omelet, Coot Liver and Gizzard Pilau, and Utterly Deadly Southern Pecan Pie.

More than an avocation, however, her interest in food came also from a conviction that the good things of the table are truly gifts from the earth. An underlying theme in all her descriptions of the region is the dependence of the people on the land that feeds them, and the meals of the local people, festive and ordinary, are described in great detail. She told the truth that country people know and city people are often distanced from: hunger is always just a growing season away. In *The Yearling*, for example, the boy Jody finally learns through a bout with near-starvation that home, family, and the land that sustains them all are not just sources of comfort but essentials of life.

Though one of the main themes of Rawlings' writing is that humans must recognize and honor the source of their lives, she generally expressed an environmentalist ethic indirectly, staying out of specific political arguments. Just after she finished editing *Cross Creek Cookery*, however, she set out on a five-thousand-mile drive through the southeastern states, "looking at timber," as she described it, for an article eventually published as "Trees for Tomorrow." Rawlings used the journalistic style she had learned in her early days to describe the devastation wrought in American forests by indiscriminate clear-cutting, and proposed a national law establishing a system of controlled cutting. She described both the evil results of "that combination of greed and thoughtlessness" and the wisdom of intelligent, planned selective cutting. She dealt with the cutting by small landholders as well as by large companies, describing "two small owners of timber [who are] wise and farsighted Americans. One is a white man and the other is black" (p. 24). Both owners look to the future of their tree crops as well as of their families. As in all her writing, Rawlings emphasizes her theme of the earth: "On this earth, man and the products of earth are bound up together. While the earth and its products would continue to exist, and very comfortably, without us, we could not exist without them" (p. 14).

Rawlings' life following the achievements of *The Yearling* and *Cross Creek* was a time of increasing acclaim for her writing. Her reputation grew steadily, with other honors regularly added to the Pulitzer Prize she won in 1939 for *The Yearling*. She was invited to stay at the White House and had tea with Eleanor Roosevelt. Her financial worries were over, and her relationship with her husband, Norton, was both supportive and independent. In 1947, she began to spend winters in Florida and summers in a little house she had bought and renovated in Van Hornesville, New York.

Meanwhile, however, work on her last novel, *The Sojourner*, went slowly and badly. *The Sojourner* is set on a farm in the area of New York where she had bought her summer house, but the novel never shows the depth of understanding of the landscape she had achieved with her Florida works. Thus, while the central character, Ase Linden, is deeply connected to the land, the land itself goes undefined and undescribed. When finally published in 1953, *The Sojourner* sold reasonably well—probably due to the Rawlings name—but it lasts today more as a moral fable about endurance and faith than as a classic piece of fiction.

Conclusion

Endurance was the characteristic most required of Rawlings during her final ten years. Her husband enlisted to serve with the American Field Service in World War II, and he came home severely ill. During the war she carried on a vast and time-consuming correspondence with many American servicemen, and she herself had several serious bouts of illness. Her normal drinking had turned into severe alcoholism, and the "perfect maid" Idella Parker could no longer provide the emotional support that had seen Marjorie through increasing mood swings. Eventually, Parker left. Max Perkins died in 1947, while Rawlings was working on *The Sojourner*, and it was a devastating loss, for she had come to depend on their interchanges and his advice. As she pushed herself to work harder, she drank harder. She suffered a heart attack in 1952, finished *The Sojourner*, and immediately began intensive work on her biography of Ellen Glasgow. Finally, illness and the strains of her life caught up. She died of a cerebral hemorrhage in Saint Augustine on 14 December 1953. Her husband wrote the epitaph on her tombstone: Through Her Writings She Endeared Herself to the People of the World.

Perhaps the message Marjorie Kinnan Rawlings would have most wanted to leave, however, is the passage that was read at her funeral, from the chapter of *Cross Creek* titled "Who Owns Cross Creek?"

Who owns Cross Creek? The red-birds, I think, more than I, for they will have their nests even in the face of delinquent mortgages. And after I am dead, who am childless, the human ownership of grove and field and hammock is hypothetical.... It seems to me that the earth may be borrowed but not bought. It may be used, but not owned. It gives itself in response to love and tending, offers its seasonal flowering and fruiting. But we are tenants and not possessors, lovers and not masters. Cross Creek belongs to the wind and the rain, to the sun and the seasons, to the cosmic secrecy of seed, and beyond all, to time. (p. 368)

Selected Bibliography

WORKS OF MARJORIE KINNAN RAWLINGS

NOVELS

South Moon Under (New York: Scribners, 1933); *Golden Apples* (New York: Scribners, 1935); *The Yearling* (New York: Scribners, 1938); *The Sojourner* (New York: Scribners, 1953).

NONFICTION

Cross Creek (New York: Scribners, 1942); *Cross Creek Cookery* (New York: Scribners, 1942).

SHORT STORIES

"The Reincarnation of Miss Hetty," in *McCall's Magazine* (August 1912); *When the Whippoorwill* (New York: Scribners, 1940); "Mountain Prelude," in *Saturday Evening Post* 219 (26 April–31 May 1947), serialized novella in six installments; *Short Stories by Marjorie Kinnan Rawlings*, ed. by Rodger L. Tarr (Gainesville: Univ. Press of Florida, 1994).

POEMS

"The Miracle," in *Wisconsin Literary Magazine* 17 (October 1917); "Having Left Cities Behind Me," in *Scribner's Magazine* 98 (October 1935); "Mountain Rain," in *Scribner's Magazine* 104 (July 1938).

ESSAYS AND ARTICLES

Editorial on Vachel Lindsay, in *Wisconsin Literary Magazine* 17 (April 1918); "I Sing While I Cook," in *Vogue* 93 (15 February 1939); "In the Heart," in *Collier's* 105 (3 February 1940), rev. and repr. in *Cross Creek*; "Regional Literature of the South," in *College English* 1 (February 1940); "Sweet Talk, Honey!" in *Vogue* 100 (1 December 1942); "Cross Creek Breakfasts," in *Woman's Home Companion* 69 (November 1942); "Trees for Tomorrow," in *Collier's* 117 (8 May 1943); "Florida: A Land of Contrasts," in *Transatlantic* 14 (October 1944); Introduction to *Katherine Mansfield Collection*, ed. by John Middleton Murray (Cleveland: World, 1946); "About Fabulous Florida," in *New York Herald Tribune* book review section (30 November 1947), review of Marjory Stoneman Douglas' *The Everglades: River of Grass*; "Portrait of a Magnificent Editor as Seen in His Letters," in *Publishers Weekly* 157 (1 April 1950).

CHILDREN'S BOOK

The Secret River (New York: Scribners, 1955).

LETTERS

Selected Letters of Marjorie Kinnan Rawlings, ed. by Gordon E. Bigelow and Laura V. Monti (Gainesville: Univ. Presses of Florida, 1983).

PAPERS

The primary archive of Marjorie Kinnan Rawlings' papers is housed in Special Collections, Univ. of Florida Libraries, Gainesville, Florida. The collection includes manuscripts, correspondence, and miscellaneous papers, as well as her published works. There are also holdings of Rawlings material in the Scribner Archives of the Princeton Univ. Library and smaller holdings at Yale Univ., the Univ. of Virgina, and the Univ. of Georgia.

FILMS AND PLAYS BASED ON RAWLINGS' WORKS

The Yearling, produced by Sidney Franklin and directed by Clarence Brown (MGM, 1946); *The Sun Comes Up*, directed by Richard Thorpe (MGM, 1949), based on "Mountain Prelude"; *The Yearling*, Broadway musical adapted by Herbert E. Martin and Lore Noto, music by Michael Leonard, lyrics by Herbert Martin (opened 10 December 1965, closed early 1966); *Gal Young 'Un*, directed by Victor Nunez (independently produced, 1979); *Cross Creek*, produced by Robert Radnitz and directed by Martin Ritt (Universal, 1983); *The Yearling*, television movie produced for CBS by Robert Halmi, Sr., and directed by Clarence Brown (1994).

BIOGRAPHICAL AND CRITICAL STUDIES

One major resource for contemporary studies of Rawlings' work is the *Marjorie Kinnan Rawlings Journal of Florida Literature*, published annually since 1988 by the Marjorie Kinnan Rawlings Society, Department of English, Illinois State Univ., Campus Box 4240, Normal, Illinois 61790-4240. Materials particularly helpful to the study of Rawlings as a nature writer include the following: Patricia Nassif Acton, *Invasion of Privacy: The Cross Creek Trial of Marjorie Kinnan Rawlings* (Gainesville: Univ. of Florida Press, 1988); Samuel I. Bellman, *Marjorie Kinnan Rawlings* (New York: Twayne, 1974); A. Scott Berg, *Max Perkins: Editor of Genius* (New York: Dutton, 1978); Gordon E. Bigelow, *Frontier Eden: The Literary Career of Marjorie Kinnan Rawlings* (Gainesville: Univ. of Florida Press, 1966, 1989), and "Marjorie Kinnan Rawlings' Wilderness," in *Sewanee Review* 73 (spring 1965); Gordon E. Bigelow, ed., "Marjorie Kinnan Rawlings' 'Lord Bill of the Suwannee River'," in *Southern Folklore Quarterly* 27 (1963), contains a five-page introduction; Julia Scribner Bigham, introduction to *The Marjorie Rawlings Reader* (New York: Scribners, 1956); Thomas Dukes, " 'Place in Fiction': Marjorie Kinnan Rawlings and Eudora Welty," in *Marjorie Kinnan Rawlings Journal of Florida Literature* (1991); Harry Evans, "Marjorie Kinnan Rawlings," in *Family Circle* (2 pts., 7 May 1943 and 14 May 1943); J. T. Glisson, *The Creek* (Gainesville: Univ. Press of Florida, 1993), reminiscence of a Cross Creek neighbor; Lloyd Morris, "A New Classicist," in *North American Review* 246 (September 1938); Sally Morrison, *Cross Creek Kitchens* (Gainesville, Fla.: Triad, 1983), the park ranger who lived at the Rawlings farmhouse gives local recipes and tells how the site was opened to visitors; David J. Nordloh, "Circular Journeys in *The Yearling*," in *Marjorie Kinnan Rawlings Journal of Florida Literature* 4 (1992); Idella Parker, with Mary Keating, *Idella: Marjorie Rawlings' "Perfect Maid"* (Gainesville: Univ. Press of Florida, 1992); "Marjorie Kinnan Rawling," in *Los Angeles*

Times (24 April and 3, 4, 10, 17, and 24 May 1953), account constructed from Rawlings' replies to a questionnaire, presented as autobiographical; Rebecca Richie, "The St. Johns River in the Work of Marjorie Kinnan Rawlings," in *Marjorie Kinnan Rawlings Journal of Florida Literature* 5 (1993); Anne E. Rowe, *The Idea of Florida in the American Literary Imagination* (Gainesville: Univ. Press of Florida, 1992), and "Rawlings on Florida," in *Marjorie Kinnan Rawlings Journal of Florida Literature* 5 (1993); Louis D. Rubin, Jr., et al., *The History of Southern Literature* (Baton Rouge: Louisiana State Univ. Press, 1985), a useful reference for Rawlings' background and contemporaries; Elizabeth Silverthorne, *Marjorie Kinnan Rawlings: Sojourner at Cross Creek* (Woodstock, N.Y.: Overlook Press, 1988); Hiroshi Tsunemoto, "A Famous Writer, an Unknown Book: Marjorie Rawlings' *Cross Creek* in Japan," in *Marjorie Kinnan Rawlings Journal of Florida Literature* 3 (1991), describes *Cross Creek* as "another kind of Walden"; John Hall Wheelock, *Editor to Author: The Letters of Maxwell E. Perkins* (New York: Scribners, 1950); Lamar York, "Marjorie Kinnan Rawlings's Rivers," in *Southern Literary Journal* 9, no. 2 (1977).

CHET RAYMO
(b. 1936)

FRED TAYLOR

IN *The Soul of the Night,* Chet Raymo describes the astronomer Harlow Shapley, who first proposed the contemporary model of the Milky Way galaxy, as a person who "dreamed a grand dream," which "enlarged the universe a thousand times." I first encountered Shapley's dream years ago in his little volume *Of Stars and Men,* which states the cosmic relationship thus: "small but magnificent man face to face with enormous and magnificent universe."

Years later, when I first read *The Soul of the Night,* these words came to mind again. Raymo's writing not only evokes the enormous magnificence of the universe but also gives rich expression to the modest but no less extraordinary magnificence of the human. And he captures brilliantly the "face to face" of which Shapley writes, describing in vivid prose the encounter between the human spirit and the vast reaches of the cosmos. Raymo, too, "dreams a grand dream" by linking fact and poetry, science and the spirit. Blending a wealth of scientific background with a vivid narrative style found in the best of nature writers, he brings a unique voice to the field of nature writing.

Born in Chattanooga, Tennessee, on 17 September 1936, Raymo grew up exploring the woods behind his home. Of greatest impact, however, were the times when his father took him outside at night to look at the stars. In a recollection published in *Orion* magazine,

Raymo writes of his first memory of the night sky, when his father woke him in the middle of the night to see a comet. They never saw it, but he carried from that night his "first memory of the stars, nameless, uncountable, flung like a cold net across the pines, beautiful and frightening" (p. 33).

As his father taught him the names of the stars, the patterns of the constellations, and the myths and stories associated with them, he planted the seeds of Raymo's career, not only as a scientist but also as a writer. For "his lessons were more than exercises in connect the dots. The sky was a textbook of history, science, mathematics, myth. And, of course, religion. For my father, the stars were infused with unfathomable mystery" ("Pocketful of Stones," p. 34). He continues: "Now, half a century later, my own response to nature is informed by science, respectful of order, material agency, and design. It is also tempered by awe, agog with mystery" (p. 34). This balance he traces to the "lessons I learned from my father on a badminton court in Tennessee, tented by night, searching for patterns and mysteries among the stars" (p. 34). Knowledge and wonder, science and religion, patterns and mysteries: on the boundary between these two complementary universes, Raymo sought his home. His books inspire and challenge readers because he writes on this boundary—juggling, balancing, integrating. To appreciate that balance fully, it is helpful to know that the synthesis did not come easily. In fact, it was only with the writing of his books that Raymo discovered that the boundary between science and mysticism need not be a struggle; it could also be a dance.

His recollections of religion in his childhood years were less pleasant than those of astronomy. Religion, as it was taught in Raymo's Catholic family, church, and school, was a matter of following rules and memorizing formulas. It left him with a legacy of dualistic thinking that required effort to overcome. In time, he came to see the splits between body and soul, good and evil, natural and supernatural, as meaningless dichotomies, and to go about the work of seaming together the halves of what had been torn apart.

Raymo's academic training led him into the world of science. He majored in electrical engineering at Notre Dame, then did graduate studies in physics, first at UCLA and then at Notre Dame, where he received his Ph.D. in 1964. In graduate school the contradictions between the religion of his youth and his scientific training provoked a crisis of faith. He describes his shifting views of religion and science in the introduction to *Honey from Stone* (1987). Faced with the universe as described by contemporary science, "the narrowly anthropomorphic forms of traditional theology seemed inadequate. Nothing of what I had been taught in my religious education seemed quite capacious enough to encompass what I learned in science" (p. x).

During this time Raymo discovered the work of the French Catholic priest and scientist Pierre Teilhard de Chardin, which had a profound impact on him. For the first time, he saw that it was possible to be dedicated to science and at the same time to be a mystic. Although he never returned to Catholic faith, he began reading a new breed of Catholic writers, including Thomas Merton and the French intellectuals Georges Bernanos and François Mauriac. He also began to rediscover medieval mystics: Meister Eckhardt, Julian of Norwich, John of the Cross. But now he found their appeal not in their theology but in something more universal than religious

dogma: their sense of connectedness to the natural world, and the depth that lies hidden there.

Raymo describes how, following this renewal of interest in religious questions, his life proceeded to move along two parallel tracks. In his professional life, he became a professor of physics and astronomy, which he has taught since 1964 at Stonehill College in North Easton, Massachusetts. For the most part, he kept his mystical inclinations out of his academic work. His religious life continued to develop apart from the traditions and institutions of the church, in a direction that he describes as mystical or pantheist.

Raymo's first books were scientific in subject matter, and straightforward in style and approach. Between 1982 and 1984 he published three books on geology and astronomy, written in highly readable prose for the general reader. Perhaps the most popular was *365 Starry Nights: An Introduction to Astronomy* (1982), which followed the sky through each night of the year, and explained a variety of celestial phenomena in easy-to-understand language oriented toward the lay person.

In 1985 Raymo published *The Soul of the Night*, which he describes as the biggest breakthrough of his writing life. After living on two parallel tracks for twenty years, teaching and writing as a scientist, thinking like a mystic and poet, he tried writing in a way that would bring these two worlds together. Largely through writing the book, he discovered the power of this process of "making connections." Reviewers recognized the importance of this book, comparing Raymo's style to Loren Eiseley and Lewis Thomas. *The Soul of the Night* established Raymo as an important new voice in nature writing.

Following this breakthrough, Raymo wrote another book in a similar style, this time exploring a more recently discovered landscape. He and his wife had spent a year on the Dingle Peninsula of southwest Ireland in 1972 and almost immediately felt at home. They had since returned each summer, and they bought a home there in 1980. Raymo was fascinated with the Irish landscape, which is infused with the dynamic of converging

Chet Raymo at his summer home in County Kerry, Ireland

land, sea, and air. Intrigued with the predominance of stone, he set about exploring both the geology of the landforms and the stones shaped by humans: the megaliths and stone circles of pre-Christian times, and the stone remains of early Christian churches, monasteries, and hermitages. Here he also found a Catholicism that appealed more to his imagination than did the religion of his birth, a Catholicism rooted in the world of its pagan forebears with their magic stones, pools, and wells. Surrounded by a landscape that its inhabitants saw as sacred, Raymo wrote to explore this more hidden dimension. The resulting book, *Honey from Stone*, focuses explicitly on the question that had been occupying him for years: the convergence of the perspectives of science and religion.

Raymo's next book, *In the Falcon's Claw: A Novel of the Year 1000* (1990)—his first work of fiction—marked another important development in his life as a writer. He sees this shift as less of a breakthrough than was *The Soul of the Night*, more as a natural evolution in his work: another way to engage in the process of making connections.

In the Falcon's Claw, for example, explores the theme of the relation between science and religion through the story of Aileran, an Irish monk living in solitude around the year 1000. Aileran seeks God through nature, and his descriptions of the natural world are breathtaking. But his views get him into trouble with Pope Sylvester, a friend and companion from his youth who now staunchly defends the church's position that God is visible in nature only through miracles. Sylvester chastizes, and eventually excommunicates, Aileran for his heretical views that miracles such as comets and shooting stars are not miracles at all, but natural expressions of the cosmic order. For Aileran, all the events of nature are miracles, "signs of the mysterious power of God at work in nature.

Because of the fullness of Creation, all natural things are filled with the 'miraculous'" (p. 29). The interactions between Aileran and the pope, and the drama of their conflicting ideas, enable Raymo to explore the complexities of the relation between science and religion while telling an engaging and thought-provoking tale.

Raymo's second novel, *The Dork of Cork* (1993), explores complex questions of beauty and ugliness, suffering and love, through his favorite metaphor of the night sky. After having written all his life about the beauty of the natural world, a review of *Honey from Stone* challenged him with the realization that what he had left out of the book was the human drama and tragedy of that landscape. And so in this novel he explores the question of beauty through the story of Frank Bois, an amateur astronomer and writer who loves looking at the stars through his telescope, and is obsessed with the question of beauty: he is a dwarf, and considered ugly. Frank is the bastard son of a French mother and an unknown American sailor who has come, by a bizarre series of circumstances, to live in Cork, Ireland. His story, told in his own words in a complex narrative of many layers, recounts the painful and often humorous episodes of his childhood and youth, and his attempts as an adult to find love and acceptance. The novel, rich with poetic descriptions of the beauty of the night sky, also explores in an unusual and compelling manner the complexities of not-so-beautiful aspects of human experience. In 1995 it was made into a full-length motion picture, a distinction claimed by few nature writers.

One other aspect of Raymo's multidimensional work is important to note. Since 1985, he has been a science columnist for the *Boston Globe*, each week generating a thought-provoking "musing" on the human questions of science. In 1991, he collected many of these reflections into *The Virgin and the Mousetrap: Essays in Search of the Soul of Science*. This book offers a wealth of information about the scientific world Raymo inhabits: not only astronomy and geology but also the natural history of sea squirts and pear thrips, the conflicts between animal rights activists and scientific research,

the risks and dangers of radiation research and genetic engineering. Since its style and content place it more in the genre of the science essay, I will not consider it in depth here. Raymo's *The Soul of the Night* and *Honey from Stone* possess a literary sophistication and a narrative style that distinguish them as important contributions to the field of nature writing. It is to a detailed consideration of those two works that I now turn.

The Soul of the Night

Because its primary subject is astronomy and the night sky, *The Soul of the Night* is a unique book in the field of nature writing. But its style and approach are much closer to Henry David Thoreau's *Walden* or Annie Dillard's *Pilgrim at Tinker Creek* than to anything in the popular literature of astronomy. If the night sky is Raymo's landscape, he re-creates it here in a way that makes it vivid and concrete for readers, enabling them to enter the world of black holes and quasars, dark matter and nebulae, with as much sense of immediacy as one might feel from a description of a pond in the woods or a mountain meadow. By introducing us to a landscape that is normally hidden, Raymo shifts our frame of reference radically, so that the world becomes a different place. As one of my students exclaimed: "Is this stuff real? It's certainly not the world I usually live in. But if it's really true, it would change my whole life!"

Raymo successfully renders this landscape of the sky, and leads us into this life-changing intimacy, through a variety of stylistic conventions often appearing in the work of nature writers: personal narratives, accounts of scientific fact and research, metaphorical language, and allusion. Each essay focuses broadly on one astronomical theme: a particular phenomenon such as the black hole, or a question, such as "Why is the night sky dark?" or "How will the universe end?" By weaving together a variety of materials and stylistic elements around each theme, the essays create a rich texture of meanings, and vividly render aspects of the universe that are normally quite distant and abstract.

Personal narrative provides a starting point for each essay. The majority of these narratives describe one of Raymo's experiences observing or searching for something in the night sky. "Often I have gone stalking the dark spaces of Ursa Major for galaxies" (p. 37), he muses, in wording more suggestive of a natural history field expedition than an extended time with an eye pressed to a telescope.

One of Raymo's most engaging descriptions is his account of watching through a telescope the rising of a crescent moon, capturing each shift in the moon's position and the changing landscape it brings into view. At first he was unaware that the dark side was already above the horizon; then, "quite suddenly, there was a scintillation on the black line of the ridge," like a "pagan festival of bonfires and torches." He describes, in turn, each feature of the moonscape as it appears: the line of light as it "gently sagged across my field of view," followed by a succession of mountains, "seas," and deserts. Raymo's descriptions have the flavor of an earthly landscape; for instance, he says of the lunar Apennines: "their great steep eastern flanks catching the full light of the sun." Several times he heightens the immediacy by describing the scene as if he were immersed in it: "I was out of the shadows now and onto the brilliant sunlit eastern plains" (pp. 165–166).

By drawing out the changing details of the scene, Raymo also re-creates his own perceptual process, which he then makes explicit: "The rising had seemed long and ponderous," but "the whole spectacular show took only a minute." He reflects that "the telescope had somehow slowed time as it fattened space. When the rising was over, I took my eye from the scope, and the moon quite suddenly shriveled to become a distant dot of light" (p. 166). By revealing the shifts in his own frame of reference in both space and time, he re-creates the perceptual experience of the astronomer and opens up new dimensions of reality.

Interwoven with these personal narratives are extensive descriptions of scientific research that has led to our present understanding of the universe. Even the most complex concepts are described so clearly that one need not have a background in astronomy or physics to become drawn into the drama.

One of the most fascinating examples is Raymo's discussion of a simple question with fascinating implications: Why is the night sky dark? "Black night is a paradox," he begins. "Let me explain." We settle in for a good story. First we learn of the debate between Galileo and Johannes Kepler over whether the universe is infinite. Kepler maintained that if it were so, then the entire sky would blaze with light. Raymo explains with an analogy: "In an infinite universe, no matter which way we looked, our line of sight must eventually terminate on a star, just as a person in a wide forest must in any direction eventually see the trunk of a tree" (p. 35). He guides us through several hundred years of debate on the issue, bringing us to the position asserted by Heinrich Olbers in 1826, which came to be known as Olbers' paradox: "If the universe is infinite and uniformly sprinkled with stars, then there should be no night" (p. 36).

This paradox left astronomers with a puzzle they could resolve only by accepting that the universe was either finite or so young that the light from distant stars had not yet had time to reach the earth. For the resolution of the paradox, Raymo takes us through a complex series of research questions that led to the hypothesis that the universe had a finite beginning fifteen billion years ago, and has been expanding ever since. Because there are no stars more than fifteen billion light-years away, there is not enough light from the distant ones to fill the sky with light. Then a story of scientific discovery leads to a stunning conclusion: *"the night is dark because the universe is expanding.* . . . The universe is too young for the night sky to blaze with light" (p. 40).

This is a characteristic move for Raymo: leading readers carefully through a straightforward analysis of the facts to a new understanding that leaves them "agog with mystery." Science is no less the sphere of the miraculous than is religion. "The light of science may be more cautiously received than the light of the mystics, but the quest is no less heroic. There are visions in the new astronomy grand enough to blow the gods from their celestial thrones" (p. 17).

Some of the power of Raymo's narratives can be attributed to his unusually rich metaphorical language, more similar to that of natural history writers than to the customary style of astronomy writing. His metaphors not only make observations or concepts more vivid but also suggest some of the larger implications, as in his description of the expanding universe. If space is "blowing up like a balloon, swelling like a loaf in the pan," then the galaxies are moving away from each other "like dots painted on the surface of the inflating balloon or raisins in the rising loaf" (p. 47).

Sometimes these metaphors help the reader to visualize the unimaginable, as in a chilling description of the infinite dispersal that is one possible scenario for the end of the universe: the earth "seared and left to freeze in darkness," "galaxies of dark starlike masses" whirling unseen, "cold, ghostly pinwheels, black on black," and the eventual diffuse gas of subatomic particles, "drifting ever farther apart, the candle of Creation snuffed, the wick crushed between the fingers, the soot blown to the wind" (pp. 195–196). Here the metaphors help us feel, imaginatively, the immensity of an event trillions of billions of years in the future: the end of the universe, our home.

Perhaps the most unique characteristic of Raymo's writing is his extensive use of allusion. Woven into his narrative of personal stories, accounts of scientific research, and vivid metaphorical language, are a wealth of allusions that give the essays much of their depth and texture. Here is where Raymo's gift for making connections becomes especially apparent. As we read, we come upon the poetry of Rainer Maria Rilke, Theodore Roethke, and Sylvia Plath; the *Odyssey* of Homer; the plays of Shakespeare; passages from the Bible; quotes from Thoreau and Herman Melville, Antoine de Saint Exupéry and Max Picard, and the fourth-century Chinese

poet T'ao Ch'ien. The literary references are worth the challenge, for they add such depth and richness to the work that one cannot grasp what the book is about without some understanding of the way they work.

Perhaps Raymo's most straightforward use of allusion is to amplify a scientific concept or natural phenomenon by suggesting its resonance with a mythological, literary, or historical image, as in "The Monster in the Pool," the scientific subject of which is the black hole. He begins by introducing us to the monsters Scylla and Charybdis of Homer's *Odyssey*, the Great Kraken of Norwegian lore, and the giant squid and great white whale of Melville's *Moby-Dick*. After shifting into a discussion of the research that led to the discovery of black holes, Raymo suggests that they may be our contemporary "monsters." "Not even Odysseus could have dreamed of a monster more bizarre than the object that resides at the center of the Milky Way spiral, a kernel of matter dense and dark beyond imagining, feeding upon stars" (p. 112). Here, the allusions not only add to the sense of mystery but also suggest that such images, whether from myth or from science, are an important aspect of the world in which we live. "The black hole, the white whale, the monster in the pool: The image won't go away" (p. 116). By linking the concepts of astronomy with mythological images, Raymo leads us through science to the mysteries of existence, thus giving "soul" to the night.

Another frequent form of allusion is the brief quotation of a line of poetry. Often these lines appear without comment or explanation, simply to amplify the imagery of the text, as when, in "Night Creatures," Raymo slips in a few lines from Sylvia Plath to enhance the imagery of darkness and its appeal to the human imagination. Other times, poetry serves to advance a particular idea more directly, often amplifying a philosophical perspective. "In a Dark Time," another essay about the allure of the dark, weaves in quotes from Roethke's poetry to suggest how darkness often gives birth to new vision. " '*In a dark time the eye begins to see.*' And this is the paradox: that black is white, the darkness is the mother of beauty, that the extinction of light is revelation" (p. 20). Then Raymo returns to an earlier reference to a concept of vision held by the ancient Greeks: that the eye sent out a pale light into the world, which then "returned again as a traveler bearing gifts." Thus the eye "was both illuminator and receiver." As the essay proceeds to its conclusion, the Greek image and the Roethke lines play off one another, the meanings gathering and deepening. "But then, unexpectedly, the Greek truth emerges. The light of the mind returns bearing extraordinary gifts. 'A Man goes far to find out what he is'" (p. 20).

Personal narrative, scientific description, metaphorical language, and literary allusion: these are key ingredients of Raymo's writing in *The Soul of the Night* that work together to create a rich texture of meaning, much in the manner of other philosophically complex nature writings, such as those of Thoreau, Eiseley, and Dillard. But Raymo's manner of blending these elements is unique, and to fully appreciate the complexity and style of the book, it is helpful to follow one essay closely and see how it works. I have chosen "The Silence" because it successfully integrates a variety of sources, styles, and perspectives, and skillfully orchestrates them around a single theme: the silences of the universe.

Raymo begins with an anecdote, not from astronomy but about an incident he observed on Boston Common. A young man on a skateboard collided with a child, who went flying through the air and was injured upon landing. From a distance, the entire incident seemed to occur "in perfect silence. . . . It was as if the tragedy were happening on another planet. I have seen stars exploding in space, colossal, planet-shattering, distanced by light-years, framed in the cold glass of a telescope, utterly silent. It was like that" (p. 3). He suggests that the silence of Boston Common and the silence of the universe are not so different; "it is a thin membrane that separates us from chaos."

Raymo follows immediately with a question, as he often does to suggest larger meanings without pinning them down: "How are we to understand the silence of the universe?" He explores this with a series of examples: meteors falling from the sky, stars exploding, even the big bang itself—all utterly silent.

There follows a leap so abrupt that the reader may wonder if he or she has missed something: "In Catholic churches between Good Friday and Easter Eve the bells are stilled." Such leaps are common in Raymo's writings: without transition or preparation, they thrust the reader into a parallel world. The effect of such abrupt transitions is striking, even exhilarating. Not gradually emerging insights, these connections set off fireworks of their own through the sheer drama of their explosion. Then Raymo slowly elaborates the connection. Here, he explains the twelfth-century European custom of sounding wooden clackers and other noisemakers instead of bells to remind the worshipers of "the terrifying sounds that were presumed to accompany the death of Christ. It was unthinkable that a god should die and the heavens remain silent." This suggestion of a moral universe that responds to tragedy with outcry is countered by returning again to the incident of the child. "I listened. I turned the volume of my indignation all the way up, and I heard nothing" (p. 4).

Raymo then leaves the moral and spiritual questions and returns to the physical, recalling a high school experiment with an electric bell in a glass vacuum jar to illustrate how without air there is no sound. He describes in vivid metaphorical language how the air was pumped from the jar until the bell became silent, as the class "watched the clapper thrashing silently in the vacuum, like a moth flailing its soft wings against the outside of a window pane" (p. 5). If the bell in the vacuum jar was silent, how much more so are the vast empty spaces of the universe.

Another sudden shift brings Raymo back to the moral question: "The physical silence of the universe is matched by its moral silence. A child flies through the air toward injury, and the galaxies continue to whirl on well-oiled axes" (p. 7). Shifting again, he describes the Queset Brook that meanders through a marsh near his town, a place that in November is "as silent as the space between the stars." As this image develops, silence begins to take on a positive connotation, and we are in a world of meanings where complexity has multiplied. Often Raymo adds such counterpoint meanings that keep us from settling into easy conclusions. Now silence bears the gift of reflection, as is suggested by a reference to Thoreau, who celebrated the deepened silence between the hoots of an owl as " 'a vast and undeveloped nature which men have not recognized.' " As Thoreau "rejoiced in that silent interval," so Raymo "rejoices in the silence of the November marsh" (p. 8).

The positive meaning of silence is amplified as Raymo recalls an idea from Max Picard's *The World of Silence*: that silence is "the source from which language springs," and to which it must "constantly return to be recreated." What from one perspective appears to be the cruel indifference of the universe, the essence of meaninglessness, from another point of view is the ground out of which language and meaning emerge.

In a brilliant synthesizing passage that recapitulates all of these allusions, Raymo pulls together ideas and images from the entire essay.

> It is for this silence, so treasured by Picard, that I turn to the marsh near Queset Brook in November. It is for this silence that I turn to the stars, to the ponderous inaudible turning galaxies, to the clanging of God's great bell in the vacuum. The silence of the stars is the silence of creation and re-creation. It is the silence of that which cannot be named. (p. 8)

It is in such silences that he finds "the soul of the night."

Raymo concludes with a suggestion of his own continuing quest for the meaning of silence in the midst of these paradoxes. Drifting down the brook in his canoe, he listens, perhaps only for a "scrawny cry," in the words of the poet Wallace Stevens. "I don't ask for the full ringing of the bell. I don't ask for a clap of thunder that would rend the veil in the temple. A scrawny cry will do, from far off there among the willows and the

cattails, from far off there among the galaxies" (pp. 8–9). Then Raymo returns to the scene on Boston Common, pondering again that pause in the action when all was still. "How long did my heart thrash silently in my chest like the clapper of a bell in a vacuum?" The images of the essay continue to play off one another as the ripples spread.

One might question if Raymo is trying to encompass too much in this essay, including as he does a current event and an ancient religious rite, a high school science class and a French philosopher, radio telescopes and Henry David Thoreau. Yet the reader's impression is not one of chaos or overload of images, but one of absolute precision and control. The images of the essay circle around the theme of silence as elegantly as the planets circle the sun, held in their orbits by an artful gravitation that enables each to be in relation to the other, exerting its pull on the other without displacing it. Dramatic leaps may startle the reader, but never upset the delicate balance of the whole. And although the essay explores phenomena and concepts of astronomical dimensions and transcendental implications, the recurring reminders of the down-to-earth tale of a child anchor us in the everyday world.

As Raymo explores the immense universe, he touches on profound questions that give "soul" to the night as well as to the book. Writing about his youthful crisis of faith, he compares the disappearance of his God to the flight of "God's sacred plover crying into the upland rain" (p. 55). He muses that "in God's absence I have tried to make a sort of theology of ornithology," seeking, like the mystics, the direct experience of "the radiance of Creation." As he affirms the "divinity of the world," he suggests the directions of his continuing search.

Raymo's explorations also reveal profound truths about the nature of the interactions between this "divine world" and the humans who inhabit it. In an essay about names and naming, he suggests that as we come to understand the universe through our observation and study of its phenomena, we transform it and make it our own: "It is we ourselves who give the stars their invisible reality, beyond the visible. By watching. By naming" (p. 147). Thus, the human is an essential, if infinitesimal, dimension of the universe Raymo describes. Recalling Shapley's words, as the "small but magnificent" human is faced with the "enormous and magnificent universe," we create it, give "soul" to it, by every act of encounter. Once a student asked Raymo if he ever felt overwhelmed and insignificant in the face of the universe he described. No, he replied, for that just made him all the more amazed at the human mind and heart, that we can contain it all.

Honey from Stone

In *Honey from Stone*, Raymo picks up the question that has been implicit in his life and writing, and makes it the central, explicit focus of the book: How is the knowledge of science compatible with the life of the mystic? The title is taken from a letter of Bernard of Clairvaux, the twelfth-century founder of the Cistercian monastic order. In it he encourages one of his abbots to write a book, in spite of the abbot's protestations that he lacks the learned background to complete such a project. Bernard assures him that not all learning can be gotten from books: "More things are learnt in the woods than from books; trees and rocks will teach you things not to be heard elsewhere. You will see for yourself that honey may be gathered from stones and oil from the hardest rock. . . ."

In the introduction to the book, Raymo suggests that after he left behind the forms of traditional theology for many years, the physical and spiritual geography of the Dingle Peninsula may have inspired him to "reinitiate the religious quest": the stones are what inspired him to search for deeper meanings. He develops the quest motif in contrast to the style of metaphysical or theological writing: this book is to be "a kind of serendipitous adventure, a spiritual vagabond's quest." He hints at the contingent nature of its goal in words that set the tone for the book: "When I called out for the Absolute, I was answered by the wind. If it was God's voice in the wind, then I heard it" (p. xii). This tentative consideration of the possibility of encountering the divine in nature creates an openness throughout the book, a capaciousness that enables images of transcendence and mystery to arise quite naturally out of his concrete descriptions, free of theological definition.

The elements out of which Raymo fashions his journey are similar to those in his earlier book: personal narrative, scientific background, metaphor, and allusion. But the manner in which he weaves these elements together here is distinctly different, suggesting a maturing style and a more complete mastery of the art of integrating and structuring diverse materials. One might characterize *Soul of the Night* as a series of meditations, essentially self-contained and only loosely knit together into a larger whole. By contrast, *Honey from Stone* is a carefully orchestrated whole that invites the reader on a more intentional pilgrimage that grows in power and depth, with images, questions, and ideas building and playing off each other through the entire book.

Although the full impact of the book's unity comes only after considerable analysis, several easily recognizable features suggest it is worth looking for. The chapters are arranged by design, structured around the Book of Hours of the medieval monastic tradition. Where the monks observed a specific liturgical rite at each appointed hour of the day, Raymo observes a specific natural occurrence at approximately that same time: a comet at Matins in the dark before dawn, sunrise at Lauds, and sunset at Vespers, for instance.

The book's unity is also heightened by the quality of the personal narrative, which is more fully developed than in *Soul*, and more effective as an organizing thread: each chapter begins and ends with a vivid present-tense account of Raymo's observations, with a strong narrative line and sustained personal voice running throughout. The tone is more that of an "excursion" rather than a meditation; in it the writer leads us on a journey, bringing us to certain discoveries as we follow the path along the physical landscape.

The prominence of the landscape of Dingle heightens this concrete sense of the physical quest, and also helps to unify the book. Raymo's narratives lead us along easily recognizable roads—up paths to the top of mountains or along particular stretches of coastline—to specific sites described with vivid immediacy: churches, megalithic tombs, or islands covered with nesting birds. By the end of the book, we feel we have gained a familiarity with the landscape of Dingle and its features.

As in *Soul*, Raymo's descriptions point beyond themselves to the unseen dimension that lies behind the visible landscape: the patterns, histories, and invisible threads that bind together the elements of land, sea, and sky. What begins as a description of a walk in a snowstorm leads to a reflection on the complexity of snowflakes and the forces that determine their formation and structure; a description of an old stone church explores the geological history revealed in the different layers of stone used to build it. Even when describing the visible landscape, Raymo does so with the eye of the physicist, geologist, and astronomer, seeking the invisible dimension that lies behind and holds together the visible world.

As we turn to a closer examination of the book, more subtle aspects of its unity become apparent. Each chapter centers on one primary point of focus in the physical landscape: a snowstorm on Mount Eagle, the birds on the rocky Skellig Islands, the layers of rocks observable along the shore at Ferriter's Cove. Parallel to this physical landscape is a corresponding spiritual motif that gradually unfolds as the physical is explored. Sometimes it develops through a poetic allusion or personal story. Frequently it appears with quotations from Christian mystics such as Meister Eckhardt, Julian of Norwich, or St. John of the Cross. One need not, however, be familiar with Christian mystics, nor accept the tenets of their belief, to appreciate their importance in the essays. Raymo is more interested in their way of seeing than in the content of their belief. For instance, after acknowledging the huge gap between his world and the sixteenth century of St. John of the Cross, he reflects that "still, across the intervening centuries, John speaks to *this* dark night; his verses stand free of religious allegory, free of theological commentary; they are great free-standing arches of praise" (p. 182). This quality of the mystics' praise emerges as a central theme through their words and stories.

The sense of a well-orchestrated progression through a series of parallel physical and spiritual motifs gives the book its underlying thematic unity, and helps to orient the reader on an intentional pilgrimage. Questions and motifs play off one another, building in depth and power as they develop. Since the spiritual focus of each chapter builds on what has gone before, the results of the search are cumulative. Frequent references to previous chapters heighten the almost musical sense of developing themes, so that on reaching the end, we feel that the whole journey has been necessary to bring us to this point. The last chapter gathers and recapitulates earlier motifs, giving the attentive reader a sense of completing the circle.

Though it is impossible to convey fully in a short space the development of these parallel themes, a consideration of how several chapters build on one another may add to an appreciation of the process. In the first chapter, "Put on Your Jumping Shoes," a quote from Meister Eckhardt sets the tone for the book by suggesting how the complementary perspectives of science and mysticism provide the necessary footwear for the journey: "Put on your jumping shoes, which are intellect and love" (p. 19). The essay centers on Raymo's observations of meteorites in the dark, predawn hour: the monastic hour of Matins. It is the morning of the feast of Saint Lawrence, and the meteors are the Perseid shower, called the Tears of St. Lawrence in many parts of rural Europe. The story of the saint poses the first and perhaps central spiritual question of the book. When the Roman Emperor Decius demanded that he worship the ancient gods, Lawrence responded accusingly with a question: "Whom should I adore, the Creator or the creature?"

As the essay proceeds, Raymo adds narrative touches about his night of watching meteors, amplifies the legend of St. Lawrence, and explains how astronomers first discovered that meteor showers occur when the earth passes through the trajectory of a comet, filled with discarded matter from the comet's tail. Further back in the history of science, the story of Galileo poses the central problem that the book attempts to resolve. When Galileo was forced by the church to renounce his belief that the sun, not the earth, was the center of the universe, a monumental split opened up between science and religion, which Raymo suggests had disastrous consequences for both. The church was cut off from "one of the great adventures of the human spirit—the flight of the human imagination with the soaring Earth into a universe of unanticipated majesty and mystery" (p. 17). It also lost its opportunity to enrich the scientific voyage of discovery with its mystical traditions. Science and religion were both impoverished as each went its separate way. Now, as he attempts to overcome that split, Raymo seeks in the description of the scientist and the reflections of the mystic that rich "language of praise" that has been lost.

The words of Meister Eckhardt prepare the way for the culminating insight of the essay. "My eye and the eye of God are one eye, one vision, one knowledge, and one love" (p. 17). This enables Raymo to consider St. Lawrence's question from a new perspective: " 'Whom should I adore,' asked Lawrence, 'the Creator or the creature?' And I am struck dumb; the question has no meaning. My eye and the eye of God are one eye—one vision, one knowledge, one love" (pp. 22–23). The bold assertion of the mystic answers the troubling question of the saint and renders it meaningless. By letting one religious text speak to a question posed by another, Raymo sets up a dialogue within the tradition that enables us to see beyond its limitations into a new sense of its possibilities.

In the next chapter, "The God That Makes Fire in the Head," spirituality enters more directly into dialogue with science, creating a space for this new "language of praise." At the dawn hour of Lauds, Raymo watches the sunrise on the morning of the vernal equinox from atop a megalithic tomb. He tells about the nature and origin of the sun, as well as its importance for pre-

Christian sun worshipers and Christian celebrants of Easter: "On my sandstone bed I roll with the turning Earth toward the equinoctial fire, the Paschal flame, an incandescent globe of hydrogen and helium" (p. 32). He links the vision of pagan, Christian, and scientist more explicitly, noting how this "recurring theme, this murmur of resurrection" is "grounded in the mystery of the world." The quest of the scientist can also be the quest of the mystic because the mysteries of the spirit are "grounded in the mysteries of the world" (pp. 33–34).

The parallel between scientist and mystic is clarified through the figure of Aristarchus, a Greek scientist of around 200 B.C.E. who, with his calculations of the relative size of the sun and the earth, suggested the dimensions of an infinite universe. Raymo compares Aristarchus' assertions with the "sin" of Job; each spoke of "those things that exceeded his knowledge." Job's audacity was chastised by the voice of God from the whirlwind: *"Have you since your birth commanded the morning, and shown the dawning of the day its place? . . . Where were you when the dust was poured onto the earth, and the clods fastened together?"* (p. 38). But Raymo praises the "heresy" of Aristarchus: his bold theorems and mathematical propositions are "the language of praise." By the bold suggestion that "the creation was not measured on a human scale," Aristarchus enabled the human imagination to stretch "to encompass an infinite creation." The discovery of the scientist is indeed compatible with the perspective of the mystic.

Another mystic's hymn, the Song of Amergin from the earliest poetry of Ireland, deepens the resonances and completes the circle. "I am the god that makes fire in the head," sings Amergin. As Raymo watches the sun rise over Dingle Bay, the words of this ancient song ring from the hills. *"Who levels the mountain? Who announces the age of the moon? Who has been where the sun sleeps? Who?* asks Amergin, *if not I?"* (p. 45). With this song we see how depth and complexity build through this counterpoint of mystic and scientific voices. The Song of Amergin echoes the ancient language of the Book of

Job, but answers the questions asked by God in a very different manner, implying that all who explore and praise the creation are one with the Creator. This also echoes the words of Meister Eckhardt from the previous chapter: "My eye and the eye of God are one eye." Eckhardt, Job, Amergin, Aristarchus, Galileo: as the mystic, poet, or scientist reaches to encompass the mystery and infinity of the universe, each embodies the vision of God. While some readers might question such assertions from a theological point of view, Raymo orchestrates them so skillfully that we are left not with theological questions, but with rhapsodic assent to the deepest mysteries of the universe.

Chapter 3 tells of Raymo's walk to the top of Mount Eagle in a snowstorm one morning during the hour of Prime. Again, his observations of the landscape lead into a scientific discussion that opens out into mystical affirmation. Raymo discusses the history of snowflake theory and observation: Kepler's theory of hexagonal structures; Wilson "Snowflake" Bentley's observations and photographs of over 5,000 flakes; and the assertions of contemporary physics that vibrations may be the means by which crystals organize themselves.

Yet for Raymo even such knowledge is but "an island in a sea of mystery," and this, he suggests, is the "ground of his faith." After having studied four centuries of theory and research on snowflakes, "still every snowflake upon my sleeve is a cipher." All we have learned about the nature of the snowflake does not lessen its mystery: "it grounds it in a deeper, broader mystery that envelops my partial knowledge as the cloud envelops the mountain, as the sea envelops the land" (p. 59). Scientific knowledge is not inimical to mystery: it extends and deepens it.

Chapter 5 explores the rugged coastal Skellig Islands where medieval monks built hermitages and lived alone in a world of rock and sea. The islands are rookeries for numerous species of seabirds: gannets, "streamlined as a sunbeam," who "wheel and dive . . . like the swirling aftermath of a pillow fight" (pp. 96–97); storm petrels, who at night "emerge from their hiding places, like bats from a dark cave, to frolic about the island, close above the sea, their tiny webbed feet dangling so low that they appear to be running upon the water" (pp. 104–105).

Inspired by the solitude of the island, Raymo recalls the words of Richard Rolle, who in the fourteenth century retreated into solitude to seek "a perfect knowledge of God." Raymo wonders if he found "in solitude a kind of pure knowledge, a participation in what simply *is*, a storm petrel's kind of knowledge . . . a knowledge that — as Rolle insists — has its source not in speculation but in intuition?" (p. 112). Yet whereas Rolle sought to be ravished by "things unseen," Raymo, as scientist, asserts that if he is to encounter God, "it must be as the ground for 'things seen.'" Here, he feels more a kinship with the monks of the Skellig hermitages, who "did not live in a 'cloud of unknowing,' but in a very real Atlantic mist," who "clamped their anchorage to the rock and listened to the song of the wind," who "found the Absolute in the elements and took their pleasure and their knowledge from *things seen*" (p. 113).

This emphasis on the visual is highlighted by a phrase from the Irish poet Seamus Heaney: "description is revelation." Raymo asserts that "The act of description is pure and sharp and satisfying, and whatever it is that is sure in this world . . . is all about me on the Great Skellig." His italicized descriptions now become the mystic texts. *"Listen, there, to the chatter of sea birds and the squeak of the wind. And look, there, where a cloud of kittiwakes follows a shoal of invisible fish"* (p. 101). Here, surrounded by rock and sea and sky and thousands of birds, Raymo embraces a mysticism of the concrete, giving shape to the "theology of ornithology" he hinted at in *The Soul of the Night*.

In his final chapter, "The Knowing That Unknows," Raymo artfully gathers together the threads he has been setting in place, and brings his "naturalist's search for God" to its culmination. This chapter occurs at Compline, the last of the evening monastic hours. He is outside in the world he loves best — "the world lit by starlight" where "surfaces are transparent . . . and the soul sees into objects and beyond" (p. 168).

This hour that brings the monastic day to a close, and the astronomer to his beloved night sky, also reveals to the mystic and seeker the depth that lies behind the surface of things.

As he looks up at the star Vega, he ponders the miracle of the human brain that enables him to receive and process the light from 10,000 stars, sorting each in its proper place and opening "my soul to a universe whose length and breadth exceed my wildest imagining." And then another miracle strikes him: that his eye is made of the same substance as the star it observes: "an astonishing revelation of the relatedness of everything that exists." This "wound-up universe" is as compact as the hazelnut that Julian of Norwich saw revealed to her in a vision as "all that is made." Yet this universe that is held together by interconnections is also ultimately mysterious, full of "rabbit holes" like those of Alice's Wonderland: "Every star is a rabbit hole into another world," and the night sky is a "thousand rabbit holes leading to Infinity."

As the essay and the book come to a close, the words of the mystics enter the dialogue once again. Raymo recalls the verses of St. John of the Cross, which speak of the darkness of the soul when the believer feels separated from God. For Raymo, this "knowledge of the evening" is not just a prelude to a final revelation: it is all that he has, and all that he asks for. "I cannot pray. I can only praise." Here he finds a new language of mysticism, one that does not depend on the conceptions of God and religion that he had abandoned in his youth. Instead, as scientist and mystic, Raymo reaches out into the darkness and mystery of the creation, and finds there his inspiration for praise.

In the wake of this realization, the key metaphors that have led Raymo along the path come flooding back. First, the question of Lawrence returns: " 'Whom shall I adore, the Creator or the creation?' And the night sky answers: *The creation!* Beautiful. Terrifying. Deep" (p. 184). Then he remembers climbing Mount Brandon in a fog, and how, as he climbed above the fog onto the summit, he recalled the metaphor of the island: "*Knowledge is an island surrounded by a sea of mystery.* On Brandon's cloud-truncated summit, the metaphor was made startlingly clear" (pp. 184–185). Finally the line from Heaney's poem enters the flow of his meditation: "*Description is revelation. Seeing is praise.*" As these and other references from earlier chapters weave together, each insight marks a stage in the journey, each is needed to bring us to the present moment.

Raymo closes by reaffirming the unknowability of the ultimate. Speaking of the possibility of encountering God along the expanding shoreline of our knowledge, he acknowledges that the word "God" may no longer "have currency in an age of science," but it may still stand "like a distant horizon, like a foreign shore." This awareness is similar to what John of the Cross calls "this knowing that unknows." Thus, the quest of the scientist and that of the mystic alike lead to a shore on the edge of a vast sea. The same humility that leaves the scientist struck dumb before the infinity of a rabbit hole universe, also haunts the mystic with the sense that the ultimate can never be known. For Raymo, as for St. John of the Cross, there is "Nowhere a bottom." The naturalist's search for God has brought him everywhere, and nowhere. For the pilgrim who is open to a vision grounded in the stuff of stones and stars, Raymo leads the way to a new kind of knowing that is both scientifically viable and mystically profound.

Conclusion .

This "knowing" that is also an "unknowing," the revelation that cannot ultimately be named, puts Raymo in the company of other great mystic naturalists of the twentieth century: Eiseley and Dillard especially come to mind. For all three writers, the mystics are an important source of inspiration, not as they point to any ultimate knowable reality but as they embody a way of knowing, a way of being connected to the world. We might call this "revelation without theology," which stops short of identifying what the revelation is *of*, wisely recognizing that to make such an identification is to watch the reality slip away. These writers give us metaphors and stories that suggest, but never define, the deeper reality to which the natural world points. This "mysticism of the concrete" leads us to contemplate the deepest mysteries and meanings of existence by entering fully into the particulars of the natural world.

The spirit of Raymo's unique contribution as a nature writer is well expressed in the chapter of *Honey from Stone* in which he recalls the struggles of his father on his deathbed to reconcile the "two great excluding poles of his life," God and science. As he fingers a stone with a fossilized brachiopod, Raymo reflects: "If there is an incarnation, then this is it. If there is a resurrection, this brachiopod has found it. If we are made in the image and likeness of God, then *this* is his image" (p. 136). In his writing, Raymo gives us stones and stars, snowflakes and black holes, storm petrels and comets. Passionately committed to the facts of existence and to the search for spiritual meanings, his writing is animated by the faith that the spiritual emerges out of the physical and is intimately bound up with it. This, indeed, is gathering "honey from stone."

Selected Bibliography

WORKS OF CHET RAYMO

BOOKS

365 Starry Nights: An Introduction to Astronomy (Englewood Cliffs, N.J.: Prentice-Hall, 1982); *The Crust of Our Earth: An Armchair Traveler's Guide to the New Geology* (Englewood Cliffs, N.J.: Prentice-Hall, 1983); *Biography of a Planet: Astronomy, Geology, and the Evolution of Life* (Englewood Cliffs, N.J.: Prentice-Hall, 1984); *The Soul of the Night: An Astronomical Pilgrimage* (Englewood Cliffs, N.J.: Prentice-Hall, 1985); *Honey from Stone: A Naturalist's Search for God* (New York: Dodd, Mead, 1987); *Written in Stone: A Geological History of the Northeastern United States* (Chester, Conn.: Globe Pequot, 1989); *In the Falcon's Claw: A Novel of the Year 1000* (New York: Viking Penguin, 1990); *The Virgin and the Mousetrap: Essays in Search of the Soul of Science* (New York: Viking, 1991); *The Dork of Cork* (New York: Time Warner, 1993).

ARTICLES

"An Examination of Consciousness," in *Notre Dame Magazine* 21 (fall 1992); "Is Science Really Necessary—or Is It Just a Means to an End?" in *Boston Globe* (14 September 1992); "Dr. Seuss and Dr. Einstein," in *Orion* 12 (spring 1993); "On the First Day There Was a Big...," in *Boston Globe* (6 December 1993); "A Pocketful of Stones: Memories of Childhood," in *Orion* 12 (spring 1993); "The Shape of Air," in *Sanctuary* 32 (January/February 1993); "In Search of the Soul," in *Boston Globe* (17 January 1994).

HOPE RYDEN

SYDNEY LANDON PLUM

I IS ONE of those paradoxes that mark humankind's place in the natural world that Hope Ryden has a temperamental propensity for stillness—part of what makes her a gifted observer of wildlife—but that the breadth and accuracy of her observations, and the eloquence with which she sets them forth, call her into a life of activism. Ryden declines publication of her birthdate. In the 1960s she established herself as a freelance documentary film producer and writer. Since 1970, she has focused her patient eye and her camera closely on animal subjects, producing book-length studies of mustangs, coyotes, bobcats, key deer, and beaver; as well as briefer or photographic studies of animals she has encountered in her careers as a naturalist, documentary filmmaker, and inhabitant of the woodlands of downstate New York.

These works, directed to various audiences, exhibit the careful observation of the naturalist and the attention to depicting life in the wild truly; they also detail the intersection of the lives of animals and humans. From the physiology of the American mustang to the diaspora of a beaver family, Ryden chronicles animal life from birth to death, with particular attention to the care of the young. In each work she marks the points at which human activity—agricultural, sportive, and as mindless as only we can be—determines and undermines the patterns of these creatures' lives. She examines the preconceptions, the fears, and the prejudices that shape our interaction with the animal world, often to its disadvantage. Out of this mindfulness of the ecology of the mustang's and coyote's lives on the range, the bobcat's wilderness hermitage, the deer's island dependency, and the beaver's wetland industry, she writes with authority and conviction, and actively proclaims the ruthlessness of industrialized society. Her knowledge and concern have made her a spokesperson at government hearings during heated debates, and give her works an enduring forcefulness.

Serendipitous Subjects

Hope Ryden, the daughter of Ernest E. Ryden, a minister, and Agnes Johnson Ryden, was born in St. Paul, Minnesota, and grew up in western Illinois. She spent her summers in the woods of northern Wisconsin at the family's summer cabin. The "Author" page of *The Little Deer of the Florida Keys* (1978) shows a photograph of a three-year-old Hope meeting her first deer. A biographical essay by Patricia Curtis tells of her encountering one of the last wolves in northern Wisconsin during a summer visit when she was nine. Ryden said, "That wild animal struck a deep note in me." These encounters must indeed have stayed with her on some level. After receiving a B.A. from the University of Iowa,

Ryden was a free-lance documentary film producer and writer in the 1960s and 1970s. A 1970 film, *Missing in Randolph*, was nominated for a Screen Writers Guild award. In 1978, a television documentary, "Angel Dust: Teenage Emergency," won Emmy, Clarion, and Society of Silurians awards. A lead from John Walsh, a special agent for the International Society for the Protection of Animals, led to the film *Operation Gwamba*, a documentary on an animal rescue project in the flooded jungles of Surinam. Walsh also interested Ryden in filming a food drop to starving huskies in the Arctic Circle.

In 1968, when a call came from Walsh about the plight of a herd of wild horses in the Pryor Mountains of Montana, Ryden and her film crew flew there. The results were a film, Ryden's first book—*America's Last Wild Horses* (1970)—and a lifelong commitment to telling the stories of the animals who share our environment. During the years she spent photographing and studying the mustangs of the West, Ryden became interested in another maligned Westerner, the coyote. *God's Dog: A Celebration of the North American Coyote* was published in 1974. Her next project was *The Wellsprings*, a documentary on coastal wetlands during the filming of which Ryden became intrigued by the small deer living in the Florida Keys, an interest that led to another book in 1978. Her next topic was a native species of wildcat. This study took on different dimensions than first planned because of the bobcat's skittishness, causing Ryden to comment (to Curtis) that she would not have attempted it had she known how "furtive and reclusive bobcats are." Still, in typical fashion, she persevered and improvised. *Bobcat Year* was published in 1981. Her most recent book-length study is of the beavers of Lily Pond, near her cabin in New York state.

Concurrent with these well-researched studies, Ryden has put together photographic studies. These books, from *Mustangs: A Return to the Wild* (1972) and *The Wild Colt* (1975), to *Your Cat's Wild Cousins* (1991) and *The Raggedy Red Squirrel* (1992), are for audiences of all ages, although most of them are designed as children's books. An interview conducted early in 1994 for this essay revealed that Ryden was working on other books for young audiences, several to be published in 1994. And she was preparing a photographic study of insects, learning both about these creatures that are in everyone's lives and about the macrophotographic techniques necessary to capture their images. One day she was working on a photograph of a cockroach. Because cockroaches are nocturnal, and flee into the dark when the lights are turned on, Ryden had to find a way to keep one still in the light needed for the photograph. She put a cockroach briefly into the freezer, to lower its metabolism. When removed from the cold and placed on a piece of bread, the cockroach began eating—not running away—and Ryden was able to shoot a roll of film. But then she was confronted by another problem: what to do with a slightly cool cockroach in a New York City apartment. Showing the respect for life forms apparent in all of her writing and photography, Ryden released the cockroach outside her apartment.

It is perhaps no accident that this anecdote concerned the welfare of a creature widely considered a nuisance. Ryden's studies have often focused on animals that are persecuted because so many consider them nuisances, or worse: mustangs, coyotes, bobcats, beavers. Ryden's studies look first at the animals, with the detail that can come only from a long time spent in the field, sitting very still. However, she also confronts the network of ideological, economic, and political circumstances that place animals in jeopardy. The dissemination of information about these animals, the rhythms of their lives, and their synergism with other species and the environment is also their defense. Ryden has been both an expert witness and amicus curiae in legal cases involving these animals and their habitats. Although she finds this kind of public and institutional speaking unnerving, she does it because she feels she "owes it to the animals." After years of fieldwork among different species, Ryden feels the connection between the life forms on the planet. She does not expect the animals to like her; however, when they start to tolerate her, she feels that she has been included. Out of this feeling comes the impetus for her activism, which is supported by her patience—the special knack for sitting quietly that her friends think is genetic.

The activism of Ryden's various studies is multifaceted. Although it is of tantamount importance to know the animals, it is also important to show them in their environment, to know the special burdens they carry, the onus of their existence. Ryden's studies accomplish this. The writings work to keep a balance between emotional responses to the animals and objective observation, between anthropomorphism and reporting on animal lives, the desire to defend wildlife and the need for some detachment in order to be heard, between mystery and knowledge; and they reveal the central imbalance that motivates the writing: between humankind's power and animal needs. These works follow in the medieval tradition of social criticism by holding a mirror up to mankind.

Ryden poised to photograph wild horses in Hawes Valley, Nevada, 1970

America's Last Wild Horses

Ryden began her twenty-five-year involvement with the American mustang by filming a herd of wild horses that was about to be rounded up by the U.S. Bureau of Land Management, the federal agency responsible for managing public lands. At the time, the mustang—designated neither as domestic livestock nor as native wildlife—was denied grazing privileges on public lands, and Bureau officials perceived it as their duty to remove them by whatever means possible. The wild horses, harassed by airplanes, were rounded up from their mountainous retreats. During these roundups many animals were injured or killed, foals unable to keep up fell behind and were left to starve, mares aborted, horses stumbled and broke their legs. Those captured were trucked to rendering plants and slaughtered.

Ryden's concern for the plight of these animals led her to learn more about them. She tracked wild horse history and studied the politics and ecology of the public rangelands; and she spent time in the field observing and photographing the horses. Two books resulted from her intense research: *America's Last Wild Horses* (1970) and *Mustangs: A Return to the Wild* (1972). The impact of the first, arousing and coalescing public concern, was such that within months of its publication the U.S. Congress passed the Wild and Free-Roaming Horse and Burro Act, which designated the wild horse a national heritage species and mandating that it be given a place on public lands.

The second book focuses more on the social pattern of a horse herd: the relationship between stallions and their mares, the maternal care given by the mares, the reckless lives of the young stallions, and the solitary lives of the older horses. The test is interspersed with pictures of mustangs in their natural setting—with no signs of humanity marring these wild reaches of the American West. One argument Ryden posits for legitimizing the horses' return to the wild is that "Simply by meeting nature's harshest test, the survival of the fittest, the wild horse, whatever its pedigree, has earned the right to be

783

respected as a wild and free creature" (*America's Last Wild Horses*, p. 39).

The reference to pedigree is quite important. Ryden's observations of these animals and her photographs of their conformations and coloration, in combination with research by Henry Schipman and others that supports skeletal evidence for a recessive trait peculiar to horses of Spanish origin, link the wild horses to a rich piece of history, the Spanish Conquest. The unskilled husbandry of the Native Americans allowed the proliferation of the Spanish-bred buffalo runners and war ponies, uncounted numbers of which later took their freedom. The first explorers of the Western plains reported enormous herds of wild horses mingling with the bison. Ryden found that many modern-day inhabitants of the West had little sense of this past. Many dismissed any suggestion that the wild horses could be anything but runaway stock. Bureaucrats in charge of public land management were single-minded in their insistence that the wild horses were of no historical worth. Because Ryden believed in the heritage of the American mustang, she presented the arguments strongly and clearly in *America's Last Wild Horses*. In the 1990s, DNA mapping is confirming that many wild horses are clearly of Spanish lineage.

Ryden's involvement with wild horses did not end with the publication of *America's Last Wild Horses*. She continues to monitor them and periodically visits her favorite herd in the Pryor Mountains, on the Wyoming–Montana border, to spot descendants of the horses she first encountered. On several occasions she has appeared in federal court as an expert witness on behalf of the mustangs. When stockmen and hunting groups challenged the constitutionality of the Wild Horse and Burro Act, she defended the horses in an amicus curiae brief before the U.S. Supreme Court, which unanimously upheld the act.

America's Last Wild Horses does much more than present the portrait of an animal or show its place in the ecosystem of the plains. It is also a history of the settlement and destruction of the Great Plains. Americans have turned their backs on the horses who shared in their early experience of the land. Ryden quotes one horse lover: "If you can't eat it, or sell it, or mount its head, it just doesn't get to live!" (1990 ed., p. 237). This attitude mirrors that of the business interests who now control the Great Plains and whose overriding concern is how to make them profitable. Ryden knows there are no easy solutions for the future protection of the wild horse, and she understands the complexities of the historical and current situation of the American West; the forces at work are portrayed as what might be termed a modern Four Horsemen of the Apocalypse: "Mismanagement, ignorance, greed, and politics had all played a part in the despoiling of the West" (p. 208).

Like the plains across which the American wild horse flees with flowing tail, Hope Ryden's first book is stunning in its breadth. The history of the land from which much of the ethos and mythos of the United States was created is blended with a researched study of the wild horse and a patient depiction of the political, social, and economic forces that now shape the West in the way that wind, rain, and fire once did. The story is very big, but the voice is hushed, as if in awe—of the land, the horses, and the ravages of modern settlement.

America's Last Wild Horses won an Oppie award as the best book in the Americana category in 1970. It also received a *Library Journal* citation as one of the 100 best science/technical titles of 1970. The 1990 edition contains two "postscripts." The first, part of the 1978 edition, gives information on the aftermath of the first publication, which was an outpouring of public concern leading to legislative measures protecting the wild horses. After passage of this legislation, Ryden received an award as Humanitarian of the Year from the American Horse Protection Society in 1979, and a Joseph Wood Krutch Award from the Humane Society of the United States in 1981. The second "update" in the 1990 edition reports on the horses' current plight, and contains heart-wrenching photographs of massacred horses. This emotional appeal from an empathic, intelligent observer bears witness to the failure of private efforts and government regulations to repair this instance of humankind's fearful treatment of the natural world.

God's Dog:
The North American Coyote

The works of Hope Ryden chart a succession of rhetorical cues and responses — interactions between the writer/naturalist and her wildlife subjects in which the delineations of "subject" and "object," of "active" and "passive," blur into a cycle. The writer notes how her world acts upon the lives of the animals; the lives of the animals act upon the consciousness of the writer. The intersections and points of impact in these currents are mapped in the writings, in the shifting perspectives and styles and decisions about audience.

The early pages of *God's Dog* map a shifting of the observer's consciousness. Ryden's early interest in coyotes is piqued by sound rather than sight. While camping in the Pryor Mountains studying mustangs, Ryden hears the coyotes at night: "raising their mournful voices to a frenetic pitch until the surrounding peaks pealed with the echoes of their sonorous wails" (p. 3). Her first attempts to get the coyotes curious enough about her to let her approach, take photographs, make some notes, are made by using a whistle to mimic the coyote voice. However, it does not take long for her to realize the limitations of this method, which had been developed by coyote hunters.

> If I were to continue to employ trapper methods, such as whistles and dogs, not only would I have to be satisfied with the briefest sightings and these always of different coyotes, but worse, I would see only one aspect of behavior, the investigatory impulse, over and over again. I was interested in knowing more than that about coyotes! (p. 11)

She would have to rely, once again, on her patience — to stalk the coyotes, to wait to learn enough about them to feel confident in the knowledge, to live next to them. She needs to be as still as a young coyote waiting at a ground squirrel hole, yet she feels she is "not the equal of the little wild canid, who seemed to have his nervous system completely under control" (p. 23). The investigatory impulse under perusal is not only the coyotes' — the naturalist is different if she comes to the coyote's call.

Whereas *America's Last Wild Horses* was a well-researched study, bringing that particularly human trait — the intellect — to bear upon the history and current problems of the mustang, early in her work with coyotes Ryden understood that a different frame of mind was necessary for the kind of writing she wished to produce. At the beginning of the paragraph in which she realizes the limitations of the whistle, she says: "The answer must have been waiting for my intellect to stop working, for it seeped into my consciousness like something I had always known but didn't know I knew" (p. 11). Indeed, the naturalist is not "the equal" of the "little wild canid." She has to find a way to release herself from *her* mind, in order to find her way to the coyotes'.

If living among the animals will change her mind, in an ontological, not political, sense, then her writing will become more sensitive to what it might take to change a reader's mind (in both senses, but perhaps the latter is needed more quickly). Ryden notes that for thousands of years the survival of these species she watches has depended upon the skills developed for reproducing and caring for their young. Thus, she decides upon careful observation and recording of these activities, particularly the nurturing and training of the young. This naturalist's method served Ryden in the years it took to put together *God's Dog*, *Bobcat Year*, and *Lily Pond: Four Years with a Family of Beavers* (1989). The titles of the latter two books express the time necessary for finding one's way into each animal's world. In *God's Dog*, Ryden eventually is able to get close enough to a coyote family to understand its "home-making," to record the rearing of their pups for one whole season — then to find the same parents the next year. This became the pattern for *Bobcat Year* and *Lily Pond*, with variations made necessary by the temperaments and reproductive patterns of the different species.

Ryden's method is similar to Jane Goodall's in Africa, and is widely used by biologists. Yet it is not without its detractors. Both those for whom the subject is anathema—those who decorate their miles of barbed wire fencing with coyote skins—and those who feel that the coyote is truly more threatened than threatening may object that Ryden is trying to present the coyote family—Gray Dog, Redlegs, Brownie, and Harness Marks—in too sympathetic a manner. Others, who seek a quantifiable objectivism, might feel similarly. Yet Ryden's coyote studies are widely and frequently cited in subsequent, scientific studies, particularly of coyote denning habits. Close observation and familiarity with the subject and its environment lead to specific findings and interpretations. In one incident included in the book, Ryden gains some valuable information from a rancher with a coyote living among his dogs.

> Everett proceeded to take an envelope from his pocket and with what remained of his cigarette he set it on fire. Then he tossed the flaming paper at the coyote, who, quick as a hare, pounced on it and began drumming the flames with her forefeet while bouncing on and off the blaze until only the edges of the envelope were gilded with dying sparks. But the coyote still was not satisfied. With her shoulder she pushed the charred scrap against the hard ground. Then, after examining it, she repeated the action with her opposite shoulder until the paper disintegrated.
> My astonishment pleased Everett.
> "How did you ever teach her to do that?" I asked.
> "Didn't. All coyotes put out fires," he said, laconically. (pp. 145–146)

The biologist to whom Ryden brings this information classes it as typical reaction to a novel stimuli, but Ryden suspects the coyotes may have developed this behavior from living with the threat of prairie fires.

Whatever argument one might have with naming the animals, as evidence of anthropo-morphic treatment, it is still the case that Ryden attempts neither to domesticate her subjects nor to insinuate herself into their lives, except as the patient observer. The hours of watching—stretching into weeks and carrying over into years—produce such a detailed narrative of coyote life that no anthropomorphic tricks are needed to keep a reader's interest. Ryden is quite sensitive to her use of terms identified with human behavior to describe coyotes' actions, and documents thoroughly the instances and intricacies of the behavior she is identifying, so that readers can judge for themselves what is going on. A pair of coyotes hunting ground squirrels together and a family unit shifting dens; pups playing "keep away" and being given chances to chase and kill rodents already captured by a mature adult; the hierarchical patterns of adult coyote society and the bonding that results from a group howl are all part of the story, as are the many references to studies by naturalists, scientists, and other interested Westerners. The strength of this book is the hundreds of pages of description. Ryden is a gifted observer, and she is sharp. Furthermore, she sees the coyotes, and all wildlife, in the context of both the natural and the human world.

Like *America's Last Wild Horses*, *God's Dog* cannot be only the story of the coyotes' lives as they mate, bear, and rear their young, and prepare them for a predator's life. The larger world of human activity threatens to put an end to the coyotes' narrative. Coyotes are the subject of violent persecution because they are sometimes predators of sheep, a source of revenue in the West. One of the purposes of *God's Dog*, and of Ryden's appearances before Senate and Environmental Protection Agency hearings, is to argue that the method of dealing with this predation—the all-out extermination of the coyote—is unacceptable.

In an approximately forty-year period before Ryden began her study, the primary method of killing coyotes in the West was by poisoning. In her revelations of the results of the use of poison, Ryden uses numbers to produce the effect of the photographs in the final pages of *America's Last Wild Horses*. "To give some idea of the devastation of wildlife inflicted by P.A.R.C. agents on behalf of the woolgrowers, one need only examine Department of the Interior figures for a single year in the 1960s" (p. 268). P.A.R.C., Predator and Rodent Control, was the name then given to a "death squad" that for a while was euphemistically renamed Wildlife Services, and is now called the Animal Damage Control (A.D.C.) Program. Ryden continues, giving these figures for animals killed on *public* lands in that one year in the 1960s:

> 89,653 coyotes; 20,780 lynx and bobcats (the lynx is endangered in the Western states); 2,779 wolves (the red wolf is endangered); 19,052 skunks; 24,273 foxes (the kit fox is endangered); 10,078 raccoons; 1,115 opossums; 6,941 badgers; 842 bears (the grizzly is slated for the endangered-species list); 294 mountain lions; and untold numbers of eagles and other rare and endangered birds. (p. 268)

Just as Ryden began her coyote study, President Richard Nixon signed a presidential order banning the use of poisons on public lands. As Ryden was working, the sheep ranchers were organizing to contest this action. Their protests led to hearings, at one of which Ryden testified. The sheep ranchers have kept up the pressure. The potent and devastating poison 1080 — responsible for many of the deaths listed above — is still banned only by presidential order; legislation has never been enacted by Congress. Moreover, various maneuverings have weakened the original ban, which is under fairly constant risk of being totally revoked. Ryden presents ample evidence of the work of those "Four Horsemen": mismanagement, ignorance, greed, and politics. She brings to the reader's attention the meaning of the term "public" land, and the importance to the survival of the human species of the particular public lands on which she has studied wild horses and coyotes.

There is more at stake in *God's Dog* than fostering an appreciation of the coyote, the legendary trickster, as a species with a life to lead. Ryden also sheds light on one vision of mankind in the natural world. In discussing "The Politics

of Poison," Ryden quotes Jack Olsen's *Slaughter the Animals, Poison the Earth*, when he identifies the trapper as one who has an oversimplified, "good-or-evil" vision of the natural world. Unwilling to understand an ecological vision, he continues to interrupt and distort nature's networks. *God's Dog* is a masterful attempt to move the reader out of the mind-set of the "trapper with his poison kit." Its strengths are the patient eye, the keen mind, the breadth of the vision of its author.

Chronicling Survival

Focusing on patterns of reproduction and on the family unit is the approach of two other book-length wildlife studies: *Bobcat Year* and *Lily Pond: Four Years with a Family of Beavers*. Although both species are threatened because they share their habitat with mankind, the dynamics of the interaction is different from that detailed in Ryden's first two studies — humankind is less actively pursuing the destruction of these species. Ryden's primary purpose, as stated in the afterword to *Bobcat Year*, is "to make clear how elegantly an animal fits into its own surroundings and to show how its behavioral adaptations serve its survival" (p. 206).

The bobcat study was plagued with difficulties from the beginning, and Ryden has admitted that had she really understood how reclusive the bobcat is, she might not have undertaken the work. The mere presence of visitors at the Arizona–Sonora Desert Museum (a "museum" for wildlife) at a crucial time results in the deaths of the kittens born to a captive female bobcat. Already committed to the study of the nurturing of those bobcat kittens, Ryden must then go into the wilds in search of subjects. The fact that she does not revise her study at this point is further evidence of her belief that the focal point for studies of how an animal fits into its environment so as to maximize survival is the parent–offspring unit. Ryden's study depicts the extreme difficulty with which two bobcat kittens survive into adolescence. In part this difficulty is due to human intervention, but it is also a result of the bobcat female's solitary maternity. There simply is not a social safety net in case of a mother bobcat's death or her inability to care for her young.

Lily Pond opens with a family tree showing the offspring of Lily and the Inspector General, the beaver pair Ryden identifies at the beginning of her research. For the first time, she is able to verify her findings about the parent–offspring unit in the wild through close observation of more than one generation. She watches as successive generations learn the tricks of "our first and foremost conservationist," as she labels the beaver. Some of the kits grow up, leave, mate, and create new ponds. One unmated three-year-old returns to help rear her parents' latest litter. The Skipper's first mate, Laurel, is killed by a car; he finds another mate. Always focusing on the welfare of the species and the network within which it survives, Ryden writes of Laurel's death: "every creature that dies from causes extrinsic to the natural system, of which and for which it was born, weakens that system" (p. 141).

In the writing of *Lily Pond*, Ryden allows herself to do what she has not done before: she becomes attached to one specific animal, Lily, the matriarch of the multigenerational family of beavers whose activities remake the landscape of the corner of the state park where they live. She makes contact with Lily and does what she has always forbidden herself—she feeds Lily in the last months of her life, for Lily is partially crippled as well as elderly. Lily's death is recorded in graceful phrasing that might be used by any of us to record the losses we are experiencing in the natural world: "In the dark, the stark forms of the other beavers continued to move about like Arctic icebreakers, still visible against the white snow. It was a beautiful sight, but all I could think of was how painful it is to give up what you love, even when it has already changed into something else" (p. 239).

The caring attitude toward these animal families and the depth of Ryden's response to Lily's death do not come at the expense of clarity or breadth of observations, or of the intelligence of the conclusions drawn. Rather, this slight shift in tone signals a movement toward a different kind of communication.

Learning a Dynamics of Activism

In putting together the photographs and text for *The Little Deer of the Florida Keys*, Ryden articulates a further refinement of her purpose in these studies: "to concentrate on making Americans aware of the plight of wild animals in danger of extinction in North America" ("Author" page). The key deer are barely known to anyone not living on the coast of the southeastern United States. Their plight has nothing to do with their being deemed nuisances to other forms of animal life, either wild or domestic—as is the case with mustangs and coyotes.

"How did they get here? Why are they so small? How do they survive in such a marinelike environment? What are their habits? And why do we Americans know so little about this animal that is unique to our land?" (p. 10). These are the questions that Ryden articulates early in *The Little Deer*, again with the awareness of the limitations of the audience foremost in her mind. Their answers will in some way involve an unraveling of the complex relationship between human activity and awareness, and animal life.

This book relies heavily on photographs to tell the story of the key deer. Ryden photographs the deer primarily alone, in the swampy growth of their island homes. The photographs depict the protective coloration of the fawn, and the text explains how the doe's absence is another form of protection. As was the case with the earlier work on mustangs, this book tells of the fight to have the key deer recognized as unique so that it could be protected, but this story is given almost in outline. The eye is focused on the deer amid their habitat. And, along with the photographs of their small, island refuges, Ryden lists the other endangered species of the keys: the southern bald eagle, great white heron, reddish egret, roseate spoonbill, mangrove cuckoo, West Indian nighthawk, eastern pelican, American osprey, white-crowned pigeon, green sea turtle, key blacksnake, American alligator, and American crocodile. What the photographs of the animal habitat cannot express is the threat posed by the habits and continued growth of another population of the key islands — the human population.

Rather than shift the focus of the camera away from the deer, Ryden published an article in *Audubon* in tandem with the book's publication. This article tells in detail of the long struggle to recognize the key deer and establish a refuge for it in the Florida Keys. Four separate bills had to be introduced in the Congress before passage of the bill establishing the National Key Deer Refuge in August 1957. Writing of the key deer twenty years later, Ryden reports that the deer is still listed as endangered, and that "some obstacles may prevent" the herd's reaching sufficient numbers to warrant removal from the list. Looking forward in time, and taking into account the pressures exerted on wildlife, Ryden knows that in the past, "natural hazards such as hurricanes, droughts, accidents, disease, and old age" kept the herd balanced. In the future, their numbers will be decimated by "highway accidents, dog kills, poaching, and habitat destruction" (p. 102).

These predictions were entirely accurate. In 1983, Ryden published an article in *Wilderness* titled "Conflict and Compatibility: When Does Use Become Abuse?" This piece, a report on the troubles in the National Wildlife Refuge System, begins and ends by updating the status of the key deer. Ryden reports on the aerial application of pesticides on the keys to control mosquitoes — one example of people pressure. She is caught in a spraying. Holding her breath, covering her face, she wonders how this "bath of poison" will affect the endangered mangrove cuckoo, the West Indian nighthawk, the key deer. Ryden's questions serve to remind her audience to loosen itself from the mind-set of the trapper described by Jack Olsen and included by Ryden in *God's Dog*. It probably cannot be overdemonstrated that for the most part humanity's vision of the natural world is focused on use. Thus, Ryden must return to this point, again with descriptions of individual cases supported by the numbers that she has learned drive home the point.

"More than 600,000 acres of refuge forestland in the lower forty-eight states await only a rise in the economy before they can be fully exploited for their timber. In the Fish and Wildlife Service 'Threats' report . . . 260 refuges reported poaching problems, 189 agricultural and urban encroachments, 163 difficulties with off-road vehicles, 79 severe overcrowding" (p. 31).

Yet one might wonder if publishing these articles in *Audubon* and *Wilderness* might be a case of preaching to the converted. Looking closely, one finds that Ryden has taken yet another rhetorical tack in her constant reassessment of the most effective way to work her patient activism. At the end of the *Audubon* article she notes that "it was not so much expert opinion that swayed legislators as the blitz of mail and petitions from ordinary citizens that piled up on their desks" (p. 102). In the *Wilderness* article she is drawing attention to a terrible irony in the ebb and flow of activism. A great deal of energy is expended to get laws passed, but once this happens, the activists and animal protectors lessen their vigilance. The laws are often ignored, however, or new pressures are exerted to weaken the laws or their enforcement. Thus, at the end of this second article, she chides herself for thinking that "the National Wildlife Refuge System was as sound as Noah's Ark. A little probing of the ship's hull, however, has since revealed that the craft itself may be endangered" (p. 31). She concludes this piece by quoting Rachel Carson's call to constant vigilance: "Like the resource it seeks to protect, wildlife conservation must be dynamic, changing as conditions change, seeking ways to become more effective. We have much to accomplish" (p. 31).

Different Audiences

The note on the author at the end of the *Wilderness* piece states that Ryden "is currently working on several children's books on wildlife and conservation." Her first book for young readers, *The Wild Colt*, was published in 1972, so this note is an announcement not of her taking on something new but of a shift toward concentrating her efforts in this area.

By 1983, Ryden had produced books for young readers on colts, pups, and the bobcat. *The Little Deer of the Florida Keys* might also be considered a work for young readers, based on the ratio of photographs to text. It is comparable with the magnificent photographic essay *Mustangs: A Return to the Wild*, and both fall within a category of books difficult to define but with wide appeal. Ryden seeks not to categorize but to reach out to several audiences with material that merits both immediate and enduring attention.

The books for young readers are not simply picture books with excerpts from other texts. They are purposefully and skillfully wrought to bring wildlife to the attention of this audience in a way that will appeal to them, and such that they will see the hard lessons that are there to be learned. Thus, the books on mustangs and coyotes are on the young of these species. The series *Bobcat* (1983), *America's Bald Eagle* (1985), and *The Beaver* (1986) might well be used as handbooks to teach about animal adaptation within an ecosystem—with notes as to how poorly humanity accomplishes this. *Bobcat* explains the Darwinian concept as "the survival of the fittest traits," and gives examples of selective changes in different species that allow them to find their niche in the environment. *The Beaver* discusses how this animal was hunted nearly to extinction in the eighteenth and nineteenth centuries. *America's Bald Eagle* highlights the important work of naturalists and activists, notably Charles Broley and Rachel Carson, in identifying the threat to the bald eagle posed by the use of DDT.

The introduction to *Wild Animals of Africa ABC* (1989) states that to "understand an animal, it is important to know where it lives." This note applies equally to *Wild Animals of America ABC* (1988). Ryden presents photographs of a reclining wolf peering through the grass; two grizzlies in a mountain meadow; mother and child vervet monkeys in the bushes; and a xoxo frog symmetrically poised atop the rocks of what might be a streambed (but is actually the bottom of an aquarium).

Although it is certainly true that we need to see animals in their environment, it is also true that we need to see how animals must work to ensure the continuation of their species, despite humankind's rapacious growth. What Ryden shows all of her readers, in these photographic presentations and elsewhere, is not the hunt for its own sake, not the thrill of the chase, but the search for food to feed the young. Her practiced eye is turned upon creatures great and small, even a red squirrel Ryden observes when foot problems immobilized her. In *The Raggedy Red Squirrel* (1992), Ryden notes of this common animal, "*Tamiasciurus hudsonicus* mothers devote many weeks and much energy to the rearing of a small number of well-developed offspring" (p. 154). This is unlike other rodents, which have a succession of large litters with few survivors. *Raggedy Red Squirrel* continues Ryden's tradition of focusing on the family unit.

Another book for young readers is *Your Cat's Wild Cousins* (1991). The book presents feline traits exemplified by the domestic and wild branches of the family, with questions to pique in her readers the habits of observation that have served Ryden so well in her studies. "Does your cat catch and eat bugs like her cousin the black-footed cat?" asks Ryden. And "When your cat hides in underbrush, do you see her ears?" The questions asked are neither rhetorical nor patronizing; they require that attention be paid to the common house cat, and to the wild cats described briefly. The descriptions focus on the trait chosen for comparison and photographed. A final note gives the scientific name for each cat and some mention of their present status. The ocelot is threatened, and the puma is in decline. The tiger is seriously endangered. The last jaguar within the borders of the United States was shot in New Mexico in 1903. The cheetah is on the endangered species list and may soon become extinct.

The reason for the threat to the cheetah is its coat. As she has in the past, Ryden holds a mirror up to those whose actions have led to this sad state: "Some people think that by wearing the cheetah's fur coat, they will look as elegant as it does. What do you think?" (p. 17). One can only hope that young readers will look into this mirror and choose a different course of action, one that will allow the cheetahs to live. That is, of course, the point of writing for the future activist. Ryden — with her years of experience as an activist, expert witness, and friend to wildlife in court — says: "I don't know if writing your Congressman helps, but writing to and for children works."

In the Balance

Writing natural history that works to change the minds of its readers is a balancing act, just as Ryden's life must balance the work of the naturalist and of the activist. It requires patience, and she seems to have a store as vast as the sky above the mustang's range. Perhaps she has learned it from watching the animals. One winter in the Lamar Valley, a few old bull elks have not moved to the higher elevations, remaining in the slushy snow with a pair of coyotes. Ryden knows the coyotes will not attack healthy bull elks. Yet every time an elk moves, a coyote leaps into the vacated place in the snow. Then she sees why. The much heavier elk break through the snow, which the slighter coyote cannot penetrate. The coyotes are going after the mice that "wintered in a wedge of air between the earth and the snowpack." This passage illustrates the genius (in its more antiquated sense, as an inhabiting spirit) of Ryden's writing. From her patient watching on a winter afternoon, enriched by weeks and months of watching and by research, comes insight into the lives of the coyote — or, at another time, another place, the mustang, the bobcat, the beaver, the key deer. Through her art, Ryden gives the reader the chance to see what is truly happening, with an eye unprejudiced by misrepresentations of animals' lives.

She is as artful as the coyote. Knowing that "the presentation of objective facts by themselves seldom has motivated human beings to behave more sanely toward the natural world" (*God's Dog*, p. xvi), she re-creates the natural world for us to see on a late winter afternoon.

As the sun's long rays filtered through the wintry sky, the snow took on a golden cast, and the coyotes, their hunger appeased, moved thirty yards from the bulls and curled up. When not in movement, they appeared indistinguishable from the tops of the giant sage that tufted the snowy fields. Even the reclining elk with their branched antlers resembled the upper portion of protruding vegetation. I wondered how many creatures that I failed to see actually studded the vast panorama! I learned to look and look again. (p. 59)

Objective facts — the number of animals killed, refuges in danger, the truth of how coyotes live — cannot by themselves get people to act, Ryden knows. What she needs is to evoke "that profound feeling for the natural world that Albert Schweitzer called *Ehrfurcht*, reverence for life" (p. xvi).

Ryden has stood on high plains amid the dust and heavy hooves of the wild mustangs; spent an afternoon floundering through chest-high snow during the winter in Yellowstone National Park; slogged through swamps, been bitten by mosquitoes, and been sprayed with insecticide to photograph the key deer. Yet these experiences receive short shrift in her writing. Ryden has been overcome by the emotional pain of leaving the beaver world she had watched and enumerated for four years, and by the pain of all the animal deaths both in the scheme of things and through human self-interest, cruelty, and fear. However, this pain does not cloud her vision.

Ryden's work has not progressed straight toward some preconceived goal. She has allowed the spirit of the wildlife to capture her interest and lead her. And even then, there have been times when their lives have become unbalanced and Ryden's work has had to take a different tack. And Ryden has herself revised her rhetoric, changing both the scope of her subject and her targeted audience over time. In the mid 1990s she is writing to teach the powers of observation and to incubate a young person's affinity for other creatures, more than to detail the lives of a specific creature and to make older audiences mend their ways.

Yet Ryden would not be able to win anyone over, to seeing or to thinking and acting differently, if she did not express love. She freely admits to her love for the wild horse, to being thrilled at the "silhouette of an arrogant stallion poised atop a ridge." This is a sight that has thrilled many, and will remain on the Western horizon — if it does — in good part due to the work of Ryden. It is one thing to be thrilled by the mustang on the horizon. It is another to be thrilled by the soulful wail of the nearby coyote, when you are alone in the high country. Still, she is not afraid; she can experience *Ehrfurcht*:

> As time passed the pack began to raise its common voice to a cobalt sky, seemingly for no other purpose than to celebrate being alive in Jackson Hole. In June the days were so perfect I wanted to sing along with them. The air smelled of summer grass, which by then was long and iridescent and concealed ground sparrows whose unexpected burbles of song brightened my solitary life inside the van. Along the slope the quaking aspen fluttered as if in perpetual dance. This was a happy time for the coyotes. The weather was perfect, food was easily obtainable, and pups were underfoot. But it was also passing quickly. (*God's Dog*, p. 242)

Selected Bibliography

WORKS OF HOPE RYDEN

BOOKS

America's Last Wild Horses (New York: Dutton, 1970; rev. and updated, New York: Lyons & Burford, 1990); *Mustangs: A Return to the Wild* (New York: Viking, 1972); *The Wild Colt* (New York: Coward, McCann and Geoghegan, 1972); *God's Dog: A Celebration of the North American Coyote* (New York: Coward, McCann and Geoghegan, 1974; repr., New York: Lyons & Burford, 1989); *The Wild Pups* (New York: Putnam's, 1975); *The Little Deer of the Florida Keys* (New York: Putnam's, 1978); *Bobcat Year* (New York: Viking, 1981); *Bobcat* (New York: Putnam's, 1983; repr., New York: Lyons & Burford, 1990); *America's Bald Eagle* (New York: Putnam's, 1985; repr., New York: Lyons & Burford, 1992); *The Beaver* (New York: Putnam's, 1986; repr. New York: Lyons & Burford, 1992); *Wild Animals of America ABC* (New York: Dutton, 1988); *Lily Pond: Four Years with a Family of Beavers* (New York: Morrow, 1989); *Wild Animals of Africa ABC* (New York: Dutton, 1989); *Your Cat's Wild Cousins* (New York: Dutton, 1991); *The Raggedy Red Squirrel* (New York: Dutton, 1992); *Backyard Rescue* (New York: Morrow, 1994); *Joey: The Story of a Baby Kangaroo* (New York: Morrow, 1994); *Your Dog's Wild Cousins* (New York: Dutton, 1994); *Out of the World* (New York: Dutton, 1995).

ARTICLES

"Good-by to the Bobcat?" in *Reader's Digest* 109 (November 1976); "Saga of the Toy Deer," in *Audubon* 80 (November 1978); "Following the Shadowy Trail of the Cat That Walks by Itself," in *Smithsonian* 12 (June 1981); "Conflict and Compatibility: When Does Use Become Abuse?" in *Wilderness* 47 (fall 1983); "A Red Squirrel's Life Is More Than Just a Tempest in a Treetop," in *Smithsonian* 22 (November 1991).

BIOGRAPHICAL AND CRITICAL STUDIES

"Beaver Behaviors Surprise Scientist: Naturalist Hope Ryden Takes You on a Visit to Explore the Fascinating World of Beavers," in *Current Science* 75 (January 1990); Patricia Curtis, "Wide, Wild World of Hope Ryden, Bedroll Naturalist," in *Smithsonian* 11 (November 1980); David L. Wilson, "Legend of the Pacific White Mustang," in *Folklore* 90, no. 2 (1979).

SCOTT RUSSELL SANDERS
(b. 1945)

WILLIAM NICHOLS

IN HIS ESSAY "At Play in the Paradise of Bombs," Scott Russell Sanders describes life at the Ravenna Arsenal, a military reservation in northeast Ohio where he spent part of his childhood and youth. He portrays a landscape and community that seem unlikely to produce a nature writer. He points, for example, to a difference between his background and that of Huckleberry Finn's creator: "At the age when Samuel Clemens sat on the bank of the Mississippi River smitten by the power of steamboats, I watched rockets sputter on their firing stand, I sat in the gutted cockpits of old bombers, hungry to pilot sky ships" (*Paradise of Bombs*, pp. 12–13). But Sanders is not claiming a handicap. Instead, he suggests that his own imagination springs from a "place that concentrates the truth about our condition more potently than any metropolis or suburb" (p. 3). For we all live, he says, in a "fenced wilderness devoted to the building and harboring of instruments of death" (p. 4). Most of Sanders' essays, novels, and stories examine this grim predicament, seeking to know how we came to inhabit such a place and how we might transform it.

Despite the haunting presence of the "fenced wilderness" in Sanders' work, there is much room for hope and beauty. He writes lyrically and knowledgeably about rivers, forests, his neighborhood in Bloomington, Indiana, and the influence of landscapes on the people he calls "unmemorialized common folks." He writes about love among people and between people and the places where they live. Although he continues to be haunted by the violence stored in the Ravenna Arsenal, Sanders writes essays and fiction about the sacred possibilities he finds where nature and culture meet.

Sanders believes that with words we might chart our way beyond civilization's capacity for destruction. The story of his coming to this belief probably begins well before his family moved into the arsenal, perhaps even before he was born on 26 October 1945 in Memphis, Tennessee, to parents—Greeley Ray Sanders and Eva Solomon Sanders—who were at home in rural landscapes and accustomed to hard physical work. But the shape of the story first becomes visible in his account of the summer of 1962, when he was sixteen. Intellectually, he was focused on science then, as he would be for a few more years. Then Sanders met Ruth Ann McClure, fifteen, at a summer science camp, and they began a five-year correspondence that led to their marriage (27 August 1967). "During those five years," he says in his essay "Letter to a Reader,"

we saw one another in the flesh no more than a dozen times. And yet, after exchanging a thousand letters, I knew this woman more thoroughly, understood more about her values and desires, and loved her more deeply than I would have if I had been living next door to her all that while. Even more than the keeping of a journal, that epistolary courtship revealed to me the possibilities in writing.

During the years of his correspondence with the woman who would become his wife, Sanders moved from physics to literature at Brown University (B.A., 1967), although his interest in science is still visible in his writing more than twenty years later. After finishing college and getting married, he studied literature at Cambridge University (Ph.D., 1971). During four years in England, Sanders began to write and publish short stories, some of which later appeared in *Fetching the Dead* (1984). But the focus of his work at Cambridge was a study of D. H. Lawrence, one of the great explorers of a theme that must have been at the center of Sanders' correspondence with McClure: the mysteries of deep, embodied love.

D. H. Lawrence: The World of the Major Novels (1974) was Sanders' first book, and his subsequent writing suggests that it was a kind of apprenticeship to Lawrence. Sanders has continued to work with some of Lawrence's themes, including the power and mystery of sexual love, the complex relationship between nature and culture, the fear of society's corrupting power, and the hope that we might build a "more humane social order." Sanders has been fascinated, too, by the British writer's effort to express those parts of human experience that least conform to language. "Over against the conscious, isolated self," he says of Lawrence, "he set the unconscious, undifferentiated being, the natural process, the matrix of life out of which the individual emerges" (p. 16). This interest in the "nature in human nature" continues to be one of Sanders' preoccupations. He often describes people as the natural issue of the landscapes they inhabit. One can say of the varied characters in Sanders' essays and fiction what he wrote of the people in Lawrence's fiction: "Like birds and wildflowers, his characters are prey to the forces and subject to the laws of the natural order." Still, when Sanders' charac-

ters encounter trouble, the destructive capacities of civilization are likely to figure in their fate.

Nonfiction

Stone Country (1985), revised as *In Limestone Country* (1991), was Sanders' first book of nonfiction after *D. H. Lawrence*. It differs from John McPhee's books on geology. Whereas McPhee explains complex geological processes in loving detail, profiling scientists who have developed theories to explain how North America came to its present state, Sanders describes the limestone quarries near his home in southern Indiana and the common people who work in them. At the Indiana Statehouse, he points out, there are many plaques and memorials to people of influence and fame, "but you will not find a word anywhere about the men who dug or cut or laid up the stone for this twelve-acre building" (p. 34). That is what interests Sanders. In the early 1980s, he set out with Jeffrey A. Wolin, whose photographs appear in the 1985 edition, to know the source of the stone for many of the United States' most important buildings, including the Pentagon, the Empire State Building, and the National Cathedral. "We were hunting a place," he says of one trip into the quarries, "that would give us a feel for what the life of a quarry hand might have been like in the long-gone days" (p. 34).

Along the roads among the quarries, Sanders finds stories of violence and terrible accidents, evidence of hard use of the land and the people. He watches three drunk men empty pistols again and again into a quarry where he is resting in a crevice. "They might have killed me by accident," he reflects. "But they might also, I was convinced, have killed me on purpose" (p. 48). Still, he finds a certain comfort in the primal world of the quarries: "At a time when our own lethal inventions could erase within the space of an hour everything our species has ever made, when the poisons we spew into air and water begin to snuff us out, when our multiplying mouths threaten to eat us out of house and planet, I find keen comfort in the enduringness of limestone" (pp. 172–173).

Local people offer comfort, too, especially those who have learned endurance from the land. Even a conversation with Ed Bennett, a scarred, suspicious old quarrier implicated in poisoning the local water by letting people dump capacitors in a quarry he owns, becomes the occasion for a surprisingly lyrical moment. When Bennett begins to tell stories about his home in Hunter Valley, he talks about a traditional winter custom of leaving stoves burning in limestone processing mills to warm hermits living in the quarries. Hearing this, his wife comes out of the kitchen to tell of a mill fire and of her love for Bennett. She remembers exactly the date of a fire at the Consolidated Mill in 1921, she says, because she and Bennett had been married just three weeks. "I was cooking with Momma," she reminds Bennett, "and we went outside to look at the fire. All I could think about was you being down there in it. My uncle was working on the traveler, and my father on the planer. But all I could think about was you" (p. 62). Such memories are one kind of treasure Sanders seeks in his explorations of local landscapes and communities.

Sanders' next nonfiction book, *The Paradise of Bombs* (1987), is a collection of personal essays. Crafted so beautifully that they have been mistaken for short stories, these essays often teeter on the edge of despair, as though Sanders were unsure of finding enough light to counter the darkness he describes. In "Listening to Owls," he recounts rising before dawn to hear mysterious birdcalls, but his meditation on the humanlike features of owls leads to this grim aside: "Aha, we think, here are feathered, midget versions of ourselves; they must be smart. I supposed the owls, noting the same resemblance, would assume we are expert killers, and they would be right" (p. 41). In "Coming from the Country" he suggests that an urban perspective might find the virtues of rural life "small potatoes," adding, "in the long cold winter of cruelty and want that lies ahead for the world, we'll need all the potatoes we can find" (p. 132). Even his account of a hike in Oregon, "Feasting

on Mountains," turns grim. What begins as a successful effort to brighten his melancholy mood by walking up Mount June is brought up short by the spent cartridges Sanders finds at the summit. People carrying guns to the top of a mountain, he suggests, must have wanted to kill something: "But what death could they have envisioned from up here? And why would they have fired aimlessly into the void?" (p. 64). In "Death Games," Sanders reflects on our society's confused love affair with violence as it is expressed in a toy store, a gun shop, and a day's headlines.

But if *The Paradise of Bombs* is one of Sanders' darkest books, it also reveals much about the resources he calls upon to find light and order in our violent society. "The Inheritance of Tools," like "At Play in the Paradise of Bombs," is a powerful meditation on his childhood and youth. It is about Sanders' father—his death, his legacy as a teacher of carpentry, and his ways of showing his son the importance of craft. This essay exemplifies Sanders' densely metaphorical style, his effort to ground language in the solidity of earth and body, the disciplines of home and community. On the morning his mother called to announce his father's death, Sanders says, "ice coated the windows like cataracts." He listened to his mother, "the long distance wires whittling her voice until it seemed too thin to bear the weight of what she had to say" (p. 102). He was doing carpentry that morning, as his father was when he died, and before his mother called, Sanders had banged his thumb with a hammer. "A week or so later," he recalls, "a white scar in the shape of a crescent moon began to show above the cuticle, and month by month it rose across the pink sky of my thumbnail. It took the better part of a year for the scar to disappear, and every time I noticed it I thought of my father" (p. 102). This is a writer who interprets the world not so much through the filters of ideas as from the ground of concrete memories, metaphorical connections. In "The Inheritance of Tools" he crafts memories and metaphors to accomplish what Robert Frost once asked of a poem—that it be a "momentary stay against confusion."

Secrets of the Universe (1991), another collection of personal essays, opens with "Under the Influence," which can be read as a shocking companion piece to "The Inheritance of Tools." "My father drank," Sanders begins, almost as though he were adding a fact he forgot to mention in the earlier essay. "He drank as a gut-punched boxer grasps for breath, as a starving dog gobbles food—compulsively, secretly, in pain and trembling" (p. 3). Sanders has said that this essay, which first appeared in *Harper's Magazine* in 1989, is more about family secrets than about alcoholism. But it is also about "the nature in human nature," a theme from Lawrence. There are haunting echoes of Lawrence's novel *Sons and Lovers*, particularly the story of Paul Morel's father, in this account of the Sanders family's struggle with Greeley Ray Sanders' alcohol addiction. In *Sons and Lovers*, Paul, his mother, and even Lawrence himself seem to condemn Paul's father for his ignorance and drunken behavior, but they also associate him with the mysterious power of nature. Sanders' father, a skillful athlete and patient teacher of carpentry, was sometimes taken over by a wild, ungovernable part of his own being, something closer to nature than to culture: "Drowsy, clumsy, unable to fix a bicycle tire, throw a baseball, balance a grocery sack, or walk across the room, he was stripped of his true self by drink" (p. 17). Sanders writes this essay, he says, in the hope of sparing his children the kind of pain that comes with assuming the grief of a parent, for he believes his own moods and his addiction to work have begun to weigh on them. The crafting of words, then, becomes for Sanders a way of caulking the boat of our foundering society for the next generation.

"Reasons of the Body" focuses on Sanders' relationship with his son, Jesse, an athlete. It is about the transmission of knowledge held in the body as much as in the mind. Here Sanders appears to be seeking a replacement for the lore of hunting and farming that men once shared with their sons. "The lore of sports," he admits, "is a step down from that of nature, perhaps even a tragic step, but it is lore nonetheless, with its own demigods and demons, magic and myths" (p. 33). Exploring such knowledge of the body, Sanders sometimes seems to be in dialogue with Lawrence. In "Looking at Women" the dialogue becomes explicit when Sanders laughs at Lawrence's view of the penis as a god. It is more like a railroad signal, Sanders suggests, or "an ill-trained circus dog." And the "force field of sex," he insists, is formed as much by culture as by nature.

One difference between *The Paradise of Bombs* and *Secrets of the Universe* is a comic, self-effacing voice in parts of the latter. In "The Singular First Person," a meditation on the personal essay, Sanders compares himself with a soapbox orator and calls his essays "naked, lonely, quixotic letters-to-the world." In the title essay he tells of his nostalgic return to his old discipline in a book called *Physics Made Simple*. He discovers, he says, that *he* has been made simple since "he last spoke physics with ease."

But this matter of discipline is deeply serious, too, in *Secrets of the Universe*, for Sanders has concluded that the discipline of craft is not enough, given the task he has set for himself. In "Landscape and Imagination" he seeks a way of knowing the world that seems un-American, given the high value we place on mobility: "It is a spiritual discipline to root the mind in a particular landscape, to know it not as a visitor with a camera but as a resident, as one more local creature alongside the red-tailed hawks and sycamores and raccoons" (p. 94). This impulse to ground the self locally, as much a way of life as a literary theme, is important in most of the essays in *Secrets of the Universe*, and it is at the very heart of Sanders' next book of nonfiction, *Staying Put*.

Staying Put: Making a Home in a Restless World (1993) is perhaps the crucial book, so far, for understanding the work of Sanders. As he explains in the preface, it is an account of his effort to root his life "in household and community, in knowledge of place, in awareness of nature, and in contact with that source from which all things rise" (p. xiii). It is a story of a search that is both practical and spiritual. *Staying Put* begins and ends with descriptions of the rural land outside the Ravenna Arsenal in northeast Ohio, where Sanders lived from 1956, after his family moved off the military reservation, until 1963, when he went to college. "After the Flood" tells of his return to this land many years after it was covered by water impounded behind a "boondoggle dam." This chapter is a meditation on loss, although Sanders insists his is a small one compared with those of Native Americans, African-Americans, refugees, migrant workers, and the homeless. Our society, he suggests, is impoverished by such losses in ways we do not fully comprehend: "We are slow to acknowledge the pain in yearning for one's native ground, the deep anguish in not being able, ever, to return" (p. 14). This elegiac chapter makes a case for nostalgia as a feeling more complex and important than just sentimental longing for an idealized past.

The next two chapters, "House and Home" and "Earth's Body," emphasize both the despair and the joy to be found in fully acknowledging our physicality. Sanders describes the house he and his wife bought for $25,000 in 1974, and the work and attention it has required since then, as they have slowly transformed it into their home. Echoes of Henry David Thoreau's *Walden* are apparent in this chapter, but Sanders' emphasis is different. Thoreau reminds readers in an increasingly materialistic society that shelter does not demand a large investment of time and wealth. In a mobile society that places little value on physical work, Sanders points to the disciplines needed to resist the effects of entropy: "A house is a shell caught in a surf that never stops grinding" (p. 23). "Earth's Body," the next chapter, begins with entropy. Sanders speaks of a fear that comes in the night with the certainty of his own annihilation, the "square root of nowhere and nothing." Recognizing that "risky, roving thought" takes him into this terrifying chaos, Sanders goes into his yard to embrace a tree and the earth itself. He struggles in the darkness to know the world physically. "For the flesh there is no past or future," he says, "there is only this instant of contact, here, now" (p. 44). In the knowledge of the body Sanders finds as he explores his yard in darkness there is a wonder-

ful paradox: "The eternal life I seek is not some after time, some other place, but awareness of eternity in this moment and this place" (p. 54). This consolation, found in one's capacity to live fully in the here and now, is another connection between *Staying Put* and *Walden*.

The next three chapters—"The Force of Moving Water," "Settling Down," and "Ground Notes"—reveal how far Sanders' impulse to inhabit a place is from parochialism. "The Force of Moving Water" examines concretely the meaning of bioregionalism by considering the significance of living one's life in the watershed of the Ohio River. "Chances are," Sanders tells his reader, "your own life and the history of your place are braided with the current of a river, as my life and place are braided with the Ohio. When we figure our addresses, we might do better to forget zip codes and consider where the rain goes after it falls outside our windows" (pp. 61–62). Our troubled relations with rivers, he suggests, reveal our deep ambivalence about all wildness.

In "Settling Down," Sanders sets himself against a part of the modernist sensibility that chooses to homogenize the earth. He quotes from John Berryman's poem "Roots":

O really I don't care where I live or have
  lived.
Wherever I am, young Sir, my wits about
  me,
memory blazing, I'll cope & make do.

                                    (p. 103)

Berryman ultimately chose not to live; his suicide, Sanders says, suggests that none of us can live utterly uprooted from place and community. Similarly, the novelist Salman Rushdie, a migrant, has celebrated the "migrant sensibility," rooted more in ideas and memories than in actual places. Sanders' response to Rushdie is stern: "Wholesale displacement may be inevitable; but we should not suppose that it occurs without disastrous consequences for the earth and for ourselves" (p. 106). These consequences Sanders refers to, advisedly, as holocaust. He describes the nightmarish effects of chain saws

Sanders under the study-window hemlock at his house in Bloomington, Indiana

himself and his own neighborhood in the context of natural history and astronomy, to fuse the great and small. But the essay reveals also a self who, having known the Holocaust and Hiroshima, has concluded that human ignorance of our connections with the rest of creation can lead us to do catastrophic damage to ourselves and the earth.

"Telling the Holy" begins with the story of Jeremiah Lofts, a fictional name for a man who first appeared in a Sanders short story, "Prophet," in 1970. During a memorable February in Sanders' childhood, this neighbor came to believe the world would end on 1 July. Preparing for Judgment Day, Lofts visited the Sanders family to warn them: "He did not rant. He delivered the news firmly and simply, as a man might tell his neighbors about a coming storm" (p. 147). Sanders was troubled by this prediction when he was a boy, and as a writer who has struggled to imagine prospects for the earth that are not utterly bleak, he is inclined to take Lofts seriously even though the world survived that particular July. Sanders, like Lofts, seeks to interpret the power that underlies the physical world. "Telling the Holy" comes from the Apache word for myth: "By telling the holy, sacred stories ground a people or an individual, not merely in a landscape, but in the power that creates and preserves the land" (p. 154). Sanders' ultimate task as a nature writer, this essay suggests, is to do what the world's religions have done—that is, "point, longingly , toward an unbroken symmetry, a primal unity."

The final chapter in *Staying Put*, "Wayland," describes Sanders' return to a literal crossroads that was a focus for much of his early life. He tells of his high school biology teacher, Fay Givens, who showed him the diverse beauty of a meadow: "She taught me that if only we could be adequate to the given world, we need not dream of paradise" (p. 186). He recalls the mysterious breeding of horses and describes a scene of powerful, confused sexual longing with his high school sweetheart in Wayland. He remembers an early encounter with death. "Wayland" is the most moving chapter in *Staying Put*,

and earthmovers on a farm near his home that is being turned into a mall in spite of the owner's attempt to save the farm in her will. This nightmare is finally, for Sanders, a spiritual matter. To find meaning in our existence, we must be "fully present" in a place. "There is only one world," he concludes, "and we participate in it here and now, in our flesh and place" (p. 121).

The sentence with which Sanders begins "Ground Notes," the next chapter in *Staying Put*, captures an important characteristic of his thought: "The dirt in my neighborhood has begun to thaw, releasing a meaty, succulent smell that is older than I am, older than humankind, older than anything I can see from my window except the sun and moon" (p. 125). Such a sentence echoes Walt Whitman, who embraces all of creation. This self longs to know perhaps because it circles back to those primal experiences, the sense of the whole or of holiness, that seem to take people beyond the reach of language. "Language is of only modest help," Sanders says near the end. But he says this in a book that uses words with great power and precision.

Like other writers who invite us to reclaim traditional virtues and values, to find our way back through the abstractions and machinery that separate us from the earth as it has been given to us, Sanders sometimes seems old-fashioned. In his fine essay about the personal essay, "The Singular First Person" in *Secrets of the Universe*, he comes close to saying that such writing puts us in touch with external truth: "I believe one writes, in essays, with a regard for the actual world, with a respect for the shared substance of history, the autonomy of other lives, the being of nature, the mystery and majesty of a creation we have not made" (p. 203). But if such a statement rings with a hint of confidence that sounds anachronistic, one need only look elsewhere in the same essay for a postmodern view of writing: "Dizzy from a dance that seems to accelerate hour by hour, we cling to the narrative line, even though it may be as pure an invention as the shapes drawn by Greeks to identify the constellations" (p. 186). Although Sanders seeks comfort in his essays, he does not turn to easy certitudes that leave out of account the powerful uncertainties at the heart of much contemporary thought.

Sanders has begun to receive wide recognition for his nonfiction. In 1986 he won the Penrod Award for *Stone Country* and in 1987, for *Paradise of Bombs*, he received the Associated Writing Programs Award for Creative Nonfiction. *Kenyon Review* gave Sanders its Award for Literary Excellence in 1991, and he won a Guggenheim Fellowship for 1992–1993. In 1995 Sanders received the Lannan Literary Award in nonfiction. Such attention suggests that Sanders' explorations of our troubled landscape, both his grim portrayal of our society's destructiveness and the hard-earned hope he finds in spite of it, have found an audience.

Fiction

Since 1971, Sanders has taught in the Enlish department at Indiana University. He has advised graduate students and served on tenure review committees during a time when his profession seems increasingly preoccupied with critical theory. Although he has not written much about the theoretical debates that often divert literary studies from literature, he has commented plainly on trends in contemporary fiction. In "Speaking a Word for Nature," an essay in *Secrets of the Universe*, Sanders criticizes much American fiction for failing to set itself against the dominant culture's obliviousness to nature. This is not a new problem, as Sanders sees it. He traces it from William Bradford through Henry James to Don DeLillo, Bobbie Ann Mason, and Raymond Carver. The absence of wild landscapes in contemporary fiction, Sanders argues, is part of a larger failure to quarrel with the dominant ways of thinking in our culture. But this is not the only problem Sanders finds in contemporary fiction. In his introduction to *The Paradise of Bombs*, Sanders explains his affection for the personal essay by criticizing fiction: "Most of the fashions in fiction of the past twenty years have led away from candor—toward irony, satire, artsy jokes, close-lipped coyness, anything but a serious, direct statement of what the author thinks and feels" (p. xiii). Contemporary fiction writers, Sanders claims, too often fail to acknowledge the ground on which they stand.

Sanders has written more fiction than essays. His narratives show the power and vulnerability of nature, the violence and greed in civilization. They reveal concerns he often expresses more directly in his nonfiction. With the exception of a few short stories set in our own time in *Fetching the Dead*, most of Sanders' fiction takes place before and after the twentieth century. *Wilderness Plots: Tales About the Settlement of the American Land* (1984) is a collection of fifty brief tales, the first of which is set in the seventeenth century. Working from "germs of fact, rather than history," Sanders imagines the lives of the people who settled the Ohio Valley. In the foreword he identifies those characters who have interested him in most of his writing: the "unmemorialized common folks, the carpenters and farmers, the fierce parents and moonstruck lovers, the sort of people who, in all ages, have actually made human history" (p. 7). These are not sentimental tales. Like many folktales, they are unembellished. They invite the audience to provide context, if only from the other tales. "Embryo Town" recounts a failed attempt to impose civility on a frontier that fostered greed and violence. "The Cold" tells of the suffering winter brings to Hames Kingsbury, his wife, and their infant son, who starves to death "in the sixtieth day of snow." "Profit and Loss" is a desolate tale of Daniel Cross, who doubles his wealth by selling a wagonload of oats and then is eaten by wolves. "Hunt" relates a township's military-style slaughter of wildlife, producing in a single day the "carcasses of twenty-two bears, seven wolves, one hundred three deer, two mountain lions, one wildcat, plus turkeys and countless smaller game" (p. 74). Like prose poems or photographs, these stories invite contemplation of the meanings that radiate from a moment in history.

The title story in *Fetching the Dead* was first published in England in 1971, when Sanders was at Cambridge University. It hints at the theme that would be central to *Staying Put* more than twenty years later. Young Ransome Morgan has left home in Mississippi to meet his older brother in Memphis, planning to go with him to Chicago. On a freight train to Memphis, an old black man who has traveled since he was fourteen tries to befriend Ransome, but the boy is too frightened, too poisoned by prejudice, to accept the friendship. As the old man leaves, still trying to protect the boy, he says: "You get on up to Memphis, son, or on to Chicago, but then you set still. Don't keep moving. There's no end of railroads. Now take it easy" (p. 30). The other stories in *Fetching the Dead* are about people who struggle desperately with the commitments involved in rooting themselves somewhere. In "Walking to Sleep," Ransome's older brother

has returned to his family in Mississippi, emotionally broken. He tells his father he must leave again if he is to get well: "But I have to get away from . . . everything." In "The Recovery of Vision" a young man traveling in Scotland with a woman he loves struggles with his fear of marriage.

Even "Prophet," the story about Jeremiah Lofts, who predicts the end of the world, becomes a tale of reconciliation with land and community. In what he takes to be the last hours for the earth, Lofts prays for its preservation, and in the morning he looks outside to see a mockingbird, evidence that the final judgment has not come. Realizing he must "go face his jeering neighbors," he nevertheless begins to think of his family and the works he will do to preserve them. "Jeremiah does not regret any of this, not the sun nor the bird nor even the sound of automobiles cruising past filled with hypocrites and blasphemers on their way to church. He has preserved every speck of it from annihilation" (p. 110). Consumed by a terrible vision of apocalypse, this man still finds himself loving the ground on which he stands.

Wonders Hidden: Audubon's Early Years was published with Ursula K. LeGuin's *The Visionary: The Life Story of Flicker of the Serpentine* (1984). In this novella, Sanders imagines the childhood and youth of the man whose drawings and paintings of bird life in America have done much to shape our conception of nature. It is a haunting story of a boy sent to France at age six to escape a slave revolt, only to find himself in the midst of the Reign of Terror. Audubon watches an execution by guillotine when he is eight and undergoes military training when he is eleven. When he leaves France at eighteen to go back to America, he is avoiding the draft for Napoleon's army. The world of Audubon's childhood is filled with more terror than Sanders' own Ravenna Arsenal.

The young Audubon, as Sanders sees him, finds luminescent mystery and meaning in the physical world. He thinks, for example, of the cathedral where his mother takes him for early mass:

Far overhead the stone vaults met in midair, a thicket of shadows, like the rafters over his bed, and on sunny mornings light streamed in, thick with dust, inflaming the saints on their pedestals, the priests at the altar, worshippers in the pews, light so substantial he imagined wrapping his arms and legs about the shaft and climbing up through the high windows into the sky. (p. 36)

Against such passages, suggesting the young Audubon's lively interest in his surroundings, Sanders sets imagined passages from "The Twilight Journal," reflections of the dying Audubon. "The birds you must nearly always kill if they are to pose for you" (p. 36), this older Audubon complains. His subsequent reflections on the power of imagination reveal his dissatisfaction with this method: "My memory is not faulty; it is fanciful. The mere fact is no more true to experience than is a dead bird: the fact, like the carcass, must be animated by imagination" (p. 50). Even before Audubon experienced the American wilderness, Sanders suggests, it had begun to work on his imagination as an antidote to the violence he had seen. *Wonders Hidden* suggests compelling sources for Audubon's disappointment in society, his eagerness to plumb the mysteries of North America, and his awareness of nature's elusiveness.

Sanders' storytelling strategy in *Hear the Wind Blow: American Folk Songs Retold* (1985), illustrated by Ponder Goembel, is closer to that in *Wonders Hidden* than to *Wilderness Plots*, where he deliberately preserves the compressed, unadorned style of folktales. In *Hear the Wind Blow*, Sanders allows himself great freedom with the narratives implied, often as fragments, in such folk songs as "Yankee Doodle," "Casey Jones," "Frankie and Johnny," "Jesse James," "Buffalo Skinners," and "Sweet Betsy from Pike." These retellings of widely known stories are fine vehicles, too, for Sanders' love of figurative language. In "Buffalo Skinners," for example, he describes a character this way: "His hair was long and straight and blacker than the inside of a cookpot at midnight. The bones of his cheeks looked like fists balled up under the skin. His eyes, dark and shiny, could have been rocks at the bottom of a creek" (p. 171). Sanders uses this invented character, Chief Mitchell, to suggest what the killing of the buffalo meant to the Plains Indians. In these stories he provides motivation and context, sometimes even happy endings. In "Frog Went A-courtin'," Miss Mouse, Uncle Rat, and Frog, who have been eaten, find their way Jonah-like out of the stomachs that try to digest them, and the newlyweds are reunited. In "The Dying Cowboy," the lugubrious cowboy in white linen turns out to have been only fooling an aspiring young author of Western novels. He is last seen alive, drinking at a bar. In four of the retellings Sanders makes powerfully explicit the dark legacy of American slavery that is implicit in the songs. *Hear the Wind Blow* is a celebration of narrative imagination and a demonstration of the complex ways folk songs bloom in the mind.

A writer who almost became a physicist might be expected to try his hand at science fiction, and Sanders has published three science fiction novels: *Terrarium* (1985), *The Engineer of Beasts* (1988), and *The Invisible Company* (1989). Still, one would not expect technological optimism from the author of *The Paradise of Bombs*. Sanders imagines worlds changed by ingenious machines, but both culture and nature are more often impoverished than enriched by them. On the other hand, these are not simple dystopias. In *Terrarium* people have withdrawn to fabricated enclosures partly because they were about to destroy wild nature with the toxic by-products of civilization. Retreating into stultifying artificiality to protect themselves, humans have given the earth a chance to heal itself. And the longing to live a life grounded in nature, attuned to seasonal change, survives.

One problem facing the protagonists in *Terrarium* is how to create an alternative to a technocratic, totalitarian government. It is a problem similar to that posed in Ernest Callenbach's *Ecotopia* (1975). Callenbach's characters solve the problem by using nuclear blackmail, allowing northern California and parts of the Pacific

Northwest to secede from the United States to form an ecologically responsible, feminist utopia. In place of nuclear threat, Sanders uses memory of place, sexual desire, and Quaker meditation. Such sources of power make for a complex but compelling plot. A young woman, Teeg Passio, remembers exploring Whale Mouth Bay on the Oregon coast as a child, before she was sent to live in the Oregon City Enclosure, which floats somewhere west of the bay. Teeg helps form a conspiracy of ten "seekers," who plan to leave the Enclosure and establish the Jonah Colony at Whale Mouth Bay. Not long before they are to leave the Enclosure, Teeg draws Phoenix Marshall into the conspiracy, partly by awakening in him a sexual desire that has been deliberately confused by social engineering in the Enclosure. In addition, Phoenix has never experienced the natural world beyond the Enclosure, so Teeg introduces him to the plants growing in her small, illegal terrarium. The "conversion" experience for Phoenix, after which he can imagine leaving the Enclosure and joining the conspiracy, comes while he is contemplating these plants. He joins the seekers in a ceremony similar to a Quaker silent meeting. Still, he is terrified by the natural world, as other citizens of the Oregon City Enclosure presumably would be, well after he has joined the conspiracy and left the Enclosure.

This novel about a kind of jailbreak is not escapist. The seekers flee into a world that has been poisoned. They take with them appropriate, advanced technologies. (Another colony of escapees, which has tried to re-enact eighteenth-century pastoral life, appears doctrinaire, brutally rigid, ridiculous.) The seekers cannot completely escape the power of those who govern the Enclosure. Their conspiracy has been gently "programmed" by Zuni Franklin, one of the architects of the Enclosure, who joins them, hoping to live out her old age in nature. Phoenix is troubled by his new sense of contingency, but Teeg tells him the Enclosure is "simply *there*, and it's going to *be* there regardless of what we do, unless humanity pulls up stakes and goes shipping off into space. So we stick out our tongues at the spy satellites and keep on planting

trees and raising fish and seek the center" (p. 272). That essentially tragic vision at the center of *Terrarium* is lightened by the fact that nature seems to be more resilient than the seekers have imagined.

The Invisible Company tells the story of Leon Ash, a fifty-year-old physicist from MIT who has made a Faustian bargain. Critically injured as a young man in an accident that killed his wife, he promised a mysterious organization to take a journey someday in exchange for the expensive medical procedures required to save his life. When the novel begins, he has been sent on the journey he promised to take. He is on his way to Paradise Island, a "gaudy theme park for wealthy Americans who were frightened of traveling abroad." The plot unravels with the intricacy of a good detective story as Ash sets out to discover why he has been sent to Paradise Island. Along the way, Sanders explores a future in which highly privileged people live exclusively vicarious lives. He imagines a kind of disembodied technological immortality. But the most lyrical sentence in the book suggests that against his portrayal of this nightmarish Disneyworld of the future, Sanders balances the same hope of being grounded in a place that underlies *Staying Put*:

> Here as well as anywhere the universe balanced, at this still point, a man and woman afloat on a winking blue eye of water, embedded in a green sacrament of lawns and flower beds and trees, the garden surrounded by a picket of glass towers, the towers by a necklace of houses and streets, the city by fields and woods and ocean, and the spinning earth embraced by ring upon ring of light. (p. 313)

If the sentence seems cryptic in the novel, in the context of Sanders' other work it promises that any place can be sacred ground, even part of a big city.

Most of *The Engineer of Beasts* takes place in New Boston, an enclosed city similar to the Oregon City Enclosure in *Terrarium*. The protagonist is a thirteen-year-old girl, Emitty Harvard Tufts, a test-tube child formed from the germ cells of two Nobel Prize–winning scientists. Until she earns another name late in the story, however, she goes by Mooch for her ability to pick locks, outwit alarm systems, and move with uncanny stealth. Like Huck Finn, she refuses to be civilized. The engineer of beasts is Orlando Spinks, a man in his seventies who owns and operates a "disney," a menagerie of mechanical animals. The conjunction of Mooch, committed to authentic wildness, and Spinks, who has lived by building mechanical caricatures of the wild, produces much of the excitement in this novel.

Mooch is perhaps Sanders' finest comic creation. Like Huck, she sees and says things clearly, and her ardent commitment to wildness gives her great comic energy. The satire in *The Engineer of Beasts* is very funny, unlike that in *The Invisible Company*, which is grim. Besides Mooch and Orlando Spinks, there are other fine comic characters in the novel: Garrison Rathbone, a gawky teenager who loves Mooch; Bertha Dill, the sour director of Mooch's orphanage; and Humphrey Tree and Grace Palomino, an aged couple devoted to stashing untold tons of junk in a simulated mountain. There is hope in this novel, too, that misdirected science and technology have only limited influence on the human mind and heart. And there is the mysterious power and resilience of nature outside New Boston, poisoned as it has been by civilization:

> During the silence that followed, Mooch noticed the silver blades of minnows veering in the shallows. She could not stop trembling. The minnows turned and darted, their sides glinting. Back at the Home [the orphanage], and back among the sullen, clumsy beasts on the Farm [a prison farm for juvenile delinquents], she would never have dreamed that anything so tiny could possess such wisdom of motion. (p. 166)

This story affirms the possibility that nature and civilization might recover from the violence and destruction we have visited upon ourselves.

Bad Man Ballad (1986), another novel with a young protagonist, is set in the early years of the nineteenth century, shortly after Lewis and Clark returned from their exploration of the West. Ely Jackson, a teenager orphaned on the Ohio frontier, sets out from Roma, Ohio, with Owen Lightfoot, a Quaker lawyer from Philadelphia, to track down the giant Iron Man. This mysterious, powerful "bad man" of the title has been accused of murder. He seems to represent a primal force in humanity, the wild nature in human nature: "His eyes reminded onlookers of the indifference of snowstorms and fevers and floods" (p. 198). Ely and Owen are an unlikely pair for such a mission. Although the lawyer has dreamed of becoming an explorer, he finds the discomfort and danger of frontier travel nearly overwhelming. At night, during a thunderstorm on a muddy trail to Marietta, Ohio, he indicts nature: "It was impossible to believe that nature worked without malice. How could blind forces have contrived a medium more foul for tramping through than this clinging mud, more foul for breathing than this sodden air?" (p. 58). Ely, on the other hand, although he reluctantly acknowledges the need for the rule of law, considers himself an "expert at living on the outside edge of things, scorned by everybody."

Ely has a much darker sense of the frontier's history than does Owen. One day he asks the lawyer why they have encountered no Indian villages on their long journey through Ohio, and Owen speaks of treaties. Ely is scornful: "Is that what they say in Philadelphia? Treaties? Money paid down fair and square to whatever drunk chiefs they can round up, and General Wayne's army there just to act as witnesses? No, sir, Mr. Lightfoot, what cleared this territory was gunpowder and lead" (p. 61). One of the questions implicit in *Bad Man Ballad* is whether the lawyer and the orphan, with their opposing visions of nature and civilization, can find common ground. The rich portrayals of Iron Man and Rain Hawk, the "bad man" and a young woman Ely's age who has been cast out of the Shawnees, offer fascinating complications.

Sanders has written two children's books based on tales in *Wilderness Plots*. The first, *Aurora Means Dawn* (1989), recounts the Sheldon family's arrival in Ohio. In writing the story,

Sanders explains to his young readers, "I knew only that Mr. and Mrs. Job Sheldon and their seven children had been caught within a few miles of their destination by a terrible storm; and that Aurora, far from being an established village as they had been led to expect, was an unbroken woods." This version of the story emphasizes the child's view of frontier life. *Warm As Wool* (1992) celebrates a frontier mother's resourcefulness and tenacity in raising sheep and weaving wool to clothe her family. Both children's stories offer a rather complex, unsentimental view of life on the border between civilization and wild nature.

The mysteries on that border continue to interest Sanders. He writes increasingly about the social arrangements that could take us beyond "fenced wilderness," beyond the Ravenna Arsenal, his metaphor for the violent, destructive capabilities of civilization. He describes communities that include both human and nonhuman inhabitants. He makes imaginable the disciplines that sustain families and neighborhoods in a time when crucial elements of our social order seem to be flying apart.

Selected Bibliography

WORKS OF SCOTT RUSSELL SANDERS

NONFICTION

D. H. Lawrence: The World of the Major Novels (New York: Viking, 1974); *Stone Country* (Bloomington: Indiana Univ. Press, 1985), repr. as *In Limestone Country* (Boston: Beacon, 1991); as ed., *Audubon Reader: The Best Writings of John James Audubon* (Bloomington: Indiana Univ. Press, 1986); *The Paradise of Bombs* (Athens: Univ. of Georgia Press, 1987; repr., New York: Touchstone, 1988, and Boston: Beacon, 1993); *Secrets of the Universe* (Boston: Beacon, 1991; repr., 1992); *Staying Put: Making a Home in a Restless World* (Boston: Beacon, 1993; repr., 1994).

FICTION

Wilderness Plots: Tales About the Settlement of the American Land (New York: Morrow, 1983; repr., Columbus: Ohio State Univ. Press, 1988); *Fetching the Dead* (Champaign: Univ. of Illinois Press, 1984); *Wonders Hidden: Audubon's Early Years* (Santa Barbara, Calif.: Capra, 1984); *Hear the Wind Blow: American Folk Songs Retold* (New York: Bradbury, 1985); *Terrarium* (New York: Tor Books, 1985); *Bad Man Ballad* (New York: Bradbury, 1986); *The Engineer of Beasts* (New York: Orchard Books, 1988); *Aurora Means Dawn* (New York: Bradbury, 1989); *The Invisible Company* (New York: Tor Books, 1989); *Warm as Wool* (New York: Bradbury, 1992).

ESSAY

"Letter to a Reader," in *My Poor Elephant: 27 Male Writers at Work*, ed. by Eve Shelnutt (Atlanta: Longstreet, 1992).

ERNEST THOMPSON SETON
(1860–1946)

LISA KNOPP

"NOW AND AGAIN there comes an individual whose gifts are so diversified that we hardly know what to call him," writes Canadian author and critic Patricia Morley. "Ernest Thompson Seton was such a man. To many, he is the writer of animal stories beloved in youth and age alike. To others, he is an artist and illustrator. To still others, a naturalist, a scientist of international repute" (1977, p. 9). Indeed, Seton's legacy speaks of many gifts. He wrote forty-odd books, most of which he illustrated himself, including collections of short stories, novels, woodcraft guides, animal biographies, an autobiography, books of Indian "lore," scouting manuals, and his magnum opus, the four-volume *Lives of Game Animals* (1925–1928), for which he was awarded top scientific honors. In addition, Seton wrote hundreds of articles, founded the Boy Scouts, was a conservationist who fought for hunting limits, and was a champion of Native American economic rights and cultural independence. Artist. Scientist. Naturalist. Conservationist. Writer. Raconteur. Seton's success, says S. E. Read, "came from his extraordinary ability to fuse into a unified and an artistic whole his manifold gifts" (p. 56). That is the genius of the man.

Life and Early Works

Seton was born as Ernest Evan Thompson on 14 August 1860 in South Shields, Durham, England, the eighth of the ten sons of Joseph and Alice Thompson. As the boy's Scottish ancestors, the Setons, were on the losing side in the Stuart rebellion of 1745, a price had been placed on the head of Seton's paternal grandfather, Alan Cameron Seton. He fled to England, entered the shipping industry, and changed his name to Thompson so he would not be as easily identified by his enemies. Ernest's father felt it pointless to change the family name back to Seton; but in 1901, Ernest legally adopted his father's family's original surname. Joseph Thompson was a prosperous shipowner of the English merchant marine before he suffered financial losses because of maritime accidents. In 1866, he moved his family to a hundred-acre tract of forest near Lindsay, Ontario, and established himself as a gentleman farmer.

Young Seton reveled in the raw frontier life, but was frustrated that neither he nor anyone else could name many of the wild creatures of the woods and prairies. In his autobiography, *Trail of an Artist-Naturalist* (1940), Seton writes,

All my nature craved for knowledge of these things, but there were neither books nor bird-men to help me. I wonder if other boys suffer so from that heart hunger. When I glimpsed some new bird, some wonderful unknown kind, I got a curious prickling in my scalp. Something clutched my throat; and when the bird flew off leaving me dark as ever, it was like a swift blackness with a vague sense of sorrow and of loss. (p. 43)

Seton says that "the beginning and foundation" of all his work as a "wild-animal story writer" occurred when he observed a bird no bigger than a sparrow yet brave enough to drive off an eagle. Seton was shocked when his brother George, who had been learning from the backwoodsmen, identified the creature as a kingbird, since "the authorities all made it [the kingbird] so far away...found in Africa, or South America, or some vague tropical place, whose name was strange, or maybe it inhabited only 'the books'" (p. 25). Each year Seton learned more about the brave little bird. In 1876, he wrote a heroic poem about it, "The King Bird: A Barnyard Legend." It was published in 1879 — Seton's first publication.

Seton's father failed as a farmer and moved his family to Toronto when Ernest was nine. But that was not the last Seton would see of the farm. Twice, poor health necessitated country living, and he stayed there with the Blackwells, the new owners of the farm. There he shot and dissected birds so he could study their anatomy and diet. Seton coveted A. M. Ross's *Birds of Canada* (1872), which cost one dollar at Pidding-ton's, the local book store. To earn the dollar, Seton chopped and carried stovewood for months, and he sold his pet rabbits, marbles, and dime novels. Three or four years after he bought the book, he concluded that it was "practically worthless" and attempted to bring it up to date by writing corrections in the margins and by coloring the illustrations. On the last page of the lining and inside the back cover, he wrote his "Key to the Hawks and Owls," "which was wholly my own invention and the first germ of the plan which I later developed into *A Key to the Birds of Canada*" (*Trail of an Artist-Naturalist*, p. 99).

Seton's father was staunchly opposed to his son's plan to become a naturalist; since Joseph Thompson had artistic talents himself, he wanted his son to become an illustrator. Seton later described his father as a principled, but selfish man. When Seton returned from his studies in London at age twenty-one, his father presented him with a bill for what it had cost to bring him into the world and "keep him": $537.50. From that date forward, interest accumulated at 6%. This further deepened Ernest's resentment toward his father. He paid his debt and resolved to change his last name.

Seton had complied with his father's demand that he study art. At fourteen, he was the youngest student to win a two-year scholarship to Collegiate High School in Toronto. Seton was a good student; school also offered escape from his father. It was to appease his father that the sixteen-year-old Seton took a job as a portrait-ist's apprentice. He prepared the artist's palette; he put photographic negatives into a stereopti-con lantern, projected them onto a screen, and then traced the faces with a red pencil; he put makeup on boxers' black eyes. When Seton realized that the portraitist was not teaching him anything, he enrolled in night classes at Cana-da's best art school — the Ontario School of Art — where his work earned him the gold medal, the school's highest honor.

The next step in his artistic training was the Royal Academy School of Painting and Sculpture in London. The entrance exam was quite competitive. Seton's first submission, a drawing of Hermes, was rejected. His second — a drawing of Michelangelo's Satyr — was picked from hundreds of applications, earning a seven-year scholarship for the twenty-year-old Seton. In addition to studying art in London, he read the writings of the great naturalists — John James Audubon, Alexander Wilson, Thomas Mayo Brewer, Robert Ridgway, John Burroughs, Henry David Thoreau — at the library of the British Museum, and sketched and studied animals at the London Zoo.

But Seton did not complete his seven years at the Royal Academy. He began hearing voices, which some biographers attribute to his spartan lifestyle (Seton had little money for food), his deep religiousness, or his extensive reading. For whatever reasons, Seton heard a voice which directed him to leave London: "A year from now you will be living on the Plains of western Canada.... Your future will be, not in Canada or London, but in New York, where, as an illustrator and writer, you will make your fortune. Go to Canada, and rejoice in life on the Plains. But do not stay too long. Go soon to New York, and there you will find your way" (*Trail of an Artist-Naturalist*, p. 147). Seton did as he was told.

At twenty-one, Seton lived with his brothers Arthur and Charles near Carberry, Manitoba, on prairie newly opened to white settlers. In addition to farm work, Seton collected and measured specimens and wrote commentary on their peculiarities, diet, and diseases. He learned to track and read trails, he observed bird behavior, and most important, he kept a journal. His first entry, dated 13 November 1881, recorded that he "saw three robins over the White Bridge." Seton noted that in the sixty years that followed the first entry he accumulated "fifty fat leather-clad volumes, most of them over-fat, and still increasing" (*Trail of an Artist-Naturalist*, p. 165). In his later years when young naturalists came to him for advice, he always told them, "Keep a full and accurate journal; and remember always Science is measurement" (p. 165). The following journal entry, dated 30 October 1882, attests to Seton's attention to these principles:

I made a careful count of the feathers on a Brewer's grackle:

Head		226
Back of neck	285	
Front of neck	300	
All Below		1000
Back		300
Each thigh	100	200
Each wing	280	560
Flight feathers		44
		4915

(By a Thousand Fires)

The sketches Seton made in Manitoba contained "instantaneous recognition features" of birds in air and on water. Ornithologist Roger Tory Peterson used them in the 1930s when drawing his field guides, and they are still in use today. To support himself during this period, Seton began publishing excerpts from his incomplete manuscript on birds. The first of these, "The Life of the Prairie Chicken," appeared in the *Canadian Journal* in February 1883. Seton's first book, *A List of Mammals of Manitoba* (1886), was based on his Manitoba field work.

As Seton's inner voice had directed him "not to stay too long" on the plains, in November 1883 he went to New York, with less than three dollars in his pocket. He worked by day in an advertising firm, studied evenings at the Art Students' League, and wrote animal stories, which he sold to such journals as *St. Nicholas, Forest and Stream*, and *Century Magazine*. In addition, he received a commission from Dr. C. Hart Merriam to make accurate animal sketches for *The Century Dictionary* (1886). But in the spring of 1884, the prairies called and Seton answered. Back in Manitoba, he set to work trapping, skinning, and sketching specimens. The following fall, Seton returned to New York, where he was in great demand as an illustrator of periodicals, scientific works, and children's books. He showed the manuscript and illustrations for his book about the birds of Manitoba to publishers. They were impressed, but believed it would be too costly to produce a book with such a limited audience.

Again, Seton went abroad, this time to study at Julian's Academy on the Faubourg St. Denis in Paris. There Seton was inspired by newspaper accounts of a hunter in the Pyrenees Mountains who had been killed by wolves after having himself killed several members of the pack. Seton's preliminary sketches of the incident took two months. Then, on a canvas so large he could not keep it in his room, he painted the scene: wolves gnawing on a skull, peasant clothes strewn on the ground. *The Triumph of the Wolves* was rejected at Paris Grand Salon of painting, though *The Sleeping Wolf*, a painting of a captive wolf in the Jardin des Plantes Menagerie, was accepted. This and Seton's other wolf paintings received mixed reactions in both Paris and Toronto because of their realism.

Once back in Canada, Seton submitted *The Triumph of the Wolves* to the 1893 Chicago

Seton with one of his taxidermy specimens, ca. 1921

World's Fair. It was rejected by one vote on the grounds that it gave a bad image of Canadian life. L. R. O'Brien, president of the art committee, wrote to the newspapers that the Canadian exhibit contained "enough sloppy milk-and-water stuff...I for one would be thankful to see some virile art" (quoted in Garst, p. 138). O'Brien's letter created such a controversy that Seton was given a place of honor at the exhibit.

In 1893, Louis Fitz-Randolph, a wealthy New Mexican cattle rancher, hired Seton to exterminate the wolves which were killing his herds. Though his five months of trapping wolves didn't eradicate the "wolf menace," Seton gathered a tremendous amount of information about wolves, coyotes, antelope, prairie dogs, bears, and other mammals, which he later used in *Lives of Game Animals*. Seton felt a special kinship for the wolf, in part because legend tells that one of his ancestors killed the last wolf in Scotland. Seton incorporated the wolf print into his signature and wrote numerous stories about wolves, including "Badlands Billy: The Wolf That Won," "The Winnipeg Wolf," and "Lobo, the King of Currumpaw."

In 1894, Seton returned to France to work on *Studies in the Art Anatomy of Animals*. This volume, published in 1896, was the first book of animal anatomy written specifically for artists. In his autobiography, Seton wrote that during the years he was illustrating *The Century Dictionary* he was "continually faced with problems of animal and bird anatomy; and found that there were no books treating of the same from the artist's point of view. There were plenty of works on animal dissection and dead animals, but these had little bearing on my needs and the needs of all artists who depict animals" (p. 291). As a result, he planned his anatomical study to be "a careful analysis of the *visible forms* and proportions of the *living* animal, which includes the feather shapes and overlaps in the birds and the fur of animals. Color does not enter in, but measurements do." John G. Samson observes that the study is so precise and detailed that it could serve as a textbook for veterinary medicine.

The Nature-Fakers Controversy

Wild Animals I Have Known, a collection of Seton's animal stories, appeared in October of 1898. The book became an instant best-seller: the initial two thousand copies sold out within three weeks; by Christmas, three large printings sold out; within eight years, it went into a twentieth printing. As a result, Seton was in demand as a lecturer; his fame and financial well-being were secure.

This collection is worth examining in detail not only because it is Seton's best-known work and has probably sold more copies than any other Canadian book, but also because it created such a controversy. The collection contains the stories of eight animals Seton claims he knew personally, including Lobo, the timber wolf he tracked in New Mexico; Bingo, his dog in Manitoba from 1882 to 1888; Redruff the partridge, and the trapper who killed him. All of the animal stories in this collection and in the many that followed have several characteristics in common. First, Seton's animal protagonists are composites, "pieced together" from the traits of several different animals; they embody in one animal everything that had been done or might have been done by that species. Wully, for instance, is a compound of two mongrel dogs, both with some collie blood and raised as sheepdogs. In a sense, his protagonists are larger than life. Second, Seton's accounts are entirely subjective. As critic Michel Poirier notes, "The animals in his works are always seen through the eyes of the writer.... [Seton shows] a marked partiality to his heroes, due to his sympathy for animals and also to his desire of increasing the interest of his tales; he rejoices at their triumphs, bewails their sufferings, calls the impassable forces of nature to their help" (p. 305).

A third common characteristic is that each creature reasons, feels, and acts like a human. Seton was a Darwinist, at least in some respects, who believed that "we and the beasts are kin. Man has nothing that the animals have not at least a vestige of, the animals have nothing that man does not in some degree share." Thus in the birds and animals, Seton finds "the beginnings of all sorts of human manners and capabilities; the rudiment of speech, of musical sense, of the making of a home, decoration and amusements, elementary systems of sanitation, the adoption of laws of marriage and property, and the bases even of the morality which found its eventual expression in the Ten Commandments" (*Spectator*, 1 October 1910, p. 488).

Despite their human faculties, Seton's animals are much more realistic than those found in other animal tales. Margaret Atwood says that anyone who has read Kipling's Mowgli stories, Kenneth Grahame's *The Wind in the Willows*, or Beatrix Potter's tales can see that these animals, like the white rabbit in *Alice in Wonderland*, are really "Englishmen in furry zippered suits, often with a layer of human clothing added on top. They speak fluent English and are assigned places in a hierarchical social order which is essentially British. . . . Of note also are the invariably happy endings" (p. 73). Seton's stories are realistic in that he shows how animals live in nature, which necessitates tragic endings. In "Raggylug, the Story of a Cottontail Rabbit," Seton writes, "No wild animal dies of old age. Its life has soon or late a tragic end. It is only a question of how long it can hold out against its foes." When Lobo realizes that he cannot "hold out against [his] foes," he chooses intentional starvation to death in captivity. Silverspot the crow is killed by an owl. Vixen the fox poisons her captured pup as an act of mercy. Redruff the partridge dies slowly in a trap.

A particularly controversial trait in Seton's animal stories is that animal parents teach their offspring how to survive. In "The Revolt Against Instinct: The Animal Stories of Seton and Roberts," Robert H. MacDonald says that in 1900, "one of the most important controversies in the biological sciences was the question of animal behaviour: did animals act instinctively, or were they capable of learning? What was the nature of an animal's knowledge: was it inherited, or was it acquired? Were animals capable of reason? Did they learn from experience, did they teach each other?" (p. 19). Most scientists and writers of the time favored inheritance and instinct. Seton, Charles Roberts, and a few

others believed that animals reasoned, educated their young, and obeyed laws. For instance, of Silverspot, the leader of a band of crows headquartered near Toronto, Seton writes,

> Twice each day in March and part of April, then again in the late summer and the fall, he passed and repassed, and gave me chances to see his movements, and hear his orders to his bands, and so, little by little, opened my eyes to the fact that the crows, though a little people, are of great wit, a race of birds with a language and a social system that is wonderfully human in many of its chief points, and in some is better carried out than our own.

Each June, Silverspot assembles the young crows in a woods "that is at once their fortress and college." They are taught to distinguish an umbrella from a gun; to count to six (Silverspot can count "nearly to thirty"); and to respond to a series of commands: fly, mount, bunch, scatter, form line, descend, forage, a man with a gun.

In "Real and Sham Natural History," published in the March 1903 *Atlantic Monthly*, the United States' then most prominent naturalist, John Burroughs, viciously attacked Seton's animal stories. Burroughs held rigidly to a mechanistic, behavioristic view of animal nature. He took particular issue with those stories of Seton's in which the animals exhibit the ability to reason and learn. Burroughs said that in the forty years he had watched crows, he had never seen anything that resembled leadership among them nor had he ever observed the behaviors Silverspot displays. Nor did he believe animals teach their offspring, though they may set examples. Seton's position was clear. In "Redruff, the Story of the Don Valley Partridge," he writes that partridge chicks graduate from instinct to rational behavior:

> Their start in life was a good mother, good legs, a few reliable instincts, and a germ of reason. It was instinct, that is, inherited habit, which taught them to hide at the word from their mother; it was instinct that taught them to follow her, but it was reason which made them keep under the shadow of her tail when the sun was smiting down.

Seton concludes, "from that day reason entered more and more into their expanding lives." Burroughs's position was equally clear, though he refused to debate whether or not animals learned: "Of course it is mainly guesswork how far our psychology applies to the lower animals. That they experience many of our emotions there can be no doubt, but that they have intellectual and reasoning processes like our own, except in a very rudimentary form, admits of grave doubt. But I need not go into that vexed subject here" ("Real and Sham Natural History," pp. 299–300). Theodore Roosevelt, who praised Burroughs' attack on the "nature-fakers," tried unsuccessfully to moderate Burroughs' position: Roosevelt believed that learning and instinct varied among animals. Monkeys, for instance, were more capable of learning than salamanders.

Burroughs' greatest complaint against Seton isn't anthropomorphizing, however, but that Seton deceives his readers: "I am bound to say that the line between fact and fiction is repeatedly crossed, and that a deliberate attempt is made to induce the reader to cross, too, and to work such a spell upon him that he shall not know that he has crossed and is in the land of make-believe" (p. 300). Burroughs cites several tales to support his charges. While foxes will run through a flock of sheep to shake a hound, it is incredible that Seton's Springfield Fox should actually ride several hundred yards on the sheep's back. While a fox will sometimes walk the rails "with the vague notion of eluding his pursuers" it is unbelievable that Seton's fox lures hounds onto the trestle at the exact time a train is passing. When Vixen realizes she cannot release her captured offspring from his chains and so brings him poison as an act of mercy, Burroughs charges Seton of "pushing the romantic to the absurd" (p. 301). In Seton's "Note to the Reader" that prefaces *Wild Animals I Have Known*, he says, "These stories are true. Although I have left the strict line of historical truth in many places, the animals in this book were all real characters. They lived the lives I have depicted." Burroughs counters, "True as romance, true in their artistic effects, true in

their power to entertain the young reader, they certainly are; but true as natural history they certainly are not" (p. 300). Burroughs suggests that a more appropriate title for Seton's collection would be *Wild Animals I* Alone *Have Known*.

Seton's part in the nature-fakers controversy was resolved in part at a dinner party Andrew Carnegie gave, to which fifty prominent writers were invited, including Burroughs and Seton. Seton arranged to be seated beside Burroughs. Throughout the meal, Seton interrogated Burroughs on his experience with wolves. When Seton learned that Burroughs had none, he asked how Burroughs felt competent enough to attack Seton's stories. Burroughs accepted an invitation to visit Seton's home in Connecticut, where he viewed Seton's museum of thousands of bird and mammal specimens, his five-thousand-volume library, his two thousand animal photographs, and his stacks of field notes. Burroughs agreed that Seton was a qualified naturalist but still maintained that his stories were deceptive: "Mr. Thompson Seton, as an artist and *raconteur*, ranks by far the highest in this field, and to those who can separate the fact from the fiction in his animal stories, he is truly delightful" ("The Literary Treatment of Nature," p. 42).

Burroughs' position on animal behavior is too extreme in the light of current biological theories, though so, too, is Seton's. In 1900, the choices were simple: behavior was either instinctive or learned. Scientists in the late twentieth century do not find the alternatives that simple. Even the terminology has changed. Robert MacDonald explains that instead of nature or nurture we now speak of innate or acquired characteristics and environmentally stable or environmentally labile behavior. We contrast imprinting, the process by which certain young animals respond as a species to certain stimuli, with adaptive learning. The mental processes of animals are not always automatic, mechanical, or simply instinctive. Apes, for instance, have learned to communicate with people through American Sign Language. Higher mammals may have mental experiences and perhaps even conscious awareness. But the Burroughs-Seton debate has wider implications than just animal behavior; Ralph H. Lutts says that this controversy foreshadowed the current debate in the environmental movement: "It is a tension between the desire to apply rational, scientific, and managerial approaches to analyzing and solving our environmental problems and the perception of these problems' non-rational, aesthetic, religious, and emotional facets that must also be addressed if we are to implement long-term solutions."

What is important in all of Seton's realistic animal stories — *Lives of the Hunted* (1901), *Animal Heroes* (1905), *Wild Animal Ways* (1916), *Woodland Tales* (1921), and others — is that, through them, Seton sought to gain sympathy and protection for wild animals: "My chief motive, my honest earnest underlying wish has been to stop the extermination of harmless animals; not for their sakes but for ours, firmly believing that each of our native wild creatures is in itself a precious heritage that we have no right to destroy or put beyond the reach of our children" (quoted in Poirier). Yet Seton's stories and actions speak of an ambivalent attitude toward wildlife. He continued to hunt. Never in his stories, says Alec Lucas, did he denounce a hunter or trapper as long as he disclosed a "fellow feeling" for wild creatures. The narrator of "Lobo," for instance, is acceptable because he shows remorse for having killed the great wolf.

The strategies Seton used to achieve his professed goal are similar in all his animal stories. He had greater faith in sympathy than reason, and believed sympathy was to be won with sentiment. In "Raggylug, the Story of a Cottontail Rabbit," Molly, the mother rabbit, jumps into a pond to escape a fox, but driving wind and snow keep her from reaching safety. "Poor little Molly Cottontail! She was a true heroine, yet only one of unnumbered millions that without a thought of heroism have lived and done their best in their little world, and died" (p. 83). He also won sympathy through direct and didactic appeals. In "Redruff, the Story of the Don Valley Partridge," when Redruff is caught in a trap by one leg and dies a slow death, Seton asks, "Have the wild things no moral or legal rights? What

right has man to inflict such long and fearful agony on a fellow-creature, simply because that creature does not speak his language?" (p. 215).

Seton attempted to popularize natural history through his animal stories. He believed that animals could best be understood by studying the unique characteristics of the individual, whereas the scientists of his day placed their emphasis on the characteristics of the species. The natural history they wrote was vague, general, dry. In his introduction to the 1977 edition of *Wild Animals I Have Known*, Alec Lucas writes that Seton wanted to preserve his living individuals "from *belles-lettres* refinements, Thoreauvian transcendentalism, and the lifeless cataloguing of the nature study guide, and to replace life histories of species with specific biographies of animals he had known." The result was Seton's simple, straightforward, and highly readable hybrid of literature and natural history.

Seton also insisted that animals are moral creatures. Consequently, he endowed his animal heroes with human virtues — motherly love, fidelity, obedience, dignity, wisdom, sympathy, discrimination, desire for freedom — and encouraged readers to better themselves by studying the animals. In *The Natural History of the Ten Commandments* (1907), Seton goes so far as to say that animals observe the last six commandments. That they sometimes "throw themselves on the mercy of some other power" suggests the beginnings of a spiritual life. Thus, Seton's animals rise above mere instinct and reach the rational, ethical, and spiritual.

Indeed, Seton does create sympathy in his readers for his animal heroes, but at the same time his depiction of "good" animals and "bad" (the squirrel who tries to prey on Redruff's brood is a "red-haired cutthroat" who has a "strange perverted thirst for birdling blood") works against an ecological perspective. Like Seton, the great ecologist Aldo Leopold went to the Southwest to eradicate wolves and coyotes, but reached different conclusions regarding predator-prey relationships than did Seton. The policy of the newly created U.S. Forest Service, of which Leopold was an employee, was to "protect" deer for the hunters by killing off predators. Yet without the predators, the mountain wrinkled with deer trails; every edible bush and seedling was browsed to death; trees were defoliated. Leopold observed, "in the end the starved bones of the hoped-for deer herd, dead of its own too-much" (p. 140). Thinking ecologically, says Leopold, demands "think[ing] like a mountain" (p. 140), objectively recognizing the necessity of each creature in an ecosystem. Bloodthirsty squirrels are as essential as heroic partridges.

The Scouting Movement

The scouting movement was born in 1900 when the boys who lived near Seton's Greenwich, Connecticut, estate destroyed his fences, shot his animals, and painted "improper" pictures on his gate. All summer long Seton made repairs, but the depredations continued. Seton believed that urbanization led to such "degeneracy." In *The Manual of the Woodcraft Indians* (1915) he wrote, "We know all too well that many Americans...have become arrogant, ignorant and, consequently, degenerate. We know money grubbing, mundane politics, degrading sports, cigarettes, town life of the worst kind, false ideals, moral laxity and lessening, in a word 'city rot' has worked evil in the nation" (quoted in Shi, p. 384). For Seton and other progressive moral reformers, including Theodore Roosevelt, the antidote was a return to nature.

Seton went a step further and called for the youths to learn woodcraft and what he considered to be "Indian ways." He went to the village school and invited all male students over the age of twelve to visit his "Indian Village" the following Friday, where he had boats, canoes, teepees, firewood, and food waiting for them. The forty-two who showed up (Seton had invited twelve) competed athletically, learned "campercraft" (making a fire by rubbing sticks together, measuring the width of a river without crossing it), learned hunting and tracking skills, and were organized into what Seton considered to be an "Indian society," electing each other to the offices of Chief, Medicine Man, War Chief, Keeper of the Tally (Secretary), Keeper of the Wampum (Treasurer), and Council of Twelve. Seton gave his scouts a code of laws and a constitution— "The laws forbade rebellion against the Council, firearms in camp, wildfire, smoking, whiskey, destruction of songbirds, or squirrels, breach of game laws, pointing of weapons at any one; and made chivalry, kindness, courage, and honor the cardinal virtues"—and a motto: "The best things of the best Indians" (*Trail of an Artist-Naturalist*, pp. 383–384). The organization's charter and bylaws were published in the May 1902 *Ladies' Home Journal*, and chapters sprang up all across the country. Groups similar to Seton's organization (Daniel Beard's Sons of Daniel Boone and the Boys' Brigade) also appeared.

Seton believed his scheme worked so well because boys are "cavemen" until they reach sixteen or seventeen; they are in the clan period during which loyalty to the gang surpasses all other loyalties. The Woodcraft Indians exploited this allegiance to the group and the power of peer pressure. Seton explained that activities "were all prepared, and lying in wait with their insidious appeal to the primitive nature of these very primitive young persons. There was sanity in every part of the scheme, because it had *picturesqueness*; it made the boys *govern themselves*, and it gave them definite *things to do*; but, above all, it never failed to play on the master power of the savage, the love of glory; that was always kept in mind" (pp. 384–385). The overriding aim of the organization was not scholarship, patriotism, or conformity, but "character building."

Seton claimed to have "invented" scouting, but so, too, did Lieutenant General Sir Robert Baden-Powell. During a lecture tour in England in 1906, Seton suggested that something similar to the Woodcraft movement be established in England, and offered *The Birch Bark Roll of the Woodcraft Indians* (1906) and other published works about his organization. Baden-Powell adopted Seton's handbook, substituting military titles and ideals for Indian ones to which Seton seriously objected. In 1908, Baden-Powell's

Scouting for Boys appeared and the Boy Scouts was "founded."

Seton was hurt and angered that Baden-Powell appropriated his ideas and gave them new names without a word of acknowledgment. Yet he chose not to protest Baden-Powell's actions because he believed the scouting movement was of primary importance. Controversy would cast a bad light upon it. In 1910, Seton, as Chief Scout, headed the committee that organized the Boy Scouts of America; his Woodcraft Indians were incorporated into the larger organization. He wrote the first American scout manual, the *Boy Scouts of America Handbook* (1910)—a perennial best-seller in the United States, with sales second only to the Bible—forever leaving his mark on the organization.

Seton's criticism of Baden-Powell is somewhat ironic when one considers that Seton appropriated Indian names and concepts for his organization without acknowledging the tribes or individuals from which he had taken them. Moreover, Seton's understanding of Native American cultures is questionable. For example, he refers to Indians as a homogeneous group instead of acknowledging the hundreds of culturally diverse tribes of North America. One could argue that it is more honest and ethical to borrow from a system one understands and has been part of, as Baden-Powell borrowed from the military.

Seton disliked the militaristic flavor of uniforms, drills, officers, and regimentation Baden-Powell had introduced to scouting. Gradually, he watched the emphasis of scouting shift from nature recreation to vocational preparation to militarism and nationalistic jingoism, according to David E. Shi. When Seton, Daniel Beard, and others voiced their objections during World War I, Roosevelt threatened to withdraw his public support and resign his post if the Boy Scouts did not rid itself of "certain leaders ... [who] have used the Boy Scout organization as a medium for the dissemination of pacifist literature and ... as a propaganda for interfering with the training of our boys to a standard of military efficiency" (quoted in Shi, p. 389). Consequently, Seton was dropped from the organization in 1915,

the excuse being that he was not an American citizen.

Seton wrote two scouting and Indian "lore" novels: *Two Little Savages* (1903) is based on Seton's fifteenth summer, which he spent with the Blackwells on the Ontario farm; *Rolf in the Woods* (1911) is set between 1812 and 1814, when Rolf, a white orphan, is befriended by an Indian. Other scouting books Seton wrote and illustrated include *American Woodcraft for Boys* (1902); *The Birch Bark Roll* (1906); *Scouting for Boys* (1910); *Forester's Manual* (1912); *The Book of Woodcraft and Indian Lore* (1912); *Manual of the Woodcraft Indians* (1915); *The Woodcraft Manual for Girls* (1916); *The Woodcraft Manual for Boys* (1917) and *Sign Talk* (1918).

Lives of Game Animals

Seton's great scientific contribution was *Lives of Game Animals*, four volumes published from 1925 to 1928, which include fifty-two animal species, fifteen hundred illustrations, sixty-eight distribution maps, and one hundred color plates. Into this work he incorporated his earlier *Life Histories of Northern Animals* (1909) and sixty years' worth of field notes. Despite the subtitle of the work—"An Account of those Land Animals in America, north of the Mexican Border, which are considered 'Game,' either because they have held the Attention of Sportsmen, or received the Protection of Law," some species described in it (moles, shrews, and armadillos, for instance) were neither hunted nor protected.

Lives of Game Animals is more than just a textbook. It is natural history in the vein of John James Audubon's *The Viviparous Quadrupeds of North America* (1845–1853) or *Ornithological Biography* (1831–1839)—scientific, anecdotal, autobiographical. The following excerpt, from "Life XXXI—The Wolverine," illustrates Seton's ability to blend scientific observation with colorful description:

Picture a Weasel—and most of us can do that, for we have met that little demon of destruction, that small atom of insensate courage, that symbol of slaughter, sleeplessness, and tireless, incredible activity—picture that scrap of demoniac fury, multiply that mite some fifty times, and you have the likeness of a Wolverine.

Even in his most scientific work, Seton is still a storyteller:

> The scarcity of game on his winter range during off-years for Rabbits, often compels him to a step that amounts to suicide. As already pointed out, the famished Wolverine had no chance to learn discretion in the matter, and when he meets a Porcupine, he slays the dull Quill-pig, revels in its blood and meat. This stays his hunger—yes. But the arrows of death are in him, and a week or two later, the Quill-pig's revenge is complete.

And still, he casts animals in human terms:

> The Wolverine is a tremendous character. No one can approach the subject of his life and habits, without feeling the same sort of embarrassment one would feel in writing of Cromwell or Tamerlane. Here, we know, is a personality of unmeasured force, courage, and achievement, but so enveloped in mists of legend, superstition, idolatry, fear, and hatred, that one scarcely knows how to begin or what to accept as fact.

Seton was more than just the author of animal stories. Both Burroughs and Roosevelt praised *Lives of Game Animals*, and it won many significant awards, including the Daniel Girard Elliot Gold Medal of the National Academy of Sciences (1928) and, ironically, the John Burroughs Gold Medal.

Conclusion

Seton was twice married. He and Grace Gallatin, a travel writer, met in 1894 on a voyage to France. They married in 1896, and their one child, Anna (Anya Seton, author of *The Turquoise*, 1946, *Katherine*, 1954, *Avalon*, 1965, *Green Darkness*, 1972, and other novels), was born in 1904. Gallatin preferred the city social life, but Seton preferred the country; gradually they saw less and less of each other. In 1918, Seton met Julia M. Buttree Moss, who became his secretary and was the author of books on mysticism and Indians. In 1930, he sold his Connecticut estate and bought twenty-five hundred acres near Santa Fe, New Mexico, and divorced Gallatin. In 1935, Seton and Moss married; three years later, they adopted a daughter, Beulah. Together, they worked on his books and on his College of Indian Wisdom, the purpose of which was to preserve Indian lore, religion, and craft.

After more than three thousand lectures, Seton retired from the lecture circuit, though he continued to write and paint until 23 October 1946, when he died of cancer at his home in Santa Fe. *Time* compared his death to "the falling of a forest tree." In its obituary, the *New York Times* dubbed Seton "the dean of American naturalists."

Selected Bibliography

WORKS OF ERNEST THOMPSON SETON

NONFICTION

A List of Mammals of Manitoba (Toronto: Oxford Press, 1886); *A Key to the Birds of Canada* (New York: D. Appleton, 1895); *Studies in the Art Anatomy of Animals* (New York: Macmillan, 1896); *The Birch-Bark Roll of the Woodcraft Indians* (Garden City, N.Y.: Doubleday, Page, 1906), also pub. as *The Book of Woodcraft and Indian Lore* (1912); *The Natural History of the Ten Commandments* (New York: Scribners, 1907); *Life Histories of Northern Animals*, 2 vols. (New York: Scribners, 1909); *Boy Scouts of America Handbook* (Garden City, N.Y.: Doubleday, Page, 1910); *The Arctic Prairies* (New York: Scribners, 1911; repr., New York: Inter-University Press, 1943); *Sign Talk*, with Hugh Lenox Scott (Garden City, N.Y.: Doubleday, Page, 1918; repr. Santa Fe, N.Mex.: Seton Village Press, 1938); *Lives of Game Animals*, 4 vols. (New York: Doubleday, Page, 1925–1928); *Great Historic Animals* (New York: Scribners, 1937); *Gospel of the Red Man: An Indian Bible*, with Julia M. Seton (Los Angeles: Willing Publishing, 1948); *Animal Tracks and Hunter Signs* (Garden City, N.Y.: Doubleday, 1958).

NOVELS

The Trail of the Sandhill Stag (New York: Scribners, 1898); *The Biography of a Grizzly* (New York: Century, 1900; repr., Lincoln: Univ. of Nebraska Press, 1987); *Krag, and Johnny Bear* (New York: Scribners, 1902); *Two Little Savages* (New York: Doubleday, Page, 1903; repr., New York: Dover, 1962); *Monarch, the Big Bear of Tallac* (New York: Scribners, 1904); *The Biography of a Silver Fox* (New York: Century, 1909; repr., Lincoln: Univ. of Nebraska Press, 1988); *Rolf in the Woods* (New York: Grosset & Dunlap, 1911); *The Preacher of Cedar Mountain* (Garden City, N.Y.: Doubleday, Page, 1918); *Bannertail: The Story of a Gray Squirrel* (New York: Scribners, 1922); *The Biography of an Arctic Fox* (New York: Appleton-Century, 1937); *Santana, the Hero-Dog of France* (Los Angeles: Phoenix, 1945).

SHORT STORY COLLECTIONS

Wild Animals I Have Known (New York: Scribners, 1898; repr., New York: Doubleday, Page, 1913; New York: Bantam, 1946; New York: Viking Penguin, 1987); *Lives of the Hunted* (New York: Scribners, 1901; repr., Berkeley: Creative Arts Books, 1987); *Animal Heroes* (New York: Scribners, 1905; repr., New York: Grosset & Dunlap, 1905; Berkeley: Creative Arts Books, 1987; Lincoln: Univ. of Nebraska Press, 1987); *Woodmyth and Fables* (New York: Century, 1905); *Wild Animal Ways* (Garden City, N.Y.: Doubleday, 1916; repr., New York: Looking Glass Library, 1959); *Woodland Tales* (Garden City, N.Y.: Doubleday, Page, 1921).

SCOUTING MANUALS

American Woodcraft for Boys (n.p., 1902); *Boy Scouts of America: A Handbook of Woodcraft Scouting, and Life-Craft* (Garden City, N.Y.: Doubleday, Page, 1910); *Forester's Manual; or, The Forest Trees of Eastern North America* (Garden City, N.Y.: Doubleday, Page, 1912); *The Woodcraft Manual for Girls* (Garden City, N.Y.: Doubleday, Page, 1916); *The Woodcraft Manual for Boys* (Garden City, N.Y.: Doubleday, Page, 1917); *The Book of Woodcraft* (Garden City, N.Y.: Doubleday, Page, 1921).

AUTOBIOGRAPHY AND JOURNALS

Trail of an Artist-Naturalist: The Autobiography of Ernest Thompson Seton (New York: Scribners, 1940); *By a Thousand Fires: Nature Notes and Extracts from the Life and Unpublished Journals of Ernest Thompson Seton*, ed. by Julia M. Seton (Garden City, N.Y.: Doubleday, 1967).

BIOGRAPHICAL AND CRITICAL STUDIES

H. Allen Anderson, *The Chief: Ernest Thompson Seton and the Changing West* (College Station: Texas A&M Univ. Press, 1986); "Animals of North America," review of *Life Histories of Northern Animals*, in *Spectator* 105 (1 October 1910); Margaret Atwood, "Animal Victims," in her *Survival: A Thematic Guide to Canadian Literature* (Toronto: Anansi, 1972); Fred Bodsworth, "The Backwoods Genius with the Magic Pen," in *Maclean's Magazine* 72 (6 June 1959); Lawrence J. Burpee, "Biographical Studies of Wild Animals," in *Dial* 48 (16 April 1910); John Burroughs, "Real and Sham Natural History," in *Atlantic Monthly* 91 (March 1903), and "The Literary Treatment of Nature," in *Atlantic Monthly* 94 (July 1904).

Wayland Drew, "Seton: Selected & Reprinted," in *Journal of Canadian Fiction* 35/36 (1986); Warren Garst and Shannon Garst, *Ernest Thompson Seton: Naturalist* (New York: Julian Messner, 1959); Betty Keller, *Black Wolf: The Life of Ernest Thompson Seton* (Vancouver: Douglas & McIntyre, 1984); Aldo Leopold, *A Sand County Almanac with Essays on Conservation from Bourd River* (New York: Ballantine Books, 1966); Charles Lilliard, review of *Selected Stories of Ernest Thompson Seton*, ed. by Patricia Morley, in *Malahat Review* 49 (January 1979); Alec Lucas, intro. to *Wild Animals I Have Known*, by Ernest Thompson Seton (Toronto: McClelland and Stewart, 1977); Ralph H. Lutts, "The Nature Fakers: Conflicting Perspectives of Nature," in *Ecological Consciousness*, ed. by Hughes Schultz (Lanham, Md.: University Press of America, 1980).

Robert H. MacDonald, "The Revolt Against Instinct: The Animal Stories of Seton and Roberts," in *Canadian Literature* 84 (spring 1980); Patricia Morley, "Seton's Animals," in *Journal of Canadian Fiction* 2 (summer 1973), and intro. to *Selected Stories of Ernest Thompson Seton*, ed. by Patricia Morley (Ottawa: Univ. of Ottawa Press, 1977); Donald Culross Peattie, "Nature and Nature Writers," in *Saturday Review* 26 (28 August 1937); Michel Poirier, "The Animal Story in Canadian Literature: E. Thompson Seton and Charles G. D. Roberts," in *Queen's Quarterly* 34 (January 1927); James Polk, "Lives of the Hunted," in *Canadian Literature* 53 (summer 1972); S. E. Read, "Flight to the Primitive: Ernest Thompson Seton," in *Canadian Literature* 13 (summer 1962); Charles G. D. Roberts, "Ernest Thompson Seton," in *Bookman* 45 (December 1913).

Malcolm J. Rohrbough, "A Dedication to the Memory of Ernest Thompson Seton: 1860–1946," in *Arizona and the West* 28 (spring 1986); John G. Samson, *The Worlds of Ernest Thompson Seton* (New York: Knopf, 1976); "Seton's Animal Book," in *Nation* 89 (2 December 1909); David E. Shi, "Ernest Thompson Seton and the Boy Scouts: A Moral Equivalent of War?" in *South Atlantic Quarterly* 84 (autumn 1985); "The Cunning of Criminal Animals," in *Spectator* 81 (29 November 1898); "Wild Animal Ways," in *Spectator* 117 (23 September 1916); Farida A. Wiley, intro. to *Ernest Thompson Seton's America*, ed. by Farida A. Wiley (New York: DevinAdair, 1954).

LESLIE MARMON SILKO
(b. 1948)

THOMAS K. DEAN

THE LAND AND the people are inseparable: this is an idea commonly seen as fundamental to much Native American thought. Generally, this attribution is true enough. Yet the idea is more complex than it appears at first glance. Inherent in it are centuries of culture, immense responsibilities, beautiful hopes, and nightmarish possibilities. Leslie Marmon Silko's works, perhaps more than those of any other contemporary Native American writer, help readers experience Native American cultural relationships with the land, leading to an understanding of nature that is at the same time visionary, apocalyptic, integrative, frighteningly pessimistic, and boundlessly optimistic.

Silko's relationship with her tribal land is intimate. She was born 5 March 1948 in Albuquerque, New Mexico, and grew up in a rock-and-adobe house at the edge of the Old Laguna pueblo, a symbol of the partial marginalization of her mixed-blood family from the community. Silko is of Laguna, Mexican, and Anglo ancestry. Her mother, Virginia, was a Plains Indian from Montana; her father, Lee H. Marmon, was a Laguna. Despite the suspicion directed toward the Marmons because of their white ancestry, family members were prominent in the community—her father was once elected treasurer of the Laguna pueblo, for example. Silko's great-grandfather, Robert Gunn Marmon, was a white government surveyor who came to the Laguna

pueblo in 1872 and married a Laguna woman, Marie Anaya. The greatest influences on Silko were the matriarchs of the family. Because her mother had to work, Silko was cared for by her great-grandmother Marie ("Grandma A'Mooh"), an inveterate storyteller. "Aunt Susie," her father's aunt, also provided Silko with stories that would later become crucial to her work.

Silko attended a Laguna school run by the Bureau of Indian Affairs where the Laguna language was not allowed to be spoken, and later a private school in Albuquerque. In 1969, she earned a B.A. in English from the University of New Mexico and published her first short stories ("The Man to Send Rain Clouds" and "Tony's Story"). At this time, she also married (though she later divorced) and gave birth to her first son. Silko attended law school at the University of New Mexico with the intent of filing land claims suits, but she gave that up in order to devote her time to writing after receiving a National Endowment for the Humanities Discovery Grant. At about this time, her second son was born.

In the mid 1970s, Silko published several short stories and a collection of poetry, *Laguna Woman* (1974), while teaching at Navajo Community College in Tsaile, Arizona. From 1976 to 1978, she lived in Ketchikan, Alaska, where she completed her first novel, *Ceremony*, published in 1977. Silko moved to Tucson, Arizona, in 1978 and began to teach at the University of

Arizona. Her eclectic collection of stories, poems, sketches, and photographs, *Storyteller*, was published in 1981, the year she won a MacArthur Foundation fellowship that enabled her to give up teaching and devote herself to writing the novel *Almanac of the Dead*, which was published in 1991.

"Landscape, History, and the Pueblo Imagination"

No consideration of Silko as a writer concerned with nature, environment, land, and landscape can begin without an understanding of her seminal essay "Landscape, History, and the Pueblo Imagination." Very few printed documents more succinctly and eloquently express the intimate and complex relationship between nature and culture. Early on in the essay, Silko insists that the term landscape is inadequate to describe a proper human relationship with the land. "Landscape" implies distance and separation, a view of natural surroundings perceived from far away. According to Laguna belief, humanity is just as connected to the land as the animals, plants, and rocks: "Viewers are as much a part of the landscape as the boulders they stand on" (p. 84). Humanity is invested with a spirit that originates from the earth, just as the rocks, plants, and animals are. This sense of equality between humanity and all other objects of creation, as well as the sense that all key elements of creation are inherent in any individual created being, fosters a reverence that forbids the idea that nature can be improved upon by humans. It also fosters the possibility of access to the spirit world; ritual (and magic) can help humans make contact with the spirits inherent in all particular things, be they squash blossoms or elk.

Pueblo peoples have a particular reverence for the natural objects within their landscapes because of the fragility of the desert, leading to an especially profound and persistent, careful attention to the natural environment. In fact, "survival depended upon harmony and cooperation not only among human beings, but among all things—the animate and less animate" (p. 86). The Pueblo way of life is nurtured by a landscape that is austere. Most important to life are the "riches realized from interaction and interrelationships with all beings above all else," and overabundance tends "to lure human attention away from what is most valuable and important" (p. 94). In the vast barrenness of the desert, every plant, every rock, every creature is significant, and therefore not taken for granted. Life—all life—is precious, an ethic that is easily emphasized, practiced, and celebrated in the arid environment of the Laguna pueblo.

Stories and storytelling play an important role in the creation and perpetuation of Silko's cultural relationship with her land, and in the essay she is masterly in her explanation of the process. In a landscape that is in some sense "empty," the Laguna people maintained a communal storytelling tradition that was rich and full. All experience is included in the people's stories, and all experience, and thus culture, becomes a story. These stories have physical contact points in the manifested world. For example, a giant sandstone boulder north of Silko's pueblo marks the spot where the heart of the giant Estrucuyo landed after the Twin Hero Brothers cut it out and threw it away in their quest to save Kochininako, Yellow Woman. Passing this boulder elicits the retelling of that story and thus the continuation of the culture.

The road this boulder is on is the road between the Laguna and Paguate villages, which also follows the route of the migration of the Laguna people after the Emergence, the time when people emerged onto this plane, the Fifth World, after a journey through the four worlds below. Everyday use of this route, then, resonates with the "spiritual or mythic dimension of the Pueblo world even today" (p. 91). For Silko although these stories and these places are as "true" as they can be, they also are ritualistic and mythic. The source of culture is in the imagination, not in rocks and boulders. The Emergence, for Silko, is thus not an actual event located in a specific time and place; rather, it is an "emergence into a precise cultural identity." The Emergence Place, the source of a cultural life, is, for ritual purposes, a natural spring near Paguate village, which also is literally the source of physical life in this desert landscape. Therefore, the eight miles between Paguate and Laguna, with their mythic/ritualistic boulders, springs, and mesas, "are actually a ritual circuit or path which marks the interior journey the Laguna people made" (p. 91). This "interior process of the imagination," which is ongoing, nurtures the understanding that the people are from and of the earth, yet have "emerged" into a distinct culture that maintains an intimate and essential relationship to the earth. Again, culture maintains that relationship with the land through story.

The stories about the animals assisting the humans in the Emergence illustrate these ideas well. Emergence, and thus cultural survival, happened only through interdependence with the animals. Once they were on the plateau landscape of the Fifth World, humans understood themselves as

> sisters and brothers to the badger, antelope, clay, yucca, and sun. Not until they could find a viable relationship to the terrain, the landscape they found themselves in, could they *emerge*. Only at the moment the requisite balance between human and *other* was realized could the Pueblo people become a culture, a distinct group whose population and survival remained stable despite the vicissitudes of climate and terrain. (p. 92)

Story, then, is essential to maintaining a culture that depends for its survival on a reverent, cooperative relationship with the land and all the creatures that inhabit it. Silko's written stories contribute in many ways to the survival of her culture, but they can also help all readers, even those outside her Laguna culture, understand the important links between art, culture, and nature as well as the ethics of a respectful, nurturing relationship between humanity and its natural environment.

Ceremony

Tayo, the main character of Silko's novel *Ceremony*, is a mixed-blood Laguna who has wandered very far from his Native American culture, and thus very far from a healthy relationship with the earth. The novel opens with Tayo returned from fighting in the Pacific in World War II, very ill. He had enlisted in the army with his cousin, Rocky, with whom he grew up as a brother. Tayo's mother, a prostitute, abandoned him at age four, giving the child to her older sister, Rock's mother. Tayo grew up with "Auntie" as his mother and Uncle Josiah, Auntie's brother, a rancher, as his father. Auntie clearly favored her son, Rocky, cultivating him to be a "success" in the white world, in part to regain respect for the family after the disgrace of Tayo's mother. Rocky became the high school football hero; his teachers told him, " 'Nothing can stop you now except one thing: don't let the people at home hold you back'" (1986 ed., p. 51).

Tayo's youth was marked by great ambivalence. Growing up, he was alienated from his entire family, yet, especially through the influence of Josiah, he maintained some respect for traditional ways at the same time that he was trying to emulate Rocky. While Rocky tries to initiate Tayo into the world of drinking and sex, Josiah inculcates such beliefs as " 'This [land] is where we come from. . . . This earth keeps us going'" (1986 ed., p. 45). A telling incident is a short scene where Rocky and Tayo are deer hunting. Tayo sprinkles cornmeal on the dead deer's nose to feed and honor its spirit, to the scorn and embarrassment of Rocky.

As enlisted men in the U.S. Army, Rocky and Tayo garner a certain amount of respect from the white culture. Rocky is killed in the war. While slogging through the rainy jungle on the way to a Japanese prison camp, Tayo prays for a hundred years of dry air. When he returns home after the war, physically debilitated and mentally ill, his desert home is experiencing a lengthy drought, and Tayo takes responsibility for it. He remembers Josiah's warning: " 'The old people used to say that droughts happen when people forget, when people misbehave'" (1986 ed., p. 46). The withdrawal of life-giving water from his land is indicative of his parched soul, and Tayo feels almost literally incorporeal—in the army hospital, he perceived himself as smoke. The whites' medicine had "drained memory out of his thin arms and replaced it with a twilight cloud behind his eyes" (1986 ed., p. 15). The world, and Tayo, are out of balance, and the novel becomes a ceremony by which Tayo will experience reintegration with himself, his culture, and his land.

As Silko explains in "Landscape, History, and the Pueblo Imagination," stories, especially traditional stories, are integral to the ritualistic re-creation, perpetuation, or, in Tayo's case, healing of the culture as well as the self. *Ceremony* establishes this fact early on, as it opens with a brief recounting of the creation story: Ts'its'tsi'nako, Thought-Woman, also known as Spider-Woman, is thinking, and whatever she thinks, appears. The end of this verse story says she is "thinking of a story now," and this novel, this ceremony, is that story. Before the story of Tayo begins, however, another mythic voice enters, insisting that stories are "all we have to fight off / illness and death." The evil of the world, although strong, will try to destroy the stories through confusion and forgetfulness, so it is the duty of the people to keep the stories alive, for in the life of the story is the life of the people.

Throughout the ceremonial progress of the novel, Tayo hears and recalls, and the narrator tells, a number of traditional tales that reconnect Tayo, and the reader, to the mythic foundations of the world, both cultural and natural. An understanding of how to proceed in life must be found in such archetypal stories, which contain wisdom. For example, very early on, Tayo bears the burden of guilt for the drought through the Reed Woman/Corn Woman story. Reed Woman, indulging in a luxurious river bath, raises the ire of her sister Corn Woman, who is working to grow the food. Corn Woman's anger, analogous to Tayo's anger at the jungle rains, causes Reed Woman to withdraw to the First World, taking her water with her, and blighting the earth with drought.

Tayo is guilty of more than simple anger, however. He also has strayed from his culture by not keeping the white world enough at bay, including his stint in the army. In other words, he is not attending to the needs of his people or his land in the tenacious way necessary for cultural survival. Tayo is reliving the story of the Pa'caya'nyi, the Ck'o'yo magician, which is interspersed throughout much of the novel as Tayo moves toward reintegration during the ceremony. The magician deflects the people's attention from their duties through flashy magic tricks and sideshow antics. Nau'ts'ity'i, one of Thought-Woman's sisters, disgusted by the people's inattention, withdraws her care, taking with her the plants, grass, animals, and rain clouds. Panicked, the people send a hummingbird and a series of other animals to the First World to ask for Nau'ts'ity'i's forgiveness.

Tayo, in late-twentieth-century America, is not about to go looking for hummingbirds to speak to the gods. He is sent to Old Betonie, a mixed-blood medicine man, who lives in the foothills north of the Gallup Ceremonial Grounds. Tayo marvels at the collection of junk in the old man's place: old newspapers, empty Coke bottles, medicine pouches, telephone books, railroad calendars. The elder insists, " 'All these things have stories alive in them.' " Betonie's methods are just as untraditional and eclectic as his surroundings. He insists that the old ceremonies were adequate for their time, but the shift in the world since the arrival of the white man calls for new ceremonies. He claims that growth and change are necessary to avoid death and stagnation.

The witchery is the force that exploits death and stagnation, that ultimately seduces the people away from their culture and the land, leading to cultural and environmental apocalypse. A world in balance is one where the forces of the witchery and the good are in check. The contemporary world is out of balance, and the witchery reigns. According to Betonie, a new paradigm is needed. The people cannot simply return to the old ways, for " 'that's what the witchery is counting on: that we will cling to the ceremonies the way they were, and then their power will triumph, and the people will be no more' " (1986 ed., p. 126). Tayo wishes to believe that Old Betonie is correct, but he wonders what power Indian ceremonies, even new ones, can have against white wars, bombs, and lies. Betonie cautions that the witchery wants the people to believe that all evil dwells within whites, but such an obsession only deflects attention from the true source of evil. White people are only the tools of the witchery.

What follows in the novel is a story fundamental to Silko's thought regarding the relationships between Europeans, environmental destruction, and Native American cultural genocide. The tale tells of a witches' gathering, a contest to see who can concoct the most horrid thing possible. One witch offers a story, the story of the destroyers. The destroyers are people who grow away from the earth, the sun, and the plants and animals. Nature is not life in their eyes, but object. They fear the world and destroy it in that fear. They bring disease and weapons of death across the waters, killing all they fear, poisoning the water, shedding the blood of the people, stealing the land. Ultimately, the destroyers will destroy each other by laying a "final pattern" in the "rocks with veins of green and yellow and black," laying it across the world and exploding everything. Horrified, the other witches urge their colleague to take the story back, but the triumphant witch, revealing the power of story, says, "It's already turned loose. It's already coming. It can't be called back" (1986 ed., p. 138).

In these latter days, the destroyers, the agents of the witchery, are clearly manifested in Europeans and their imperialistic enterprises, which will end not only in environmental destruction but also in nuclear holocaust. Betonie takes Tayo out into the hills for several days and nights of ritual and story that culminate in a vision that the old man passes on to his charge. Unknowingly, Tayo has already begun his ceremony and is part of a larger ceremony of purification. Likewise, the reader discovers that the novel has been enacting this ceremony all along, and the plots, subplots, and characters already encountered have been part of the larger novelistic pattern that is only now being perceived. In Tayo's ceremony, the mythical patterns, the stories, are clearly playing themselves out in the manifested world, and he must participate in the story to save both himself and the world. Betonie warns him that if he does not complete his own personal ceremony of reintegration, the circle will be broken and the witchery will have won. Betonie leaves Tayo with a vision he saw in the stars of spotted cattle, a woman, and a mountain.

In essence, Tayo discovers that life itself is a ceremony. He has been part of this larger mythic pattern all along, and his new awareness, provided by Betonie, reveals the correct choices to make in order to integrate the pattern of his life with the pattern of a healthy world and universe. The cattle mentioned by Betonie were, in Tayo's mind, clearly Uncle Josiah's spotted cows. Josiah had acquired this herd of Mexican cattle, a particularly hardy breed, in anticipation of the coming drought. Josiah was told of the possibility of acquiring these cattle by Night Swan, a retired Mexican prostitute in Cubero with whom Josiah had sexual liaisons. Josiah's quest throughout the novel is following the herd back to Mexico in order not to lose them, for as soon as they were delivered to the ranch, they began an inexorable march back to their homeland. After his experience with Betonie, Tayo knows that he must finish his now dead uncle's unfinished quest of reclaiming the spotted cattle as part of his ceremony.

Tayo also realizes that Night Swan was a manifestation of the "woman" he must encounter. Some years earlier, when Josiah was alive, Tayo himself had a sexual encounter with Night Swan. As Tayo left her place in Cubero, Night Swan bid him a cryptic farewell: " 'But remember this day. You will recognize it later. You are part of it now' " (1986 ed., p. 100). Now, in the midst of the ceremony, this message makes sense to Tayo: his encounter with Night Swan was an encounter with the feminine earth power with which he must reintegrate. In quest of the cattle after visiting Betonie, Tayo ends up at Mount Taylor, the Laguna sacred mountain, during an evening when he sees Betonie's pattern of stars in the sky. He is housed and clothed by a woman, Ts'eh, whose blue shawl links her with the blue accoutrements of Night Swan and Betonie's grandmother. All of these powerful women — Ts'eh, Night Swan, and Betonie's grandmother — are manifestations of Ts'its'tsi'nako, or Thought-Woman. The sexual encounter between Tayo and Ts'eh, then, leads to the subsequent nurturing rain that the Mother needs to bring back to the people.

Eventually, Tayo recovers the cattle; their proper integration with the landscape, signaling a partial fulfillment of the ceremony, is indicated as Tayo views "their spotted hides blending into the sandy talus of the big mesa. . . . He could see Josiah's vision emerging, he could see the story taking form in bone and muscle" (1986 ed., p. 226). Ts'eh and Tayo tend the cattle together, spending the summer in the natural landscape of the ranch, apparently in harmony with it. Tayo's family, however, urges him to return home, worried that he is becoming mentally unstable again. Ts'eh warns Tayo that this is the work of the destroyers, wanting to change the story so that Tayo does not come to integration but goes mad in the hills and must be hospitalized again.

Ts'eh points specifically to Emo as the perpetrator of this false tale of the destroyers. Emo, along with Harley, Leroy, and Pinkie, are Native Americans who, like Rocky, have been seduced by the forces of the destroyers. Emo, especially, is contemptuous of the old traditional ways, citing white urban technological achievement as the locus of value and power in the world. His perverted sexuality and alcoholism are by-products of this corrupted vision. The stories claim that the whites will destroy themselves more quickly than the Native Americans, but it is imperative that the latter, and Tayo personally, retake control of the story and make sure the forces of destruction rebound on the destroyers.

Remembering Old Betonie's image of the patterns of destruction etched in the veins of the land, Tayo realizes that the place of ultimate destruction, and the place of possible reclamation of the universe through ceremony, is the uranium mine. The Europeans, through this mine, had extracted natural forces and twisted them to their own incomprehensibly destructive ends, culminating in the atomic destruction of Hiroshima and Nagasaki. At the mine shaft, Tayo knows the "pattern of the ceremony was completed," both the anti-ceremony of the destroyers and the reclamation ceremony he himself is undertaking. The Europeans had

taken these beautiful rocks from deep within earth and they had laid them in a monstrous design, realizing destruction on a scale only *they* could have dreamed.

He carried the relief he felt at finally seeing the pattern, the way all the stories fit together—the old stories, the war stories, their stories—to become the story that was still being told. He was not crazy; he had never been crazy. He had only seen and heard the world as it always was: no boundaries, only transitions through all distances and time. (1986, p. 246)

The destroyers arrive: Harley, Pinkie, Leroy, and Emo. In an orgy of vandalism, they enact an anti-ceremony of destruction. Most horribly, Harley is tortured by the others in a manner reminiscent of the witchery contest that wrought the advent of the destroyers in the first place, and he is eventually killed. Tayo is tempted to jump Emo and kill him, in order to save Harley, by driving a screwdriver into his skull, but he realizes that would be the end of the story that the destroyers themselves want. The destroyers must destroy themselves, and Tayo's holding back of his own destructive impulses lets the forces of life in him triumph. The stars above him, "existing beyond memory," hold together, and Tayo helps to hold together the coherence of the universe: "The story goes on with stars of the old war shield; they go on, lasting until the fifth world ends, then maybe beyond. The only thing is: it has never been easy" (1986 ed., p. 254).

Tayo has succeeded. The ceremony is complete; he has reintegrated himself into his culture and his land. For now, the destroyers' power is dead. For now. Although the novel ends in rain and sunrise, the universe in Laguna conception is cyclic. The power balance will shift again.

Storyteller

Silko's collection of myths, short stories, poems, autobiographical sketches, and photographs, because of its nonlinear structure, illustrates even more vividly than *Ceremony* the cyclic nature of the balance of forces. Even the fact that the collection includes a number of her previously published stories and poems, some of them the myths told in *Ceremony*, suggests that the mythic patterns on which Silko has based her previous work are eternal. The telling of a story, the performance of a ceremony, the reading of a book do not end in closure. The patterns of existence are recursive, and *Storyteller* can be seen either as a bundle of works that are sliced out of the infinite or as a single infinite work: the works can be read in any order and through any number of repetitions, for a literally endless series of possibilities, or they can be read continuously, with a return to the beginning once the end is reached, causing the book to grow in structural coherence. The book also suggests both the infinite gulf and the intimate ties between the individual or particular (photographs of Silko's family captured in specific moments in time) and the eternal (the mythic, endless story of the witchery retold from *Ceremony*). In this way, such tales as "Tony's Story," which tells of the murder of a state trooper by two young Native American men, become understandable in the context of the eternal struggle against the destroyers.

Scattered throughout the book are pieces that suggest both the reverence for and the destruction of the land. For example, a short poem titled "The Time We Climbed Snake Mountain" briefly recounts a climb with such lines as "I grab the warm parts of the cliff/and I feel the mountain as I climb" (p. 76), suggesting an intimacy with the land. Aware of a yellow spotted snake sleeping on a rock nearby, the speaker cautions the fellow climbers/readers to watch out and not step on the snake, for the "mountain is his." "Storyteller" in large part illustrates the lace of ethics that accrues from exploitation or rape of the land in the white oil workers' sexual exploitation of a Native American woman. More generally, their introduction of a material attitude toward landscape in the land of the Eskimos "rapes" the Alaskan Native American culture as well.

The story "Yellow Woman" is at the center of a more complex web of stories that runs

Leslie Marmon Silko

throughout *Storyteller*. Its basic theme, like that of *Ceremony*, is contemporary Native Americans' necessary reconnection to the spirit worlds of the earth and their confusion over such opportunities when they present themselves. To provide the rich context of this tale, Silko scatters retellings of other Yellow Woman stories throughout the book ("Cottonwood: Parts One and Two," "What Whirlwind Man Told Kochininako, Yellow Woman," and others). Traditionally, the Yellow Woman tales involve a human woman going to a river to draw water; meeting a manifested *ka'tsina* spirit, often near a cottonwood tree; going away with him; entering into a relationship with him for a number of years; and returning to her people with something that will help perpetuate the life of the people. Often this something is twin boys who continue the life of the people and protect them, for they could be manifestations of the Twin Heroes. In "Cottonwood Part Two: Buffalo

Story," Kochininako goes away with Buffalo Man, another common pattern. Her husband, Arrowboy, becomes jealous and threatens to kill the Buffalo People, whom he perceives as having kidnapped his wife. In actuality, the reason for the events was to provide the people with food during a drought. After Arrowboy kills the buffalo who have appeared on the plains because of his wife's new relationship, he also must kill Yellow Woman, for she has grown to love her life with the Buffalo People. Although the story ends tragically in this sense, Yellow Woman has fulfilled her sacrificial purpose: in her absence and, in this case, death, she has provided for the continuance of her people.

Again, the point of these Yellow Woman stories is the recurring need for humanity to maintain its contact with the animal and spirit worlds in order to sustain life. The contemporary Yellow Woman of the story of the same name is confused about events that resemble the Kochininako stories. She meets a handsome stranger, apparently a Navajo, while getting water at the river, and proceeds to spend several days and nights with him. She tells herself that this all seems like a Yellow Woman story, but " 'what they tell in stories was real only then, back in time immemorial.' . . . I live now and I've been to school and there are highways and pickup trucks that Yellow Woman never saw" (p. 56). Nevertheless, Silva, the Navajo, calls her Yellow Woman throughout their affair.

Silva turns out to be a cattle rustler, and on the way to Marquez to sell some meat, the couple encounters a white rancher who intends to turn them in to the state police. At Silva's prodding, Yellow Woman bolts away on the horse and never sees Silva again. She returns to her home but brings nothing with her. The willow leaves on the riverbank where she first met Silva are withered, suggesting no renewal from her experience. Although she believes Silva will return and she will be waiting for him, this Yellow Woman experience, perhaps because of her own ambivalence about the spiritual power of the pattern of events, yields nothing, not even a story. In the last lines she says, "I was sorry that Old Grandpa wasn't alive to hear my story

because it was the Yellow Woman stories he liked to tell best" (p. 62).

The storytelling tradition is not being maintained here, and the ramifications could be deadly. Without a belief in the story, there is no belief in the renewing power of the encounter with the animal spirits, and thus there is no cultural or environmental renewal. On the other hand, Silva exhibits a number of characteristics of the Coyote trickster, linking this tale to a number of others in the collection (such as "Coyote Holds a Full House in his Hand"), perhaps suggesting that Coyote is up to his usual tricks in distracting the people from tending to what they should. Even if this were the case, however, Yellow Woman is still unaware that she has gained access to the animal spirit world through Coyote, and cannot act accordingly. She has not committed herself to the necessary traditional belief, as Tayo does in his ceremony.

However, "Yellow Woman" cannot be taken out of the context of the intricate web that is *Storyteller*, and the thematics of the story, although it has received much critical attention, should not be projected as a singular idea onto the whole book. The moments of pessimism and defeat are part of the cycle, the ebb and flow of experience, both physical and spiritual, that will ultimately end in the return of the proper relationship between the people and the land.

Almanac of the Dead

The war between the forces of life and destruction take an epic and apocalyptic turn in Silko's most recent novel, the ambitious *Almanac of the Dead*. The same philosophies of the inevitability of the destroyers and of a return of the people to their land found in *Ceremony*, and to some extent *Storyteller*, inform this novel as well. The novel seems slightly futuristic because, in the narrative, the indigenous battles against the powers of the controlling European destroyers in Central and South America that occurred in the 1980s have filtered into Mexico. The United States is preparing for military protection of its economic and political interests in Mexico, so the Western Hemisphere is on the brink of war.

The novel presents a vast array of narrative lines, most of which focus on the absolute corruption of a people totally alienated from the powers of the earth. A capitalist ethic that objectifies everything on the earth and makes it a commodity has led to environmental destruction, war, a seemingly universal dependence on drugs, unimaginable sexual perversions, paranoia, and a total disregard for all life. Just a sampling of the collection of misfits will suggest the depths of degradation that the world depicted in the novel has come to: the insurance company executive turned mobilizer of a private army who has a fetish for his bulletproof vest, the drug dealer whose sideline is pornographic snuff and films of medical operations, the judge who raises basset hounds for sexual companions, and the plasma center operator who kills the homeless by draining their blood in order to harvest their organs for a sideline "biomedical materials" business.

Clearly, these perverts and misfits are the destroyers, some of them Native Americans who have been led astray; like Emo and the rest in *Ceremony*, they are quickly destroying themselves. In fact, many do die in the novel, usually violently, at least perversely, at the hands of their own kind. Yet underlying all this horrible activity suggesting that the world is heading for apocalypse, the forces of the indigenous people and other disfranchised are rallying to reclaim what was/is theirs: the land. Not all of these subversives are on the side of good, however. Serlo, who is establishing an institute to develop "Alternative Earth" modules, frighteningly like the real Biosphere 2 project, that will orbit the earth, is a neo-Nazi who wishes to preserve only the purest of northern European stock. The International Holistic Healers Convention toward the end of the novel is, on the whole, nothing more than a collection of "eco-terrorists" ("deep ecologists" who are a " 'symptom of what had become of the Europeans who had left their home continent to settle in strange lands'" [p. 689]) and New Age hucksters. The Cuban

Communists are just as corrupt as the corporate powers of North America.

The seemingly true force of life and goodness is represented by those closest to original culture and those with the simplest, yet most profound respect for the land. Among the various factions vying for power and prominence in this brewing cauldron about to explode are El Feo and his twin brother Wacah. The two are never explicitly identified as the Twin Hero Brothers of Pueblo legend, but clearly they represent the forces that will deliver the people back to their land and back to a peaceful, balanced relationship with the earth. They receive their instructions, appropriately, from animal totems, macaws who direct them to make the people walk north with them, rather than via destructive technology. Their message is simple: "Home" is where the ancestor spirits are, and that is in the home*land*. A return to that homeland will come about through patience, waiting for the earth's natural forces, which are already set loose, to rebalance themselves. In the meantime, just as Tayo must protect his ceremony in order that the destroyers do not wrest it from him, the people must protect the earth from destruction. This will be accomplished if people "let go of a great many comforts and all things European; but the reward would be peace and harmony with all living things. All they had to do was return to Mother Earth. No more blasting, digging, or burning" (p. 710).

An accounting of all the characters and plot lines in the novel is impossible in a short space, but ultimately that does not matter. The novel ends neither in apocalypse nor in nirvana. In fact, despite the epic sweep of the novel, it concludes its message by coming back down to one individual, as all things must when the earth, culture, and the people are at stake.

Sterling is a character introduced early in the novel. He is Laguna but is estranged from his tribe. Growing up, he never paid particular attention to the traditional ways. He spent most of the time reading true crime magazines, memorizing the history of gangsters and other assorted criminals (certainly destroyers) in vast particular detail. "Beer and big women bouncing in water beds" are his other diversions, as is the case for most whites portrayed in the novel. A Hollywood movie studio begins filming on the reservation, and Sterling is assigned by the elders to make sure the cast and crew do not desecrate anything. While the filming is in progress, a stone serpent, perceived as a mystical sign, appears on the land. The crew films it, and Sterling's carelessness in allowing the serpent to be filmed earns him excommunication from the tribe. He drifts about and ends up working as a gardener for a couple of old Native American women, one of whom, Lecha, is transcribing pages allegedly from the Almanac of the Dead.

The almanac was a desperate attempt to save indigenous culture hundreds of years ago. As Old Betonie warned Tayo in *Ceremony*, the whites are not the witchery and are not the whole of the destroyers. This becomes clearer in *Almanac of the Dead* as Silko deepens her history of the destroyers. Sorcerers among the Native Americans of what is now Central and South America, called Gunadeeyahs, were in fact destroyers, with a voracious appetite for blood, even their own people's, and sexually thrilled by killing. Montezuma was one of these sorcerers, and it was his complicity with the Spanish conquerers that led to the destruction of the Native American peoples. Many of the latter fled north to escape the Gunadeeyahs, and these people are the ancestors of the Southwestern desert peoples. Many of these people, fearing the destruction, or at least dispersion, of their culture, attempted to preserve as much as possible in almanacs, records of traditions, customs, astrological calendars, and so on.

By the end of the book, the ranch, corrupted by drug trade, is no longer viable, so Sterling is on his own again. As he wends his way back to his tribal homeland and his people, he gains a new appreciation for what Lecha was trying to do in preserving what she thought was an ancient almanac. Sterling is silently accepted back into the community, and the novel ends with him traversing the tribal grounds, searching for meaning in the same landmarks Tayo seeks: Mount Taylor, the sacred mountain, and the uranium mine, the zenith and nadir of Laguna

relationships with the land. Sterling stumbles upon the stone snake and notices that it has changed: its head is raised, its jaws are opened, and it is pointing south. In this visionary moment Sterling, and we as readers, understand all; the last line of the novel is "The snake was looking south, in the direction from which the twin brothers and the people would come" (p. 763). Sterling, in casting off the patina of European culture and in remembering and honoring the spirit of the homeland, serves as an example of what Natives need to do to save the earth. In this sense, the novel is boundlessly optimistic: the people, and thus the earth, *will* return.

No doubt Silko would not dub herself a "nature writer." But it is clear that underlying all her work is a philosophy, her tribal philosophy, that is so suffused with ideas about human relationships with the earth that ethical issues regarding humanity's destruction of the earth cannot help but emerge. Perhaps the greatest gift that Silko's work provides is an understanding of how culture and nature are inseparable, and degradation of one is degradation of the other. She also provides a solution to such degradation: the maintenance of story. Memory and its transmission through story are the highest honorific. Although the immediate future looks bleak, Silko nurtures a calm assurance for her people that both they and the earth can survive. But this will happen only when the people accept the responsibility to nurture the story of life.

Selected Bibliography

WORKS OF LESLIE MARMON SILKO

POETRY

Laguna Woman: Poems (Greenfield Center, N.Y.: Greenfield Review, 1974).

BOOK-LENGTH PROSE

Ceremony (New York: Viking Penguin, 1977; repr., New York: New American Library, 1978, and New York: Penguin, 1986); *Storyteller* (New York: Arcade, 1981); *Almanac of the Dead* (New York: Simon and

Schuster, 1991); *Sacred Water* (Tucson, Ariz.: Flood Plain Press, 1993).

ESSAYS

"Leslie Silko, Laguna Poet and Novelist," in *This Song Remembers: Self-Portraits of Native Americans in the Arts*, ed. by Jane B. Katz (Boston: Houghton Mifflin, 1980); "Language and Literature from a Pueblo Indian Perspective," in *English Literature: Opening Up the Canon*, ed. by Leslie Fiedler and Houston A. Baker, Jr. (Baltimore: Johns Hopkins University Press, 1981); "Landscape, History, and the Pueblo Imagination," in *Antaeus* 57 (autumn 1986); "Interior and Exterior Landscapes: The Pueblo Migration Stories," in *Landscape in America*, ed. by George F. Thompson (Austin: Univ. of Texas Press, 1995).

LETTERS

The Delicacy and Strength of Lace: Letters Between Leslie Marmon Silko and James Wright, ed. by Anne Wright (St. Paul, Minn.: Graywolf, 1986).

BIOGRAPHICAL AND CRITICAL STUDIES

Paula Gunn Allen, "The Feminine Landscape of Leslie Marmon Silko's *Ceremony*," in Allen, ed., *Studies in American Indian Literature: Critical Essays and Course Designs* (New York: Modern Language Association, 1983); Thomas K. Dean, "Teaching Leslie Marmon Silko as Nature Writer," in *The American Nature Writing Newsletter* (fall 1994); Richard F. Fleck, "Sacred Land in the Writings of Momaday, Welch, and Silko," in *Entering the 90s: The North American Experience: Proceedings from the Native American Studies Conference at Lake Superior University, October 27–28, 1989*, ed. by Thomas E. Schirer (Sault Ste. Marie, Ontario: Lake Superior Uni-

versity Press, 1991); Reyes Garcia, "Senses of Place in *Ceremony*," *MELUS* 10 (winter 1983); Melody Graulich, ed. *"Yellow Woman,"* by Leslie Marmon Silko (New Brunswick, N.J.: Rutgers Univ. Press, 1993), casebook with text, interviews, and critical articles; Kenneth Lincoln, *Native American Renaissance* (Berkeley: Univ. of California Press, 1983); Mick McAllister, "Homeward Bound: Wilderness and Frontier in American Indian Literature," in *The Frontier Experience and the American Dream*, ed. by David Mogen, Mark Busby, and Paul Bryant (College Station: Texas A&M Univ. Press, 1989).

Robert M. Nelson, *Place and Vision: The Function of Landscape in Native American Fiction* (New York: Peter Lang, 1993); Christopher Norden, "Ecological Restoration as Post-Colonial Ritual of Community in Three Native American Novels," in *SAIL: Studies in American Indian Literatures* 6 (winter 1994); Catherine Rainwater, "The Semiotics of Dwelling in Leslie Marmon Silko's *Ceremony*," in *American Journal of Semiotics* 9, nos. 2–3 (1992); Lee Schweninger, "Writing Nature: Silko and Native Americans as Nature Writers," in *MELUS* 18 (summer 1993); Patricia Clark Smith and Paula Gunn Allen, "Earthy Relations, Carnal Knowledge: Southwestern American Indian Women Writers and Landscape," in *The Desert Is No Lady: Southwestern Landscapes in Women's Writing and Art*, ed. by Vera Norwood and Janice Monk (New Haven, Conn.: Yale Univ. Press, 1987); Edith Swan, "Healing via the Sunwise Cycle in Silko's *Ceremony*," in *American Indian Quarterly* 12 (fall 1988), and "Laguna Symbolic Geography and Silko's *Ceremony*," in *American Indian Quarterly* 12 (summer 1988); Alan R. Velie, *Four American Indian Literary Masters: N. Scott Momaday, James Welch, Leslie Marmon Silko, and Gerald Vizenor* (Norman: Univ. of Oklahoma Press, 1982).

GARY SNYDER
(b. 1930)

PATRICK D. MURPHY

BEFORE HE HAD established his reputation as a poet, Gary Snyder had already been made famous as one of the leading figures of the Beat Generation by Jack Kerouac. In 1958 Kerouac published *The Dharma Bums*, a thinly disguised roman à clef with a wisdom-trickster figure named Japhy Ryder. Reviewers, critics, and other authors were quick to point out that Japhy Ryder was modeled on Gary Snyder. Over the years, Snyder has sought to distance himself from the character, pointing out that Japhy Ryder is indeed fictitious and that readers and critics should not be treating *The Dharma Bums* as if it were his biography. Nevertheless, it would be decades before a very different view would emerge in the public eye, that of Snyder as one of the preeminent ecological poets of the United States.

Snyder also has drawn a sharp distinction between the Beats and the San Francisco Renaissance, dissociating himself from the former label and identifying himself with the latter movement. Despite Kerouac's exaggerated fictionalization of the people and events shaping his life in the 1950s, he did make an evaluation that has been borne out over the decades since *The Dharma Bums* was published: Gary Snyder and Allen Ginsberg have proven to be the most lasting and productive of the New York and San Francisco literati collectively known as the Beats. Today, far more people think of Snyder as an environmentalist rather than as a beatnik, but the two should not be seen as a contradiction. The Beats were a formative influence on the hippies, and both movements defined themselves as being against the military-industrial complex, centralized government, and the destruction of the wild. The Beat and San Francisco Renaissance writers were mostly born in the late 1920s and early 1930s and came of age during World War II and the Korean War. While their parents' generation was participating in the economic prosperity, technological transformation of industry, and suburban sprawl of the 1950s, these writers were developing critiques of the consumer society, cultural stability, and social conformity that defined the mainstream American values of that decade.

Early Life

What were the factors of his early life that positioned Snyder to become a poet in his twenties and to make nature a crucial, integral component of his life philosophy and his writing? Like the other individuals who generated the counterculture movements of the 1950s that grew into the civil rights, antiwar, communal, and environmental movements of the 1960s, he is a child of the Great Depression. On 8 May 1930, Gary Snyder was born in San Francisco.

829

During her pregnancy, Snyder's mother, Lois Wilkie Snyder, lived part of the time with relatives while her husband, Harold Snyder, scoured the West Coast, looking for employment. After a short stint working for a grocery company, Harold moved his family to Washington State, where they survived by raising chickens, doing a little farming, and cutting shake shingles from logging stumps while he remained more or less unemployed for about seven years. During that time the Snyders had a daughter, Anthea. The family made do with a house covered with tar paper.

Although his family apparently was poorer than most of their neighbors, Snyder claims to have felt no sense of deprivation. Early in life he learned the appreciation of work through helping his father; the imaginative pleasure of reading with his mother; and the physical satisfaction of outdoor recreation, such as hiking, camping, and climbing, largely on his own.

World War II generated jobs in the United States for the men and women who did not join the armed forces. Snyder's parents found work in Portland, Oregon, in 1942. A few years later they separated, the children staying with their mother. In high school, Snyder joined the Wilderness Society and the Mazamas mountaineering club, and worked summers at a YMCA camp near the base of Mount St. Helens, the site of his first snow-peak ascent. In the winters he worked as a copyboy for the *Oregonian*, the newspaper where his mother was employed. He also began experimenting with expressing his feelings through poetry, an interest he continued and expanded in college.

Snyder stayed in Portland to attend Reed College, where he majored in literature and anthropology, and became involved with a literary group. This group, which worked on the student magazine *Janus*, provided him with several life-long friends, such as the authors Lew Welch and Philip Whalen. *Gary Snyder: Dimensions of a Life* (1991), edited by Jon Halper, includes reminiscences about Snyder by Reed College teachers and fellow students. These indicate that Snyder remained poor and maintained a fairly ascetic, if

highly social, lifestyle. In 1951, Snyder graduated after writing a complex undergraduate thesis titled "He Who Hunted Birds in His Father's Village." In this work Snyder integrates anthropology and literature to produce a serious study of Pacific Northwest Native American beliefs and traditions. He was briefly married to Alison Gass, whom he divorced in 1952, and began practicing Buddhist meditation.

It becomes clear from Snyder's correspondence with his Reed College friends and from later interviews that he engaged in ongoing discussions over the future of American poetry, debating the significance of such writers as William Carlos Williams, Ezra Pound, D. H. Lawrence, and Robinson Jeffers. Snyder, Welch, Whalen, and some of the others were interested not only in modernist poets but also in environmental ones, such as Jeffers; they were particularly interested in exploring any connections between this literature and East Asian philosophy and spirituality. Throughout the 1950s, Snyder and Whalen carried on a spirited correspondence over the merits of Buddhism, modernist poets, the antimodernist Jeffers, and social change. Like other aspiring writers of his generation, such as Welch and Ginsberg, Snyder was torn between pursuing a career in academia, through attending graduate school, or following the vocation of a writer. Although he enrolled in graduate school at Indiana University, poetry called him away after one semester, and he returned to the West Coast. Given that Snyder worked at a YMCA camp, participated in a Park Service archaeological dig while in high school, and had become a skilled mountaineer and backpacker, it should be no surprise to learn that he worked for the U.S. Forest Service as a seasonal fire lookout in 1952.

When younger, Snyder had been interested in traditional Native American cultures because of their environmentally aware and harmonious lifestyles. But he realized their spiritual and cultural pathways were not open to nonnatives. So while continuing to develop his knowledge of Native American beliefs and practices after college, Snyder increasingly turned his attention to another spiritual pathway: Mahayana Buddhism. Early in his life Snyder had been impressed by Chinese landscape painting, and in college he read Chinese and Japanese poetry in translation. On and off from 1953 through early 1956 he studied Chinese and Japanese at Berkeley, which led to his translation of the poems of Han Shan.

By 1954, Snyder had in effect completed one phase of his life and was poised to initiate a second phase, during which he wrote a considerable amount of poetry and some prose. At age twenty-four, he had made a commitment to poetry and had deepened his commitment to and practice of an environmentally conscious and antimaterialistic lifestyle. He also had determined that the next phase of his life would require studying Buddhism in Japan.

Crisscrossing the Pacific

From 1956 through 1968, Snyder crisscrossed the Pacific Ocean several times, developing his reputation as a poet and an ecological thinker on the West Coast, and his spiritual practice as a Buddhist, primarily through study at a Rinzai Zen temple, in Japan. While working in Yosemite on a trail crew in the summer of 1955, he made a breakthrough into a poetics that he felt represented his own voice, less derivative than the various styles found in his earlier work. He participated, that October, in the famous Six Gallery poetry reading in San Francisco at which Allen Ginsberg first performed "Howl." Both senior poets, such as Kenneth Rexroth, and other young poets identified Snyder as one of the major voices of the new generation of poets, and his poetry began appearing in literary magazines around the country that were promoting the Beats.

The next May, Snyder set off from San Francisco to study Buddhism in Kyoto. He left behind the manuscript of a poetic sequence, written between 1952 and 1956, called *Myths and Texts*, and took with him the Yosemite poems he had written the previous summer. It took four years

for this sequence to see print, and by then Cid Corman had printed in Japan a collection titled *Riprap*, which contained those 1955 Yosemite poems and several more written in Japan and during the eight months he spent aboard an oil tanker, weaving its way from Yokohama to the Persian Gulf and eventually to California.

Myths and Texts is a complex, highly allusive sequence written under the evident stylistic influence of Ezra Pound's ideogrammatic method, enhanced by Snyder's growing knowledge of the Chinese written language. Despite the modernist influence, the sequence clearly displays Snyder's syncretic philosophy and life experiences, which provided him with an orientation toward life, work, and culture very different from that found in high modernist poetry. Originally published by Totem Press in 1960, it was reprinted several times and reissued in 1978 by New Directions.

The sequence begins and ends with allusions to Thoreau, appropriate for multiple reasons. For one, Snyder is re-visioning what inhabitation might mean for the migrant peoples who have become the dominant culture in the United States. For another, he had studied Thoreau during the period he was writing the sequence. And Snyder, like Thoreau, blends a deep respect for Native American practices with an interest in Eastern metaphysics. In various articles, Sherman Paul has addressed the connections between Snyder and Thoreau; these works contribute to an appreciation of the ecological vision that carries Snyder philosophically beyond the modernism reflected in the aesthetic features of the sequence.

Myths and Texts is a three-part poetic sequence that engages in mythopoeia, specifically attempting to generate a new myth that can guide inhabitation in contemporary North America by the nonnative populations. Snyder's claims about myth in *He Who Hunted Birds in His Father's Village*, the published version of his undergraduate thesis, are quite instructive for a reading of this mythopoeia. At the beginning of the study, Snyder declares, "Original Mind speaks through little myths and tales that tell us how to *be* in some specific ecosystem of the far-flung world" (p. x); toward the end of the study he concludes,

> Myth is a "reality lived" because for every individual it contains, at the moment of telling, the projected content of both his unarticulated and conscious values: simultaneously ordering, organizing, and making comprehensible the world within which the values exist. One might even reformulate the statement to say "Reality is a myth lived." (pp. 109–110)

Snyder strings together a series of "little myths and tales" that cumulatively move toward a reconceptualization of humanity's relationship to the rest of the world and a reconceptualization of the relationship of the conscious and unconscious parts of the human mind with the rest of the human body.

In the first section of *Myths and Texts*, "Logging," Snyder critiques the world-as-commodity mentality of contemporary industrialized societies, with emphasis on the United States. He identifies this mentality as developing out of the Western Judeo-Christian tradition, and uses frequent allusions to Eastern and Native American values to suggest alternative myths and practices to counter the destructive character of modern economics. This section ends with a poetic segment blending Pacific Northwestern and Hindu myths that looks to "rebirth" rather than reform for ending the anti-environmental, earth-destroying practices that have been identified and condemned.

In the second section, "Hunting," Snyder emphasizes Native American stories and practices that provide an inhabitory and bioregional alternative to the culture condemned in "Logging." Toward the end of "Hunting," he begins to infuse the Native American-based stories with Buddhist imagery, linking the positive characteristics of both mythic interpretations of reality. The third section, "Burning," synthesizes Native American beliefs and shamanistic practices with Buddhist precepts and bodhisattva practice, which is to say being on the path to enlightenment and seeking to enlighten others as a part of that path.

Throughout these three sections, Snyder alternates myth fragments with realistic images and stories, one often providing an interpretation or implementation of the other. In the final segment, "Burning 17," he brings these two disparate forms of knowledge together by depicting a forest fire put out by a rainstorm in both mythic and realistic imagery. Although humans are fighting the forest fire, it is nature's own interaction that extinguishes the blaze. Myth and reality interpenetrate as each represents an interpretation of human participation in the world. And the perception of that human participation is clearly, if complexly, an ecological one. It emphasizes the specificity of human experience in an event that is regenerative rather than consumptive.

Riprap was first published in 1959 by Cid Corman's Origin Press. In 1965, Snyder's translations of Han Shan poems from the Chinese, which had appeared in *Evergreen Review* in 1958, were added and the Four Seasons Foundation of San Francisco published *Riprap and Cold Mountain Poems*. In 1990, North Point published a new edition based on the reset 1969 Four Seasons text. Through the 1960s *Riprap* defined Snyder's poetics to a new generation of American readers.

The highly metonymic poems have a distinctive style emphasizing observation and reflection without an emphasis on the persona of the observer. In this respect they are strongly anti-romantic, and thus a departure from the dominant tradition within modern nature poetry. And, although personal, the poems are not confessional; thus they mark a break with a prominent trend in contemporary American poetry. The lines tend to be short and highly rhythmical, with frequent pauses, as in the opening of "Piute Creek": "One granite ridge/A tree, would be enough/Or even a rock, a small creek." The pauses slow the pace of reading. They encourage attention to the singular natural entities being identified, as if the speaker were stopping to touch each one in reverent awe, and the reader should reflect on them in the same manner.

The poems in *Riprap* have received more critical attention as individual poems than almost any others in all of Snyder's many volumes. The poetics revealed here recurs throughout Snyder's books published since 1959 and may be defined as his bedrock aesthetic. But even within this volume, a range of poetic styles appears. "Mid-August at Sourdough Mountain Lookout" and "Piute Creek" are examples of a meditative lyric, frequently of two stanzas, that consists almost entirely of a depicted image, with a philosophical comment wedded to that image in the second stanza. For example the phrase "that / Which sees is truly seen," in "Piute Creek," establishes a reciprocity and similitude, although not an identity, between the speaker and the nonhuman animals sharing the experience of the event and place imaged in the first stanza.

Other poems are more narrative, such as "Milton by Firelight" and "Hay for Horses." The former continues the practice of direct philosophical statement found in the meditative lyrics, but the latter poem does not. In general, one finds that with more narrative there is less philosophizing. Determining a meaning for the story in "Hay for Horses" depends entirely upon what the reader makes of the character's reported speech about the nature of his life. The interpretive possibilities for this kind of poem by Snyder are often significantly enlarged by the thematic context generated by the other poems. They resonate with more meaning as part of the book than they do when standing alone.

Although many of these poems have deservedly been celebrated and interpeted individually, *Riprap* is more than just a group of poems. The volume, treated as a loose sequence, traces a journey from the West Coast to Japan and back again that culminates in a philosophy and a poetics, as exemplified by the title poem, "Riprap," placed at the end. In this poem, the act of riprapping a mountain trail—laying down loose rocks wedged together to form a hard trail bed—depicts the processes of building a poem, living a life, and participating in a universe. Mental and physical being are identified as manifestations and events in a single cosmic process, the universal flow of nature.

In the mid 1960s two full-length books of Snyder's poetry were published by Fulcrum Press in London. The first, *A Range of Poems* (1966), reprinted *Riprap and Cold Mountain Poems* and *Myths and Texts*, plus a group of poems titled "The Back Country" and Snyder's translations of poems by Miyazawa Kenji, an early-twentieth-century Japanese poet who paid particular attention to place and nature. The second, *The Back Country* (1967), consisted of an expanded and reorganized version of that section of the previous book, with about twice as many poems in it. The first American edition of *The Back Country* was published by New Directions in 1968, set directly from the Fulcrum Press text, with the Miyazawa Kenji translations added because they had not previously appeared in the United States. The 1971 edition, completely reset, remains in print. *The Back Country* is much larger than either of Snyder's previous collections, and brings together poems written over a much longer span of time. Snyder remarked to bibliographer Katherine McNeil, "I arranged it very deliberately, section by section, but it's mixed, a very diverse gathering of poems, and some of them are much better than others" (p. 35). It contains eighty-nine poems by Snyder plus the eighteen translated poems.

Like *Riprap, The Back Country* can be read as a loose sequence recounting a circular journey from the U.S. West Coast to East Asia, to India, then back to the West Coast. The subtitles of the sections complicate the geographical motif, however. "Far West" and "Far East" are simple enough, but the last two sections are "Kālī" and "Back," suggesting that the journey is as much spiritual and psychic as it is geographical; or perhaps it would be better to say that place informs mind throughout this journey. It is interesting to note that whereas the poems were written over fifteen years, the book was put together over a period of two years and went through some transformations. The subtitles were not added until the New Directions edition was published in 1968. The decision to name the fourth section "Back" reflects Snyder's decision to return permanently to the United States.

Although Snyder has remarked in interviews that he always knew he would return to the United States, the timing of that return seems to be based mainly on three significant events in Snyder's life that occurred in 1966 through 1968, after the poems in this book had been written and most of them published in various journals: Oda Sessō Roshi, Snyder's Zen master, died in 1966; Snyder married Masa Uehara on 8 August 1967 in Japan; and in 1968 Gary and Masa's first son, Kai, was born. Significant changes in the cultural and political climate in the United States no doubt also influenced his decision. The antiwar and Black Power movements were gaining strength, and the hippie movement was peaking. Snyder had been in San Francisco briefly in early 1967 and had participated in the Great Human Be-In at Golden Gate Park. It was certainly a propitious time for a counterculture activist and poet to settle in northern California.

The Back Country is framed by two poems that emphasize celebrating and feasting in a spirit of carnival and plentitude: "A Berry Feast" and "Oysters." "Far West" opens with "A Berry Feast," which Snyder performed at the Six Gallery reading at which Ginsberg introduced "Howl." An obviously pre-Japan poem, its mythic tropes are based on Native American Coyote and Bear stories, including the story of the woman who married a bear, to which Snyder returned some twenty-five years later in *The Practice of the Wild*. Natural fecundity and human sexuality are repeatedly linked throughout the poem, and mythic time is figured as the eternal present; the present-time reality of the urban industrialized world is depicted as transient and aberrational. In much the same style as *Myths and Texts*, mythologized events and realistically portrayed events are juxtaposed for thematic development. Through identification with the mythic beliefs of native North Americans, the poet imagines that he and his companions are capable of becoming tricksters. Through becoming Coyote and Bear they participate in the feast of the wild, rather than domesticated, world.

Whereas "A Berry Feast" has very much an us-versus-them, Beats-versus-squares dichotomy to it, "Six-Month Song in the Foothills" has an "us-together" quality of solitary, yet cultured, human experience in the midst of wild nature. In "The Importance of Nothing," Jody Norton captures the spirit of this poem: "In their home-in-nature neither being interferes with the other, bird and man pursuing separate works, separate ends without destructiveness or hostility" (p. 58).

The second part of *The Back Country*, "Far East," contains poems that mainly emphasize cultural and political considerations as a result of immersion in an extremely different society. "Eight Sandbars on the Takano River," however, is an example of the kind of poem more prevalent in *Regarding Wave* (1969), the poetry volume published soon after *The Back Country*, in which Snyder depicts and interprets specific Japanese landscapes and human interaction with them. Such relationships are most fully realized in the thirteen-part sequence, "Six Years," which closes this section. In conversation with Katsunori Yamazato, who recorded the remark in "Seeking a Fulcrum," Snyder said that the use of Japanese words here forms a record of "actually trying to enter the whole taste and flavor of the country and culture," whereas earlier Japanese allusions, as Yamazato notes, had focused on myth and literature (p. 80).

Although the title of the third section of *The Back Country*, 'Kālī,' obviously identifies it with India, relatively few of the poems are about that place. Rather, it is the character of this mythic figure that defines the section. Kālī is one of the manifestations of the female goddess, consort of Shiva, and in her the creative and destructive principles are one and the same. She is like the food chain: to be in it means you are both predator and prey; another creature is your dinner, but you also are another's lunch. The poems in "Kālī" were written over a decade, and India seems to have been more a catalyst for realization about Snyder's own life and psyche than a locus for inspiration or insight about nature and culture. Many of these poems are about past sexual relationships, meditations on the transience of human relationships and lives.

"Back" radically reverses the tone of "Kālī" and returns at times to the ecstatic celebration found in "A Berry Feast." This section opens with "The Old Dutch Woman"; and Snyder focuses on her and his grandmother, who were attentive gardeners. Women and nature are linked here, but the attention to gender seems designed to suggest the diversity of nature rather than to make a women-nature connection, which Snyder does employ elsewhere. The Dutch woman causes Snyder to reflect on the different human perceptions of nature that exist and the positive variety of the relationships such perceptions can bring. Most important here is Snyder's recognition that nature is not limited to the wild mountain regions by which he had defined it in the past, but consists of all nodes of the biosphere. By extension, he recognizes that his methods of engaging nonhuman nature are no more authentic than the Dutch woman's backyard studies or his grandmother's pruning of loganberry bushes.

"For the West" returns to depictions of modern industrialized Western societies, European and North American, as transient. "America" is imaged as "the flowery glistening oil blossom/ spreading on water" until it thins into dissolution. The last four poems of this section express, at least in part, Snyder's love, both ideally and erotically, for the western United States from the San Francisco Bay area to the Uinta Mountains of Utah. "Through the Smoke Hole" and "Oysters" most specifically link Snyder's philosophy and a sense of a place-based spiritual practice to the American West and to the spiritual and ecological practices of its indigenous inhabitants.

Building a Household

After his permanent return to the United States, Snyder first brought out a collection of prose, *Earth House Hold* (1969), which will be dis-

cussed in the section on prose works. Also in 1969 he published a limited edition poetry volume, *Regarding Wave.* The following year Snyder published an expanded edition with New Directions. This version contains the three "Regarding Wave" sections of the first edition, plus two others titled "Long Hair" and "Target Practice." Most of the poems in this volume were written in 1967 and 1968, with the majority of the "Regarding Wave" poems centered on Snyder and Masa's relationship and the birth of Kai. Their human to human erotic relationship is interwoven with a larger individual to community nurturing relationship, as represented by the Banyan Ashram collective in which they participated, and an even larger human to nonhuman sensuous relationship of interpenetration and interbirth, what Buddhists would define as "dependent co-origination."

The poem "Burning Island" best epitomizes the human to human erotic relationship; it is a song celebrating Gary and Masa's wedding day. Significantly, it begins with a focus on immersion in the place, rather than in each other, where their relationship develops and is ritually recognized. The individual to community relationship is represented in the poem "Rainbow Body," which again begins with a celebratory description of place and closes with a description of communal labor and a communal meal. The larger realm of human within the nonhuman is treated in all six of the "song" poems in "Regarding Wave II." The title poem of the volume, which ends "Regarding Wave III," unites ecology and human marriage through Buddhist metaphysics by invoking "The voice of the Dharma." In "True Communionism," Julia Martin explains "Regarding Wave" in this way: "The poem invites the audience to participate, not only in ideas *about* Vak, the interconnectedness of phenomena, of 'self' and 'universe,' but also in the direct experience of union which reciting the mystic syllables [at poem's end] is believed to evoke" (p. 69).

The sections "Long Hair" and "Target Practice" round out this volume with poems written during and just after the period of the poems in the "Regarding Wave" sections. "Long Hair" links Snyder with the hippie movement; many of these poems are more politically oriented in relation to social transformation than the earlier ones. "Revolution in the Revolution in the Revolution," "The Trade," and "In the Night, Friend" are easily labeled "political" poems, but others are more complex. In "Poke Hole Fishing After the March," the activists find a common ground of action and conversation with a roofing contractor. Snyder ends the poem by contrasting the rocks of low tide with the fish of high tide. In the poem "Long Hair," he depicts "Deer" as a trickster figure subverting the existing anthropocentric structures from within and proposing spiritual transformation rather than militant confrontation as the way to effect deep cultural change. The small poems of "Target Practice" suggest the influence of the haiku form and the paradoxical, enigmatic character of Zen koans. Many of them focus on human-nature conflicts and the wild versus the domesticated. In some ways, in "Target Practice" the poet has become the Deer of "Long Hair," a trickster upending received opinions and settled values.

Published by New Directions in 1974, *Turtle Island*, Snyder's next volume of poetry, won the Pulitzer Prize the following year. Whereas Snyder had already built a strong following on the West Coast and among American countercultural movements, *Turtle Island* generated national prominence. Seen as an ecological manifesto, and praised and criticized simultaneously as such, it became required reading for environmentalists, one of the best-selling volumes of contemporary American poetry. The poems in this volume were all written after Snyder's permanent return to the United States, and reflect his settling into a homestead on San Juan Ridge, near Nevada City, California. Katsunori Yamazato has written a detailed account of Snyder's homestead and ridge community in his essay "Kitkitdizze, Zendo, and Place," which provides a valuable historical context for these poems. Yamazato contends that Kitkitdizze and *Turtle Island* initiate Snyder's increasing commitment and attention to "reinhabitation."

Turtle Island is divided into four unequal sections, three of poems and one of prose pieces. The volume, which generates a vision for leading an ecologically and physically balanced daily life, takes the continent's original human inhabitants as its primary source of inspiration. The introductory note makes this point explicitly: "Turtle Island—the old/new name for the continent, based on many creation myths of the people who have been living here for millennia. . . . A Name: that we may see ourselves more accurately on this continent of watersheds and life-communities. . . . The poems speak of place, and the energy-pathways that sustain life." Much of the volume has a political directness and emphasis that some long-time Snyder readers found disconcerting and considered poor poetry.

The first section, "Manzanita," consists of eighteen poems originally published as a chapbook in 1972 and not sold, at Snyder's request, east of the Rockies, perhaps to emphasize the bioregional character of reinhabitation. The first poem, "Anasazi," pays tribute to an early indigenous people of the Southwest. Snyder envisions them as "sinking deeper and deeper in earth," molding themselves to the shape of the environment in which they cultivated their food and their culture.

Whereas "Anasazi" is mythic in its dimensions, other poems are placed in the present-day world of poet and reader, such as "The Dead by the Side of the Road" and "Steak." The former depicts practices of appropriate respect for all other animals and the importance of utilizing as much of them as possible after they have died. The latter depicts the wasteful world of commercial feedlots and steak houses, where cattle are not recognized as other living beings but are only economic units, products to market. "Spel Against Demons" emphasizes the linkages between Buddhism, indigenous cultural history, and ecological living in the present through a syncretic mythopoeia. Using the mantra for a Japanese deity who can be traced back to the nature-worship religion *Shūgendo*, Snyder playfully links this retributive figure with a critique of left-wing militant political organizations, which he views as muddying the waters of change. (Snyder discusses the spiritual practice behind this poem in his 1993 essay "Walking the Great Ridge, Omine, on the Womb-Diamond Trail.")

Even more overtly political is "Front Lines," in which Snyder states explicitly that it is time to "draw / Our line" in the battle against the ecological destruction wrought by "Amerika." (This spelling, popular in the antiwar and Black Liberation movements, uses the "k" to link the United States, as imperialist, colonialist, and racist, with the Nazis.) "Control Burn" appears immediately after "Front Lines," and their association encourages a political reading of this poem as well. In it Snyder expresses the desire to set fire to all of the second growth and "logging slash" choking the forest. After such a controlled burn, the United States would be more like "when it belonged to the Indians."

In several poems in "Manzanita," Snyder brings family experiences into the politics of ecology and balanced living. "The Bath," however, promotes the concept of a harmonious family life with no overt political overtones. Nevertheless, Julia Martin has observed in "True Communionism" that giving this much "attention to bathing indicates a deliberate making of community, and a definition of family-as-energy-network that is radically different from the familiar nuclear structure" (p. 66). And in "The Call of the Wild," Snyder explores what he and his children are up against when he contemplates the likelihood of their being able to hear the coyotes howling in the hills, their being able to remain immersed in the wild. They must stand against not only the ranchers, miners, and loggers who fear wilderness and wild animals, but also "ex–acid heads from the cities," former LSD users who know nothing of the place in which they have established their quick-to-fail communes. And, finally, they must stand against the government, which wages not only a war against the Viet Cong and the wild jungles that hide them, but also "a war against earth" itself. Snyder's ending of the poem, warning

against the desire to imagine that the coyote song will live on through human memory even if the animal becomes extinct, orients the reader away from elegy and toward militancy. To remember is insufficient; one must resist the destruction.

The second section of *Turtle Island*, "Magpie's Song," contains some of the militancy and explicit rhetoric of "Manzanita," but more frequently emphasizes the positive actions of humans and animals that portend victory for the wild and its reinhabitants. This is particularly the case in such poems as "Night Herons," "By Frazier Creek Falls," "Black Mesa Mine #1," and "It Pleases." "Mother Earth: Her Whales," however, one of the most affective poems of this volume, bristles with anger. Snyder wrote it about a month after returning from a U.N. conference on the human environment, and it was published in the *New York Times* (13 July 1972). As Hwa Yol Jung and Petee Jung note in "Gary Snyder's Ecopiety," the *New York Times* printing of it "began with a terse foreword which said that everyone came to Stockholm not to give but rather to take.... The poem meant to defend all the creatures of the earth" (p. 76).

Three poems at the heart of "For the Children," the third section of *Turtle Island*, may be said to be Snyder's vision rendered as prophecy. These are "Tomorrow's Song," "What Happened Here Before," and "Toward Climax." In "Tomorrow's Song," the vision of the future is predicated upon the dissolution of the United States for failing to include the nonhuman in its conception of democracy. In a postindustrial, postpetroleum culture, people will establish a set of nature-based values that include adaptations of indigenous labor and cultural practices.

In order to develop such values, today's children will need to know the history of the place, this Turtle Island, that they are inhabiting. "What Happened Here Before" sets out such a history of the western rim of the continent over the past 300 million years or so. Snyder sets the appearance of humans at the 40,000-year mark, which emphasizes the degree to which the inhabitory practices of native peoples have been established over a far more vast stretch of human history than the current social practices of a paltry few centuries. All of this history comes down to the question of who is preparing for the future, who today has the vision to move beyond the present growth-model expansionist economy into a steady-state system. Snyder prophetically declares: "WE SHALL SEE/WHO KNOWS/HOW TO BE."

"Toward Climax" begins to delineate the character of the inhabitory knowledge that Snyder endorses in opposition to the destructive knowledge that guides contemporary economics. This poem echoes numerous earlier poems in the volume that criticize contemporary American life and returns to the imagery of forests and clear-cutting that Snyder used in "Front Lines."

Snyder concludes *Turtle Island* with a set of prose pieces titled "Plain Talk." The most famous of these, "Four Changes," was distributed as a pamphlet nationwide in 1969. In *Turtle Island*, Snyder reprints the 1969 version, with various parenthetical emendations in each of the sections: "Population," "Pollution," "Consumption," and "Transformation." He not only analyzes each of these conditions but also proposes specific actions in the realms of the "social/political" and the "community." Perhaps the most famous line from this essay is "no transformation without our feet on the ground." Other prose pieces here elaborate on the philosophy presented in the poetry and also on specific poems. "The Wilderness" and "What's Meant by 'Here'" establish a clear bioregional perspective in Snyder's thinking at this time.

Turtle Island has generated more critical debate than any of Snyder's other books. Some critics who had previously praised Snyder, such as Charles Altieri, criticize him for subsuming the aesthetic to the political and substituting the improper poetic role of "prophet" for the proper one of "seer." Other critics, such as Charles Molesworth, cite what Altieri criticizes as precisely the strengths of the book. And Sherman Paul, years later in *In Search of the Primitive*,

remarked, "This political book is remarkably joyous, and serene; hence, its authenticity" (p. 282).

Handing Down the Practice

Nearly a decade passed between the publication of *Turtle Island*, which deeply rooted Snyder's national reputation, and that of his next full-length volume of poetry, *Axe Handles* (1983). By this time Snyder had found a new publisher and, in a significant number of the poems, a new tone. Certainly this volume strikes a far less apocalyptic and confrontational stance than *Turtle Island*. It displays the surety and confidence of a deepening maturity, of a parent able to see that the "children" are indeed learning the important lessons necessary to build a new, inhabitory culture.

Axe Handles begins with a twenty-five-poem section titled "Loops." Julia Martin, in "The Pattern Which Connects," interprets the title as reflecting "a recursive sense of history and tradition." This claim serves as an interpretation of the title poem of the collection as well. Roger Schultz and David Wyatt have accurately noted that "instruction," the handing down of the traditions of a life practice, is the guiding concept for this volume; "Axe Handles" provides an example of and commentary on instruction as imitation and apprenticeship. The poem consists of a story about Snyder helping his son make a hatchet handle by using a working hatchet and instructing his son to rely on imitating the shape of the carving hatchet to form the new one. Intertwined with this instruction is Snyder's own epiphanic recollections of previous scenes of instruction, when he was the apprentice and others the master. Snyder recognizes that he has gone from being a "handle" to being an "axe," and that his son is now "a handle, soon/To be shaping again." Cultural transmission is a process of being shaped and of shaping. The role of the poet, or master, is to understand the process, articulate it, and act creatively within the process so that cultural

Snyder atop Matterhorn Peak, Yosemite National Park, 1986

continuity always includes conscious efforts at positive change.

Many of the rest of the poems in this section of *Axe Handles* embody instruction, cultural conservation, and shaping. In "River in the Valley," the speaker is engaged in a process both of understanding the place of humans within natural cycles and articulating that understanding to his sons. In this poem Snyder emphasizes both the diversity of natural cycles and the importance of conceptualizing them heterarchically rather than hierarchically, as mutually cocreating and interdependent. Whereas "River in the Valley" begins with attention to a specific place and spirals out from that to a cosmic perception of relationship, other poems, such as "Berry Territory" and "Painting the North San Juan School," focus exclusively on the particularities of place. These are, as Katsunori Yamazato and others have noted, poems of "inhabitation." Snyder does not go out to nature for experiences to render poetically, but rather makes poems of the daily life of human immersion in the nonhuman.

The next section of *Axe Handles*, "Little Songs for Gaia," originally appeared as a 1979 Copper Canyon chapbook, and is best read as a single unit rather than as individual poems. The use of Gaia here refers to the scientific Gaia hypothesis popularized by James Lovelock and developed by him and others, which argues that the earth's biosphere is actually a single, living organism. But it also invokes a spirituality and religious awe originating in the myth of the goddess Gaia, the Earth Mother. Some of these poems are virtually prayers; others, mythic dreams; and others, poetic personifications of nonhuman nature as a living, larger-than-human life entity.

The third section of the volume, "Nets," is subdivided into four parts. Woody Rehanek claims that "the four parts of 'Nets' are roughly equivalent to four layers of healing songs defined in 'Poetry, Community & Climax,' the final chapter of *The Real Work*" (pp. 11–12). They are unity with nature, humanity with others outside one's group, speaking for the unconscious, and expressing a "climax" state of mind. The poems of "Nets I" tend to continue the attention to the sacred, with the spiritual presence of Gaia very much in evidence. "Nets II" focuses on events pulling the speaker into the morass of human culture and ideology, which are counterbalanced in "Nets III" by poems about the local community in which Snyder participates, San Juan Ridge. "Nets IV" consists of a medley of poems looping back to various themes expressed throughout *Axe Handles*. In so doing, this final section of Part III, and of the entire volume, weaves together the various strands of Snyder's poetic themes in *Axe Handles* to create a carrying bag of "instructions" for the children who are coming of age, like Snyder's own sons, to learn to build a stable and healthy inhabitory community.

Left Out in the Rain: New Poems 1947–1985, published in 1986 by North Point Press, prints for the first time poems written over the course of Snyder's adult life but omitted from his other books. Although there are strong poems here, there are also many weak ones: experiments, imitations, prototypes of other poems, playful fragments, and verse jokes. The poems have been minimally revised, and as a volume provide a record of an individual poet's artistic growth. As such, they are mainly of interest to readers already familiar with Snyder's other volumes. *Left Out in the Rain* is not meant, and should not be used, as an introduction to Snyder's poetry. Another more recently published volume serves that purpose.

For years, Snyder deflected suggestions that he organize a "selected poetry" volume by pointing out that all of his individual poetry books remained in print. But finally, in 1992, he brought out *No Nature: New and Selected Poems*, with Pantheon Books. A generous selection, it reprints a major portion of Snyder's previous collections.

Snyder included fifteen new poems in *No Nature*. Of these, "Kušiwoqqóbī," "Off the Trail," "Word Basket Woman," "At Tower Peak," and "Ripples on the Surface" are of the most interest from an ecological perspective. They repeat established philosophical positions and human–nature relationships, yet do so in fresh ways. "Kušiwoqqóbī" and "Word Basket Woman" link contemporary inhabitory practice with the history of indigenous peoples; the latter also contains a critique of Robinson Jeffers' poetry. "Off the Trail" opens with the line "We are free to find our own way," and later alludes to the *Dao De Jing* axiom that "the trail's not the way."

"At Tower Peak" is reminiscent of the early poems of *Riprap*. Here, Snyder contrasts the rejuvenating experience of mountain climbing with the increasingly urbanized world where "Every tan rolling meadow will turn into housing." But he does not end with the illusion of the individual being able to separate from the rest of humanity through ascetic retreat to some pure, wild, place. He observes near poem's end, "It's just one world," and the contradictions must be worked through from within. Snyder reinforces this one-world image in the final poem of the volume, "Ripples on the Surface." He opens it with a quotation distinguishing different kinds of ripples on the water, and in midpoem remarks: "Nature not a book, but a *performance*, a / high old culture." He concludes by deconstructing the dichotomy of house and wild, of human and nonhuman, announcing: "No nature / Both together, one big empty house." The final line echoes the Buddhist image of the world as illusion. Or, in the words of *The Diamond Sutra*, a

Buddhist text very important in Snyder's Zen training, "As to any Truth-declaring system, Truth is undeclarable; so 'an enunciation of Truth' is just the name given to it."

In addition to writing individual poems, Snyder continues to work on a poetic sequence that he began in the late 1950s, *Mountains and Rivers Without End*. The title is based on a famous sutra, or talk, given by the thirteenth-century Zen master Dōgen, "Mountains and Waters Sutra." It is also indebted to the Chinese scroll landscape paintings that Snyder first encountered as a boy visiting the Seattle Art Museum. In 1965 Snyder brought out *Six Sections from* Mountains and Rivers Without End, and five years later published *Six Sections from* Mountains and Rivers Without End *Plus One*. Over the years he also has published poems that he has indicated in readings, or has otherwise suggested, comprise sections of the sequence. In 1973, for example, Shaman Drum published the limited edition chapbook *The Fūdō Trilogy*, which some have assumed is part of *Mountains and Rivers*. It was not until 1993, however, that Snyder specifically labeled another collection as part of that sequence. Like *The Fūdō Trilogy*, *North Pacific Lands and Waters: A Further Six Sections* is a limited-edition, small-press publication consisting of fewer than 300 signed copies. Snyder has completed a draft of the entire sequence and is planning to publish it in late 1996. To date, Anthony Hunt has provided the most thorough analyses of individual sections of this highly allusive mythopoeic sequence.

Prose Collections

Snyder has published five volumes of prose and dozens of essays, forewords, reminiscences, and talks over three decades. Although the prose at the end of *Turtle Island* has received considerable attention, only two of his entirely prose volumes have been widely read: *Earth House Hold* and *The Practice of the Wild*. Yet it seems likely that in the years to come, Snyder will place even greater emphasis on prose texts, as is in-dicated by the frequency with which he has been publishing essays.

In *Earth House Hold: Technical Notes and Queries to Fellow Dharma Revolutionaries*, published by New Directions in 1969, Snyder collected prose pieces written between 1952 and 1968. Although a rather eclectic set of pieces, it was designed as a unified book, poetically rather than rhetorically structured, indicating major components of Snyder's life education. Whereas Sherman Paul has compared it with *Walden* and the journal sections bear the influence of that text, I would argue that *Earth House Hold* is more indebted to Ezra Pound and books such as his *ABC of Reading*. Snyder, like Pound, is concerned with informing the reader of his poetry about the education of the poet, in part to create a more literate reader but more significantly to create a more enlightened world citizen. Snyder identifies the primary audience for the book in its subtitle and educates them about the formative influences on his interconnected attitudes toward nature, spiritual transformation, and social revolution.

Snyder's attitudes toward nature are mainly developed in the journal entries, particularly from his fire lookout days in the early 1950s. These are the parts of *Earth House Hold* that most directly inform readings of his poetry, and are the most widely quoted and referenced. Spiritual transformation receives the most attention, both through discussion in the journal entries and through material on Buddhism. Social revolution becomes the focus of the latter part of the volume, with Buddhism and ecological activism intertwined. The asceticism and nonharm precepts of Buddhism are defined as forms of environmental conservation and as politically subversive because they undermine capitalist economics. Finally, Snyder's ideas about "tribe," family, and community integrate all three concerns through a utopian envisioning of a more nature-centered, inhabitory way of life.

The Old Ways, published by City Lights Books in 1977, consists of six essays of uneven quality and significance. The most substantive of these continue discussion of the topics raised in the "Plain Talk" section of *Turtle Island*. "The

Politics of Ethnopoetics" and "Re-Inhabitation" are the two essays in *The Old Ways* that are most frequently quoted. The former focuses on Snyder's support for the 1970s project of ethnopoetics because it would study the poetry of peoples who have ecosystem, rather than biosphere, cultures. Here Snyder develops his vision of cultural continuity and inhabitory community along bioregional lines in opposition to centralized governments and expansionist economic systems. Snyder also makes specific reference to the Gaia hypothesis in this essay. In "Re-Inhabitation," Snyder first defines the term "inhabitation" and then identifies some of the kinds of practices that need to be implemented for Americans to become inhabitants of, rather than migrants across, Turtle Island. "The Yogin and the Philosopher" and "The Incredible Survival of Coyote" are also of interest in terms of Snyder's efforts at synthesizing Native American and shamanistic beliefs for the purpose of creating a regenerated mythopoeia.

Passage Through India was published by Grey Fox Press in 1983. A somewhat different version originally appeared as "Now India" in the poetry journal *Caterpillar*, edited by Clayton Eshleman, in 1972. It is Snyder's journal of the six-months trip he and Joanne Kyger, his second wife, took to India in 1961–1962, and provides background for some of the poems published in *The Back Country*. It has received virtually no critical attention and does not seem to have been widely read, even by devoted fans of Snyder's poetry. I would expect this lack of attention to continue.

Earth House Hold is very much a youthful work; *The Practice of the Wild* very much a mature work. There is no other way to describe this book than to say that it is a very complex, but uncomplicated, presentation of knowing "how to be" in this world at this time, and of directions for the future. Although many of the chapters have been separately published as essays, *The Practice of the Wild* is thematically unified around the interrelationships of freedom and responsibility, wilderness and wildness, humanity and nature, mind and body, conscious and unconscious, thought and action, perception and practice. In the interview with David

Robertson published in *Critical Essays on Gary Snyder*, Snyder remarked: "I would like to see the book be political in the sense of helping people shape the way they want to live and act in the world" (p. 262). The topics for the chapters of *Practice* indicate what Snyder believes people need to understand in order to engage in such shaping.

"The Etiquette of Freedom" engages in defining a series of concepts in such a way that freedom and responsibility are recognized as complementary rather than oppositional. In order to come to terms with, and enable the continuation of, wild nature and the freedom it generates, humans have to learn their responsibilities toward "Nature, Wild, *and* Wilderness." Building on this sense of responsibility toward the wild, Snyder next focuses on "The Place, the Region, and the Commons" in order to work up the importance of human rootedness in place in order to reclaim inhabitory relationships with the rest of nature. Recognizing that his foregoing discussions of wildness and inhabitation have relied heavily on etymology and definitions of terms and concepts, in "Tawny Grammar" Snyder treats the significance of language and language use in the epistemological development of life philosophies. The issue of cultural continuity is also addressed through his concern for oral and written transmissions of cultural wisdom.

In "Good, Wild, Sacred" Snyder moves from the realm of epistemology to that of ontology, investigating the spiritual practices of inhabitory peoples and ecosystem cultures. The spiritual realm is entered even further in the next essay in *Practice*, "Blue Mountains Constantly Walking," as Snyder returns to the importance of Zen Buddhism for his own inhabitory practice. This chapter is the least accessible for most readers, because it builds on a meditation about Dōgen's "Mountains and Waters Sutra" and demands a greater knowledge of Buddhism than most readers are likely to have. A key distinction is made in this chapter, however, that is pertinent to the rest of the book: there is no *nature* as a discrete object; rather, there is *naturing*, a dynamic process of interaction, transformation, and cocreation, in which all humans participate as one configuration of energy among multiplicitous other configurations: rocks, trees, streams, stars, and galaxies.

The next two chapters, "Ancient Forests of the Far West" and "On the Path, off the Trail," emphasize various types of spiritual and meditative practices that are nature oriented. In the former, Snyder emphasizes logging and related "economic" activities that contribute to the destruction of the wild. In the latter, he emphasizes the individual process of finding one's "way" through life, the path to follow for right living. This discussion returns to issues, such as freedom and responsibility, raised in the first chapter. In the penultimate chapter, "The Woman Who Married a Bear," Snyder retells this Native American tale, bringing together in the process tradition and innovation, myth and experience, spiritual and physical life. Knowing and retelling the original stories becomes part of learning the inhabitation of a place. Snyder ends *Practice* with "Survival and Sacrament," in which he emphasizes the difference between death and extinction. Humans are responsible for tremendous suffering in this world and, from a Buddhist perspective, will have to bear the consequences of that in the future.

In the opening chapter, Snyder raises the idea of a "compact" between humans and the rest of nature, and in his conclusion he introduces the idea of a "covenant." This covenant requires "embracing the other as oneself" and developing a "culture of the wilderness" that will preserve the biodiversity of the planetary ecological web. Snyder argues that human survival depends on recognizing our participation in food chains and life cycles as a sacrament involving thanks, reciprocity, and reverence. A deeply moving and profound book, *The Practice of the Wild* has the potential to become the text by which the largest number of the next generation come to know Snyder, rather than by his poetry.

There is one other type of text through which many readers have learned about Snyder's ideas and practices: the transcribed interview. Snyder has been interviewed dozens of times over the years and continues to give interviews, particularly when on the road doing readings and promoting new books. A group of these have been edited and collected into a single volume by William Scott McLean, *The Real Work: Interviews and Talks 1964–1979*. A few of them are what is known as "craft interviews," in which the interviewer focuses on aesthetic and stylistic questions about the writing of poetry, occasionally revealing considerable ignorance about Snyder's background and intellectual development. Most, however, are substantive interviews that get at the mind and instruction behind the poetry, with considerable attention to environmental issues and ethics and the interrelationship between Buddhism and ecology. The main limitation of the volume is its cutoff date of 1979; many interviews since then remain uncollected and often are not readily accessible.

Conclusion

Literary and philosophical criticism of Snyder's poetry and prose is amazingly contradictory; much of it reveals more about the predilections and values of the critic than it provides insights into readings of particular poems or the philosophy and life behind the writing. Whereas Charles Altieri criticizes Snyder for becoming too political and prophetic in *Turtle Island*, Charles Molesworth praises that turn in his poetry but complains that Snyder is not adequately in touch with the urban working class, and Sherman Paul celebrates the joyful quality of Snyder's polemics. Whereas one critic claims Snyder as part of the Romantic tradition of nature writing and identifies him with Wordsworth and Whitman, another confuses antihumanism or, perhaps more accurately, posthumanism with misanthropy, and attacks Snyder as hating humanity. Others attempt to embrace Snyder's environmental ethics while ignoring his Buddhist metaphysics, even as critics such as Julia Martin and Katsunori Yamazato demonstrate the synthesis of the two in Snyder's poetry and prose. Finally, there are critics who write exclusively about Snyder's poetics, his field composition, his modernist techniques and elliptical compression. Others claim that he is not a great poet because he is more concerned with ideas than with form.

Snyder is a complex thinker, widely read, and international in his learning and experience. His poetry and his prose reflect the diversity of his intellectual interests, life experience, and social commitments. His commitment to learning how humans can best inhabit this planetary home can be found throughout his writings, from the opening poems of *Left Out in the Rain* through his final remarks about "grace" in *The Practice of the Wild*. This commitment is represented through myriad examples and images, from backhoes to mandalas, from mountain peaks to mushrooms; they are crafted through an array of styles, from simple anecdotes to Zen meditations, from singular images to mythopoeia, and voiced in a range of tones, from the jeremiad to the dithyramb, from serious statement to trickster wordplay.

From his earliest publications, Snyder was hailed as a significant new poetic voice in American literature. Academic recognition followed belatedly on the heels of acclaim by fellow poets. Critics, reviewers, and readers recognized his attention to environmental issues and his writing of a kind of nature poetry very different from that practiced by his predecessors. With the publication of *Turtle Island*, he was widely acclaimed as the preeminent living nature poet, in terms of both his popularity and the sophistication of his themes. He continues to write poetry that not only pleases but also educates and motivates. With *The Practice of the Wild* Snyder has also become a significant nature essayist, from whom readers may expect even more in the future.

Selected Bibliography

WORKS OF GARY SNYDER

POETRY

Riprap (Ashland, Mass.: Origin Press, 1959); *Myths and Texts* (New York: Totem Press, 1960; repr., New York: New Directions, 1978); *Riprap and Cold Mountain Poems* (San Francisco: Four Seasons Foundation, 1965, 1969; repr., San Francisco: North Point Press, 1990); *Six Sections from* Mountains and Rivers Without End (San Francisco: Four Seasons Foundation, 1965; London: Fulcrum Press, 1967), enl. ed., *Six Sections from* Mountains and Rivers Without End *Plus One* (San Francisco: Four Seasons Foundation, 1970); *A Range of Poems* (London: Fulcrum Press, 1966); *The Back Country* (London: Fulcrum Press, 1967; rev. and enl. ed., New York: New Directions, 1968, 1971); *Regarding Wave* (Iowa City: Windhover Press, 1969, a limited ed.; rev. and enl. ed., New York: New Directions, and London: Fulcrum Press, 1970); *Cold Mountain Poems: Twenty-four Poems by Han Shan Translated by Gary Snyder* (Portland, Oreg.: Press 22, 1970); *Manzanita* (Bolinas, Calif.: Four Seasons Foundation, 1972); *The Fūdō Trilogy* (Berkeley, Calif.: Shaman Drum, 1973); *Turtle Island* (New York: New Directions, 1974); *Songs for Gaia* (Port Townsend, Wash.: Copper Canyon, 1979); *Axe Handles* (San Francisco: North Point Press, 1983); *Left Out in the Rain: New Poems 1947–1985* (San Francisco: North Point Press, 1986); *No Nature: New and Selected Poems* (New York: Pantheon, 1992); *North Pacific Lands and Waters: A Further Six Sections* (Waldron Island, Wash.: Brooding Heron Press, 1993), a limited ed.; *Sixteen T'ang Poems*, trans. by Gary Snyder (Hopewell, N.J.: Pied Oxen Printers, 1993), a limited ed.

PROSE BOOKS

Earth House Hold: Technical Notes and Queries to Fellow Dharma Revolutionaries (New York: New Directions, 1969; London: Jonathan Cape, 1970); *The Old Ways: Six Essays* (San Francisco: City Lights Books, 1977); *He Who Hunted Birds in His Father's Village: The Dimensions of a Haida Myth* (Bolinas, Calif.: Grey Fox Press, 1979); *Passage Through India* (San Francisco: Grey Fox Press, 1983); *The Practice of the Wild: Essays by Gary Snyder* (San Francisco: North Point Press, 1990).

ARTICLES

"Walls Within Walls," in *The CoEvolution Quarterly* 37 (spring 1983); "Coming into the Watershed," in *San Francisco Examiner* (1 and 2 March 1992), repr. in Scott Walker, ed., *Changing Community* (St. Paul, Minn.: Graywolf, 1993); "Walking the Great Ridge, Omine, on the Womb-Diamond Trail," in *Kyoto Journal* no. 25 (fall 1993).

INTERVIEWS

Donald Allen, ed., *On Bread and Poetry: A Panel Discussion Between Gary Snyder, Lew Welch, and Philip Whalen* (Bolinas, Calif.: Grey Fox, 1977); Uri Hertz, "An Interview with Gary Snyder," in *Third Rail*

7 (1985–1986); Catherine Ingram, "The Legacy of the Wild: An Interview with Gary Snyder," in *The Sun* no. 173 (April 1990); Julia Martin, "Coyote-Mind: An Interview with Gary Snyder," in *TriQuarterly* no. 79 (fall 1990); James McKenzie, "Moving the World a Millionth of an Inch: Gary Snyder," in Arthur Knight and Kit Knight, eds., *The Beat Vision: A Primary Sourcebook* (New York: Paragon House, 1978); William Scott McLean, ed., *The Real Work: Interviews and Talks 1964–1979* (New York: New Directions, 1980); Nicholas O'Connell, "Gary Snyder," in his *At the Field's End* (Seattle, Wash.: Madrona, 1987); Frances Phillips, "Urgent Time: An Interview with Gary Snyder," in *Hungry Mind Review* no. 24 (winter 1992–1993).

BIBLIOGRAPHY

Katherine McNeil, *Gary Snyder: A Bibliography* (New York: Phoenix Bookshop, 1983).

BIOGRAPHICAL AND CRITICAL STUDIES

BOOKS AND DISSERTATIONS

Tim Dean, *Gary Snyder and the American Unconscious: Inhabiting the Ground* (New York: St. Martin's, 1991); Jon Halper, ed., *Gary Snyder: Dimensions of a Life* (San Francisco: Sierra Club Books, 1991); William J. Jungels, "The Use of Native-American Mythologies in the Poetry of Gary Snyder" (Ph.D. diss., SUNY at Buffalo, 1973); Jack Kerouac, *The Dharma Bums* (New York: Viking, 1958); James W. Kraus, "Gary Snyder's Biopoetics: A Study of the Poet as Ecologist" (Ph.D. diss., University of Hawaii, 1986); Howard McCord, *Some Notes to Gary Snyder's* Myths and Texts (Berkeley, Calif.: Sand Dollar, 1971); Charles Molesworth, *Gary Snyder's Vision: Poetry and the Real Work* (Columbia: Univ. of Missouri Press, 1983); Patrick D. Murphy, *Understanding Gary Snyder* (Columbia: Univ. of South Carolina Press, 1992), and, as ed., *Critical Essays on Gary Snyder* (Boston: G. K. Hall, 1991); Bob Steuding, *Gary Snyder* (Boston: Twayne, 1976); Katsunori Yamazato, "Seeking a Fulcrum: Gary Snyder and Japan (1956–1975)" (Ph.D. diss., University of California, Davis, 1987).

ARTICLES AND BOOKS WITH CHAPTERS ON SNYDER

Charles Altieri, *Enlarging the Temple: New Directions in American Poetry During the 1960's* (Lewisburg, Pa.: Bucknell Univ. Press, 1979), and "Gary Snyder's *Turtle Island:* The Problem of Reconciling the Roles of Seer and Prophet," in *Boundary* 2, no. 4 (1976); Lee Bartlett, "Gary Snyder's *Myths and Texts* and the Monomyth," in *Western American Literature* 17 (summer 1982); David Carpenter, "Gary Snyder's Inhumanism, from *Riprap* to *Axe Handles*," in *South*

Dakota Review 26, no. 1 (1988); Michael Castro, *Interpreting the Indian: Twentieth-Century Poets and the Native American* (Albuquerque: Univ. of New Mexico Press, 1983; repr., Norman: Univ. of Oklahoma Press, 1991).

Michael Davidson, *The San Francisco Renaissance: Poetics and Community at Mid-century* (New York: Cambridge Univ. Press, 1989); John Elder, *Imagining the Earth: Poetry and the Vision of Nature* (Urbana: Univ. of Illinois Press, 1985); Ekbert Faas, ed., *Towards a New American Poetics: Essays and Interviews* (Santa Barbara, Calif.: Black Sparrow Press, 1979); L. Edwin Folson, "Gary Snyder's Descent to Turtle Island: Searching for Fossil Love," in *Western American Literature* 15, no. 2 (1980); Woon-Ping Chin Holaday, "Formlessness and Form in Gary Snyder's *Mountains and Rivers Without End*," in *Sagetrieb* 5, no. 1 (1986); Anthony Hunt, " 'Bubbs Creek Haircut': Gary Snyder's 'Great Departure' in *Mountains and Rivers Without End*," in *Western American Literature* 15, no. 2 (1980), and " 'The Hump-Backed Flute Player': The Structure of Emptiness in Gary Snyder's *Mountains and Rivers Without End*," in *ISLE: Interdisciplinary Studies in Literature and Environment* 1, no. 2 (1993).

Hwa Yol Jung and Petee Jung, "Gary Snyder's Ecopiety," in *Environmental History Review* 14, no. 3 (1990); Robert Kern, "Clearing the Ground: Gary Snyder and the Modernist Imperative," in *Criticism* 19 (1977); Sanehide Kodama, *American Poetry and Japanese Culture* (Hamden, Conn.: Archon Books, 1984); Tom Lavazzi, "Pattern of Flux: The 'Torsion Form' in Gary Snyder's Poetry," in *American Poetry Review* 18 (July/August 1989); Yao-fu Lin, " 'The Mountains Are Your Mind': Orientalism in the Poetry of Gary Snyder," in *Tamkang Review* 6, no. 2, and 7, no. 1 (1975–1976); Thomas J. Lyon, "The Ecological Vision of Gary Snyder," in *Kansas Quarterly* 2 (spring 1970), repr. in Patrick D. Murphy, ed., *Critical Essays on Gary Snyder* (Boston: G. K. Hall, 1991).

Julia Martin, "Practising Emptiness: Gary Snyder's Playful Ecological Work," in *Western American Literature* 27, no. 1 (1992), and "True Communionism: Gary Snyder's Transvaluation of Some Christian Terminology," in *Journal for the Study of Religion* (South Africa) 1, no. 1 (1988); Patrick D. Murphy, "Beyond Humanism: Mythic Fantasy and Inhumanist Philosophy in the Long Poems of Robinson Jeffers and Gary Snyder," in *American Studies* 30 (1989), *Literature, Nature, and Other* (Albany: State Univ. of New York Press, 1995), and "Penance or Perception: Spirituality and Land in the Poetry of Gary Snyder and Wendell Berry," in *Sagetrieb* 5 (1986); Rudolph L. Nelson, " 'Riprap on the Slick Rock of Metaphysics': Religious Dimensions in the Poetry of Gary Snyder," in *Soundings* 57, no. 2 (1974).

Jody Norton, "The Importance of Nothing: Absence and Its Origins in the Poetry of Gary Snyder," in *Contemporary Literature* 28, no. 1 (1987), repr. in Patrick D. Murphy, ed., *Critical Essays on Gary Snyder* (Boston: G. K. Hall, 1991); Sherman Paul, "From Lookout to Ashram: The Way of Gary Snyder," in *Iowa Review* 1, no. 3 (1970) and 1, no. 4 (1970), *In Search of the Primitive: Rereading David Antin, Jerome Rothenberg, and Gary Snyder* (Baton Rouge: Louisiana State Univ. Press, 1986), and *Hewing to Experience: Essays and Reviews on Recent American Poetry and Poetics, Nature and Culture* (Iowa City: Univ. of Iowa Press, 1989); Woody Rehanek, "The Shaman Songs of Gary Snyder," in *Okanogan Natural News* no. 19 (1984); David Robertson, "Gary Snyder Riprapping in Yosemite, 1955," in *American Poetry* 2 (1984); Eric Paul Shaffer, "Inhabitation in the Poetry of Robinson Jeffers, Gary Snyder, and Lew Welch," in *Robinson Jeffers Newsletter* no. 78 (1990); John Whalen-Bridge, "Gary Snyder's Poetics of Right Speech," in *Sagetrieb* 9, nos. 1–2 (1990); David Wyatt, *The Fall into Eden: Landscape and Imagination in California* (New York: Cambridge Univ. Press, 1986); Katsunori Yamazato, "Kitkitdizze, Zendo, and Place: Gary Snyder as Reinhabitory Poet," in *ISLE: Interdisciplinary Studies in Literature and Environment* 1, no. 1 (1993).

THEODORA COPE STANWELL-FLETCHER
(b. 1906)

MARCIA MYERS BONTA

"NATURE'S OWN CHILD," her husband Philip Gray once called her. And so she is. Theodora Cope Stanwell-Fletcher, known to her family and friends as Teddy Gray, still keeps a daily bird list, as she has since childhood. She also snowshoes in the winter and walks in the woods the rest of the year, taking a daily picnic lunch to one of her favorite secluded spots on top of her northeastern Pennsylvania hillside.

Despite a life of travel and high adventure, Gray always came home again to her family's 610-acre estate in remote Susquehanna County, where she spent some of her happiest hours. The only child of Francis R. Cope, Jr., and Evelyn F. Morris, both of whom came from distinguished Philadelphia families prominent in early American history, she was part of the extended Cope clan, with companionable cousins instead of siblings, a continual parade of visiting aunts and uncles, and a resident grandmother.

Theodora Cope was born in Germantown, Pennsylvania, on 4 January 1906. Soon after, her father decided to move to the family home in Susquehanna County, called Woodbourne, which was built by his father, Alexis T. Cope, in 1883, near rural Dimock. There Francis Cope started an orchard business, planting eighteen acres of apple trees in 1910.

Cope, like several of his relatives, including a third cousin—the famous nineteenth-century paleontologist Edward Drinker Cope—was a naturalist and teacher. His special passion was birds, and he became an expert self-taught ornithologist. Both he and his wife loved the out-of-doors and communicated that love not only to their daughter but to her cousins and the local farmers' children. As part of their commitment to educate children about the natural world, the Copes conducted their informal Dimock Nature Study Camp every summer, camping in the two-hundred-acre virgin forest tract at Woodbourne, and later at East Fishing Creek on North Mountain, in a valley below a virgin tract owned by Cope's friend Colonel Bruce Ricketts. There they taught camping skills and natural history as well as lessons in personal ideals and behavior.

Those ideals were based on the Cope family's long tradition of Quaker idealism and public service. A great-great-grandson of Quaker merchant Thomas P. Cope, who with his brothers Jasper and Israel had founded a line of fast-sailing packet ships between Philadelphia and Liverpool in 1821, Francis Cope also embraced and transmitted to his daughter the value Quakers place in peace and tranquillity. When Gray lived with her Quaker grandmother and aunts in Germantown in order to attend Germantown Friends' School, they continually asked her, "Has thee made a little quiet time for thyself today?" She took this query seriously, and throughout her life, sparsely inhabited, quiet places maintained a hold on her, leading to her later sojourns in remote British Columbia and the Canadian Arctic.

Still another strong influence on Gray was the emphasis her extended family placed on reading aloud every evening. She grew up surrounded by books—books on Arctic exploration, forestry, ornithology, evolution, and fruit farming, as well as poetry, literary novels, and the classics. She also played the piano and the harp.

Except for attending kindergarten and two years of high school at Germantown Friends' School, Gray received her childhood education at the Dimock four-room schoolhouse, which had excellent teachers, perhaps in part because her father was on the school board. An advocate of rural education, Francis Cope became an adviser to Governor Gifford Pinchot regarding Pennsylvania's schools. Some of Gray's fondest memories are of traveling to school, usually by horse and buggy except during the winters, when she either snowshoed with friends (a skill she learned when she was six years old) or rode on a bobsled pulled by a team of horses.

Gray stayed with Foote relatives, a distinguished New England family, on Mt. Desert Island, Maine, for several weeks each summer. Trips to New York City with her parents and Evans cousins (prominent Philadelphia Quakers), especially her visits to the American Museum of Natural History and the theater, were also high points of her girlhood. When she turned eight years old, her father helped her to start keeping bird lists (a list of birds one observes on any given day) and recording observations on the plant and animal life at Woodbourne.

In 1924 Gray entered Mount Holyoke College, an all-female school in South Hadley, Massachusetts. Its isolated, beautiful settings suited her perfectly. She majored in economic geography because of her interest in the interrelationship of nature and humanity, an interest her family had imparted to her through their emphasis on connections among all organisms—what we today call ecology. The classes that most strongly influenced her were Mignon Talbot's economic geography course and an outstanding literature class taught by Ada Snell. She was admitted to the latter as a freshman, on the basis of an essay about her camping experiences with her parents. Snell helped to develop Gray's skills as a writer. Twenty-four years later, when Gray's *The Tundra World* (1952) was published, Snell reviewed it favorably for the *Mount Holyoke Alumnae Quarterly*, citing the author's "rare gift of words."

After her graduation from college, Gray's father took her to the Orient and the South Pacific for a year; they visted such remote places as Fiji, Java, and Sumatra, as well as New Zealand and Australia, in search of rare birds. That trip not only nurtured her lifelong passion for travel but also introduced her to a succession of fascinating male explorers and scientists. She decided that the college boys she had known were too narrow in their interests. She wanted a husband with a broader range of experience who was "doing something" valuable in the out-of-doors.

Academic Works

Encouraged by her parents, Gray entered Cornell University in 1930 to study for a Master of Science degree. She loved her years at Cornell, delighting in the many field studies and the atmosphere of a large, prestigious university. There she was elected a member of Cornell's Sigma Chi and was a founding member of the Cornell Laboratory of Ornithology. Her master's thesis was titled "Some Observations of the Vertebrate Ecology of a Pennsylvania Mountain Farm." She conducted her fieldwork for the thesis during the summer of 1931 and the spring of 1932, although she based much of her study on earlier notes and observations she had made under her father's tutelage. She discusses, for instance, the flying squirrel and two raccoons, a gift from a fellow student, that she kept and then released at Woodbourne. Other vivid descriptions include watching a pileated woodpecker nest, a red fox den, a mink installed in an old woodchuck den, and the behavior of muskrats. She also cited observations made by her father.

Gray's thesis constituted a potpourri of animal and bird observations, the history of the Cope family and farm, her own background, and the conservation efforts and goals of her parents, in addition to the obligatory lists of observed plants, fish, reptiles, birds, and mammals. This inclusive approach was encouraged by Gray's Cornell professors, who included Albert H. Wright and Arthur A. Allen. Gray acknowledged Wright's influence in the thesis, stating that he allowed her "to pursue a rather unusual type of study in the field instead of by the more conventional methods" (p. 5). She described her field technique as "personal observation of the species in their natural haunts... backed by the collection and identification of specimens whenever possible" (p. 4). She also relied on information from several local observers.

In the midst of the required scientific jargon, Gray's evolving literary style and philosophy emerges. For instance, in the section titled "Present Appearance of the Farm," she evokes the seasonal beauty of the view seen from her front porch, which could be observed

> on a green summer day, or in the radiant gold and red of autumn, in the bleak gray of November, in the white snows and drifts of winter, which pile against the old stone walls and hide the ugly new barb wire fences, or on a sparkling day in spring when the woods and fields are a harmony of greens and the deep rose of new buds. Always, no matter what the season, time of day, or weather, it looks surprisingly beautiful and seldom fails to call forth an exclamation of pleasure, whether you are seeing it for the first or thousandth time. (p. 14)

But she pauses to describe with disgust "some ugly signs of civilization such as tractors, telephone poles, and a state concrete road down which cars go 60 miles an hour" (p. 14). This dislike of technology has remained a recurrent theme throughout her life. So has the general longing expressed in her conclusion, for "the early days of great forests, where encounters with panthers, wolves, and bears were a common occurrence" (p. 15).

For her master's thesis, Gray conducted bird censuses in the virgin forest at Woodbourne. On one chilly thirty-eight-degree day in May, she counted twenty-three species. She performed similar censuses on other sections of the varied property, concluding that "the numbers of species of birds [at Woodbourne] is relatively large. ... It is thought that the large number of birds are due to the relatively large amount of forest land which has been allowed to remain on this farm, thus helping to furnish the birds with plenty of shelter and food" (p. 152). Furthermore, "the owners of the Cope Farm are endeavoring to save as much of their remaining native forest land as possible and to reforest the cleared areas which do not make profitable farm regions" (p. 155). These twin themes of conservation of virgin forests and reforestation of marginal farmland—relatively new ideas at that time—are still being debated.

After she completed her master's thesis, in June 1932, Gray went on to obtain her Ph.D. in vertebrate ecology from Cornell with a minor in both ornithology and economic botany. Once again she turned to the familiar forests of Pennsylvania for her topic, titling her dissertation "Observations on the Vertebrate Ecology of Some Pennsylvania Virgin Forests." In addition to studying Woodbourne's two-hundred-acre virgin forest, she chose three other virgin forest tracts—a six-hundred-acre, semivirgin tract at Silver Lake, also in Susquehanna County; an eight-hundred-acre virgin forest at her old camping spot on North Mountain; and the forty-three-hundred-acre Tionesta Tract in northwestern Pennsylvania's Allegheny National Forest.

In a 1934 article she coauthored with Arthur S. Hawkins of Cornell University in the journal *Forest Leaves*—"A Preliminary Survey of the Flora and Fauna of the East Tionesta Virgin Forest, Pennsylvania"—she acknowledges "the continued help and encouragement of Mr. Francis R. Cope, Jr., Vice-President of the Pennsylvania Forestry Association, who made the study of this area possible and assisted greatly in the census of plants and animals" (p. 23). She further acknowledges her father's inspiration in her thesis, claiming that he "has been largely instrumental in giving to the writer a love of Natural History and the desire for scientific learning, and without whose unfailing sympathy and help in acquiring information, such a study could not have been accomplished" (p. 5). Her mother, too, provided "never failing encouragement" (p. 5).

Gray's Ph.D. dissertation, like her master's thesis, is filled with fascinating vignettes of animal behavior that illustrated her talent for closely observing wild creatures. She shows empathy for the despised, such as rattlesnakes ("Like most other snakes and all wild animals the rattlesnake is not harmful unless molested," p. 133), snapping turtles ("most adaptable. They learned to always appear in a certain spot to take food off a fork," p. 134), and little brown bats ("This bat made a very pleasant pet and became sufficiently tame to eat out of the writer's hand after two or three days," p. 167).

Gray's observations led her to conclude that animals are individuals with differing dispositions, and that their activities and habits are not always utilitarian: "It is the writer's belief that some of their time may be spent in carrying on a certain activity for the pure pleasure of it, or else in doing nothing at all" (pp. 127–128). She is convinced that the adult black bears she had observed "wrestling and boxing with perfect amicability for an hour in a woodland opening" (p. 28) were playing.

As a naturalist/observer Gray obviously enjoyed her relationships with wild creatures, but she also performed her scientific duties. She examined the stomach contents of a rattlesnake and found two large field mice still in an undigested state, recorded the mating activities of spotted salamanders, collected a rare bog lemming at Woodbourne, and faithfully listed and described the woody and herbaceous plants, fishes, reptiles, amphibians, breeding birds, and mammals living in each virgin forest tract.

Several of Gray's conclusions—that habitats which are varied contain an abundance of species; "that much may be learned from Nature's methods of growing trees and all forms of plant and animal life, and that these methods may well be superior to those employed by man" (p. 74); and that predators, such as bobcats, "may well be more beneficial than harmful in helping to maintain a balance of healthy wild animal life in any given year" (p. 185)—are now widely accepted tenets of wildlife and forestry management.

One reason Gray gave for writing her dissertation was to leave a record for future naturalists of what such remnants of virgin timber contained "before [they] had been ruthlessly changed by the hand of man," thereby providing the kind of baseline data that has been mostly lost in the eastern forests. To have foreseen the need for such records in the 1930s illustrates her scientific acumen. But what was most obvious in both her master's thesis and her Ph.D. dissertation was her longing to live in a natural area untouched by humanity.

Driftwood Valley

Shortly after she received her doctorate in 1936, Gray had her chance. Two years previously, she had spent a part of the summer studying the birds and plants around Churchill, Manitoba, as part of a team of Cornell University scientists and students, an experience she later fictionalized in *The Tundra World*. There she met John Stanwell-Fletcher, a young Englishman, who was a capable and resourceful explorer, hunter, and trapper with years of survival experience in the Canadian Arctic.

They were married on 4 January 1937, and almost eight months later they arrived in Hazelton, British Columbia, in search of "virgin territory . . . untouched wilderness" where they could build a home, live a peaceful, simple life, and study the flora and fauna in natural conditions throughout all the seasons. To give scientific credibility to the venture, they agreed to collect plant and animal specimens for the British Columbia Provincial Museum.

From the time they started their grand adventure on 26 August 1937, Gray kept a detailed record. She had not set out to be a writer, but she felt compelled to share her unusual experiences with others. The diary she kept about her life as a pioneer became her first book, *Driftwood Valley* (1946), after the remote region she and her husband found with the help of a knowledgeable Indian. This valley became their home. At that time the area was unmapped and unknown to white men. It was some 200 miles northeast of the southern tip of Alaska; the nearest telephone, railroad, and road were 240 miles away. No humans had ever lived in the valley, although a few Indians had traplines in the area. Their encounters with other human beings were scarce. They had no means of communicating with "the outside" for months at a time, nor means of obtaining help when needed. It was a place with a "gift of quiet . . . one which inhabitants of the civilized world don't possess" (p. 99).

With the help of a couple of Indians and a Danish trapper, they managed to build their cabin, which overlooked Tetana, a mile-long jewel of a lake, before winter set in, but it was rough work. Gray collected gunnysacks of sphagnum moss every day for a week to chink the logs and kept everyone fed, while her husband and his helpers—with axes, hammers, two saws, and a few nails—designed and erected a twenty-by-thirty-foot cabin in a month and a half.

By 24 November, the snow was three feet deep and the temperature fifteen to twenty degrees below zero at dawn. In addition to digging out after every snowfall and keeping the cabin roof snow free, Gray had to haul water up a steep bank from the lake, on snowshoes, while her husband spent much of his time cutting firewood. They needed to burn two or three trees, twelve to fourteen inches in diameter, every twenty-four hours to keep their cabin warm. They had not had time to stockpile firewood, and cutting the wood and hauling it to the cabin as the snow deepened and the cold intensified proved to be a Herculean task. To survive such severe conditions required unceasing, self-imposed discipline, not only in mental attitudes but in everyday actions—they had to, for instance, clean any remnants of snow off their clothes every time they entered the cabin to keep ice from forming on the floor, check their snowshoes carefully before setting out on them, and make certain they were properly dressed and carried survival equipment for even short periods outside in the cold.

Gray quickly learned that "wilderness teaches patience and endurance" (p. 163). She was able to snowshoe sixteen to twenty miles a day through soft snow, and she assisted in shooting grouse for food, hauling in the meat of the moose her husband killed, fishing, and carrying logs on her shoulders. "Sometimes I struggle along far behind J., tears streaming down my face from sheer physical pain" (p. 81). Several times they were in precarious situations, yet they always survived. Such tales of struggle made her book extremely popular; it was the ultimate wilderness adventure, what many people dream about but few venture to try—the perfect vicarious armchair experience.

To a naturalist like Gray, though, the real adventure was in the privilege of living in and observing the natural world. Despite having to gather specimens for the museum, the Stanwell-Fletchers resolved not to do any of their collecting near their cabin, reserving Tetana and the territory immediately surrounding it as "a kind of sanctuary for observation purposes" (p. 32).

And what sights they saw from their cabin windows: singing dippers in an open patch of lake water one bitter night when the ground was covered with two feet of snow; ducks fighting and mating on the lake in the early spring; timber wolves that came to the lake in August to feast on kokanee, a small, landlocked salmon that migrates seasonally up the Driftwood River, turning the water gold as they cram it from shore to shore. The Stanwell-Fletchers also saw and heard the wolves during the winter of 1937–1938. With the advent of these animals, the valley became "a concert hall filled with wolf music" (p. 151). According to Gray the wolves sang most actively on beautiful nights, and she reiterated her belief that "much of an animal's time must be spent in the sheer joy of living, the sheer pleasure of physical sensations" (p. 144). The wolves, she maintained, had a sense of beauty that led them to lie atop a hill that overlooked the distant mountain ranges, a place that the Stanwell-Fletchers named Wolf Hill and that they, too, were partial to.

Theodora Cope Stanwell-Fletcher (Teddy Gray) with her two dogs at the cabin in Driftwood Valley, British Columbia

In their championing of wolves as intelligent predators deserving respect from humans the Stanwell-Fletchers were ahead of their time. Before Adolph Murie's important book *The Wolves of Mount McKinley* was published in 1944, the Stanwell-Fletchers were observing wolves, writing about them for *Natural History* magazine, and photographing them. Wolves, Gray maintained, never kill for the sake of killing, as sportsmen do, and seldom waste what they kill.

The occasional talk from some ignorant authority or, worse, a supposedly intelligent scientist, about an actual extermination of wolves here or in Alaska, on the ground that unless wolves are done away with there will be no game animals left, fills us with helpless wrath . . . by what right does man, who after all forms only one small branch of all the great world of vertebrate and invertebrate animals, decree that another form, because it must prey for its livelihood on other live things, shall no longer exist? (p. 141)

In the end, both she and her husband arrived at remarkable conclusions regarding the potential for interspecies coexistence: "The wolves are well aware of our presence and habits, and like us! They even allow their young to be near us. With their remarkable gift of understanding, they have apparently come to realize that there is nothing to fear from us, that we like them, that we are interested in their welfare" (p. 354).

She believed that the wolves, like other animals she had observed in Pennsylvania, possessed individual personalities.

Gray is also at her best when describing birds. Those winter-visiting dippers wove a spell of enchantment with their "crystal tinkles, which matched so perfectly the icy purity of the winter night" (p. 72); ruby-crowned and golden-crowned kinglets "hang every dark green spruce with chains of bubbling, rippling melody" (p. 182); and the "voice of the Pacific loon—that ghostly, haunting, wailing 'oh-h-h-h, oh-h-h, ooh-ooh.' Like a woman crying hopelessly, endlessly. . . . Like a far-off foghorn of a ship at sea.

Like the mournful sign of wind in a pine tree" (pp. 214–215).

Perhaps Gray's most lyrical passages concern the aurora borealis displays, especially the one of 17 April 1938: "Last night at 2 A.M., I saw a miracle!" she writes. "Great, bright scarlet clouds were rolling over the pinewoods. . . . I could never have even imagined such a sight! It was all unbelievable, the sort of thing that happens only in fairy stories" (pp. 175–176).

During their time in the wilderness, the Stanwell-Fletchers managed to make valuable contributions to science. They were assisted at long distance by Ian McTaggart Cowan, professor of zoology at the University of British Columbia and director of the British Columbia Provincial Museum. Their correspondence and sacks of specimens had to await the occasional Indian trapper, and took as long as two months to reach the nearest trading post. Cowan wrote letters of encouragement, coaching them in the techniques of collecting from an unknown region, telling them what they needed to obtain more of, and identifying what they had found. Gray's plant collection for the museum contained several specimens of every woody and herbaceous plant she could find—180 kinds. It was "a man-sized job carrying an oilskin bag around all summer to keep the flowers fresh till I got them home, putting them in the plant press, and writing notes about each one" (p. 223).

While collecting in the Driftwood Mountains the Stanwell-Fletchers devoted every afternoon to skinning specimens and pressing plants.

This means hours of back-breaking toil, crouched inside our tiny tent, smoke blowing through and smarting our eyes. No matter how careful we are with the netting, a few mosquitoes and flies always get in. Flies attack the smelly bloody skins, mosquitoes attack one's neck, or ear, or arm just as one reaches the crucial and most difficult part of the job. (p. 320)

They found mountain maple far north of its known range; extended the range of northern skunks, pygmy owls, and evening grosbeaks considerably; were the first to record kokanee in the region; discovered an abundance of tawny lemmings; and set a new record for the northern range of cougars. Altogether they produced an annotated list that included 280 plants, 13 fishes, 4 amphibians, 139 birds, and 41 mammal species and subspecies.

One day in June 1938, Francis and Evelyn Cope appeared in a motorboat piloted by local Indians on the flooded, supposedly unnavigable Driftwood River and stayed for two months. This was a happy surprise, because the Stanwell-Fletchers had had no communications from the Copes for months. Despite the demonic appearance of mosquitoes whose "thrum" "from five o'clock on . . . drowns out all bird song" (p. 197), Francis Cope helped with the collecting and listing, and Evelyn "tramp[ed] the forests with me like a girl of sixteen" (p. 193). They were the only visitors, other than Indians and an occasional trapper, that the Stanwell-Fletchers had during their first stay in Driftwood Valley, which ended on 4 January 1939.

After a hiatus of almost two years, during which Gray gave birth to a daughter, Patricia, at Woodbourne, their wilderness adventures continued when Theodora flew into Tetana on 18 February 1941 to join her husband, who had arrived a month earlier to fix up the cabin.

They stayed only until 16 September 1941 and made several expeditions with the Indians to nearby mountain ranges to do more collecting. By then, they both knew not only how to survive but also how to thrive under rugged conditions, including those presented by winter camping. Back in December 1938, Gray summed up her philosophy, much of which had been developed by her experiences in Driftwood Valley.

Man talks much about serving his fellow men, very little about serving the earth which has served him faithfully throughout the centuries of his being, and without whose cooperation he could not even exist. It is very humbling to learn how much better a natural area gets on without the inevitable interference or exploitation of man—to realize that while birds, for example, can exist perfectly without man, man, because birds keep down the insects which might otherwise dominate this earth, very possibly could not exist without birds. And it is rather appalling when one has watched the manifestations of a primeval land and its wild inhabitants to realize the depths of the arrogance and ignorance displayed by most human beings toward the character, mind, and behavior of the animals. (*Driftwood Valley*, p. 249)

But with World War II on the horizon and a baby daughter back at Woodbourne, they were forced to cut their time in the valley short. Still, they planned to return as soon as they could, and asked the Indians to guard their cabin as if it were their own and to respect Tetana as a sanctuary for wildlife, birds, animals, and plants.

Gray concluded, "I look toward the Frypans and Driftwood Mountains, now so remote and far-off, keeping watch over Tetana and our beloved wilderness, forever steadfast and serene, undisturbed by the comings and goings and distresses of mere man. Keep safe, Tetana, until we come again" (p. 369). But they never returned. John Stanwell-Fletcher went off to war and then conducted a series of Arctic explorations, dying many years later; Theodora went home to Woodbourne to raise their daughter, write three books, and take her own trips to the north country.

Driftwood Valley was published in 1946 and became a best-seller; in 1947 it received the John Burroughs Medal for outstanding literary work in the field of natural history. Over the years, the book has gone through twenty-seven printings in its first hardcover edition, and numerous later printings by other publishers, including paperback editions. New generations continue to read the book and to visit Driftwood Valley. Surprisingly, the remote region was still relatively untouched at the close of the twentieth century, and Tetana has kept safe, so far.

Natural History "Fiction"

For her next book, Gray decided to describe her experiences as a Cornell student in the Arctic;

first she returned to Churchill in 1949 to do futher research on the place and its people. She also relied on her husband's help "to acquire the general atmosphere and background of the life of northern men." Because some of the people in *The Tundra World* objected to her portrayal of them, she fictionalized names and appearances. Nevertheless, it is obvious that the narrator, Rosamund Reeves, is Gray and that trapper Eric Grey is her husband. Dr. Stevens is modeled on one of her "best-loved teachers" at Cornell, the ornithologist Arthur A. Allen, and Rosamund's friend Sue is patterned after Gray's friend A. Marguerite Baumgartner, who was the first American female college student to work completely on her own at Churchill studying tundra birds, and who inspired Theodora to travel there.

Gray again used the journal style. She believed it to be "an ideal form for expressing natural history observations [because] accuracy in dates and timing, and freshness of detail, are important to naturalists" (p. ix). She also sprinkled the narrative with the scientific names of wildflowers "because many of the plants here don't have common English names; also I want the scientific ones for future reference" (p. 79), and frequently included footnotes on birds and bird articles. The book, written in the enthusiastic, innocent voice of a young woman new to the Arctic and its people, both white and native, has no real plot. But the situation and cast of characters were so unusual for the time that the book held the general reader's interest.

The fictional material of the book is merely background for the star of the show—the natural world. Like *Driftwood Valley*, *The Tundra World* is filled with excellent and accurate descriptions of the landscape, birds, animals, and plants. In one such passage, birds called old-squaws are depicted as

clowns of the tundra. . . . As they rush past you, their cry is a ludicrous "owl-owl-omelette, owl-owl-omelette," rather like a travesty on an automobile horn, emphasis on the "om." And their plump brown bodies with white patchings in disorderly array (they've not yet entirely acquired their full summer plumage), the two elongated tail feathers of the male, the almost bald appearance of the white splotched heads, the funny, excited way they take off from water or flounder sideways as they land, their odd courting habit of snapping the head back and jerking the body forward, all remind one exactly of a clown. (pp. 32–33)

American golden plovers are "one of the world's greatest of travelers (bird or human!), whose marvelous yearly journeyings to and from the nesting grounds make naturalists wax lyrical, and must inspire any perceptive human with reverence at the ways of animal life" (p. 39). On a later visit to Churchill she observes a golden plover whose numbered leg band shows it has made yearly migrations to wintering grounds in Africa, returning on approximately the same date for years to its former nesting grounds at Churchill. Collared lemmings have "little black shoe-button eyes [that] twinkle at you from behind stones and low plants. If you keep very still they sit up and stare—funny squashy little figures with large front paws draped on fat chests" (p. 111).

Gray's usual themes—her love for the untouched natural world, appreciation of peace and quiet, upset over humanity's despoliation of nature, and disgust with "a soulless, mindless, machine-controlled existence" (p. 46)—are in evidence throughout the book. The character Rosamund Reeves spends much time observing beluga whales in Hudson Bay. She believes that "these whales must be highly organized creatures, capable of great suffering" (p. 54), an unusual sentiment given that this was written long before the animal rights' movement.

At several points she is harsh in her criticism of human attitudes toward the natural world and voices ideas that again have a modern ring to them. "Strange how shortsighted men are, as well as selfish. What foundation is there for thinking that the entire earth is man's to use or abuse exactly as he may choose?" (p. 142), she writes when discussing the exploitation of the eggs and down of common eiders, a supposedly protected species. "Like the sad history of our own states there will appear to be unlimited supplies of everything till it's too late" (p. 142).

She continues this theme when she explains the recent extermination of caribou with high-powered rifles.

More and more you become impressed, especially when you contact true wilderness areas, with the *stupidity* of man—his ignorance and lack of understanding and ridiculous inability to get on with other forms of life which were put here in this world just as surely as he was, and form such an essential part in the whole scheme of things.... The crime lies in the fact that man has so needlessly exterminated whole races of animals, when he might have used carefully a limited supply: the wholly unnecessary and terrible suffering he causes, when he might just as easily (and for his own profit) have exercised careful handling and respect for their welfare; his utter lack of appreciation so often not only for their usefulness but for the very great beauty and pleasure and inspiration contributed by so many of them. (pp. 164–165)

At the end of the book, Rosamund Reeves reaches an understanding with Eric Grey as she prepares to return home. He will come down to the States the following year to take her back to the North. And although she realizes the risks in such a life and partner, given her genteel upbringing among people steeped in "book-learning, the sciences, cultural and intellectual things," she concludes: "For a long time I've sensed dimly that all this wouldn't quite do for me.... I have to know more, though sometimes it must be far easier and safer and pleasanter not to know, to believe in the best, have little to do with the hard and the sordid and the ugly [all of which she witnessed during her summer in the Arctic]" (p. 263). So she decides to "chance it. Perhaps if I do I shall lose out, experience great unhappiness. But I've done just enough mountain climbing to be aware that to know the real heights you must also know the depths. To know great things, you must have great courage, take a great risk. And I want to try, at least, to know the great things" (pp. 263–264). Certainly a summary not only of the heroine's philosophy of life but also of Teddy Gray's.

The Tundra World was published in 1952 and also sold well—not as well as *Driftwood Valley* but well enough to encourage Gray to write a third book. That same year she was one of twenty-eight career women honored by Mount Holyoke College at the conclusion of a two-day convocation on science and human values. Her citation, presented to her by college president Roswell G. Ham, read: "Distinguished for your ability to translate scientific fact into literature, you have created unforgettable pictures in your books—*Driftwood Valley* and *The Tundra World*—books which materially increase our knowledge of wild life in Canada and which spiritually alert us to the beauty and mystery of the world of nature everywhere." She also received the Distinguished Daughters of Pennsylvania medal, was elected to the Society of Woman Geographers, and later became a member of the Philadelphia branch of the Explorers' Club.

Her third book, *Clear Lands and Icy Seas: A Voyage to the Eastern Arctic* (1958), was based on two summer trips she made to the eastern Arctic in 1952 and 1953 on the Hudson's Bay Company supply ship M.V. *Rupertsland*. Again she fictionalized most of the characters, except for the ship's officers and her friend Hazel R. Ellis, professor of biology at Keuka College in New York State, who had accompanied Gray on her 1949 trip to Churchill.

This "novel" has an even thinner plot than *The Tundra World*. Of all Gray's books, *Clear Lands and Icy Seas* is most purely a book steeped in natural history, with evocative descriptions of the north country and the challenges it presents to its people and its wild creatures. She succeeds admirably in what she sets out to do: "to paint ... a clear picture of the special value and atmosphere as a whole of that wonderful, still relatively little known area of the North American Arctic" (p. vii).

She boards the *Rupertsland* at Montreal and is off to the far north, ostensibly to discover

whether its human inhabitants, as well as its wildlife, would show striking evidence of

greater happiness and health in an environment that forced them to closer contact with elemental and natural forces instead of man-made, machine-age ones.

But, most of all, I simply longed for the North again! ... You never quite forget, or stop wanting, and needing, that great quietness and cleanness, the deep pure colors, the indescribable tonic of air from vast, cold spaces. (pp. 4–5)

The 190-foot *Rupertsland*, powered by two three-hundred-horsepower diesel engines, slowly makes its way from Montreal down the St. Lawrence River, up the Atlantic coast along Labrador, through the great ice fields of Hudson Strait and Ungava Bay, along the southern coast of Baffin Island, halfway down the eastern coast of Hudson Bay to Port Harrison, and across the bay to Churchill, stopping at remote Hudson's Bay Company posts throughout the Arctic to deliver yearly supplies and pick up freight.

In addition to dangers the ship faces in its journey, including ice fields, there are many uneventful hours in which Gray gets to know her fellow passengers and the crew. Gray and a scientist, "Dr. Henderson," debate conservation issues and moral dilemmas. Henderson decries humanity's "doctrine of abusing, instead of carefully using and preserving resources which don't belong wholly to him" (p. 129). He goes on to offer a possible explanation for such abuse:

I often wonder if many of the churches in their narrow interpretation of Christianity aren't actually the chief and most short-sighted sinners in this respect. The church lays such enormous stress on man's importance and superiority above everything—it seems to forget that, according to the Christian doctrines, if the individual's lot is to be bettered, the earth environment on which he depends for life must be kept intact for future generations. (p. 129)

The idea that the Christian viewpoint may have contributed to Western humanity's rapaciousness toward the natural world became a hot topic of debate nine years after *Clear Lands and Icy Seas* was published, when Lynn White, Jr., published his thought-provoking "The Historical Roots of Our Ecologic Crisis" in *Science* (10 March 1967). His article concludes: "We shall continue to have a worsening ecologic crisis until we reject the Christian axiom that nature has no reason for existence save to serve man." Furthermore, he counsels that Christians should look to "the profoundly religious, but heretical, sense of the primitive Franciscans for the spiritual autonomy of all parts of nature" (p. 1207). Both statements sound very much like "Henderson's" thinking.

Gray also discusses overpopulation on the basis of her reading of Henry Fairfield Osborn's *Our Plundered Planet* (1948) and William Vogt's *Road to Survival* (1948). She recognizes that

> not only unlettered natives of unexploited regions, but also the average educated inhabitants of civilized places, still have little or no comprehension either, it seems, of the simple, vital fact that the purity of the actual air we breathe, as well as the earth's basic resources, which cannot be duplicated by synthetic or machine products, are slowly but certainly being exhausted by the ever-expanding human population . . . on an earth that is *not* expanding. (p. 151)

At the close of the twentieth century, humanity had not come to grips with the common sense inherent in Gray's remark, and the world population continued to increase while resources dwindled.

Not all of Gray's time on the *Rupertsland* is spent philosophizing with fellow passengers. She and Ellis take every possible chance to get off the ship when it docks and explore the natural world. Near Payne Bay, a small settlement in northern Quebec on Ungava Bay, they follow two young Eskimo boys on a trek to photograph a gyrfalcon nest. She and Hazel, "cumbered with rubber boots far heavier than sealskin ones, jackets, raincoats, lunches, cameras, glasses" (p. 176) have a difficult time keeping up with the boys as they clamber up a rock-strewn, steep hillside. But the reward of seeing the landscape close up is worth the effort: The "low-lying, spread-out rocks on those hills of Payne Bay [were] painted with vivid orange lichen; and

every earth or gravel-filled nook and cranny was bedded deep with bright moss and flowers. All moist areas along streams and pools and warmer southern slopes were covered with whole gardens of Arctic plants" (p. 178). They do not find the nest, but later, various Eskimos take them to a nearby bird island—"a high, steep, little island, about three quarters of a mile in circumference . . . an enchanting place. . . . We had come to a bird world of wheeling forms and swishing wings and screaming voices" (p. 192). In order to photograph a rough-legged hawk nest, they have to crawl down a steep incline to the edge of a precipice and lie with their heads pointing downward. In addition, Gray counts eleven common eider nests, which the Eskimos and the local Hudson's Bay Company people carefully protect and collect for winter clothing only after the young birds have left.

She also makes remarkable observations on board the ship. Most memorable is her description of common murres.

> As is the habit of murres, they flew continually in straight, single lines, each bird exactly behind the other, veering this way or that, in graceful, perfect unison, like trained figures of a ballet. Slanting light rays, vividly picking out the white of each body, turned the flying lines of birds into giant strings of iridescent pearls, or waving ribbons of white. All over the sea, and all through the air, and all round our ship, the gleaming necklaces and ribbons were flung, and swayed, in the lovely light. (p. 233)

As they approach the Wolstenholme cliffs on the northwest point of the Ungava Peninsula, they see that the cliffs "were enveloped in whirling snow flurries, this time not thousands, but millions of murres. It dizzied you to watch them, as it makes one dizzy to stare at whirling snowflakes" (p. 234).

Not only does Gray write evocatively about the birds of the North, she also tries to convey the "terrible beauty" of icebergs even when the *Rupertsland* is in danger of being crushed by ice, the "deep, strong color" of the landscape, the "soft, steady roar of cold winds," and the ever-changing sky. She concludes *Clear Lands and Icy Seas* with a description of a spectacular aurora borealis over Churchill:

> Facts of modern science could make it seem no less of a great and awesome presence; something alive and breath-takingly lovely; indescribably mysterious and utterly remote. Again and again it brushed with luminous white and palest of phosphorescent green, the moving ice, that mighty factor of Northern seas, which had been so constant, so beautiful, so dangerous a companion of that voyage with the *Rupertsland*. (pp. 260–261)

Although *Clear Land and Icy Seas* was not the commercial success Gray's other books had been, it is, in many respects, her best nature book. Her natural history descriptions are most fully developed, and so is her philosophy both toward the natural world and toward humans' relationship with it. She also reveals a little of her private sorrows—due, she admits "perhaps to my own stubbornness, lack of worldly wisdom, or a too-adventurous romantic spirit" (p. 186). She and Henderson "philosophize . . . on ethics and wisdom in particular. We both had been struck with the fact that the hardest people to deal with in this world are often the exceptionally charming or talented, who at the same time may lack a moral stamina which makes for true success" (p. 186).

Private Life

All the while she was writing and researching her books, Gray was also a full-time mother. According to her daughter Patricia, her mother gave her the same kind of upbringing she herself had had. Writing in the third person, she says she "took Pat camping from an early age—at first in the apple orchards, then in the depths of the virgin forest at Woodbourne. They read poetry, listened to owls, lit natural firecrackers by touching a match to dry *Lycopodium sporangia*, picnicked . . . as far as possible from roads and people, walked in the forest in the blackest night holding phosphorescent fungi, identified birds

[and] found rare salamanders under stones" (Patricia Bidlake, letter).

Shortly before the publication of *Clear Lands and Icy Seas*, Gray met and married biologist Lowell Sumner, a fan of *Driftwood Valley*. She and Pat moved to California, where Sumner worked for the National Park Service. This marriage ended after several years, while Pat was at Scripps College in Claremont. Then Gray moved to Claremont to be near her daughter and some special friends and to do research on several western areas. She especially liked the Southwest desert because it reminded her of the North and the "great open quiet places which I loved." She and Pat traveled to Alaska, where they visited the University of Alaska at Fairbanks (Pat later took her M.S. in plant ecology there). They also visited Camp Denali in Denali National Park. Another year, Gray and her daughter voyaged on a Norwegian passenger freighter around the Lofoten Islands and the North Cape.

In 1966, Gray married the recently widowed Philip Hayward Gray, a distinguished professor of English at Scripps College as well as a talented writer and outdoorsman. At the age of sixty, she found great joy, and by all accounts the marriage was idyllic. She loved the rich cultural life of Claremont and the college students, and led Girl Scout troops on nature study hikes in the nearby San Gabriel Mountains. She and her husband went camping whenever they could, observing nature in the deserts, the high mountains, and on the California coast.

After Philip Gray's retirement, they divided their time between his summer home near Greensboro, Vermont, and Woodbourne, when they were not studying wildlife in such places as Great Britain, Kenya, Tanzania, the Gaspé peninsula, Tahiti, Moorea, the Everglades, and the Florida Keys. They picnicked at all seasons of the year, shared their common love of poetry, and explored the natural world.

At Woodbourne, Gray amazed her husband with her ability to read animal tracks in the snow; she easily identified those of white-footed mice, red-backed voles, lemmings, and shrews. Whenever they came home from a hike or a ride, she consulted her bird guide and wrote up her notes. In one of many books of poems Philip Gray wrote for her, he made it clear that her love of and curiosity about nature never waned: "I'm an ecologist: To my nature-mill, everything's grist," he heard her say.

In 1956, Gray's father, her stepmother, Margaret, and Gray herself had donated 478 acres of Woodbourne to the then fledgling Nature Conservancy. That donation included the virgin forest area. In 1965 they gave an additional 72 acres, which included a 9.6-acre pond with several floating bog islands and some rare plant and insect species. A year before Philip Gray's death in 1978, he and Gray donated another 52 acres. By then, the area, renamed the Woodbourne Forest and Wildlife Sanctuary, was the largest virgin woodland in eastern Pennsylvania. At Philip Gray's summer home in Vermont, he and Gray set up the Bar Hill Nature Preserve and donated it to the Nature Conservancy.

Since Philip Gray's death, Gray has led an increasingly quiet and retired life, but she still attends the regular meetings of the Woodbourne Management Committee, and she entertains local community groups as well as her extended family throughout the year. Her daughter, Pat, who married Canadian wildlife biologist Larry Bidlake, lives in Brandon, Manitoba, with their son and daughter. Several times a year they visit Woodbourne Orchards. According to her daughter, Gray has passed on to her grandchildren her ideals, her attitudes toward nature and the environment, her love for animals, and her delight in books and poetry. Most of all, she seems to have passed on a love of Woodbourne Forest. Her greatest desire is to have the property maintained as her father and all her family wished it to be—intact and undeveloped—and to keep the house built by her grandparents attractive and in good repair so that her many friends and family members can, as Bidlake says, "stay in the peace of an old and beautiful house filled with books, surrounded by magnificent views of Pennsylvania hills and valleys, in the setting of lawns and shrubs and surrounding woodlands" (Bidlake letter).

Perhaps Gray's life as a naturalist is best summed up in a humorous poem Philip Gray wrote about her, "Bird Lover Misses Heaven," included in a privately published collection titled *For Teddy* (1980). It concluded:

"Just wait five minutes, please, until I see
What kind of birds flew in that big spruce
   tree.
I'll just skip back and get my glasses,"
True ornithologist! She'd rather miss
Her likely chances of eternal bliss
Than quit while unnamed species passes.

Selected Bibliography

WORKS OF THEODORA COPE STANWELL-FLETCHER

BOOKS

Driftwood Valley (Boston: Little, Brown, 1946; repr., New York: Penguin, 1989); *The Tundra World* (Boston: Little, Brown, 1952); *Clear Lands and Icy Seas: A Voyage to the Eastern Arctic* (New York: Dodd, Mead, 1958).

ACADEMIC WORKS

"Some Observations of the Vertebrate Ecology of a Pennsylvania Mountain Farm" (master's thesis, Cornell Univ., 1932); "Observations on the Vertebrate Ecology of Some Pennsylvania Virgin Forests" (Ph.D. diss., Cornell Univ., 1936).

ARTICLES

"A Preliminary Survey of the Flora and Fauna of the East Tionesta Virgin Forest, Pennsylvania," in *Forest Leaves* 24 (1934), with Arthur S. Hawkins; "Naturalists in the Wilds of British Columbia: Part 1, Our Wilderness Home and Life in Winter," in *Scientific Monthly* (January 1940), with John F. Stanwell-Fletcher; "Naturalists in the Wilds of British Columbia: Part 2, The Ending of Winter and Coming of Spring," in *Scientific Monthly* (February 1940), with John F. Stanwell-Fletcher; "Naturalists in the Wilds of British Columbia: Part 3, The Summer and Preparations for Our Second Winter," in *Scientific Monthly* (March 1940), with John F. Stanwell-Fletcher; *Some Accounts of the Flora and Fauna of the Driftwood Valley Region of North Central British Columbia*, British Columbia Provincial Museum Occasional Paper 4 (1943); "On Knowing Our Natural Environment," in *Mount Holyoke Alumnae Quarterly* 35 (August 1951).

BIOGRAPHICAL AND CRITICAL STUDIES

Stanleigh Arnold, review of *Clear Lands and Icy Seas*, in *San Francisco Chronicle* (30 April 1958); Peter Freuchen, review of *The Tundra World*, in *New York Times Book Review* (17 August 1952); Philip H. Gray, *For Teddy: Poems Grave and Merry* (privately pub., 1980); Eliza Cope Harrison, ed., *Philadelphia Merchant: The Diary of Thomas P. Cope* (South Bend, Ind.: Gateway, 1978); M. L. Kinnard, review of *Clear Lands and Icy Seas*, in *Christian Science Monitor* (8 May 1958); Ada Snell, review of *The Tundra World*, in *Mount Holyoke Alumnae Quarterly* 36 (August 1952); John F. Stanwell-Fletcher, "Three Years in Wolves' Wilderness," in *Natural History* 49 (March 1942); George R. Stewart, "Wilderness Adventure," in *New York Times Book Review* (15 September 1946), review of *Driftwood Valley*; George Miksch Sutton, review of *The Tundra World*, in *New York Herald Tribune Book Review* (17 August 1952); Edwin Way Teale, review of *Driftwood Valley*, in *Weekly Book Review* (25 August 1946).

WALLACE STEGNER
(1909–1993)

NEIL B. CARMONY

THE WRITING OF Wallace Stegner first came to my attention in the early 1960s. Living in Arizona, a state with an important Mormon heritage, I had become interested in the history and special culture of the Latter-day Saints. However, I discovered that books on the subject that were not undermined by bias were hard to find. Then a friend suggested I read *Mormon Country* (1942) by Wallace Stegner. This was good advice. Not a harsh denunciation of Mormon beliefs nor a pious defense of the faith, *Mormon Country* proved to be a balanced and graceful evocation of life in a Mormon community in the American West. Wallace Stegner became and remains one of the writers and thinkers I admire most.

Stegner is best known as a writer of fiction. During his long career he produced thirteen novels. *Angle of Repose* (1971) won a Pulitzer Prize, and *The Spectator Bird* (1976) received the National Book Award. His short fiction garnered the O. Henry Prize on three occasions. Stegner's standing as a major American novelist is secure. However, more than most creative writers, he made important contributions to nonfiction disciplines. He produced insightful works of history and biography, and composed essays on a vast array of topics from literary criticism to conservation.

Although certainly not a writer of "Westerns" in the tradition of Zane Grey, Stegner is properly identified as a Western writer—almost all of his works focus on the American West. From 1945 until his death in 1993, he made his home in Los Altos Hills, California, a suburban community near Palo Alto. (Stegner taught at Stanford University from 1945 until his retirement in 1971.) Nonetheless, the West Coast was not the region or cultural environment he felt he knew best. The northern Great Plains, the Rocky Mountains, and especially the intermountain region known as the Great Basin and Colorado Plateau, the places where he spent his youth, remained "Stegner country" throughout his life. No one has written about this region with more elegance and understanding. However, Stegner's writings were never provincial—he used the West as a springboard for exploring large themes of universal relevance.

It might surprise some of Wallace Stegner's admirers to find him included in a volume devoted to "nature writers," but he truly deserves this title as well as that of novelist and biographer. Stegner's training was in literature, not in the biological sciences, and he never presumed to be an authority on natural history. Therefore, his approach to the natural environment was not as a chronicler of the life cycles of plants and animals or as an interpreter of biological processes. It was the complex land-man relationship that fired his imagination and inspired some of his best writing. (The term "land" as used here does not refer to mere acreage but to a region's entire system of soils, waters, plants, and animals.) That people have an impact on the land upon which they live has long been recognized. That the land affects people and helps shape their cultures, even in modern industrial societies, is also not a novel concept. It is obvious, therefore, that bad land-use practices can devastate both the land and the lives of its inhabitants. However, Stegner believed that the importance of these truths and the negative consequences of an unhealthy man-land relationship were poorly understood by most people. To ventilate the problems resulting from the careless management of the resources of the American West, and to explore the cultural roots of these imprudent actions, were Stegner's goals as a native writer. To see America move away from thoughtless resource exploitation and adopt a healthy, responsible land ethic was Wallace Stegner's goal as a conservationist.

A Stegner Chronology

Hilda Paulson Stegner gave birth to Wallace Earle Stegner, her second of two children, on 18 February 1909, in Lake Mills, Iowa, while she, her husband, George, and their two-year-old son, Cecil, were visiting her parents. At the time the Stegners were living in Grand Forks, North Dakota. They soon returned home but did not stay in Grand Forks for long. George Stegner was a footloose wanderer who had no capacity for putting down firm roots.

The Stegners moved several times during the next five years. They spent some time in the state of Washington, and in 1914 found themselves in East End, Saskatchewan (the little town is shown as Eastend on recent maps). George Stegner had taken a homestead, hoping to convert a parcel of the semiarid Canadian plains into a profitable wheat farm. For six years, until Wallace was nearly twelve, the Stegners were sod-busting pioneers in southwestern Saskatchewan, a few miles north of the Montana border. Success eluded them, however. When the

rains failed to come for three summers in a row, their farming venture went bust.

The Stegners spent the next fifteen months in Great Falls, Montana, then in 1921 moved to Salt Lake City. The following decade in Utah was one of relative stability for Wallace, although the family lived in a dozen different houses during those years. He attended high school in Salt Lake City, then enrolled in the University of Utah. Literature had become his passion, and he graduated with a B.A. degree in English in 1930. Wallace's brother, Cecil, died suddenly of pneumonia that year.

Although the Stegners were not Mormons, life in Utah was generally pleasant for Stegner. He was something of an outsider, yet was not rejected by his neighbors and classmates. He often attended youth activities sponsored by the Mormon Church and was made to feel welcome. Stegner came to respect much of what he observed about the Mormon way of life but never adopted their religious beliefs as his own. Many years later he wrote two distinguished books devoted to the Mormon experience in settling the West.

Having determined to pursue a career as a teacher and writer, Stegner began graduate studies in English at the University of Iowa. He received an M.A. degree in 1932 and the Ph.D. in 1935. His mother, to whom he had been very close, died of cancer in 1933, at the age of fifty. She had little formal schooling but was intelligent and an avid reader, and Stegner credited her with nurturing his love of literature. Stegner took time off from his studies to nurse his mother through the final stages of her illness.

Stegner married Mary Page, a fellow graduate student at the University of Iowa, on 1 September 1934. Now a family man needing to make a living, he took his first teaching job at Augustana College in Rock Island, Illinois, before completing his doctorate. The administrators of this small religious school soon became disenchanted with Stegner's lack of piety, and his time there was brief. The Stegners returned to Salt Lake City, and Wallace began teaching English at the University of Utah. He completed his doctoral dissertation in 1935. It was a study

Stegner at his home in Los Altos Hills, California, 1981

of the career of Clarence Dutton, a geologist who had assisted John Wesley Powell in his surveys of the Colorado Plateau in the 1870s.

In 1937 Stegner accepted a position on the faculty of the University of Wisconsin. That year the Stegners' only child, a son named Page, was born. The year 1937 also saw the publication of Wallace's first major work of fiction, a short novel titled *Remembering Laughter*. The novella won a $2,500 prize offered by the publishing house Little, Brown — big money during the Great Depression.

In 1939 Stegner was recruited to teach creative writing at Harvard University. It would seem that no greater opportunity could come to an academician than to bask in the radiance of this most prestigious citadel of learning, but Stegner later recalled that he did not find the six years he spent at Harvard especially memorable. Yes, he made friends with many important literary figures, including Robert Frost and journalist and historian Bernard DeVoto, but when he received an offer to teach at a school in the West, he gladly accepted it.

A few months after arriving in Cambridge, Stegner received the news that his father had committed suicide in a seedy Salt Lake City hotel. To Wallace, this seemed the final sad chapter in a spiritually bankrupt life. It is an understatement to describe the father-son relationship as strained; they had little contact after Hilda Stegner died. George Stegner had some good qualities, but he could be harsh, insensitive, and domineering, and he had a vicious temper. In *Conversations with Wallace Stegner* (1983), Wallace said of his father: "There were times when one could feel very proud of him; other times when one would have willingly strangled him" (p. 8). He felt that his father would have been happier if he had been born fifty years earlier, because he was a rough and rowdy frontiersman at heart. George Stegner was a restless man who was always on the lookout for a get-rich-quick scheme, but he never discovered one that paid off. He never found a situation that suited him, and his family suffered as a result.

The Big Rock Candy Mountain, Stegner's fifth novel, was published in 1943. This highly autobiographical work remains one of his most popular novels. When interviewed on the subject, Stegner always emphasized that *The Big Rock Candy Mountain* was a work of fiction, and readers should approach it as that. He acknowledged, however, that the story grew out of his own experiences during childhood and youth, and in many ways it was fairly straightforward family history. He based the principal characters on himself and his relatives: Bo and Elsa Mason have undeniable resemblances to George and Hilda Stegner; their children, Chet and Bruce, can only represent Cecil and Wallace. Part of the story takes place in the village of Whitemud, Saskatchewan, a thinly disguised version of East End. *The Big Rock Candy Mountain* is required reading for anyone interested in Stegner's early life and the family relationships that helped shape his personality.

In 1945 Stegner left Harvard and accepted the challenge of directing Stanford University's new creative writing program, which he launched the following year. This graduate-level course of study, supported by grants and endowments, was designed to hone the skills of young writers of proven ability. Participants were not required to pursue degrees, only to write and write well. A full professor for the first time, Stegner super-vised the Stanford program until his retirement in 1971. Among the writers who spent time under Stegner's tutelage were such diverse talents as Larry McMurtry, Wendell Berry, Thomas McGuane, and Edward Abbey.

At Stanford, not all of Stegner's time was spent in teaching. He devoted much energy to his own writing, and received fellowships that allowed him to study and lecture at institutions all over North America and as far off as Tokyo, Rome, and Athens. After his retirement, his literary output increased. A steady stream of books and articles continued to flow from his fertile mind, and he was much in demand as a guest lecturer throughout the United States and Canada. In 28 March 1993, at the age of eighty-four, he was in Sante Fe, New Mexico, to deliver a speech when he was involved in an auto accident. Stegner died on 13 April 1993, from pneumonia and other complications brought on by the injuries he suffered in the collision. He was vigorous and productive until the end.

Life in Saskatchewan

It may seem odd that Wallace Stegner, an erudite man of letters, found more inspiration in the six years he spent on the Canadian plains than in the six years he spent on the Harvard faculty, but such was the case. The time Stegner spent in East End, Saskatchewan, caused him forever after to think of himself as a farm boy who became a writer and teacher, rather than as a learned professor who managed to rise above his humble origins. Saskatchewan was so pivotal in shaping his values and worldview that his life there is worthy of examination.

The little town of East End is located in the southwestern corner of Saskatchewan, about forty miles north of the international boundary. It is at the "east end" of an upland region known as the Cypress Hills. The Frenchman River flows past the village, a sluggish, small stream at that point near its headwaters. The local people called it the Whitemud River in the old days, the name referring to the white clay deposits along its course. The surrounding countryside is rolling grassland. Average precipitation is about thirteen inches per year, too dry for forests. The landscape is not the spectacular kind that attracts tourists. Southern Saskatchewan is at the northern end of the physiographic region known in the United States as the Great Plains. In Canada the district is often called the Prairies. The elevation of East End is about 3,000 feet, and it is very cold in the winter—temperatures far below zero are common. The zone suitable for growing crops does not extend for very many miles to the north. All in all, it is a harsh environment for agriculture, but strains of wheat developed specially for the region's climate have helped farmers to cultivate the land successfully where local conditions are favorable.

Saskatchewan ceased being a territory and became a province within the Dominion of Canada in 1905. The human population was tiny at that time (it is not large now), and the government had enacted generous homestead laws to promote settlement of the vast, empty prairies. The Stegners were among the thousands of hopeful immigrants lured to Saskatchewan by the offer of free farmland.

East End was just getting started as a town when the Stegner family arrived in 1914. A section of the Canadian Pacific Railroad had been completed through the area the previous year, opening up the district to farmers and land speculators. The fledgling community had fewer than 200 residents, dirt streets, and a ragtag assortment of businesses, homes, and shacks. The population was a conglomeration of nationalities and creeds, and these diverse people made a lasting impression on young Wallace. Like George Stegner, most were intent on developing wheat farms, but there was also boastful talk of drilling for oil and mining coal. The possibilities seemed endless, and there was much excitement in the air. East End attracted dreamers, and few of the new settlers were prepared for the realities of life there.

George Stegner rented a place in the town to shelter his family while he built a frame house on a lot he had purchased. The 320-acre homestead he selected was not close to East End but forty miles to the south, on the Montana border. George Stegner was not an experienced farmer, and the land he picked out was not the best cropland available—he had a knack for beginning a project with two strikes against him. He built a cabin on the farm, and during the summer the family stayed there for several days at a time, returning to town for supplies. The boys helped with the farming chores that were within the scope of children their age. It was their job to trap and poison the Richardson's ground squirrels that invaded the fields—no small task because the squirrels reproduced prodigiously. During the long, cold winters, the family stayed in town and the boys attended the one-room elementary school. Wallace thrived on schoolwork and looked forward to the beginning of school each fall.

In his book *Wolf Willow* (1962), Stegner characterized his life in Saskatchewan as that of a "little savage." What he meant was that he and his brother spent much time out-of-doors, engaged in totally unsupervised activities. When they were in town, a five-minute walk took them into an untamed countryside where they were on their own with no adults to restrict their adventures. On the farm, the wilderness began at their doorstep. Although big game was scarce—the bison were long gone and pronghorn antelope were rare—smaller wildlife was abundant. Every boy in town had a .22 rifle, and Cecil Stegner was allowed to use his father's twelve-gauge shotgun at the age of ten. He and Wallace shot ducks on the sloughs now and then, and on rare occasions bagged a sharp-tailed grouse or two on the prairie. In those days every hawk was a "chicken hawk" that needed killing. The boys often roasted a rabbit or duck over a campfire, celebrating their hunting prowess with a feast. These cookabouts were of dubious culinary merit but gave the boys the satisfying feeling of living off the land. During the winter Wallace and Cecil trapped weasels, muskrats, and minks along the river and sold their skins.

George Stegner planted his first wheat crop in the spring of 1915. Conditions were favorable that summer, just the right mix of sun and rain, with no insect outbreaks or damaging storms.

Every farmer in the area had a bumper crop. The war in Europe had pushed wheat prices up, and profits were generous. It was a time of plenty and rejoicing. Rains were heavy in 1916, and although the wheat grew well at first, rust, a disease encouraged by the damp weather, destroyed the Stegners' entire crop. Not a bushel of wheat was harvested. The next three summers were hot and dry, yields were poor, and the Stegners and many other farmers were wiped out. In 1920, George Stegner sold his property in town for a pittance, abandoned his homestead, and took his family back to the United States.

Despite the bleak living conditions and ultimate failure of the farm, Stegner remembered life in Saskatchewan with fondness. His testimony supports the common belief that life in small towns and rural settings can be especially enriching for children, even if that life in a material sense is spartan. However, Stegner knew that the six years of struggle on the Canadian prairie were terribly hard on his mother. He wrote in *Wolf Willow*, "For her sake I have regretted that miserable homestead....But on my own account I would not have missed it—could not have missed it and be who I am" (p. 281). He remembered East End as a town he liked living in, and recalled he was sorry to leave it. He also noted that as an adult he would not live on those windswept plains if you paid him a thousand dollars an hour to do so. For Stegner, southwestern Saskatchewan was "as good a place to be a boy and as unsatisfying a place to be a man as one could well imagine" (p. 306).

Although he was not quite twelve when his father loaded his family into the Ford and drove south across the border into Montana, the time he spent in Saskatchewan left a deep and permanent impression on Stegner. Throughout his life he maintained an interest in Canada and an appreciation for things Canadian. He once remarked that if southern Saskatchewan averaged about two more inches of rainfall per year, he might have remained a Canadian for the rest of his life. Studying the history of the settlement of the Canadian West as well as that of the American West yielded insights to Stegner that were unavailable to most American writers.

Reflecting on his family's activities in Saskatchewan was an exercise in humility for Stegner as he matured and became interested in conservation issues. He had witnessed firsthand the consequences of an unhealthy man-land relationship. The heedless rush to put the prairie to the plow took a heavy toll on the land and the people who worked it. The result was not a prosperous farming community but a ghost town in the midst of a dust bowl. Stegner never minimized his family's culpability in this crime, and expressed his feelings of guilt in *Wolf Willow*: "Because of us, quite a lot of the homestead's soil lies miles downwind. Because of us, Russian thistle and other weeds . . . have filled the old fields and choked out the grass" (p. 273). He observed that they had not been farmers but wheat miners depleting the soil's fertility. The Saskatchewan debacle prevented him from taking a sanctimonious view regarding similar misadventures by others.

Probably because of his farm-boy youth, Stegner was not a purist in his approach to questions regarding the best use of the public lands in the West. To him, rural lifestyles that were based on healthy relationships with the land were perfectly acceptable, even desirable. For example, he did not oppose grazing livestock on the public domain if stocking rates were modest, if grazing was limited to lands that could support it without being degraded, and if lessees did not exert undue influence on land management agencies. Stegner viewed ranching (especially a family operation) as a legitimate activity, but only if healthy native plant communities and wildlife populations were maintained on the range, and if unnatural soil erosion did not result. He realized that the ranching enterprises in the West that met these criteria were not abundant, however, and many areas were simply too arid to be grazed without sustaining damage.

Another rural activity with which Stegner could sympathize was hunting. Whereas he saw little value in trophy hunting, people who hunted and used wildlife in more traditional ways did not offend him, as long as their hunts were sensibly controlled and wildlife populations were not depleted. He later described some of his own youthful assaults on wildlife as "brainless," but he did not feel the need to apologize for them—they were a normal part of growing up on a frontier homestead. His family's failed farm in Saskatchewan taught him that the plow could be more deadly than the gun. Although he gave up his predatory ways, Stegner did not feel that hunting and wildlife conservation were necessarily incompatible. In *Conversations with Wallace Stegner* he noted, "One way to get to know a good deal about wildlife is to hunt it. Obviously that's one of the reasons why hunters and fishermen have very often been close to the conservation movement. . . . They often know the animals better than the people who are trying hard to save them from hunters" (p. 167).

Stegner and the Conservation Movement

Wallace Stegner's writings about the natural environment, about the land in "Stegner country" and the people who use and often abuse it, consistently have a conservationist's point of view. He had an inborn sensitivity to landscapes, to the seasons and weather, to the special light, sounds, and smells that characterized a place. It was natural for him to be saddened and angered when, later in life, he came to realize that much land in the West was carelessly abused.

As a young man Stegner's approach to conservation was much like that of John Wesley Powell, a pioneer geologist and hydrologist he had come to admire. A government scientist who explored the canyon country of eastern Utah in the 1860s and 1870s, Powell fought for the efficient use of land and water in the arid West. He despised the wasteful, reckless schemes of speculators that threatened to dissipate natural resources and squander public capital. However, like most people at that time, he did not see the importance of the West as open space, as a vast reservoir of natural beauty where the human spirit could find inspiration and rejuvenation.

During his years in Cambridge, Stegner became a close friend of Bernard DeVoto, an estab-

lished writer and literary critic who had taught at Harvard in the early 1930s. The two men had much in common. Both were Westerners—DeVoto was born and raised in Utah—and both were deeply interested in the history of the American West. Their views on life and the values they held dear were much alike. DeVoto became something of a mentor to his younger friend, and the two men remained in close contact after Stegner left Harvard in 1945.

For many years, DeVoto wrote an influential opinion column, "The Easy Chair," for *Harper's* magazine. From 1947 until his death in 1955, he devoted many of these columns to conservation issues, particularly efforts by stockmen to gain increased control of public grazing lands in the West. On one occasion Western politicians introduced legislation in Congress that would greatly reduce the authority of the Forest Service to manage grazing on the national forests. DeVoto railed against what he saw as a greedy landgrab by the livestock industry. He pointed out that the proposed law could eventually result in most federal lands going into private and corporate ownership without the full knowledge and approval of the American public. The legislation was defeated, and DeVoto was at least partly responsible. This selfless and spirited campaign by his friend encouraged Stegner to use his own writing skills for similar purposes. His biography of DeVoto, *The Uneasy Chair*, was published in 1974.

Shortly after moving to California in 1945, Stegner joined the Sierra Club. This conservation organization now is well known throughout the country. Then it was a small group based in San Francisco, and most of its members were Californians. John Muir and some of his friends founded the club in 1892 for the primary purpose of fighting for the protection of the scenic wonders of the Sierra Nevada and to save what was left of the redwood forests. In the 1940s, a goodly percentage of the club's members were professionals, academics, and intellectuals.

One of the most dedicated members of the club was David Brower, then an editor at the University of California Press. In 1952, Brower left his job at the press and became the Sierra

Club's executive director. Stegner got to know David Brower well, and the fiery conservationist had a great influence on the scholarly professor. During the next two decades, Brower became the best-known conservation activist in the country.

The two men were brought even closer together in the mid 1950s as a result of a proposal by the U.S. Bureau of Reclamation to build two dams on the Green River in Dinosaur National Monument. The monument, administered by the National Park Service, was located in northeastern Utah, in the heart of Stegner country. The lakes to be formed by the dams would flood Echo Park and the Canyon of Lodore, places of superb natural beauty. Conservationists around the country banded together to fight what they viewed as the opening battle in a war with the dam builders, with the future of the nation's entire system of national parks and monuments at stake. Bernard DeVoto hammered at the dams in some of his last columns, and David Brower enlisted Stegner to edit a book (the text to be written by others) extolling the virtues of the national monument. The book, *This Is Dinosaur: Echo Park Country and Its Magic Rivers*, was published in 1955. The Sierra Club sent copies to every senator and congressman, and to newspaper and magazine editors around the country. This was Stegner's first active participation in a conservation struggle, and his work brought him to the attention of national leaders. Arizona congressman Stewart Udall admired Stegner's writing about the West, and when Udall became secretary of the interior in 1961 he persuaded Stegner to take several months off from teaching to serve as his adviser on conservation matters.

The odious dams in Dinosaur were defeated, but ultimately at great cost. As an alternative to the Dinosaur dams, Congress funded Glen Canyon Dam downstream on the Colorado River, and work on the massive project began immediately. It was completed in 1963. There was some opposition to the dam in Glen Canyon, but it was feeble and ineffective. The area did not have any special park or monument status, and the reclamation juggernaut was very powerful in the 1950s. Conservationists—including Steg-

ner, who was one of the few people who had floated through the canyon—have regretted the inundation of beautiful Glen Canyon ever since.

Stegner continued to write fiction but kept his novels and conservation ideals mostly separate. He explained why in *Conversations with Wallace Stegner*:

> As for conservation, it's a cause. It means joining, it means activism, and I don't think fiction should really have proselytizing as its purpose. Fiction ought to be concerned with the perception of truth, the attempt to get at the concerns of the human heart. It has to do with human relations, and human feelings, and human character, and not with things that you could join. . . . That's probably why I haven't put any outright conservationists into my fiction. (p. 172)

Throughout his later years, Stegner maintained memberships in the Sierra Club and a number of other conservation organizations, both national and local. He lent his support to them whenever he could, and wrote some of the most intelligent essays on conservation ever published. Few worked harder for passage of the Wilderness Act of 1964, and his writings on the value of wilderness were profoundly moving. The nonfiction books discussed below contain these writings and others that illuminate the path we have taken in the settlement and development of "Stegner country." They disclose where we have done things right and, sadly, where we often have behaved irresponsibly. Stegner was a masterful stylist, but the power of his works comes from the fact that he truly loved his subject—the American West.

Beyond the Hundredth Meridian

Prior to publication of *Beyond the Hundredth Meridian* in 1954, John Wesley Powell (1834–1902) was known to Americans primarily as the man who led the first expedition to explore the Grand Canyon by boat. After publication of Stegner's acclaimed biography, Powell was also recognized as one of the most original thinkers ever to study the arid lands of the West.

Stegner described his book as a study of Powell's career, not of his personality. Therefore, the author does not spend much time discussing Powell's childhood or private life. The subject is Powell's work as a public servant, a government scientist of extraordinary competence. What drew Stegner to Powell was not merely his intellect or the fact that he had explored and mapped the canyon country of Stegner's beloved Utah, but his idealism. Stegner saw him as a model government official, a person who put the welfare of the nation ahead of his own career. Powell's is not a story of unqualified success, however; it is also one of failure. His most prescient ideas were ultimately rejected by the politicians he was paid to advise. Readers should approach *Beyond the Hundredth Meridian* not only as a biography but also as a history of the development of federal policy regarding the public lands and water of the West. The effects of these policies are still felt in the region and are at the core of many ongoing environmental and conservation debates. Stegner's thoughts on Powell's life and times are as relevant today as when he published them.

John Wesley Powell was a geology professor at Illinois State Normal University when he led a party of ten men in four wooden boats down the Green and Colorado rivers in 1869 (one man soon left the company and one boat was lost in the Green River). The expedition was funded by the government, but the participants were independent adventurers, not federal employees. When the bedraggled party emerged from the Grand Canyon, they were hailed as heroes and Powell came to the attention of important politicians in Washington. During the 1870s, the one-armed former major (he lost his right arm at the battle of Shiloh during the Civil War) was given the responsibility of supervising additional explorations of the region known as the Colorado Plateau. In 1879, all of the various federal surveys and mapping programs being conducted in the West were placed under a single new bureau, the U.S. Geological Survey. Powell became the second director of the agency in 1881

and was the person who built it into a respected scientific organization. He resigned as director of the Geological Survey in 1894.

In Stegner's view, Powell's most impressive achievements as a thinker were not in the field of geology but in the ideas contained in his *Report on the Lands of the Arid Region of the United States*, which he presented to the secretary of the interior in 1878. Powell understood as few of his contemporaries did that the essential fact of the West, those lands lying beyond the hundredth meridian, was aridity. The settlement and development of the West would be ruled by a scarcity of water, and irrigation systems and water management policies would determine the region's future, for good or for ill. Powell was the first to enunciate these truths, and Stegner was the first to give him full credit for doing so.

The recommendations in Powell's report were revolutionary. He had been impressed with the success of Mormon farming settlements that he had visited in Utah and used them as something of a model. The Mormons placed a priority on cooperative community efforts, much more so than was common in the East. Powell became convinced that the local political institutions and land and water laws that worked well in the humid East had to be discarded. Totally new governing bodies designed around the special demands of an arid environment needed to be created. Laws ensuring equitable water distribution had to be passed. To facilitate sensible water management, Powell recommended that political boundaries in the West be drawn to coincide with drainage basins. The rivers of the West should be carefully studied by experts and the best sites for storage dams identified. Lands suitable for irrigation should be inventoried and water delivery systems designed. Much to the consternation of boosters of the West, Powell urged that the homestead laws then in place be scrapped and a new, conservative system for carefully parceling out only federal lands deemed to be suitable for farming or stock raising be instituted. Powell's method was to go slowly, study the situation thoroughly, and plan for the long term.

Powell's goal was the efficient use of both the West's water resources and federal dollars. As a responsible public servant, he could not sit by and see them needlessly squandered. The myth that the American frontier was a Garden of Eden had to be debunked, and scientific assessments of its agricultural potential needed to be made. To allow unrealistic homestead laws and reckless boosters to lure thousands of settlers onto parched acres where they had no hope of success would be to participate in a cruel hoax. He argued that viable communities with adequate water supplies, places where people could prosper and reach their full potential, were what the government should strive to foster. Places where such communities could be developed were few in the arid regions and had to be selected with care.

Over the next decade, Powell battled to convince Congress to adopt his plans and had some successes. In 1888 his irrigation survey of Western rivers was authorized, and the public domain was temporarily closed to homesteaders soon after. However, Western politicians dedicated to rapid growth at any cost were outraged by the moratorium and quickly took the offensive. Within months the public domain was reopened to settlers and, as an additional rebuke, Powell's budget was slashed. His influence greatly diminished, Powell resigned from the Geological Survey a few years later. These were some of the main features of Powell's career. In his biography, Stegner deftly analyzed their significance, and explored the cultural and political climate that brought Powell to prominence and subsequently defeated him.

Readers should keep in mind that John Wesley Powell was not a conservationist in the modern sense of the term. He felt that every drop of water in the West should be put to practical use, and did not consider or appreciate the costs to wildlife or natural beauty. The U.S. Bureau of Reclamation, the dam-building agency with which conservationists have been at odds so often, was created by Congress in 1902 in fulfillment of some of Powell's recommendations. As he should, Stegner judged Powell by the standards of his time and against his contemporaries. Because of this and because it was thoroughly researched and beautifully written, *Beyond the Hundredth Meridian* remains a great book.

Wolf Willow

A portion of Wallace Stegner's 1943 novel *The Big Rock Candy Mountain* describes life in a small town in Saskatchewan in the early 1900s. Clearly based on his own early experiences, the novel deals with the complex world of family relationships. In his 1962 book *Wolf Willow* (named for a shrub that grows on the northern plains), Stegner examined southwestern Saskatchewan as a physical place, and explored the history of the people who have been drawn to its grassy sweeps. It is a fascinating study of what people have done to the region, and what it has done to them. The lessons to be learned from taking a close look at this small piece of a Canadian province have universal applications. The book is both history and autobiography because Stegner himself participated in a chapter of the region's story.

Like his biography of John Wesley Powell, *Wolf Willow* required considerable historical research. However, although some of his admirers might disagree, Stegner never considered himself a historian. He was a dedicated student of the history of the West but was not confined by a formal, academic approach to the subject. In the early chapters of *Wolf Willow*, Stegner follows the successive waves of invaders who fought with and eventually displaced the Indians native to the region: explorers, trappers, bison hunters, stockmen, and homesteaders like his father. The early stockmen and farmers ultimately failed, defeated by cold and drought, and the author examines the messages their mistakes have for us. Stegner explores the puzzling question of why his father and many like him foolishly tried to farm unsuitable land. He is convinced that answer lay in their belief in the popular myth that the West was a land of milk and honey where fortunes were easily made. Stegner notes that modern versions of this myth are still believed by some.

In one chapter of the book Stegner uses fiction to illustrate the harsh realities of raising cattle in such a climate. The device works well. What could be a dry listing of the number of cows that were lost during the terrible winter of 1906–1907, and of the number of ranchers who were devastated by the loss, becomes a compelling story that gives meaning to such a catastrophe. Not many writers could make such an unconventional approach work.

In preparation for writing *Wolf Willow*, Stegner traveled to Saskatchewan in 1953 and visited the little town of East End, where he had spent six years of his youth. Memories came flooding back as he walked along the streets and lanes he had not seen for thirty-three years. There were some reminders of the old days—he even ran into some people who had been in East End when the Stegners lived there. Of course, there were many changes and some signs of modest prosperity, but the population was still far less than a thousand people. He had the feeling that the prairie hamlet had not achieved a nourishing cultural life, but was encouraged to note that its residents were bravely striving to do so. Stegner wove many stories from his own childhood into his narrative, and these add special poignancy to the book. He visited what had been the Stegners' homestead and found the fields had gone back to grass. It was obvious that the grass did not grow as luxuriantly there as on adjacent areas that had never been farmed. Damage inflicted on arid land can take a long time to heal.

The Sound of Mountain Water

Stegner was a brilliant essayist—his best essays have the charm and vigor of well-crafted short stories. However, the periodicals in which such works are published are ephemeral. No matter how fine the writing in them may be, they soon are found only in library archives. It is therefore a boon to readers when authors of exceptional ability rescue their best magazine and journal articles from obscurity and publish them in book form. *The Sound of Mountain Water* (1969) is just such a collection. It includes fourteen essays written from 1946 to 1967.

The subject of the essays collected in *The Sound of Mountain Water* is the West, both as a tangible entity and as an idea, an abstraction with special meaning for Americans. The book is divided into two parts. The first contains Stegner's thoughts about the land—the mountains and forests, the rivers and canyons, the plains—and its beauty and fragility. Part II is dedicated to writing and Western literature. In these essays Stegner discusses the impact of the West on writers and analyzes the works of some of his favorite authors. Part I contains the essays that most qualify as nature writing.

Stegner was interested in subjects of broad significance and usually avoided trendy topics of no lasting importance. As a result, his early nonfiction has much to say of relevance to present-day Americans. Not that he did not change his mind over time—he was always reassessing his ideas. In "The Rediscovery of America: 1946," an account of a trip by car through "Stegner country," he told how thrilled he was when he first saw Hoover Dam on the Colorado River. He described it as a "sweeping cliff of concrete," and he admired what he then saw as its "efficient beauty." Like most people at that time, he applauded the growth that the water and power provided by the engineering marvel was bringing to the region. However, in a few years his attitude changed. He realized that dam building in the West had become a pleurisy and that "growth" came at a terribly high price. In "Glen Canyon Submersus," an essay written twenty years after he first admired Hoover Dam, he reflected with great sadness on the submerging of Glen Canyon under Lake Powell. He had floated through Glen Canyon before the Bureau of Reclamation arrived on the scene, and knew something more magnificent than any dam had been lost.

In 1964, the U.S. Congress passed the Wilderness Act. The law mandated that the national forests and other public lands be inventoried for roadless tracts suitable for preservation as wilderness. The act gave lands previously set aside as wildernesses by the Forest Service legal protection. All of this capped many years of hard work by conservationists around the country. Stegner came to believe that wilderness was profoundly important to our national well-being and that its preservation was essential. In a letter written in 1960, he expressed his feelings on the matter to a government official involved in the tedious hearings and debates that are part of the lawmaking process. The lengthy letter is reproduced in *The Sound of Mountain Water.* Whether the bureaucrat was moved by its eloquence cannot be known, but any modern reader who loves the backcountry will find Stegner's observations on wilderness as powerful now as when they were written. Here is an excerpt from his letter:

> We need wilderness preserved — as much of it as is still left, and as many kinds — because it was the challenge against which our character as a people was formed. The reminder and the reassurance that it is still there is good for our spiritual health even if we never once in ten years set foot in it. It is good for us when we are young, because of the incomparable sanity it can bring briefly, as vacation and rest, into our insane lives. It is important to us when we are old simply because it is there — important, that is, simply as idea. (p. 147)

American Places

The collection of essays titled *American Places* features the talents of both Wallace Stegner and his son, Page. Eight of the thirteen chapters are by Wallace Stegner, four by Page Stegner, and one is a combined effort. Some of the chapters in *American Places* were first published in periodicals, but many were written specially for the book, published in 1981. Those by Wallace Stegner are the product of a person able to reflect on his favorite landscapes with the perspective that only decades of thought can produce. Rural America is the subject, and only those places the authors know and love well are addressed. By examining small pieces of North America, Wallace and Page Stegner disclose the larger picture of how we are treating our once-virgin continent.

Vermont is the subject of a chapter by Wallace Stegner titled "The Northeast Kingdom." He and his wife bought a summer home in Greensboro, Vermont, in 1939, and over the decades came to know the region well. It was the one state east of the Great Plains where Stegner truly felt at home. The approach to life of the rural people there seemed to him to be much different from that of the people who lived in the West. They did not have a frontier get-rich-quick mentality, the culture of growth was poorly developed among them, and boosters were not held in high esteem. Vermonters farmed, harvested trees in the forest, hunted, and fished, but did not abuse the land. They seemed to know in their bones the difference between use and exploitation. The farms and forests they passed down from one generation to the next were fertile and rich with wildlife, not depleted and sterile. Stegner felt that much could be learned about how to use land wisely from the people of this green New England state.

"Crow Country" by Wallace Stegner is a gem. It is an assessment of the ranching culture of southwestern Montana, and includes both history and personal observations. Over the years Stegner had become acquainted with a number of ranching families in the area, responsible people who wanted to do right by the land. During the 1970s making a profit was becoming increasingly difficult for small stock outfits, and the pressure to sell out to corporations and real estate developers was strong. Like the Crow Indians before them, the ranchers were gradually being dispossessed, and the future of Crow country was in doubt. Stegner was distressed by the prospect of Montana rangeland passing into indifferent corporate ownership, but he found no easy solution to the problem.

In "High Plateaus" Wallace Stegner pondered the future of his beloved southeastern Utah, the canyon and plateau country first surveyed by John Wesley Powell. The dam builders, having flooded Glen Canyon, were no longer actively promoting new projects, but fumes from coal-fired power plants were a threat to the region. National parks now gave the canyons upstream from Lake Powell much-needed protection.

However, they attracted tourists by the thousands, and pressure to build new roads through the backcountry was growing. Stegner found Utah's wildness and natural beauty under siege but not defeated.

There is much rich reading in this handsome, large-format book that is lavishly illustrated with photographs by Eliot Porter. It is no trivial coffee-table book, however; the writing is even more beautiful than the color photos. Page Stegner's chapters are also worthy contributions. He has followed his father's path as a writer, teacher, and lover of wild country.

One Way to Spell Man

The essays in *One Way to Spell Man* (1982) span three decades of Stegner's career as a contributor to magazines and journals. Most are devoted to writing, writers, and American culture, not natural history. The book deserves mention here because it contains an elegant essay titled "The Gift of Wilderness." Written in 1981, it surveys the history of the wilderness preservation movement and gives the author's appraisal of the importance of wilderness to Americans, from the earliest explorers to his own grandchildren.

Thinking back many decades, Stegner remembers his own first taste of wildness, one that grew in significance as his understanding grew and matured:

In June 1915 my father took my brother and me with him in the wagon across fifty miles of unpeopled prairie to build a house on our homestead. . . . Night overtook us, and we camped on the trail. Five gaunt coyotes watched us eat supper, and later serenaded us. I went to sleep to their music. Then in the night I awoke, not knowing where I was. Strangeness flowed around me; there was a current of cool air, a whispering, a loom of darkness overhead. In panic I reared up on my elbow and found that I was sleeping beside my brother under the wagon, and that a night wind was breathing across me through the

spokes of the wheel. It came from unimaginably far places, across a vast emptiness, below millions of polished stars. And yet its touch was soft, intimate, and reassuring, and my panic went away at once. That wind knew me. I knew it. Every once in a while, sixty-six years after that baptism in space and night and silence, wind across grassland can smell like that to me, as secret, perfumed, and soft, and tell me who I am. (pp. 175–176)

Wallace Stegner concluded his essay on the value of wilderness with these thoughts: "We need to learn to listen to the land, hear what it says, understand what it can and can't do over the long haul; what, especially in the West, it should not be asked to do. To learn such things, we have to have access to natural wild land" (p. 177).

Conversations with Wallace Stegner on Western History and Literature

In 1980 and 1981, writer and scholar Richard W. Etulain conducted a series of ten interviews with Wallace Stegner. He recorded their conversations, and transcribed and edited them into a remarkable book published in 1983. Most of the words in the book are Stegner's, and he is listed as coauthor. The subject of their talks was Stegner himself and his literary works, as well as his views on other writers, history, American culture, and, of course, the West, past, present, and future. Fans of Stegner's books will find these conversations fascinating.

One of Stegner's strengths was that he knew his limitations and stayed within his zone of expertise. He was a modest man, despite all the honors he received during his career, and did not have an exaggerated opinion of his talents. When talking about himself, he emphasized his mistakes more than his triumphs. Stegner knew full well that one learns more from mistakes than from successes. The fact that the United States as a nation has not yet learned to use land wisely despite the lessons of past blunders saddened him and inspired much of his nature writing. Nevertheless, Stegner was not a pessimist and felt lucky to be American, especially one who grew up and lived most of his life in the West. A revised edition of the book, which includes a new chapter in which Stegner gives his thoughts on the 1980s, was published in 1990.

Where the Bluebird Sings to the Lemonade Springs

Where the Bluebird Sings (1992) was the last book of Stegner's to be published during his lifetime (posthumous publication of other writings is, of course, a possibility). It is a fitting final statement by one of our great writers. A collection of essays and lectures produced during his last decade, it covers many subjects and is divided into three parts. The chapters in part I are autobiographical. Part II is devoted to the arid West, its history, its literature, its present land-use problems, and its prospects for the future. Part III concerns writing and writers whom Stegner admired.

Could Stegner find something new to say about the West after writing about it for a lifetime? Yes, because the West is always changing. In the essays in part II of this collection, Stegner summarizes the history of land use and water management in the West, examines the present situation and possible future trends, and attacks the myth of the wild "cowboy" West that often distorts our thinking. He observes that Americans still have not learned to live with aridity, and continue to fight it, to the detriment of the land and its people. Large additions have been made to the wilderness system, and all conservationists can take satisfaction in this. Yet poorly managed urban sprawl and rapid population growth are eroding the West's greatest resources—open space and natural beauty. Stegner reminds us that despite notable conservation achievements, those who love the West and its wild, unspoiled places must never become complacent.

Selected Bibliography

WORKS OF WALLACE STEGNER

NOVELS

Remembering Laughter (Boston: Little, Brown, 1937); *The Potter's House* (Muscatine, Iowa: Prairie, 1938); *On a Darkling Plain* (New York: Harcourt, 1940); *Fire and Ice* (New York: Duell, Sloan and Pearce, 1941); *The Big Rock Candy Mountain* (New York: Duell, Sloan and Pearce, 1941; repr., Lincoln: Univ. of Nebraska Press, 1983, and New York: Viking Penguin, 1991); *Second Growth* (Boston: Houghton Mifflin, 1947; repr., Lincoln: Univ. of Nebraska Press, 1985); *The Preacher and the Slave* (Boston: Houghton Mifflin, 1950), repr. as *Joe Hill* (Garden City, N.Y.: Doubleday, 1969; repr., New York: Viking Penguin, 1990); *A Shooting Star* (New York: Viking, 1961); *All the Little Live Things* (New York: Viking, 1967; repr., New York: Viking Penguin, 1991); *Angle of Repose* (Garden City, N.Y.: Doubleday, 1971; repr., New York: Viking Penguin, 1992); *The Spectator Bird* (Garden City, N.Y.: Doubleday, 1976; repr., Lincoln: Univ. of Nebraska Press, 1979, and New York: Viking Penguin, 1990); *Recapitulation* (Garden City, N.Y.: Doubleday, 1979; repr., Lincoln: Univ. of Nebraska Press, 1986); *Crossing to Safety* (New York: Random House, 1987; repr., New York: Viking Penguin, 1990).

COLLECTED SHORT FICTION

The Women on the Wall (Boston: Houghton Mifflin, 1950; repr., Lincoln: Univ. of Nebraska Press, 1981); *The City of the Living, and Other Stories* (Boston: Houghton Mifflin, 1956); *Collected Stories of Wallace Stegner* (New York: Random House, 1990; repr., New York: Viking Penguin, 1991).

NONFICTION BOOKS

Mormon Country (New York: Bonanza, 1942; repr., Lincoln: Univ. of Nebraska Press, 1981); *One Nation* (Boston: Houghton Mifflin, 1945), with the editors of *Look* magazine; *Beyond the Hundredth Meridian: John Wesley Powell and the Second Opening of the West* (Boston: Houghton Mifflin, 1954; repr., New York: Viking Penguin, 1992); *This Is Dinosaur: Echo Park Country and Its Magic Rivers* (New York: Knopf, 1955; repr., Boulder, Colo.: Roberts Rinehart, 1985), Stegner as editor; *Wolf Willow: A History, a Story, and a Memory of the Last Plains Frontier* (New York: Viking, 1962; repr., Lincoln: Univ. of Nebraska Press, 1980, and New York: Viking Penguin, 1990); *The Gathering of Zion: The Story of the Mormon Trail* (New York: McGraw-Hill, 1964; repr., Lincoln: Univ. of Nebraska Press, 1992); *The Uneasy Chair: A Biog-*

raphy of Bernard DeVoto (Garden City, N.Y.: Doubleday, 1974; repr., Salt Lake City: Peregrine Smith, 1989); *The Letters of Bernard DeVoto* (Garden City, N.Y.: Doubleday, 1975), Stegner as editor; *Conversations with Wallace Stegner on Western History and Literature* (Salt Lake City: University of Utah Press, 1983; rev. ed., 1990), with Richard W. Etulain.

COLLECTED ESSAYS

The Sound of Mountain Water (Garden City, N.Y.: Doubleday, 1969; repr., New York: Dutton, 1980, and Lincoln: Univ. of Nebraska Press, 1985); *American Places*, ed. by John Macrae III (New York: Dutton, 1981; repr., Moscow: Univ. of Idaho Press, 1983), written with Page Stegner, with photographs by Eliot Porter; *One Way to Spell Man* (Garden City, N.Y.: Doubleday, 1982); *The American West as Living Space* (Ann Arbor: Univ. of Michigan Press, 1987; repr. as part of *Where the Bluebird Sings*); *Where the Bluebird Sings to the Lemonade Springs: Living and Writing in the West* (New York: Random House, 1992; repr., New York: Viking Penguin, 1993).

BIOGRAPHICAL AND CRITICAL STUDIES

Anthony Arthur, ed., *Critical Essays on Wallace Stegner* (Boston: G. K. Hall, 1982); Nancy Colberg, *Wallace Stegner: A Descriptive Bibliography* (Lewiston, Idaho: Confluence, 1990); David Dillon, *Wallace Stegner: An Interview* (Dallas: New London, 1978); Merrill Lewis and Lorene Lewis, *Wallace Stegner* (Boise, Idaho: Boise State College, 1972); Forrest G. Robinson and Margaret G. Robinson, *Wallace Stegner* (Boston: Twayne, 1977).

GENE STRATTON PORTER
(1863–1924)

SYDNEY LANDON PLUM

WHERE GENE STRATTON PORTER made her life a determined, headlong charge toward a constant goal, critics and commentators of the twentieth century have stumbled, grumbled, or turned away, faced with what they have seen as the contradictory impulses of her many-faceted career. There has been a tendency to treat the novelist and the naturalist as a literary Mr. Hyde and Dr. Jekyll. Critical attention to the novels has tended to be dismissive, and study of the nature writing sparse. Even Paul Brooks's 1980 article in *Audubon*, "Birds and Women," uses the novels, not the nonfiction works, to compare Stratton Porter's work with that of ornithologists Olive Thorne Miller, Mabel Osgood Wright, and Florence Merriam Bailey. Gene Stratton Porter's practice was to hyphenate her maiden and married names. However, in the years since her death, it has become bibliographic practice to drop the hyphen.

Stratton Porter was a gifted storyteller who used episodes from her life and the lives of family members as starting points for her famous early novels. In later life, she wrote autobiographical sketches that may have been embellishments of the truth, but the image she provided of the natural world was never distorted. One can view her life—marked by the manic construction of a series of beautiful homes—and her work—with its alternating series of sentimental novels and nature studies grounded in years of careful study of her surroundings—as interdependent parts of a whole. The houses and the books both depended upon successive, intense, intimate relationships to a home. Her life and her works are as closely related as the birds and moths of the Limberlost Swamp, the blue-eyed grass and sycamore trees of Sylvan Lake, the dry grasses and turbulent waters of coastal southern California.

The Popular Author

Gene Stratton Porter died of injuries sustained in an automobile accident on 6 December 1924. At the time of her death she had published ten novels, seven books of nature writing, two book-length poems, two children's books, and a myriad of essays. Another long poem, "Euphorbia," had been serialized. She had overseen the screen writing for and production of two motion pictures based on her novels—for which she had formed her own production company—and was working on a third. Two novels—*The Keeper of the Bees* and *The Magic Garden*—and two essay collections—*Tales You Won't Believe* and *Let Us Highly Resolve*—would appear posthumously. She was a dedicated letter writer, as well. Although several of the nature books are slightly edited versions of previously published material, this is a prodigious output.

Her death was widely mourned. Yet today it is difficult to find copies of her books in print. The potential worth of Gene Stratton Porter as a naturalist and nature writer has continued to be overshadowed, if not totally obscured, by the popularity and financial success of her early novels. Even with the decline in sales after her seventh novel for adults *Michael O'Halloran* (1915), Stratton Porter continued to be an enormously popular and influential writer. Her fiction sold well enough to support her nature writing, the building projects, and an extended family. She wrote novels primarily in order to share with others the remarkable benefits of a life in tune with the natural world, to inspire in others something of the wonder she felt in her almost daily contact with the elements.

Keeper of the Bees (1925) was dictated by Stratton Porter to a secretary as she lay in a hammock among the flowers, butterflies, and hummingbirds at the vacation home she had recently built on Catalina Island. By contrast, the early work had been written out in longhand during the stolen hours available to the mother of a young child, the wife of a prominent banker. The settings of the novels, which were usually written during the winter and delivered to her publisher in the spring—to leave her free for nature studies and photography during the remainder of the year—are reliable indicators of the movements of Stratton Porter's life. The nature writings, which were the culmination of years of fieldwork, seem almost eulogies for lives and places now lost forever under the bulldozers of American social progress. However, the natural world is not simply a setting for the novels. Stratton Porter wrote so vividly of place, envisioned her stories in such a way, that the setting itself becomes a character.

Early Years and the Limberlost

Gene Stratton Porter's first six novels are set along the Wabash River and in the Limberlost Swamp: her particular stamping ground. Geneva Grace Stratton was born on 17 August 1863, the youngest of twelve children born to Mary Schallenberger and Mark Stratton on their large and fairly prosperous farm in northeast Indiana. When Geneva was a toddler, her mother became seriously ill with typhoid, and was never completely well again. Geneva, loosely supervised by her older siblings and father, spent her childhood wandering around out-of-doors. She remembered that she had often napped under a fence post while her father and brothers worked the fields. Her mother was a gifted gardener and herbalist, and seems to have passed on the gift to her youngest child, who had her own garden into which she transplanted all manner of interesting flowers and herbs she found in her meandering.

A headstrong child, she was upset when her father and brothers killed the birds that ate the orchard fruits or threatened the poultry, and tried in various ways to intervene on behalf of the birds. She wore her father down, and in a gesture that probably shaped her entire life, he gave over to her the care of all the birds who nested on the farm. Thus she began a lifetime of locating birds' nests, developing their trust, learning their songs and habits, feeding them, caring for their injuries (including adopting birds too injured to live in the wild)—all of which contributed to her success in photographing and making written records of birds in their natural habitat.

In 1872 a string of personal and financial hardships added to the strain of Mary Stratton's failing health, and by 1874 the family had moved to the town of Wabash. For the next thirteen years, Geneva Stratton lived there, in boardinghouses, with relatives, or in the small, dark house to which her husband took her at their marriage. She did not have a garden, and she was able to have her pet birds only for the first few years in town. Her adventures in the natural world were limited to her brief, summer visits to the chautauquas on Sylvan Lake, about sixty miles to the Northwest, where, in 1884, she attracted the attention of Charles Dorwin Porter, then thirty-four and a successful druggist. Mr. Porter, as she continued to call him for years, initiated a correspondence with her. Her sprightly letters, in which she invented the lovers "Gene" and "Mr. Porter," won him over completely, and they were married on 21 April 1886. Their daughter, Jeannette, was born in August 1887.

With her idyllic childhood, it is small wonder that Stratton Porter committed herself early in her married life to creating the best rural nest possible for herself. First she persuaded Charles to move them to a house in Geneva, Indiana, with a sizable garden. Then in 1894, after a trip to the Chicago Exposition, they began building the home called "Limberlost Cabin" just off the main street of Geneva, near the Wabash River. Modeled after the Foresters Building at the Exposition, the cabin has a log exterior and a gracious, Victorian-style interior. This magnificent house was possible due to Charles's business acumen—he had started a bank by then—and Gene's drive.

In 1895, with her new home completed, Gene began serious ornithological studies. An early article was rejected because she lacked illustrations, and she refused to use pictures of dead birds. For Christmas 1895, Jeannette and Charles gave her her first camera. Charles was able to get the developing chemicals easily and cheaply through his drugstore, and through diligent practice and experimentation, Stratton Porter invented her own techniques for creating her lifelike photographs. In 1900, her articles started appearing in *Recreation* and *Outing* magazines. From February 1900 through May 1901, Stratton Porter wrote the column "Camera Notes" for *Recreation*, receiving equipment as compensation.

In 1901, her short story based on a childhood experience of her brother Laddie was published in the *Metropolitan Magazine*. Stratton Porter delighted in telling of the acceptance of this piece, which she acknowledged as her first published story. In her biography of Stratton Porter, Judith Reick Long makes the case that she had written and had published anonymously another anthropomorphic story of animals before *The Song of the Cardinal*. This story, "The Strike at Shane's," was entered in a competition sponsored by the American Humane Society in 1892,

which required that all entries be anonymous.[1] The story did not win a prize, but was so liked by the chairman of the Humane Society and one of the judges that it was published later—billed as "a sequel to Black Beauty" because a horse is the protagonist. Stratton Porter never acknowledged authorship of this story, although she did sometimes refer to earlier, lost works.

In later writings, Stratton Porter told of falling asleep at night while sitting on her father's lap, her head against his chest, as he read the Bible or told his stories. Other evidence supports her claim that her father was a great storyteller, and she was aware at an early age that she had inherited, or absorbed, his gift—and that it could be used to her advantage. Toward the end of her rather undistinguished school career, Stratton Porter was given the assignment of preparing a paper on mathematical law for oral presentation before the school and parents. She was incapable of comprehending the material, but she was at the time enthralled with an Italian novel one of her sisters had allowed her to read, *Picciola* by Xavier Boniface Saintine. She prepared a review of the novel for her presentation.

She began speaking, and was soon interrupted by the principal, who asked her to wait while he fetched the superintendent. Stratton Porter, assuming the worst, stood her ground; when the two returned, she was asked to begin again. Her substitute program was well received. Reflecting on this experience later, in an essay entitled "What My Father Meant to Me," she wrote of realizing that "I might be able to bring to others beauty that I had learned for myself; I might teach to others what I had been taught of persistence, patience. . . . I would reach my goal through the satisfaction of a something in my soul that would make things possible to me through my own effort."

Her first novel, *The Song of the Cardinal*, was published in 1903. Although its close and careful observation of the habits and habitat of the cardinal, straightforward style, and lifelike illus-

1. Reprinted by Judith R. Long Antiquarian Books, Marietta, Ga., 1984.

trations might almost lead it to be considered an early example of her nature books, this work is classed as a novel because of its anthropomorphic portrayal of the courtship and mating of a pair of cardinals. This treatment, although critically disparaged then and now, is tempered by the realism of Stratton Porter's descriptions. The cardinals do not have names, nor are they given dialogue or thoughts unsuitable to their natural activities (they think about food and worry about predators), and when several of their young die before maturing enough to leave the nest, there is no great rise in the emotional tenor. Wildlife and natural setting are portrayed with the clarity and understanding made possible by a deep and immediate knowledge.

Stratton Porter did not continue in this genre. Her next novel, which followed closely in 1904, was the story of a young, one-armed orphan guarding the valuable timber of the Limberlost Swamp. *Freckles*, usually listed as a book for juveniles, is now considered something of a minor classic. However, it took three years to catch on with the public. Stratton Porter did not sit around and wait; she worked on a series of articles on birds and wrote her next novel, *At the Foot of the Rainbow*, which was published in 1907. Critics both then and now prefer this novel to *Freckles*. It also depicts an outdoor life, but less sentimentally. In 1909, Stratton Porter published the novel that continued the story of the great Limberlost Swamp begun in *Freckles*, the story that made her famous in her own time and kept her name, and to a certain extent her other works, alive to readers: *A Girl of the Limberlost*. Her next, best-selling novel, *The Harvester* (1911), was also set in the Limberlost.

Creating Wildflower Woods

The Limberlost Swamp was Gene Stratton Porter's outdoor home: it was the natural world she studied and photographed and wrote about, the source of her inspiration. Along with the Wabash River and its banks, the swamp was the background for her childhood and most of her married life. However, by 1912 the clearing of the Limberlost Swamp for lumber and to make way for oil drilling had progressed to the point where the old swamp was nearly gone. Stratton Porter had continued to visit Sylvan Lake, near Rome City, Indiana, during the summer, and in 1912 she purchased a cottage there. The cottage was only a toehold. By the end of the summer she had purchased a large piece of lakefront property and begun building what would become Wildflower Woods. The next novel was set in Stratton Porter's past, at Hopewell Farm, her home before the Limberlost cabin. *Laddie* (1913) was primarily autobiographical and chronicled the further adventures of Gene's beloved brother, who drowned when he was a young man.

The creation of Wildflower Woods, into which she moved in 1914, was an enormous undertaking. Stratton Porter envisioned it as not only her home but also as a sanctuary for the wildlife and native flowers fast disappearing from the Indiana she had known as a child. Wildflowers were set in beds by color, radiating outward from the cabin. Of the more than fourteen thousand botanical specimens represented, nearly all were planted by Stratton Porter. She hired Frank Wallace, a tree surgeon who later became the Indiana state entomologist, to direct conservation efforts and the work of a corps of men. Later she had the help of Bill Thompson, a young man whose departure for the war she took very much to heart. By 1915, several acres of wildflowers were established, and Stratton Porter had written another novel, *Michael O'Halloran*. This novel attempts to depict something of city life, in order to point up the benefits of the country, but the author's work in this regard proved unsuccessful.

In 1917, Stratton Porter was stricken with poison ivy, and a movie, with which she was not pleased, was made of *Freckles*, and war raged abroad. Yet by the spring of 1918, continuing her rhythm of writing during the winter and delivering a manuscript in time to get outside when the weather allowed, she had written the novel some consider her best, *A Daughter of the Land*. Set in a rural Indiana of large-scale farms, *Daughter of the Land* tells of the struggles of Kate Bates to acquire on her own the same amount of acreage granted by her wealthy father to each of her brothers. *Daughter of the Land* did not do as well as earlier novels, however. Also in 1918, Stratton Porter's daughter was going through a painful divorce from her husband, an alcoholic and drug abuser. Wildflower Woods, which had been intended as a retreat for herself as well as a refuge for the birds, was constantly overrun by visitors and tourists, who picnicked on the banks of the lake—leaving their litter and often destroying flower beds. Many came up to the house, expecting admittance. Stratton Porter never turned away anyone with a sick or injured bird or animal, and she did not want to turn away others. Yet these visitors interrupted her work, took mementos from the house, and published fabricated descriptions of their visits and the contents of her home. In 1918, Stratton Porter went east to a sanitorium in upstate New York for a complete checkup and rest. She was fifty-four. Assured of her good health and with her boundless energy restored, she returned home after a month. But the winter of 1918–1919 was the winter of the great flu epidemic, and Stratton Porter began to look for a healthier, happier place to be. She had many relatives in and around Los Angeles, so she went for a visit.

By the middle of 1919 Stratton Porter had settled affairs in Indiana. She established trusts for her sisters Florence and Ada, and, having sold all her Indiana real estate except Wildflower Woods, set up housekeeping in a bungalow in Los Angeles. The next year Jeannette's divorce was final, so she brought Jeannette and her two granddaughters to Los Angeles, buying a large colonial house with a garden containing over seventy varieties of roses. Charles, still running his business, continued to spend at least part of the year in Indiana visiting his family during the winter.

California

In Los Angeles, Gene Stratton Porter belonged to a community for the first time. Her new friends included the financier Charles Brown and his wife, Helen; Edward Sheriff Curtis, the famous photographer; Charles Lummis, scientific authority and librarian; and the artist Jack Wilkinson Smith. She had always been outside the narrowly described social circles of Geneva and Rome City, Indiana, where people did not really know what to do with a middle-aged woman who spent most of her time dressed in drab pants, toting heavy photographic equipment through swamps and up and down ladders. Southern California was still undeveloped and unspoiled, a paradise of different plants and birds for her to know.

In 1921 she published the novel *Her Father's Daughter*, which was set in southern California. The plant lore for the book had been supplied by her nephew-in-law, James Sweetser Lawshe, to whom the book is dedicated. In the fall of 1921 she formed an alliance with Thomas Ince, who had the film rights to *Michael O'Halloran* and options on five other novels. The director chosen for these projects was James Leo Meehan, an actor and journalist whom Gene liked and trusted (and who married Jeannette in 1922). *Freckles* had been filmed by Paramount in 1921, and Stratton Porter was not pleased with the movie. With Ince and Meehan, the author formed Gene Stratton Porter Productions, which filmed *Michael O'Halloran* in 1923 and *A Girl of the Limberlost* in 1924. After the author's death, the production company re-formed as Film Booking Offices and brought out films based on *The Keeper of the Bees* (1925), *Laddie* (1926), *The Harvester* (1927), *The Magic Garden* (1927), and *Freckles* (1928).

She had begun writing columns on homemaking for *McCall's* at the request of Harry Burton, the magazine's editor. She had always wanted to write poetry, and in rapid succession wrote three long narrative poems. *The Fire Bird*, inspired by Curtis' photographs of Native Americans, was published in book form in 1922. In 1923, "Euphorbia" was serialized in *Good Housekeeping* and *Jesus of the Emerald* was published. She had purchased land on Catalina Island for a vacation home and cottage that were completed early in 1924. There she dictated the novel *Keeper of the Bees*. Much of her last year was spent overseeing the construction of Floraves — her hillside home for "the flowers and the birds" in Bel Air — but she died before it was finished.

Naturalist as Novelist

Gene Stratton Porter wrote fiction in order to write about the natural world. Early in her career as a writer it became clear to her that fiction would have a much wider readership than the pieces she was contributing to *Recreation* and *Outing* magazines. She wanted people to see the birds and moths, the whole ecology of the Limberlost Swamp, as she saw them. Thus, her first novel was a bird's story. The novel *Freckles* grew out of an encounter Gene and Charles had with a vulture chick. Elnora, the girl of the Limberlost, is steeped in the knowledge of moths; David Langston, the harvester, in the study of medicinal herbs. Throughout the novels are scattered passages that describe the setting, the birds and their songs, the moths and their colors, the varieties of bees, and the flowers to which each species is attracted. There are passages that explain the delicate balance of the whole, and the benefit to humanity of maintaining the balance.

In nearly every novel there is an example of how a healthy regime of outdoor living repairs the sick. These passages on medicinal cures, physical workouts, vitamin cures obtained through proper diet, and water and mud baths show her to have been an early forerunner of Euell Gibbons and Adele Davis. That Stratton Porter's knowledge of the medicinal uses of plants was accurate is evidenced by Ruth R. Mann's article "Botanical Remedies from Gene Stratton Porter's *The Harvester*."

Stratton Porter espoused a life harmonious with the natural world for reasons beyond nature's salubriousness. She was convinced that there were moral lessons in the stories of the birds and moths, and the people who lived, gently and wisely, among them. David Langston, the Harvester, says about living in the woods: "You not only discover miracles and marvels in them, you not only trace evolution and origin of species, but you get the greatest lessons taught in

all the world ground into you early and alone — courage, caution, and patience" (p. 31).

She focused her vision on the nest, the place where she saw many of the lessons the natural world has to offer. She believed that humanity needed lessons about making a home, so she translated what she learned from the nest to her stories and essays. Most of her novels are about men and women making homes. The romances, which made the novels popular, are courtships preliminary to nesting — a pattern set forth in her first novel, *The Song of the Cardinal*. Her essays for *McCall's* collected and published posthumously as *Let Us Highly Resolve* (1927), are also for the most part lessons for the home — "The Good Old Institution of Home," "How to Make a Home," and "No Lazy Man Can Make a Garden" are examples — set forth without the intermediary of the nature story.

Stratton Porter's writing was criticized because her characters were idealized. Still, that was the point. She was writing at a time when there was a good deal of latent anxiety about the kinship of humans with animals, and she tried to describe what she saw as the morality, even the natural nobility, of the birds. As society became less agrarian, there were fears that people would lose the values attributed to the agricultural life and associated with the foundations of the United States. Many of Stratton Porter's most avid admirers were not only removed from a life in the natural world, but also demoralized. She maintained that she "wrote *Girl of the Limberlost* to carry to workers inside city walls, to hospital cots, to those behind prison bars, and to scholars in their libraries" ("Why I Wrote *A Girl of the Limberlost*"). Stratton Porter was able to transport her readers out of their particular confinements and into the freer air out-of-doors. She was able to convince her readers that good still existed, in them and in the natural world. She was, as many have seen, the right writer for her time.

Disaffection for the sentimentalism and idealism in the Stratton Porter novels has tended to preclude critical recognition of the objective knowledge which these characters have of their natural settings. Furthermore, Stratton Porter weaves plots that demonstrate the mutual benefits to mankind and nature of homes built in a harmony guided by intelligence, sensitivity, and good conscience. In this respect, the lives of the characters mirror the life of the novelist. Stratton Porter freely admitted her idealism—even writing an article entitled "Why I Always Wear My Rose-Colored Glasses" (1919)—but she did not work or live as if it were at odds with her zeal for knowing the natural world. Stratton Porter's romances are played out in the carefully drawn settings of the Limberlost Swamp, the banks of the Wabash River and Sylvan Lake, and amid the hills of southern California. It is the reader who must accommodate the "double vision" provided by the novelist who looked at the world through "rose-colored glasses" and the naturalist who waded through the poisonous snakes of the Limberlost Swamp to leave carrion for the vulture chicks she photographed.

It has been said that in her novels, Gene Stratton Porter created gardens without snakes: a comment on both her idealism and the low level of dramatic conflict in her books. However, snakes are not absent from her work—after all they were everywhere in the Limberlost. In her nonfiction there are stories of encounters between Gene or Jeannette and snakes. Gene's primary method of dealing with the very serious threat posed by the massasauga, the poisonous snake of the Limberlost, was not to give fear a chance to attract the snake. She often told of the time she watched one of these snakes crawl between the legs of an oblivious baby Jeannette as she picked flowers. Gene did nothing to alarm her daughter, did not shout or move or snatch her daughter up, because she knew the fright would signal the snake to attack. She herself had several similar encounters.

The evil in the gardens created by Gene Stratton Porter was not the snake. These are not stories of mankind's struggle against the powerful, inhuman forces of nature. The evil in her stories is the gun, as carried by the hunter in *Song of the Cardinal*. The gun is the threat from outside the natural world, a mechanized means of killing, a symbol of a humanity so blind to the morality, nobility, and wonder of the natural

world as to be oblivious to its destruction. The figure with the gun, or the ax, or a legal claim to a piece of property for which he or she has no love, is seen repeatedly in Stratton Porter's writings. In the novels these figures are reformed or tricked out of their claims, or they conveniently die. In the nature writings the truth is more squarely faced, the destruction happens, and the losses are recorded.

Bird Woman

Disregarding *Song of the Cardinal*, which straddles two genres, Stratton Porter's first book-length nature study was *What I Have Done with Birds*, published in 1907. The book was a compilation of articles written for the *Ladies Home Journal*, detailing her experiences making photographs that accurately recorded the nests and habits of birds common to her locale. This work continued what she had begun in her bird studies for *Outing* magazine, for which she spent hours in the field, collected legends regarding the various birds from local and literary sources, and supported her work with material from her scientific readings. The birds illustrated in *What I Have Done with Birds* include the rail, wood thrush, owl, killdeer, black vulture, loggerhead shrike, purple martin, catbird, belted kingfisher, yellow-bellied cuckoo, blue heron, mourning dove, cowbird, cardinal, robin, blue jay, hummingbird, and quail. Ten years later this work was updated and reissued as *Friends in Feathers*, with the addition of chapters on the tanager, indigo finch, goldfinch, wren, and kingbird. In her introductory notes, Stratton Porter underscores the purpose of her study:

The whole value of a natural-history picture lies in reproducing atmosphere, which tells the story of outdoor work, together with the soft high lights and velvet shadows which repaint the woods as we are accustomed to seeing them. It is not a question of timing; on nests and surroundings all the time wanted can be had; on young and grown birds, in motion, snap shots must be resorted to; but frequently, with them, more time than is required may be given. It is a question of whether you desire to reproduce *nature* and procure a natural-history picture, or whether you are going to insert a background and make a sort of flat Japanese, two-tone, wash effect, suitable only for decoration, never to reproduce nature. (*Friends in Feathers*, p. 10)

Stratton Porter's "courage, caution, and patience" came not only from her knowledge of the techniques of photographing birds but also from a familiarity with the birds developed through an entire lifetime. "This is the basis of all my field work: a mute contract between woman and bird" (*Friends in Feathers*, p. 2). Each chapter tells of the painstaking efforts made to get a true photograph, the physical hardships and misadventures as well as the joys. In describing this process, Stratton Porter is also relating a good deal of information about the habits of the birds that are her subjects. She finds a wood thrush nest made from the roots of red raspberries and nettles. She distinguishes between the song of the bluebird and its relative the robin. She pinpoints the particular brand of inquisitiveness exhibited by the catbird, and discovers how quickly a heron can capture and swallow a frog. Interwoven with the bird lore are the descriptions of places traversed and discovered in the process of finding each species. The photographer makes a very different guide into and spokesperson for the natural world than the novelist. The writing is as clear as the air, as the waters of the Wabash, as the song of the wood thrush.

Nature Writer

What I Have Done with Birds was published by Bobbs-Merrill of Indianapolis. Her next nonfiction work was *Birds of the Bible* (1909), published simultaneously by Jennings & Graham and Easton & Mains, religious publishers. Jennings & Graham did such a good job with the photographic reproductions for *Birds of the Bible* that Stratton Porter published her next nature book with them. *Music of the Wild: With Reproductions of the Performers, Their Instruments, and Festival Halls* (1910) required special, clay-coated paper for its 120 photographs. After *Music of the Wild* was published, Stratton Porter worked out a contract with Doubleday. Frank Doubleday, aspiring to establish his company as the publisher of books on country life and values, wanted to publish her novels. He was less optimistic about the sales potential of the nature works, but he wanted to represent her exclusively. Stratton Porter believed that the nature writing would have a more lasting appeal and worth, and was anxious to see it published—and published according to her sometimes demanding specifications. They worked out an agreement whereby the novels and nature works were to be published alternately.

Gene Stratton Porter wrote easily. She did not do extensive revisions—if, in fact, she did any revising at all. She realized that this was somewhat unusual for a writer, and apparently she valued this talent for giving her the time she needed to produce so much on several different fronts. Nonetheless, there was not a nature book published for every novel. *Moths of the Limberlost*, the result of several years' work, was published in 1912. The next nature book was *Friends in Feathers*, the revision of *What I Have Done with Birds*, published in 1917. In 1919, *Homing with the Birds* came out. Subtitled "The History of a Lifetime of Personal Experience with the Birds," this collection is autobiographical in the sense that it begins with her childhood experiences with birds and continues as the story of the growth and development of her knowledge. In 1923, Doubleday brought out *Wings*, a selection of chapters from the three "bird books." Two final collections of Stratton Porter's nonfiction were published posthumously. The pieces in *Tales You Won't Believe* (1925) had all been previously published: one in *Outdoor America*, and the remainder in *Good Housekeeping*. *Let Us Highly Resolve* (1927) consists of essays first published in McCall's, many of them reaching print only after her death.

Doubleday, Page doubled its business between 1910 and 1913, at least in part due to the success of *The Harvester*, the number one best-seller of 1912. Yet, while Stratton Porter wrote eight more novels (including *The Harvester*), she produced only three more nature studies, two of them collections of short pieces. Only *Moths of the Limberlost* has the singleness of purpose and focus of thought and creativity, expressed through both photography and writing, of the earlier nature studies. *Homing* weaves her life and love for birds together, and provides sketches on bird behavior in response to the photographer.

Music of the Wild

Music of the Wild, published in 1910 by Jennings & Graham, is very nearly a photographic essay. There are 120 photographs, more than in any other of Stratton Porter's works except the expanded *Friends in Feathers*. There are photographs of birds, but there are also crickets and bats, hop toads and dragonflies. There are trees, flowers, and even grasses. There are several photographs of rural roads and winding rivers trailing off into a distant vanishing point. The photographs for *Music of the Wild* were taken in the Sylvan Lake area, because the destruction of the Limberlost was already under way during the years Stratton Porter collected the material for this book. An elegiac tone pervades all three sections of the book: "The Chorus of the Forest," "Songs of the Fields," and "The Music of the Marsh."

It is possible that her choice of a religious publisher influenced the language and sentiment of the opening section of the book, written in hushed and worshipful tones: "begin at the gate and find your road slowly, else you will not hear the Great Secret and see the Compelling Vision" (*Music of the Wild*, p. 35). This attitude of religious awe contrasts with the vision of the naturalist, and is not typical of Stratton Porter's style. And eventually her tone smooths into something more akin to her earlier descriptions of working with the birds: "Sometimes when taking pictures I get more than I intend. In making this study of papaw leaves and fruit a ray of sunshine crept through an interstice of the forest and fell across my subject. So long as the

Gene Stratton Porter

picture lasts the sunbeam lives" (*Music of the Wild*, p. 84).

Although the book's subtitle, *With Reproductions of the Performers, Their Instruments, and Festival Halls*, gives the full scope of this work, it almost seems as if the play of light on papaw and oat field, the wind in the forest and the orchards, the difference in the yellows of the flowers of the field could all be considered "music" in the author's mind. When, years later, friends spoke of their confusion in response to a new book of poetry, *The American Rhythm* by Mary Hunter Austin (1923), Stratton Porter wrote that she had no problem understanding the words of a woman who, as a child, had talked to God under a tree. In "Books for Busy People" (*McCall's*, January 1924), she wrote that the book "was about the life we lead in this great land of ours—the song of the axe stroke, the sweep of the scythe, the hum of life where it strikes in measured rhythm that I have heard all of my life" (p. 28).

There are several passages written in the voice of the conservationist in *Music of the Wild*. One extols the virtue of leaving the flowers to cheer another weary soul along the path. Another spells out the meteorological relationship between draining the swamp and decreasing rainfall. Stratton Porter is serious about protecting the environment, and will pull out all the stops to make her point. At the end of the twentieth century, we are still using both poetic and scientific appeals to defend our natural environment, but perhaps neither is as powerful as Gene Stratton Porter's elegant photographs of a time and place now lost, and the generous passages of lucid prose in this work.

Moths of the Limberlost

In the introductory remarks in the first chapter of *Moths of the Limberlost*, Stratton Porter distinguishes between Naturalists and Nature Lovers. The former "have impaled moths and dissected, magnified and located brain, heart and nerves." They are concerned with "minute detail" of anatomy, "couched in resounding Latin and Greek terms they cannot possibly remember." Throughout this work and elsewhere, Stratton Porter is at odds with "the authorities" over their methods of study, the accuracy of their findings, and the obscurity of their reporting. Yet this is not to imply that her own studies are without discipline, a desire for accuracy, and intelligence. Her audience is those who look to nature "for rest and recreation"; who "would be delighted to learn the simplest name possible for the creatures they or their friends find afield, and the markings, habits and characteristics by which they can be identified" (p. 19).

They want a book that will teach them how to identify the moths they find, explain whether they are creatures of light or darkness, whether they feed or accomplish their mission without nourishment, where it is probable they can be found, what their habits are, how to identify their eggs and caterpillars, whether to look for their winter quarters in a cocoon on a twig or outbuilding, under the bark of a tree, among the leaves of earth, or in a case in a hole in the ground; that will give to them a name that there is some possibility of remembering, and coloured illustrations to guide in identification.

In *Moths of the Limberlost*, Stratton Porter pursues the desire that moved her to write her novels: to bring an understanding of and appreciation for the natural world to a wider audience.

Perhaps the greatest challenge to the success of this endeavor was the creation of her extraordinary illustrations. Anxious to produce a study of moths for which no moths had to be destroyed, and convinced that the colors of these fantastic creatures faded and changed—sometimes to the point of making them unrecognizable—after death and when exposed to chemicals, Stratton Porter devised her own photographic and illustrative method for this book. She found a way to make her photographic paper extremely sensitive, so that it took and held only the merest image of the photographed moth. Then she painstakingly hand-painted this photographic ghost. The greater part of this work had to be done in the few hours it took for the moth to emerge from its cocoon and dry its wings. After that, she released the subject rather than have it fly around indoors and damage itself. Her patient and detailed illustrations amplified her written descriptions of each subject.

Moths of the Limberlost might be a nature writer's primer. (Indeed, Annie Dillard included it on a list compiled for *Antaeus* of important nature books.) Although the author claims there is no particular order to the chapters, certain transitions show a studied artistry. The anecdote at the end of the section on the Yellow Emperor, *Eacles imperiales*, shows Jeannette alone among a social gathering of highly educated people—representative perhaps of the naturalist scholars for whom Stratton Porter felt awe, mixed with contempt for their ignorance of the everyday—able to identify this common moth. The next chapter, on the moth *Deilephila lineata*, which is called the Lady Bird, describes the young

Stratton Porter's empirical study of this native, during the course of which she discovers that what she pursues is not a kind of hummingbird—as her father had taught her—but a moth. Her firsthand knowledge infuses the early chapter on eggs and caterpillars and winter quarters, in which she classifies moths according to when they appear. She reviews the scientific studies on moth antennae and compares them to what she has seen herself. She constantly emphasizes the necessity for close observation, exemplifies it with anecdotes, and makes observation concrete through description and illustration. The first moth to which she devotes a chapter is one that can be found in cities, and is easy to identify and study: "The Cecropia moth resembles the robin among birds; not alone because he is gray with red markings, but also he haunts the same localities. The robin is the bird of the eaves, the back door, the yard and the orchard. Cecropia is the moth" (p. 130). She details the relationship between the moths and their environment, including in the chapter on *Hyperchiria Io* a passage on corn cultivation that ought to be a part of every Midwesterner's, perhaps every American's, education. The passage details the life of the cornfield and those who depended upon it, including the author as a child.

For I always had played among the corn. Untold miles I have ridden the plow horses across the spring fields, where mellow mould rolled black from the shining shares, and the perfumed air made me feel so near flying that all I seemed to need was a high start to be able to sail with the sentinel blackbird, that perched on the big oak, and with one sharp "T'check!" warned his feeding flock, surely and truly, whether a passing man carried a gun or hoe. Then came the planting, when bare feet loved the cool earth, and trotted over other untold miles, while little fingers carefully counted out seven grains from the store carried in my apron skirt. . . .

Then father covered them to the right depth, and stamped each hill with the flat of the hoe, while we talked of golden corn bread, and slices of mush, fried to a crisp brown that cook would make in the fall. We had to plant

enough more to feed all the horses, cattle, pigs, turkeys, geese, and chickens, during the long winter, even if the sun grew uncomfortably warm, and the dinner bell was slow about ringing. (*Moths*, pp. 219–220)

Stratton Porter came to study moths through her surprise at finding so many of their cocoons during the long hours she waited in the woods and fields for certain bird photographs. It is also possible, as Bertrand Richards suggests, that she chose to study moths, not butterflies, because their nocturnal habits meant that they were not in direct competition with the birds for her attention. For whatever reason, she threw herself wholeheartedly into the study. Jeannette describes the impact of this study upon the household:

Almost any place in our house you might find a glass turned down over a little patch of moth eggs on a rug to protect them; you might find a little strip of paper pinned on a window curtain to protect another batch; . . . you might find several different size boxes containing baby caterpillars just hatched, feeding on the particular kind of leaves that they ate; you might find cocoons pinned almost anywhere, and newly emerged moths and butterflies flying through the house and feeding on the flowers in the conservatory. (Meehan, pp. 119–120)

With moths, Stratton Porter had a subject for study that defied an anthropomorphic treatment; thus she developed literary skills to support her powers of observation. Passages on the life process of the moth, her husband's discovery of the pupa case of a *Protoparce celeus* while digging for fishing worms, and the wing development of a *Citheronia regalis* are remarkable for their clarity and control.

Homing with the Birds

The subtitle of *Homing with the Birds* (1919) makes it clear that the intent of this collection is autobiographical: *The History of a Lifetime of*

Personal Experience with the Birds. The essays record events that add to the reader's knowledge of the author's life and understanding of her way of doing fieldwork. Stratton Porter was an active sixty-one when she died, five years after *Homing with the Birds* was published. Had she lived, she might have written another autobiography; instead she left pieces of her story throughout her writings. Certain episodes appear again and again, like the notes of the birds' songs.

This collection contains the story of Mark Stratton's handing over the care of the birds on the farm to the young Geneva, as well as stories of her mother's working around the birds who nested near the house and garden. She remembers the birds on the banks of the Wabash as they were in her childhood, a childhood of "slow time," of discovery, observation, and care. The tenor of the relationship she was building was stewardship, not domination.

There are also numerous anecdotes about the author's encounters with birds. She tells of a red-winged blackbird being eaten by a bass and of a crow who tries to steal one of her camera lenses. In addition to stories, there are tips for those who would photograph the birds, and for those who would help birds who have been immersed in crude oil. There are calls for the conservation of resources that provide homes for the birds — and one vehement cry for controlling the English sparrow. There are discussions of the evolution of birds and the place of birds in the ecological balance. There are reflections on, and some indictments of, the methods and findings of ornithological authorities.

In *Homing with the Birds*, Stratton Porter often speaks of pursuing an intimacy with the birds. The term "intimacy" appropriately describes the relationship she sought. In her accounts of moving through the grass and trees, climbing ladders, taking photographs, what Stratton Porter describes is only partially a search for factual knowledge. Ultimately, she strives to be accepted into the birds' lives, into their nests: "I have come to know the birds more intimately and to understand their ways

better than those of my fellow men, with whom I have had no such contact" (p. 67).

"A Wonder Tale"

Tales You Won't Believe (1925) is also a collection of stories spanning the years and familiar places of Gene Stratton Porter's life. Like *Homing with the Birds*, it reveals the inner qualities that made her respond to nature as she did. Here, too, there is a feeling of intimacy in the stories told and the images depicted. The first piece, "A Wonder Tale," tells of her fascination with moths and the process by which she studied them. The "wonder" is in the story of her being accidentally sprayed with the substance by which the female moth attracts the male. She stood one night in the apple orchard at the cabin on Sylvan Lake, in her nightgown, as the moths came in great numbers to alight on her: "the night became a vibrant thing, a thing of velvet wings, of velvet sound and brilliant colour" (p. 12).

This collection of essays has a coherence beyond the autobiographical: all the tales are tales of wonder. The stories tell of strange happenings, things difficult to believe, rare appearances in nature, idiosyncrasies of people and wildlife — and all work to re-create the sense of wonder that was the particular gift of Gene Stratton Porter. The effect is produced not by exaggerated emotion but by the careful description of the closely observed. "When the Geese Fly North" is the story of the passing of an enormous flock of geese one February night. In order to document the size of the flock, she stood for an hour on the porch of the cabin, watching. "During all that time, from three to five abreast, a steady procession of feeding geese went hurrying around our shore line" (p. 23).

There is a stillness at the heart of several of these essays. Stratton Porter's eyes are turned back in time, her own and nature's. Most of the stories she tells are from her experiences at Wildflower Woods. By 1924, she had already begun the process that would transform her lakeside retreat into an Indiana state historic site, and she had lived for five years in California. Yet the California countryside is the topic of only one essay, the last.

There is a stillness in listening for absent sounds as in the essay "The Last Passenger Pigeon." "The Bride of Red Wing Lake" tells of the author's amazement at discovering a wood duck on Sylvan Lake, during the summer she was looking for just the right piece of property for Wildflower Woods. She spent hours observing the duck—whose name, "Aixsponsa," means bride, although it is the male of the species whose markings are spectacular—drawing his portrait and getting the color of his markings just right. Then one day, as she watched, a man in a boat shot the duck. She berated him up one side and down the other, until he was suitably depressed by the finality of his act, for even then the wood duck was a rarity. Indeed, Stratton Porter did not see another during her years at Sylvan Lake.

Often the stillness in this collection is awe. Of moths, she writes: "We do not realize that the present form of these fragile and exquisitely coloured creatures, so delicate and fine that the lightest touch of a finger tip brushes the feathers of velvet down from their wings, is the shortest link in the chain of their existence" (p. 3).

The same sense of morality that drove the novels is at work in these essays, but here there is less didacticism, more sadness. There are several dramatic confrontations with those who would destroy nature. For eight years Stratton Porter's nearest neighbor on Sylvan Lake put out poisoned chickens to rid himself of the great horned owls nesting on his side of their common property line. For eight years, she retrieved the poisoned chickens to save the owls. Hunters and farmers, those who drill for oil and drain the swamps, all are confronted against the backdrop of the natural wonders they destroy. There is a special sharpness reserved for those who do not see the wonders right in front of them; they are like those who stand in the grass and do not see it, let alone marvel at the richness of its variety.

During the winter of 1914, Stratton Porter lost a good friend, a large beech tree, and a bed of white strawberries she had created from cuttings from the friend's strawberry bed. She was almost at the point of asking the heirs if she could get another set of cuttings when she discovered a patch growing in the wild, near where the beech had been:

> The squirrels had been feeding on the white strawberries and . . . they had sowed the seed . . . and when the tree was removed and the earth was raked smooth, and when the snows blanketed it and the sun shone and the rains fell, all these little seeds in their fertilized coats germinated and sprang up and gave back to me my lost and dearly loved wild white strawberry bed. Nature returned to me my lost gift. (p. 244)

Gene Stratton Porter's gaze was rarely turned upon the past for long. She did not muse in nostalgic longing for a natural world beyond recovery. Her life and works were devoted to activism. She developed her career as a popular novelist in order to create a greater audience who would listen to the "music of the wild." Both novels and nature writings blend an appreciation for the everyday in our natural world—the cardinal and the cecropia, the blackbird and the white strawberry—and an understanding of the process by which these forms of life exist, and coordinate with our own.

Stratton Porter's emphasis, in her writings, was not on what had been lost but on what might be found. Her eyes were always in focus, her hands busy, her intelligence sharp—so that her sense of wonder was continually aroused. Wonder and knowledge work together to inform the best of her writing. It is unfortunate that the past popularity of the novels has created a situation in which her other writing is all but lost, and is perhaps diminished by association. Yet, as she demonstrates in the tale of the wild strawberries, what has been lost may not be truly lost. Gene Stratton Porter's life was committed to the exploration and documentation of the natural subjects of her wonder.

Selected Bibliography

WORKS OF GENE STRATTON PORTER

NOVELS

The Song of the Cardinal (Indianapolis: Bobbs-Merrill, 1903); *Freckles* (New York: Doubleday, Page, 1904; Bloomington: Indiana Univ. Press, 1986; New York: Dell, 1988); *At the Foot of the Rainbow* (New York: Outing, 1907); *A Girl of the Limberlost* (New York: Doubleday, Page, 1909; Dell, 1986; Signet Books, 1988); *The Harvester* (Garden City, N.Y.: Doubleday, Page, 1911); *Laddie: A True Blue Story* (Garden City, N.Y.: Doubleday, Page, 1913); *Michael O'Halloran* (Garden City, N.Y.: Doubleday, Page, 1915); *A Daughter of the Land* (Garden City, N.Y.: Doubleday, Page, 1918); *Her Father's Daughter* (Garden City, N.Y.: Doubleday, Page, 1921); *The White Flag* (Garden City, N.Y.: Doubleday, Page, 1923); *The Keeper of the Bees* (Garden City, N.Y.: Doubleday, Page, 1925); *The Magic Garden* (Garden City, N.Y.: Doubleday, Page, 1927).

POETRY

The Fire Bird (Garden City, N.Y.: Doubleday, Page, 1922); *Jesus of the Emerald* (Garden City, N.Y.: Doubleday, Page, 1923); "Euphorbia," in *Good Housekeeping* (January, February, March 1923).

NATURE STUDIES

What I Have Done with Birds: Character Studies of Native American Birds Which Through Friendly Advance I Induced to Pose for Me, or Succeeded in Photographing by Good Fortune, with the Story of My Experiences in Obtaining Their Pictures (Indianapolis: Bobbs-Merrill, 1907), rev. and enl. as *Friends in Feathers* (Garden City, N.Y.: Nelson Doubleday, 1922); *Birds of the Bible* (Cincinnati: Jennings and Graham, and New York: Eaton & Mains, 1909; Cutchogue, N.Y.: Buccaneer Books, 1986); *Music of the Wild: With Reproductions of the Performers, Their Instruments and Festival Halls* (Cincinnati: Jennings and Graham, and New York: Eaton & Mains, 1910); *Moths of the Limberlost* (Garden City, N.Y.: Doubleday, Page, 1912; repr. without photos, Greenport, N.Y.: Harmony Raine, 1980; Cutchogue, N.Y.: Buccaneer Books, 1986); *Homing with the Birds: The History of a Lifetime of Personal Experience with the Birds* (Garden City, N.Y.: Doubleday, Page, 1919; Cutchogue, N.Y.: Buccaneer Books, 1986); *Wings* (Garden City, N.Y.: Garden City, 1923; repr., Muncie, Ind.: Rollin King, 1976), contains selected and edited chapters from previously published books; *Tales You Won't Believe* (Garden City, N.Y.: Doubleday, Page, 1925); *Coming Through the Swamp: The Na-ture Writings of Gene Stratton Porter*, ed. by Sydney Landon Plum (Salt Lake City: Univ. of Utah Press, forthcoming).

MISCELLANY

After the Flood (Indianapolis: Bobbs-Merrill, 1911; repr., Muncie, Ind: Rollin King, 1975), children's book; *Morning Face* (Garden City, N.Y.: Doubleday, Page, 1916), children's book; *Let Us Highly Resolve* (Garden City, N.Y.: Doubleday, Page, 1927), essay collection.

ARTICLES AND SHORT STORIES

"A New Experience in Millinery," in *Recreation* 12 (February 1900); "Camera Notes," in *Recreation* 12 (February 1900; April 1900), 13 (July 1900), 14 (January 1901; February 1901; March 1901; May 1901), bylined column; "From the Viewpoint of a Field Worker," in *The American Annual of Photography and Photographic Times Almanac for 1902*, ed. by Walter E. Woodbury (New York: Scoville Manufacturing Co., 1901); "Bird Architecture," in *Outing* 38 (July 1901); "Laddie, the Princess, and the Pie," in *Metropolitan Magazine* 14 (September 1901); "Photographing the Belted Kingfisher," in *Outing* 39 (November 1901); "How Laddie and the Princess Spelled Down at the Christmas Bee," in *Metropolitan Magazine* 14 (December 1901).

"A Study of the Black Vulture," in *Outing* 39 (December 1901); "Under My Vine and Fig Tree," in *The American Annual of Photography and Photographic Times-Bulletin Almanac for 1903*, ed. by W. I. Lincoln Adams (New York: Scoville Manufacturing Co., 1902); "The Birds' Kindergarten," in *Outing* 40 (April 1902); "When Luck Is Golden," in *Metropolitan Magazine* 15 (April 1902); "The Real Babes in the Woods," in *Metropolitan Magazine* 16 (August 1902); "The Music of the Marsh," in *Outing* 40 (September 1902); "Bob's Feathered Interloper," in *Metropolitan Magazine* 17 (November 1903); "The Camera in Ornithology," in *The American Annual of Photography and Photographic Times-Bulletin Almanac for 1904*, ed. by W. I. Lincoln Adams (New York: Scoville Manufacturing Co., 1903).

"Freckles' Chickens," in *Ladies Home Journal* 21 (November 1904); "The Call of the Wayside," in *The American Annual of Photography and Photographic Times-Bulletin Almanac for 1906*, ed. by W. I. Lincoln Adams (New York: Scoville Manufacturing Co., 1905); "Why I Wrote *A Girl of the Limberlost*," in *World's Work* 19 (February 1910); "Hidden Treasures: Moths of the Limberlost," in *Country Life in America* 22 (June 1912); "My Work and My Critics," in *Bookman* [London] 49 (February 1916); "My Life and My Books," in *Ladies Home Journal* 23 (September 1916); "Why I Always Wear My Rose-Colored Glasses," in *American Magazine* 88 (August 1919); "What My Father Meant to Me," in *American Magazine* 99 (February 1925); "The Healing Influence of Gardens," in *McCall's* (December 1927).

BIBLIOGRAPHY

David G. MacLean, *Gene Stratton-Porter: A Bibliography and Collector's Guide* (Decatur, Ind.: Americana Books, 1976).

BIOGRAPHICAL AND CRITICAL STUDIES

Jane S. Bakerman, "Gene Stratton-Porter: What Price the Limberlost?" in *Old Northwest* 3, no. 2 (1977), and "Gene Stratton-Porter Reconsidered," in *Kate Chopin Newsletter* 2 (winter 1976–1977); Paul Brooks, "Birds and Women," in *Audubon* 82 (September 1980); Frederic Taber Cooper, "The Popularity of Gene Stratton-Porter," in *Bookman* (August 1915); Deborah Dahlke-Scott and Michael Prewitt, "A Writer's Crusade to Portray the Spirit of the Limberlost," in *Smithsonian* (April 1976), repr. as "Elder of the Tribe: Gene Stratton-Porter," in *Backpacker* (16 August 1976); Jan Dearmin Finney, ed., *Gene Stratton-Porter, the Natural Wonder: Surviving Photographs of the Great Limberlost Swamp by Gene Stratton-Porter* (Mattituck, N.Y.: Amereon, and Indianapolis: Museum Shop, Indiana State Museum, 1983), foreword by William E. Story.

Ellen Hoekstra, "The Pedestal Myth Reinforced: Women's Magazine Fiction, 1900–1920," in *New Dimensions in Popular Culture*, ed. by Russel B. Nye (Bowling Green, Ohio: Bowling Green Univ. Press, 1972); Edward Ifkovic, "The Garden of the Lord: Gene Stratton-Porter and the Death of Evil in Eden," in *Journal of Popular Culture* 8, no. 4 (1975); "In Memoriam Gene Stratton-Porter," in *McCall's* (February 1925); Rollin Patterson King, *Gene Stratton-Porter: A Lovely Light* (Chicago: Adams Press, 1979); Judith Reick Long, "Gene Stratton-Porter: The Hum of Life," in *Traces of Indiana* 2 (summer 1990), and *Gene Stratton-Porter: Novelist and Naturalist* (Indianapolis: Indiana Historical Society, 1990); Ruth J. Mann, "Botanical Remedies from Gene Stratton Porter's *The Harvester*," in *Journal of the History of Medicine* (October 1975).

Jeannette Porter Meehan, "My Mother," in *McCall's* 52 (January 1925), and *The Lady of the Limberlost: The Life and Letters of Gene Stratton-Porter* (Garden City, N.Y.: Doubleday, Doran & Co., 1928); Lisa Mighetto, "Science, Sentiment, and Anxiety: American Nature Writing at the Turn of the Century," in *Pacific Historical Review* 54, no. 1 (1985); "Mrs. Porter and Nature," in *Bookman* 35 (August 1912); Mary DeJong Obuchowski, "Gene Stratton-Porter: Women's Advocate," in *Midamerica: The Yearbook of the Society for the Study of Midwestern Literature*, vol. 17 (East Lansing, Mich.: Midamerica, 1990); Grant M. Overton, "Naturalist vs. Novelist: Gene Stratton-Porter," in *American Nights Entertainment* (New York: D. Appleton & Co., 1923).

Kathryn Thompson Presley, "Neglected Popular Fiction of the Gilded Age: A Quest for Certainty" (Ph.D. diss., Texas A & M Univ., 1991); Bertrand F. Richards, *Gene Stratton-Porter* (Boston: Twayne, 1981); Peter J. Schmitt, *Back to Nature: The Arcadian Myth in Urban America* (New York: Oxford Univ. Press, 1962), and "Wilderness Novels in the Progressive Era," in *Journal of Popular Culture* 3, no. 1 (1969); Frank N. Wallace, "Afield with Gene Stratton-Porter," in *McCall's* (June 1926); W. Tasker Witham, *The Adolescent in the American Novel* (New York: Frederick Ungar, 1964).

EDWIN WAY TEALE
(1899–1980)

STAN TAG

THE NINETEENTH-CENTURY American naturalist and artist John James Audubon wrote: "Time is ever precious to the student of nature." That was certainly true for Edwin Way Teale. More than anything else, Teale longed for days without time, days to linger in the slow rhythms of nature, days to watch insects emerging from egg sacs, or hawks riding wind currents, or stars arcing across the night sky. He spent much of his lifetime writing about and photographing nature—in all, he wrote thirty books, and over 250 articles, and took over twenty thousand photographs. He kept journals, diaries, extensive lists and notes, and was a prolific letter writer. Honest, vivid, accurate nature writing, Teale believed, preserved something valuable about our lives and the natural world in which we live. "In my writings," Teale stated in *The American Seasons* (1976), "I have thought of myself less as a teacher than as a Pied Piper leading people into the out-of-doors. And . . . through all my books, there has been an undercurrent of an unstated hope, the hope of stirring to life a sense of wonder" (p. xv).

Dune Boy

Teale's childhood memories of nature never lie very far beneath the surface of his books. Like trout, they filter the constant flow of his life and writing through their gills. Sometimes they even dimple the surface or leap into the air. As a boy, Teale explored the natural world with zeal and wonder and insatiable curiosity. As an adult, he did the same. He told naturalist Ann Zwinger that he suspected the secret to a long and happy life rested in "never quite growing up."

Teale was born in Joliet, Illinois, on the western bank of Hickory Creek. On that late spring day, 2 June 1899, his parents, Clara Louise Way and Oliver Cromwell Teale, christened him Edwin Alfred Teale. Later, at the age of twelve, Teale changed his middle name to Way, his mother's maiden name; Alfred, he said, was "too commonplace" for a future writer. His mother had been raised at Lone Oak Farm in the dune country of northern Indiana, where her parents, Edwin Franklin and Jemima George Way, had settled in the fall of 1867. Teale's father, an Englishman, left Ravensthorpe, Yorkshire, in 1884. He came to the Midwest, met and married Clara Way, and in Joliet, a steel and rail center, found work in the Michigan Central roundhouse. Teale described his parents as "sincere, hard-working, religious people. They tended to be conciliatory and gentle" (*Dune Boy*, p. 8). The Teales lived near the railroad tracks on Washington Street "in the kind of neighborhood," he later told his publisher and biographer Edward Dodd, Jr., "where boys put rocks in their snowballs" (*Of Nature, Time and Teale*, p. 8).

Teale's sooty, paved Joliet neighborhood provided few places to explore the natural world, but he did find some wild spaces in the gravel pit that stretched for hundreds of acres across the street from his house, and among the muskrats, bullheads, cattails, willows, and redwing blackbirds on the edges of nearby Brown's Pond. When Teale returned to Joliet in 1952, during his autumn journey across America, the place fondly triggered "memories of swimming holes and sunfish and hellgrammites under stones in the riffles, memories of butternut and walnut and hickory trees, memories of lowland stretches yellow with marsh marigolds in the wake of melting snow, of Davison's Woods carpeted with spring beauties in the time of returning warblers" (*Autumn Across America*, p. 79). One of his earliest discoveries in natural history occurred in Joliet during the fall of 1907, when Teale was in the second grade. His teacher had assigned the students to bring in brilliant autumn leaves. Teale enthusiastically brought in a large bouquet of what turned out to be poison ivy. Neither he nor his teacher was at school the following week.

For the most part, though, when Teale remembered his childhood, he thought of his summers at his grandparents' farm in the Indiana dune country. It was there at Lone Oak Farm (where he spent every summer until he was fifteen) that the great mysteries and wildness of nature indelibly "stirred his imagination." Like Huck Finn, Teale lived outdoors from morning until night; he ran barefoot, wore overalls, watched swallows, followed snakes, listened to cicadas, and explored every corner of that semi-wild farm, time and time again. As his friend Roger Tory Peterson later recognized, Teale never lost this childlike enthusiasm for the natural world; he was "always vital, always interested in everything that grows, crawls, walks, swims, or flies" (*Natural History*, p. 452).

In Teale's classic memoir of his early years, *Dune Boy* (1943), we see his passion for nature taking root, growing, and blossoming under the kind care of his grandparents, Gramp and Gram, as he called them. Gramp was a good-natured Civil War veteran who loved jokes, worked ex-

tremely hard, and, as Teale put it, "desired existence plain and simple" (p. 17). Gram read books aloud nearly every evening, wasn't afraid to show her emotions, and "never compromised with the wickedness of the world" (p. 23). "The debt I owe my grandparents most of all," Teale concluded, "is the freedom they gave me, freedom to roam the acres of corn and wheat and potatoes, the woods and swamps, and to make this world my own" (p. 26).

Increasingly, the world Teale made at Lone Oak Farm looked more and more like the laboratory of a young naturalist. One summer he started a natural history museum in a corner of the wagonshed. Teale filled it with a wide assortment of objects: birds' nests, arrowheads, twisted sticks, leaves, bark, acorns, wasps' nests, roots, snakeskins, hundreds of stones, small bottles of dirt and sand, and, his most-prized possession, the skeleton of a cow.

At the age of seven, Teale felt his first urgings to write. He began scribbling down notes on things he noticed while wandering through the fields, and making lists of all the creatures he had seen at Lone Oak. These nature notes and lists eventually grew into stories. At the age of nine, having decided that he wanted to be a naturalist for the rest of his life, Teale began to write his first book: "Tales of Lone Oak." The twenty-five-chapter book (which took him eighteen months to complete) describes Teale's outdoor adventures with his boyhood friend Verne Bradfield, in and around Lone Oak.

Lone Oak not only spurred Teale's beginnings as a writer, it provided the means for his initiation into photography. At the age of eleven, his heart set on a box camera from the Sears, Roebuck catalog, Teale singlehandedly picked twenty thousand strawberries for his grandfather in order to earn the $3.75 it cost for the complete outfit of camera, film, developing kit, and printing material. Teale took his first photograph of a young wild cottontail he had been training to sit still. It was to that same dune-country cottontail that Teale later dedicated his first book on photography, *The Boys' Book of Photography* (1939). The final picture on that first roll (all taken the same morning) showed the farmhouse with the lone oak rising behind it. Those first, clumsy prints were the quiet beginnings of Teale's lifelong love of photography, which, in later years, brought him international recognition.

For Teale, "all the days at Lone Oak were like golden islands in a stormy sea" (*Dune Boy*, p. 273). In high school Teale continued to write and take photographs, but he also directed much of his creative energy into public speaking. He entered many oratorical competitions and eventually became Indiana's state debating champion. After graduating from high school in 1918, Teale enrolled in the Student Army Training Corps at the University of Illinois. He was on the point of being transferred to the Air Corps when the Armistice was signed on 11 November.

Soon after, Teale entered Earlham College in Richmond, Indiana, a small, coeducational Quaker school whose president happened to be his uncle, David M. Edwards. Oddly, the naturalist-to-be took no courses in botany or zoology or any other science. Instead, Teale studied literature, majoring in English; he received the B.A. in 1922. He met some of his college expenses by selling photographs, and by cleaning and repairing furnaces. Edward Dodd, Jr., claimed that Teale's chief activities at Earlham were weightlifting, debating, and Nellie Donovan, whom he met in 1921 and married two years later.

Born in Colorado Springs, Nellie Imogene Donovan had spent her childhood summers in rural Michigan and shared Teale's passion for literature and the outdoors. She majored in English at Earlham and loved to watch birds, able to spot them more readily than he. In Nellie, Teale found a fellow naturalist, an inspiring friend, and his lifelong companion. She traveled with him, read the drafts of his books aloud to him, and shared in his adventures in every way. Teale's poetic dedication to Nellie in *A Walk Through the Year* (1978) expresses the deep love he felt for her: "Dedicated / To the sun and the moon/ and Nellie; / To the pasture rose and the / bluebird and Nellie; / To the starlight and the rainbow / and Nellie; / To all that means the most to / me at Trail Wood — / especially / Nellie."

Two months before he was married, Teale set out with his college friend Bob Kellum on a rowboat excursion down the Ohio River. They talked of rowing from Louisville, Kentucky, to New Orleans. As it turned out, Kellum accompanied Teale for only two days. Undaunted, Teale decided to go on alone, rowing downriver to Cairo, Illinois, where the Ohio meets the Mississippi, some three hundred miles away. Teale describes these adventures in three chapters of *The Lost Woods* (1945). It was on this journey that Teale first picked up and read a copy of Thoreau's writings. "Rowing down the river in the days that followed," he later told the Thoreau Society, "I would pull out into the middle of the stream and let the boat drift with the current for half an hour at a time, reading as I drifted" ("Henry Thoreau and the Realms of Time," p. 1). Thus began another lifelong journey for Teale, a journey of the mind and spirit into the sinuous and startling world of Thoreau's prose.

After Nellie and Edwin were married on 1 August 1923, they drove their first car, a black Model T, to Wichita, Kansas, where Teale began his second year of teaching English and public speaking at Friends University, and Nellie her first. In 1924 they moved to New York City so that Teale could be closer to the publishers. He still dreamed of making a living as a writer. Teale entered the master's program at Columbia University and began working as an editorial assistant for Dr. Frank Crane, a widely syndicated columnist noted for moralist and inspirationalist writings. Teale had been sending Dr. Crane ideas for years. In 1926 Teale received his master's degree.

But in 1927 the world seemed to come crashing down all around the Teales. Later, in a letter to Ann Zwinger, Teale explained the events of "that dreadful year." Oliver Teale, his father, was very ill and finally died in 1928. The Teales' infant son David had an abscess in his ear that had possibly ruptured the ear drum. Nellie had acute appendicitis. Edwin went to the hospital with a high fever and blood poisoning. They were running out of money, and Teale lost his job when Dr. Crane died. The Teales survived by reading *Don Quixote* every evening. "For us," Teale wrote to Zwinger, "it is the greatest book ever written, such a wonderful combination of the ridiculous and the noble, the wise and the absurd" (*A Conscious Stillness*, p. xiii).

Popular Science

With a letter of recommendation from Frank Crane in his pocket, Teale walked the streets of New York City looking for a writing job. It was a tough and exhausting market to crack. Teale was once so tired that he fell asleep in the waiting room of the *New Republic*. When Teale finally met the editor of *Popular Science* magazine, in 1928—as Edward Dodd, Jr., tells the story—he reached into his pocket to pull out Dr. Crane's letter, but it was not there. Teale had changed his suit before the interview. Perhaps, concluded Dodd, it "was just as well because a flustered young human being appealed more strongly to the scientific editor than an inspirational writer. He was hired" (*Of Nature, Time and Teale*, pp. 10–11).

Teale worked as a staff writer for *Popular Science* magazine for thirteen years. His first article, "South Sea Colony Reveals New Facts about Heredity," appeared in the October 1928 issue. In all, Teale wrote over 130 articles for *Popular Science*. The magazine sent him down into a submarine, up in an airplane with a test pilot, underwater in a diving suit, on an all-night adventure with the New York City police radio patrol, and on a five-thousand-mile trailer trip through the South. Teale interviewed model-car racers, detectives, scientists, bomb experts, photographers, doctors, whittlers, inventors, explorers, fiddlemakers, divers, pilots, and goldfish breeders. He wrote over 20 *Popular Science* articles on crime and detectives, under titles such as "Weird Unseen Rays Trap Master Crooks," "Auto Stealing Now $50,000,000-a-Year Racket," and "Laundry-Mark Detective Solves Mysterious Crimes."

Aviation was the other frequent topic of Teale's *Popular Science* articles. Teale had been fascinated with flight all his life. As a young boy on his grandparents' farm, he used to lie on his back gazing at the cumulus clouds and imagine himself floating through the air currents. His eyes caught the swift darts and loops of the barn swallows, and his spirit often soared when the great winds rolled in from the northwest. "Some deep need of the spirit," Teale wrote in *Dune Boy*, "some inheritance of untold centuries, was finding release in this contact with the sky-wind" (p. 123). He grew up at a time when aviation was still in its infancy, and he read anything he could find about flying.

At the age of ten, Teale determined he would build his own glider and soar into the sky above Lone Oak Farm. However, it was not until 1914, after five years of building and testing model planes and gliders, that young Teale finally got his chance to soar. That summer he finished constructing the Dragonette, a huge gliding biplane with wheels; Teale's father, grandfather, and Dolly (his grandfather's horse) helped him launch it. It did fly, for one brief moment. That night, however, a storm tossed his glider across the farm, dashing it to pieces.

It is no surprise, then, that Teale's first published book concerned gliding: *The Book of Gliders* (1930). Five of his *Popular Science* articles on gliding had appeared during the year prior to the book's publication, and America's glider champion, W. H. Bowlus, wrote the introduction. In the book, Teale describes various types of gliders, the history of gliding, some of the most famous flights, and mostly how to get started—including chapters on choosing sites, flying, getting a pilot's license, constructing gliders, and organizing glider clubs and meets.

In his years at *Popular Science* Teale did get some opportunities to write about natural history topics: insects, stars, tides, fog, spider webs, horned toads, the sea, goldfish, pigeons, bamboo, flowers, cicadas, bats, and falcons. These articles gave Teale a chance to hone his skills as a nature writer. He learned how to show his readers the fascinating connections between the natural world and their own lives; in short, he learned how to make science popular. Likewise, *The Book of Gliders* and *The Boys' Book of Photography* were practical guides, written to inspire and to equip his readers to get out and experience the natural world—to fly through it, to see it, to enjoy it.

During World War II, Teale's publisher, Dodd, Mead, released his quintessential book in this genre: *Byways to Adventure: A Guide to Nature Hobbies* (1942). Dedicated to Teale's father, *Byways to Adventure* addresses nature hobbyists, as Teale calls them; chapter by chapter it describes how to look for and learn about birds, weather, stars, insects, reptiles, trees, plants, rocks and minerals, animals, fossils, and fish; how to collect shells, use a microscope, take nature photographs, get involved in conservation; and which natural history museums to visit. "The simple things of the natural world," Teale reminded his readers, "take on added appeal in times of tension and trouble" (*Byways to Adventure*, p. 1).

An Insect Garden

In October 1929, a year after the publication of Teale's first article in *Popular Science*, the stock market crashed and the Great Depression began in earnest. Although Teale dreamed of traveling to Africa or Australia to write natural history articles on exotic wildlife and birds, economic reality necessitated that he stay home and continue to write and photograph for *Popular Science*. Like J. Henri Fabre, the famous French chronicler of insect life, Teale narrowed his horizons and began to explore the natural world in and around his home in Baldwin, Long Island. Hardly a fifteen-minute walk away, Teale found exactly what he had been looking for: an old hillside apple orchard that sloped down into a swamp. There, he discovered, nearly every kind of insect in the region could be found. The old apple trees alone provided habitat for over five hundred species of insects. For ten dollars a year Teale purchased the "insect rights" to the hillside, and thus began his first great adventure as a naturalist: the exploration of an insect garden.

Teale planted wildflowers and cultivated plants, shrubs, and vines on the hillside—anything to attract insects and encourage them to stay. He set out bits of decaying meat for carrion beetles, dead twigs for robber flies to perch on, and pans of muddy water for wasps and butterflies. Teale spent many hours in his hillside garden taking notes, observing, and photographing insects. Such activity, he wrote in *Grassroot Jungles: A Book of Insects* (1937), "is like making a Gulliver's journey into another world" (p. 1). At first, his neighbors weren't quite certain what to think of Teale's odd behavior. He "soon learned . . . that a full-grown man peering into a grass clump, or stretched out prone to watch an ant-lion at work, is inevitably an object of curiosity and concern" (*Near Horizons*, pp. 1–2).

"Dinosaur of the Insect World" was Teale's first natural history essay to appear outside of *Popular Science*. The February 1935 *Travel* magazine article became the prototype for almost all of his subsequent natural history essays. It combined his stunning photographs of praying mantises with personal anecdotes of mantis behavior, clear descriptions, pertinent historical and scientific information, staggering statistics, stories from around the world, and, most importantly, an inviting tone of wonder, fascination, and sheer delight at the strange life of this creature.

Between 1937 and 1962 Teale published eight insect books. His friend and fellow naturalist John Kieran once stated that when it comes to insects, "Edwin Way Teale never found too many to suit his tastes." Nor, it seems, too many insect *books*. Teale's first insect book, *Grassroot Jungles*, was an immediate success. On 19 December 1937, Teale's mesmerizing photograph of a praying mantis loomed across the front page of the *New York Times Book Review*. In his review of the book, John Kieran said that he did "not know which to admire more, [Teale's] science or his art." At its heart, *Grassroot Jungles* is a book of wonder. Its photographs and prose mark Teale's awakening to the world of insects. He insists that "we cannot ignore insects" or "dismiss them as insignificant," and his book encourages us to open our eyes and enter that world for ourselves. "If the world is dull," Teale wrote in the chapter on crickets, "it is because we are blind and deaf and dumb; because we know too little to sense the drama around us" (*Grassroot Jungles*, p. 178).

The success of *Grassroot Jungles* spurred *Popular Science* to publish the first feature article ever written on Teale. In April 1938 Robert E. Martin's portrait of the "insect explorer" appeared, illustrated with Teale's black-and-white photographs of a praying mantis, an ant's head, a Polyphemus moth, a monarch butterfly's face, a battle between a praying mantis and a black widow, and Teale himself looking through a magnifying glass at a bumblebee on a sunflower. After ten years of taking photographs and writing for *Popular Science*, Teale had finally become the subject of his own scientific adventure story.

In 1939, Dutton published Teale's second insect book: *The Boys' Book of Insects* (revised as *The Junior Book of Insects* in 1953). A year later, Teale's book about bees, *The Golden Throng*, appeared. Maurice Maeterlinck—Belgian poet, naturalist, and author of *The Life of a Bee*—declared that *The Golden Throng* would become "the Bible of the bees." "These insects," Teale writes, "with their harmonious, golden cities of wax, hold a perennial fascination for us. . . . For there is beauty as well as mystery in the life of the bee" (*The Golden Throng*, p. 9). Like *Grassroot Jungles* before it, *The Golden Throng* expresses the dimensions of that beauty and that mystery through the interplay of Teale's photographic images and words. "It is," as Teale said about Maeterlinck's bee classic, "a book [for bee lovers] to own, to read, and to read again" (*The Golden Throng*, p. 174).

By 1941, it had become clear to Teale that his explorations of his hillside insect garden had not only psychological and spiritual rewards, but financial benefits as well. His longtime dream of becoming a full-time nature writer finally came true when he quit his staff writing job at *Popular Science* on 15 October, the day he forever after celebrated as "independence day." In 1942 alone, Teale became a contributing editor to *Audubon* magazine (a position he held for the rest of his life); published two books, *Byways to Adventure* and *Near Horizons*, and twelve magazine articles, in *Nature*, *Natural History*, the *New York Times Magazine*, *Better Homes and Gardens*, and *Audubon*; he also welcomed the British edition of *The Golden Throng* and was invited to lecture on his insect adventures at the Explorers' Club in New York City.

Near Horizons: The Story of an Insect Garden, as Teale put it, "is the travel book of a man who stayed home" (p. vii). Like Fabre and Thoreau, who "travelled a good deal in Concord," Teale discovered that the mysteries of life swirled in surprising fullness right in his backyard. *Near Horizons* won Teale the John Burroughs Medal for nature writing in 1943. It reflects the depth and maturing of Teale's vision of nature: nature, he concluded in the book, is not only an expression of wonder and beauty and mystery, but "in all her acts, [she] reflects her faith in the future" (p. 309).

Teale wrote four additional insect books: an edited collection of Fabre's writings, *The Insect World of J. Henri Fabre* (1949); two children's books, *Insect Friends* (1955) and *The Bees* (1961); and the book that Annie Dillard, in *Pilgrim at Tinker Creek*, said she "couldn't live without": *The Strange Lives of Familiar Insects* (1962). But it was among the knotholes, cattails, apple cores, and wildflowers of Teale's Long Island insect garden that he really began his "adventures in viewpoint" (*Near Horizons*, p. 41). It was there that he first watched rat-tailed maggots hatching from eggs, froghoppers making bubble houses, and wasps sleeping on dried iris leaves. For Teale, the insect garden "revealed a whole new silent world of activity, a world unseen and unappreciated by the casual eye" (*Near Horizons*, p. 42).

The American Seasons

In November 1940, *Popular Science* sent Teale to Philadelphia to report on a meeting of amateur scientists who had been gathering natural history data. There he met and interviewed University of Pennsylvania botanist Dr. John M. Fogg, Jr., who told him that spring moves north at an average rate of about fifteen miles a day. "Riding home on the train," Teale later remembered, "I beguiled myself by imagining what it would be like to drift north with the spring, keeping pace with its long advance" (*The American Seasons*, p. ix). Thus, the seeds were planted for Teale's second great adventure as a naturalist: his twenty-year, four-volume, seventy-six-thousand-mile attempt to chronicle the natural history of the American seasons.

During World War II, Nellie and Edwin looked forward to their spring trip. While their son, David, served as an infantryman with General Patton's troops in Europe, the Teales gathered maps, pored over books, and carefully planned their route. As soon as the war was over, David, who loved the outdoors as much as his parents did, planned to join them. The great tragedy of their lives was that David never returned home from the war. As Roul Tunley tells the story in his November 1969 *Audubon* article on Teale: "One night, two months before the end of the war, [David] volunteered for a night reconnaissance patrol. He crossed the Moselle near Koblenz on a raft. In midstream, David, who was only nineteen, caught a sniper's bullet. Only four of the twelve-man patrol got back, and David was not among them" ("His Backyard," p. 126). The army reported him "missing." For a year the Teales didn't know whether he had been killed or captured. In the years between their initial dream of the spring trip and the finality of accepting David's death, "the world changed," Teale wrote in *North with the Spring* (1951), "and our lives changed with it" (p. 2). They dedicated all four books in the American Seasons series to their son, "Who Traveled with Us in Our Hearts."

North with the Spring marks a significant shift in Teale's career as a nature writer. The backyard explorer becomes a roving naturalist, traveling wide and far. The Lilliputian worlds of Teale's insect garden—the knotholes, puddles, and plant stems—are replaced by an entirely different dimension of natural environments and processes: mountain ranges, flyways, watersheds, the instincts of hibernation and migration, and the all-encompassing movement of the seasons across the American continent. This transition from the Teale of *Near Horizons* to

the Teale of *North with the Spring* is reflected, most particularly, in two books: *The Lost Woods* (1945) and *Days Without Time* (1948), each subtitled *The Adventures of a Naturalist*. Each book comprises a collection of nature essays loosely tied together through the themes of memory and time. Neither book possesses the compelling unity of Teale's insect books or his series on the American seasons. But they do contain intriguing individual essays and provide Teale an opportunity to expand his subject matter into the larger, more diverse, horizons of natural history.

In 1947 Nellie and Edwin finally took their long-awaited trip north with the spring, the first of their four journeys through the American seasons. They began in the Everglades and finished three months later in the White Mountains of New Hampshire. In the autumn of 1952, a year after *North with the Spring* was published, the Teales took their second journey, this time heading west from Monomoy Island, Cape Cod, to Point Reyes, California. Like latter-day pioneers they followed the well-trodden trails of earlier explorers and naturalists: Lewis and Clark, Thomas Nuttall, John K. Townsend, and John James Audubon. Their account of this westward migration, *Autumn Across America*, was published in 1956.

The Teales' summer trip took place in 1957 and began where the spring trip had ended, on a bridge just north of Franconia Notch in the White Mountains of New Hampshire. Ten years earlier they had watched the sun set there; in 1957 they watched the sun rise over the mountains to the east. Again they headed west, this time to explore the Great Lakes, the Midwest, and the mountain country of Colorado. They ended their summer trip on the summit of Pikes Peak, facing east, watching the mountain's great shadow stretch toward the horizon to end the day, and the summer season. Teale's account of the trip, *Journey into Summer*, appeared in 1960. On their final trip across America the Teales reversed their direction and began in the West at Silver Strand, a spit of land that forms the western edge of San Diego Bay. Traversing the continent, they completed their winter jour-

Edwin Way Teale

ney in March 1962, in northern Maine, north of Caribou.

The publication of *Wandering Through Winter* in 1965 brought many accolades to Teale. On the front page of the *New York Times Book Review*, Roger Tory Peterson called Teale's series on the American seasons "the major work of his life." "There is something of all the great nature writers in Teale," wrote Peterson, "something of W. H. Hudson, of John Muir, of Henry Thoreau" ("Time of Rest," p. 36). In *The Atlantic*, Edward Weeks placed Teale in the company of Audubon, Thoreau, Muir, and Teale's nature writing contemporaries Sally Carrighar, Joseph Wood Krutch, and Rachel Carson. "Every one of those I have mentioned," wrote Weeks, "has opened the minds and the eyes of thousands to wonders they would otherwise have missed in this country" ("Peripatetic Reader," p. 134).

Lewis Gannett felt that Teale's writing and photography deserved "a special niche in American literature." So did many others. In 1966 *Wandering Through Winter* won the Pulitzer Prize for general nonfiction, the first nature book to do so.

Teale was humbled by his journeys through the American seasons. He realized that no matter how much he had read about or paid attention to the natural world in the places he and Nellie visited, he would never experience and understand the local landscapes the way those who had inhabited those places did. "Everywhere we went," he wrote in *North with the Spring*, "we encountered people who had spent their lives reading from one particular shelf in nature's library. They knew more about it—more about their area and their particular field—than we could ever hope to know. We could but sample the books they had time to read in detail" (pp. 223–224). Teale greatly admired the local people they met on their journeys—people like Mrs. Toy Miller, who gathered herbs in the Blue Ridge Mountains; Connie Hagar, the "birding wizardess of the Texas coast"; and Leslie C. Peltier, the Delphos, Ohio, stargazer and comet collector. They are the quiet heroes of Teale's great adventure.

"The way to become acquainted with an area intimately, to appreciate it best," Teale wrote in *Journey into Summer*, "is to walk over it. And the slower the walk the better" (p. 6). This was one of the great dilemmas of Teale's entire project. How could he become intimate with the American continent while driving a car seventy-six thousand miles through it in only a year's time? John Muir had had time to notice the subtle rhythms and changes in the landscape on his thousand-mile walk to the Gulf of Mexico in 1867. Peter Jenkins stopped and worked for weeks at a time during his walk across America in the 1970s. But Teale wanted to do the impossible: grasp each season by the collar and the tail and shake it until it somehow fit onto the framework of two naturalists wandering their way through the endless folds of its fabric. On one hand, Teale failed. At the end of *North with the Spring* he admits that "spring is like life. You never grasp it entire; you touch it here, there; you know it only in parts and fragments" (p. 336). Teale knew that he could never really encompass the natural history of a season. But the marvel of his American seasons books is that he tried, and that his grand, four-volume attempt successfully weaves the fragments of natural history, experience, photography, feature writing, science, and memory into an enduring tapestry of the American continent and its seasons.

Edward Weeks said that "Teale grew with the undertaking." One of the ways he grew, during his twenty years of exploring the American seasons, was in his reading. The words and wisdom of the great naturalists reverberate through every chapter of Teale's books on the American seasons: Thoreau, Muir, Audubon, Charles Darwin, Lewis and Clark, William Bartram, W. H. Hudson, Richard Jeffries, John Burroughs, Gilbert White, Mary Hunter Austin, Robert Ridgway, Rachel Carson, Thomas Nuttall, David Douglas, and Alexander von Humboldt, among many others. In 1952, the year of Teale's autumn journey, Dodd, Mead published his marvelous anthology *Green Treasury: A Journey Through the World's Great Nature Writing*. Two years later, after visiting Yosemite, Teale edited a collection of Muir's writings, *The Wilderness World of John Muir*; and in 1964 Viking published Teale's *Audubon's Wildlife*. Teale also wrote articles on W. H. Hudson, John Burroughs, Gilbert White, and J. Henri Fabre, as well as book reviews of Roger Tory Peterson's *Wild America* (1955), Sigurd Olson's *The Lonely Land* (1961), and Edward Abbey's *Desert Solitaire* (1968). Of the latter, Teale wrote, Abbey's "is a passionately felt, deeply poetic book. It has philosophy. It has humor. It has sincerity and conviction. . . . [all] set down in a lean, racing prose, in a close-knit style of power and beauty" (p. 7).

Though W. H. Hudson was Teale's favorite nature writer, the writings of Thoreau seemed to permeate nearly everything Teale wrote. From his first encounter with Thoreau's writings during his rowboat excursion down the Ohio River to his final collaborative book project with Ann Zwinger, *A Conscious Stillness: Two Naturalists on Thoreau's Rivers* (1982), Teale lived, breathed, and worked in the best spirit of Henry David Thoreau. In *The Lost Woods* Teale included two essays on Thoreauvian pilgrimages. Those pilgrimages led to Teale's 1946 edition of *Walden*, illustrated with 142 of his black-and-white photographs. Thoreau scholar Walter Harding, whom Teale had met and befriended in 1943 at a meeting of the Thoreau Society, called Teale's edition of *Walden* "the edition we have dreamed of and never hoped to see." E. B. White, however, cautioned that despite Teale's "beautiful photographs," "*Walden* is, of course, not a book that can be illustrated. . . . Thoreau was writing not about beans but about the meaning of beans—which is hard to photograph" (*New Yorker*, 28 December 1946).

In July 1957 the Thoreau Society elected Teale president. The following summer, Teale canoed at dawn with Walter Harding, and later that morning gave his presidential address to the Thoreau Society, "Henry Thoreau and the Realms of Time." In 1962, Dodd, Mead published Teale's *The Thoughts of Thoreau*. And three years later, at nearly the same time as the publication of *Wandering Through Winter*, Harding dedicated his biography, *The Days of Henry Thoreau*, to Martin Luther King, Jr., and Edwin Way Teale, "who although they lead widely disparate lives have both found inspiration in Henry David Thoreau." Thoreau inspired Teale because, as Teale put it in *The Lost Woods*, "He knew that it is not birds alone, nor animals alone, nor plants alone, nor insects alone that has the greatest claim upon us in the out-of-doors. It is the whole of Nature with its sanity and health" (p. 283).

Trail Wood

By the mid-1950s the Teales' home in Baldwin, Long Island, no longer provided the sanity or health it once had. The city had grown up around them. So Edwin and Nellie began searching for a wilder place to live—a place with woods, a stream, a swamp, lots of birds, and a Cape Cod–type farmhouse. On the last day of April 1959, they found it: a country house nestled on a hilltop in the woods near Hampton, in northeastern Connecticut. Trail Wood, as they named it, became the home Edwin and Nellie lived in for the rest of their lives. In time, like White's Selborne, Thoreau's Walden, Burroughs' Slabsides, and Aldo Leopold's Sand County, Trail Wood became the natural and spiritual center of Teale's world.

About two hundred yards from the farmhouse, Teale built an outdoor study under a huge pile of branches and brush. There he could work on his books while secretly watching animals and birds near the waterfall, the meadow, and the woods beyond. Once, he told newspaperman Lawrence Willard, within a few moments he saw a kingfisher dive near his study, then a heron appeared, then a broad-winged hawk swooped down by the stream, hunting for frogs. Such occurrences appear frequently in *A Naturalist Buys an Old Farm* (1974), Teale's gentle description of his and Nellie's outdoor adventures at Trail Wood. It is a quiet but powerfully affirmative book about what it means to inhabit a place, to live within its rhythms, and to love it as one loves the earth, "*this* earth," Teale says, "the only earth we know" (p. 298).

According to Ann Zwinger, Teale's books never became "environmental writing," but over the years his love of the earth did compel him to speak out for nature and against human destruction of wild places. In 1945, six years after the introduction of DDT and seventeen years before Rachel Carson's *Silent Spring*, Teale cautioned the readers of *Nature Magazine* that DDT could cause a "winter stillness [to] fall over the woods and fields." Seven years before Congress passed the Wilderness Act (1964), Teale wrote an article in *Audubon* magazine urging the passage of a bill then before Congress, to establish a National Wilderness Preservation System. He felt the time was right "for putting wilderness philosophy into law." In *Wandering Through Winter*, years before the passage of the Convention on International Trade in Endangered Species (1973), Teale proposed that the time would soon come for a wildlife bill of rights. "It is the conservationist," he insisted, "who is concerned with the welfare of all the land and life of the country who, in the end, will do most to maintain the world as a fit place for human existence as well" (*Wandering Through Winter*, p. 162).

In the last years of his life, Teale continued to make the world a fit place to live—for himself, for Nellie, for others, and especially for the insects, fish, birds, and trees that happened to share Trail Wood with him. The final book he completed, *A Walk Through the Year* (1978), is as much a walk through the country of Teale's mind as it is a reflective tribute to the rhythms and seasons at Trail Wood. Like its earlier counterpart, *Circle of the Seasons: The Journal of a Naturalist's Year* (1953), it is a day-by-day chronicle; it begins in the spring, and ends in anticipation of the spring. For Teale, there always was more day to dawn, and the sun truly was a morning star.

In 1979 Edwin and Nellie celebrated his eightieth birthday by canoeing on the Sudbury, one of Thoreau's rivers, and they deeded Trail Wood to the Connecticut Audubon Society. Edwin died the following autumn, on 18 October 1980. In autumn "there is death in the air," wrote Thomas Hardy (one of Teale's favorite writers). "Life would come again in the spring," added Teale, in *Autumn Across America*, "but not *this* life, not to *these* flowers, not to *these* leaves, not to *these* crickets and grasshoppers" (p. 88). Nor to *this* Edwin Way Teale. Though he measured his life by the "sunrise and moonset and the turning of the seasons," the conscious stillness of his presence will always reverberate through his words and photographic images, into the lives and memories of all who come to his books seeking to know nature. "Memory," he wrote in *Days Without Time*, "is the soul of time" (p. 4).

Selected Bibliography

WORKS OF EDWIN WAY TEALE

BOOKS

The Book of Gliders (New York: Dutton, 1930); *Grassroot Jungles: A Book of Insects* (New York: Dodd, Mead, 1937); *The Golden Throng: A Book About Bees* (New York: Dodd, Mead, 1940; repr., Sherborne, U.K.: Alphabooks, 1981); *Byways to Adventure: A Guide to Nature Hobbies* (New York: Dodd, Mead, 1942); *Near Horizons: The Story of an Insect Garden* (New York: Dodd, Mead, 1942); *Dune Boy: The Early Years of a Naturalist* (New York: Dodd, Mead, 1943; Lone Oak ed., with 3 new chaps., 1957; repr., New York: Bantam, 1968 and Bloomington: Indiana Univ. Press, 1986); *The Lost Woods: Adventures of a Naturalist* (New York: Dodd, Mead, 1945); *Days Without Time: Adventures of a Naturalist* (New York: Dodd, Mead, 1948); *North with the Spring* (New York: Dodd, Mead, 1951; repr., New York: St. Martin's Press, 1990).

Circle of the Seasons: The Journal of a Naturalist's Year (New York: Dodd, Mead, 1953; repr., 1987); *Autumn Across America* (New York: Dodd, Mead, 1956; repr., New York: St. Martin's Press, 1990); *Journey into Summer* (New York: Dodd, Mead, 1960; repr., New York: St. Martin's Press, 1990); *The Strange Lives of Familiar Insects* (New York: Dodd, Mead, 1962); *Audubon's Wildlife* (New York: Viking, 1964); *Wandering Through Winter* (New York: Dodd, Mead, 1965; repr., New York: St. Martin's Press, 1990); *Springtime in Britain* (New York: Dodd, Mead, 1970); *Photographs of American Nature* (New York: Dodd, Mead, 1972); *A Naturalist Buys an Old Farm* (New York: Dodd, Mead, 1974; repr., 1987); *A Walk Through the Year* (New York: Dodd, Mead, 1978; repr., 1987); *A Conscious Stillness: Two Naturalists on Thoreau's Rivers* (New York: Harper & Row, 1982; repr., Amherst: Univ. of Massachusetts Press, 1984), written with Ann Zwinger.

BOOKS FOR YOUNGER READERS

The Boys' Book of Insects (New York: Dutton, 1939), rev. and repr. as *The Junior Book of Insects* (New York: Dutton, 1953; 2nd rev. ed., 1972); *The Boys' Book of Photography* (New York: Dutton, 1939); *Insect Friends* (New York: Dodd, Mead, 1955); *The Bees* (Chicago: Children's Press, 1961); *The Lost Dog* (New York: Dodd, Mead, 1961).

ANTHOLOGIES

Adventures in Nature (New York: Dodd, Mead, 1959); *The American Seasons* (New York: Dodd, Mead, 1976).

EDITED BOOKS

Walden, by Henry David Thoreau (New York: Dodd, Mead, 1946); *The Insect World of J. Henri Fabre*, trans. by Alexander Teixeira de Mattos (New York: Dodd, Mead, 1949; rev. ed., Greenwich, Conn.: Fawcett, 1956; repr., Boston: Beacon Press, 1991); *Green Treasury: A Journey Through the World's Great Nature Writing* (New York: Dodd, Mead, 1952); *The Wilderness World of John Muir* (Boston: Houghton Mifflin, 1954); *The Thoughts of Thoreau* (New York: Dodd, Mead, 1962; repr., 1987).

BOOK REVIEWS

"Naturalists' Grand Tour," review of *Wild America*, by Roger Tory Peterson and James Fisher, in *New York Times Book Review* (16 October 1955); "This Was—and Is—the North at Its Best," review of *The Lonely Land*, by Sigurd Olson, in *New York Times Book Review* (9 April 1961); "Making the Wild Scene," review of *Desert Solitaire*, by Edward Abbey, in *New York Times Book Review* (28 January 1968).

ARTICLES

"Dinosaur of the Insect World: The Praying Mantis, Tyrant and Destroyer," in *Travel* 64 (February 1935); "Gilbert White," in *Audubon* 47 (January 1945); "DDT," in *Nature Magazine* 38 (March 1945); "W. H. Hudson's Lost Years," in *Saturday Review of Literature* 30 (12 April 1947); "Fabre: The Explorer Who Stayed Home," in *Coronet* 29 (February 1951);

"John Burroughs: Disciple of Nature," in *Coronet* 31 (March 1952); "Land Forever Wild," in *Audubon* 59 (May 1957); "Henry Thoreau and the Realms of Time," in *Thoreau Society Bulletin* 64 (summer 1958).

MANUSCRIPTS AND PAPERS

The Edwin Way Teale Archives, in the Homer Babbidge Library, Univ. of Connecticut, Storrs, include Teale's papers, lists, notes, journals, diaries, letters, articles, and books.

BIOGRAPHICAL AND CRITICAL STUDIES

Edward H. Dodd, Jr., *Of Nature, Time and Teale* (New York: Dodd, Mead, 1960); Lewis Gannett, "Lots of June in January," review of *Wandering Through Winter*, in *Book Week* 3 (17 October 1965); Frank Graham, Jr., "The Last Naturalist," in *Audubon* 83 (January 1981); Walter Harding, "Edwin Way Teale," in *Thoreau Society Bulletin* 154 (winter 1981) and 156 (summer 1981); John Kieran, "About Edwin Way Teale," in *Audubon* 54 (May 1952); Roger Tory Peterson, review of *Autumn Across America*, in *Natural History* 65 (November 1956); "Time of Rest, Rebirth and Hope," review of *Wandering Through Winter*, in *New York Times Book Review* (24 October 1965); Roul Tunley, "His Backyard Was a Passage to Fame," in *Audubon* 71 (November 1969); Edward Weeks, "The Peripatetic Reader: The Four Seasons," in *Atlantic* 216 (December 1965); E. B. White, "Walden," in *New Yorker* (28 December 1946).

CELIA THAXTER
(1835–1894)

VERA NORWOOD

CELIA LAIGHTON THAXTER was one of the nineteenth century's most famous American female poets and writers. She numbered among friends New England's most influential literati, including John Greenleaf Whittier and Sarah Orne Jewett. Her poetry and prose appeared in *Century*, *Scribner's*, *Harper's*, and the *Atlantic Monthly*. Embracing the visual arts as well, she was acquainted with the painters Childe Hassam, William Morris Hunt, and Ellen Robbins. This group shared an interest in depicting the natural landscapes along America's northeastern coast as an important aspect of the national heritage, to be cherished and preserved. Valuing a pastoral, middle landscape over both city and wilderness, the writers and artists in Thaxter's set worked to bring a broader public to share their appreciation of such space as the proper home for America's republican spirit.

Thaxter herself came to symbolize the importance of such a landscape not only through her writings but also in a portrait of her done by Childe Hassam. Completed in 1892, *Celia Thaxter in Her Garden* remains one of America's most famous paintings of the landscape and a citizen's place in it. In this painting, Celia Thaxter stands at the edge of a gate separating her garden from the surrounding untamed coast. Rather than a formal cultivation, the garden suggests the naturalized designs favored by famous landscape architects of the period, such as

Frederick Law Olmsted. There are no distinct boundaries between the natural world in the garden and that outside the gate. Cultivated hollyhocks and Shirley poppies in the garden spill outside the fence, mingling with free-growing wildflowers. Dressed in a rather plain white frock, Thaxter makes no intrusive human presence in the landscape. Rather, she appears simply as a tall flower, cultivated for her plain style and native civility. The painting suggests that, after almost three centuries of effort, Euro-American immigrants finally had made some peace with the place—that, in fact, the mark of their civilization was the balance they were able to achieve between wild and cultivated nature.

It would not have been lost on the viewer of such a painting that the subject was female. Identification of nature as female and females as close to nature has a long tradition in European thought, a tradition whose beginning historian Annette Kolodny has traced, in America, to the sermons delivered in the New World by the Puritan fathers. William Gerdts's studies of landscape paintings link this image to depictions of women in their gardens, and outline a lineage proceeding from the European impressionist painters to nineteenth-century American artists. A woman at her ease in the garden symbolized nature under a certain amount of cultivation. In America such images took on the additional weight of suggesting a wilderness landscape that had been domesticated but not eradicated. That a proper Victorian woman (whose purity was testified to by that white dress) defined her civility in this pastoralized balance of native and domesticated plants underscored the value of maintaining such places as domestic retreats from the uncivilized challenges of the wilderness and the city.

Celia Thaxter in Her Garden is painted from the viewpoint of the male expedition leader or captain of industry who returns from the frontiers of wilderness or city to find a haven of domesticity that he longs to reenter. Such a model situated women within a particular natural world while positioning men outside that space. Like her friend Sarah Orne Jewett, Thaxter shared her culture's celebration of Victorian women's perceived empathy with a romantic, pastoralized nature. Her poetry's popularity came in part from her ability to articulate these popularly accepted gender-role differences. She often wrote her poems in a male voice, as in the piece "Alone," which appeared in her poetry collection *Drift-weed* (1878). Here Thaxter takes on the persona of a male suitor who stands outside a garden wall, watching a lovely woman. The woman in the garden relaxes among her roses and lilies. The flowers seem to respond to her touch—one even leans into her hand in a state of "bliss." The suitor's one desire is to become for a moment the rose that earns her love. But, as in much romantic poetry, he is caught forever alone at the gate in unrequited passion for the woman in her garden.

To leave Celia Thaxter ensconced so firmly in the nineteenth century's images of nature and women's place in nature, such as that presented by Hassam, however, would be to forfeit a complete understanding of her life and work. Unlike the woman who frustrated her suitor in "Alone," Thaxter did invite her admirers through her garden gate, and then spun many tales of her deep love for the plants and animals of her domestic life. Her most significant contribution to American nature writing was made in her autobiographical writings detailing her lifelong efforts to make her home in the unpromising, decidedly ungenteel, landscapes of a group of lonely islands off the coast of New Hampshire. In Thaxter's autobiographical nature essays, the character in Hassam's tableau comes to life and sets in motion the struggles and rewards of a life defined through the natural world.

Youth

Born Celia Laighton on 29 June 1835, in Portsmouth, New Hampshire, Thaxter was the daughter of Eliza Rymes and Thomas B. Laighton, a lumber merchant and importer who held several local offices before losing his bid for selectman in 1839. In that year he made a move that forever changed Celia's life. Thomas Laighton took on the post of lighthouse keeper at White Island, a three-acre outpost that is part of the chain called the Isles of Shoals, off the coast of New Hampshire. In 1841 the family moved again, to Smutty-nose Island, where Laighton rented rooms in his house to island visitors. By 1848 he had moved a last time, building a summer hotel on Appledore, the largest of the Isles of Shoals, and settling into the life of host to the rising tide of upper- and middle-class urban tourists who escaped to the countryside in search of rejuvenation in nature.

Thaxter's childhood on White Island and Appledore shaped her landscape preferences and contributed to her becoming a writer. Her first major prose publication, *Among the Isles of Shoals* (1873), ostensibly was written to answer questions about the natural and human history of the islands, which generations of tourists brought to the keepers of Appledore House. Much of the narrative is taken up with descriptions of geology, climate, plants, and native animals of the chain, explaining along the way the odd names of each island. Thaxter also offers a brief ethnography of the earlier settlers, many of whom seemed to fall away from the religious virtues and social graces of their class. The locals'—or, as she calls them, "natives' "—loss of civility was due, she argues, in large part to the isolation and hard life on these wind-swept, apparently barren rocks. Thaxter also contends, however, that the wild landscapes of the islands could forge a specially attentive love of nature and spark the creative voice.

This last point was particularly important in the time period in which *Among the Isles of Shoals* appeared. As Peter Schmitt has documented in his *Back to Nature*, between 1880 and 1940 American popular culture was filled with messages encouraging citizens to get back in touch with America's remnant natural landscapes, which offered an escape from, and the best hope for countering, the pressures of urban life. *Among the Isles of Shoals* spoke eloquently to a generation of tastemakers who feared that urban life was robbing children of experiences in the natural world that would make them good citizens. The book mirrored the belief that close observation of nature's processes would help the next generation maintain spiritual values in an increasingly materialist age.

In *Among the Isles of Shoals*, Thaxter wrote that as a child she knew little of the great affairs of history. History on White Island was measured by the turn of the seasons, not the arrival of the newspaper. The return of human life to the islands, as summer visitors came back to the inn, was noted by Celia and her younger brothers only as part of the return of all sorts of animal and plant life—a sort of absolute version of republican egalitarianism. In the book, Thaxter casts herself as something of a "wild" child because of the family's year-round tenancy on a spot otherwise deserted for most of the year. However, she uses the terms "wild" and "native" interchangeably, to mean those aspects of life most closely in touch with the natural history (as opposed to the human history) of the islands. She often compares herself to the animals native to the place—most often to the sandpipers. It was, Thaxter argues, the enforced isolation of her childhood on the islands that drew her to nature: "To the heart of Nature one must needs be drawn in such a life; and very soon I learned how richly she repays in deep refreshment the reverent love of her worshipper" (p. 123).

The Laighton children engaged in exactly the sort of playing and learning in nature that educational professionals of the late nineteenth century, appalled at the ignorance of nature displayed by urban children, were developing into a popular nature-study curriculum for the schools. In fact, the only school that Thaxter reports attending in *Among the Isles of Shoals* is that offered by nature. She and her brothers explored the shoreline each day, in the process learning a great deal about the flora and fauna of their home. Such knowledge made them serious where other children might be frivolous: "I remember in the spring kneeling on the ground to seek the first blades of grass that pricked through the soil, and bringing them into the house to study and wonder over. Better than a shop full of toys they were to me!" (p. 128).

Vera Norwood's *Made from This Earth* documents how women of the mid-to-late nineteenth century were encouraged to study botany and ornithology, fields that allowed them to pursue knowledge within the confines of home and neighborhood and that could be passed on easily to children in the daily domestic round. Young Celia, evidencing a "natural" call to the endeavors of girls of her class, showed a decided predilection for identifying and studying the wildflowers and migrating birds of her home. Such knowledge led her to value and respect those aspects of her natural heritage that many of her generation felt were threatened with destruction by urban growth. For example, she took a properly protective, nurturing role toward the island wildflowers—reporting that she felt somewhat guilty for killing individual flowers as she picked them, and would gently lay the spent blooms to rest in secluded places on the island. Thus, her childhood in the natural spaces of the lonely islands, as she described it in *Among the Isles of Shoals*, supported a growing popular sentiment that the best hope for creating a responsible citizenry was to get them back to nature.

The increasingly materialist, consumer culture of middle-class Americans in the late nineteenth century seemed to threaten spiritual values. A hike in the local woods or along the shore could offer the opportunity to meditate upon larger questions, to ponder the meanings of life and death, to reconnect with the Maker of the world. Thaxter's childhood offered her many occasions to confront forms of power and beauty that reminded her of her place in the universe. Living, as she put it, like a "little cockleshell" on a toehold island at the mercy of the fierce storms of the Atlantic Ocean, she could never forget the fragility of her life and its place in a much larger environment. In counterpoint to the changeless image of the woman safely sheltered in a rose garden, *Among the Isles of Shoals* offers the truer narrative of a young girl's life (which represented all life) as she struggles through adversity and finds momentary peace. Thaxter reports that many times she worried about the seabirds during the vicious winds and rains that broke across the islands, only to discover that they were made to weather such storms. Her understanding of how the beauties and terrors of nature fit together led her to appreciate what she called the "infinite harmony" expressed in nature.

This direct, unsheltered experience of nature first called Thaxter to the life of the writer. In *Among the Isles of Shoals* she asserts that a particular August thunderstorm and the ensuing stunning calm first awoke in her an ambition to relay what she witnessed:

> Ever I longed to *speak* those things that made life so sweet, to speak the wind, the cloud, the bird's flight, the sea's murmur . . . the manifold aspects of Nature held me and swayed all my thoughts until it was impossible to be silent any longer, and I was fain to mingle my voice with her myriad voices, only aspiring to be in accord with the Infinite harmony, however feeble and broken the notes might be. (pp. 141–142)

Marriage and Literary Success

Thaxter and her brothers were not quite so free from the rigors of book learning as the memoir she constructed in *Among the Isles of Shoals* suggests. Thaxter, in particular, found a vehicle for her strong feelings for nature in the literary education provided by her tutor and future husband, Levi Lincoln Thaxter. Thaxter came from a wealthy, intellectual Boston family. After finishing his education at Harvard, he sought a career that would allow him to spend more time on the Isles, whose natural beauties initially attracted him as they had Celia. He and Thomas Laighton were partners in the building of Appledore House, but Levi found himself unsuited to the task of running a hotel and the partnership dissolved. He stayed on, however, as the Laighton children's tutor, serving in this capacity from the time Celia was twelve until their marriage on 30 September 1851, when she was sixteen and he was thirty-one.

First as her tutor, then as her husband, Levi Thaxter introduced Celia to the pleasures of literature. Himself something of a Browning scholar, he read her the English poets, instilling in her his love of verse. Celia's letters document their joint exploration of some of the key literature forming the aesthetic tastes and opinions of the intellectuals of the day. She read Charlotte Brontë's novels "with rapture," and spoke of the "wonder and admiration" she felt for John Ruskin's works. The importance of nature to so many of the authors she studied combined with her childhood immersion in the native landscape of White Island to produce in Thaxter a genuine affinity for the Romantic poets so popular among the intellectual elite. In fact, the one hint she gives in *Among the Isles of Shoals* that a more formal education succeeded her tutorials in nature was a comment on how her youthful passion for flowers led to her strong appreciation for John Keats's poetry.

But Thaxter did not break through as a writer who combined her education in nature and her education in literature until her husband forced her to abandon the native landscape that was her home. Levi Thaxter had been unable to settle upon a profession. In the early years of their marriage, he and Celia led a peripatetic existence, moving back and forth between the mainland and the islands as Levi pursued a variety of occupations. He did, however, maintain his home on Appledore until an accident forever changed his feelings about the Isles of Shoals. As Celia pointed out in her narrative, the waters around the islands were often difficult to navi-

Celia Thaxter

gate. *Among the Isles of Shoals* tells many a tale of horrible shipwrecks. One near tragedy occurred in 1855, when Levi almost lost his life while sailing in a storm. His fear of the sea and the islands as a result of this accident led him to move the family permanently to the mainland. Thus, in 1856, at the age of twenty-one, Celia found herself beached in Newtonville, Massachusetts, with two small sons, Karl (who was mentally ill throughout his life) and John. Two years later her last child, Roland, was born.

Thaxter's remove from friends and family on the islands resulted in a tide of letters, which were edited and published in 1895 by her Boston friends Annie Fields and Rose Lamb. They reveal a young wife whose lifestyle was at first dictated by the tastes and social sphere of her more mature, more educated husband. In part because of Levi's family connections, the couple quickly found a place among Boston's literary establishment and Celia gained a reputation as a hostess. But her letters of the late 1850s give voice to a dawning realization that she was homesick for her island life, and that she and her husband did not always share the same beliefs and values. During this time, Thaxter recognized that the family would face economic struggles due to Levi's inability to settle on a profession.

Over this stream of life Thaxter tried to find a bridge through poetry. Her first published piece was a poem given by an acquaintance to James Russell Lowell. Lowell liked the poem so much that he gave it a title and in 1861 published it in the *Atlantic Monthly*. "Land-Locked" poignantly conveyed the loss Thaxter felt at being denied her home on the sea-encircled islands. The poem's narrator watches a river that runs into the sea and wishes she could follow. Aware that she should not be "ungrateful" for the full life she leads inland, she still cannot help but "crave / The sad, caressing murmur of the wave / That breaks in tender music on the shore" (*Letters*, p. xiv). This piece set the stage for the best of Thaxter's poetry—works that sprang from her emotional connections to the natural worlds on the islands.

Thaxter was taken up by John Greenleaf Whittier, who encouraged her to write and publish more. He served as her literary guide for many years. During the 1860s and 1870s, Thaxter published in numerous magazines, including inspirational nature poems in children's magazines like *St. Nicholas*. Her poems appeared in two collected volumes in the 1870s, one of which (*Poems*) was in its twentieth edition by 1894. Such literary success finally allowed Thaxter the opportunity to use the voice she discovered in her childhood rambles in nature. Her work also gave her a means to contribute to the family's income. According to her niece, Rosamond Thaxter, whose biography of Celia, *Sandpiper*, provides the most extensive account of her life, her income was a much-needed addition.

Thaxter's literary education made her mistress of many popular forms. But she knew that her most honest, effective statements were those that came from the center of her life among the plants and animals of the Isles of Shoals. As she confessed to her friend and editor, James T.

Fields, after sending him some less than successful works: "I believe, I am *afraid*, I never can put my heart into anything that doesn't belong to the sea" (*Letters*, p. 24). Thaxter was well aware that the subject matter giving her voice wings was to be found on the islands, but her personal circumstances during the 1860s and 1870s made it very difficult for her to focus her attention on the natural world. She was responsible for running a household with three growing boys and a husband who began experiencing health problems that would last for the rest of his life. The mental disability of her eldest boy, Karl, drained her attention. There was little money to pay for help and free her time for writing. During these years her parents died. As the only daughter in the family, Thaxter felt obligated to spend time away from her family to help care for her parents during their last illnesses.

However, her husband's ailments and her parents' decline also presented Thaxter with the opportunity to return for extended periods to her beloved Appledore. After his first bout of serious ill health in the winter of 1868–1869, Levi went to Florida with the two youngest sons for seven months, and Celia was free to return with Karl to the islands. This pattern of extended separations, in which Levi left for a climate that might support his health while Celia returned to Appledore, defined their marriage until his death in 1884. Although Thaxter's letters reveal that she was disappointed in this fragmentation of her family, and missed having a settled home life with her husband, she also finally felt released to return to the natural pleasures the islands proffered.

Her letters also speak of a rift between Celia and Levi that made the physical separations acceptable. Although Celia apparently enjoyed domestic life with her husband and children, and the intellectual life of elite Boston and her literary friends, she did not share the assumptions of Levi's wealthy family and associates. In particular, the extravagant lifestyle of his circle was not always appealing to a woman who had grown up in constrained circumstances. For example, in an 1868 letter to a friend, she noted that she was pleased to have missed a ball in Boston that Levi had attended: "the flowers alone cost fifteen hundred dollars...and the poor children in the streets of Boston barefoot and squalid!" (*Letters*, p. 36). When a relative brought her a silver service early in her marriage, she knew she was supposed to treasure it, but wrote to a friend that it really represented more domestic work by requiring polishing. She allied herself with another advocate of the simple life and one of her favorite authors when she defended her feelings about this gift: "Give me my iron jug and iron spoon, say I with Mr. Thoreau" (*Letters*, p. 17). In her own dress, she was remembered for her plain style—wearing white, gray, or black with a necklace or bracelet of seashells.

Her attire was in part a political statement that indicated, perhaps, her deepest disagreement with her husband on a single issue. Like many nature-loving women of her generation, Thaxter was horrified at the massive killing of birds in order to provide feathers for women's fashions. She joined with women in the newly emerging Audubon societies to educate female consumers about the devastation of native bird populations caused by millinery preferences. Her poems often took up the issue, as in "The Kittiwakes" (in *Drift-weed*), a children's poem that casts the boatmen who kill such birds for the market as "evil" men senselessly murdering "fair, pathetic creatures." Although she generally eschewed making direct public statements on political causes, she wrote a pamphlet on the issue titled *A Woman's Heartlessness*.

Although much of Thaxter's anger at hunters was directed at the specific slaughter of birds for the fashion market, this concern reflected her deep-seated disapproval of the killing of any native animals. Here she took a stance that was obviously at odds with her husband's views. Like many educated, male, amateur naturalists of his generation, Levi Thaxter was an avid hunter. He often took John and Roland on extended hunting expeditions to bag birds and other native species. Women of this period often parted company with men on hunting and worked to limit the collecting done by their fathers and husbands, even that done in the name of science. Thaxter agreed with what she saw as this "woman's way

of viewing" all hunting. She hated watching the men in her family "go murdering round the country," and was relieved when she could escape to the island while her husband was in Florida, "shooting all the crocodiles, parrakeets, mockingbirds, herons, flamingoes, white ibises and every other creature, feathered or otherwise, that chance to fall in their way" (*Letters*, pp. 39–40).

So, although Thaxter's periodic returns to Appledore in the 1870s signaled separations from her husband and two of her sons, and were often occasioned by the illnesses of her parents, the island represented a native landscape that sheltered her from the artificiality of mainland life and provided a refuge for all the aspects of nature that she loved and that nurtured her own creativity. The first direct evidence of the importance of the island to Thaxter's life as a writer was the publication of a series of articles on life on the islands in the *Atlantic Monthly*. They were later issued as *Among the Isles of Shoals* (1873).

As well as containing a memoir of her childhood, *Among the Isles of Shoals* argues that Thaxter, and any other individual for whom the islands were home, could thrive nowhere else. Speaking for the "natives, or persons who have been brought up here," Thaxter points out that they literally die of homesickness when pulled off the island: "No other place is able to furnish the inhabitants of the Shoals with sufficient air for their capacious lungs; there is never scope enough elsewhere, there is no horizon; they must have sea-room" (pp. 16–17). This is true not only for humans and other animals, but for plants as well. Speaking metaphorically for herself as well as for her flowers, Thaxter notes that even domesticated garden plants fare better on the islands than on the mainland: "When you plant [garden flowers] in this soil they fairly run mad with color. People say, 'Do give me some seeds of these wonderful flowers', and they sow them in their gardens on the mainland, and they come up decorous, commonplace, and pale, like their sisters in the same soil" (pp. 27–28). With comments such as this, Thaxter sets herself apart from mainlanders, announcing that she had returned home. The comment also acknowledges that her return was paid for in part by taking on the role of native host to touring mainlanders. If *Among the Isles of Shoals* served to give Thaxter a vehicle for her personal creativity, it also, like most of her published work, helped to bring in much-needed money for both the Thaxter family on the mainland and her Laighton relatives whose livelihoods depended on attracting tourists to the islands.

Rosamond Thaxter's biography of Celia charts how the family's inns became favorite summer places for many New England writers and artists, including Nathaniel Hawthorne, Ralph Waldo Emerson, and Mark Twain. Some, like Whittier and Lowell, who had first encouraged Celia to publish her work, were drawn to the source of her inspiration. Her book on the islands continued to draw new summer visitors to Appledore House and her family's other hotel on Star Island. With *Among the Isles of Shoals* as their guide, visitors not only shared in the geological and human history of the island, but also could seek out Celia's old haunts and use her descriptions of native plants to identify the wildflowers they found there. Or they could sit on the beach at sunset, watching and listening for the comings and goings of the various birds she recounted seeing on similar evenings. If they were very lucky, they might even have the famous author as a companion. They were more likely, though, to meet her hard at work in the island garden that became the primary recipient of her creative energies from the 1880s on.

Although Thaxter continued to write poetry, and published seven volumes during her life, it is not this work, but the chronicle of her devotion to the garden at Appledore House, that has earned her an enduring place in the canon of literary naturalists. It is not without reason that the best-known portrait of Thaxter is Hassam's painting; but the painting, because it resonates so powerfully with the traditional image of a woman in the garden, also masks the specific value of that green space to the individual woman. Thaxter's main contribution to nature writing was in evoking for generations of gardeners and nature lovers the particular meanings that the well-loved plants of home engender in their caretakers.

Garden Literature

Thaxter's first garden sprang directly from the constrained circumstances of her childhood on White Island. Besides roaming the island in search of her precious wildflowers, as a girl Thaxter had a small flower bed of her own. Less than a yard square, it was filled with pot marigolds that she remembered as "rich in color as barbaric gold." Thaxter's mother enjoyed gardening and instilled a passion for flowers in her daughter. Thaxter remembered that one of the female duties in her parents' household was to take care of the ornamental plants, both indoors and out. During the long, isolated winters, indoor plants brought much joy to the Laighton household.

When her husband moved the family inland, Thaxter kept a garden wherever she lived. Her letters are filled with references to her gardening activities in the 1860s and 1870s. She was always on the lookout for native and cultivated plants that could be imported into her gardens, as when she wrote to a friend asking her to gather harebell seeds along a riverbank, "for I want to get the dear lovely bells to grow here by our river as well as by yours" (*Letters*, p. 17). Specific plants, like this harebell, were important to Thaxter not only for their beauty but for their associations with friends and family. Some of her most intense feelings were reserved for plants her mother loved. When Eliza was on her deathbed, Thaxter daily brought her the flowers she loved most, filling her sickroom with them. After Eliza's death in 1877, Thaxter always planted her mother's favorite flowers in the garden at Appledore.

Yet Thaxter's talents were not hidden in a secluded garden enjoyed only by family and close friends. Although the island remained a personal retreat from the artificiality of mainland life, Thaxter's letters indicate that such seclusion was limited and earned at a price. She complained about having to give up wearing her old clothes when the tourists arrived, and to suffer silently the sight of "women with carcasses of the birds I love borne in simple vanity above their faces" (*Letters*, p. 176). In fact, the seemingly private garden on Appledore served as a public space frequented by guests of the Laighton family's inn. After their parents' death, Celia's brothers took over the hotels, but Celia helped out by designing and planting gardens each year. It was in the gardens at Appledore and Star Island that Thaxter gained a reputation as an expert plantswoman.

The painter Ellen Robbins remembered being very impressed with Thaxter's gardening creations on one of her summer visits to Star Island. Watching Thaxter in the garden inspired Childe Hassam to paint not only the portrait but also a series of landscapes that immortalized the cultivated landscapes around Appledore House. As she pointed out in *Among the Isles of Shoals*, guests often asked her for plant cuttings and seeds to carry home, and consulted her for advice on their own garden designs.

Landscape historians Ann Leighton and John Stilgoe have documented the rise of ornamental gardening activities as more Americans joined the ranks of the home-owning, suburban middle class in the later nineteenth century. Seedmen and nurserymen experienced burgeoning plant sales by the end of the century. Popular magazines encouraged Americans to beautify their yards and join in civic efforts to create a greater number of public green spaces. Women of all classes, but particularly the supposedly leisured wives of the middle and upper classes, were encouraged to take on the responsibility of designing beautiful green spaces around the home. For example, the 1869 edition of Catharine Beecher and Harriet Beecher Stowe's influential *The American Woman's Home* included in its frontispiece a prominent illustration of the genteel woman gardener (appropriately sheltered from the sun by a servant holding a parasol) and three chapters on gardening. Following the 1872 publication of Anna Warner's *Gardening by Myself*, women's gardening books dominated the market. When Thaxter decided in the 1890s to turn from poetry to a gardening book, she knew she had a ready audience and an important topic. And, as with her best poetry and prose, the subject struck a balance between the passions of her private life and the tastes of an educated class of Americans.

For many of the women to whom Thaxter's garden book was addressed, keeping an ornamental garden was part and parcel of their general interest in nature study and preservation. In order to design a successful garden, one had to be familiar with the climate and soils of the region and to study a bit of botany. For those concerned with the loss of native plants, particularly wildflowers, the garden could become a new home for local varieties. Gardens also served as habitats for small animals—particularly sheltering the native birds that women in the Audubon clubs were working to preserve. Thaxter's gardens attracted many of the native birds she extolled in her poetry and in the prose pieces in *Among the Isles of Shoals*. Robin Doughty's *Feather Fashions and Bird Preservation* notes that women wrote many of the popular books about common birds of home and neighborhood. In her later years, Thaxter corresponded with one of the most famous of these women—Olive Thorne Miller, whose books encouraged women to take up ornithology as a properly female way to study nature. This intertwining of her love of plants and birds also drew the famous naturalist Bradford Torrey into extended correspondence with Thaxter as she described for him the comings and goings of birds to the islands.

Of course, not all gardens or their owners were as tied to their natural setting as Thaxter and her friends were. In the later nineteenth century there were also gardening fads for exotic plants and extravagant designs that were antithetical to the surrounding natural landscape and often threatened its very existence. Women like Thaxter and Miller published their observations about the flora and fauna of home in order to counter what they saw as an industrialized, urbanized, mass-produced culture rapidly losing touch with its roots in the land. In this crusade, Thaxter was supported and advised by another important literary friend, Sarah Orne Jewett.

913

Jewett used her novels and short stories to document the overall decline of the small-scale, land- and ocean-based communities of coastal New England in the late nineteenth century. She argued that it was women's role to preserve the regional landscapes in danger of being overwhelmed by mass culture. Championing the pastoral middle landscape of preindustrial America as its best (and now most threatened) heritage, Jewett's short stories offered a fictional version of the simple life that Thaxter lived on her island. When Thaxter took up the task of writing her garden book, she and Jewett corresponded about the manuscript. Jewett served as a valuable reader and editor, helping Thaxter infuse her gardening guide with a sense of the values such spaces supported. Like her compatriots Miller and Jewett, Thaxter wrote in order to bring her readers into a more compassionate relationship with the natural world.

Thus, the garden at Appledore was not a space separate from the rest of nature but played an active part in Thaxter's relationship with the native flora and fauna of the island. Although her book about that garden, *An Island Garden* (1894), served as a guide to the production of a space that might seem outside the ken of the traditional "nature" experience, it was in fact the space in which Thaxter and many women of her generation had their most intense relationships with the plants and animals of their homes and neighborhoods. In this sense, garden books like *An Island Garden*, which chronicle this aspect of human/nature interactions, exemplify an important genre of nature writing.

The garden from which Thaxter wrote her guide seems unprepossessing in both size and design. The bed was a rectangle fifteen by fifty feet, off the piazza and running the length of her private cottage at Appledore. The plan was a simple pattern of formal paths with beds, reached by the steps off the piazza. Two gates led out—one of them to the sea, on the south. The whole was fenced, with banks of less formally organized flower plantings bordering the outside of the enclosure. But the fences were permeable boundaries, allowing cultivated and wild plants to intermingle. Similarly, the distinction between garden and house was blurred. Thaxter grew vines along the piazza and kept water lilies in tubs on the porch. The room that opened directly onto the piazza was filled throughout the summer with cut flowers from the garden. The flowers Thaxter grew in her beds included an informal mix of native plants and imports, annuals and perennials, organized mostly in complementary color combinations.

A hotel guest who happened to pass by as Thaxter rested on the shady porch in the heat of a summer day might have been forgiven if he entertained a romantic conception of a woman for whom such an apparently self-generating garden framed a life spent in leisurely, passive contemplation of nature. Such were the woman and the garden Childe Hassam captured in his paintings, but such was not the relationship Thaxter had with her plot of land. For her, the most important moment of the day came when she took her first step off the piazza and into her garden in the dawn light, as she set out to take part in the renewal of the green world each day. The garden's major joy for Thaxter was in its upkeep—in getting a seed to sprout, in the accomplishment of setting out a hundred sweet pea seedlings, in a thorough job of close hand-weeding, and even in the humbling battles lost with various plant pests. The most important lesson of *An Island Garden* is that in order to know nature, one must work with and respect flora and fauna on their own terms.

Thaxter notes in the "Prefatory" to her garden biography that she wrote it at the behest of friends who kept asking how she had cultivated such a pretty place. Like most garden books, *An Island Garden* contains a great deal of information on the daily round of the gardener. Often rising at four o'clock in the morning so that she could get household chores done in time to be out in the garden at sunrise, Thaxter offers good advice on the necessity of soil preparation and improvement ("many people make a compost heap," p. 13), on how to transplant tender seedlings (Iceland poppies grow best when sprouted in eggshells), on the best fertilizers for specific plants (wallflowers "thrive marvelously if fed with a mixture of old plastering in the soil," p. 41), and discusses in detail a method for killing the garden slugs that are her nemeses ("I carry a large pepper-box filled with air-slaked lime and shake it over them everywhere," p. 62).

Thaxter gives advice on how to plan a garden that will have something green and growing in it throughout the year. And, for her readers with limited financial resources, little actual experience, and a small garden space, she offers specific guidance on plants that are easy to grow, on the basic plans for a garden, and on the virtue of organic fertilizers over more costly, mass-produced products ("I have . . . never found anything to equal barn manure"). Most important, *An Island Garden* expresses the sense of achievement that comes from a task well done in the garden:

It took the whole afternoon to stick [stake] the Peas, and I enjoyed every moment of it. Before putting the dry brittle branches in the ground, with a small, light hoe I went all over and through the earth about the Sweet Peas . . . till there was not a weed to be seen near them. When night fell I had only just finished this pleasant work. (p. 59)

The friends who asked Thaxter to tell them how she made her garden were often members of the educated, influential New England literati she had counted as friends and colleagues for over thirty years. Fortuitously, as had been the case in her first poetic successes, her own preferences as a gardener (driven as much by financial necessity as by personal choice) were in tune with the romantic visions of the pastoral life favored by this tastemaking elite. Thaxter's plant preferences as a young woman were nurtured by the traditional, simple tastes of her mother. As an adult, she discovered that John Ruskin and his gardening compatriot Gertrude Jekyll were horrified by the Victorian craze for conspicuous consumption of annuals in massive, temporary plantings designed to look like oriental rugs. Ann Leighton's *American Gardens of the Nineteenth Century* documents the alternative style that Ruskin, Jekyll, and other founders of the arts-and-crafts movement espoused: a "cottage garden" based on the small perennial beds of rural England. Such spaces mirrored the gardens of Thaxter's mother. Ever mindful that the audi-ence for *An Island Garden* included a literary group influenced by the back-to-nature aesthetic of their English colleagues, Thaxter made a point to note that she shared the values of this elite group, that her garden style was not driven solely by her lack of financial choices:

I have not room to experiment with . . . ribbon-borders and the like, nor should I do it if I had all the room in the world. For mine is just an old-fashioned garden where the flowers come together to praise the Lord and teach all who look upon them to do likewise. (p. 71)

An Island Garden is filled with references to nature appreciation shared with other important writers of the day, including Hawthorne, Emerson, Alfred Lord Tennyson, and Gilbert White, the English parson/naturalist whose chronicles of the natural world in his home and neighborhood in eighteenth-century England had become something of a bible for European Americans seeking a similar feeling of settlement in North America. *An Island Garden* thus contributed to the literature that suggested Americans could return to their true republican and spiritual selves by brief sojourns in the preindustrial, pre-mass-produced remnant spaces left in isolated settings like the Isles of Shoals.

But, finally, *An Island Garden* turns its back on such sentiments, just as Thaxter turned her back on the social whirl of intellectual Boston and on the idea that anyone could understand nature by spending a few summer weeks at Appledore House. Although she makes the proper bows to her literary friends, Thaxter's most compelling voice in her garden biography is the one that situates her in the community most important to her—the plants and animals of the Isles of Shoals. In a letter written while she was on the island, Thaxter observed that she did not truly experience nature in the same way as such New England worthies as Emerson and Thoreau. Casting both as intellectual naturalists who enjoyed "a walk for a walk's sake," she contrasted her own best contacts with "Nature" as those that "flash[ed] on me in some pause of work" (*Letters*, p. 54).

Thaxter's garden, finally, was a vehicle into nature. Rather than sheltering her from the outside world, it connected her to its most important community—the rest of creation. Her best nature writing documents those moments when she shares in the seasonal, regionally specific cycle of nature on Appledore. Thus, in the first week of May, Thaxter always set out her pansies and gillyflowers. As she made her spring return to the garden, so the barn swallows and the sandpipers returned to the Isles of Shoals, and the martins and song sparrows began nesting and singing, and the sea continued the "gentle lapping of waves from the full tide, for the sea is only a stone's-throw from my garden fence" (p. 21). Together, Thaxter, the flowers, the birds, the island rock, and the ocean created the natural world.

In 1880 Celia and Levi sold their house in Newtonville and spent the times they were together at their son John's farm in Kittery Point, Maine. She also spent some time during the winters in Boston or Portsmouth, but her primary residence for the rest of her life was the private cottage on Appledore. Thaxter continued to contribute to family finances through her writing and also took up china painting, creating miniature landscapes on her pieces and selling them. Levi died in 1884, and many of the friends who had become frequent visitors to Appledore also passed on. Debilitating illnesses in her fifties left Thaxter facing her own death. These losses weighed heavily on her and made the natural community she shared on Appledore all the more important. Acknowledging her age, she opened An Island Garden with the consolations that her flowers offered her: "Because of tender memories of loving eyes that see them no more, my flowers are yet more beloved and tenderly cherished" (p. vii). Thaxter died on 26 August 1894 while in residence at Appledore. She was buried on the island near her parents.

Although Thaxter produced more volumes of poetry than of prose, it is her prose narratives about life on the islands that have contemporary appeal. Americans continue to be drawn to stories about the daily lives lived in the remnant rural settings that bespeak the continent's pastoral heritage. The mesh of cultivated garden with native flora and fauna that makes Thaxter's narrative so captivating occurs in nature writing of the late twentieth century as well. Many of the best garden biographies continue to be produced by women who create green spaces that shelter humans, all sorts of other animals, and an astonishing variety of plants.

Among New Englanders who are today following Thaxter's path is Sara Stein, whose delightful My Weeds: A Gardener's Botany, recounts her struggles to deal with what Thaxter described as some wild plants' tendency to overstep their bounds. And Eleanor Perènyi, in Green Thoughts: A Writer in the Garden, carries on the specific literary tradition, giving her readers a tour through many of the Romantic writers whom Thaxter read and who continue to influence nature writers today. Perènyi also details the losses of native plants and animals that once frequented her rural garden in Connecticut. When Perènyi laments the decline of martins as a result of "pollution, pesticides and the slow destruction of their habitats" (p. 29), the reader who has never seen such birds may return to Thaxter's world and understand much better what we have lost since 1894 and what we must protect for the future:

As I stand pruning the Rosebushes, there is a flutter of glad wings, and lo! the first house martins! Beautiful creatures, with their white breasts and steel-blue wings, wheeling, chattering, scolding at me, for they think I stand too near their little brown house on the corner of the piazza eaves. . . . All through April and May I watch them . . . we do not interfere with each other; they have made up their minds to endure me, but I adore them! (Island Garden, pp. 19–20)

Selected Bibliography

WORKS OF CELIA THAXTER

POETRY

Poems (New York: Hurd and Houghton, 1872; new, enl. ed., 1875); Drift-weed (Boston: Houghton, Osgood, 1878); Poems for Children (Boston: Houghton Mifflin, 1882); The Cruise of the Mystery and Other

Poems (Boston: Houghton Mifflin, 1886); *Idyls and Pastorals* (Boston: Lothrop, 1886); *My Lighthouse, and Other Poems* (Boston: Prang, 1890); *Verses* (Boston: Lothrop, 1891).

PROSE

Among the Isles of Shoals (Boston: Osgood, 1873; Boston: Houghton Mifflin, 1901; Sanbornville, N.H.: Wake-Brook House, 1962; Bowie, Md.: Heritage Books, 1978); *A Woman's Heartlessness* (Audubon Society of Pennsylvania, 1897); *An Island Garden* (Boston: Houghton Mifflin, 1894, 1904, 1988; Bowie, Md.: Heritage Books, 1978; Ithaca, N.Y.: Bullbrier, 1985).

LETTERS

Letters of Celia Thaxter, ed. by Annie Fields and Rose Lamb (Boston: Houghton Mifflin, 1895).

POSTHUMOUS PUBLICATIONS

Stories and Poems for Children, with a Biographical Sketch and Portrait (Boston: Houghton Mifflin, 1896; Freeport, N.Y.: Books for Libraries, 1971); *The Heavenly Guest, with Other Unpublished Writings by Celia Thaxter; with Reprints of Essays by Friends and Contemporaries*, ed. by Oscar Laighton (Andover, Mass.: Smiths and Coutts, 1935).

BIOGRAPHICAL AND CRITICAL STUDIES

Robin Doughty, *Feather Fashions and Bird Preservation: A Study in Nature Protection* (Berkeley: Univ. of California Press, 1975); Thomas R. Dunlap, *Saving America's Wildlife* (Princeton, N.J.: Princeton Univ. Press, 1988); William H. Gerdts, "The Artist's Garden: American Floral Painting, 1850–1915," in *Portfolio* 4 (July–August 1982); Annette Kolodny, *The Lay of the Land: Metaphor as Experience and History in American Life and Letters* (Chapel Hill: Univ. of North Carolina Press, 1975); Ann Leighton, *American Gardens of the Nineteenth Century: "For Comfort and Affluence"* (Amherst: Univ. of Massachusetts Press, 1987); Deborah Nevins, "The Triumph of Flora: Women and the American Landscape, 1890–1935," in *Antiques* 127 (April 1985); Vera Norwood, *Made from This Earth: American Women and Nature* (Chapel Hill: Univ. of North Carolina Press, 1993).

Eleanor Perènyi, *Green Thoughts: A Writer in the Garden* (New York: Random House, 1981); Ellen Robbins, "Reminiscences of a Flower Painter," in *New England Magazine* 14 (June/July 1886); Peter J. Schmitt, *Back to Nature: The Arcadian Myth in Urban America* (New York: Oxford Univ. Press, 1969; repr., Baltimore: Johns Hopkins Univ. Press, 1990); Beverly Seaton, "The Garden Autobiography," in *Garden History: The Journal of the Garden History Society* 7 (spring 1979); Sara Bonnett Stein, *My Weeds: A Gardener's Botany* (New York: Harper & Row, 1988); John Stilgoe, *Borderland: Origins of the American Suburb, 1820–1939* (New Haven, Conn.: Yale Univ. Press, 1988); Rosamond Thaxter, *Sandpiper: The Life of Celia Thaxter* (Sanbornville, N.H.: Wake-Brook House, 1962); Ola Elizabeth Winslow, "Celia Laighton Thaxter," in Edward T. James, ed., *Notable American Women, 1607–1950* (Cambridge, Mass.: Harvard Univ. Press, 1971).

LEWIS THOMAS
(1913–1993)

ALISON R. BYERLY

WHEN LEWIS THOMAS DIED on 3 December 1993, the obituaries seemed to write themselves. His death, while naturally regrettable, could not be viewed as tragic. There was a peculiar grace to his passing that was consistent with the poised directness of his writing. One of Thomas' most famous essays, "The Long Habit," from *The Lives of a Cell*, criticizes our culture's assumption that the proper job of medicine is to delay death as long as possible. If medicine finally succeeds in eradicating all diseases, Thomas suggests, "we will perhaps terminate by drying out and blowing away on a light breeze, but we will still die." Having known since 1988 that he was afflicted with Waldenström's disease, a cancer of the lymph system, Thomas had talked openly about his approaching death. With rare detachment, he viewed his own death as part of the natural cycle that makes life itself a privilege. "Our individual coming to an end," he told an interviewer in November of 1993, "may have some connection with the continuity of the species. It may be as important for us to die as it is for plant life to die. So we die and live in our successors" (Rosenblatt, p. 53). Lewis Thomas' essays celebrate the wonder of life in an elegant, economical form that portrays each detail of biology as an expression of nature's own elegance and economy. It seems appropriate, then, that his own life should achieve the kind of thematic closure that makes his essays so compactly profound.

Lewis Thomas is a difficult figure to categorize. His ability to make difficult scientific concepts accessible to the general reader places him in the company of science writers like anthropologist Loren Eiseley and biologist Stephen Jay Gould. As a writer who was also a practicing doctor, he belongs to a literary tradition that includes nineteenth-century Russian dramatist Anton Chekhov, twentieth-century American poet William Carlos Williams, and contemporary doctor-essayists like Richard Selzer and Oliver Sacks. Although he became known to the public through his popular essays, he was already internationally famous in professional circles for his medical research and administrative work. His medical career culminated in his appointment as president and chief executive officer of the Memorial Sloan-Kettering Cancer Center in Manhattan, one of the world's premier cancer research centers. Few people achieve success in two such distinct fields of endeavor. But one cannot say that Thomas' two vocations, doctor and writer, were in competition with each other. Thomas' writing would have been impossible without the scientific training that fostered his inquisitiveness and provided his unusual perspective. Conversely, the breadth, cogency, and synthetic thinking that typify his writing undoubtedly contributed to his medical expertise.

At first glance, Thomas' essays may not seem to be "nature writing" in the traditional sense. He does not recount his explorations of the wilderness or describe the beauties of landscape. He does write about plants and animals, but not, generally speaking, plants and animals his readers have met. Cells, pheromones, bacteria, viruses—these are the organisms that stimulate Thomas' awe of nature. Part of his project is to enlarge our sense of what we mean when we talk about "nature." In "Comprehending My Cat Joeffry," from *The Fragile Species*, Thomas complains, "Nature itself, that vast incomprehensible meditative being, has come to mean for most of us nothing much more than odd walks in the nearby woods, or flowers in the rooftop garden, or the soap opera stories of the last giant panda or whooping crane." For Thomas, nature is not a place, or a particularly rare animal. Nature is a force—and a force to be reckoned with.

Medical and Literary Career

Lewis Thomas was born on 25 November 1913 in Flushing, New York, the son of a doctor, Joseph Simon Thomas, and a nurse, Grace Peck Thomas. Throughout his childhood, he accompanied his father on house calls, an experience that would permanently shape his view of the medical profession. Thomas attended Princeton University and Harvard Medical School, graduating cum laude in 1937. He held a variety of posts before being commissioned as a lieutenant in the U.S. Naval Reserve. Thomas would write in *The Youngest Science* that World War II was "the guiltiest of wars" for him, because he thoroughly enjoyed the research he conducted while stationed in Guam and Okinawa as a virologist.

Thomas' medical appointments are too numerous to list here. He held professorships in pediatrics, medicine, pathology, and biology, and was dean of both the New York University and Yale schools of medicine. As a researcher, he was noted for his work in immunology; endotoxins (toxins produced by certain bacteria); and histocompatibility (the study of immune reactions such as those involved in transplants). It was during his tenure at Yale, as professor and chief of pathology at Yale–New Haven Hospital in

1969–1972, and finally as dean of Yale University School of Medicine in 1972–1973, that he began his essay-writing career.

Thomas had written while at school and had even published a poem in the *Atlantic Monthly* when he was an intern. In 1970, as Thomas recalled in his memoir, *The Youngest Science*, he gave the keynote address at a symposium on inflammation. The appealingly informal style of his presentation impressed an old friend and former mentor, Dr. Franz Ingelfinger, who was then editor of the prestigious *New England Journal of Medicine*. Ingelfinger proposed that Thomas write a short monthly column for the journal, and "Notes of a Biology Watcher" was born.

The succinct, witty columns that Thomas wrote on biology, medicine, and other topics quickly attracted the attention of many nonscientists. Novelist Joyce Carol Oates, for example, photocopied several essays for discussion in her writing classes, and wrote Thomas a letter urging him to collect them in book form. Several presses contacted Thomas, but he was reluctant to take the time to lengthen and connect the essays. However, Viking Press agreed to print them just as they were, and *The Lives of a Cell: Notes of a Biology Watcher*, containing twenty-nine of the thirty essays published in the *New England Journal of Medicine* between May 1971 and February 1974, appeared in 1974.

To the astonishment of everyone involved, *The Lives of a Cell* was an immediate success. It received simultaneous laudatory reviews in *Time* (22 July 1974) and *Newsweek* (24 July 1974). Joyce Carol Oates wrote a lengthy appreciation of it in the *New York Times Book Review*, claiming that to look at *The Lives of a Cell* as either a collection of essays on " 'science' " or as "masterpieces of the 'art of the essay' " would be to misjudge it: following the book's emphasis on evolution, she calls the book itself a higher form that "anticipates the kind of writing that will appear more and more frequently, as scientists take on the language of poetry in order to communicate human truths too mysterious for old-fashioned common sense" (p. 3). In a long *New*

Yorker review, novelist John Updike praised Thomas as a "lively, thoughtful writer" (p. 83), though he found the book's emphasis on advantageous symbiosis among organisms to be overly optimistic. *The Lives of a Cell* won the National Book Award for 1974, having been nominated in the categories of both arts and sciences. It sold very well and within five years of its publication had been translated into eleven languages.

Subsequent columns from the *New England Journal* were collected into a second book, *The Medusa and the Snail: More Notes of a Biology Watcher* (1979). While thematically connected to *The Lives of a Cell* in its emphasis on symbiosis, it is a more eclectic series of essays, touching on many nonscientific topics. Now an established voice rather than an impressive newcomer, Thomas rated a front-page discussion by biology writer Stephen Jay Gould in the *New York Times Book Review*. Gould admired Thomas' "kind and humane vision," but admitted that he "cannot view it as nature's voice.... Nature is much more complex and ambiguous." Nevertheless, Gould writes that he "cannot remember when [he] appreciated a book so much in the face of such fundamental disagreement in intellectual perspective" (pp. 32–33).

Thomas' recognition that his audience was largely composed of nonscientists was reflected in his decision in 1980 to begin writing for *Discover* magazine instead of the *New England Journal of Medicine*. He retired as president of Sloan-Kettering in 1980, though he maintained research affiliations elsewhere. Thomas received many awards and honorary degrees during this period, ranging from a Book of the Month Club Award in 1986 for his "distinguished contribution to American letters," to the 1989 Albert Lasker Medical Research Award (which was announced together with the award to Étienne-Émile Baulieu, the creator of the French "abortion pill"). The most unusual honor bestowed upon him was the construction of a $29 million molecular biology facility at Princeton named the Lewis Thomas Laboratory. In deference to Thomas' enthusiasm for interdisciplinary re-

Lewis Thomas

search and information exchange, the interior laboratory space was specially designed to facilitate collaborative work.

Thomas now had time to pursue his literary interests. His memoir, *The Youngest Science: Notes of a Medicine-Watcher* (1983), was commissioned as part of an Alfred P. Sloan Foundation series on the lives of distinguished contemporary scientists. Poised uneasily between autobiography and commentary on the medical profession, it tends to disintegrate into separate essays. It was recognized, however, as a charming and provocative reflection on the development of modern medicine. In 1985, he published *Could I Ask You Something?*, a book of poems that are perhaps less interesting as verse than as meditations on some of the same subjects that Thomas discusses in his essays. He also continued his lifelong interest in language with a series of philological explorations published as *Et Cetera, Et Cetera: Notes of a Word-Watcher* (1990).

As he became less directly involved in biological research, Thomas became more preoccupied with public policy issues. His collection *Late Night Thoughts on Listening to Mahler's Ninth Symphony* (1983), which includes some *Discover* essays as well as miscellaneous pieces from other magazines, reflects the tense atmosphere fostered by the Reagan administration's emphasis on nuclear deterrence through the Strategic Defense Initiative ("Star Wars"). Several of the pieces, including the much-anthologized title essay, present a physician's perspective on the threat of nuclear war. Throughout the 1980s, Thomas assumed the role of spokesman for the scientific establishment, lecturing on environmental concerns, the population crisis, and health care reform. His final collection, *The Fragile Species* (1992), discusses such contemporary issues as AIDS, drug abuse, global warming, cancer, health maintenance organizations, senile dementia, world hunger, species extinction, and the continuing threat posed by nuclear weapons. It nevertheless maintains what some reviewers felt was unwarranted optimism about the human species and the fate of the planet.

The Unity of Life

Thomas' essays are best discussed collectively, rather than one book at a time, because of the extraordinary thematic coherence of his works. While one might say that the general trend of Thomas' writing from *The Lives of a Cell* onward is to focus somewhat less on strict biology with each subsequent book, all of them cover a startlingly miscellaneous array of subjects. They nevertheless hold together because Thomas' writing is not centered on subjects; it is centered on concepts. His subjects range from computers to olfactory receptor cells to Bach and back again, as he circles around each idea, bringing up different examples and then returning to his starting point. The same key concepts, however, underlie all of his discussions.

The central theme of *The Lives of a Cell* reappears in all of Thomas' books: organicism, the belief in the interconnectedness of living things. Thomas sees the simplest organism, the cell, as a model for the workings of human society and even the planet as a whole. He offers insight into systems as diverse as insect colonies, language, and research laboratories by treating them as living entities that develop something like a mind of their own. Thomas sees "cooperation" or "collaboration" as the key characteristic of all successful organisms. His use of these social terms to describe the behavior of nonsentient forms of life illustrates his thesis that many "lower" forms of life, when combined, are capable of behaving like a higher form of life. Fortunately, this is as true of humans as of anybody else.

Thomas' confidence that humans can work together is the source of what one critic has called Thomas' "relentless" optimism about the fate of the planet. In spite of his recognition of the dangers humankind poses to the earth, he does not fear that "Modern Man" will "detach himself from nature." In fact, he writes at the beginning of *The Lives of a Cell*, "Man is embedded in nature." He is part of a living, breathing organism known as Earth:

Aloft, floating beneath the moist, gleaming membrane of bright blue sky, is the rising earth. . . . If you could look long enough, you would see the swirling of the great drifts of white cloud, covering and uncovering the half-hidden masses of land. If you had been looking for a very long, geologic time, you could have seen the continents themselves in motion, drifting apart on their crustal plates, held afloat by the fire beneath. It has the organized, self-contained look of a live creature, full of information, marvelously skilled in handling the sun. ("The World's Biggest Membrane")

Thomas speculates that "an extraterrestrial embryologist," looking at this planet, "would probably conclude that the morphogenesis of the earth is coming along well, with the beginnings of a nervous system and fair-sized ganglions in the form of cities, and now with specialized dish-shaped sensory organs, miles across, ready to receive stimuli" ("Ceti"). Humankind, he suggests in "The Youngest and Brightest Thing Around," from *The Medusa and the Snail*, may have a special role to play in the evolution of this organism; "we may be engaged in the formation of something like a mind for the life of this planet." If this is so, he comments wryly, it is the mind of an adolescent.

Thomas reinforces his claim that human societies function like organisms (and vice versa) by metaphorically connecting the two. He frequently applies sociological language to nonhuman forms. Bacteria, for example, are "social animals" that "live by collaboration, accommodation, exchange, and barter." Insects are a favorite example of lower creatures that seem at times to engage in human behavior. Two essays from *The Lives of a Cell*, "On Societies as Organisms" and "Antaeus in Manhattan," spin this idea out at length. Ants, Thomas writes, "are so much like human beings as to be an embarrassment. They farm fungi, raise aphids as livestock, launch armies into wars, use chemical sprays to alarm and confuse enemies, capture slaves. They exchange information ceaselessly. They do everything but watch television." Both essays are classic examples of the way in which Thomas' deliberately simple language situates his ideas halfway between seriousness and whimsy. He describes the collective action that creates the semblance of thought in the ant colony: "A solitary ant, afield, cannot be considered to have much of anything on his mind; indeed, with only a few neurons strung together by fibers, he can't be imagined to have a mind at all. . . . Four ants together, or ten, encircling a dead moth on a path, begin to look more like an idea." If we consider the entire group of ants an organism, he suggests, then the organism begins to look very familiar.

Thomas works this same metaphoric connection in reverse, using the language of science to characterize human behavior. In "The MBL," an essay from *The Lives of a Cell* on the famous Marine Biological Laboratory in Woods Hole,

Massachusetts, Thomas describes the development of this institution as a kind of evolution. The MBL is "possessed of a life of its own, self-regenerating." Moreover, he explains, "the place was put together, given life, sustained into today's version of its maturity and prepared for further elaboration and changes in its complexity, by what can only be described as a bunch of people." Thomas' self-deflating conclusion to the sentence emphasizes that the scientists who contribute to this life are not of individual significance. It is as a collaborative group that they constitute the larger organism that impresses Thomas.

The essential connection between all of the entities that Thomas discusses is the way in which cooperation between different parts helps to sustain and improve the organism. Thomas' books are full of examples of the unexpected forms of symbiosis that demonstrate the interdependence of all living creatures. The title essay of *The Medusa and the Snail* describes two creatures living in the Bay of Naples: the nudibranch, a common sea slug, and the medusa, a jellyfish that is parasitically attached to it. Thomas sees this pair as emblematic of life in general. "Like a vaguely remembered dream," he writes, "they remind me of the whole earth at once." *The Lives of a Cell*, too, emphasizes the "tendency for living things to join up, establish linkages, live inside each other . . . get along, whenever possible" ("Some Biomythology"). Again, his casual mixing of human social language ("join up," "get along") with references to nonhuman organisms ("establish linkages," "live inside each other") reinforces the similarity between all living things, us and them.

Thomas feels a certain affinity and even respect for the living parts of his own body. In *The Fragile Species*, he returns to a subject he had first discussed in *The Lives of a Cell*—the importance of mitochondria, the energy-producing portions of the cells of which we are made: "We are symbionts, my mitochondria and I, bound together for the advance of the biosphere, living together in harmony, maybe even affection. For sure, I am fond of my microbial engines, and I assume they are pleased by the work they do for me." If his imposition of human feeling onto the mitochondria seems somewhat patronizing, Thomas himself is aware of the problem, adding: "Or is it necessarily that way, or the other way round? It could be, I suppose, that all of me is a sort of ornamented carapace for colonies of bacteria that decided, long ago, to make a try at real evolutionary novelty" ("The Art and Craft of Memoir"). The microcosm is not less important than the macrocosm; the two are equal partners.

Thomas frequently uses such reversals of perspective to suggest that all organisms have the same intrinsic value. He makes a similar joke about the relation between himself and his cells in "Organelles as Organisms" in *The Lives of a Cell*: "I could be taken for a very large, motile colony of respiring bacteria, operating a complex system of nuclei, microtubules, and neurons for the pleasure and sustenance of their families, and running, at the moment, a typewriter." The facetiousness of Thomas' scenario renders this radical shift in perspective so comprehensible that it seems almost obvious.

Most of Thomas' ideas, in fact, are based on the simple notion that every organism *is* fundamentally like us in its basic motivations—it plans to live, reproduce if possible, and die with a minimum of fuss. It therefore makes a certain amount of sense to consider the "point of view" of creatures to which we do not normally attribute sentience. Individually, Thomas admits, they do not think; but collectively, they function as if they did. In his essay "Germs" (from *The Lives of a Cell*) for example, Thomas refers to our fear of germs as "paranoid delusions on a societal scale," pointing out that the vast majority of bacteria encountered in modern life do not cause infection because it is not to their advantage to do so. He notes that "there is nothing to be gained, in an evolutionary sense," by a parasite's capacity to cause the death of its host. In fact, quite the reverse: "The man who catches a meningococcus is in considerably less danger for his life, even without chemotherapy, than meningococci with the bad luck to catch a man."

Differences between organisms, then, are simply a matter of scale. A mitochondrion, a cell, a human being, a society, a planet—each organism is both a conglomeration of the smaller organisms and a constituent part of the next item on the list. Understanding how the pieces of the puzzle fit together requires a constant adjustment in our microscopes. We zoom in for a closer look, then we widen our focus, trying at all times to retain a sense of the whole. It is this constant shifting of perspective and alteration of scale that gives Thomas' writing its understated wit. The classic strategy of satire, of course, is to make the big seem little and the little seem big. Jonathan Swift's *Gulliver's Travels*, for example, literalizes this reversal of scale by showing Gulliver first as a giant to be swarmed over by the Lilliputians, then as a pygmy beside the Brobdingnagians. Swift's defamiliarizing device forces the reader to see accepted aspects of society in a new way. Thomas' gentler satire underlines the hubris of our assumption that we are the only organisms that count.

The Celebration of Life

Thomas uses the model of the organism to illuminate nonbiological structures as well. The sensitivity to language that is evident in his highly literate writing style is also reflected in his many comments on the function and development of language. He sees language as the single most distinctively human trait, something that "marks us all genetically, setting us apart from all the rest of life." Language itself, he writes in *The Lives of a Cell*, is "like an active, motile organism":

> Parts of it are always being changed, by a ceaseless activity to which all of us are committed; new words are invented and inserted, old ones have their meaning altered or abandoned. . . . The underlying structure simply grows, enriches itself, expands. Individual languages age away and seem to die, but they leave progeny all over the place. . . . Two languages may come together, fuse, replicate, and give rise to nests of new tongues. ("Social Talk")

He suggests that the linguists' distinction between "dead" and "living" languages is more than a metaphor. It shows a recognition that existing languages are indeed living things in their capacity for growth, in the way that they form mutations and hybrids.

Thomas' sense of language as an evolving organism is very apparent in *Et Cetera, Et Cetera: Notes of a Word-Watcher*, which explores the etymologies of hundreds of words, following each word back through its parents to its original progenitors and then showing the genetic links between it and its various relatives. Even in *The Lives of a Cell*, Thomas makes a point of the fact that the word "human" comes from the Indo-European *dhghem*, meaning "earth," which became *guman* in Germanic and *gumen* in Old English before arriving in Latin as *humanus*, from which we have human. This link between humanity and the earth is also apparent in the word "world," which can be traced back through *weraldh* in Germanic to *wiros*, meaning "man," in Indo-European. As Thomas demonstrates, words do not appear from nowhere, they evolve out of earlier meanings.

It is important to note that Thomas does not imply that languages are like organisms—to him they *are* organisms. His definition of life embraces a wide variety of things because he sees life not as a specific biological quality but as a condition of change; almost any kind of system that has the capacity to change itself in response to its environment is in effect an organism. A language changes in response to the needs of its speakers. Once a word of a language is no longer useful, no longer communicates anything that needs to be said, it dies.

Thomas sees a similarity in all systems of communication, biological and nonbiological. The work performed by a strand of DNA is not very different from the work performed by a sentence: both of them present pieces of information. In a key essay from *The Fragile Species*, "Comprehending My Cat Jeoffry," Thomas makes these connections explicit. "The kingdom of bacteria," he writes, "is engaged in something like artificial intelligence," transmitting pieces of information back and forth as if

part of "an idealized AI [artificial intelligence] machine." He gives an example: "Recently, when the notion of how to resist certain antibiotics popped into the plasmids of bacteria in some New York City hospitals, in almost no time the news had spread like gossip to similar bacteria in Peru, Australia, and Japan. Bacterial viruses can do this, carrying information from place to place, quicker than overnight mail." Given this similarity, what, he asks, separates bacteria from computers? Do either of them achieve something that we could call intelligence? Thomas considers the nature of consciousness, wondering what, if anything, separates the mind of his cat from the mind of a cricket—or, for that matter, his own mind. Typically, he does not come up with concrete answers, only questions.

In his essay "Ceti," from *The Lives of a Cell*, Thomas discusses scientific efforts at interstellar communication. He points out that a great deal of attention has been directed at methods of establishing communication with any life that may exist elsewhere, but little thought has been given to what we will say if we succeed. "What on earth are we going to talk about? . . . The barest amenities, on which we rely for opening conversations—Hello, are you there?, from us, followed by Yes, hello, from them—will take two hundred years at least." This means that whatever news of ourselves we send must have "durability of meaning." Any discussion of current political situations would be hopelessly out of date, and any science would seem embarrassing in two hundred years. Thomas' solution is to send an expression of ourselves that is at once complex and timeless: music. "This language may be the best we have for explaining what we are like to others in space, with least ambiguity." In fact, he is even more specific: "I would vote for Bach, all of Bach, streamed out into space, over and over again. We would be bragging, of course, but it is surely excusable for us to put the best possible face on at the beginning of such an acquaintance. We can tell the harder truths later."

The idea of music as an authentic expression of the human soul is deeply embedded in Western culture, particularly since the early 1800s. The British Romantic poets of that period, and the philosophers who followed later in the century, saw music as the most purely expressive of the arts. Music is in general nonrepresentational; unlike painting or literature, it does not portray anything in particular, nor does it "say" anything one could define. For Thomas, it would be the perfect message to send because it is not a message at all. It is simply a manifestation of the complex human spirit, evidence of human life.

Music is an important source of metaphor in all of Thomas' writings. He sees it not as a decorative embellishment to human endeavor, but as a fundamental part of our existence. In "The Music of *This* Sphere," from *The Lives of a Cell*, he describes the terrestrial harmony of birds, crickets, and whales singing together, claiming that the desire to express oneself through music is felt by most living things: "If, as I believe, the urge to make a kind of music is as much a characteristic of biology as our other fundamental functions, there ought to be an explanation for it." He then introduces his own explanation with typical humility: "Having none at hand, I am free to make one up."

Thomas briefly presents Harold Morowitz's hypothesis that the energy of the sun mandates the reordering of the matter it encounters. Solar energy, according to this hypothesis, does not simply dissipate; the "clustering of bonded atoms into molecules of higher and higher complexity" means that "it is thermodynamically inevitable that [solar energy] must rearrange matter into symmetry, away from probability, against entropy." The rhythmic sounds produced by living things are a primal memory that "recapitulat[es]" this process, "a score for the transformation of inanimate, random matter in chaos into the improbable, ordered dance of living forms." For Thomas, music is emblematic of the invisible and implausible forces that dictate our presence here. In "Things Unflattened by Science," from *Late Night Thoughts*, he suggests that "music (along with ordinary language) is as profound a problem for human biology as can be thought of." While language and music

are both forms of communication, it seems that the information they communicate, and celebrate, is the simple fact of our aliveness.

The Study of Life

Unresolved questions are typical of Lewis Thomas' methodology. His essays are full of admissions of ignorance, and seldom come to a triumphant conclusion. On the contrary, Thomas' essays often end on a self-effacing, anticlimactic note that, paradoxically, has the effect of reinforcing his authority. You have to trust a writer who ends by saying, "it would do for what I have in mind," "but there it is," "What a way to talk," and even, "The thought of such things is something else to worry about, but perhaps not much worse than the average car radio." He so clearly is not trying to impress you. Thomas emphasizes, again and again, that science is founded on inquiry. What you know is much less interesting than what you suspect.

In "The Hazards of Science," from *The Medusa and the Snail*, Thomas writes that the only "solid piece of scientific truth" about which he is completely confident is "that we are profoundly ignorant about nature." But this does not depress him. In fact, he regards this as the major discovery of biological science in the past hundred years. His chief worry about the future of science is that economic pressures will force scientists to turn from basic research to applied science. Thomas suggests that any effort to pursue "useful" knowledge is bound to be fruitless, because genuine scientific inquiry requires that you *not* head in a specific direction. "It is hard to predict how science is going to turn out," he notes, "and if it is really good science it is impossible to predict." The reason for this is simple: "If the things to be found are actually new, they are by definition unknown in advance, and there is no way of telling in advance where a really new line of inquiry will lead." Thomas makes the same point in "Natural Science," from *The Lives of a Cell*, when he suggests that "what must be planned for" in laboratories is the "totally unforeseeable."

The single most important sign of truly distinguished scientific research, Thomas feels, is surprise at the results. Applied research requires goals, while in basic research, "what you need at the outset is a high degree of uncertainty." This is, after all, the way nature itself proceeds—through trial and error, with the emphasis on error. Our own development as individuals and as a species depends on this process, as Thomas explains in "To Err Is Human," from *The Medusa and the Snail*. (Several Thomas essays point out that the word "error" comes from the Latin *errare*, to wander; in *The Youngest Science* he notes that "error" is also related to the Old Norse *ras*, "rushing about looking for something.") In "The Wonderful Mistake," also from *The Medusa and the Snail*, Thomas points out that evolution would not occur if DNA molecules were not programmed to make small mistakes that would later turn out to be improvements. Improvement requires change, and change requires deviation from the norm. The element of unpredictability, of randomness, is what propels things forward, in science as in life. This is why, moral considerations aside, Thomas does not consider military research to be "real science": "It has nothing whatever to do with a comprehension of nature; it is not an inquiry into nature. Its only possible outcome will be the destruction of nature itself," he insists in "Sermon from St. John the Divine," from *The Fragile Species*.

In "Humanities and Science," from *Late Night Thoughts*, Thomas makes some radical recommendations about the way science should be taught. Instead of beginning with the basics, he suggests, begin by teaching what is *not* known. Do not show how biology is "useful" or "profitable": "Teach instead that there are structures squirming inside all our cells, providing all the energy for living, that are essentially foreign creatures, brought in for symbiotic living a billion or so years ago. . . . Teach that we do not have the ghost of an idea how they got there." He gives examples of several such questions, claiming that the most important tool a young scientist needs is the desire to know more. An essay from *The Fragile Species*, "In Time of Plague," prescribes the same exploratory strategy for AIDS research. While Thomas supports such temporary remedies as sex education and needle distribution to drug addicts, he emphasizes that in the long run AIDS is not a social problem but a problem for biomedical science.

The unpredictability of nature is the source of its fascination for Thomas. His sense of wonder at human life is exactly that—not just admiration but *wonder*, surprise, that we exist at all. As he points out in "On Probability and Possibility," from the *Lives of a Cell*: "Statistically, the probability of any one of us being here is so small that you'd think the mere fact of existing would keep us all in a contented dazzlement of surprise." This is true of our species as well as of our selves. The chances that we would evolve were very small, but here we are.

Thomas feels that our pride in our own scientific accomplishments often overwhelms our appreciation of the more impressive accomplishments of nature. In "On Embryology," from *The Medusa and the Snail*, Thomas derides all of the hoopla surrounding the birth of the first "test-tube baby" in 1978. This achievement, he points out, is ultimately a "minor technical modification of the general procedure." Really, "the older surprise, which should still be fazing us all, is that a solitary sperm and a single egg can fuse and become a human being under any circumstance, and that, however implanted, a mere cluster of the progeny of this fused cell affixed to the uterine wall will grow and differentiate into eight pounds of baby." Furthermore, this astonishing process is a complete mystery to us. We have no idea how the single cell that derives from the coupling of sperm and egg manages to encode "all the information needed for learning to read and write, playing the piano, arguing before senatorial subcommittees, walking across a street through traffic." All of the human capacities that we take for granted, including the capacity to make scientific discoveries, we owe to nature.

While Thomas lauds the unpredictability of nature as a whole, he has tremendous respect for the stability of individual organisms, including the human body. He is constantly amazed at what our bodies can do. In "Autonomy," from *The Lives of a Cell*, Thomas gently pokes fun at the mid-seventies vogue for using mental techniques to attempt to control one's own bodily functions. Even if it were possible to train your brain waves to run your body, he asks, would that be such a good idea? He admits to a lack of confidence in his own ability to make the kinds of decisions his body makes all the time: "If I were informed tomorrow that I was in direct communication with my liver, and could now take over, I would become deeply depressed. I'd sooner be told, forty thousand feet over Denver, that the 747 jet in which I had a coach seat was now mine to operate as I pleased; at least I would have the hope of bailing out." He ruefully concludes, "Nothing would save me and my liver, if I were in charge." The body, Thomas insists, is a wonderfully self-regulating mechanism that should be interfered with as little as possible.

In fact, Thomas feels that medicine has often been counterproductive in its useless "meddling." In his essay "On Meddling," from *The Medusa and the Snail*, Thomas points out that the effects of intervening in large systems, such as cities, are impossible to predict because the complexity of the system introduces so many variables. The human body often functions in the same way. Many of the classic medical treatments for disorders like syphilis and tuberculosis probably did more harm than good, he claims, because the real nature of the disease was imperfectly understood.

Many of Thomas' discussions of medical science suggests that real medicine is a very recent invention. In "Medical Lessons from History," from *The Medusa and the Snail*, he calls the history of medicine an "unrelievedly deplorable" story. After centuries of pointless, even destructive, treatments, a real breakthrough finally occurred around the 1830s with the realization that "the greater part of medicine was nonsense." Doctors began to notice that many patients recovered by themselves if left alone, and realized that death was not the inevitable conclusion of every illness. As Thomas tells the story in "1933 Medicine," from *The Youngest Science*, the birth of modern medicine involved a long period of careful observation and diag-

nosis. For many decades this was the major goal of medical science: "Explanation was the real business of medicine. What the ill patient and his family wanted most was to know the name of the illness, and then, if possible, what had caused it, and finally, most important of all, how it was likely to turn out." Most hospital care was essentially "custodial": very sick patients were made comfortable while they either recovered or not.

Real advances in medicine came only after considerable resources were devoted to "basic science": research into the role of bacteria and viruses in illness. By the late 1930s immunization was possible for diphtheria, tetanus, and lobar pneumonia. Furthermore, the development of antibiotics ushered in an exciting new era in medicine when, for the first time, very serious illnesses could be prevented or cured with relative ease. Thomas comments in a number of essays on the fact that improved public sanitation as well as common immunizations allow us to take for granted the virtual nonexistence of diseases that used to be a terrifying threat: tuberculosis, rheumatic fever, polio. He uses this as evidence for his continual argument that basic research into the causes of disease is ultimately much more effective than expensive interventions like repairing or replacing damaged organs. Thomas' late essays on the future of health care are relentless in their emphasis on one point: money spent now on research, even research whose utility is not apparent, will ultimately pay handsome dividends. He points out that we have already reaped unexpected benefits from the products we have developed. For example, Thomas notes that at about the time syphilis became treatable, it also became dramatically rarer: fewer people came in to receive treatment for it. He theorizes that this may have been a side effect of the widespread prescription of penicillin for a variety of minor ailments. Similarly, he attributes the documented drop in cardiac ailments from the 1950s to the present to the rise of television, with its frequent commercials for aspirin (which was discovered to exert a beneficial effect on the arteries).

In a way, Thomas seems to suggest, medicine has become the victim of its own success. We have come to expect a level of general health that has never before been obtainable. Thomas points out that even a designation like the current "HMO" — health maintenance organization — helps to foster the illusion that everyone's health can be "maintained," all the time, indefinitely. Surprisingly, Dr. Thomas is somewhat skeptical of what he calls "the ideology of healthy living." (Or perhaps this is not so surprising in a lifelong smoker.) "On Magic in Medicine," from *The Medusa and the Snail*, questions the medicinal value of making alterations in one's personal lifestyle. He criticizes the conclusions drawn from a famous study of the effects of diet and exercise on the progress of certain illnesses, claiming that the variables are too numerous to establish a direct cause-and-effect correlation.

The doctrine that illness is caused by "not living right," and hence is in some sense your own fault, seems to Thomas a vast simplification of the mechanisms of disease. Thomas is amused to consider the "Seven Healthy Life Habits" that were widely recommended in the wake of the diet and exercise study. He agrees that not smoking and not drinking are likely to improve your health, and that exercising might make you feel better, but draws the line at eating breakfast: "It is hard to imagine any good reason for dying within five years from not eating a good breakfast, or any sort of breakfast." This kind of advice is damaging because it establishes a mythology about health, creating the illusion that we have more control over our bodies than we do. While Thomas is clearly an optimist, he is also a fatalist. He believes that, inevitably, many people will get sick of illnesses we cannot cure, and some of them will die. In fact, he reminds his readers, we all will die; no matter how advanced medicine becomes, that is one fact it cannot change. Medical science, he suggests, should concentrate on improving life — not extending it.

The End of Life

It is something of a shock to realize how much this "relentless optimist" has written about death. Lewis Thomas' essays on the subject are among his best-known pieces: "The Long Habit" and "Death in the Open," from *The Lives of a Cell*; "On Natural Death," from *The Medusa and the Snail*; the title essay of *Late Night Thoughts on Listening to Mahler's Ninth Symphony*. All of these essays emphasize the idea that death is not an aberration: it is the most natural thing in the world.

"The Long Habit" takes its title from Sir Thomas Browne, a seventeenth-century author who wrote that "The long habit of living indisposeth us to dying." Thomas suggests that this habit has become "an addiction" in our culture. Our increased life span makes us less ready than our forebears to accept the inevitability of death; we are "hooked" on living, even when life has lost its "zest." Most of his friends, he writes, see death as something that happens because we get sick, and assume that "if we did not have our diseases we might go on indefinitely." Now that serious illnesses result in hospitalization, very few of us have actually seen death close at hand, so it has become terrifyingly unfamiliar. Thomas makes a similar point in "Death in the Open": he notes that, while everything in nature dies, you do not see a lot of dead animals lying around everywhere. Animals instinctively seek privacy in death, and their remains are quickly recycled. This makes "the process of dying seem more exceptional than it really is, and harder to engage in at the times when we must ourselves engage." Death has become abstract to us, but in fact, Thomas reminds us, it is the one thing we all have in common: "There are 3 billion of us on the earth, and all 3 billion must be dead, on a schedule, within this lifetime."

Thomas points out that as the world's population continues to expand, death will become harder to ignore. He certainly does not advocate that we become indifferent to unnecessary death. Writing eighteen years later, in his essays "Obligations," from *The Fragile Species*, Thomas asserts that of the 4.5 billion humans now alive, only one-third enjoy "reasonably good health" and the expectation of living the current maximum life span. The majority "have less than half a chance at that kind of survival, dying earlier and living miserably for as long as they do live." He therefore sees the central foreign policy question of our time as: "what should the relatively healthy 1.5 billion human beings be doing to bring the other 3 billion into the twentieth (or twenty-first) century?" But in thinking about our own deaths, he writes in "Death in the Open," we must abandon the notion that death is "detestable, or avoidable, or even strange." Instead, we must remember that all of life requires a "trade," the living for the dead. The fact that it happens to everyone should be some comfort: "we all go down together, in the best of company."

Although Thomas preaches the acceptance of natural death, he is deeply troubled by the specter of unnatural death raised by nuclear arms. Several Thomas essays, such as "The Unforgettable Fire," from *Late Night Thoughts*, discuss nuclear arms as scientific creations and as public policy. "Late Night Thoughts on Listening to Mahler's Ninth Symphony," however, presents Thomas' feelings about the threat of nuclear war in starkly personal terms. In this classic essay, Thomas meditates on a favorite piece of music, using it as a touchstone for his changed perspective on the world. He writes that he used to hear the final movement of Mahler's Ninth Symphony as "an open acknowledgement of death" that conveyed "a quiet celebration of the tranquillity connected to the process." But he interrupts this reminiscence with a blunt assertion: "Now I hear it differently. I cannot listen to the last movement of the Mahler Ninth without the door-smashing intrusion of a huge new thought: death everywhere, the dying of everything, the end of humanity." The piece used to remind him of the continuing cycle of life and death. Now, faced with the prospect of the destruction of all life in a nuclear war, he is unable to hear the same comforting message.

Thomas contrasts his own feelings as a young man with what he imagines a young person might feel today. "If I were very young, sixteen or seventeen years old," he writes, "I think I would begin, perhaps very slowly and imperceptibly, to go crazy." Young people who grow up in the shadow of nuclear weapons are robbed of the power to imagine a future. Instead, they must imagine the possibility that the perpetual cycle of life and death will stop, forever, with them. Growing up like that, Thomas thinks, would make him "want to give up listening and reading." We saw earlier that Thomas considers music and language to be humanity's way of expressing its pleasure in living. He proposed sending Bach as a messenger into space because music like Bach's represents the best of what we have to offer. To reject the joy of listening and reading, then, is to disown humanity. To Thomas, this is the only response to humanity's evident desire to disown itself.

Thomas believes that the driving force behind all life—including, and especially, human life—is the desire to continue. The individual will even sacrifice itself for the continuation of the species; the mode of behavior that he calls "cooperation," "symbiosis," or "altruism" reflects an organism's recognition of its obligation to ensure the perpetuation of its kind. Planning the destruction of our own "family," even if we hope that these plans are never followed, violates our deepest genetic impulses. It is the most unnatural act Thomas can imagine.

In his essay "Altruism," from *Late Night Thoughts*, Thomas extends the idea of "family responsibility" to encompass all the earth's life, suggesting that we are equally obligated to protect our "cousins," the "sandworms, dolphins, hamsters, and soil bacteria." To disregard their future by polluting the atmosphere, burning up the forests, and generally "rampaging at large through nature as though we owned the place" is essentially self-destructive. It threatens to dull our awareness of our most precious gift; what Thomas calls, in *The Fragile Species*, the "sense of being alive."

Selected Bibliography

WORKS OF LEWIS THOMAS

BOOKS

The Lives of a Cell: Notes of a Biology Watcher (New York: Viking, 1974); *The Medusa and the Snail: More Notes of a Biology Watcher* (New York: Viking, 1979);

Late Night Thoughts on Listening to Mahler's Ninth Symphony (New York: Viking, 1983); *The Youngest Science: Notes of a Medicine-Watcher* (New York: Viking, 1983); *Could I Ask You Something?* (New York: Library Fellows of the Whitney Museum of American Art, 1985), poetry; *Et Cetera, Et Cetera: Notes of a Word-Watcher* (Boston: Little, Brown, 1990); *The Fragile Species* (New York: Collier, 1993).

ARTICLES

In addition to some two hundred medical articles published in scholarly journals, Lewis Thomas published over one hundred essays in literary journals and popular magazines. Many of these were reprinted in essay collections without revision. No essays appeared after the publication of *The Fragile Species* in 1993.

INTERVIEWS

Jeremy Bernstein, "Profiles: Biology Watcher," in *New Yorker* 54 (2 January 1978); David Hellerstein, "The Muse of Medicine," in *Esquire* 101 (March 1984); Roger Rosenblatt, "Lewis Thomas," in *New York Times Magazine* (21 November 1993); Sally Squires, "Poet Laureate of Twentieth-Century Medical Science," in *Washington Post Health* (17 October 1989).

BIOGRAPHICAL AND CRITICAL STUDIES

Andrew J. Angyal, *Lewis Thomas* (Boston: Twayne, 1989); Marilyn Berger, "Lewis Thomas, Whose Essays Clarified the Mysteries of Biology, Is Dead at 80," in *New York Times* (4 December 1993), sec. A.; Jeremy Bernstein, "Lewis Thomas: Life of a Biology Watcher," in his *Experiencing Science: Profiles in Discovery* (New York: Basic Books, 1978); Stephen Jay Gould, "Biological Musings," review of *The Medusa and the Snail*, in *New York Times Book Review* (6 May 1979), and "Calling Dr. Thomas," review of *The Youngest Science*, in *New York Review of Books* 30 (12 July 1983); Paul Gray, "In Celebration of Life," review of *The Medusa and the Snail*, in *Time* 113 (14 May 1979); Spencer Klaw, "A Celebrant of Life on Earth," review of *The Medusa and the Snail*, in *Natural History* 88 (June/July 1979).

Christopher Lehmann-Haupt, "Optimism (Relentless) on Humanity," review of *The Fragile Species*, in *New York Times* (16 April 1992), sec. C.; Howard Nemerov, "Lewis Thomas, Montaigne, and Human Happiness," in his *New and Selected Essays* (Carbondale: Southern Illinois Univ. Press, 1985); Joyce Carol Oates, "Beyond Common Sense: *The Lives of a Cell*," in *New York Times Book Review* (26 May 1974); Chet Raymo, "The Consortium That Is Ourselves," in *Boston Globe* (27 December 1993), and "Thoughtful Reflections on Man and His World," review of *The Fragile Species*, in *Boston Globe* (26 April 1992), sec. B.; John Updike, "A New Meliorism," review of *The Lives of a Cell*, in *New Yorker* 50 (15 July 1974); Steven Weiland, "'A Tune Beyond Us, Yet Ourselves': Medical Science and Lewis Thomas," in *Michigan Quarterly Review* 24 (1985); George F. Will, "In Death, a Return to Randomness," in *Washington Post* (12 December 1993), sec. C.

HENRY DAVID THOREAU
(1817–1862)

LAWRENCE BUELL

WHEN HENRY DAVID THOREAU died of tuberculosis on 6 May 1862 at the early age of forty-four, his mentor Ralph Waldo Emerson declared, "The country knows not yet, or in the least part, how great a son it has lost" (*Complete Works*, vol. 10, p. 484). He was right. Although during Thoreau's lifetime and for a half century after his death his reputation was overshadowed by Emerson's, in the twentieth century Thoreau's "Resistance to Civil Government" (also called "Civil Disobedience") and other social reform papers have had worldwide impact, and he has become America's most famous and influential nature writer. His most important book, *Walden*, which describes his two years and two months living in a self-built cabin in the local woods, is today more frequently taught in college and university American literature courses than any other text; it has been translated into many languages, from Bulgarian to Japanese; and it has inspired countless latter-day quests to simplify the terms of our increasingly complicated modern civilization.

Thoreau lived virtually all his life in the town where he was born, Concord, Massachusetts, twenty miles from New England's metropolis, Boston. All of his writings in one way or another relate to this fact: either Concord was his direct subject, as in *Walden* and the voluminous journal that he religiously kept during the twenty-five years of his adult life, or it was the reference point against which he measured everything else. Before Thoreau's birth, Concord was already rich in historical association. It was New England's first inland town, founded in 1635. It was where the first battle of the American Revolution was fought in 1775, when the "minutemen" (the militias from Concord and neighboring towns) repulsed the "redcoats" and thereby "fired the shot heard round the world," as Emerson put it in his "Concord Hymn" sung at the dedication of the Concord Battle Monument in 1837, the year Thoreau graduated from college. (Thoreau was a member of the choir.) Considering how distant his life now seems from ours, more than a century and a quarter after his death, it is all the more important to stress that the history of Concord began almost two centuries before Thoreau's birth. For Concord's historic character was both a source of great pride to him and a source of irritation, impatient as he often was with neighbors who unthinkingly relied on tradition and habit as a substitute for facing the present.

This ambivalence was not unique to Thoreau, and it reflects the fact that Concord, and America, was changing rapidly during his lifetime. Between the War of 1812 and the Civil War—two major upheavals that roughly mark the beginning and end of Thoreau's life—the United States expanded from the Mississippi Valley to the shores of the Pacific, and then broke in two. The industrial revolution transformed the American economy and thereby made the antebellum period the first age of what is now called "future shock." A good example of technological innovation during this period is the railroad, which reached Concord (via the west end of Walden Pond) in 1844, the year before Thoreau moved to Walden. Suddenly people and commodities could be whisked across the landscape and remote places brought temporally much closer together. Concord youth could now envision, as never before, the possibility of making their fortune elsewhere (Thoreau himself considered both Maine and Illinois); and it ensured that Concord would sooner or later become a suburb of Boston, first as a market town and then as a bedroom community. Immigrant labor brought more ethnic diversity to Concord and other northeastern communities. These major changes were regarded by Thoreau and some others as a crisis of modernization, a crisis that involved the natural environment as much as it did the village center. Economically, the old, small-scale, self-sufficient farm now seemed obsolete. Ecologically, the Concord landscape was being exploited as never before (or since): swamps were being drained to increase arable land and pasture, and the percentage of wooded land reached an all-time low just about the time of Thoreau's Walden experiment (the deforestation would doubtless have worsened had coal stoves not replaced wood burners as the preferred means of heating).

In the 1990s, despite intensive suburbanization, Concord is far more leafy and environmentally protected than it was in Thoreau's lifetime—a situation for which Thoreau deserves partial credit. Although Thoreau could not exactly be called an environmental activist, his writings posed a direct challenge to the fast-growing American cult of bigness and had the effect of raising readers' consciousness of the beauty and importance of unspoiled nature as a natural resource.

Early Life and Education

Thoreau's family was respectable but not illustrious. His father, John Thoreau, was an unprosperous storekeeper who only in later life found success as a manufacturer of pencils, thanks in part to Henry's engineering skills. His mother, Cynthia Dunbar Thoreau, augmented the family income by running a boarding house. Henry was the third of four siblings, none of whom married and two of whom died young: Helen (1812–1849), of tuberculosis—which ran in the family as in many a pre-twentieth-century New England clan—and John Jr. (1815–1842), to whom Henry was very close, who died of lockjaw after nicking himself while shaving. Both John and Sophia (1819–1876) shared Henry's keen interest in natural history, which seems to have been "inherited" from their parents. (Sophia would co-edit with William Ellery Channing, Henry's *The Maine Woods* and *Cape Cod*.) According to a local report, one of the Thoreau children "narrowly escaped being born" during a parental botanical expedition.

Unlike 95 percent of the young men of his day, Thoreau received a college education—at Harvard, which required a considerable financial sacrifice from his family. Though he barely passed the entrance examinations in 1833, in 1837 he graduated nineteeth in his class of forty four, a strong enough record for him to be given a speaking part at his Commencement. He then began work as a teacher in the Concord Center School, which was not a bad start, considering that the country was in the midst of a severe depression. But now Thoreau's independent-mindedness started to assert itself. Within two weeks, he resigned rather than follow the school committee's policy of flogging students periodically to keep order. He also inverted his name, from his baptismal "David Henry" to the "Henry David" that posterity knows him by. Probably at Emerson's suggestion, he started keeping what became *The Journal of Henry Thoreau*, a repository for idealistic aspirations of a dreamily individualistic and anti-social kind ("Let not society be the element in which you swim," "How can a man sit down and quietly pare his nails, while the earth goes gyrating ahead?"). The *Journal* was also Thoreau's source of first resort in the composition of *Walden* and most of his other works as well. In short, Thoreau was trying to find himself—to find a vocational path that would satisfy his spirit, even though it might not be one a young man with a college degree typically pursued (such as law, medicine, the ministry, teaching, or commerce). For some time, he continued to look for a school position, enlisting the help of President Quincy of Harvard among others. When this effort failed, he opened a private school in Concord in 1838; his brother, John, signed on as preceptor a few months later. By using innovative teaching methods such as field trips, the school enjoyed considerable success for almost three years until John became seriously ill. Throughout Thoreau's venture in private education, he wrote lectures, essays and poems intended for a larger audience. He made his debut at the local "lyceum" (a forum for speakers, debates, and discussion organized by Concord and many other Yankee towns in the nineteenth century) with a lecture on "Society" in the spring of 1838; he became the secretary and curator of that body the same fall.

Emerson and Transcendentalism

Thoreau's intellectual ferment was partly caused, partly intensified, and partly calmed by his increasing association with the so-called transcendentalist movement, in which the leading inspirational force was Ralph Waldo Emerson (1803–1882), a former Boston minister who had settled in his ancestral town of Concord in the mid-1830s in order to pursue a career as a freelance lecturer and man of letters. Emerson preached a gospel of "self-reliance," which was based on the idea that every person had immediate access to divine truth if only he or she would listen aright to the voice of the authentic Self within. This was especially calculated to appeal to an earnest young person of poetic bent like Thoreau, and all the more so considering that Emerson took a special interest in nature. His first book, *Nature* (1836), a copy of which Thoreau bestowed upon a college classmate as a graduation present, was a poetic-didactic meditation on the romantic theme that the right intuitive understanding of physical nature is the key to interpreting human nature, society, and history. Thoreau eventually pursued the study of

nature in a much more rigorously empirical way than Emerson did, but Emerson's combination of amateur interest in science, romantic faith in nature's salubriousness and spiritual significance, and commitment to a personal and creative rather than a conventionally objective and systematic form of writing remained fundamental to Thoreau's own approach to nature study and nature writing.

Soon after they became acquainted in that fateful year of 1837, Emerson became Thoreau's chief adviser and patron. He engaged Thoreau in long conversations and walks, prizing his satirical wit and prowess as raconteur. Emerson was particularly struck by Thoreau's combination of a passion for intellectual and scholarly labor with a talent and relish for woodsmanship, carpentry, and other practical arts; in handicraft, Thoreau's skills far surpassed the older man's. Emerson introduced Thoreau to a much wider range of acquaintance, and he enlisted Thoreau in various literary projects. It was Emerson who prompted Thoreau to undertake his first exercise in natural history writing, a long 1842 review for the transcendentalist magazine, the *Dial*, of a series of recent "scientific" surveys commissioned by the Commonwealth of Massachusetts. The *Dial* also printed a number of Thoreau's poems and prose pieces.

Emerson also helped Thoreau in more material ways. After the Thoreau brothers closed their school, Henry moved into the Emerson home for a two-year period of free room and board in exchange for work in the garden and around the house, as well as occasional child care. (Emerson's whole family was very fond of Thoreau; his younger son, Edward, later wrote a memoir of Thoreau, and Thoreau and Emerson's wife, Lydian, had such a close Platonic relationship that some have argued that he was in love with her.) This live-in arrangement, though surprisingly successful given Thoreau's typical cantankerousness and Emerson's characteristic reticence, also contributed to the later discord that caused a distinct cooling of the relationship in the late 1840s, when Thoreau came to resent what he took to be Emerson's growing conventionalism and halfhearted support for his writing; for Thoreau's status as a dependent in the Emerson household inevitably cast him in the role of factotum, reinforcing the difference in social status between the two men that was already manifest to the tight little world of Concord, and rigidifying Emerson's inclination to picture Thoreau as the practical exemplar of his own ideas rather than as an independent agent. It is significant that Thoreau began during these years to feel more at ease with another unsuccessful aspiring poet of nature about his own age who had also been patronized by Emerson: William Ellery Channing II (1818–1901). Channing became Thoreau's most frequent walking companion and the "poet" mentioned in *Walden*.

In 1843, Emerson arranged for Thoreau a venture to New York, where he could try his luck at the center of the American publishing industry while residing in Staten Island in the home of Emerson's lawyer-brother William, serving as tutor to his son. This was the one time in Thoreau's life when he seriously tried to relocate. The experiment lasted only six months. Thoreau became homesick; he disliked New York; his literary ventures all failed in the short run, for he could not quite bring himself to produce the popular journalistic pieces that would sell well; he found William Emerson stiffish and his son unappealing. But he did make one invaluable literary contact in Horace Greeley, the endlessly energetic and reform-minded editor of the New York *Tribune*. Greeley seems genuinely to have believed in Thoreau's genius, and even in its marketability. He served as Thoreau's literary agent for a number of years, promoted his work, and helped to make possible the modest commercial success of *Walden* by enthusiastic notices (starting as early as 1848) of the Walden experiment, on the lectures of life at Walden that Thoreau gave in various northeastern towns, and by printing advance excerpts from the book itself.

Altogether, Thoreau was far more fortunate in his literary contacts than the vast majority of literary unknowns. He was backed first by Emerson, then by Greeley, and finally by the leading literary publishing house in America, Ticknor and Fields, which published (and vigorously promoted) *Walden* and the various posthumous books derived from his manuscripts.

The Walden Experience and Its Impact

Returning to Concord in November of 1843, Thoreau went through a period of indecisiveness lasting more than a year before undertaking the two-and-a-half-year adventure that became the turning point of his personal life and his career as a writer: his bivouac at nearby Walden Pond. In a small cabin he set up on a rustic tract that Emerson had recently purchased, Thoreau conducted what he described in his book as an experiment in simplifying the terms of existence, paring down his material necessities in order to better cultivate his spiritual, aesthetic, and environmental senses. As many other environmentally sensitive people have favorite spots to which they love to return again and again, so, for Thoreau, Walden always had a magnetic attraction. Being brought there at the age of four was, he wrote in *Walden* "one of the oldest scenes stamped on my memory" (1971 ed., p. 155). In an early *Journal* entry, Thoreau imagined going there to live. But just why he did so exactly when he did so is an insoluble question that Thoreauvians love to ponder. One biographer has described the Walden episode as a "moratorium," a calculated retreat from purposefulness in order to take stock of his life. Others have suggested that Thoreau's purpose was essentially literary: he had started work on what was to become his first book, a travel-meditation based on a two-week excursion taken by him and his brother to the White Mountains of New Hampshire; and he needed a block of uninterrupted time in which to compose. One psychobiographer, Leon Edel, has claimed that Thoreau retreated to Walden out of chagrin, licking his wounds after a disastrous accidental burning of hundreds of acres of Concord woods when a campfire he and a companion set in a very dry season flared out of control. Though improbable, this thesis does point to the fact of Thoreau's increasing social alienation. By 1845, he knew that this life was not likely to have any of the outcomes expected of a Harvard graduate, that he was destined to be considered odd by most Concordians, that he had nonetheless committed himself to remaining at Concord, and that he would live his life as much as possible on his own terms, regardless of local gossip. The move to Walden was the confirmation and symbol of his independence, for in those days the only people who voluntarily lived on the outskirts of town were farmers and socially marginal folk: the free blacks and the broken-down alcoholic described in the "Former Inhabitants" chapter, the hapless immigrant laborer of "Baker Farm," the French Canadian woodchopper of "Visitors," and impoverished railroad workers the likes of which sold Thoreau the boards for his shanty.

Thoreau himself was probably somewhat uncertain of his own motives. Shortly after he moved in (significantly, on Independence Day, 1845—though in *Walden* he insisted that this was a coincidence), Thoreau wrote in his journal, "I wish to meet the facts of life. . . . who knows what it is, what it does? If I am not quite right here, I am less wrong than before" (1981 ed., vol. 2, p. 156). This was the wobbly origin of the eloquent passage in *Walden* that declares, "I went to the woods because I wished to live deliberately, to front only the essential facts of life, and see if I could not learn what it had to teach, and not, when I came to die, discover that I had not lived" (1971 ed., p. 90). He wanted, without doubt, to strip his life of nonessentials—to become self-sufficient, to live a purposeful life—but to just what end he initially could not and finally preferred not to state precisely. This leaves us with a biographical puzzle, but perhaps the indefiniteness is all to the best: it allows us more easily to adapt the terms of his unique life-experiment to our own.

In any case, Thoreau's *Journal* entries from his pastoral retreat glow with an exuberance that also appears in *Walden*. Before long, Thoreau had settled into a casual, unorthodox routine: a little farming; a little day labor (Thoreau found that he could make as respectable a living from land surveying as from the family pencil factory);

a great deal of reading and meditating and roaming (including a two-week trip to the Maine woods); frequent returns to town for supplies, meals, socializing, and (on one occasion) the one-night stint in jail for tax resistance that led him to write "Resistance to Civil Government"; and, eventually, some local lecturing as Thoreau discovered that audiences were interested in hearing about his practical application of Emersonian self-reliance.

Most important, from posterity's standpoint, Thoreau wrote a great deal at *Walden*. Indeed, he did more concentrated writing there than at any other time in his adult life. He came close to completing what later became his first book, *A Week on the Concord and Merrimack Rivers*, and he wrote the first draft of *Walden*. When he left the pond for a nine-month residence as caretaker for the Emersons during Ralph Waldo's extended lecture tour abroad, he had almost transformed himself from a very minor poet and writer of minor descriptive essays to a major prose writer on both social and environmental themes.

But his publications proceeded to meet with a disappointing reception. What was to become his most famous political essay, "Resistance to Civil Government," was dismissed in 1849 as a piece of anarchism too radical to be taken seriously, even though Thoreau appealed to the time-honored acts of the founders of the American republic in order to justify his theory of protest against arbitrary taxes supporting slavery and an unjust foreign war (against Mexico). A New York periodical published one of the best of Thoreau's many extended travel essays, "Ktaadn," a descriptively rich and poetically intense account of his ascent of New England's second-highest mountain (more commonly known as "Katahdin"); but *Union Magazine* quickly folded, and Thoreau was only partially reimbursed. And *A Week on the Concord and Merrimack Rivers* (1849) met with a mixed critical reception and minuscule sales.

Today, Thoreauvians think much better of *A Week*, but it is easy to see why the larger antebellum public did not care much for this particular kind of debut from an almost unknown

Daguerreotype of Henry David Thoreau, 1856

knew; and his might also have been popular had it maintained the levity and brevity that were expected. But Thoreau, as always, staunchly resisted such trivialization, for which he was slighted in his own day but has been honored in ours.

There were some of Thoreau's contemporaries, however, who did appreciate the lingering penetration of his gaze as he meandered simultaneously among the riparian landscapes of New England, among aspects of the Puritan and Native American past associated with them, and among the wealth of reading at his command. "It seems to us," declared an anonymous reviewer in the *New Hampshire Patriot*, that American society's "fidgeting, itching, hustling turn of mind might frequently with profit be exchanged for a meditative and thoughtful habit" like Thoreau's: "he turns the mental eye inward and endeavors to read the mysterious page of his own soul," and he surveys the "objects around which meet his senses" with such perceptiveness that "the very stones preach sermons and the reeds become eloquent." Today, readers of *A Week* who look closely at the catalogue of fish in "Saturday," the discussion of the nature of scripture in "Sunday" and of work in "Monday," the narrative of Thoreau's ascent of Mount Saddleback in "Tuesday," the chronicle of Hannah Dustan's revenge of her Indian captors in "Thursday," and the closing meditation on silence in "Friday" will understand some of the many attractions of this unusually ambitious first book—wordy and repetitious though it often is, overloaded with agendas sometimes ineptly dovetailed, and more transparently Emersonian than anything Thoreau wrote thereafter. Despite its flaws, *A Week* stands next to Emerson's *Nature*, Thoreau's own *Walden*, and the first edition of Walt Whitman's *Leaves of Grass* as the most complex and capacious literary expression of the spirit of American transcendentalism. In Thoreau's hands, the brothers' voyage becomes not only a rich descriptive chronicle but also a symbolic quest, a historical and primordial investigation and an emblem of a whole life's passage. It was both a young man's exuberant intellectual summa and an elegiac

author. Despite a number of eloquent passages and episodes, this five-hundred-page reminiscence about a short pleasure excursion is a rather ponderous read. Thoreau's initial version of the book was a straightfoward narrative sketch of an 1839 excursion with his brother, John, to Mt. Agiocochook (Mt. Washington) and back. But to this he added innumerable descriptive, meditative, polemical, and historical side-glimpses (including an extended discussion of religion that distressed its few readers by contrasting Judaeo-Christianity unfavorably with Greek myth and Hindu scripture); and he threw in a series of extended set pieces on literature (Chaucer, Ossian, Aulus Persius Flaccus), on the nature of friendship, and on other excursions he had taken elsewhere. Tossed-salad literary travelogues were popular fare in those days, as Thoreau well tribute to his late brother, with whom he enjoyed a more intimate and unguarded relation than with any other person he ever knew.

Although Thoreau originally hoped and expected that *Walden* would be published soon after *A Week*, he was set back in both his finances and his morale by his first book's failure. It took him nearly five additional years to ponder and complete *Walden*, which thus became one of the most revised major works in American literary history, going through no less than eight stages of composition from the first draft (1846–1847) to the final version, issued in the summer of 1854. This was trying for Thoreau, but good for posterity. Had *Walden* been published as originally planned, it would have been remembered as a provocative autobiographical reminiscence and an incisive critique of conventional ways of making a living, but not as the intricate and challenging work of close description and knotty philosophical-poetic reflection that it became. Several interrelated developments in Thoreau's life contributed to this deepening.

First, it was not until 1850 that Thoreau became a really serious, systematic student of natural history, making long records in his journal of his almost daily walks around Concord, joining the Boston Society of Natural History as a "corresponding member" (exempt from annual dues, but granted library privileges), collecting specimens for the Society and for Harvard scientists like Louis Agassiz, compiling a comprehensive "Kalendar" of predictable seasonal phenomena, conducting a study of the phenomenon of forest succession and has led him to be acclaimed as a pioneer of the yet-unbaptized science of ecology, and serving on Harvard's Committee for Examination in Natural History. When he died, his occupation was officially listed as Natural Historian, and he was eulogized in the Boston Society's *Records* "for the great accuracy of his observations"—as a "highly esteemed" botanist and as an "unrivalled" observer of the habits of animals.

To be sure, Thoreau's natural history interests were already evident in the meticulous detail with which the first draft of *Walden* described

his encounter with a field mouse (recapitulated in "Brute Neighbors") and his surveyor-ish sounding of Walden Pond ("The Pond in Winter"). But the proportion of naturalistic detail to meditative reflection increased greatly during the course of *Walden*'s composition, as the erstwhile transcendental poet became more earthbound. Much of "The Ponds" chapter and the last third of the book (from "Brute Neighbors" on) were added after 1849. Thoreau could not, for example, have written the climax of his chronicle of the cycle of the natural year—his description of winter giving way to spring in *Walden*'s next-to-last chapter—without repeated visits to the pond after he "left" it, visits that were informed by a growing interest in the minutiae of natural processes.

This pattern of revisitation is itself a second significant fact about the way *Walden* took shape. Between the Walden experience and the publication of the book, Thoreau committed himself beyond all possibility of change to Concord as his once-and-future community and to a certain pattern of living there as a lifetime tenant in the family home. His *Journal* entries during the 1850s consistently indicate this commitment. He would never enter a conventional profession; instead, he would work only for short stints, as financial or family exigency required, making pencils or surveying land. ("Apollo keeping the flocks of Admetus" was his favorite image for this sort of practical compromise.) He devoted himself to reading, thinking, writing, and nature study, remaining close to home apart from occasional trips around the New England region, balancing his day between his study and his field trips. The final text of *Walden* is deeply ingrained with the marks of Thoreau's reiterative pattern of daily existence. The woods, the ponds, the creatures he describes not as once-seen objects but as objects seen and pondered and internalized over a long period of time. The time of fullest immersion (the years of the Walden experiment proper) is both distinguished from the aftermath (the years of continued rambles throughout the region) and also intermixed. One sign of *Walden*'s temporal complexity is the ease with which Thoreau moves back and forth from the present to the past tense, suggesting a mood of habitual action or even an eternal present, so that many of the actions described (bathing in the pond, fishing, "nooning" in front of his cabin, keeping a wintertime appointment with a particular tree) seem to take on a ritual quality. Altogether, *Walden*'s call to simplify the terms of one's material existence—for many readers, the book's most important dimension—expresses not only Thoreau's stripped-down lifestyle during the years at Walden but the simplicity of the life he elected thereafter, when (as he wryly puts it in the first paragraph) he became "a sojourner in civilized life again." This is the best answer to those dogged literalist skeptics who discount *Walden* (either the book, the life, or both) on the ground that Thoreau did not keep the experiment up but left after a "mere" two years.

Interestingly, Thoreau also vigorously presents himself in *Walden* as the opponent of all routinization: of mindless devotion to the work ethic, of following in the footsteps of one's seniors. He professes shock at realizing that he had worn a path between his cabin and the village. The resolution of this paradox is of course that freshness of perspective, independence of vision, is what counts for Thoreau, rather than the mechanical variation of routine. He would have dismissed the idea that insight is dependent on variety; indeed, for Thoreau, the more often he looked intently at something, the more luminous it became, the more he saw in it.

Thoreau did indeed worry, during the last decade of his life, that his sensitivities were being blunted by age and habit. One of the ways in which he held onto the sense of freshness of vision, even as he sometimes fretted about the loss of it as he grew older and as his naturalist's passion for accuracy threatened to overshadow his romantic quest for visionary immediacy, was through the keen half-prideful, half-painful sense of outsiderness that never left him. Thoreau was both invigorated and wounded by the awareness that most of his townsmen thought of him as an eccentric who perversely eschewed the normal responsibilities of work and citizenship. *Walden* reflects this awareness,

particularly in the adversarial tone of the first and last chapters ("Economy" and "Conclusion") and in Thoreau's continual emphasis on how his cabin was, in effect, as far away from the village as the prairies or the tundra were. These touches were partly done out of wish-fulfilling romantic exoticism, but they also mirrored how Thoreau saw himself in the public eye. They show the occasional combativeness of *A Week* quietly but pervasively ingraining itself as a settled disposition, as well as the kinship between *Walden* and Thoreau's series of more overtly political essays starting with "Resistance to Civil Government." Some have claimed that, following *Walden*'s opening chapter, "Economy"—which dominated the first draft even more than the finished work—Thoreau's comparative disengagement from direct confrontation with social issues (particularly the turn toward nature beginning in the "Sounds" chapter) signifies a retreat from the social and political arena into privatism. But it would be truer to conceive of Thoreau's turn to nature in *Walden* and his critique of the political order in "Resistance to Civil Government" as complementary sides of the same sensibility. Thoreau did indeed sometimes turn to nature in order to escape from society's corruptions, as even "Resistance to Civil Government" demonstrates: in the conclusion to his narrative of being jailed for civil disobedience, he makes a point of stressing that he took off for the hills to become the captain of a huckleberry party. But he would have argued that to flout the work ethic for the sake of pursuing his private "business" with nature was for him as mystifyingly obnoxious an act of bad citizenship as his tax resistance was to his townsmen.

Reading *Walden*

As Thoreau revisited Concord, he revisited *Walden* (eight times in all). The result is a work of exceptional density and intensity, demanding of its reader what Thoreau thought all classic literature demanded: "a training such as the athletes underwent, the steady intention almost of

Walden Pond (Concord, Massachusetts) from the site of Thoreau's hut, 1908

the whole life to this object" (1971 ed., p. 101). During *Walden*'s lifetime in print—and it has never gone out of print since 1862, the year of Thoreau's death—it has been subjected to thousands of "close readings" by professional and amateur critics. The best of these, many of which are listed in the bibliography below, are very illuminating. But rather than rely on them exclusively, it is more important to bring to *Walden* concentrated thought of one's own. To invoke one of Thoreau's favorite words, read this book "deliberately." Slow yourself down. Carefully read, phrase by phrase, a single paragraph—any paragraph—in the first few chapters. Then read it again, this time aloud. Notice anything that starts to take on a different meaning or tonality when read aloud. (Thoreau often italicizes words that he intends to use with a double meaning, or in an ironic way.) Notice cases where Thoreau seems deliberately paradoxical or mysterious, cases where he seems to be suggesting two different or opposite ideas at

once. Reflect on why he might have done so. Notice how Thoreau intermixes plain, even colloquial language with learned language and references. Try to visualize the descriptive parts, and to paraphrase the argumentative parts of the passage in your own words. Notice where Thoreau understates or exaggerates for the sake of effect; notice what the text has especially emphasized or otherwise, seemingly understated or left out. Assume that the author knew pretty much what he was doing even if he had a few blind spots: reflect on why he might have made the choices he did; consider how the book might appear had he arranged certain things differently. If you notice and think about most of these issues carefully, you will not come away with a tidy bottom-line impression of the book or any of its passages—that's not the point—but you will have begun to appreciate the depth of Thoreau's thinking and the subtlety of his art.

These reading suggestions apply no matter which of the many dimensions of *Walden* specifically interests you. And indeed *Walden* has meant many different things to different people. Some have read it as a literal recipe for the healthfully simple life. Others have read it as a pastoral idyll or poem, a work of art rather than a straightforward guide for the would-be experimenter in self-sufficiency. Still others have read it as a philosophical book, either with a view to absorbing or critiquing what they believe to be its main arguments or as a collection of wise observations and sayings, like "The mass of men lead lives of quiet desperation." Again, some consider *Walden* autobiographical; others emphasize how Thoreau's selectivity and exaggerations of certain details have the effect of creating a fictive persona, a first-person epic (or mock-epic) hero who should not be mistaken for the flesh-and-blood Thoreau. Some have read *Walden* as a satire on economic entrepreneurialism; others have stressed its implication in the commercial order it criticizes—was not the book itself a commercial venture, for instance? This essay, then, will unavoidably narrow the field of possibilities in approaching *Walden* as a work about the Concord environment, particularly its natural environment.

Roughly speaking, *Walden* marks the crossroads in Thoreau's unfolding as a writer from his early transcendental phase—when his interest in nature tended to be subordinate to his interest in the realms of literature, meditative thought, and personal introspection—to his late adulthood, when he subordinated mental investigation to comparatively minute and objective environmental observation. Although *Walden* has no "plot" in the ordinary sense of the word, no continuous narrative line, at least in a figurative sense it tells the story of Thoreau's life-transition: a story of environmental awakening, as it were. The book becomes less self-focused and more engaged with environmental detail as it proceeds. The pivotal chapters are "Sounds," "The Ponds," and "Brute Neighbors." Before "Sounds," Thoreau presented the pond and its surroundings in broad brushstrokes, almost as a glimmering abstraction; so far, the book has been overwhelmingly preoccupied with his

"quest for meaning." Now, however, the writer lets us for the first time catch him in the act of responding to the array of stimuli around him. In "The Ponds," which stands in the exact center of the book, Thoreau looks with unprecedented intensity on the central defining feature of his habitat. The writing here is more extrospective, more outward looking, than anything that precedes it, even his sometimes meticulous but also rather dreamy chapter on bean-farming. Several chapters later, in "Brute Neighbors," the book signals decisively that it has become more interested in environment than in self. At this point, significantly, Thoreau switches from the method of ordering his chapters in topical pairs ("Solitude" vs. "Visitors") to the method of ordering in terms of nature's cycle, from autumn through spring. The chapters become increasingly laden with descriptive detail. The result is not an autobiographical tale of the author's transformation from tenderfoot to woodsman, but an increasing immersion of both the author and the sympathetic reader in the tones and textures of the Concord landscape. This process of immersion parallels the change occurring in Thoreau's own life during the nine years that he worked on his book.

"Process" is the key word here, surely. For *Walden* only begins to approach Thoreau's later grasp of the details of natural history, his proto-ecological sense of the relationship among different life-forms (why certain kinds of trees take over from others and what animals have to do with this process, for instance), and his sense of environmental imperilment and the need to counteract the despoliation of nature that was proceeding virtually unchecked in nineteenth-century America. For example, although *Walden* contains several passages that mourn the incursions of the railroad and tree-harvesting near the pond, Thoreau tends to repress these potentially alarming signs of change for the sake of celebrating Walden as "perennially young," "the same woodland lake that I discovered so many years ago." Green radicals may find *Walden* too timid or compromised as a result. But in light of the conceptual difficulties that faced Thoreau at a time when the idea of conservation had just begun to take root in America, it would be fairer to see *Walden* as a heroic struggle to deal with one's own cultural baggage, as Thoreau's transition from his youthful state of Emersonian pastoral idealism to a more solidly eco-centric ethic and aesthetic.

Walden fared much better with the public than *A Week*, which sold so badly that the cost of publication put Thoreau in debt for a number of years. Upon *Walden*'s publication, it was widely and, by and large, very favorably noticed, as "one of those rare books that stands apart from the herd of new publications under which the press absolutely groans," to quote one reviewer. *Walden* did not make Thoreau's fortune; it took the rest of his lifetime for the first edition of two thousand copies to sell out. But this was the beginning of a real measure of fame for him, the making of a reputation—independent of Emerson's—as a trenchant albeit offbeat philosopher-practitioner of economic and moral self-sufficiency, and as a keen and eloquent student of nature. During the next six months, Thoreau lectured in Philadelphia on moose hunting; in Providence and New Bedford and Nantucket, he delivered the jeremiad against materialistic and trivial living ("The ways by which you may get money almost without exception lead downward") that later became the essay "Life without Principle." These topics roughly typify the two characteristic directions of his work of the 1850s.

Reform Papers, The Maine Woods, Cape Cod

His condemnation of thoughtless, materialistic society led to a series of "reform papers," as his editors have called them, lecture-essays mostly on anti-slavery topics in the spirit of "Resistance to Civil Government." The most powerful were got up for special occasions: "Slavery in Massachusetts" as a 4 July 1854 denunciation of the arrest in Boston of a fugitive slave; "A Plea for Captain John Brown" (1859) and two other lectures on Brown as, respectively, a defense of Brown's moral character during his imprisonment, a eulogy at the time of his death, and a commemorative address on the Independence Day following. These works leave no doubt as to the strength of Thoreau's anti-slavery convictions and his social radicalism generally, although at the same time they also show that his political activism was periodic rather than continuous and that he generally reserved his concentrated political statements for moments of crisis. Thoreau believed that it was better to spend one's energies in the effort to disengage from complicity with social evil rather than in crusading against it. "It is not a man's duty, as a matter of course," he wrote in "Resistance to Civil Government," "to devote himself to the eradication of any, even the most enormous, wrong; he may still properly have other concerns to engage him; but it is his duty, at least, to wash his hands of it, and, if he gives it no thought longer, not to give it practically his support" (*Reform Papers*, p. 71). It is no accident that the "reformist" lecture Thoreau gave most often, "Life without Principle," mainly uses "slavery" metaphorically ("What is it to be free from King George and continue the slaves of King Prejudice?" [p. 174]); but it is also no accident that Thoreau denounced the literal institution of slavery in the process.

But it was the second topic, nature and life in the outdoors, that became the dominant one for Thoreau. Much of the writing he intended to publish focused on either two of New England's outbacks (the Maine woods and Cape Cod) or a variety of Concord flora.

Before *Walden* was published, Thoreau had already taken two trips to each of the New England regions, written up two of the three parts of what became *The Maine Woods*, and begun lecturing on Cape Cod. He published the first chapters of *Cape Cod* as magazine articles in the mid-1850s. Thoreau never quite finished either book. His health failed after 1860, but even if it had not, Thoreau's perfectionism and the ever-increasing intricacy of his narrative web of encounters (with regional geography and inhabitants, with the literature of their natural and human history) made it unlikely that he could meet the challenge of completing both projects. Still, both manuscripts were well enough along at the point of his death to be published almost immediately thereafter and make eminently readable books that have proven over the years to have an appeal—especially for devotees of nature writing—at least as enduring as *A Week on the Concord and Merrimack Rivers*, if not *Walden* itself.

The Maine Woods narrates Thoreau's three trips in chronological order. *Cape Cod* conflates Thoreau's different visits into a single excursion from Cohasset to Provincetown. Both include a much more distinct narrative line and are written in a much more spare and direct prose style than either of Thoreau's first two books, and they begin more graphically, as Thoreau chronicles an exciting ascent of Mount Katahdin *(Maine Woods)* and a tragic shipwreck at Cohasset. It is clear that Thoreau originally intended a magazine readership for these books. After the first third of each book, however, the pace slows rapidly, reflecting Thoreau's evolution toward a more densely descriptive style of environmental writing.

In *The Maine Woods*, this is particularly the case with the third section, "The Allegash and East Branch," which in fact comprises more than half of the entire book. This section is cast in diary format with a botanical appendix, and it dwells extensively on Thoreau's transactions with Joe Polis, the Indian guide whose woodsmanship Thoreau admired (and also relished correcting when he could). Whereas the second section, "Chesuncook," is built upon an extended narrative of moose hunting that Thoreau portrays with both satire and enthusiasm for environmental detail, the third section is a combination of natural history and amateur anthropology. It is almost an informal monograph on Native American cultural practices based on Thoreau's observation of Polis and enhanced by Thoreau's wide reading in Native American history and ethnography. (His many "Indian notebooks" remain even today in manuscript, published only in facsimile that Thoreau's semi-legible penmanship makes very rough going.)

In *Cape Cod*, Thoreau and his companion proceed rather quickly to within twenty-five miles of the Cape's end, but then take two-thirds of the book to cover the last quarter of the way. The first third of the book, five of ten chapters, contains some of Thoreau's most striking prose ("The Shipwreck") and also some of his most droll and racy, particularly his portrait of an old salt, "The Wellfleet Oysterman," a fountain of anecdote and local lore, "the merriest old man that we had ever seen" (1988 ed., p. 71). The balance of *Cape Cod*, which takes the travelers through the Cape's two remaining townships, engages the reader with its comprehensiveness. It is replete with lingering seascapes and landscapes, scientific and historical information: anecdotes of previous landings and shipwrecks, actual and mythical; glimpses of the daily lives of fisherfolk; the vistas at each turn and height. The companions linger, for instance, as they approach Provincetown "to admire the various beautiful forms and colors of the sand" and to consider "an interesting mirage, which I have since found that Hitchcock also observed on the sands of the Cape" (p. 150). This mirage was produced by a series of pools that "appeared to lie by magic on the side of the vale, like a mirror left in a slanting position." According to Thoreau, "It was a very pretty mirage for a Provincetown desert, but not amounting to what, in Sanscrit, is called 'the thirst of the gazelle,' as there was real water here for a base, and we were able to quench our thirst after all" (p. 151). This is a typically small but detailed example of Thoreau's attempt in *Cape Cod* to describe just how the landscape looked as the hikers shifted their position. The synthesis of superfine observation with wide and sometimes esoteric learning is a combination we find in *Walden* also, but in the later chapters of *Cape Cod* the environmental textures are brought out with even greater subtlety.

Indeed, both *The Maine Woods* and *Cape Cod* manage splendidly to convey the impressions of an informed and observant outsider exposing himself to districts ecologically and culturally very different from his own. Each book was one of the first of its kind about its chosen region, and neither has been surpassed. Their obvious qualities are due to Thoreau's inquisitiveness and his talent for descriptive prose. Equally memorable, though, is their complex tone: a mixture of the prosaic, the idiosyncratic, the compellingly exotic, the perplexing, and the irretrievably forlorn. The north woods' and the Cape's very different forms of "primitivism" — or so Thoreau considered it—both appealed strongly to his imagination and returned him with a certain sense of relief to his home base in Concord.

It has often been said, and with justice, that Thoreau's preferred form of writing was "the excursion." Travel writing was certainly his favorite kind of contemporary literature, and when it came to setting down his impressions of the environment, whether in a daily journal entry or for a piece of formal writing, his first approach was to organize his material chronologically. His four major books all follow the excursion form, at least if one takes seriously Thoreau's characterization of *Walden* as the result of "travel[ing] a good deal in Concord" (1971 ed., p. 4). Several of Thoreau's shorter magazine pieces are explicitly excursive: "A Walk to Wachusett" (1843), "A Winter Walk" (1843), and "A Yankee in Canada" (1853). Indeed, one of Thoreau's favorite lectures, "Walking," is a meditation on the nature of the kind of travel that most interested him. The essay focuses on two themes of special importance to him: first, that the proper sort of walking is "sauntering" and as such a kind of pilgrimage (Thoreau playfully derives "saunter" from "*Sainte Terre*," Holy Land); and, second, that the right destination for Thoreau's sensibility is "the West," which "is but another name for the Wild" (*Excursions*, 1863 ed., pp. 161–162). It isn't out of any desire to imitate the forty-niners that Thoreau's mental compass takes him southwestward on his walks; rather, Thoreau walks as an act of faith: "I believe in the forest, and in the meadow, and in the night in which the corn grows" (p. 185). Thoreau sums up what his pilgrimage-walking means for him in the phrase that many

environmentalists remember him by, the phrase the Sierra Club has taken as its motto: "in Wildness is the preservation of the World" (p. 185).

But it was not describing what he saw on his excursions ("*my* walk") that increasingly interested Thoreau so much as articulating the meaning of what he saw there: the forest, the meadow, the night, and the corn. From his own standpoint, his most important work after *Walden* was his extended scientific-poetic-analytic study of a range of natural phenomena based chiefly on a combination of wide reading and years of observation within the Concord region: seasonal change, moonlight, the colors of fall, seed dissemination, and the natural history of wild fruits. On all of these subjects Thoreau composed and, in some cases, delivered lectures. (For example, he gave a salty 1860 lecture entitled "The Succession of Forest Trees" at a local county fair [or "cattle show," as it was called].) None of them did he bring to full consummation. It was probably this body of work to which Emerson was referring in his funeral address, which still stands as the most probing short profile of his former disciple, when he declared, "The scale on which [Thoreau's] studies proceeded was so large as to require longevity. . . . It seems an injury that he should leave in the midst his broken task, which none else can finish" (vol. 10, pp. 484–485). Yet some of Thoreau's findings have made it into print. Recently, the unfinished manuscript from which the "Forest Trees" lecture came, "The Dispersion of Seeds," has been published in *Faith in a Seed* (1993). In the penultimate year of his life, after his health had begun to fail, Thoreau came close to completing a long essay on huckleberries, which he intended as a lecture but never delivered; it was finally published in 1970. This was a spinoff of another very ambitious study, related to "Dispersion," he called "Wild Fruits," which he left in an inchoate condition. He did compose two significant late lecture-essays, "Autumnal Tints" and "Wild Apples." These, together with "The Succession of Forest Trees" and fragments from a mid-1850s lecture, "Night and Moonlight," were collected along with

"Walking" and four earlier pieces as *Excursions* the year after Thoreau's death.

Later Work—Legacy

All this later work, like the latter chapters of *Cape Cod* and *The Maine Woods*, survives today in a form less rigorously worked through and revised than had Thoreau not been forced to abandon it or "finish" it hurriedly for publication in the face of imminent death. None of it, as it stands, can seriously challenge *Walden* as Thoreau's masterpiece. Some Thoreauvians have gone so far as to assert that even had he lived he could not have come close to rivaling *Walden*, because hyperfocus on natural history detail had clotted his prose and curtailed his creative suppleness. On the other hand, admirers of the later work emphasize its much firmer command of the scientific knowledge of his day, including at least a partial assimilation of Darwin, whose *Origin of Species* (1859) Thoreau read sympathetically soon after publication. They also point to the fact that Thoreau was still capable of the lyric enthusiasm and the cross-grained tonalities that make the persona of *Walden* so interesting. Certainly the "environmentalist" Thoreau emerges much more forcefully in later passages, such as the eloquent outline of an ambitious program for a five hundred-acre park in every Massachusetts township, and Thoreau expresses himself as a canny, observant "ecologist" in his accounts of how pines and squirrels conspire to colonize open tracts. But just as the belittler of the late Thoreau cannot prove that he suffered from an irretrievable creative blockage, so the defender cannot prove that he would in fact have been able to complete another literary classic when his interests were seemingly in the process of veering slowly but steadily away from literature toward natural history.

Perhaps it is just as well that this debate about the merits and promise of the later Thoreau is insoluble. It helps to promote him not as the Shakespeare of American nature writing—not as a single, monumental figure—but as a prophet and harbinger of what American nature writing might become: he is inspiring for what he did, and did not, achieve. The odyssey-like quality of his slow and somewhat belated progress from transcendentalist romantic of limited nature knowledge to the full-fledged natural historian mirrors the kind of quest that most readers and writers of environmental literature themselves must undertake, a quest that they undertake (as Thoreau did) with the awareness that there is too much to know, feel, and perceive ever to understand comprehensively.

In some ways, then, the best work to remember Thoreau by is his late lecture-essay, "Wild Apples," which was in fact the last work that he sent off for publication before he died. Thoreau loved the wild apple both because the apple was an anciently valued fruit, brought to North America by New England's early settlers, and because apples can also thrive in unexpected, wild places, producing odd-shaped trees and (to Thoreau's palate, anyhow) tartly delicious flavors. "Who knows," he ruminates, "but this chance wild fruit, planted by a cow or a bird on some remote and rocky hillside, where it is as yet unobserved by man, may be the choicest of all its kind?" (*Excursions*, p. 287). Thoreauvians have been quick to identify the wild apple as a personal insignia. Indeed, he himself makes this point when he observes that the American wild apple "is wild only like myself, perchance, who belong not to the aboriginal race here, but have strayed into the woods from the cultivated stock" (p. 280). This apparently offhand remark can stand as a pretty fair summary of his life's aspiration: to stray from the village, become more feral, find a spiritual if not literal home in some half-hidden nook where he could interact with an environment more sylvan than his own point of origin, and yield for his reader the kind of fruit he celebrates in this essay—the "natural raciness, the sours and bitters which the diseased palate refuses" (p. 295).

In one of the essay's most delightful passages, Thoreau describes with comic gusto his delighted discovery of edible windfalls as late as mid-November: from their "lurking-places" under fallen leaves, "I draw forth the fruit . . .

perhaps with a leaf or two cemented to it (as Curzon an old manuscript from a monastery's mouldy cellar), but still with a rich bloom on it, and at least as ripe and well-kept, if not better than those in barrels, more crisp and lively than they" (pp. 300–301). He might have been describing the experience of discovery that many admirers of nature writing have had when reading Thoreau, particularly during the period of his relative obscurity, before he became "canonized" (as students of literary history like to put it) in the early twentieth century. During his lifetime and, indeed, for almost a century after his death, Thoreau was not reckoned the unique treasure of premodern American nature writing that he is today (in spite of the fact that his work was kept in print and increasingly publicized by the most prestigious literary publishing house in America: Ticknor and Fields and its successor, Houghton Mifflin). A number of Thoreau's predecessors and near-contemporaries who wrote about the countryside and wilderness were treated with equal respect: William Bartram, John James Audubon, Susan Cooper, Wilson Flagg, John Burroughs, and others. Only the cranky wild-apple harvesters of the late-Victorian intellectual world were prepared to argue that Thoreau was a writer fully the equal of his great contemporaries Emerson and Hawthorne.

In the twentieth century, it has been much more respectable to value Thoreau's work. Since 1941, there has been a Thoreau Society, which today is the largest and most flourishing society devoted to memorializing an individual author. It meets annually, in Concord, on the Saturday in midsummer closest to Thoreau's own birthday (July 12); it maintains a museum and a bookstore; and it will soon open a research center on an estate near Walden Pond recently made available to the Society. Yet, the general public is still unaware of much of Thoreau's work. *Walden*, "Resistance to Civil Government," and perhaps the essay on "Walking" are known far more widely than the other 95 percent of Thoreau's writings. Partly because Thoreau fully polished for publication only a small percentage of what he wrote, partly because he (like Emerson) was inherently stronger

as an artist of passages than of larger, extended units, the Thoreauvian of today can look forward to the prospects of finding unappreciated fruit among the leafage.

Nowhere is this more strikingly the case than with the journal that Thoreau kept with increasing, almost religious devotion for nearly a quarter of a century. An immense, two-million-word work, *The Journal of Henry Thoreau* can make for dry, redundant reading, particularly in the later years, but at any moment it can also electrify the reader with pithy dicta, wonderfully sensitive descriptions of encounters with animals, striking historical anecdotes and excerpts from books Thoreau has read, deft portraits of local character and landscapes realized with an exquisite painterly touch. Most of what Thoreau wrote up in a formal way can be seen in embryo here, but much in the *Journal* is also unique. Some have even claimed the *Journal* to be Thoreau's most important work, more so even than *Walden*. Although he apparently began his journal as an exercise in self-scrutiny (in the Puritan tradition that older transcendentalists like Emerson and Bronson Alcott and Margaret Fuller continued), and then used it as a source-book from which to quarry ideas and cannibalize passages for *A Week* and the early drafts of *Walden*, after 1850 the journal increasingly became a literary project in its own right, even as Thoreau continued to rifle it for usable passages and jot down in it some of his rough drafts. In particular, the journal became Thoreau's most intimate, most objective, and certainly most extended record of his perceptions of nature's phenomena, structure, and meaning. The fact that these perceptions kept repeating and renewing and complicating themselves until Thoreau's death was not so much a sign of Thoreau's inadequacies as an observer or writer about nature—though of course it is true that he was limited by the inadequacies of the scientific theory of his day—as it was a sign of what all students and lovers of nature quickly come to feel: the inexhaustibleness of nature.

As Thoreau matured, his conception of nature changed somewhat. At first, during his transcendental period, roughly before 1850, he was strongly influenced by Emerson's theory of the mystical "correspondence" between natural and spiritual phenomena, a theory that allowed a poetic-idealistic temperament like the young Thoreau's to presume that nature worked according to a spiritually meaningful design and that its seasons, events, and individual life-forms had some sort of spiritual significance that the informed and sensitive eye could potentially decode. In time, this idealism began to yield to Thoreau's empiricism, which indeed had also been present from the start in his passion for gathering and classifying data, for making lists and charts. Later, Thoreau became adept at making generalizations about natural phenomena, at perceiving what a later generation would call "ecological" relationships, especially in the areas of seasonal concurrence and plant succession. But Thoreau never abandoned his idealism in his gradual commitment to empirical data and relations; for example, he always remained attracted to the myth of nature's spiritual meaningfulness and coherence, even in the face of skepticism and the lack of evidence. Thoreau's sense of the bounty and mystery of nature animates the *Journal* from beginning to end and has continued, partly through his example and direct influence, to animate American nature writing.

Thoreau's increasing devotion to nature, based on the quite personal reverential bond he felt for nature throughout his adult lifetime, has been both an inspiration and an enigma to Thoreau watchers in his day and ours. Particularly in our highly urban and technological contemporary civilization, it is hard for many to understand Thoreau's passion for nature except in terms of some other factor—such as that it was a fashionable thing for a member of the Euro-American intelligentsia during the nineteenth century to love nature, that he was socially maladroit, that he could not fit into the conventional workplace, that he was disappointed in love, or that he was more homosexually than heterosexually inclined and felt compelled to sublimate his erotic passion. And indeed all of these hypotheses probably have some truth to them; all of them point to certain or likely traits

of Thoreau's character that might well have influenced his pursuit of nature. None of them, however, not even the whole group of them taken together, suffice to explain why nature became for Thoreau such an overwhelmingly strong preoccupation, why he felt such a strong desire to understand nature comprehensively, why he felt such a strong bond to nature and such a strong desire to see nature cherished and protected by his contemporaries. The mystery of Thoreau's own nature may be why Thoreau's works are likely to continue to speak to future generations of readers and writers of literature.

Selected Bibliography

WORKS OF HENRY DAVID THOREAU

A Week on the Concord and Merrimack Rivers (Boston: James Monroe, 1849), scholarly ed. by Carl Hovde, William L. Howarth, and Elizabeth Hall Witherell (Princeton, N.J.: Princeton Univ. Press, 1980); *Walden* (Boston: Ticknor and Fields, 1854), scholarly ed. by J. Lyndon Shanley (Princeton, N.J.: Princeton Univ. Press, 1971); *Excursions* (Boston: Ticknor and Fields, 1863), repr. with intro. by Leo Marx (New York: Corinth, 1962), includes Emerson's "Thoreau" as the introductory "Biographical Sketch"; *The Maine Woods*, ed. by William Ellery Channing and Sophia Thoreau (Boston: Ticknor and Fields, 1864), scholarly ed. by Joseph J. Moldenhauer (Princeton, N.J.: Princeton Univ. Press, 1972); *Cape Cod*, ed. by William Ellery Channing and Sophia Thoreau (Boston: Ticknor and Fields, 1865), scholarly ed. by Joseph J. Moldenhauer (Princeton, N.J.: Princeton Univ. Press, 1988).

The Journal of Henry Thoreau, ed. by Bradford Torrey and Francis H. Allen, 14 vols. (Boston: Houghton Mifflin, 1906), scholarly re-edition by John C. Broderick, Robert Sattelmeyer, et al., 4 vols. to date (Princeton, N.J.: Princeton Univ. Press, 1981–); *The Correspondence of Henry David Thoreau*, ed. by Walter Harding and Carl Bode (New York: New York Univ. Press, 1958); *Collected Poems of Henry Thoreau*, ed. by Carl Bode, enl. ed. (Baltimore: Johns Hopkins Univ. Press, 1964); *Reform Papers*, ed. by Wendell Glick (Princeton, N.J.: Princeton Univ. Press, 1973); *Early Essays and Miscellanies*, ed. by Joseph J. Moldenhauer and Edwin Moser, with Alexander Kern (Princeton, N.J.: Princeton Univ. Press, 1975); *The Natural History Essays*, ed. by Robert Sattelmeyer (Salt Lake City: Peregrine Smith, 1980); *Faith in a Seed: The Dispersion of Seeds and Other Late Natural His-*

tory Writings, ed. by Bradley P. Dean (Washington, D.C.: Island/Shearwater, 1993).

BIBLIOGRAPHIES

The Thoreau Society Bulletin (see next section for details); *American Literary Scholarship*, ed. by James Woodress and successors (Durham, N.C.: Duke Univ. Press, 1964–), annual volume of bibliographical essays, includes a section appraising studies of Thoreau; William Howarth, *The Literary Manuscripts of Henry David Thoreau* (Columbus: Ohio State Univ. Press, 1974), describes the manuscripts and indicates where they are deposited; Walter Harding and Michael Meyer, *The New Thoreau Handbook* (New York: New York Univ. Press, 1980), succinct overview chapters on Thoreau's life, work, and reputation indicating the important studies in each area as of the late 1970s; Gary Scharnhorst, *Henry David Thoreau: An Annotated Bibliography of Comment and Criticism Before 1900* (New York: Garland, 1992).

BIOGRAPHICAL AND CRITICAL STUDIES

Charles Anderson, *The Magic Circle of Walden* (New York: Holt, 1968), detailed discussion of *Walden's* literary form and style, with considerable attention to main themes; Lawrence Buell, *The Environmental Imagination: Thoreau, Nature Writing, and the Formation of American Culture* (Cambridge, Mass.: Harvard Univ. Press, 1995), posits that Thoreau's work, especially *Walden*, is central to the major forms and emphases of American environmental writing; Joan Burbick, *Thoreau's Alternative History: Changing Perspectives on Nature, Culture, and Language* (Philadelphia: Univ. of Pennsylvania Press, 1987), explores Thoreau's interest in natural history as a key to his interest in human history; Sharon Cameron, *Writing Nature: Henry Thoreau's Journal* (New York: Oxford Univ. Press, 1985), examines the quest for understanding nature in Thoreau's *Journal* as his central intellectual endeavor.

Stanley Cavell, *The Senses of Walden* (New York: Viking, 1972), a thoughtful, sensitive examination of Thoreau's thought and language; William Ellery Channing II, *Thoreau, the Poet-Naturalist*, enl. ed., ed. by Franklin B. Sanborn (Boston: Charles E. Goodspeed, 1902), rev. version of the earlier full-length biography of Thoreau, by a friend who knew him intimately; Edward Waldo Emerson, *Henry Thoreau as Remembered by a Young Friend* (Boston: Houghton Mifflin, 1917), fond memoir of Thoreau by Emerson's youngest child, sole surviving son, and editor.

Ralph Waldo Emerson, *The Complete Works of Ralph Waldo Emerson*, 12 vols., ed. by Edward Waldo Emerson (Boston: Houghton, Mifflin, 1903–1904; repr., 1994); Steven Fink, *Prophet in the Marketplace: Thoreau's Development as a Professional Writer* (Princeton, N.J.: Princeton Univ. Press, 1992); Peter A. Fritzell, *Nature Writing and America: Essays upon a Cultural Type* (Ames: Iowa State Univ. Press, 1990), close examination of the work of Thoreau and other American nature writers; Frederick Garber, *Thoreau's Fable of Inscribing* (Princeton, N.J.: Princeton Univ. Press, 1991), a difficult but probing study of Thoreau's theory and practice of art in relation to other forms of making.

Robert A. Gross, "Concord, Boston, and the Wider World: Transcendentalism and Urbanism," in *New Perspectives on Concord History*, ed. by William M. Bailey et al. (Concord, Mass.: Foundation for Humanities and Public Policy, 1983), puts Thoreau's moment in the context of the history of (sub)urbanization, and " 'The Most Estimable Place in All the World': A Debate on Progress in Nineteenth-Century Concord," in *Studies in the American Renaissance 1979*, ed. by Joel Myerson (Boston: Twayne, 1978), Thoreau in relation to other loyal nineteenth-century Concordians' sense of the town's nature and future; Walter Harding, *The Days of Henry Thoreau*, rev. ed. (Princeton, N.J.: Princeton Univ. Press, 1982), the classic factual biography of Thoreau; John Hildebidle, *Thoreau: A Naturalist's Liberty* (Cambridge, Mass.: Harvard Univ. Press, 1983), Thoreau as an unconventional natural history writer; William Howarth, *The Book of Concord: Thoreau's Life as a Writer* (New York: Viking, 1983), an interpretative factual biography that places strong emphasis on Thoreau's natural history interests.

Richard Lebeaux, *Young Man Thoreau* (Amherst: Univ. of Massachusetts Press, 1977), first of two biographical studies of Thoreau from the standpoint of Eric Erikson's theory of human development through life stages, and *Thoreau's Seasons* (Amherst: Univ. of Massachusetts Press, 1984), the sequel to *Young Man Thoreau*; James McIntosh, *Thoreau as Romantic Naturalist: His Shifting Stance Toward Nature* (Ithaca, N.Y.: Cornell Univ. Press, 1974), Thoreau's ambivalence toward nature seen in relation to romantic tradition; Robert Milder, *Reimagining Thoreau* (Cambridge: Cambridge Univ. Press, 1995), careful study of the development of Thoreau's thought and writing; Joel Myerson, ed., *The Cambridge Companion to Thoreau* (New York: Cambridge Univ. Press, 1995), excellent collection of essays on different aspects of Thoreau, including several on Thoreau's interest in nature; Leonard Neufeldt, *The Economist: Henry D. Thoreau and Enterprise* (New York: Oxford Univ. Press, 1989), probing study of Thoreau, particularly *Walden*, in relation to contemporary economic thought and discourse.

Sherman Paul, *The Shores of America: Thoreau's Inward Exploration* (Urbana: Univ. of Illinois Press, 1958), classic scholarly study of the development of

Thoreau's thought and art; H. Daniel Peck, *Thoreau's Morning Work: Memory and Perception in A Week on the Concord and Merrimack Rivers, the Journal, and Walden* (New Haven, Conn.: Yale Univ. Press, 1990), probing examination of how Thoreau organized and dramatized his sense of nature's spatial and temporal order; Robert D. Richardson, Jr., *Henry Thoreau: A Life of the Mind* (Berkeley: Univ. of California Press, 1986), a factual and interpretative biography that illuminates especially well how Thoreau synthesized direct life experience with his extensive reading; David M. Robinson, " 'Unchronicled Nations': Agrarian Purpose and Thoreau's Ecological Knowing," in *Nineteenth Century Literature* 48 (1993): 326–340, examines Walden (both the experience and the book) as a kind of agrarian experiment.

Robert Sattelmeyer, "The Remaking of *Walden*," in *Writing the American Classics*, ed. by James Barbour and Tom Quirk (Chapel Hill: Univ. of North Carolina Press, 1990), succinct summary of the process of *Walden*'s composition, and *Thoreau's Reading: A Study in Intellectual History with Bibliographical Catalogue* (Princeton, N.J.: Princeton Univ. Press, 1988), overview of Thoreau's major reading interests, with a list of what he is known to have read; Robert Sayre, *Thoreau and the American Indians* (Princeton, N.J.: Princeton Univ. Press, 1977), judicious study of the degree to which Thoreau came to understand Native American culture; Edmund A. Schofield and Robert C. Baron, ed., *Thoreau's World and Ours: A Natural Legacy* (Golden, Colo.: North American, 1993), a collection of scholarly and appreciative essays that contains much on Thoreau's natural history interests and on the natural history of Concord; J. Lyndon Shanley, *The Making of Walden* (Chicago: Univ. of Chicago Press, 1957), valuable for its reprinting of the first draft of *Walden*; *The Thoreau Society Bulletin*, ed. by Walter Harding (1941–1991) and Bradley P. Dean (1991–), a quarterly publication of news, scholarly articles, and memorabilia of interest to both amateur and professional students of Thoreau, including the most complete available annotated bibliographies of books and articles about Thoreau.

JOHN C. VAN DYKE
(1856–1932)

PETER WILD

AT THE TURN of the twentieth century, John Charles Van Dyke's book *The Desert* (1901) launched the genre of desert writing with a prose that has not yet been surpassed in its convincing lushness. Until that time, America's deserts were all but universally condemned as useless, as "God's mistakes" in the making of Creation. There were good reasons for the negative attitude. Settlers from the humid East were seeking lush green lands on which to stake out their farms and build their homes. Rows of bare lava peaks shimmering in the 110 degree heat over seemingly endless expanses of cactus flats inhabited by rattlesnakes repelled the pioneers. They looked on the barren scenes as horrid obstacles between them and more welcoming places. Yet to Van Dyke, desert sands were not the dreaded wastes faced by travelers on their way to the abundant allure of California; they were objects of beauty:

> The long line of dunes at the north are just as desolate, yet they are wonderfully beautiful. The desert sand is finer than snow, and its curves and arches, as it builds its succession of drifts out and over an arroyo, are as graceful as the lines of running water. The dunes are always rhythmical and flowing in their forms; and for color the desert has nothing that surpasses them. In the early morning, before the sun is up, they are air-blue, reflecting the sky overhead . . . at sunset they are often flooded with a rose or mauve color. (*The Desert*, p. 53)

Through such writing Van Dyke described the exotic region, its strange plants and animals and vivid sunsets. He wrote with enthusiasm about lizards that bleed from the eyes and about dust storms that whirl up and turn the sky golden. Although his approach marked a radical shift in desert perception from utilitarian to aesthetic, it came naturally to him.

Roaming the Southwest in midlife, in hopes of curing his respiratory problems, art critic Van Dyke also followed an old habit. Wherever he wandered, he applied his theories of beauty to the landscapes about him, in this case to a despised landscape. In particular, his outlook derived from the Art for Art's Sake movement. This offshoot of Romanticism, gauzy in its tenets, was especially favored by the upper classes of the time. Adherents often took aloof positions toward the public. From his lofty perch as an authority, for example, Van Dyke insisted that a thing was beautiful simply because he declared it so. Whatever the vagaries that gave individuals the license to tailor its theories to serve their own whimsies, basically Art for Art's Sake held that the enjoyment of beauty was life's highest good.

951

Furthermore, along with some other devotees, Van Dyke held that the greatest beauty was to be found not hanging on the walls of the world's art museums but revealed in the forms and colors of wild nature. Such believers despised the realism and functionalism of art popular among the masses. Thus, in Van Dyke's coterie of elitists, it mattered not at all that sand dunes were noxious obstacles to the settlers who had to labor through them. As Van Dyke whizzed across the Southwest in a lavish Pullman car, he saw the waves of sand in quite a different light. To him, they were not wastes but objects of beauty to be appreciated by people of fine sensibilities. The dunes were valuable "simply because they are beautiful in themselves and good to look upon" (*The Desert*, p. 232). He meant for the wealthy to look upon.

As might be guessed, strong social prejudices often lay behind such a view. At the turn of the century, immigrants by the millions were pouring into the nation from Europe. Mostly uneducated, they flocked into many American cities, and although the growing slums provided convenient pools of cheap labor for wealthy industrialists, the resulting social turmoil and violent labor strikes threatened the privileged status of the well-off. Many wealthy people looked on the jungles of the recently created slums in their cities and threw up their hands in despair. As the problems grew by the year, such people turned their backs on conditions appearing to be beyond remedy. Instead, they escaped to nature, not only to the clean air and bright landscapes of their country homes but also to the nonthreatening nature they might enjoy in their leisure. These artistic and social attitudes lie at the heart of Van Dyke's "nature writing." More accurately, they represent his escape from fetid humanity and his way of seeing beauty in the forms and colors of the outdoors. In effect, they are largely aesthetic treatises using nature as their vehicle. Among such works are *The Opal Sea* (1906), *The Mountain* (1916), *The Grand Canyon* (1920), *The Open Spaces* (1922), and *The Meadows* (1926).

Aesthetics and Nature

Van Dyke stated the link between art and nature early on, in *Nature for Its Own Sake* (1898), a title that significantly echoes the name of the movement central to his aesthetic views. As he emphasizes in the preface:

> What, then, is the object of the book? Simply to call attention to that nature around us which only too many people look at every day and yet never see, to show that light, form, and color are beautiful regardless of human meaning or use, to suggest what pleasure and profit may be derived from the study of that natural beauty which is everyone's untaxed heritage, and which may be had for the lifting of one's eyes. (p. x)

Clear as Van Dyke is in such assertions of purpose, readers have for the most part ignored two others. A rebel at heart, Van Dyke boldly states that although he will include a few "scientific facts" now and then, as curious points of interest concerning nature, his book "has no direct bearing upon any branch of science." Rather, his pages are simply "records of personal impressions," perhaps "warped" by his personal outlook.

With that statement, the wily Van Dyke has done two things. He has given fair warning that he cares not one whit about objectivity. To the contrary, he has given himself license to follow the lead of his often whimsical impressions and to say whatever he pleases about nature, accurate or not. Unfortunately, in their enthusiasm for his heady passages, readers tend to overlook this second aspect of Van Dyke's writing— and this to their peril, for as will be seen primarily in the discussion of *The Desert*, with his impressionistic waywardness Van Dyke not only creates a good deal of factual mischief but also apparently takes perverse delight in doing so.

On the surface, however, Van Dyke's books appear to offer reliable rundowns of nature's beauties. *Nature for Its Own Sake* is a survey of those beauties, its chapters musing on the artistic effects of running water, of sunlight playing on cloud formations, the shapes and folds of hills, and so on. In fact, the concluding sentence of the preface announces that this overview launches a series of books whose individual volumes will cover specific aspects of nature in greater detail.

The Opal Sea follows suit. Referring to the variegated play of light and color of the semiprecious stone, the title is well chosen. Van Dyke's preface states his case for the choice:

> All the oceans are one. North or south of the line, at the equator or at the poles, around Iceland or around Formosa there is but the one water. And up and down the vast expanse, everywhere over its shining surface, with summer suns and rosy atmosphere, there spreads the violet light, the pearly color, of the Oriental stone. Therefore I ask again: Why not the Opal Sea? (p. viii)

And he follows the pattern previewed in *Nature for Its Own Sake*. Each chapter is a study of an aspect of the sea: its currents, winds, breakers, birds. Yet the treatment of the material shows that Van Dyke's interest is not so much in the facts of the matters before him as in the aesthetic pleasure he derives from observing their effects. For example, a night scene of wind-driven waves crashing against a cliff combines the artist's eye with the poet's thrill:

> Ghost-like in the dim light reel and toss the white riders of the storm. Onward they come. Swash! Booooooom! Sssssss-ss! And the great cauldron under the cliff having flung forth its spume, halts, hesitates, sinks back upon itself, sucks out in a great undertow, then rises into a new crest higher than ever. (pp. 136–137)

Van Dyke's intent is far more than to pass on memorable word pictures spun from the natural world. Very much in line with his version of Art for Art's Sake, he wants to show man as puny,

overwhelmed by the power of surrounding nature. In such a way, humans can feel "part of the universal whole" and reverberate with those emotions of harmonious oneness Freud spoke of as oceanic. Found throughout the series, that romantic notion can easily sacrifice content for vague if lush shivers, but an age much like ours, blessed with the luxury of having the time to feel jaded by the very comforts industrialization had brought, welcomed Van Dyke's approach.

Following the method already established, and reflecting Van Dyke's addiction to travel, *The Mountain* surveys the aesthetic pleasures derived from highlands and ranges around the world, from the Rocky Mountains to the Carpathians, the Apennines to the Caucasus. Again, each chapter is devoted to a specific feature, such as foothills, waterfalls, the play of light over snowfields. And again, Van Dyke's preface makes clear that in his view, science is secondary to the purpose, merely the incidental factors generating the loveliness before him. The writing that follows bears this out. Although Van Dyke has some things to say about geology and the physics of light, the prose that captures his passionate seeing illustrates the quest for visual excitements that propels him. In Alaska, he gapes, stunned, at the "wonderful blues and greens" of a glacier: "The hue is exquisite, jewel-like, and in depth unsurpassed," he gasps (p. 153). At such moments, the traveling aesthetician becomes almost vertiginous, overwhelmed by the landscape before him.

Yet the concluding book in the series shows Van Dyke capable of playing more complex chords, adding the wisdom of maturity to their timbre. Written in the last decade of his life, *The Meadows* is at once a relaxed ramble and a tribute to the gentle fields and woodlands surrounding Van Dyke's native New Brunswick, New Jersey. Here the excitement is controlled, refined through contemplation and sobriety as the stroller eyes the interlocking tracery of bare trees silhouetted against a winter sky. And when, out prowling in a snowstorm, he stands across the river to look back on the ghostly

Van Dyke (far right) during his travels in the desert of northern Mexico

patterns of college steeples rising through the snowy mist, one feels the mixture of giddiness and profundity in Van Dyke's accomplishment.

The Desert

However, far more famous than any other volume in the series is Van Dyke's widely misunderstood *The Desert*. Frequently hailed as a breakthrough, it was the result of what Van Dyke often did when he traveled, that is, he picked up his pen and described the landscape about him, whatever it happened to be. Much of the book's originality, then, lies not in his approach but in its application to a novel subject, the despised desert. Whatever the complexities lying behind it, *The Desert* took the nation by the ears, especially people who lived in cities and tended to idealize life in the outdoors. Not forced

to deal with the uncomfortable realities of desert life—its heat, poisonous scorpions, and lack of water—from far off they saw the nation's arid lands as desirable places, as places of freedom and romance. Instructed by Van Dyke that they were beholding the "most decorative landscape in the world, a landscape all color, a dream landscape" (p. 56), they could see the distant lands of mesas and sandy vastness with new, romantic eyes. Out there a delicate veil of lilac air hung over the stark peaks by day, and at night the moon turned the endless creosote flats an eerie gold. *The Desert* was a large publishing success, reprinted many times and remaining available throughout Van Dyke's life.

Although *The Desert* went out of print at about the time of Van Dyke's death, the book was not forgotten either by desert devotees or by historians. In 1950, Franklin Walker's *Literary History of Southern California* praised Van Dyke as the man who first "discover[ed] the beauties of the desert." In our own age of environmental activism, with its concerns over the rapid loss of the Southwest's natural heritage, almost predictably the man who first sounded the trumpet blast that "the deserts should never be reclaimed" but "preserved forever" once again has come into his own. Since 1976 *The Desert* has appeared in three reprints, marking a rebirth of Van Dyke's popularity.

In fact, given Van Dyke's self-projected image as the lone romantic who manfully braves the unknown and rides off "beyond the wire fence of civilization," in the eyes of moderns yearning for the open spaces of wilder days he has almost achieved the status of a desert saint. Critics have ascribed to him the virtues of the superb outdoorsman combined with the sensitivities of a traveler so attuned to nature that he is having a "love affair" with the desert. Indeed, few are the serious desert lovers who do not have the name of this early traveler on their lips—and rightly so, given the power of Van Dyke's book.

Considering the worshipful atmosphere surrounding such a figure, an atmosphere that has been passed on all but unquestioned through the decades, it probably comes as something of a surprise to discover that Van Dyke displayed far more than his share of human foibles. Worse, he likely faked most of his desert forays. According to recent scholarship, he hardly rode off into the unknown with a pistol strapped to his side, as he implies in *The Desert* and boldly states in his autobiography. In contrast, the aristocratic Van Dyke likely viewed the region through the windows of Pullman cars and from the verandas of first-class hotels. Of course, in aesthetic terms the circumstances of a book's writing should make no difference in the judgment of its worth. Still, although *The Desert* remains the best book on the subject, the deception involved in its creation cannot help but leave many readers feeling somewhat betrayed.

The standard excuses hardly help. To be generous, it could be said that the West of Van Dyke's day was a rambunctious place, a fertile ground for entertaining tall tales in the mode of Mark Twain and other humorists. Yet the facts

that *The Desert* is written with apparent high seriousness, has been important historically, and has been dear to people's hearts for nearly a century are circumstances weighing against easy forgiveness. But in Van Dyke's case, righteous indignation could be counterproductive. For the deception latent in *The Desert*, Van Dyke's most popular book, was not at all an isolated case. Rather, it is but one example of a pattern of trickery running not only through many of his works but also through Van Dyke's life. In this sense, the unveiling of the fraud surrounding *The Desert* is a fortunate event. Now readers can see that the man emerging from his desert myth is far more fascinating than the plaster saint of the popular imagination. And released from the clichés of heroism, people can begin to appreciate that many of Van Dyke's books, particularly *The Desert*, are far more intricate than previously understood.

John C. Van Dyke was born at Green Oaks, the family mansion on the outskirts of New Brunswick, New Jersey, on 21 April 1856. His father, John Van Dyke, was, variously, an attorney, bank president, congressman, and justice of the New Jersey Supreme Court. His mother, Mary Dix Strong, was the daughter of Theodore Strong, who taught at Rutgers College and was one of the best-known mathematicians of the day. For reasons still not entirely clear, in 1868, when Van Dyke was twelve, his father moved the family to Minnesota. There, both from the public schools and from tutoring by his elder brother, Theodore, he received an excellent education in languages and literature. Turning down an appointment to West Point, he instead went east to attend Columbia Law School and was admitted to the bar in 1877. But Van Dyke never practiced. The youth had taken fire with the Art for Art's Sake movement, and, returning to New Brunswick, within commuting distance of New York City, he immersed himself in the world of art.

As the years passed and Van Dyke published volume after volume of art criticism, nature writing, and travel, he found himself in ever more comfortable circumstances. Professionally well situated, he prided himself on his meticulous Rembrandt scholarship. He came to be considered an arbiter of public taste in art. Some years after his return east, he was concurrently holding two prestigious positions. He was the librarian of the New Brunswick Theological Seminary and the first professor of art history at nearby Rutgers. For all the busyness, his official duties at the two institutions must have been light. An avid traveler both of the globe and through fashionable society, Van Dyke moved with ease among such major figures of his day as Theodore Roosevelt, Mark Twain, and Woodrow Wilson. He hunted ducks with railroad presidents while discussing the fine points of art. Having crossed the Atlantic to vacation at Andrew Carnegie's castle in Scotland, Van Dyke fished for trout while advising the industrialist about purchasing new paintings for his collection. He was at home among elegance and erudition, in a world of servants, conversations in French, and tinkling crystal.

However, his life had a dark side as well. Although matters of others' faith lie beyond human access, both Van Dyke's life and his writings indicate that he, like many other late Victorians, had abandoned the traditional Protestantism of his youth but had found no organized religion to replace it. In consequence, a heavy sense of loss masked by cynicism dogged him. Significantly, Van Dyke's *Autobiography* opens by grumbling about the long and ineffectual family prayers of his youth, then moves on to a deeper sarcasm about religion: "Everyone attended church, and if there were doubters they sat in the square pews, smothered their doubts, and bowed their heads" (p. 27). *The Desert* leaves no doubt about its author's Darwinism and mechanistic view of a universe governed not in God's love but in a ruthless competition for survival marked by bloodstained fangs and claws. Of the animals Van Dyke sees in the desert, he observes: "The warfare is continuous from the birth to the death." He continues the rather overdramatized view of Darwinism: "Everything must fight, fly, feint, or use poison; and every slayer eventually becomes a victim" (p. 171). Nonetheless, Van Dyke turns the ruthlessness and meaninglessness of the natural

world to his literary ends by celebrating what he calls the "grandeur of the desolate." That is, nature may be heartless in human terms, but for all that, it is supremely thrilling in its impersonal beauty that soars far beyond human concerns. In this way Van Dyke uses personal despair as a device to build his image as a doomed romantic wandering worshipfully in a cruel but exhilarating world.

The stance played well to the romanticism of the day, as it does to a certain extent to ours. However, some of Van Dyke's passages are of such intensity as to signal genuine pain in his unyielding nihilism. From *The Open Spaces*:

> The entire belt of the Milky Way is supposed to be moving as a mass through space. Whither? Whence the measureless energy that started or keeps such colossal bodies in motion? And where and what are we in this mighty scheme of things? Are we anything more than petty animalculae clinging to a cold discarded fragment of a sun? You turn over in your blankets and listen to the yap of a distant coyote. Along that Milky Way lies madness. (p. 19)

Such an aesthetic of horror mixed with beauty, for Van Dyke and others who shared his views, became a secular religion, a substitute for traditional faith. Yet as Van Dyke teetered, vertiginous, at the edge of stability, it was just such potential for madness that kept his breast in productive turmoil.

This may well have a great deal to do with the pain turned into bitterness that often fuels cynicism. In Van Dyke's case it produces a tone with an edge ranging from a fairly harmless and sometimes humorous mockery to railing spite. In the first instance, *The Open Spaces* pokes gentle fun at campers who so fear the moon and howling wolves that they slink off into their tents at night. In contrast, *The Money God* (1908) is a prolonged tantrum against the depravity of immigrants, unions, professors, businessmen, and a host of other types whose greed and mean spirits are responsible for the sorry condition of the world. Why, then, did Rutgers and one of the most prestigious seminaries in the nation tolerate such a wayward man? The answer is twofold. Although theologically conservative, the seminary was open to questionings and tolerant of divergent views. Second was Van Dyke's value to the institutions. As a nationally known writer and a skillful fund-raiser, Van Dyke was a "star" property. The two schools acknowledged this by granting many favors. The seminary provided a house for Van Dyke on the campus, and both schools gave him generous leaves of absence for his travels.

If there is any truth to the saw that the cynic is a disillusioned romantic, Van Dyke was quite capable of becoming one while remaining the other. This scene from his childhood, typical of his yearning for a better past, leaves no doubt that Van Dyke was imbued with the sentimentalism of his day:

> Among my earliest memories was that of the long music room at Green Oaks, with my mother seated at a blue-and-red-piped organ singing "Long, Long Ago." I can see myself seated on the floor playing with toys, the room darkened to keep out the heat, and my mother dressed in white. There was a large glass chandelier hanging from the ceiling, and a stray sunbeam striking the prisms threw a halo of color about her head. I have always remembered that picture and the sadness of "Long, Long Ago" and "Gaily the Troubadour," which she sang out of a large music book. (*Autobiography*, p. 26)

Moreover, Van Dyke was aware of the excess in himself, although he could not control it. This is revealed in the John Charles Van Dyke correspondence. Here, writing to his editor at Scribners, William C. Brownell, Van Dyke says repeatedly that he cannot trust his own writing instincts (letter of 1 May 1898) and all but goes to his knees in thanking Brownell for his literary guidance (letters of 7 January 1893 and 11 March 1914[?]). They are astounding admissions of vulnerability from a writer who almost everywhere else boasts of his own rectitude and stubbornness. Brownell was a good man for the job. Like Van Dyke wealthy and refined, yet suspicious of "excessive individualism" and

chary of the "romantic ideal" running free, Brownell was able to rein in Van Dyke and save him from his literary excesses. The extent of the favor, both to Van Dyke and to his readers, comes clear in *The Story of the Pine* (1893), a maudlin tale about a love affair between two trees, and in *The Raritan* (1915), a family history eulogizing New Brunswick with talk of the "Golden River in Elfland." These were books in which Brownell did not have a hand.

Yet as far as subject matter and the imagination as functions of literary style are concerned, Van Dyke's romanticism often took on positive dimensions. In response to the uncertainties of the times and to cultural self-doubts, many people idealized the vigorous life in what was left of the wildness the nation had mostly tamed. Van Dyke happily filled their demand for appropriate literature. Probably his most relaxed and enjoyable book, *The Open Spaces* spins yarns about his adventures in the outdoors. It presents Van Dyke as the aesthete who also has the toughness to get the drop on five horse thieves marauding along the Mexican border and to subdue a raging drunk. If the anecdotes likely are manufactured, they take the author out of his musty academic provinces to delight in fiction passed on as fact.

However, the impulse had a less savory, though perhaps understandable, side. Unable to stop at forgivable literary playfulness, Van Dyke began thumbing his nose at his readers. He wanted people to believe that he spent his boyhood in Minnesota growing up with "wild" Indians, the Sioux. There, so he leads people to believe, he learned the frontier skills that years later enabled him to strike out on his own across the desert that others feared. Following suit, the first chapter of *The Mountain* offers a rollicking account of Van Dyke's boyhood adventures when he rode with a band of Dakota Sioux for hundreds of miles westward over the plains, hunting buffalo. Here, the descriptions of the warriors and their bareback plungings are colorful and memorable: "What a picture, those half-naked Sioux silhouetted against the blood-red twilight, each one bunched over his pony's shoulder and peering catlike into the gathering gloom!" (p. 4). But the Minnesota that Van Dyke shows in his *Autobiography*, with its local high school and Ladies' Circulating Library in the nearby town, was hardly a land of skin-of-the-teeth survival, and his story of participating in a buffalo hunt is so historically improbable that the ruse becomes transparently far-fetched.

It is difficult to read Van Dyke's intent in such matters. Possibly he was chuckling up his sleeve at the gullibility of his readers over his derring-do; possibly, too, given the webs he wove around both his personal and his writing lives, he began to believe his own fantasies. Whatever the case, he kept perpetrating the fictions until his dying day, elaborating on his adventures as a cowboy and frontiersman and blurring the line between his actual and fantasy lives. That is not to say that Van Dyke's stratagems cannot be effective and highly sophisticated literary devices. *The Mountain*, a highly serious study of the aesthetics of mountain ranges, contains a number of unattributed passages of poetry, apparently to support the statements in the text—a feature easily glided over with little note. Some of the verses obviously are by Shelley and Goethe, whereas others defy identification. Finally, years after publication of the book, Van Dyke admitted with a chuckle that he was "pushing into" *The Mountain* snatches of his own poetry. However, there is more than a boyish prank going on here. A careful rereading of the book in this ironic light shows that the poetry is used for a quite different reason than is first apparent. It is used to show that even the finest work by the world's poetic geniuses (including that by Van Dyke) pales in comparison with the beauties of nature.

Which is to say that when considering all the above-mentioned features, the success of Van Dyke's writing depends not on logic, consistency, or objective truth but on the emotional power of his prose, which obliterates such concerns. And it is also to say that Van Dyke's writing is all the more intriguing for the deceptions and pitfalls artfully crafted into it, but only recently discovered. Fortunately, the foremost example also is his most famous book, *The Desert*. As so often occurs in the works of Van Dyke, it is not at all the book that it has been perceived to be by generations of desert lovers, and the deceptions are perpetrated on purpose.

Literary Hoodwink

Through his various ways of pulling the wool over people's eyes, the body of Van Dyke's writing gains a complexity it otherwise would not have. This manipulation of readers can range from gentle literary play through sarcasm to contempt for his audience. There can be little doubt in the matter. His *What Is Art?* (1910) damns "anything that is of popular interest." In the sophisticated joke of *The Desert*, Van Dyke plays mostly on the bitter end of the spectrum.

This is not an overstatement. That Van Dyke's famous book is largely make-believe—based not on the hard-won desert experience of its author, as he leads us to believe, but on train trips available to any traveler at the turn of the century—is forgivable. As earlier mentioned, the book would fit in with the tall-tale hoodwinking not uncommon to other volumes of the day written about the West. Still, unlike most such works, the tone of *The Desert* is so serious, and its avowed purpose so earnest—to help people see the arid lands with the new eyes of appreciation and then support desert preservation—that the gross deceit of the book's making cannot help but undercut its authority.

On this score, readers of Van Dyke's day trying to educate their tastes perhaps became too accustomed to accepting the pronouncements of a man whose articles in the leading magazines told them what was beautiful and what was not. That they did, despite his lack of a consistent system, is something of a measure of their need for an authority at a time when powerful crosscurrents in art left people adrift and confused. Then, too, most readers of the early editions of *The Desert* were Easterners who had never seen the Southwest. Van Dyke, the experienced travel writer, acted as their guide, and they had no reason to disbelieve what he said about the region. Such is not true today, and it is a comment on human nature and our avidity for desert heroes that over the better-educated generations not one person, not one scientist or devoted desert enthusiast, has appeared to challenge in print what obviously is bad information.

It appears with such frequency—in dozens of instances throughout the text—and is offered with such high-handed disregard for the truth that the mistakes cannot possibly be the errors that can creep into any book. They are, rather, intentional, the writer's deliberate insults to his readers. A few illustrations of the many possible: rattlesnakes are "in fact sluggish," the saguaro cactus has a "purple" flower, the coyote "seldom runs after things." Even schoolchildren with a fairly casual knowledge of the desert could give the lie to such "facts." In truth, rattlesnakes can strike with great speed, the saguaro's flower is white, and coyotes survive by catching rabbits and other fleet-footed prey.

What could have possessed the man? Certainly the charge of laziness could not be laid at the door of a writer who published over forty titles and, to ensure the accuracy of some of his art texts, spent years researching them. Given Van Dyke's waywardness and an unpredictable temperament, a mean spirit seems closer to the truth. However, on closer examination, *The Desert* is not merely the child of maliciousness, but an elaborate literary hoax. By purposely misleading the mass of readers, the book makes essential statements about the author's views of art and nature.

Van Dyke not only covered his tracks, he often laid a false trail. The latter lies in the expansive invitational tone of Van Dyke's preface to *The Desert*, urging "you," the reader, to shed the strictures of civilization and join him in exploring the freedom and beauties of the wilderness. However, a careful reading of the pages shows that in midstride Van Dyke shifts from "you" to address a specific person, as evidenced by references to events they shared. In fact, then, Van Dyke abandons his mass audience in favor of a particular friend and his small coterie of Art for Art's Sake sympathizers. In Van Dyke's opinion, they alone have the refinement and intelligence to appreciate the delicacies of nature.

If, despite the internal evidence, such a reading seems far-fetched, we have a letter from Van Dyke to Brownell crowing that the manuscript Van Dyke is sending on is so good that the audience will be "only a few thousand, thank God." Although Van Dyke was wrong about the size of his readership, he may have taken a certain smug satisfaction that his vast audience badly misunderstood his book, seeing it not as a treatise on art but rather as a travel guide that, as one reviewer put it, "should be in the travelling-bag of every transcontinental tourist by Central and Southwestern routes" ("In the Western Wastes," p. 23). But the backfiring also must have been a taunt to elitist Van Dyke as he saw the tourists he had helped to inspire overrunning the Southwest.

In the preface, the individual Van Dyke addressed as "you," also the A.M.C. of his dedication, was hardly a champion of the people. He was none other than the nature-wrecking industrialist Andrew Carnegie, the richest man in America. Carnegie probably qualified for the honor in Van Dyke's mind because he enjoyed strolling the moors around his castle in Scotland and indulged his friend Van Dyke with lavish entertainments.

Carnegie and Van Dyke

The mention of Carnegie raises two questions. Working himself into a high froth of sarcasm over the sacrifice of nature by greedy men, Van Dyke stormed in *The Desert*: "The 'practical men,' who seems forever on the throne, know very well that beauty is only meant for lovers and young persons—stuff to suckle fools withal. The main affair of life is to get the dollar, and if there is any money in cutting the throat of Beauty, why, by all means, cut her throat" (p. 60). Was Van Dyke, then, sincere when he thundered the often-quoted words "The deserts should never be reclaimed. They are the breathing-spaces of the west and should be preserved forever" (p. 59)? As a man focused on the passions of the moment, yes. Also, the sentiment makes excellent literary pyrotechnics in a heady passage echoing the powerful imagery of John Muir's earlier article "The American Forests." Yet, unlike Muir, Van Dyke elsewhere rarely hints at preservation, and no evidence suggests that he took an active part in supporting the growing conservation movement. No doubt, to Van Dyke the desert indeed was a beautiful place; thus it should be protected—much as a collection of priceless paintings should be protected—lest the aesthete's pleasures be ruined. In this sense, rather like a lover with the appropriate words ready on his lips, Van Dyke said what seemed right for the moment, then moved on. In view of his vast capacity for rationalizing and overlooking contradictions, making his good friend Carnegie a dedicatee was not an obstacle.

Second, wouldn't the clutch of Eastern readers for whom Van Dyke intended his book be offended by the flagrant inaccuracies concerning desert ecology? The answer is a solid no. Along with most of the book's readers, Van Dyke's small audience would not have been aware of the deliberate errors, and if they had, they probably would not have cared. Their object was to enjoy the loveliness of nature, not the scientific aspects of nature that generated it. Van Dyke states the attitude directly in *The Mountain*: "My interest is with the beauty of the mountains rather than the science" (p. vii). Or, as he bluntly puts it in *Principles of Art* (1887), the purpose of art "is to give pleasure, not to inculcate truth."

Last, there was one almost unknown aftereffect of *The Desert*. Van Dyke published the book when he was forty-five, but he was not done with the region either personally or literarily. Although the exact dates of his comings and goings thereafter are not known, he kept returning to the place of his original arid-land experience, southern California, where brother Theodore lived. Furthermore, his visits spanned the decades, for the last in a series of photographs of Van Dyke taken at Theodore's ranch in the Mojave desert clearly shows him in his advanced years. Curiously, he penned only one article about his desert forays, "The American Desert." Nonetheless, something must have been troubling Van Dyke, dogging him with a sense of incompleteness. The *Autobiography* reveals a tantalizing tidbit. Van Dyke wrote a novel with the rather fearsome title "The Jaws of the Desert." This—or so he claims—tells the "truth"

about his desert experiences. Unfortunately, the manuscript, kept "in a table drawer," has never been found. Yet its mention is a strange grace note to the desert experiences of a man with a mind so unpredictable that surprises are expected. Van Dyke represented *The Desert* as fact, whereas the book is largely fiction, then claimed he used a work of fiction to tell the truth about the subject.

Although one cannot explain what psychological urges drove Van Dyke into his duplicity, all the twists and turns may not have been necessary to begin with. Surely he possessed the talent to write very fine books without enlisting dupery as his ally. Concerning Van Dyke's personal life, it would seem that a man who rubbed shoulders with Twain, James McNeill Whistler, and Roosevelt would not have been so starved for excitements that he felt compelled to engage in the rather boyish antics of secret codes on rings. For instance, among its pages of pasted-up articles, printed invitations, and photographs, Van Dyke's scrapbook drops two startling morsels. James Bertram, Andrew Carnegie's secretary, writing to Van Dyke on 20 October 1921, refers to a past kidnapping threat in Taos, New Mexico, and a separate, equally intriguing, though veiled, story about "Andy." No amount of research places Van Dyke in Taos, although, in view of this letter and his wide scurryings around the West, he likely visited this enchanting mountain village. The kidnapping threat remains a complete mystery.

However, the reference to the story about Andrew Carnegie points to a convolution underlying the many convoluted circumstances of the nation's first desert paean. That is the possibility that assumptions about what took Van Dyke to the desert in the first place, like so many other things in his life, prove suspect. To begin with, Van Dyke himself is elusive about his motives. I have already discussed the image of the lone romantic wanderer created in the preface. Turned into a "lover" by his encounter with the desert, he is a man burning with a mission: to redeem the abused reputation of his mistress. Because he viewed *The Desert* as a treatise on nature as art to be kept free of what the *Autobiography* calls the "human element"—that is, personal storytelling—it is understandable that Van Dyke saves the personal details of his travels for his *Autobiography*. Here he tells us that he was ill, probably of a respiratory condition, and sought out the curative powers of the desert's climate—as had his brother, Theodore, before him.

Well and good, it is the old story of the health seeker who falls in love with his new landscape. Yet other elements of Van Dyke's story do not add up. While in the desert, he fell into depression, suffered from blackouts, and yearned for civilization—yet for a reason he skirts, he says that he continued pushing into the wilderness. Then his account, particularly of his months in Mexico, lapses into the vagueness that often is a sign of a dissembling writer. Finally, Van Dyke says he didn't much enjoy his stay in the desert after all. He so waffles on the details of his journey that we are not convinced he's telling the whole truth about his motives for one of the major events in his life.

Indeed, it is likely that impulses beyond his search for health lay behind the trip to the Southwest that produced the most famous work about the desert. They have little to do with Van Dyke's widely vaunted love of nature. Carnegie's autobiography, edited by Van Dyke after the industrialist's death, recounts a supposedly chance, yet rather strange meeting in Mexico between the professor and a Carnegie enemy. A recently discovered letter from Carnegie to Van Dyke in the latter's scrapbook gives further evidence. Van Dyke traveled to the Southwest at least partly to make a payoff for Carnegie in one of the many complicated dealings contributing to the steel magnate's success. Pile on this yet a further convolution—that during this period life was getting awkward for Van Dyke in New Brunswick, perhaps because of a row over an illegitimate daughter—and we have a conjunction of plots worthy of a thriller movie. (Van Dyke died in New Brunswick on 5 December 1932.) Strange as such things may at first seem, they match any number of schemes in the secret life of a man who apparently enjoyed moving through subterfuges.

Yet he quite gleefully turned the chuckles of his private life into the public veneer of his artistic reputation, much of it casting the writer as a paragon of political correctness far ahead of his time. Representing himself as the selfless nature lover, Van Dyke tells us one more unlikely story. While supposedly braving the dangers of the desert in his search for beauty, he also supposedly found gold. He rushes to add, "but that did not greatly interest me. I was not seeking gold" (*Autobiography*, p. 120)—the implication being that the promise of mere riches could not distract the aesthete from his high-minded quest.

Selected Bibliography

WORKS OF JOHN C. VAN DYKE

NATURE WRITINGS

Nature for Its Own Sake: First Studies in Natural Appearances (New York: Scribners, 1898); *The Desert: Further Studies in Natural Appearances* (New York: Scribners, 1901); *The Opal Sea: Continued Studies in Impressions and Appearances* (New York: Scribners, 1906); *The Mountain: Renewed Studies in Impressions and Appearances* (New York: Scribners, 1916); *The Grand Canyon of the Colorado: Recurrent Studies in Impressions and Appearances* (New York: Scribners, 1920); *The Open Spaces: Incidents of Nights and Days Under the Blue Sky* (New York: Scribners, 1922); "The American Desert," in *Mentor* 12, no. 6 (1924): 1–22; *The Meadows: Familiar Studies of the Commonplace* (New York: Scribners, 1926).

OTHER WRITINGS

The Story of the Pine (New York: Authors Club, 1893); *The Money God: Chapters of Heresy and Dissent Concerning Business Methods and Mercenary Ideals in American Life* (New York: Scribners, 1908); *The Raritan: Notes on a River and a Family* (New Brunswick, N.J.: privately published, 1915); *The Autobiography of John C. Van Dyke: A Personal Narrative of American Life from 1861 to 1931*, ed. by Peter Wild (Salt Lake City: Univ. of Utah Press, 1993).

PAPERS

The John Charles Van Dyke correspondence with Charles Scribner's Sons, with related papers, is in the Charles Scribner's Sons archives, Special Collections, Princeton Univ. Library. His scrapbook is in the archives of the Gardner A. Sage Library, New Brunswick Theological Seminary.

BIOGRAPHICAL AND CRITICAL STUDIES

"In the Western Wastes," a review of *The Desert*, in *Dial* 32 (1 January 1902): 22–23; Zita Ingham and Peter Wild, "The Preface as Illumination: The Curious (If Not Tricky) Case of John C. Van Dyke's *The Desert*," in *Rhetoric Review* 9 (spring 1991): 328–339; Lawrence Clark Powell, "John C. Van Dyke: *The Desert*," in his *Southwest Classics: The Creative Literature of the Arid Lands* (Los Angeles: Ward Ritchie, 1974); Peter Wild, *John C. Van Dyke: "The Desert"* (Boise: Boise State Univ., 1988), "Van Dyke's Little Trick: Catching the Wily Esthetician in a Net of Poetry—Some of It (Probably) His Own," in *New Mexico Humanities Review* 32 (1989): 116–128, "Curmudgeon or Campus Ornament?: Focusing the Images of John C. Van Dyke, Librarian/Professor," in *New Jersey History* 108 (spring/summer 1990): 31–45, and " 'My Dear Van Dyke'; 'My Dear Brownell': New Perspectives on Our Foremost (and Most Coy) Desert Writer," in *New Mexico Humanities Review* 35 (1991): 131–148; Peter Wild and Neil Carmony, "The Trip Not Taken: John C. Van Dyke, Heroic Doer or Armchair Seer?," in *Journal of Arizona History* 34 (spring 1993): 65–80.

Peter Wild, "Interviews and Notes Regarding John C. Van Dyke," is in the Special Collections, Alexander Library, Rutgers Univ.; the archives of the American Academy of Arts and Letters, New York City; the archives of the Gardner A. Sage Library, New Brunswick Theological Seminary; and the Special Collections, Univ. of Arizona Library. It is sealed until 2009.

DAVID RAINS WALLACE
(b. 1945)

MICHAEL KOWALEWSKI

"MY INTENTION IN writing," David Rains Wallace once told a Berkeley editor, "is to continue the tradition Thoreau established when he stated his profession as 'Inspector of Snowstorms.' But it would be old fashioned to call myself that, more appropriate terms might be 'Twilight Quality Indexer' or 'Sunrise Intensity Impact Analyst'" ("The Making of a Naturalist"). Wallace's six books of natural history, along with his two ecological mystery novels and his occasional essays and criticism, have placed him in the forefront of contemporary quality indexers in American nature writing. Along with such authors as Barry Lopez, Terry Tempest Williams, Richard K. Nelson, Gary Nabhan, Rick Bass, Gretel Ehrlich, and Scott Russell Sanders, Wallace began publishing after the appearance of a more ecologically aware post-1960s audience concerned with environmental issues. His work acknowledges the presence of that audience, and just as often assumes the need to tutor it, to revise and complicate certain popular conceptions of nature—even well-meaning ones—some of them perpetuated by other nature writers.

In particular, Wallace questions the role of the nature-elegist who laments disappearing wilderness or the destruction of habitat with either excess yearning or self-righteous indignation. Some authors, he says in his essay "The Nature of Nature Writing," seem to have accepted the notion that wilderness will eventually disappear. "They write like undertakers: an elegy on every page." "It's important for us to know how bad things are, but. . . . As dealers in myth," Wallace asserts, "writers ought to know better than to let technocrats and salesmen mesmerize them into believing that civilization can conquer nature. They should understand that this is a myth too, what one might call the myth of nature as loser" (*Untamed Garden*, p. 117). Nature is not a loser, he reminds us, "because it is not a competitor." The assumption that the shrinkage of wilderness and the growth of land development will somehow entail an end of wildness is, as he says in his second book, *Idle Weeds: The Life of a Sandstone Ridge* (1980), a "misapprehension of reality."

> Wildness is not an Eden or Chaos that can be repealed by the extirpation of large wild animals or the removal of forest. It is a fundamental condition of the biosphere.
> . . . The cycling of water, minerals, and gases, which makes life possible, is wild, as are the lesser organisms—bacteria, fungi, algae, protozoans, and invertebrates—which make life possible for the greater. These phenomena are at once too vast and too detailed for any but peripheral human control. (*Idle Weeds*, p. 165)

The fact that the earth retains a fundamental

wildness does not, of course, preclude a concern for ecological diversity. Although the planet's essential wildness may remain intact, its quality of life is crucially impoverished when entire landscapes of plants and animals are destroyed. Wallace neither downplays nor ignores the havoc wreaked by modern urban growth and development (themselves terms, he notes, that land speculators have appropriated from the vocabulary of biologists). He advocates a creative, nondestructive relationship with nature, and since the early 1980s he has worked as a writer and editor for a number of conservation agencies, citizens' groups and educational institutions, publicly promoting environmental conservation. His work appears regularly in *Sierra, Wilderness,* and other environmental periodicals.

Nevertheless, Wallace remains healthily wary of the ways in which the verbal conventions of protest and advocacy can become overly convenient or unimaginative. He often uses clear-eyed understatement to express his disapproval of reckless human tampering with insufficiently understood landscapes. His remark about the impending fate of a particularly enthralling hermit thrush in his first book—*The Dark Range: A Naturalist's Night Notebook* (1978), a study of nocturnal ecology in the Yolla Bolly–Middle Eel wilderness of northern California—can be taken as representative in this regard. Wallace admits that he actually heard the thrush outside rather than within the Yolla Bolly wilderness, but he then goes on to note that "after listening for an hour to this Caruso of hermit thrushes, I walked on a few steps and ran into a line of red plastic ribbons for a newly surveyed logging road. The thrush's grove was about to be cut out from under him. I've moved him into the wilderness so he can keep singing, at least on paper" (p. 111).

The fact that the very paper containing this description of the thrush ultimately originated in logging activities like those destroying the bird's habitat is not lost upon Wallace. Yet the way in which he presents this inherently complicitous circumstance suggests a cast of mind capable of acknowledging such ironies without being paralyzed by them. Wallace does not ignore the fate of the bird, but neither does he engage in cloying

lamentation. His narrative restraint and balance of tones in this moment can be taken as a parallel to the complex forces of nature evoked in his books. On the one hand, the realization that nature is "at once too vast and too detailed for any but peripheral human control" applies to writerly control as well as to other forms of human management, and should instill humility. On the other hand, humility does not have to mean self-diminishment. Human beings are not simply perceivers of nature but participants in it. Observation, Wallace suggests, is by its very nature a form of participation. An observer of nature alters what is observed, but he also, and perhaps more importantly, mirrors what is perceived. "The eye that looks through the microscope," as he puts it in *The Klamath Knot: Explorations of Myth and Evolution* (1983), "teems with more cellular life than the water drop on the slide" (p. 37).

If Wallace's name is less familiar to a general reader than that of other naturalists, it may have to do, oddly enough, with the very strengths of his writing. His work displays an independence of mind that remains as wary of environmentalist cant or eco-theology as of overzealous developers or clear-cut loggers. "A humanity destined for demonic holocaust by its manipulative cleverness is a mirror image of the more popular evolutionary myth of a humanity destined for godlike triumph," he says in *The Klamath Knot.* "If the four billion years of evolution demonstrate one thing, it is that humanity is not *destined* for anything. Evolution has always been open to new possibilities. . . . Every organism continually confronts a galaxy of evolutionary choices" (p. 133). Wallace's willingness to explore "new possibilities" in his own work, to cross the boundaries of genre, and to question the term "naturalist" itself does not encourage pat categorization. Neither too technically narrow nor too insistently lyrical, his distinctive narrative voice displays a restlessly inventive verbal intelligence, one that attempts to keep pace, on paper, with the ingenuity and infinite variety of nature.

Wallace—who was named after his great-great-grandfather, a Confederate cavalry officer during the Civil War—was born on 10 August

1945 to Sebon Rains Wallace, a psychologist, and Sarah Hahn, in Charlottesville, Virginia. Shortly thereafter, his family moved to Burlington, Connecticut (an area he has lovingly described in his essay "Lost Worlds of the Connecticut"), where he spent his childhood and adolescence. He majored in English at Wesleyan University, graduated in 1967, and then moved to New York City, where he took classes at the Columbia University film school and spent time in the American Museum of Natural History. He left in 1969 and traveled to San Francisco, where he worked for six months as a cabdriver on the night shift (5 P.M.–2 A.M.) during the height of the Zodiac killings of cabdrivers (an experience he said was valuable in preparing himself for his work on nocturnal nature).

Wallace then moved to the Sonoma area of California and worked as an orchardist. It was there that he began his night prowlings in the country with a flashlight. His time in Sonoma was followed by several years of creative vagrancy, hitchhiking through Mexico, Guatemala, British Honduras, then up to British Columbia, the Yukon, and southeast Alaska. His first nature essay was published in 1971. The following year he enrolled at Mills College in Oakland, California, and wrote his M.A. thesis in 1974, a work that would later be published as *The Dark Range*. Wallace is an autodidact, at least in terms of scientific training. *The Dark Range* includes an index to plants and animals, but he informs his first readers that he has no degree in biology: "The knowledge I've used is accessible to anybody who's willing to poke around in libraries and biological abstracts, with a little pestering of biologists on the side" (p. 112). The book won a silver medal from the Commonwealth Club of California in 1979.

Wallace married Ann (Betsy) Kendall, an artist, on 3 July 1975. After leaving Mills, Wallace went to Ohio to be a public information specialist for the Columbus Metropolitan Park System. He lived for much of his three years there in Carroll, just north of Lancaster. His stint as a naturalist formed the basis for his second work, *Idle Weeds*, which recounts the natural history of a year on an "ordinary" wooded outcropping, Chestnut Ridge, in central Ohio. "A battered dwarf of wildness," Chestnut Ridge is a piece of remnant wilderness that economists and planners call "marginal land." By following the seasonal and atmospheric changes on the ridge, however, Wallace not only suggests the "powerful loveliness" of this seemingly unprepossessing place. He also suggests that our future may depend more crucially upon how we treat places like Chestnut Ridge than on our treatment of more highly touted wilderness areas.

Wallace's third book, *The Klamath Knot*, marked a substantial widening of concerns in his work. An extraordinary synthesis of research and naturalist observation, the book focuses on the Klamath Mountains in northwest California and southwest Oregon, an area that prompts philosophical and psychocultural reflections on evolution, which Wallace provocatively calls the "great myth of modern times." Probing the deeper meanings of evolutionary processes, Wallace contends that wilderness "leads the mind back to stories of origins and meanings, to imagining the world's creation" (p. 8). Exploring everything from the area's geological enigmas to legends of Sasquatch, or Bigfoot, a giant hominoid said to live in the Klamaths, Wallace sees evolution as expressing an ancestral mythic resonance wherein a "bear is not simply a black, shaggy animal but a wave of animals surging up through abysses of time from the original one-celled beings" (p. 134). The book attracted national attention, earning widespread praise and the John Burroughs Medal for Nature Writing in 1984, as well as drawing sharp criticism from some readers who thought Wallace should have kept poetry and science separate and who saw science not as a form of mythology but as an alternative to it.

The Klamath Knot was followed by *The Wilder Shore* (1984), which uniquely blends literary criticism and personal memoir. A study of the influence of landscape on California writers, the book also includes impressionistic journal entries from locations appropriate to the regions of the state that Wallace discusses. *The Wilder Shore* was meant to be a collaborative verbal and visual exploration of California; the text is accompanied by large-format photographs by noted West Coast photographer Morley Baer. Unfortu-

965

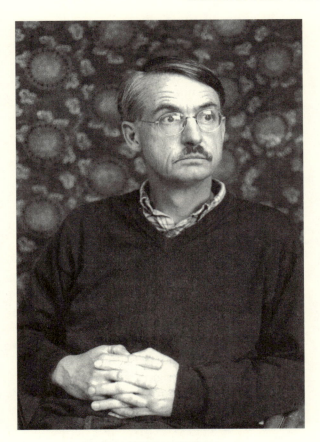

David Rains Wallace

(one a five-foot-tall parrot that likes fettuccine and reads the *Los Angeles Times* classifieds) was seen as fatuous by some readers and intriguingly disorienting by others. If nothing else, both novels established Wallace's willingness to use unorthodox means in attempting to raise ecological awareness among readers who would not normally be attracted by naturalist writing.

Wallace's occasional essays on gardening, wildlife, and conservation, over half of which originally appeared in "The Naturalist" column of *The Berkeley Monthly*, were collected in *The Untamed Garden* (1986). It is a strong, diversified collection that contains pieces on Japan, Montana, and Alaska and several on the ecology of various sites in northern California. This was followed by *Life in the Balance* in 1987, a large-format companion volume to an Audubon Society Public Broadcasting System series on wildlife conservation. The year 1989 saw the publication of another full-length work of natural history, *Bulow Hammock: Mind in a Forest*. The book explores the "warm, spicy" environment of a woodland grove near Daytona, Florida. Beset with freeways and resort communities, Bulow Hammock nevertheless provides Wallace with an occasion for drawing parallels between the ecology of this partly tropical, partly temperate swampland and the evolution of human consciousness. "The question that agitates us the most," he says, "is not how the human body evolved but how the human brain did" (p. 42). Once again using a very specific location as a catalyst for far-ranging questions about the dynamics of evolution and the structure of the human mind, Wallace interweaves childhood memories, local history, and the work of such notable naturalists as William Bartram and John James Audubon as he explores the ecological and evolutionary dimensions of the Florida landscape.

His most recent book, *The Quetzal and the Macaw* (1992), combines a study of Central American ecology with the institutional practices of conservation in detailing the history of the Costa Rican national park system. Wallace examines the natural history of the parks, but he also profiles such individuals as Mario Boza,

nately, the "exhibit format" apparently encouraged readers to view this important study of the literary geography of California as primarily a "coffee-table book," and the book has not received the kind of close attention it deserves.

The following year saw the publication of Wallace's first novel, *The Turquoise Dragon*, dubbed an "eco-thriller" and set largely in the Trinity Alps of northeastern California and the Kalmiopsis wilderness of southern Oregon. It was the first mystery novel published by the Sierra Club. The book received mixed reviews but sold well and was subsequently published in British and Japanese editions. It was followed in 1991 by a sequel set in Big Sur and the highlands of northern Mexico, *The Vermilion Parrot*, which features the same detective narrator, former marijuana grower George Kilgore. The implausibility of the latter's events and characters

Alvaro Ugalde, Olof Wessberg, and Antonio Zuñiga, who were instrumental in helping establish the park system. He focuses more upon the human story of conservation in this book than he has in any of his previous naturalist writings. This is partly, no doubt, because Costa Rican history is largely unfamiliar to readers in the United States. But it also seems to signal Wallace's increased willingness to address the bureaucratic aspects of wilderness preservation. He emphasizes the research, discussion, lobbying, and political maneuvering that have accompanied the making and maintaining of national parks in Costa Rica and elsewhere. The Costa Rican park system embodies an exemplary, innovative fusion of environmental protection and sustainable development. But that system was implemented only after a tangled history of negotiation, compromise, and mishaps. (One of the first park wardens in Costa Rica, for instance, was an alcoholic who killed the last ten spider monkeys on the Cabo Blanco reserve for the oil in their fat.)

In his previous work Wallace tended to address legal and ethical questions about nature — why certain species have a more privileged legal status, for example, or why individual organisms are more highly valued than ecosystems — as outgrowths of certain impoverished metaphors and habits of mind. *The Quetzal and the Macaw* more directly acknowledges the inescapably political and legalistic ground upon which all contemporary environmental issues are decided, and not only in developing countries. He reminds us that such compromises and negotiations are not new in the history of conservation, but that they have often been ignored or misunderstood by naturalists and a nature-loving public impatient with what it takes to be uninteresting political gerrymandering useful only for arousing outrage and indignation. A naturalist's trained eye, this book suggests, can highlight and decode ideas about nature, land management, and conservation that manifest themselves in institutional structures and practices just as readily as it might interpret a natural environment. An informed interest in nature, Wallace implies, must now involve nearly as much time in the library or in legislative archives as in the field, though "collecting mosquito bites," as he says in "The Nature of Nature Writing," will always "go with the job."

One of Wallace's primary goals as a naturalist is to emphasize the stubborn and ingenious persistence of nature in our lives. That ingenuity cannot be fully appreciated without noting how natural phenomena, when closely observed, complicate or contradict conventional scientific notions as often as they reinforce them. Wallace relishes this devious and unpredictable aspect of nature, despite the taxonomical headaches it can inspire. "Evolution, at least in the Klamath Mountains," he says in *The Klamath Knot*,

> is less a tidily consecutive array of increasingly advanced organisms than a leapfrogging mob of plants, animals, and dubious beings such as fungi, all earnestly photosynthesizing, feeding, respiring, and reproducing without much respect for hierarchy or direction. It is less a progression than a cyclic accretion wherein organisms appear or disappear for reasons that often are obscure or mysterious, and not readily applicable to scientific concepts. This is not to say that science is wrong, only that it is incomplete, as any scientist worth the name will agree. (p. 16)

Wallace acknowledges that the incompleteness of scientific knowledge also limits "emotional knowledge": "We can't fully imagine a tree's existence because we don't know how, or if, a tree experiences its life" (p. 137). Yet, incomplete as it is, science has opened a potential for the imaginative interpretation of nature, not in human terms but in multiple forms of consciousness that we can attempt to describe by careful observation and inspired analogy.

The fact that people both alter and are altered by natural environments establishes an intricate reciprocity in Wallace's work, one that evokes a sense of nature as a fragile but also surprisingly resilient network of forces that both compete and cooperate. This partly explains Wallace's predilection for overlooked or underappreciated natural areas (though he would undoubtedly assert that most natural areas, whether suburban

967

or rural, are underappreciated). He tends to es- chew spectacular, more ingratiating landscapes for less well-designated places (like the Yolla Bolly Mountains or the Kalmiopsis wilderness) or for vulnerable remnant areas (like Chestnut Ridge or Bulow Hammock) whose proximity to urban or suburban development makes their wilderness seem unexpected, even unlikely, but whose marginal status offers illuminating les- sons about the dangers of thinking about nature in terms of "margins" and "centers."

The seemingly unremarkable features of the places Wallace studies belie a uniqueness and complexity that make them, paradoxically, rep- resentative in their very distinctiveness. The abiding value of Chestnut Ridge, he contends in *Idle Weeds*, is not as "a museum piece sur- rounded by urban sprawl." If it were, its "fabric of beeches, oaks, asters, and goldenrods" would be reduced to the status of a "mere rarity," and its value, he says in an adept reversal of conven- tional wisdom, "would decline to that of gold and gems. Important as it is to save rare plants and animals, it is even more important to per- petuate common ones. The fact that there are still thousands of 'idle' or gently used places like it engaged in cycling water, minerals, and gases through the biosphere is what gives Chestnut Ridge its main significance, because it is this fact that makes the 'World' of human culture pos- sible" (p. 166). Even Wallace's interest in the Klamath wilderness — which he calls the strang- est landscape he has ever seen — stems not from the area's pristine scenic beauty but from its rougher, more elusive quality of venerability and from the evolutionary quandaries the area dramatizes.

Wallace's primary achievment as a naturalist has been to create a narrative style congruent with his view of nature as a devious, constantly mobile, and adaptive set of life forces. He has fashioned a style of reportage that is, by turns, observant and playful, fussy and genial, scientific and literate. He is as likely to quote Dante, John Milton, Leo Tolstoy, Sir Arthur Conan Doyle, or T. S. Eliot as he is John Muir or Aldo Leopold; he is as liable to refer to Mr. Mole in *The Wind in the Willows* as to a scientific tome. Wallace

clearly loves language as much as he does nature, and he sees the two as metaphorically bound at the spine. He delights in the metaphorical or aural extravagance of naturalist etymology, in the pure fun of referring to resurrection ferns, pillow basalts, filmy dome spiders, mayapples, quillwort, tuco-tucos, and kidneyleaf crowfoot, or in pointing out that "petro-oleum" literally refers to rock oil. Yet he does so even as he reminds us that such phenomena are, after all, the precise coordinates by which to locate a particular ecosystem. They offer both flashes of whimsy and a functional tool, a naturalist's stock-in-trade.

What makes nature writing distinctive for Wallace is its expression of an appreciative aes- thetic response to a scientific view of nature. The most daunting challenge facing nature writers today, he contends, is that of translating ever- burgeoning reams of data and information into feelings and visions. This endeavor involves at- tempts to widen the potential audience for natu- ral history, which Wallace has done both in his fiction and in large-format books, such as *Life in the Balance* or his work with Philip Hyde in *Drylands* (1987). But he is also at pains to ensure that such efforts to make nature more accessible to a larger audience do not, in the process, caricature the science involved or let the clarity of observation that has always characterized the best nature writing slip into soft focus.

Wallace examines the difficulties of populariz- ing natural history, given the often ludicrously undifferentiated visions of nature encountered in American popular culture, in an entertaining essay on "television ecology" titled "Ecological Imperialism." In it, he examines how flora and fauna are constantly scrambled and rearranged through the ignorance or indifference of televi- sion producers and technicians. Citing an epi- sode of "The Waltons" by way of example, Wallace observes that when John Boy and his father go to visit some hillbilly relatives deep in the Blue Ridge Mountains of Virginia, they find the cabin of their kin in a typical California forest of ponderosa pine and manzanita (an eco- system conveniently close to the Hollywood stu- dios filming the series). This incongruously

968

located environment would certainly "have taken Appalachian hill people of the pre-television 1930s by surprise," Wallace notes, and it obviously compromises the "relatives' fierce love of their native hills, around which the episode was built" (p. 101). Like the tape loops of birdsong that are used out of context to help sell organic shampoos, body creams, and whole-grain cereals, this kind of perceptual inattention to nature might, in a lesser writer, inspire mournful words about the ecological impoverishment of modern technology. But the "antiquity of the house cricket probably argues against such a conclusion," Wallace asserts with a note of wry hope. "The cricket has sung cheerfully through the demise of dinosaurs and wooly mammoths, and I see no reason why it shouldn't continue when the last television aerial is buried under five hundred feet of sedimentary rock. . . . An ecosystem as simplified and random as what we see on television . . . would in all likelihood not be an ecosystem capable of producing something so rich and intricate as a television set" (p. 104).

Wallace works to correct not only popular homogenized versions of nature but also anthropocentric ways of thinking about it. He tends to organize his books around local biotic markers or seasonal changes. *The Dark Range* is divided into three parts—"The Digger Pine," "The Sugar Pine," and "The Foxtail Pine"— each of which details the unique qualities and characteristics of an altitudinal life zone exemplified by those trees. The tripartite structure of *Idle Weeds* involves temporal divisions ("Past Time," "Present Time," and "Future Time"), but the bulk of the book focuses on the present and the impact of seasonal change on plant and animal life. *The Klamath Knot* and *Bulow Hammock*, as their subtitles suggest, are looser and more meandering in their structure, but they, too, focus upon basic elements of the landscape—rocks, water, trees, grass, animal life, bacteria—as stabilizing structural principles.

This does not mean that Wallace ignores human history and culture: he discusses the earthen mound culture of woodland Indians in Ohio, slave plantations in Florida, and miners in the Klamath Mountains. He does suggest, however, that there is something unimaginative about evolutionary hierarchies that suggest that the size of a life-form should determine our interest in it. Too much emphasis on larger life-forms, especially in evolutionary thinking, obscures the fact that animals, particularly vertebrates, are relative latecomers in the evolutionary process and are vastly outnumbered by other organisms, particularly one-celled organisms, which are much more fundamental to the evolutionary process. Like Lewis Thomas, Wallace expands the focal length of his narratives to include microbial life-forms and cellular activity. Discussing the remarkable durability of lichens in *The Klamath Knot*, Wallace says, a "species of lichen is more of a monument than the peak it encrusts. . . . Organisms outlast mountain ranges because they work much harder at existing than rocks do" (pp. 27, 30). Even the simplest organisms, he points out, do not adapt passively to their environments. To some degree, they all adapt their environments to themselves. Green algae, slime molds, and fungi in the deserts, he says in his introduction to Hyde's *Drylands*, have not merely adapted to arid desert soil, they have actually helped make it, "changing its sand and clay from stacks of quartz grains and laterite particles into networks of mycelia and nitrogen-fixing bacteria without which creosote bushes could not live" (p. 23).

This kind of evolutionary ingenuity and adaptation—much of it still mysterious and not fully explainable by science—encapsulates the genius of natural systems that Wallace finds so endlessly engaging. Nature everywhere consists of forms of energy that embody what one might call "a history of restlessness" (Wallace's term for the plant distribution of North American deserts). It is a quality that animates all of the natural systems he presents in his books. Nature is seen as embodying, in effect, a perpetual present, a time warp of immediate means and destinations, active and alive. Over and over, a flurry of concentrated action and intention occupies Wallace's full attention as his animals and insects forage, frolic, breed, or engage in defensive maneuvers.

Furthermore, supposedly "inanimate" forms of life take on a richly textured sensual life. Winds toss tree branches, rustle plant cover, and wave insect antennae; snow tunnels, earthworm chambers, and root systems not only help support the life that teems within them, they also feature their own intricate texture and architecture; false dawn and foxfire (small chips of phosphorescent fungi that cause decaying wood to glow) create shifting sensory effects; the acoustic qualities of silence or the nuances of darkness differ subtly at different elevations; the shape of methane marsh bubbles surfacing in a lake varies according to water conditions and the chemistry of exhalation; fluctuations in temperature alter animals' metabolic rates, as when shortening autumn nights in Ohio stimulate the nervousness of a yellow-billed cuckoo; and soils, whether in swamp-marsh or hardpan, "interact" with a hiker's foot. (Wallace actually walks across an oozy lake in *The Klamath Knot* without touching bottom; he feels only buried tree branches that prick his feet and the "green ooze" into which he sinks "until the water's buoyancy neutralized my weight.")

These sensory phenomena take on a precisely calibrated lyricism in Wallace's work. The beauty and energy of living systems are appreciated in their own right and are made more immediate by his habit of describing a sound, smell, or glimpsed motion first, and then, once we have imaginatively experienced it in purely sensory terms, identifying its source and cause. These phenomena are always placed in context, however, and are always seen as constituent elements of overlapping, multilayered patterns of interdependence. One set of animal activities constantly leads into or violently interrupts another, either in peaceful, sometimes puzzled coexistence or in predatory action. This sense of crisscrossing, interactive life is offered as a fundamental precondition of existence, a part of the natural depth of individual ecosystems. That this interaction can be deadly as well as enlivening for the flora and fauna involved is also made apparent. A January ice storm on Chestnut Ridge, complete with icicles laced with sulfuric acid from the polluted air of the Ohio lowlands,

wreaks havoc on the local bird life in *Idle Weeds*: "A red-bellied woodpecker lay head down, its beak thrust into the snow. A cardinal sprawled with its neck broken from falling off its perch. A dead junco was already half eaten by an opossum, its feathers scattered. The survivors of a quail covey huddled in an ice-enameled honeysuckle thicket and made low, heartbroken sounds" (p. 27).

Yet although Wallace does not disregard the harsher struggle for existence in the food chain, neither does he excessively focus upon it. He uses it as one more opportunity for evoking precisely visualized details that take on a life of their own, even as he reminds us that no life in nature is ever on its own. ("A longing for complete self-sufficiency" is a peculiarly human yearning, he reminds us in *Bulow Hammock*, one that "is almost the same as a longing for complete integration, for a solitude so perfect it is not lonely" [p. 9]) Natural processes, as Wallace presents them, are not only relentlessly continuous and interactive, they are also accretive. They gain a cumulative momentum that gradually helps collapse the distinction between foreground and background in his work.

For Wallace, nature is always local and always in simultaneous motion. What he captures in his writing is the metabolism, as it were, of a local environment, which consists of nothing less than the sum total of all the interacting metabolisms of its individual elements. He transforms local landscapes from a falsely passive background to a dynamic ecology with a "sensurround" dimension. "The *depth* of a wilderness interests me far more than its height," he avers in *The Klamath Knot*.

The perceptual depth and expansion in Wallace's writing spring partly from the paradox that although the energy and motion in nature are fragile and transitory (most life-forms die within a year), they are also continually self-replenishing or, in the evolutionary timescale, easily replaced. "The elk and panthers devoured by our factories and emporiums," Wallace says in *Idle Weeds*, "are presently being excreted as pariah dogs and sewer rats in our inner cities" (p. 167). Yet however ephemeral its existence, the ceaseless simultaneity of nature in Wallace's work serves to remind his reader that all this activity is ongoing, that it continues after the narrator has looked away. The conventional linearity of narrative and naturalist description, in other words, often does not lend itself to adequately "deep" or "thick" descriptions of nature.

At the end of *Idle Weeds*, Wallace notes that the traditional organization of time into past, present, and future (the organization that governs the way he has divided that book) "really has more relevance to the five-thousand-year-old earth of the seventeenth century than it does to the five-billion-year-old one of the twentieth" (p. 168). Past and future require "certain limitations and symmetries to be meaningful—there must be a plot or at least a story"; and if time is a story, the present is merely an insignificant and diminished "hiatus between the significant events that were and will be." But time really is not much like a story, Wallace asserts. It is more like an "ocean current that rises from imperfectly perceived depths and flows into unseen distances" (p. 168). In such a view, the present is not less important than other moments, "any more than a single water molecule in an ocean is less important than the others. In a sense each living moment is the whole of time—an eternal present—because it can't be set apart from all the other moments" (p. 169).

This insight inspires a new direction in Wallace's work after *Idle Weeds*, particularly in *The Klamath Knot* and *Bulow Hammock*. In those books, temporal depth is superimposed on the spatial depth of particular ecosystems to create a kind of fourth dimension in which "deep" descriptions of local ecology become depth soundings into the origins and history of evolution and consciousness. Looking at nature in the present simultaneously involves peering into time's depths. Living landscapes are projected onto primeval ones (or vice versa) in order to illuminate life's history. Time does not exist for certain aspects of human consciousness, Wallace reminds us, for childhood memories can be as "present" as those of five minutes ago for an individual's unconscious brain. The same may hold true, he suggests in *Bulow Hammock*,

for the human mind more generally, which "evolved in warm, spicy places." Thus, when Wallace says that he wants to understand his mind "in relation to trees" (echoing Thoreau's lovable but serious declaration in *Walden* that he was determined to "know beans"), he means to understand the connections and parallels between the instincts and perceptual reflexes of the human mind and the original environments that shaped those processes.

Similarly, in *The Klamath Knot*, Wallace sees the Klamath Mountains as something more than simply a puzzling "knot" of geological evidence. What particularly interests him is the fact that the past and the present have not been as sharply severed in the Klamaths as in most of North America. The scrambled geology of the area is matched by the diversity of a forest that does not conform to Western life-zone patterns. Rugged terrain and a special climate have allowed species of trees to grow together that elsewhere are segregated by altitude or latitude. The result is a rare remnant forest that contains a rich gene pool of all Western forests, a "community of trees at least forty million years old." Likewise, the organisms in the bacteria-rich Klamath lakes are even more ancient. Some microbial inhabitants of these mountain lakes are akin to life-forms that may go back four billion years, preceding the earliest fossils, even the earliest known sedimentary rocks in Greenland. In the context of such ancestral biological and geological lineages, Wallace envisions evolution as a living continuum, a vital, ever-active process rather than a remote occurrence. The animals, trees, and plants of the region not only inhabit this area, they quite literally embody a "treasury of evolutionary stories," each of which mimics the "entire history of life, from the first cells to form in primal ooze . . . to the drying, cooling world of the great mammals, our world" (p. 13).

Imagining genetic resonances in wilderness that parallel these age-old physical dimensions of the Klamaths, Wallace places human consciousness in the "ancient continuum of bears and forests" (p. 8). "Wilderness generates mythological thinking," he says. "The symbiotic superconsciousness I vaguely sense in forests is not outside scientific possibility" (p. 136), and neither is the possibility that Sasquatch may actually exist. These are the kinds of mythic or legendary possibilities that have struck some of his readers as overly mythopoetic, and one wonders if George Kilgore, the wry, self-deprecating freelance forester who narrates Wallace's novels, *The Turquoise Dragon* and *The Vermilion Parrot*, might not be partly designed to counterbalance this side of Wallace's sensibility. Yet despite his veneer of jaded skepticism, Kilgore is sensitively attuned to the natural world, and these novels, despite their action-packed surfaces and outlandish plot twists, express an informed concern with ecological issues. The action in *The Turquoise Dragon* revolves around an intriguing evolutionary concept, a previously undiscovered species of salamander found to exist only in the Kalmiopsis wilderness. *The Vermilion Parrot* features a nonhuman but sentient character who lived on the planet seventy million years ago, comes back, and offers ecological insights (sometimes while drinking Italian wine or picking fresh morels). However successfully these concerns mesh with the conventions of hard-boiled detective fiction, they attest to the offbeat distinctiveness that has characterized Wallace's naturalist writing from the beginning.

"We need new ways of connecting human sympathies to our nonhuman relatives," Wallace wrote at the end of *The Dark Range*. His willingness to take risks in exploring "new ways of connecting," new ways of communicating his own "deep vision" of nature, stands as testimony to the creative improbabilities he so admires in the natural world. The elegance and mythic insight of his writing have earned it a place of lasting importance in American nature writing.

Selected Bibliography

WORKS OF DAVID RAINS WALLACE

NATURAL HISTORY

The Dark Range: A Naturalist's Night Notebook (San Francisco: Sierra Club, 1978); *Idle Weeds: The Life of a Sandstone Ridge* (San Francisco: Sierra Club, 1980), repr. as *Idle Weeds: The Life of an Ohio Sandstone Ridge* (Columbus: Ohio State Univ. Press, 1980); *The Klamath Knot: Explorations in Myth and Evolution* (San Francisco: Sierra Club, 1983); *Life in the Balance: Companion to the Audubon Television Specials* (San Diego: Harcourt Brace Jovanovich, 1987); *Bulow Hammock: Mind in a Forest* (San Francisco: Sierra Club, 1989); *The Quetzal and the Macaw: The Story of Costa Rica's National Parks* (San Francisco: Sierra Club, 1992).

NOVELS

The Turquoise Dragon (San Francisco: Sierra Club, 1985); *The Vermilion Parrot* (San Francisco: Sierra Club, 1992).

LITERARY CRITICISM

The Wilder Shore (San Francisco: Sierra Club, 1984).

COLLECTED ESSAYS

The Untamed Garden and Other Personal Essays (Columbus: Ohio State Univ. Press, 1986).

INDIVIDUAL ESSAYS

"Mystery and Evolution in a Rain Shadow," in *Drylands: The Deserts of North America*, by Philip Hyde (San Diego: Harcourt Brace Jovanovich, 1987); "Sand County's Conservation Prophet," in *Sierra* 22 (November/December 1987); "The Next Four National Parks," in *Mother Jones* 14 (July/August 1989); "Of Buccaneers and Biodiversity," in *Wilderness* 53 (winter 1989); "The Klamath Surprise," in *Wilderness* 56 (winter 1992); "The Crowded Desert Islands," in *Manoa: A Pacific Journal of International Writing* 1 (winter 1993); "The Writer's Notebook," in *Zyzzyva* 9, no. 4 (1993); "Burros and Mustangs: Literary Evolutionism and the Wilderness West," in *Reading the West: New Essays on the Literature of the American West*, ed. by Michael Kowalewski (New York: Cambridge Univ. Press, 1996).

BIOGRAPHICAL AND CRITICAL STUDIES

Karen Klaber, "The Making of a Naturalist," in *Berkeley Monthly* 9 (18 January 1979); John Murray, "David Rains Wallace: A Profile," in *Bloomsbury Review* 8, no. 4 (July/August 1988); John M. Muste, foreword to *The Untamed Garden and Other Personal Essays*, by David Rains Wallace (Columbus: Ohio State Univ. Press, 1986).

TERRY TEMPEST WILLIAMS
(b. 1955)

LORRAINE ANDERSON

TERRY TEMPEST WILLIAMS is pictured in a 1993 *Life* magazine special issue on the Wild West standing between two shoulder-high hunks of igneous rock in the shallows of a gray blue Great Salt Lake. Her black-clad figure stands out starkly against a fog that blends seamlessly with the water; her dark hair curls back from her face and her fringed shawl hangs down behind her like wings. Her red-gloved hands resting on the rocks on either side of her provide a startling splash of color, like the epaulets on a red-winged blackbird. Eyes closed and face tilted skyward, Williams seems to be listening intently to a revelation. She proclaims in the accompanying text: "We are connected consciously and unconsciously to the places we live."

Deeply rooted in her ancestral home ground, Williams writes with a vivid awareness that stories can bring a landscape alive and that stories from the land can in turn nourish and heal us. Her intimate relationship with the wetlands and deserts of the Great Basin and the Colorado Plateau is informed by the stories of four generations of Mormon forebears as well as the native cultures of the area. It is also informed by the fact that she is a woman—a woman who at thirty-four became the matriarch of her family. The combination of her rootedness in family and place, her sensitivity to the power of story, and her feeling for the particular bond between women and nature makes hers a strikingly original voice in contemporary nature writing.

What is also striking about Williams is her evolution from a writer concerned primarily with a "poetics of place" to one passionately espousing a "politics of place" growing out of an "erotics of place." As her books have become increasingly outspoken and personal, she has evolved from a woman writing safely within the bounds of traditional gender roles to one risking more and more pointed challenges to the status quo. This evolution has placed her in an increasingly paradoxical situation within the Mormon culture that nurtured her.

Indeed, like Coyote in the Native American stories she loves so well, Williams is an embodiment of paradox. In *Life* magazine she describes herself as a "radical soul in a conservative religion." She is also a feminist in a patriarchal religion, an environmentalist in one of the very few American religions that in the 1990s has not embraced ecological values, a woman who has been arrested for civil disobedience in a religion that holds obedience to civil authority as an article of faith, a childless woman in a pronatalist religion. While she has asserted that "the most radical act we can commit is to stay home" (*An Unspoken Hunger*, p. 134), she is increasingly in demand as a speaker and teacher at locales as far-flung as the Bread Loaf Writers Conference in Vermont and the Ojai Foundation in California.

And while Williams writes as a skilled observer of the natural world—one who sees herself as "a naturalist first and a writer second"—her writing just as surely conveys a belief in a spiritual world where meaning resides. Inspired by the magical worldview at the root of her religion, she sees angels in rainbows, magic in yucca, and messages in the visits of animals to the backyard. Further, her writing addresses what she called in a 1988 public dialogue with fellow naturalist Robert Finch "this yearning to heal the fragmentation and divisions that separate us from nature, that separate us from ourselves, that separate us from God or the mysteries" (in Lueders, ed., p. 43). By juxtaposing natural fact with myth, dreams, symbols, and personal stories, she seeks to present the world whole.

In the lineage of nature writing, Williams carries on the spirit of Mary Austin and Rachel Carson. Like Austin, she insists on the validity of a feminine way of seeing and feels an affinity for arid landscapes that ask us "to redefine what is beautiful" (in Lueders, ed., p. 51). Like Carson, whom she has named as her foremost role model, she merges the imagination of a creative writer with a belief in the eloquence of facts and writes prose suffused with the lyric grace of poetry. Like Carson, she is a passionate woman who threatens to undermine the status quo. "I want to carry a healthy anger inside of me and shatter the complacency that has seeped into our society," she wrote in an *Audubon* magazine essay honoring Carson (p. 107).

But her own special genius is in articulating—and living—a way of life in spiritual and physical dialogue with landscape. Williams finds metaphors in the natural world that tutor her in how to live and illuminate inner truths: seasonal variations in the land reflect her own cyclic nature, the land's wildness calls forth her own. Landscape sometimes become a second skin: "I am desert. I am mountains. I am Great Salt Lake," she proclaims in *Refuge* (p. 29). Her physical dialogue with landscape is carried on in solitary visits to the field—visits that often find her lying on the earth or immersed in water—and sealed by ritual. A scar meandering down the center of her forehead "like a red clay river," the result of a tumble down a talus slope in the

desert, is a mark of that dialogue. She understands that her own natural history lies in the elders who have taught her and the landscape that has marked and mentored her.

No other American naturalist—aside, perhaps, from Wendell Berry, to whom Williams has paid tribute in an essay—has written with such a deep sense of tradition in a particular place. In writing about the arid wilderness lands of Utah, Williams follows in the footsteps of John Wesley Powell, Wallace Stegner, and Edward Abbey, but they were foreigners to the territory. For her, generation upon generation of family stories enliven the Utah landscape, and the history of her religion there lends special resonance. She commented in her dialogue with Robert Finch: "Brigham Young said 'This is the place,' and there are those of us who still believe that" (in Lueders, ed., p. 42). She and her husband make their home in Emigration Canyon, through which Young led his followers into the Salt Lake Valley in 1847. "It is a matter of rootedness," she writes in *Refuge*, "of living inside a place for so long that the mind and imagination fuse" (p. 21).

With her fierce loyalty to family, community, and place, Williams is an increasingly visible figure in what *Newsweek* called "the war for the West," the political and cultural battle over what remains of the wilderness in the eleven western states. A 1991 article in *Newsweek* listed Williams as one of twenty "leading movers and shakers in the West," calling her "one of the West's most striking new writers." She serves on the boards of directors of several organizations concerned with the future of the West, including the Southern Utah Wilderness Alliance and the Northern Lights Institute, and has been an outspoken opponent of the nuclear testing conducted in the Nevada desert. Her writing often reflects her sense that the faraway eastern power base desperately needs to be educated about the real West, so that "a blank spot on the map" is not translated to mean "empty space, space devoid of people, a wasteland perfect for nerve gas, weteye bombs, and toxic waste" (*Refuge*, p. 241). Unwittingly underscoring the extent of eastern ignorance about the West, both the 1991

Newsweek article and the 1993 *Life* article mentioning Williams erroneously reported that there are nuclear test sites in Utah (the only nuclear test site in the United States is in southern Nevada).

And contrary to the *Newsweek* label, in 1991 Williams was hardly a "new" writer about the West. Her writing first won a national audience in 1991 with the publication of *Refuge*. But in two children's books, a volume of creative nonfiction and a volume of stories, a poetry chapbook, and numerous essays prior to *Refuge*, she had established a reputation as a storyteller concerned with environments that are fragile and often misunderstood. In 1990, she was the youngest writer anthologized in *The Norton Book of Nature Writing*, proof of the stature she had already attained and harbinger of achievements yet to come. From her first book in 1984, her work can be seen as a record of the unfolding natural history of a woman seeking to become a whole human being, one participating fully in nature and committed to describing her experience in a feminine voice.

Early Life and Influences

Terry Lynn Tempest was born in Salt Lake City, Utah, on 8 September 1955, a century after her Mormon ancestors crossed the plains and mountains from Illinois. She was the first child of Diane Dixon Tempest and John Henry Tempest III, to be followed by three boys. The men of the family had been digging in the Utah soil for three generations, laying pipe; her father, her uncles, her grandfather, and her great-grandfather all worked for the Tempest Company, the family's pipeline-contracting business, as would her brothers. She recalled in her conversation with Robert Finch, "My father taught us at an early age that nothing is as it appears, that you must dig deep, make test holes, and find out for yourself. I remember as a small child standing with him as he would calculate and read the landscape and talk to us about what we saw and what was really there" (in Lueders, ed., p. 43).

This sensitivity to what is hidden but nonetheless real was reinforced in her upbringing by the Mormon belief in a spirit world that precedes and follows physical existence on earth. Her family, engaged with the natural world in its work, taught her that "God can be found wherever you are, especially outside" (*Refuge*, p. 14), an idea reinforced by the example of church founder Joseph Smith, who received his original revelation while kneeling in a grove of trees. Mormon family life also taught her the importance of ritual acts, from the informal ritual of "family home evening" to temple rites of baptism and marriage, while the Book of Mormon taught her the power of story, of homeland, and of the personal spiritual quest.

Learning what it meant to belong to a people and a place with a tradition, she also learned what it meant to be female in that tradition. While her father took the boys rabbit hunting on family camping trips, she and her mother would stay in camp talking. When the men returned, her mother would cook dinner. In *Pieces of White Shell* she recalls observing the "wild enthusiasm" her father and her brothers shared as hunters over finding deer tracks in their yard. "Feeling out of place and out of touch," she "went back inside and shut the door" (pp. 99–100). A Mormon woman's role was clearly within the domestic sphere, nurturing her family and her community.

Wallace Stegner, whom Williams has singled out in an interview with David Petersen as "perhaps my greatest teacher, because he has defined the American West as 'living space,'" wrote in *The Sound of Mountain Water* (1969) that during his Salt Lake City boyhood he was drawn to the mountain canyons behind the city. Terry was drawn in the opposite direction. She recalls in *Refuge* that the childhood days she loved most were those spent with her paternal grandmother Kathryn Blackett Tempest ("Mimi") at the Bear River Migratory Bird Refuge, a wetland on the delta of the Bear River, which pours into the northeastern arm of Great Salt Lake near Brigham City, Utah. They would walk along the road with binoculars around their necks and watch birds, hundreds of birds of different shapes and colors. The sight captured the imagination of this intense child used to the dull green tones of the Great Basin's sagebrush plains.

When she was five, her grandmother gave her a copy of Roger Tory Peterson's expanded *Field Guide to Western Birds* (1961), in which she jotted notes, beginning the journal keeping that she would later call "the bedrock of my voice" (Petersen interview). Mimi was a fountain not only of natural-history information but also of myth and legend, seeding the young girl's imagination with a language of metaphor and symbolism. Under Mimi's tutelage, Terry learned to record and interpret dreams. Mimi introduced her to the work of Rachel Carson; turned her intensity toward creative activities such as collecting shells, dancing, and painting to music; and taught her to value "beauty, awe, and curiosity." Summer afternoons spent floating in Great Salt Lake were also instructive: "For hours we floated on our backs, imprinting on Great Basin skies. It was in these moments of childhood that Great Salt Lake flooded my psyche," she remembers in *Refuge* (p. 33).

At the University of Utah, Terry wanted to study both literature and biology, but the English department refused to let her major in "environmental English" and the biology department refused to let her major in "literary biology," so she ended up majoring in English and minoring in biology. During the summer of 1974, after her first year of college, she met naturalist Ted Major at the Teton Science School in Jackson Hole, Wyoming, where she had a grant to study tourist behavior. Major, an expert in winter ecology, became an important mentor, showing her "the power of questioning, and that for every question there's an answer waiting in the natural world" (Petersen interview). At the school, where she returned the following summer to teach ecology and biology, she also met Mardy Murie, wife of wildlife biologist Olaus Murie and a crusader for wilderness in her own right. Terry was inspired by finding in Murie's tale of life in Alaska, *Two in the Far North* (1962), "an independent woman's voice rooted in family and landscape" (*An Unspoken Hunger*, p. 92). Murie would also become an important mentor and friend.

Early in college, Terry worked part-time at Sam Weller's Zion Bookstore in downtown Salt Lake City, a serious bookstore whose Mormon owner had liberal leanings. She read widely and copiously, expanding her world far beyond the confines of Mormon Utah and laying the foundation for the allusion to other literary works that would characterize her own. She met a customer at the bookstore who showed that he was a kindred spirit by buying her favorite books. Brooke Williams was also from a Mormon family with deep roots in Utah; he worked in the family construction business founded by his grandfather. Having earned a degree in biology, he shared Terry's passionate love of nature. Terry and Brooke were married "for time and all eternity" in the Mormon temple in Salt Lake City on 2 June 1975. She was nineteen, wearing a garland of wildflowers in her hair; he was twenty-three. Nearly twenty years later, Terry Tempest Williams would name her marriage as "the single most significant influence" on her life and work, telling interviewer David Petersen that the solidarity she finds there enables freedom in her relationships "with the land and with other people."

While pursuing a master's degree in environmental education at the University of Utah, Williams spent time with Navajo children as a teacher at Montezuma Creek, Utah, "curious to see the desert from the children's perspective." By exploring narrative in the Navajo culture, she saw "a correspondence between language and landscape" and found a way to integrate her passions for the natural world and literature through story. Professor Florence Krall, a woman who came to feminism by way of deep ecology, was a strong influence. Barry Lopez, whom she met when she was twenty-three, tutored her in the importance of story. The writers Simon Ortiz, Linda Hogan, and Louise Erdrich inspired her as native voices of the land. *Pieces of White Shell*, her second book, would grow out of her master's thesis.

Finding a Voice:
The First Three Books

Hired in 1979 as curator of education at the Utah Museum of Natural History, Williams was charged with outreach to the schools. In a pattern typical of earlier female naturalists who had shaped their work to conform with gender roles, she began writing as an outgrowth of her work with children and collaborated on her first book, *The Secret Language of Snow* (1984), with her mentor Ted Major. Although Williams is listed as the lead author, Major had previously published a book on snow ecology and provided the impetus for the project. The collaboration was a successful one: the book was named the best children's science book of 1984 by the New York Academy of Sciences.

The Secret Language of Snow explores winter ecology through the language and stories of the Inuit people of the Kobuk Valley in northwestern Alaska. In twelve chapters, each of which begins with a free-verse poem, the authors discuss the importance of snow and of the language used to describe it, the lives and environment of the Inuit people, and ten distinctly different kinds of snow named by the Inuits. The snow chapters correspond roughly to the seasonal round, beginning with the first snowfall of the season and ending with the melting snow of spring, and weave together scientific information and lore about the geography, plants, and animals of the Arctic.

Williams had visited Alaska with Brooke soon after their marriage and had worked to support the Alaskan Lands Bill in the late 1970s, so the setting of her first book held personal meaning for her. Already in this book she was focusing on themes and developing a style that would be important in her later writing. The theme of finding identity through story is glimpsed briefly in a mention of the function of storytelling in Inuit culture. A distinct subtext of this book and Williams' later writing is that accurate naming is essential to accurate seeing, that language enables heightened perception of the natural world. Her trademark melding of the poetic and the scientific is already in evidence: the writing is graceful and engaging, marrying fact with metaphor. And although the text conveys an abundance of scientific information, it also appeals to the reader's own sensory experience of the world for corroboration and acknowledges that mysteries exist outside the realm of science.

Her second children's book focuses on a landscape much more familiar to her: *Between Cattails* (1985) describes the plant and animal life of the marsh. Although not specifically about the wetlands of Great Salt Lake, it is firmly grounded in Williams' early trips to the Bear River Migratory Bird Refuge with Mimi, to whom the book is dedicated. (Ironically, the book's publication coincided with the drowning of Great Salt Lake's marshes, chronicled in *Refuge*.) Written in free-verse form, the brief book evokes the beauty of wetlands while conveying facts about the complex interrelationships among life forms there and urging concern for marsh habitat. On the first page, it invites readers to enter into a physical dialogue with the marsh by separating the cattails, stepping down, and watching "murky water seep into our shoes."

Emphasizing the domestic round of the permanent inhabitants of the marsh rather than drawing attention to the dramatic migration of seasonal visitors, *Between Cattails* reflects the traditional concerns of woman's sphere. Williams' focus on the domestic meanings of wetlands is clear from the way she frames the book: it opens and closes with the cry of red-winged blackbirds, "singing about home—their home of willow greens, lily greens, and water." By describing what one might see on a particular day in the marsh, she gives readers a sense of its inhabitants as individuals. When she writes of Green-winged Teal and Great Blue Heron as if these were personal and not generic names, it is clear that the birds have become like relatives to her, members of a wider family.

Williams' first book for adults, *Pieces of White Shell: A Journey to Navajoland* (1984), was also anchored in her work with children. Published after *The Secret Language of Snow* and before *Between Cattails*, it had been in the writing since she worked with Navajo children during graduate school. With this book Williams began to establish an identity as a Mormon storyteller inspired by native voices and arid landscapes. In a prose style that Rhoda Yerburgh called "alternately luminous with insight and purple as sage" (p. 2155) she shows us the Four Corners region of Utah, Arizona, New Mexico, and Colorado through the stories and rituals of its Navajo inhabitants as well as through tales of her own experiences as a teacher there. She writes that she has trusted Navajo stories as her guides across the desert because she could find no others. "They are rooted in native soil. To these people they are sacred. Truth. To me, they are beacons in a nation suspicious of nature" (p. 3).

In the book's prologue, Williams draws parallels between her own Mormon people and the Navajo: both are relative newcomers to the land who have a strong sense of locale; both are spiritual people who believe in "a power that moves us, directs us, cares for us"; both have family ties that are extended and strong; both find themselves caught between modernization and tradition. Still, there are differences, and the book is meant as a vehicle for cultural exchange, as indicated by its title. Pieces of white shell, as Williams points out in the chapter of the same name, serve as "currency between cultures" (p. 40). There is also paradox in the title, for in a literal view of the world, pieces of white shell are associated not with the desert but with the ocean. It is only through Navajo eyes, free from "biological rules and constraints," that one might expect to see pieces of white shell in the desert.

The first and last chapters of *Pieces of White Shell* ground the book in Williams' role as curator of education at the Utah Museum of Natural History. Spread out on her desk, objects from her curatorial pouch — such as a sprig of sage, a bouquet of feathers bound by yarn, a bone from Black Mountain — evoke chapter topics just as individual seashells do in Anne Morrow Lindbergh's 1955 classic *Gift from the Sea*. Each chapter examines a different facet of the Navajo

Terry Tempest Williams

relationship to the land: beliefs about the origins of things, the deities that guide the people's course, the uses of plants, the teachings and sustenance provided by animals, the ways of their vanished Anasazi predecessors, and the vital role of story and ritual. Each chapter weaves together Williams' own experiences, knowledge gathered personally from the Navajo, and lore from published sources.

When Williams relates Navajo stories, she is also learning her own craft. "The Navajo taught me to listen in a way I had never imagined," she writes in a chapter entitled "The Storyteller" (p. 131). It is apparent from her own stories that the Navajo taught her other skills as well: to be ambiguous and suggestive, to find significance in ordinary things, to recognize the existence of sacred time and space, to blur the distinction between what is real and what is imagined, to challenge the idea that the land and the self are separate entities. In the chapter "Turquoise, Obsidian, and Coral," she writes, "The warm desert winds blow through me. . . . I may be here for days. Perhaps I shall be an arch tomorrow" (p. 30).

There are echoes here of Mary Austin, another maverick storyteller who learned her craft from native peoples, the Paiute Indians. In her autobiography, *Earth Horizon* (1932), Austin credits "the study of Indian verse, strange and meaningful; of Indian wisdom, of Indian art" with teaching her to write. An immigrant to the desert regions of southern California, she worked at first like Williams as a traveling teacher, illustrating natural-history lessons with stories and in turn learning to know the West through the eyes of children. Like Williams, she focused in her writing on the interrelations among humans, landscape, and culture; like Williams, she was a solitary wanderer in the desert, a curious and patient observer of desert flora and fauna, seeking to understand their patterns of life. "The land holds stories . . . that come to us and sing the mysteries which surround us," writes Williams in *Pieces of White Shell* (pp. 136–137). "The palpable sense of mystery in the desert air breeds fables," writes Austin in *The Land of Little Rain* (1903, p. 7). Each book represents the author's attempt to find a vocabulary and a style to describe a land of unconventional beauty that captivates her.

Williams is also akin to Austin in her preoccupation with what it means to be a woman in relationship to nature. Contemplating the myth of Changing Woman, who "holds the mysteries of earth and the promise of fecundity," Williams is reminded that "earth goddesses dwell at the heart of every culture" and that in European cultural histories, "women and earth have always been bonded." She asks herself: "Where are our earth goddesses today?" (p. 44). Walking in a Salt Lake City park, she and a friend are discussing this when they encounter a woman clearing vines from a tree that she says she has been visiting since she was transplanted from Germany twenty-seven years earlier. They have found their contemporary earth goddess.

Williams is beginning to test the bounds of her role as a woman and to feel the contradictions inherent in her life. Many times in the book we see her engaged with children, her students, but just as often we see her wandering off alone into the desert, like a heroine in one of Mary Austin's stories. The woman who writes so lovingly in the prologue of the ritual of trimming the Christmas tree with her extended family also finds it essential to her nature to sit on the canyon's edge and watch a desert sunset in solitude, to spend the better part of a day in a wildflower-studded meadow in the company of Great Horned Owl, and to step alone into a room of an ancient Anasazi dwelling at Chaco Canyon. In the room, she reads female energy in handprints streaked across the whitewashed walls and wants "to talk, listen, share, spend entire afternoons in womanly conversation about her life, mine" (p. 127). When she and a Navajo woman immerse themselves in the San Juan River at daybreak and "dance obeisantly around the gentle rapids—arms outstretched, waists turning, breasts loose" (p. 134), she is creating a ritual to honor what is wild in her nature, outside woman's traditional sphere.

Thus, *Pieces of White Shell* is a quietly subversive book. Intending to school the Navajo in white ways of perceiving nature, Williams instead returns with an appreciation for what the Navajo can teach "a nation suspicious of nature." She questions her own culture's orthodoxies, in the chapter titled "A Bouquet of Feathers Bound by Yarn," when she compares the egocentricity of the Anglo nomenclature for birds—"Wilson's snipe," "Swainson's thrush," and such—with the Navajo way of naming birds based on "perception and thoughtful observation"; for instance, the Navajo name for the marsh hawk is *ch'il taat'agii*, meaning "one-flying-close-to-the-woods." Underlying the book is a critique of the loss of connection to landscape through story and ritual that characterizes contemporary technological culture. "A story keeps things known—and in the case of the natural world, few are literate" (p. 137), Williams writes of today's urban dwellers. When she exhorts readers to "let go of cultural biases and societal constraints, taking the time to experience earth as it is, raw and self-defined," to "confront the mysteries of life directly by involving ourselves, patiently and quietly, in the day-to-day dramas of the land," and to "imagine ourselves flying on the backs of owls" (pp. 136 and 137), she is issuing a wake-up call.

Still, in this volume Williams has not yet begun to turn a critical eye on her own Mormon culture. In the chapter entitled "Wool," which explores the importance of sheep to the Navajo economy and way of life, she sharply criticizes the U.S. government's sheep-reduction program as "a striking example of a dominant culture's insensitivity and ignorance toward Native People's ways" (pp. 112–113). Yet she does not question the Mormon church's Indian Placement Service, which recruits young Indians to live in white foster homes with the goal of assimilating them into white society as Mormons. At the end of the chapter she encounters two Navajo boys taking the bus home to New Mexico from their Mormon foster home in Idaho. The boys are going home because their grandmother, the one who taught them to butcher sheep and weave wool into beautiful rugs, has died. They enthuse to Williams about the beauty of New Mexico, the pleasure of herding sheep, the stories their grandparents tell them about the old days. Her last admonishment to them is to "remember your grandparents." The reader may wonder how they are to remember their grandparents and the ways of their homeland when they are being raised in a Mormon home in Idaho, but this Williams does not address.

Nevertheless, she has come a long way. Drawn to the Navajo when she "had no tales to tell," in *Pieces of White Shell* she now has stories to give away. As if to symbolize the roots of her craft, a bracelet of Navajo silver given to her by her mother and Mimi will hereafter hold the wrist of her writing hand. Ultimately, however, she realizes that although Navajo stories can serve as examples, "we must create and find our own stories, our own myths, with symbols that will bind us to the world as we see it today" (p. 5). In *Pieces of White Shell* we see her glean-

ing ideas about story not only from the Navajo but also from the Kalahari bushmen, Barry Lopez, Aldo Leopold, Simon Ortiz, Gregory Bateson, and Esther Harding. These ideas work in her as she finds her way to her own voice, until in 1989 with *Coyote's Canyon* she presents "a new mythology for desert goers, one that acknowledges the power of story and ritual, yet lies within the integrity of our own cultures" (p. 16).

Pieces of White Shell received the 1984 Southwest Book Award for creative nonfiction but attracted little notice outside the West. Throughout the 1980s, Williams honed her skills as a teacher both in her work for the Utah Museum of Natural History and as an adjunct professor at the University of Utah, where she taught courses in ornithology as well as on women and nature. In 1985 she went with a group of women from Utah to the International Women's Decade conference in Nairobi, Kenya. This experience gave rise to her essay "In the Country of Grasses," reprinted in *The Norton Book of Nature Writing* (1990) and later in *An Unspoken Hunger* (1994), and introduced her to some inspiring models of environmental activism, including Wangari Maathai, founder of the women's Green Belt Movement in Kenya. In 1986 she traded her position as curator of education at the museum for naturalist-in-residence to gain more time in the field, more time to write, and more time to spend with her mother, who had been diagnosed with ovarian cancer in 1983. Distracted by her mother's illness and eventual death in 1987, Williams did not publish another book until *Coyote's Canyon* in 1989.

A New Mythology: *Coyote's Canyon* and *Earthly Messengers*

A collaboration with photographer John Telford, *Coyote's Canyon* is a celebration in story and photograph of the wild lands of southern Utah, where "the blood of the rocks gives life to the country." Williams writes in the preface that she means the book as a reminder that "beauty is not found in the excessive, but in what is lean and spare and subtle." John Telford's photographs reveal a fantastic landscape of scoured red rock and windswept red sand, of stone arches and bridges, spires and pinnacles, buttes and domes, sandstone monoliths and slot canyons, looping rivers and meandering streams, Anasazi pictographs and cliff dwellings, fern grottoes and stands of box elder. Set against this backdrop, Williams' seven very short stories are crafted with a sure hand, in prose that is as "lean and spare and subtle" as the landscape.

The first story, "Lion Eyes," is a perfect segue from *Pieces of White Shell*. Williams is riding at dusk in the back of a pickup with Navajo children as they are being delivered home from a field trip. A mountain lion runs in front of the truck and disappears. The kids scare themselves with talk of the dangers of mountain lions and then, after a subdued interval, begin chanting together until they have "sung themselves back to hozho, where the world is balanced and whole." After this reminder of Navajo ritual, the following stories go on to suggest new rituals that might grow out of this place and time. A woman retreats to a desert canyon and fashions a clay bowl and figurines while she comes to terms with the demands of her family role; an archaeologist buries poems in the desert to pique the locals' interest in their town's history and prehistory; friends conspire to return an ancient juniper ladder from a museum to the Anasazi kiva where it belongs; a woman dances in the desert to celebrate and honor its plants and animals; a man and a woman spend a day in joyful play on a riverbank, creating a spiral of stones.

Williams dedicates *Coyote's Canyon* to the Coyote Clan—the "hundreds, maybe even thousands, of individuals who are quietly subversive on behalf of the land." Thus, this book of exquisite beauty that creates a "poetics of place" also hints at a "politics of place." The political battles over the fate of southern Utah, increasingly threatened by development schemes since Glen Canyon Dam was completed in 1963, have been heated and acrimonious and sometimes played out on a national stage. *Slick-*

rock: Endangered Canyons of the Southwest (1971) by Edward Abbey and Philip Hyde, Wallace Stegner's introduction to *Wilderness at the Edge: A Citizen Proposal to Protect Utah's Canyons and Deserts* (1990), and the essay "Love or Power?" by Terry's husband, Brooke Williams, in *Northern Lights* (fall 1991) serve as primers on the debate.

Coyote's Canyon represents a striking departure from the polemical debate that preceded it and that was sure to follow. Williams' strategy toward those who would despoil sacred land in the name of profit is distinctly feminine: instead of bludgeoning them with reason, she will seduce them with beauty and magic. She will tempt them with buried poems to tune in to their own innermost dreams and imaginings. In stories about the joyful and fierce members of the Coyote Clan, she will make them recognize their own longings for freedom. The same strategy is at work in her poetic narration of "The Canyon's Edge," a mixed-media paean to the beauty of canyon country that began running at a theater in Moab, Utah, in 1988.

Coyote's Canyon gives other evidence of Williams' continuing quest to envision a feminine way of being that is true to nature both within and without. In the preface she suggests that enough "pilgrimages to the slickrock" will result in "separation from society's oughts and shoulds." The heroine of Mary Austin's "The Walking Woman" also found this to be so—by wandering in the desert she "walked off all sense of society-made values." This is the healing that Williams imagined for her mother in "The Bowl." She had seen in her mother's face "the pallor that comes when everything is going out and nothing is coming in," the position she was placed in too often as a wife and mother. In the story, the woman returns to the small desert canyon where in her childhood "she last remembered her true nature." Alone in this beautiful place, she sheds her clothing, her inhibitions, and her overburdening sense of responsibility toward her family.

The woman who dances in the desert in "A Woman's Dance" is Williams herself. She comes to the desert in a long red skirt, gathers a variety of plants, and places them in a circle on the red soil.

> Movement surrounded her. The wind, clouds, grasses, and birds—all reminded her that nothing stands still. She held up the hem of her skirt in both hands and began walking briskly around the circle. Deep breaths took the aroma of mint and sage down to her toes. Her long, spirited stride broke into short leaps with extended arms as she entered the circle dancing, without guile, without notice, without any thought of herself. She danced from the joy of all she was a part.
>
> Pronghorn Antelope entered the circle through her body. She danced Eagle, Raven, and Bear. The Four Seasons sent her swirling as she danced to ignite the Moon. She danced until gravity pulled her down, and then she rested, her eyes closed, with nothing moving but her heart and lungs, beating, breathing, against the hot, dry desert.

Here is a woman who knows her own power and recognizes that it flows from her connection to the natural world. Here is a passionate woman determined to love what is sacred in the world and to honor it through ritual. Here is a woman experiencing "an unspeakable joy in being fully present and responding totally to the moment." Here is a woman who realizes that life is a dance, that life and death are entwined in the dance, and that the dance is everything. Like the Greek goddess Artemis, Williams embodies the wisdom of the wild. Like the heroines in Mary Austin's stories, she is a desert woman invigorated by contact with wilderness.

If *Coyote's Canyon* explores a public landscape, *Earthly Messengers*, a handmade chapbook published in a limited edition by a Salt Lake City art gallery the same year, explores a private one. Dedicated to Brooke "in this landscape of marriage," this very personal book contains nine poems inspired by creatures that visit a couple in the bedroom of their humble mountain house. Their bed's white-pine posts are "each carved in the shape of a beehive," emblem of the Mormon church. Their bedroom's large French doors are open at night to a view of a small aspen grove. Through the doors come a moth, a white dove, a hummingbird, a deer mouse, a bat, glimpses of mule deer and porcupine, a black widow, a lizard.

The book's epigraph, from Joseph Campbell's *The Power of Myth* (1988), provides a key to interpreting the text: "The images of the myth are reflections of the spiritual potentialities of every one of us. Through contemplating these, we evoke their power in our own lives." Thus, each creature is a metaphor for a spiritual potentiality in the marriage: illumination, love, joy, accountability, fear, reciprocity, acceptance, ambiguity, and commitment. These words, blind engraved on the last page of the book, name landmarks in the uneven terrain of marriage. As the couple navigates this uneven terrain,

> a sense of goodness
> filled them, humbled them, kept them
> moving towards passion.
> And they never stopped
> dreaming or wondering about love.

Earthly Messengers, like so much of Williams' work, defies conventional boundaries. The French doors thrown open to let "the outside in" extend the boundaries of the home to encompass the land, plants, and animals, making nature a third party in the marriage. Further, the book implicitly challenges conventional definitions of nature writing by showing that even writing focused primarily on the most intimate of human relationships can belong to the genre. Applying metaphors from nature can enable us to see human institutions and relationships in a new light. Thus, at the same time that Williams is enlarging woman's traditional sphere to encompass all of nature, she is also drawing nature writing into woman's traditional sphere.

She explores the landscape of marriage further in her 1992 essay "A Love That Is Wild," which grapples with the question of how to stay true to one's own nature within the confines of social and religious institutions. Her husband wants to dissolve the marriage vows they made "as kids" and commit to a renewed marriage "within a context of experience" that is "about improvising each day." He proposes burning their marriage certificate. Terry is reluctant, but at dawn the next day they set their marriage certificate aflame on the shore of Great Salt Lake and hurl their wedding bands into the lake. With this ritual they proclaim that they have chosen to respect the natural integrity of the relationship more than the institution. "I realize the courage it takes to love, especially to love in a way that defies tradition," writes Terry. She declares that what she loves about Brooke, a writer himself who occasionally comes into view in her stories as a companion in the field, is "his reliability and his insistence in shattering established forms." The two are clearly soulmates, smashing icons together.

Crossing the Line: *Refuge*

While Williams was making a name for herself in the West with the five books published during the 1980s, she was harboring a painful personal story that she would relate in the pivotal book of her career. In the spring of 1983, at the age of fifty-one and twelve years after a bout with breast cancer, Williams' mother was diagnosed with ovarian cancer. At the same time, Great Salt Lake was on the rise due to an unusually wet winter. The diagnosis devastated the family just as the rising waters threatened to devastate Terry's beloved Bear River Migratory Bird Refuge. "The landscape of my childhood and the landscape of my family, the two things I had always regarded as bedrock, were now subject to change," she writes in *Refuge: An Unnatural History of Family and Place* (1991, p. 40).

This memoir chronicling the years between 1983 and 1990 in Williams' life grew out of the twenty-two journals she filled as first her mother and then her two grandmothers died and as she witnessed the drowning and resurrection of the bird sanctuary. *Refuge* weaves together classic natural-history writing about a fluctuating Great Salt Lake and its birds with stories from Mormon history, family tradition, and personal experience. It represents Williams' attempt to heal herself through story, as she writes in the pro-

logue, but it also reads as a historical record of natural cataclysm, a meditation on mortality and death, an exploration of a woman's identity as it is shaped by family and place, and a challenge to cultural and religious orthodoxies.

Williams' characteristic determination to see the world whole, with the eyes of a poet as well as a scientist, is evident throughout. As often as she counts birds for the scientific record, she prays to them because she believes they will carry the messages of her heart upward. When she comes across a storm-battered whistling swan dead on the shores of Great Salt Lake, she lies down next to it and imagines the drama of its migration, just as she later lies down next to her dying mother to help her work with her pain. We see her in dialogue with landscape, buried in desert sand, licking the salt water of the lake off her fingers, keening in a sacred cave where a spring bubbles up.

Seeing the world whole, Williams cannot separate her family's story from the land's. Her family, the lake, and its birds are part of the same natural history unfolding. One natural—or unnatural—process becomes a metaphor for another. As her mother goes through months of chemotherapy, the Utah state legislature debates how best to control the rising lake. As she starts radiation treatments, the state breaches a railroad causeway to equalize water levels in the north and south arms of the lake. As the lake level drops temporarily in the summer of 1984, Terry's mother and father enjoy a momentary reprieve in Switzerland. When her mother's health again declines and she grows to accept her cancer, state officials finally close the offices of the bird refuge, surrendering to the advancing waters. After her mother's death in January 1987, the refuge becomes ocean and the birds abandon it altogether.

As her grandmother Mimi is diagnosed with cancer in mid-1987, the governor of Utah proclaims that the state is finally in control of the lake with the completion of the West Desert Pumping Station, which will pump excess lake water into the desert to the west. Shortly after Mimi dies in June 1989, the state turns off the pumps. The flood is over. Williams is left to cope with an enormous grief that encompasses the loss of her mother and two grandmothers as well as the displaced birds, the pumped lake, and the flooded desert. She slowly and painfully comes to the realization that refuge is not to be found in a person or place outside herself. She writes: "My refuge exists in my capacity to love. If I can learn to love death then I can begin to find refuge in change" (p. 178).

Birds provide a unifying theme. *Refuge* begins with the poem "Wild Geese" by Mary Oliver (we later learn that wild geese are her mother's favorite bird) and ends with a list of the more than two hundred bird species associated with Great Salt Lake. The chapter titles, with one exception ("Birds-of-Paradise," for the flowers she places on her mother's grave), are drawn from this list. As Williams charts how the lake's rise affects various bird species, she also looks for the birds' metaphoric meanings and applies avian metaphors to herself and others. At one point she admits that she wants to be a bird; elsewhere she writes, "I am a woman with wings" (p. 273). Chastened by her illness, her mother is "the bird touching both heaven and earth, flying with newfound knowledge of what it means to live" (p. 136). The birds' displacement from the lake is the same displacement Terry experiences in the landscape of her life; when she at last finds the birds again at Malheur National Wildlife Refuge in southeastern Oregon, she is inspired to hope that she too can find the courage to move on.

At the heart of *Refuge* is the special bond shared by three generations of women: Terry, her mother, and her grandmother Mimi. Woven through the book like a silver cord is the spiritual instruction Terry receives from her female elders as they live and die. All three grapple with what it means to cultivate a self in a culture bent on repression of women and women's values. All three read Eastern religious thought and Jungian psychology and come to trust personal revelation more than religious orthodoxy. All three find healing in time spent alone in nature. Yet it is clear that Terry will come to a fuller realization of her beliefs and aspirations than was possible for her elders. Where her mother was never able

to resolve fully the tension she felt between her need for solitude and her obligations toward family, Terry considers the possibility of not having children in order to protect her solitude, her time to retreat and create. Where Mimi could only challenge her conditioning covertly, by developing and expelling an abdominal tumor, Terry has in writing *Refuge* made an open declaration of her challenge to the social and religious orthodoxies she was raised with. As the book's startling epilogue—"The Clan of One-Breasted Women"—makes clear, she believes that her life depends on doing so.

The epilogue, which stands alone as an essay first published in *Northern Lights* and later in *Ms.* magazine, describes the event that made Williams decide to write *Refuge*. A year after her mother's death, she told her father of a recurring dream of seeing a flash of light in the nighttime desert. When her father revealed that she had indeed witnessed a nuclear explosion in the Nevada desert when she was barely two, sitting on her mother's lap as the family drove home from California, she suddenly put together the mastectomies of nine women in her family (and the eventual cancer deaths of seven) with the fact that they were "downwinders"—members of the population exposed to fallout from the government's nuclear-testing program. At that moment, "my poetics of place evolved into a politics of place," she told interviewer David Petersen.

Soon after, Williams trespassed with other antinuclear demonstrators at the Nevada Test Site and was arrested for civil disobedience, an act documented both in the epilogue and in the 1993 film *Bound by the Wind*, written and produced by David L. Brown. *Bound by the Wind* is the story of the victims of nuclear testing and the movement galvanized by the survivors. Williams is one of several downwinders interviewed in the film, which shows her ducking through barbed wire to enter the test site, then bending to touch a flowering plant tenderly before trotting off into the desert in her long red skirt. As the camera follows her, her voice-over narration describes the act of civil disobedience as a gesture of respect for her own elders as well as those of the Shoshone tribe on whose land the atomic testing takes place. "Once I crossed that line—physically, at the Nevada Test Site, as well as psychologically in recognizing that the price of obedience is too high—I could never go back, back to the same place in the family, the same place within the Mormon culture," she told David Petersen. In the epilogue to *Refuge*, Williams writes that she must now question everything, even if it means losing her faith.

And question she does, in a number of subtle and not-so-subtle challenges to her religion throughout *Refuge*. She makes several references to the exclusion of women from the Mormon priesthood. She says her prayers no longer bear the "proper" masculine salutation and suggests that "if we could introduce the Motherbody as a spiritual counterpoint to the Godhead, perhaps our inspiration and devotion would no longer be directed to the stars, but our worship could return to the Earth" (p. 241). Her worship already has: while her fellow Mormons from around the world gather "to hear the latest council and doctrine from the Brethren" at the church's annual conference, she drives past the meeting and out to Great Salt Lake, "a spiritual magnet that will not let me go." She declares: "Dogma doesn't hold me. Wildness does" (p. 240).

Yet at the same time she cannot help but affirm her Mormon background and faith. She acknowledges her debt to the magical worldview and the belief in personal revelation and individual authority at the root of Mormon religion. She celebrates the sense of family and community that is the cornerstone of the religion. She gives thanks for the "generational history of belief Mormon ritual holds," for the way it empowers its members to heal themselves and each other. Still, as she explains to Petersen, she hopes to provoke with "both love and criticism" a "revolution of the spirit" in the church. She questions the patriarchal repression of women in the Mormon church "because it ultimately has to do with how we treat the land: the repression of women parallels the repression of the earth."

Clearly, Williams' concern with women and nature has evolved into an ecofeminist con-

sciousness. *Refuge* reflects this consciousness both implicitly, in the way it juxtaposes her mother's story with the lake's, and explicitly, in comments about how women's bodies and the body of the earth have been mined and how the health of the planet reflects that of women. Throughout, she identifies nature with women. Both Great Salt Lake and women are cyclic. "I want to see the lake as Woman, as myself, in her refusal to be tamed" she writes (p. 92), pointing out that although the State of Utah may try to control her waters, the lake will outlive the state. With her mother gone, Williams finds a new genealogy as a daughter of the earth:

I am reminded that what I adore, admire, and draw from Mother is inherent in the Earth. My mother's spirit can be recalled simply by placing my hands on the black humus of mountains or the lean sands of desert. Her love, her warmth, and her breath, even her arms around me—are the waves, the wind, sunlight, and water. (p. 214)

In the epilogue, she describes a dream in which women from all over the world—women "who understood the fate of the earth as their own"—circle a blazing fire in the desert and infiltrate the test site to reclaim the desert for their children.

Aside from its ecofeminist message, *Refuge* contains the same subtle critique of our loss of connection to and destruction of nature as *Pieces of White Shell*. Williams' intimate account of her mother's process of dying exposes our culture's impulse to keep death hidden and masked as just one more way in which we are estranged from nature. Reflecting on swarms of starlings at the dump, she muses that although we loathe them, we are taking over the world just like they are, and by destroying the habitats of other birds we are encouraging them. She pleads for the preservation of wetlands as bird habitat, her words echoing those of Rachel Carson: "Marshes all across the country are disappearing without fanfare, leaving the earth devoid of birdsong" (p. 112).

Indeed, in crossing the line from poetics into politics, *Refuge* is closely akin to *Silent Spring*.

The tribute Williams pays Carson in her essay "The Spirit of Rachel Carson" could apply to her own work as well. Like *Silent Spring*, *Refuge* grew out of a woman's bearing witness to death and speaking out on behalf of the land. Like *Silent Spring*, *Refuge* required emotional and intellectual stamina of its author, the "ability to endure the pain of the story she was telling." In the face of vehement criticism, Carson stood her ground as a female voice; in writing *Refuge*, Williams learned to do the same. Carson "spoke her truth at great personal cost"; the cost to Williams of speaking her truth may be to become "a member of a border tribe" among her Mormon people.

Refuge was a pivotal book in Williams' career not only because it crossed from poetics into politics but also because it won her a national audience. It was reviewed favorably in newspapers on both coasts and in magazines with a national readership. It caught the attention of women in the growing women's spirituality movement as well as those interested in ecofeminism. It provoked the Los Angeles–based Lannan Foundation to award her in 1993 a fellowship worth $50,000, given to "writers of distinctive literary merit who demonstrate potential for outstanding future work." Called "a modern masterpiece" by Dave Foreman (of Earth First! fame) in his "Books of the Big Outside" catalog, *Refuge* was named one of the twenty best books about the earth in the 1994 *Information Please Environmental Almanac*. Williams suddenly was in great demand as a speaker and teacher.

A forceful presence in person, Williams is a captivating storyteller with a sense of drama and humor, a mellifluous voice, and an aura of mystery and beauty, strengths she has capitalized on by extending her work to audio and video media as well as the lecture circuit. In 1990 she recorded selections from *Pieces of White Shell* and *Coyote's Canyon* on an audiotape called *Coyote's Canyon*. In 1992 she recorded an audio version of Mary Austin's *Land of Little Rain*. In 1993 she recorded *Refuge* on audiotape and wrote, hosted, and narrated *A Desert Sea*, a documentary on the natural and human history of Great Salt Lake. Her narration draws on some historic literature by others, a foreshadowing of *Great and Peculiar Beauty: A Utah Reader* (1995), which she edited with Thomas J. Lyon of Utah State University (editor of the 1989 nature-writing anthology *This Incomperable Lande*).

Among the Mysteries: *An Unspoken Hunger* and *Desert Quartet*

An Unspoken Hunger: Stories from the Field (1994) begins with this quotation from Argentine writer Clarice Lispector: "So there was no going back: she had to fight for survival among the mysteries of life. And what human beings want more than anything else is to become human beings." Having challenged cultural and religious orthodoxies, Williams cannot go back: she must now trust her own experience as never before as she continues her journey toward wholeness. As recounted in *An Unspoken Hunger*, that journey has begun to carry her away from home ground. In eighteen short essays and stories, she visits the Serengeti Plains of Africa, the wetlands of Pelham Bay Park in the Bronx, a wildlife refuge within the borders of an Air Force bombing range in Arizona, the high desert of southeastern Oregon, the timber-producing Willamette National Forest, Yellowstone National Park.

Some landmarks are familiar. She honors mentors: her grandmother Mimi, Georgia O'Keeffe, an uncle whose brain was damaged during a breech birth, Edward Abbey, Mardy Murie, bears, the land itself. Her "politics of place" continues: she carries on her antinuclear protest in the face of the Gulf War, describes the sacrilege of military maneuvers in a desert wildlife refuge, testifies before a congressional subcommittee on behalf of Pacific yew management, and questions the internment of Japanese Americans during World War II at Topaz, Utah, and Heart Mountain, Wyoming. Her devotion to her female lineage continues with the book's dedication to her three nieces.

And her special interest in women and nature continues, now drawing her squarely into the controversy within the feminist movement over women's "true nature." The essays "Undressing the Bear" and "The Wild Card" make categorical statements about women's traits and concerns, in line with Mary Austin's contention that women see the world "in some other way." This brand of feminism, popularized by Harvard psychologist Carol Gilligan in her 1982 book *In a Different Voice* and generally known as radical or cultural feminism (and in academia as essentialism), has wide appeal to women in the 1990s but is by no means universally embraced. Some feminists see it as a modern-day version of the Victorian cult of true womanhood, assigning men and women to separate spheres and making women the carriers of compassion, emotionality, and caregiving. In "The Wild Card," Williams asks women to turn these traditional womanly virtues to the service of the environment, as Rachel Carson often did when speaking to women's organizations.

Her radicalization continues. "The Wild Card" demands that women's issues—centered on the health and integrity of family, community, and the land—no longer be considered peripheral. It suggests that women carry wild cards and use them to challenge the status quo; for instance, if a woman "found herself in a board of directors meeting and the truth as she felt it was not being told, she would place all her cards on the table as a sign that the games of men are not the games of women" (pp. 134–135). Williams served on the board of directors of the Wilderness Society, in whose magazine this essay first appeared, from 1989 through 1993. The kind of struggles hinted at in the essay prompted her to resign from the board when she concluded that as a woman she could not work within that political system.

An Unspoken Hunger also articulates a new theme: an "erotics of place." In "Winter Solstice at the Moab Slough" and "Yellowstone: The Erotics of Place," Williams develops the idea that how we relate to each other in our most intimate relationships directly affects how we relate to the land. If we restrain our passionate nature due to fear, we abandon the wild. If we desire to control the land or others, we lose feeling. Conversely, when we love the land and honor its mysteries, "we are lovers, engaged in an erotics of place" (p. 84). In 1991 Williams told interviewer David Petersen, "Like death, I think our sensuality is something we're afraid of. . . . I am interested in taboos, because I believe that's where the power of our culture lies." Taking off masks and naming what is hidden is for her a healing act.

Desert Quartet: An Erotic Landscape (1995) continues this healing. In a series of four short essays, each taking one of the elements of earth, water, fire, and air as its theme, Williams portrays herself making love to the canyon country of southern Utah. "I come to the rock in a moment of stillness, giving and receiving, where there is no partition between my body and the body of Earth," she writes. Reflections about the power of passion in human relationships intertwine with descriptions of the landscape she passes through on her journey. The prose is daring and revealing; it breaks new ground in applying the language of desire to the natural world.

Williams will no doubt continue to "hold the questions of a woman's life" in her bones, the questions she raises in *An Unspoken Hunger* in "The Wild Card": "Am I an activist or an artist? Do I stay home or do I speak out?" She will no doubt continue to struggle with "the obligations of a public life and the spiritual necessity for a private one." In her own Mormon culture she seems destined to play the trickster, about whom she wrote in *Pieces of White Shell*: "Coyote frees them from cultural restrictions as they break taboos vicariously. Yet at the same time, Coyote is a form of cultural affirmation" (p. 78). Whether there is room in Mormon culture for a Coyote figure remains to be seen. What is certain is that by repeatedly risking herself, writing with honesty and generosity of spirit, Williams has articulated through story a unique vision of a passionate, fully embodied relationship with the land. Her books, like the Navajo tales she first took as her guides, stand as "beacons in a nation suspicious of nature."

Selected Bibliography

WORKS OF TERRY TEMPEST WILLIAMS

CHILDREN'S BOOKS

The Secret Language of Snow, with Ted Major (San Francisco: Sierra Club/Pantheon, 1984), illus. by Jennifer Dewey; *Between Cattails* (New York: Scribners, 1985), illus. by Peter Parnall.

NONFICTION

Pieces of White Shell: A Journey to Navajoland (New York: Scribners, 1984), illus. by Clifford Brycelea.

ESSAYS AND STORY COLLECTIONS

Coyote's Canyon (Salt Lake City: Peregrine Smith, 1989), photographs by John Telford; *An Unspoken Hunger: Stories from the Field* (New York: Pantheon, 1994); *Desert Quartet: An Erotic Landscape* (New York: Pantheon, 1995), illus. by Mary Frank.

POETRY

Earthly Messengers (Salt Lake City: Western Slope, 1989), limited ed. of 150 copies handbound on handmade paper.

EDITED WORK

Great and Peculiar Beauty: A Utah Reader, ed. by Terry Tempest Williams and Thomas J. Lyon (Salt Lake City: Peregrine Smith, 1995).

MEMOIR

Refuge: An Unnatural History of Family and Place (New York: Pantheon, 1991).

SELECTED ESSAYS

"A Naturalist's Notebook," in *Desert News* (Salt Lake City), weekly column, 1984–1986; "A Full Moon in May," in *Wendell Berry*, ed. by Paul Merchant (Lewiston, Idaho: Confluence, 1991); "A Love That Is Wild," in *Northern Lights* 8, no. 1 (winter 1992); "The Spirit of Rachel Carson," in *Audubon* (July/August 1992); review of *The Moon by Whale Light* by Diane Ackerman, in *Orion* 11, no. 4 (autumn 1992); "A 'Downwinder' in Hiroshima," in *Nation* (15 May 1995).

AUDIO AND VIDEO RECORDINGS

"The Canyon's Edge" (Moab, Utah: Canyonlands Field Inst., 1988), narration for multimedia presentation; *Coyote's Canyon* (Audio Press, 1990), 2 cassettes, selections from *Pieces of White Shell* and *Coyote's Canyon* read by Terry Tempest Williams; *Land of Little Rain* by Mary Austin (Audio Press, 1992), 2 cassettes, read by Terry Tempest Williams; *A Desert Sea* (Salt Lake City: KUED Television, 1993), narration for video documentary, distrib. by the Univ. of Utah Press; *Refuge* (Audio Press, 1993), 2 cassettes, read by Terry Tempest Williams.

INTERVIEWS

Edward Lueders, ed., "Dialogue Two: Landscape, People, and Place," in *Writing Natural History: Dialogues with Authors* (Salt Lake City: Univ. of Utah Press, 1989); David Petersen, "Memory Is the Only Way Home: A Conversational Interview with Terry Tempest Williams," in *Bloomsbury Review* 11, no. 8 (December 1991); David L. Brown, producer, *Bound by the Wind* (Energon Films, 1993), video documentary, distrib. by the Video Project, 5332 College Avenue, Suite 101, Oakland, Calif. 94618; Mickey Pearlman, "Terry Tempest Williams," in *Listen to Their Voices: Twenty Interviews with Women Who Write* (New York: Norton, 1993).

BIOGRAPHICAL AND CRITICAL STUDIES

ARTICLES

James N. Baker, "Rhinos and Desert Bombs," in *Newsweek* (2 May 1994), review of *An Unspoken Hunger*; James N. Baker, John Taliaferro, and Patricia King, "Who's Who: 20 for the Future," in *Newsweek* (30 September 1991); Marilyn R. Chandler, "Unnatural Disasters," in *Women's Review of Books* (March 1992), review of *Refuge*; Nancy Bray Cardozo, "Clan of the One-Breasted Women," in *Audubon* (January/February 1992), review of *Refuge*; Grace Lichtenstein, "Consolations of Nature," in *Washington Post Book World* (29 September 1991), review of *Refuge*; Thomas J. Lyon, "Reviews," in *Sierra* (September/October 1991), review of *Refuge*; John Hanson Mitchell, "Mother Earth," in *New York Times Book Review* (4 September 1994), review of *An Unspoken Hunger*; Melissa Stanton, "Terry Tempest Williams: Chronicler," in *Life* (5 April 1993); Rhoda Yerburgh, review of *Pieces of White Shell*, in *Library Journal* (15 November 1984); Susan Zwinger, review of *Refuge*, in *Orion* 11 (summer 1992).

ANN ZWINGER
(b. 1925)

PETER WILD

FOR SOME TENSE minutes as she paddles along, the noise from around the bends in the river ahead keeps getting louder. She paddles more slowly, more carefully, having been warned about the canoe-crunching rapids. All at once, before there's enough time to react as she desperately tries to line up her canoe with the speeding current, the river before her simply disappears—and Ann Zwinger shoots over a waterfall, out of control, past boulders and through a crazed, thrashing chaos of icy water. Luck is with her. "Fortunately we are lined up right with the tongue. As the canoe shoots through I take a deep breath, sure I am going out and under. The bow points straight down. Water pours in. The canoe stabilizes in the calm water just beyond. Awash and amazed, we look back . . . " (*Run, River, Run*, pp. 137–138).

Memorably described as such unnerving moments can be in Ann Zwinger's works, they are more the adrenaline thrills of dramatic relief than the essence of her writing. Closer to the heart of Zwinger are the contemplative moments, the fruits of quiet observation, the "mature cell of a thunderhead [that] cauliflowers up" (p. 216) or the drops of water dripping off the tip of her paddle that "spatter into pinheads, skittering across the surface like motes of mercury" (p. 45). As she glides farther down the Green River, she sees "an orange butterfly . . . imprinted like a triangle of orange tissue paper" on a boulder (p. 21). Sliding still farther, through the remoteness of southwestern Wyoming, Zwinger looks down through the water to the pebbles on the bottom. Patched with green algae, they look "like old Indian-head pennies" (p. 49). As will be seen, however, even such delicate and striking descriptions rendering the physical world into prose are not at the core of Zwinger's intentions.

Zwinger prefers that critical emphasis be placed on her writing rather than on her personality. Despite her modesty and self-effacement, however, the link between her work and the person behind it is clear. Zwinger has lived what she has called a "traditional life" (Rea, p. 33); that life, however, has provided the security for the psychic (and in Zwinger's case, the physical) risk-taking in the act of creation that every writer must chance if she is to be remembered for the singleness of her vision.

Early Life

Ann Zwinger was born Ann Haymond in Muncie, Indiana, on 12 March 1925. As a child, although she did her share of exploring the countryside, she never felt completely "at home" in the nearby woods. In fact, she jokes, at the time "my greatest literary creations were trying to persuade my mother to bring me home from camp . . ." (Rea, p. 32). Nonetheless, she was from early years sensitive to the world about her. She remembers her usually mild father, William Thomas Haymond, fuming when a crew appeared one day and in an abortive effort at flood control cut down the trees along a nearby river; in addition to that first lesson in ecological awareness, her father (an attorney) also passed on to his daughter a meticulousness that characterizes her work, a trait she also ascribes to her myopia and her consequent fascination with detail. Picking up on this early on, her mother, Helen Glass Haymond, encouraged her daughter's interest in art.

Indeed, Zwinger devoted much of her youth and early adulthood to the pursuit of such a career. In 1946 she received her bachelor of arts degree (with honors) in art history from Wellesley College and in 1950 her master of arts degree in the same field from Indiana University. Thereafter, she did Ph.D. work at Radcliffe, and she has been an instructor of art at various institutions, including Indiana University and Smith College. From this background emerges a related characteristic of her work, the urge to teach, to point out to her readers what they otherwise would not see. In 1952, Ann Haymond married Herman Zwinger, an Air Force pilot. They raised three daughters and, a buoyant military family, made the most of periodic moves necessitated by Herman's service. They enjoyed the "Florida ocean, an Arkansas farm, the big city and the small town, the bests of many worlds" (*Beyond the Aspen Grove*, p. 7).

Beyond the Aspen Grove

When Herman Zwinger retired, the couple settled in Colorado Springs, at the base of the Rocky Mountains and with the dramatic cordillera in full view. The move foreshadowed an unexpected change. Spacious Colorado held out the openness the couple wanted, both for themselves and for their children. As part of the new freedom, the Zwingers bought forty remote forested acres with a lake up in the pines and set about building an idyllic summer home while pausing to watch the ducks, moose, and other abundant wildlife. One day Marie Rodell, the literary agent of a friend, visited Colorado Springs and asked to see the mountains. A serendipitous moment that earnest writers daydream about but rarely experience was about to happen: obliging Zwinger took the agent up to the summer place, and in the course of the pleasant day of wandering, Rodell asked Zwinger, "Why don't you do a book on Colorado ecology?" (*Beyond the Aspen Grove*, p. ii). Zwinger laughed at the idea. Until then, the housewife had continued her drawing for her own enjoyment, but she had done little serious writing. Eventually, however, she decided to give the idea a try, and she naively sent off a brief outline and two pages of her writing. Astoundingly, on that slight basis, Random House offered a contract. Nine months later, Zwinger, then in her midforties, completed the manuscript of her first book, *Beyond the Aspen Grove* (1970).

With more than a dozen books now to her credit, Zwinger may look back with a certain amused chagrin at *Beyond the Aspen Grove*. "I was a Johnny-come lately . . . to nature writing," she reflects in "Writers of the Purple Figwort" (p. 143), and her first book clearly bears signs of a writing voice searching for its tenor as well as indications of its mature potential. Showing some of the nervous chatter of the beginner starting at the obvious place, the opening chapter introduces readers to the Zwinger family, its background, and its way of living at Constant Friendship, the name the Zwingers gave to their summer refuge. In later pages we see such as the antics of Mad Ludwig, the resident muskrat. This is an approach with popular appeal, establishing a vicarious link with readers, but it hardly rings with Zwinger's later sophistication.

A stream crossing the property predictably chatters, and a weak passive voice sometimes shows the hand of a writer still in the process of learning her craft. Lifting a piece of old wood from the ground and accidentally disturbing an ant colony, Zwinger muses:

Such Lilliputian activity seemed to be very proper in the Persian miniature world, where moths nuzzle columbine, hummingbirds sip of scarlet gilia, and small children believe that fairies dance on midsummer's eve. After all, the circles of gray-green lichen on the rocks mark where a fairy tripped and spilled a bucket of moonbeams. (p. 267)

Despite such peccadilloes, Zwinger was a quick learner, and what truly impresses is how swiftly she left the occasional patches of dangerously precious writing well behind her and concentrated instead on her strengths. *Beyond the Aspen Grove* bears signs of this future promise.

As is true to one degree or another of almost all her works, Zwinger uses a fairly simple organization, the book as an account of exploration. Thus, the various chapters of *Beyond the Aspen Grove* take us on an investigative tour of Constant Friendship, its lake, meadows, forest. At each stop, Zwinger pauses to point out the natural history, both of the general picture before us and its minute detail. Through brief lessons in geology, her sweep takes in the ancient making of the place, and, more immediately, she tells why certain trees, and not others, grow in the forest. Thus armed to understand the context, the reader is ready to appreciate—and at times be amazed at—how the details of nature fit into the larger scheme. Exploring the lake, Zwinger notes the delicate conditions of temperature and water quality necessary to maintain trout and comments that every pound of the fish eaten has its origin in about one thousand pounds of algae consumed by the trout. Or later, taking us along a stream, she focuses our seeing on the remarkably complex eye of the dragonfly, containing twenty-eight thousand facets and capable of seeing twelve to fifteen feet.

Zwinger's alternately lengthening and shortening scope varies the pace of the writing, and it also takes in the human history of Constant Friendship. Briefly Zwinger describes the past mining activity in the mountains and the difficulties of obtaining an accurate survey of the steep terrain. Zwinger is a passionate and intelligent person who lives intimately with the land. She knows it both firsthand and through extensive research, a convincing overall effect of her

book. Her purpose, both as a person and as a writer, is to understand her mountain world, to understand the "land's total pattern of existence" (p. 9). By the end of the work readers, having gained such intimacy, feel they have become familiars of the place.

Expanding a Literary Territory

Some of the elements of Zwinger's writing style evolve, others change radically: gone will be hummingbirds that sip and small children believing in fairies—replaced by frogs that simmer an evening background noise (*Run, River, Run*) and a beaver in quiet water that "sleeks along downstream" ("The Flip Side of River Travel," p. 14). Other word choices similarly become more sophisticated, at once surprising and demanding of her readers' intelligence, yet aesthetically appropriate in risks, resulting in an airy rightness.

If Zwinger is a controlled writer, she also knows when to throw restraint to the winds in daring choices. Walking through thick woods back from a loud river, she notices that its roar "is reduced to wistfulness" (*Run, River, Run*, p. 25). She doesn't hesitate, either, to challenge her readers by making references to literature and art. Struggling to set up his camera on a steep slope, Herman finally succeeds, helped along by a "Chaucerian vocabulary" ("The Day Before Spring," p. 19). Preternatural cliffs looming in shadow remind her of the operatic setting for Richard Wagner's *Der fliegende Holländer*, while the delicate reflections in placid water echo those in a Pierre-Auguste Renoir canvas. Topping the challenge of such references and catching the changing seasons, "In spring, violets make a Botticelli carpet" (p. 177)—ah, just so. It may take a moment to realize the trick. The reference is to the Italian painter's delightful *Primavera*. The completion of the image takes place in the reader's mind, not on the page—a superb accomplishment. And if readers don't happen to know the painting, that's their own misfortune.

991

Guides hardly come without personalities, though the Zwinger persona in *Beyond the Aspen Grove* is fairly translucent. Here, she's an instructor, a gentle, capable, and motherly type. Throughout her books Zwinger continues the guiding role, but her personality will change somewhat. Zwinger stays at the edge of the natural scenes under consideration, but her character becomes more complex and pronounced. Whether or not owing to the urgings of editors pushing their writers to massage readers along by developing identifiable personalities — an idea Zwinger resists — she will become more developed and colorful, and admirably even-tempered schoolmarm who nonetheless shows that in moments she, too, is capable of mood swings into fear, awe, and disgust. She even has her cranky days. Then she can be sarcastic, if often about her own foibles.

As for Constant Friendship and the cold waters of the lake, relished by some, she describes herself inching into the chill depths, "protesting, shivering," one of the "vocal people who share their suffering with those who still wait" (*Beyond the Aspen Grove*, p. 23). That's a pretty light touch. Later, however, mocking people around her, she can show her shirty side. Pausing for lunch on a hot day of hiking, Zwinger turns up her nose at food, at her cheese that "has reached the consistency of putty" and salami that tastes like "grout." Weary and in no good mood, she then turns an acid eye on those less-restrained souls about her who didn't bring enough to eat. After ransacking their own packs, they glance over at her untouched food and "make clutching sounds of unsatisfied hunger" (*Wind in the Rock*, 1978, p. 153). After the gentle, teatime grace of *Beyond the Aspen Grove*, Zwinger will have the confidence to reveal herself not only with gentle sarcasm but also in moments of passion, of genuine, high-voltage ecstasy. Nonetheless, though Zwinger comes more to the fore, her main focus continues to be on nature. The raftsmen and ranchers and other people who drift through her pages — again perhaps at an editor's behest — will remain largely incidental and undeveloped, attendant accidents as her explorations unfold.

Yet other features of Zwinger's work change into a richer complexity. As in *Beyond the Aspen Grove*, Zwinger's drawings continue to illustrate her books and articles, as does, less often, the photographic work of her husband. Because her subject is nature, and as a teacher Zwinger wants to equip readers for further discoveries on their own, her books come with an apparatus, variously consisting of glossary, bibliography, index, notes. Taken together, the aesthetic features and the science undergirding it lead to Zwinger's ultimate goal, lying beyond everyday wonder and intelligent perception, yet the consequential reward of both, the freeing wonder of nature. She embodies this wonder in a moment when, alone, afraid of heights, she claws "nearly nauseated with fear" across a high ledge. Then she stands before a great cliff:

> To me there is an enchantment in these dry canyons that once roared with water and still sometimes do, that absorbed the voices of those who came before, something of massive dignity about sandstone beds that tell of a past long before human breathing, that bear the patterns of ancient winds and water in their crossbeddings. (*Wind in the Rock*, p. 7)

Her lesson is clear. The greatest moments of ecstasy need to be earned, both physically and psychically. Her books may thrill her readers vicariously, but they are merely renditions of the far more valuable thing itself, Zwinger's own experience. Thus, though secondhand to the events, her books ring with the intensity of their first cause.

In book after book Ann Zwinger rambles with intense seeing through the wilderness of the Southwest, her happy raison d'être, introducing readers to the region's history and natural wonders. Talent rarely feels comfortable confined to a groove, however; one feature of creative writers is their active plasticity, their compulsion to explore new literary territory, to stretch out and exercise themselves by trying new styles, approaches, and subjects. Yet in practical terms, both publishers and literary agents make money by selling books. On the one hand, publishers

992

and agents know the value of their authors' establishing a comfortable predictability with the book-buying public. But predictability also can become deadening. At a certain indefinable point, a writer's following will fade, and along with it the sales of her books, if volume after volume seems dipped out of the same literary barrel. A good publisher, along with a good agent, will allow a promising writer a certain leeway in the balancing act between the value of the familiar and the appeal of novelty, hoping that if one book doesn't sell, others will compensate for the loss by turning a profit over the long run.

Although in Zwinger's case the details of such shifting dynamics are not known, *Beyond the Aspen Grove* apparently sold well. Her first book caught the swing of the environmental movement and the public's renewed enthusiasm for the outdoors as a balm for the stresses of civilization. As depicted, the Zwinger family, seemingly "at one with nature" in their intriguing wilderness hideaway, no doubt appealed to a jangled, urbanized public as enjoying an ideal situation. Reviewers applauded the book, and Zwinger received many appreciative letters from her audience. In purely marketing terms, a repeat performance would have seemed in order for her second volume.

A Scholarly Absorption

Her next work, however, coauthored with Beatrice E. Willard, didn't follow suit. A tome of nearly five hundred pages, *Land Above the Trees* (1972) explores the natural history of the regions above timberline, those remote, rarely visited lands of rock and snow and intensely adapted plants found on the highest peaks of the United States. *Land Above the Trees* assembled such information in one place for the first time, with diagrams and hundreds of Zwinger's drawings of plant specimens and with a long appendix of scientific information. The hefty volume is quite thoroughly a scientific text, and it certainly illustrates the admirable scientific interest and fix-

ation on detail underlying Zwinger's popular works, though it is hardly a book designed to catch a fickle public's imagination.

Other of her works also reflect the scholarly bent. In fact, Zwinger claims to enjoy her research far more than the drudgery of converting her original excitements into the pages appearing between hard covers. In an ideal world she would gladly divide her time between scouring books for the scientific underpinnings of nature and then marveling at the real thing on her strolls. Looking forward to doing a volume on the natural history of the Grand Canyon, she elates: "The research will be marvelous and compelling to do — to me, research is what books are all about." As to the step after that, she quips, "Writing is for peasants" (Rea, p. 35).

In line with her enthusiasm for the dusty alcoves of scientific history is an article coauthored with librarian Julie Jones-Eddy, "In-House Preservation of Early U.S. Government Maps." A technical piece with an important message, the article tells how to humidify the desiccated charts drawn by nineteenth-century explorers now crumbling in archives. Then, step by step Zwinger tells how to preserve them for the use of future generations. Once again, such precision shows the depth of knowledge Zwinger draws upon to create her popular writing. Related to this virtue are two edited volumes, *John Xántus: The Fort Tejon Letters, 1857–1859* (1986) and *Xántus: The Letters of John Xántus to Spencer Fullerton Baird from San Francisco and Cabo San Lucas, 1859–1861* (1986). Concerning an obscure naturalist of the last century, the companion books are all but guaranteed not to sell to a wide market. Historians both amateur and professional, however, will clap their hands at Zwinger's having brought to light valuable manuscripts that have lain ignored for years.

Zwinger's work on Xántus illustrates another aspect of her personality: her own vicarious pleasure. Xántus was a rapscallion on the run from the Hungarian army who lied his way into the halls of science. As a collector, he nonetheless did invaluable work, laboring in the bleak and remote desert of Baja, California. Groan though he might over the world's lack of appreciation for his genius, he sent barrel after barrel of plant and animal specimens back to the Smithsonian Institution in Washington, D.C. This pathological liar and misfit was about as different from Zwinger as a personality could be. Yet Zwinger was "enthralled to see what an irascible, flamboyant, difficult, abrasive man emerged" from her research (Rea, p. 27). If there's any truth to the old saw about the attraction of opposites, one begins to understand Zwinger's vicarious pleasure in her enthusiasm for Xántus' antics.

The bulk of Zwinger's magazine articles show a relationship close to her writing as found in the core of her books. As with the books, her articles are spun off from her wandering motif, but she clearly adjusts such shorter pieces to fit purposes not necessarily emphasized overtly in her books. For *Audubon*, the publication for the environmentally concerned members of the National Audubon Society, she wrote "The Eagle's Fate and Mine Are One." In this long piece, Zwinger visits a refuge for golden eagles, red-tailed hawks, and other raptors in a canyon of Idaho's Snake River. Hiking through a desert refuge as "godforsaken as it is gorgeous" (p. 58), Zwinger investigates the health of this delicate, arid-land ecosystem.

With her sharp reporter's eye she evaluates the Bureau of Land Management's stewardship of the refuge. Then she goes on to alert her readers to the ranchers, the gun-toting public, and revelers on off-road vehicles threatening the preserve. An investigation piece of admirable thoroughness, again in line with the magazine's purpose, here Zwinger's writing is designed both to increase appreciation of nature and through that appreciation to arouse her audience to more active support for the good cause of preservation. In the course of things, Zwinger reveals an unusual heat contributing to the effectiveness of her writing. The article runs a grim photograph of dead animals slung over a barbed-wire fence, slaughtered by teenagers out on a shooting spree. Commenting on the lenience of local judges, who casually levy low fines for such "minor" offenses, Zwinger seethes: "I find myself think-ing more in terms of stringing up by the thumbs over a fire ant nest than an insignificant monetary fine" (p. 76).

The revelatory outbursts are rare in Zwinger. When it comes to conservation issues, however burning, the well-bred writer is not one to rally the troops and lead a charge to the barricades, though she admits a little guiltily that she admires those who do. Accepting her scholarly absorption, she concedes, "I'm not a very activist person" (Rea, p. 28). In an astute comparison she makes between heself and another popular Southwestern writer, the pyrotechnic, monkey-wrenching Edward Abbey, Zwinger faces the reality of their differences:

Ed Abbey is an absolutely superb writer, a legend in his own time, the quintessential curmudgeon. He is such a versatile writer, with a marvelous gift of irony, akin to Swift's "Modest Proposal," and I think that's one thing that really sets him apart. He says he's not a nature writer (which is what I am, pure and simple) and he's probably right. Still, when he writes about nature there's nobody better. I suspect that the fierceness in our point of view may be much the same, we just go about it differently. If I could write like Ed Abbey I'd die happy, but I can't. I'm me — he writes like Ed Abbey and I write like Ann Zwinger. I respect what he does and I hope he respects what I do. (pp. 29–30)

That doesn't mean she isn't effective in her own way. She prefers the less aggressive role of the teacher showing people how to see nature more appreciatively in the hope that they'll respond by respecting what they now admire. Recalling her encounter with a woman exhilarated by her mindless, sand-splashing, and environmentally destructive ride in a dune buggy, Zwinger ponders how to "get her to see the beauty *without* the dune buggy" (Rea, p. 28). Noting that "courtesy goes a lot farther in getting a point across than dogmatic confrontation," she expands on her own attitudes about reforms, attitudes reflecting, as she herself hints, perhaps too sanguine a faith in human nature:

Ann Zwinger

ful and challenging teacher with an imagination sometimes swinging off toward the surreal; she's devoted to her profession and through a combination of pedagogical allures and dares, has the best interests of her students at heart as she encourages them to stretch their mental legs. This attitude certainly applies to her mainline articles. Another one for *Audubon*, "The Day Before Spring," takes readers wandering into the Rocky Mountains on an "elusive, contrary, quixotic" day when winter has not yet ended, though spring is about to begin. A cheery piece, it pokes fun at husbands who grow impatient at "dawdling wives who poke under every knot of dead leaves" (p. 14). Down on her knees, Zwinger delights at a tiny clover leaf, "brilliantly green," and crossing the still-frozen lake to her cabin notes that the ice cracks underfoot "like an old screen door banging" (p. 15). Such relaxed and graciously entertaining pieces also can instruct. In "The Art of Wandering," she says that idling through nature "is, on the surface, frittering away one's time" (p. 6). It can be a deeply productive frittering, however. It takes us away from the worst of the world and brings us to the best of ourselves. During her rambles, she feels intense serenity, a heightened sense of being as she drifts in the alpha state, opened to the surprises of nature's constantly changing pleasures. "The hours when the mind is absorbed by beauty are the only hours when we really live," she wisely reminds us (p. 9).

The chain of principles upon which I operate are simple—or, if you will, simplistic. If you can entice someone to look at a facet of nature they may get curious. If they get curious they may make an attempt to learn something about what they're seeing. If they learn something, that becomes an irrevocable part of their experience. If it becomes part of your experience you are more likely to appreciate and enjoy it. If you appreciate and enjoy, you're less likely to destroy. It becomes "yours" in the *only* way anything can be owned—in your head. And at the very best, you come to have an understanding of the worth and intricacy of the natural world and man's place in it. ("Writers of the Purple Figwort," p. 150)

In the main, then, Zwinger's words give the impression of a somewhat flinty-edged, yet hope-

The Essential Zwinger

Such a discussion leads to two central and related issues. Which Zwinger books form the core of her work? And in literary terms, how does Zwinger stand out from the abundance of contemporary nature writers to make her particular contribution? Understandably, most writers would like to think of their last book as the best and to expect their next book will be better still. It is the thrill of such a pursuit that keeps them chained to their desks. Thus, to single out a work, or a cluster of works, in a person's oeuvre as typical may be thought something of an insult. Despite this, many nature writers are rightly associated with certain locations. Although they traveled widely for their day, when we think of Mary Austin, we think of her musing as she roams the deserts of southern California; of John Muir, his exhilarated rompings across the Sierra Nevada, his self-celebrated "Range of Light"; of Henry David Thoreau, his intimate absorption over decades with the gentle woods around the village of Concord, Massachusetts. For some nature writers, then, place is all-important. And often, though not always, they do their best work in their locales because psychically they feel "at home." They perceive a deep and sympathetic bond between their chosen stomping grounds and what they consider the depths of their innermost selves.

Place, then, becomes a major identifying marker. Added to the theme of intelligent, sensitive wandering, this is true of Zwinger. She not only was a Johnny-come-lately to nature writing, she also was a Johnny-come-lately to the Southwest. The two coincided, and the bond with the region is so great that she says she "can imagine living nowhere else" ("Writers of the Purple Figwort," p. 143). Her books reflect the fascination. Of her fourteen titles, all but *Land Above the Trees* and *A Conscious Stillness* (1982), a book written with Edwin Way Teale about canoeing in Massachusetts, concentrate on that region. For instance, the two Xántus books, though atypically works of editing letters, nonetheless bring one of the Southwest's historical figures to light. Of the twelve, nine are accounts of Zwinger's avid travels through the region. Here, her method is pretty much the same: Zwinger, the keen and kindly docent, takes us along on explorations of her adopted homeland.

Such an approach could easily wear thin, yet the Southwest is so large and its landscape varies so widely—ranging from fourteen-thousand-foot peaks to deserts below sea level, from sand dunes running into the sea to vast forests with lions and bears—that her prose, catching the excitements of such changes, soars above cliché. Zwinger seizes the advantage of a landscape that encourages different physical approaches, resulting in varied literary renditions. One Zwinger book may take readers racing down the length of a river through desert labyrinths, another meditatively hiking through the isolated canyons dotted with Indian ruins in rarely visited southeastern Utah. In such ways, each Zwinger book has what Ezra Pound said all good writing must have, a sense of newness.

A closer look at these "core" books in the larger body of Zwinger's works bears this out. After the promising incipiency of *Beyond the Aspen Grove*'s gentle and revealing tour of nature around Constant Friendship and the impressive grasp of science found in most of her work but especially revealed in *Land Above the Trees*, her *Run, River, Run* (1975) combined the two in a tone and method that established the main direction of her work. From here on out, Zwinger's writing would admirably fulfill the Latin exhortation to be sweet and useful: her books would be gracious and entertaining guides that also brooked no nonsense when it came to knowledge of the particular landscape being explored. With the prize-winning *Run, River, Run*, recipient of the John Burroughs Medal, Zwinger trimmed her sails and set her course.

Run, River, Run

In the spring of 1869, the nation had held its breath as one-armed John Wesley Powell paddled off down the Colorado River toward the unknown labyrinths of the Grand Canyon. Naysayers shook their heads at the folly, predicting that he and his small crew would meet their end sailing over giant waterfalls believed to be roaring in the unseen bowels of the earth. When Powell emerged from the dark maws of the Great Chasm a hundred days later, he became a national hero, the first man in recorded history to survive the maddened waters of the Grand Canyon.

For roughly a century after, few men cared to risk duplicating Powell's exhilarating feat. The industrialized tourism of the late twentieth century, however, tends to depreciate his brave accomplishment. Technical knowledge of the river and vastly improved equipment have made the trip relatively safe. Each year people by the thousands, watched over by experienced and duly licensed boatmen, speed down the West's rivers in relative safety. In fact, "running" the West's whitewater rivers has become almost de rigueur for modern celebrants of the outdoors with enough money to take such tours. In literary terms, this creates a dilemma. Hundreds of travel books have been written on the subject. The writer of yet another faces a dual problem. Such a book almost by necessity must follow a standard organization, the physical progress of the trip. But what can a writer say that hasn't been said many times before about the thrills of plunging through watery haystacks and the adrenaline rush of being sucked by tons of rushing water between menacing boulders?

Zwinger solves the problem in several deft ways. She writes not about the popular Colorado but about a tributary, the Green River. Rising in southwestern Wyoming and twisting through varied landscapes to meet the Colorado in southeastern Utah, the Green at the time was not as widely known to the public as it is today. Furthermore, though there are heart-in-the-mouth episodes aplenty in the book's pages, this is not a usual rendition focusing mainly on the excitements of a watery roller-coaster ride through the wilderness. Respecting both her readers and the land, Zwinger sets out to do far more. She begins her book where the river itself begins, as a stream seeping from a glacier high in Wyoming's Wind River Range. From there, she takes us the full length of the watercourse. As the Green twists through three states, Zwinger not only explores the river but reveals its lore along the way, the peoples both ancient and modern forming its history, its plants, animals, and geology. What we get, then, is both emotionally and intellectually comprehensive, an instructive yet intimate portrait rather than a fast tour, and beyond that, as the book successfully risks the clichéd feelings about nature, a convincing sense of a woman blessedly, if momentarily, "at one" with the land. In overview, *Run, River, Run* is an act of engagement. "The river," says Zwinger, "becomes a way of thinking" (p. 100)—a state-

ment, it turns out, that applies equally to the book deriving from it.

Even though up until publication of *Run, River, Run*, the Green had not received such full treatment, it would be glib to suppose that the novelty of the material was the book's main selling point. It is said that there is no such thing as a boring person, and likewise there is no such thing as a vapid landscape. But just as it takes a skilled writer to turn her raw material, people, into a forceful novel, it takes an alert mind and a special talent to transform the story of a place into a book compellingly followed by readers. After all, once the Green sluices out of the high mountains, it twists and carves its way through what appears to be unmitigated desert. The scenery, with its sheer canyons, can be dramatic enough in places, but to the unpracticed eye it is largely repetitive, one desert scene after another. Zwinger counters this problem by picking up on both the area's subtleties and its unsuspected background, and her prose swings back and forth from large panoramas to specific details.

As it happened, for example, the region was a favorite haunt of mountain men. Around the 1830s, the white adventurers forged into a new country, lured by the values of pelts, to be shipped back east, from the beaver along the streams. Zwinger fills in the historical background of the trade, noting that the new fashion in gentlemen's beaver hats back East and in Europe kept driving up the price of pelts, then livening up the history by telling a hair-raising story or two about escapes from Indians. In discussing an individual trapper's gear of Hawken rifle, lead, and knife, she pauses on the particular kind of knife the mountain man was likely to carry. An all-purpose tool in the wilderness, it was known as a Green River knife. And here we're in for the kind of small surprise that delights the scholarly minded. An expression of the day, "up to Green River," derived from the act of plunging the knife in deeply, up to its trademark on the blade. From that the meaning of the expression expanded: it referred to doing something thoroughly, as we might say, "up to the hilt." That trademark had "Green River" stamped into the steel, but the words referred not to the location of the knife's popular use but to its maker, a company in Green River, Massachusetts. The mini-lecture presents just one of the many ironies, one of the many memorable twists and turns, throughout a book that becomes a record of surprises, whether about the river's peculiar history or about its rare beauty.

In a similar vein, but on an entirely different topic, as the course of her trip proceeds Zwinger pauses after lush descriptive passages of the land formations to feed in the geological events—the rising of mountains over millions of years and the sediments depositing in vast lakes over eons—responsible for the specific scene presently before our eyes. Typically, her information is backed up by notes at the end of the book referring the interested to further reading. Typically, too, Zwinger doesn't ignore the immediate details. Taking a break to stretch her legs and explore Kendall Warm Springs, back from the river a quarter of a mile, she explains why the water bubbling out among rocks is warm. Delving into chemistry, she tells why its calcium content supports stonewort, a large alga, along with other plants and animals not abundant elsewhere in the area (p. 48). And careening around a bend, she explains the physics of stream dynamics, why the river's fast current cuts a bank on the outer curve of a bend, while leaving a deposit of silt on the inner curve, where the water runs more slowly (pp. 57–59, 90).

In control of her prose and aware of her readership's needs, Zwinger varies the pace. She realizes that *Run, River, Run* is not *Land Above the Trees*; it is not a textbook. Teacher though she is at heart, she knows what all good teachers know, that she must vary her tone and the approach to her subject or risk losing her audience. Thus she keeps bringing her account back to the river and waking her audience up as her craft speeds into the dangerous challenge of yet another cauldron of boulders and thrashing water. In such ways, her pages sway between contemplative instruction and physical excitements.

She alters the pace in a number of other ways so appropriate to her story that there's hardly a jolt in the change. Meanwhile, she mixes in, variously, elements of humor, pathos, and the transport of sheer beauty. Zwinger followed the length of the Green not on one extended excursion but through several trips over the years. Different people accompanied her, and this allows their injection into the story, the diversion of the human element. At one point, a rare opportunity appears; La Barge, a small town with a café, offers the chance to take a break from the river fare, and here Zwinger creates a warm vignette of the local, friendly people. The passage ends when the café owner says good-bye, offering the canoeists both free candy bars and wishes for their good luck in surviving the notorious whirlpool ahead (*Run, River, Run*, p. 108).

The subtlety of Zwinger's humor is well represented in *Run, River, Run*. Her husband, Herman, accompanied her on one leg of the trip, and he brought along the irritants that come even with good marriages. At the end of one long, hot day on the river, the two start fussing about the choice of a campsite. Finally, Herman finds one acceptable. It turns out to be infested with mosquitoes. Worse, the wind starts blowing, a condition, as we've earlier seen, sure to put Zwinger on edge. But Herman doesn't seem to be aware of any problem:

> In the quieter layer of air near the ground the mosquitoes speckle my hands when I try to pound in a tent stake. Letting go to swat means starting all over again and recapturing the elusive tent loop; bedrock lies so close to the surface that the stakes will not hold by themselves. . . . It is dark by the time I get the tent secured, and the wind still blows and the mosquitoes still whine and I seriously question what I am doing here, and there is murder in my heart when Herman, freshly fortified with repellent and a generous drink, asks if the tent is ready for his sleeping bag. (p. 202)

Cranky people, however, don't make good teachers. Usually, Zwinger's humor either is gently or self-mocking. One hazard to canoeists on the Green is the barbed wire that ranchers have strung across the river. It's both hard to see and potentially decapitating:

When fence posts appear on either side of the river it pays to look carefully into the future. Accepted procedure is to hold the paddle up vertically in front of your face, letting the wire slide up the shaft as your head goes under. Being a craven coward, I simply get out of the canoe and crawl under on hands and knees, in a foot of water, following the same procedure that I would were I on land, enduring much ridicule. (p. 96)

Deceptively innocent on their surface, the words strike a nice balance between very real danger and comic relief.

Abandoned homesteads dot the length of the river. The stops to poke through the fallen walls and scattered equipment, the physical remains of ruined hopes, provide another parallel thread holding Zwinger's text together. They also offer Zwinger the opportunity to give another lesson, this time on the misunderstood West. Government-sponsored homesteading failed because it was based on a tragically flawed concept. The west was not at all the treasure house of agricultural abundance that hopeful congressmen back East liked to imagine. Instead, the region's aridity militated against settlement by crop-raising individuals on the small plots mandated by the Homestead Act. Farmers by the thousands wore their fingers to the nubs, failing despite their brave efforts as they avidly participated in the mass fantasy. Rummaging through the shambles left behind, Zwinger stops and captures the pathos in a detail: "At my feet shards of a blue bowl lie, convex sides up, pale sky blue." She remembers the human suffering as well as its historical perspective. Returning to the river and drifting off, she gives a backward glance. The cabin "does not seem abandoned, only waiting" (p. 224).

The essence of Zwinger's writing, however, lies beyond her able manipulation of readers through convincing literary theatrics as she takes them through a range of emotions. What is far more accomplished is that she achieves what novelist Joseph Conrad demanded of himself in his famous preface to *The Nigger of the "Narcissus"* (1897). "My task," he says, ". . . is,

before all, to make you *see*. That — and no more, and it is everything." The alchemy that leads to this is inenarrable, which makes the manifestation as striking as it is rare. It comes with a near passionless rightness, passionless because it has an aesthetic truth beyond the immediate individual self. Floating quietly through Horse Canyon, Zwinger gawks up at formidable cliffs soaring thirteen hundred feet as they loom above the river's course. Domed and notched and spired, they take on bizarre shapes. "Corteges of deformed animals cross the skyline, bawling who knows what brayings and barkings that are sheared away by the high wind" (p. 273). Later, as the landscape changes, she notes quite different cliffs, "pale peach, the color of the inside of a conch shell" (p. 278). Zwinger's best writing in all her books, whether she's climbing a peak in Mexico or watching the trembling green colors of aspen leaves in Colorado, is about the things of nature immediately before her, whatever the wider context provided. No doubt this is because such things of nature are themselves what most excite her; the act of seeing leads in turn to efforts toward understanding, both by Zwinger and her audience, of the entire matrix. This is the heart of Zwinger's contribution to nature writing.

An Old-Fashioned Naturalist

"I am a naturalist," says Zwinger ("The Art of Wandering," p. 6). She clarifies, "My focus is nature" (Rea, p. 25). The two statements seem axiomatic and unnecessary. Of course, naturalists are people who study nature. Nature writers are people who both study nature and write about it for a wide audience. In an earlier time, this hardly would bear saying. Clearly, Zwinger combines the two pursuits, studying and writing about the natural world while also supplying its human history. In light of a shift in emphasis taking place over the past century and a half, however, a shift becoming more accelerated in the past few decades, Zwinger's comments take on the radical cast of a confident writer bucking a popular fad.

Eighteenth-century naturalists went into the outdoors with a sense of excitement at discovering the secrets of nature. Under the influence of romanticism, with its emphasis on the self, however, writers excited about nature next became excited about their own reactions to it. In recent times, nature has become not the goal but rather a means of self-awareness; it has become but the convenient stage on which troubled people perform self-therapy as they try to resolve their problems. On the first page of his *Seeking Awareness in American Nature Writing*, Scott Slovic describes this change as exhibited in four well-known contemporaries: "Such writers as Annie Dillard, Edward Abbey, Wendell Berry, and Barry Lopez are not merely, or even primarily, analysts of nature," but rather are on quests of self-discovery. Many recent nature writers could be added to Slovic's list. Far from isolated, the circumstance reflects the larger phenomenon of the culture's present self-absorption (discussed by Robert N. Bellah et al. in *Habits of the Heart*).

One might praise the change as an expansion of nature writing or see the shift as a sign of the genre's degeneration. In any case, in literary terms there is a very real danger here. When the writer himself becomes his own focus, he has severely limited his subject, and to call such results "nature writing" is at best a questionable use of the term. Nonetheless, time and again one beholds the spectacle of writers gaining mountaintops or strolling through the woods, only to turn their backs on the scenes about them to reflect on the unresolved conflicts of their childhoods, the sad state of their marriages, and other personal concerns having little to do with the natural world about them. Expressing disappointment as a reader at the short shrift given to nature, Elaine Tietjen observes, for instance, that Annie Dillard's actual subject is not nature but rather the "unresolved experiences" (p. 108) of Dillard's "idiosyncratic life" (p. 106).

This Ann Zwinger adamantly refuses to do. She refuses to be trendy. To her, "naturalists find out about what goes on in the natural world through observation" ("The Art of Wandering," p. 6). Clearly she admires those naturalists of the past who put aside their personal problems as minor concerns by comparison to the greater excitements of the world before them ("A World of Infinite Variety"). In this regard she admires the precision of scientific illustrators of the last century: "Early scientific illustrators were unparalleled for their portrayals of details and their understanding of the natural world," she praises. "For a wonderful afternoon, spend it looking at the illustrations in the Pacific Railroad Surveys. They are of the highest quality—exquisite, precise, and informative" (p. 38). Following this tradition, Zwinger sees herself as an "old-fashioned naturalist in today's world" (p. 43). Ironically, then, as a traditionalist she has become a rebel in terms of current fads. She has chosen the more difficult path. It is easy, after all, to write about one's problems, but it takes a far keener talent to analyze the complex world of nature and teach readers to see it in new ways. Long after current fashions have gone their way, generations hence will doubtless continue to look beyond themselves to delight in seeing the natural world memorably through Ann Zwinger's eyes.

Selected Bibliography

WORKS OF ANN ZWINGER

BOOKS

Beyond the Aspen Grove (New York: Random House, 1970); *Land Above the Trees: A Guide to American Alpine Tundra* (New York: Harper & Row, 1972), with Beatrice E. Willard; *Run, River, Run: A Naturalist's Journey Down One of the Great Rivers of the West* (New York: Harper & Row, 1975); *Wind in the Rock: The Canyonlands of Southeastern Utah* (New York: Harper & Row, 1978); *A Conscious Stillness: Two Naturalists on Thoreau's Rivers* (New York: Harper & Row, 1982), with Edwin Way Teale; *A Desert Country Near the Sea: A Natural History of the Cape Region of Baja California* (New York: Harper & Row, 1983); *John Xántus: The Fort Tejon Letters, 1857–1859* (Tucson: Univ. of Arizona Press, 1986) and *Xántus: The Letters of John Xántus to Spencer Fullerton Baird from San Francisco and Cabo San Lucas, 1859–1861* (Los Angeles: Dawson's Book Shop, 1986), companion volumes ed. by Zwinger; *The Mysterious Lands: A Naturalist Explores the Four Great Deserts of the Southwest* (New York: Dutton, 1989).

ESSAYS AND ARTICLES

"The Day Before Spring," in *Audubon* 74, no. 3 (May 1972); "The Eagle's Fate and Mine Are One," in *Audubon* 79, no. 4 (July 1977); "The Flip Side of River Travel," in *Adventure Travel* 2, no. 1 (June 1979); "A'Aly Waipia," in *Audubon* 83, no. 3 (May 1981); "Becoming Mom to an Infant Word Processor," in *Smithsonian* 12, no. 11 (February 1982); "The Art of Wandering," in *Orion Nature Quarterly* 5, no. 1 (winter 1986); "A World of Infinite Variety," in *Antaeus* 57 (autumn 1986); "Drawing on Experience," in *Orion Nature Quarterly* 6, no. 1 (winter 1987); "Writers of the Purple Figwort," in *Old Southwest/New Southwest: Essays on a Region and Its Literature*, ed. by Judy Nolte Lensink (Tucson: Tucson Public Library, 1987); "In-House Preservation of Early U.S. Government Maps," in *Government Publications Review* 15 (January/February 1988), with Julie Jones-Eddy.

BIOGRAPHICAL AND CRITICAL STUDIES

Robert N. Bellah, *Habits of the Heart: Individualism and Commitment in American Life* (Berkeley: Univ. of California Press, 1985); Edward Lueder, ed., "Dialogue Three. Field Notes: The Literary Process," in *Writing Natural History: Dialogues with Authors* (Salt Lake City: Univ. of Utah Press, 1989); Paul W. Rea, "An Interview with Ann Zwinger," in *Western American Literature* 24 (May 1989); Scott Slovic, *Seeking Awareness in American Nature Writing* (Salt Lake City: Univ. of Utah Press, 1992); Elaine Tietjen, "Perceptions of Nature: Annie Dillard's *Pilgrim at Tinker Creek*," in *North Dakota Quarterly* 56, no. 3 (1988); Stephen Trimble, ed., "Ann Zwinger," in *Words from the Land: Encounters with Natural History Writing* (Salt Lake City: Gibbs M. Smith, 1988); Peter Wild, *Ann Zwinger* (Boise: Boise State Univ., 1993). Ann Zwinger appears in *Contemporary Authors*, new rev. ser. 13, ed. by Linda Metzger (Detroit: Gale, 1984).

AFRICAN AMERICANS, WRITING, AND NATURE

DAVID LIONEL SMITH

I am sure none of these things would ever have happened to me had I limited the subject matter of my poems to roses and moonlight. But, unfortunately, I was born poor—and colored—and almost all the prettiest roses I have seen have been in rich white people's yards—not in mine. That is why I cannot write exclusively about roses and moonlight—for sometimes in the moonlight my brothers see a fiery cross and a circle of Klansmen's hoods. Sometimes in the moonlight a dark body sways from a lynching tree—but for his funeral there are no roses. (Langston Hughes, *Good Morning, Revolution*, p. 143)

WHO ARE the black nature writers? Even the question sounds silly. Although African-American writers have not been oblivious to the beauties of the natural world and have sometimes invoked nature in their works, nature writing as a genre has been conspicuously absent from the world of African-American letters. The attitude voiced by Langston Hughes in the passage quoted—a somewhat high-handed dismissal of nature writing as effete and racially privileged, a white indulgence contrasted to black oppression—represents one extreme that not even Hughes could embrace with consistency. (Hughes's intention in this essay is to attack the ideology of nature writing, not to

dismiss nature. Many of his poems contain lovely descriptions of natural phenomena, but always, from his most famous poem, "The Negro Speaks of Rivers" [1920] on, he presented nature as a site of human activity, thereby rejecting "nature" as a distinct and separate category.) Yet there is an element of truth in Hughes's statement that makes it quite pertinent in helping us understand the curious absence of nature writing from the various genres of African-American literature. This absence is not merely coincidental. It follows inevitably from the hegemonic conceptions of "race" and "nature" in American culture.

"Nature" and "civilization" have commonly been understood in American culture as opposite, hierarchical concepts. Civilization is viewed as superior to or advanced beyond nature. For a complex set of historically specific reasons, the "Negro race" has been relegated traditionally to a "natural," "primitive," or "less advanced" position within this conceptual hierarchy. The conceptual hierarchy is not just a pattern of ideas, of course; it reflects quite accurately the relationships that our society has created and maintained through the fabrication of racial categories and the assignment of specific human beings to those categories. Thus, virtually by definition within our culture, whites are civilized and blacks are natural. Civilization is self-conscious and literate; nature is unreflective (or spontaneous) and nonverbal, if not mute. Given this underlying cultural predisposition, nature writing is an oxymoron, and black nature writing is doubly oxymoronic.

Apart from this theoretical problem, nature writing as a genre poses two obvious dilemmas for black writers. To write about nature is to invite the invidious associations of presumptive inferiority and backwardness that black writers as a class have been especially anxious to avoid. Furthermore, black nature writing is inherently dubious as a genre, because our culture has understood nature as that which has no voice (or literary voice) of its own and, thus, requires the intervention of the civilized to render its being into writing. The reality of black literacy, in other words, belies the ideology of black natural-ness. Black nature writing would render this anomaly of nature writing nature all the more explicit. Writers need not apprehend these ideo-logical problems explicitly in order to be disin-clined toward nature writing as a genre. Indeed, the implicit injunction against black nature writ-ing works much better if it remains at the level of common sense and is not subjected to self-conscious scrutiny. In other words, a given topic, such as nature, is not addressed because it does not seem worthy of consideration, and if it is considered, it produces a sensation of vague discomfort that dissuades one from pursuing it further. In this respect, the absence of black nature writing is integral to the common sense of our culture. (By "common sense" I mean to designate what Antonio Gramsci called the " 'folk-lore' of philosophy." This folklore is not an explicit ideology but rather the miscellaneous and invisible a priori assumptions that consti-tute the premises of premises. See "Critical Notes on an Attempt at a Popular Presentation of Marxism by Bukharin.")

In conjunction with the offensive entailments of being defined as folkish, undifferentiated, and natural, African-American writers have, on the other hand, inherited a distinctive social stand-point. Regardless of their personal orientations or preferences, their own legitimacy as writers is challenged by the hegemonic ideology of nature. This being the case, black writers have had both the motivation and the perspective to recognize the negative implications of the nature/culture dualism and to develop a conception of nature that is neither dismissive nor uncritically ro-mantic. In some instances this endeavor has resulted in a conception of nature that makes it integral, not oppositional, to the conscious self. Even so, presenting alternative views does not necessarily unsettle the dominant consensus.

Some of our best writers have addressed this invidious association of blacks and nature ex-plicitly—none more pointedly than Herman Melville in *Benito Cereno* (1855). This astonish-ing novella presents one of the most complex, densely compacted examinations of racial atti-tudes and racial constructions ever written by an American novelist. It is the story of a Yankee captain, Amasa Delano, who encounters a Span-ish ship in distress, the *San Dominick*, and boards it to offer assistance. He finds the Spanish captain, Benito Cereno, to be weak, distracted, and evasive, and the general situation aboard the *San Dominick* appears to him anarchistic, bewil-dering, and vaguely menacing. He blames the dismal situation on Cereno, whose weaknesses he perceives as manifestations of a dainty and effete Spanish racial character. He never realizes that the *San Dominick* is in fact caught up in a slave insurrection and that the rebellious Afri-cans are in control of the ship. Delano's rac-ism—along with a heavy dose of stupidity—prevents him from understanding the situation accurately. Ironically, this obtuseness saves his life.

A major factor in that racism is his chauvinist conviction that blacks are subhuman and there-fore incapable of complex behavior. As the nar-rator remarks: "Captain Delano took to negroes, not philanthropically, but genially, just as other men to Newfoundland dogs" (p. 279). He likes Negroes because he regards them as cute, child-ish, and entertaining. He takes an immediate liking to Babo—apparently Cereno's personal servant but actually the leader of the rebellion—because he perceives Babo's face as being "like a sheperd's dog," exhibiting "sorrow and affection . . . equally blended." The most egregious example of Delano's equating blacks with animals is his observation of a black woman nursing her baby,

> like a doe in the shade of a woodland rock. Sprawling at her lapped breasts, was her wide-awake fawn, stark naked, its black little body lifted from the deck, crosswise with its dam's; its hands, like two paws, clambering upon her; its mouth and nose ineffectually rooting to get at the mark; and meantime giving a vexatious half-grunt, blending with the composed snore of the negress. . . . There's naked nature, now; pure tenderness and love, thought Captain Delano, well pleased. (pp. 267–268)

Delano's mixing of metaphors is doubtless intended by Melville to comment unfavorably upon the quality of the captain's intelligence.

In the quoted passage, the baby begins as a fawn, but Delano compares its hands to paws, thus changing the analogy from deer, which have hooves, to some other animal—dogs, perhaps. Almost immediately he describes the baby as rooting and grunting, terms associated with pigs, and implicitly figures the mother's breasts as a patch of ground. In addition to garbling his metaphors, Delano makes incongruous comparisons—asserting, for example, that "most uncivilized women" are "unsophisticated as leopardesses; loving as doves" (p. 268). That Delano is deluded should be obvious. We eventually learn, for instance, that the women have been among the most murderous of the insurgents. Furthermore, Delano's resolute presumption that whites "by nature were the shrewder race" prevents him from comprehending the sinister designs that Babo conceals beneath his masquerade of servility. As Melville demonstrates, the dehumanizing equation of blacks with animals is not only despicable, it is dangerous.

Not surprisingly, black writers have been painfully aware of this common American tendency to depict African Americans as natural objects. Alice Walker's *Meridian* (1976) characterizes such narratives aptly as "those Southern epics about the relationship of the Southern white man to madness, and the closeness of the Southern black man to the land" (p. 176). The white man, in other words, is defined in terms of his mind, whereas the black man is associated with nature. Ishmael Reed's protagonist in *Flight to Canada* (1989), a fugitive slave named Raven Quickskill, makes a similar point, complaining: "Whitman desires to fuse with Nature, and here I am, involuntarily, the comrade of the inanimate, but not by choice. . . . I am property. I am a thing. I am in the same species as any other kind of property. We form a class, a family of things" (pp. 63–64). As Raven realized, being equated with animals and reduced to a commodity are two versions of the same dehumanization. Given the pervasiveness of this racist tendency, it should be easy to understand why black writers have not embraced nature writing. Indeed, black writers have often addressed nature in terms of their alienation from it.

This alienation has taken a variety of forms. African-American writers have often used conventional nature symbolism, although frequently with the intention of developing a dissenting view of the conventions. For example, Richard Wright, in his story "Big Boy Leaves Home," initially represents nature in Edenic terms, as a group of black boys cavort in youthful innocence. Soon, however, innocence and immersion in nature prove to be their downfall; a white woman stumbles upon them swimming nude. She panics when they emerge naked from the pond, and when her fiancé dashes to the rescue, a deadly fight ensues, resulting in the deaths of two black boys and the white man. The boys have no sexual designs on this woman, nor is she their temptress. Perhaps she is instead the serpent in their garden. Nature, in any case, turns out to be the site of their destruction rather than a place of refuge. Later in the story, nature is depicted as entirely sinister. For instance, Big Boy has to fight and kill a monstrous rattlesnake to secure his underground hiding place from a lynch mob. Subsequently, a dog attacks Big Boy in his den, and after a fierce struggle, Big Boy strangles the dog. Big Boy's salvation becomes possible when he leaves the country behind and hops a truck bound for Chicago.

This latter detail reflects another common form of alienation. Euro-American writers frequently spurn urban civilization and seek redemption in rural, or natural, environments. The common pattern in African-American writing is the exact opposite. For black people, farm life has often been associated with slavery, and folk culture with superstition and backwardness. These modes of life represent a closeness to nature that many black writers have preferred to shun. A familiar example of this tendency is the movement of Ralph Ellison's protagonist in *Invisible Man* (1952) from the rural South to New York. The protagonist associates the black folk of the South with nature and with dark, primitive urges. Thus, when the protagonist first mentions Jim Trueblood, the incestuous griot of the novel, he recalls the loathing of the college students for the "primitive spirituals" sung by black country folk like Trueblood: "We were embarrassed by the earthy harmonies they sang, but since the visitors were awed we dared not laugh at the crude, high, plaintively animal sounds Jim Trueblood made as he led the quartet" (1989 ed., p. 47). Ironically, it is white people who appreciate black vernacular music, whereas the college students, the protagonist, and his cronies hold such singing in contempt because it is "earthy" and, in their view, not cultured. Concluding his reminiscence, the protagonist reflects, with a hint of self-criticism: "How all of us at the college hated the black-belt people, the 'peasants,' during those days! We were trying to lift them up and they, like Trueblood, did everything it seemed to pull us down" (p. 47). Not only are these peasants antithetical to the aspirations of the black professional class, but their connection to the earth itself—to nature—is a bond that the black elite wish to transcend.

When the protagonist reaches New York City, his antipathy toward nature and folk life emerges in new and more complicated forms. Shortly after his arrival he encounters a blues-singing man who calls himself Peter Wheatstraw—the name of an immensely popular 1930s blues artist. The singing evokes disconcerting memories of his own repressed past, "things I had long ago shut out of my mind." When Wheatstraw accosts him, the protagonist becomes "embarrassed and angry," because he does not like being associated with such an ignorant, country black person—especially not in public. The imagery of Wheatstraw's song and conversation underscores his association with nature. For example, paradoxical animal images express the intensity of his sexual passion:

> *She's got feet like a monkey*
> *Legs like a frog—Lawd, Lawd!*
> *But when she starts to loving me*
> *I holler Whoooo, God-dog!* (p. 173)

Needless to say, the protagonist cannot understand what this song implies about the joyful irrationality of sexual passion. He puzzles: "Was it about a woman or about some strange sphinx-like animal? . . . And why describe anyone in such contradictory words? . . . What kind of woman could love a dirty fellow like that, anyway? And how could even *he* love her if she were as repulsive as the song described?" (p. 177). The poetic power of these similes derives from the apt exaggeration of describing a woman in animal terms, at once acknowledging the animal nature of man and asserting the power of sexual passion to undermine rationality and transgress social boundaries and taboos. This scene dramatizes once again that the protagonist's contempt for black folk and his alienation from nature are two versions of the same problem: his narrow fixation on rationality necessitates his refusal to acknowledge that nature and the folk are part of himself.

Ellison recognizes, however, that this rift cannot be healed easily. In another scene the protagonist encounters a man selling yams on the street. Smelling them overwhelms him with nostalgia. Impulsively, he buys one and begins to eat it, which brings him a feeling of transformation:

Zora Neale Hurston (1901–1960), author of *Their Eyes Were Touching God*

"I walked along, munching the yam, just as suddenly overcome by an intense feeling of freedom — simply because I was eating while walking along the street. It was exhilarating. I no longer had to worry about who saw me or about what was proper" (p. 264). For a brief, intense moment, he imagines that he has purged his inhibitions. Consuming this natural object, he thinks, has reconnected him with the South and the folk. The fantasy ends abruptly and distastefully, however, when he buys two more yams and finds them both frostbitten. Thus, alienation is not so easily resolved; eating yams is no panacea.

Such ambivalent attitudes toward nature are common in the work of African-American writers. Nevertheless, nature plays a therapeutic or redemptive role in some African-American texts. For instance, it has a complex and central role in Zora Neale Hurston's *Their Eyes Were Watching God.* An important moment of epiphany occurs early in the novel as the protagonist, Janie, watches a bee in a pear blossom.

She was stretched on her back beneath the pear tree soaking in the alto chant of the visiting bees, the gold of the sun and the panting breath of the breeze when the inau-

1007

dible voice of it all came to her. She saw a dust-bearing bee sink into the sanctum of a bloom; the thousand sister-calyxes arch to meet the love embrace and the ecstatic shiver of the tree from root to tiniest branch creaming in every blossom and frothing with delight. So this was a marriage! She had been summoned to behold a revelation. Then Janie felt a pain remorseless sweet that left her limp and languid. (pp. 10–11)

This is one of the most celebrated and frequently analyzed passages in African-American literature. Observing the bees and blossoms provides Janie an analog that allows her to understand and to exult in her own awakening sexuality. Throughout the novel, this moment serves as a touchstone for Janie's quest to attain fulfillment as a woman. "Oh to be a pear tree," she thinks repeatedly, "*any* tree in bloom!" This wishful utterance implies that attaining a natural state is the way to achieve happiness. Revealingly, this naive idea is Janie's first, not her wisest, articulation of what womanly fulfillment might entail. Indeed, the novel immediately proceeds to invalidate the simple equation of naturalness and happiness.

Janie's formulation implies that any bee can bring to any blossom that ecstatic shiver of orgasmic gratification. She is soon disabused of this notion when her grandmother arranges her marriage to a local farmer, an old and unattractive man named Logan Killicks. Janie finds no satisfaction in this union. She complains: "His belly is too big too, now, and his toe-nails look lak mule foots. And 'taint't nothin' in de way of him washin' his feet every evenin' before he comes tuh bed" (p. 23). No one can deny that Logan is a natural man. He looks like a mule and brings the topsoil to bed with him, yet he is no bee to Janie's blossom. Rather, he reminds her of "some old skullhead in de grave yard." The problem is not simply that Janie has misinterpreted the bee/blossom scenario. As Hurston makes clear, the belief that such a natural process could provide an adequate analogy for human experience is itself erroneous.

The novel also demonstrates that the corresponding impulse to achieve social gratification by joining the folk is similarly erroneous, although most critics of the book have failed to comprehend this point. With very few exceptions, critics have assumed that Janie's—and Hurston's—ultimate objective is to achieve full integration into the black community. Janie does in fact state this desire, just as she states a desire to become "*any* tree." We ought not, however, to confuse premises with conclusions. The novel begins with Janie returning from her adventures and snubbing the townsfolk who are congregated on her porch. Despite her frequent claims that she wants to join the community, which is symbolized by the porch talk, she returns at the end of her travels and declines to share her story with them, instead going directly into the house. Much critical energy has been wasted in futile attempts to explain that Janie does not really intend to spurn the black folk community, but through her experiences, Janie has outgrown her need for porch talk, just as she has transcended her desire to be a blossom for any passing bee. She has arrived at an individualized understanding of her relationship to other people, and unlike so many critics of the novel, she has ceased to romanticize an undifferentiated mass called the "community" or the "folk." Such concepts are, as I have argued, the social equivalents of "nature."

Hurston dramatizes her understanding of this convergence between nature and the folk in her chapters detailing Janie's life in the Everglades region known as the "muck." Within the novel the movement of Janie and her husband, Tea Cake, from Eatonville to the muck is tantamount to moving from civilization into nature. The novel lays this out explicitly:

To Janie's strange eyes, everything in the Everglades was big and new. Big Lake Okechobee, big beans, big cane, big weeds, big everything. Weeds that did well to grow waist high up the state were eight and often ten feet tall down there. Ground so rich that everything went wild. . . . People wild too. (p. 123)

In the Everglades they encounter exotic animals, such as alligators and panthers, and exotic, primitive people as well: Native Americans, West Indians, and other migrant workers. The latter Hurston describes as "people ugly from ignorance and broken from being poor." In this wild realm Janie escapes from the social conventions and strictures that have hitherto constrained her life. Tea Cake teaches her to shoot and hunt, and she volunteers to join him in harvesting beans. She even learns to accept and apparently relish a beating as an expression of love. If Hurston intended simply to extol the return to nature, she could do no better than to leave her protagonist to live happily ever after in the Everglades.

Needless to say, the design of this narrative is not nearly so simple. Life on the muck brings Janie the greatest freedom, passion, and contentment she has ever experienced, but, on the other hand, here she also discovers less appealing passions, such as jealousy and class chauvinism. Ironically, it is nature, in the form of a hurricane, that drives them from this paradise and their socialization—Tea Cake's faith in white people—that prevents them from escaping in advance of the storm. Hurston shows, in other words, that nature is not benign and socialization cannot be stripped away simply by going into the wilderness. Before the storm the Seminoles, the animals, and the Bahamians begin to leave. When one of the latter invites Tea Cake to join the exodus, he retorts: "Indians don't know much uh nothin', tuh tell de truth. Else dey'd own dis country still. De white folks ain't gone nowhere. Dey oughta know if it's dangerous" (p. 148). Despite his resourcefulness and free spirit, Tea Cake retains the same social attitudes. He is in the muck, but not of the muck. Consequently, he is impervious to the lessons that nature and people close to nature might teach him. During his flight from the hurricane, Tea Cake is bitten by a rabid dog, which leads to his death. Driven mad, he attempts to shoot Janie, and she, using skills she has learned from him, kills him in self-defense.

Janie returns home to Eatonville after Tea Cake's death, which is where the novel begins. Her experience on the muck does not persuade her to "go native." Rather, it teaches her how to be independent and self-sufficient. She no longer needs to join the folk. As she tells her friend Pheoby, "Ah done been tuh de horizon and back and now Ah kin set heah in mah house and live by comparisons" (p. 182). Her experience on the muck was an essential part of her education, but it is not the end of her journey. *Their Eyes Were Watching God* appears at first to be a novel concerned with becoming "natural" and joining the folk. In the end, it is about recognizing how experiences with nature and the folk can contribute to self-knowledge.

Thus described, *Their Eyes Were Watching God* appears to have a great deal in common with the long tradition of nature hermitage works, typified by *Walden*, in which narrators take up temporary residence in natural (or "primitive") settings and use their encounters with nature as the basis for narratives later to be recollected in civilized tranquillity. In a strictly formal sense, it is indeed related to that genre. The substantive differences, however, ought not to be ignored. In Hurston's novel Janie learns lessons from nature; one of the most important is that nature is not where she belongs. Her separation from nature is not ultimately a form of alienation to be lamented or reversed. Hurston does not present nature or the folk as a repository of higher truths or exemplary virtue—quite the contrary. Superficially, *Their Eyes* appears to be quite different from *Invisible Man*, because the central movement of the latter is toward the urban North and modernity, whereas the predominant movement of the former is southward, toward the natural and the primitive. In the end, however, the two works converge, because they both celebrate the development of the individual who has evolved away from the folk community and has become instead a self-conscious author of sophisticated autobiographical narrative.

Accordingly, both novels end with their narrators alone in personalized, enclosed spaces, recounting their own experiences and uncertain when or if they will emerge to reenter the community. Unlike authors who seek, in the tradition of Ralph Waldo Emerson, to read the truths embedded in nature, Hurston and Ellison are both, in their own distinctive ways, committed to the assertion of culture. The protagonist of *Invisible Man* acknowledges this point explicitly when he recalls his English professor's comments regarding James Joyce's Stephen Daedalus:

> "Stephen's problem, like ours, was not actually one of creating the uncreated conscience of his race, but of creating the *uncreated features of his face.* Our task is that of making ourselves individuals. The conscience of a race is the gift of its individuals who see, evaluate, record. . . . We create the race by creating ourselves and then to our great astonishment we will have created something far more important: We will have created a culture." (p. 354)

For writers belonging to a group that has always been associated with nature rather than culture, and defined in terms of an undifferentiated, folkish mass rather than individuals, the emphasis on individual pursuits of culture and on the use of writing to demonstrate cultural achievement ought not be surprising.

The place of nature in African-American writing is not always so vexed. Even in black folk culture, however, the representation of nature differs from the conventions of European-American nature writing. The African-American folk tradition has tended to humanize nature; or, to be more precise, black folk culture has generally not conceived nature in such stark terms of opposition between self and other. Animals, for example, are often depicted in African-American folklore in human terms or as part of a social continuum that comprises both humans and animals. The Brer Rabbit stories, for instance, depict the interactions of animal characters as a reflection of human society, but without sacrificing a sense of the particular species personality of rabbits, foxes, bears, terrapins, and such. These tales belong to an oral tradition that has been traced to African origins, but they also resemble trickster tales from Native American and other cultures. Furthermore, they have entered our literary tradition through the work of Joel Chandler Harris, whose mediation makes the interpretation of these stories as African-American artifacts especially problematic.

Black folk songs and ballads also manifest this tendency to humanize animals, as these stanzas from "Boll Weevil Song" illustrate:

> De first time I seen de boll weevil,
>   He was a settin' on de square.
> De next time I see de boll weevil, he had all
>   of his family dere,
>   Jus' a-lookin foh a home, jus' a-lookin'
>   foh a home.
>
> De farmer say to de weevil:
>   "What make yo' head so red?"
> De weevil say to de farmer, "It's a wondah
>   I ain't dead,
>   A-lookin' foh a home, jus' a-lookin' foh a
>   home."
>
> De farmer take de boll weevil,
>   An' he put him in de hot san'.
> De weevil say: "Dis is mighty hot, but I'll
>   stan' it like a man,
>   Dis'll be my home, it'll be my home."
>
>   . . .
>
> And if anybody should ax you
>   Who it was dat make dis song,
> Jus' tell 'em 'twas a big buck niggah wid a
>   paih o' blue duckin's on.
>   Ain' got no home, ain' got no home.
>   (Botkin, pp. 916–918)

Clearly, this ballad refers to the boll weevil infestations during the early years of the twentieth century and the migrations of farmworkers that were caused by this and other calamities. This fascinating song conflates the boll weevil, which destroys cotton crops, with black people, who depend on cotton for their livelihood. This complexly ironic conception completely nullifies any simple binary opposition between the human and the animal. One finds the same tendency in African-American mule tales, a staple of black folklore. Hurston incorporates an example of this genre in *Their Eyes Were Watch-*

ing God. By identifying animals in human terms, such tales break down the boundaries of difference that in much conventional nature writing define animals as inscrutably other. In these stories, animals are no more inscrutable to human observers than other people are.

We might conclude, then, that both African-American writing and folklore have resisted the tendency to regard nature as the "other" of culture. When writers have accepted this oppositional frame of reference, they often have opted for culture over nature, but most black writers have ultimately rejected this opposition and have instead articulated conceptions of culture that incorporate an engagement with nature (or the folk) as integral to the definition of culture. Both Hurston and Ellison, as we have seen, recognize an essential role for nature and the folk in the articulation of their cultural visions.

A final example demonstrates that this incorporation of nature has manifested itself even in African-American texts that do not appear to have any concern with nature. In *The Hidden Wound* (1989), Wendell Berry cites a passage from *The Autobiography of Malcolm X* (1965) concerning the garden plot that Malcolm's mother gave him to tend when he was a child. Malcolm describes the care with which he cultivated, planted, weeded, and eradicated pests. He concludes: "And sometimes when I had everything straight and clean for my things to grow, I would lie down on my back between two rows, and I would gaze up into the blue sky at the clouds moving and think all kinds of things" (p. 84). Any reader of Berry will immediately recognize the most obvious reason why this passage would appeal to him. The description of agricultural activity provides a connection between these two intellectual activists.

This, however, is not the point that Berry wishes to make in discussing the passage. Instead, he uses the passage to illuminate his understanding of Malcolm X as a heroic figure. Malcolm, he asserts, "was a heroic figure not so much because of what he did, but because of the thorough involvement of a powerful intelligence in all that he did." For Berry, the passage provides a clue to what sustained Malcolm in his passionate, exhausting political quest. Berry's response to this question is speculative but compelling:

> Part of the strength of that passage is that it is probably the only really serene and happy moment in the whole book. He doesn't say what were the "all kinds of things" he thought, but it is hard for me to avoid the suspicion that the experience — lying there as low as he could get, against the earth, his mind free — filled him with a rich sense of the possibilities of life in this world that never left him, and that served him as a measure of the destructiveness and sterility of racism. The passage throws the resonance of myth over the book: it is the myth of Antaeus, the giant of Libya, the son of Earth, who could not be conquered so long as he touched the ground. (p. 85)

One might quibble with some details of Berry's interpretation. A few other moments in the narrative, for example, could be described as "serene and happy." This claim, however, is not crucial to Berry's argument. His main point, that Malcolm can be understood as an Antaeus figure whose childhood intimacy with the earth — with nature — engenders in him a sense of human possibility that sustains him in his subsequent life of political struggle, is a brilliant and very compelling interpretation.

Whether Berry is right or wrong about Malcolm X and the importance of gardening in his life is not what matters here. The importance of Berry's argument, rather, is that it provides a useful and suggestive model for how we might inquire regarding the place of nature in African-American writing. Berry has identified a passage that has probably escaped the notice of most readers of *The Autobiography*, and he uses it to challenge our common understanding of Malcolm X. Berry's interest in farming and in nature is what prompts him to notice this fleeting episode. It may well be that if we raise a different set of questions, we will begin to discover a presence of nature in African-American texts that we have not noticed before.

Alice Walker provides a striking testimonial about her experience as a Southerner that confirms the validity of Berry's argument as it might apply to her:

Perhaps my Northern brothers will not believe me when I say there is a great deal of positive material I can draw from my "underprivileged" background. But they have never lived, as I have, at the end of a long road in a house that was faced by the edge of the world on one side and nobody for miles on the other. They have never experienced the magnificent quiet of a summer day when the heat is intense and one is so very thirsty, as one moves across the dusty cotton fields, that one learns forever that water is the essence of all life. In the cities it cannot be so clear to one that he is a creature of the earth, feeling the soil between the toes, smelling the dust thrown up by the rain, loving the earth so much that one longs to taste it and sometimes does. . . .

No one could wish for a more advantageous heritage than that bequeathed to the black writer in the South: a compassion for the earth, a trust in humanity beyond our knowledge of evil, and an abiding love of justice. We inherit a great responsibility as well, for we must give voice to centuries not only of silent bitterness and hate but also of neighborly kindness and sustaining love. (*In Search of Our Mothers' Gardens*, 1983, pp. 20–21)

This passage seems worth quoting at length because it speaks so pertinently to the point argued throughout this essay: that African-American writers tend to see nature as integral to their own identities. Walker argues, in addition, that such groundedness in the natural landscape provides one with a moral standpoint, an implicit understanding of the proper place of human beings in relationship to the world and to each other. Whether we accept these claims as valid or not, they clearly represent a significant tradition of thinking about humanity's relation to nature. This set of questions has hardly been addressed in the study of African-American writing. Perhaps it is time for such an inquiry to begin.

Selected Bibliography

Wendell Berry, *The Hidden Wound* (San Francisco: North Point Press, 1989); Benjamin Albert Botkin, ed., *A Treasury of American Folklore* (New York: Crown, 1944); Ralph Ellison, *Invisible Man* (New York: Vintage Books, 1989); Antonio Gramsci, *The Modern Prince, and Other Writings* (New York: International Publishers, 1967), trans. by Louis Marks; Langston Hughes, *Good Morning, Revolution: Uncollected Social Protest Writings* (New York: Lawrence Hill, 1973); Zora Neale Hurston, *Their Eyes Were Watching God* (New York: Harper Perennial, 1990); Herman Melville, *Benito Cereno*, in *Great Short Works of Herman Melville*, ed. by Warner Berthoff (New York: Harper Perennial, 1969); Ishmael Reed, *Flight to Canada* (New York: Atheneum, 1989); Alice Walker, *Meridian* (New York: Washington Square Press, 1976), and "The Black Writer and the Southern Experience," in her *In Search of Our Mothers' Gardens: Womanist Prose* (New York: Harcourt Brace Jovanovich, 1983); Richard Wright, "Big Boy Leaves Home," in his *Uncle Tom's Children* (New York: Harper Perennial, 1993).

BIOREGIONALISM IN NATURE WRITING

DAVID ROBERTSON

A BIOREGIONAL STUDY of literature attempts, self-consciously and rigorously, to fuse three disciplines: literary criticism, ecology, and religious studies. These disciplines are academic codifications of three distinguishable but interrelated modes of human awareness and practice: the aesthetic, the scientific, and the religious. Each is characterized by a supreme effort to make connections between the parts of a whole system. At the broadest level of generalization, the whole is the universe, or Nature (with a capital *N*). Thus, the principal motive behind the study of literature from a bioregional perspective is to understand how Nature functions in the life of the author and in his or her work.

BIOREGIONAL DICTIONARY

Nature: (capitalized) the universe, everything that exists; **a:** the material universe, on the supposition that everything is material and that the so-called spiritual is an aspect of the material; **b:** the material plus the spiritual worlds, on the supposition that these two worlds are related but separable aspects of the universe as a whole.

Except during rare moments of transcendence, human beings are unable to take in the entire universe. So, in imitation of the god of Genesis 1, let us divide the universe into two parts. The first is what human beings find as given. The term "nature" (with a small *n*) will do to designate this part. The second is that which human beings make. The term "culture" is an acceptable designation of this part. A bioregional study of literature is, in this more modest version, an attempt to see how culture is related to nature, or, to see how nature gives rise to and is expressed in culture.

BIOREGIONAL DICTIONARY

nature: (not capitalized) all of the universe except the products of human activity.

culture: the products of human activity.

Human beings, bifurcated as they are, have a foot in each half of Nature, causing themselves much consternation and academics who study them much confusion. Both the anguish and the ambiguity are apparently endemic to the human condition. Perhaps Paleolithic peoples considered their cultures "natural." Some of our contemporary interest in them is motivated by a desire to peer into a Stone Age Eden, in the hope that we ourselves might reenter. Bioregionalists, both those who practice bioregionalism and those who study it, hope that attention to place will make culture more natural and thereby more wholesome for its members. Perhaps at some time in the future a culture will arise that will be accepted by its members as wholly natural. In the meantime, the nature-culture dichotomy endures. As a result, no editor can make a Bioregional Dictionary precise. Beneath the words lie huge paradigmatic plates that slip by each other, causing great mental edifices to shake and sometimes to shatter.

The study of the whole of nature and all of culture is still unmanageably large for most of us. So we continue to divide. We reach in and pick "art" out of culture with one hand and pick the "land" out of nature with the other. Literary critics simplify the task even further by skimming "literature" off the top of art and by selecting only a small part of the landmass of the earth to examine. *What* part of the earth is crucial. Critics interested in the study of literature and land have usually confined their studies within the borders of a nation-state (as in American literature, where "American" includes the United States and excludes Canada and all territory south of the Mexican-American border). Selection of a particular region of a nation-state (as in the literature of the South) is also common. The bioregional approach is a development of the late twentieth century.

BIOREGIONAL DICTIONARY

art: a part of culture; specifically, imaginative works of all types, including writing, visual arts, crafts, and three-dimensional pieces, such as sculpture and architecture.

literature: a part of art; specifically, imaginative writing of all types, including poetry, fiction, drama, and nonfiction.

the land: a part of nature; specifically, the surface of the earth, including its geological structure, atmosphere, and biological inhabitants.

landscape: a part of the land; specifically, its visible topography.

The Bioregion

"Bioregion" is no easier to define than the other entries in our Bioregional Dictionary. A literalist of the lexicon might say that the term means "life region" or even "region that is alive." From the beginnings of ecology as an independent science, practitioners have frequently employed organic metaphors to illustrate the functioning of ecosystems. Ecoparts relate to ecosystem as body parts to organism, making the whole greater than the sum of the parts. From the point of view of bioregionalist literary critics, such metaphors are particularly apt, for we are interested, finally, in the unity of being. Unquestionably the most obvious and dramatic examples of parts working together as wholes are multicellular organisms at the top of the evolutionary scale. We must recognize, however, that many contemporary ecologists are skeptical. They point to a considerable body of evidence that suggests that organism is, at best, a rough analogy to ecosystem and, at worse, downright misleading. Interrelation is crucial to ecosystem. How this interrelation happens, however, and whether it happens organically are debatable.

This theoretical discussion still leaves us with the practical problem of defining bioregion or, at least, of giving some advice on how to choose a unit of study. A manageable bioregion will usually be the solution to the following equation: Geography + Biology + Culture = Bioregion. Imagine making three maps, in the form of transparencies, of a region chosen as a general area of study. The first uses geographical considerations to determine the boundaries within which ecoparts interact, the second biological, and the third cultural. The area common to all three maps, when the transparencies are placed on top of each other, constitutes the core bioregion. Around it are three other zones: where two maps overlap, where one map only is represented, and everywhere else. Bioregional study will concentrate on the core. Some considerable attention, however, will have to be paid to all three zones outside the core. Given the earth's systems of transportation, decisive influences on an ecosystem may come from hundreds if not thousands of miles away. Los Angeles smog floats toward the Sierra Nevada, and Sierra Nevada snow, once melted, flows via aqueducts in the opposite direction.

BIOREGIONAL DICTIONARY

bioregion: a part of the land that functions as an ecosystem, specifically, a region whose boundaries are defined by a combination of cultural and natural factors and that functions as an interrelated system of the living and the nonliving.

As one moves from geography to biology to culture, subjectivity increases. Since the geographical map is the most straightforward, it is best to begin with it. The trend at present is to set bioregional boundaries by watershed (the area drained by the Ohio River, let us say) or landmass (such as the Colorado plateau or the Great Basin). The biological map is an overlay with information about vegetation types and animal ranges. The cultural map is an additional overlay that takes into account political, economic, and social borders.

I can most easily illustrate how one might solve the bioregion equation by referring to my own work. Broadly put, I am interested in the literature of northern California, especially the literature of the Sierra Nevada. In delineating the geographical boundaries of my study, I previously directed my attention to the boundaries of the Sierra's three major national parks, Yosemite, Kings Canyon, and Sequoia. Now my concerns are mainly bioregional, and I find myself drawn to less spectacular landscapes. For reasons that are largely coincidental, having to do, for example, with the people I happen to know, I discovered that poems were coming out of the hills around the old mining town of Nevada City in the northern Sierra the way gold nuggets used to. Nevada City is about sixty miles northeast of Sacramento, just north of Interstate 80, which crosses the Sierra Nevada by the historic and infamous Donner Pass. It is a major stop on Highway 49, the route established by the state of California to make tourist money out of the state's gold-bearing region. It is within two hours of my home, a practical consideration of no small import.

Nevada City lies in the watershed of the Yuba River, one of many rivers draining the western slope of the Sierra Nevada. On the south is the American River, where gold was discovered in January 1848. On the north is the Feather River. The Yuba begins at the Sierra crest and empties into the Feather just before the Feather in turn flows into the Sacramento. Its course is, for the most part, westerly. Across it, running in a north-south direction, are a series of vegetation belts that change with altitude; the definitions and boundaries of these are indistinct. Because the crest of the Sierra in the Yuba drainage is relatively low (seven thousand to nine thousand feet), the uppermost band of vegetation is particularly mixed, consisting of many elements that, at other places in the range, are more distinct. Mostly one sees lodgepole and Jeffrey pines, red fir, and mountain hemlock. Below this is a belt of lodgepole pine and red fir (fifty-five hundred to seventy-five hundred feet). At elevations of two thousand to fifty-five hundred feet the dominant tree is the ponderosa pine, although Douglas fir, white fir, and black oak are also abundant. Farther down, in the foothills, forests give way to woodlands of gray pine, blue oak, and interior live oak and to a dense chaparral of chemise, ceanothus, and manzanita. Foothills gradually level off to the plain of the Sacramento River valley.

In the valley are farms and orchards, a couple of towns in the process of becoming small cities, and an air force base. Cattle and deer share the foothills with a few people in widely scattered homes. Most of the people live at or about an elevation of twenty-five hundred feet, clustered in Nevada City and Grass Valley near the South Yuba, but spread across Nevada, Yuba, and Sierra counties, where forests of ponderosa pine meet the woodlands. To Californians, this is the Gold Country. The economy of this region has depended, more or less in order, on acorns, gold, timber, and tourism. Several relatively distinct populations can be identified: Native Californians; old-timers (that is, descendants of the early miners and loggers); ranchers; reinhabitory groups, whose migration to the area began in the late 1960s; and colonies of retired people, whose numbers have steadily increased since the 1970s. Because the snow line is typically between thirty-five hundred and four thousand feet, above those altitudes people become fewer and forest more dense.

When geography is overlaid with biology and culture, a core bioregion becomes clear. The watershed of the Yuba River forms distinct boundaries on the north and south, while the limits of concentrated human populations, roughly at the lower edge of the conifer forest and at the upper edge of the oak-pine woodlands, provide indistinct but workable borders on the east and west. But to the north for about fifty miles and to the south for several hundred miles, a similar band of vegetation, history, and culture stretches across the lower- to mid-elevations of the Sierra Nevada, sliced into ridges by one river after another. This is the natural and cultural ecoregion of which the Nevada City area is most immediately a part. Out to the west, across the great valley of California and across the Coast Ranges, are San Francisco and the larger Bay Area, whose peoples and culture have dramatically influenced Sierra ecosystems.

Ecology and the Unit of Study

The study of literature by bioregion is essentially synecdochic. The part stands for the whole. Literature stands for art, which stands for culture, which is a part of the universe. Bioregion stands for the land, which stands for nature, which is a part of the universe. All of these divisions are ultimately arbitrary and false. We have taken a knife to the universe for heuristic purposes, to simplify the task. This simplification seems advisable, but it is also ironic. After all, we were initially persuaded to enter the territory of bioregion because we were convinced that everything touches everything else in the context of the whole. In a sense, bioregionalists are trying to learn two types of languages. One

type is like English: it splits. The other type is like German: it lumps. The assignment is not only to be bilingual, to speak two languages, but to speak them at the same time.

A bioregional approach to literature is distinctive, first of all, because of the way the territory is identified. It is not the nation, not the region that is our concern, but the bioregion. It is also distinctive because of its assumption of interrelationship between all things, not just writer to other writers, not just literature to other arts, not just literary communities to other human communities. The unit of study is the bioregion, and that means human to animal to vegetable to mineral communities. This point must be stressed, otherwise one will make an understandable but crucial mistake in methodology. Bioregional literary study does not intend to be for the bioregion what national literary study has been for the nation and regional literary study has been for the region. Typically, when the borders are national or regional, the literary tradition is isolated and examined for its own sake, or it is at most placed in the context of other human activities. Bioregional literary study does not wish to draw new boundaries only to ask old questions.

Bioregional literary critics want to understand the relationship between literature and Nature. In order to make such a galactic enterprise more manageable, they allow local nature to represent, or stand in for, cosmic nature. They define local nature as the bioregion and make *it*, not a poem, nor an author, nor a movement, the unit of study. It is at this point, perhaps more than at any other, that literary scholars will look to ecology for instruction and advice. All ecologists are interested in the relationship of parts to a whole. Some address this problem from the point of view of the whole. They may, for example, study the input and output of energy in order to chart the history of an ecosystem. Is it expanding, contracting, or in a state of equilibrium? Others take a different approach. They focus on a part, in the short run to understand the role of that part in the whole, and in the long run to allow an accurate addition of parts into a whole. Borrowing a metaphor from economics, one might say that these ecologists want to know how an organism makes a living in a particular ecosystem and how that occupation affects the dynamics of the system as a whole. From the point of view of an organism, the ecosystem where it is located is its habitat. How it makes its living, its "profession," as it were, is its niche within that habitat.

Almost certainly it is to the second group of ecologists that literary critics will look, for they, too, are interested in approaching the whole from the point of view of an organism. In this case the organism is Homo sapiens, subspecies *litteratus*. They want to identify and understand the niche of writers in their bioregional habitat. They want to know how writers make a living. The social sciences are concerned with how groups of human beings make a living. Yet only a few of these disciplines (one thinks of economics, geography, and anthropology) are likely to pay sustained attention to other animals, plants, and the inorganic world in which humans are situated. Enter human ecology. Its niche within the academic habitat is, systematically, to link the social with the biological sciences, that is, to take the human animal in environmental context and to describe the interchange between animal and context. It will try to answer the question of how human beings make a living, when making a living refers to all dimensions of living that human beings count as significant: the physical, the emotional, and the spiritual.

A bioregional approach to literature is a subdiscipline of human ecology. It seeks to know how a writer makes a poetic living in his or her local environment. "Poetic" here stands for all forms of imaginative writing; "living" refers not to monetary compensation but to the interchange of writer and locale that eventuates in a creative work. I am fond of the word "negotiation." We can imagine discussing how a farmer negotiates with the soil and weather to produce a crop or how an eagle negotiates with air and cliffs and tree to make an aerie. Correspondingly, the bioregional literary critic wants to know how a writer negotiates with a local environment, its plants, animals, and rocks, its geological forces,

its slope and prospect, its weather, to produce a work. Inelegantly put, making a poetic living is the process by which writers get written whatever it is they write.

Forming Hypotheses and Collecting Data

In order to understand how writers make a poetic living, bioregional literary critics need to accomplish a number of tasks. One task is to learn as much as possible about the discipline of ecology, including how ecologists identify relevant environments, collect data, and formulate and test hypotheses. A second task is the selection for study of one or more bioregions. In making these choices, practical considerations will play an important part: accessibility of the bioregion, its role in history, the career and personal predilections of the critic, and so forth. Critics should, in choosing regions for intensive study, have some inkling that their methods will produce significant results. The rationale here is simple: time invested in research should have a decent chance of paying off. If a group of astronomers believe they have discovered a new method for measuring the value of the Hubble constant (a number that places the velocity of an extragalactic astronomical object in relation to its distance from the Milky Way), they do not apply it at random to cosmic entities. Instead, they select a group of entities most likely to yield significant results. Similarly, Freudian literary critics turn first to literary works with characters and plots. Dramas and novels lend themselves more to psychoanalytic readings than do lyric poems. Correspondingly, bioregional critics should look to regions that support a sizable population of writers in active negotiation with the land.

The third and fourth tasks are hypothesis formation and data collection. Currently a debate rages over inductive versus deductive methods of scientific procedure. Historians want to know how science has been done, philosophers want to know how it ought to be done in order to sustain claims of validity, and scientists want to know, from a practical point of view, how best to proceed on their next project. None of them have arrived at any clear-cut conclusions. From the perspective of a scientific layperson, examples exist of sound results being achieved through both inductive and deductive methods. Literary critics should be aware of this debate and even, perhaps, put in a word or two about it, but should not get locked into either methodology. The best advice is, do what works. Eventually, data have to be collected and hypotheses formulated and tested.

Before data collection (proceeding deductively) or during and after data collection (proceeding inductively), literary critics must formulate ideas about the relationship between literature and place. Has a particular body of literature come into being as a result of a negotiation between writer and locale, and if so, how? I have devised several hypothesis about how writers make a poetic living in a specific bioregion, and I plan to use them to guide my initial field research. I put them forward here, not as hypotheses others should adopt, but as examples of the process. All bioregional critics will have to do this work in their own distinctive way.

Hypothesis One: Writers negotiate with a place by identifying within it a number of especially powerful locations that they visit habitually, or periodically (perhaps at certain times of the year), or in times of celebration, or in times of stress. I expect to find that these locations are not necessarily prominent when measured on a scale of the sublime, or even the picturesque. They may be distinctive, however, in terms of some combination of their geology, weather, soil, and the biological communities they support. In California, such a place might be an outcropping of serpentine rock that supports a fine stand of Sargent cypress, a conifer especially adapted to serpentine.

Hypothesis Two: Writers make a poetic living in a place by devising rituals that situate their community in that place. Rituals are an important means by which human beings negotiate with transhuman powers. In Western culture, these powers are customarily thought of as transnatural. Westerners readily grasp that the

Eucharist is, for example, an instrument for negotiating with the transcendent Christian deity. Since this god has no locale, it is appropriate that place be irrelevant to Christian rituals. I believe that a bioregional community of writers invents place-based rituals that facilitate the transfer of natural power to its members.

Hypothesis Three: Sometimes bioregional writers engage in rituals that have community support but are performed in isolation. The way native peoples of California train their doctors provides a helpful analogy. Prospective healers in a typical northern California tribe might go out by themselves to a place well known for its power and engage there in a series of actions that make available to them healing powers. They might, for example, fast, dance around a heap of stones, or dive into a lake. We will find, I think, that contemporary communities of bioregional writers fashion similar rituals for the purpose of gaining inspiration.

Hypothesis Four: Writers make a poetic living in a place by imitating the way plants and animals of that locale make a living. It is even possible that writers mimic the way the inorganic entities of a region behave. The way rock and hawk function in the poetry of Robinson Jeffers comes immediately to mind here. This hypothesis seems rather more far-fetched than the previous three, and I confess that I have considerable doubts about it. I am not even confident I would recognize relevant data to support it. Perhaps it is only intuition that tells me this hypothesis may be worth paying attention to. In any case, it highlights the importance of bioregional critics heeding both plant and animal communities as well as the inorganic setting of the bioregion.

Hypothesis Five: Writers in different cultures on the same land will make a similar poetic living and will produce works that bear some fundamental similarity to each other. The difference in cultures may be diachronic. All bioregions in the Americas support cultures that are, historically, at least two-layered: an exotic European-based culture comes after and mostly supplants an indigenous culture. For most American places, the situation is considerably more complex. The native culture itself may be multilayered, and populations from Africa and Asia may have contributed significantly to the exotic culture. The difference in cultures may, on the other hand, be synchronic: more than one culture may inhabit the same area at the same time. In the late twentieth century, for example, the Sierra Nevada bioregion supports remnant populations of Native Californians and gold miners alongside immigrant populations of reinhabitory peoples and retirees. My hypothesis is that, over time, the process and products of the writers of these different cultures will bear a resemblance to each other that is a function of the land.

To test their hypotheses, bioregional critics need data. Methods of collection are numerous. The following remarks are meant to be suggestive, not exhaustive. Critics need to explore their bioregions, by plane, by automobile, by bike, but mostly by foot. "Nature literacy" is important. Elementary nature education is a sine qua non of successful bioregional study. Bioregionalists must pause for plants and patiently observe the animal populations, dig down through the soil to the bedrock, and look up through the air at the weather-bearing clouds.

The history of human habitation of a bioregion and the stories human beings tell about a region need to be studied. An understanding is needed of the conventional ways human beings have subsisted in a place. Land ownership and patterns of land use must be investigated, as well as the political entities that have come into being to promote and protect those patterns. What communities of writers have come into being? What have they produced and how? How have they interacted with other human communities? The list of subjects and questions is potentially infinite, limited finally by the attention span (it is to be hoped not the life span) of the critic.

Some of the needed data can be collected in traditional ways. Museums and libraries maintained by local historical societies are likely to be especially helpful. Often the people who run these institutions are invaluable sources of information about the location of both archival

materials and community experts. Bioregional critics will probably find themselves frequently resorting to the interview. To develop and fine-tune skills in qualitative data collection, consultation with colleagues in sociology and anthropology can be useful.

In the bioregion there is literature both written and oral, both published and unpublished, both famous and obscure, both serious and frivolous, both happy and sad. Bioregional critics will embrace it all. Bioregional criticism is, finally, an inclusive enterprise: everyone and every work are represented in the canon. No one and no work are cast out as irrelevant or inferior. How good an understanding of an ecosystem would we have if biologists investigated only glamorous plants and animals, such as redwoods and grizzly bears? Bioregional critics will be wary of qualitative distinctions. Such discriminations usually presume that the unit of study is literature, not literature in relation to community. Moreover, those who render such judgments may be members of an elite with a social and political agenda that has relatively little use for the provincial and the local. The utterance "This is no good; I'll not waste my time on it" might be a reliable sign that the reader has exited the bioregion for some other area of criticism. In the final analysis, bioregional critics are likely to be more concerned with describing a *process* than with evaluating a *product*.

Mandala in Buddhism

I began this essay by claiming that bioregional study combines three disciplines. I included religious studies along with the more obvious two, literary criticism and ecology, partly because religions so clearly attempt to see human activity through the widest possible lens. There was an additional motive. In many of the religions of the world, belief and practice and land are three threads of a closely woven garment worn by worshipers. That land is relatively unimportant in Christianity may cause occidental scholars to overlook its centrality elsewhere. An instructive example for bioregional criticism is esoteric Bud-

Detail from a Buddhist "womb" mandala

dhism and its use of mandalas. Mandalas are concentric diagrams (mandala means "circular" in Sanskrit) that depict the interrelationships between fundamental Buddhist concepts and states of mind. They are used as aids in study and in meditation and can be drawn, printed, or woven. In design and in use they are analogous to the sand paintings of various native North Americans.

As seen by a Westerner looking in from the outside, mandala has multiple meanings. It seems, for example, to designate at least three different spaces. It is, at first, a visual representation of the spatial order of the physical universe. From the perspective of the philosopher Thomas Kuhn, it is, at this level of meaning, a paradigm, like a diagram of the solar system according to Copernicus. Next, mandala creates a space for dharma practice, the purpose of which is the attainment of enlightenment within the spatial order of the universe. The second space of mandala allows human beings to position themselves in the first space in a way that allows them to know the truth about themselves

and the world. Finally, mandala is the sacred space that comes into being at the moment of enlightenment. It is true space, the ultimately real universe.

The Judeo-Christian heritage disposes most Westerners to think of the relation between the actual world and the ultimately true world as spatially discontinuous and temporally sequential. Heaven is up there, not here, and it is then, not now. When we impose this dualism on the meanings of mandala, we conclude that at some moment in time, the moment of enlightenment, the third space of mandala somehow replaces or cancels out the first space. The practitioner uses the second space of mandala, the space for dharma practice, in order to escape the first space, samsara (the cycle of birth, death, and rebirth), and arrive at the third space, Buddhahood. Samsara has been transcended. We are in Buddha Heaven.

Practitioners of esoteric Buddhism tell me, if I understand them correctly, that we Westerners have made a serious, though understandable, mistake. In fact, this universe and the true universe are one and the same, although one does not know it at the start. From the perspective of enlightenment, heaven is here, eternity is now. This world, as it is, is sacred space. And so, the first and third meanings of mandala join and become one. The process of unification does not end there, however. The space created by mandala for dharma practice can be none other than the spatial order of the true universe, which is in turn the spatial order of the real universe. Therefore, in the most final of analyses, namely, from the perspective of Buddhahood, all three spaces are the same. The geometry of this world, the geometry of the world created for dharma practice, and the geometry of the sacred world are all equal to each other.

An important corollary of mandalic geometry is this: if the space for dharma practice is the space of the actual here-and-now world, then one can practice dharma in the real space made by the tree-growing, mountain-building, and water-recycling land we live in. In other words, land can be mandala. Proof that this corollary is not just theoretical is provided by the *yamabushi* of the Japanese religious order Shugendō.

Shugendō is a syncretic religious movement that first achieved coherence toward the end of the twelfth century. It combines elements of an ancient pre-Buddhist "mountain practice," *sangaku shinkō* in Japanese, with the doctrine and ritual of esoteric Buddhism. Its practitioners and its priests are called *yamabushi*, or "those who lie down in the mountains." From about A.D. 800, *yamabushi* were solitary men and women who practiced severe austerities in the mountains in order to gain special magical powers. By the seventeenth century, *yamabushi* had mostly settled down in villages as resident exorcists and healers, functioning somewhat the way priests do in a Roman Catholic parish. Shugendō was proscribed in 1873 by the Meiji government as a part of its effort to separate pure Shintō, the traditional religion of Japan, from baser Buddhist ores. In 1945, under the Occupation Government, it underwent something of a revival and continues in attenuated form today.

In 1987 the poet Gary Snyder contributed two woven mandalas of Japanese origin to an exhibit of Buddhist art in the Ring of Bone Zendo, a place of worship and practice for the Zen Buddhist community on San Juan Ridge, Yuba River Watershed, Sierra Nevada Bioregion. On either side of the Zendo's altar, Snyder had hung the two mandalas. To the right was a mandala of the Vajra Realm, or *Kongokai* in Japanese. He explained that it depicted the Universal Mind of the mandala's central figure, Dainichi Nyorai, the grand, cosmic Buddha of the Sun. To the left was a mandala of the Womb Realm, *Taizokai*, as the Japanese call it. On it was Dainichi Nyorai's diagram of her-his own body. The two realms together made up the totality of the universe. After describing in some detail the contents of the two mandalas in a pamphlet entitled *Contributions to the Ring of Bone Zendo Dharma Art Exhibit September '87 from the Kitkitdizze House*, Snyder turned to the *yamabushi*:

The Yamabushi regard the landscape itself as the mandala, and feel that mountain peaks are the Vajra realm, valleys and ravines the Womb realm. In particular the 60-mile-long Omine ridge, sacred to their practice, with its main peak at the center, is their Vajra Realm mandala. Completing ceremonies on the summit, and walking the many miles to the Kumano valley and the ancient Kumano ("Bear Meadow") Shinto shrine they conduct another ceremony, for the Womb Realm, at the valley bottom.

The gender dualism of the *yamabushi* mandalic landscape disturbs my twentieth-century Western mind, placing it on the tip of an intellectual pin. Nevertheless, I don't want to let my discomfort get in the way of appropriating for bioregional criticism an important insight from long ago and far away. The insight is that land can be mandala.

Diagram in Ecology

Fundamentally, mandala is a diagram of the universe. Open an ecology text, almost any one will do, and you will find comparable diagrams. (Good examples are the three illustrations on energy flow on pages 62 and 65 of the second edition of Eugene P. Odum's *Ecology*, and the predator-prey triangle on p. 138.) Ecologists make diagrams to represent physical reality as they understand it. These diagrams encode, by means of graphs, charts, and explanatory words, the world as ecologists think it actually operates. In other words, these diagrams, and the theories behind them, are mandalas.

Making mandalas out of ecological diagrams is unproblematic when we limit our conception of mandalas to representations of the physical universe. We can believe, not without some epistemological doubts, to be sure, that these graphs plot what really happens on this planet. When we move to a more philosophical understanding of the term, however, we become far more skeptical. We might allow that an ecological theory creates a space for our minds to practice clear and distinct thinking about interdependent relationships within the universe. We might even go further and admit that straight thinking might lead us to an enlightened understanding of our place in the universe. But we would be inclined to limit this practice to the intellectual. The emotional and the spiritual would have little or no place in it. And it would be rare indeed, even in our wildest moments of eco-enthusiasm, for us to affix the label "sacred" to anything found within the covers of an ecology book. Ecological paradigms might create spaces for scientists to practice in, to devise experiments and test them, but it would be stretching matters for most of us to say that this practice had significant religious dimensions, except in the sense that scientists might devote themselves to the task religiously.

We can comprehend how both mandala and ecological theory diagram the universe. We can imagine how Buddhists on the one hand and scientists on the other accord the status of truth to their respective models. We might not agree with these claims in either or both cases, but the logic is clear enough. It is difficult for us to grasp, however, how a scientific theory can lay out a field for religious practice, by which I mean a practice that includes and involves the entire person, the same person that the reading of literature engages. And it is difficult in the extreme for us to understand how such a theory, at the moment of comprehension, might become the universe it diagrams. In other words, we in the Western world can understand how scientific equations can be true (although we may tie our tongues in knots trying to defend this claim), but we can hardly imagine such formulas becoming sacred, in the sense of becoming vehicles for religious awareness.

Reenter the land, not the mountains of Japan where the *yamabushi* walk, but land in the shape of North America. Americans can conceive of land as creating a space for the spiritual imagination to practice in. What is difficult for Americans, shaped by Western intellectual values, to imagine is how any particular landscape can be a visual representation of the universal order. While they recognize intellectually that all the forces operating in the universe are also operating at the local level, they find it hard to visualize it, and, of course, visualization is what allows mandalas to work.

Bioregion and Mandala

Ecology can help Americans with the practice of visualization. If ecologists were going to choose a unit, a piece of the world, and say, "This is the unit that best illustrates how the whole is working," might not that unit be the bioregion? Ecology can, I think, by getting us to look at land bioregionally, enable us to visualize a particular landscape as the part that effectively stands for the whole, as that which on the local level is representative of the order that exists in the universe. We can then consider a bioregion as a unit of space where, by locating ourselves there, we place ourselves in a physical, mental, and spiritual relationship with the whole. At the moment that relationship is felt, not just grasped with the intellect, the moment it is realized, not merely postulated, bioregion will become sacred space. Bioregion will be mandala in all of its meanings.

Mandalas need to be set in the context of tantric practice, the religious life and tradition in which they are most fully developed. To one so untutored as I am, to venture very far on the trail of tantric discipline would take me light-years beyond my understanding. So let me follow the lead of Roger Corless, who has written the best primer of Buddhism I have read, *The Vision of Buddhism: The Space Under the Tree*. Corless makes a distinction between tantra and sutra:

> The primary meaning of the word tantra is similar to that of sutra. Both mean a thread or connection, that is, a link with the true teaching of the Buddhas. A sutra is an exoteric thread and is, in form, generally something like a sermon. It is an explanation or exposition of a doctrine. A tantra is a liturgy *(sadhana)*. One listens to a sutra in order to understand it. One learns a tantra in order to perform it. The tantra will contain [mandalas], mudras, and mantras, that is, visualizations, gestures, and sounds. When it is performed correctly by the properly prepared practitioner, a phenomenon that the Japanese Tantric teacher Kobo Daishi calls *sammitsu-kaji* takes place: the synergy *(kaji)*, or linking of energy between sentient beings and Buddhas. (p. 263)

Put simply, I am suggesting that as we practice bioregional criticism, we consider ecological diagrams not only as sutras, which comes easily and keeps us safely in the world we are used to inhabit. Let's also take them in the tantric sense, as liturgical directions, in which diagrams of bioregions (and ecosystems) are used as aids in visualizing our interconnection with all other things. The purpose of the liturgy is the linking of energy between one inhabitant of a bioregion and all other living and nonliving beings of the same bioregion. The ultimate goal would be, simply put, "living in place," where place is, for me, the Putah Creek watershed, Shasta nation, Turtle Island, Earth, air, fire, water, the Universe. Your list will begin differently and end the same.

Mandala and Metaphor

We have now come full circle. We began, by means of metaphor, with bioregion as Nature's local habitation and name. We end, by means of mandala, with bioregion as a local diagram of the real and the true universe. Both metaphor and mandala are members of the set of things that stand for other things. Even though we in the West are more comfortable with metaphor, mandala, as expressed in esoteric Buddhism, has some advantages over metaphor for the bioregional critic. Of some significance is the fact that mandalas are visual, making them, we hope, less abstract and easier to follow. In addition, one can, and this point is of greater significance, more easily compare mandalas with the diagrams and theories of ecology, thereby facilitating literature and ecology's joining hands in bioregional space. From a broad philosophical point of view, of course, one can argue that all scientific hypotheses are metaphors, but this is not the way we habitually think about them. Normally, scientific theories seem to be "true" in a way that metaphors are not. And so we arrive at the third advantage of mandala over metaphor, the one with the greatest significance. Mandalas implicitly contain a claim to truth the way scientific theories do, and these truths concern the realms of emotion and spirit as well as the realm of matter. In fact, with mandalas, it is impossible to separate the three realms. This

indivisibility is helpful for bioregional critics, who venture into bioregional territory precisely because of a belief that all things are ultimately one.

Bibliographical Essay

The cultivation of bioregion as fruitful ground for thought and action on planet Earth is, for the most part, a phenomenon of the second half of the twentieth century. The study of literature in a bioregional context was undertaken only in the last decades of that century, as the availability of works on this subject reflects. I recommend beginning with four very basic books on ecology. *Ecology*, by Eugene P. Odum, is a good textbook for the person relatively untrained in the natural sciences. Donald Worster in *Nature's Economy* gives an excellent account of the history of ecological thinking. It is helpful to supplement Worster with an account of the rise of ecology as an independent scientific discipline. My choice for this purpose is *The Background of Ecology*, by Robert P. McIntosh, although the nonspecialist will find it dense with complexity and detail. It should be read straight through fairly rapidly, concentrating on the fundamental issues that ecologists have dealt with. Finally, *Foundations of Ecology*, edited by Leslie A. Real and James H. Brown, is a collection of classic papers that have helped define the discipline.

The best single statement of a bioregional point of view is Jim Dodge's essay "Living by Life." It is most readily available in *Home! A Bioregional Reader*. This volume contains numerous other foundational essays, as does *Reinhabiting a Separate Country* and issues of the journal *Raise the Stakes*, both also published by Planet Drum Foundation in San Francisco. *Co-Evolution Quarterly* (winter 1981) and *The New Catalyst* (spring 1986) have published special issues on bioregionalism. Kirkpatrick Sale in *Dwellers in the Land* presents a basic argument for bioregionalism and a history of the movement. *Home!* contains a helpful annotated bibliography. The student serious about a bioregional approach to literature can write Planet Drum Foundation requesting a catalog of publications and a directory of bioregional organizations. The address is P.O. Box 31251, San Francisco, Calif., 94131. Another excellent source of information and publications is *The New Catalyst*, P.O. Box 189, Gabriola Island, British Columbia, V0R 1X0, Canada.

It has become increasingly apparent that ecofeminism and bioregionalism are often allies in philosophy and social action. Susan Griffin's *Woman and Nature* is a foundational essay. Because of its ecological perspective, *The Death of Nature*, by Carolyn Merchant, is an especially valuable book for bioregional literary critics. *Healing the Wounds*, edited by Judith Plant, is a good anthology of ecofeminist essays.

Roger Corless's primer on Buddhism, *The Vision of Buddhism*, is thorough and imaginative and is superior to most books written from the point of view of comparative religion because, although the audience is Western, the structure and categories of presentation are informed by Buddhist values. *A Religious Study of the Mount Haguro Sect of Shugendo*, by Byron Earhart, is a full-length, scholarly study of contemporary *yamabushi* practice.

My recommendation is that a bioregional study of literature begin with the bioregion, not with writers who have espoused a bioregional philosophy. Nevertheless, the desire to read authors associated with the movement, in order to form some idea of the shape and content of bioregional literature, is not unreasonable. I suggest beginning with Mary Austin's *Land of Little Rain*, the poetry and prose of Gary Snyder, and the novel *Always Coming Home*, by Ursula Le Guin, and then moving on to Terry Tempest Williams and Gary Nabhan. Of course, any and all of the writers discussed in the present collection provide a helpful context for bioregional thinking about literature.

Selected Bibliography

Van Andruss, Christopher Plant, Judith Plant, and Eleanor Wright, eds., *Home! A Bioregional Reader* (Philadelphia: New Society Publishers, 1990); Mary Austin, *The Land of Little Rain* (Boston and New York: Houghton Mifflin, 1904; many reprints available in paperback); Peter Berg, ed., *Reinhabiting a Separate Country* (San Francisco: Planet Drum Foundation, 1978); Roger J. Corless, *The Vision of Buddhism: The Space Under the Trees* (New York: Paragon House, 1989); Jim Dodge, "Living by Life: Some Bioregional Theory and Practice," in *The Co-Evolution Quarterly* (winter 1981), repr. in *Home! A Bioregional Reader*; H. Byron Earhart, *A Religious Study of the Mount Haguro Sect of Shugendo* (Tokyo: Sophia Univ., 1970); Susan Griffin, *Woman and Nature: The Roaring Inside Her* (New York: Harper & Row, 1978); Ursula K. Le Guin, *Always Coming Home* (New York: Harper & Row, 1985); Robert P. McIntosh, *The Background of Ecology: Concept and Theory* (New York: Cambridge Univ. Press, 1985); Carolyn Merchant, *The Death of Nature: Women, Ecology, and the Scientific Revolution* (New York: Harper & Row, 1980).

Gary P. Nabhan, *The Desert Smells Like Rain: A Naturalist in Papago Indian Country* (San Francisco: North Point, 1982), and *Gathering the Desert* (Tucson: Univ. of Arizona Press, 1985); Eugene P. Odum, *Ecology* (New York: Holt, Rinehart and Winston, 1963; 2d ed., 1975); Judith Plant, ed., *Healing the Wounds: The Promise of Ecofeminism* (Philadelphia: New Society Publishers, 1988); Leslie A. Real and James H. Brown, eds., *Foundations of Ecology: Classic Papers with Commentaries* (Chicago: Univ. of Chicago Press, 1991); Kirkpatrick Sale, *Dwellers in the Land: The Bioregional Vision* (San Francisco: Sierra Club, 1985); Gary Snyder, *Earth House Hold: Technical Notes and Queries to Fellow Dharma Revolutionaries* (New York: New Directions, 1969), *The Practice of the Wild* (San Francisco: North Point, 1990), and *Turtle Island* (New York: New Directions, 1974); Terry Tempest Williams, *Refuge: An Unnatural History of Family and Place* (New York: Pantheon, 1991); Donald Worster, *Nature's Economy: A History of Ecological Ideas* (San Francisco: Sierra Club, 1977).

CANADIAN NATURE WRITING IN ENGLISH

REBECCA RAGLON

CANADIAN NATURE WRITING, like its American counterpart, has its origins in the land. All too often, however, Canada has been portrayed as little more than a hard, cold land of perpetual snow, populated by Mounties, sled dogs, and hewers of wood. Edmund Wilson expressed a typical view when commenting in *O Canada* (1964) that Americans tended to imagine Canada "as a kind of a vast hunting preserve convenient to the United States." Even a superficial survey of its main features, however, modifies this impression of the "Great White North," for Canada also includes the green fecundity of the Pacific coast, the orchards and valleys of Nova Scotia and New Brunswick, the fishing villages of Newfoundland and Prince Edward Island, the Laurentian Shield country of Ontario, the interlake regions of Manitoba, the prairie of Saskatchewan, and the mountains of Alberta.

There are seventeen major ecosystems in Canada, ranging from the tundra in the north to the deciduous forests in the south. Nevertheless, much of the country is covered by the huge boreal forest that runs from the Yukon Territory through the top halves of the prairie provinces, before dipping south of Hudson Bay and on through the northern portions of Ontario and Quebec. Composed of black spruce forests, muskeg, rivers, and bogs, it is a land that has been thoroughly studied and explored by Europeans comparatively recently. Canada is embraced by three oceans, it has more coastline than any other nation, and its almost four million square miles of territory contains 22 percent of the world's remaining wilderness areas. Some of its mightiest rivers flow north: the Mackenzie and Yukon rivers, which empty into the Beaufort Sea, and the Saint Lawrence, which connects the Great Lakes with the Atlantic Ocean. More than 500 species of birds migrate to Canada every spring to breed and raise their young, grizzly bears and wolves still roam many parts of the country, and on both coasts salmon still migrate in some of the world's most extensive salmon runs.

The great variations in the natural landscape provide the underpinning for strongly defined regional cultures that include the Maritimes, Quebec, Ontario, and the Arctic as well as the provinces that collectively make up the "West." Nevertheless, the majority of the Canadian population resides within 100 miles of the U.S. border, a fact that has cast the northern part of the country in the role of a modern-day Ultima Thule, the "farthest land" of the imagination, a land that both beckons and terrifies. The ability of the land to crush or swallow the human is a common theme in Canadian literature, and it is a fear that haunts certain aspects of Canadian nature writing. Positioned against an enormous amount of space, human concerns often appear very small and insignificant, and, in a sense, much that is distinctive in Canadian nature writing confronts this idea of unimaginable space.

It is a theme that emerged very early in Canadian writing about the land and continues to the present day. For example, George D. Warburton, a retired British soldier, pauses for a moment in *Hochelaga; or England in the New World* (1846) seemingly awestruck by the immense "desert" that stretches between the last signs of human activity and the distant North Pole. There is a silence in this distance that fires the imagination of many Canadian nature writers. Grey Owl (Archie Stansfeld Belaney), in his book *The Men of the Last Frontier* (1929), comments on the silence that follows the eerie howls of wolves, a silence that settles down layer by layer, "and the frozen wastes resume their endless waiting; the Deadmen dance their grisly dance on high, and the glittering spruce stand silently and watch" (p. 44). Wallace Stegner, in a similar poetic vein, recalls his early boyhood on a family homestead near the Frenchman River in Saskatchewan. One winter night in 1914, while he is sledding, he finds himself alone on a snowy hill under the northern lights. He writes in *One Way to Spell Man* (1982): "I stood there by myself, my hands numb, my face stiff with cold, my nose running, and I felt small and insignificant and quelled, but at the same time exalted. Greenland's icy mountains, and myself at their center, one little spark of suffering warmth in the midst of all that inhuman clarity" (p. 175).

The imagination confronted by a land that seems to go on forever is a central feature of Canadian literature. There is a loneliness in the vision, but also a certain beauty, for it suggests the wisdom of coming to terms, finally, with human limitations. Whereas fiction writers and poets might be tempted to portray a harsh land that crushes human aspirations, nature writers seem able to step back and assess the human place in the world more dispassionately. Not infrequently, they seem to imply that the human place is not and cannot be a large one. This sense can manifest itself variously in terms of awe or of fear or by jostling humans from center stage altogether. Thus in *Dancing on the Shore* (1987) Harold Harwood portrays himself as sitting in a canoe in the Bay of Fundy, aware that his life is merely a flicker in the vasts depths of time, and in *A Wing in the Door* (1993) Peri Phillips McQuay realizes, after her frightening encounter with a deer, that it is she who is an intruder in the deer's home. Theodora Stanwell-Fletcher, in the depths of a northern British Columbia winter, discovers that the snow which makes travel so difficult for humans is a blessing for other types of life. She writes of one of her winter camping trips in *Driftwood Valley* (1946):

> So I spent the rest of that long night awake by the fire. Heat had melted a great circular space; I was in a small hot room surrounded by crystal walls five feet high; where snow had melted completely away just in front of the fire there was a tiny patch of bare ground; green vines and leaves, fresh and unharmed sparkled in red light. This great, wonderful, terrible mass of white stuff was not just beauty or danger to men of the Northland; it was also protector and guardian to animals and plants which hid beneath it; the mice and squirrels and bears, the tiny flowers of the forest floor, all those live things too small or clumsy to be abroad during winter. (pp. 104–105)

One of the key ways Canadian nature writing has muted the centrality of the human, however, is in the construction of animal stories in which the central "character"— the privileged "I" staring out at the world—is not human at all, but an animal or bird. In the process of confronting the fierceness and loneliness of a northern wilderness, Canadian nature writers have discovered the common bonds they share with other creatures making their home in a difficult land.

European Explorations

The first nature writing about Canada is found in the records of the earliest European explorers.

Initially, exploration involved the charting of Canada's coastal and inland waters, and accounts of the voyages of Jacques Cartier, Henry Hudson, and Samuel de Champlain contain early impressions of Canadian lands. Most of the very early British explorers were less interested in Canada itself, however, and far more interested in finding a passage through Canada to China. By far the most detailed accounts of the early exploration and settlement of Canada are in French, in the work of Marc Lescarbot and de Champlain and among the seventy-three volumes that compose the travels and explorations of the Jesuit missionaries in New France (*The Jesuit Relations and Allied Documents*, 1896–1901, edited by R. G. Thwaites). At this early stage, however, European assessment, both English and French, was contradictory. On one hand, there is astonishment at the sheer abundance of plant and animal life in the new land. On the other hand, there were genuinely harsh conditions to face as ships were forced to winter in icy Arctic conditions or to confront the storms of the Atlantic. On John Cabot's 1497 voyage the rich fishery of the Grand Banks was discovered, and soon English and French fleets joined those of Spain and Portugal in fishing Canadian waters. Although Basques had been fishing off Newfoundland since the thirteenth century, no permanent European settlement had been established during the intervening years, and when Cartier navigated the Saint Lawrence River in 1534, he is reported to have said that the Gaspé area was "the land God gave to Cain" (quoted in Cook, p. 10).

An early account that carefully notes the plants and wildlife of the new land is provided by the chronicler of Sir Humphrey Gilbert's Newfoundland voyage in 1583. After commenting on the cold and the snow of this northern island, Edward Hayes provides a long list of the land's "commodities" in Richard Hakluyt's *Voyages to the Virginia Colonies* (1986):

Touching the commodities of this country, serving either for sustenation of inhabitants, or for maintenance of traffic, it seems Nature has recompensed that only defect of some sharp cold, by many benefits: viz. with incredible quantity and variety of kinds of fish in the sea and fresh waters, as trout, salmon and other fish to us unknown. Also cod, which alone draws many nations thither, and is become the most famous fishing of the world. . . . Concerning the inland commodities, as well to be drawn from this land. . . . Namely, resin, pitch, tar, soapashes, dealboard, masts for ships, hides, furs, flax, hemp, corn, cables, cordage, linen-cloth, metals and many more. . . . Upon the land divers sorts of hawks, as falcons, and other by report; partridges most plentiful. . . . Birds some like blackbirds, linnets, canary birds, and others very small. Beasts of sundry kinds, red deer, buffalo or a beast, as it seems by the track and foot very large in manner of an ox. Bears, ounces or leopards, some greater and some lesser, wolves, foxes, which to the northward a little further are black, whose fur is esteemed in some countries of Europe very rich. Otters, beavers, martens . . . we could not observe the hundredth part of creatures in those uninhabited lands. (pp. 36–37)

This passage hints at what would become one of the grand motifs of English Canadian history: a land forged not by the dreams of settlers longing for a free land or a better life or by dreams of creating a "New France," but by a desire to extract wealth in the form of fish, fur, and timber from a land conveniently perceived as "uninhabited." From the point of view of a European settler wishing to farm, the northern half of North America was distinctly disappointing and could not be portrayed as a second Eden.

By the late eighteenth century much of the Canadian eastern seaboard had been mapped. European explorers then turned their attention to the vast space in the center of the country. This land, extending west and north of the Saint Lawrence River was known as Rupert's Land, and much of it had been ceded to the Hudson's Bay Company. For Canadians this land became a potent metaphor for their experience, similar to the idea of the "West" in American culture. The difference between the two metaphors, however, lies in the fact that Rupert's Land remained a place permanently beyond the influence of civilization, a place not for optimistic new beginnings but, rather, one that could swallow or destroy those who intruded too deeply. This was a land for fur traders, not settlers, an impression confirmed by many of the early explorers of Canada. Alexander Mackenzie, who completed a transcontinental journey at Bella Bella on 22 July 1793, fourteen years before Meriwether Lewis and William Clark began their explorations, believed that there was little land in the Canadian interior fit for cultivation and that the climate was too harsh for settlement. Perhaps the most haunting of all exploration accounts was John Franklin's *Narrative of a Journey to the Shores of the Polar Sea* (1823). Attempting to chart the Arctic coastline, Franklin became stuck in ice. His struggle to survive (which included cannibalism) has forever haunted Canadian impressions of the far north.

First Literary Impressions

Because of harsh geographical features and other difficulties, including intermittent fighting between the British and the French, much of Canada was deemed not suitable for settlement. Because of this early history, a very different relationship to the land developed from that forged in the United States. At issue was not the conversion of an entire land into a "New Jerusalem," but rather how the wild interior might be most favorably administered and exploited. As late as the eighteenth century the interior of Canada was viewed as a severe and difficult place permanently beyond the influence of European civilization; a place where fur traders might forever pursue their prey. The early concerns of the British, in particular, were not for building a new society, for saving souls, or for bringing the "advantages" of civilization to the native inhabitants: the London Committee of the Hudson's Bay Company did not concern itself with the questions of religion or the delivery of justice in the territories it governed. Rather, it was interested in trade with the native inhabitants, in fur, in profit, and in effectively administrating a vast and thinly populated territory.

Settlement of central Canada began to occur more rapidly, however, during the American Revolutionary War, when loyalists left the United States to settle in New Brunswick and Quebec. Soldiers demobilized in British North America were entitled to land. In spite of the liberalization of laws granting land to settlers, and in spite of the dozens of travel books published in the early years of the nineteenth century that extolled the virtues of Upper Canada (pointing out, among other things, that the winter climate was not nearly so severe as previously reported), settlement in Canada continued slowly, and early settlers in the colonies frequently revealed a deep ambivalence to the land surrounding them.

A gap existed between the imported language and the land these early settlers confronted. The German, British, Irish, and Scottish immigrants had inherited an aesthetic that valued the picturesque, and the first literary impressions of Canada are appreciative of the "sublime" aspects of Canadian nature, commenting again and again on the "grandeur" of the mountains, the rivers, and Niagara Falls. Such writings are also caught up many times in sentimental notions of a benevolent natural order and clearly find evidence of God's order in flowers, sunsets, and seasonal change. It was when nature was viewed in terms of the particular elements of day-to-day life, however, that the settlers' antipathy began to emerge. Many of these early writers found the trees crowding in on their clearings oppressive, the insects difficult, the cold daunting, and the split-rail fences that seemed to surround every homestead unattractive. Over and over again, in both fiction and non-fiction, the sense of the "oppressive" forest emerges. In one of the most extreme examples, the novelist John Richardson compares the forest to a type of prison in his *Wacousta* (1832).

In time, however, these British expatriates found that the Canadian landscape had become "home." French Canadians, unlike the British settlers, had long held a deep-seated belief in a special connection their communities had to the "land," and a habitant literature glorifying this relationship developed throughout the nineteenth century, finding its most romantic expression in Louis Hemon's *Maria Chapdelain* (1916). Eventually English-speaking Canadians, too, began to see that their "special identity"—neither European nor American—was somehow linked to the land.

English Canadians, however, even while investigating this "special relationship," retained a certain unease, perhaps even distrust, of the land that was their home. They never seemed as confident as their American neighbors in the regenerative good to be reaped by hard work or as seduced by the lure of "freedom" in the backwoods. Nor did they seem as inclined to celebrate "wildness" in the way that Americans from Henry David Thoreau to Edward Abbey have. Canadians were and are more inclined to call their wilderness territory the "bush," a term that conveys a complex mixture of affection, contempt, and fear. Nature writing is only one strain among the many that provide a collective testimony of the Canadian relationship with the land, yet it is a strain that allows for a more equitable relationship to emerge. Nature writing offers a corrective to an unbalanced metanarrative haunted by storms, hardships, and freezing cold. In its earliest stages it also offered a path toward reconciliation with a land that was frequently misunderstood.

In all of Canadian letters there is no example that illustrates the reconciling possibilities of nature writing more concretely than that of the two sisters who settled in Upper Canada in the 1830s. Susanna Moodie, in *Roughing It in the Bush* (1852), reveals a woman who looked forward to seeing the "solemn grandeur" of nature in North America and who was bitterly disappointed by the somber pine woods, charred stumps, piles of brushwood, and split-rail fences she found. Beauty in nature, if it was to be perceived at all, was seen in the abstract and from a distance. Moodie writes about her trip down the Saint Lawrence: "Never shall I forget that short voyage from Grosse Isle to Quebec. I love to recall, after the lapse of so many years, every object that awoke in my breast emotions of

astonishment and delight. What wonderful combinations of beauty, and grandeur, and power, at every winding of that noble river!" (p. 27). But when she tried going for a walk in the woods near her home, she was afraid of the wild animals that might be lurking behind the somber pine trees. Disgusted by the charred and blackened stumps and piles of brushwood lying everywhere waiting to be burned, she concludes unhappily that "there was very little beauty to be found in the backwoods."

Catherine Parr Traill, Moodie's sister, was equipped with different expectations of nature as well as with different skills—before immigrating to Canada, she had published *Sketches from Nature: or, Hints to Juvenile Naturalists* (1830). Whereas Susanna lamented the landscape she had left behind, Catherine worked diligently to become an accomplished naturalist in Canada and eventually produced books dealing with native plants and flowers. She frequently lamented the fact that she had not paid more attention to her botanical studies in England, because they would have been helpful to her in identifying the unknown plants of the Canadian bush. Although Traill's was a hard life, her writing about the "backwoods" of Canada nevertheless reveals a woman deeply touched by the natural beauty around her. One of the first gifts given to her by her husband upon arrival in North America was a bouquet of flowers, a gift that could not have been more appropriate for a woman who years later published *Canadian Wild Flowers* (1868) and, at age eighty-three, *Studies of Plant Life in Canada* (1885).

Traill remained steadfastly optimistic in her writing partly because of her personality and partly because she believed in a benevolent natural order. Although determined to carry on cheerfully, whatever hardships she might face, she is realist enough to be aware of the loneliness of the backwoods, particularly for women. In *The Backwoods of Canada* (1836), her collection of letters to relatives in England, she comments on many of the unlovely results of land clearing and makes the usual complaints about the oppressively warm summer weather, the troublesome blackflies and mosquitoes, and the annoying smoke from the smudges lit to keep them away. But she also notes the order of forest succession, enjoys the antics of a red squirrel, and, unlike her sister, has a few kind words to say about her "Yankee" neighbors. Although always longing for the spring and summer, when the flowers she loved so much would come into bloom, eventually she comes to appreciate even the winter, long and severe as it was.

What is particularly interesting about Traill is the keenness of her observations about nature. Unlike her sister, who had only the most general adjectives at her disposal and who was clearly frustrated when the gap between reality and expectation was so great, Traill was able to write very concretely about particular experiences with the natural world. Because she was a naturalist, and because she had taken the time to become acquainted with the plants and animals in the "bush" surrounding her homestead, she gained a new vocabulary and, with it, the ability to talk about her new surroundings. It is difficult to make much of Moodie's "enchanting scenes" or "glorious rivers," but it is possible even now to share a moment with Traill when she talks about pausing on her walk to inhale the fragrance from a cedar swamp on a sunny day or describes a winter scene with its dark pines and the "deep leaden tint" of a half-frozen lake. She writes about sumac, water lilies, violets, grass, ferns, and wild roses. In *The Backwoods of Canada*, she lingers over sensual experience, such as the scent of her favorite flowers:

> The flowers that afford the most decided perfumes are our wild roses which possess a delicious scent; the milkweed which gives out a smell not unlike the night flowering stock; the purple monarda, which is fragrance itself from the root to the flower, and even after months' exposure to the winterly atmosphere its dried leaves and seed vessels are so sweet as to impart perfume to your hands or clothes. (p. 91)

In addition to reporting in such detail the sights, scents, and sounds of her new home, Traill seems to embark on a type of "edible" communion with nature that is reminiscent of Thoreau's later experiments. But she is far more thoroughgoing in her quest, looking at the uses of both wild and domestic plants, providing recipes, medicinal advice, instructions, hints, and suggestions in *The Female Emigrants Guide* (1854), which was reprinted as *The Canadian Settler's Guide* (1855). It is a book that reveals a thorough and intimate knowledge of the plants in her new surroundings. Although Traill could take a very practical view of her surroundings, she also found inspiration and solace in nature and was one of the first Canadian writers to ground her aesthetic sense in what was locally available. Over and over again she encourages new settlers to make use of native plants to beautify their stark houses, urging them to plant hedges and to train the vines of native grape or ivy to climb up the porches of their log homes. She hoped her book *Pearls and Pebbles; or Notes of an Old Naturalist* (1894) would become a popular and inspirational household book similar to Gilbert White's *Natural History of Selborne* (1789).

Traill was one of the first nature writers in Canada, and her accomplishments are made even more impressive by the fact that women's efforts in natural history study were generally ignored in Victorian Canada. Although Traill has on occasion been deemed less interesting than her sibling, her writing nevertheless has a vivacity and concreteness that have worn very well and that place her in the front ranks of early nature writers.

Canadian Wilderness Theories

Natural history studies, both institutional and social, were a part of the intellectual climate in most English-speaking countries during the nineteenth century, and Canada was no exception. For many Canadians, nature was merely the "bush" — a mass of impenetrable scrub that hemmed in their clearings. For those with scientific curiosity, however, a great deal of interest could be found in the Canadian wilderness. The impetus for the study of the Canadian bush was provided in the form of innumerable natural history clubs and societies that were established during the 1850s. Field excursions became scientific and social events in which both men and women participated. More formal acknowledgment of the importance of natural history study came with the establishment of chairs in natural history at several Canadian universities. The Royal Society of Canada was formed in 1882; textbooks dealing with Canadian geography, plants, and animals were written; and journals such as the *Canadian Naturalist* were founded.

All of this scientific activity, however, could not mask the fact that in terms of a literary response to their northern landscape, Canadians retained peculiarly ambivalent attitudes. Northrop Frye attempted to fashion a national myth from Canadian literature, theorizing that the Canadian identity was made by a shared "garrison mentality." Unlike the Americans, who marched confidently forward, intent on improving, developing, and ultimately converting their wilderness, Canadians, faced with an even more formidable wilderness, huddled down, looked inward, sought comfort from one another. Americans regarded their land with a certain amount of affection for what it could be; Canadians, on the other hand, looked at their land with terror because the bush seemed to resist "humanization." Frye writes in *The Bush Garden* (1971):

> I have long been impressed in Canadian poetry by a tone of deep terror in regard to nature. . . . It is not a terror of the dangers or discomforts or even the mysteries of nature, but a terror of the soul at something that these things manifest. The human mind has nothing but human and moral values to cling to if it is to preserve its integrity or even its sanity, yet the vast unconsciousness of nature in front of it seems an unanswerable denial of those values. (p. 225)

Frye also suggests that the writers who spend their time describing a white wasteland, howls of wolves, a limitless sense of space receding off into the Arctic share an almost neurotic sense of "spiritual responsibility" for this landscape. Canada is also a place that always fears its own disappearance, according to Frye. Beginning with the early explorers, who wanted only to get past the Canadian land by finding a way through it, to more contemporary fears of being swallowed by American culture, Canadians seem always to be testing the viability of their continued existence. This ongoing anxiety over the Canadian identity is at least partly due to the Canadians' experience of their land. According to Frye, the "empty spaces" of Canada—the unknown forests, lakes, and rivers—have resulted in a type of "obliterated environment" that produces "imaginative dystrophy."

The Canadian novelist Margaret Atwood picked up and developed some of Frye's themes in her *Survival: A Thematic Guide to Canadian Literature* (1972). She attributed her experience of an "obliterated environment" not to the physical environment as such but to a lack of guides, and found that when she began reading Canadian fiction, particularly the animal stories of Charles G. D. Roberts and Ernest Thompson Seton, she had entered, at last, a familiar territory. Atwood attempts to define the "Canadianness" of certain books by identifying a central symbol for American, British, and Canadian literature. She believes a central symbol for America is the Frontier and its associated ideas of new beginnings. For England the central symbol is the Island and its associated ideas of the body politic. The central symbol for Canada, however, is survival, *la survivance*, in all its physical, cultural, and political forms. The main idea behind survival, moreover, is hanging on and staying alive.

> Our central idea is one which generates, not the excitement and sense of adventure or danger which The Frontier holds out, not the smugness and/or sense of security, of everything in its place, which The Island can offer, but an almost intolerable anxiety. Our stories are likely to be tales not of those who made it but of those who made it back, from the awful experience—the North, the snowstorm, the sinking ship—that killed everyone else. The survivor has no triumph or victory but the fact

of his survival; he has little after his ordeal that he did not have before, except gratitude for having escaped with his life. (p. 33)

Atwood notes that given a choice of using a negative or a positive aspect of a natural symbol, Canadian writers not only show a preference for the negative but will even work to contrive spectacular failures. Such fictions, according to Atwood, merely restate the whole Canadian experience with land—beginning with the explorations that didn't "find" anything or that led to doom and death. Death by nature is an event that occurs with such regularity in Canadian narratives that Atwood wonders if Canadians have a will to lose that mirrors Americans' will to win.

Even more curious, according to Atwood's thesis, is that once humans do start to "win" in Canadian literature, sympathy switches from the victor to the victim. Once humans appear on the verge of "conquering" nature, in other words, sympathy begins to be extended to the whole natural world. Nature is seen to be filled with fellow victims, and from this insight evolves the archetypal Canadian animal story. Unlike the animal stories of Beatrix Potter or Kenneth Grahame, however, where toads and bunnies are presented as dressed animals, and unlike such American hunting stories as William Faulkner's *Bear*, Canadian writers such as Seton and Roberts tell stories from the point of view of a realistically portrayed animal. As Atwood points out, "English animal stories are about 'social relations,' American ones are about people killing animals; Canadian ones are about animals *being* killed, as felt emotionally from inside the fur and feathers" (p. 74).

Building on the work of both Frye and Atwood, Gaile McGregor makes the case that Canadians have a very different relationship to nature than do Americans. She sees even in the most celebrated group of Canadian "nature" painters, the Group of Seven, a type of uneasiness in the face of nonhuman nature. This uneasiness has prevented Canadians from developing a celebratory relationship to the "wild." In part this is because of a different type of geography, a differ-

ent history, and a different time frame—rather than a seventeenth-century millennial reading of nature, Canada's early settlers were saddled with a Wordsworthian concept of nature that was inadequate when faced with the reality of their northern frontier.

Canada, like the United States, might be a frontier society; nevertheless, McGregor argues in *The Wacousta Syndrome* (1985) that there are important cultural divergences between the American West and the Canadian North:

A western frontier, depending on one's perspective, is the *limit of knowledge* or the *limit of control*, and as such denotes a temporary and arbitrary boundary that may not only be transcended but actually redefined—moved, advanced, or even eradicated—by human effort. To "go beyond" a western frontier, therefore, is both a commendable achievement in public terms and an exhilarating experience on the private level. A northern frontier, in contrast, denotes the *limits of endurance*. It is, in brief, an intangible but ineradicable line between the "self" and the "other," between what is and is not humanly possible. While the western frontier is simply a culturally defined interface, the northern frontier is an existential one. (p. 59)

Whatever the explanation advanced, it is nevertheless true that Canadians, unlike their American counterparts, have not produced a body of wilderness prose that could be comparable to the wilderness writings of Henry David Thoreau, John Muir, or Abbey. Although Frye's thesis might be overstated, most writers who have attempted to grapple with the Canadian perception of nature have noticed a lingering sense of caution when confronted with the wider aspects of the land. Nor is this strictly a European response, as awesome spirits such as D'Sonoqua or Windigo arising from a variety of native cultures can attest. Perhaps there is less wilderness rhapsodizing simply because there still *is* some wilderness territory in Canada.

Paradoxically, however, wilderness imbues much of Canadian literature. As Bruce Littlejohn and Jon Pearce point out in their anthology

Marked by the Wild (1973), *"If there is one distinguishing element that sets Canadian literature apart from most other national literatures, it is the influence of the wild"* (p. 11). Even Frye's "garrison mentality," in other words, is best seen as constructed within a reciprocal relationship with the surrounding wilderness. The striking fact remains, however, that overt discussions of the wild, so prevalent in American nature writing, is not a prominent feature in Canadian nature writing.

Animal Stories

Canadians have written about the land in all the major variations in nature writing. They have had their explorers, their sportsmen, their naturalists. They have had books of rambles and books of adventures. There have been innumerable celebrations of country life, farming, and fishing. More recently, strong environmental perspectives have emerged in Stan Rowe's *Home Place* (1990), Don Gayton's *The Wheatgrass Mechanism* (1990), and John Livingstone's *The Fallacy of Wildlife Conservation* (1981). The complexities of different cultural perspectives are handled in Hugh Brody's remarkable book *Maps and Dreams* (1981), which deals with native hunting societies in northern British Columbia and the conflicting ways in which the area has been "mapped." Michael Poole's *Ragged Islands* (1991), an account of a canoe trip along the Inside Passage of British Columbia, examines the decline of many of the natural resources in one area, which seems to parallel the decline of small permanent settlements, both native and nonnative. Nature writers have emerged from all areas of the country, and there are strong regional voices linked to certain geographies in the way that Muir is linked to the Sierras: Andy Russell and the Rocky Mountains; Emily Carr and Roderick Haig-Brown with the Pacific coast; Harold Harwood and Nova Scotia; Louise de Kiriline Lawrence with northern Ontario; Frederick Philip Grove and prairie trails; Farley Mowat and the North.

In surveying the literary, scientific, and natural backgrounds of nature writing in Canada, however, it seems that the unique contribution Canadians have made to the genre resides in the animal story. American writers have taught their readers to value what is wild in nature, and the British portray and extol a rural sensibility. Canadians, on the other hand, have excelled in conveying a deeply felt sense of kinship with other creatures. What emerges from Canadian animal stories is not only a finely honed appreciation for "fellow creatures" but also a reexamination of human values. In the stories of Seton and Roberts, the human no longer resides in the center. Since it is possible only to imagine the activities that collectively make up the story of any animal's life these works are technically "fiction." Yet by insisting that animals not only learn but also feel, these stories retain a contemporary relevance and interest.

Animal stories in the form of fables, legends, and myths are universal in all cultures, but Canadian writers developed a new version when they linked their stories to natural history studies. Seton, in particular, was a respected naturalist, and one of his proudest accomplishments was a survey of wildlife, published as the *Mammals of Manitoba* (1886), undertaken for the government of Manitoba in his capacity as that province's "official naturalist."

There are various implications that derive from making nature a "storied" place rather than a place that is a treasure-house of fact. Seton addresses the issue in his first collection of animal stories, *Wild Animals I Have Known* (1898), when he defends his use of story line by asserting that "natural history has lost much by the vague general treatment that is so common" (p. 9). Seton's flare for the dramatic had been well developed before he turned to writing: he had early combined his career as a naturalist with illustration, and in 1892 had the distinction of having a major canvas titled *The Wolves' Triumph* rejected by both the Paris Salon and a Toronto selection committee charged with putting together an exhibit for the Chicago World's Fair. *The Wolves' Triumph* pictured wolves feeding on human remains, and the Toronto committee worried about what kind of message such a picture might convey about life in Canada. By the time Seton turned to writing, however, the "triumph" of wolves had been converted into a concern for the essential tragedy of the lives of animals in the wild. Seton had homesteaded in Manitoba during the early 1880s and when he returned for a visit in 1892, he was struck by the changes: the diminished birds and wildlife, the drained marshes, and new crops growing where prairie grasses had once thrived.

"The life of a wild animal *always has a tragic end*," Seton wrote in *Wild Animals I Have Known*. He pointed out in his next collection of stories *Lives of the Hunted* (1901), that the only way to avoid the tragic end would be to stop before the last chapter. Seton was convinced that the "truth" of an animal's life could be seen only when it was portrayed as an individual being, with an individual's fate, rather than in an abstract way, as an interchangeable member of a species. It was also by focusing on the individual that Seton could further what he saw as the "moral purpose" of natural history, that is, to teach the truth that humans and animals are kin. In Seton's view, natural history should be colorful, lively, and full of incident, because in essence such writing reflected the reality of the lives of birds and animals. There was no reason why humans should arrogantly believe that they were the only ones to have life stories. In addition, natural history contained profound moral lessons. In *Lives of the Hunted*, Seton took the opportunity to elaborate on his dramatic brand of nature writing:

> My chief motive has been to stop the extermination of harmless wild animals; not for their sakes, but for ours, firmly believing that each of our native wild creatures is in itself a precious heritage that we have no right to destroy or put beyond the reach of our children. . . . I have tried to stop the stupid and brutal work of destruction by an appeal—not to reason: that has failed hitherto—but to sympathy, and especially the sympathies of the coming generation. (p. 13)

Roberts, a distinguished Canadian poet, outlined an anatomy of the animal story in *The Kindred of the Wild* (1902), suggesting that there has been a type of progressive movement toward this new genre. According to Roberts, the animal story is as old as literature itself, originating in hunting stories and based upon the desire to overcome or conquer an animal. These stories were enthralling but concentrated less on the existence of the animal and more on the adventure of the chase and the final triumph of the human actor. The next step in the evolution of the animal story occurred when animals were turned into symbols of human vices and virtues and thus became the basis of legends and fables. In this development, Roberts clearly sees a widening line being drawn between humans and animals—as humans became more and more engrossed in a world of their own making, the real nature of the animals surrounding them became more and more obscure.

Interest in the true nature of animals is indicative of an ongoing spiritual revolution, according to Roberts. Feeling that Christianity was at odds with the natural world, Roberts believed that scientific pursuits marked a significant broadening of human intellectual and spiritual interests. Furthermore, as people began to observe their pets and domestic animals more closely, they would see that these "irrational" creatures at times acted in ways that could not be explained entirely by theories about animal instincts. According to Roberts, humans had hardly even begun to think about animals, but once they did, their relationship to both animals and the wider world of nature would be transformed:

> Looking deep into the eyes of certain of the four-footed kindred, we have been startled to see therein a something, before unrecognized, that answered to our inner and intellectual, if not spiritual selves. We have suddenly attained a new and clearer vision. We have come face to face with personality, where we were blindly wont to predict mere instinct and automatism. It is as if one should step carelessly out of one's back door, and marvel to see unrolling before his new-awakened eyes the peaks and seas and misty valleys of an unknown world. (pp. 23–24)

Roberts' true interest and originality lay in what he called "animal psychology." In its best form, the animal story was a "psychological romance constructed on a framework of natural science." It was the scrupulous adherence to fact that differentiated Roberts' and Seton's work from other romances, for according to Roberts, a story such as *Black Beauty* was predicated upon human psychology. In contrast, Roberts believed that his work, as well as Seton's, was devoted to finding the true motive behind an animal's or bird's action. To do so was both to enlarge the world humans live in and to court emancipation: "The animal story, as we now have it, is a potent emancipator. It frees us for a little from the world of shop-worn utilities, and from the mean tenement of self of which we do well to grow weary" (p. 29).

This sense of kinship is developed in a number of ways, including dealing with the idea of an animal as an individual with a complex life history. Because most observations of wild animals are by necessity mere "glimpses," descriptions of animals in nature writing are usually presented as slice-of-life vignettes. Seton and Roberts, as well as the others who followed them, presented animals and birds as creatures that must be considered in terms of a continuous life history. Because of their focus they included in their work the heretical idea that animals have intelligence and can think, reason, and learn. Most important, however, the animal heroes in Seton's and Roberts' works can feel. The fox in Roberts' *Red Fox* (1905) is by turn apprehensive, filled with anger, cautious, puzzled, astonished, playful, or elated. Red Fox is not a victim, however; rather, he is portrayed as a triumphant survivor who time and again outwits the humans bent on destroying him.

Similarly, Seton's Redruff, the Don Valley partridge, feels the thrill of spring just as surely as he feels the cruelty of the poacher's snare in *Wild Animals I Have Known*:

Have the wild things no moral or legal rights? What right has man to inflict such long and fearful agony on a fellow-creature, simply because that creature does not speak his language? All that day, with growing, racking pains, poor Redruff hung and beat his great, strong wings in helpless struggles to be free. All day, all night, with growing torture, until he only longed for death. But no one came. The morning broke, the day wore on, and still he hung there, slowly dying; his very strength a curse. The second night crawled slowly down, and when, in the dawdling hours of darkness, a great Horned Owl, drawn by the feeble flutter of a dying wing, cut short the pain, the deed was wholly kind. (pp. 357–358).

There are "laws of nature" in the work of both Roberts and Seton, but these laws do not mean that animals must be presented as devoid of some of the same feelings, thoughts, and motivations as humans or that their lives lack events that give them interest, meaning, and the possibility to learn.

Archie Stansfeld Belaney, an Englishman who emigrated to Canada in 1906 and became first a trapper and then a conservationist, lived an entire life that was a type of fiction. Nevertheless, under the name Grey Owl, he wrote deeply empathic accounts of animals and attributed his conversion from a trapper to a conservationist to the influence of his native wife, Anahareo. He was vaguely aware that the land he loved was trapped out, yet he recounts in *Pilgrims of the Wild* (1935) that he went on a spring hunt to clean out a family of beaver. Although, he said, he had scruples about hunting in that season, "like too many of my kind, I salved my conscience by saying that I may as well to clean them out before someone else stepped in and took them" (p. 27). The mother was killed, but two kittens remained, and a vague sense of the need for atonement resulted in Grey Owl and Anahareo adopting them, taking the two beavers literally into their home and their lives.

In the same book, Grey Owl recounts becoming more and more horrified by the cruelties of trapping, in one instance finding a mother beaver nursing a kitten while held by one foot in the trap and whimpering in pain:

These inhumanities aroused in me a strange feeling; it was that these persecuted creatures

Grey Owl (Archie Stansfeld Belaney) shares his canoe with a member of his adopted beaver family, from *The Men of the Last Frontier.*

no longer appeared to me as lawful prey, but as co-dwellers in this wilderness that was being so despoiled, the wilderness that was so relentless yet so noble an antagonist. They too fought against its hardships and made their home in it; we all, man and beast, were comrades-in-arms. (pp. 49–50)

Grey Owl's beavers, Jelly Roll and Rawhide, like Grey Owl himself, eventually became famous: a great success in film, on the lecture circuit, and through his other books, *The Adventure of Sajo and Her Beaver People* (1935) and a book of essays, *Tales of an Empty Cabin* (1936).

Roberts, Seton, and Grey Owl wrote at a time when it was still possible to speculate about the possibility of animal personalities. It would be easy enough, perhaps, to dismiss such writing as sentimental or too anthropomorphic for modern tastes, except for the immense dignity and passion with which these writers press their claims for a renewed sense of "fellow creature." Later in the century, Fred Bodsworth would feel less secure in this matter, and his book *Last of the Curlews* (1955) contains a certain amount of scientist language that mars the deeply felt, elegiac tone. Particularly dramatic moments in the curlew's incredible annual pole-to-pole migration, for example, are undercut by talk of an "instinctive behavior code," a "rudimentary brain," or the "outpouring of hormones." Bodsworth is far more hesitant that his predecessors when it comes to considering the bird's "loneliness" or fatigue or capacity for joy. For Bodsworth there is no insistence on reasoning or intelligence; rather, the curlew is presented as responding to wider patterns or physiological changes. Nevertheless, the enormity of Bodsworth's topic makes his one of the most moving of all animal stories. Bodsworth writes from the point of view of an individual curlew, but it is a curlew that is also one of the last of his species.

Farley Mowat injects a welcome humor into the animal tale in his *Never Cry Wolf* (1963). Although the book is not written from the animal's perspective, Mowat has no hesitation in anthropomorphizing the wolves he studied in the Barren Grounds of the Northwest Territories, although to maintain the pretext of scientific objectivity, he refers to "George," one of his favorite wolves, as Wolf "A" in his official notebook. He has a great deal of pleasure in poking fun at the entire scientific enterprise, which insists on "objectivity." He pictures himself as ludicrously encumbered with an "arsenal" of scientific equipment or taking part in mock-serious experiments to see whether a diet of mice can sustain large carnivores. In part he does this because he is attempting to overthrow "scientific" notions about wolves current at the time. In one particularly amusing scene he finds himself unceremoniously displaced from the central role of official human "watcher" when he discovers that he has become an object of interest for the wolves.

Other animal "biographies" written by accomplished naturalists include Roderick Haig-Brown's *Ki-Yu: A Story of Panthers* (1934) and *Return to the River* (1941); R. D. Lawrence's *Cry Wild* (1970) and *The Ghost Walker* (1983), and, most recently, the Canadian poet Lloyd Abbey's *The Last Whales* (1989). Abbey's novel tells of a remaining blue whale searching for his mate and surviving calf; it is scrupulously researched and beautifully written, but almost unbearably poignant when it becomes clear that the fate of the blue whale is tied to oceans now contaminated by nuclear waste. Another variation of the animal story is the tale written about the domestic animals. One of the best known in this genre is Sheila Burnfold's *Incredible Journey* (1961).

Conclusion

It is indeed difficult to speak of "Canadian" nature writing—nature, after all, does not acknowledge national boundaries. What is "Canadian" about species of birds, animals, or plants that make their home across the entire North America continent? How can one speak of the "Canadian" prairies or "Canadian" Rockies without sensing that such distinctions are at best arbitrary, and at worst, harmful, in terms of understanding broader patterns within the natural world? Nevertheless, Canadians have claimed "Northernness" as one of their distinctive features. Northernness is like wildness, only with an edge; in the American context it is Thoreau on top of Mount Katahdin rather than Thoreau at Walden Pond. Certainly there has been a great deal of mythmaking about the True North, a difficult land that hones stalwart men and women. In reality, most Canadians, huddled along their nation's southern border, are as likely as most Americans to be indifferent to the huge land that stretches out above them.

Legends about frightening spirits, stories of doomed exploration, poems about survival, theories about a garrison mentality together have constructed the "Canadian North." Nature writers are not immune to literary climates any more than they are immune to the weather, but they have made a different, wiser use of the mythology. An awestruck awareness of immense space, once perhaps a fairly common human experience, is today rare, and the testimony of that experience seems strange and unsettling. Nature writing is credited with helping humans adjust to a wider sense of home, and it seems churlish and old-fashioned of these Canadian writers to insist on the utter strangeness of the universe. It seems something of a luxury to face loneliness or to be able to experience profound silence.

Any survey of Canadian nature writing must concede that however favorably an author views "nature," what emerges is nevertheless a portrait of a formidable land. R. D. Lawrence writes in *Where the Water Lilies Grow* (1968) that the winter season is full of "harshness and fear and solitude, and an eerie silence during its short days; and a cold impassiveness during its long nights" (p. 74). On the other hand, summer offers no Edenic reprieve, for summer is the season of insects. Beginning with Catherine Parr Traill and continuing down to Chris Czajkowski, Canadian nature writers have been well aware of the swarms of insects that are a part of northern life. In *Cabin at Singing River* (1991) Czajkowski writes about the abominable horseflies that mar an alpine hike in British Columbia:

> Huge and sluggish, they descend upon us in swarms. Even their startlingly beautiful emerald eyes cannot endear them to us. Their sharp feet prickle our skin, and they crawl in our hair, buzzing and rubbing our nerves ragged. It is hard to suppress the desire to flail our arms in a frenzy to drive them away. They are easy to kill, but it is so unpleasant to feel their juicy bodies crush beneath our fingers and in the end, we let them alone and pull raincoats and hoods tightly over our heads in an effort to shut them out. (p. 50)

Nature writing, however, is a literary form that has an ultimate loyalty to a larger world than one that is solely human. In spite of discomforts and dangers, nature writers work to reconcile the human world with the natural world by acting as sensitive witnesses. The difficulties the land imposes frequently are presented as a type of trial through which the writer must pass in order to be worthy of greater insight. So Lawrence, after commenting on the harsh, fearful, and lonely wilderness, is rewarded for his perseverance in the face of such obstacles by a fleeting sight of wolves playing in the snow. Czajkowski, climbing a mountain on a hot, sunny day, wrapped in a raincoat, is rewarded by the sight of range upon range of mountains emerging from a fog. The more difficult the approach, it seems, the more sublime the revelation.

The luxury of sensing that human concerns are but a small part of a much larger reality is a wisdom that has been derived most fully from Canadian land. Accompanying such insight is a reaching out toward the "others" who live in the North, the animals and birds that share the same difficulties and joys as the humans. The animal story has been claimed most fully by Canadian cultural historians, but it is also a curious sidebar in the history of nature writing. In part the marginalization of the animal story has to do with the issue of the legitimacy of different kinds of knowledge—works about nature, after all, are supposed to be nonfiction, factual, full of information. Subjectivity in the form of emotive responses to events is allowed, but can be claimed only by the human observer. Canadian nature writers have so regularly broken the rules that their peculiar talents have been to a large extent ignored in the history of the genre. Yet they have been among the first to recognize other creatures as "subjects" and have broken down the observer–observed dualism by creating a "storied" version of nature. Such an accomplishment surely is not trivial, no matter how uncomfortable the issue of "anthropomorphism" has become.

The curious development and persistence of the animal story in the Canadian context challenges notions of what can really be "known" about the natural world. And although many writers have dealt with human arrogance toward the natural world, none have dealt as effectively with it as the animal stories in which the whole center of the world has shifted and it is viewed, as Atwood suggests, from within "feathers and furs." Nature, in the Canadian context, has not been completely tamed; it is a storied place, full of mystery, danger, and drama. Writers such as Grey Owl and Mowat are among the most flamboyant and colorful of all nature writers, and it is because their very lives are a type of fiction.

Finally, Canadians have had to come to terms with a northern land. They can curse the snow or discover its beauty; they can flee from the cold or linger. There is no doubt that nature writers have helped Canadians reconcile themselves to the difficulties of living in the North. Frederick Philip Grove, a novelist and accomplished nature writer, focuses on his fascination with cold lands in both *Over Prairie Trails* (1922) and *The Turn of the Year* (1923). He writes eloquently of his determination to stay and witness the approaching winter in *The Turn of the Year:*

Nature to us is not a fleeting incident nor a brief recreation: it is the one great experience of our lives. The poplars are still green, though their leaves have darkened, hardened, and become brittle: but here and there an ash has turned yellow; and here and there a clump of dogwood slowly assumes its purplish, warmly glowing red. Like poplar, ash, and dogwood we linger and look. It is from choice that we do not close ourselves in and that we do not close winter out. We want to live life as it is; we want to react to all of what exists; and we want to measure our lives by the largest unit, by the slowest and mightiest pulse which nature provides. (p. 232)

It is the desire to come to terms with the "mightiest pulse" of nature that characterizes the best Canadian nature writing.

Selected Bibliography

PRIMARY WORKS

Chris Czajkowski, *Cabin at Singing River* (Altona, Manitoba: Camden House, 1991); Frederick Philip Grove, *The Turn of the Year* (Toronto: McClelland and Stewart, 1923); Grey Owl, *Pilgrims of the Wild* (Toronto: Peter Davies, 1935; repr., Toronto: Macmillan, 1990); R. D. Lawrence, *Where the Water Lilies Grow* (London: Michael Joseph, 1968), and *The Natural History of Canada* (Toronto: Key Porter, 1988); Susanna Moodie, *Roughing It in the Bush; or, Life in Canada* (London: Richard Bentley, 1852), repr., ed. by Carl Ballstadt (Ottawa: Carleton Univ. Press, 1988); Charles G. D. Roberts, *The Kindred of the Wild: A Book of Animal Life* (Toronto: Clark, 1902); Ernest Thompson Seton, *Wild Animals I Have Known* (New York: Scribners, 1898; repr., New York: Penguin, 1987), and *Lives of the Hunted* (New York: Scribners, 1901); Theodora Stanwell-Fletcher, *Driftwood Valley* (Boston: Little, Brown, 1946); Wallace Stegner, *One Way to Spell Man* (Garden City, N.Y.: Doubleday, 1982); Catherine Parr Traill, *The Backwoods of Canada* (1836; repr., Toronto: McClelland and Stewart, 1966).

ANTHOLOGIES

Gerald M. Craig, ed., *Early Travellers in the Canadas 1791–1867* (Toronto: Macmillan, 1955); Wayne Grady, ed., *Treasures of the Place: Three Centuries of Nature Writing in Canada* (Vancouver: Douglas and McIntyre, 1992); Richard Hakluyt, *Voyages to the Virginia Colonies* (mod. vers., London: Century, 1986), ed. by A. L. Rowse; Bruce Littlejohn and Jon Pearce, eds., *Marked by the Wild* (Toronto: McClelland and Stewart, 1973); Germaine Warkentin, ed., *Canadian Exploration Literature* (Toronto: Oxford Univ. Press, 1993).

SECONDARY WORKS

Margaret Atwood, *Survival: A Thematic Guide to Canadian Literature* (Toronto: House of Anansi Press, 1972); Carl Berger, *Science, God, and Nature in Victorian Canada* (Toronto: Univ. of Toronto Press, 1983); Ramsay Cook, *The Voyages of Jacques Cartier* (Toronto: Univ. of Toronto Press, 1993); Northrop Frye, *The Bush Garden: Essays on the Canadian Imagination* (Toronto: House of Anansi Press, 1971); W. J. Keith, *Literary Images of Ontario* (Toronto: Univ. of Toronto Press, 1992); Marcia B. Kline, *Beyond the Land Itself: Views of Nature in Canada and the United States* (Cambridge, Mass.: Harvard Univ. Press, 1970); Alec Lucas, "Nature Writers and the Animal Story," in *Literary History of Canada*, ed. by Carl F. Klinck (Toronto: Univ. of Toronto Press, 1965); Robert MacDonald, "The Revolt Against Instinct: The Animal Stories of Seton and Roberts," in *Canadian Literature* no. 84 (spring 1980); Gaile McGregor, *The Wacousta Syndrome: Explorations in the Canadian Langscape* (Toronto: Univ. of Toronto Press, 1985); T. D. MacLulich, "Reading the Land: The Wilderness Tradition in Canadian Letters," in *Journal of Canadian Studies* 20 (summer 1985); James Polk, "Lives of the Hunted," in *Canadian Literature* 20, no. 53 (summer 1972), and *Wilderness Writers* (Toronto: Clarke, Irwin, 1972); Susan Joan Wood, *The Land in Canadian Prose 1840–1945* (Ottawa: Carleton Monographs in English, 1988).

CONTEMPORARY ECOFICTION

NICHOLAS O'CONNELL

AMID THE CONFUSION of the contemporary literary scene, it is easy to overlook trends that offer hope for a new coherence in American literature. One such trend is the growing body of ecofiction, which represents one of the most promising directions for American writing in some time. Ecofiction is a hybrid genre combining the concerns of nature writing with those of narrative fiction. In borrowing liberally from both categories, it attempts to achieve a fuller and more comprehensive scope than that available to either genre separately.

Like nature writing, ecofiction calls for a new relationship between people and place, a relationship that emphasizes the spiritual dimensions of landscape and the need for people to treat the land with respect and reverence. But while nature writing focuses primarily on the individual's relation with the natural world, ecofiction adds a social dimension. Most nature writing is autobiographical; the writer narrates his or her firsthand experiences of the natural world. The prototypical example is Henry David Thoreau's *Walden* (1854), but there are numerous contemporary examples as well, including Edward Abbey's *Desert Solitaire: A Season in the Wilderness* (1968), Annie Dillard's *Pilgrim at Tinker Creek* (1974), and Gretel Ehrlich's *The Solace of Open Spaces* (1985).

Works of ecofiction are typically concerned not only with the relationship between the individual and nature but also with the relationship between the individual and society. In this regard, ecofiction resembles traditional fiction writing, which focuses primarily on human relationships. Social conflict forms the basis of most modern short stories and novels, in which one protagonist or more attempts to achieve resolution with human society.

Works of ecofiction seek to synthesize the concerns of the two genres, resolving the conflict of the human heart in relation to others and to the environment, thus reconciling the individual with both society and nature. Ecofiction serves as a promising direction for literature because it demonstrates how individuals and society can find harmony with the environment. Thus it presents an appealing vision of human life on the planet.

This essay will examine four examples of contemporary American ecofiction: *Ceremony* (1977) by Leslie Marmon Silko, *A River Runs Through It* (1976) by Norman Maclean, *Housekeeping* (1981) by Marilynne Robinson, and *Always Coming Home* (1985) by Ursula K. Le Guin. It will suggest how these works are representative of contemporary ecofiction and how they and other works in this genre have grown out of the larger American narrative tradition.

Concern with landscape is certainly not a new issue in American literature. In *A Writer's America: Landscape in Literature* (1988), Alfred Kazin argues that behind all American writers "lies some everlasting background that we call 'Nature,'—land, the land that was here before there was anything else" (p. 8). Much of American literature addresses the subject of nature and the desire to come to terms with it as a society. In the early nineteenth century, Ralph Waldo Emerson argued eloquently for this aspect of the American tradition. In his introduction to *Nature* (1836), he calls for an American society "embosomed for a season" in the natural world, "whose floods of life stream around and through us, and invite us, by the powers they supply, to action proportioned to nature." In this and other essays, Emerson argues that American society should be based on nature in general and the American landscape in particular.

But such a society was by no means easy to achieve, especially since the terms "society" and "nature" are mutually exclusive in much American culture and literature. In the five novels that make up James Fenimore Cooper's *Leatherstocking Tales* (1823–1841), Natty Bumppo's frontier lifestyle seems incompatible with encroaching settlements. Likewise, Herman Melville's *Moby-Dick* (1851) ends not with a reconciliation between society and nature, but with the destruction of society in the form of a ship, the *Pequod*, by nature in the form of a white whale. And Mark Twain's *The Adventures of Huckleberry Finn* (1884) concludes with Huck's decision to "light out for the Territory ahead" to avoid being civilized by his Aunt Sally. If a desire to come to terms with nature represents an important aspiration of nineteenth-century American society, this aspiration was rarely resolved in its literature.

In the early twentieth century, however, this began to change, as writers responded to the growing evidence of an ecological crisis. Works such as Willa Cather's *O Pioneers!* (1913) and *The Professor's House* (1925), H. L. Davis' homesteading novel, *Honey in the Horn* (1935), and William Faulkner's short story collection *Go Down, Moses* (1942) set the stage for an emerging American tradition of ecofiction. Picking up the thread of these earlier works, novels such as A. B. Guthrie's *These Thousand Hills* (1956),

Wendell Berry's *A Place on Earth* (1967), N. Scott Momaday's *House Made of Dawn* (1968), as well as short stories by Wallace Stegner and futuristic tales such as Frank Herbert's *Dune* (1965) and Ernest Callenbach's *Ecotopia* (1975) developed the genre further, paving the way for the authors of ecofiction discussed below.

Ceremony

Since its publication in 1977, Leslie Marmon Silko's *Ceremony* has been hailed as one of the pioneering works of contemporary ecofiction. Like the other works in this genre, it illustrates how people can achieve reconciliation with each other and with the land by developing a new relationship with the environment, a relationship that acknowledges the spiritual dimension of landscape. *Ceremony* accomplishes this by adapting the Native American storytelling tradition to the forms of Western fiction to create a new kind of narrative, a hybrid novel that speaks to people everywhere, regardless of their background or ethnic origin. The book built on such works as N. Scott Momaday's *House Made of Dawn* and paved the way for such important contemporary novels as Craig Lesley's *Winterkill* (1984), James Welch's *Fool's Crow* (1986), and Louise Erdrich's novels and stories. *Ceremony* has helped spark a renaissance in Native American–influenced fiction, both by Indian and non-Indian authors.

Silko herself is of mixed ancestry—Laguna Pueblo, Mexican, and white. She was born in 1948 in Albuquerque, New Mexico, and grew up on the Laguna Pueblo Reservation, where she has spent much of her adult life. Many of her works concern the land and people of this area, including a book of poems (*Laguna Woman*, 1974), a book of stories (*Storyteller*, 1981), and another important novel (*Almanac of the Dead*, 1991). These works have won her a wide audience, but she remains best-known for *Ceremony*, her most celebrated novel.

As the scholar Scott Slovic pointed out in his essay "Nature Writing and Humor," *Ceremony* is essentially a conversion narrative. In the course of the novel, Tayo, a young half-breed, undergoes a change of mind and spirit, overcoming his despair of contemporary reservation life by rediscovering the rich history of Native American culture. He escapes the cycle of alcohol and senseless violence that traps many of his friends by experiencing the power of ancestral stories firsthand and then finding a way to adapt them to his present life. Throughout *Ceremony*, Silko treats the activity of storytelling as a powerful act, one that does much more than simply entertain or inform, and in fact can shape human lives and worlds. Early in the book, the narrator calls attention to the importance of stories.

> I will tell you something about stories,
> [he said]
> They aren't just entertainment.
> Don't be fooled.
> They are all we have, you see,
> all we have to fight off
> illness and death. (p. 2)

At their best, stories are the cement that binds people to each other and binds them to the land. At their worst, they encourage disharmony between people and dislocation from the land. Stories in *Ceremony* are never merely neutral; they always serve an ethical function.

In the early part of the book, Tayo is out of sync with his surroundings and out of touch with his Indian ancestry. After serving as a soldier in World War II, Tayo is sent to a veteran's hospital to recover from the trauma of his wartime experiences. The army doctors can do little to help him, so Tayo returns to Laguna Pueblo.

To pass the time and get some relief from battle fatigue, Tayo spends his time drinking beer and swapping tales with the other Indian war veterans. Drinking helps ease his pain, but the war stories only make matters worse. These stories concern the men's combat experiences and sexual conquests while on leave but do not help the men to come to terms with their present lives. In fact, the stories alienate them from the land and society around them. Tayo and his friends precisely lack the kind of story that could give order and meaning to their present lives.

Most of his friends, such as Harley, Pinkie, and Leroy, are content with these alienating stories, but Tayo grows increasingly frustrated with them, though he doesn't completely understand why. There is an implicit comparison at this point in the novel between Tayo and the Hereford cattle that his uncle Josiah describes as being out of touch with the land. "Cattle are like any living thing," Josiah says. "If you separate them from the land for too long, keep them in barns and corrals, they lose something" (p. 74). Like the Herefords, Tayo has been away from the land too long, partly because of his combat experiences, but mostly because of the stories he has chosen to guide his life.

When his grandfather suggests that he see an old Navaho medicine man about his condition, Tayo reluctantly agrees. The medicine man, Betonie, lives in a hogan north of Gallup, New Mexico. On meeting him, Tayo immediately notices Betonie's ease in his surroundings: "There was something about the way the old man said the word 'comfortable.' It had a different meaning—not the comfort of big houses or rich food or even clean streets, but the comfort of belonging with the land, and the peace of being with these hills" (p. 117). This sense of belonging with the land is inextricably bound up with the kind of stories Betonie tells. The first night at the hogan, Tayo hears a number of these stories. Unlike those of his barfly friends, Betonie's stories give Tayo a sense of hope. Among other things, they fault modern American civilization for cutting people off from the earth.

> Then they grow away from the earth
> then they grow away from the sun
> then they grow away from the plants and
>   animals.
> They see no life
> When they look
> they see only objects.
> The world is a dead thing for them
> the trees and rivers are not alive

1043

the mountains and stones are not alive.
The deer and bear are objects
They see no life. (p. 135)

Contemporary American civilization too often sees the land in materialistic terms. In such terms, the land has economic value but no spiritual dimension. Tayo recognizes that he has internalized this view, which has encouraged the psychological dislocation he now confronts. Though he has had intimations of a more animistic view of the world, he has not been able to fully realize it. He now seeks to do so through the ceremony Betonie agrees to perform.

The ceremony takes place over several days and includes certain "tests," points where Tayo must confront troubling aspects of his past, present, or future. Some aspects of the ceremony are the same no matter who is undergoing them; others are tailored to the individual and his particular problems or needs. The ceremony begins with storytelling. Betonie interprets the current world problems in the light of Native American mythology. He doesn't so much blame the whites for these problems as claim that they have been manipulated by evil deities, the destroyers of Navaho mythology. The only way to return himself and eventually the world to a sense of balance and harmony is by participating in the old ceremonies against the witchcraft of the destroyers.

In describing this ceremony, Silko mixes contemporary novelistic techniques such as scene-by-scene construction with those of Native American storytelling traditions. Native American storytelling is an oral tradition, lacking the concrete detail and scenic construction of modern fiction. It relies heavily on dream-visions, and includes stories peopled by mythic creatures such as Coyote. It is just such a fusing of narrative traditions, one white, one Indian, that makes possible Tayo's eventual healing. For the ceremony not only puts him back in touch with his Indian ancestry, it also allows him to reconcile that ancestry with his present circumstances. To this end, the ceremony includes not only generalized rituals but ones that apply to him personally.

After the second day of the ceremony, Tayo falls into a deep sleep and dreams of his Uncle Josiah's herd of speckled cattle, a dream that serves as the key link between the stories of his Navajo ancestors as represented by Josiah and his own ongoing personal narrative. When he wakes, he feels the healing effects of the dream. The distress that has plagued him for so long begins to loosen its grip; he starts to get back in touch with his surroundings: "He breathed deeply, and each breath had a distant smell of snow from the north, of ponderosa pine on the rimrock above; finally he smelled horses from the direction of the corral, and he smiled. Being alive was all right then: he had not breathed like that for a long time" (p. 181).

From that point on, Tayo remains firmly within the footsteps of the ceremony and begins to see his and Josiah's dream become a reality. Josiah's dream is to breed and raise the herd of speckled cattle he has purchased early in the book. What started as a half-formed desire to carry out Josiah's vision becomes a deep conviction and an integral part of the ceremony. Tayo sets out to find and retrieve the cattle. Once he has accomplished this, he realizes that the ceremony is nearing completion; his vision is merging with Josiah's vision and bringing him in touch with his ancestry and with the land: "Tayo's heart beat fast; he could see Josiah's vision emerging, he could see the story taking form in bone and muscle" (p. 226).

Tayo must pass one final test before the ceremony is complete. By instinct, he heads for a uranium mine not far from his aunt's house. The mine is particularly significant because ore from it provided fuel for the world's first atomic bomb. Thus it was here that the fate of his people became linked with that of all the world's peoples: "From that time on, human beings were one clan again, united by the fate the destroyers planned for all of them, for all living things; united by a circle of death that devoured people in cities twelve thousand miles away, victims who had never known these mesas, who had never seen the delicate colors of the rocks which boiled up their slaughter" (p. 246).

In this way, the stories of the Navajo, whites, and other peoples of the world have been knit together into one large story. Tayo begins to understand the enormous dimensions of the ceremony, its potential to change his own life as well as that of the entire human and natural world.

> He cried the relief he felt at finally seeing the pattern, the way all the stories fit together—the old stories, the war stories, their stories—to become the story that was still being told. He was not crazy; he had never been crazy. He had only seen and heard the world as it always was: no boundaries, only transitions through all distances and time. (p. 246)

Tayo's realization of the awesome significance of the ceremony allows him to see more deeply into everything. He recognizes how the stories told by his drinking buddies were not harmless or trivial, but in fact encouraged bitterness and despair, playing into the hands of the destroyers. He now understands that his uncle's dream of raising the herd of speckled cattle offers him a very personal vision of wholeness and completion, which includes a sense of connection with his Native American ancestry and a deep sense of identification with his surroundings. When all this has registered on him and the ceremony is finally complete, Tayo staggers home:

> His body was lost in exhaustion; he kept moving, his bones and skin staggering behind him. He dreamed with his eyes open that he was wrapped in a blanket in the back of Josiah's wagon, crossing the sandy flat below Paguate Hill. The cholla and juniper shivered in the wind, and the rumps of the two gray mules were twin moons in front of him. Josiah was driving the wagon, old Grandma was holding him, and Rocky whispered "my brother." They were taking him home. (p. 254)

By completing the ceremony, Tayo realizes that in putting his own life in order he has helped bring hope to his people, whose larger story is intimately connected with his own, and by implication to all the world's peoples, whose many and varied narratives have been knit inextricably together by events such as the detonation of the atomic bomb. *Ceremony* opens with an invocation of the sunrise and finally ends with a prayer to the next sunrise and all it promises for Tayo and the rest of the world's people: "Sunrise, / accept this offering, / Sunrise" (p. 262). In completing his ceremony, he has also helped complete the circle of hope for all humanity.

The repetition of the word "sunrise" calls attention to the circularity of *Ceremony*'s narrative. This structure emphasizes the cyclicity as much as the progress of time, and shows how Tayo's working through the ceremony leads him toward a kind of eternal present. In the later stages of the ceremony, Tayo becomes so intensely aware of the beauty of the earth that his sense of the passage of time diminishes; he becomes content merely to contemplate creation and his place within it. The novel reflects his change in consciousness by devoting less time to describing action and more to detailing the splendor and diversity of the earth. In so doing it calls attention not only to the progress of time and the importance of human action, but also to the round of the seasons and the infinite complexity of the natural world.

In this and many other ways, *Ceremony* demonstrates its status as a new kind of novel. In its structure, *Ceremony* is a hybrid book, a blend of the contemporary realistic novel and Indian storytelling traditions. Examples of Indian storytelling techniques include repetition of certain key phrases, dream-vision structure and talking animal characters such as Coyote, which imply connection between the world of animals and the world of human beings. *Ceremony* uses the techniques of realistic fiction such as flashback, scene, dialogue, and characterization, but it also incorporates Native American stories, which comment on and complicate the action taking place within the realistic narrative. It successfully and unapologetically brings together both traditions. As Betonie says of stories, they must keep changing, they cannot stay the same:

the wisdom of white culture must be added to the wisdom of Native American culture.

Leslie Silko has taken this advice. Using the techniques of modern realistic fiction and the tradition of Indian storytelling, she has managed to fashion a story that synthesizes both traditions as it illustrates a reconciliation of society and the environment. This sense of reconciliation is aided by the animistic nature of Native American stories and by the relatively close relationship between Laguna Pueblo society and the land. In demonstrating a reanimation of the natural world and a healing of the division between people and place through storytelling, *Ceremony* serves as an outstanding example of contemporary ecofiction.

A River Runs Through It

Like *Ceremony*, Norman Maclean's novella *A River Runs Through It* (1976) calls attention to the spiritual dimensions of landscape and suggests that appreciating these dimensions is necessary to achieving a respectful relationship with the natural world and with human society. But whereas Silko uses Native American tales to emphasize this dimension of landscape, Maclean adapts biblical stories to this purpose. Maclean uses the Judeo-Christian tradition as the basis for a deep and abiding identification with place. *A River Runs Through It* begins amid the rugged mountains and powerful rivers of western Montana, but in adapting biblical mythology it speaks to all those seeking a new relationship with landscape.

While in *Ceremony* Silko treats Christianity as part of the problem in spiritualizing landscape, Maclean sees it as an important part of the solution. The view of Christianity presented in *Ceremony* is largely polemical and serves mainly to make Native American spirituality seem preferable by contrast. Maclean has no such axe to grind. He understands the complexity of the Christian tradition and uses it to serve his own storytelling purposes. In his hands Christianity becomes a religion of nature, with fly-fishing serving as an equivalent of the Chris-

tian liturgy. In this way, *A River Runs Through It* uses a Christian mythology and the activity of fly-fishing to dramatize the spiritualization of landscape. Though it chooses a different means, the novella aims for and achieves similar effects as *Ceremony*.

A River Runs Through It and the other stories in the collection of the same name bring together Maclean's practical knowledge of fishing, logging, firefighting, and woodsmanship with his deep sensitivity to the language and prose rhythms of the Bible as well as of Shakespeare, Wordsworth, Browning, Frost, Hemingway, and the entire tradition of English and American literature. Born in 1902 in Clarinda, Iowa, Maclean spent much of his youth in and around Missoula, Montana. While in his teens, he began working for the United States Forest Service, but he eventually chose to pursue a career as a college English professor. He earned his Ph.D. from the University of Chicago in 1940 and taught there from 1930 until his retirement in 1973. After retiring, he took up writing full time, publishing *A River Runs Through It* in 1976 and working on a nonfiction account of the 1949 Mann Gulch forest fire until his death in 1990. This account, *Young Men and Fire*, was published in 1992.

In his work, Maclean shows himself to be both an experienced outdoorsman and an astute literary craftsman. Practical details of human activity in the natural world are related with an ear finely attuned to poetic rhythms. Such an approach gives his work an integrity of fact and a suggestiveness of feeling that helps dramatize the sometimes mysterious connections between humans and the environment. According to Maclean in "The Hidden Art of a Good Story," the stories in *A River Runs Through It* rest on three closely related aspirations:

(1) to depict the art and grace of what men and women can do with their hands in the region of the country that I was brought up in and know best; (2) to impart with a description of these arts something of the feeling that accompanies their performance or, indeed, of intelligently watching them performed; and

(3) of seeing in the parts of nature where they were performed something like the beauty, structure, rhythm and design of the arts themselves. (p. 29)

This threefold approach to narrative underlies all of the stories in the collection, which depend on the realistic and dramatic descriptions of life in western Montana to make clear the link between the human and the natural world. Maclean's writing pays scrupulous attention to physical details of people and place; in this, he shows his allegiance to the naturalistic tradition in American fiction writing and demonstrates a particular debt to the work of Ernest Hemingway. In *At the Field's End: Interviews with Twenty Pacific Northwest Writers*, Maclean makes clear this debt to Hemingway.

Hemingway's influence is felt throughout Maclean's works, but perhaps nowhere more strongly than in *A River Runs Through It*. The parallels between the novella and Hemingway's stories such as "Big Two-Hearted River" are clear and deliberate. Maclean follows Hemingway's lead in providing the physical details that produce in the reader the feeling of actually participating in the action. In meticulously rendering such details, Maclean is able to describe and dramatize actions simultaneously, and so suggest the connections between humans and landscape.

But unlike Hemingway, Maclean is as much interested in fishing's ability to test and perfect character as he is in its pastoral qualities of rest and repose. In "Big Two-Hearted River," Nick Adams goes fishing to get away from the memories of the war and get back in touch with the innocence and simplicity of his former life. In *A River Runs Through It*, Norman and his brother, Paul, go fishing to get away from the troubles of their family, but they also see in fishing a way to prove their manhood. In the novella, fishing serves as a point of struggle between men and the environment. The brothers earn their right to identify with the landscape by proving themselves tough enough to stand up to it.

In this way Maclean shows his affinity with other Western realistic novelists such as A. B.

Guthrie, H. L. Davis, James Stevens, and Ivan Doig. Like them, Maclean gained his understanding and appreciation of the wilderness by working within it and struggling against it. Stories in this tradition often exhibit an adversarial relation with nature, with characters earning their identification with place not by surrendering themselves to it but by engaging themselves with it.

Such is the case with Norman and Paul. They count themselves as strong at least partly because they are the products of a strong country and an especially strong river. The Big Blackfoot is no meandering brook.

It isn't the biggest river we fished, but it is the most powerful, and per pound, so are its fish. It runs straight and hard—on a map or from an airplane it is almost a straight line running due west from its headwaters at Rogers Pass on the Continental Divide to Bonner, Montana, where it empties into the South Fork of the Clark Fork of the Columbia. It runs hard all the way. (p. 12)

Like most writers of ecofiction, Maclean is interested in the merge, the point where humans feel a sense of oneness with the landscape. But while some authors emphasize the need for people to surrender themselves to landscape to achieve this, Maclean suggests instead that this sense of oneness comes by struggling with the environment. By learning to outwit the powerful and discriminating trout of the Big Blackfoot River, Norman and Paul earn their sense of oneness with the landscape. This sense of identification does not come easily or naturally, but only as the result of great and sustained effort.

This desire for unification with landscape is embodied and made concrete through the activity of fly-fishing. In the novella, fly-fishing plays a role similar to that of storytelling in *Ceremony*; it serves as the activity that links people with each other and binds them to place. More than just a sport or pastime, fly-fishing is a religion, a ritual through which humans are reconciled to each other and to the world around them. From the very first line of the novella, Maclean makes this clear: "In our family, there was no clear line between religion and fly-fishing" (p. 1).

Fly-fishing attempts to bridge the gap between humans and the natural world, but it does not always succeed in this. The relationship between people and place always remains vulnerable to a principle of disarray. Whereas Silko blames contemporary American civilization for this principle, Maclean sees it as a fundamental flaw of human nature. He cites his father's belief in original sin as an explanation for why it occurs: "As a Scot and a Presbyterian, my father believed that man by nature was a mess and had fallen from an original state of grace" (p. 2).

Modern civilization is not the problem; human nature is the problem. As a consequence, humanity must struggle to regain this sense of grace and perfection and oneness with landscape. This will not come easily, but only through great effort. This is especially the case with fly-fishing, one of the most artful and difficult ways of catching fish, but one which imitates God's rhythms and thereby holds out the hope of reestablishing an ideal relationship with landscape: "As for my father, I never knew whether he believed God was a mathematician but he certainly believed God could count and that only by picking up God's rhythms were we able to regain power and beauty" (p. 2).

Norman and Paul follow their father's example in seeking to pick up God's rhythms through fly-fishing. The novella is organized around five fishing trips on which Norman seeks and finally achieves this sense of oneness. As Maclean says of himself: "Something within fishermen tries to make fishing into a world perfect and apart—I don't know what it is or where, because sometimes it is in my arms and sometimes in my throat and sometimes nowhere in particular except somewhere deep" (p. 37).

On the first of these trips, Norman falls far short of perfection. He catches one big trout, thereby achieving some measure of harmony with the river, but he remains alienated from his brother. Paul may be a genius with a fly rod, but he is also a drinker, a fighter, and a gambler, and increasingly this behavior has been landing him in jail. Norman understands that his brother needs help, but does not know how to help him.

On the second of these trips, Norman comes a bit closer to perfection, at least with regard to his brother. Norman manages to talk to Paul about his problems and even offers to help him with money. Paul doesn't respond directly, but clearly appreciates Norman's efforts. Norman feels reconciled with his brother, though not with the river, as his fishing proves unsatisfactory.

On the third trip, Norman attains a sense of unity with the river, but not with his family. His brother-in-law, Neal, invites himself and Rawhide, a woman he picked up in a bar, along with Norman and Paul, thus violating the family code against bringing women fishing. Norman and Paul simply leave the two of them to their bait fishing and go off fly-fishing. After catching several large trout, Norman takes a break from casting and sits down to watch the river and distance himself from the difficulties of his family:

> I sat there and forgot and forgot, until what remained was the river that went by and I who watched. On the river the heat mirages danced with each other and then they danced through each other and then they joined hands and danced around each other. Eventually the watcher joined the river, and there was only one of us. I believe it was the river. (p. 61)

Norman achieves a sense of oneness with the river, but only by blocking out the problems with his family. This sense of harmony is shattered when he and his brother discover that Neal has not been fishing but instead has been having intercourse with Rawhide on a sandbar of their family river. Both Norman and Paul are furious at this violation of their family river, but they take their anger out not on Neal who is protected by Norman's mother-in-law, but on Rawhide. The incident blots out any sense of perfection Norman might have achieved on the bank of the river.

On the fourth fishing trip, accompanied by his father and Paul, Norman finally achieves the sense of oneness with family and nature he has long sought. Norman easily outfishes his brother on the first large hole. He does so well that he receives the "rock treatment": Paul tosses several rocks into the pond so that Norman cannot fish it any further. Rather than being angry, Norman considers this the highest compliment, since it happens so infrequently that he can outfish Paul. On the following hole, Paul regains his form and hooks many more fish than Norman. He refuses to gloat, however, and comes back across the river to tell Norman what fly to use. With Paul's advice, Norman is able to continue catching fish. Thus Norman achieves a perfect sense of unity; he feels at peace with his family and at peace with God's creation. The difficulty inherent in this achievement makes the moment immensely satisfying: "So on this wonderful afternoon when all things came together it took me one case, one fish, and some reluctantly accepted advice to attain perfection" (p. 88).

He has long sought reconciliation with his family and creation and finally attains it in this one shining moment. The rest of the novella has served as prologue for this transcendent scene. This experience of perfection stands outside time and gives him intimations of eternity, as he says, "Poets talk about 'spots of time' but it is really fishermen who experience eternity compressed into a moment" (p. 44).

But in a fallen world, such moments of perfection are impossible to sustain. Shortly after the fishing trip, the police find Paul in an alley, beaten to death with a gun butt, with no explanation as to the cause or perpetrator of the crime. Though Paul's death profoundly shocks Norman and the rest of his family, it does not detract from the reality of their last fishing trip together. Instead, the subsequent events make that trip seem even more luminous.

The sequence of fishing trips serves as a good example of the narrative method Maclean employs throughout the novella. All of the story's major scenes operate by contrast: the climactic moment is accompanied by its opposite; tragedy closely shadows any triumph. In this respect, Maclean's work shows the influence of the great Shakespearean tragedies, such as *King Lear* and *Hamlet*, in which humor and comedy serve to heighten the dark moments. Both the tragic and transcendent elements of the narrative stand out more strongly by contrast.

For both Maclean and Shakespeare such an approach is more than simply a formal device. It suggests a vision of life in which the tragic and the transcendent can be reconciled into a deeper sense of union. This reconciliation assumes an essentially Christian character in the novella. Just as the suffering and death of Jesus precede his final resurrection, so the death of Paul and the suffering it causes the Maclean clan make possible the narrator's final transfiguration at the end of the book.

In the final scene the narrator fishes the Big Blackfoot River as an old man and experiences an even deeper sense of perfection than he felt on his final fishing trip with his father and Paul. His vision of life at the book's end comprehends not only that final transcendent fishing trip but also his brother's tragic death, which it has taken him most of his life to come to terms with. Norman now feels both a oneness with creation and a oneness with the fallen nature of the human condition: "Eventually, all things merge into one, and a river runs through it. The river was cut by the world's great flood and runs over rocks from the basement of time. On some of the rocks are timeless raindrops. Under the rocks are the words, and some of the words are theirs" (p. 104).

All of the events and memories of his past life merge together in this one moment and join with the waters of the Big Blackfoot River to connect up with all of creation. The words of his brother and father are gathered with those of the Gospel to underlie this creation and animate it. The novella's final line, "I am haunted by waters," demonstrates that Norman has assimilated the outer landscape of the Big Blackfoot into this inner landscape. He uses the term "haunted" to suggest that this experience of oneness with the river and with his family includes both a sense of transcendence and a sense of tragedy. This double vision allows him to achieve the final perfection of feeling at one with nature and at one with human life in the form of his family.

In dramatizing the way human beings achieve union both with nature and with society, *A River Runs Through It* shows its affinity with other works of ecofiction. As is the case with Tayo in *Ceremony*, Norman's sense of oneness with nature and society in the form of his family is the product both of personal effort and the adoption of a tradition that emphasizes the spiritual nature of landscape. The novella differs from *Ceremony*, however, in that reconciliation with society is presented as secondary to reconciliation with nature and family. This difference results at least in part from the nature of the two societies described in the books. Modern American society, of which the Maclean clan is a part, remains larger, more complex, and more separated from the land than the smaller, tribal, regionally based society of which Tayo is a member. As such, resolution with nature and society presents more difficulties in the novella than it does in *Ceremony*. But, like *Ceremony*, *A River Runs Through It* suggests that personal commitment to a tradition that emphasizes the spiritual dimensions of landscape is key to developing a dignified and satisfying relationship with the land, family, and ultimately human society.

Housekeeping

Marilynne Robinson's novel *Housekeeping* (1981) calls for a reorientation of the relationship between people and place by adopting elements of the Judeo-Christian tradition to spiritualize landscape and so break down the division between humans and environment. It does so by illustrating the change in consciousness of the book's narrator, Ruth, who first sees a sharp distinction between human society and the natural world and later comes to believe that such distinctions are illusory. This change in consciousness is dramatized through the change in her approach to housekeeping, an activity

through which she and the book's other characters express their attitudes toward human society and the natural world.

The activity of housekeeping in this novel serves a similar purpose to that of fishing in *A River Runs Through It* and storytelling in *Ceremony*: it makes concrete the characters' attitudes toward society and the surrounding environment. Housekeeping as an activity assumes particular significance in the novel due to Robinson having chosen the genre of the foundling's tale as the basis for her story. A foundling's tale concerns a child or children who are abandoned by their parents and left to be brought up by relatives or others. Such tales trace the development of these orphans and show how they overcome their difficulties and achieve a stable life. The home figures prominently in this genre, representing stability and security such as is provided by the mansion in Charles Dickens's nineteenth century classic *Bleak House* (1852–1853). In this and other examples of the genre, the home serves as a place of refuge and remains sharply distinct and separate from the hostile world outside of it.

Robinson accepts no such distinction. If she appropriates key elements of the foundling's tale, she refuses to accept the ideology that typically accompanies them. Rather than emphasizing the division between home and world, her version of the foundling's tale dramatizes the breakdown of this division and its replacement with a sense of continuity. Thus, she adapts the form of the foundling's tale to demonstrate the potential unity of human life and the natural environment.

Like many foundling's tales, *Housekeeping* begins with the story of an ancestor, in this case a grandfather, Edmund Foster. As was the case with many of those who moved west around the turn of the century, he was a dreamer. He had grown up in the Midwest and had come to Fingerbone, the fictional town in the novel, to see mountains. In this and some other respects, the novel reflects the experience of Robinson's own family; her maternal grandfather came west because he wanted to see mountains. He settled there and raised a family, including a daughter,

Robinson's mother. Robinson's father worked in the timber industry, and in the course of his career the family moved to various places around the inland Northwest.

Robinson was born in Sandpoint, Idaho, in 1944. After graduating from high school, she went east to attend Brown University and later returned to the Northwest to complete a Ph.D. in English at the University of Washington in Seattle. Since finishing *Housekeeping*, she has published *Mother Country* (1989), a book-length exposé of the Sellafield Nuclear Plant in Britain, some short stories, and an occasional book review in the *New York Times*.

Her own family's story and that of the family in *Housekeeping* intersect at several points, but Robinson warns that it is unwise to interpret the novel too literally in terms of her own life. She said in an interview, "There's no point really in thinking about experience as if it would translate straightforwardly into artistic behavior, because it simply never does" (O'Connell, p. 228).

After arriving in Fingerbone, Edmund Foster gets a job with the railroad, marries, and eventually fathers three daughters. Shortly thereafter, he dies in a spectacular train wreck, in which a locomotive, followed by the rest of the cars, jumps the track and plunges into the icy waters of the lake, thus leaving all of the daughters fatherless.

In this way, the story follows the conventional formula of the foundling's tale. There is the death of a parent, bereavement, upheaval, and eventual readjustment. His death necessitates a change in housekeeping, one which the grandmother selflessly undertakes:

She had always known a thousand ways to circle them all around with what must have seemed like grace. She knew a thousand songs. Her bread was tender and her jelly was tart, and on rainy days she made cookies and applesauce. In the summer she kept roses in a vase on the piano, huge, pungent roses, and when the blooms ripened and the petals fell, she put them in a tall Chinese jar, with cloves and thyme and sticks of cinnamon. (pp. 11–12)

The grandmother's housekeeping emphasizes the division between the home and the outside world. She is steadfast in maintaining this distinction, and when one of her daughters commits suicide, she devotes herself with equal devotion to caring for the two granddaughters left behind: "For five years my grandmother cared for us very well. She cared for us like someone reliving a long day in a dream. . . . She whited shoes and braided hair and fried chicken and turned back bedclothes, and then suddenly feared and remembered that the children had somehow disappeared, every one. How had it happened?" (pp. 24–25).

The physical structure of the house is the centerpiece of the grandmother's housekeeping. In Fingerbone, this structure is constantly under siege from the elements, especially that of water. The town is subject to heavy snowstorms, power outages, and floods that recall those in the Old Testament. In many ways, the environment around Fingerbone not only belittles human constructions and human society, but also seems to actively destroy them. It frequently intrudes on the story, and not as a passive, submissive, docile, pastoral landscape, but as an active, strange, and sometimes malevolent force that disregards the orders human beings construct for themselves.

For the grandmother, life is a constant struggle against such forces of ruin and decay. She works diligently to keep the physical structure of the house intact, and thus keep the elements outside. She sees the world in dualistic terms, with the home representing the inner world, and the environment the outer. For her there is real separation between the two worlds, and she does her best to keep the distinction clear.

Eventually the grandmother dies, and the girls' aunt Sylvie arrives to take over their care. Sylvie's approach to housekeeping contrasts greatly with that of her mother. Her style of housekeeping recognizes and acknowledges the continuity between the home and the world. Rather than emphasizing the separation between interior and exterior, she permits such a distinction to break down, allowing wind, leaves, and crickets inside the house: "Thus finely did our house become attuned to the orchard and to the particularities of weather, even in the first days of Sylvie's housekeeping. Thus did she begin by littles and perhaps unawares to ready it for wasps and bats and barn swallows" (p. 85).

For Sylvie, the division between self and environment, between inner and outer, is illusory. Her sense of housekeeping would include all the world, not simply the part contained within the shell of the house. These two approaches to housekeeping represent two distinct ways of seeing the environment and of viewing the self. The first posits a distinction between the self and the environment. In such a view the subject tries to distance herself from it, carefully maintaining the physical structure of the house to keep out the cold, darkness, insects, and creatures of the night. The second view seeks to erase the distinctions between inner and outer, letting the physical structure of the house, its boundaries, deteriorate.

During Sylvie's tenure as housekeeper, Ruth undergoes a change in consciousness whereby she becomes aware of the continuity between nature and human life. This change in consciousness takes place gradually. It is prepared for by Ruth's somewhat diffuse personality: "It was a source of both terror and comfort to me then that I often seemed invisible—incompletely and minimally existent, in fact. It seemed to me that I made no impact on the world, and that in exchange I was privileged to watch it unawares" (pp. 105–106).

Her undefined sense of self makes it possible for Ruth to accept Sylvie's housekeeping. By contrast, the personality of her sister, Lucille, is hard-edged and sharply defined. She has little compunction about rejecting what she considers her aunt's incompetent approach. When the three of them are sitting in the dark before dinner one night, Lucille abruptly switches on the light: "The window went black and the cluttered kitchen leaped, so it seemed, into being, as remote from what had gone before as this world from the primal darkness. We saw that we ate from plates that came in detergent boxes, and we drank from jelly glasses" (p. 100). This is the beginning of Lucille's disaffection with her fam-

ily. Eventually it leads to open revolt, but in the early stages of Sylvie's tenure as head of the household, Lucille remains loyal, and she and Ruth are inseparable. It is during this time that they spend a night out in the woods, a night that becomes a turning point for both of them.

In a scene reminiscent of Mark Twain's *Huckleberry Finn*, the two set out to go fishing, intending to return home before dark, but they stay too late, and end up having to build a makeshift shelter in which to spend the night. The sisters react very differently to this experience. Lucille defiantly tries to maintain the integrity of their driftwood hut, insuring the distinction between inner and outer: "For a while she sang 'Mockingbird Hill,' and then sat down beside me in our ruined stronghold, never still, never accepting that all our human boundaries were overrun" (p. 115). By contrast, Ruth comes to understand that the division between self and environment is an illusion, that at base, the two are one entity, an entity symbolized by the darkness.

> I simply let the darkness in the sky become coextensive with the darkness in my skull and bowels and bones. Everything that falls upon the eye is apparition, a sheet dropped over the world's true workings. The nerves and the brain are tricked, and one is left with dreams that these specters loose their hands from ours and walk away, the curve of the back and the swing of the coat so familiar as to imply that they should be permanent fixtures of the world, when in fact nothing is more perishable. (p. 116)

As soon as the sky lightens, Lucille insists on leaving the camp. She refuses to speak to Ruth on the way back. After this night out, Lucille goes her own way. She begins reading fashion magazines, seeking to adopt the look and attitudes shared by the other girls in the town, for whom human culture and society remain separate and distinct from the immense landscape surrounding them. Ruth seems incapable of "improving" herself in this way and adopts Sylvie as her model, mentor, and eventually surrogate mother. This new relationship is expressed physically during the trip Ruth takes with her across the lake in a stolen boat: "She stood up and turned around and stooped to hold the gunwales, and I crawled under her body and out between her legs" (p. 146).

After this trip out to an abandoned homestead, which provides an example of a house open to the elements, Ruth gives herself over to a view of the world that is like Sylvie's. She strives to break from a dualistic conception that sees the self and human society as separate from the world. She recognizes the continuity between self and nature, and undertakes to structure her life in accord with it. The boat trip comes to symbolize the way her life will be led. She and Sylvie will travel through the world lightly, with only minimal separation between themselves and the environment around them. They will not be encumbered by a house or possessions; the lack of such encumbrances will allow them to live close to nature and will in fact protect them: "The immense water thunked and thudded beneath my head, and I felt that our survival was owed to our slightness, that we danced through ruinous currents as dry leaves do, and were not capsized because the ruin we rode upon was meant for greater things" (p. 162).

Here, as elsewhere in the book, the lake comes to symbolize infinity, the ground of being, the well from which all things come and to which they return. It is only in acknowledging the existence of this substance underneath the superficial distinctions created by the visual world that one may reorder one's life so as to live lightly in the world. Sylvie helps Ruth take a step in this direction by suggesting that they ride the freight train back into town from the lake, thus taking the first step toward a life of transience, Sylvie's former lifestyle, and the one they both will now follow.

When the townspeople find out about this trip, they immediately take action. In a town as shallow-rooted as Fingerbone, evidence of such transience combined with Sylvie's lackadaisical attitude toward housekeeping is seen as a threat to the community. They begin legal proceedings to strip Sylvie of guardianship.

But they act too late: by this time Ruth has decided never to return to the town. When the sheriff tries to lure her away from Sylvie with the promise of apple pie and a good home environment—what he considers the attractions of conventional housekeeping—Ruth turns him down. Shortly thereafter, Sylvie's housekeeping takes an ironic turn: to preserve the privacy of the house from prying neighbors, she and Ruth destroy it by setting it afire.

In ending the book in this way, Robinson turns the conventional structure of the foundling's tale on its head. Though *Housekeeping* deals with the usual material of such a story—parental deaths, wills, probate courts, the ancestral mansion—it doesn't follow the classic pattern of such a tale. The novel could never be mistaken for a book like Dickens's *Bleak House*, which ends with the family home, a symbol of stability and permanence, intact.

By changing the ending of the foundling's tale, Robinson profoundly changes its meaning. No longer does the form assume that there is a clear distinction between the home and the outer world. Her version of the foundling's tale focuses on dissolution and merges home and world, demonstrating an essential indivisibility of human life and environment.

Ruth achieves harmony with the natural world by adjusting her life so as to live lightly on the earth. This necessitates a rejection of the conventional approach to home and community life and its replacement by a life of transience with Sylvie. The book ends with the two of them traveling around the West working as itinerant waitresses.

In this way Ruth achieves only partial reconciliation with family and only minimal reconciliation with human society. Like many other western American heroes, Ruth and Sylvie find it nearly impossible to experience unity with both society and nature. The book suggests that American society's frontier-like attitude toward the environment is largely to blame for this. Though Ruth and Sylvie yearn for a full reconciliation with family and at least a partial reconciliation with human society, the attitude toward nature prevailing in Fingerbone makes this diffi-

Ursula K. Le Guin, author of *Always Coming Home*

cult for them to achieve. For Ruth and Sylvie, any reconciliation between family, society, and nature must begin with a rejection of the present division between nature and society. *Housekeeping* is a darker book than any of the others discussed here because it suggests that a complete reconciliation between society and nature will not be possible without a radical revision of American society, the sort of revision presented in Ursula K. Le Guin's futuristic tale, *Always Coming Home*.

Always Coming Home

Like the novels previously discussed, Ursula K. Le Guin's *Always Coming Home* (1985) is above all interested in establishing a new relationship between people and place. Le Guin seeks to do this by animating the natural world and by enlarging the sense of home to include more than simply a house, neighborhood, or city, but

instead an entire ecosystem, in this case the Napa Valley of northern California in the distant future.

Though ecological themes are common throughout Le Guin's work, this is the first of her novels in which ecology takes center stage. The theme of people living in harmony with the land appears in other of her novels, such as *The Word for World Is Forest* (1972), *The Dispossessed* (1974), and the Earthsea trilogy, but in *Always Coming Home* it becomes the dominant subject. Le Guin takes it up directly to create an ecologically exemplary society that fits seamlessly within its environment.

To invent such a society, she borrows heavily on anthropological reconstructions of American Indian life. This is by no means a new strategy, as many of her other novels show a similar approach. She has long been fascinated with anthropology, an interest inherited from her parents. Le Guin's father, Alfred L. Kroeber, was a renowned anthropologist, who did much of his work on the Northwest coastal tribes. Her mother, Theodora Kroeber, was the author of the bestselling *Ishi in Two Worlds: A Biography of the Last Wild Indian in North America*.

Le Guin herself was born in Berkeley, California, in 1929. She received a B.A. in French from Radcliffe College in 1951 and an M.A. in romance languages from Columbia University in 1952. She first made her mark as a writer of science fiction, winning the Hugo Award three times, but eventually she branched out to write realistic fiction and nonfiction. Her interest in anthropology has always proved useful in her creation of imaginary societies in distant galaxies and on Earth.

Always Coming Home closely resembles an anthropological reconstruction of a society, but in this case it is an entirely fictional one. Much of the book consists in description of the daily life of the Kesh, a predominantly agricultural people who are one of many small, distinct, local cultures that have followed the breakdown of industrial civilization as we know it. Although the Kesh society is clearly based on Native American models, it also contains elements of contemporary American civilization. It's an unusual hybrid, a remarkable mix of high and low tech, and provides a glimpse of what life might be like in the twenty-first century or beyond.

If this society is ecologically exemplary, it is by no means perfect in other ways. Le Guin goes out of her way to emphasize that this society is not a standard utopia dehumanized in its perfection, such as that depicted in B. F. Skinner's *Walden II* or Ernest Callenbach's novel *Ecotopia*. The character Pandora seems to speak for the author when she remarks, "I never did like smartass utopians. Always so much healthier and saner and sounder and fitter and kinder and tougher and wiser and righter than me and my family and friends. People who have the answers are boring, niece. Boring, boring, boring" (p. 335).

In Kesh society, there are still wars, disappointment, petty behavior—the usual stock-in-trade of human experience. Indeed, Le Guin realizes the impossibility of permanently removing evil and suffering from the world. As one of the Kesh warriors observes, "I have come to think that the sickness of Man is like the mutating viruses and the toxins: there will always be some form of it about, or brought in from elsewhere by people moving and travelling, and there will always be the risk of infection" (p. 411).

But despite its imperfections, Kesh society does achieve harmony with its environment. Le Guin devotes much of the novel to describing how the Kesh accomplish this. In its extensive use of exposition, *Always Coming Home* resembles nineteenth-century novels such as *Moby-Dick*, which allow ample room for digression. *Always Coming Home* is loosely constructed, a collection of fragments rather than a unified work of art. There is little progress in the novel, at least in a temporal sense, since the Kesh don't see time as linear but as a continuum. The narrative passages of the novel are not consecutive; they are separated by exposition on everything from Kesh poetry to Kesh pottery. The book achieves coherence by incorporating passages from the life of Stonetelling, a young Kesh girl, whose struggle to come to terms with her family and her place in Kesh society links the parts of the book together.

Unlike in the novels previously discussed, the characters here experience no real conflict with their environment; they fit within it so well that no disjunction between them and it occurs. Instead, the story's main dramatic conflict revolves around Stonetelling and her need to reconcile the influences of her two very different parents and find her place in Kesh society. Her father is a military officer for the Condor people, a warlike, imperialistic tribe who seek dominion over the Kesh and other peoples. Her mother is Kesh and eventually divorces her husband when he returns to the city of the Condor. Stonetelling's story is broken up into three sections: her early life in the valley, her journey away from the valley with her father to visit the Condor people, and finally her return to the valley. It is this cycle of departure and return that serves as the basis for her story.

The descriptions of Stonetelling's early life demonstrate how completely the Kesh have subsumed themselves within the local environment. They are a post-apocalyptic people, who have learned from the mistakes of their ancestors, whom they call the Backward-Head people. Those people had no vision for the future, and did not see how their actions would contribute to the destruction of the planet.

In contrast to their ancestors, the Kesh see no sharp distinction between themselves and the surrounding environment. They treat the land respectfully, taking only what they need from it: "With ceremony, with forms of politeness and reassurance, they borrowed the waters of the River and its little confluents to drink and be clean and irrigate with, using water mindfully, carefully. They lived in a land that answers greed with drought and death. A difficult land: aloof yet sensitive" (p. 55). Though the Kesh revere the valley, they are not a particularly religious people and do not see any kind of spirit underlying it. Instead they see the valley as a living organism, and themselves as part of it.

I think it is one another whom we greet, and bless, and help. It is one another whom we eat. We are gatherer and gathered. Building and unbuilding, we make and are unmade;

giving birth and killing, we take hands and let go. Thinking human people and other animals, the plants, the rocks and stars, all the beings that think or are thought, that are seen or see, that hold or are held, all of us are beings of the Nine Houses of Being, dancing the same dance. (p. 325)

The Kesh worldview owes much to American Indian culture, even if it lacks its pervasive animistic element. In adapting this culture to her fiction, Le Guin shows her kinship with many other contemporary writers such as Leslie Marmon Silko. But Le Guin distinguishes herself from these writers by mixing these Native American materials with elements of high technology. As a science fiction writer, Le Guin lacks the romantic contempt of technology common to many writers, especially nature writers. Though she clearly has a tempered view of technology, she does not reject it out of hand. She sees science and technology as an extension of the human ability to make tools, and understands that technology becomes dangerous only when it is emphasized to such a degree that it dehumanizes or threatens mankind.

In leaving progress to the machines, in letting technology go forward on its own terms and selecting from it, with what seems to us excessive caution, modesty, or restraint, the limited though completely adequate implements of their cultures, is it possible that in thus opting not to move "forward" or not only "forward," these people did in fact succeed in living in human history, with energy, liberty, and grace? (p. 406)

By drawing from her background in science fiction, Le Guin can create an ecologically harmonious society without getting bogged down in the primitivism that limits much American nature writing. In *Always Coming Home*, Le Guin describes the Exchange, a vast computer network linking all of the towns and cities of the world. Information is shared through the Exchange, but only one person per city is generally initiated into its use. The Exchange is not despised in the valley, but it holds no particular fascination for

people, either. It is merely a tool, not a religion. It is in balance with the rest of life.

The Exchange plays a crucial role in the defeat of the Condor people, an oppressive group who seek control over the surrounding societies, as they seek to tame and control their environment. The smaller towns and villages repel the advance of the Condors by passing information and organizing resistance through the Exchange. It becomes a vast command-and-control center that allows the smaller cultures to harass, weaken, and finally defeat the larger Condor army.

Le Guin provides an in-depth view of the Condor people by having Stonetelling accompany her father on a visit to the city of the Condor. Their cold, northern capital city contrasts greatly with the warm, sunny valley of the Kesh, and Stonetelling soon becomes homesick. She eventually escapes from the city of the Condor and makes her way back to the valley.

Although she rejoices when she first sees the valley, she has some difficulty fitting back into Kesh society. To facilitate this transition, she performs the Kesh songs and dances, which strengthen her sense of her place in Kesh society and celebrate the Kesh's place in the valley and the surrounding natural world. These songs and dances emphasize the union between Kesh society and the other creatures of the valley. One such song is the Initiation Song from the Finders Lodge, a song that applies especially to Stonetelling: "Walk carefully, well loved one, / walk mindfully, well loved one, / walk fearlessly, well loved one, / Return with us, return to us, / be always coming home" (p. 428). The song suggests that living in one place can be a process of continuous discovery. If the Kesh treat the valley with respect and pay careful attention to it, they will always be discovering new things about it. For the valley is always changing, always revealing new things, always providing them with new ways to come home to it.

This song and others help Stonetelling reintegrate herself into Kesh society, a society caught up in the rhythms of the larger valley life. Gradually she becomes ready to dance the World Dance, the Kesh's celebration of "human participation in the making and unmaking, the renewal and continuity, of the world" (p. 484). Once human society assumes its proper relation to the environment, it can participate in the making and remaking of the world without destroying or polluting the planet in the process. Since the Kesh consider human society as a part of nature rather than as separate from it, they see human beings as playing a necessary role in the creation and recreation of the world. There is a balanced reciprocity in the Kesh's relationship with nature; human culture and nature are mutually interdependent, with neither one overwhelming the other since both are needed to fully complete the world.

In this way, the novel envisions human society as achieving a harmonious relationship with place. Instead of seeing human society as separate and distinct from nature, *Always Coming Home* emphasizes that human society should be integrated within nature, so that human beings can play their proper role in the drama of creation. By combining Native American materials with those of modern American culture, the novel creates a realistic and hopeful vision of the future.

Conclusion

Works of ecofiction seek to reconcile the individual with society and nature by calling for a new relationship between people and place, a relationship that sees human society as a part of nature rather than as separate from it. Authors of ecofiction seek to spiritualize landscape by adapting Native American or biblical stories to their fiction, or by otherwise emphasizing a more unified vision of the relationship between people and place.

This unity of society and nature is a complicated proposition, one limited by the nature of the traditions these writers borrow from and the character of the societies they describe. Le Guin and Silko successfully reconcile community and nature by using animistic Native American stories to underpin their work and by describing societies that have not yet lost touch with the surrounding landscape. Maclean and Robinson, on the other hand, manage mainly to reconcile family and nature in their novels and only partially to reconcile community and nature. This results partly from their use of Judeo-Christian tradition to ground their narratives, a tradition less obviously rich in ecological materials than that of Native American mythology, and partly from their decision to write about societies that see a clear separation between themselves and the surrounding environment. And yet if *A River Runs Through It* and *Housekeeping* fail to achieve the fullness of unity between community and nature demonstrated by *Always Coming Home* and *Ceremony* they ultimately may do more to ground ecofiction within the tradition of American literature by borrowing and adapting materials from within that tradition rather than from outside of it.

If works of ecofiction are not always successful in bringing about the unity of individual, society, and nature, the very fact that they strive for this overall synthesis distinguishes them from other works of contemporary literature. Unlike traditional nature writing, which seeks union between an individual and nature, or traditional fiction, which seeks union between an individual and society, works of ecofiction such as *Ceremony*, *A River Runs Through It*, *Housekeeping*, and *Always Coming Home* seek a more comprehensive sense of unity—between an individual, society, and nature. This wider scope in turn makes possible a hopeful and promising vision of what human life can be like on this planet.

Selected Bibliography

PRIMARY SOURCES

Ernest Callenbach, *Ecotopia: The Notebooks and Reports of William Weston* (Berkeley, Calif.: Banyan Tree, 1975); Charles Dickens, *Bleak House* (1852–1853; repr., New York: New American Library, 1964); Ralph Waldo Emerson, *Selections from Ralph Waldo Emerson*, ed. by Stephen E. Whicher (Boston: Houghton Mifflin, 1957); Ernest Hemingway, *The Short Stories of Ernest Hemingway* (New York: Scribners, 1938); Ursula K. Le Guin, *Always Coming*

Home (New York: Harper & Row, 1985); Norman F. Maclean, *A River Runs Through It and Other Stories* (Chicago: Univ. of Chicago Press, 1976); N. Scott Momaday, *House Made of Dawn* (New York: Harper & Row, 1968); Marilynne Robinson, *Housekeeping* (New York: Farrar, Straus & Giroux, 1980); Leslie Marmon Silko, *Ceremony* (New York: Viking, 1977).

SECONDARY SOURCES

Mary Catherine Harper, "Spiraling Around the Hinge: Working Solutions in *Always Coming Home*," in *Old West—New West: Centennial Essays*, ed. by Barbara Howard Meldrum (Moscow, Idaho: Univ. of Idaho Press, 1993); Alfred Kazin, *A Writer's America: Landscape in Literature* (New York: Knopf, 1988); Glen A. Love, "Revaluing Nature: Toward an Ecological Criticism," in *Old West—New West: Centennial Essays*, ed. by Barbara Howard Meldrum (Moscow, Idaho: Univ. of Idaho Press, 1993); Norman Maclean, "The Hidden Art of a Good Story: Wallace Stegner Lecture," in *Norman Maclean*, ed. by Ron McFarland and Hugh Nichols (Lewiston, Idaho: Confluence, 1988); Nicholas O'Connell, *At the Field's End: Interviews with Twenty Pacific Northwest Writers* (Seattle, Wash.: Madrona, 1987); Marilynne Robinson, "My Western Roots," in *Old West—New West: Centennial Essays*, ed. by Barbara Howard Meldrum (Moscow, Idaho: Univ. of Idaho Press, 1993); Wallace Stegner, "Haunted by Waters," in *Norman Maclean*, ed. by Ron McFarland and Hugh Nichols (Lewiston, Idaho: Confluence, 1988); Scott Slovic, "Nature Writing and Humor: David James Duncan's Parodic Narrative of Environmental Conversion" (essay presented at the College English Association Convention, San Antonio, Tex., 1991); Frederick Turner, *Spirit of Place: The Making of an American Literary Landscape* (San Francisco: Sierra Club, 1989).

Early Romantic
Natural History Literature
(1782–1836)

MICHAEL P. BRANCH

During the half-century between the publication of Hector St. John de Crèvecoeur's *Letters from an American Farmer* (1782) and Ralph Waldo Emerson's *Nature* (1836), natural history writing was a flourishing discipline that helped nurture awareness of an emergent American culture's unique dependency upon the land. This period has received little attention from scholars of nature writing, who more often focus upon Henry David Thoreau and his literary descendants—a distinguished lineage that includes figures such as John Muir, John Burroughs, Aldo Leopold, Edward Abbey, and Annie Dillard. However, Thoreau is also the descendant of a literary tradition as much as he is the progenitor of one, and nature writing from *Walden* onward is prefigured in and indirectly influenced by a rich tradition of late-eighteenth- and early-nineteenth-century natural history writing.

I wish to survey early Romantic ideas about nature in the New World, raising questions about the status and function of American natural history writing around the turn of the nineteenth century. How is the early Romantic enthusiasm for natural history a product of the changing intellectual climate of the period? If natural history writing is viewed as both science and belles lettres, what is the larger relationship between American natural history studies and the rise of a distinctively American culture during the early Romantic period? How do naturalists' representations of the relationship between human and nonhuman nature contribute to the environmental awareness that has inspired and sustained the American nature writing tradition?

Using illustrations from the work of Crèvecoeur, Thomas Jefferson, Alexander Wilson, and John James Audubon, I suggest that early Romantic natural history writers introduced a number of concerns that are essential to the post-Thoreauvian literature of nature. In addition to turning American attention toward the cultural possibilities of the land and speaking for the divinity of wilderness, these writers valorized the dual urge to document wild nature and to express concern regarding its critical endangerment by human development.

The early Romantic affinity for the land was preconditioned by a series of important historical changes in the way Americans viewed nature. Colonists in the seventeenth century had little affection for wild nature. To the Puritans, who interpreted their experience in the New World according to biblical typology, wilderness existed only as an impediment to Christian civilization. Thus, William Bradford described the lush forests of the American continent as a "hideous and desolate wilderness"—an ugly and threatening obstacle to the prosperity of God's chosen people. In *God's Controversy with New England*, Puritan poet Michael Wigglesworth described the unsettled land as a moral vacuum: "A waste and howling wilderness, / Where none inhabited / But hellish fiends, and brutish men / That Devils worshipped" (p. 83). By carrying the moral law of their settlements deeper into the ungodly forest, the Puritans were doing the work of the righteous, preparing the New Canaan for the millennium.

Although descriptions of nature in the southern settlements were less theologically inflected, it is owing primarily to the rhetorical goals of the extant accounts. Much seventeenth-century writing in the southern colonies takes the shape of promotional tracts, hyperbolic descriptions of Edenic plenitude calculated to attract Englishmen to the struggling settlements of the New World. The touchstone of such writing is the idea that a man could make his fortune with ease in the rich soil of the American colonies. Even as malaria, Indian attacks, and famine continually threatened the colony at Jamestown, Captain John Smith could write that in America

every man may be master and owner of his own labour and land; or the greatest part in a small time. If hee have nothing but his hands, he may set up this trade; and by industrie quickly grow rich; spending but halfe that time wel, which in England we abuse in idleness, worse or as ill.

If northern wilderness was conquered in God's name, southern wilderness was conquered in the name of Mammon. In neither region was genuine love of nature an aesthetic or a moral imperative. After all, it was John Winthrop's "city upon a hill" that seventeenth-century America envisioned as its destiny — not the hill itself.

During the eighteenth century the confluence of several currents of European thought helped mitigate the American aversion to wild nature. Of primary importance was the influence of deism, the rationalist "natural religion," which held that the Creator's hand was evident in the intricate perfection of the natural world. Behind the deist association of God and nature were the century's vast accomplishments in natural science, which continued to reveal the complex precision of geological and astronomical systems. Natural theologians such as John Ray and William Paley had already begun to accord nature a kind of scriptural status, as is apparent from the title of Ray's influential book, *The Wisdom of God Manifested in the Works of the Creation* (1691). According to deism, the "wilderness pleases" because it is the landscape least encumbered by humans and therefore most directly illustrative of their Creator.

The new perspective on nature was carried to America in the writings of such deists as Anthony Ashley Cooper, Earl of Shaftesbury, and Alexander Pope, who were widely read in the colonies. Shaftesbury's passion for wild nature prompted him to reject the "feigned wilderness" of palace gardens, and Pope, in his *Essay on Man*, encouraged readers to "look up through nature to Nature's God." In America, where Puritan orthodoxy had been a primary source of enmity toward wilderness, deist theology precipitated a radical revision of the human relationship to nonhuman nature.

Once deism had introduced the maxim that nature was an expression of divinity, a revision of the seventeenth-century notion of "howling wilderness" became inevitable. A primary catalyst for change came in 1757, with the publication of Edmund Burke's *Philosophical Enquiry into the Origin of Our Ideas of the Sublime and Beautiful*. Reviving Longinus' concept of the sublime from antiquity, Burke's influential distinction of sublimity from beauty reshaped conventional aesthetic categories to include as ennobling the feelings of awe and terror. Burke's sublime enjoyed great currency in America and was soon joined by William Gilpin's concept of the "picturesque." Like the sublime, the idea of the picturesque was widely disseminated in American culture, and Gilpin's work was known to nineteenth-century authors, including Emerson, Thoreau, Nathaniel Hawthorne, and Edgar Allan Poe.

In one sense, the reintroduction of the sublime was simply a backlash against highly controlled eighteenth-century aesthetics; like the vogue for literary and architectural Gothic, and the popular interest in primitivism as espoused by Jean-Jacques Rousseau and Daniel Defoe, the rise of the sublime was a reaction to the rationalist sensibility of the age. But in addition to challenging the severity of neoclassical aesthetics, Burke's thesis legitimized the feelings so often induced by the vast, untamed wilderness of the New World. Significantly, the concept of the sublime also shifted emphasis from the qualities of the landscape toward the feelings that the landscape engendered in the observer. As the fear produced by Niagara's magnificent cataract came to seem more worthy than the repose occasioned by the impeccably ordered gardens of Versailles, the aesthetic of the sublime established a dynamic, emotional connection between the human spirit and the grandeur of wild nature.

Beginning in the late eighteenth century, an atmosphere of intense nationalism fueled Americans' urge to view their country as "nature's nation." In the years following the Revolution, a young America was struggling to find its identity, to discover a source of national pride that would galvanize movement toward what it considered its destiny as a great nation. The "promised land" motif projected upon the continent by the early settlers created a legacy of great expectations, and by the turn of the nineteenth century the need to proclaim American genius had become a national obsession. Fears about the inadequacy of American culture were intensified by Americans' paradoxical "neocolonial insecurity complex": although they needed to distinguish their culture as independent from British influence, Americans continued to judge their efforts according to European standards. A familiar concern was that America—barren as it was of royal blood, ruined castles, and ancient cultural monuments—lacked the resources necessary to produce great art. Although Americans wanted a Homer, a Virgil, or a John Milton to legitimate their infant nation and express its emergent national identity, efforts at indigenous cultural forms were necessarily doomed by their imitation of European styles.

It was not until the early years of the nineteenth century that Americans finally discovered a fit subject for their national literature. This subject was more ancient than the Revolution, broader than all of Europe, and the embodiment of America's national destiny. It represented wealth, strength, freedom, and sublime beauty. Best of all, it was a subject endemic to the United States, one that Europe lacked and could never procure. The subject was, as it had to be, the vast and unexplored wilderness of the American continent. Whereas one might object that Europe had nature of its own, its sheer expanse was considerably less than America's, and its character was decidedly rural compared with the unmediated wilderness of the New World. As Leo Marx suggested in *The Machine in the Garden* (1964), European pastoralism functioned as an aesthetic convention, whereas the American pastoral was reality rather than a trope.

Although the American land had been there all along, it was not until the early nineteenth century that changes in the intellectual climate rendered it fully fit for artistic inhabitation. The aesthetic of the sublime had opened the way for these changes, and deism's supposition that God was manifest in nature inadvertently supported the idea that America—itself a remarkable expanse of wild nature—might enjoy a moral advantage over Europe. Other factors also came into play. The pristine quality of the American landscape compared favorably with the filthy and overcrowded cities of "civilized" Europe, and Americans were quick to assert that their land would protect them against the vices of excess civilization so evident in England and France.

At the same time, America's budding natural science confirmed the amazing variety, vigor, and unspoiled beauty of the land that was to support the immense weight of American faith. Futhermore, the aesthetic program of English and continental romanticism had begun crossing the Atlantic, suggesting the spiritual and artistic potential of nature. Johann von Goethe, for example, helped direct America toward the rich resource of its own land and warned American poets to "guard well in all they do/Against knight-robber-and-ghost-story." Far from being a liability, America's lack of history came to represent freedom from the burden of the past and promise for the realization of a great future; in the American imagination, the land itself became inseparable from the national character and destiny.

If the national faith was to be based upon the vast, uncorrupted wilderness of the new continent, it became imperative to explore, survey, and describe that wilderness as a means of both appraising and expressing American prospects. Just as Jefferson suggested that the diversity and size of American animals was emblematic of the republic's rising glory, turn-of-the-century America looked increasingly to natural history as an index of American possibilities. The call for a national literature—which was ubiquitous in the late eighteenth and early nineteenth centuries—was consistently expressed in terms of American nature. In an impulse we might call the "topographical imperative," Americans demanded a culture that would be commensurate with the greatness of the land: as expansive as its prairies, as lofty as its mountains, as prolific as its forests. Thus, natural history writing functioned as an expression of America's need to discover the means by which its national destiny would be enacted.

Of course, there were other important reasons for the growth and influence of American natural history studies. The work of establishing America's independence had been finished, and citizens could devote more atention to the arts and sciences. This leisure was also manifest in the vogue for "scenic tours" and for dabbling in naturalism, such as the casual bird-watching so popular during the period. Before the end of the eighteenth century, a gentleman or lady would not have considered natural history within the domain of their proper affairs, but since then deism and Enlightenment science had widely disseminated the idea that nature could be learned from, as well as about. From every corner of Western culture the nexus of natural history and literature was receiving the blessing of romanticism. Samuel Taylor Coleridge in England, Goethe in Germany, and Rousseau in France

were exemplars of how provocative and productive the blend could be. Thanks largely to the influence of Gilbert White's *Natural History of Selborne* (1789) in England and William Bartram's *Travels* (1791) in America, toward the turn of the century the nature essay began to develop into a genre of its own—an informative and stylistically accomplished convergence of science and romanticism.

To some extent, the early-nineteenth-century turn to the land functioned as an apology for a lack of American culture, and to some degree the vogue for natural history expressed a need to compensate for a dearth of cultural history. But as the anxiety over European influence began to wane, there grew in Americans a very real sense that—however unlikely the concept—wilderness would itself inspire culture. The American continent had long been viewed as regenerative, and just as seventeenth-century Americans believed that an oppressed Protestant might begin anew in Massachusetts or that an impoverished laborer might do the same in Virginia, so nineteenth-century Americans believed that culture itself could begin anew, that its seed would germinate and flourish in the rich soil of the New World.

In order to prosper, however, American natural history writers first needed to liberate themselves from the colonial impulse to defer to British authority in the field. Until the late eighteenth century, most Americans assumed that British museums were the proper repository for specimens gathered on either side of the Atlantic, and the idea of maintaining permanent natural history collections in America was entertained by only a few. By the early nineteenth century, however, Americans were demanding of their science—just as they were demanding of their art and literature—a purging of European influence and a turning to the uncorrupted cultural resources of the American land. One critic urged naturalists to "study and examine for themselves, instead of blindly using the eyes of foreign naturalists, or bowing implicitly to a foreign bar of criticism" (Curti, p. 253).

As an artistic and literary correlative to the idea of Manifest Destiny, the topographical imperative enjoined a literature commensurate with the greatness of the land; thus, American natural history writers were urged to construct cultural monuments that would "rise beautifully as our hills, imperishable, and lofty as their summits, which tower sublimely above the clouds" (Curti, p. 253). By the early nineteenth century, Americans had concluded that indigenous species should be studied and housed in America and that funding for conducting surveys, creating permanent collections, and publishing natural history at home was essential to nurturing the emergence of American culture. Efforts to establish American natural history were successfully carried forward on a wave of Romantic nationalism, and the opinion that wilderness was both a natural and cultural resource finally took root in the literary imagination of the young republic.

The work of Crèvecoeur, Jefferson, Wilson, and Audubon illustrates the important contributions made by natural history writers during the early Romantic period; many of their characteristic thematic concerns became essential to both nineteenth- and twentieth-century nature writing. First, their brand of natural history helped define a uniquely American subject and style; these writers turned west in an attempt to define the "distinctively American" in terms of the impressive geography, flora, and fauna of the young nation. Second, these natural history writers helped relocate divinity in wilderness; elaborating upon the deistic presupposition that the Creator is manifest in nature, they began to affirm America's moral advantage over domesticated Europe by emphasizing God's sublime presence in the New World landscape.

Third, these writers were partly motivated by an impulse to document the natural history of an evanescent frontier and its nonhuman inhabitants; early Romantic naturalists attempted to delineate a wilderness and to mourn its irrevocable loss before the march of westward expansion. Finally, Crèvecoeur, Jefferson, Wilson, and Audubon—and other authors of early Romantic natural history—cultivated a new ethical sensitivity to nonhuman nature; through emphasis upon a feeling of membership in a natural community and upon the morally regenerative qualities of the natural world, these writers helped introduce a tradition of environmental concern into American intellectual history.

Hector St. John de Crèvecoeur (1735–1813)

Crèvecoeur's primary contribution to the nature-writing tradition is his *Letters from an American Farmer* (1782), the first book to imaginatively construct the American experience in nature according to a fully Romantic sensibility. Although Crèvecoeur's agrarian ideology anticipates Jefferson's *Notes on the State of Virginia*, his romanticized wilderness also prefigures Thoreau's Walden Pond, Melville's South Pacific, and Faulkner's Big Woods. Crèvecoeur's timely query "What is an American?" helped set the agenda for American literature, and his claim that the answer to this perennial question would be found in the land clearly resonates through the work of such later nature writers as Emerson, Thoreau, and Muir.

We might well ask how a Frenchman's paean to rural life has done so much to adumbrate and to shape our national literature. To begin with, Crèvecoeur perspicaciously raised the question of American identity at a historical moment in which national character was nascent and ill-defined. His *Letters* focuses upon the environmental as well as the social differences between Europe and America, thus providing readers on both sides of the Atlantic with a new means by which to measure the distance separating them. Like John Woolman's *Journal* (1774) and Benjamin Franklin's *Autobiography* (1793), Crèvecoeur's *Letters* nurtured the emergence of an American culture by projecting the American as a "new man"—an independent, self-reliant individual reborn into the New World landscape.

What ultimately distinguishes Crèvecoeur's vision from that of his contemporaries is the essential presence of the land and the extent to which the cultural icon of the "American" is inexorably contingent upon it. As D. H. Lawrence wrote in his incisive essay about

Crèvecoeur: "NATURE. I wish I could write it larger than that. NATURE. Benjamin [Franklin] overlooked NATURE. But the French Crèvecoeur spotted it long before Thoreau and Emerson worked it up" (p. 29). Crèvecoeur's own classic definition of the American as someone "who leaving behind him all his ancient prejudices and manners, receives new ones from the new mode of life he has embraced" explicitly asserts that the "new mode" is a life in close contact with the natural world. "He becomes an American," Crèvecoeur continues, "by being received into the broad lap of our *Alma Mater*" (pp. 54–55). Americans of heterogeneous descent (whom he likens to transplanted plants) are to be unified in the Alma Mater, the nurturing mother that is the earth itself. Metaphors of transplantation, mothering, and husbanding punctuate the *Letters*, where they function to reinforce the idea that American laws, social order, and identity are contingent upon the land.

To see how Crèvecoeur's belief in the cultural preeminence of nature engenders American literary possibilities, we need look no further than Letter I, "Introductory Letter" in *Letters from an American Farmer*. This letter, which explains the epistolary structure of the book as the correspondence from Farmer James to Mr. F. B., a learned and wealthy European, also explores the trepidation with which James approaches the act of writing. Although F. B. requires only that the correspondence describe the American farmer's manner of life upon the frontier, James is driven to a "fit of astonishment" both by the idea that he should "write" rather than "work" and by the suggestion that his vernacular frontier experience is worthy of record. James's wife functions as the consummate voice of American cultural insecurity:

James, wouldst thee pretend to send epistles to a great European man, who hath lived abundance of time in that big house called Cambridge; where, they say, that worldly learning is so abundant, that people get it only by breathing the air of the place? Wouldst not thee be ashamed to write unto a man who has never in his life done a single day's work, no,

not even felled a tree. . . . If thee persistest in being such a fool hardy man, said my wife, for God's sake let it be as great a secret as if it was some heinous crime. . . . I would not have thee James pass for what the world calleth a writer. (pp. 3, 16, 17–18)

The wife's response both represents and helps define American anxieties about basing a homegrown literature upon New World nature, for while Mr. F. B. extols James as the "farmer of feelings," James's wife fears that her husband will earn the epithet the "scribbling farmer."

If the wife's voice dramatizes the shame surrounding James's—and, by implication, Crèvecoeur's—performance as a literary naturalist, the counsel of James's minister provides an alternative interpretation of the literary experiment at hand. By asserting that both natural beauty and political felicity make American life an appropriate subject for art, the minister imaginatively constructs an audience for American nature literature:

Although [Mr. F. B.] is a man of learning and taste, yet I am sure he will read your letters with pleasure: if they be not elegant, they will smell of the woods, and be a little wild. . . . [they] will have the merit of coming from the edge of the great wilderness, three hundred miles from the sea, and three thousand miles over that sea: this will be no detriment to them, take my word for it. (pp. 5, 10)

The minister's confidence that the American wilderness will spontaneously inspire both James's writing and his audience is consequently a statement of faith in American literary naturalism. "The smell of the woods" describes a uniquely American subject and style that is found not only in the idiomatic dialect of James Fenimore Cooper's Natty Bumppo and Mark Twain's Huck Finn but also in the most polished prose of Thoreau and Muir.

The minister's exhortation to James may be seen as a version of the topographical imperative—that indefatigable American desire for a national literature commensurate with the greatness of the land. Optimism about James's prospects as a writer are continually linked to the richness of New World nature. For example, the minister tells James:

> You will appear to [Mr. F. B.] something like one of our wild American plants, irregularly luxuriant in its various branches, which a European scholar may probably think ill placed and useless. If our soil is not remarkable as yet for the excellence of its fruits, this exuberance is however a strong proof of fertility. . . . Were I in Europe I should be tired with perpetually seeing espaliers, plashed hedges, and trees dwarfed into pigmies. Do let Mr. F. B. see on paper a few American wild cherry trees, such as nature forms them here, in all her unconfined vigour, in all the amplitude of their extended limbs and spreading ramifications — let him see that we are possessed with strong vegitative embryos. (pp. 14–15)

When we consider how thoroughly Crèvecoeur's use of the biological metaphor conflates vegetable and cultural growth, it becomes apparent that only the American wilderness is uniquely grand enough to nurture both. What has inspired James to undertake the correspondence, and what sustains him throughout it, is his interest in the natural environment he inhabits. Read as a parable of the would-be American nature writer, Letter I dramatizes both the anxieties and the possibilities of a home-grown American culture. A seminal accomplishment of the *Letters* is the way in which the American farmer — and through his agency, Crèvecoeur himself — demonstrates that American literature is itself a forest product.

Although Crèvecoeur's importance as a Romantic author is widely acknowledged, his talent as a natural history writer has been overlooked. Many of his important achievements were in the field of natural history: he promoted Franco–American seed exchange and was responsible for introducing several new plants to the republic; he helped found botanical gardens in Connecticut and New Jersey; his invaluable contributions on American natural history informed the French *Encyclopédie* (1751–1772) article on the United States; and, in recognition of his contri-

butions to natural science, he was made a member of the French Academy of Sciences and the American Philosophical Society.

Within the textual world of the *Letters*, the privileging of natural history is most important in the adulation of colonial botanist John Bartram, father of William Bartram, one of America's earliest and most accomplished nature writers. Letter XI is devoted entirely to the visit of a Russian gentleman to Bartram's famous garden outside Philadelphia. In this letter, Crèvecoeur shapes Bartram into the ideal type of the American — an American Farmer par excellence. Bartram incarnates only the best aspects of political freedom, religious tolerance, and pragmatic ingenuity; he is an industrious man who has maintained the rustic virtues of honesty and simplicity even as he wins the admiration of Linnaeus and the patronage of Queen Ulrica of Sweden.

According to Crèvecoeur, the character of Bartram perfectly delineates the prospects for the American Farmer. Like James, Bartram's patrimony was a small farm that his industry has transformed into a respectable inheritance for his children, and his humble beginnings make him suspicious that intellectual projects will compromise his proper labor. Also like James, though, Bartram's anxiety about devotion to culture (botany and writing) as well as to agriculture is eclipsed by his enthusiasm for making a record of the land and his life upon it. Crèvecoeur suggests that James's secret to success is inscribed over Bartram's greenhouse door: "Slave to no sect, who takes no private road, / But looks through nature, up to nature's God!" (p. 265).

In addition to casting the yeoman naturalist as the Romantic hero of his New World narrative, Crèvecoeur writes natural history with all the charm and color of Gilbert White or William Bartram. The second chapter of *Letters*, "On the Situation, Feelings, and Pleasures of an American Farmer," is one of the earliest mature examples of the natural history essay in America. In this letter James's curiosity and powers of observation lead to questions about the formation of frost, the life cycles of trees and insects, the mating rituals and migration patterns of birds, and the social intelligence of honeybees. In all his ruminations upon nature, James preserves the inquisitive openness and sense of wonder that is indispensable to the Romantic naturalist. Far from being an effete aesthetic pose, his admiration for the "sublimity" and "miracles" of nature becomes the occasion for genuinely engaged nature study. As a backyard ethologist, James learns a great deal about interspecific competition among birds, and his understanding of the behavior of bees is remarkably sophisticated. On several occasions he examines the contents of the crops of birds in order to speculate upon their diet, nesting grounds, and flight speed.

When considering Crèvecoeur's approach to natural history, we should acknowledge how anthropomorphic that approach can be—how often, for example, he uses nature simply as a vehicle for political analogy. Nevertheless, James's sense of membership in the natural community demonstrates his genuine environmental concern. His respect for nature manifests itself primarily in his Franciscan love for animals, both domestic and wild. He shares his food with quail during freezing weather, and he congratulates the compassionate farmer who saves the entire quail species by giving sanctuary to the remnants of the population during an unusually hard winter. He builds shelters for songbirds and honeybees, and he celebrates animal "art" and "intelligence" at every turn:

> the whole economy of what we proudly call the brute creation, is admirable in every circumstance; and vain man, though adorned with the additional gift of reason, might learn from the perfection of instinct, how to regulate the follies, and how to temper the errors which the second gift often makes him commit. (pp. 40–41)

Although James's environmental ethic is consistently one of paternalistic stewardship, his sense of moral community with nature demonstrates an incipient environmental concern—a concern that is essential to the work of most later nature writers. His sensitivity to environmental processes and the ecological interre-

lationships among them seasons the *Letters* with that broader sensibility the Romantics identified as love of nature. Crèvecoeur approached the natural world with reverence, as a living testament of the Creator; indeed, the American farmer avers this natural divinity with the acknowledgment that "I know no other landlord than the lord of all land, to whom I owe the most sincere gratitude" (p. 24).

Thomas Jefferson (1745–1826)

Published two years after his friend Crèvecoeur's *Letters from an American Farmer*, Thomas Jefferson's *Notes on the State of Virginia* (1787), a significant contribution to American natural history writing, is widely recognized as one of the most important American books of the Revolutionary period. Received with enthusiasm both at home and in Europe, *Notes* distinguished Jefferson as one of the finest minds of his age, a man well versed not only in architecture, law, political philosophy, and statesmanship but also in many aspects of natural history, a pursuit that had become a primary focus of Enlightenment thinking.

Of the contributions that *Notes* made to American natural history, the most significant is Jefferson's justly famous emendation of the French naturalist Buffon's theories concerning nature in the New World. Rivaled only by Linnaeus as the premier natural historian of the eighteenth century, Georges-Louis Leclerc, Comte de Buffon, was court naturalist to Louis XV, and the forty-four volumes of his *Histoire naturelle générale et particulière* (1789–1804) had given him nearly unassailable authority in the field. Nevertheless, not even the most illustrious credentials could prevent Jefferson from challenging a theory of the degeneration of New World animals that, as an American, he found particularly repellent. According to the theory, species common to Europe and America were said to be smaller and weaker in the latter, and species carried from the Old World to the New were described as having succumbed to a progressive degeneration of their stock. For Jefferson, who knew of the huge bison, bear, and elk living in the fecund wilds of his home country, the idea that American animals were enfeebled was a national insult as well as simply bad science.

The patent absurdity of Buffon's thesis, however, did little to discourage the encomiums of Europeans, who rather appreciated its aristocratic implications. The most insidious extrapolation from the theory of degeneration—and one that was supported, in varying degrees, by scholars as illustrious as Louis Daubenton; Constantin Chasseboeuf, Comte de Volney; and, especially, Abbé Guillaume Raynal and Corneille de Pauw—claimed that humans also degenerated when transplanted from the Old World to the New. In his *Histoire philosophique* (1770), Raynal had implied that Buffon's theory might explain what he perceived as the cultural impoverishment of America. According to Jefferson, Raynal claimed that America had not "produced one good poet, one able mathematician, one man of genius in a single art or a single science" (*Notes*, p. 64). In an uninformed diatribe published in his *Histoire naturelle*, Buffon himself concluded that "man makes no exception" to the theory of degeneration (vol. 6, p. 252).

Jefferson recognized that Buffon's theory was prejudicial to America and that it was based upon exiguous evidence. At the same time, America's fledgling natural history studies could offer him only a modicum of support, because most of the American continent remained unsurveyed. Nevertheless, Jefferson's own assiduous studies of natural history led him to believe that he could disprove the degenerative theory, and he did so in Query VI of *Notes*, "Productions Mineral, Vegetable, and Animal." By drawing upon his knowledge of paleontology, he challenged Buffon's misidentification of mastodon bones as those of the elephant, thus suggesting that America had been home to the world's largest quadruped mammal. Using data from meteorological studies he conducted in Williamsburg and at Monticello, he refuted the climatological basis of Buffon's theory.

By drawing on his extensive knowledge of Native American culture, he exposed the many inaccuracies in Buffon's derisive description of the Indian—an "afflicting picture," Jefferson wrote, "which, for the honor of human nature, I am glad to believe has no original" (p. 59). By pointing to salient logical inconsistencies in the *Histoire Naturelle*, Jefferson questioned the methodological certitude of Buffon's conclusions. Furthermore, he carefully constructed a series of tables comparing the weights of Old and New World quadrupeds, thereby decisively refuting Buffon's theory and in fact subtly suggesting that fauna were actually larger and more numerous in America. Finally, Jefferson bolstered the credibility of his data on the "economy of nature" with references to William Bartram, Pehr Kalm, and Mark Catesby, New World naturalists whose work he had studied with care.

Having successfully completed his defense of nature in the New World, Jefferson had a copy of *Notes* and an unusually large panther skin delivered to Buffon in June 1785. Like the book, the skin was calculated to instruct, because it forced Buffon to concede that the panther was not, as he had previously maintained, identical to the cougar. Along with the antlers of several large mammals, including the caribou and elk, Jefferson later sent Buffon the entire skeleton and hide of a seven-foot-tall moose: an animal under whose belly, Jefferson once boasted, the European reindeer might walk upright. Buffon, who had held the moose and reindeer to be the same animal, was again forced to capitulate.

Seen in light of the period's intense nationalism and faith in the symbolic and aesthetic possibilities of American wilderness, Jefferson's challenge to Buffon appears less esoteric. Because his agrarian ideology caused him to associate the land with national prospects, he was compelled to defend America's natural features as energetically as he defended its political institutions. Thus, the query nominally concerned with animals, vegetables, and minerals also argues vigorously against Raynal's application of the degenerative theory to American culture. Pointing to George Washington, Benjamin Franklin, and David Rittenhouse as indicative of American genius, Jefferson writes that "of the geniuses which adorn the present age, America contributes its full share" (p. 65). His challenge to Buffon's thesis was, like the thesis itself, fraught with symbolic significance; if Buffon wished his theory to suggest the inevitability of European cultural superiority, Jefferson likewise wished to measure American prospects by the antlers of a moose.

Although his joust with Buffon underscored Jefferson's accomplishments in the empirical study of nature, it is equally significant that *Notes* helped introduce into American letters a new emotional response to nature. Consider, for example, the often-quoted description of Virginia's Natural Bridge, which Jefferson considered "delightful in the extreme":

> It is impossible for the emotions, arising from the sublime, to be felt beyond what they are here: so beautiful an arch, so elevated, so light, and springing, as it were, up to heaven, the rapture of the Spectator is really indescribable! (p. 25)

In order to experience fully the sublimity of the Bridge, Jefferson insists that you must "fall on your hands and feet, creep to the parapet and peep over it" (pp. 24–25).

Another passage—that of the Potomac River through the Blue Ridge Mountains—further illustrates Jefferson's affective response to the American landscape:

> [It] is perhaps one of the most stupendous scenes in nature. You stand on a very high point of land. On your right comes up the Shenandoah, having ranged along the foot of the mountain an hundred miles to seek a vent. On your left approaches the Patowmac [*sic*], in quest of a passage also. In the moment of their junction they rush together against the mountain, rend it asunder, and pass off to the sea. . . . But the distant finishing which nature has given to the picture is of a very different character. It is a true contrast to the fore-ground. It is as placid and delightful as that is wild and tremendous. For the mountain being cloven asunder, she presents to your eye, through the cleft, a small catch of smooth blue horizon, at an infinite distance in the plain country, inviting you, as it were, from the riot and tumult roaring around, to

pass through the breach and participate in the calm below. . . . This scene is worth a voyage across the Atlantic. (p. 19)

These passages constitute an incipient romanticism that is extraordinary in an eighteenth-century American book. Indeed, Jefferson's voice conveys a genuine enthusiasm, and aesthetic immersion, a sense of appreciative involvement impossible in the work of a pedagogue such as Buffon. The wonders of nature are viewed as awe-inspiring and inviting, and a significant emphasis is placed upon the aesthetic and emotional response of the spectator. Even more remarkable is that these passages bloom upon the stalk of the most exacting natural history. Just as Thoreau would later measure Walden Pond both physically and metaphysically, Jefferson likewise measures the Natural Bridge both in feet and in sublimity; similarly, Jefferson's exhilaration at the spectacle of the Potomac's passage is yoked to speculation about the formation of mountains, the probable existence of ancient inland seas, and the erosive force of rivers. *Notes* exist on the cusp of a new era in the American understanding of nature, for it is at once a work of Enlightenment science and an early Romantic paean to the beauty of nature.

Despite Jefferson's thoroughly Enlightenment sensibility, we need not be too surprised to find *Notes* expressing so direct an emotional response to nature. He was near the center of the cultural changes that informed the late-eighteenth-century shift toward a love of nature. As an eminent naturalist he contributed to the body of scientific knowledge that helped put humans in contact with the workings of their environment; like his friend Franklin, whose zeal for swimming and experimenting with lightning helped convert American fear of nature into enthusiastic curiosity, Jefferson insisted that the once "howling wilderness" would reveal itself to the rational and emotional faculties of humankind. As his description of the Natural Bridge demonstrates, he was also familiar with the concept of the sublime and applied it without hesitation to features of the American landscape.

As a deist, Jefferson firmly believed in nature as a testament of the Creator; his consequent faith that the rural life enjoyed a moral privilege over the urban became the substance of his agrarian ethos, which held that contact with the land would protect the "sacred fire" of American virtue. As a patrician humanist and sworn advocate of natural rights, he thoroughly associated the natural with principles of justice and liberty; in the Declaration of Independence he had argued that Americans were entitled to freedom by the "Laws of Nature and of Nature's God." The praise of wilderness in *Notes* was made possible, then, by significant changes in the American approach to nature. The fact that Jefferson could, in the Age of Reason, describe the land as "delightful," "sublime," "rapture[ous]," "stupendous," and "inviting" shows how pervasive those changes were and how directly *Notes* prefigures the love of nature that would inform nineteenth- and twentieth-century nature writing in America.

Jefferson's devotion to natural history writing is evident in the fact that his only book is largely a study of American landscape and its vital relationship to American culture. It was Jefferson who articulated the belief that contact with the land—whether agricultural, scientific, or literary—was an ennobling pursuit that would help unify the nation. Jefferson was an early supporter of Charles Willson Peale's Philadelphia Museum and a powerful advocate for the establishment of permanent collections of natural history in America. As president, he effected the Louisiana Purchase in part because he recognized the scientific value of the acquisition. The Lewis and Clark expedition was conducted at Jefferson's direction, and many of the specimens sent back from that journey were maintained at his Poplar Forest estate. Above all, Jefferson assuaged national anxieties by redressing the offense Buffon had given to New World nature and, by extrapolation, to hopes for American culture.

Alexander Wilson (1766–1813)

William Bartram was a remarkable nature writer and an invaluable mentor to naturalists such as Benjamin Barton, Thomas Nuttall, and François

Michaux; his most accomplished scientific and literary protégé, however, was the ornithologist Alexander Wilson. Like Crèvecoeur, Wilson was a European whose faith in nature resulted in a literary gift to his adopted homeland. In many ways Wilson resembles the vernacular American hero "Andrew the Hebridean," in Letter III of *Letters from an American Farmer*. In 1794, at the age of twenty-eight, Wilson emigrated from Scotland, where he had been a weaver, reformer, poet, painter, and peddler in the mill town of Paisley. In 1802 he had the good fortune to secure employment teaching at the Union School outside Philadelphia, close to Bartram's botanical garden. Wilson quickly became friends with Bartram, from whom he received encouragement and instruction in drawing and in the study of natural history. Immediately inspired by the beauty and diversity of American birds, Wilson soon devoted his life to their study, traveling many thousands of miles on foot in search of undiscovered species. By the time of his death eleven years after meeting Bartram, Wilson was the nation's foremost authority on birds and had completed nearly all nine volumes of his monumental *American Ornithology* (1808–1829).

Wilson's prodigious literary and ornithological accomplishments were motivated largely by his desire to help ground American culture upon the land. Even before he became an American citizen in 1804, Wilson had delivered an "Oration on the Power and Value of National Liberty" to celebrate Jefferson's election to the presidency and had composed a popular song entitled "Jefferson and Liberty." Like Jefferson and Bartram—both of whom he acknowledged as ornithological predecessors in the introduction to his *American Ornithology*—Wilson found Buffon's unflattering opinions to be "ridiculous and astonishing," and his research joined Jefferson's and Bartram's in refuting the theory of degeneration.

Wilson assumed very deliberately that his momentous study of the birds was a contribution not only to natural history but also to the cultural identity of the nation. According to historian Robert Elman's *First in the Field: America's Pioneering Naturalists* (1977), Wilson expressed a "somewhat mystical belief . . . that the living riches of America's wilderness formed a common heritage—a kind of natural unifying fabric—linking all the peoples of diverse ancestry and background to a single destiny in a young, vigorous nation" (p. 65). Wilson had promised that if the "generous hand of patriotism be stretched forth to assist and cherish the rising arts and literature of our country . . . [they will] increase and flourish with a vigor, a splendor and usefulness inferior to no other on earth" (Porter, p. 47). President Jefferson and Thomas Paine, both of whom were early subscribers to Wilson's unprecedented volumes, would have agreed that the "unifying fabric" of American nature was a crucial determinant of the republic's evolving national character.

Wilson's considerable scientific acumen was always entwined with an engaged literary sensibility. If he was a weaver by trade and a peddler by necessity, he was a poet by inclination and had published his verse long before he began his study of birds. Wilson's ornithological opus is itself a literary accomplishment, for in addition to eloquent prose describing the appearance and habits of the birds, it interpolates lyrics of his own composition. Like earlier naturalists, including Linnaeus, Wilson understood the study of nature to be an ennobling pursuit that spontaneously engendered a poetic response.

Wilson's "poetics of natural history" is most evident in *The Foresters*, the Romantic narrative poem describing his 1,200-mile journey on foot to the falls of Niagara. Over 2,200 lines long, the poem was published serially from July 1809 through March 1810 in the Philadelphia *Port Folio* and was well received. Although literary history does not remember Wilson as a poet, *The Foresters* is an excellent example of how thoroughly enmeshed were his impulses as a writer and a naturalist. The poem's exordium invites readers to "explore / Scenes new to song, and paths untrod before":

> To Europe's shores, renowned in deathless
> song,
> Must all the honours of the bard belong?
> . . .

> While bare bleak heaths, and brooks of half
> a mile
> Can rouse the thousand bards of Britain's
> Isle? . . .
> Our western world, with all its matchless
> floods,
> Our vast transparent lakes and boundless
> woods. . . .
> Spread their wild grandeur to the
> unconscious sky,
> In sweetest seasons pass unheeded by;
> While scarce one Muse returns the songs
> they gave,
> Or seeks to snatch their glories from the
> grave.
> *(Poems*, pp. 147–148, st. 2)

The poem reaches its crescendo at Niagara, where the travelers gaze with "holy awe" upon the sublime falls, which recall the walls of Mecca. Both as ornithologist and as Romantic poet, Wilson responded to the beauty of the American wilderness by leading readers on a pilgrimage into the heart of their own country.

Wilson's writing was often informed by an implicitly environmentalist critique of human pretensions to control nature. For example, in "Verses, Occasioned by Seeing Two Men Sawing Timber in the Open Field, in Defiance of a Furious Storm," he criticized the seemingly indefatigable human urge to destroy nature, regardless of the consequences. The speaker of this poem tries in vain to save two sawyers who, bent upon their work and the harvest they have come to reap, refuse to desist from their labors during a mounting gale. Heedless of the speaker's warnings and of the force of the nature they believe they can dominate, the men are crushed beneath the falling tree:

> Now see, ye misbelieving sinners,
> Your bloody shins—your saw in flinners,
> An' roun' about your lugs the ruin,
> That your demented foly drew on.
> *(Poems*, p. 67, st. 2)

Although Wilson's verse here is mediocre, his objection to the sawyers' self-destructive folly is patent: rather than walking with humility in the natural world, these men have been literally crippled by the "sin" of their arrogant determination to destroy that world.

Wilson's literary brand of natural history also displayed an incipient ecological sensibility, especially in its emphasis upon the crucial role each species plays in the "economy of nature." For example, in his treatment of the bluebird in *American Ornithology*, Wilson includes a poem explaining to readers that the bird "drags the vile grub from the corn he devours" and should therefore be suffered to visit their crops unmolested. As an early conservationist, he made pioneering studies of wildlife populations and projected the devastating impact that human settlement would have upon native habitat. Because Wilson could identify and appreciate the singing of individual birds in his neighboring woods, he was uniquely qualified to remark and lament the extirpation of species that inevitably followed the westward movement of the American frontier.

Wilson was also capable of activism on behalf of the birds. In 1807, when good sense would not prevail upon merchants who were killing thousands of robins to satisfy the palates of genteel Philadelphia, he sent an unsigned article to city newspapers explaining that robin flesh was unhealthy because of the birds' heavy diet of pokeberries; though Wilson knew the claim to be entirely false, it effectively curtailed the slaughter of robins for the Philadelphia market. Because Wilson, like his mentor William Bartram, understood nature study to be the "contemplation and worship of the *Great First Cause*," he viewed natural history writing as a devout mission and protection of fellow creatures as an article of faith (*American Ornithology*, p. 2). Believing that what he studied would inspire America and its poetry because it was inspired by God, Wilson devoted both his scientific and his literary talents to recording the national treasure of America's birds.

John James Audubon (1785–1851)

The idyllic vision of America as a regenerative wilderness had a remarkable incarnation in Jean

Audubon's depiction of the snowy owl, from *The Birds of America*

Jacques Rabin Fougère Audubon, the aristocratic Frenchman reborn in America as John James Audubon, the self-styled "American Woodsman." Like Wilson, who had come to America to avoid the Scottish mill masters determined to silence his socialist poetry, Audubon came to the land of the second chance as a wayward youth, leaving behind the history of his illegitimate birth to a French slave trader and his Creole mistress. Audubon arrived in America in 1803, then weathered business misfortunes and poverty for a quarter-century while painting the birds of his adopted homeland. Like Bartram and Wilson before him, he traveled thousands of miles through wilderness in order to discover, study, and document native species in both paint and ink. Finally, in 1826, he made his startlingly successful debut before the artistic community: the next twelve years saw the momentous publication of the 435 plates of the unprecedented double elephant folio edition of *The Birds of America*.

Although his considerable fame has rested upon his outstanding accomplishments as an artist, Audubon was also a talented writer whose colorful descriptions of life on the frontier deserve a permanent place in our literature. In style as well as subject, Audubon's "Episodes" are an especially important contribution to the literature of the period. Later published under the title *Delineations of American Scenery and Character* (1926), his "Episodes" were sixty short essays covering his travel adventures from 1808 to 1834. They provide remarkable glimpses of the evanescent phenomenon of the frontier and clearly show why this renowned "naturalist" should be seen in the context of American Romantic literature.

"Kentucky Sports," for example, tells of a competition between candle-snuffing, nail-driving masters of the long rifle and is similar to the marksmanship scenes in Cooper's *Pioneers*. "The Turtlers" is a detailed account of that mysterious beast Herman Melville was to record in "The Encantadas." In "Niagara" we read of Audubon's adventures at the cataract so celebrated by William Cullen Bryant and other Romantic poets. The rough justice administered to an apprehended confidence man in "The Regulators" recalls the misadventures of the King and the Duke in Twain's *Adventures of Huckleberry Finn*. In "Scipio and the Bear," the exciting details of the hunt prefigure the mature treatment Faulkner would give the subject in "The Bear." Many of the essays illustrate how his use of lore, tall tales, boasting, and pranks makes him a relative of the Southwest Humorists, writing in the same region at the same time. Throughout the "Episodes," Audubon blends natural and social history into narrative tales that teach us about life in the American wilderness.

Like his predecessors Crèvecoeur, Jefferson, and Wilson, Audubon understood that the role of natural historian was complementary to that of Romantic author. In "The Ohio," the first of his "Episodes," he makes explicit his vision of the link between American literary accomplishments and the need for documenting a disappearing wilderness condition:

> I feel with regret that there are on record no satisfactory accounts of the state of that portion of the country, from the time when our people first settled in it. This has not been because no one in America is able to accomplish such an undertaking. Our Irvings and our Coopers have proved themselves fully competent for the task. It has more probably been because the changes have succeeded each other with such rapidity, as almost to rival the movements of their pen. However, it is not too late yet. . . . I hope. . . . [t]hey will analyze, as it were, into each component part, the country as it once existed, and will render the picture, as it ought to be, immortal. (*Delineations*, p. 5)

Audubon's painting and prose were dedicated to just such a project, and in recognition of his artistic talent and objectives, Washington Irving sought government patronage for his work in 1836. Like the work of Irving, Bryant, and Cooper, Audubon's writing is unmistakably characterized by elements of early romanticism in America: a fondness for the picturesque in natural scenery; a powerful attraction to "the American sublime"; a propensity for melodramatic sentimentality; an enduring interest in Native Americans and in the quotidian existence of settlers, trappers, and woodsmen; an incipient impulse to distinguish nature as a source of moral authority; a stylistic tendency to romanticize characters; and a dramatic inclination to set the scene of his stories in the liminal zone between wilderness and civilization.

Also interesting is the peculiar way in which Audubon connects Romantic literature and natural history by casting the naturalist in the role of Romantic hero. Like William Bartram, whose *Travels* influenced Coleridge, and like Wilson, who was probably the model for William Wordsworth's peddler in "The Excursion," Audubon was the type of the solitary wanderer whose vision led him on a Romantic pilgrimage into the wilderness. In fact, distinctions between the period's romanticized folk heroes and its itinerant natural history writers often blur. William Bartram's woodsmanship and belief in the divinity of wilderness also distinguish the character of Cooper's Natty Bumppo. Wilson's extensive and perilous explorations are reminiscent of Meriwether Lewis, whose mysterious death Wilson investigated in 1810. The tireless Audubon, forever in search of adventure, resembles the mythicized figure of Daniel Boone, with whom the naturalist claimed to have hunted in Kentucky.

Audubon provides the most fascinating study of the naturalist as Romantic hero because he so self-consciously cultivated the identity. Like Crèvecoeur, Audubon could by turns play the diplomat or the rustic. Just as Michael-Guillaume-Jean (Hector St. John) de Crèvecoeur emerged from the romantic chrysalis of the *Letters* as the "American Farmer," so Jean Jacques Rabin Fougère Audubon metamorphosed into the self-styled "American Woodsman." Following the lead of his own hero, Benjamin Franklin, who played the noble American rustic to great effect at the French court, Audubon's success depended largely upon his mastery of the role of American Woodsman. Although taught to excel at the aristocratic arts of dancing, fencing, and sporting finery, he visited European drawing rooms clothed in fringed buckskin, carrying a walking stick, and wearing his hair long and dressed with bear grease. In a letter to his wife (from Edinburgh, 22 December 1826), Audubon commented that "My hairs are now as beautifully long and curly as ever and I assure thee do as much for me as my Talent for Painting (p. 16).

An enthusiastic reader of Lord Byron and Sir Walter Scott as well as of Cooper and Irving, Audubon knew—in his various roles as a Romantic writer, naturalist, painter, and public figure—how to satisfy his audience's appetite for the wilderness. In many of the "Episodes," Audubon writes himself into the leading role of narratives he heard while traveling the riverboats, wagon paths, and Indian trails of the old

Southwest. It is not surprising, therefore, that he has been received into American culture according to the romantic persona he projected. Eudora Welty's short story "A Still Moment" (1943), Jessamyn West's play "A Mirror for the Sky" (1948), Robert Penn Warren's poem series *Audubon: A Vision* (1969), and Scott Russell Sanders' novel *Wonders Hidden* (1984) all commemorate and perpetuate the image of Audubon the romantic.

In *The Bicentennial of John James Audubon* (1985), Alton Lindsey coined the term "ornitheology" to denote bird study as the "popular faith" of which "John James Audubon [was] the original prophet" (p. 137). Although he was an accomplished scientific naturalist who pioneered bird-banding experiments and contributed to our knowledge of the nesting, mating, feeding, and migration habits of birds, Audubon is perhaps best remembered as a purveyor of "ornitheology." Through his paintings and prose, he effectively brought the vanishing wilderness before a popular audience. Although many critics fault him for his zealousness as a hunter, his message from the wild remains one of devout enthusiasm and concern—a genuine love of nature tempered by a scrupulous fear for its destruction. Indeed, Audubon's ecological anxieties often resulted in what has been called an "interrupted idyll"—a narrative moment in which the pastoral enjoyment of nature is invaded, in this case by a disconcerting awareness of its inevitable disappearance.

For example, the Episode "Scipio and the Bear" energetically relates the story of a bear hunt, but ends abruptly by lamenting the needless cruelty of humans toward their fellow creatures. After hounding a family of bears that sometimes visited a farmer's field, the hunting party ends by "smoking" two of the bears in the tree where the animals had retreated for safety:

At length the tree assumed the appearance of a pillar of flame. The Bears mounted to the top branches. When they had reached the uppermost, they were seen to totter, and soon after, the branch cracking and snapping across, they came to the ground, bringing with them a mass of broken twigs. They were cubs, and the dogs soon worried them to death.

The [hunting] party returned to the house in triumph. . . . But before we had left the field, the horses, dogs [. . . and] fires, had destroyed more corn within a few hours, than the poor bear and her cubs had, during the whole of their visits. (*Delineations*, pp. 109–110)

Audubon leaves little doubt that the crop damage done by the bears in no way warrants the cruel treatment the animals receive. Indeed, the fact that the hunters are more destructive to their fields than the bears are suggests that the hunt is motivated primarily by a desire to subjugate nonhuman nature. In response to the very real loss of wildlife represented in such tales, Audubon became an early advocate of government intervention as a means of halting the "war of extermination" waged upon native species; he often despaired that "Nature herself seems perishing."

Much of Audubon's writing laments the swiftness with which wilderness was being lost. Consider this poignant passage in which he reflects upon his early rambles along the Ohio River:

When I think of these times, and call back to my mind the grandeur and beauty of those almost uninhabited shores; when I picture to myself the dense and lofty summits of the forest, that everywhere spread along the hills, and overhung the margins of the stream, unmolested by the axe of the settler . . . when I see that no longer any Aborigines are to be found there, and that the vast herds of elks, deer and buffaloes which once pastured on these hills and in these valleys, making for themselves great roads to the several salt-springs, have ceased to exist; when I reflect that all this grand portion of our Union, instead of being in a state of nature, is now more or less covered with villages, farms, and towns, where the din of hammers and machinery is constantly heard; that the woods are fast disappearing under the axe by day, and the fire by night . . . when I remember that these extraordinary changes have taken place

in the short period of twenty years, I pause, wonder, and, although I know all to be fact, can scarcely believe its reality. (*Delineations*, p. 4)

As Audubon correctly recognized, the impulse toward domination and extermination of wild nature was fast becoming the ecological legacy of the American frontier.

Audubon's sensitivity to the natural world and his concern for its preservation form an essential precursor to modern American nature writing and to the ethic of environmental concern that sustains it. Like Crèvecoeur, Jefferson, and Wilson before him, Audubon was inspired by the divine beauty of nature, and his study of natural history resulted in contributions to nature writing and environmental awareness as well as to painting and ornithology. Audubon's life in America (1803–1851) spanned the most active years of frontier expansion, a time when wilderness and its settlement were fiercely competing interpretations of a single landscape. By the time Thoreau—who wrote that he read Audubon "with a thrill of delight"—had removed himself to Walden Pond, the American Woodsman had already asked in his journal: "Where can I go now, and visit nature undisturbed?"

As we have seen, the early Romantic period's combination of republican nationalism with Romantic values created a perfect matrix for the growth of natural history literature. The topographical imperative set the American cultural agenda in terms of the land and nurtured a distinctively American brand of literary naturalism that arose to explore and express the possibilities of the wilderness. Nevertheless, it is important to distinguish the proto-ecological sensibility of Crèvecoeur or Audubon from the genuinely ecocentric ethic that informs the work of many twentieth-century nature writers. The early Romantic literary naturalists studied nature with greater attention than had their predecessors, and they expressed the sense of loss that attended the settlement and subjugation of the wilderness. They also nurtured the environmentally sensitive vision of nature as a community of interrelated beings among which humans have a place.

Unlike later nature writers, these authors based their love of wilderness largely upon a nationalistic faith that nature could generate a distinctively American culture. Although they often argued for a spiritual and aesthetic use of nature as well as a strictly economic use, their environmental ethic rarely called for a nonanthropocentric recognition that nature is not made for human use. The important bridge from an instrumental to an intrinsic valuation of the natural world would be built by later nature writers such as Thoreau, Muir, and their literary descendants.

Selected Bibliography

PRIMARY SOURCES

ST. JOHN DE CRÈVECOEUR

Gay Wilson Allen and Roger Asselineau, *St. John de Crèvecoeur: The Life of an American Farmer* (New York: Viking, 1987); Bernard Chevignard, "St. John de Crèvecoeur in the Looking Glass: *Letters from an American Farmer* and the Making of a Man of Letters," in *Early American Literature* 19 (fall 1984); St. John de Crèvecoeur, *Letters from an American Farmer* (London: T. Davies, 1782; repr., New York: Fox, Duffield, 1904), *Journey into Northern Pennsylvania and the State of New York*, trans. by Clarissa Spencer Bostleman (Ann Arbor: Univ. of Michigan Press, 1964), and *Sketches of Eighteenth-Century America: More Letters from an American Farmer*, ed. by Henri L. Bourdin, Ralph H. Gabriel, and Stanley T. Williams (New York: Benjamin Blom, 1972); Everett Emerson, "Hector St. John de Crèvecoeur and the Promise of America," in *Forms and Functions in American Literature: Essays in Honor of Ursula Brumm*, ed. by Winfried Fluck, Jürgen Peper, and Willi Paul Adams (Berlin: Erich Schmidt, 1981); Norman S. Grabo, "Crèvecoeur's American: Beginning the World Anew," in *William and Mary Quarterly* 48 (April 1991).

James L. Machor, "The Garden City in America: Crèvecoeur's *Letters* and the Urban-Pastoral Context," in *American Studies* 23 (fall 1982); Thomas Philbrick, *St. John de Crèvecoeur* (New York: Twayne, 1970); Doreen Alvarez Saar, "The Revolutionary Origins of Thoreau's Thought: An Examination of Thoreau in Light of Crèvecoeur's *Letters from an American Farmer*," in *Mid-Hudson Language Studies* 7 (1984); Tsutomu Takahashi, "The Myth of the Land and Crèvecoeur's Vision of Self in *Letters from an American Farmer*," in *Studies in English Language and Literature* 40 (February 1990).

THOMAS JEFFERSON

Silvio A. Bedini, *Thomas Jefferson: Statesman of Science* (New York: Macmillan, 1990); Noble E. Cunningham, *In Pursuit of Reason: The Life of Thomas Jefferson* (Baton Rouge: Louisiana State Univ. Press, 1987); Edward E. Edwards, ed., *Jefferson and Agriculture* (Washington, D.C.: U.S. Dept. of Agriculture, 1943); Eugene L. Huddleston, *Thomas Jefferson: A Reference Guide* (Boston: G. K. Hall, 1982); Thomas Jefferson, *The Complete Jefferson, Containing His Major Writings, Published and Unpublished, Except His Letters* (New York: Duell, Sloane and Pearce, 1943), *Notes on the State of Virginia* (1787; Chapel Hill: Univ. of North Carolina Press, 1955), and *The Garden and Farm Books of Thomas Jefferson* (Golden, Colo.: Fulcrum, 1987); Georges-Louis Leclerc, Count of Buffon, *Natural History, General and Particular*, trans. by William Smellie, 20 vols. (London: T. Cadell, 1812); Christopher Looby, "The Constitution of Nature: Taxonomy as Politics in Jefferson, Peale, and Bartram," in *Early American Literature* 22 (1987).

Edwin T. Martin, *Thomas Jefferson: Scientist* (New York: Henry Schuman, 1952); Barbara McEwan, *Thomas Jefferson, Farmer* (Jefferson, N.C.: McFarland, 1991); Charles A. Miller, *Jefferson and Nature: An Interpretation* (Baltimore: Johns Hopkins Univ. Press, 1988); Frank Shuffelton, "From Jefferson to Thoreau: The Possibilities of Discourse," in *Arizona Quarterly* 46 (spring 1990); Randall Willard Sterne, *Thomas Jefferson: A Life* (New York: Holt, 1993).

ALEXANDER WILSON

Robert Cantwell, *Alexander Wilson: Naturalist and Pioneer* (Philadelphia: Lippincott, 1961); Clark Hunter, *The Life and Letters of Alexander Wilson* (Philadelphia: American Philosophical Society, 1983); George Ord, *Sketch of the Life of Alexander Wilson* (Philadelphia: Harrison Hall, 1928); Alan Park Paton, *Wilson the Ornithologist: A New Chapter in His Life* (London: Longman's, Green, 1863); Irving N. Rothman, "Niagara Falls and the *Port Folio*," in *Aldus* 11 (November 1973); Alexander Wilson, *American Ornithology; or, The Natural History of the Birds of the United States*, 9 vols. (Philadelphia: Bradford and Inskeep, 1808–1829) and 3 vols. (Philadelphia: Porter & Coates, 1870), *The Foresters: A Poem, Descriptive of a Pedestrian Journey to the Falls of Niagara, in the Autumn of 1804* (Newtown, Pa.: Siegfried and Wilson,

1818), *Memoirs of Alexander Wilson* (Philadelphia: Carey & Lea, 1831), *The Poetical Works of Alexander Wilson* (Belfast: J. Henderson, 1857), and *The Poems and Literary Prose of Alexander Wilson*, ed. by Rev. Alexander B. Grosart (Paisley, Scotland: Alexander Gardner, 1876).

JOHN JAMES AUDUBON

John James Audubon, *The Birds of America* (London, 1827–1838; New York: Macmillan, 1946), *Ornithological Biography*, 5 vols. (Edinburgh: A. Black, 1831–1839), *Delineations of American Scenery and Character* (New York: G. A. Baker, 1926), *Journal of John James Audubon, Made While Obtaining Subscriptions to His* Birds of America, *1840–1843* (Cambridge, Mass.: Business Historical Society, 1929), *Journal of John James Audubon Made During His Trip to New Orleans in 1820–1821*, ed. by Howard Corning (Boston: Club of Odd Volumes, 1930), *Letters of John James Audubon, 1826–1840*, 2 vols., ed. by Howard Corning (Boston: Club of Odd Volumes, 1930), *Audubon and His Journals*, 2 vols., ed. by Maria R. Audubon, with notes by Elliott Coues (New York: Scribners, 1897; Dover, 1986), and *The 1826 Journal of John James Audubon*, ed. by Alice Ford (New York: Abbeville Press, 1987); John James Audubon and Rev. John Bachman, *The Viviparous Quadrupeds of North America*, 2 vols. (New York: J. J. Audubon, 1845–1848); Maria R. Audubon, *Audubon and His Journals*, 2 vols. (New York: Scribners, 1897; repr., New York: Dover, 1986).

Desmond Sparling Bland, *John James Audubon in Liverpool, 1826–1827* (Liverpool: Univ. of Liverpool Press, 1977); John Burroughs, *John James Audubon* (Boston: Small, Maynard, 1902); Nancy Cluck, "Audubon: Images of the Artist in Eudora Welty and Robert Penn Warren," in *Southern Literary Journal* 17 (spring 1985); James H. Dorman and Allison Heaps de Pena, eds., *Audubon: A Retrospective* (Lafayette: Center for Louisiana Studies, Univ. of Southwestern Louisiana, 1990); Mary Durant and Michael Hargrove, *On the Road with John James Audubon* (New York: Dodd, Mead, 1980); Edward H. Dwight, "The Autobiographical Writings of J. J. Audubon," in *Bulletin of the Missouri Historical Society* 19, no. 1 (1962); Daniel G. Elliott, "The Life and Services of J. J. Audubon," in *Transactions* 13 (1893); Alice Ford, *John James Audubon: A Biography* (New York: Abbeville Press, 1988), and, as ed., *Audubon, by Himself* (Garden City, N.Y.: Natural History Press, 1969); W. Fries, *The Double Elephant Folio: The Story of Audubon's* Birds of America (Chicago: American Library Association, 1973).

Francis Hobart Herrick, *Audubon the Naturalist: A History of His Life and Time*, 2 vols. (New York: Appleton, 1917); Alton A. Lindsey, *The Bicentennial of John James Audubon* (Bloomington: Indiana Univ. Press, 1985); Suzanne Marrs, "John James Audubon in Fiction and Poetry: Literary Portraits by Eudora Welty and Robert Penn Warren," in *Southern Studies* 20 (winter 1981); John Francis McDermott, ed., *Audubon in the West* (Norman: Univ. of Oklahoma Press, 1951), and *Up the Missouri with Audubon: The Journal of Edward Harris* (Norman: Univ. of Oklahoma Press, 1965); Davy-Jo Stribling Ridge, *A Load of Gratitude: Audubon and South Carolina* (Columbia: Thomas Cooper Library, Univ. of South Carolina, 1985); Constance Rourke, *Audubon* (New York: Harcourt, Brace, 1936); Scott Russell Sanders, ed., *Audubon Reader: The Best Writings of John James Audubon* (Bloomington: Indiana Univ. Press, 1986); Shirley Streshinsky, *Audubon: Life and Art in the American Wilderness* (New York: Villard, 1993).

OTHER

John Smith, *The Complete Works of Captain John Smith (1580–1631) in Three Volumes*, vol. 1, ed. by Philip L. Barbour (Chapel Hill: Univ. of North Carolina Press, 1986); Michael Wigglesworth, *God's Controversy with New England*, in *Proceedings of the Massachusetts Historical Society* 12 (1871).

SECONDARY SOURCES

Marcia Bonta, *Women in the Field: America's Pioneering Women Naturalists* (College Station: Texas A&M Univ. Press, 1991); Lawrence Buell, "American Pastoral Ideology Reappraised," in *American Literary History* 1 (spring 1989); Robert Clark, "The Absent Landscape of America's Eighteenth Century," in *Views of American Landscapes*, ed. by Mick Gigley and Robert Lawson-Peebles (Cambridge: Cambridge Univ. Press, 1989); Merle Curti, *The Growth of American Thought*, 2d ed. (New York: Harper & Bros., 1951); Rose Marie Cutting, *John and William Bartram, William Byrd II and St. John de Crèvecoeur: A Reference Guide* (Boston: G. K. Hall, 1976); Ernest Earnest, *John and William Bartram, Botanists and Explorers* (Philadelphia: Univ. of Pennsylvania Press, 1940); Frank N. Egerton, "Ecological Studies and Observations Before 1900," in *Issues and Ideas in America*, ed. by Benjamin J. Taylor and Thurman J. White (Norman: Univ. of Oklahoma Press, 1976), and, as ed., *History of American Ecology* (New York: Arno Press, 1977); Arthur A. Ekirch, Jr., *Man and Nature in America* (New York: Columbia Univ. Press, 1963); Robert Elman, *First in the Field: America's Pioneering Naturalists* (New York: Mason/Charter, 1977).

Edward Halsey Foster, *The Civilized Wilderness: Backgrounds to American Romantic Literature, 1817–1860* (New York: Free Press, 1975); Clarence J. Glacken, *Traces on the Rhodian Shore: Nature and*

Culture in Western Thought from Ancient Times to the End of the Eighteenth Century (Berkeley: Univ. of California Press, 1967), and "Culture and Environment in Western Civilization During the Nineteenth Century," in *Environmental History: Critical Issues in Comparative Perspective*, ed. by Kendall E. Bailes (New York: Univ. Press of America, 1985); John C. Greene, *American Science in the Age of Jefferson* (Ames: Iowa State Univ. Press, 1984); Wayne Hanley, *Natural History in America: From Mark Catesby to Rachel Carson* (New York: Demeter Press, 1977); Brooke Hindle, *The Pursuit of Science in Revolutionary America, 1735–1789* (Chapel Hill: Univ. of North Carolina Press, 1956); Hans Huth, *Nature and the American: Three Centuries of Changing Attitudes* (Lincoln: Univ. of Nebraska Press, 1957).

D. H. Lawrence, *Studies in Classic American Literature* (New York: Penguin, 1977); Thomas J. Lyon, *This Incomperable Lande: A Book of American Nature Writing* (Boston: Houghton Mifflin, 1989); Leo Marx, *The Machine in the Garden: Technology and the Pastoral Ideal in America* (London: Oxford Univ. Press, 1964); John C. McCloskey, "The Campaign of Periodicals After the War of 1812 for a National American Literature," in *PMLA* 50 (1935); Perry Miller, *Errand into the Wilderness* (Cambridge, Mass.: Harvard Univ. Press, 1956); Lee Clark Mitchell, *Witnesses to a Vanishing America: The Nineteenth-Century Response* (Princeton, N.J.: Princeton Univ. Press, 1981); Roderick Nash, *Wilderness and the American Mind* (New Haven, Conn.: Yale Univ. Press, 1967); Max Oelschlaeger, *The Idea of Wilderness from Prehistory to the Age of Ecology* (New Haven, Conn.: Yale Univ. Press, 1991); Charlotte M. Porter, *The Eagle's Nest: Natural History and American Ideas, 1812–1842* (University: Univ. of Alabama Press, 1986).

Pamela Regis, *Describing Early America: Bartram, Jefferson, Crèvecoeur, and the Rhetoric of Natural History* (De Kalb: Northern Illinois Univ. Press, 1992); Bernard Rosenthal, *City of Nature: Journeys to Nature in the Age of American Romanticism* (Newark: Univ. of Delaware Press, 1980); Paul Semonin, " 'Nature's Nation': Natural History as Nationalism in the New Republic," in *Northwest Review* 30, no. 2 (1992); Bruce Silver, "William Bartram's and Other Eighteenth-Century Accounts of Nature," in *Journal of the History of Ideas* 39 (October–December 1978); Richard Slotkin, *Regeneration Through Violence: The Mythology of the American Frontier: 1690–1860* (Middletown, Conn.: Wesleyan Univ. Press, 1973); Benjamin T. Spencer, *The Quest for Nationality: An American Literary Campaign* (Syracuse, N.Y.: Syracuse Univ. Press, 1957); Cecelia Tichi, *New World, New Earth: Environmental Reform in American Literature from the Puritans Through Whitman* (New Haven, Conn.: Yale Univ. Press, 1979); Donald Worster, *Nature's Economy: A History of Ecological Ideas* (Cambridge: Cambridge Univ. Press, 1985).

THE FORMS OF AMERICAN NATURE POETRY

CHRISTOPHER MERRILL

ON THE ISLAND of Maui, more than two thousand miles from the nearest continent, the poet W. S. Merwin has planted on eighteen acres of land countless palms, many of which are either endangered or extinct in the wild. Merwin collects seeds from palm growers around the world, and in his nursery hundreds of seedlings twist upward toward the sun. To walk in this burgeoning preserve is to be reminded of the seemingly infinite tones of green nature offers; only the blue of the sea in the distance and of the sky filtered through palms, mangoes, and a stand of bamboo distract the eye. American nature poetry is very like Merwin's palm garden—green, endangered, and vital. It is that "force that through the green fuse drives the flower," as Dylan Thomas sang. The forms it takes are shades of green that have been with us for millennia.

"The world is emblematic," Ralph Waldo Emerson announced in *Nature*, a founding document of the American literary tradition. Indeed, the New World teems with emblems and omens—natural facts that our poets turn into musical phrases. Mountains and rivers, deserts and plains, forests and swamps, tundra and tropics—the sheer abundance and variety of landscapes in North America boggle the imagination even as they summon poems in their praise. Just as the land is blessed with a myriad

of life forms, so American poets employ a bewildering range of verse forms to sing and say their surroundings into aesthetic life. "Deep calls unto deep," said Emerson in that same essay, and our best poets chart the depths of language, of nature, of the world.

If, as Emerson believed, "nature is a discipline" that instructs and governs, then poets learn from it not only how to live but also how to pass along its lessons. "I feel the universe is full of glorious energy," Richard Wilbur remarked in a 1977 interview, "that the energy tends to take pattern and shape, and that the ultimate character of things is comely and good." This, of course, influences his formal strategies, the decisions—prosodical and rhetorical, conscious and unconscious—by which a poet reveals his or her epistemological concerns. "My feeling is that when you discover order and goodness in the world," he continued, "it is not something you are imposing—it is something which is likely really to be there, whatever crumminess and evil and disorder there may also be. I don't take disorder or meaninglessness to be the basic character of things" (*Conversations with Richard Wilbur*, 1990, pp. 190–191). Not surprisingly, Wilbur's poetry is marked by formal elegance and beauty—"the compressed expression of the whole of one's experience, all at once," as he defines it.

But what of other American poets? What patterns and shapes do they find in their surroundings? Do they enjoy what Emerson called in *Nature* "an original relation to the universe"? If so, how do they enact that in their work? Examined in the following pages are some of the multitudinous ways in which the glorious energy of the universe manifests itself in American poetry — in the emblems, that is, of human settlement of America, an ongoing process in which poetry plays an essential, though often overlooked, role.

A Poetry Commensurate with Place

In February 1844 Emerson completed "The Poet," an ambitious essay delineating the qualities required for American poetry to be equal to the landscapes of the New World. "A rhyme in one of our sonnets should not be less pleasing than the iterated nodes of a seashell," he suggested, "or the resembling difference of a group of flowers." Nevertheless, in his view America had yet to produce a poet capable of such rhymes; despite the example set by their colonial forefathers — declaring independence from England, waging the Revolutionary War, drafting the Constitution — the bards of this young country were still tethered to the past. They needed to break with the linguistic, aesthetic, and spiritual habits of the old order. They needed to establish original contact with their new surroundings. "Yet America is a poem in our eyes," Emerson concluded with his customary optimism; "its ample geography dazzles the imagination, and it will not wait long for metres."

His essay was prophetic: within two decades, Walt Whitman (1819–1892) and Emily Dickinson (1830–1886) revolutionized the national literature. The father of American poetry, "Walt Whitman, an American, one of the roughs, a kosmos," as he described himself, took Emerson to heart, affirming in the preface to his seminal book, *Leaves of Grass* (1855), that "the largeness of nature of the nation were monstrous without a corresponding largeness and generos-

ity of the spirit of the citizen." Though he had no use for Emerson's idea of poetry as "a metre-making argument," since the traditional meters shackled his particular form of genius, he readily adopted the essayist's belief, as delineated in "The Poet," that a poem should express "a thought so passionate and alive, that, like the spirit of a plant or an animal, it has an architecture of its own, and adorns nature with a new thing." The new thing Whitman added to nature was the notion that "the United States themselves are essentially the greatest poem."

His formal contribution? Versets, which combine the cadences of the King James Bible with Homeric catalogs: a flexible form in which "his thoughts are the hymns of the praise of things." These lines from the thirty-first section of "Song of Myself," his — and the nation's — poetic anthem, illustrate Whitman's methods and concerns:

I believe a leaf of grass is no less than the
     journeywork of the stars,
And the pismire is equally perfect, and a
     grain of sand, and the egg of the wren,
And the tree-toad is a chef-d'oeuvre for the
     highest,
And the running blackberry would adorn
     the parlors of heaven,
And the narrowest hinge in my hand puts
     to scorn all machinery,
And the cow crunching with depressed
     head surpasses any statue,
And a mouse is miracle enough to stagger
     sextillions of infidels,
And I could come every afternoon of my
     life to look at the farmer's girl boiling
     her iron tea-kettle and baking
     shortcake.

I find I incorporate gneiss and coal and
     long-threaded moss and fruits and
     grains and esculent roots,
And am stucco'd with quadrupeds and
     birds all over,
And have distanced what is behind me for
     good reasons,
And call any thing close again when I
     desire it.

It is as though Whitman translated into American versets William Blake's revelation in "Auguries of Innocence"—

To see a World in a Grain of Sand
And a Heaven in a Wild Flower,
Hold Infinity in the palm of your hand
And Eternity in an hour

—and then developed it in an expansive fashion. "The known universe has one complete lover and that is the greatest poet," he proclaims in the preface to *Leaves of Grass*. "Song of Myself" enumerates the loving ways by which this poet knows the world(s). "I celebrate myself," he begins, "And what I assume you shall assume,/ For every atom belonging to me as good belongs to you." In fifty-two sections—one for each week of the year—he presents a poetic almanac, cataloging as much of life as he can take in, sounding his "barbaric yawp over the roofs of the world." And what a yawp it is:

Smile O voluptuous coolbreathed earth!
Earth of the slumbering and liquid trees!
Earth of departed sunset! Earth of the
    mountains misty-topt!
Earth of the vitreous pour of the full moon
    just tinged with blue!
Earth of shine and dark mottling the tide of
    the river!
Earth of the limpid gray of clouds brighter
    and clearer for my sake!
Far-swooping elbowed earth! Rich apple-
    blossomed earth!
Smile, for your lover comes!

The initiating poem in American literature, then, is a paean to the universe, which after all gave rise to a country, Whitman wrote, "with veins full of poetical stuff." Emerson immediately recognized Whitman's achievement: "I am not blind to the worth of the wonderful gift of *Leaves of Grass*," he wrote in a letter to Whitman, which the poet took the liberty of reprinting in the preface to the 1856 edition of his book. "I find it the most extraordinary piece of wit and wisdom that America has yet contributed." That is, Whitman had become the poet whose "spirit responds to his country's spirit"—his (and Emerson's) ideal—because "he incarnates its geography and natural life and rivers and lakes." Indeed, his work gives voice to the voiceless—to slaves, prostitutes, thieves, "fog in the air and beetles rolling balls of dung," in short, to the whole of life—and thus outlines a central theme for American poetry: the sacred bond between the land and the people. "I bequeath myself to the dirt to grow from the grass I love," Whitman asserts in the final section of his poem, "If you want me again look for me under your bootsoles."

A nation founded by revolutionaries, who were determined to make freedom a guiding principle as well as a religious imperative, was perhaps destined to create a poetic tradition indebted to civic and religious forms. If "Song of Myself" is the United States' poetic Declaration of Independence, Emily Dickinson's 1,775 short poems correspond to Lincoln's Emancipation Proclamation and Gettysburg Address, crucial texts for the American experiment in democracy. And Whitman's versets are balanced by Dickinson's use of common meter, the medieval folk ballad stanza that filled the pages of the hymnal she sang from in the Congregational Church—a form that, like the rolling cadences Whitman heard in the Psalms, had a civic as well as a religious meaning by the advent of the Civil War.

Dickinson was at first glance Whitman's opposite: chaste, retiring, reticent. Her life in Amherst, Massachusetts, was as cloistered as his was worldly, her verse as carefully measured as his was capacious. He was a consummate self-promoter (writing, for example, at least three laudatory reviews of *Leaves of Grass*); she published only a handful of poems in her lifetime. Yet in the American imagination these singular artists are forever linked. They are Emerson's "liberating gods," the sources of a nation's tradition; their representative poems, at once ecstatic and meditative, put side by side recall the figure of Janus, the Roman god of doorways and beginnings, the deity who looks in both directions. Male and female, light and dark, yin and yang, they belong together "by the Right of the White Election," in Dickinson's phrase, an accession crowned by "the Royal Seal" of poetry: their complete works.

The pivotal year in the War Between the States was 1862. After spectacular Confederate victories in the Shenandoah Valley and at the Second Battle of Bull Run, in the fall Union forces regrouped to stop the army of General Robert E. Lee. Neither side won the Battle of Antietam waged on September 16–17, but Lee was forced to abandon his Maryland campaign and retreat to Virginia, prompting Lincoln to issue his Emancipation Proclamation early the following year, freeing the slaves. And 1862 marked another emancipation: Dickinson completed, on average, a poem a day that year— hers was a "Soul *at the White Heat*," as she wrote. (Interestingly, almost half of her work— some 850 poems—dates from the Civil War.) A poem unites two things that have heretofore been apart, as in this poem from Dickinson's, and the nation's, fateful year (in *The Complete Poems of Emily Dickinson*, 1890), which relies on a figure from nature—embedded in common meter—to describe the war:

The name—of it—is "Autumn"—
The hue—of it—is Blood—
An Artery—upon the Hill—
A Vein—along the Road—

Great Globules—in the Alleys—
And Oh, the Shower of Stain—
When Winds—upset the Basin—
And spill the Scarlet Rain—

It sprinkles Bonnets—far below—
It gathers ruddy Pools—
Then—eddies like a Rose—away—
Upon Vermillion Wheels—

The dashes function as rest notes, disrupting the regular beat of each line. The capitalized nouns are equally unnerving, since written English ordinarily reserves that feature for references to God. It is as if the poet is in church, gazing out a stained glass window, repeatedly losing her place in her hymnal as her fellow parishioners sing "A Mighty Fortress is Our God": the syn-copation of these lines unsettles the reader who, like the believer, may focus on the one looking out the window. What does she see?

A narrow Fellow in the Grass
Occasionally rides—
You may have met Him—did you not
His notice sudden is—

The Grass divides as with a Comb—
A spotted shaft is seen—
And then it closes at your feet
And opens further on—

He likes a Boggy Acre
A Floor too cool for Corn—
Yet when a Boy, and Barefoot—
I more than once at Noon

Have passed, I thought, a Whip lash
Unbraiding in the Sun
When stooping to secure it
It wrinkled, and was gone—

Several of Nature's People
I know, and they know me—
I feel for them a transport
Of cordiality—

But never met this Fellow
Attended, or alone
Without a tighter breathing
And Zero at the Bone—

Here is an American version of Milton's *Paradise Lost*. In Dickinson's Garden of Eden, however, the religious—and civic—lesson is a function of prosody: the deceptive ease with which the regular fourteeners—alternating four- and three-beat lines—give way to strict trimeter quatrains by the last two stanzas, which also contain the poem's only examples of true rhyme, shorten the reader's breathing and focus his or her attention—in this case, on the key pairings of "me/cordiality" and "alone/bone"—in the same way that a chance encounter with a snake will cause most humans to freeze. This is a real snake, not an emblem of evil. Dickinson's work, and American poetry in general, is a study in convergences with nature, some of which end in terror, others in "transport[s] / Of cordiality." It is a matter of discovering, again and again, the truth of Emerson's maxim in "The Poet": "Every touch should thrill." In this way a community—indeed, a nation—of readers is created: "The Soul selects her own Society," said Dickinson. And just as the Gettysburg Address turned *these* United States into *the* United States, according to historian Gary Wills, so her poems contribute to the cementing together of disparate strands of humanity. One of her last works is exemplary:

> To make a prairie it takes a clover and one
> bee,
> One clover, and a bee,
> And revery.
> The revery alone will do
> If bees are few.

Remaking Traditional Forms

Robert Frost (1874–1963) structured his reveries in iambic pentameter, the most common line in English poetry. Now that trails had been blazed into the New World, so to speak, this poet-farmer was free to explore more conventional prosodical means, albeit in a wholly original fashion. What he heard in the speech rhythms of his New England neighbors led him to reinvigorate blank verse: " 'Fred, where is north?' " a woman asks her husband in "West-Running Brook" (in *The Poetry of Robert Frost*, 1969). " 'North? North is there, my love,' " he replies. " 'The brook runs west.' " To which she answers:

> "West-Running Brook then call it."
> (West-Running Brook men call it to this
> day.)
> "What does it think it's doing running
> west
> When all the other country brooks flow
> east
> To reach the ocean? It must be the brook
> Can trust itself to go by contraries

> The way I can with you—and you with
> me—
> Because we're—we're—I don't know what
> we are.
> What are we?"

Her question lies at the heart of most poetic and philosophical explorations, yet in Frost's rephrasing it sounds altogether new. He did not consider himself to be a nature poet; rather, he used the figures of nature to address mankind's dilemmas. Thus a brook running west instead of east becomes an occasion to meditate on the vagaries of marriage. For in his view, "Poetry is simply made of metaphor. . . . Every poem is a new metaphor inside or it is nothing."

"The sound of sense"—that was Frost's idea of what a poem's prosody should enact. Consider the opening lines of "Directive":

> Back out of all this now too much for us,
> Back in a time made simple by the loss
> Of detail, burned, dissolved, and broken off
> Like graveyard marble sculpture in the
> weather,
> There is a house that is no more a house
> Upon a farm that is no more a farm
> And in a town that is no more a town.

The poet and critic Joseph Brodsky has said that an English poem declares its metrical intentions in its first line, an American poem in its second. Though "Directive" is a good example of Frost's "strict iambics," as he called them, readers will not know that before the second or even the third line. "Back out of all this now too much for us" is an earful; in ten words—ten syllables—readers hear at least seven stresses and eight different vowel sounds: it is a cacophony the poet listens to in alarm. He wishes to direct readers away from it, toward "A brook that was the water of the house, / Cold as a spring as yet so near its source, / Too lofty and original to rage." Frost's directions to this brook, a metaphor for poetry, depend on his prosodical and rhetorical abilities to create "a time made simple," another Garden of Eden where civilization's accoutrements have been "burned, dissolved, and broken off." Thus he moves this

Robert Frost reading his poetry for a Library of Congress recording project

house from its historical setting into the realm of myth, where in regular meters he can say: "Here are your waters and your watering place. / Drink and be whole again beyond confusion."

Robinson Jeffers (1887–1962) had a more elemental view of Paradise—a world cleansed of man. Formally, he redoubled Frost's efforts, as it were, often laying blank verse lines back to back, as if to call into question the usefulness of the very structures he employed in order to proclaim what the poet Czeslaw Milosz calls "an inhuman thing," as in the closing "couplet" of "Continent's End," where he addresses the sea in a remarkable fashion: "Mother, though my song's measure is like your surf-beat's ancient rhythm I never learned it of you. / Before there was any water there were tides of fire, both our tones flow from the older fountain."

It is his faith in that older source that prompts him to rage against the excesses of modern life.

In "The Purse-Seine" (in *The Selected Poetry of Robinson Jeffers*, 1927), watching sardine fishermen haul in their net, he says:

> I cannot tell you
> How beautiful the scene is, and a little
>   terrible, then, when the crowded fish
> Know they are caught, and wildly beat from
>   one wall to the other of their closing
>   destiny the phosphorescent
> Water to a pool of flame, each beautiful
>   slender body sheeted with flame, like a
>   live rocket
> A comet's tail wake of clear yellow flame;
>   while outside the narrowing
> Floats and cordage of the net great sea-lions
>   come up to watch, sighing in the
>   dark; the vast walls of night
> Stand erect to the stars.

This scene he compares to a city's "colored splendor, [and] galaxies of light," certain that for mankind "there is no escape." Born only five years after Emerson died, Jeffers is a dark counterweight to the optimistic author of "The Poet." Foreseeing anarchy and disaster, he writes of civilization's narrowing net. "The Purse-Seine" concludes:

These things are Progress;
Do you marvel our verse is troubled or
    frowning, while it keeps its reason? Or
    lets it go, lets the mood flow
In the manner of the recent young men
    into mere hysteria, splintered gleams,
    crackled laughter. But they are quite
    wrong.
There is no reason for amazement: surely
    one always knew that cultures decay,
    and life's end is death.

No wonder Jeffers, enormously popular early in his career and then forgotten, was rediscovered by the environmental movement in the last decades of the twentieth century. Notwithstanding his misanthropy, readers delight in his exact and gorgeous descriptions of the natural world, and it may be argued that his long narrative poems, dismissed in many circles, have inspired a number of younger poets keen on resurrecting the form.

Another questioner of traditional poetic means was Marianne Moore (1887–1972), who wrote in syllabics, a formal structure the ear cannot discern, in order to discover "imaginary gardens with real toads in them," as her famous verse description in "Poetry" puts it. Uncovering reality, in as many of its disguises as possible, she examined the things of this world, swans and elephants and quartz clocks, which in her poetry take on lives of their own. Hers was a penetrating gaze — *Observations* was the revealing title of her first book — and in her work "nothing loses its identity because of the composition," William Carlos Williams noted. "The Fish" (in *The Complete Poems of Marianne Moore*, 1967), for example, incorporates the title into the body of the poem, blurring yet another conventional line of poetic demarcation:

The Fish

wade
through black jade.
    Of the crow-blue mussel-shells, one
    keeps adjusting the ash-heaps;
        opening and shutting itself like

an
injured fan.
    The barnacles which encrust the side of
    the wave, cannot hide
        there for the submerged shafts of the

sun,
split like spun
    glass, move themselves with spotlight
    swiftness into the crevices —
        in and out, illuminating

the
turquoise sea
    of bodies. The water drives a wedge of
    iron through the iron edge
        of the cliff; whereupon the stars,

pink
rice-grains, ink-
    bespattered jelly-fish, crabs like green
    lilies, and submarine
        toadstools, slide each on the other.

All
external
    marks of abuse are present on this
    defiant edifice —
        all the physical features of

ac-
cident — lack
    of cornice, dynamite grooves, burns, and
    hatchet strokes, these things stand
        out on it; the chasm-side is

dead.
Repeated
    evidence has proved that it can live on
    what can not revive
        its youth. The sea grows old in it.

Moore's rhymes do not obscure the eccentric nature of her prosody. Her stanzas close — or

1085

open?—with an unrhymed line, that measure of experience which will not fit into a poetic scheme. Her poem, like the fish itself, is a "defiant edifice" in which the sea—a source of poetry—"grows old," and yet something—"the chasm side"?—eludes us. Her hymn of praise depends on a recognition of limits as arbitrary as the decision to make the first line of each stanza one syllable in length. To see the world anew, her work reminds us, one must invent new formal structures.

This was an idea dear to Moore's friend William Carlos Williams (1883–1963). "The commonest situations in the world have the very essence of poetry if looked at correctly," he asserted in *I Wanted to Write a Poem* (1958), and so he looked long and lovingly at his surroundings, which furnished him with enough material for scores of books. He wanted to create "a new form of poetic composition, a form for the future"; believing that "rhyme belonged to another age," he decided early on that his poetics would depend on rhythm and precise observation of the world. "When I came to the end of a rhythmic unit (not necessarily a sentence) I ended the line," he explained, and those rhythmic units were based on what he heard in America, in contradistinction to his more renowned colleagues, T. S. Eliot and Ezra Pound, who looked to the Old World for inspiration. A general practitioner of medicine in Rutherford, New Jersey, Williams listened closely to his patients and acquaintances, then turned their speech patterns into free verse. In "A Sort of a Song" (in *The Selected Poems of William Carlos Williams*, 1968), Williams outlines his poetic program:

> Let the snake wait under
> his weed
> and the writing
> be of words, slow and quick, sharp
> to strike, quiet to wait,
> sleepless.

> —through metaphor to reconcile
> the people and the stones.
> Compose. (No ideas

> but in things) Invent!
> Saxifrage is my flower that splits
> the rocks.

Drawing an analogy between the word and the object, the signifier and the signified, Williams recalls Emerson's assertion in "The Poet" that "language is fossil poetry." The poet awakens our memory to the poetic origins of each word, breathing new life into the language. "The poet names the thing because he sees it," Emerson continued, "or comes one step nearer to it than any other." And that naming, which was Adam's first task in the Garden of Eden and which remains the poet's primary responsibility, that "abandonment to the nature of things," is what revitalizes our perception of the world: a poem makes what is familiar strange. Alive. Thus Williams insists that a description of a snake, say, imitate its movements so completely that the words themselves slither across the page. His ars poetica embodies a moral imperative, reconciling us to our surroundings, if only for the duration of the poem—to the stones that may be sundered by the invention—or invocation?—of a flower.

Poets across America have taken Williams' advice to speak "straight ahead about what concern[s] us," and free verse has become one of the glories of American poetry. At his best Williams restores a sense of magic to the mundane; as in the title poem of *Spring and All* (1923):

> By the road to the contagious hospital
> under the surge of the blue
> mottled clouds driven from the
> northeast—a cold wind. Beyond, the
> waste of broad, muddy fields
> brown with dried weeds, standing
> and fallen

> patches of standing water
> the scattering of tall trees

> All along the road the reddish
> purplish, forked, upstanding, twiggy
> stuff of bushes and small trees
> with dead, brown leaves under them
> leafless vines—

Lifeless in appearance, sluggish
dazed spring approaches—

They enter the new world naked,
cold, uncertain of all
save that they enter.

Williams teaches his readers how to see that new world: no small feat for a poet living in an age, as Pound rightly observed in the poem "Hugh Selwyn Mauberley," which "demanded an image / Of its accelerated grimace."

Wallace Stevens (1879–1955), who worked in both free and fixed forms, provided many such images, none more relevant to the matter at hand than "Anecdote of the Jar" (in *The Collected Poems of Wallace Stevens*, 1954). In this beguilingly simple poem variations from a strict metrical norm provide the underpinning for Stevens' argument, which proposes to reconcile—through the agency of a jar, a metaphor, that is, for poetry and culture—Americans and their "slovenly wilderness":

I placed a jar in Tennessee,
And round it was, upon a hill.
It made the slovenly wilderness
Surround that hill.

The wilderness rose up to it,
And sprawled around, no longer wild.
The jar was round upon the ground
And tall and of a port in air.

It took dominion everywhere.
The jar was gray and bare.
It did not give of bird or bush,
Like nothing else in Tennessee.

"Slovenly," of course, is the key word in this poem. Rhythmically, it upsets the regular iambic tetrameters, introducing to these orderly quatrains a careless note, a quality of indifference not unlike that which is integral to the natural world. Though Stevens' jar tames the wilderness, it does so at a price: there are two beats missing in the last line of the first stanza, and their absence pulls the reader up short, as if to suggest the limits of any cultural endeavor. Likewise, Stevens drops a beat from the second line of the final stanza, reinforcing his notion that the jar is only a partial solution to the problem of finding "a supreme fiction" adequate to this sprawling continent.

This recognition of limits in no way vitiates Stevens' poetry, which is predicated on the possibility of "the imagination's new beginning" in a world bereft of conventional religious belief. For such knowledge is what both disciplines and liberates the poet: form, like marriage, is a prison only to the unimaginative. And what is more indispensable to a society resolute on destroying every form and ritual in its endless questing after the new? "The death of Satan was a tragedy / For the imagination," according to this insurance executive, yet he devoted his life to transforming that loss into poetry that celebrates the pleasures of the physical world and of the imagination— "the thesis scrivened in delight, / The reverberating psalm, the right chorale." In "The Idea of Order at Key West," for example, a blank-verse extravaganza containing some of the most beautiful lines in the English language, Stevens presents a woman who "sang beyond the genius of the sea." She is a figure for poetry, a siren on the beach:

It was her voice that made
The sky acutest at its vanishing.
She measured to the hour its solitude.
She was the single artificer of the world
In which she sang. And when she sang, the
  sea,
Whatever self it had, became the self
That was her song, for she was the maker.
  Then we,
As we beheld her striding there alone,
Knew that there never was a world for her
Except the one she sang and, singing,
  made.

Her song enchants the night, or so the speaker thinks; aching to hear more, he turns to his companion and cries,

Oh! Blessed rage for order, pale Ramon,
The maker's rage to order words of the sea,
Words of the fragrant portals, dimly-starred,

And of ourselves and of our origins,
Ghostlier demarcations, keener sounds.

Those "keener sounds" are what drive poets mad, or—as in Stevens' case—coax poems from them.

A windrose, a circular figure on ancient navigators' charts, is "a whole of the air in motion," according to Brewster Ghiselin (1903–), "multifoliate rose of the winds of the earth that flow about us and enfold." It is also an emblem for Ghiselin's poetic achievement, much of which is collected in *Windrose: Poems 1929–1979* (1980). Though he is not well known, Ghiselin is one of the most spirited and inspiriting navigators of American poetic waters, a man avid to lead what he calls "the life of discovery." His work is, indeed, a record of his discoveries both within himself and in the world at large. "People tell me again and again, when we go out in the wild, that I notice things nobody else does," he once said. "But that is not because I'm a nature lover, it's because I'm interested in the world" (personal interview).

As with most poets who turn to nature for inspiration and subject matter, that interest dates from his childhood, which he divided between Missouri and California. "I collected and properly labeled a clutch of eggs," he recalls in an autobiographical essay, "white, nearly round, from the hollow in a sycamore tree that a screech owl had deserted."

I learned to call the owls to their chorus of dusk on the hill where I lived for a while in Marin County. And from the high school that I attended, some miles by electric train toward San Francisco, I used to walk home up the steep south slope of Mount Tamalpais, across the peak from which I could see the far Farallones in the glitter of the westward ocean, before I turned to run down the roll-rock slither of the firebreak toward home.

I had little understanding of the course I followed, yet knew it was an escape from constrictions. (*Contemporary Authors Autobiography Series*, vol. 10, p. 129)

The urge to transcend "established limits of custom and habit" led Ghiselin to write "a poet's poems" revered for their aural and visual qualities, such as "Rattlesnake" (in *Windrose*):

I found him sleepy in the heat
And dust of a gopher burrow,
Coiled in loose folds upon silence
In a pit of the noonday hillside.
I saw the wedged bulge
Of the head hard as a fist.
I remembered his delicate ways:
The mouth a cat's mouth yawning.
I crushed him deep in dust,
And heard the loud seethe of life
In the dead beads of the tail
Fade, as wind fades
From the wild grain of the hill.

A variation on the theme of D. H. Lawrence's poem "Snake," Ghiselin's compressed and considerably more violent version of the story of mankind's fall from grace is a formal wonder. The juxtaposition of sibilants with long vowel sounds—"sleepy," "silence," "ways," "deep," "seethe," "beads," "fades"—calls to mind Williams' method: Ghiselin's literary construction moves and sounds like a real rattlesnake. Meanwhile, the accentual or stress-based rhythmic pattern, derived from Anglo-Saxon verse, places the action in an elemental context. The snake's slow and heavy syllables—"loose folds," "wedged bulge," "head hard"—weigh on the speaker, as if to underscore the tension between his passivity and sudden action. This is a sinister encounter, in both aural and visual terms. Nor is the speaker absolved by his confession, his poem, for what he loses in the end is "the loud seethe of life"—the snake's as well as the promise of his own.

Elsewhere, however, Ghiselin writes of being "saved from commitment to a life of intellectual specialization by the savor of original salt in the thoughtless ocean"—the Pacific, that is, in which he swam "by day and night [and] learned the ways of the waves in all weathers" (*Contemporary Authors Autobiography Series*, vol. 10, p. 130). There he gathered material for his masterpiece, "Sea" (in *Windrose*), a long poem which is among the handful of necessary literary works from our time. Here is the penultimate section:

> I can foretell no form: before us lie
> Horizons empty as the heart's expectation
> On the shore of morning, the sea's clear promises
> Until the end. If end. Our language questions
> Mainly itself, a tangled theorem spread
> Straining in the elemental tide
> To take those glittering shoals that swarm and pass.

> And all these names are lies: the gannet's bath,
> The Pacific, the Dark, the User. That sea is not
> What we believe, but something past belief;
> That tone we love most is its cry of escape
> Out of our categories as it names
> Forever a new name for namers' ears:
> Never itself. O word, where is thy sting?

In these blank verse lines Ghiselin writes "music to name our needs," which ultimately escapes our impulse to categorize. While Stevens praises a woman singing on the beach, Ghiselin plunges into the vast of the sea, where he finds the "original salt": poetry.

Janet Lewis (1899–) is another poet whose work deserves a wider readership. Best known as the author of several acclaimed novels, including *Against a Darkening Sky* and *The Wife of Martin Guerre*, in *Poems ¹Old and New: 1918–1978* (1981) Lewis reveals her genuine poetic originality and importance. The concluding couplet of "The Earth-Bound," a sonnet dating from the 1920s, sums up her attitude to the planet that sustains us: "Tangled with earth all ways, we move,/And sleep at last in heaven that is a grove." Lewis revives an old form—standard practice for a good poet—in the hope of discovering new meaning from her walk in the sun. She turns to the sonnet, with its long history of singing the beloved's praises, to write a love poem to the earth.

In the freer measures of a much later poem, "Snail Garden" (in *Poems Old and New*), Lewis explores the same morally ambiguous terrain Brewster Ghiselin described in "Rattlesnake," the shifting ground between the human and nonhuman realms of existence:

> This is the twilight hour of the morning
> When the snails retreat over the wet grass
> To their hidden world, where my dreams, retreating,
> Leave me wondering what wisdom goes with them,
> What hides in mouldering earth.

> Softly they go, the snails,
> Naked, unguarded, perceptive
> Of the changing light, rejoicing
> In their slow progress from leaf to stem,
> From stem to deeper darkness.
> Smoothness delights them.

> What do they hear? The air above them
> Is full of the sharp cries of birds.
> Do they see? The lily bud,
> Three feet above the soil on its leafy stalk,
> Is known to them at midnight
> As if it were a lighthouse. Before sunrise
> They have gnawed it half in two.
> Toothless mouths, blind mouths
> Have turned the leaf of the hollyhock to lace,
> And cut the stem of the nasturtium
> Neatly, just below the blossom.

> The classic shell, cunningly arched, and strong
> Against the hazards of the grassy world
> Is nothing before the power of my intention.
> The larks, also, have had their fun,
> Crashing that coiled shell on stone,
> Guiltless in their freedom.

> But I have taken sides in the universe.
> I have killed the snail that lay on the morning leaf,
> Not grudging greatly the nourishment it took
> Out of my abundance,
> Chard, periwinkle, capucine,

Occasional lily bud,
But I have begun my day with death,
Death given, death to be received.
I have stepped into the dance;
I have greeted at daybreak
That necessary angel, that other.

Our knowledge of "that necessary angel" is our peculiar burden as a species, and it is poets who remind us that although we may not ignore the invitation of "that other"—extended at our birth—we may join in the great dance of life and death, wondering, in fear and awe, "what hides in mouldering earth."

Theodore Roethke (1908–1963) dug deep into that nether world. The son of a nurseryman, in his characteristic work he returns to the greenhouse and its "full cargo of roses." "We all know that poetry is shot through with appeals to the unconsciousness," he once declared, "to the fears and desires that go far back into our childhood, into the imagination of the race" (*On the Poet and His Craft*, 1965). And his work is a study in those appeals. Whether he remembers, as in the poem "Child on Top of a Greenhouse," "the half-grown chrysanthemums staring up like accusers," or near the end of his life finds himself "dream[ing] of journeys repeatedly" ("The Far Field"), Roethke is in some sense always marveling at the mystery of the world, which he first glimpsed in his father's root cellar, forcing house, and flower dump.

Roethke's method of writing was to abandon himself to the language—"Believe me, knot of gristle, I bleed like a tree," is how he begins "Give Way, Ye Gates," a process he imitated in his first drafts of a poem—and then to turn his scribbled notes, which encompassed childish babble, surrealist imagery, and high rhetoric, into memorable verse. Approaching the problem of form in an inventive spirit, he incorporated into his poetry the full range of his thoughts and feelings. Thus "The Shape of the Fire" (in *The Collected Poems of Theodore Roethke*, 1966), includes zany flights—"Mother me out of here. What more will the bones allow? / Will the sea give the wind suck?"—and serious considerations:

Morning-fair, follow me further back
Into that minnowy world of weeds and
    ditches,
When the herons floated high over the
    white houses,
And the little crabs slipped into silvery
    craters.
When the sun for me glinted the sides of a
    sand grain,
And my intent stretched over the buds at
    their first trembling.

Roethke's commitment to both traditional and open forms is a function of his conviction that "the soul has many motions" ("The Motion"). Indeed, his work is a brief for availing oneself of all poetic structures and resources at hand. "Is that dance slowing in the mind of man / That made him think the universe could hum?" he asks in "Four for Sir John Davies." His reply is instructive:

The great wheel turns its axle when it can;
I need a place to sing, and dancing-room,
And I have made a promise to my ears
I'll sing and whistle romping with the
    bears.

Roethke might "take this cadence from a man named Yeats," but he did not stop there; for as he wrote his way into American literature he heard "other tunes and other wanton beats," everything from nursery rhymes to Whitman's catalogs. And when he danced to them, he made the poetic universe hum.

Elizabeth Bishop (1911–1979) was even more adept at exploiting a variety of poetic forms. Though in a half-century of writing she published only 101 poems, her reach is nothing short of astonishing. Nova Scotia, Key West, Boston, and Brazil—these are the coordinates of her literary imagination, a world she mapped with rigor and exhilaration. She wrote sonnets, a double sonnet, rhymed and unrhymed triplets and quatrains, songs, sestinas, a villanelle, prose poems, light verse, and free verse, all with the grace that comes only with the mastery of one's craft. A painstaking artist—"The Moose," one of her most famous poems, was twenty years in the making—Bishop is blessed with a painter's eye, an ear for speech rhythms, and a large spirit, qualities prized by younger poets who have made her their model.

Poetry resides in the tension between what the poet knows and what remains unknown—that is, in the ongoing dialogue between the inherited forms and traditions the poet lives by and the adventure offered by a new poem, the creative possibilities the poet seizes on to make his or her work spring to life. Much of Bishop's free verse plots a course between elegant iambics and the vagaries of speech, now steering toward the rhythms of George Herbert—the seventeenth-century metaphysical poet whose sculpted verse she admired above all others—now sailing near the colloquial. In her freest moments we still hear what Eliot called "the ghost of some simple metre," as in the last lines of "At the Fish-houses" (in *The Complete Poems, 1927–1979,* 1979):

> I have seen it over and over, the same sea,
>   the same,
> slightly, indifferently swinging above the
>   stones,
> icily free above the stones,
> above the stones and then the world.
> If you should dip your hand in,
> your wrist would ache immediately,
> your bones would begin to ache and your
>   hand would burn
> as if the water were a transmutation of fire
> that feeds on stones and burns with a dark
>   gray flame.
> If you tasted it, it would first taste bitter,
> then briny, then surely burn your tongue.
> It is like what we imagine knowledge to be:
> dark, salt, clear, moving, utterly free,
> drawn from the cold hard mouth
> of the world, derived from the rocky breasts
> forever, flowing and drawn, and since
> our knowledge is historical, flowing, and
>   flown.

Poetry is at once a search for knowledge—of the world, of one's self, of language—and a formal structure in which knowledge both secretes and reveals itself: it celebrates and stimulates consciousness, sharpening our awareness of what it means to be alive. Bishop's epistemological meditation focuses on the sea, an apt symbol for consciousness, and so its lulling rhythms and repetition of key words—"same," "stones," "free," "ache," "burn," "taste," "dark," "knowledge," "drawn," "flowing"—imitate the movements of the sea, which often looks the same even as it undergoes fantastic changes. In Bishop's poem waves of meaning wash over the reader.

Denise Levertov (1923–) is freer yet in her prosody, believing that "the metric movement, the measure, is the direct expression of the movement of perception" (*The Poet in the World,* 1973, p. 11). Hers is organic verse (Emerson wrote in "The Poet": "The expression is organic, or the new type which things themselves take when liberated."), the rhythms improvised beat by beat; like jazz compositions, her poems continually surprise the reader listening for a regular metrical scheme: a pleasurable change, free verse in the last half of the twentieth century came to dominate American poetry. It was Ezra Pound who commanded, "As regarding rhythm . . . compose in sequence of the musical phrase, not in sequence of a metronome" (*Literary Essays* [1935], repr. 1968, p. 3). In *O Taste and See* (in *Poems, 1960–1967,* 1983) Levertov can be seen as one of Pound's truest heirs:

> The world is
> not with us enough.
> *O taste and see*
>
> the subway Bible poster said,
> meaning *The Lord*, meaning
> if anything all that lives
> to the imagination's tongue,
>
> grief, mercy, language,
> tangerine, weather, to
> breathe them, bite,
> savor, chew, swallow, transform
>
> into our flesh our
> deaths, crossing the street, plum, quince,
> living in the orchard and being
>
> hungry, and plucking
> the fruit.

This poem inverts the proposition of the famous Wordsworth sonnet that begins, "The world is too much with us." Levertov strings a single sentence over fourteen lines—a free-verse sonnet within the poem?—in which she offers an altogether different idea about our response to the world (or lack thereof). In this nonce form she translates a line from the Psalms—"O taste and see that the Lord is good"—into a psalm for the earth, insisting that the Garden of Eden is as close as the orchard across the street. The fruit that Levertov plucks—plum and quince, life and death—is what schools her "imagination's tongue," and quickens her response to the world.

Religious Forms in Nature Poetry

William Everson (1912–) approaches the theme of paradise on earth from a religious angle in his "Canticle to the Waterbirds," written for the Feast of Saint Francis of Assisi. Published in *The Crooked Lines of God* (1959) when Everson, then known as Brother Antoninus, belonged to the Dominican Order of the Catholic Church, this long poem illustrates the vitality of religious forms in American poetry. Here are its opening lines:

Clack your beaks you cormorants and
    kittiwakes,
North on those rock-croppings finger-jutted
    into the rough Pacific surge;
You migratory terns and pipers who leave
    but the temporal clawtrack written
    on sandbars there of your presence;
Grebes and pelicans; you comber-picking
    scoters and you shorelong gulls;
All you keepers of the coastline north of
    here to the Mendocino beaches;
All you beyond upon the cliff-face
    thwarting the surf at Hecate Head;
Hovering the under-surge where the cold
    Columbia grapples at the bar;
North yet to the Sound, whose islands float
    like a sown flurry of chips upon the sea;
Break wide your harsh and salt-encrusted
    beaks unmade for song
And say a praise up to the Lord.

Everson's catalogs and long lines recall both Whitman and Jeffers, but his praise is profoundly religious in a traditional sense. He does not praise the self, America, or a version of nature safe from human beings. Rather, he sings a hymn to the creatures of the earth in order to praise God. His Song of Songs is a testimony to the "freshwater egrets east in the flooded marshlands skirting the sea-level rivers, white one-legged watchers of shallows; / Broad-headed kingfishers minnow-hunting from willow stems on meandering valley sloughs;" and all the other waterbirds whose "ways are verved with the secret skills of His inclinations." Thus he restores to the world a measure of its sacred nature, and though his beliefs may seem old-fashioned, the power of his verse makes clear the old-fashioned power of faith, which, in the hands of a competent craftsman, may be translated into lasting poetry.

Gary Snyder (1930–) is also a religious poet whose life and work grow out of an ancient tradition—in his case, that of Zen Buddhism. One of America's most popular poets and an eloquent spokesman for the environmental movement, Snyder is revered as much for his way of life, his determination to live in right relation to the land, as for his writings. In a collection of essays, *The Practice of the Wild* (1990), he reminds us that "It has always been part of basic human experience to live in a culture of wilderness. There has been no wilderness without some kind of human presence for several hundred thousand years. Nature is not a place to visit, it is *home*—and within that home territory there are more familiar and less familiar places. Often there are areas that are difficult and remote," he concludes, "but all are *known* and even named" (p. 7). In his work he explores our relationship to that home; what he names is what we have forgotten.

Believing that philosophy is "a place-based exercise," Snyder declares his faith in our home in the largest sense, the planet Earth. In "For All" (in *No Nature: New and Selected Poems*, 1992), he uses a civic form—the Pledge of Allegiance to the flag—to give his testimony:

Ah to be alive
    on a mid-September morn
    fording a stream
    barefoot, pants rolled up,
    holding boots, pack on,
    sunshine, ice in the shallows,
    northern Rockies.

Rustle and shimmer of icy creek waters
stones turn underfoot, small and hard as
      toes
    cold nose dripping
    singing inside
    creek music, heart music,
    smell of sun on gravel.

I pledge allegiance.

I pledge allegiance to the soil
    of Turtle Island,
    one ecosystem
    in diversity
    under the sun
With joyful interpenetration for all.

Snyder salutes an idea much larger than that of the nation-state, and he does so with a sense of humor.

A search for pattern in nature, Snyder's work demonstrates, shapes a poet's experiences, conditioning his or her responses to the world. It is as well a search for origins—of the self, of America, of the divine—a search that in our time may assume any form. Richard Wilbur (1921–) returned to the source of English poetry, for instance, to write "The Lilacs" (in *New and Collected Poems*, 1988), discovering in the heavily alliterative hemistiches of Anglo-Saxon verse new energy with which to address the things of the world. An elegant formalist who likens his way of writing to the improvisatory practices of a poet working in free verse, in these lines Wilbur introduces a strange sound into contemporary poetry, a rhythm borne "out of present pain / and past terror," which echoes in our memory, connecting us to the scops who performed their poems, their dark miracles, in mead halls a thousand years ago:

Those laden lilacs
      at the lawn's end
Came stark, spindly,
      and in staggered file,
Like walking wounded
      from the dead of winter.
We watched them waken
      in the brusque weather
To rot and rootbreak,
      to ripped branches,
And saw them shiver
      as the memory swept
      them
Of night and numbness
      and the taste of nothing.
Out of present pain
      and past terror
Their bullet-shaped buds
      came quick and bursting,
As if they aimed
      to be open with us!

Indigenous Voices and Forms

W. S. Merwin (1927–) has likewise used hemistiches in his search for poetic truth, which he calls "a vibrancy of life." Indeed, his formal range is among the broadest in American poetry, for he writes not only in almost every possible English form but also in the forms he finds in his extensive work as a translator from French, Spanish, German, Italian, Russian, Latin, Greek, Chinese, Japanese, Malayan, and various indigenous languages. In short, he listens to the world and turns it into poetry.

In "Learning a Dead Language" (in *Selected Poems*, 1988) he tells us that "what you remember saves you. To remember / Is not to rehearse, but to hear what never / Has fallen silent." Here the language may be Greek or Latin, but Merwin's understanding of what is required for our salvation includes the languages of the plant and animal kingdoms. "I am trying to decipher the language of insects," he writes in "After the Alphabets" (in *Rain in the Trees*, 1988), "they are the tongues of the future." What is more, "they are wholly articulate / they are never important they are everything." Though we may not learn to speak with plants and animals—our true significant others—Merwin believes our only hope of surviving the environmental catastrophe we have created lies in our learning to honor that which surrounds us. Hence his urgency: "I want to tell what the forests/were like," he says in "Witness" (in *Rain in the Trees*), "I will have to speak/in a forgotten language."

Of all the forms in which Merwin has approached the natural facts of America, none calls into question so much the meaning of poetic form as the prose poetry of *The Miner's Pale Children*. First published in 1970, in the preface to a 1981 edition of the book he describes the surprise and excitement he felt when these prose pieces came to him. "As I wrote," he recalls,

> I was listening for recognizable but perhaps scarcely noticed or unacknowledged or emergent forms and conventions in current use. I recalled what I thought were precedents—fragments, essays, journal entries, instructions and lists, oral tales, fables. What I was hoping for was akin to what made a poem seem complete. But it was prose that I was writing, and I was pleased when the pieces raised questions about the boundary between prose and poetry, and where we think it runs.

"Unchopping a Tree" offers one of Merwin's most dazzling conceits: our destruction of the natural world may be reversed, he suggests, one damaged area after another, through a healing process at once magical and forbidding. "You"—the writer, the reader—must gather all the leaves, twigs, nests, and branches from a felled tree, then reassemble it. "Even in the best of circumstances it is a labor that will make you wish often that you had won the favor of the universe of ants," Merwin warns, "the empire of mice, or at least a local tribe of squirrels, and could enlist their labors and their talents. But no," he adds, "they leave you to it. They have learned, with time. This is men's work." This work is, of course, impossible—and absolutely necessary. "Others are waiting," after all. "Everything is going to have to be put back."

Merwin's political activism, which came of age during the national protests against the Vietnam War and which in the next two decades focused primarily on environmental issues, coincided with a general awakening to the cultural resources of indigenous peoples, the primitive poetry of those who first settled the New World. Jerome Rothenberg's *Technicians of the Sacred: A Range of Poetries from Africa, America, Asia, & Oceania* (1968) is an invaluable introduction to the old ways of seeing and singing, poetic and philosophic forms of being which have exerted a strong influence on contemporary poetry. In this Zuni text, which appears as the frontispiece of Rothenberg's book, we may glimpse what Frederick Turner calls "an aboriginal sense of America":

> Come, ascend the ladder: all come in: all sit down.
> We were poor, poor, poor, poor, poor,
> When we came to this world through the poor place,
> Where the body of water dried for our passing.
> Banked up clouds cover the earth.
> All come four times with your showers:
> Descend to the base of the ladder & stand still:
> Bring your showers and great rains.
> All, all come, all ascend, all come in, all sit down.

Because many poets have accepted this ancient invitation, John Elder notes in *Imagining the Earth: Poetry and the Vision of Nature* (1985), that "the oldest stories and myths of North America flow into current nature poetry along with Dickinson and Frost." Janet Lewis was inspired by Ojibway Indian themes, chants, and narrative structures, David Wagoner has written versions of Northwest Coast Indian tales, and Galway Kinnell's "The Bear" is a renowned "translation" of an Eskimo story. Moreover, in the last thirty years Native American poets and writers like N. Scott Momaday, Leslie Marmon Silko, Simon Ortiz, Linda Hogan, and Ray Young Bear have created a genuine literary renaissance. Rooted in the oral tradition, they have revived the art of storytelling, which had all but disappeared from American poetry. Louise Erdrich's "I Was Sleeping Where the Black Oaks Move" (in *Jacklight*, 1984) is a short story in the form of a free-verse poem:

We watched from the house
as the river grew, helpless
and terrible in its unfamiliar body.
Wrestling everything into it,
the water wrapped around trees
until their life-hold was broken.
They went down, one by one,
and the river dragged off their covering.

Nests of the herons, roots washed to bones,
snags of soaked bark on the shoreline:
a whole forest pulled through the teeth
of the spillway. Trees surfacing
singly, where the river poured off
into arteries for fields below the
    reservation.

When at last it was over, the long removal,
they had all become the same dry wood.
We walked among them, the branches
whitening in the raw sun.
Above us drifted herons,
alone, hoarse-voiced, broken,
settling their beaks among the hollows.

Grandpa said, *These are the ghosts of the
    tree people, moving above us, unable
    to take their rest.*

Sometimes now, we dream our way back to
    the heron dance.
Their long wings are bending the air
into circles through which we fall.
They rise again in shifting wheels.
How long must we live in the broken
    figures
their necks make, narrowing the sky.

A Scientific Nature

Native American myths are not the only cultural manifestation informing contemporary poetry. Scientific discoveries increasingly stimulate American poets to new and exciting work. Pattiann Rogers writes: "The world picture we hold today has for the most part been given to us by science." Therefore, "[we] must learn how to grasp our cosmology fully and to infuse it with a sustaining spirituality. . . . We must possess our cosmology fully rather than being possessed *by* it" (pp. 4, 8). James Merrill (1926–) makes such an effort in *The Changing Light at Sandover* (1982), the poetic record of his nights hunched over a Ouija board. "POEMS OF SCIENCE," commands Ephraim, his familiar spirit, and though Merrill would rather write almost anything else, he soon realizes that "on the dimmest shore of consciousness/Polypeptides—in primeval thrall/To what new moon I wonder— rise and fall" (p. 110). He gives himself over to the "God of Biology" and writes a sacred poem for the scientific age.

"The poet alone knows astronomy, chemistry, vegetation and animation," Emerson wrote in "The Poet," "for he does not stop at these facts, but employs them as signs." A. R. Ammons (1926–) uses those signs throughout his poetry, which is a sturdy bridge to the findings of his colleagues in the natural sciences. "Corsons Inlet" (in *The Selected Poems, 1951–1977*, 1977), Ammons' ars poetica, is a description of a walk by the sea. "The walk liberating, I was released from forms," he rejoices,

from the perpendiculars,
    straight lines, blocks, boxes, binds
of thought
into the hues, shadings, rises, flowing
    bends and blends
        of sight . . .

Free to recognize that "in nature there are few sharp lines," he sees the world afresh:

the news to my left over the dunes and
reeds and bayberry clumps was
fall: thousands of tree swallows
gathering for flight:
an order held
in constant change: a congregation
rich with entropy . . .

Such a revelation, a product of the scientific revolution, demands new forms, and so at the end of his walk Ammons says,

> I see narrow orders, limited tightness,
> but will not run to that easy victory:
>   still around the looser, wider forces work:
>   I will try
> to fasten into order enlarging grasps of
>   disorder, widening
> scope, but enjoying the freedom that
> Scope eludes my grasp, that there is no
>   finality of vision,
> that I have perceived nothing completely,
>   that tomorrow a new walk is a new walk.

What Richard Kenney calls "new forms of worship" for the scientific age — that is what many American poets now are writing, none more exuberantly than Pattiann Rogers (1940–). Combine Whitman's catalogs, an Adamic zeal for naming, and a zoologist's training, and you will have a poet unlike any other working today: "What is it I don't know of myself, / From never having seen a crimson chat at its feeding / Or the dunnart carrying its young?" Rogers asks in "Second Witness" (in *Firekeeper: New and Selected Poems*, 1994), which, like much of her work, is a hymn to complexity. Her answer is brimful of possibility:

> It must be imperative
> That I watch the entire hardening of the
>   bud
> Of the clove, that I witness the flying fish
>   breaking
> Into sky through the sun-smooth surface of
>   the sea.
>
> I ask the winter wren nesting in the clogged
>   roots
> Of the fallen oak to remember the
>   multitoned song
> Of itself in my ears, and I ask the
>   short-snouted
> Silver twig weevil to be particular and the
>   fishhook
> Cactus to be tenacious. I thank the distinct
>   edges

> Of the six-spined spider crab for their
>   peculiarities
> And praise the freshwater eel for its graces.
>   I urge
> The final entanglement of blade and light
>   to keep
> Its secrecy, and I beg the white-tailed kite
>   this afternoon,
> For my sake, to be keen-eyed, to soar well,
>   to be quick
> To make me known.

Her imperative holds for us all.

Conclusion

And the future? In the wake of two centuries of formal experimentation, American poets know there are countless ways to probe the glorious energy of the universe. In traditional forms and nonce patterns, free verse and prose, our poets are exploring their surroundings in a passionate manner, mindful of the ways in which their formal decisions condition their search for meaning. While the nation's first poets celebrated the natural riches of the New World in their meditations on the experiment in democracy, in the chaos of the new world order American poets turn to nature to learn, once again, how to live "*at the White Heat*," where we may discover how to survive our folly. "Mirror of the fraternity of the cosmos, the poem is a model of what human society might be," Nobel laureate Octavio Paz writes in *The Other Voice* (1990), a defense of poetry. "In the face of the destruction of nature, it offers living proof of the brotherhood of the stars and elementary particles, of chemicals and consciousness" (p. 158). We ignore that proof at our peril.

Selected Bibliography

PRIMARY SOURCES

A. R. Ammons, *The Selected Poems, 1951–1977* (New York: Norton, 1977), and *Selected Longer Poems* (New York: Norton, 1980); Elizabeth Bishop, *The Complete Poems, 1927–1979* (New York: Farrar,

Straus and Giroux, 1979), and *The Collected Prose*, ed. by Robert Giroux (New York: Farrar, Straus and Giroux, 1984); Emily Dickinson, *The Complete Poems of Emily Dickinson*, ed. by Thomas H. Johnson (Boston: Little, Brown, 1890); Ralph Waldo Emerson, *Selections from Ralph Waldo Emerson*, ed. by Stephen E. Whicher (Boston: Houghton Mifflin, 1957); Louise Erdrich, *Jacklight* (New York: Henry Holt, 1984); William Everson (writing as Brother Antoninus), *The Crooked Lines of God: Poems 1949–1954* (Detroit: Univ. of Detroit Press, 1959); Robert Frost, *The Poetry of Robert Frost*, ed. by Edward Connery Lathem (New York: Holt, Rinehart and Winston, 1969); Brewster Ghiselin, *Windrose: Poems 1929–1979* (Salt Lake City: Univ. of Utah Press, 1980), and *Flame* (Salt Lake City: Univ. of Utah Press, 1991).

Robinson Jeffers, *The Selected Poetry of Robinson Jeffers* (New York: Random House, 1938); Richard Kenney, *The Invention of the Zero* (New York: Knopf, 1993); Denise Levertov, *The Poet in the World* (New York: New Directions, 1973), *Poems, 1960–1967* (New York: New Directions, 1983), and *New and Selected Essays* (New York: New Directions, 1992); Janet Lewis, *Poems Old and New, 1918–1978* (Chicago: Swallow Press, 1982; Athens: Ohio Univ. Press, 1982); James Merrill, *The Changing Light at Sandover* (New York: Atheneum, 1982); W. S. Merwin, *The Miner's Pale Children* (New York: Atheneum, 1970; 2d ed. 1981; Henry Holt, 1994), *Selected Poems* (New York: Atheneum, 1988), and *Rain in the Trees* (New York: Knopf, 1988); Marianne Moore, *The Complete Poems of Marianne Moore* (New York: Macmillan, 1967); Ezra Pound, *Literary Essays*, ed. by T. S. Eliot (New York: New Directions, 1935; repr., 1968); Pattiann Rogers, *Firekeeper: New and Selected Poems* (Minneapolis: Milkweed Editions, 1994).

Theodore Roethke, *On the Poet and His Craft: Selected Prose of Theodore Roethke*, ed. by R. J. Mills, Jr. (Seattle: Univ. of Washington Press, 1965), and *The Collected Poems of Theodore Roethke* (New York: Anchor Books, Doubleday, 1966); Gary Snyder, *The Practice of the Wild: Essays* (New York: North Point, 1990), and *No Nature: New and Selected Poems* (New York: Pantheon, 1992); Wallace Stevens, *The Collected Poems of Wallace Stevens* (New York: Knopf, 1954); Walt Whitman, *The Portable Walt Whitman*, ed. by Mark Van Doren (New York: Viking, 1945), and *Walt Whitman's Leaves of Grass: The First (1855) Edition*, ed. by Malcolm Cowley (New York: Viking, 1959); Richard Wilbur, *New and Collected Poems* (San Diego: Harcourt, Brace, Jovanovich, 1988), and *Conversations with Richard Wilbur*, ed. by William Butts (Jackson: Univ. Press of Mississippi, 1990); William Carlos Williams, *Paterson* (New York: New Directions, 1958), *I Wanted to Write a Poem: The Autobiography of the Works of a Poet* (Boston: Beacon, 1958), and *The Selected Poems of William Carlos Williams* (New York: New Directions, 1968).

SECONDARY SOURCES

John Elder, *Imagining the Earth: Poetry and the Vision of Nature* (Urbana: Univ. of Illinois Press, 1985); Leo Marx, *The Machine in the Garden: Technology and the Pastoral Idea in America* (New York and London: Oxford Univ. Press, 1964); Christopher Merrill, ed., *The Forgotten Language: Contemporary Poets and Nature* (Salt Lake City: Peregrine Smith, 1991); Sherman Paul, *Hewing to Experience: Essays and Reviews on Recent American Poetry and Poetics, Nature and Culture* (Iowa City: Univ. of Iowa Press, 1989); Octavio Paz, *The Other Voice: Essays on Modern Poetry*, trans. by Helen Lane (New York: Harcourt, Brace, Jovanovich, 1990); Robert Pinsky, *The Situation of Poetry: Contemporary Poetry and Its Traditions* (Princeton, N.J.: Princeton Univ. Press, 1976); Pattiann Rogers, "Twentieth-Century Cosmology and the Soul's Habitation," in *Connotation* (fall/winter 1993); Jerome Rothenberg, ed., *Technicians of the Sacred: A Range of Poetries from Africa, America, Asia, and Oceania* (Garden City, N.Y.: Doubleday, 1968); Frederick Turner, *Spirit of Place: The Making of an American Literary Landscape* (San Francisco: Sierra Club, 1989); Helen Vendler, *Part of Nature, Part of Us: Modern American Poets* (Cambridge, Mass.: Harvard Univ. Press, 1980); Hyatt H. Waggoner, *American Visionary Poetry* (Baton Rouge: Louisiana State Univ. Press, 1982).

LITERARY THEORY AND NATURE WRITING

MICHAEL P. COHEN

The cowboy, injured and rebellious, cried out blindly into this fog of mysterious theory. "Well, I didn't do anythin', did I?"
— Stephen Crane, "The Blue Hotel"

Sometime in the late 1860s, Albert Bierstadt (1830–1902) painted a spectacular and monumental landscape known as "Looking Up the Yosemite Valley," or "Sunset in Yosemite Valley." Oil on canvas, $35\frac{1}{2}$ by $51\frac{1}{2}$ inches, this image of the valley—which includes no human being—is bathed in celestial golden and red light. For Bierstadt, Yosemite was itself a "vision," though the light in his painting was invented by himself; he was criticized by some at the time, not only for his geological inaccuracy but also for the bombastic, exaggerated, and sentimental quality of his depictions. Nevertheless, his eye-catching inventiveness was popular with the large, unsophisticated public audience and with most critics; a writer for the *Boston Post* said of one such painting, "It is the perfect type of the American idea of what our scenery ought to be, if it is not so in reality."

More than a century later, Nicolai Cikovsky, Jr., curator of American art at the National Gallery of Art, attempted to place Bierstadt's image of the landscape in a historical context. This image, he noted, was inspired and produced during the era when Yosemite Valley was re-

served as a state park. Cikovsky invoked Freud's *General Introduction to Psychoanalysis* to explain that "nature preserves were themselves manifestations of fantasy in the face of the reality of civilization." Freud wrote, "The 'reservation' is to maintain the old condition of things which has been regretfully sacrificed to necessity everywhere else." Cikovsky declared that "anyone painting unspoilt wilderness in America by the 1860s was painting myth, not reality; agencies of human enterprise . . . were by then leaving their traces everywhere." Consequently, Bierstadt "painted neither reality nor scientific truth, but fantasy." A contemporary critic agrees remarkably with the writer for the *Boston Post* that Bierstadt's paintings are valuable to us because they represent a "recognition of the actual condition and psychological meaning of wilderness in late nineteenth-century America."

A sympathetic viewer who believes that he has seen, in person, in the Yosemite of the late twentieth century what Bierstadt painted a century ago is faithful to the fantasy Bierstadt painted and has shared the "vision." But the viewer is also inaccurate, because wishing to believe that world was "out there," he has mistaken it for something "in here," for some shared desire or idea, one that is particularly American. Those who believe, with Thomas J. Lyon, that nature writing provides an "essential connection . . . in attitude, mind, allegiance—something going on at the heart, something that might render cosmopolitan criticism trivial," are similar to the sympathetic viewer. What they share with him is a nostalgia, which Adrienne Rich defines as "amnesia turned inside out."

This parable about the personal responses and critical responses to a painting has a simple lesson: A critical response to a work of art is not the same as a personal response to it. Yet they are related, even as theory intervenes. As SueEllen Campbell has written, "Theory helps me to step back from myself, to *think* about desire." One would not read American nature writing without a desire to see the land as Barry Lopez, Aldo Leopold, or Annie Dillard saw it. But if one is to bring more than a personal response to nature writing, neither amnesia nor nostalgia will serve well. What we have been taught through critical method about literary art—about the worlds in which it is created, the ways in which it is written, and the many ways in which a text can be said to have meaning—impinge on our personal readings and alter them. Modern critical theory is cosmopolitan, and modern environmental problems are global in scope. One cannot escape modern cosmopolitan critical theory or its set of difficulties. Offering precious few unambiguous answers, it generates interesting and pertinent questions. What follows is an attempt to sort, arrange, and organize these issues.

Is American Nature Writing a Genre?

To think of nature writing as more than simply an assortment of love songs and sermons, one must subject the conception of its genre to critical scrutiny. The fundamental questions about genre are about form, technique, and sometimes subject matter. For us, as post-Romantics, literary kinds have no ideal existence, nor do they obey universal laws of kind. Instead, they have conventions: arbitrary rules agreed upon by a community of readers and writers. *Natural* is normally contrasted to *conventional*. But the topic at hand is writing; all writing has conventions.

What are the conventions of nature writing? To begin with this question is to ask about the implicit agreements between these texts and persons, about the culture of this phenomenon. For instance, when someone recommends a book of nature writing, we expect it to be something like the following: somebody wrote a story, wherein the narrator is the main or perhaps only character. It is set in the outdoors. More often than not, it is structured by seasons, that is, naturally. The style is informal and tends toward clarity and sincerity. If it is a wilderness narrative, which is one kind of nature writing, we expect it to include the experience of solitude and perhaps other experiences, such as wonder, awe, even reverence. We expect it to be about being "in" nature, and so it will include "sleeping out." We expect to find description predominating over introspection, of "untrammeled" nature. In other words, we are already thinking within a genre. Generic assumptions shape the work and the way the reader interprets the work. One must step outside this agreement between reader and writer to perceive the constitution of this implicit agreement.

Does Nature Writing Preach to the Converted?

The culture of nature writing has always been didactic, marked by exhortation, focused on sanctioned places and favored beasts, and including sermons about the right treatment of them. Do these sermons change minds or confirm what the speaker and auditor share? What has *not* been asked about nature writing, about what is in it, who it addresses, and what it does not reveal? To what extent do its conventions rest on time-bound premises? These are questions about the rhetorical situation, including the willing suspension of disbelief enacted by the reader. It is precisely the accessibility, the pedestrian mode of nature writing, that it is earth-bound, slow of pace in its lyrical and measured narrative, consisting of plain storytelling, which has made it so popular. Lyon says, ". . . the fundamental goal of the genre is to turn attention outward to the activity of nature." It seems so simple, to turn one's attention away from one's self, outward. "All you have to do is pay attention," Lopez announces.

Such simplicity is deceiving, though the deception may be part of the pleasure, since many of these texts are, in the end, inspired and passionate. This "hidden agenda," according to Anna Bramwell in *Ecology in the Twentieth Century* (1989), allows a critic to use the term *ecology* in a politically normative sense. She establishes an "ethnic map" of the area where ecological beliefs are held, marking a Protestant region, a triangle between San Francisco, Zurich, and Stockholm. She says, "Ecologism is a political box," whose formative cultural roots have led a movement advocating a "return to isolation, and the abandonment of treasure and knowledge to tribes and nations in foreign lands who pose no threat to us. Consciously or otherwise, this is a death-wish." To argue so vehemently that nature writers have an offensive political agenda! Sooner or later one must confront the delicate issue of authorial intention.

What Is a Nature Author?

Nevertheless, why not begin with the most basic question, about the production of the texts of nature writing? How is nature writing authored? This question should be asked in practical terms first. Who sits in front of a computer? Or, as literacy critics are fond of saying, what is the site of writing? In 1988, Wendell Berry, a man who has been known to plow his hundred-acre farm in Kentucky with horses and who claims to write with a pencil or a pen and a piece of paper, published a short essay titled "Against PCs." The second paragraph begins, "My wife types my work on a Royal standard typewriter bought new in 1956, and as good now as it was then." Berry goes on to write, "We have, I think, a little cottage industry that works well and pleasantly." Finally, he had a list of compelling reasons for his practice. This short piece called out a re-

markable controversy, because Berry had focused attention on the following fact: writers do not work alone, and the tools they choose — consciously or unconsciously — have a thematic relationship to their work and have a real effect on other people.

There are other questions about the process of authoring. Who works from journals? Where do nature writers get their facts and information? Do they, like John McPhee, use informants? Do they, like Ann Zwinger, use guides? Do they, like Lopez, wheedle information out of federal employees? How is the writer's experience inscripted, transcribed, published? The place of publication itself can be significant, if the author prepares the writing for it. For example, *Scribner's*, the *Atlantic*, the *Century Magazine*, *Orion*, *Outside*, the *North American Review* — all have had their own criteria for publication. Do the writer's forays into nature actually precede writing, or are they a result of it? In other words, is writing produced by the exposure to nature or to culture or to the market?

It is a short step to more theoretical issues of authoring. Literary theorists often portray the problem of the woman writer in Virginia Woolf's terms, as a need for a room of one's own and later, perhaps, a publisher. Annette Kolodny, who wrote *The Lay of the Land* (1975) and *The Land Before Her* (1984); Carolyn Merchant, author of *The Death of Nature: Women, Ecology, and the Scientific Revolution* (1980); and other women who are also historians have made the issue global and taken it outdoors. Men and women experience the environment in very different ways, they argue. As a result of this challenge, one male historian concedes, ". . . one cannot hope to understand the way a culture relates to an environment without examining the ways it engenders the world." If, for instance, one wishes to read a wide range of nature writing by nineteenth-century American women, one must read diaries and letters, not simply lectures at the lyceum.

Some modern theorists would inspect all the gaps in the lists of authors, finding the omissions more significant than the included names. They would argue that the unpublished perceptions of people in nonliterary cultures, people of different races, genders, and cultures, constitute a much wider set of perceptions than have yet been read and that these "other" perceptions perhaps have forms which do not fit preconceptions about nature writing as a genre.

Is Nature Writing Nonfiction?

Generations of cultural historians have asked whether it is really possible to write nature, and they have sometimes answered as does Raymond Williams: "Ideas of nature . . . are the projected ideas of men." To say this is, at the least, to ask, "Is Nature writing really *nonfiction*, or is it a form of autobiography?" (Williams, a British writer, figures prominently as a literary theorist, as the author of *The Country and the City*, 1973, and other works on the cultural history of conceptions of nature.) Critics have always studied nature writing as a form of autobiography. Recently Scott Slovic, in *Seeking Awareness in American Nature Writing* (1992), has followed Sharon Cameron in suggesting that "to write about nature is to write about how the mind sees nature, and sometimes about how the mind sees itself." For him, "awakening," "awareness," or "watchfulness" are the very goals of nature writing. For John P. O'Grady, author of *Pilgrims to the Wild* (1993), what draws the writer to nature is not a conscious, but unconscious world, sought by the writer, an "erotic space" that is reached through the crossing of a threshold into a state described as "liminality."

Yet many writers do not like to be called nature writers. Stephen Trimble, assembling the anthology *Words from the Land: Encounters with Natural History Writing* (1988), found that "so-called nature writers acknowledge their love of landscape but they define themselves as writers." He found that Lopez claimed to be on the inside of his writing, while the critic was on the outside; Robert Finch said that it was a business manager who made him put the word "nature" on the front cover of his book; Edward Abbey heartily denied being a naturalist; and David Quammen called himself a "science journalist." Trimble found some contemporary writers disdaining the label "environmentalist." Why? Is it because they feel that their work would be judged deficient by purely scientific criteria? Or is it that they prefer that their work—indeed their lives—be seen as individual, as their own, as autonomous?

Behind these questions is a shifting concept of literary authoring, marked by a groundbreaking essay, "What Is an Author?," published in 1969 by Michael Foucault. Foucault, described in the *New York Review of Books* as the "most famous intellectual figure in the world" at his death in 1984, reminds us that the idea of individual authors or literary works is a contemporary and perhaps ephemeral idea, associated with the ownership of texts. All literary work is an act of appropriation, he argues, directing us to view literature as a socially determined discursive practice and asserting that a text is never the product of a unified consciousness, but that rather it consists of several socially determined roles, or "author-functions." Foucault finds the "man and his work" criticism anachronistic. Using Samuel Becket's line "What does it matter who is speaking?," Foucault argues that the "author does not precede the work, [but is] the ideological figure by which one marks the manner in which we fear the proliferation of meaning."

Foucault sheds considerable doubt on the qualifications of nature authors as autobiographers. We ask, how does such an author establish authority? By the depth of his or her exploration, the distance of the pilgrimage, the qualities of mind developed, the observations, the verifiability of the discoveries? And Foucault would answer that these authors are socially constructed. The writers are created by their audience, they speak of and to the audience's expectations. They are not professional naturalists because the readers are not. Nor should they be; any academic conference, whether on literary theory or on ecology, dramatizes the failure of experts to relate to humans and the need for translation.

But why do American readers of nature writers avidly devour interviews of these authors? Perhaps, Foucault would answer, they satisfy the American need to believe in individualism. Long ago, literary scholars learned to trust the tale, not the teller. One wonders, particularly since nature writing is supposed to be so outer-directed and even nonanthropocentric, why there are cults of dead writers, such as Henry David Thoreau, John Muir, Mary Austin, and why huge crowds have appeared at performances by Abbey, Gary Snyder, Terry Tempest Williams. Why does the reading public have such an insatiable desire for interviews, as if a nature writer somehow lived a more authentic life than the reader—as if it were so impossible to live an authentic life that it seemed a miracle when it happened—or the life was more important than the writing?

After Foucault, the critic's understanding of American autobiography has grown more sophisticated; see, for instance, the volume edited by John Paul Eakin, *American Autobiography: Retrospect and Prospect* (1991). The deindividualization of authors, explorers, and scientists, however, is found in much modern cultural history. William Goetzmann, in *Exploration and Empire* (1966), argues, in a thesis similar to Foucault's, that scientific exploration, as a mission, was always "programmed" by some older center of culture. Foucault's theory has also been compared to that of Thomas Kuhn in *The Structure of Scientific Revolutions* (1962), which contends that scientists work within a paradigm of "normal science." Such a paradigm is, according to Kuhn, socially constructed. In the ensuing decades there has grown up a considerable literature written on the social construction of scientific knowledge and writing. Critics of nature writing should surely take cognizance of this trend in scholarship.

Do Nature Writers Write About Nature?

If one gets past the vexing question of authorship and readership one is still left with the texts themselves: What is their subject? Nature? John

Hay has written, "You might think, after many years of teaching a class called 'Nature Writers,' that I would know what nature meant, but I do not." Surely few are prepared to claim that the theory of evolution is *only* the "projected ideas of men." Yet linguistic theory has distanced language from its object in precisely this disturbing way.

In the widely used system of Ferdinand de Saussure (1857–1913), one is exposed to the modern conception of the linguistic sign, which is dual, composed of an arbitrary relationship between signified and signifier. We can never pierce rotten diction or attach words to things, because meaning in language is created only by relationships between signifiers and signifieds, and also between signs. In Saussure's system, as it has been used by subsequent theorists, language itself is a closed set of conventions, constantly changing yet unattached to the world, floating and self-referential. Such a world has been described as the "prisonhouse of language."

Scientific theories of nature seem as fluid as language, suggesting that there will never be a certain and secure informational foundation for nature writing. Change is evident especially in the biological realm, where ecology is not yet ready to offer a settled and uncontroversial picture of the world. Nature may be an irreducibly ambiguous sign. Yet for humans it must have meaning. As Herman Melville's Ishmael says, "Some certain significance lurks in all things, else all things are little worth, and the round world itself but an empty cipher, except to sell by the cartload." And humans must decipher it. This problem of meaning seems to divide, and then divide again. The first epistemological problem is "Can we separate nature and culture?" In a now-classic essay, "Structure, Sign, and Play in the Discourse of the Human Sciences," Jacques Derrida disassembled the structuralist anthropological arguments of Claude Lévi-Strauss. He did so on a ground directly relevant to nature writing, by choosing Lévi-Strauss's opposition of nature and culture, pointing out that such a scheme is part of the anthropologist's desire to separate method (like culture, a system of regulating norms) from truth (like nature, something universal and spontaneous). At the end of this "deconstruction" of Lévi-Strauss, one is left with the "joyous affirmation of the free-play of the world and without truth, without origin, offered to an active interpretation."

Deconstruction's world of networks and free play shares a great deal with ecology. (The concept of "freeplay," as Derrida develops it, suggests the impossibility of separating any single meaning of a literary structure from the set of antithetical meanings. Thus "nature" and "culture" play upon each other.) As Campbell has noted, both might be described as "subversive science." They both offer a revolutionary questioning of authority, an insistence that truth is multiple, and a critique of the dream of an objective scientific method. The ethnographer Paul Shepard welcomed ecology as a form of free play. "Ecological thinking," he believed, "requires a kind of vision across boundaries." For example, he points out, the "epidermis of the skin is ecologically like a pond surface or a forest soil, not a shell so much as a delicate interpenetration."

What is this ecological science, for which Shepard had such high hopes and upon which nature writing has come to depend? In *The Order of Things*, Foucault identifies "immature sciences"—"too tinged with empirical thought, too exposed to the vagaries of chance or imagery, to age old traditions and external events, for it to be supposed that their history could be anything other than irregular." He might have been describing the discourse of 1960s ecology. Its language of climaxes and etymological households, webs of life, diversity, and complexity, its expressions of organic wholeness, suggest in no uncertain terms that this science has been exposed to the vagaries of chance and imagery. Ecologists themselves have recognized that the language of their discipline has misled many writers. Daniel Botkin, in *Discordant Harmonies* (1990), provides a critique of this discourse. Foucault believed that in such sciences, when they matured, there would be no deep or shallow.

What Is Environmental History?

Environmental historians—whose interests parallel those of literary students absorbed by the relationship between literature and the natural environment—have studied changes in theories of nature and have come, somewhat grudgingly, to apply contemporary critical methods. Like scholars of nature writing, their writing is itself a genre, about ideas about nature and the way such ideas influence or direct social development. Preeminent among them is Donald Worster. His history of ecological science, *Nature's Economy: The Roots of Ecology* (1977), is the standard text. More recently, he has expressed his concern that the persistent enthusiasm for ecology, represented on T-shirts or in movements such as "deep ecology," suggests a hope that the science can offer a "pathway to a kind of moral enlightenment." Most of the political slogans of the "ecology movement" come from the language of Eugene P. Odum's *Fundamentals of Ecology* (1953). In studying the actual changes in science—rather than the slogans that have come out of it—however, Worster has seen a diversity of conflicting theories of ecological change. And he concludes, in part, that "ecology today, no more than in the past, can be assumed to be all-knowing or all-wise or eternally true."

Worster is not alone in his concerns. In fact, environmental historians have carried out an extended inquiry into the dialectic between cultural ideas of nature, the alterations of biological environments, and social change. A minimal reading list would include, in addition to Merchant and Worster, William Cronon's *Changes in the Land* (1983), Alfred Crosby's *Ecological Imperialism* (1986), Arthur McEvoy's *Fisherman's Problem* (1986), Martin V. Melosi's *Garbage in the Cities* (1981), Stephen J. Pyne's *Fire in America* (1982), and Richard White's *Roots of Dependency* (1983).

These historians remind us that what nature writing teaches about nature is testable by science in a limited way. "Which nature, what science, when, and where?," we must ask. What it teaches about humans is testable, too, but linked to the limits of the science, art, philosophy, history, politics, or ideology that at first seem only to inform the writing, but are inescapably formative of it. This is the legacy of modern, poststructuralist literary theory. Historians of nature writing have begun to consider this problem. A history of the coevolution of bears and humans, *The Sacred Paw* (1985), has been written by the human ecologist Paul Shepard. A history of American literary bears, from the bears of Meriwether Lewis and William Clark through Ernest Thompson Seton, including William Faulkner, and leading to the avalanche of modern bear stories, remains to be written.

Agassiz and the Fish: Does Nature Writing Have an Ideology?

One remembers the parable told by Ezra Pound of "Agassiz and the Fish," as the "proper method" for studying literature. Louis Agassiz (1807–1873) was the most influential American naturalist of his day. He introduced the method of careful firsthand examination and comparison of specimens. A postgraduate student came to him for "final and finishing touches." "The great man offered him a small fish and told him to describe it." He replied that it was only a sunfish. Agassiz again asked him to describe it. The student went to the library and came back with a textbook description. Agassiz told him to look at it. And so on, until, at the end of several weeks, the "fish was in an advanced state of decomposition, but the student knew something about it." The way Pound tells it, all you have to do is pay attention and describe, yet his anecdote turns out to describe neither the methods of contemporary science nor the methods of contemporary literary study. Furthermore, we worry about the decomposition of the fish and fear that the world or its text may be disappearing while we are studying it. So it is that ideological considerations intrude on literary study.

As environmental historians have pointed out, science will not give us absolute answers; scholars of nature writing will always be faced with questions of ideology. What is the political and economic environment for nature writing? How is this environment reflected in the writing? At present, in the midst of a social and perhaps biological crisis, one must consider the political scene wherein people read nature, write nature, read nature writing.

One highly influential ideological book is George Sessions and Bill Devall's *Deep Ecology: Living As If Nature Mattered* (1985). Sessions has consistently described deep ecology, as a "total view—a world view—which involves not only our way of acting in daily life but also our relationship to Nature, our basic values, and our beliefs about what is of ultimate importance in life." Sessions' implication that there is only one "relationship" to Nature allows for his premise that "Deep Ecology provides a philosophical basis for the Green movement." Sessions is a philosopher and an advocate of an ideology. As a student of nature writing, as literature, one is supposed to think about literary works, not simply advocate their theses. To that extent, a literary critic must speak from inside and outside the genre. Is it possible, if the critic is inside a particular ideology, such as deep ecology? David Rothenberg, a leading American expert on this philosophy, says of its founder, Arne Naess, that he "likes him best when he celebrates skeptical inquiry."

One would not study nature writing if one did not feel its themes were vital; however, students in the late twentieth century should be cautious, and go in fear of monolithic ideological stances, remembering what happened to those unfortunate American critics who began by writing of social injustices in the American political and economic system and ended by becoming social Darwinists or, more recently, literary Stalinists. The past decade has seen a variety of ideologically based critical methodologies particularly directed toward nature writing. Deep ecology is one. Ecofeminism is another, as represented by two influential anthologies, Judith Plant's *Heal-*

ing the Wounds: The Promise of Ecofeminism* (1989) and Irene Diamond and Gloria Feman Orenstein's *Reweaving the World: The Emergence of Ecofeminism* (1990). The term *ecofeminisme*, as Carolyn Merchant describes its history in her essay "Ecofeminism and Feminist Theory" in Diamond and Orenstein's collection *Reweaving the World* (1990), "was coined by the French writer Françoise d'Eaubonne in 1974 to represent women's potential for bringing about an ecological revolution to ensure human survival on the planet. Such an ecological revolution would entail new gender relations between women and men and between humans and nature." A most powerful American version of this ideology is represented by Susan Griffin in *Woman and Nature: The Roaring Inside Her* (1978). These anthologies demonstrate ecofeminism's considerable promise, as practiced by these women and others (including Ynestra King) and also as practiced by men such as Michael E. Zimmerman and Yaakov Jerome Garb.

What happens when one imagines that nature writing has no ideology, that it is about nature's influence, whatever that is, and not about the influence of humans? Can one think determinatively of the influence of nature, by focusing on place alone? Snyder has suggested such a project: "What I'm working on now is the quixotic idea of replacing ethnicity, ideology, nationalism, race, religion, class with place as primary sense of identity. That," he says, is the "long-range hope of bioregionalism." In fact, bioregionalism, or "reinhabitation," as it is sometimes called, is itself an ideology. Roderick Nash, in *The Rights of Nature: A History of Environmental Ethics* (1989), defines it thus: "People would cultivate love for a particular region and structure their style of life so as to live gently in that place" (p. 148). Max Oelschlaeger, in a more congenial study, *The Idea of Wilderness: From Prehistory to the Age of Ecology* (1991), thinks of this process of personal and social transformation as an "old-new way of being." Such a culture is "rooted in the land rather than some a priori ideology," Oelschlaeger argues. Is such an idea too all-encompassing and paradoxically too narrow? Is it too naive?

Is There a Canon of Nature Writing?

Canon is the term originally applied to the authorized or accepted list of books belonging to the Christian Bible by virtue of having been declared divinely inspired. In a figurative sense, the term implies a standard of judgment, a criterion. The process of canon formation has been much discussed in literary circles since the early 1980s. This process, which always includes certain writers, making them central, and excludes others, making them marginal, is most dramatically represented in the making of literary anthologies. In the 1990s, the most popular of these in the realm of nature writing included Ann Ronald's *Words for the Wild: The Sierra Club Trailside Reader* (1987), Lyon's *This Incomperable Lande: A Book of American Nature Writing* (1989), and Finch and Elder's *Norton Book of Nature Writing* (1990). The first includes selections from the writings of nineteen men and four women, all Caucasian Protestant Americans. In the second, the numbers for these groups are twenty and two, respectively. In the Norton anthology, which is largely British and American, there is slightly more diversity, including seventy-eight men and fifteen women with three selections from Native American perspectives.

The numbers speak for themselves, and would seem to reflect an assumption that the culture of nature writing has a single "center," or ideology. American literary scholarship has yet to open up the canon of nature writers and expose all writers to contemporary methodologies of history, philosophy, and criticism. Such a process would lead to a certain degree of relativism and to the question "Is it possible at all to create a taxonomy of American nature writing?" There have been many attempts.

Traditionally, American perceptions of landscape have been explored through their Jeffersonian premises. Henry Nash Smith's *Virgin Land: The American West as Symbol and Myth* (1950), Leo Marx's *The Machine in the Garden: Technology and the Pastoral Ideal in America* (1964), and Nash's *Wilderness and the American Mind* (1967) represent pioneering work in this branch of what came to be called American studies. The approach here is probably indebted to William Empson's *Some Versions of Pastoral* (1935), which sees the strategy of the pastoral genre as "putting the complex into the simple." Centering on the pastoral or middle landscape as ideal, these American studies also feature a triune structure of landscapes, with the pastoral ideal bracketed by the garden on one side and the wilderness on the other. Lawrence Buell has provided a thorough review and extension of these issues in "American Pastoral Ideology Reappraised" (1989).

Consequently, one might segment American nature writing in terms of gardeners, such as Jamaica Kincaid, Lewis H. Lapham, and many anonymous westering American women. Pastoralists are legion, including Thoreau, Gretel Ehrlich, Dillard, Berry. Then come the hard-line wilderness writers—Muir, Lopez, Zwinger. If nature writers are the children of Linnaeus, as some argue, then a taxonomy by subject is appropriate. If they are straying children, as Lyon has suggested, then they can be categorized by the degree to which they wander from their source of information about natural history, toward personal responses, and finally toward philosophical interpretations. Such a scheme, which Lyon tabulates in *This Incomperable Lande*, includes a continuum from field guides and professional papers, natural-history essays, and rambles to solitary and backcountry living, travel and adventure, farm life, and finally to the role of humans in nature. Such systems are approximations, and like the biological systems that give, at best, a snapshot of evolution at a particular moment in its ongoing process, their primary function for a student is the preliminary organization of data.

What is wrong with the taxonomic approach? In what Dillard has called the "best book ever written about nature," Melville argues that Americans have a secret motto or monomania. "Ego non baptizo te in nomine patris, sed in nomine diaboli" ("I do not baptize you in the name of the father, but in the name of the devil"), deliriously howls Ahab. *Moby-Dick* is great American nature writing, and Pip, its fool, is the supreme relativist. "Have you seen the White Whale?" is the text's repeated question, and Pip's answer is "I look, you look, he looks; we look, ye look, they look." *Moby-Dick*, multiple in perspective and in literary genre, itself eludes literary classification. The questions we ask shape the range of answers we can hope to get. What if we are asking only one question? Many renderings perhaps, but still one text. Perhaps a widening canon will eliminate singleness of vision, or at least dispel certain singular myths.

Is the West Another Name for the Wild?

Traditionally, one of the purposes of the study of history is to explode untenable myths. This was the intention of Smith's *Virgin Land*. To understand American mythology, one must understand something of the late-twentieth-century controversies in American, and especially western American history. A singularity of American nature writing is its tie to American history and, in particular, to western American history. "The West of which I speak is but another name for the Wild," wrote Thoreau. And every portion of the American continent has been, at one time or another, the West.

Many historians are no longer willing to depict the West as a place of solitary frontiersmen and separate individuals. Nevertheless, many wilderness advocates, sometimes in their roles as nature writers, have done so. Their view places them in the transcendentalist tradition, as represented by Ralph Waldo Emerson and Thoreau. In his essay "Transcendentalist Self-Examination and Autobiographical Tradition" (1973), Buell has observed that the "most egoistic movement in American literary history produced no first-rate autobiography, unless one counts *Walden*." He notes a strange paradox, that "they attached great theoretical importance to the self," yet "most of what they themselves wrote seems quite impersonal, including their own private journals." Surely, a discussion of works written in this tradition must confront the formative influence of this paradox and must recognize the formative effects of Transcendental ideas about self and nature as well as those of the West.

Emerson's "Nature" (1836), which has been called America's intellectual declaration of independence, asks, "Why should not we also enjoy an original relation to the universe?" And to answer this question, he must create a sharp distinction between "Nature and the Soul." Yet Emerson surely created a mythology of the insular American individual (one developed by Thoreau). The American writer is led out of the library and into solitude, at night, to look at the distant and separate stars. "The first in time and the first in importance of the influences upon the mind is that of nature," he intones in "The American Scholar." But nature is separate from us, a spectacle. Under Emersonian circumstances, is it possible to have a defensible theory of nature writing? Or a theory of nature?

These questions about transcendentalism, which I have only outlined, constitute a parallel inquiry to that taken by western American historians in the late twentieth century who have begun to inspect the so-called frontier thesis of Frederick Jackson Turner (1861–1932). One essay by Turner—"On the Significance of the Frontier in American History"—seems to constitute the solid basis of their discipline. The frontier, for Turner, was a theoretical line separating savagery and civilization, or what we might call nature and culture. Cronon (1987) underlines the importance of Turner's theoretical line: it "set American space in motion and gave it a plot." Patricia Limerick has summarized that plot in *The Legacy of Conquest: The Unbroken Past of the American West* (1987). She refers to its narrative with some humor as the American "origin myth." In it, the American migration from Europe to take new land is "as elemental as a law of physics." The process of conquest, repeated sequentially from Atlantic to Pacific as the line moved across the continent, brought civilization to displace savagery, recreated the social contract from scratch, stripped the European trappings from the pioneers, and produced a new national character. It is as if there were no Americans before Europeans arrived. At the conclusion of this chapter of North American history, the frontier ended. Indeed, says Cronon (1987), in this narrative scheme, the "whole point of the frontier had been to vanish." There is a monumental geographical determinism in Turner's theory. Richard White begins *"It's Your Misfortune and None of My Own": A New History of the American West* (1991) quite simply by asserting that "geography did not determine the boundaries of the West; rather, history created them."

At root, the new western historians are asking, "What if Turner's thesis was not a description of American history but a self-fulfilling thesis?" (One would like to hear literary historians asking the same question about Thoreau's "Walking.") Although many western historians, along with many scholars of American nature writing, still cling to the Turnerian story, there has been considerable dissent. Modern historians point out that the West became, by the 1880s, the most urbanized part of the United States. The West might be, as Limerick or White argue, the site of multicultural intercourse, the place where we met each other. We might imagine that the land shaped North American society, but such works as Cronon's *Nature's Metropolis: Chicago and the Great West* (1991) argue not only that there are linkages between economics and ecology, the country and the city, human enterprises and natural resources but also that a "second nature," created by humans, determined the course of Chicago's development as much as "first nature." Nevertheless, so much discourse has subsumed the Turner myth that the West of which we speak is *intertextual*, in a term created by Julia Kristeva, who says, "Every text builds itself as a mosaic of quotations, every text is absorption and transformation of another text." Western writers speak in a language created by Emerson, Thoreau, Walt Whitman, William Lloyd Garrison, and Frederick Turner, though altered by more recent authors.

Boundaries: Mapping American Nature Writing

Like Melville's "two sides to a tortoise" in *The Encantadas*, American nature writing as a totality presents two sides. Its back—which is its surface and at first appears as a dark side we might name "first nature"—calls for a shedding of multidisciplinary light. Changes in the disciplines of ecology, western American history, environmental history, literary criticism, and art criticism reveal a complex, though perhaps symmetrical, web of premises shared by an audience and an author, the seams in texts, which are rarely discussed. The second, or other, side of nature writing, an inescapable consequence of the first—but hidden—has a bright promise that can be revealed by enlarging the canon with the writings of marginal groups as nature writers in their own right. For it is not immediately clear where the boundary lies between that which constitutes the theory of this activity and that which constitutes its practice. On that boundary or edge where the two sides fuse, there one finds American nature writing—a consequence of social convergence, not a consequence of geographical region. Why not situate the beginning of the problem of boundaries precisely at the edge, which is either a high ascending ridge or a deep and appalling chasm?

The Ethics of Representation

Representation is the most traditional and perhaps most basic of literary issues. Feminists, for example, have focused on this issue with regard to women as objects subjected to the male gaze and the male pen. Modern discussions of representation are concerned with the power relations between the person who represents and the object. The way this issue applies to the nature writer and his or her object is perhaps obvious, a problem as old as the writing of books, structured by the linked dilemmas of naming or not naming, saying or not saying, saving or sharing.

Because writing is a business, one notices this issue in strange contexts. One day, I listened to a set of writers discuss the ethics of naming in magazine articles one particular slot canyon on the Colorado Plateau or one particular campsite in the Wind Rivers. We were in Ogden, Utah, in a state with a birthrate sometimes described as equaling that of a Third World country. Just west of us sat the largest storage area for lethal nerve gas on the planet, and we were in a region downwind from three decades of nuclear testing in the state of Nevada. One wonders about the importance of our particular examples.

Naming has always been associated with appropriation, taking possession. In "The Stone Horse," Lopez, by attempting to refrain from the activity of naming, illustrates many of the problems of representation. The horse in question, an intaglio found somewhere in the Imperial Valley, is not strictly speaking natural, though it is described as something wild. The essay is equally difficult to locate; it both names and refuses to name, describes but refuses to describe, locates and refuses to locate its object, and finally writes about and refuses to write about the image of the horse. The narrator himself might be, and might not be, Lopez himself.

The horse, made several hundred years ago by clearing spaces between the dark stones of desert pavement, is an archeological site. The narrator is directed to it by a Bureau of Land Management archaeologist, who makes a "gesture of wonder at its existence." How our narrator knew to ask about the horse we are not told. Perhaps by reading of it or hearing a story. The archaeologist gives topographical directions "with understandable reluctance." Ostensibly, this reluctance stems from his concern about the possibility of vandalism. This narrator, whose text represents himself as a writer, assures the archaeologist that he will not tell anyone how to find this horse. "I waited until I held his eye," he writes. Is this a conspiracy of which we read, or a deception of one man by another?

After several hundred words, the essay approaches its object, using various metaphors, including that of a library and those of art. To the narrator it is a historical object and a piece of art, an "admirably accurate representation," as he says, and evidence of a certain quality in the artist. He assumes the artist was interested in "realistic" representation and "reads" the meaning of the image thus: This unknown artist observed his object, a "real" horse, very closely, so that one who knew enough about horses, which the narrator does not though he has been a cowboy, could tell the breed. Furthermore, the narrator suggests that anyone who wishes to find any meaning in this representation must pay attention *as he has done*, and watch the image bathed by shifting light for many hours and from many vantage places. Indeed, the reader suspects that the narrator's discourse is less about the horse and its maker than about himself, as a maker of the essay at hand. There is self-congratulation here: the narrator admires his own attentiveness as he gazes "wordlessly" for hours, and he wants the reader to do so too.

Following the description of the image itself is a delineation of an endless network of representations of horses in history, which is to say a description of the "postmodern reality" of horses. History, the narrator concludes, is "inscribed everywhere in the face of the land," at least where it has not been destroyed by vandals, whom he calls "people who devour history."

There is something explicit about the ethics of representation here. The narrator finds a stone tool where he is sitting and says it is hard to resist the desire to steal it. More important, he makes no notes while he is "with" the horse, because it "would have seemed disrespectful" and would have called for "another kind of attention." Only after he has paid respect to the "horse, its maker, and the history of us all," only after he is back in his motor vehicle, does he patiently drain his memory of "details it had fastened itself upon." Of course, he knows that he steals the horse when he writes it, and has known all along, as we have. And he knows something worse, as his language suggests, that he has devoured it and now he is expressing his

memories—or abstractions—onto paper for others to consume.

What do we think of him finally, who knows how to make an archaeologist reveal a secret treasure, who will tell us there is a wonderful intaglio horse in the desert and will not tell us how to find it? Intaglios, he tells us, "were meant to be seen by people on the ground, over a long period of shifting light." When he recounts his own ecstatic encounter with this wonder, is he not saying to the reader, I am qualified to see these things, but you are not? I will represent them—indeed, you will find their value represented in me—but I will not take the risk or responsibility for sharing them with you.

Who knows the world best, we must ask, and who is capable of speaking with the great clarity of art? How can a critic distinguish the intermingled human desires to possess and display? The subject of nature writing is not a simple knowledge, and it is complicated by problems of language, represented perhaps by the ambiguous signs that confront us at the bottom of poststructuralist theory. "Permits must be obtained to enter this wilderness," we read, though we know the wilderness would be better off without our entry, better protected if there were a "flaming sword which turned every way, to keep the way of the tree of life." And what are the consequences of communicating or acting upon our knowledge? There is a man with a name painfully close to my own who wrote a book entitled *How Nature Works* (1988). Most of us are not so audacious. More to the point, the other Michael Cohen has not written literature; representation gives us not nature, but literature.

What Light Does American Nature Writing Reflect?

My inquiry ends, provisionally, with the validity of nature writing's claims as a reflective medium: What, finally, are the benefits of what a friend of mine has named "meditations on a plover's egg"? What does the study of nature give to the living of our lives? Do we return from the mountains enlightened? Two major works on wilderness, by Nash and Oelschlaeger, disagree on precisely this subject, while Joyce Carol Oates has argued, in "Against Nature" (1986), that "[Nature] inspires a painfully limited set of responses in 'nature writers'—REVERENCE, AWE, PIETY, MYSTICAL ONENESS." But in the same essay she shows those who wish to defend nature writing how to refute her argument, by their own less-certain, more-skeptical reading of the canon. She quotes Nietzsche: "We all pretend to ourselves that we are more simple-minded than we are: that is how we get a rest from our fellow men." It is for the student of American nature writing to investigate that pretense.

Do we read nature to know Nature or to know ourselves? The annoying recurrence of this issue in almost all of the questions a theorist must ask about nature writing suggests, in all probability, that it is the key theme that marks the presence of a unique genre worthy of critical scrutiny. No doubt the genre includes a great many texts that have not yet been accepted into the canon. As they grow to be accepted, the canon will grow sufficiently complex that it will scarcely serve to provide a single unitary image of ourselves. We should not be afraid if we find it more difficult to see ourselves clearly in this mirror. It is, finally, possible to have a criticism of American nature writing that is both cosmopolitan and committed, one that allows no easy answers or easy fitting of modern humans into their environment. As Limerick has written,

New Western Historians surrender the conventional, never-very-convincing claim of an omniscient, neutral objectivity. While making every effort to acknowledge and understand different points of view, [they] admit that it is OK for scholars to care about their subjects, both in the past and in the present, and to put that concern on record. ("The New Western History," ca. 1990)

In this case, doubt may serve as a prelude to responsibility for a re-constructive task, good for the literature and good for the world that inspires it.

Selected Bibliography

This bibliography is meant to be discordant, unsettling, disruptive, provocative perhaps, or evocative; in order to suggest the dilemmas and predicaments that surround nature writing. Consequently it is to some extent polemical and personal. It is neither representative of conventional approaches to nature writing, nor is it a complete survey. It is meant to suggest the scope of discussion of the tangled literary, political, historical, and aesthetic issues that surround nature writing. The quotations from the authors mentioned in the body of the essay can usually, but not always, be found in these works. I have eschewed page references within the text. I do not cite individual pages because, in my personal view, literary theory is not about individual or isolated statements, but about the structure, the method of literary thinking.

Wendell Berry, "Against PCs," in *Harper's Magazine* (September 1988), repr. incl. letters and Berry's reply in *The Dolphin Reader*, 3d ed., ed. by Douglas Hunt and Carolyn Perry (Boston: Houghton Mifflin, 1993); Daniel B. Botkin, *Discordant Harmonies: A New Ecology for the Twenty-first Century* (New York: Oxford Univ. Press, 1990); Anna Bramwell, *Ecology in the Twentieth Century* (New Haven, Conn.: Yale Univ. Press, 1989); Lawrence Buell, "American Pastoral Ideology Reappraised," in *American Literary History* 1 (spring 1989), and "Transcendentalist Self-Examination and Autobiographical Tradition," in *Literary Transcendentalism: Style and Vision in the American Renaissance* (Ithaca, N.Y.: Cornell Univ. Press, 1973); SueEllen Campbell, "The Land of Language and Desire: Where Deep Ecology and Post-Structuralism Meet," in *Western American Literature* 24 (November 1989); Nicolai Cikovsky, Jr., "On the Cover," in *Journal of Forest History* 33, no. 1 (January 1989); Michael J. Cohen, *How Nature Works: Regenerating Kinship with Planet Earth* (Walpole, N.H.: Stillpoint, 1988); Michael P. Cohen, *The Pathless Way: John Muir and American Wilderness* (Madison: Univ. of Wisconsin Press, 1984); William Cronon, *Changes in the Land: Indians, Colonists, and the Ecology of New England* (New York: Hill and Wang, 1983), "Revisiting the Vanishing Frontier: The Legacy of Frederick Jackson Turner," in *The Western Historical Quarterly* 18 (April 1987), *Nature's Metropolis: Chicago and the Great West* (New York: Norton, 1991), and "A Place for Stories: Nature, History, and Narrative," in *Journal of American History* 78 (March 1992). Alfred Crosby, *Ecological Imperialism: The Biological Expansion of Europe, 900–1900* (New York: Cambridge Univ. Press, 1986); Jacques Derrida, "Structure, Sign, and Play in the Discourse of the Human Sciences," in *Contemporary Literary Criti-*

cism, 2d ed., ed. by Robert Con Davis and Ronald Schliefer (New York: Longman, 1989); Bill Devall and George Sessions, *Deep Ecology: Living As If Nature Mattered* (Salt Lake City: Peregrine Smith, 1985); Irene Diamond and Gloria Feman Orenstein, eds., *Reweaving the World: The Emergence of Ecofeminism* (San Francisco: Sierra Club, 1990); John Paul Eakin, ed., *American Autobiography: Retrospect and Prospect* (Madison: Univ. of Wisconsin Press, 1991); William Empson, *Some Versions of Pastoral* (London: Chatto & Windus, 1935); Robert Finch and John Elder, eds., *The Norton Book of Nature Writing* (New York: Norton, 1990); Michel Foucault, *The Order of Things: An Archaeology of the Human Sciences* (New York: Pantheon, 1970), and "What Is an Author?," repr. in *Contemporary Literary Criticism*, 2d ed., ed. by Robert Con Davis and Ronald Schliefer (New York: Longman, 1989).

William Goetzmann, *Exploration and Empire: The Explorer and the Scientist in the Winning of the American West* (New York: Knopf, 1966); Susan Griffin, *Woman and Nature: The Roaring Inside Her* (New York: Harper & Row, 1978); C. Hugh Holman and William Harmon, *A Handbook to Literature*, 6th ed. (New York: Macmillan, 1992); David Couzens Hoy, ed., *Foucault: A Critical Reader* (New York: Basil Blackwell, 1986); Annette Kolodny, *The Lay of the Land: Metaphor as Experience and History in the History of American Life and Letters* (Chapel Hill: Univ. of North Carolina Press, 1975), and *The Land Before Her: Fantasy and Experience of the American Frontier* (Chapel Hill: Univ. of North Carolina Press, 1984); Thomas Kuhn, *The Structure of Scientific Revolutions* (Chicago: Univ. of Chicago Press, 1962); Vincent B. Leitch, *Deconstructive Criticism: An Advanced Introduction* (New York: Columbia Univ. Press, 1983); Frank Lentricchia and Thomas McLaughlin, eds., *Critical Terms for Literary Study* (Chicago: Univ. of Chicago Press, 1990); Patricia Nelson Limerick, *The Legacy of Conquest: The Unbroken Past of the American West* (New York: Norton, 1987), and "The New Western History" (mimeographed, ca. 1990); Barry Lopez, "The Stone Horse," in *Crossing Open Ground* (New York: Scribners, 1988); Edward Lueders, *Writing Natural History: Dialogues with Authors* (Salt Lake City: University of Utah, 1989); Thomas J. Lyon, "Part 1: A History," in *This Incomperable Lande: A Book of American Nature Writing* (Boston: Houghton Mifflin, 1989).

Arthur F. McEvoy, *The Fisherman's Problem: Ecology and the Law in the California Fisheries* (New York: Cambridge Univ. Press, 1986); Leo Marx, *The Machine in the Garden: Technology and the Pastoral Ideal in America* (New York: Oxford Univ. Press, 1964); Martin V. Melosi, *Garbage in the Cities: Refuse, Reform, and the Environment, 1880–1980* (College Station: Texas A&M Univ. Press, 1981); Carolyn Merchant, *The Death of Nature: Women, Ecology, and the Scientific Revolution* (San Francisco: Harper & Row, 1980), *Ecological Revolutions: Nature, Gender, and Science in New England* (Chapel Hill: Univ. of North Carolina Press, 1989), and, as ed., *Major Problems in American Environmental History* (Lexington, Mass.: D. C. Heath, 1993); Roderick Nash, *Wilderness and the American Mind* (New Haven, Conn.: Yale Univ. Press, 1967), and *The Rights of Nature: A History of Environmental Ethics* (Madison: Univ. of Wisconsin Press, 1989); Joyce Carol Oates, "Against Nature," in *Antaeus* 57 (autumn 1986); Eugene Odum, *The Fundamentals of Ecology* (Philadelphia: Saunders, 1953); Max Oelschlaeger, *The Idea of Wilderness: From Prehistory to the Age of Ecology* (New Haven, Conn.: Yale Univ. Press, 1991); John P. O'Grady, *Pilgrims to the Wild* (Salt Lake City: Univ. of Utah Press, 1993); Judith Plant, ed., *Healing the Wounds: The Promise of Ecofeminism* (Philadelphia: New Society, 1989); Ezra Pound, "Agassiz and the Fish," in *The ABCs of Reading* (New York: New Directions, 1934); Stephen J. Pyne, *Fire in America: A Cultural History of Wildland and Rural Fire* (Princeton, N.J.: Princeton Univ. Press, 1982).

Ann Ronald, ed., *Words for the Wild: The Sierra Club Trailside Reader* (San Francisco: Sierra Club, 1987); David Rothenberg, *Is It Painful to Think? Conversations with Arne Naess* (Minneapolis: Univ. of Minnesota Press, 1992); Paul Shepard, "Introduction: Ecology and Man—A Viewpoint," in *The Subversive Science: Essays Toward an Ecology of Man*, ed. by Paul Shepard and Daniel McKinley (Boston: Houghton Mifflin, 1969); Paul Shepard and Barry Sanders, *The Sacred Paw: The Bear in Nature, Myth, and Literature* (New York: Viking, 1985); Scott Slovic, *Seeking Awareness in American Nature Writing* (Salt Lake City: University of Utah Press, 1992); Henry Nash Smith, *Virgin Land: The American West as Symbol and Myth* (Cambridge, Mass.: Harvard Univ. Press, 1950); Gary Snyder, *The Practice of the Wild* (San Francisco: North Point, 1990); Theodore Stebbins, Jr., Carol Troyen, and Trevor Fairbrother, *Masterpieces of American Painting 1760–1910* (Boston: Museum of Fine Arts, 1983); Toby Thompson, "The Happy Buddha of Kitkitdizze," in *Outside* 17 (November 1993); Stephen Trimble, ed., *Words from the Land: Encounters with Natural History Writing* (Salt Lake City: Gibbs M. Smith, 1988); Frederick Jackson Turner, "On the Significance of the Frontier in American History," in *Annual Report of the American Historical Association for the Year 1893* (Washington, D.C.: Government Printing Office, 1894).

Richard White, *The Roots of Dependency: Subsistence, Environment, and Social Change Among the*

Choctaws, Pawnees, and Navajos (Lincoln: Univ. of Nebraska Press, 1983), and *"It's Your Misfortune and None of My Own": A New History of the American West* (Norman: Univ. of Oklahoma Press, 1991); Raymond Williams, *The Country and the City* (London: Oxford Univ. Press, 1973), and "Ideas of Nature," in *Problems in Materialism and Culture* (London: Verso, 1980); Donald Worster, Richard White, William Cronon, and Stephen Pyne, "A

Roundtable: Environmental History," in *Journal of American History* 76 (March 1990); Donald Worster, *Nature's Economy: The Roots of Ecology* (San Francisco: Sierra Club, 1977), *The Ends of the Earth: Perspectives on Modern Environmental History* (New York: Cambridge Univ. Press, 1988), and "The Ecology of Order and Chaos," in *Environmental History Review* 14, nos. 1–2 (spring/summer 1990).

LITERATURE OF MOUNTAINEERING

MIKEL VAUSE

I t's hard to imagine an arena where man has fewer claims and less authority.
　　—John Long, *Rock Junction*, p. 103

The greater mountains, wherein sublimity so much excels our daily things, that in their presence experience dissolves, and we seem to enter upon a kind of eternity.
　　—Hilaire Belloc, quoted in Styles, p. 153

MOUNTAIN TRAVEL HAS inspired an exceptionally strong literature. This is true not only of British and European mountain writing but of American as well. In order fully to appreciate American mountaineering literature, it is important first to examine its roots. American mountaineering literature, like other genres of American literature, is much indebted to its British and Western European antecedents. Yet artistic recognition of and response to mountain environs is far older than these literatures. According to Michael Tobias, in his essay "A History of Imagination in Wilderness" (in *The Mountain Spirit*, 1979), ancient Chinese mystics entered the mountains in search of religious experiences and recorded them in paintings. The climbing of mountains appears in many texts that date back to 2350 B.C. It is also quite evident from the recent discovery of the "ice man" in the Swiss Alps, as recorded in David Roberts'

article "The Ice Man," that early inhabitants of mountainous regions had trade and hunting routes through the high passes leading from one valley to another.

According to Jeremy Bernstein, in his slim, but important volume *Ascent*, mountaineering as a sporting activity is generally thought to have begun in 1741 with a young Englishman William Windham, who undertook an expedition into the valley above Chamonix, France. A year earlier, Horace-Bénédict de Saussure, whom Bernstein credits as being the first "real" mountain climber and mountain writer, was born. Saussure spent a good deal of his youth rambling around the mountains and in time became a geologist and meteorologist. Gaston Rébuffat, one of France's most famous modern mountaineers and author of eleven books on mountaineering, including *Starlight and Storm* (1954) and *On Ice, Snow, and Rock* (1954), called Saussure the "founder of our family." Saussure had great interest in Mont Blanc, which was thought to be the highest mountain in the world. Around 1760 he offered a reward to the first men to reach its summit. The recipients of the reward in 1786, were Michel Paccard, a village physician, and Jacques Balmat, a climbing guide and hunter. With their history-making effort, many myths were dispelled. As they stood on the 15,000-foot summit, they found only snow and rock and saw only the valley below. The monsters and demons thought to inhabit the high peaks were nonexistent.

Mountains have always been at the center of human mythmaking, as is evidenced in much of classical literature. Representing the abode of the gods and places of special powers, they have served as archetypes in human intellectual and spiritual development. They are the starting points for much folklore and legend. In Britain's mountainous areas there are ancient stone rings, sometimes call "Druid rings," such as Castlerigg, near Keswick, Cumberland, where early inhabitants are said to have practiced astronomy and to have held religious ceremonies. Also common are ancient trails and paths leading through the mountains, some crossing the summits of Britain's highest peaks. Scotland has always been known for the mountain adventures of the highland tribes. One of the great historical events in Scottish annals occurred at Glencoe, the "vale of tears," possibly one of the most beautiful mountain settings in the world. Here the Campbells massacred the MacDonalds, on the orders of King William III of England, in 1692. It has been said that at certain times, Glencoe is still visited by the restless spirits of the murdered MacDonalds.

Scottish mountains are at the center of much of the myth and lore of supernatural events. One of the most famous legends is that of Fear Liath Mor, the "great Grey Man" of Ben Macdhui. The legend goes that climbers of Ben Macdhui are sometimes followed on their ascents by an apparition in the form of a very large man. Fear Liath Mor stalks only those who are climbing either in fog and mist or at night. John Norman Collie, the eminent English scientist and professor, encountered the Grey Man sometime in the 1890s during a night ascent of Ben Macdhui, but did not publicly mention it until many years later while addressing the annual dinner of the Cairngorm Club. His meeting with the Grey Man so frightened Collie that he refused to visit Ben Macdhui again. After his speech he was approached by a number of individuals in the audience who had had similar encounters with this apparition.

In North America, the Indians were regular visitors to the remote mountains, where they sought medicine dreams and communion with their animal relations. This tradition is clearly illustrated in the great Crow tribal chief Plenty Coups's "Vision in the Crazy Mountains": "I decided to go afoot to the Crazy Mountains, two long days' journey from the village. The traveling without food or drink was good for me, and as soon as I reached the Crazies I took a sweat-bath and climbed the highest peak" (p. 224). Even though Plenty Coups's experience occurred in the mid-nineteenth century, it is representative of the Native American tradition of travel in and reverence for Earth's high places.

Nearly every culture, either in its oral histories or in its written literature, makes reference to mountains either as actual physical places or as metaphorical or philosophical "symbols." The British seem to have had the greatest impact on mountaineering literature. Chris Bonington, for example, is the most prolific British mountaineer in both actual climbing and producing books on the subject. He has written eleven major books and hundreds of articles over his forty-year career, including *I Chose to Climb* (his autobiography), *Everest the Hard Way*, *Annapurna South Face*, *Mountaineer*, and *The Climbers*.

There are many notable mountain writers from around the world who have made extremely important contributions to the literature of mountaineering. *Nanga Parbat Pilgrimage*, by Hermann Buhl, a leading Austrian mountaineer, and *Annapurna*, by Maurice Herzog, the leader of the successful 1950 Annapurna expedition, are classics of the genre. They are stylistically strong, excite the emotions, and invite the reader to both intellectual and physical participation. Another important European mountain writer is Heinrich Harrer. He and Anderl Hechmair made the first ascent of the north face of the Eiger. In the *White Spider*, Harrer records his and Hechmair's success, along with well-researched accounts of the many tragic attempts preceding theirs. Harrer also includes accounts of both successful and disastrous climbs that came after his, in 1936. Harrer later wrote *Seven Years in*

Tibet, which recounts his seven years in the Tibetan Himalayas after escaping from a British prisoner-of-war camp during World War II.

Most mountain writing began merely as reports of adventures to satisfy either the scientific world or the world of industry. Seldom did early accounts of mountain ascents hold any literary interest. The few exceptions are those of the British Lake poets: William Wordsworth, Samuel Taylor Coleridge, and John Ruskin. In the mid-1800s the sport of climbing mountains gained popularity, although the effect of mountains on the development of literary and philosophical ideas showed up much earlier. Wordsworth and his friend and fellow poet and mountain rambler Coleridge, were constantly climbing the mountains in the Lake District of England. Their visits were not limited to the lower valleys; both men were avid summit seekers and thought nothing of going for several 1,000-meter summits in a day. Coleridge takes the mountain experience even further with the record of his famous "circumcursion" of the lakes recorded in his notebooks under the dates 1–9 August 1802.

It was not until mountaineering became a leisure activity, practiced by the educated upper classes of Western Europe, that climbing accounts developed into a literary form. In England it was through the writings of such literary notables as Sir Leslie Stephen, the editor of the *Dictionary of National Bibliography*. One of Britain's leading mountaineers, he produced a number of excellent works dealing with the sport of ascent. Stephen is most remembered for *The Playground of Europe* (1871). He was followed by Albert F. Mummery, a mathematician, and Geoffery Winthrop Young, a Cambridge don. Mummery was killed in an attempt on Nanga Parbat in 1895, the same year his delightful book *My Climbs in the Alps and Caucasus* was published.

Young was a leader in British climbing. His exploits began while he was still an undergraduate at Cambridge. He was quite involved in climbing the buildings and, in fact, wrote a guidebook titled *The Roof-Climber's Guide to Trinity* (1905). Young lost his leg as a result of injuries he received in battle during World War I, but he continued to climb until 1935. His contributions to the literature of mountaineering are many, but he is most remembered for *Mountain Craft* (1920), sometimes referred to as the "Climber's Bible," and for his outstanding autobiography, *On High Hills*, and his verse. In 1956, Young delivered the W. P. Ker Memorial Lecture at the University of Glasgow. Titled "The Effects of Mountains upon the Development of Human Intelligence," it is an important historical examination of the part mountains have played in human intellectual development.

The influence of such poets as Wordsworth and Coleridge on writers, not only in their native England but also in America, is substantial. Their transcendental philosophies had far-reaching effects on many writers in many countries, but possibly the greatest influence was upon Americans, in particular Ralph Waldo Emerson. Emerson, through his magnum opus *Nature* (1836), laid the foundations of American nature writing. *Nature* was the vehicle for expounding Emerson's philosophy that Frederic Ives Carpenter called "pragmatic mysticism." This philosophy argued that humans have the potential to unite the "ideal" and the "actual" by frequent visits to wilderness. The more one ventures out, the more likely one is to make that ideal union. From a mountaineering standpoint, Doug Scott's essay "On the Profundity Trail" (in *Mirrors in the Cliffs*, 1983) is in clear agreement with Emerson:

> If big wall climbing is pursued in a more hostile environment and for longer periods, or if the big-wall climber climbs alone, as Bonatti did on the Dru, then the doors of perception will be opened wide. The climbers involved may experience a more lasting state of heightened awareness, and may even reach a truly visionary, if not mystical state of being which transcends normal human comprehension. Most of us will never make such climbs, but that is not to say that less demanding climbs could not have a similar effect. The climber who is willing to extend himself to the limit of his technical skill and endurance on any long climb is en route up the profundity trail. (p. 51)

David Mazel, in his book *Pioneering Ascents: The Origins of Climbing in America 1642–1873* (1991), documents the works of some of the earliest American explorers. They include William Bradford, Darby Field, John Lederer, Robert Fallam, William Byrd, Alexander Spotwood, and William Bartram. The writings of these writer/explorers deal with the mountains and wilderness areas of the eastern United States. It can be argued that American mountaineering literature begins with an adventure on one of the great mountains in the eastern United States, Thoreau's famous climb of Katahdin. Although his climb was not a technical climb, and he certainly was not the first to make the ascent (Charles Turner was the first, in 1804), from a literary and philosophical perspective is still it an important account of the activity of ascent.

Thoreau, experimenting in "living life deliberately," took Emerson's ideas and applied them by living a life of extreme simplicity. During his time at Walden (1845–1847), he, his brother, John, and friends made a number of wilderness trips to the woods of the region and floated for a week on the Concord and Merrimack rivers in Massachusetts. In addition to visits to Cape Cod, he took many solo walks throughout Massachusetts. Upon the completion of his Walden experiment, Thoreau declared, "I left the woods for as good a reason as I went there. Perhaps it seemed to me that I had several more lives to live, and couldn't spare any more time for that one" ("Walden," p. 562). Yet it is clear that he continued to walk and explore for as long as his health would let him. In his essay "Walking," Thoreau gives his readers a challenge: "We should go forth on the shortest walk, perchance, in the spirit of undying adventure, never to return, prepared to send back our embalmed hearts only as relics to our desolate kingdoms" (p. 593).

In the essay "Ktaadn," Thoreau takes the reader with him to the summit of the mountain: "There stood Ktaadn with distinct and cloudless outline in the moonlight" (p. 124). Thoreau starts the expedition with a happy heart at 6 A.M., on what he estimates to be a fourteen-mile trek. After crossing the "open-land stream"

on logjams and rocks, Thoreau and his team "struck for the highest peak." He willingly accepts the role of lead climber: "Here it fell to my lot, as the oldest mountain-climber, to take the lead" (p. 124). But as the climb proceeds, and Thoreau and his team leave the green, living valley, his descriptions of the landscape become increasingly sublime, until the mountain becomes a place almost unnatural: "The mountain seemed a vast aggregation of loose rocks, as if some time it had rained rocks, and they lay as they fell on the mountain sides, nowhere fairly at rest, but leaning on each other, all rocking-stones with cavities between, but scarcely any soil or smoother shelf" (p. 129).

Upon reaching the summit, Thoreau is almost terrified. He declares:

> The tops of mountains are among the unfinished parts of the globe, whither it is a slight insult to the gods to climb and pry into their secrets, and try their effect on our humanity. Only daring and insolent men, perchance, go there. Simple races, as savages, do not climb mountains,—their tops are sacred and mysterious tracts never visited by them. Pomola is always angry with those who climb to the summit of Ktaadn. (p. 131)

Thoreau, having reached the summit of Katahdin, provides the reader with the following insights: "This was that Earth of which we have heard, made out of Chaos and Old Night. Here was no man's garden. . . . Man was not to be associated with it. It was Matter, vast, terrific,—not his Mother Earth that we have heard of, not for him to tread on, or be buried in" (p. 135).

Even though Thoreau sees his visit to the summit of Katahdin as an intrusion into a part of the world not meant for humans, he returns to the lowlands changed and more insightful:

> I stand in awe of my body, this matter to which I am bound has become so strange to me. I fear not spirits, ghosts, of which I am one,—that my body might,—but I fear bodies, I tremble to meet them. What is this Titan that has possession of me? Talk of

mysteries! Think of our life in nature, — daily to be shown matter, to come in contact with it, — rocks, trees, wind on our cheeks! the *solid* earth! the *actual* world! the *common sense! Contact! Contact! Who* are we? *where* are we? (p. 135)

John Muir, a follower of Emerson's nature philosophy, was greatly influenced by the writings of Thoreau. Whereas Thoreau put Emerson's ideas to a somewhat limited test at Walden, Muir extended the experiment to a lifetime in the High Sierra of California. Just as Scott argues in "On the Profundity Trail" that the rewards of the experience are compounded by deeper commitment, so Muir is rewarded with a more positive and heightened experience on Mount Ritter than it seems Thoreau had on Katahdin.

Muir's account of his climb of Mount Ritter, in *The Mountains of California* (1894), is one of the best and earliest literary accounts of heightened awareness, in the Emersonian sense, coming from contact with extreme wilderness:

> I succeeded in gaining the foot of the cliff on the eastern extremity of the glacier, and there discovered the mouth of a narrow avalanche gully, through which I began to climb, intending to follow it as far as possible, and at least obtain some fine views for my pains. . . . I thus made my way into a wilderness of crumbling spires and battlements, built together in bewildering combinations, and glazed in many places with a thin coating of ice, which I had to hammer off with stones. The situation was becoming gradually more perilous; but, having passed several dangerous spots, I dared not think of descending; for, so steep was the entire ascent, one would inevitably fall to the glacier in case a single misstep were made. Knowing, therefore, the tried danger beneath, I became all the more anxious concerning the developments to be made above, and began to be conscious of a vague foreboding of what actually befell; not that I was given to fear, but rather because my instincts, usually so positive and true, seemed vitiated in some way, and were leading me astray. At length, after attaining an elevation of about 12,800 feet, I found myself at the foot of a sheer drop in the bed of the avalanche channel I was tracing, which seemed absolutely to bar further progress. . . . After scanning its face again and again, I began to scale it, picking my holds with intense caution. After gaining a point about half-way to the top, I was suddenly brought to a dead stop, with arms outspread, clinging close to the face of the rock, unable to move hand or foot either up or down. My doom appeared fixed. I *must* fall. There would be a moment of bewilderment, and then a lifeless rumble down the one general precipice to the glacier below.
>
> When this final danger flashed upon me, I became nerve-shaken for the first time since setting foot on the mountains, and my mind seemed to fill with a stifling smoke. But this terrible eclipse lasted only a moment, when life blazed forth again with preternatural clearness. I seemed suddenly to become possessed of a new sense. The other self, bygone experiences, Instinct, or Guarding Angel, — call it what you will, — came forward and assumed control. Then my trembling muscles became firm again, every rift and flaw in the rock was seen as through a microscope, and my limbs moved with a positiveness and precision with which I seemed to have nothing at all to do. Had I been borne aloft upon wings, my deliverance could not have been more complete. . . . How truly glorious the landscape circled around this noble summit! (*The Mountains of California*, pp. 63–65)

Muir transcends the actual world by going deeper and deeper into wilderness and is enlightened both during and after the climb. This sort of experience, which became the center of most mountaineering writing, represents the justification for "going out." The British climber/writer Wilfrid Noyce argues that humans are adventurous by instinct:

> If adventure has a final and all-embracing motive, it is surely this: we go out because it is our nature to go out, to climb mountains, and to paddle rivers, to fly to the planets and plunge into the depths of the oceans. When man ceases to do these things, he is no longer man. (quoted in Schultheis, p. 33)

There are a number of other important nineteenth-century works that support mountaineering as an important aspect of American exploration and represent excellent mountain writing. One is Lucy Crawford's *The History of the White Mountains* (1846). Crawford was the wife of Ethan Allen Crawford, a mountain pioneer in the northeastern United States. Crawford's work was followed by Thomas Starr King's *The White Hills: Their Legends, Landscape, and Poetry* (1860), which includes a record of an ascent of Mount Washington. King later moved to California, where Mount Starr King in Yosemite National Park is named for him. Another important contributor is Frederick H. Chapin, known as the father of Colorado mountaineering and leader of several first ascents in the Mummy Range. In 1889 he published *Mountaineering in Colorado: The Peaks About Estes Park*, which includes a description of an early ascent of Long's Peak, the highest mountain in Colorado.

American mountain writing gained popularity partly because the writings of explorers were published in major newspapers and magazines, providing readers with vicarious excitement and adventure. In 1872 two members of the Hayden Survey, James Stevenson and Nathaniel Langford, claimed the first ascent of what has sometimes been referred to as Mount Hayden but is most generally called Grand Teton. Langford sold the written account to *Scribner's Monthly*. The *Scribner's* article sparked increased interest in climbing in America with the vivid account of the successful ascent of the "American Matterhorn":

Laying hold of the rocky points at the side of the ice sheet, we broke with our feet in its surface a series of steps, up which we ascended at an angle deflecting not more than twenty degrees from the vertical line one hundred and seventy-five feet to its topmost junction with the rock.

The peril to which this performance exposed us was now fully revealed, and had we seen it at the foot of the ice sheet, the whole world would not have tempted us to the effort we had made. Why the entire mass of ice, yielding to our exertions, was not detached from its slender fastenings and hurled down the mountain is a mystery. On looking down through the space which separated it from the rock, I could see half a dozen icy tentacles, all of small size, reaching from wall to wall. Seemingly the weight of a bird would have loosened the entire field. We felt, as we planted our feet on the solid mountain, that we had escaped a great peril and, quenching our thirst from one of the numerous little rivulets which trickled down the rock, we set resolutely at work to clamber over the fragments and piles of granite which lay between us and the summit. This was more tedious than difficult, but we were amply rewarded when, at three o'clock P.M., after ten hours of the severest labor I ever experienced, we stepped upon the highest point of the Grand Teton. Man measures his triumphs by the toil and exposure incurred in the attainment of them. We felt that we had achieved a victory and that it was for ourselves to know—a solitary satisfaction—that we were the first white men who had ever stood upon the spot we then occupied. Others might come after us, but to be the first where a hundred had failed was no braggart boast. (quoted in Bonney and Bonney, *The Grand Controversy*, pp. 34–35)

Another early contributor to American mountain literature is Clarence King, a Western explorer who recorded his adventures in several articles and in his book *Mountaineering in the Sierra Nevada* (1872). A Yale graduate, he first worked as an assistant geologist to Josiah Whitney. At age twenty-five he was appointed director of the Geological and Geographical Exploration of the Fortieth Parallel Survey, and in 1878 he was named director of the newly formed U.S. Geological Survey. King saw his writing as an experiment in natural history writing. Although he was influenced by the literary style of Ruskin, he was not concerned with producing aesthetic literature. He was more concerned with providing an awareness of American wilderness and his concerns for its future.

King's accounts of his climbs are enticing. He revels in the wild natural beauty of the high mountains of the American West. Of the early American mountain writers, he is possibly the most exciting, as is illustrated in the following passage from *Mountaineering in the Sierra Nevada*:

> The rock was so steep that we descended in a sitting position, clinging with our hands and heels.
>
> I heard Cotter say, "I think I must take off these moccasins and try it barefooted, for I don't believe I can make it." These words were instantly followed by a startled cry, and I looked round to see him slide quickly toward me, struggling and clutching at the smooth granite. As he slid by I made a grab for him with my right hand, catching him by the shirt, and, throwing myself as far in the other direction as I could, seized with my left hand a little pine tuft, which held us. I asked Cotter to edge along a little to the left, where he could get a brace with his feet and relieve me of his weight, which he cautiously did. I then threw a couple of turns with the lasso round the roots of the pine bush, and we were safe, though hardly more than twenty feet from the brink. (pp. 73–74)

There were a number of other significant works produced during the period between 1840 and 1900. Joseph Le Conte's *Journal of Ramblings Through the High Sierras of California* (1875) recounts an 1870 camping trip taken by Le Conte and a group of his students from the University of California. Muir was a member of this party for a short time. This was the first of many such trips on which Le Conte would lead his students during the next thirty-two years. His name is closely associated with Yosemite and the Sierra Nevadas. Another mountain writer of importance is William H. Brewer. Brewer was a field leader of Whitney's First Geological Survey of California (1860–1864). He was a meticulous note-taker, and his journals record his many adventures during the four years he wandered up and down mountains, through valleys, and along the coast of California. Brewer's journals, more than sixty years after he wrote them, were published under the title *Up and Down California in 1860–1864, the Journal of William H. Brewer* (1930). Francis P. Farquhar edited this important volume. Farquhar went on to publish his own *History of the Sierra Nevada* (1965); he is a noted scholar and literary craftsman as well as a great mountaineer.

The turn of the twentieth century saw a great deal of interest in exploration, particularly in Robert Peary's attempts to reach the North Pole. It was also during this time that Dr. Fredrick Cook claimed the first ascent of Mount McKinley, as recorded in his book *To the Top of the Continent: Discovery, Exploration, and Adventure in Sub-Arctic Alaska. The First Ascent of Mount McKinley, 1903–1906* (1908). Although Cook was later proved a fraud, the interest in topping out on high mountains was now in the forefront of exploring. The first few years of the twentieth century saw the American explorer Annie Smith Peck making important climbs in South America, particularly her first ascent of Huascarán. Peck's book *A Search for the Apex of America* was published in 1911. Peck was not the only American with an eye on the high mountains of South America. Hiram Bingham, who discovered Machu Picchu, the lost city of the Incas in 1911, waited almost three years before reporting his find because he considered it secondary to his attempts to reach what he thought was the high point of the Southern Hemisphere, Coropuna.

It was also during the early part of the twentieth century that Americans began taking climbing, simply for the sake of climbing, seriously. The poet Robert Frost questioned the purpose of climbing in "The Mountain":

> "It doesn't seem so much to climb a
>   mountain
> You've worked around the foot of all your
>   life.
> What would I do? Go in my overalls,
> With a big stick, the same as when the
>   cows
> Haven't come down to bars at milking
>   time?
> Or with a shotgun for a stray black bear?
> 'Twouldn't seem real to climb for climbing
>   it."

Regardless of the skepticism of the speaker in Frost's poem about climbing, there was a great

Pete Sinclair

deal of climbing going on in the Tetons and Yosemite, not to mention the northeast. But most of the writing about this climbing was more of the guidebook variety—descriptions of routes, the type of equipment needed for ascent, the amount of time required to make the climb.

One of the most active Teton climbers was Fritiof Fryzell, author of *The Teton Peaks and Their Ascents* (1932), which for many years was the only guide to the Teton Range and was also the first book on technical climbing in the Tetons. Other important figures of the early period are R. L. M. Underhill, Glenn Exum, Paul Petzoldt, and Phil Smith. The Tetons have continued to be home to many of America's most active mountaineers. They have included Willi Unsold (killed on Mount Rainier), Yvon Chouinard (author of *Climbing Ice* [1978]), Mort Hemple, Jake Breitenbach (killed during the 1963 American Everest expedition), Gary Cole, Gary Hemming, Dick Emerson, Dick Pittman,

Tim Bond, and Leigh Ortenburger (author of *A Climber's Guide to the Teton Range* [1965]). Ortenburger, widely accepted as the expert on nearly all aspects of Teton history, died in a fire in 1991, and much of his valuable research and many of his records were destroyed.

Pete Sinclair is another member of the 1950s–1970s group of Teton climbers involved in the ascents that took place in what is now referred to as the "Golden Age of Teton Mountaineering." In his book *We Aspired: The Last Innocent Americans* (1993), Sinclair provides his recollections of climbing in the Tetons and Alaska (including the first ascent of the south face of Denali). His work is an excellent example of mountain writing. He combines the excitement of a young mountaineer with the skill of an experienced literary scholar in producing a work that is both factual and poetic:

I didn't need much, but the world appeared to be constructed to have me use all my time and energy just to survive. Having to struggle to survive was not an unattractive prospect in itself. In the context of climbing mountains or of settling the last frontier in Alaska, surviving was purpose enough. But the Territory of Alaska no longer existed, and living only to climb didn't quiet the voices in my mind. I had some kind of responsibility to other people on the one hand, and on the other, the kind of purposes I had seen in many of my peers at Dartmouth didn't seem to be mine. I remembered one case in particular, that of a classmate who had studied business. Business as a poker game on a larger scale seemed okay to me. I could understand why somebody might want to do that. This classmate had two job opportunities upon graduation. One was an offer to manage a new branch of a small but expanding company; the other was a job as a very junior executive with a large corporation. He took the job with the corporation, not because there were bigger fish to fry, but because it "has a better retirement plan." My consciousness of my mortality didn't work that way. . . . We chose our route according to the angle of the moon, moving in a pool of moonlight as if God held a lantern for us. (pp. 85–86, 94)

The most dangerous part of writing this type of essay is that the author has to be somewhat arbitrary in the use of illustrations and therefore faces the danger of leaving certain important figures out while favoring others. Since the mid-1960s there have been a number of extraordinary American climbers-writers adding to this growing canon. Chris Jones, a transplanted Englishman, contributed *Climbing in North America* (1976), an extremely well-written history. David Brower, former executive director of the Sierra Club and an avid climber, is noted for his efforts in environmental preservation. In the first volume of his autobiography, *For Earth's Sake* (1990), he tells wonderful tales concerning his mountain exploits with the likes of Ansel Adams and the great Sierra climber Norman Clyde. Certainly one of the most active and most literary of the mountaineering wordsmiths is David Roberts. Roberts began his climbing career as a Harvard undergraduate in the 1960s and has published quite a few important books and essays, among them *The Mountain of My Fear* (1968), *Deborah: A Wilderness Narrative* (1970), *Like Water and Like Wind, Great Exploration Hoaxes* (1982), and *Moment of Doubt and Other Mountaineering Writing*.

In Roberts' essay "The Mountain of My Fear," excerpted from his book of the same title, he tells a touching story of a successful expedition to Mount Huntington that is marred by the death of one of his companions during the descent. Roberts' narrative intermeshes with the transcendental qualities of the mountain experience—truth, reality, and beauty—and is then coupled with an almost Hardyesque fatality as it ends in tragedy. Roberts is philosophical as he describes the meaning of his reaching the summit after weeks of effort:

If only this moment could last, I thought, if no longer than we do. But I knew even then we would forget, that someday all I should remember would be the memories themselves. . . . And that someday I might be so old that all that might pierce my senility would be the vague heart-pang of something lost and inexplicably sacred, maybe not even the name Huntington meaning anything to me, nor the names of three friends, but only the precious sweetness leaving its faint taste mingled with the bitter one of dying. And that there were only four of us (four is not many), and that surely within eighty years and maybe within five (for climbing is dangerous) we would all be dead, the last of our deaths closing a legacy not even the mountain itself could forever attest to. (quoted in Bergon, pp. 362–363)

Roberts' thoughts on the summit foreshadow the death of Ed, who has a family and the most to lose in case of an accident. Ed dies while rappeling, the result of a failed carabiner. Roberts, trying to come to grips with Ed's death, reflects on all the events of the day, from the summit to the accident and then the tragic irony: "My recollections had stuck on a remark he had made in the Nose Camp as we rested after the summit. I had told him that it had been the best day I'd ever had climbing. Ed had said, 'Mine too, but I don't know if I'd do the whole thing again'" (p. 369).

Yet even with this sad ending, Roberts is able to remain philosophical and somewhat optimistic: "We had spent forty days alone there, only to come back one man less, it seemed. We had found no answers to life: perhaps only the room in which to look for them" (p. 372). This "room to look" is a recurrent theme in mountain writing, and it seems that the "room" comes only after a great deal of commitment and sacrifice.

Another important contemporary American mountain writer is Jonathan Waterman, one of the most knowledgeable Alaskan mountain scholars. He worked as a guide and climbing ranger on Denali for many years and is the author of *Surviving Danali* (1991). According to Bradford Washburn, quoted on the dust jacket of the book, "*Surviving Denali* should be read, in fact its text almost memorized, by every climber who attempts the ascent." Waterman has three other books to his credit: *High Alaska: Denali, Foraker, and Hunter* (1988); *Cloud Dancers: Portraits of North American Mountaineers* (1993); and *In the Shadow of Denali* (1994).

In the Shadow of Denali does an excellent job of dealing with the technical points of mountaineering, but Waterman does an even better job of telling stories. He guides the reader through a series of personal experiences in an informal and personal way. The book reads more like a conversation in a tent or around the fire after a climb than like an autobiography. In Chapter 5, "Denali in Winter," Waterman describes the suffering that is a big part of climbing big mountains. At this point in the story, suffering from frostbite and the early effects of pulmonary edema, he is trying to keep pace with his two partners:

> I caught up with them at eighteen thousand feet only because they had stopped. We chopped out a platform, then set up the tent, continually looking over our shoulders at the sky.
>
> Now everything had changed. I felt ever conscious of my earlier premonition of death. I performed the only option left: Hidden inside my sleeping bag I assumed a praying position and whispered, "Please, please, please, please give us one more good day." In the grip of forces beyond your control, righteousness and prayer come to agnostic lips as if you had been born bible thumping. Such alchemy is frequently denied afterward, but during the heat of action, it shrinks your skin with all the swiftness of a frigid baptism. Nor could anyone deny that Denali rose higher and whiter than any church on earth. (p. 136)

Pat Ament may well be the one true starving artist in the world of American mountaineering. Having purposely chosen the life of the writer, he depends on his writing to provide for all his expenses and has dedicated himself to furthering the cause of art and literature. He has produced books ranging from his classic *Master of Rock: The Biography of John Gill* (1976) to *Rock Wise* (1978), a philosophical "how-to" book. He has published a total of eighteen books, including four books of essays and six guidebooks, as well as dozens of articles in both climbing and literary magazines. Ament is also the founder and past editor of *Climbing Art*, a magazine centering on the artistic and literary aspects of mountaineering. He is widely recognized as one of the finest literary artists in climbing. Ament has continued to climb at a very high standard, having made hundreds of first ascents in both Colorado and Yosemite. His collection of essays titled *High Endeavors* contains some of the finest mountain prose in print, such as "A Brief Supremacy." In this essay Ament conveys to a reader the child-like excitement and discovery that come from climbing:

> We drove up the canyon, past the main climbing area of Eldorado, to the provocative, hidden crack piercing the south side of a quartzite slab. Dave had a grin on his face instead of the usual austere look. In his mind he was seeing me swing off the crack on his old, white, hopelessly frayed Diamond Rope, about which he was sentimental. Dave scrambled the easy way to the top, doubled the rope down from a piton anchor, returned, and had me tie in. He sat down with the rope around him, half knowing the route would go. A fall meant a sixty-foot swing above the river, and the bottoms dropped out of our stomachs when we thought about it. Instructed to practice the swing in order to get rid of fear of it, I made a move upward, reluctantly, glanced with wide eyes at Rearick's happy face, was overcome with a weak, hysterical sensation, and let go. I was like a ball of gum spinning slowly away from him on a strand of hair. When it was his turn, Dave much preferred climbing up and jumping off to giving the crack a serious attempt. Every kid sooner or later finds a rope to swing on—Tarzan style—across a river. Rearick was in his thirties. (p. 31)

Another of the important contemporary climbers/writers in American mountaineering is Greg Child. Child was born in Australia but has lived in the United States since 1980. His book *Thin Air* (1988), the story of his climbs in the Himalayas, is another excellently crafted work that draws the reader into participation with the text, a participation so vivid it seems the reader is involved in the climb.

Mountaineering and mountain writing rely on historical perspective. Very few stories about climbs or climbers escape a contextual setting. Each climb is compared with other recorded climbs, and each climber tries to establish some sort of contextual bond to other climbers. In reading Chris Bonington's book *Everest the Hard Way* (1976), one is placed on the mountain among such historical figures as Hamish MacInnes. His account of MacInnes being hit by a large spindrift avalanche on Everest's southwest face sends shivers down the reader's spine. Then, to assess the price MacInnes pays—his lungs are burned and he is denied a chance to reach the summit—the reader comes face to face with the high costs of climbing mountains. Several years after reading *Everest the Hard Way*, I was myself caught in a spindrift avalanche during an ice climb. My first response to this experience was to compare it to the MacInnes incident. In Chapter 18, "The Gamble," Child is on Gasherbrum IV. He weighs his chances of surviving a bivouac at high altitude with no provisions by reflecting on the experiences of others:

> We have nothing but the clothes on our backs. No water, food, or stove. I'd read long ago about Hermann Buhl sitting out a night just below the summit of Nanga Parbat. It seemed to me then something only a superhuman could endure or a madman conceive. I'd also heard the separate tales of Nazir Sabir and Jim Wickwire, both of whom had sat out nights near the summit of K2. Nazir had suffered memory loss for months. Jim's bivouac had cost him a piece of lung when fluid had frozen in his chest. And there was Bonatti and Mahdi on K2. Even with an oxygen cylinder, Mahdi had lost his feet. A bivouac here would be harsh, but at the same time I felt our chances were good; the weather was clear, and we still had some strength left. Instinct condoned the idea, the ambition put words in my mouth.
>
> "I'll risk it," I hear myself say. (p. 163)

Historically, women's opportunities in the world of mountaineering have been somewhat limited; but that has started to change. Since the 1970s women have established themselves in the climbing world. There have been all-woman expeditions to the highest and most remote peaks, and women have achieved extremely high standards of rock and ice climbing. As a result, women are now producing some of the very best climbing literature. Although not always well enough recognized, there have in fact always been talented women in the mountaineering world. One only need look at the writings and adventures of Isabella Bird, the first woman to ascend Long's Peak in Colorado (1873); she subsequently rode a bicycle across the Sahara Desert. Her modest account of climbing Long's Peak is found in her book *A Lady's Life in the Rocky Mountains* (1881). One also must consider Annie Smith Peck's efforts in the high mountains of South America. Elizabeth Knowlton, famous for her climbs in South America, accompanied the 1932 German-American expedition to Nanga Parbat as a reporter. This was the first expedition to attempt Nanga Parbat since the ill-fated 1895 British expedition on which Mummery was killed. Her account of the expedition, a classic in the genre, is titled *The Naked Mountain*.

Another important contributor to the literature of mountaineering is Arlene Blum. The author of numerous articles, she is most recognized as the organizer and leader of the 1974 all-woman expedition to Annapurna. Her book, *Annapurna: A Woman's Place* (1980), is an excellent and important contribution to the literature of the mountains. It is both an expedition report that deals with the technical aspects of a major expedition and a personal narrative taking the reader inside the hearts and minds of the expedition members. The honesty of emotion in this book makes it very comparable to Herzog's *Annapurna*. Both are accounts of first ascents on the same mountain, both successful and both tragic. Blum's account of clearing the mountain psychologically is in line with Roberts' *Mountain of My Fear*, where dear friends are left on the mountain and those who have survived are forced to face up to the loss:

> Soon the team was together at Base Camp. Looking up at the remote summit, it was hard to believe that any of us had ever stood there, even harder to comprehend the great loss that accompanied our achievement. But we had gained something more

than the summit. The years of planning and the months of climbing together had changed and strengthened us. We had survived the hardest physical and psychological stresses and found that as a team we could do great things. Each woman had contributed her abilities and effort in full measure, and each was rewarded with the knowledge that her contribution had helped us attain our goal. In addition, we had gained a friendship and warmth that now united us. (Blum, *Annapurna*, p. 236)

The honesty of Blum's writing is echoed in the writing of many women climbers. In 1990 I edited the first anthology of mountaineering essays by women. *Rock and Roses* contains sixteen essays by some of the best climbers in the world, "women bold enough to break the old ideological mode set for them by society and go seeking adventure" (p. 1). This anthology brings together the works of Ruth Dyer Mendenhall and Elizabeth Woolsey, who were heavily involved in the American climbing scene well before climbing was considered appropriate for women. Woolsey talks of hiding bruised legs and scraped hands under opaque stockings and white gloves, and Mendenhall remembers her courtship with John, her future husband, centering on climbing. One cannot help but be moved to tears as Linda Givler writes of going with her friend Diana Jagerski to help in the recovery of the bodies of their husbands, Al Givler and Dusan Jagerski, after their fatal accident in Alaska, holding on to a flicker of hope that their loved ones would somehow still be alive:

Flying into Glacier Bay National Monument and seeing the flags at half mast did not deter our thinking in the least little bit. "It's a holiday," I explained to Diana, "they always put the flag at half mast on holidays." . . . Maybe it was the sight of the person with the black zippered bag triggered something in me; it was then that I realized that he had in there small pieces of skin and bones and hair that used to be those two wonderful, very alive, human beings who should have been there, too. (p. 56)

Another very honest response to the mountains and the difficulties faced by climbers is in the essay in *Rock and Roses* titled "Horizons," by Cherie Bremer-Kamp, author of *Living on the Edge* (1987). In this essay Bremer-Kamp reflects on the death of her husband, Chris Chandler, as well as the loss of most of her fingers and toes after an alpine-style winter ascent of Kanchenjunga. After returning home she faces dealing with the reality of her losses:

Climbing encompasses that concept of grasping the meaning of life through certain crucial experiences: the death and grief of war, accidents, passionate loves, or great catastrophes of earthquakes and volcanic eruptions. The "calamity theory" is that people evolve through conflict and struggle. Having led the adventurous life—survived the battleground, debilitating illness or earthquake that wrenched us into awareness—we could be now free to sit back in what may easily become smug complacency, or on the other hand, lured once more to taste the drug of action, as both opiate and stimulant. (p. 72)

This argument of "going back out" after facing severe difficulty or tragedy, in order to reestablish one's mental and physical well-being, complements the Romantic theories in which mountaineering literature is rooted. In the introduction to my collection of essays titled *On Mountains and Mountaineers*, I argue that the literature of mountaineering is an extension of the "Romantic essay." The careful reading of mountain writing, particularly that dealing with ascent, clearly illustrates that climbers are more than athletes; they are artists, poets, and philosophers. Like Emerson, Wordsworth, and other great thinkers and poets who believe in the divine nature of humans, they reach their full potential through such challenges as those found climbing, not only in the wild backcountry of the remote mountain ranges of the world, but many times on local crags as close to home as Walden Pond was to Thoreau's Concord.

The literature of mountaineering is transcendental. Because language is limiting, each climbing story or essay is inevitably an incomplete record of the climber/writer's sojourn in the ideal world. Yet although it is incomplete, that piece of writing provides the reader with a vicarious account of enlightenment achieved by the climb, a written vision of the climber's art achieved through travels in Earth's wild places, and a record of the physical exhilaration felt by the climber fortunate enough to reach the summit. It matters not if it be the first ascent or the hundredth visit to the top. The experience is the end in itself.

The climber, by providing the record of the climb, acts as a proxy for those who, for various reasons, are unable to go into the wilds. One philosophy of the mountaineer is very clearly presented by the Italian climber Walter Bonatti, who explains the psyche of the climber as being set for high achievement, unwilling to settle for the mediocrity so commonly found among industrialized humans; the climber willingly takes risks, not for anything material but for the uplift of the inner spirit that directs the character of humans in all of their aspects. This is not to say that the climber is superhuman or semidivine, but rather that the climber's philosophical perspective is an explanation and justification for such risks. The climber, according to Bonatti, is rebelling against the morbid effects of a collective industrial/technical society. The actual physical experience helps develop individuals who are more spiritual and ultimately more responsible. The climber is given over to the spiritual, intrinsic betterment that comes from increased personal awareness and self control in all situations.

According to Bonatti, it is the climber's goal to reject a self-indulgent, self-centered society that receives uplift only through gratification of worldly appetites and materialism. The writings of the rebellious therefore become their Romantic declarations for change. Basically, it is a Romantic tendency—this emphasis on individuality, on close contact with nature as a spiritual matter, and on the release and freedom that come from this kind of experience. And all this tends to be put in an elevated language, a kind of inspirational "chant." The literature of mountaineering is made up of elevated ideas that are the result of serious craftsmanship by serious artists and writers.

Selected Bibliography

Pat Ament, *High Endeavors* (La Crescenta, Calif.: Mountain 'n Air Books, 1991); Jeremy Bernstein, *Ascent: Of the Invention of Mountain Climbing and Its Practice* (Lincoln: Univ. of Nebraska Press, 1965); Arlene Blum, *Annapurna: A Woman's Place* (San Francisco: Sierra Club, 1980); Orrin H. Bonney and Lorraine Bonney, *The Grand Controversy* (New York: American Alpine Club Press, 1992); Cherie Bremer-Kamp, "Horizons," in *Rock and Roses*, ed. by Mikel Vause (La Crescenta, Calif.: Mountain 'n Air Books, 1990); Greg Child, *Thin Air: Encounters in the Himalayas* (Salt Lake City: Peregrine Smith, 1988); Plenty Coups, "Vision in the Crazy Mountains," in *The Wilderness Reader*, ed. by Frank Bergon (New York: Mentor, 1980); Robert Frost, "The Mountain," in *The Poetry of Robert Frost*, ed. by Edward Connery Lathem (New York: Holt, Rinehart and Winston, 1969); Linda Givler, "The Other Love," in *Rock and Roses*, ed. by Mikel Vause (La Crescenta, Calif.: Mountain 'n Air Books, 1990); Heinrich Harrer, *The White Spider* (London: Paladin Grafton Books, 1985); Clarence King, *Mountaineering in the Sierra Nevada* (New York: Penguin, 1989); John Long, *Rock Junction* (Evergreen, Colo.: Chockstone Press, 1994).

David Mazel, *Pioneering Ascents: The Origins of Climbing in America, 1642–1873* (Harrisburg, Pa.: Stackpole, 1991); John Muir, *The Mountains of California* (Berkeley, Calif.: Ten Speed Press, 1977); David Roberts, "The Mountain of My Fear," in *The Wilderness Reader*, ed. by Frank Bergon (New York: Mentor, 1980), and "The Ice Man: Lone Voyager from the Copper Age," in *National Geographic* 183 (June 1993); Rob Schultheis, "The Adventurers," in *Outside* (January 1981); Doug Scott, "On the Profundity Trail," in *Mirrors in the Cliffs*, ed. by Jim Perrin (London: Diadem, 1983); Pete Sinclair, *We Aspired: The Last Innocent Americans* (Logan: Utah State Univ. Press, 1993); Showell Styles, *The Mountaineer's Week-End Book* (London: Seeley Service and Co., 1960); Henry David Thoreau, "Ktaadn," in *The Wilderness Reader*, ed. by Frank Bergon (New York: Mentor, 1980), and "Walden" and "Walking," in *The Portable Thoreau*, ed. by Carl Bode (New York: Penguin, 1981); Michael Charles Tobias, "A History of Imagination in Wilderness," in *The Mountain Spirit*, ed. by Michael Charles Tobias and Harold Drasdo (Woodstock, N.Y.: Overlook, 1979); Mikel Vause, *On Mountains and Mountaineers* (La Crescenta, Calif.: Mountain 'n Air Books, 1993), and, as ed., *Rock and Roses* (La Crescenta, Calif.: Mountain 'n Air Books, 1990); Jonathan Waterman, *Surviving Denali* (New York: AAC, 1991), and *In the Shadow of Denali* (New York: Delta Expedition Series, 1994).

MODERN BIRDWATCHING LITERATURE

DEBORAH STROM GIBBONS

Beginnings of Birdwatching Literature

Birdwatching literature is an invention of modern times. Nature writers of the nineteenth century frequently included bird observations as subject matter. Thoreau, for example, made a great deal of that loon on Walden Pond, but typically for his time he turned the loon into a spiritual symbol. The ornithologist Frank Chapman, a founder of the Audubon Society and head of the bird department at the American Museum of Natural History, wrote a handbook for amateur bird students that was a popular forerunner of our modern field guides. He also wrote several charming autobiographical travelogues, but they are mainly descriptions of scientific expeditions to study birds. Writers like Gene Stratton Porter incorporated a love of nature—in particular birds and moths—into her novels for young readers. For her, nature was a vehicle for redemption rather than a protagonist at the center of a drama. A new form of literature centered on bird appreciation was invented as the bird conservation movement, focused increasingly in the Audubon Society. At the turn of the twentieth century, this literature filled the pages of the journals published by local Audubon Societies and in the national society's *Bird-Lore*, precursor of today's *Audubon Magazine*. The Audubon movement was born when a handful of ornithologists and nature lovers noticed that market hunting, recreational gunning, and, most importantly, plume hunting were killing North American birds at an alarming rate. The plumers sold the feathers of wild birds to milliners, who used them to decorate women's hats.

The spectacle of these hats at the close of the nineteenth century is difficult to imagine. Women of all ages and classes routinely wore hats adorned with the feathers of dead wild birds. Entire stuffed birds or amputated wings perched rakishly on forms of straw or felt. American plume hunters supplied European markets as well. Since the most sought-after plumes, the egret's aigrettes, only develop on birds during breeding season, the plumers slaughtered the adults in their rookeries while they incubated eggs and raised young, wiping out the breeding birds and leaving the young to die untended, the eggs to addle in the sun. By 1900 only a few isolated rookeries had escaped the gunners. Entire populations of terns, gulls, herons, and egrets, as well as songbirds like robins and bluebirds, were under continuous and deadly pressure. The survival of North American avian populations was in serious doubt.

The heroic campaign to save North American bird life was waged cleverly and effectively on several fronts. Nature-loving lawmakers introduced bills in state legislatures and in the Congress forbidding trade in plumes. The Audubon Society established wildlife sanctuaries, which were guarded from hunters by wardens who were necessary because the plumers were violent and untrammeled. Two wardens were murdered while patrolling rookeries. Significantly for the development of birdwatching literature, bird conservationists waged a saturation campaign to convince women not to wear feathers. If the market for plumes dried up, they argued, the birds might be left alone. Women were encouraged in the pages of *Bird-Lore* and the many local Audubon societies' newsletters to go outside and observe birds, to learn to love their animated spirits, their vivacious charm.

The Audubon Society started clubs in many communities and on college campuses, especially women's colleges like Mount Holyoke and Vassar. The modern sport of birdwatching was born. Women were discouraged from actual ornithological study, but their keen observations flooded the pages of *Bird-Lore* and local journals. Children joined Audubon school clubs, mostly led by women teachers. A powerful group of women birdwatchers helped to implement this successful effort to reeducate the American public about the value of avian life.

For men, competitive birding was meant to substitute for sport hunting or for the popular hobby of collecting birds for private curio cabinets. Frank Chapman invented the Christmas bird count, still a National Audubon Society annual event, to replace the Christmas bird hunt, a recreational shoot in rural areas that took place after Christmas dinner often, ironically, consisting of roast goose or turkey. Count them, don't kill them; observe them, don't wear them was the constant message delivered in magazines and preached from lecterns by earnest female bird conservationists.

Many of these Audubon club women had grown up in the temperance movement and were politically savvy as well as articulate publicists. Middle-class women had the time and energy to fight for a just cause. Their audience was eager to don galoshes and mackintoshes, grab a pair of binoculars, and take off for social bird walks with other women.

Much of modern birdwatching literature developed out of this journalism. John Burroughs was America's foremost nature writer and an old man when the Audubon movement was born. Frank Chapman occasionally enlisted his pen for *Bird-Lore* but his style was ill-suited to a publicity blitz. Mabel Osgood Wright, novelist and nature writer, was Chapman's first lieutenant in the literary campaign to encourage birdwatching, and her chatty birding columns, which appeared in every issue of *Bird-Lore*, helped spawn written work that began to pour forth from the pens of both men and women birdwatchers.

Wright, born in 1859, was the daughter of a prominent New York City Unitarian minister. Typically, for a woman writer of her day, she carefully kept the details of her personal life from her readers. We know that she was married to an antiquarian bookseller and that she had a child. She lived with her family on a farm in the then almost entirely rural community of Fairfield, Connecticut. From this base she wrote ten rather superficial social novels, founded the Connecticut Audubon Society, served for eleven years as associate editor of *Bird-Lore*, and established a bird sanctuary called Birdcraft on her farm, which is still operated by the Connecticut Audubon Society. In 1895 she produced one of the earliest and most popular guides for birdwatchers, *Birdcraft: A Field Book of Two Hundred Song, Game, and Water Birds*, which was reissued eleven times. Wright was an effective spokeswoman for bird conservation and her writings for children about birds are humorous and educational. Unfortunately, her bird essays for adults are written with a heavy hand and are dependent for their style on the work of John Burroughs. But in her monthly columns for *Bird-Love*, Wright perfected a chatty voice, a charming blend of humor and bird appreciation. This style, which she confined to her columns, had enormous influence.

Birdwatching Literature Through the Mid Twentieth Century

Two other birdwatching writers, Florence Page Jaques and Helen Gere Cruickshank, epitomized the fruits of the Audubon movement. Florence

Page Jaques was married to Francis Lee Jaques, one of the greatest bird artists of the twentieth century and a staff artist, under Chapman, at the American Museum of Natural History, where he painted landscape backgrounds for the remarkable dioramas that still grace the museum. Florence Jaques was born in 1890 and came of age with the Audubon movement. A midwesterner like her husband, she moved to New York City in 1923 to study literature at Columbia University. She married Lee Jaques in 1927, thus beginning a fruitful literary partnership that resulted in several entertaining travelogues about birdwatching, with text by Florence and superb scratchboard illustrations by Lee.

Jaques's writing can easily be undervalued. Her first book, *Canoe Country*, which appeared in 1938, was in fact a literary invention. Jaques chronicled a canoe trip to the Minnesota lake district, which she undertook with her husband shortly after their marriage. Lee was obsessed with ducks and geese. A Minnesotan by birth, he never lost his love of the northern lakes and their avian life and in this regard shared territory with Sigurd Olson, who also drew his inspiration from Minnesota's superbly wild watery woodland. *Canoe Country* stands apart from other birdwatching literature because of its intimate tone. Jaques altered the style of the nature travelogue invented by Henry Thoreau to include her marriage at its center. The love Lee Jaques offered to her through his love of birds serves as the thematic center of *Canoe Country*, and Jaques grants the reader access to her personal life while she travels in search of birds. This fusion of personal revelation with outdoor adventures would have been unthinkable twenty years earlier. Burroughs, Wright, Chapman, and other late Victorians kept their personal lives out of their writings about birds and as a result their feelings are obscure to the reader.

But with Florence Jaques's writing we know right from the start that we are in for some fun. Arranged as a journal, *Canoe Country* begins with a conversation between the author and her husband during which Lee suggests the camping trip that is the subject of the book. Florence humorously demurs and then allows herself to be convinced to go on what proved to be a rugged but uplifting pilgrimage. Lee offers Florence the enticement of sharing something he loves with Florence, his love: " 'I'd like you to see the pines and tamaracks in three feet of snow. You ought to hear the snow screech under the sled runners, and trees crack in the silence, at twenty below zero.' 'I'll go in summer,' I said firmly."

Florence includes mundane details like the groceries they took along, their surprisingly skimpy camping kit, and their reading material, including eighteenth- and nineteenth-century travel accounts of the area and some paperback novels. Florence frequently includes observations made by early explorers, along with her own modern ones. The chronicle of this trip, offered in the first person, is meant to be educational as well as entertaining. It is meant to teach the reader about birds, about the Minnesota wilderness and the importance of preserving it, and, most particularly, it is meant to encourage women and men to go out of doors and experience the liberation that the wilderness can provide, a message she delivers early in her chronicle:

> Before I left New York, I had wondered whether it would not seem a little desolate to sleep on the ground in a tent, and if the night noises would keep me awake and restless. . . .
>
> But now, as I crept between the blankets, I was far too drowsy to realize I was sleeping out of doors for the first time in my life. I went to sleep without a thought for my surroundings.
>
> But this morning, the white mist about us, the exultant laughter of the loons (Lee's favorite bird in this country), made me feel I was really in a different land. . . .
>
> The loons are flying above us, still laughing. I would like to laugh as jubilantly, at all the people who said I wouldn't like a canoe trip! (pp. 19–21)

Canoe Country is a slim volume, almost a picture book, sumptuously illustrated with Lee's drawings, a format that is a complete departure from any earlier birdwatching books. In her spare chronicle Jaques tells of an adventure-filled yet gentle odyssey during which the author's discovery of the wilderness is inextricably linked to the warmth of her husband's love. "It's threatening rain tonight, and Lee is making the tent snug, seeing that the wall canvas is tucked under the floor cloth on every side, and digging a shallow trench around us" (p. 32). Florence Jaques is often funny, particularly when describing her own silly doubts and foibles, weaving an elegant tapestry of natural history lore and personal revelation in the following passage: "An osprey circled over the lake searching for fish. Then he sat in the top of a pine and looked down meditatively into the water. *Le Penseur*. I don't know what he caught, but I caught four pike, a bass, and a water lily as lovely as an ivory carving" (p. 33). Jaques could also be a beguiling stylist. Seemingly without artifice, her writing is gentle and refined. She is particularly adept at landscape description, painting evocative scenes with a few well-chosen words as in the following passage in which she describes a foggy morning in the canoe: "After a time we got the vaguest of shore lines; by then the lake was so thick with rushes that we slid along through them as if we were paddling in a grassy meadow. We found the mouth of the phantom river and went along, surprising a flock of black ducks and two great blue heron" (p. 34).

Florence Jaques went on to write a few more travelogues of her outdoor adventures, all illustrated by her husband. In them she often describes how her husband perfected his visual knowledge of the birds that he was asked to illustrate. Lee went to extraordinary lengths to sketch every species of duck and goose in various flight configurations, trying to learn their characteristic methods of landing on water, taking off from land or water, flocking in formation or grazing on land. His scrupulous honesty had stupendous results for his art, which has no equal among bird art today. Florence Jaques's language retains a remarkable freshness and immediacy for today's reader. Because her travelogues have at their center a loving marriage as well as birds they describe, they are infinitely more alive for us than Burroughs' or Wright's more dispassionate nature worship. Her work,

moreover, ushered in a whole new era of excellence in American birdwatching literature.

Helen Gere Cruickshank was a close friend of the older Florence Jaques. They occupied a similar ecological niche, the nonprofit conservation organizations in New York City in the years before and after World War II. Cruickshank was born in 1907 and graduated with a science degree from Pennsylvania State in 1927. She was teaching high school science in Rye, New York, when she met and married Allan D. Cruickshank in 1937. Allan was a staff educator and photographer for the National Audubon Society. After their marriage Helen became Allan's photographic partner and taught at his side every summer at the Audubon Society camp on Hog Island, in Muscongus Bay off the coast of Maine.

Allan was one of the greatest bird photographers who ever lived and Helen herself became adept with a still camera. Because of her science background, Helen shared her husband's career to a greater degree than Florence Jaques shared Lee's. The Cruickshanks were frequently on the road for the Audubon Society, making films and still photographs of nesting birds to be used by Audubon lecturers. Allan was obsessed with documenting the life cycles of endangered birds, especially the exotic waders that had been nearly extirpated by plumers only a few years earlier. His exacting methods and his endless zeal for adventure led the Cruickshanks into remote habitats rarely visited by anyone but Audubon wardens and the plumers themselves. Out of these exciting and exhausting expeditions came Helen Cruickshank's brilliant books about birds.

Helen Cruickshank's first book, *Bird Islands Down East*, appeared in 1941 and, like all her later volumes, this early effort was illustrated with Allan's magnificent photographs. Her friend Florence Jaques had suggested that she give writing a try, and in many ways Cruickshank's books derive their form directly from Jaques. *Bird Islands Down East* tells of the visits to bird colonies the couple made in Maine, and although competent and amusing, Cruickshank's first effort broke little new ground. After a seven-year silence due to World War II, during which Allan served with the army overseas,

Helen Cruickshank wrote *Flight into Sunshine*, which won the John Burroughs award in 1949. Published on crude postwar paper and with Allan's photographs unfortunately clustered behind the text, the book nonetheless expresses a graceful intelligence and delicate spirituality.

Flight into Sunshine tells the stories of the Cruickshanks' odyssey to study and photograph the exotic birds of Florida. Most of the adventures Cruickshank describes took place before the war, in the years when the fruits of the Audubon movement were just beginning to be harvested. Each rookery they visited represents a miraculous salvation, a thrilling victory for conservationists and bird lovers. This exhilaration enlivens Cruickshank's pages.

The format of the book is elegantly simple; each species studied is the subject of a separate chapter and the photographs themselves serve as partners with the birds as subject. How the photographs came to be made is the narrative armature holding together the two subjects. Cruickshank takes us on a treasure hunt in which the birds and Allan's photographs are the prizes. The rookeries are always almost impossible to reach and Cruickshank spares us none of the gory details. She is neither indefatigable nor endlessly insouciant, unlike her husband, and often dreaded the mucky process of arrival especially since Allan never gave up once his prey was in reach.

In her chapter on the American egret colony at Dildo Key, Cruickshank devotes a full third of the narrative to chronicling the horrible journey out to the rookery. The couple, while rowing through a shallow lagoon to a mangrove island near Cape Sable, became mudbound while still a half-mile from the rookery:

"We will have to wade and push the skiff ahead of us," Allan decided, "I don't want to risk carrying the cameras that distance and we certainly couldn't carry the blind too."

I did not like the idea at all. I pointed to an olive-green stingaree lying just an inch or so beneath the surface and reminded him that whip rays, too, might be around. Moreover, this was ideal habitat for sand sharks. No, I did not want to wade in that muddy, grass-choked water. Allan pointed out that it was a case of getting into the water or giving up. We had no other choice. So with shrinking muscles I stepped into the tepid water after Allan. Our feet sank down several inches in the soft marl mud. The grasses brushed softly but clingingly against our legs. Those horrid, sickly green grasses effectively hid from sight any dangerous creatures lurking in the expanse of water around us.

"Just shuffle along," Allan encouraged me. "And any sharks or rays near you will be scared away."

I nearly climbed right back into the skiff. Just how could I shuffle along when I found it hard work just to pull my feet out of the clutching mud? I thought of all the tales I had read of infections caused by sting and whip rays, of stories fishermen told of toes being mangled and torn by sand sharks. I was not at all happy as the mud sucked and squelched around my feet and the grasses swished around my ankles.

Slowly the distance between us and Dildo grew less. Occasionally we came to strange round areas sunk down like the rounded bottoms of great whale oil kettles. These measured perhaps ten feet in diameter. Some were as much as six feet deep in the center. The grass stopped short at the edge of these circular depressions and the curving sides were smooth and bare. When we came to one of them, we could climb into the skiff, give it a shove and float across. We wished there were more. Unfortunately we could not only float and see the bottom but we could see all the creatures living there. None of the fish appealed to me as pleasant water companions. Once a sand shark actually darted over the basin ahead of us and went into the grasses on the other side where it raised a cloudy trail like a plume of smoke in the water as it stirred the soft mud. Its pasty, whitish, unhealthy-looking presence was not at all welcome. I think it only fair to confess, however, that while I have often been scared in Florida, such fright was almost always merely the result of inexperience rather than real danger. Red bugs, often called chiggers, are the only creatures in Florida that have caused me real discomfort and they are microscopic. But each time we floated across an open basin, I was more reluctant to get back into that warm, cloudy water with its mud bottom and dense growth of soft, clinging grass.

We pushed and rested, pushed and rested, approaching Dildo at a snail's pace. I was glad we had a boat to push because we could sit in it whenever another step was almost impossible. Moreover, the boat was a haven of safety in which I could leap in case danger showed itself.

It grew hotter and hotter. My tired muscles rebelled but were forced on. I looked at Allan. His shirt was dark with perspiration and little rivulets ran down his face. It is always tiring to walk long distances in water but this was particularly difficult for the bottom was so soft and clutched tenaciously at every step. It released its suction only after a real tug and the waving grasses further impeded our movements. The heat and glaring intensity of the sun, magnified by its reflection on the water, made me dizzy. Nor could I find relief by splashing water on myself. The water was too warm to refresh. (pp. 115–117)

This is a pretty great story. The reader learns something about Florida marine ecology but is also held fast to a genuine drama. Not all hunts resulted in success. On Dildo Key the Cruickshanks' work was interrupted by untimely visitors from the mainland who scared off all the birds. But most of their days in the field were halcyon. Cruickshank is entranced with the paradisal quality of Florida's wilderness, with the outdoor life into which these birds of paradise lead her, and with her partnership with Allan.

Cruickshank is more of a scientist than her friend Florence Jaques. She provides the reader with detailed descriptions of the appearance and behavior of each species, yet she never seems didactic. In this passage, she uses her gently instructive style to impart some facts about the white ibis:

The ibises were just beginning to mate and many of them were going through nuptial ceremonies. Often birds would drop from great heights, tipping from side to side like

Helen Cruickshank in the field, sometime during the 1950s

falling leaves. Occasionally, sudden clouds of them would rise from the colony when some impulse seized them. Most of the time they just stood around, often holding twigs in their bills. No attempt at nest-building was made and the sticks were soon dropped. Fights were frequent but no harm ever resulted. (p. 66)

Cruickshank is a master at letting the drama of the birds fill the center of her essays. Yet she includes many of her personal responses to the creatures and their habitats and these revelations keep this book alive for today's reader. The obsessive dedication at the center of this story is a remarkable third protagonist who shares the stage, albeit unwittingly, with the birds and the photographs.

Helen Cruickshank's career spanned several decades. She edited a lovely compendium of Thoreau's prose about birds in 1964 and four years later published her most ambitious book, *A Paradise of Birds*, a travelogue of bird and nature watching in Texas. Although the result of several separate trips to Texas, Cruickshank's lengthy chronicle is seamless and timeless. In this, her finest achievement, she weaves an astonishingly rich tapestry of bird lore, botany, geography, geology, mammology, anthropology, and ecology. Unlike her earlier book about Florida, *A Paradise of Birds* is a hefty octavo richly illustrated with Allan's photographs which accompany each chapter. Allan Cruickshank died in 1974 and Helen retired to Florida, where she continued to photograph and watch birds until her death in 1994.

The format invented by Florence Pages Jaques and perfected by Helen Cruickshank continues to be popular today. Mary B. Durant and Michael Harwood are two contemporary writers whose marital and literary partnership has had felicitous results for birdwatching literature. Harwood, who died in 1989, made a strong reputation for environmental writing with his well-regarded 1973 chronicle of birdwatching called *View from Hawk Mountain*. After his marriage to Durant, a novelist, he joined her in two literary outings, the delightful *A Country Journal*, which narrates their rediscovery of na-Iture when the couple quit their jobs in New York City and moved to Durant's family homestead in western Connecticut. There is much about birds in this classic back-to-nature saga. Their monumental effort, *On the Road with John James Audubon*, was published in 1980 and takes the birding travelogue several steps farther. The couple set out to trace the American voyages of Audubon, following his restless pilgrimage in search of birds. The text consists of journal entries by three writers, Audubon, Durant, and Harwood. This format allowed the authors to include a great deal of contrast between the untamed frontier of Audubon's day and the often heartbreaking urbanization and habitat destruction of the late twentieth century. Audubon, the birds, the American landscape — cultural and physical — natural history, and folklore emerge in tantalizing bites from each journal entry. Weaving the whole together is Durant and Harwood's gentle, sometimes quixotic quest for knowledge, for understanding, for natural beauty, and for each other.

Erma Fisk and Louis Halle

Jaques, Cruickshank, Harwood, and Durant were writers who wove together birding and human adventures into classic natural history travelogues. The journal form was a particularly well-designed vehicle for their literary voyages. Cruickshank avoided the diary format but her chronicles were obviously pieced together, however skillfully, from her travel journals. Erma (Jonnie) Fisk, who died in 1990, was an exceptionally adept practitioner of the birdwatching journal but is distinguished from her predecessors by the extreme degree to which she was willing to expose herself to the reader. Hers is a voice of modern self-exploration, particularly appropriate for older readers in that she wrote her first book when she was over seventy years old. Widowed in her late fifties, Fisk was left with decades of time to fill. Even before her husband's death, she had dabbled in bird banding, but after her bereavement she became a full-time ornithologist, banding and studying nesting behavior in Florida, on Cape Cod (to which she eventually retired), in Arizona for the Nature Conservancy, in Belize, in Trinidad, and wherever else her skills and expertise were needed. Of this amazingly fruitful career she modestly wrote in her first book, "At heart I am a nester, a housewife. My ornithological career budded only after my man's death, when the world of people had been too close, too abrasive for me to reenter" (p. 24). Fisk was responsible for recognizing the plight of the least tern, a species whose nesting habitat was disappearing to beachfront condominiums on the Atlantic coast. Her efforts to save this beautiful bird were heroic.

In 1978 Fisk was sent to census the avian population of a remote cattle ranch in the mountains south of Tucson, Arizona, which had recently been acquired by the Nature Conservancy. She lived largely alone and cut off from communication with the outside world for six months. She was seventy-three years old. From this experience came her first book, published in 1983, a journal of her time spent forty-five hundred feet above the desert floor. She called the book *The Peacocks of Baboquivari*, after the

1135

highest mountain she could see from her cabin porch and after the feral peacocks with whom she shared a front yard.

Fisk is disarmingly self-deprecatory about her skill with birds and the breadth of her ornithological knowledge. Arranged in the now familiar journal, the book is a fascinating mix of personal history, bird lore, and travel adventure. She is a genuine rebel against the strictures of old age, and yet the aging process possesses her consciousness as she slips and slides down rugged canyons and sloshes through teeming streambeds. She writes of how she came to Baboquivari and quotes her letter to the Nature Conservancy seeking out this unlikely job:

> If you know of a cabin in a canyon where an old crone is needed to count hummingbirds and tanagers outside the window I might easily be tempted. I can think of a dozen reasons why not, but then I have never been a reasonable woman. I'm not as young as in 1945 when I first visited Arizona, and I am not a real ornithologist, just a pseudo, with probably only two or three more years to dig out useful data. So this is only a dream . . . (p. 30)

Fisk is an experienced educator and knows the best ways to impart information about birds without using confusing technical language. Here she describes her first good catch in her mist nests:

> I catch my first Arizona bird, a pyrrhuloxia. Pronounce it any way you want. These are regional differences in bird name pronunciation. I say *locksia*, out here they say *locksha*. By either one it is a finch, cousin to the cardinals, in the family of *Fringillidae*, the largest family of North American birds. That's the family that takes in grosbeaks, buntings, and those darned sparrows I don't know one from another. I better learn fast; there are plenty of them on these hills.
>
> Birds don't have teeth. Seed-eating finches crack the tons of weed seeds they eat as a boon to gardeners with the edges of their bills. Cousin cardinal can raise a blood blister even on my tough hands. (pp. 70–71)

She is a wry observer of human foibles, especially her own:

> Setting up a net in this rocky soil with only one pair of hands, knees, and set of teeth is not as easy as the finished product appears to the visitors who think I lead a cushy life. The task involves pick, shovel, sledgehammer, rake, a ball of nylon twine, adrenalin, and cuss words. Unsecured, a pole tips, the net slackens into a patch of nightshade with pretty yellow berries and branched stems. These berries are so evil that even the peacocks don't eat them. (p. 137)

Although she published her first book in her eighth decade, Fisk writes with great texture and color. She is particularly moving about the depression and despair which accompany her through a life without her husband. The beauty of birds and their habitat are palliatives to this human agony, which deepens as Fisk ages. In her second book, *Parrots' Wood* (1985), we find Fisk surveying birds in the rain forest of Belize and she is older, sadder, and less intrepid. She wrestles with these demons and we are rubbed sore:

> I sulked in my tent all morning. . . . I don't know why I am sulking, either, unless my digestion is rebelling against the steady heat and humidity here. . . .
>
> Actually I am surly—I force myself to look at myself, at reality—because it is time I found something new to work at, and I don't know what. Maybe my patron Saint, Anthony, will slip something into my mail. The newcomers have brought us stories of storms, closed highways, and airports they were glad to leave behind. Today I would gladly trade these against the enervating heat, the warnings of deeper mud, more insects where we are to work tomorrow. My age is showing. This upsets my digestion too. (pp. 192–193)

Fisk's originality lies in her willingness to expose her inner self to the reader. This is a disturbing journal, powerfully scented with mortality and fear. The birds emerge as mysterious, inchoate beings whose silence Fisk contrasts with the clamorous raging of her own thoughts. Somewhat more mellow, Fisk awaits death in the last volume of her autobiographical trilogy, *A Cape Cod Journal*, published posthumously in 1990. She is back with her beloved songbirds on the Cape, busy with lectures to promote her books, with banding demonstrations, with family visits and small projects. It is a narrower life than the wilderness of Arizona or Belize, but Fisk enjoys it all with a gentle nod to mortality.

This survey of birdwatching literature was not intentionally focused on women writers. Serendipity played the strongest role in the emergence of three superior female writers and no feminist polemic can be implied by the selection of Jaques, Cruickshank and Fisk to delineate the course of American birdwatching literature in the twentieth century. But this essay closes with a description of Louis Halle's birdwatching essays and his is an undeniably male voice. Every so often a writer is born with a clearer and more resonant voice than others of his generation. Halle is more articulate and more complex, more probing and more disturbing than any other bird writer of the twentieth century.

Born in 1910, Halle has been a railroad executive in Latin America, a diplomat in Washington, D.C., and for most of his maturity an academic, teaching and writing about international relations and political theory in Geneva, Switzerland, where in 1995 he still watches birds and writes about them. His mind is restless, hungry for truth, and alarmingly creative. These qualities dominate his several books on birds which appeared in the last half of the twentieth century. Birds are Halle's hobby and his obsession. His first book about birds appeared in 1938 and won the John Burroughs medal. Called *Birds Against Men*, the book is strongly focused on a theme that Halle returned to in all his later writings about birds: man's relationship to birds, the strangeness and mystery of birds and their incomprehensibility to man.

In this work, Halle muses on man's inability to comprehend the mind of the bird. He tells the stories of several birds he domesticated in his home and his attempts to understand them. Pitting his ability to reason against the existential reality of his bird companions, Halle ruefully admits his own defeat.

Unlike Cruickshank or Fisk, Halle gives us little information about his life—no details of arrivals or departures, no glimpses of wife, children, work. But his books are no less personal for these omissions. Halle's intellect serves as the exclusive protagonist of his books, and it is a mind of rich complexities and imaginings, of disturbing questions and beguiling answers, of rebellions against canon and of acute sensitivity to beauty. The reader finds the landscape of Halle's mind on every page of his books. His belief in the life of the mind is complete, as he declares in *Spring in Washington*, published in 1947 with beautiful illustrations by Lee Jaques: "I take it that the noblest trait of the human mind, which marks the difference between man and beast, is its capacity for contemplation and understanding. . . . Having the power, however, a man must exercise it, or he will lose it and become a sick man because he is not a whole man" (pp. 59–60).

In *Spring in Washington*, Halle ostensibly reports on the arrival of spring in and around the capital, a phenomenon he views daily from the seat of his bicycle or on foot in the city's numerous parks. Loosely organized as a journal, the book is really a series of intellectual ramblings, part sermon, part nature lecture, part reportage. In this regard it closely resembles *Walden*, especially in its central theme, man's alienation from his natural surroundings:

> I should like to have called the attention of the senators on Capitol Hill to these geese overhead, as to the violets that had grown up without a by-your-leave in the parkway. (Geese have before this been a portent to senators.) Here, in a way, the geese above and the lawmakers below, are earthly travelers that pass each other as if they belonged to other dimensions. There is no exchange of signals, no correspondence, no recognition between them—the aboriginal and eternal wilderness on the one hand, on the other the passing carnival of civilization. How many city dwellers, in their somnambulistic preoccupation, ever know that wild geese are

overhead, or violets underfoot in the crack of the pavement? The city is threatened with invasion from every side. (p. 93)

Forty years later, ineluctably, Halle, an octogenarian, returns to the same theme in *The Appreciation of Birds*, published in 1989: "In some cases, the human population of our cities seems not to be aware of what it harbors in its midst.... I think most people in Geneva, if they notice them at all, assume that the wildfowl in the city are domestic fowl of some kind" (p. 39).

Another theme with which Halle is obsessed is Darwin's theory of evolution. His brilliance allows him to rethink many of the implications of Darwin's ideas, and like him, Halle excels at sorting out observations on the behavior and appearance of natural objects. Because Halle is not a scientist in any respect he remains rebelliously independent of methodology, leading him to some surprising and original conclusions. In this passage from *The Appreciation of Birds* he muses about beauty and evolution:

> I now come to a point that scientists are bound to disregard because, while it has a certain self-evidence, it is hardly susceptible of testing or proof—and, indeed, it does not belong to the domain of science at all....
>
> The point is that, where immature and adult plumages differ, the adult plumages are the more beautiful. (p. 79)

Scientists are likely to find this kind of reasoning infuriating, and the reader who seeks pleasure as well as enlightenment from essays on birds will often be left behind, for Halle is often boxing with ghosts unknown to others. The resemblance to Thoreau is strong.

Halle follows an inverse progression as he gets older. He becomes more intense as time goes by rather than less; he never mellows. In *The Appreciation of Birds* he elegantly argues for the remaking of man's relationship to birds in light of massive avian habitat destruction. He points out that several species are already sharing man's spaces and that many others can be induced to find our cities hospitable: "We must hope to limit the macadamization of the world, but, to the extent that we do not, we must hope that birds and mammals of the wild can become adapted to living in such a world" (p. 46).

Halle's mind takes odd twists and turns that can be stimulating or infuriating depending on the reader's willingness to go along on his restless voyage of self-discovery. He often raises questions that disturb, such as why mute swans never notice any other kind of life, including the men who feed them or the gulls that ride on their backs. This observation leads him to ask if men notice other creatures, and so into the domain of anthropology. Halle is particularly fond of seabirds and their unending circumpolar flights. Flight is a phenomenon that grabs his attention incessantly—how do birds fly, what makes them fly endlessly over the ocean waves, what does it sound like to have the wind rushing by if you are a bird in flight? Halle's birdwatching books are closer to the transcendental meditations on nature of Henry Thoreau than any other writer's today, but this is no ersatz Thoreau. Halle includes more actual scientific data and information than his nineteenth-century model and is less dogmatic. His writings are completely bound within his own imagination and intellect but he pays no lip service to the entertainment of his readers nor their edification. His books are an odd sort of personal journal, but they can be classified in no other way. Halle's writings are the inevitable evolutionary development of birdwatching literature for our times. Like other writers Halle uses birdwatching as a springboard for the vital life of the mind by which he defines his humanity and his spirit.

Selected Bibliography

PRIMARY SOURCES

HELEN GERE CRUICKSHANK

Bird Islands Down East (New York: Macmillan, 1941); *Flight into Sunshine* (New York: Macmillan, 1948); *John and William Bartram's America* (New York: Devin Adair, 1957), as ed.; *Thoreau on Birds* (New York: McGraw-Hill, 1964), as ed.; *A Paradise of Birds* (New York: Dodd Mead, 1968).

MODERN BIRDWATCHING LITERATURE

MARY DURANT AND MICHAEL HARWOOD

A Country Journal (New York: Dodd Mead, 1974); *On the Road with John James Audubon* (New York: Dodd Mead, 1980).

ERMA J. FISK

The Peacocks of Baboquivari (New York: Norton, 1983); *Parrots' Wood* (New York: Norton, 1985); *Cape Cod Journal* (New York: Norton, 1990).

LOUIS J. HALLE, JR.

Birds Against Men (New York: Viking, 1938); *Spring in Washington* (New York: William Sloane, 1947), illus. by Lee Jaques; *The Storm Petrel and the Owl of Athena* (Princeton, N.J.: Princeton Univ. Press, 1970); *The Sea and the Ice: A Naturalist in Antarctica* (Boston: Houghton Mifflin, 1973); *The Appreciation of Birds* (Baltimore: Johns Hopkins, 1989).

FLORENCE PAGE JAQUES

The Geese Fly High (Minneapolis: Univ. of Minnesota Press, 1939); *Birds Across the Sky* (New York: Harper, 1942); *Snowshoe County* (Minneapolis: Univ. of Minnesota Press, 1944); *Canadian Spring* (New York: Harper, 1947); *As Far As the Yukon* (New York: Harper, 1951).

SECONDARY SOURCES

Felton Gibbons and Deborah Strom, *Neighbors to the Birds: A History of Bird-watching in America* (New York: Norton, 1988); Joseph Kastner, *A World of Watchers* (New York: Knopf, 1986); Donald Culrose Peattie, *A Gathering of Birds: An Anthology of the Best Ornithological Prose* (New York: Dodd, 1939); Roger Tory Peterson, *The Bird Watcher's Anthology* (New York: Harcourt, 1957); Deborah Strom, ed., *Birdwatching with American Women: A Selection of Nature Writings* (New York: Norton, 1986).

NATURE IN NATIVE AMERICAN LITERATURES

HERTHA D. WONG

IN 1969, for the first time, the Pulitzer Prize for literature was awarded to an American Indian writer. N. Scott Momaday's receipt of the prestigious award for his novel *House Made of Dawn* (1968) initiated what some scholars have called a Native American Renaissance, a period of renewed interest in and publication of American Indian writers. Whereas Vine Deloria, Jr., has noted that fascination with American Indians seems to ebb and flow in twenty-year cycles, interest in literature by Native American writers has been growing consistently since the 1960s. The importance of place, the narrative dimensions of history, the potency of storytelling, the possibility of (re)connection to cultural traditions, the struggle to define Indian identity, the translation of oral literatures into print, the interconnectedness of all forms of life, the sacredness of the earth, and the insistence on the power of language to articulate and influence are all central aspects of contemporary Native American literatures. Because indigenous people have long been written about (particularly by anthropologists) but less often have written for themselves, because educators are increasingly committed to a broadly multicultural curriculum that reflects the diversity of the United States, and because some of those concerned with the challenges of the postmodern age (such as environmental destruction and spiritual skepticism) seek alternative models to those originating in

Western Europe, it seems likely that Native American literatures will continue to grow in appeal.

The association between nature and Native American cultures is well known. A wide array of Indians and non-Indians—from environmentalists to spiritualists, from academics to history buffs—routinely invoke a vaguely defined "love of Mother Earth" and a kinship with all living things as defining features of Native American modes of thought. Even though there is great diversity of culture, language, and geography throughout the hundreds of nations in Native North America, a sense of intimate connection to the land is central to most, and such a geocentric perspective is reflected in Native American literatures. What follows is an attempt to sketch in very broad strokes the inclusive conception of nature shared by many indigenous peoples. More particularly, the focus here is on how place—precise geographic locations and the network of relations enacted within them—is important in American Indian literatures.

Definitions and Terminology

Before considering how the natural world is represented in Native American literatures, it is important to clarify a few terms and ideas used throughout this essay. The term "Native American," for instance, is used interchangeably with "American Indian." Both are used to denote indigenous people, that is, descendants of those culture groups who have lived longest in a particular region. Since many Native Americans refer to themselves simply as "Indians" subverting the European misnomer to make it their own, "Indian" is used occasionally as well. Also, in this discussion, "Native American," "American Indian," or "Indian" refers to persons indigenous to what is now the United States rather than to the Americas generally. Although "indigenous" is associated with an intimate connection to a specific geography, the term applies also to nomadic peoples and to those who have been dispossessed of or removed from their homelands, because people can be linked to a particular place (via tradition, history, memory, or story, for instance) even when physically separated from it.

Native American Perceptions of Nature

The distinction between Western and non-Western notions of nature has often been noted. Although any generalization has limitations and an element of misrepresentation, it is true to say that, in general, European Americans consider themselves separate from, and often superior to, nature, whereas indigenous people see themselves as part of the interconnective web of the natural world. As a consequence of such culture-specific assumptions, European Americans have seen naure as a potent force to be subdued and as a valuable resource to be used, whereas Native Americans have viewed nature as a powerful force to be respected and as a nurturing Mother to be honored. In contrast to the hierarchical Judeo-Christian tradition, Native American traditions emphasize egalitarianism. Native people, says Laguna Pueblo writer and English professor Paula Gunn Allen, "acknowledge the essential harmony of all things and see all things as being of equal value in the scheme of things" (*Studies*, p. 5). "Even a rock has spirit

or being," explains Leslie Marmon Silko, "although we may not understand it" ("Landscape," p. 84). Nature, then, which includes all celestial bodies, animals, plants, rocks, and minerals, is not separate from humans.

Native American cultures and the narratives they generate both arise from and refer to specific geographic sites. Just as European Americans often define themselves in relation to a specific social geography, so Native Americans often define themselves in relation to a precise physical geography that is mapped in a network of social relations (such as kinship and clan relations). A set of binary oppositions (itself a western mode of thought) oversimplifies the issue and might better be replaced by a spectrum of positions that reflect the diversity of perspectives within both groups. Nevertheless, the contrast between European American and Native American perceptions of nature accurately describes some of the basic assumptions that illuminate the dominant behavior of these two sets of cultures.

Indians and Environmentalism

Although pre-Columbian indigenous people in the Americas lived intimately and respectfully with the plant and animal life of their environments (what we call today an ecological awareness), pre-twentieth-century indigenous people would not have considered themselves "environmentalists." First, the term suggests a separation between humans and the rest of the natural world that many Native people would not have acknowledged. Second, the term is specific to a particular historical period and is used most accurately to reflect a twentieth-century philosophical and political awareness of the interrelatedness of all aspects of nature and the simultaneous fear of global destruction. Historians caution against interpreting the past from the point of view of the present (a practice not entirely avoidable; historians, of necessity, interpret and construct the past from the present moment) because such a strategy ignores the political, economic, and social conditions of a previous period. What we interpret today as indigenous environmentalism did not arise from fear of the human destruction of the natural world but rather from a pragmatic understanding of the reciprocity between humans and all living beings (including, for example, kinship with celestial bodies, land, animals, and plants). And such reciprocity was due, at least in part, to how human survival depended on precise knowledge of the properties of plants, the habits of animals, and the configurations of the geography within which they all existed.

Environmentalists have often looked to Native American cultures for models of living in harmony with nature. Sometimes non-Indians have used Indians as images of a people living in an Edenic, pretechnological era; sometimes they have even revised the words of Native speakers to suit their own political agendas. The history of the so-called environmental speech of Chief Seattle (Seeathl), researched by Rudolf Kaiser, is a good example of how Indians have sometimes been reinvented and (re)presented to suit the interests of the dominant society. In this case, Seattle has been presented as a natural ecologist. The ecological speech so popular in the United States and Europe is, in fact, primarily the work of several non-Indians. The fourth version of Seattle's speech, displayed at the 1974 world's fair in Spokane, Washington, is a poetic adaptation of the third. The third version was rewritten substantially in 1970–1971 by scriptwriter Ted Perry. Perry's version, in turn, was inspired by the second version—William Arrowsmith's revision in 1969 of the "original" record of the 1854 speech. But the "original" speech is really a written record of what Dr. Henry A. Smith remembered of Chief Seattle's address several days after having heard it. In short, Perry rewrote Arrowsmith's revision of Smith's remembered reconstruction of Chief Seattle's words. Such an editorial history makes it difficult to know with any certainty precisely what Chief Seattle said. It seems clear, however, that Chief Seattle was reconstructed as an environmental spokesperson in the 1970s.

Similarly, some writers, artists, environmentalists, spiritual seekers, and consumers of popular culture have invented the "Indian" in the preferred images of the dominant society, often transforming complex and diverse Native people into a monolithic cultural commodity whose signs (feathers, beads, and ecological orations, for instance) can be exchanged in a market economy. Many non-Natives seek inspiration and vision from indigenous cultures; as a result there have been discussions of if, when, and how such cultural borrowings are appropriate. Given the devastating effects of colonialism on indigenous people, some Native people fear that, not satisfied with Native land, non-Indians now want Native knowledge. Non-Indians' gleaning what they want (and often only superficially understand) from Indian knowledge and culture, they conclude, amounts to cultural theft, an act that participates in cultural genocide. Others, believing that a paradigm shift is necessary for global survival, choose to share their beliefs, traditions, and narratives with anyone genuinely interested. Momaday, for instance, suggests that the Kiowa "regard of and for the natural world" could be used as a model by all Americans who are afflicted with a "kind of psychic dislocation" ("Man," pp. 162, 166). That this is not a simple matter is reflected in the ever-growing legal battles that are part of an attempt to define intellectual (and cultural) property and the ongoing debates to clarify the ethics of representation.

Some Native Americans scholars and writers have written in response to western nature writers and historians, critiquing, correcting, and refining terminology and, in the process, expanding culture-bound perspectives. Alfonso Ortiz, an anthropology professor and San Juan Tewa Indian, has critiqued the term "frontier," for instance, because "one culture's frontier may be another culture's backwater or backyard" ("Indian/White Relations," p. 3). Similarly, "wilderness," a term dear to seventeenth-century colonists, nineteenth-century historians, and twentieth-century environmentalists and one associated historically with Indians, reflects a colonist's point of view. In the early days, wilderness and Indians were both depicted by Europeans as "wild." But "Only to the white man was nature a wilderness," says Luther Standing Bear in *Land of the Spotted Eagle*

(1993; 1978 ed., p. 26). The wilderness may have been unknown and frightening for new-comers, but it was home to those who lived there. Now, more often than not in popular culture, wilderness and Indians represent a physical and spiritual retreat, respectively, into a pristine past in which humans and nature lived harmoniously and where a promise for the future may be found. Native American critiques of European American environmentalist terminology should not suggest that Native people are unconcerned about environmental issues, but rather that they are acutely aware that both the destruction and the protection of the earth, air, and water have been dominated by European-American self-interest. Ironically, although they have been made the symbols of environmentalism by some non-Natives, Native Americans often find themselves at odds with environmentalists, particularly when indigenous rights to hunt or fish may be at stake.

Although "frontier" and "wilderness" take on entirely new meanings (and histories) when considered from the "other" side of the frontier or from a home situated *within* the "wilderness," less obviously colonizing terminology is being challenged as well. Silko has suggested a reconsideration of the word "landscape," for instance, because "scape" insists on a perceiver who is separate from, outside the world being viewed. Landscape, then, with its linguistic split between human observer/nature observed cannot convey a "human consciousness [that] remains *within* the hills, canyons, cliffs, and the plants, clouds and sky" ("Landscape," p. 84). Similarly, in *Place and Vision*, literary scholar Robert M. Nelson criticizes the term "sense of place" because it "privileges the process of human identification" and, in so doing, diminishes the importance of nature as it is. These terms imply that the natural world has value "only as it enhances and serves our human lives" (p. 8) rather than affirming, as Chickasaw writer Linda Hogan thinks they should, that all parts of the natural world are "invaluable not just to us, but in themselves" ("What," p. 16). Such interrogations of the very categories and perspectives imposed by language make it clear that language is not a neutral medium for, but rather a partisan constructer of, the world—and, more significantly, that the recovery and maintenance of Native languages are important contributions to reenvisioning human relationships with the rest of the natural world.

Brief Overview of Native American Literatures

Three basic categories of Native American literatures have been outlined: (1) oral literatures, including myth, ritual dramas (such as ceremonies, songs, and rituals), narratives (myths, tales, and histories, for instance), and oratory; (2) life histories that were often recorded and translated by a non-Native amanuensis-editor; and (3) written literatures that (leaving aside picture writing) began in the eighteenth century. These three categories suggest the historical span and the formal diversity of Native American literatures.

Oral literatures, with roots in pre-Columbian times, continue to be told and performed today. Like life histories, many were recorded, translated, and edited by European (American) historians, ethnographers, government and military officials, clergy, journalists, and others. Although accounts of indigenous life have been produced since first contact, intensive and systematic recording of oral literatures and personal narratives began in the late nineteenth century and continues, to some degree, in the late twentieth. Many oral narratives, performed and interpreted in their own cultural and historical contexts, were meant to be heard and seen collectively rather than read individually. The written texts, then, are translations or "retranslations" of oral performances.

In fact, the written versions of Native American oral literatures recorded by non-Indians are the result of multiple translations: from speech to print, often from a Native language to English, from performance to page, and from one cultural community to another. The resulting ethnographic document is always a translation, a version of a single (or several) performance(s) from a specific historical moment in a precise place shaped by a singular audience and reconfigured by a (usually) European American amanuensis-editor. Rather than being viewed as static, "authentic" sources, written translations of myths, songs, and stories are better considered recorded versions of continuing but ever-adaptive practices of oral narration.

Some scholars believe that in such collaborative texts any Native American voice is erased or suppressed; only the voice of the editor, usually a member of a colonial power, remains. Others insist that these cross-cultural texts constitute a third space that both distinguishes and connects cultural and literary boundaries, allowing readers to apprehend both the voice of a Native American speaker and the pen of a European American editor. Literary scholars have theorized about such collaborations as the "textual equivalent[s] of the frontier" (Arnold Krupat), "literary boundary cultures" (Hertha Wong), or "contact zones" (Mary Louise Pratt) — all ways to talk about a bicultural site of literary and cultural interaction.

Today both written literatures (such as poetry, fiction, nonfiction, and drama) and oral literatures (such as stories, songs, and spoken life histories) are thriving. Although most Native American writers-performers write or speak in English, others, like Rex Lee, write in Native languages or, like Luci Tapahonso and Ray A. Young Bear, compose bilingual texts. Oral literatures continue to be performed in many Native communities, both reservation and urban.

Nature in Oral Literatures

Of the many forms of oral literature, origin myths reveal most clearly a people's orientation to the land. Among Native North American origin myths, three basic types, each delineating a specific relationship with the natural world, have been outlined. Earth Diver myths, Emergence myths, and Earth Created myths. Many times, these creation myths are followed by migration narratives in which the people locate and/or create their physical and cultural home. In all three myth types, a portion of creation often exists prior to the creation of humans; then humans and animals cocreate or shape the rest of the world. The active engagement in a series of creative acts and the collaborative efforts of human-people and animal-people foster a sense of responsibility and reciprocity, a sense of everything as interrelated and sacred. With their non-human colleagues, humans take responsibility for shaping the earth and interacting respectfully with all living beings.

In Earth Diver myths (common in the Northeast), for instance, a spirit being (often Sky Woman) descends from the sky to a water-covered earth. Animals volunteer to dive deep to the bottom of the water to retrieve some soil upon which Sky Woman may rest. Often after four attempts involving great effort and sacrifice, a tiny morsel of soil is brought up. (In many indigenous cultures, four is a sacred number associated with the four cardinal directions, the four elements, the four ages of human beings, the four seasons, and so on.) In the Northeast, Turtle offers her strong, round back as the support for the soil, the reason earth is often referred to as Turtle Island.

In Emergence myths (common in the Southwest), prehumans move up within the earth, changing form and consciousness as they move from one world to another, until they emerge into this world, the Fifth World for many cultures. The Kiowa are said to have emerged into this world through a hollow log. The Navajo describe a series of emergences. They began in the First World as insectlike Air-Spirit People, then moved successively into the Second World of Swallow People, the Third World of Yellow Grasshopper People, and the Fourth World of People Who Live in Upright Houses. In the Fourth World, First Man and First Woman were created simultaneously from two ears of corn, the people learned agriculture, and they resolved to do "nothing unintelligent" that would create disorder. Finally, they emerged into the Fifth World of Earth-Surface People in which we live today. Emergence can be understood in psychological as well as physical terms; over time, humans transform from one state of being into another until they emerge into their current cultural identity. In some cultures, male spiritual leaders meet in a kiva, a subterranean ceremonial room sometimes described as representing the womb of Mother Earth. Descending into a kiva is a symbolic return to their origins. Each time the participants emerge from the kiva, they reenact the Emergence, thus reminding the gathered community of their connection to the earth and their shared origins.

In addition to Earth Diver and Emergence origin narratives, some creation myths describe how human beings are created from the clay on earth's surface. In one version from the northern Plains, Trickster experiments with constructing humans from clay and baking them. He proceeds by trial and error until he has baked humans in various hues. Similarly, the red pipestone deposits of what is now southwestern Minnesota are sometimes described as the congealed blood of the ancestors—a link to familial and cultural history through a specific site and a particular collection of narratives associated with it.

Finally, some creation cycles combine more than one type of origin narrative. According to Young Bear, before the "Mesquakie or Red Earth People . . . were sculpted from the earth," *Okima*, a "human being who came from the very flesh and blood of Creator's heart" was brought into being to guide the people through creation (p. 95). Like *Okima*, Earthdiver (Muskrat) contributed to the beginnings of the earth. Whether humans emerge from, dive for, or are created from it, Earth is at the center of indigenous self-definition. Thinking of origin myths may help explain why Allen says that for a Native person to say "I am the earth" is not a metaphor.

Native American myths are enacted in ceremonies, and both myth and its ritual reenactment in ceremony articulate an orientation to the natural world. As noted earlier, Native Americans often see themselves in relation to, not separate from, the earth, its creatures, and its cycles; they envision reciprocity (between and among living beings) rather than hierarchy (in which humans have dominion over animal and plant life). But these are ideals, not always reali-

ties; thus, ceremonies are necessary to restore harmony, the natural and desired state. Ceremonies, then, are a means to reconnect to self, community, nature, and the cosmos. The patterns and symbolism of ceremonies are not arbitrary. Rather, they arise from a specific landscape. Throughout the arid Southwest, for instance, water is central to most ceremonies. The parallelisms and variable repetitions of songs may be arranged into desirable meteorological patterns, particularly those that bring rain, thus ensuring crops and the continued well-being of the people.

Even when the ceremony is performed to heal an individual, because one person is intimately interconnected to everything, it is understood that the ceremony will restore balance to the community and the entire natural world as well. For example, in the Night Chant, a nine-day Navajo healing ceremony, the singer calls forth "dark clouds," "abundant showers," male rain, female rain, and the fecund results of rain, such as "abundant vegetation," "abundant pollen," "abundant dew"—all central to survival in a dry land (Bierhorst, p. 295). By the end of the ceremony, described by John Bierhorst, through the power of ritual language and action, *hozho*—*harmony, beauty, order*—has been restored for individual, community, and cosmos. Oral traditions reflect how an intimate relationship with the natural world is central to a Native American sense of identity. Equally important is how oral literatures (ceremonies and narratives) teach each generation how to restore and maintain balance—how, as Abenaki writer and storyteller Joseph Bruchac says in "The Circle Is the Way to See," to "recognize our place as part of the circle of Creation, not above it" (p. 263).

Written Literatures

A sense of place continues to be a fundamental theme in literature written by Native Americans in the twentieth century. On the one hand, the land is associated with home (often homeland) and tradition; on the other hand, land is a reminder of the loss of land, life, and culture under colonialism. More often than not, when protagonists of Native American novels return to their homelands, the homecoming is a means to find their Indian identities, to reconnect to their histories and cultures.

"The story of my people and the story of this place are one single story," a Taos Pueblo man is reported to have said (Ortiz, "Indian/White Relations," p. 11). For Native writers, said Bruchac in a lecture, autobiography and nature writing are basically the same thing, because "you can't tell your story without telling the story of the earth." He cites the example of studies of Native American kindergarten children who drew pictures in which they were depicted as tiny figures in a vast natural setting that included animals and plants. The fact that non-Indian psychologists interpreted the children's drawings as indicative of "low self-esteem" suggests the wide gap between European American and Native American notions of nature. A Native interpretation, according to Bruchac, is that the children show a healthy sense of themselves as part of, not dominant over, the natural world. This may be one reason so many of those who related their life stories to European American amanuenses in the late nineteenth and early twentieth centuries refused to speak of their experiences after removal onto reservations. How could they tell their life stories when they were removed from the land that animated their entire histories and cultures?

According to many Native American writers past and present, the land itself is storied. Hunting stories may have been entertaining, but they also educated listeners about animal migration paths, water holes, and geographic landmarks. As Silko explains in her essay "Landscape, History, and the Pueblo Imagination," such tales mapped a terrain and the relationships upon and within it. These stories literally assisted survival. A landmark noted in the narrative might serve as a map to help the listener to find his or her way home. Perhaps more important, stories of place contain the entire history of a nation. When a narrative about the origin of a specific mountain or rock formation is told, the people are connected to a land, a culture, and a history.

Just as stories educate the people about geography, history, and culture, so a specific geographic site recalls these tales to the people. Ortiz tells a story about the time he took a trip to southwestern Colorado with a fellow Tewa Pueblo Indian who had never been in that part of the country. At a certain point, his friend began to recognize the terrain from the stories he had heard all his life from the elders. He repeated "tale after tale of events in the early life of our people" that had taken place in that area. We "began to realize," says Ortiz, "that we were retracing a portion of the ancient journey of our people." Finally, the distinction between present and past was blurred as the two men thought of their ancestors who had made similar pilgrimages. "He had heretofore never journeyed here," explains Ortiz, "but now it was as if he had come home" (Beck and Walters, *The Sacred*, p. 78; Ortiz, "Look to the Mountaintop," pp. 89–90). Place, animated by story, links past and present, departed ancestors and the living.

Whereas Ortiz links the land to San Juan Pueblo history, Silko relates the land to Laguna Pueblo mythology. She tells the story of a "giant sandstone boulder about a mile north of Old Laguna," a place that always evokes the "story about Kochininako, Yellow Woman, and the Estrucuyo, a monstrous giant who nearly ate her" ("Landscape," p. 89). The Twin Hero Brothers killed the giant, cut his heart out, and threw it as far as possible. The "monster's heart landed there," explains Silko, as if she is pointing it out to us, "where the sandstone boulder rests now" (p. 89). Of course, she admits, the boulder may have excited the people to compose an etiological tale, but that does not account for why *that* particular boulder has a story and many others do not. It is not possible to determine which came first, the story or the land. Finally, Silko concludes that unlike European Americans, for Pueblo people, place (not time) is central to narrative.

Allen's essay "The Autobiography of a Confluence" illustrates both Ortiz's sense of the narrative mappings of the earth and Silko's insistence on the centrality of place in narrative. The land, the people, and the history are linked by spatial networks — particularly highways — and by temporal networks — the stories, not official metanarratives but rather human-interest stories, what some might refer to as gossip, stories that link over time and space. Allen literally maps her past, present, and future, all linked by three central themes: the land, the family, and the road. She describes the Southwest (where she grew up on the Cubero Land Grant, in New Mexico) as the "confluence of cultures." Allen's New Mexico is not simply the tricultural state (Natives, Chicanos, and Anglos), as it has been called in travel brochures, but a mixture of "Pueblo, Navajo and Apache, Chicano, Spanish, Spanish-American, Mexican-American . . . Anglo," including "Lebanese and Lebanese-American, German-Jewish, Italian-Catholic, German-Lutheran, Scotch-Irish-American Presbyterian, half-breed (that is, people raised white-and-Indian), and Irish-Catholic" (Swann and Krupat, *I Tell You Now*, p. 145).

Situating herself at the house in which she grew up, Allen's persona scans the horizon, noting the mountain to the north, the hills to the east, and the paved road to the south. She follows the road, which traces the contours of the land — in this case, along the arroyo — until it parts from the arroyo; then she traces how the arroyo joins the "San Jose River [that] eventually meets the Rio Puerco, which, in its turn, joins the Rio Grande" on its way south to Mexico and the Gulf (p. 146). Returning to the road, she follows it from Albuquerque east through Tijeras Canyon, stopping to point to Texas, Oklahoma, the Plains and the East beyond.

In the next section, Allen sets out on the road again, guiding the reader along "Old Highway 66," noting landmarks:

If you go right on the old highway out of Cubero, from the cattle guard southwest of the village, you will pass King Cafe and Bar, where the wife shot the husband a few years ago and got out on $10,000 bail; next comes Budville, once owned by the infamous Bud, who was shot in a robbery. The main robber-murderer later married Bud's widow. They

were living happily ever after, the last I heard, and it served old Bud right. Or so most people around there believed. (p. 148)

She points out the Dixie Tavern, the Villa (which includes a café, motel, and general store), Bibo's, and many other places. These are not historical or geographical landmarks but places where people gather, just off the highway, for rest and replenishment. What is particularly striking is that these places are inhabited by people and stories, past and present. Allen's detailed descriptions of the land are interspersed with those of the landmarks. Occasionally, she will stop at the top of a hill, for instance, and describe the vista. All are connected, not only by the road but also by the stories of those who lived there in the past and live there in the present.

In this section Allen also turns west, describing key towns and cities — Grants, Milan, Gallup. Then, just as she invokes the monolithic East at the conclusion of the last section, she describes the West represented by California, a place where edges and extremes converge. By the end of the essay, having mapped her physical, cultural, and spiritual geography, Allen describes herself as living in the "confluence" — the space between West and East, the coming together of many cultures. The Road "has many dimensions," she says; "it exists on many planes; and on every plane it leads to the wilderness, the mountain, as on every plane it leads to the city, to the village, and to the place beneath where Iyatiku waits, where the four rivers meet, where I am going, where I am from" (p. 154). Here she provides an image of overlapping communities, notes her ability to reside in or traverse those communities (unlike others, who feel stuck between them), links past and future with the autobiographical present, reconciles opposites, and illustrates that the first-person construction is always plural — connected to people and place.

Although an intimate connection to a particular place is crucial for Native American identity, historical dispossession and removal make it not always possible for Native people to know a sense of place by living in their homelands. In fact, the metanarrative of American history—that Europeans marched across the continent, naming and claiming the land of American Indians as part of the grand scheme of Manifest Destiny—relies on the idea of a conveniently "vanishing" (because "savage") Indian. For those many American Indians who live in urban settings or who have no established homelands to which to return, a memory of place often suffices. Rather than a specific homeland, such writers may, as Rayna Green suggests for Native women writers, present the Road—a place that suggests continually being on the way—as home. That may be why memory is a central theme of contemporary poetry and prose by Native American writers. An identification with the land, then, is based not only on where one resides but also on an orientation to that land or to the memory or history of that place.

William Bevis offers one of the most insightful and comprehensive considerations of the depiction of nature in Native American writing. "Native American nature," he concludes, "is urban." That is to say, the "woods, birds, animals, and humans are all 'downtown,' meaning at the center of action and power, in complex and unpredictable relationships" ("Native American Novels," p. 601). Ultimately, nature is home. It is not surprising, then, that as Bevis notes, in Native American novels the protagonists are all returning home (or at least trying to do so), whereas in European American novels (by men), they are leaving home, lighting out for the territory, in search of new frontiers. In her forthcoming essay, "Recollections," Inés Hernández-Ávila situates this discussion in feminist terms when she explains that for many Native American female writers and activists, the "concern with 'home' involves a concern for homeland." When colonizers displaced indigenous people, they disrupted Native homes so that the "domestic sphere of home" necessarily became the public sphere. Forcible relocations resulted in leaving not only a homeland but also a home language. Hernández-Ávila argues that "this relocation home," both physical and linguistic, can be a "site of contestation and reconciliation."

Many scholars have commented on the optimism of contemporary Native American novels, how writers suggest the potential for reconciliation, the possibility of reconnecting to a past that was violently wrenched from Native control and to indigenous religions and cultures that were suppressed or outlawed. Whereas modern and postmodern novels by European American writers generally emphasize fragmentation, alienation, and emptiness that remain perpetually unresolved, many Native American novels suggest, even if only faintly, the possibility of renewal and reconnection. Usually this transformation occurs through a return to one's homeland and ancestral culture.

Momaday's novel *House Made of Dawn*, patterned in part after the Navajo Night Chant, tells the story of a returning World War II veteran. The novel begins with Abel's return to Walatowa, the ancient name of Jemez Pueblo in New Mexico. In his drunken state, Abel does not recognize his grandfather, one sign of his spiritual blindness. Furthermore, he is inarticulate, lacking a voice to define or even acknowledge his own existence. After killing a man and serving time in prison, Abel returns again to Walatowa, where, after his grandfather's death, he joins the ceremonial runners, thereby hinting at the beginning of his healing, that is, his eventual reintegration into the community. By the end of the novel, he begins to see the land (and himself) more clearly, and he finds at least a faint voice in ceremonial song.

Like *House Made of Dawn*, Silko's novel *Ceremony* (1977) centers on the experiences of a World War II veteran, a mixed-blood Pueblo Indian, who returns to his reservation. Tayo begins the novel as white smoke, invisible and voiceless. His illness is due not only to war fatigue but also to his separation from self, community, and earth, which began before the war. His mixed-blood status and his family's shame at his mother's off-reservation life colored by too much alcohol and too many men are symptomatic of a much more expansive illness: a disconnection of cosmic proportions. Throughout the novel, Tayo's story is connected to Laguna Pueblo myth, and both are connected to the earth. Silko tells a multilayered story on two levels: the mythic in poetry form and the contemporary narrative of Tayo in prose. Just as his illness is reflected in the drought, so Tayo's healing parallels the healing of the earth.

It takes a collective effort to help Tayo. The old-time medicine man, Ku'oosh, is unable to assist him. Although he is trained in traditional healing, he was never prepared to cure a warrior who is not even sure he killed someone. New diseases need new medicine, so Ku'oosh refers Tayo to the mixed-blood Navajo healer Betonie, who lives in a hogan crammed with calendars and phone books in the foothills overlooking Gallup. Betonie begins the ceremony that Tayo, with the help of many—particularly Night Swan and Ts'eh—must complete. Ts'eh, an embodiment of Yellow Woman, or a spirit being from the northern mountains, teaches Tayo about medicinal plants and caring for the earth and other people. Their lovemaking is described in images of earth, as if his union with Ts'eh is a reunion with Mother Earth (from whom the people have become disconnected, as reflected in the drought). Tayo's journey parallels the mythic journey to restore balance to the earth. Personal, community, and cosmic healing are related and impossible to bring about in isolation.

In all his work Momaday invokes the power of place and the memories it inspires. For Momaday, as for Silko, the "events of one's life, take place, *take place*" (*The Names*, p. 142). That is to say, life experiences are rooted in the earth. Although he was born in Oklahoma, he grew up at Jemez Pueblo in New Mexico. "I existed in that landscape, and then my existence was indivisible with it" (*The Names*, p. 142), he explains. In *The Way to Rainy Mountain* (1969), using three narrative modes, Momaday recalls several journeys: mythic, historical, and personal. He begins by recalling the Kiowa emergence myth. Then he retraces the Kiowa migration from the Yellowstone into the southern Plains, to his grandmother Aho's house in what is now Oklahoma.

In addition, Momaday explains the origin of Devils Tower and the Big Dipper. One day, he says, a little boy and his seven sisters were out

Representation by Al Momaday of the Devils Tower and Big Dipper creation story, from *The Way to Rainy Mountain* by N. Scott Momaday

playing. As the boy chased his sisters, he was pretending to be a bear, and as his sisters ran, they pretended to be afraid. But soon the boy metamorphosed into a real bear, and the girls' pretend fear turned to genuine terror. To escape the claws of their brother-turned-bear, the girls jumped onto a tree stump. When the bear-brother got too close, the stump grew tall, elevating the sisters to safety. The brother reached up to grasp his sisters, scoring the tree with his huge claws. The miraculously tall tree stump, its circumference scored all around by the bear's scratches, turned into Devils Tower, and the seven sisters, elevated into the sky, became the seven stars of the Big Dipper. "From that moment, and so long as the legend lives," writes Momaday, "the Kiowa have kinsmen in the night sky" (*Way*, p. 8). The tale links the Kiowa to both terrestrial and celestial relations, just as the emergence and migration narratives do. In the process of retelling these stories, Momaday links himself to the land as well as to Kiowa history and culture.

Momaday continues his emphasis on the shaping influence of the land in his autobiography, *The Names: A Memoir* (1976), published seven years after *The Way to Rainy Mountain*. He describes his visit to Tsoai, better known today as Devils Tower—the monolith dominating the plains of northeastern Wyoming. By contact with that place and the stories it embodies, he is linked to his Kiowa ancestors. As he did in *The Way to Rainy Mountain*, Momaday begins with the Kiowa origin myth. This time, though, in the epilogue he describes his imaginative journey back to his source, stopping along the way at Devils Tower, finally arriving at his destination: the "hollow log there in the thin crust of the ice" (*The Names*, p. 167). If *The Way to Rainy Mountain* is the story of Momaday's journey of return to his grandmother's house, to Oklahoma, and to Kiowa history, here Momaday tells the story of his return to the site of Kiowa origin, a place both geographic and imagined that links the writer to a mythic, historical, and cultural past reimagined in the present. A specific place, like Devils Tower, may initiate personal memories, but, more important, as Charles Woodward notes, such a place embodies and evokes profound cultural memories (*Ancestral Voice*, p. 211).

Louise Erdrich, a Turtle Mountain Ojibwa–German American writer, is best known for her set of novels: *Love Medicine* (1984; enl. ed., 1993), *The Beet Queen* (1986), *Tracks* (1988), and *The Bingo Palace* (1994). In her tetralogy, referred to by some scholars as a family saga reminiscent of William Faulkner, land is most often discussed in terms of its historic loss. Together the novels tell the multivoiced story of several generations of Ojibwa and German American relatives and community members in North Dakota. Through a variety of narrative voices, *Love Medicine* describes the life of several Ojibwa families on and near a North Dakota reservation from 1934 to 1984. In *The Beet Queen*, Erdrich presents a series of parallel stories taking place from 1932 to 1972. The focus

is on German American characters (with a few mixed-blood characters) in the small town of Argus, North Dakota. *Tracks*, narrated by only two voices—Nanapush and Pauline—relates the history of a few Ojibwa family members from the great influenza epidemic of 1912 to the federal government's granting of citizenship to Indians in 1924. In *The Bingo Palace*, Erdrich gathers together all the reservation families in the present by focusing on Lipsha Morrissey, who is related by blood or adoption to many of the characters. In all four books the land is central. All the characters are shaped by the flat, wide-open spaces and the dramatic weather of North Dakota. Erdrich's interlocking stories focus on relations with land, community, and family and on the power of these relations—remembered, reimagined, and narrated—to resist cultural loss. The goal, she says, is to "tell the stories of the contemporary survivors while protecting and celebrating the cores of cultures left in the wake of catastrophe" ("Where I Ought to Be," p. 23).

As in so many other Native American novels, homecomings are important in Erdrich's novels. If, as she has said, "people and place are inseparable," the desire to return to family and community may be strong, even though it is not always possible. *Love Medicine* begins with June Kashpaw, a "long-legged Chippewa woman" (p. 1993 ed., p. 1) who ran away from home, leaving behind the reservation, an abusive husband, and a child. Living in anonymous poverty, disconnected from her past, her family, and herself, June seeks comfort with men, hoping each time that this one "could be different" (p. 3). Finally, after the latest in a series of disappointing white lovers in the "oil boomtown, Williston, North Dakota," a somewhat intoxicated June decides to walk home during an early spring snowstorm. "The snow fell deeper that Easter than it had in forty years," the narrator explains, "but June walked over it like water and came home" (p. 7). In the next section, the reader learns that June never reached home; her death in the snowstorm provides the occasion for all the characters to gather together. Henry, Jr., returns home from the war, then commits suicide. Lipsha, on the other hand, leaves briefly to discover who he is. By the end of the novel, like his mother (June) before him, Lipsha travels across the water to return home. Unlike June, he is successful. Lipsha has a second homecoming in *The Bingo Palace* with far more ambiguous success. Although he does not succeed in business or love, he learns to truly care for another when he bundles an accidentally kidnapped baby into his jacket as he presumably freezes (just as his mother died in the snowstorm long ago, and just as his father followed June's ghost into the blizzard moments before). A few other characters leave and return to the reservation (most notably Albertine, who is going to nursing school in the nearby Twin Cities), suggesting the possibility of moving between the European American and Ojibwa worlds.

But even more pervasive than homecomings are leave-takings, in particular, forced removals and relocations. Forced removal from the land results in the breakdown of family, clan, and community relations. In *Tracks*, Fleur loses her land. After allotment, Native people had to pay taxes on their land. When they were unable to pay owing to lack of money or lack of familiarity with a cash economy or for numerous other reasons, the land was taken from them. The pressures of this arrangement take their toll. Fleur gives her land tax to Nector, who is to deliver the payment, but Nector puts Fleur's money toward his own mother's land instead. "Legally," then, Fleur's land can be confiscated. When she refuses to vacate her land so the lumbermen who purchased the site can cut down the trees, the government arranges for her forced removal. In *The Bingo Palace*, Fleur regains her land by appealing to what the white dispossessor, the Indian agent, knows best: greed. He trades her the deed to her "worthless" deforested land for an expensive, shiny automobile. Fleur retreats to her land to live on the edge of the lake, far from the most populated part of the reservation. But by the end of the novel, it is again one of her own who threatens her land. Lyman Lamartine, reservation entrepreneur, has big plans for a Las Vegas–style bingo palace to be built on the site of Fleur's cabin.

Lulu Lamartine, Lyman's free-spirited mother, who in her senior years turns into an activist for Indian rights, has always been suspicious of how Europeans measure everything. "Numbers, time, inches, feet," Lulu reasons, are "just ploys for cutting nature down to size" (*Love Medicine*, 1993 ed., p. 281). "If we're going to measure land, let's measure right," she concludes. "Every foot and inch you're standing on, even if it's on the top of the highest skyscraper, belongs to the Indians" (pp. 281–282). But such an assessment does not take into consideration the limited economic opportunities for reservation Indians or the results of colonization.

Like Erdrich's *Tracks*, Chickasaw writer Hogan's first novel, *Mean Spirit* (1990), focuses on Indian-white interactions and the theft of Native land. As one way to illustrate Indian-white perspectives, Hogan presents three viewpoints of a dramatic explosion at a local oil refinery. In the first, a white woman called China learns "that earth had a mind of its own," that the "wills and whims of men were empty desires, were nothing pitted up against the desires of earth" (p. 183). Father Dunne hears the "sound of earth speaking," (p. 186) but assumes it is God's voice. Michael Horse, an Indian man, disagrees: that "wasn't the voice of God," he counters, but the "rage of mother earth" (p. 187). While the two European American characters are being transformed by Native perceptions (at least they begin to think of the earth as having a voice), Horse offers an ironic corrective to the priest's analysis.

Not all whites are transformed, like China and the priest, by their interactions with Native people. Based on historical research into the scandalous dealings with the Osage and the Oklahoma land grab, Hogan tells a murderous story of a world in which human life, particularly Indian life, is expendable for the black oil bubbling below the surface of the earth. Even the Hill people, who have tried to live peaceably apart from the white community, have come down from the hills to try to allay the violent changes they sense but do not fully understand. After they make heroic efforts to resist removal from their home and to stay alive, the Graycloud family's home is blown up in the middle of the night. Although the family survives the blast, the fire line moves "like the blood of the wounded earth" and consumes everything. The family disappears into the inferno-lit night with only their memories.

Another dramatic exception to the dominant Native American vision of the possibility of healing through reconnecting to Earth and tradition is Silko's novel *Almanac of the Dead* (1991). It is as if the Destroyers, who in her earlier novel *Ceremony* were subdued (not destroyed), have been unleashed and rage unchecked throughout the world, creating havoc and ruin on a global scale. A network of crime and violence, rather than ceremony and narrative, links the world. The land is still central, but now the focus is on its degradation and loss. Politicians, real estate dealers, developers, miners, and other international criminals divide land into parcels, an image mirrored in the trade in human body parts carried on by a seedy character named Trigg. The dismemberment and consumption of the earth and of humans are clearly linked.

But this is not merely a literary image of postmodern fragmentation and alienation; rather, it is a critique of colonialism's "vampire capitalism." Silko's almost 800-page novel is an exhaustively scathing critique of international colonialism that imposes vampire capitalism, a network of distorted power relations that survives by sucking the lifeblood of the people and the land. This is not a book of doom and despair if there is comfort in a vision of hemispheric revolution. Angelita, the Mayan revolutionary known as La Escapia, believes that "Marx had recited the crimes of slaughter and slavery committed by the European colonials who had been sent by the capitalist slave-masters to secure the raw materials of capitalism—human flesh and blood" (p. 315). By the end of the book, the dispossessed of the world—the homeless, veterans, and indigenous people—move independently toward the southern border of the United States for a final confrontation.

Maps are important throughout *Almanac* precisely in proportion to how they overlay artificial boundaries onto the land. Maps, tools of capitalism, impose the illusion of individual ownership

and national boundaries. Architect Alegria designs a palatial home built on the edge of the diminishing rain forest; Leah Blue has grand plans to build New Venice, a town of green golf courses and flowing canals, in the Arizona desert. Such selfish and arrogant misuse of the land reflects the Destroyer sensibility that land is only one of many resources to be exploited for short-term personal gain.

Specific strengths and truths are within the land itself, Silko is reported to have said, and they one day will be heard. Just as many Native elders have said that the prophecies instruct the people to wait patiently for the colonizers to destroy themselves, so Silko suggests that all things European (not all Europeans) will pass away. By the end of the book, she makes it clear that the earth is really not in danger (although its inhabitants may be). Sterling, a Laguna Pueblo Indian who seems the closest thing to a voice for Silko in the novel, returns to the uranium mines located on the pueblo and muses that "humans had desecrated only themselves with the mine, not the earth. Burned and radioactive, with all humans dead, the earth would still be sacred. Man was too insignificant to desecrate her" (p. 762). This is an opinion she repeats in a collection of personal prose and nature photographs titled *Sacred Water* (1993).

In *Sacred Water*, Silko seems to return to a more positive vision when she uses the hyacinth and datura as metaphors for the purifying capacities of the earth. Hyacinths "digest the worst sorts of wastes and contamination"; they can even "remove lead and cadmium from contaminated water" (p. 72). And the datura can "purify plutonium contamination" (p. 75). The pollutants from uranium mines and underground nuclear test sites and the chemicals and heavy metals from mines pollute the water. "But," concludes Silko, "human beings desecrate only themselves; the Mother Earth is inviolable. Whatever may become of us human beings, the Earth will bloom with hyacinth purple and the white blossoms of the datura" (p. 76). Although this may be considered a positive interpretation of the self-purifying capacities of Mother Earth as larger and more significant than mere polluting humans, it is optimistic only insofar as humans are seen as separate from the natural world.

It would be inappropriate not at least to mention that the inclusive sense of the natural world elicited by most Native American writers challenges another western category, another binary opposition: the natural versus the supernatural. Rather than viewing them as opposites, what the West calls "supernatural" might better be understood as part of the natural, at least for those whose orientation and training prepare them to experience beyond the five senses or beyond what the West refers to as rationality. This may be why the spirit(ual) world is so evident in much Native American literature. Ghosts, transformations (of people into bears, for instance), and visitations are all part of an inclusive sense of the natural world. They are not borrowed literary devices, like magical realism, but a fundamentally different way of perceiving the world.

For the Kiowa writer Momaday, a "deep, ethical regard for the land" is central to Indian identity and necessary for all humans. Such regard demands an expansive vision, considering not only the consequences of human actions seven generations into the future, as the Iroquois recommend, but also the ramifications of our actions throughout the entire (super)natural world. "We Americans need now more than ever before," he insists, "to imagine who and what we are with respect to the earth and sky" ("Man Made of Words," p. 166). To reconceive an "American land ethic," Momaday suggests that each individual observe the natural world with careful regard:

> Once in his life, a man ought to concentrate his mind upon the remembered earth.... He ought to give himself up to a particular landscape in his experience, to look at it from as many angles as he can, to wonder about it, to dwell upon it. He ought to imagine that he touches it with his hands at every season and listens to the sounds that are made upon it. He ought to imagine the creatures there and all the faintest motions of the wind. He ought

to recollect the glare of noon and all the colors of the dawn and dusk. (*The Way to Rainy Mountain*, p. 83)

To concentrate on, to surrender to, to experience with all the senses in every season, to imagine and to remember the earth and their position on it are, for many Native American writers, essential acts of recuperating a connection to history and culture via a relationship with the earth.

Selected Bibliography

PRIMARY SOURCES

John Bierhorst, ed., "The Night Chant," in *Four Masterworks of American Indian Literature* (New York: Farrar, Straus and Giroux, 1974); Joseph Bruchac, "The Circle Is the Way to See," in *Story Earth* (San Francisco: Mercury House, 1993), repr. in *Family of Earth and Sky*, ed. by John Elder and Hertha D. Wong (Boston: Beacon Press, 1994); Louise Erdrich, *Love Medicine* (New York: Holt, Rinehart and Winston, 1984; new and enl. ed., New York: Harper-Perennial, 1993), "Where I Ought to Be: A Writer's Sense of Place," in *New York Times Book Review* (28 July 1985), *The Beet Queen* (New York: Holt, 1986), *Tracks* (New York: Holt, 1988), and *The Bingo Palace* (New York: HarperCollins, 1994); Rayna Green, ed., *That's What She Said: Contemporary Poetry and Fiction by Native American Women* (Bloomington: Indiana Univ. Press, 1984); Linda Hogan, "The Kill Hole," in *Parabola* 13, no. 3 (1988), repr. in *Family of Earth and Sky*, ed. by John Elder and Hertha D. Wong (Boston: Beacon Press, 1994), *Mean Spirit* (New York: Atheneum, 1990), "Walking," in *Parabola* 15, no. 2 (1990), and "What Holds the Water, What Holds the Light," in *Parabola* 15, no. 4 (1990).

D'Arcy McNickle, *The Surrounded* (New York: Dodd, Mead, 1936; Albuquerque: Univ. of New Mexico Press, 1978); N. Scott Momaday, *House Made of Dawn* (New York: Harper & Row, 1968), *The Way to Rainy Mountain* (Albuquerque: Univ. of New Mexico Press, 1969), *The Names: A Memoir* (New York: Harper & Row, 1976), and "The Man Made of Words," in *The Remembered Earth: An Anthology of Contemporary Native American Literature*, ed. by Geary Hobson (Albuquerque: Red Earth Press, 1979), repr. in *Family of Earth and Sky*, ed. by John Elder and Hertha D. Wong (Boston: Beacon Press, 1994); Simon Ortiz, *Woven Stone* (Tucson: Univ. of Arizona Press, 1992); Leslie Marmon Silko, *Ceremony* (New York:

Viking Press, 1977), *Storyteller* (New York: Seaver Books, 1981; New York: Arcade, 1989), "Landscape, History, and the Pueblo Imagination," in *Antaeus*, no. 57 (1986), repr. in *Family of Earth and Sky*, ed. by John Elder and Hertha D. Wong (Boston: Beacon Press, 1994), *Almanac of the Dead* (New York: Simon and Schuster, 1991), and *Sacred Water* (Tucson, Ariz.: Flood Plain Press, 1993); Luther Standing Bear, *Land of the Spotted Eagle* (Boston and New York: Houghton Mifflin, 1933; Lincoln: Univ of Nebraska Press, 1978); Brian Swann and Arnold Krupat, eds., *I Tell You Now: Autobiographical Essays by Native American Writers* (Lincoln: Univ. of Nebraska Press, 1987); James Welch, *Winter in the Blood* (New York: Harper & Row, 1974), and *Fools Crow* (New York: Penguin, 1986); Ray A. Young Bear, *The Invisible Musician* (Duluth, Minn.: Holy Cow! Press, 1990).

ANTHOLOGIES

Paula Gunn Allen, ed., *Spider Woman's Granddaughters: Traditional Tales and Contemporary Writing by Native American Women* (Boston: Beacon Press, 1989); Beth Brant, ed., *A Gathering of Spirit: A Collection by North American Indian Women* (Rockland, Maine: Sinister Wisdom Books, 1984; New York: Firebrand Books, 1988); George W. Cronyn, ed., *American Indian Poetry: The Standard Anthology of Songs and Chants* (New York: Liveright, 1934); Arthur Grove Day, ed., *The Sky Clears: Poetry of the American Indians* (New York: Macmillan, 1951; Lincoln: Univ. of Nebraska Press, 1964, 1971); John Elder and Hertha D. Wong, eds., *Family of Earth and Sky: Indigenous Tales of Nature from Around the World* (Boston: Beacon Press, 1994); Andrea Lerner, ed., *Dancing on the Rim of the World: An Anthology of Northwest Native American Writing* (Tucson: Sun Tracks/Univ. of Arizona Press, 1990); Craig Lesley, ed., *Talking Leaves: Contemporary Native American Short Stories* (New York: Laurel, 1991); Duane Niatum, ed., *Carriers of the Dream Wheel: Contemporary Native American Poetry* (New York: Harper & Row, 1975), and *Harper's Anthology of 20th-Century Native American Poetry* (San Francisco: HarperSanFrancisco, 1988; Bernd C. Peyer, ed., *The Singing Spirit: Early Short Stories by North American Indians* (Tucson: Univ. of Arizona Press, 1989); Kenneth Rosen, ed., *The Man to Send Rain Clouds: Contemporary Stories by American Indians* (New York: Random House, 1975); Frederick W. Turner III, ed., *The Portable North American Indian Reader* (New York: Viking/Penguin, 1973); Alan R. Velie, ed., *American Indian Literature: An Anthology* (Norman: Univ. of Oklahoma Press, 1979; rev. ed., 1991), and *The Lightening Within: An Anthology of Contemporary American Indian Fiction* (Lincoln: Univ. of Nebraska Press, 1991).

SECONDARY SOURCES

Paula Gunn Allen, *The Sacred Hoop: Recovering the Feminine in American Indian Traditions* (Boston: Beacon Press, 1986), and, as ed., *Studies in American Indian Literature: Critical Essays and Course Designs* (New York: Modern Language Association, 1983); Gretchen M. Bataille and Kathleen Mullen Sands, *American Indian Women: Telling Their Lives* (Lincoln: Univ. of Nebraska Press, 1984); Peggy V. Beck and Anna L. Walters, *The Sacred: Ways of Knowledge, Sources of Life* (Tsaile, Ariz.: Navajo Community College, 1977); William Bevis, "Native American Novels: Homing In," in *Recovering the Word*, ed. by Brian Swann and Arnold Krupat (Berkeley: Univ. of California Press, 1987); Joseph Bruchac, ed., *Survival This Way: Interviews with American Indian Poets* (Tucson: Univ. of Arizona Press, 1987); H. David Brumble III, *American Indian Autobiography* (Berkeley: Univ. of California Press, 1988); Abraham Chapman, ed., *Literature of the American Indians: Views and Interpretations* (New York: New American Library, 1975); Laura Coltelli, ed., *Winged Words: American Indian Writers Speak* (Lincoln: Univ. of Nebraska Press, 1990); Inés Hernández-Ávila, "Relocations," in *American Indian Quarterly* 19 (fall 1995); Dell Hymes, *"In Vain I Tried to Tell You": Essays in Native American Ethnopoetics* (Philadelphia: Univ. of Pennsylvania Press, 1981); Rudolf Kaiser, "Chief Seattle's Speech(es): American Origins and European Reception," in *Recovering the Word*, ed. by Brian Swann and Arnold Krupat (Berkeley: Univ. of California Press, 1987); Karl Kroeber, ed., *Traditional Literatures of the American Indian* (Lincoln: Univ. of Nebraska Press, 1981); Arnold Krupat, *For Those Who Come After: A Study of Native American Autobiography* (Berkeley: Univ. of California Press, 1985), and, as ed., *New Voices in Native American Literary Criticism* (Washington, D.C.: Smithsonian Institution, 1993).

Kenneth Lincoln, *Native American Renaissance* (Berkeley: Univ. of California Press, 1983); Lauren Muller, "Map Making as Speculation in *Almanac of the Dead*: Mapping the News" (unpub., 1994); Robert M. Nelson, *Place and Vision: The Function of Landscape in Native American Fiction* (New York: Lang, 1993); Alfonso Ortiz, "Look to the Mountaintop," in *Essays on Reflection*, ed. by E. Graham Ward (Boston: Houghton Mifflin, 1973), and "Indian/White Relations: A View from the Other Side of the 'Frontier,'" in *Indians in American History: An Introduction*, ed. by Frederick E. Hoxie (Arlington Heights, Ill.: Harlan Davidson, 1988); Louis Owens, *Other Destinations: Understanding the American Indian Novel* (Norman: Univ. of Oklahoma Press, 1992); Mary Louise Pratt, *Imperial Eyes, Travel Writing and Transculturation* (London: Routledge, 1992); John Lloyd Purdy, *Word*

Ways: The Novels of D'Arcy McNickle (Tucson: Univ. of Arizona Press, 1990); Jarold Ramsey, *Reading the Fire: Essays in the Traditional Indian Literature of the Far West* (Lincoln: Univ. of Nebraska Press, 1983), and, as ed., *Coyote Was Going There: Indian Literature of the Oregon Country* (Seattle: Univ. of Washington Press, 1977); A. LaVonne Brown Ruoff, *American Indian Literatures: An Introduction, Bibliographic Review, and Selected Bibliography* (New York: Modern Language Association, 1990); Greg Sarris, *Keeping Slug Woman Alive: A Holistic Approach to American Indian Texts* (Berkeley: Univ. of California Press, 1993); Brian Swann, ed., *Smoothing the Ground: Essays on Native American Oral Literature* (Berkeley: Univ. of California Press, 1983); Brian Swann and Arnold Krupat, eds., *Recovering the Word: Essays on Native American Literature* (Berkeley: Univ. of California Press, 1987); Gerald Vizenor, ed., *Narrative Chance: Postmodern Discourse on Native American Indian Literatures* (Albuquerque: Univ. of New Mexico Press, 1989); Andrew O. Wiget, *Native American Literature* (Boston: Twayne, 1985), and, as ed., *Critical Essays on Native American Literature* (Boston: G. K. Hall, 1985); Hertha D. Wong, *Sending My Heart Back Across the Years: Tradition and Innovation in Native American Autobiography* (New York: Oxford Univ. Press, 1992); Charles L. Woodard, ed., *Ancestral Voice: Conversations with N. Scott Momaday* (Lincoln: Univ. of Nebraska Press, 1989).

New Voices in
American Nature Writing

LORRAINE ANDERSON

BROWSING IN THE nature section of any well-stocked bookstore or library today reveals an astonishing array of new authors and titles. Indeed, the number of new books on nature seems to be growing in direct proportion to the urgency of the environmental crisis. When the Worldwatch Institute announced in 1994 that the planet had reached the limits of its biological carrying capacity, humans were, as never before, putting pen to paper to celebrate connections with plants and animals, to muse on the farmer's relationship to the land, to report travels to distant frontiers where wilderness can still be found, to lament the loss of places and species dear to them, to ponder the cultural and philosophical and economic roots of the worsening crisis, and to praise some little corner of the earth where daily life still maintains contact with what is good, wild, and healthy.

The basic message in this flood of books is that in the closing decade of the twentieth century we are—all of us, not just the hermits and the mystics—in the throes of working out a new relationship with nature. How well we succeed will determine the fate not only of our own species but of countless others as well. Nature writers are on the front lines of this endeavor, addressing the perennial question "How, then, shall we live?" in light of new evidence from the frontiers of science.

Their task is not without its paradoxes. As John Daniel writes in *The Trail Home* (1992), "Because I write these words on the stuff of trees...because dead trees carry John Muir's thoughts across a hundred years to my eyes" (p. 84), he cannot discount the need to cut trees to fill human requirements. Recognizing their own complicity in the knot they seek to untangle creates a certain discomfort even if it lends psychological complexity and interest to the work of nature writers. Another paradox of the profession is that the more distressing the news from the ecological front becomes, the less people want to read about it. Whereas works of a celebratory sort may hope to attract a reasonable number of readers, only the most committed environmentalists seem open to reading critiques of the shopping mall culture.

All this adds a certain pessimistic undercurrent to much new writing about nature. Still, writing a book is an expression of hope, and the fact that so many talented new authors are writing about nature adds hope to hope. Four of the most promising new voices belong to Bill McKibben, Sharman Apt Russell, John Daniel, and Susan Zwinger, who give some idea of the vitality and diversity of new nature writing.

In this age of discontinuities, it is comforting to contemplate the continuities in the lineage of nature writing represented by these authors. All four cite classics that have inspired them and continue to inform their lives. McKibben is a disciple of Edward Abbey and Wendell Berry; Russell's reading of Aldo Leopold marked a turning point in her life; Daniel was inspired and supported by Wallace Stegner and Wendell Berry; Zwinger admires Rachel Carson and carried Muir's work with her on a trip to Alaska. With their roots firmly in tradition, then, these writers communicate a sense that the hour is late and the need for change is pressing.

Life in a Postnatural World: Bill McKibben

The 1980s were a pivotal time in our understanding of nature's limits. In 1985 British researchers in Antarctica reported a huge hole in the ozone layer above the South Pole. In 1987 an international team of scientists established beyond the shadow of a doubt that the ozone loss was caused by man-made chemicals: the chlorofluorocarbons. Between 1983 and 1988, a dramatic decline in the health of West German forests was noted by researchers, a decline almost surely caused by acid rain. In June 1988 a U.S. Senate committee heard testimony from scientists that they could discern a global warming trend due to a buildup in the atmosphere of greenhouse gases—gases produced largely by human activity. That their testimony came in the midst of a drought in America's grain belt and a heat wave in the urban East lent credibility to what they said and viscerally predisposed the senators and the public to accept their findings.

The hot summer of 1988 also helped crystallize the thinking of twenty-seven-year-old McKibben, who for some time had been traveling the country talking to conservationists and pondering the environmental decline that had accompanied his coming of age. Part of the first American generation to have more limited material prospects than their parents, he understood that the bill from the Industrial Revolution was at long last coming due; he also understood

with the clear vision of youth the "inertia of affluence" that keeps American culture mired in its environmentally destructive ways. So he decided to write a wake-up call. His first book, *The End of Nature* (1989), so dramatically captured the environmental anxieties of the time that it was read and reviewed more widely than any other nature book since Carson's *Silent Spring* (1962). Not one to shy away from large themes, McKibben took on in his second book, *The Age of Missing Information* (1992), the most ubiquitous medium of our age—television—and traced its complicity in the environmental crisis.

The End of Nature is a clear exposition of the global atmospheric changes humankind has wrought, an examination of the possible consequences and ways of coping, and a plea to change our mode of thinking about ourselves and nature in response. In it, McKibben proclaims that nature is at an end and we now live in a "postnatural world." He hastens to explain that by the "end of nature" he doesn't mean the end of the world. He means the end of a "certain set of human ideas about the world and our place in it," and in particular "our sense of nature as eternal and separate" (p. 8). He suggests that we have crossed a threshold as important as that identified by Frederick Jackson Turner when he announced to the American Historical Association in 1893 that the frontier was closed. Both ideas have "faith-shattering effects," says McKibben, who is fond of the Book of Job for its defense of "nature free from the hand of man."

He is by no means the first American nature writer to have been haunted by the vision of a world in which the last shred of wild nature has come under human control. Henry David Thoreau, for instance, asked in his essay "Walking," "What would become of us, if we walked only in a garden or a mall?" Nor is McKibben the first nature writer to have sounded an alarm about the path toward ecological ruin taken by industrial society and to have called for a change in our ways of life and thought. A spate of writers did so around the first Earth Day in 1970. Earlier, there was *Silent Spring*; even earlier, William Vogt's *Road to Survival* and Fairfield Osborn's *Our Plundered Planet*, both published in 1948, pointed to ecological degradation around the globe and pleaded for a reasoned response. George Perkins Marsh foreshadowed all of these writings with his *Man and Nature* (1864).

But these previous writers conveyed the message that although damage to soil, water, forests, and wildlife had been done, with a change of course it could be repaired. McKibben, writing about damage to the atmosphere, likely to be the major environmental issue of the twenty-first century, is perhaps the first nature writer to proclaim that the hour is already too late, the damage is irreparable, the greenhouse effect has been set into motion, and there is no turning back. To prevent the accelerated climatic changes in store for us, he notes, "we would have had to clean up our collective act many decades ago" (p. 45)—presumably when Vogt was warning that "by excessive breeding and abuse of the land mankind has backed itself into an ecological trap" and Osborn was proclaiming that "the time for defiance is at an end."

Aimed at a general readership, *The End of Nature* reached a very large audience with its alarming message. Portions of it were serialized in the *New Yorker*, in the tradition of the earlier tocsins *Silent Spring* and Jonathan Schell's *Fate of the Earth* (1982). It was reviewed in such sober publications as the *Wall Street Journal*, the *Wilson Quarterly*, and *Nature* as well as in the popular press and has been translated into seventeen languages. Its popular appeal owes as much to McKibben's style as to the timing of his titillatingly ominous prophecy. His smooth journalistic prose presents arcane scientific findings in readily understandable terms and doesn't burden readers with scholarly details (there is an index but neither bibliography nor notes). The book unfolds easily and at times becomes downright chatty, as when McKibben describes his own lifestyle and jaunts into the woods around his home in the Adirondacks. The bad news is peppered with ironic humor: for instance, he summarizes scientists' findings about ozone de-

pletion as the "vision of a nation underarm-deodorizing its way to total destruction, expiring not with a bang but with a floral hiss" (p. 41).

The End of Nature makes its argument in two parts. Part I, "The Present," contains two chapters. "A New Atmosphere" presents the scientific evidence that we have substantially altered the earth's atmosphere, tracing the idea of a greenhouse effect back to the eighteenth-century scientist Jean-Baptiste Joseph Fourier and forward through the various computer models projecting carbon dioxide levels and climatic changes, also mentioning the research on ozone depletion and acid rain. The second chapter, "The End of Nature," laments the loss of a wild nature beyond the reach of our self-centered tinkering and argues that we have demolished the idea of nature. McKibben summarizes his argument thus: "We have changed the atmosphere, and thus we are changing the weather. By changing the weather, we make every spot on earth man-made and artificial. We have deprived nature of its independence, and that is fatal to its meaning. Nature's independence *is* its meaning; without it there is nothing but us" (p. 58). This seems to be essentially an extension of the complaint made by E. B. White, another *New Yorker* writer, in his essay "Sootfall and Fallout," referred to by McKibben in this chapter.

Part II, "The Near Future," starts with "A Promise Broken," which points out that nature's promise—that change will occur slowly enough for us to adapt—has expired, and we are in for a future of increasingly rapid and disorienting change. The chapter imagines various scenarios, from a rise in global sea level to disruptions of agriculture and impacts on human health. "The Defiant Reflex" explores how we might ameliorate or adapt to the effects of global warming. McKibben suggests that defiance will be our reflex: rather than giving up our comfortable, fossil-fueled lifestyles, we will search for new ways to continue dominating nature. The most promising new way, he writes, is biotechnology, which to him represents the "second end of nature." "A Path of More Resistance" describes the other road McKibben sees open to us: one of humility rather than defiance. In this chapter he discusses deep ecology, imagines a future in which we curtail our use of fossil fuels and trim our material desires, and declares his own intention to live a life of voluntary simplicity.

McKibben is at his best when translating science into language and concepts the average American can understand. He helps readers imagine the reality of atmospheric change thus: "If you'd climbed some remote mountain in 1960 and sealed up a bottle of air at its peak, and did the same thing this year, the two samples would be substantially different. Their basic chemistry would have changed" (p. 18). He locates the responsibility for this state of affairs as follows: "We have done this ourselves, by driving our cars, building our factories, cutting down our forests, turning on our air conditioners" (p. 45). Global warming becomes much less abstract an idea when we read that "summer will mean something new in Omaha if the temperature is above 95 degrees fifty days instead of the current thirteen" (p. 127). McKibben is also good at interpreting and bringing to bear the words of a host of important nature writers, from William Bartram to Mary Austin to Abbey.

What McKibben does less well, some of his reviewers point out, is to argue on philosophical themes. Charles E. Little, writing in *Wilderness* magazine, found McKibben's basic argument less than convincing: "Obviously, no species can 'kill' nature—the idea is absurd, for it is nature, not a species, that does the killing" (p. 56); he also found the book to be "concerned not so much with the facts of the case, as with [McKibben's] personal complaints about them" (p. 56). Peter Wild groused in *Sierra* magazine, "If the future is as hopeless as the author paints it, it's a little puzzling that McKibben would waste his time writing the book" (p. 145). Michael Grubb, reviewing the book in *Nature* magazine, accused McKibben of setting up a biotechnology straw man and refusing to talk about trade-offs. On balance, though, reviewers took the book seriously and found its argument reasonable.

Its main argument aside, *The End of Nature* is interesting as a chronicle of the conversion to

deep ecology of a "child of the suburbs" with "only a tenuous understanding of the natural world" (p. 69). William Ernest McKibben was born on 8 December 1960 in Palo Alto, California, the first of two sons of Gordon C. and Margaret Hayes McKibben. His father is a journalist whose career has encompassed stints at the *Wall Street Journal, Business Week*, and the *Boston Globe*; his mother was also a journalist at *Business Week* before retiring to family life. If journalism runs in the family, so does love of nature: McKibben's father grew up in the Pacific Northwest and imparted his love of mountains and woods to the boys. The family moved to Altadena, California, when McKibben was very small and thence to Toronto, where he spent his school years through fifth grade. The family then moved to Lexington, Massachusetts; McKibben graduated from Harvard University with a B.A. in government in 1982.

Hired as a staff writer for the *New Yorker* that year, McKibben wrote hundreds of pieces for "Talk of the Town" and also served as an editor until 1987, when he became a freelance writer. While he was at the *New Yorker*, he was assigned to edit an article on homelessness by a former Rhodes scholar named Sue Halpern; they married in 1988 and moved to the Adirondacks, a move chronicled in Halpern's book *Migration to Solitude* (1992). In 1993 their daughter, Sophie, was born. McKibben serves as a volunteer member of the Garnet Lake Fire Department and a lay leader and Sunday school director for the Johnsburg United Methodist Church. He writes articles on nature for such national publications as *Rolling Stone*, the *New York Review of Books*, and *Audubon*.

McKibben concedes in his second book, *The Age of Missing Information*, that he grew up watching a lot of television. His move to the Adirondacks, where television reception is poor to nonexistent, made it possible for him to gain enough distance from the medium to think critically about it. In particular, he began to wonder why, in this so-called Age of Information in which television is the chief way that most people tap into the larger world, our behavior is so obviously out of step with the urgent messages being sent by the biosphere and such books as *The End of Nature*. Could it be that the information we're getting from television isn't the information we really need? To find out, McKibben undertook the heroic task of comparing the information obtained by watching all of the programming shown on the ninety-three stations of the Fairfax, Virginia, cable system (the largest in the country at that time) during one twenty-four-hour period with that gleaned from one twenty-four-hour period spent camping on a mountaintop by a small pond a mile from his house. His perhaps predictable conclusion is that the mountaintop offers all sorts of information unavailable on the tube, information we need to live sustainable, fully human, and truly satisfying lives.

For McKibben, one of the biggest problems with television is that the lives we see modeled there are lives from the 1950s, 1960s, 1970s, and 1980s, when America was on an unprecedented resource binge. These lives seem normal to us but in fact are utterly abnormal. Another problem is that television news cannot capture the worst disasters, such as environmental decay and poverty, because they move too slowly. "You can't dash off in a helicopter to track down global warming—you need to sit calmly in a chair and think," he points out (p. 157). Even nature shows get across less information about living systems than a person could glean by taking a long, observant hike. Television also dishes out the misinformation that economic growth is an unalloyed good, that buying consumer products is the way to happiness, and that humans are at the center of the universe, among other messages identified by McKibben. As he gives an hour-by-hour account of what was on television on 3 May 1990, the reader is struck by how trivial it all seems.

By contrast, the "one great logoless channel" offers information about how much is enough (which McKibben calls the "most important question of the late twentieth century"), what sensual pleasure and comfort are, what God is, how living systems function, what an appropriate pace of life might be, what beauty is, the inevitability of death, and our insignificance in the whole scheme of things. It offers, says McKibben, the information we need in order to understand our situation so deeply and thoroughly that we begin to question the way we live, something that the relentless flood of television information seems unable to bring about. But, McKibben warns, information from the world of nature is growing fainter as species are lost and ecosystems altered. At the close of *The Age of Missing Information*, as in the final chapter of *The End of Nature*, he urges a change. He points out that with so many tools available to us, "this society could pick and choose those things that would create a life both sustainable and rich" (p. 244).

Both sustainable *and* rich—here at last we get a glimpse of McKibben's driving philosophy: that environmental sanity and personal satisfaction lie in the same direction. His third book, *The Comforting Whirlwind: God, Job, and the Scale of Creation* (1994), urges this philosophy in the context of an environmentalist interpretation of the Book of Job. Aimed at a Christian audience, this brief volume incorporates material from *The End of Nature* and *The Age of Missing Information* while challenging the religious orthodoxy that places humans at the center of creation. McKibben contends that environmental destruction, if unchecked, will lead to a "convulsive crisis of faith"; he poses the question, "When you live in a shopping mall where everything bears a human imprint, who do you worship?" (p. 83). Still, he believes that the church, because of its professed values, is the only institution left that can mount a challenge to our consumer culture and inspire deep change, by proclaiming "the real joy of God and creation" (p. 86).

McKibben's fourth book, *Hope, Human and Wild* (1995), documents examples from Brazil, India, and the United States of places that give him hope for an environmental recovery. His vision of life in a postnatural world, then, is not unremittingly grim. His work seems to testify that in such a world, finding reason to hope may be the most useful skill of all.

New Stories for a New West: Sharman Apt Russell

Sharman Apt Russell moved to the Mimbres Valley of southwestern New Mexico with her new husband, Peter, in 1981. The two had met during graduate school in Missoula, Montana, and were determined to create a self-reliant life close to the land. They wanted to grow all their own food; build their own house from adobe bricks made by their own hands; have chickens and goats, a composting privy, and home births for their children. As youthful dreams gave way to the lessons of experience, their original vision altered to take into account their own natures and the practicalities of earning money and parenting children. Sharman got a job teaching writing at Western New Mexico University in Silver City, and Peter tried teaching high school and then worked as a freelance photographer and wilderness outfitter, later as a city planner and conservation lobbyist. As the couple's field went to weeds, books grew instead of vegetables. In *Songs of the Fluteplayer* (1991) and *Kill the Cowboy* (1993), Russell writes with the flair of a storyteller about the complex realities of life in a southwestern landscape.

The Southwest has had more than its fair share of interpreters and mythologizers. Writers of Westerns have romanticized it as a harsh and spacious land of rugged individualism, whereas nature writers such as Austin, John Charles Van Dyke, and Joseph Wood Krutch have romanticized it as a landscape of stark and arid beauty that invites transcendental and spiritual insight. Taking a cue from Abbey, newer writers, such as John Nichols, Barbara Kingsolver, Gary Nabhan, Janice Emily Bowers, Charles Bowden, and Russell, are painting a more complex and realistic portrait of life, culture, and nature in the Southwest. In this portrait, dreams of living in close contact with the earth clash with economic reality and the fact of increasing urbanization. A fragile, arid environment shows scars inflicted by careless human use. New stories unfold as larger outside forces bring change to a timeless land.

In *Songs of the Fluteplayer: Seasons of Life in the Southwest*, a collection of nine personal essays, Russell looks back on her experiences of the past decade and calmly comes to terms with the way her life has unfolded. She reflects on the changes her little valley has seen, records her encounters with illegal aliens and the ordeal of home birth, describes the uneasy relations between neighbors on the irrigation ditch and between ranchers and environmentalists. She visits the trading posts of the past and the biosphere of the future, remembers her father (a test pilot killed in a crash in the desert), and works out an understanding of her own place in wilderness.

She comes finally to a clearer picture of what she and her husband wanted when they bought twelve acres of irrigated land—"transformation, safety, serenity"—and admits that they overestimated their ability to transform themselves, "to become more primitive, more sensual, thinner, browner, healthier" (p. 100). But still she is not willing to give up the hope that their land will yet bring them what they originally envisioned. As she and Peter watch other people leave the valley, goaded by restlessness, the burdensome aspects of the "simple life," and economic necessity, they wonder if they will ever regret their choice "to step outside what we were taught to consider the mainstream" (p. 12). But they stay, adjusting to the complications and contradictions of a back-to-the-land lifestyle, committed—for now—to making a home rooted in this place.

Russell's roots in the Southwest actually go back several generations. Her mother's grandparents moved from Texas to Arizona in the early 1900s; various members of the family engaged in "ranching and mining and horsemanship," which were the ways they knew to "anchor themselves to the land." Sharman was born 23 July 1954 at Edwards Air Force Base, California, the second of two daughters of Milburn Grant Apt and Faye Lorrie Apt. When her father, a test pilot, was killed in 1956, her mother moved the girls to Phoenix. Russell's inner landscape bears the mark of the Sonoran Desert as well as of the Kansas farm where she spent summers with her grandparents. She began writing in the fourth grade and started college as a drama major, intending to write plays, but changed her major after reading Leopold's *Sand County Almanac* (1949). Drawn to the outdoors, she backpacked a good portion of the Pacific Crest Trail one summer, much of it alone, and after earning her B.S. in conservation and natural resources from the University of California at Berkeley in 1976, she and a girl-friend spent a year traveling around the world. In 1980 she earned an M.F.A. in creative writing from the University of Montana and looked to the Southwest again to find a home. When she began writing about that arid land, it was in terms of her concern with how humans fit into the ecosystem.

Although Russell sometimes treads on controversial ground in *Songs of the Fluteplayer*, her careful and well-paced prose is consistently evenhanded. Whether discussing differing viewpoints about undocumented workers from Mexico, the Biosphere II project in the desert outside Tucson, or the "range war" pitting ranchers against environmentalists, here is a voice of moderation and reasonableness. Still, it is apparent that her own point of view is that of an environmentalist and a feminist. In her tour of trading posts, she admits that what really interests her is not the Navajo rugs for sale but "what the women say." The young male president of the local Hispanic irrigation association makes her feel excluded "as a woman, as a white woman." She feels bullied by the "hard masculine anger" expressed by ranchers at a public hearing on livestock and elk in the Gila National Forest. Her evenhandedness itself makes clear that she values the feminine skill of building community, making sure that all voices are heard and understood. This is her approach to environmental battles where the various interests are polarized and passionate.

Russell speaks for many women in her attempts to define her relationship to wilderness in the absence of appropriate role models, articulated in "Gila Wilderness." Aspiring to be her version of Daniel Boone, she tries a number of brave experiments in wilderness solitude and each time comes up with misery compounded of boredom and loneliness. Giving up the idea

of becoming a mountain man, she settles instead on becoming Leopold—"not the man who lives wilderness, but the one who manages it" (p. 116). Years later, as she accompanies her husband and two children, another family, and four horses into the Gila Wilderness near her home, site of Leopold's early lessons in ecology, she concludes: "I do not need to become more than I am to have a place in the wilderness. I do not need to love solitude more than the company of my own species. I do not need to become a man. Or a manager. The shrine is here already.... I need only walk in" (p. 120).

The wilderness realm that she of necessity traverses by herself is that of pregnancy and childbirth. "Homebirth" describes the "messy, bloody, and intensely personal" ordeal of giving birth to two children, assisted by a midwife, thirty miles from the nearest hospital. Of this initiatory experience she writes: "Growing a baby is the most exotic of lands, bordered by joy, fraught with a sense of danger, and beset by internal politics.... By the end, discomfort compels us. Like adventurers cast on some Pacific isle, we are ready to sail back to civilization" (p. 56). She remembers these home births as moments of power, when she felt "at the center." Here, then, is the raw territory that this female Daniel Boone can explore with competence and self-assurance edged with awe and a sense of mystery.

Russell's second book, *Kill the Cowboy: A Battle of Mythology in the New West*, amplifies her inquiry into the "range war" she first wrote about in *Songs of the Fluteplayer*. Despite the book's bellicose title, its mission is to foster dialogue and understanding in the volatile and increasingly polarized debate over grazing on public lands in the West. Recognizing that the debate is a complex one with many facets and no easy answers, Russell presents a number of different viewpoints. She sets the stage by acknowledging the power of the West's dominant myth—the myth of the cowboy, which incorporates our "cultural dreams of freedom and solitude, of riding a horse across golden fields as thunderclouds roll across the sky, of sleeping peacefully under the arc of the Milky

Way, of waking alone to the bitter light of dawn" (p. 2). She also documents the damage done to rangeland by overgrazing and to wildlife by predator control programs—the cowboy's "dark side."

The public lands debate comes alive as Russell skillfully profiles sincere, articulate people with diverse opinions and sometimes strong emotions. We meet outspoken opponents of grazing on public lands, conservationists who favor open dialogue with ranchers and feel a commitment to community and cooperation, a Forest Service official whose vigilant efforts to "protect the resource" have incurred the wrath of local ranchers, and ranchers who practice holistic resource management and are proud of the health of the land their cows graze. We meet a professional environmentalist who would like to see the end of predator control on public lands, a wildlife biologist for Animal Damage Control who believes ADC has a legitimate role to play in protecting livestock interests, and people involved in educating the public about wolves and getting them reintroduced.

We read about Russell's own thoughts and feelings as she encounters cows in the Gila Wilderness on a family outing. In "The Green Woman," a chapter exploring the larger cultural context of the debate, we read about the role of the Judeo-Christian heritage in our view of natural resources and meet spokespersons for various alternative forms of spirituality: a Tewa Indian who contrasts his people's view of the land and the American way, a couple committed to bioregionalism as a moral and spiritual choice, and the originator of the philosophy of goat walking—a life of nomadic pastoralism based on a covenant with the land.

Russell's own opinions are clearly stated. She would like to see a transition from viewing land as a commodity belonging to us to viewing it as a community to which we belong, Leopold's old idea. She thinks that there should be less grazing on the public range, that the health of land and wildlife should be the bottom line. She says that we need wilderness and wolves. She thinks we also need ranchers: "As our last frontier urbanizes, we need the psychic ballast of people

who make their livelihood directly from soil, grass, and water" (p. 3). She believes we need the cowboy. She believes environmentalists and ranchers can find common ground as they seek to remedy environmental ills. And she says that beyond new laws and management plans, we also need a "biodiversity of myth," new myths and role models that include "heroines as well as heroes, urbanites as well as country folk, ecologists as well as individualists" (p. 12). Her answer to the cowboy is the "green woman, an elusive dryad hidden in our hardened modern selves. A powerful green force. A generous spirit." Russell suggests that we call out this green woman and "see what she has to say about the West" (p. 193).

What Russell ultimately has to say about the West in *Kill the Cowboy* is that its "real work" may be reinvention, based on remembrance (an "acknowledgment of the past, of all that was good and all that was bad," p. 13) and repentance (a "transformation lured by the vision of what the future could be," p. 197). Reinvention, remembrance, and repentance also seem to be the impulses that motivate her own work. Her children's fantasy book *The Humpbacked Fluteplayer* (1994) envisions a parallel world in which the Sonoran Desert exists without the blight of Phoenix. *When the Land Was Young: Reflections on American Archaeology* (1996) sprang from her thrill at finding potsherds from the Mimbreno culture dating from about A.D. 1000. This book about contemporary issues in archaeology reflects her conviction that in order to understand who we are and to extend concern to future generations, we must be able to imagine the distant past and how people once lived. It reflects her intention to know, in all its dimensions, in its old stories as well as its new ones, the landscape in which she has deliberately taken root.

A Question of Belonging: John Daniel

By the time John Daniel was forty, he had lived in twenty-nine different dwellings. He was launched on this nomad existence by his father, an itinerant labor organizer who uprooted his family numerous times "because there was union organizing to be done." Daniel came of age in the 1960s, dropping out of college, resisting the draft, taking psychedelics, and holding a series of odd jobs, touched lastingly by that decade's "bloom of environmental awareness" and by a sense of sacredness that he followed "into the world and into words." When he found his vocation first as a poet and then as an essayist and environmental journalist, it was perhaps natural that the question of belonging, of trying to locate himself, would preoccupy him. Woven through *Common Ground* (1988), his first book of poetry, and *The Trail Home* (1992), a collection of literary essays, is an inquiry into finding that place of balance and belonging called home.

In *Common Ground* we get our first inkling that the idea of home is a complex and tantalizing one for Daniel. The first poem, "One Place to Begin," instructs the reader to drive west and to "forget where you thought you were going," to leave the road and travel by foot into a natural landscape, where closer kinship with earth and animals becomes possible, and to understand that this landscape never visited before "has been waiting for you to come home." "First Light" describes Daniel's sense of returning to himself as he stands at the woodpile, attentive to the day's first light and the creatures around him, imagining that he could "melt into morning like a coyote." "In this light anywhere would be home," he writes. In "Of Earth," as he witnesses the exquisite beauty of swallows, oaks, and grasses at sunset and speculates that "these could have happened a different way," he decides that "a mind thinking so is a mind wandering from home" and lets himself rejoice in the "sweet peculiar loveliness" of the reality before him. Belonging begins to seem like a matter of learning to pay attention to where one happens to be.

In *Common Ground* we also get an inkling of the literary tradition to which Daniel belongs, and in particular of the enormous influence of Stegner in his life. A complimentary quotation

John Daniel

from Stegner graces the back of the book; one of the poems is titled "The Sound of Mountain Water," an echo of the title of one of Stegner's books; and the poem "Of Earth" is dedicated to Stegner. Many of the poems in *Common Ground* were written while Daniel was a Wallace Stegner fellow and Jones lecturer at Stanford University. The poetry fellowship came as a jolt of electricity that galvanized Daniel's developing identity as a writer. Before the fellowship he had lived through his share of adolescent confusion and vocational mobility. He had tried his hand at writing short stories and noticed that his most passionate passages had to do with landscape.

Daniel was born on 25 May 1948 in Spartanburg, South Carolina, to Franz and Zilla Hawes Daniel, the second of two boys. His father was a social activist who cared more about human than natural history, but his mother's affinities were toward the natural world and influenced his own in that direction. The family moved to Charlotte, North Carolina, and then to Denver before settling in the suburbs of Washington,

D.C., where they moved from house to house throughout most of Daniel's childhood. When he was twelve, his parents bought a weekend cabin in the Blue Ridge Mountains of northern Virginia, a landscape that fed his love of "stars and streams and forest silences." He migrated west to Oregon in 1966 to attend Reed College but dropped out after four semesters, thereby losing his draft deferment. When the invitation came from the U.S. Army to participate in the Vietnam war, he refused as a matter of conscience but never formally registered as a conscientious objector.

Never indicted for draft evasion, Daniel spent the next decade working at a variety of jobs in California and Oregon. For two summers he was a choker-setter for the Weyerhaeuser Timber Company. An eight-year stint as a railroad freight inspector, first in the Bay Area of California and then in Klamath Falls, Oregon, amounted to an "extended fellowship in fooling around" and provided him with the opportunity to start writing. When Daniel was thirty, he moved to a ranch in eastern Oregon to see if he could write full-time. Although that sage and juniper steppe initially seemed bleak to him, it was the first landscape in which he invested enough time and energy to truly see it. When a friend told him about the Stegner fellowship at Stanford, he submitted a slim poetry manuscript and was chosen despite his lack of a college degree. After the one-year fellowship ended in 1983, he stayed on for five years as a lecturer in poetry and composition, simultaneously earning an M.A. in English/creative writing. In 1983 Daniel married Marilyn Matheson, whom he had met at a poetry reading in Klamath Falls.

Stegner is a palpable presence in Daniel's second book, a collection of fourteen essays, ten of which were previously published in such periodicals as *Wilderness* and *Orion*. *The Trail Home* is dedicated to Stegner "with thanks for his example as writer, conservationist, and human being." The first two and the last two essays in the book are set on Wallace and Mary Stegner's hilltop land south of San Francisco, where the Daniels rented a cottage during the years at Stanford. We hear "Wally" reminisce about the time when theirs was the only house for half a mile and the place teemed with animals. Daniel admires and envies the Stegners' "engagement with their surroundings," cultivated during forty years of watching the seasons come and go in the same place. "They know where they are in a way I probably never will," he reflects (p. 207).

The Trail Home grew from Stegner's encouragement as much as from his land. Stegner handed an early draft of Daniel's essay "Water Power" to T. H. Watkins, the editor of *Wilderness* magazine. Watkins published it, the first essay by Daniel to appear in print; the essay, in a slightly different form, is included in *The Trail Home*. (In 1988 Daniel persuaded Watkins that *Wilderness* needed to publish poetry and thus became the magazine's first poetry editor.)

Wendell Berry also had a hand in the publication of *The Trail Home*, and has been, no less than Stegner, a source of support and inspiration to Daniel. "I consider Wendell Berry the wholest and most important writer at work in America today," says Daniel. Since Daniel first wrote to him in 1979 asking for comments on his early poems, Berry has offered criticism and encouragement. Berry sent three of Daniel's essays to his editor at North Point Press, Jack Shoemaker, who then wrote to Daniel asking if he had more. He did, and thus *The Trail Home* was born.

Stegner died the year after *The Trail Home* was published, and so did poet William Stafford, another writer whose friendship touched Daniel's life. In a memorial piece on Stafford, Daniel reflects: "He had little use for the heroic, the revolutionary, the rhetorically loud. He placed his faith in little things, in subtle clues and slight changes" (p. 231). Daniel himself has learned to put a lot of store in small things. In "Desert Walking," he confesses that he used to hope for a vision in the desert, a "flash of knowing in whose light I would understand life and death, and all the hieroglyphic forms of nature" (p. 142). "I've walked some desert miles now," he writes, "and I'm beginning to think that vision is not a sudden kind of thing. Maybe it's a progress, a slow gathering of small seeings. Maybe it has to be" (p. 142). Similarly, in "Some Mortal Speculations," he writes, "My mind, like my hands, is best suited to the grasping of smaller things, things that happen close in front of me, things I can see and turn slowly in memory and see again, in imagination's second light" (p. 199). His sense of belonging, then, is necessarily constructed of small accretions of knowledge about a place, like that gained in cultivating a summer garden, an experience he records in "The Garden and the Field."

But Daniel is concerned with more than just belonging to a place; he wants to be fit to belong as well to the larger family of living things, the Earth community. Fully half of the essays in *The Trail Home* are expositions of the "environmental dysfunctions" of American culture and Americans, encapsulated in Daniel's characterization of Americans as "sure of what belongs to us but not at all sure of what we belong to" (p. 206). In these essays, what he most laments is that we have separated ourselves from nature in so many ways that we no longer understand its fate as our own; we have lost a sense of belonging to and having responsibilities toward a community larger than the human tribe. Alternating between anecdote and meditation, Daniel occasionally brings in ideas and quotations from classic conservation writings to bolster his points. His prose is always lucid, frequently lyrical, sometimes luminous; his voice is principled and idealistic.

In "The Impoverishment of Sightseeing," Daniel laments the superficial way too many of us experience the natural world: "nature as sight," a fragile basis for preserving the wild lands we have left. In "On the Power of Wild Water," he argues against the American attitude that whatever we can do with our machines and our ingenuity, we should do—in this case, put another dam on the Klamath River. "We will be a saner society," he writes, "when we remember the free and boisterous power of wild water for what it is—the song that sings its way through stone, more ancient and as filled with truth as any utterance of man, an original voice of Earth that celebrates, in its ceaseless fluid tongue, the same unfolding mystery that made us" (p. 57). "Place of Wild Beasts" praises the Wilderness Act of 1964 as, along with the Endangered Spe-

cies Act, the "boldest and most intelligent thing our society has done in regard to our relationship with wild nature" (p. 62) but decries the relative smallness of the wilderness preservation system and the fact that simply drawing a boundary around a piece of land is not sufficient to protect it from acid rain, air pollution, global warming, or the impact of too many visitors.

In "The Long Dance of the Trees," Daniel deplores the cutting of old-growth forest and suggests that "we might pause to ask, as our past perishes in the screech of saws, if we aren't at the same time clearcutting our future from the face of the earth" (p. 94). In "Among Animals," he points out that animals are at home on the land in a way that human animals have forgotten how to be and laments the fact that we have "stripped ourselves of the kinship of fellow creatures." "Marks on the Land" contrasts the restraint and discretion bespoken by the rock art left by prehistoric tribes, a signal of the reverence they felt toward nature, with the thrashing, scraping, digging, and blasting that is our distinctive signature on the land. "Remembering the Sacred Family" challenges our worship of economic growth and technological power, and encourages us to rediscover a "religious relationship to the natural world" like that of our tribal ancestors.

What saves these pieces from sermonizing is Daniel's humble inclusion of himself in the crowd of humans whose habits he so laments. His own quandaries about belonging to the Earth community come to light in the essays in the book that focus on his personal experience. In "Pack Rat," for instance, he reflects as he dumps the body of a pack rat he has killed, a former resident of his house, that although we need our human residences and the walls we put around us, "I wish we knew some other way of building them, I wish we could live in our human house without sweeping it so clean of other lives" (p. 33).

Threaded through these essays is the idea that a fundamentally different response is required of humans if we are to have any kind of future on Earth. Daniel shares with Stegner, Thoreau, Muir, Robinson Jeffers, Leopold, and McKibben a sense of disappointment with the human family and a yearning toward a future in which he and his fellows will be wiser, more alert to the real riches of the world, more willing to shoulder their responsibilities and actually begin to live a land ethic. At the same time, in "The Machine and the Grove," a strong essay on the value of radical environmentalism as a counterpart of the mainstream environmental movement, he recognizes that the "struggle for an environmentally responsible society is a large, complicated, and immensely difficult job" (p. 110). "We have been fighting well and we are losing," he admits heavily (p. 103).

Daniel seems to transcend his own pessimism in the most illuminating essay in *The Trail Home*, "The Poem of Being." Here he achieves the fullest formulation of the religious notions that figure in many of his essays and poems. Sensing a kinship between the human imagination and the "imagination of nature," he suggests that "evolution resembles the creative activity of the poet." To Daniel, both are "God's way of being born," and all forms of life are God's body and spirit "realizing itself in time." Thus, as he writes in the poem "Common Ground," "we are Earth learning to see itself, to hear, touch, taste." Taking the long view, he comes to the comforting understanding that the universe has a dynamic wholeness and will go on without us—without our individual lives and even without the life of our species—in "its forms and orders that range far past what we can know" (p. 190).

"All of us are in motion, rising out of previous forms and advancing into new ones," he proclaims in "Some Mortal Speculations" (pp. 200–201). Daniel and his wife moved from Stegner's land to Portland, and in 1994 to the Coast Range foothills near Eugene. In the same year a new book of poetry, *All Things Touched by Wind*, came out, as did an expanded paperback edition of *The Trail Home*. Daniel's literary essays and journalistic pieces regularly appear in such publications as *Wilderness*, *Sierra*, and *Orion*; in 1994 his essay "Toward Wild Heartlands" in *Audubon* won the John Burroughs Association award for an outstanding published natural history essay. Finally, Daniel's sense of home has less to do with belonging to any particular place than with belonging to the community of Earth and to a tradition of literature focused on the natural world.

Drawn to the Last Jagged Frontier: Susan Zwinger

When Susan Zwinger was forty-one, she came to a time of seismic change in her life: she had lost a significant love relationship and left a job as an art curator in Santa Fe to take up some kind of environmentally focused work in Seattle. In the hope that entering a totally unfamiliar landscape might "catalyze" her vision and put her in touch with elemental power and some deeper rhythm, she took off on a three-month road trip to Alaska, the "last jagged frontier." Equipped with a large black notebook, a hand lens, and a stack of guidebooks, she drove her small pickup truck thousands of miles, venturing north almost as far as Prudhoe Bay and south to the Kenai Peninsula, with side trips to Denali National Park and towns with such names as Hope and Chicken. Hikes into raw wilderness to gawk at landforms, plant and animal life, and weather were complemented with stops in cafes and roadhouses to tune in to the local miners, hunters, truckers, and oilmen. During the two years after her return to Seattle, she shaped 200 pages of notebook jottings into a kaleidoscopic record of her journey titled *Stalking the Ice Dragon: An Alaskan Journey* (1991), thus launching a new career as a nature writer.

The journey into wilderness with its parallel journey into some wilder part of the self is an old and venerable theme in American nature writing, dating back to Bartram's *Travels* (1791) and Thoreau's *The Maine Woods* (1864). American naturalists who have written about journeying to Alaska include Muir, whose *Travels in Alaska* (1915) Zwinger dips into on her trip; Charles Sheldon, a hunter-naturalist who explored *The Wilderness of Denali* (1930) and was the earliest promoter of national park status for the area; John McPhee, whose *Coming into the Country*

(1977) is as focused on backcountry settlers as on backcountry; and Barry Lopez, whose *Arctic Dreams* (1986) is a meditation on perception as much as an account of what he perceives. If men dominate this list, it is because journeys into wilderness involve physical hardship and risk, and very few women have dared undertake them alone.

Women who have traveled to Alaska and written about it have generally accompanied their husbands: Lois Crisler in *Arctic Wild* (1958) tells of the year and a half she and her husband spent in the Brooks Range filming the wolves and the caribou migration for a major Hollywood studio; Margaret Murie in *Two in the Far North* (1962) reminisces about her early life in Alaska, her marriage to wildlife biologist Olaus Murie, and several of their trips together into Alaskan wilderness; and Billie Wright, in *Four Seasons North* (1973), describes the experience of living for a year with her husband in a miner's cabin in the Brooks Range.

With *Stalking the Ice Dragon*, Zwinger joins the tiny pantheon of gusty women who have braved the rigors of the Arctic alone. The naturalist Sally Carrighar spent nine years in Alaska researching *Icebound Summer* (1953), a saga of the summer courtship and mating of several species of animals. Her stay there provided material for two other books: *Moonlight at Midday* (1958), a personal account of her adventures during that time, and *Wild Voice of the North* (1959), a portrait of the Siberian husky she rescued and cared for while living in Nome. And Debbie Miller spent thirteen years hiking, climbing, and kayaking in the Arctic National Wildlife Refuge on journeys described in her book *Midnight Wilderness* (1990).

If Zwinger's visit to Alaska is briefer than these other women's, she is also more explicitly interested in how gender influences her experience. She acknowledges on the first page of her book that, historically, it is the man who has left home to venture forth into the unknown; her own urges are clearly more exploratory than domestic. When she enters a restaurant alone, conversations stop and men stare at her "like deformed game." After a couple of weeks on the road she catches a glimpse of herself in the mirror and sees staring back a "wild animal, a *real* animal," instead of the carefully made-up countenance whose attractiveness she feels defines her worth in the eyes of other people. "My fear in the wilderness is substantially different from that of men I have known," Zwinger writes. "I feel part of the long continuum of life and death. I mostly fear to be disconnected—no husband, no children, no family" (p. 82). Her musings on what it means to be a woman alone in the wilderness foreshadow a collaboration with her mother in editing a book of essays by women entitled *Women in Wilderness* (1995).

But in *Stalking the Ice Dragon* Zwinger spends relatively few words on introspection and does not dwell on physical discomfort or the logistics of her trip. In the introduction she states her desire to allow this new land to permeate six senses at once, and that is the impression she lays down. In a series of journal entries dated from 6 August 1988 to 21 October 1988, she strives to capture in sensory detail the vast and rugged landscape of Alaska as it spreads itself out before her. From painterly descriptions of the sheer spectacle of it all, she spins off into tutorials on subjects as varied as plate tectonics and tundra life-forms, philosophical reflections on such topics as native people's perceptions of time and space, and flights of fantasy that have her imagining what it feels like to be a bear or to encounter a living, breathing woolly mammoth. Zwinger is as interested in the political landscape as in the geological, eagerly eavesdropping on conversations between locals peppered with such phrases as "environmentalist assholes" and registering her own outspoken disgust at policies and practices relating to mining, fishing, drilling for oil, and clear-cutting.

Although the book is oriented toward present time, Zwinger occasionally drops clues about her background, as in references to poking around abandoned Colorado mines during her girlhood and learning to use her journal seriously, as her mother does. Born 17 July 1947 in Muncie, Indiana, she is the oldest of three daughters of the nature writer Ann Zwinger and Herman Zwinger. The mountainous landscape around

Susan Zwinger

Workshop, and a Ph.D. in art education from Pennsylvania State University.

The delightful verve of Zwinger's writing owes much to her training as a fine artist and poet. She writes of herself:

> I admit to an Emily Dickinsonian character: the twitch of minutiae is as moving as volcanoes and tsunamis. The outer margins of life, like the Southwestern deserts, and the northern tundras, where the greens are never crude and robust, draw me: the subtle ranges of grays, lavenders, oranges like flute scales in Oriental quarter tones, where one sits through long, quiet observations. (p. 27)

Through the eyes of this poet and painter, a mountain three miles away "appears as an etching, and the next mountain after that a fray of wet watercolor into dry" (p. 48). A mudflat is "not barren, but broken in Paul Klee cubism, each section gleaming a different earth pastel" (p. 149). The oil pipeline is a "slug of black sludge moving rapidly through a Rousseau painting" (p. 68). Other metaphors are equally arresting: tube mushrooms "crowd out of earth like the fingers of a thousand dead men" (p. 12), hawks "rise on thermals with the slow turn of a knife peeling an apple" (p. 45), cumulonimbus clouds are "magnificent, towering giants that reduce mountains to small muttering tooths" (p. 78), golden eagles fly "followed by an entourage of disgruntled ravens, charred ladies in waiting" (p. 144).

Susan shares with her mother a "natural instinct toward observation, toward collecting, sorting and naming" (p. 31) and an admiration for Carson's sea books, but there the similarities end. Ann Zwinger's first book, *Beyond the Aspen Grove*, is as close to home as Susan's is distant. Ann keeps political concerns out of her writing and maintains an impersonal tone in much of her prose. If Susan's writing is more exuberant, Ann's is more careful. Whereas Ann's meticulously researched books show a reverence for the "holy grail of accuracy" she refers to in the preface to the 1988 edition of *Beyond the Aspen Grove*, Susan's book is marred by misspellings of

the family's summer home in Colorado, described by Ann Zwinger in *Beyond the Aspen Grove* (1970), made a strong impression on Susan's adolescent consciousness, filling her life with a "richness, a texture, and a *raison d'etre* I cannot imagine having developed anywhere else" (*Ice Dragon*, p. 77).

Although both Susan and her mother came to nature writing serendipitously in early middle age, Susan's circuitous career path resembles Carrighar's more than her mother's. Whereas her mother dedicated herself to home and family after studying art history, Susan set out to be an artist, then a humanities scholar, then an artist again, then a museum curator of contemporary art, then an art critic. She also worked as a house painter, a maid, an art packer, a salesperson, a tile layer, a furniture finisher, and a server at a deli counter in the course of earning a B.A. in art from Cornell College in Iowa, an M.F.A. in poetry from the University of Iowa Writers' a number of names (among them those of Gaia hypothesis originator James Lovelock, Representative George Miller of California, Susan Stamberg of National Public Radio, and the Porcupine caribou herd, so called because it lives in the drainage of the Porcupine River), as well as other small errors, such as conflicting reports of the date the Alyeska pipeline was started. And while Ann Zwinger's books have a straightforward linearity, *Stalking the Ice Dragon* is more like a collage, as unplanned and unpredictable as the trip's itinerary, as raw as the land it describes.

Despite its flaws, *Stalking the Ice Dragon* stands as a vivid snapshot of a great land and the human impact thereon at the end of the twentieth century. Of particular note is Zwinger's description of Prince William Sound six months before the *Exxon Valdez* oil spill. "The Sound and the shipping terminal appear to be a disaster waiting to happen," she writes with uncanny prescience (p. 160). Also notable is the unwitting evidence *Stalking the Ice Dragon* gives that we do indeed live in a "world in which all (from microorganism to president) are entangled irrevocably in each other's oxygen tubes" (p. xi)—a world in which environmentalists are entangled in the evils they decry.

Although Zwinger condemns the voracious appetite for fossil fuel that is causing our country to "devour our mother," she enjoys the unprecedented liberty provided by fossil fuel in the gas tank of her truck. Although she sees the pipeline as representative of the "clash of man and nature," she cannot keep herself from admiring "its technology, its complex response to conservation concerns, its environmental checks and balances" (p. 162). In subtle sympathy with Alaskan citizens who snarl about environmental regulations imposed by the lower forty-eight states, she sees Alaska as an "immense place to be free" and confesses that she herself has "some resistance" to following Park Service regulations in Denali. These unintended ironies are instructive for what they say about the complexity of the crisis in which we find ourselves.

Finally, Zwinger's optimism about humankind wrestles with her pessimism. Although she wants to believe that "our salvation as a species will come through the revival of the sense of beauty, our wanting it above all else," so that "we will find intolerable gravel-scraped streams and oil-humped shores" (p. 49), she also seems to feel a conviction that "we will not last as a species." The summer following the oil spill in March 1989, Zwinger returned to Alaska to work for five months as a public information officer at Kenai Fjords National Park and witnessed firsthand the wake of death left by that disaster. In the years since, her commitment to natural history fieldwork and writing has deepened: she has written the text for a photographic celebration of the lands protected by the California Desert Protection Act and has completed a book about traveling the last wild edge from the Yukon down the coast of British Columbia and northern Washington. If she thinks that beauty will lose in the end, she intends to champion it until that time.

Selected Bibliography

PRIMARY SOURCES

John Daniel, *Common Ground* (Lewiston, Idaho: Confluence, 1988), *The Trail Home* (New York: Pantheon, 1992; enl. paper ed., New York: Pantheon, 1994), "William Stafford, 1914–1993," in *Western American Literature* 28 (November 1993), "Writing Nature," in *American Nature Writing Newsletter* 5 (spring 1993), *All Things Touched by Wind* (Anchorage, Alaska: Salmon Run, 1994), "Toward Wild Heartlands," in *Audubon* (September/October 1994), and "Cuttings," in *American Nature Writing 1995*, ed. by John Murray (San Francisco: Sierra Club Books, 1995); Bill McKibben, *The End of Nature* (New York: Random House, 1989), *The Age of Missing Information* (New York: Random House, 1992), *The Comforting Whirlwind: God, Job, and the Scale of Creation* (Grand Rapids, Mich.: Eerdmans, 1994), *Hope, Human and Wild* (Boston: Little, Brown, 1995), and, as ed., *Birch Browsings: A John Burroughs Reader* (New York: Penguin Nature Library, 1992); Sharman Apt Russell, *Songs of the Fluteplayer: Seasons of Life in the Southwest* (Reading, Mass.: Addison-Wesley, 1991), *Kill the Cowboy: A Battle of Mythology in the New West* (Reading, Mass.: Addison-Wesley, 1993), *The Humpbacked Fluteplayer* (New York: Knopf, 1994), and *When the Land Was Young: Reflections on*

American Archaeology (Reading, Mass.: Addison-Wesley, 1996); Susan Zwinger, *Stalking the Ice Dragon: An Alaskan Journey* (Tucson: Univ. of Arizona Press, 1991), "The Accidental Naturalist," in *American Nature Writing Newsletter* 5 (spring 1993), and, as ed. and contributor, *Women in Wilderness* (San Diego: Harcourt Brace, 1995).

CRITICAL STUDIES

Terrell F. Dixon, "Three Examples of New Nature Writing," in *American Nature Writing Newsletter* 5 (spring 1993), reviews of *The Trail Home* by John Daniel and *Stalking the Ice Dragon* by Susan Zwinger; Michael Grubb, "This Ever-Changing World," in *Nature* 344 (26 April 1990); Charles E. Little, "Books for the Wilderness," in *Wilderness* 53 (spring 1990), and "Books for the Wilderness," in *Wilderness* 55 (fall 1992), review of *The Trail Home* by John Daniel; Peter Wild, "A Sweet Planet Gone Sour," in *Sierra* 75 (January/February 1990).

WESTERN GEOLOGISTS AND EXPLORERS
CLARENCE KING AND JOHN WESLEY POWELL

JOHN TALLMADGE

GOD MAY HAVE made the mountains and deserts of the American West, but the West as idea and symbol was made by writers. Preeminent among them were the scientists-explorers of the great government surveys undertaken in the two decades after the Civil War, when the country had turned its attention toward consolidating a sense of identity and settling the vast interior. These men sent back reports of enduring scientific and literary value, and many produced popular works that have become classics of nature writing. Two of the most famous are Clarence King's *Mountaineering in the Sierra Nevada* (1872) and John Wesley Powell's *Report on the Exploration of the Colorado River of the West and Its Tributaries* (1875). Both men engaged the exotic landscapes and peoples of the West with sensibilities disciplined by science and refined by the conventions of genteel travel writing, yet their works lead the reader to fundamentally different understandings of the relationship between nature and the self. This disparity is due in part to the differing landscapes they explored and in part to dissimilarities in character and personality. But their books attracted a wide and durable following and, more than a century later, continue to influence the ways we think and write about the West.

As scientists and writers, both King and Powell were men of their age. In the mid-nineteenth century, American natural science was energized by the excitement of new discovery, yet torn by the conflicting paradigms of mechanistic materialism and natural theology. The former was gaining ascendancy in Europe with advancing industrialism, the decline of romanticism, and the publication of Charles Darwin's *Origin of Species* (1859). But in America, still under the sway of an Emersonian romanticism, nature continued to be seen as a form of divine revelation. William Paley's *Natural Theology; or, Evidences of the Existence and Attributes of the Deity, Collected from the Appearances of Nature* (1802) was read by students on virtually every campus in the land. Louis Agassiz, that great popularizer of natural history, based his particular brand of scientific optimism on the classic argument that nature's order implied the existence of a divine Creator. "It is my hope," he declared, "to see, with the progress of intellectual culture, a structure arise among us which may be a temple of the revelations written in the material world" (quoted in Stein, p. 161). And Alexander von Humboldt, Agassiz's mentor and the most influential scientist of the age, had promoted a method that combined "rational empiricism" with the critical study of the impressions made by natural phenomena on human consciousness. It is fair to say that mid-nineteenth-century American science was inspired by a vision of systematic understanding grounded in disciplined observation that would elevate the sensibilities, vindicate Christian principles, and extend civilization, in the form of knowledge, into the most remote and exotic places.

Travel writing partook of this same cultural enterprise. As long journeys by steamship and rail became safer and more affordable, Americans began to see travel as requisite to a genteel education. For those who could not go themselves, a good book filled with curious facts, local color, and vivid landscape descriptions would do. Travel books soon became as popular as novels, and the most successful writers combined a strong narrative line with the aesthetic and moral judgments of a personable narrator whose exposure to foreign culture served to confirm a native patriotism. Travel books were a way for Americans to learn about the world while renewing their enthusiasm for building a new kind of country. And many of the best writers, like Bayard Taylor and Mark Twain, found the West as fit a subject as South America, Asia, or the Near East. To a reader ensconced in a Boston parlor, the arid West could seem as remote and strange as any foreign country.

Accounts of exploration form a visible current within this broad stream of travel writing, sharing many of its generic features while adding elements of risk, hardship, adventure, and the unknown. The setting is always exotic in the extreme, located at the farthest remove from the reader's world. The explorer's heroic motivations (generally conquest or science) contrast with the curiosity, pleasure, and desire for education that draw the traveler. If the travel book appears as a "cultivated conversation," to use Howard Mumford Jones's evocative phrase, the explorer's account is a high-stakes adventure in which character often determines the outcome. The plot structures in both forms show affinities with chivalric romance, where the hero's character is repeatedly tested by encounters with the exotic. But in exploration literature the exotic is located in wild nature or tribal culture, which resists accustomed categories of thought and makes psychic assimilation a real challenge. Both forms engage the Other, the former in a mode of observation and poised critique and the latter with a relentless intimacy born of scientific ambition and the need to survive. In King's and Powell's books we see elements of both forms. However, King's stories gravitate finally toward the paradigm of romance, which confirms rather than challenges the ego and its culture. Powell's story, in contrast, leaves us with a darker, more complex view of the world and a sense that all learning comes at a price. It moves us away from romance toward tragedy, comedy, and initiation.

Clarence King

Clarence King was born on 6 January 1842 in Newport, Rhode Island. His father, a merchant engaged in the China trade, died overseas when Clarence was still a young boy, leaving him to be raised by a doting mother. Bright and precocious, King entered Yale's Sheffield Scientific School at eighteen and graduated two years later with a degree in chemistry. At Yale he read Paley and John Ruskin, excelled at sports, and began to contemplate a career in geology. After hearing Agassiz lecture on glaciers and reading a dramatic account of the ascent and survey of Mount Shasta undertaken by William Brewer, a fellow Yale graduate employed by Josiah Whitney's California Geological Survey, King decided to head west and seek his fortune as a geologist. In 1863 he set off across the plains with a friend, and after an adventure-filled trip through the Rockies, the pair offered themselves to Brewer as volunteers. During the next four years King traveled the length and breadth of California. He surveyed Yosemite Valley, discovered the age of the gold belt, and made many first ascents in the High Sierra. Upon returning east in 1867, he persuaded the federal government to undertake a geological survey of the fortieth parallel, following the route of the Union Pacific Railroad. King's 1878 report, *Systematic Geology*, is considered a scientific and historical landmark. He had also described his Sierra adventures in a series of articles for the *Atlantic Monthly* that became an instant success when it was issued in book form as *Mountaineering in the Sierra Nevada*.

By all accounts King was a man of remarkable gifts. Charismatic, generous, and cultivated, he moved easily on every level of society, from the roaring gold camps of California to the gilded club rooms of Manhattan. A dazzling conversationalist, he could charm an audience with a discourse on Ruskin or a tale of pursuing a wounded grizzly into its den. His personal integrity and scientific acumen became the stuff of legend when he and his Fortieth Parallel Survey staff exposed the Diamond Swindle of 1872, a clever fraud involving a salted claim in the Uinta Mountains that had drawn investments of $10 million. King's timely exposé averted a financial catastrophe and made him the toast of San Francisco. King's lifelong friend Henry Adams, who accompanied him for several months during the Fortieth Parallel Survey, described him at the height of his career:

> His wit and humor; his bubbling energy which swept every one into the current of his interest; his personal charm of youth and manners; his faculty of giving and taking, profusely, lavishly, whether in thought or in money as though he were Nature herself, marked him almost alone among Americans.... He was creating one of the classic scientific works of the century. The chances were great that he could, whenever he chose to quit the Government service, take the pick of the gold and silver, copper or coal, and build up his fortune as he pleased. Whatever prize he wanted lay ready for him — scientific, social, literary, political — and he knew how to take them in turn. With ordinary luck he would die at eighty the richest and most many-sided genius of his day. *(The Education of Henry Adams*, 1918, pp. 312–313)

Adams' high hopes for his brilliant friend went unfulfilled. In 1878, when King completed his exploration of the fortieth parallel, he returned to Washington as first director of the newly consolidated U.S. Geological Survey; three years later he resigned to pursue various attractive but ill-fated business ventures. Although his tastes in art, society, and travel were expensive, the riches he secured for others seemed to elude him. For the next twenty years he lived a genteel bachelor life, traveling to Europe on an art-collecting tour, staying in expensive New York clubs, and dreaming of literary endeavors that he described in glittering detail to his friends but never committed to paper. Meanwhile, he had finally acted upon an oft-expressed fascination with exotic and dark-skinned women, entering into a secret marriage with Ada Todd, a young African American from Brooklyn, whom he supported under an assumed name; they eventually had five children. The strain of this double life and the failure of his mining and banking ventures eventually undermined his health. He died of tuberculosis at Phoenix on 24 December 1901.

Written during the meteoric ascendancy of King's career, *Mountaineering in the Sierra Nevada* is an exploration classic and one of the defining works of western American literature. Couched in an ornate but vigorous nineteenth-century prose, it appeals to a genteel audience by showing how superior willpower, intelligence, knowledge, and skill can prevail over bandits, natives, and the hostile forces of nature. King presents himself as a swashbuckling adventurer with a serious scientific mission. His Sierra is a land of breathtaking summits and dizzying chasms from which geographic truths must be wrested by force, but it is also a land of stunning beauty that calls forth deep, conflicting emotions from the observer.

King's first chapter, "The Range," offers a panoramic view of the Sierra and a digest of its geologic history as reconstructed by the Whitney Survey. The story unfolds in five acts according to a "great plan of development," whereby cycles of erosion, deposition, and uplift are succeeded by volcanism and glaciation. For King the range is a setting for heroic displays of nature's power; the more dramatic, the better. His descriptions reveal an almost decadent romanticism in the

Byronic vein: "The rent mountains glowed with outpourings of molten stone. . . . The misty sky of those volcanic days glowed with innumerable lurid reflections" (p. 3). Then, "With a tendency to extremes which 'development' geologists would hesitate to admit, nature passed under the dominion of ice and snow. . . . The whole Sierra crest was one pile of snow, from whose base crawled out the ice-rivers, wearing their bodies into the rock" (p. 4). The paradoxical image of glaciers as dragons recurs in his descriptions of Mount Shasta, Mount Whitney, and other Sierra peaks. It is consonant with other metaphors taken from epic and romance—peaks as "battlements," the range as a "fortress"—that suggest a fascination with romantic types of heroism. For King, nature mirrors the mind's own great expectations. Natural and human history (real or imagined) coincide. "The volcanoes are extinct," he concludes, "and the whole theatre of this impressive geological drama is now the most glorious and beautiful region of America" (p. 4).

These opening descriptions set the tone for the book and establish the narrator as an expert interpreter adept at word painting and literary plot construction. King's geologic paradigm is catastrophism, according to which landscapes are formed primarily by such sudden, dramatic events as earthquakes rather than by gradual, uniform processes such as stream erosion. Such a view would lead him to endorse Whitney's erroneous theory that Yosemite Valley had been formed by a great rift fault. But whatever its scientific merits, catastrophism makes for compelling literature. It not only implies that nature offers coherent stories, and so conforms to the structures of human thinking, but also prescribes a heroic role for the geologist, who must interpret those stories for the reader. The mountains, in their fierce sublimity, seem made to elicit feats of imagination and courage.

King's landscape descriptions, unrivaled for vividness and drama, show that he brought to nature not just a meticulous scientific eye, but the moral imagination of a Romantic philosopher. He was moved not only to discover the landscape's underlying system, but to experience and assess its impact on his sensibilities in the manner of Humboldt or Ruskin. As Roger Stein points out, these two impulses were often in conflict. One minute nature is seen as a grand drama of struggle and aspiration; the next it is seen as a meaningless assemblage of debris left by the workings of blind, mechanical forces. Although King's profession requires the latter view, it is the former that engages his temperament. For instance, returning from his daring climb of Mount Tyndall, he indulges in a supremely Romantic moment:

> Under the later moonlight I rose and went out upon the open rocks, allowing myself to be deeply impressed by the weird Dantesque surroundings;—darkness, out of which to the sky towered stern, shaggy bodies of rock; snow, uncertainly moonlit with cold pallor; and at my feet the basin of the lake, still, black, and gemmed with reflected stars, like the void into which Dante looked through the bottomless gulf of Dis. A little way off there appeared upon the brink of a projecting granite cornice two dimly seen forms: pines I knew them to be, yet their motionless figures seemed bent forward, gazing down the cañon; and I allowed myself to name them Mantuan and Florentine, thinking at the same time how grand and spacious the scenery, and how powerful their attitude, how infinitely more profound the mystery of light and shade, than any of those hard, theatrical conceptions with which Doré has sought to shut in our imagination. (pp. 91–92)

Here King is, first, the pilgrim of Christian epic venturing through a hostile, apocalyptic landscape where every encounter is both a challenge and a lesson. The Sierra is a type of hell: dark, overpowering, and full of dangers to the soul. Then King shifts his stance to that of an interpreter, seeing literary types in natural forms, and finally to that of an art critic using the standard of nature to disparage the work of a popular illustrator. This last turn is characteristically Ruskinian, as is the sense of atmosphere conveyed by the complex, repetitive syntax and accumulating epithets.

King returns frequently to the *Inferno* as an aesthetic touchstone, finding landscapes as varied as Mount Brewer, Yosemite Valley, and Shoshone Falls of the Snake River equally Dantesque. The landscapes of the *Inferno* are indeed characterized by rugged grandeur, darkness, howling winds, roaring waters, fire, ice, and utter sterility. To a point, then, the comparisons seem apt. But anyone who has traveled in the Sierra also remembers the abundant wildflowers; rich, green meadows; sparkling cascades; and dazzling sunshine that inspired John Muir to call it the Range of Light. King seems little interested in the living world or, indeed, in the Sierra's Edenic qualities. Perhaps this attitude is understandable for a professional geologist. But his failure to extend the comparison beyond the *Inferno* to the *Purgatorio* and the *Paradiso*, where Dante encounters both living nature and the radiance of divine grace, suggests that he is projecting his own inner landscape upon nature. He remains fixated upon the first stage of Dante's spiritual journey, where the pilgrim challenges a hostile and demonized landscape, barely escaping with body and soul intact. The *Inferno* can be read as a great adventure story that celebrates the heroic virtues of classical epic, a paradigm whose limitations are exposed by the subsequent canticles. From this point of view, one might observe that when King compares himself to the Dante of the *Inferno* alone, he is announcing his epic ambition while simultaneously revealing his own moral and literary shortcomings.

Nevertheless, King's account of the ascent of Mount Tyndall remains one of the great stories of mountaineering. It is unrivaled for vividness, suspense, and sheer drama. Ascending what they believe to be the crest of the Sierra, King's superiors are astonished to discover a higher ridge some miles to the east, separated from where they stand by a seemingly impassable gulf. They return to camp exhausted and discouraged, but King is inspired to a further effort:

> Brewer and Hoffman were old climbers, and their verdict of impossible oppressed me as I lay awake thinking of it; but early next morning I had made up my mind, and, taking

Cotter aside, I asked him in an easy manner whether he would like to penetrate the Terra Incognita with me at the risk of our necks, provided Brewer should consent. In a frank, courageous tone he answered after his usual mode, "Why not?" Stout of limb, stronger yet in heart, of iron endurance, and a quiet, unexcited temperament, and, better yet, deeply devoted to me, I felt that Cotter was the one comrade I would choose to face death with, for I believed there was in his manhood no room for fear or shirk. (pp. 50–51)

The bravado in this passage sets the moral tone for the story to come: it is a test of manhood, humans against mountains. Almost immediately the pair encounter obstacles: impassable crests, precipices, steep ice and snow, intense cold. Several times they nearly get stuck on cliffs. King never loses his composure. Each challenge seems only to energize him: " 'We're in for it now, King,' remarked my comrade, as he looked aloft, and then down; but our blood was up, and danger added only an exhilarating thrill to the nerves" (p. 67).

The energy such obstacles call forth in King seems to correlate with the energy displayed in the landscape itself, which he depicts in terms of the Romantic sublime: abrupt forms, dramatic contrasts of light and shade, blasted trees, heaps of ruins. It is a stimulating but hostile environment, and the view from the summit depresses rather than exalts:

> The serene sky is grave with nocturnal darkness. The earth blinds you with its light. That fair contrast we love in lower lands between bright heavens and dark cool earth here reverses itself with terrible energy. . . . There is no sentiment of beauty in the whole scene. . . . Silence and desolation are the themes which nature has wrought out under this eternally serious sky. A faint suggestion of life clings about the middle altitudes of the eastern slope, where black companies of pine, stunted from breathing the hot desert air, group themselves just beneath the bottom of perpetual snow, or grow in patches of cloudy darkness over the moraines, those piles of wreck crowded from their pathway by glaciers long dead. (pp. 78–79)

Significantly, this summit view provides no new insights, scientific or otherwise. It confirms the senses of self and nature that King has brought with him. Faced with such conditions, what can one do but try to survive, to get in and out in one piece? It is easy to suspect King of exaggerating the dangers and overdramatizing his account. However, having retraced his route myself — it lies wholly within Sequoia and Kings Canyon national parks — I can affirm that the landscape is as rugged and challenging as he describes; in that respect his account is both honest and accurate. More interesting from a literary point of view is the fact that he does not seem changed by the ordeal. The King who returns is the same King who set forth, except that he now carries a trophy, in the form of a first ascent enshrined in a tale that grabs one by the throat. This explorer has proved that nature cannot sway him bodily, intellectually, or spiritually. In this respect, of course, he differs profoundly from Dante the pilgrim, though he does not seem to realize it. His story is one of endurance and exertion — a triumph of the will — rather than one of redemptive learning and transformation.

King's other chapters on mountaineering depict adventures of the same type. His thematics, style, and self-characterization are the same; the only real difference is in the locale. He climbs Mount Shasta, the Yosemite Obelisk, and Mount Whitney, which, as the highest peak in the lower forty-eight states, might have offered a natural climax but instead provides only a nostalgic view backward toward Mount Tyndall. By this time the range has been mapped and named, and it no longer wears an air of mystery or sublimity. King finds himself trapped in the paradox facing all explorers: their discoveries destroy the very mysteries that allured them.

The book's other chapters, which describe encounters with people rather than landscapes, engage other features of travel writing and reveal complementary aspects of King's character. In "Kaweah's Run," our hero is pursued by Mexican bandits from whom he escapes by a combination of shrewdness, courage, and the speed of his magnificent horse. Noticing them loitering about the Wells, Fargo office as he withdraws a bag of gold, he describes his opponents in picturesque and racist terms:

> There was no especial reason why I should remark the stolid, brutal cast of their countenances, as I thought them not worse than the average California greaser. . . . The elder was a man of middle height, of wiry, light figure and thin hawk visage. . . . He wore an ordinary stiff-brimmed Spanish sombrero, and the inevitable greasy red sash. . . . His companion struck me as a half-breed Indian, somewhere about eighteen years of age, his beardless face showing deep brutal lines, and a mouth which was a mere crease between hideously heavy lips. . . . I thought them a hard couple, and summed up their traits as stolidity and utter cruelty. (pp. 112–113)

When the chase begins, King gets the same kind of rush he felt in the mountains, a "thrill of pleasure, a wild moment of inspiration, almost worth the danger to experience" (p. 118). He is equally confident of victory, "for Kaweah was a prince beside their mustangs, and I ought to be worth two villains" (p. 119). Thus the contest is set out in terms of race and class. King is the Anglo aristocrat being attacked by predatory natives of inferior breeding and character. In the end, he outruns and outwits them, circumventing their ambush, enjoying the chase, and never once losing his composure. He beats the bandits at their own game of horsemanship, which is satisfying enough, but he is also the better man. His class is being put to the test, and, like a knight of romance, he proves its virtues by winning.

Class and race issues also come to the fore when King encounters Indians and emigrants in the mountains. In "Through the Forest," his survey party camps near a band of Digger Indians, who intrigue King the aesthete with their "half-droll, half-pathetic *genre* picturesqueness." He recalls a funeral ceremony that momentarily shook him out of the "most sanguinary Caucasian prejudice." The weeping women and grief-stricken husband crowding the pyre are depicted in terms that suggest a Salvator Rosa gypsy camp:

It was all indescribably strange: monarch pines standing in solemn ranks far back into the dusky heart of the forest, glowing and brightening with pulsating reflections of fire-light; the ring of Indians, crouching, standing fixed like graven images, or swaying mechanically to and fro. . . . Buck watched with wet eyes that slow-consuming fire burn to ashes the body of his wife of many years, the mother of his group of poor frightened children. Not a stoical savage, but a despairing husband, stood before us. I felt him to be human. (p. 39)

King obviously means the last sentence to be a compliment. He begins to relate to the Indians first on the basis of their resemblance to artistic imagery and second because they display emotions he deems appropriate. But this budding sympathy vanishes the next morning when he learns that Buck has gotten drunk and taken a new wife overnight. "I went back to camp an enlightened but disillusioned man," King writes. "If driven to the wall, I will usually confess my opinion that the Quakers will have to work a great reformation on the Indian before he is really fit to be exterminated" (p. 40). Although King nursed a secret fascination for tribal cultures and dark-skinned peoples (noted by Adams and analyzed by such scholars as John O'Grady), such flagrantly racist statements must have appealed to his intended audience, for they are offered without batting an eye. His casual use of racist epithets, such as "tar-heads" and "greasers," also suggests an unself-conscious bigotry consistent with his self-presentation as a genteel aristocrat. Of course, he shows no interest in finding out more about native customs and culture; he seems content merely to classify and judge them by his own standards of conduct or beauty. The Indians might as well be just another part of the landscape.

King also meets lower-class white people in the mountains, notably in "The Newtys of Pike," where a nomadic swineherd and his family epitomize the class of "chronic emigrants" whom the "brave spirit of Westward Ho!" has left stranded all over California. King has considerable fun at the Newtys' expense, transcribing their broad country dialect and commenting with exaggerated delicacy upon their rustic manners and uncouth behavior. Here he becomes the aristocrat in disguise, venturing among the common folk and bringing back an amusing report for his audience of peers. Incongruity, caricature, and the mock-heroic define this Western anti-pastoral, where "two acres of tranquil pork" take the place of grazing sheep.

King brings his art critic's eye to bear upon the daughter, Susan, a statuesque but illiterate girl who reminds him of classical renderings of Niobe, Minerva, or Ceres. Despite her comical lack of breeding, he admires her horsemanship and strength, masculine virtues that make her seem like an Amazon. He decides to "probe" her to determine "whether there were not, even in the most latent condition, some germs of the appreciation of nature" (p. 109). He finds that there are when, after lecturing on the aesthetics and geography of the forests, he notices that a "strange new light gleamed in her eye." When the time comes to leave, Mr. Newty blurts out that the lucky man who gets Susan will also get half the hogs.

But this comic pastoral does not end in marriage. King cannot forsake his class, and he regards the Newtys, finally, with a mixture of pity and contempt. They have no future, and King confesses he "thought of it too gravely to enjoy as I might the subtle light of comedy which plays about these hard, repulsive figures" (p. 110). Like John Field, the Irish squatter of *Walden* to whom Henry David Thoreau preaches in vain about the virtues of life in the woods, the Newtys are condemned by lack of breeding and imagination to a life of squalor. They are the ironic, absurd conclusion to our Edenic dreams of the West, compelled to scratch out a living from landscapes that for people like King will always be places to visit. Just as his aristocratic virtues allow him to escape from the infernal world of the high peaks, so they permit escape from the vulgar world of bandits and swineherds into a bright, promising, and, above all, civilized future.

Although *Mountaineering in the Sierra Nevada* consists of a series of freestanding adventure narratives, it has the consistency of a picaresque novel, in which episodes linked by the same protagonist provide a cross-sectional view of society. Setting and narrator give the book its principal unity. King is a Western adventurer with an appetite for vivid sensation, a connoisseur's eye, and an overwhelming ambition to prove his worth. He escapes the charge of egotism only to the extent that he presents himself as a representative of his class. *Mountaineering* is a great read, full of spectacular feats, vivid descriptions, hard science, and memorable humor, but underneath it all is a protagonist who does not change. This seems odd for a scientist and explorer ostensibly committed to discovery. But in the end we realize that for King, science is a way of subjugating nature. In this respect, geology becomes a moral gesture akin to climbing a peak for the first time, describing a landscape in Ruskinian terms, or ranking natives on a scale of civilization. In short, it is a projection of one's own values onto the Other.

John Wesley Powell

The life and work of John Wesley Powell offer a telling contrast. His government career was closely entwined with that of King, yet the two men came from quite different backgrounds and reached quite different ends. Powell was born in the town of Mount Morris in western New York state on 24 March 1834, the oldest son of an itinerant Methodist preacher, and grew up on the Midwestern frontier. His education was improvised, self-directed, and highly effective. During his boyhood in Jackson, Ohio, he came under the influence of a prosperous farmer and amateur scientist named George Crookham, who maintained a private museum and encouraged his interest in natural science. The young Powell read voraciously and traveled widely in search of specimens. By eighteen he was teaching school. He tried various colleges but could not find the scientific training he craved, so he taught himself and by 1860 had become a principal of public schools in Hennepin, Illinois. The following year he volunteered for the Union Army; in three years of service during the Civil

War, he fought in more than ten battles, lost his right arm at Shiloh, served on Ulysses Grant's staff, and rose to the rank of major. After the war he returned to teaching and by 1866 was a professor of geology at Illinois State Normal University. The following year he went to Washington, seeking funds to support an expedition of students to the Dakota Badlands. Grant gave him rations and a small military escort. During that first summer in the West, Powell conceived the idea of exploring the Green and Colorado rivers. In 1868 he made a detailed reconnaissance of the Green and White rivers, and in 1869, in boats of his own design loaded with instruments and supplies for ten months, he set off with nine other men on his epic voyage through the unknown canyons of the Green and the Colorado. When he emerged three months later at the mouth of the Grand Canyon, he was a national hero.

For the next ten years Powell's work on the Colorado Plateau was funded by Congress. He did not publish his own account of the great river trip until 1874, when *Scribner's Magazine* commissioned a series of articles that were later incorporated into his government report, *Report on the Exploration of the Colorado River of the West and Its Tributaries*. Powell's fame as an explorer and scientist, and his astute political and managerial abilities, led to solid work and increasing appropriations. He proved to be a public servant of uncommon integrity and effectiveness. When the King, Wheller, and Hayden surveys were merged with his own in 1878, King was put in charge of the newly formed U.S. Geological Survey on Powell's recommendation, leaving the Bureau of American Ethnology to Powell. But when King resigned in 1881 to go "whoring after Mexican gold mines" (as Wallace Stegner put it), Congress turned once more to Powell, who took on both organizations and ran them with stunning efficiency for the next thirteen years.

While his able lieutenants were producing reports that changed the face of American science—Clarence E. Dutton's *Tertiary History of the Grand Canyon District* (1882) and James C. Pilling's bibliographies of Indian languages

Major Powell asking Tav-Gu for the location of the nearest water pocket, Colorado region

come to mind—Powell was conceiving massive projects: a complete set of topographic maps of the United States and a comprehensive land-use plan for the arid regions based upon reclamation and irrigation. He knew more about the West than anyone else, but his ideas proved too threatening to vested interests. When his irrigation survey, which Congress had authorized, withdrew 800 million acres from settlement pending completion of water resource studies, powerful senators and envious scientific rivals conspired to cut Powell's appropriations. It would take half a century for Powell's prophetic ideas to catch on, but by then, as Stegner describes in *Beyond the Hundredth Meridian*, the West was littered with ruined landscapes and broken dreams. Powell retired from the Geological Survey in 1894 and devoted the rest of his life to writing, lecturing, and philosophical speculation. He died at his summer home at Haven, Maine, on 23 September 1902, one of the most respected scientists and public servants of his day.

Powell's report of his canyon voyage was constructed from his field journals and the letters he sent to the *Chicago Tribune* during the first month of the trip, when the party could still make periodic contact with civilization. These documents were amplified by information gathered during the next year's journey through the canyons and overland from Utah to the Zuñi pueblos of New Mexico. The 1895 edition, *The Canyons of the Colorado*, was further revised and expanded, with lavish illustrations culled from two decades of government reports. It opens with a panoramic view of the entire Colorado River watershed, proceeds to the canyon voyage and overland journey, and concludes with a powerful analytic description of the scenery of the Grand Canyon. Taken as a whole, the book responds comprehensively to the expectations of a typical nineteenth-century reader of travel writing. It offers a blend of fact, curiosity, adventure, imaginative landscape description, and encounters with picturesque natives. But the canyon voyage forms the book's narrative and emotional core.

In his preface Powell insists that the voyage was made not for adventure but for science and that he had no intention of writing his own account until persuaded to do so by congressmen and editors. He also apologizes for his shortcomings as a descriptive writer. Such disclaimers add to the sense of immediacy and authenticity conveyed by his use of a journal format and the present tense. We seem to be reading a transcription of field notes, conspicuously rough and unadorned. But we also come to the text knowing the story and its outcome. We already know about the hopeful launch, the early losses of food and instruments, the escalating intensity of the rapids, the narrow escapes followed by blissful moments in calm water or verdant side canyons, the darkness, the danger, and the increasing strain of the Grand Canyon that finally force three men to abandon the trip just short of success, the happy ending darkened by tragedy. As readers we now want to know what all this felt like, to see these events through the eyes of the explorer himself, to experience directly how landscape and character come together to create a powerful story.

In Powell's account, adventure happens to the men in spite of themselves. They are on a serious scientific mission, and knowledge is a worthier goal than wealth, souls, or thrills, the motives that seem to have drawn Powell's various predecessors. But science and adventure prove to be indissolubly linked. Powell worries as much about the instruments as about the food: the loss of the expedition's meaning is almost as frightening a prospect as injury or death. Science is depicted throughout as a heroic enterprise, bringing orderly and systematic understanding to bear upon an exotic, alien landscape that has attracted superstition and so far has resisted the advance of civilization. It is important in this respect that Powell is an amateur, a self-educated scientist with meager institutional support. He has no pedigree, little money, and few

prospects—quite a contrast to an explorer such as King. Powell is handicapped by more than a missing arm, which makes his achievements seem even more impressive.

Doing science in the canyons requires constant bravery and endurance. Powell and his men have to take compass bearings at every bend, climb to opposing rims for simultaneous barometer readings, and measure the thickness of strata by triangulation. This tedious, exacting work is carried out under the most stressful conditions. Pursuing knowledge, Powell and his men find themselves trapped on cliffs, caught in storms, swamped in rapids, starved, battered, and intimidated by the river, yet they persevere. Powell's clear-sightedness, pragmatism, and humility are mirrored in the uniformitarian paradigm that governs his geology: a belief that even the most dramatic landscapes are formed by simple, observable processes acting steadily over vast stretches of time. Despite ample opportunities—the lava flows in the Grand Canyon, the symmetry of opposing walls that might have suggested rift faults to King—Powell never embraces catastrophism. There is a palpable sense of restraint in his science, a dogged adherence to humble facts in the faith that they alone can reveal the landscape's underlying system.

But science connects with adventure in other ways as well. By closely observing the composition, angle, and relative placement of strata, Powell learns that he can often predict conditions downriver. The worst rapids occur when the strata dip upstream, where soft rock gives way to hard, or where tributaries enter. Good science is thus bound up with survival. The more Powell learns and the more quickly he understands the system, the better his chances of making it through the canyon. Science also helps combat the fear and anxiety of heading into the unknown, which is heightened by weeks of running through the dark Vishnu Schist of the Grand Canyon's Inner Gorge. That such emotions can be lethal is shown by the fate of the three men who leave the expedition.

Powell's descriptive writing shows that he brings to the landscape an eye sharpened not only by science but also by aesthetic principles similar to those of King. The canyon country, however, does not lend itself to the usual categories of taste, and Powell is forced to invent new ones. His early descriptions convey both novelty and bewilderment.

> After dinner we pass through a region of the wildest desolation. The canyon is very tortuous, the river very rapid, and many lateral canyons enter on either side. These usually have their branches, so that the region is cut into a wilderness of gray and brown cliffs. In several places these lateral canyons are separated from one another only by narrow walls, often hundreds of feet high — so narrow in places that where softer rocks are found below they have crumbled away and left holes in the wall, forming passages from one canyon into another. These we often call natural bridges; but they were never intended to span streams. . . . Piles of broken rock lie against these walls; crags, and tower-shaped peaks are seen everywhere, and away above them, long lines of broken cliffs. . . . We are minded to call this the Canyon of Desolation. (p. 191)

It is obvious from passages such as these that Powell's descriptive writing lacks the polished elegance of King's, maintaining a reportorial stance and an expository, almost pedestrian tone. Whereas King makes extravagant and seemingly effortless use of metaphor, allusion, and sophisticated syntactic variation to conjure up a scene, Powell's writing often seems chained to the facts. Yet his text as a whole confirms Thoreau's admonition that facts tend to flower into truths. In this passage Powell seems to be grasping for metaphors, finding momentary relief in architectural images that soon come to dominate his visual descriptions. His imaginative struggle to find a coherent way of writing about the landscape parallels the intellectual struggle to understand its geology and the physical struggle of the journey itself. Description, like science, is a way of taking possession of a landscape by assimilating it to a worldview. But whereas King's smooth, polished vignettes suggest a strong element of projection, Powell's

rough takes show him wrestling with nature and being transformed in the process.

Like other explorers, Powell tries to appropriate the landscape by bestowing names. Some of these memorialize experience ("Disaster Falls"), others honor patrons or colleagues ("Henry Mountains"), and still others refer to literature or religion ("Canyon of Lodore," "Bright Angel Creek"). Names represent an extension of culture, part of the inscriptive process that converts terrain into maps and wilderness into history. Many of Powell's most memorable names achieve their resonance by the level of civilization (or artificiality) they impose. Thus "Vasey's Paradise" and "Gate of Lodore" prove to be more suggestive than the prosaic "Marble Canyon" or "Echo Park." And names embody the complex aesthetics that Powell brings to his observations. A name such as "Music Temple," for instance, combines the visual with the auditory, alluding to both the architectural landforms and the sounds in which the traveler is immersed.

Unlike King's aesthetics, which appear pictorial and largely static, Powell's incorporate sound, motion, and duration. For King, nature is often just a tableau, something to grasp in a moment of contemplation. But for Powell there is almost no such thing as a view. His perspective changes each time he rounds a bend or climbs a few feet above the river. He is always moving, and so, relatively speaking, is the landscape. A canyon lends itself more to absorption than to contemplation. It exerts a cumulative influence upon the psyche. Sound is part of this kinesthetic effect: the constant roar of the river, the rush of wind, the tinkle of rivulets, and the songs of birds. The canyon country is so vast that travel is the only way to experience it. Of the Grand Canyon, which is only a part of that country, Powell writes in conclusion:

> You cannot see the Grand Canyon in one view, as if it were a changeless spectacle from which a curtain might be lifted, but to see it you have to toil from month to month through its labyrinths. It is a region more difficult to traverse than the Alps or the Himalayas, but if strength and courage are

sufficient for the task, by a year's toil a concept of sublimity can be obtained never again to be equaled on the hither side of Paradise. (p. 397)

How different this attitude is from King's, who saw the mountains as a vast theater and whose excursions, although no less intense than Powell's, were of much shorter duration. He spent four days climbing Mount Tyndall to Powell's three months in the canyons. Perhaps that is one reason he remained "animated by a faith that the mountains could not defy us." But in Powell's story nature resists all attempts at an easy understanding. Although the systems of stratigraphy and erosion reveal themselves, the landscape as a whole remains beyond grasp. It cannot be known through a single trip, or even many trips. Thus it remains sublime. A tension between mind and nature drives the plot in Powell's account, and it is never fully resolved.

Although both King and Powell made enduring contributions to science and were equally skilled as analysts and observers, the literary qualities of their works depend upon the fundamental differences in their character. Powell's restraint, pragmatism, endurance, humility, and leadership contrast with King's extravagance, risk taking, and solitary heroics. Against the dramatic, colorful King, Powell at first appears rather dull. He plays down his courage and narrow escapes. Nor does he dwell on his anxiety, suffering, fear, hunger, or, most important, his physical handicap. The effect is to enhance his credibility and moral stature while, curiously enough, intensifying the sense of drama, for the reader is invited to imagine the details that Powell leaves out, and hence becomes more fully involved with the story. Although King may be more glamorous and entertaining as a writer, Powell's story proves more engaging.

Both writers make judicious use of comic relief, but whereas King's humor is almost always class-based, confirming the prejudices of his audience, Powell's is more like the wry wit of the oppressed, for whom laughter is one way to cope with impossible situations:

While eating supper we very naturally speak of better fare, as musty bread and spoiled bacon are not palatable. Soon I see Hawkins down by the boat, taking up the sextant— rather a strange proceeding for him—and I question him concerning it. He replies that he is trying to find the latitude and longitude of the nearest pie. (p. 213)

Here we see an endearing (and redemptive) touch of self-mockery. There is no doubt that Powell suffers along with his men. There is no hint that he feels superior to them or to nature. He knows the canyon not only can defy but also can destroy them. He and his men are not the masters here. All they can do is keep their wits about them, work hard, and learn as fast and as well as they can. Under such circumstances, aristocratic arrogance could well prove fatal.

Powell also demonstrates the humility of a true learner in his interactions with the Indians, which, not surprisingly, appear richer and more complex than King's. Powell was renowned for his success in dealing peaceably with Indians, and his account shows that he treated them with a mixture of genuine interest and respect, to which they responded in kind. Not only were his property and person never molested, but the Indians told him their myths, a sign of trust. Powell certainly does not indulge in Romantic fantasies of the noble savage. Indeed, he is unsparing in his depiction of their sometimes squalid living conditions. Nor, as an adherent of Lewis Morgan's doctrine of the three stages of culture, does he refrain from locating various tribes on a scale of civilization relative to his own. But these ethnocentric opinions appear, oddly enough, to be free of the racism so evident in King. I believe this difference may arise in part from Powell's belief that all cultures, including his own, are in process; although his may be farther along the road toward scientific enlightenment, it has by no means arrived. For another thing, Powell clearly has an ethnographer's interest in Indian culture for its own sake and not just as an occasion for flattering comparisons with his own. And finally, Powell refrains from glorifying his liberal attitudes.

The most telling instance occurs on the trip to Zuñi, when Powell finally learns that Indians ambushed the three men who left his expedition. He transcribes the dignified apology offered by the chief of the Shi'vwits, whose warriors had mistaken the men for miners who had murdered a squaw. Characteristically, Powell accepts the explanation and offer of friendship. He does not pursue vengeance or seek to apply a white standard of justice. And he does not judge the Indians. In a place we might have expected to find at least a bit of preaching, Powell's account shows his customary restraint:

> That night I slept in peace, although these murderers of my men, and their friends, the Uinkarets, were sleeping not 500 yards away. While we were gone to the canyon, the pack train and supplies, enough to make an Indian rich beyond his wildest dreams, were all left in their charge, and were all safe; not even a lump of sugar was pilfered by the children. (p. 323)

Because Powell lets the facts, and the Indians, speak for themselves, this episode stands as a powerful indictment of the racist stereotypes and class-based judgments so characteristic of the age and so evident in King's description of the Digger funeral.

As accounts of heroic exploration, King's and Powell's have few equals in American literature. Both create indelible, formative images of the West. Both illuminate with unforgettable clarity the encounter between landscape and the self. Both radiate scientific optimism. Both find in wild nature a kind of divinity. It is fitting that the paths both explorers opened should now be preserved in national parks. One can follow King's route up Mount Tyndall and Powell's down the Grand Canyon and find the land in much the same condition as they did. Yet interestingly it is Powell's story rather than King's that has inspired retelling and reenactment. Hundreds of people run the Grand Canyon each year, but few retrace King's routes in the High Sierra. I suspect that at least part of the reason

lies at the deepest level of plot, which in each case depends upon the character of the landscape and the protagonist.

Mountain topography lends itself to brief, dramatic adventures and episodic plot structures akin to those of romance and its comic inversion, the picaresque. A mountain poses an immediate challenge, requiring energy, willpower, good judgment, and decisive action. The climax most often occurs at the summit, with its god-like perspective and clarifying views. Aside from local variations, stories of mountaineering tend to resemble each other, and so books like King's embody a principle of repetition and reenactment that accords with the unchanging character of romance heroes. It is no surprise, then, to observe that King does not change as a result of his experiences, nor that, finally, his adventures appear as brief sallies into the wild followed by restful retreats into civilization, which never lies more than a few days' ride away. In Powell's story the landscape imposes conditions that lead to a fundamentally different plot. First, it takes months rather than days to run the river, and, once entered, each canyon has to be run all the way through. There is no easy out if things get rough, and no way to retrace one's steps. A much higher degree of commitment is required for this kind of travel. During the first month Powell passes a few spots where he might have walked out to civilization, but once he enters the Grand Canyon, there is no escape.

Powell's journey presents itself as a series of tests that increase in difficulty as he descends. Each rapid seems worse. The men rejoice in their survival only to face greater trials a few miles downstream. There is no rest for them. Each time they make it through a rapid they learn something, but they also lose something precious: food, instruments, degrees of morale. The canyon makes them pay for their knowledge. It offers no convenient markers of progress or success comparable to a summit view. On the contrary, the landscape withholds perspective. The river takes Powell and his men deeper and deeper into the earth, where the oldest rock makes the worst rapids of all. The Grand Canyon is oppressive and gloomy, full of danger and the ceaseless roar of water. It costs Powell a lot to get through, both physically and psychologically. Like Dante, Odysseus, and other epic heroes who descended into the underworld, he emerges worn out and permanently marked by his ordeal. He has had to keep his wits about him and learn fast enough to fend off the landscape's psychic assaults.

But in the end, knowledge alone cannot assure success. For Powell the fateful moment comes when three of his men decide to leave. Neither he nor they can know the Canyon will soon come to an end, for their barometers have been lost. The decision to stay or leave must be made on faith, and it is here that Powell's character is most tellingly revealed. He does not condemn the three men; he stays up all night worrying, and in the morning he wishes them well while resolving to stay the course. The episode is described without a trace of self-righteousness or censure. We rejoice when Powell and his remaining men emerge from the Canyon into the light and safety of open country. But the happy ending is darkened by loss. We cannot help thinking that if the others had persevered, they would still be alive. Here, as in so many of the greatest stories, the difference between a comic and a tragic outcome hangs by a thread, and that thread is character.

John Wesley Powell is a hero who suffers and learns. His experiences come at great cost, but they give him strength. Clarence King is a hero who struggles and triumphs, taking on spectacular adversaries and returning with body and mind intact. He is not a learner but an icon, and his book appeals to our heroic self-expectations, the fantasies we harbor of elegance, power, and grace under pressure. The world it projects out of the mountains and deserts of the West is a world of romance, a place for the fulfillment of dreams. But Powell's story offers a darker and more complex vision that more closely resembles the life we know. His world is full of contrasts, tension, strangeness, beauty, and power, and his progress through it is marked by suffering and change. In the end, he and his men more closely resemble ordinary people than literary heroes. We all feel maimed, ignorant, and conflicted,

facing an endless series of impossible situations with which we must cope as best we can. In the life we know there is no escape and no turning back. The only way out is to stay the course. But the darkness and gloom are relieved by intervals of beauty and peace that permit reflection, encourage learning, build strength, and renew hope. Powell's story projects a world of initiation rather than of romance. Perhaps this is why his adventure has inspired retelling and reenactment. On the deepest level it feels more real, and in that respect it is finally more redemptive.

Selected Bibliography

PRIMARY SOURCES

Clarence King, *Mountaineering in the Sierra Nevada* (Boston: James R. Osgood, 1872; repr., Lincoln: Univ. of Nebraska Press, 1970), and *Systematic Geology*, vol. 1 of *Report of the U.S. Geological Exploration of the Fortieth Parallel* (Washington, D.C.: U.S. Government Printing Office, 1878); John Wesley Powell, *Report on the Exploration of the Colorado River of the West and Its Tributaries* (Washington, D.C.: U.S. Government Printing Office, 1875), repr. as *The Canyons of the Colorado* (Meadville, Pa.: Flood and Vincent, 1895) and as *The Exploration of the Colorado River and Its Canyons* (New York: Dover, 1961), *Report on the Geology of the Eastern Portion of the Uinta Mountains and a Region of the Country Thereto* (Washington, D.C.: U.S. Government Printing Office, 1876), and *Report on the Lands of the Arid Region of the United States*, 45th Cong., 2d sess., H.R. exec. doc. 73 (Washington, D.C., 1878).

SECONDARY SOURCES

Henry Adams, *The Education of Henry Adams: An Autobiography* (Boston: Houghton Mifflin, 1918); William Culp Darrah, *Powell of the Colorado* (Princeton, N.J.: Princeton Univ. Press, 1951); Ernest L. Fontana, "Cognition and Ordeal in Clarence King's *Mountaineering in the Sierra Nevada*," in *Exploration* 4 (July 1977); William H. Goetzmann, *Exploration and Empire: The Explorer and the Scientist in the Winning of the American West* (New York: Knopf, 1966); James D. Hague, ed., *Clarence King Memoirs* (New York: Putnam's, 1904); Loren Hoekzema, "The Literary Landscape of Clarence King's *Mountaineering in the Sierra Nevada*," in *Exploration* 4 (July 1977); Howard Mumford Jones, *The Age of Energy: Varieties* of American Experience, 1865–1915 (New York: Viking Press, 1971); John P. O'Grady, *Pilgrims to the Wild: Everett Reuss, Henry David Thoreau, John Muir, Clarence King, Mary Austin* (Salt Lake City: Univ. of Utah Press, 1993); Wallace Stegner, *Beyond the Hundredth Meridian: John Wesley Powell and the Second Opening of the West* (Boston: Houghton Mifflin, 1954; repr., New York: Penguin, 1992); Roger B. Stein, *John Ruskin and Aesthetic Thought in America, 1840–1900* (Cambridge, Mass.: Harvard Univ. Press, 1967); Peter Wild, *Clarence King* (Boise, Idaho: Boise State Univ., 1981); Thurman Wilkins, *Clarence King: A Biography* (New York: Macmillan, 1958), rev. and enl. with Carolyn Lawson Hinkley (Albuquerque: Univ. of New Mexico Press, 1988).

ILLUSTRATION ACKNOWLEDGMENTS

Charles Scribner's Sons gratefully acknowledges the individuals and institutions who graciously allowed the use of photographs and illustrations protected by copyright. Every effort has been made to contact the copyright owners of photographs and illustrations in these volumes; if the holder of the copyright of an illustration has not received a formal permission request he or she should contact Scribners.

Volume I

p. 3, Jack W. Dykinga/Back Bay Books; p. 23, photo by Barbara Ball/William Morrow & Co., Inc.; p. 44, reproduced by permission of The Huntington Library, San Marino, California; p. 59, from the collection of Barbara Hastings McKee; p. 64, reproduced from the Collections of the Library of Congress; p. 77, L. L. Griffin/ Houghton Mifflin, Inc.; p. 95, photo by Dan Carraco/Twayne Publishers; p. 110, Al Flint; p. 112, courtesy of Cape Cod National Seashore; p. 131, The Bettmann Archive; p. 133, courtesy Department of Library Services, American Museum of Natural History; neg. no. 333914; p. 143, Sally Carrighar/Houghton Mifflin Co.; p. 160, Archive Photos; p. 181, Division of Rare and Manuscript Collections, Carl A. Kroch Library, Cornell University Division of Rare and Manuscript Collections; p. 191, W. G. Smith/ Syracuse University Press.

p. 201, Oregon Historical Society, #OrHi 27399; p. 220, John Montre/Twayne Publishers; p. 232, copyright © John Gillan Photography, Inc./Pineapple Press, Inc.; p. 241, M. Woodbridge Williams/United States Department of the Interior National Park Service Photo; p. 249, photo by Bill Webb; p. 260, by permission of Illinois State Museum; p. 275, The Bettmann Archive; p. 299, The Bettmann Archive; p. 311, Kathy Shorr/W. W. Norton & Co.; p. 331, photograph by Bill Wittliff/The Encino Press; p. 343, photograph copyright © Ken Norgard 1991; p. 353, Barry Donahue/Cape Codder. Copyright © 1996; p. 364, Noel Young; p. 382, photo © Gary Isaacs/Scribner; p. 396, drawing by Adrian Hoover/Alfred A. Knopf.

p. 403 copyright © Nancy Stacel/HarperCollins; p. 416, University of Nebraska Photograph; pp. 427, 433, Cathy Johnson; p. 441, copyright © 1996 the Estate of Josephine Johnson Cannon. By permission of John Fleischman, literary executor; p. 455, copyright © 1984 by Diana Kappel-Smith. Reprinted by permission of McIntosh & Otis, Inc.; p. 473, Archive Photos; p. 491, copyright © Craig Blouin/Viking Penguin USA; p. 508, copyright © Anne LaBastille. Reprinted by permission; p. 515, James L. Amos/ National Geographic Image Collection; p. 539, photo by Charles Bradley. Courtesy of the Aldo Leopold Foundation Archives; p. 558, Mike Mathers/Alfred A. Knopf; p. 579, photograph by

R. H. Martin, courtesy of Faith McNulty; p. 592, The Bettmann Archive.

Volume II

p. 611, Inge Morath/Magnum Photos, Inc.; p. 617, courtesy Enos A. Mills Cabin; p. 629, copyright © 1990 Jerry Howard. Positive Images; p. 646, photo by Jim Kalett/St. Martin's Press; p. 660, The Bettmann Archive; p. 663, Yosemite National Park Research Library; p. 675, photo copyright © Stephen Trimble; p. 690, North Point Press; p. 705, Alfred Eisenstaedt/Life Magazine. Copyright © Time Inc.; p. 718, Cynthia Foster/National Geographic Society; p. 726, copyright © Bob Peterson, Photographer; p. 737, Christopher Simons/Houghton Mifflin Company; p. 743, Jim Evans; p. 758, The Bettmann Archive; p. 769, Chet Raymo; p. 783, Dick Durrance © National Geographic Society; p. 798, Eva Sanders.

p. 808, Seton Memorial Library, Cimarron, New Mexico; p. 823, Arb/Arcade Publishing; p. 839, David Robertson; p. 852, courtesy Department Library Services, American Museum of Natural History; neg. no. 338588 (copy by Jackie Beckett); p. 863, Leo Holub; p. 885, Limberlost State Historic Site; p. 900, The Bettmann Archive; p. 909, reproduced from the Collections of the Library of Congress; p. 921, New York University Medical Center Archives; p. 938, daguerreotype by B. E. Maxham; p. 941, The Bettmann Archive; p. 954, Special Collections and Archives, Rutgers University Libraries; p. 966, Betsy Kendall; p. 978, Michelle MacFarlene/Pantheon Books; p. 995, Harper & Row, Publishers.

p. 1007, Carl Van Vechten, courtesy Photographs and Prints Division, Schomburg Center for Research in Black Culture, The New York Public Library, Astor, Lenox and Tilden Foundations; p. 1020, David Robertson; p. 1036, Grey Owl/Country Life, Ltd.; p. 1054, Marian Wood Kalisch/HarperCollins, Inc.; p. 1071. Courtesy Department of Library Services, American Museum of Natural History; neg. no. 2A13009; p. 1084, Archive Photos; p. 1122 Utah State University; p. 1134, courtesy estate of Helen Cruickshank; p. 1150, Al Momaday/University of New Mexico Press; p. 1165, Marilyn Daniel/Pantheon Books; p. 1170, Herman Zwinger/University of Arizona Press; p. 1181, The Bettmann Archive.

INDEX

Numbers in boldface refer to volume number or extended treatment of a subject.

N